SCRIBNER LIBRARY OF DAILY LIFE

ENCYCLOPEDIA OF CLOTHING AND FASHION

EDITORIAL BOARD

SCRIBNER LIBRARY OF DAILY LIFE

ENCYCLOPEDIA OF CLOTHING AND FASHION

VOLUME 3:
Occult Dress to Zoran, Index

Valerie Steele, Editor in Chief

CHARLES SCRIBNER'S SONS
An imprint of Thomson Gale, a part of The Thomson Corporation

THOMSON
GALE

Detroit • New York • San Francisco • San Diego • New Haven, Conn. • Waterville, Maine • London • Munich

Encyclopedia of Clothing and Fashion

Valerie Steele, Editor in Chief

Library of Congress Cataloging-in-Publication Data

Encyclopedia of clothing and fashion / Valerie Steele, editor in chief.
    p. cm. — (Scribner library of daily life)
Includes bibliographical references and index.
    ISBN 0-684-31394-4 (set: hardcover: alk. paper) — ISBN 0-684-31395-2 (v. 1) —
ISBN 0-684-31396-0 (v. 2) — ISBN 0-684-31397-9 (v. 3) — ISBN 0-684-31451-7 (e-book)
    1. Clothing and dress—History—Encyclopedias. I. Steele, Valerie II. Series.
GT507.E53 2005
391'.003—dc22
                                                                              2004010098

This title is also available as an e-book.
ISBN 0-684-31451-7
Contact your Thomson Gale Sales representative for ordering information.

Printed in the United States of America
10 9 8 7 6 5 4 3 2

SCRIBNER LIBRARY OF DAILY LIFE

ENCYCLOPEDIA OF CLOTHING AND FASHION

OCCULT DRESS Occultism is any nonmainstream Western system of spirituality that uses magic, the definition of magic being the way in which internal thoughts are used to effect changes in the outside world. Occultists, such as northern European Pagans (e.g., Wiccans, Druids, and witches) and ceremonial magicians (Cabalists, hermetics, and the like) practice magic as part of their religions. Occult dress is used when participating in magic rites, rituals, or ceremonies. Western occult dress has three primary functions: (1) to psychologically place the wearer in an extraordinary sense of reality; (2) to identify the status of the wearer within a social group; and (3) to indicate the beliefs of the wearer.

Clothing

Occult beliefs promote nudity as occult dress, because clothing is believed to impede the flow of magical energies through the body from the surrounding environment. Wicca practitioners and witches have traditionally performed rites in the nude to show their devotion to the Wiccan goddess. Due to modesty or weather, some occultists wear robes or tunics with bare feet and no undergarments. This latter dress is believed to still allow the flow of magical energies. Many covens and magical groups have set occult dress guidelines, using tradition or personal tastes as a basis for these guidelines. Occult dress, especially nudity, is not a common Western mode of dress, therefore it psychologically alerts and reinforces the awareness of special occasions and presence of magic for occultists. Each magical group sets the guidelines for occult dress. There is not a specific literature, although a magical group may draw inspiration from books, movies, or even more mainstream cultural practices.

Some occult groups don garments symbolically colored according to a ceremony or rite. For example, a Northern European Pagan coven may don white clothes to celebrate Yule rites and green clothes to celebrate Beltane festivals. Ceremonial magic groups, such as the Hermetic Order of the Golden Dawn, have an extensive magical color symbolism, and thus certain colored clothing is worn for a specific ritual. This is done in order to mentally link the practitioner to the rites being performed, raising awareness and effectiveness of the spiritual ritual.

Occult dress is also used to indicate status within a group. Wiccan high priestesses of Alexandrian lineages indicate status to other initiates by a colored leg garter. Also, a waist cord may be worn in the same group to indicate the wearer having taken oaths pertaining to a level of initiation. Other occult groups, such as the Order of Bards, Ovates, and Druids, who originated in England, wear colored robes denoting rank during some occult ceremonies.

Cultural disposition is another motivation for specific occult dress. For example, Asatru practitioners may don tunics and mantles of historic Germanic styles to denote their affiliation to the ancient Teutonic religion. Celtic knotwork designs on clothing and jewelry may be worn to show an affiliation to Druidism and other ancient Celtic spiritualities.

Western occult dress tends to be self-manufactured (sewn by the practitioner or by a fellow occult member), or if technical skills are lacking, utilizes existing everyday clothing for a magical purpose such as a silk bathrobe purchased at a department store that could be worn in ritual as magical raiment.

Jewelry

Jewelry is used to indicate occult status or beliefs. A Wiccan priestess may don a silver tiara or crown emblazoned with moon-phase symbols, while a Wiccan practitioner or a Witch may wear a necklace with a moon or feminine symbol. Both silver metal and the moon symbolize the Goddess and feminine energies. A Wiccan priest may wear a headdress of antlers to symbolize fertility, fecundity, and the God of Wicca. A high priest or other practitioner may wear a necklace or torc decorated with appropriate spiritual symbols.

The pentacle, a disk emblazoned with a five-pointed star known as a pentagram, is commonly worn by many occultists as a token of affiliation to a nature-based pagan religion. The pentagram's points symbolize the elements of air, earth, wind, fire, and spirit, important concepts in northern European paganism. Another common indicator of a belief in a nature-based religion, especially witchcraft, is the Egyptian ankh pendant, worn as a symbol of eternal life.

Practitioners of Teutonic religions may wear an upside-down T-shaped "Thor's hammer." This symbol is used as an overall indicator of Asatru, a name sometimes used for the Teutonic pantheon-based religion.

Tattoos

Tattoos may be used to indicate Pagan spiritual beliefs. Celtic knotwork and swirls are common designs employed as indicators of a nature-based religion. Tattoos can be utilized as proof of initiation or devotion. For example, some worshippers of Odin may get a tattoo of three interlocking triangles as a sign of their devotion to that Teutonic deity.

Contemporary Occult Stereotypes

The media generally depicts occultists wearing all-black clothing, especially black robes or cloaks, and having pentacles as jewelry. This stereotypical dress perpetuates the erroneous belief that the occultist is sinful or "evil."

"Witch" stereotype. The "witch" is an enduring stereotype of female occult dress, exemplified by the Wicked Witch of the West from *The Wizard of Oz* and the witch antagonist from various Grimm's fairy tales. The witch stereotype consists of ragged, all-black clothing, cape, conical wide-brimmed hat, and facial deformities. This stereotype originated in medieval Christianity's attempt to denigrate practitioners of Western Pagan religions. The color black and physical deformities are associated with the concepts of evil and sin, hence the witch stereotype is "covered" in sin—black clothing and warts. Around the turn of the twenty-first century, the popularity of the *Harry Potter* book series by J. K. Rowling helped to alter the stereotype of the witch, replacing it with more diversified images and connotations.

Warlock/Satanist stereotype. The "warlock/Satanist" from cinema, such as those in the 1970s' *Hammer* horror films, is another Western occult dress stereotype. The male and female Satanist stereotypes typically wear pentacle jewelry, black robes, black hair, and black eyeliner; similar dress is used for the (male) warlock. Since Western cinema has historically dressed the villain archetype in all-black clothing, dressing the occultist in black visually communicates a sinister character to the audience.

Influences on Contemporary Dress

In the late twentieth century, some occultists wishing to be recognized in mainstream religious and cultural arenas adopted stereotypical occult dress—black robes, pentacle jewelry, black hair, and black eyeliner. While controversial among occult communities, they visually publicized and communicated occult membership and beliefs by wearing this type of dress.

Occult dress has also influenced subcultures. The dark-romantic Goths, some heavy metal music fans "headbangers," and a variety of vampire subcultures utilize elements of occult dress, especially stereotypical components, such as black clothing and pentacles. Occult dress styles are more commonly worn by these subcultures as a symbol of subculture affiliation, rather than as an indicator of religious or spiritual beliefs and practices.

See also **Ceremonial and Festival Costumes; Religion and Dress.**

BIBLIOGRAPHY
Buckland, Raymond. *Buckland's Complete Book of Witchcraft.* St. Paul, Minn.: Llewellyn Publications, 1998.
———. *The Tree: The Complete Book of Saxon Witchcraft.* York Beach, Me.: Samuel Weiser, 1985.
Campanelli, Pauline. *Rites of Passage.* St. Paul, Minn.: Llewellyn Publications, 1995.
Fitch, Ed. *The Rites of Odin.* St. Paul, Minn.: Llewellyn Publications, 2002.
Raven Wolf, Silver. *Solitary Witch: The Ultimate Book of Shadows for the New Generation.* St. Paul, Minn.: Llewellyn Publications, 2003.

Thomas A. Bilstad and Theresa M. Winge

OILSKINS Oilskin is a heavy cloth that has been made waterproof by being impregnated with a hot solution of oil, gum, and wax to ensure maximum protection under extreme conditions. It has traditionally been made into the foul-weather apparel worn by sailors and fishermen.

Like many pieces of outerwear, the oilskin was born out of necessity. Life upon the high seas was never easy for those on board ship, and sailors devised a number of protective garments to deal with extreme conditions. During the early nineteenth century, it became common for sailors to smear themselves and the clothes they were wearing with oil for protection from the cold and the continuous ocean spray. One sailor at the time, Edward Le Roy, discovered that worn-out sail canvas could be recycled as outerwear. He devised a method of painting the fabric with a mix of linseed oil and wax so that it would become waterproof and suitable to be worn on deck in foul-weather conditions. By the 1830s, the oilskin had become established as essential attire for rough weather at sea for sailors, fishermen, and lifeboat men. The oilskins appeared to have a yellowish hue owing to the linseed oil used to treat them. Overcoats, hats, jackets, and trousers were also produced in this manner. When sailors came to shore they would often still be sporting their oilskin attire, and the wearing of oilskins was adapted for use by people on land. As news of the effectiveness of Le Roy's new discovery spread, oilskin coats were soon being made by colonists in Australia, and by members of the British army to protect their rifles during rainstorms.

The oilskin coat is often known as a "slicker" in the United States. Oilskin coats and trousers, now made of rubberized or plastic-coated fabric, are still widely worn by fishermen and those in other maritime occupations, and have become standard rainwear for young children. They typically are made in a bright yellow color, echoing the original linseed-oil hue of oilskin itself.

Cattle drovers in Australia developed a version with a fantail to protect the seat of the saddle and leg straps to prevent the coat billowing out or blowing off while riding in the harsh conditions of the outback. The coat, that would become known as the Driza-Bone (the name recalls the dried-out bones of animals often found in the deserts of the outback) also had extended sleeves to protect the wearer's arms when they were extended. Oilskins of this style are still worn by motorcyclists, fishermen, and water-sports enthusiasts alike; the Driza-Bone has become one of the iconic garments of Australia.

The Barbour is another version of an oiled and waxed jacket, the use of which has filtered through to the mainstream. Established in 1894, the Barbour Company's eponymous lightweight coats have become a byword for traditional British oilskins. Ideal for walking, yachting, and fishing, Barbours come in three different weights. The Barbour has also become synonymous with agriculture, owing to its durablity, functionality, and most importantly, its warmth and protection from the rain.

Not only do oilskins work as functional pieces of outerwear, they also look as good with a pair of jeans and loafers as they do with working overalls, heavy-duty boots and other protective dress.

See also **Parka; Rainwear.**

BIBLIOGRAPHY

Byrde, Penelope. *The Male Image: Men's Fashion in England, 1300–1970.* London: B.T. Batsford, Ltd., 1979.

Chenoune, Farid. *A History of Men's Fashion.* Paris: Flammarion, 1993.

De Marley, Diana. *Fashion For Men: An Illustrated History.* London: B.T. Batsford, 1989.

Schoeffler, O. E., and William Gale. *Esquire's Encyclopedia of 20th Century Fashions.* New York: McGraw-Hill, 1973.

Wilkins, Christobel. *The Story of Occupational Costume.* Poole, Dorset: Blandford Press, 1982.

Tom Greatrex

OLEFIN FIBERS Polyethylene and polypropylene are familiar to consumers who recycle as PP, HDPE, and LDPE in disposable plastic items. As fibers, the Federal Trade Commission classifies them as "olefins"; this is also the chemists' term for the ethylene and propylene used to make them. Depending on the way the polymer is made, polyethylene melts at 110° to 135°C (240° to 275°F), while the usual polypropylene melts at around 165°C (330°F). For this reason, the vast majority of olefin fibers are based on polypropylene, and even then, the low melting point is a limitation. Gel-spun polyethylene fibers are distinctly different and are discussed below.

Olefin fibers are cheap. The polymer is melted for extrusion through a spinneret into fiber. Olefin production is a relatively simple operation that small companies can undertake. Most olefin fibers have a round cross-section. They have strength comparable to nylon and polyester with a fiber tenacity of 5–7g/d (grams per denier). If olefin fibers are stretched or crushed they bounce back well; they have good resilience and recovery properties. Olefin also doesn't absorb moisture, and the fiber is the lightest of all the common fibers. Its g/cc density is 0.92 (grams per cubic centimeter). This means that fabrics of a given bulk are lightweight, and olefin materials float in water. Weather resistance is limited, but stabilizers are added to render this deficiency unimportant in practice. The fiber is undyeable, and while much research has been undertaken to achieve dyeability, few of these modifications have proved commercially successful. For this reason, most colored olefin fibers are produced by the inclusion of pigment in the melt before spinning, in a process commonly called "solution-dyeing" (although it is technically neither a solution nor a dyeing process). The undyeability can also be viewed as inherent stain resistance, and together with the good resilience, abrasion resistance, low density (i.e., good cover for a given weight), and low cost make olefin a realistic alternative to nylon for carpet fiber, and olefin is widely used in upholstery fabrics for the same reasons. The strength is sufficient to make olefin ropes and cords useful, and coupled with low biodegradability and low cost, makes olefin fibers a good choice for geotextile applications.

The lack of moisture absorption translates into "wickability," and olefin fibers have thus been used for athletic and hiking socks, cold weather underwear, and diaper liners. In many instances, polyester, which also has a very low moisture retention but is dyeable, has taken over those end-uses. Low cost renders the material disposable, and olefin has been used for disposable surgical gowns. It has tended to replace cellulosic fibers such as jute in carpet backing and in sacking.

The technique of gel spinning has been used to produce polyethylene fibers in which the polymer chains are highly aligned along the length of the fiber. One commercial example is sold as Spectra. The excellent alignment gives the material a very high strength, some 3 to 4 times stronger than polyester, and of the same order as para-aramid fibers such as Kevlar. Like Kevlar, it is thus useful in cut protection, ballistic protection, and sailcloth. While the lower weight of olefin is an advantage, the low melting point may be considered a limitation.

See also **Acrylic and Modacrylic Fibers; Fibers; Techno-Textiles.**

BIBLIOGRAPHY

Adnaur, Sabit, *Wellington Sears Handbook of Industrial Textiles.* Lancaster, Pa.: Technomic, 1995.

Cook, J. Gordon. *Handbook of Textile Fibers, Part 2: Man-Made Fibers.* 5th ed. Durham, U.K.: Merrow, 1984.

Moncrieff, R. W. *Man-Made Fibres,* 6th ed. London: Newnes-Butterworth, 1975.

Martin Bide

Women wearing dresses by Japanese designer Chiyo Tanaka. After World War II, the West showed a re-emergence of interest in other cultures, and Asian designers began to make an impact in the fashion world. © BETTMANN/CORBIS. REPRODUCED BY PERMISSION.

ORIENTALISM The Orient has been a source of inspiration for fashion designers since the seventeenth century, when goods of India, China, and Turkey were first widely seen in Western Europe. While the use of the term "Orientalism" has changed over time, it generally refers to the appropriation by western designers of exotic stylistic conventions from diverse cultures spanning the Asian continent.

Though luxury goods have been filtering into Europe from countries like China since ancient times, it was not until the great age of exploration that a wider array of merchandise from cultures throughout Asia found their way to the west. For example, the importation of Chinese ceramics exploded in the seventeenth century. Not only did these wares remain popular for centuries, they also inspired the creation of stellar ceramic compa-

nies like Sevres in France and Meissen in Germany. Even plants, like the legendary flower from Turkey that led to the "tulipmania" craze in Holland and the brewed leaf that became the status drink of the well-to-do and evolved into the ritualized "high tea," fueled the love of all things from Asia.

It was in the realm of fashion that the impact of "Orientalism" could also be profoundly felt. Platform shoes from central Asia led to the creation of the Venetian chopine in the sixteenth century. Textiles from all over Asia, primarily China, India, and Turkey, inspired the creation of fashions like the *robe á la turquerie* in the eighteenth century. This was a more extraordinary phenomenon since the fear of Turkish Islamic invaders was a constant and imminent threat. Coupled with the threat of an invasion was a diametrically opposed view: the romantic notion of a far-distant land, such as Cathay (or China), filled with genteel philosophers and lovers of art. This idealized impression of China would continue until the rise of the industrial revolution and European colonialism in the early nineteenth century. The gritty reality of ever-increasing business transactions between East and West, as well as the ever-encroaching military dominance by European powers in Asia was firmly cemented by the middle 1800s.

As Queen Victoria ascended the throne of England 1837, then the most powerful empire in the world, she oversaw an eclectic art style that would come to dominate the remainder of the nineteenth century. The Victorian era brought together many historical European styles of the past, Gothic and Rococo for example, which were sometimes surprisingly combined with elements from cultures like Japan. The end result of one amalgamation, Gothic and Japanese, led to the creation of the Aesthetic Movement. Fashion gowns reflected this blend: smocked robes like medieval chemises were embroidered with asymmetrically placed floral motifs of chrysanthemums, two distinctly Japanese design elements.

The influence of Orientalism on fashion could be seen in many other ways, both frivolous and profound. For example, the fad for harem pants from Turkey appeared in the form of fancy dress costume at balls, just as the Zouave costume of North Africa found its way into the wardrobes of some Southern soldiers fighting in the American Civil War and the closets of European ladies. On the other hand, items of dress from Asia would become essential for women through the mid-nineteenth century. Kashmiri shawls, originally woven in India then exported to the west in the late eighteenth century, became a ubiquitous part of the neoclassical costume. The shawl was often paired with a white columnar dress made of diaphanous, finely woven Indian cotton. Its popularity inspired many weaving companies in Europe to create their version of this essential nineteenth-century wrap, later known as the paisley shawl.

The Orientalism trend reached an apex in the early twentieth century, and the sources for this mania for "all things oriental" ranged from nostalgia for the legends of Persia and Arabia, as popularized by "A Thousand and One Nights," to the Paris debut of Sergei Diaghilev's Ballets Russes in 1909. This burst of Orient-inspired creativity in the realm of fashion also had lesser-known sources, including the avant-garde art movement Fauvism and Japanese kimonos made expressly for the western market.

French couturiers, such as Paul Poiret and Jeanne Paquin, were inspired by the Ballet Russes' performances of "Cléopatre," "Schéhérazade," and "Le Dieu Bleu." This Russian dance company took Paris by storm with their revolutionary choreography, music, and costume and set designs by the Russian artist Leon Bakst (1866–1924). In addition to these fantastic costume

Model in Scherrer 2004 haute couture design. Asian and other ethnic influences began finding their way back into fashion lines in the 1960s and continued to make an impact into the early 2000s. AP/WIDE WORLD PHOTOS. REPRODUCED BY PERMISSION.

shapes and opulent decorative elements, couturiers incorporated the vibrant color palette of Fauve artists such as Henri Matisse. Not only did designers create garments with Orientalist influences, so did the modistes: turbans topped with aigrette or ostrich plumes and secured with jeweled ornaments were paired with either neoclassic columnar gowns or fantastical lampshade tunics.

Clothing created more in the realm of craft by artists such as Mariano Fortuny and Monica Monaci Gallenga also fused historical European and Asian styles into cohesive aesthetic statements. Using silk velvet as a base, both Fortuny and Gallenga precisely incorporated textile patterns from East Asia and the Islamic world for their creations. The importance of craft also fueled the European and American fad for batik cloth. Both the technique for making resist-dyed fabrics like batik and the motifs perfected in cultures like Indonesia were created by artisans on both sides of the Atlantic Ocean in the 1920s.

Marie Callot Gerber (1895–1937), the venerable head of the leading couture house Callot Soeurs, was another innovator who readily embraced Orientalism. She was inspired by the kimono and created some of the earliest versions of harem pants. From 1910 to the outbreak of World War I, acclaimed beauty and woman of style, Rita de Acosta Lydig, worked with Gerber to create versions of Oriental costumes that were composed of vests made from seventeenth-century needle lace that topped trousers or one-pieced garments that were full and loose over the lower part of the torso before tapering over the calves. Often called the tango dress, after the dance craze imported from Argentina, this style was popularized by couturiers like Lucile (Lady Duff Gordon, 1863–1935) and by fashion illustrators. The house of Callot would go on to lead the 1920s trend for embellishing the columnar dresses of the era with rich embroideries that readily copied Persian and Chinese design elements.

Also influential were exhibitions and expositions geared specifically to exhibit products of France's colonies. One of the first was a major exhibition of Moroccan art installed at the Pavillion de Marsan in March, 1917. The exhibition also forecasted far larger things to come: the Exposition Coloniales, held in Marseilles in 1922 and in Paris nine years later. These shows not only generated public interest in non-Western cultures, but also projected France's commitment to imperialism. According to art historian Kenneth Silver in his publication *Esprit de Corps,* the exposition of 1922 expressed a "less than covert sense of racism." The French were still recovering from the devastating effects of World War I as late as 1925, and there is little doubt that these exhibitions and expositions allowed them to publicly display not only their high position in the modern world, but also their dominance over a vast array of Third World cultures.

Many of the centuries most noted couturiers in France were readily absorbing the influences of the Colonial Expositions of 1922 and 1931. It was the first time that many had direct access to art from such remote countries. This exposure to ethnic dress gave them a far more profound understanding of non-Western dress, primarily objects from Asia. This understanding would enable a few enlightened couturiers to create both new fashion silhouettes as well as imbue their designs with a fundamentally different construction that emphasized the textile rather than complex tailoring.

Marcel Rochas, for example, was directly inspired by dance costumes from the Balinese court, as seen in his broad-shouldered garments of the season immediately following the 1931 Exposition. His "robe Bali," a black silk dress with a broad and square collar trimmed in white pique, is interesting in that it follows the silhouette of a non-Western garment but uses typical European colors and fabrics. Madame Alix Grès also created her version of a Balinese costume in 1937. Jacques Heim designed a sarong-style bathing suit inspired by the Tahitian exhibits in the 1931 Exposition. These sarong suits, in a radical departure from contemporary bathing-suit construction, were made not of knitted wool but with draped woven

cotton. *Harper's Bazaar* made mention of these sarongs and his *pareos* from later collections. By the mid-1930s, Hollywood costumer Edith Head designed a version of the sarong for actress Dorothy Lamour in a series of comedic films starring Bob Hope and Bing Crosby. As noted earlier, all these designers' ethnic-inspired work of this period was not based on non-Western construction techniques, but rather their inspirations came from overall cultural impressions.

The output of "ethnic" garments by fashion designers was to drop off significantly during the 1940s and 1950s as the influence of exotic cultures on fashion had already begun to diminish around 1934. Inspired by the play "The Barrets of Wimpole Street" and the Hollywood film version, couturiers like Madeleine Vionnet, to cite but one of many examples, began to create modern versions of nineteenth-century Western dress. This trend dominated fashion from the late 1930s through the 1950s. The revival of historical styles offered an escape from the pressures of the Great Depression of the 1930s and helped assert the growing sense of nationalism in Europe at that time. Also a factor in the United States was strong anti-Japanese sentiment during and after World War II.

Fashion periodicals of the 1940s, 1950s, and early 1960s seem to indicate only a minimal interest in foreign dress for most designers, as compared with earlier decades. However, a strong revival of ethnic influences arose during the mid-1960s, as the fashion world responded to the purposeful rejection of standard, mass-produced fashion by young people. The young people known as "hippies" ushered in a style noted for its free-form mix of fashion elements from around the world, particularly the Middle East, India, and Native American cultures. Coupled with this renewed interest in non-Western cultures was the emergence of Asian designers. For the first time, Japanese creators like Hanae Mori not only made fashion, they began to influence the work of western designers.

After World War II, other Asian garments began to find their way into the fashion mainstream. One example is the quintessential twentieth-century Chinese dress—the *qipao* or *cheongsam.* This figure-revealing garment worn by a range of urban Chinese women since the mid-1920s has become known in the Western world as the "Suzie Wong" dress, deriving its nickname from the infamous, fictional prostitute in Richard Mason's novel, *The World of Suzie Wong,* published in 1959. Born in the tumultuous years of early Republic China, the *qipao* (meaning "banner gown" in Mandarin) or *cheongsam* (meaning "long dress" in Cantonese) is a true fashion hybrid that fused the elements of traditional Qing Dynasty court dress, Han Chinese costume, and the modern European silhouette. Despite its respectable status in China, Taiwan, and Hong Kong, the *qipao* came to represent in the Occidental mind a two-pronged, stereotypical view of Asian women—subservient, obedient, traditional, on the one hand, and exotic, sexual, even menacing, on the other. Films such as *Love Is a Many Splendored Thing* (1955) and *The World of Suzie Wong* (1960) are tales filled with textual excess whose narratives featuring Asian-Caucasian sexual liaisons use the *qipao* to uphold and sometimes subvert culturally accepted notions of race.

Perhaps it is those provocative elements of the *qipao* that have made contemporary reinterpretations of it so prevalent in the early twenty-first century. European or American designers, along with Chinese transplants like the New York–based Hong Kong native Vivienne Tam, have been creating their popular versions of Chinese-inspired fashions since the late 1990s. Examples range from the lavishly embroidered Neo-Chinoiserie gowns by John Galliano for Dior, Miuccia Prada's minimalist remake of the Mao jacket, and the body-revealing corseted mini *qipaos* by Roberto Cavalli. It is clear that the continued fascination with Orientalism continues into the twenty-first century.

See also **Japanisme; Qipao.**

BIBLIOGRAPHY

Ames, Frank. *Kashmir Shawl and Its Indo-French Influence.* Woodbridge, U.K.: Antique Collectors Club, 1988.

Barbera, Annie. Interview by author, Musee de la Mode et du Costume, Palais Galliera: Paris. January 1992.

Battersby, Martin. *Art Deco Fashion: French Designers 1908–1925.* New York: St. Martin's Press, 1974.

Beer, Alice Baldwin. *Trade Goods: A Study of Indian Chintz.* Washington, D.C.: Smithsonian Institution Press, 1970.

Burnham, Dorothy. *Cut My Cote.* Toronto: Royal Ontario Museum, 1974.

de Osma, Guillermo. *Mariano Fortuny: His Life and Work.* New York: Rizzoli, 1980.

Druesedow, Jean. Interview by author, Costume Institute, Metropolitan Museum of Art, New York. 18 December 1991.

Garnier, Guillaume, et al. *Paris Couture Années Trente.* Paris: Musée de la Mode et du Costume, 1987.

Jon, Paulette. Interview by author. Paris: January 1992.

Kirke, Betty. *Madeleine Vionnet.* San Francisco: Chronicle Books, 1998.

Koda, Harold. Interview by author, Fashion Institute of Technology, New York. January 1991.

Levi-Strauss, Monique. *The Cashmere Shawl.* New York: Harry N. Abrams, 1987.

Martin, Richard, and Harold Koda. *Orientalism.* New York: Harry N. Abrams, 1994.

Poix, Marie-Helene. Interview by author, Musee des Arts de la Mode: Paris. January 1992.

Steele, Valerie, and John S. Major. *China Chic: East Meets West.* New Haven: Yale University Press, 1999.

Tiel, Vicki. Interview by author: Paris. January 1992.

White, Palmer. *Poiret.* New York: Studio Vista, 1973.

Wichmann, Siegfried. *Japonisme: The Japanese Influence on Western Art in the 19th and 20th Centuries.* New York: Harmony Books, 1981.

Patricia Mears

OUTERWEAR Outerwear attire is worn over other garments and is generally designed to protect wearers from inclement weather or other adverse environmental conditions, although some outerwear is primarily ceremonial in function. Humans have worn outerwear garments since prehistoric times, but the word "outerwear" has been in use only since the early twentieth century as a general term for this type of clothing. Any garment worn over the day, evening, or work attire of a given period is technically an outerwear garment, with styles ranging from simple shawl-like drapes to jumpsuits that cover the entire body. Fashionable outerwear, however, does not include protective work garments, so this entry focuses only on those outerwear styles worn with regular day or evening clothes.

Although there is no definitive evidence, it seems probable that the first outerwear garments were fur skins used as final body wrap. By the late Paleolithic period (c. 40,000 B.C.E.), skins were being cut and sewn together using bone needles and thread made of animal hair or ligaments. The first sewn outer garments were probably fur capes, designed to fit over the shoulders. This assumption is supported by the existence of wooden "toggle" pieces discovered in European graves of the Magdalenean period (15,000–8,000 B.C.E.), positioned to act as the front closures for a garment worn over the shoulders. In outerwear intended for warmth, the fur was worn next to the body, whereas if the garment's function was primarily ceremonial, the fur was worn outside, as in the leopard skins seen much later in depictions of Egyptian priests of the eighteenth dynasty (1580–1350 B.C.E.).

Just as wraps of fur had done in the earliest societies, lengths of cloth draped or wrapped around the body served as outerwear garments in the early Middle Eastern, Egyptian, Greek, and Roman civilizations. In Greece, both men and women draped a length of fabric called a himation over their tunics. Soldiers wore a short cape called a chlamys, made from a fabric rectangle wrapped around the left arm, and clasped by pins at the right shoulder, leaving the edges open along the right arm. In Rome, the himation became the pallium, and semicircular as well as rectangular fabric pieces were used for capes, as in the *paenula*, which also had a hood. Another ancient outer garment was a poncho-type cape, in which a slit was cut as an opening for the head; the Roman version was called a *casula*.

As noted, capes—sleeveless garments hanging from the shoulders—date back to prehistory with various styles developing over time. In European countries, from the time of Christ to the eighteenth century, capes, cloaks, or mantles—the words are generally used interchangeably—were the primary outerwear garments for both sexes and for all ages and economic classes. These garments were variations on the forms worn since antiquity, and of different lengths and styles depending on the era and/or their

Frock coats and top hats, ca. 1916. The men depicted in this poster are wearing frock coats and suits designed by the American Century Clothing Company. Various styles are shown here, including double- and single-breasted "Prince Albert," as well as one- and two-button frock coats. © HISTORICAL PICTURE ARCHIVE/CORBIS. REPRODUCED BY PERMISSION.

wearers' rank. For example, wealthy people wore capes lined and trimmed with fur both for extra warmth and as a status symbol. Outerwear garments were also sometimes worn indoors as well as outside, for added protection against the cold in unheated buildings. Ceremonial outerwear, robes of state, and robes for chivalric orders were impressive mantles made of luxurious fabrics and furs.

Occasionally, new garments came into fashion that were part of stylish daywear with an outerwear character, such as the coat-like over-gowns worn by aristocratic men and women in the fifteenth and sixteenth centuries. The men's gown developed from the long gowns worn by men in the Middle Ages and, by the 1490s, versions were being worn over the new short doublets. The gown was open in front to show the doublet and was typically sleeveless or with short sleeves to reveal the doublet's sleeves. Portraits of Henry VIII from the 1530s show him wearing flaring, knee-length examples over elaborately slashed doublets. Like the male version, the women's over-gown was usually open in the front and sleeveless or with short sleeves so that the under-gown and its sleeves would show from beneath. The women's style was worn in the third quarter of the sixteenth century and originated from the Spanish *ropa*, which itself may have had Oriental origins. Because these gowns were part of current fashion, they were not outerwear in the same sense as capes. The gowns certainly provided additional warmth for their wearers, but, unlike capes, did not afford overall protec-

tion from the elements. For men, the gowns went out of fashion by the 1570s and for women by the 1580s.

Modern fashion trends toward complex clothing styles and rapid style changes, which were set in motion during the Renaissance, did not affect outerwear to any extent until much later. The most significant changes for outerwear took place during the eighteenth and nineteenth centuries, with sleeved coats and jackets slowly superseding capes as the primary outerwear garments for both men and women.

In men's fashion, this progression begins in the late seventeenth century with a new outerwear garment, the greatcoat, also called a surtout. The origins of the greatcoat are unclear, but it is generally thought that it developed from workingmen's clothing, possibly the *hongerline*, an overcoat worn by French coachmen in the late 1600s. It was the English, however, who popularized the greatcoat, obscuring its working-class beginnings and tailoring it into a fashionable garment. Greatcoats were worn over men's suits and were cut fuller, looser, and longer than the suit coats they covered. Over the century, as suit coats lost fullness in their skirts and sleeves, so too did greatcoats become more streamlined in cut. By mid-century, greatcoats had also acquired their most distinctive feature—tiers of two or three wide cape-like collars. Although many men still wore cloaks, greatcoats had definitely become the more stylish outerwear option by 1800.

Informal short outercoats, or jackets, were the other important development in men's outerwear in the eighteenth century. These garments, which had many style variations, also originated from working-class clothing and resembled sleeved waistcoats. Because of their obvious working-class associations, jackets did not become popular among the upper classes until the century's end. By the 1790s, however, fashionable young men were wearing jackets for hunting. One such style was the spencer, probably named after George John Spencer, second Earl of Spencer, who first sported one of the fitted, waist-length jackets.

Women's outerwear coats and jackets have their roots in the seventeenth century, when women first adopted elements of male dress for riding. In the late 1600s and early 1700s, the style of women's riding habit coats and waistcoats were taken directly from men's suit coats and waistcoats, except that the women's garments were cut to go over full skirts instead of breeches. At the beginning of the eighteenth century, women's riding coats were slightly above knee-length and when open, revealed a waistcoat of almost equal length. By mid-century, riding coats had shortened to about hip length, becoming fitted jackets, and riding habits were regarded as outerwear suitable for both riding and traveling. Women also wore a variety of jacket-style bodices for informal daywear; however, unlike riding habit jackets, these garments were not considered outerwear.

Another garment patterned after menswear, in this case the greatcoat, came into fashion for women in the late 1770s. Called a riding greatcoat or redingote, this garment was a floor-length coatdress with a fitted bodice and long, fitted sleeves. Many variations of this style were worn into the 1790s, some with the skirt attached only at the bodice back or to its sides, revealing a decorative petticoat in front. In spite of its name, the redingote was not intended for riding; it was an informal day dress that was also acceptable as outerwear for walking or traveling. At the end of the century, shawls, especially fine woolen examples imported from India, came into vogue as decorative indoor-outdoor accessories. Despite these innovations, capes persisted as the main outerwear garment for women, especially during very inclement weather.

In the nineteenth century, rapid changes in women's dress determined whether capes, coats, jackets, or shawls were the fashionable outerwear choices at any given time. While capes continued to be worn throughout the century, shawls, coats, or jackets were sometimes more in vogue than the time-honored cape. This was especially true in the early nineteenth century when shawls and innovative jacket and coat styles predominated over capes. The most important new fashions were the spencer jacket, charmingly adapted from menswear for the narrow, high-waisted dresses of this period, and long overcoats, called pelisses, that mimicked the neoclassical silhouette of the dresses beneath.

Capes resumed their former importance by 1830 because capes were more accommodating than jackets or coats over dresses whose sleeves had ballooned into the leg-of-mutton style. Even after sleeves deflated in the mid-1830s, capes, styled in a myriad of new designs, continued as the dominant women's outerwear garments for the next thirty years. Shawls were also popular for daywear into the 1860s, especially large ones with paisley designs. Jackets again came into vogue in the 1850s and 1860s, including fashions with fur-trimmed, fitted bodices and knee-length full skirts for winter and short summer styles that flared out over hooped skirts. It was also in this period that fur garments with the fur on the outside, not as a lining, were introduced. Another jacket fashion, the dolman, was cut to accommodate the bustles of the 1870s and 1880s. Although not as popular as jackets, full-length coats were worn from the 1870s to the early 1890s, later losing favor to capes during the mid-1890s revival of the leg-of-mutton sleeve. Throughout the century, muffs and tippets, fur or fur-trimmed neck wraps, accessorized stylish outerwear.

For men, the greatcoat continued as the most fashionable outerwear option until the 1840s. New styles appeared in mid-century, including the Inverness coat, a loose coat with an arm-length cape; and the paletot, a boxy, thigh-length jacket. From the 1830s to the 1890s, when men wore suits consisting of a skirted frock coat, a waistcoat, and trousers, the frock coat, although it was technically daywear, could also serve as outerwear except in severe weather. By the 1890s, the sack suit was replacing the frock suit for daywear and the sack suit jacket (the forerunner of modern men's suit jackets) was effective as lightweight outerwear. The winter overcoat of choice over both frock coats and sack suits was the Chesterfield, a topcoat cut similarly to a frock coat but longer, looser, and without a waist seam. Capes went out of style early in the century for daywear but endured as outerwear over formal evening wear.

Wool or fur outerwear provided significant protection from the cold for centuries, but similarly effective protection from rain was only made possible by technological advances in the nineteenth century. In 1823, Charles Macintosh, a Scottish chemist, patented the first viable waterproof fabric, consisting of two pieces of wool cemented together by rubber dissolved in coal-tar naphtha. This invention had great potential but had the serious drawbacks of becoming stiff in cold weather and sticky in hot. These problems were resolved when vulcanized rubber was invented in 1839 and Macintosh produced the first practical raincoats; in England, Macintosh or "Mac" raincoats are still worn today. From the mid-nineteenth century to today, further technological developments have led to man-made materials with increasingly effective waterproof and heat-retention properties, such as vinyl rainwear and acrylic furs.

Many forces shaped twentieth-century outerwear fashions. As in earlier centuries, the day and evening attire worn under the outerwear affected the look and cut of the overgarments, but sports, ethnic influences, the development of unisex styles, and new materials also played important roles. After centuries of predominance, capes were no longer the most ubiquitous outerwear garments. Men continued to wear capes for evening wear until mid-century, and women's capes were produced for both day and evening wear, but by the 1920s, capes constituted only a very minor part of the outerwear market. Throughout the century, the most basic outerwear options for both sexes were single- and double-breasted overcoats with notched collars. The men's versions often resembled their nineteenth-century precursors, while women had more diverse choices—coats fashioned in bright colors, new materials, and with contemporaneous style details such as padded shoulders.

Primarily worn by women, twentieth-century fur outerwear had a checkered record. Fur was a luxury item in the early 1900s, but fur and fur-trimmed garments became more affordable by mid-century due to the mass marketing of cheaper furs. In the 1960s, there was a fad for "fun furs"—inexpensive pelts, made up into a variety of trendy jackets and coats. However, escalating labor and material costs, plus the concerns of animal-rights activists, led to price increases and lessened popularity of real fur garments by the 1990s. Fortunately, refinements in man-made furs have allowed fur to continue its long-standing role in outerwear fashion.

The proliferation of new jacket styles for both sexes was the most significant outerwear development during the twentieth century. Whether ethnic-influenced anoraks and parkas, military-influenced pea and bomber jackets, or tailored blazers derived from men's suits, jackets are indispensable and versatile additions to everyone's outerwear wardrobe.

See also **Blazer; Coat; Duffle Coat; Jacket; Parka; Rainwear; Windbreaker.**

BIBLIOGRAPHY
There are no definitive secondary sources focusing on outerwear in all its forms. For a study of outerwear, general histories of dress plus histories of clothing in specific periods must be consulted. Some of the more helpful texts are included below.

Ashelford, Jane. *The Art of Dress: Clothes and Society, 1500–1914.* London: The National Trust Enterprises Limited, 1996. History of fashionable dress in which outerwear is regularly mentioned and illustrated.

Ashelford, Jane, ed. *The Visual History of Costume: The Sixteenth Century.* London: B.T. Batsford, Ltd., 1993.

Boucher, Francois. *20,000 Years of Fashion: The History of Costume and Personal Adornment.* New York: Harry N. Abrams, 1987. General history of costume in which outerwear garments are mentioned for each period from prehistory to 1947.

Ewing, Elizabeth. *Fur in Dress.* London: B.T. Batsford, Ltd., 1981. Provides a good overview of fur and fur-trimmed outerwear from prehistoric times to the 1970s.

The Visual History of Costume Series: *The Nineteenth Century* (Vanda Foster, 1984). London: B.T. Batsford, Ltd. Presents images with commentary on the clothing of the people in the pictures. Several images in each book depict outerwear.

Colleen R. Callahan

OXFORD MONK'S CLOTH. *See* **Weave, Plain.**

P

PAGNE AND WRAPPER The wrapper, called by the French word *le pagne* in Francophone West African countries, is a cloth about 59 inches by 98 inches (150 cm by 250 cm). In its main use, it is wrapped around the hips and rolled over on itself at the waist to form a skirt. Worn throughout West and Central Africa, it belongs to that large class of clothing that is not sewn but wrapped around the body. Found the world over, this class includes the sarong, kain, kanga, sari, shuka, and toga. Although traditionally made of strip or broadloom hand-woven cloth, wrappers can also be made of hand-dyed or factory-printed cotton, as well as silk and rayon.

Gendered and Ethnic Styles
In the seventeenth and eighteenth centuries, men wore wrappers, but by the twentieth century, they became, with a few notable exceptions, exclusively women's wear. Exceptions to this gender rule are certain ethnic groups, including the Kalabari, of Nigeria. Here men's formal dress includes an ankle-length wrapper worn with a long or short shirt, depending on one's rank. The outfit is topped with a bowler hat.

As women's wear, the wrapper usually comes to the ankle, but is worn with different upper garments in Francophone and Anglophone countries of West Africa. In Senegal and the neighboring Francophone countries Mali, Guinea, and Benin, the *pagne* is worn with elegant long garments, the *grand boubou* or a long, loose dress called the *ndoket*. A head-tie finishes the outfit. While these long garments hide most of the *pagne*, it is also worn with short garments: a loose blouse with puffed sleeves called the *marinière*, or a fitted top with a flounce at the hip and puffed sleeves called the *taille basse*. One graceful style in these countries is the two wrap or *deux pagnes*. With a *marinière* and one *pagne* worn as a long skirt, the second, matching *pagne* is wrapped tightly around the hips and tied.

Historical Changes in Style
In the early part of the twentieth century, when Senegalese women wore their *boubous* hip or knee length, the *pagne* was a stronger visual focus for both the aesthetics and the symbolism of dress. Cloth was a major form of wealth, as well as a principal medium of artistic expression. In order to show their status and taste, Senegalese women wore three *pagnes*, layered in three different lengths. The three contrasting *pagnes* were made of hand-woven, hand-dyed, and factory-printed fabrics. After World War II, the *grand boubou*, reaching almost to the ankles, came into fashion for women. The *pagne*, almost hidden, became less of a focal point. In the latter part of the twentieth century, elegant fashion demanded a single *pagne* of the same fabric as the boubou and head-tie, either richly dyed or in Holland wax.

Differences in Use of the *Pagne*
In Nigeria, where the upper garments are usually short, and where weaving and dyeing are complex arts, the wrapper has retained its strong visual focus in the overall outfit. Luxurious, handwoven either on strip looms or broad looms, intricately dyed with resist patterns, or in solid colors of rich silk, wrappers, called *Iro*, can be used in many styles. For elegant occasions they can be worn with a short overblouse of rich fabric, often of lace. In several ethnic groups, women dress for ceremonial occasions in a style called "up and down." For this outfit, two matching cloths are wrapped around the body, one at the waist, the other under the arms. They can also be wrapped at the waist, one knee length and one ankle length. In addition, urban women in Nigeria can adopt a style in which a handwoven wrapper is gathered around the middle of the body over a Western dress. The outfit is topped with a matching head-tie.

This overwrapper style differs from the *deux pagnes* in a way that epitomizes the differences in culture, nationality, and age. The overwrapper is a form of elegance worn by older married Nigerian women to demonstrate their wealth and social position, and is tied loosely around the waist to show off the expensive, heavy cloth, woven in stripes. The *deux pagnes* or two wrapper, by contrast, is made of either dyed or factory-printed cotton cloth that is lightweight, more supple, and clings to the body. The style is worn in West and Central Africa by younger women, whose body contours, graceful carriage, and swaying gait show themselves to good advantage in the tightly wrapped second *pagne*.

Cultural and Sexual Symbolism of *Pagnes*
In Senegal, a second, knee-length *pagne*, called in Wolof a *bethio*, is worn as an underskirt and seen only in intimate

meetings with a lover or husband. A focus of erotic fantasy and innuendo, the *bethio* plays a strong role in the art of seduction, for which Senegalese women are famous. It is also a product of women's craft. Usually in solid colors, and often white, the *bethio* is made of various hand-worked fabrics. One such fabric is a factory silk, or more often polyester, with hand-cut eyelet patterns and silver or gold embroidery. Another fabrication is made of percale, hand embroidered with heavy thread in bright colors. For a third fabrication, women crochet the *bethio* in fine yarn.

But most important, the *pagne* or wrapper, as an endlessly versatile piece of cloth, is symbolically fundamental to human culture itself. In Wolof, the principal African language of Senegal, the word for *pagne* is *séru*, which means simply "cloth." When a child is born, it is immediately wrapped in a *pagne*, and as an infant it is carried on its mother's back in a *pagne* wrapped around her upper body. When a woman in Senegal marries, her friends veil her head in a *pagne* before they take her on her journey to her husband's house. When a person dies, he or she must be wrapped in a white percale *pagne*. A symbol of wealth, sexuality, birth, death, and marriage, the *pagne* is a rich focus of visual aesthetics and multiple meanings.

See also **Africa, Sub-Saharan: History of Dress; Boubou.**

BIBLIOGRAPHY

Boilat, P.-David. *Esquisses sénégalaises; physionomie du pays, peuplades, commerce, religions, passé et avenir, récits et légendes.* Paris: P. Bertrand, 1853.

Eicher, Joanne Bubolz. *Nigerian Handcrafted Textiles.* Ile-Ife, Nigeria: University of Ife Press, 1976.

Eicher, Joanne Bubolz, and Tonye V. Erekosima. "Why Do They Call It Kalabari? Cultural Authentication and the Demarcation of Ethnic Identity." In *Dress and Ethnicity: Change across Space and Time.* Edited by Joanne B. Eicher. Oxford: Berg, 1995.

Heath, Deborah. "Fashion, Anti-Fashion, and Heteroglossia in Urban Senegal." *American Ethnologist* 19, no. 2 (1992): 19–33.

Mustafa, Huda Nura. "Sartorial Ecumenes: African Styles in a Social and Economic Context." In *The Art of African Fashion.* Edited by Els van der Plas and Marlous Willemson. Eritrea: Africa World Press (1998).

Perani, Judith, and Norma H. Wolff. *Cloth, Dress and Art Patronage in Africa.* New York: Berg, 1999.

Picton, John, and John Mack. *African Textiles.* New York: Harper and Row, 1989.

Picton, John, Rayda Becker, et al. *The Art of African Textiles: Technology, Tradition, and Lurex.* London: Barbican Art Gallery; Lund Humphries Publishers, 1995.

Rabine, Leslie W. "Dressing Up in Dakar." *L'Esprit créateur* 37, no. 1 (1997): 84–107.

———. *The Global Circulation of African Fashion.* Oxford: Berg, 2002.

Leslie W. Rabine

PAILLETTES. *See* **Spangles.**

PAISLEY The paisley pattern, though derived from Kashmir shawls and their European imitations, is a variant of an ancient and versatile design theme. The teardrop, or elongated oval with one end tapering to a point, can be traced back to Pharaonic, Chaldean, and Assyrian stone carvings, ancient Greek ceramics, and medieval Coptic, Central Asian, and European textiles. It features variously as lotus bud, tree-of-life, ivy or acanthus leaf, cone, palm frond or cypress, occasionally with the bent-over tip that is the paisley's defining characteristic.

As we know it today, however, the paisley emerged much later, in the shawl design of Kashmir, and perhaps contemporaneously in Persia, in the *termeh*, the woven shawls of Meshad, Kerman, and Yazd. It developed out of the single, somewhat naturalistic bloom, a restrained and graceful form that in the seventeenth century became the favorite motif of Mughal courtly art. Applied to the shawl fabrics for which Kashmir and Persia were already famous, the single flower evolved into a bush, or a bouquet of flowers, growing ever more elaborate and stylized. By about the second half of the eighteenth century, it assumed its characteristic shape, becoming, in myriad variations, the predominant motif of shawl design. In Kashmir it is usually called *buta* (Persian *boteh*, a shrub); and one version is still called *shah-pasand*, or "emperor's favorite," indicating that royal patronage may have played some part in popularizing it. It was quickly incorporated in textile design elsewhere in India, where it is known as *kalgi* or *kalga* (plume), *badam* (almond), or *ambi* (mango).

By the end of the eighteenth century, imported Kashmir shawls had become high fashion in Europe—as accessories to women's attire rather than shoulder mantles for men, Indian-style. British entrepreneurs started experimenting with "imitation Indian shawls" in the last decades of the century, first in Edinburgh, then in Norwich, copying or adapting the Kashmir designs.

As demand grew, Edinburgh shawl manufacturers started outsourcing work to Paisley which, as home to a long-established textile industry, had a pool of skilled weavers capable of drawing on the experience of Norwich, Edinburgh, and various shawl-manufacturing centers in France, and could take advantage of technological developments, particularly the Jacquard loom. This adaptability, together with good management and easy access to imported raw materials through the ports of the Clyde made Paisley shawls so competitive that in time they eclipsed those of the other British centers. By the mid-nineteenth century, in the English-speaking world, the term "paisley" had become synonymous with shawls, and by extension with the *buta* design, whether used on shawls or elsewhere.

The paisley retained its popularity even after the shawl fashion came to an end in the 1870s, partly due to the famous London store Liberty's, many of whose trademark printed fabrics used designs derived from shawl-pattern books. In the twenty-first century, it features textiles destined to be made up into clothes—from saris and shawls in India to dresses, ties, and scarves in the West—as well as on furnishing materials, bone china, and indeed almost any item that calls for a "traditional" form of decoration. Its popularity has endured across the board, from high fashion to high-street kitsch (especially in Scotland). But it does seem a pity that it has come to be known by the name of a town whose weavers—though responsible for popularizing it—made no significant contribution to its development, rather than by any of the names indigenous to the region where it originated.

See also **Asia, South: History of Dress; Cashmere and Pashmina; Shawls.**

BIBLIOGRAPHY

Ames, Frank. *The Kashmir Shawl.* Woodbridge, U.K.: Antique Collectors' Club, 1986: 2nd ed., 1997.

Clabburn, Pamela. *Shawls.* Risborough, U.K.: Shire Publications, 2nd ed., 2002.

Falke, O. von. *Decorative Silks.* London: B.T. Batsford, Ltd., 1922.

Reilly, Valerie. *Paisley Patterns: A Design Source Book.* London: Studio Editions, 1989.

Rossbach, Ed. *The Art of Paisley.* New York and London: Van Nostrand Reinhold Company, 1980.

Skelton, Robert. "A Decorative Motif in Mughal Art." In *Aspects of Indian Art.* Edited by P. Pal. Leiden: Brill, 1972.

Janet Rizvi and Jasleen Dhamija

PAJAMAS Pajamas are a garment for sleeping or lounging worn by men, women, and children. Pajamas may be one-piece or two-piece garments, but always consist of loosely fitting pants of various widths and lengths. While pajamas are traditionally viewed as utilitarian garments, they are often a reflection of the fashionable silhouette and the image of the exotic "other" in popular imagination.

The word pajama comes from the Hindi "pae jama" or "pai jama," meaning leg clothing, and its usage dates back to the Ottoman Empire. Alternate spellings include: paejamas, paijamas, pyjamas, and the abbreviated pj's. Pajamas were traditionally loose drawers or trousers tied at the waist with a drawstring or cord, and they were worn by both sexes in India, Iran, Pakistan, and Bangladesh. Pajamas could be either tight fitting throughout the entire leg, or very full at waist and knees with tightness at calves and ankles. They were usually worn with a belted tunic extending to the knees. Although the word is Hindi, similar garments are found in traditional costume throughout the Middle and Far East.

Pajamas were adopted by Europeans while in these countries, and brought back as exotic loungewear. Although the wearing of pajamas was not widespread until the twentieth century, they were appropriated as early as the seventeenth century as a signifier of status and worldly knowledge.

Pajamas as Sleepwear

Pajamas are generally thought to have been introduced to the Western world about 1870, when British colonials, who had adopted them as an alternative to the traditional nightshirt, continued the practice upon their return. By the end of the nineteenth century, the term *pajama* was being used to describe a two-piece garment: both the pajamas (trousers) and the jacket-styled top worn with them.

By 1902, men's pajamas were widely available alongside more traditional nightshirts and were available in fabrics like flannel and madras and had lost most of their exotic connotations. Pajamas were considered modern and suitable for an active lifestyle. The advertising copy in the 1902 *Sears, Roebuck Catalogue* suggested that they were: "Just the thing for traveling, as their appearance admits a greater freedom than the usual kind of nightshirts" (p. 966).

The streamlined, often androgynous fashions during the 1920s helped to popularize the wearing of pajamas by women. While men's pajamas were invariably made of cotton, silk, or flannel, women's examples were often made of brightly printed silk or rayon and trimmed with ribbons and lace. Early examples featured a raised or natural waist with voluminous legs gathered at the ankle in a "Turkish trouser" style, while later examples featured straight legs and dropped waists, a reflection of the 1920s silhouette. Throughout the century, pajamas would continue to reflect the fashionable ideal. The 1934 film *It Happened One Night*, which featured a scene in which Claudette Colbert wears a pair of men's pajamas, helped to popularize the menswear-styled pajama for women.

By the 1940s, women were wearing "shortie" pajamas, which would later develop into the "baby doll" pajama. The typical baby-doll pajama consisted of a sleeveless smock-style top with a frill at the hem, and balloon panties frilled at the leg openings. By the mid-1960s, baby-doll pajamas were standard summer nightwear for millions of girls and women.

With the popularity of unisex styling during the 1970s, pajamas were often menswear inspired. Tailored satin pajamas had been popular since the 1920s but were rediscovered during this period by both men and women. In this decade, ethnic styles based on the traditional dress of Vietnam and China were worn as antifashion and a statement about the wearer's political views. This trend toward unisex and ethnic remains to this day and is particularly apparent in women's fashions, where the division between dress and undress has become blurred.

Pajamas as Fashion

This blurring of these boundaries began long ago. Women had begun experimenting with the adaptation

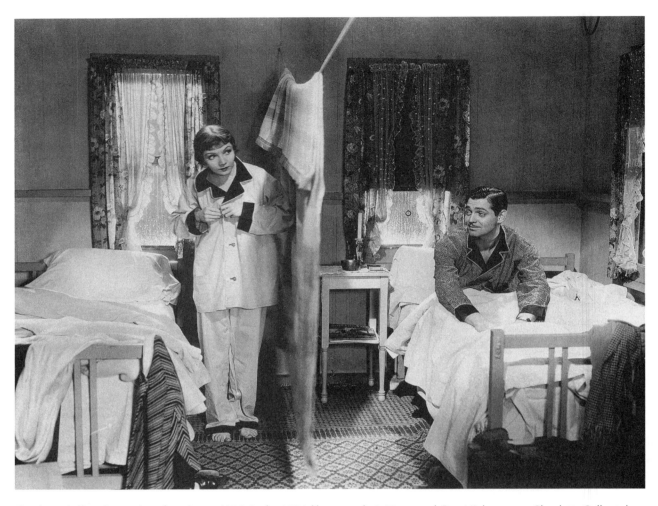

Claudette Colbert in men's-style pajama, 1934. In the 1934 film comedy *It Happened One Night,* actress Claudette Colbert dons a pair of men's-style pajamas in a bedroom scene with Clark Gable. This famous scene popularized the men's pajama look among women. © BETTMANN/CORBIS. REPRODUCED BY PERMISSION.

of pajama-style trousers since the eighteenth century, but this was associated with masquerade costume, actresses, and prostitution, not with respectable women. In 1851, Amelia Jenks Bloomer (1818–1894), an American feminist, adopted voluminous "Turkish trousers" worn with a knee-length skirt as an alternative to fashionable dress. The response to her appearance was overwhelmingly negative, and the "Bloomer Costume" failed to gain acceptance.

Pajamas began to be adapted into fashionable dress in the early years of the twentieth century when avant-garde designers promoted them as an elegant alternative to the tea gown. French couturier Paul Poiret launched pajama styles for both day and evening as early as 1911, and his influence played a large role in their eventual acceptance.

Beach pajamas, which were worn by the seaside and for walking on the boardwalk, were popularized by

Gabrielle "Coco" Chanel in the early 1920s. The first beach pajamas were worn by the adventuresome few, but by the end of the decade had become acceptable dress for the average woman. Evening pajamas, intended to be worn as a new type of costume for informal dining at home, also became widely accepted during this decade. Evening pajamas would remain popular throughout the 1930s and would reemerge in the 1960s in the form of "palazzo pajamas."

Palazzo pajamas were introduced by the Roman designer Irene Galitzine in 1960 for elegant but informal evening dress. They greatly influenced fashion during the 1960s and continued into the casual 1970s. Palazzo pajamas featured extremely wide legs and were often made of soft silk and decorated with beading and fringe. During the 1970s, eveningwear and loungewear merged, as evening styles became increasingly simple and unstructured. Halston was particularly known for his bias-cut pantsuits of satin and crepe, which he referred to as "pajama dressing." In light of this, popular magazines suggested readers shop in the lingerie departments for their eveningwear.

This increased informality of dress has made the evening pajama a staple in modern fashion, and the Asian influence on designers like Ralph Lauren and Giorgio Armani has blurred the boundaries between dress and undress even further. It is likely that this trend will continue well into the twenty-first century.

See also **Lingerie; Trousers; Unisex Clothing.**

BIBLIOGRAPHY

Calasibetta, Charlotte. *The Fairchild Dictionary of Fashion.* New York: Fairchild Publications, 1983.

Ewing, Elizabeth. *History of Twentieth Century Fashion.* Lanham, Md.: Barnes and Noble Books, 1992.

Gross, Elaine, and Fred Rottman. *Halston: An American Original.* New York: HarperCollins Publishers, 1999.

Kidwell, Claudia Brush, and Valerie Steele. *Men and Women: Dressing the Part.* Washington, D.C.: Smithsonian Institution Press, 1989.

Probert, Christina. *Swimwear in Vogue since 1910.* New York: Abbeville Press, 1981.

Sears, Roebuck Catalogue, 1902 Edition. New York: Gramercy Books, 1993 (reprint).

Wilcox, R. Turner. *The Dictionary of Costume.* New York: Macmillan Publishing Company, 1969.

Yarwood, Doreen. *The Encyclopedia of World Costume.* New York: Charles Scribner's Sons, 1978.

Clare Sauro

PANNIERS. *See* **Skirt Supports.**

PANTIES Underpants or drawers, known colloquially as "panties," were first worn during the Renaissance for function but were also used as a chastity device. They were described at the time as "helping women keep clean and protecting them from the cold, they prevent the thighs being seen if they fall off a horse. These drawers also protect them against adventurous young men, because if they slip their hands under their skirts they can't touch their skin at all" (Saint-Laurent, p. 65). As a result of their direct contact with the female genitals, underpants were considered the most risqué of garments, so much so that it was considered almost more immodest to wear them than not, as they not only concealed but also drew attention to the vagina. Thus, until the mid-nineteenth century, they were primarily worn by prostitutes and by little girls.

By 1841, however, *The Handbook of the Toilet* suggested that French drawers were "of incalculable advantage to women, preventing many of the disorders and indispositions to which … females are subject. The drawers may be of flannel, calico, or cotton, and should reach as far down the leg as possible without their being seen" (Carter, p. 46). Underpants were variously known as drawers, knickers (derived from the original knickerbocker), smalls, britches, and step-ins. Nineteenth-century drawers were designed so that each leg of the garment was separate and the crotch was either open or sewn closed. By the end of World War I, as skirts became shorter, underpants became scantier. Thus in the 1920s, underpants were much smaller than in the nineteenth century.

Outside the realm of erotica and the burlesque theater, underpants were intended to be hidden garments. During the Wimbledon Tennis Championships in 1949, tennis player Gertrude Moran took to the court wearing a short tennis dress, designed by Teddy Tinling, that revealed a pair of ruffled lace-trimmed knickers. This apparel made headlines around the world as a very daring fashion statement. One of the seminal panty moments of post–World War II film saw Marilyn Monroe revealing her underpants when a draft from a subway grating blew up her skirt in the film *The Seven Year Itch* (1955).

The 1960s saw the development of matching bra and brief sets, disposable paper panties, and the bikini brief. In the 1990s, a new fashion for thong underwear became popular. More recently, boy-style underwear briefs have come into fashion for women. By the 1990s the meaning of panties had completely changed. Previously they had to be hidden at all costs but in this decade it became fashionable to wear big waist high pants under the transparent outerwear designs of Gianni Versace or Dolce & Gabbana. The deliberately non-sexual look of the pants diffused the potential vulgarity of the clothes above.

See also **Brassiere; Lingerie; Underwear.**

BIBLIOGRAPHY

Carter, Alison. *Underwear: The Fashion History.* London: B.T. Batsford, Ltd. New York: Drama Book Publishers, 1992.

Chenoune, Farid. *Beneath It All: A Century of French Lingerie.* New York: Rizzoli, 1999.

Saint-Laurent, Cecil. *The Great Book of Lingerie.* London: Academy Editions, 1986.

Caroline Cox

PAPER DRESSES The paper dress enjoyed a brief but lively vogue in the late 1960s as a novelty fashion item. A simple, above-the-knee length chemise, constructed from nonwoven cellulose tissue reinforced with rayon or nylon, the inexpensive "paper" garment featured bold printed designs and was meant to be discarded after a few wearings.

Individual paper clothes and accessories existed as early as the nineteenth century, when paper was especially popular for masquerade costumes. The first modern paper dress is credited to the Scott Paper Company of Philadelphia, which introduced it as a 1966 mail-in promotion. Consumers were invited to send in a coupon from a Scott product, along with $1.25, in order to receive a "Paper Caper" dress made of Dura-Weve, a material the company had patented in 1958. The dress boasted either a striking black-and-white Op Art pattern or a red bandanna print. Scott's sales pitch underscored its transience: "Won't last forever…who cares? Wear it for kicks—then give it the air."

The campaign was unexpectedly successful, generating 500,000 shipments and stimulating other manufacturers to promote paper garments. Within a year of Scott's promotion, paper fashions were on sale in major department stores. Some, such as Abraham & Strauss and I. Magnin, created entire paper clothing boutiques. At the height of the craze, Mars Hosiery of Asheville, N.C., was reportedly manufacturing 100,000 dresses a week.

A big factor in the appeal of the dresses was their eye-catching patterns—daisies, zigzags, animal prints, stripes—that suggested Pop Art. Some imagery made the dresses akin to walking billboards, showcasing ads for *Time* magazine, Campbell's Soup cans, political candidates, and poster-sized photographs. Fun and fashion-forward, the dresses could be hemmed with scissors or colored with crayons. And, at about $8 apiece they were affordable, inspiring *Mademoiselle* magazine editors to exclaim in June 1967: "The paper dress is the ultimate smart-money fashion" (p. 99).

Modern, whimsical, and disposable, paper garments captured the 1960s zeitgeist. It was a time when new industrial materials like plastics and metallic fibers were making inroads, Rudi Gernreich and Paco Rabanne were pushing the limits of clothing design, and the post-World War II baby boomers were in the throes of a vibrant youth culture centered on fashion and music. Consumers accepted the notion of cheap, throwaway clothing as they embraced disposable cutlery, plates, razors, napkins, lighters, and pens. The fashion press even predicted that paper garments might take over the marketplace.

Instead, by 1968 paper dresses had lost their currency. Wearers found they could be ill-fitting and uncomfortable, the printed surfaces could rub off, and there were concerns about flammability and excessive post-consumer waste. Plus, they had simply lost their cutting-edge appeal due to overexposure.

However, the dresses' paperlike cellulose fabric was adapted as a practical and lightweight material for disposable garments for hospital and factory workers. And the legacy of the 1960s paper dress continues to inspire contemporary fashion designers like Yeohlee and Vivienne Tam, whose spring 1999 collection featured a line of clothes constructed from DuPont Tyvek, the reinforced paper used in overnight mail envelopes.

See also **Fads; Gernreich, Rudi; Rabanne, Paco.**

BIBLIOGRAPHY

Palmer, Alexandra. "Paper Clothes: Not Just a Fad," In *Dress and Popular Culture*. Ohio: Bowling Green State University Popular Press, 1991, pp. 85–105.

"Paper Profits." *Mademoiselle* June 1967, 99–101.

Szabo, Julia. "Pulp Fashion Continues to Inspire," *New York Daily News*, May 30, 1999.

Internet Resources

"Paper Dress, 1966." Available from <http://www.consumerreports.org>.

Kimberly-Clark. "1966, The Paper Caper Dress." Available from <http://www.kimberly-clark.com/aboutus/paper_dresses .asp>.

Kathleen Paton

PAQUIN, JEANNE Jeanne Paquin (1869–1936) was the first woman to gain international celebrity in the fashion business. Her design career spanned the three decades from 1891 to 1920. She was born Jeanne Marie Charlotte Beckers in l'Ile Saint-Denis, on the outskirts of Paris. As a young girl she was employed at a local dressmaker's shop and then became a seamstress at the distinguished Parisian firm of Maison Rouff. In February 1891 she married Isidore Rene Jacob *dit* Paquin (legally changed to Paquin in 1899), a former banker and businessman. One month before their marriage he founded the House of Paquin at 3, rue de la Paix, where for two years prior he was a partner in a couture business under the name of Paquin Lalanne et Cie. Creating a new business model, with Madame as head designer and her husband as business administrator, the couple built a couture business whose worldwide scope and stylistic influence were unparalleled during the early years of the twentieth century. Their innovative approaches to marketing and youthful yet sumptuous design aesthetic attracted fashionable women of the world who were poised for a new fashion image at the end of the Victorian era. The diverse and prestigious client list included famous actresses and courtesans, European royals, and the wives of American business tycoons such as Rockefeller, Astor, Vanderbilt, Ballantine, and Wannamaker. At its height the house employed more than two thousand workers, surpassing even the house of Worth. In 1907 Isidore Paquin died suddenly, leaving Jeanne Paquin to head their fashion empire alone. Her half brother, Henri Joire, and his wife, Suzanne, joined her as partners in 1911. She retired in 1920 and eleven years later married Jean-Baptiste Noulens, a French diplomat. The House of Paquin remained open under a series of designers, until it merged with Worth in 1954. Worth-Paquin closed in 1956.

Business Innovations

Astute and inventive in their approaches to doing business, the Paquins originated practices that later became standard operating procedures in the fashion world. Most sweeping was the concept of international expansion through opening foreign branches. In 1896 the house opened a full-scale branch in London, the first of its kind, where designs from the Paris house were produced in ateliers on the local premises. A branch in Buenos Aires and a fur establishment in New York followed in 1912, and a final branch opened in Madrid in 1914.

The Paquins also took bold initiatives in the areas of client relations and marketing. From the very beginning, in contrast to the aloof approach of their contemporaries, the Paquins developed personal relationships with their clients that addressed their individual personalities and scheduling needs. Harnessing from the outset the power of glamour and entertainment to promote clothing, they sent beautiful young actresses to the opera and the races dressed in their newest models, several often wearing the same dress. Later, Madame introduced all-white ballet finales at her fashion shows, and in 1913 produced "dress parades" of dresses designed specifically for dancing the tango at the popular "Tango Teas" held on Monday afternoons at the palace in London. In 1914 she sent her entire spring collection on an American tour, which included New York, Philadelphia, Boston, Pittsburgh, and Chicago. The fashions were modeled by Paquin's own mannequins who astonished the public by wearing mauve and pink wigs on the street.

Personal Image and Acknowledgments

Beautiful, chic, intelligent, and charismatic, Paquin was herself the best publicist for her own style. She always wore her own designs, and, widely admired by the public, was the first woman to become a fashion icon, establishing the precedent for Gabrielle Chanel. Equally acclaimed for her business skills, she received numerous awards and appointments, all firsts for a woman in her time. In 1900 her fellow couturiers selected her to head their first collective public display of couture at the great Paris Universal Exposition. She was awarded the Order of Leopold II of Belgium in 1910 and the prestigious Légion d'honneur in the field of commerce in 1913, and was elected president of the Chambre syndicale de la couture, the official organization of Parisian couturiers, in 1917.

Clothing Designs and Artistic Hallmarks

The house offered a full range of garments that included fashions for all occasions—chic *tailleurs* (suits) for day wear; extravagant outerwear, especially evening wraps; and sporting clothes, which were sold in a special department opened in 1912 at the London branch. Opulent furs and fur-trimmed garments were always a specialty. Paquin clothes were renowned for their imaginative design, superb craftsmanship, and incomparable artistry. A brilliant artist and colorist, Paquin created breathtaking visual effects with color, light, texture, and tonal nuance that ranged from an ethereal luminescence in the filmy, pastel dresses fashionable from 1900 to 1910, to a bold vibrancy in the Oriental-inspired creations that

Illustration of woman wearing Paquin evening dress. Jeanne Paquin's imaginative and striking designs, coupled with her savvy business acumen, made her the first female couturier to gain international renown. © STEPLETON COLLECTION/CORBIS. REPRODUCED BY PERMISSION.

followed. Extant examples of these clothes are some of the most stunning works of art in fabric ever created. Signature techniques to achieve these effects, especially in the earlier pieces, included layering, blending, and veiling filmy and textural materials of subtly varying hues; orchestrating the play of light on a garment's surface by juxtaposing trims and fabrics having differing light-reflective qualities, often outlining them with contrasting piping or chenille; and building up surface design

[Sometimes] ... it is the material that inspires me. But I get inspiration everywhere. When I am travelling or walking in the street, when I see a sunset with beautiful blendings of colour, I often get an inspiration that helps me to evolve new combinations.... Our work in some respects resembles that of the painter.

Jeanne Paquin in *Designs and Publicite*, 1913.

Woman in a day dress by Jeanne Paquin. As the fashion capital of the Western world through the eighteenth century, Paris drew wealthy foreigners who came to have their clothes tailor made to copy the latest Paris fashions. COURTESY SPECIAL COLLECTIONS, FASHION INSTITUTE OF TECHNOLOGY. REPRODUCED BY PERMISSION.

While her artistry in visual effects and composition was unsurpassed, Paquin also designed for function and comfort. Through her promotion of these principles, she was a significant force in moving fashion towards the modern style that took hold in the 1920s. She herself frequently wore a practical, ankle-length, blue serge suit for work. By 1905 she was already aggressively promoting the more natural and less restrictive empire line that established the context for Paul Poiret's radical versions of 1908. Between 1912 and 1920 she designed clothes for the active woman, such as a gown that combined tailoring with draping, so that it could appropriately be worn from day into evening, and a version of the hobble skirt that kept the narrow line but allowed for ease of movement with the invention of hidden pleats.

Paquin's contributions in the areas of business, public persona, art, and design firmly establish her place in fashion history as the first great woman couturier.

See also **Fashion Designer; Paris Fashion; Spangles; Worth, Charles Frederick.**

BIBLIOGRAPHY

Buxbaum, Gerda, ed. *Icons of Fashion: The Twentieth Century.* Munich, London, and New York: Prestel Verlag, 1999.

McAlpin, W. L. "Mme. Paquin Honoured. A Famous Dressmaker and Her Methods." In *Designs and Publicite.* By Jeanne Paquin. Volume 336. Unpublished scrapbook, 1913.

Reeder, Jan Glier. "The House of Paquin." *Textile and Text* 12 (1990): 10–18.

———. "Historical and Cultural References in Clothes from the House of Paquin." *Textile and Text* 13 (1991): 15–22.

Sirop, Dominique. *Paquin.* Paris: Adam Biro, 1989.

Steele, Valerie. *Women of Fashion: Twentieth-Century Designers.* New York: Rizzoli International, 1991.

Troy, Nancy J. *Couture Culture: A Study in Modern Art and Fashion.* Cambridge, Mass.: The MIT Press, 2003.

Jan Glier Reeder

motifs with dense encrustations of the smallest possible decorative elements, paying minute attention to size gradation and variation of placement. Endless varieties of gleaming paillettes, beads, and sequins; finely worked shirring and ruching box-pleated ribbon trim; padded appliqué; silk-wound beads; and spotted net were some of the favorite materials used to imbue the gowns with the uniquely Paquin visual quality. Other hallmarks were unorthodox combinations of materials, such as chiffon with serge in a tailored suit and strips of fur on a filmy, pastel evening gown. Always seeking novelty and individualism for her designs, Paquin frequently incorporated elements from other eras and cultures into her contemporary designs, as in a 1912 opera coat fashioned from fabric derived from the eighteenth century and draped like a Roman toga. Her signature accent color was a brilliant pink, and she was famous for her dramatic use of black, both as an accent and as a chic color in its own right. Neoclassicism was a favorite design motif.

PARIS FASHION Paris has been the fashion capital of the Western world from the seventeenth century to the twenty-first century, although other cities, such as New York, London, and Milan, also have become important centers of fashion. The clothes we wear today owe a great deal to Paris, even if they were designed (and almost certainly manufactured) elsewhere in the world.

Prior to the rise of the modern nation-state fashions were geographically dispersed, with loci in Florence and other powerful Italian city-states as well as at the courts of Burgundy and Spain. But France emerged from the end of the Thirty Years' War, in 1648, as by far the largest, richest, and most powerful state in Europe, and the rulers of France—most notably Louis XIV (reigned 1643–1715)—understood that fashion was a potent weapon in establishing France's cultural preeminence. Louis XIV exercised control over his aristocrats by requiring that all who were in attendance at his new court at Versailles be dressed in appropriate fashions. At the same time the king's chief minister, Jean-Baptiste Colbert, recognized the growing economic importance of textiles and clothing and harnessed the power of the state to France's fashion leadership.

By the eighteenth century, wealthy foreigners were traveling to Paris to have their clothes made, or they employed seamstresses and tailors to copy the latest Paris fashions (which were described in the newspapers of the day), exclaiming all the while at how quickly the fashions changed, how expensive everything was, and how outré the fashions had become. These intertwined themes—eagerness to follow the latest Paris fashions, and outrage over their extravagance, expense, and immorality—were to characterize foreigners' attitudes toward Paris fashion for centuries. Meanwhile, the high-quality tailoring of London (where men's dress was increasingly based on country and sporting clothing, rather than on "Frenchified" court fashions) began to make its influence felt on the continent, and men of fashion throughout the Western world began to dress in English style.

The leadership of Paris in women's fashions accelerated during the nineteenth century, with the rise of what became known as the haute couture. It was not merely that the arts of fine sewing, cutting, and the myriad other techniques necessary for the production of fine garments flourished in Paris. The structure of the industry also evolved, as dressmaking moved from being a small-scale craft to a big business. Prior to the middle of the nineteenth century there were no fashion designers, as such. Dressmakers, assisted by specialized skilled workers, collaborated with their clients to produce garments in the latest styles (which were widely publicized in the burgeoning fashion press). The first true couturier was the Englishman Charles Frederick Worth, a dynamic and enterprising man whose skills at clothing design and dressmaking were matched by his skills for merchandising and self-promotion. He portrayed himself as an artist and an arbiter of taste, whose function was to understand what his clients should wear and to dress them accordingly—a far cry from the old system under which dressmakers basically executed their customers' orders. Meanwhile, the new Paris of grand boulevards shone even more brightly as the setting for fashionable display.

Worth was the first of many designers who took Paris fashion in the direction of the haute couture, the pinnacle of custom dressmaking. But fashion also evolved simultaneously toward the production of *confection*, ready-made dresses, and other garments made for sale in the innovative department stores where items were attractively displayed and clearly marked with fixed prices. In these stores, shopping became a form of recreation that made affordable versions of fashionable dress available to a broad segment of the city's population. By the late nineteenth century, the garment industry, embracing both couture and *confection*, and including ancillary activities such as distribution, merchandising, journalism, and illustration, was one of Paris's most important industries,

Paquin day dress, 1903. Jeanne Paquin established a successful couture business that enjoyed unparalled influence during the first half of the twentieth century. COLLECTION OF VALERIE STEELE. PHOTOGRAPH BY JOHN S. MAJOR. REPRODUCED BY PERMISSION.

employing tens of thousands of workers and making a major contribution to the French national economy. This was recognized in French government backing for efforts to publicize Paris fashions in world markets; for example, fashion was prominently featured in numerous international exhibitions held in Paris.

Paul Poiret was the most influential fashion designer of the early twentieth century, to be followed in the 1920s by Gabrielle (Coco) Chanel, whose dresses redefined elegance as understatement. Chanel had many competitors, however, including Madeleine Vionnet, Jeanne Lanvin, and Elsa Schiaparelli. In the years between the two wars designers (mostly women) created styles that were feminine and body-conscious, and imitated all over the world.

New techniques contributed to the rapid dissemination of Paris fashions throughout the world. Whereas in the nineteenth century clients were shown sample dresses and fitted for their own garments in the privacy of couturier's showrooms, by the early twentieth century the fashion show, with its now-familiar parade of models wearing the season's new outfits, had become the standard means by which designers introduced their new collections. News of the latest fashions was quickly relayed to magazines and newspapers abroad, and copyists worked overtime to sketch the new designs for production in less expensive ready-to-wear versions. Fashion photography, which by the end of the 1930s had decisively displaced fashion illustration as the preferred means of representing fashion in editorial and advertising copy, also gave rapid publicity to new designs.

World War II and the German occupation of Paris dealt a severe blow to Paris's fashion leadership. Many couture houses shut down for the duration of the war. Those that remained in business found both materials and customers in short supply. Even worse, the vital American market threatened to go its own way, as sportswear designers such as Claire McCardell made a virtue of "the American Look" during this hiatus in Parisian fashion leadership. With the end of the war, the reestablishment of the fashion industry was one of the top priorities of the new French government. With Christian Dior and the creation of the New Look in 1947, Paris found its champion of reasserted fashion leadership.

Dior and his contemporaries, such as Jacques Fath and Hubert de Givenchy, represented a new development in the fashion business. Unlike many of the women designers of the between-the-wars years, whose companies were often very small, these male designers (and a few women, most notably Chanel) were at the helm of large, well-funded corporations, equipped to compete in a new climate of international trade and finance. In addition to their couture collections, they also licensed their names to American manufacturers who produced less expensive lines and ancillary products.

The new reign of Paris did not last long, however. In the early 1960s the "Youthquake" fashions of Carnaby Street turned all eyes on London. Self-taught English designers such as Mary Quant popularized the miniskirt and other "mod" styles. Since the French lacked a youth culture comparable to that of England and America, French couturiers, such as André Courrèges, had to develop a stylistic equivalent. At first, the future served as a metaphor for youth, in the space-age styles of Courrèges and Pierre Cardin. Ultimately, however, the most successful designer to emerge in Paris was the young Yves Saint Laurent, who had formerly worked for Dior.

Saint Laurent was attuned to influences coming from "the street" and from popular culture. Over the next decade, he introduced a number of radical styles, including trouser suits for women, pop-art dresses, safari jackets, pea coats, and other styles derived from vernacular clothing, and, perhaps most importantly, ethnic styles, which drew on the antifashion sensibility of the hippies. Saint Laurent also recognized that many of the women who most appreciated his clothes were too young (and not rich enough) to buy couture, so he also launched a

ready-to-wear line called Rive Gauche (Left Bank). At the same time, however, he reinvigorated the French couture at a time when it seemed to many to be increasingly irrelevant. The 1970s also witnessed the flourishing of Paris *Vogue*, which published controversial fashion photographs by Guy Bourdin and Helmut Newton.

Nevertheless, both New York and Milan became increasingly important centers of fashion during the 1970s. French fashion was regarded as creative and prestigious, but many international consumers preferred the luxurious sportswear created by Italian designers such as Giorgio Armani and the minimalist styles associated with Americans such as Halston. Meanwhile, new subcultural styles—notably punk—developed in London, where Vivienne Westwood dressed bands like the Sex Pistols in deliberately aggressive styles. Paris began to seem a little old-fashioned.

Yet Paris came to the forefront again in the 1980s and 1990s, both because of the revival of famous French brands, and because designers from around the world chose to show their collections in Paris. The house of Chanel, which had been in the doldrums even before Chanel herself died in 1971, became fashionable again in 1983, when the owners hired the German-born designer Karl Lagerfeld. Lagerfeld irreverently revised Chanel's iconic images, exaggerating details and introducing new materials, such as denim and chiffon, to a house long associated with proper tweed suits. Simultaneously, Paris witnessed the invasion of avant-garde Japanese designers such as Yohji Yamamoto and Rei Kawakubo of Comme des Garçons, who launched a radically new style, featuring oversized, asymmetrical, black garments, which were enthusiastically adopted by an influential minority of men and women, mostly associated with the arts. Christian Lacroix launched a new couture house in 1987, showing pouf skirts inspired by Westwood's mini-crinis.

Similarly, in the 1990s, houses such as Dior and Givenchy imported designers from London. John Galliano almost single-handedly transformed Dior with his wild yet commercially successful styles. Alexander McQueen, on the other hand, left Givenchy to establish his own company (backed by Gucci). Significantly, however, McQueen almost always chose to show his collections in Paris, because the Paris fashion shows attracted more journalists than the shows in New York or London. After Saint Laurent retired, the American Tom Ford briefly took artistic control at the famous French house, while also maintaining control at the Italian fashion company Gucci. A host of Belgian designers also showed in Paris, and even many Italian designers, such as Versace and Valentino, moved back and forth between Milan (or Rome) and Paris. As fashion becomes ever more international, the Paris shows now include increasing numbers of designers from countries as diverse as Brazil and Korea.

The globalization of textile and garment manufacturing is changing the economics of the entire fashion system, but the couture, which really exists only in Paris, retains its prestige and helps to drive an array of luxury goods from perfume to handbags and ready-to-wear lines. Continuing a tradition established many years ago by the Englishman Charles Frederick Worth and the Italian Elsa Schiaparelli, many of the most influential designers in Paris (such as Karl Lagerfeld and John Galliano) are not French. But whatever their country of origin, these designers live and work in Paris. Fashion journalists today have become accustomed to making an exhausting round of fashion shows in New York, Milan, Paris, and London. Even though another city might become paramount during some seasons, Paris remains generally acknowledged as the most important fashion city.

See also **Haute Couture; Italian Fashion; London Fashion; New Look.**

BIBLIOGRAPHY

Milbank, Caroline Rennolds. *Couture: The Great Designers.* New York: Stewart, Tabori, and Chang, 1985.

Steele, Valerie. *Paris Fashion: A Cultural History.* 2nd ed. Oxford: Berg, 1998.

Valerie Steele and John S. Major

PARKA A parka is a loose-fitting hooded piece of outerwear invented in prehistoric times by the Inuit people living near the Arctic Circle. Traditionally, and most commonly, made from caribou and sealskins, parkas are also known to have been made from polar-bear fur, bird skins, fox fur, and salmon skins. Today, parkas worn in the non-Inuit world are usually made of nylon, polyester/cotton blended fabric, cotton, or wool, and given a water-repellent coating. The parka has become an item of fashionable winter wear.

History

Although the design is of Inuit invention, the word *parka* is of Russian derivation, meaning "reindeer fur coat." With the Inuit people of Canada's Arctic region living in some of the planet's most extreme climates, the parka, like many pieces of outerwear, was originally designed to provide warmth for its wearer. Often two parkas would be worn together (one with the fur facing outward, the other, fur inward) to allow for better insulation and air circulation even in the coldest of temperatures. But although several layers may be worn, the parka remains a fully functional garment, as Betty Kobayashi Issenman explains in *Sinews of Survival*:

> The cut and tailoring of Inuit costume create garments that are loose yet fitted when necessary and that admirably meet the requirements of hunter and mother. Hood construction with its close fit and drawstring, ensures clear peripheral vision. Capacious shoulders allow the wearer to carry out complex tasks (p. 40).

It was this ease of movement and the ability to withstand subzero temperatures that led the U.S. army to adopt and adapt the Inuit-styled parka to suit its own needs during World War II.

The prototype field cotton parka was a long skirted, hooded jacket that formed the windproof outer shell for severe conditions. The field parka . . . was standardised after shortening to raise the lower closure to waist level. The longer version was modified by adding fur trimming to the hood (p. 188).

The later nylon-cotton mix M1951, available in olive and white colors, was developed to include a removable mohair liner, snap-fastened fly front, adjustable cuffs, and split lower-back sections, and was filled with quilted nylon.

In the mid-1960s, benefiting from fabric developments initiated by the U.S. Army, the nylon parka, worn with tapered stretch pants, became a fashion staple on European ski slopes. Parkas with reversible quilting, corduroy, leather trims, and leather shoulders were all available in a multitude of colors and patterns. Some skiers went for the longer parka while many preferred the shorter version as it was more versatile on the slope as well as for après ski.

During the early to mid-1960s, some of the pioneers in the mod subculture adopted the original army parkas as protection for their much-prized bespoke suits while on their scooters. This helped to move the parka off the ski slopes and into the conventional wardrobe. The parka has remained a winter-fashion constant since the 1960s.

See also **Coat; Inuit and Arctic Dress; Outerwear; Windbreaker.**

BIBLIOGRAPHY

Amies, Hardy. *A,B,C of Men's Fashion.* London: Cahill and Company Ltd., 1964.

Byrde, Penelope. *The Male Image: Men's Fashion in England, 1300–1970.* London: B.T. Batsford, Ltd., 1979.

Chenoune, Farid. *A History of Men's Fashion.* Paris: Flammarion, 1993.

De Marley, Diana. *Fashion for Men: An Illustrated History.* London: B.T. Batsford, Ltd., 1985.

Issenman, Betty. *Sinews of Survival: The Living Legacy of Inuit Clothing.* Vancouver: University of British Columbia Press, 1997.

Schoeffler, O.E., and William Gale. *Esquire's Encyclopedia of 20th Century Fashions.* New York: McGraw-Hill, 1973.

Stanton, Shelby. *U.S. Army Uniforms of World War II.* Harrisburg, Penn.: Stackpole Books, 1991.

Tom Greatrex

PASHMINA. *See* **Cashmere and Pashmina.**

PATOU, JEAN Jean Patou (1880–1936) was born in Normandy in northwestern France in 1880. His father was a prosperous tanner who dyed the very finest leathers for bookbinding, and his uncle, with whom he went to work in 1907, sold furs. In 1910 Patou opened a dressmaking and fur establishment that foundered, reportedly

Jean Patou, 1926. Patou opened his first dressmaking shop in 1910. Though the shop failed, within a few years Patou's designs became popular on both sides of the Atlantic, and he was a leading courtier into the 1930s. © HULTONARCHIVE/GETTY IMAGES. REPRODUCED BY PERMISSION.

due to insufficient funding, although he was able to open a tailoring business in Paris the following year. In 1912 he opened Maison Parry, a small salon located at 4, Rond-Point des Champs-Elysées, which offered dressmaking, tailoring, and furs. Patou's designs were striking for their simplicity in comparison to the prevailing fashions, although his biographer quoted him as stating that this change was the result of ignorance rather than any great fashion instinct. In 1913 a major New York City buyer known as the elder Lichtenstein praised Patou as an innovator and purchased the designer's entire collection, presaging his future popularity in the United States.

Early Career
In 1914 Patou established a couture house at 7, rue St. Florentin, near the rue de la Paix. Although his first collection was prepared, it was never shown, as he went to serve as a captain in a French Zouave regiment during World War I. Following the cessation of hostilities Patou became a leading international couturier. He commissioned his fellow officer Bernard Boutet de Monvel, who was working for several fashion magazines, to illustrate many of his advertisements. Patou's salon was dec-

orated by the leading art deco designers Louis Süe and André Mare, who painted the interior and upholstered the furniture in a color described as ash-beige, and installed huge mirrors to accentuate the building's elegant eighteenth-century proportions. At the same time that Patou was a shrewd businessman, however, he was also a playboy and a heavy gambler.

Patou did not regard himself as a skilled draftsman; he claimed that not only could he not draw, but also that a pair of scissors was a dangerous weapon in his hands. Each season he provided the designers in his "laboratory" with various antique textiles, fragments of embroidery, and documents annotated with special instructions for the styles and colors he wanted to develop. His staff would then develop these ideas and present him with *toiles* (sample garments made using inexpensive fabric to check cut and fit), which Patou modified until he was satisfied. At the height of Patou's career in the mid-1920s, he made around six hundred models each season, which he refined down to some three hundred. A collection of this size would be considered enormous by contemporary standards, as the Chambre Syndicale de la Couture Parisienne specifies that a couture collection must comprise a minimum of only fifty models.

The Early Twenties
Patou's early 1920s garments, like those of his archrival Chanel, were embellished with colorful folkloric Russian embroidery. His bell-skirted, high-waisted evening dresses, often made in georgette crêpe, were beaded—he particularly liked diamanté—delicately embroidered, or embellished with fine lace, which he felt was more youthful than heavy lace. Beige was Patou's primary color for spring–summer 1922, and his collection was received with acclaim. A gown of beige kasha cloth featured a deep V-neckline that was emphasized by a lingerie-style collar, while beige chiffon was combined with kasha to form pleated side panels and full undersleeves that were finished with a tight cuff. Patou was an exceptional colorist, and this season he offered a high-collared evening cape in an unusual shade of beige verging on green; its sole trimming was twisted silk openwork. A beige jersey costume was self-trimmed with bias-cut bands around the collar, cuffs, and hem of the hip-length coat.

Patou and Chanel were the leading exponents of the *garçonne* look that dominated the fashions of the 1920s. Patou was particularly well-known for his geometric designs. Most famous are the sweaters he designed from 1924 with cubist-style blocks of color inspired by the paintings of Braque and Picasso. This ultramodern motif was then applied to matching skirts, bags, and bathing costumes. Although Patou was influenced by the fine arts, he was emphatic that he himself was not an artist, and that a successful couturier did not have to be one. "What is needed is taste, a sense of harmony, and to avoid eccentricity" (Etherington-Smith, p. 38). His eminently wearable sweaters, with horizontal stripes in contrasting colors teamed with box-pleated skirts, were regularly featured in *Vogue* magazine.

Although Patou was renowned for his smart daywear, his *robes d'intérieur* (negligées) were unashamedly romantic. In 1923 he offered a design in rose-pink satin draped with silk lace dyed to match, and trimmed with clipped brown marabou. British *Vogue* described the gown as shown with "sabot" slippers with upturned toes in white glacé kid, decorated with red leather cutwork and red heels. Another robe was of crystal-embroidered satin worn with Turkish trousers, a "Capuchin hood" and fringed mules of orange and gold brocade. Patou's shoes were made by Greco (January 1923, p. 45).

Patou's sportswear. Patou's brother-in-law Raymond Barbas introduced the designer to the world of sport and many of its champions. On meeting the androgynous, smartly elegant tennis star Suzanne Lenglen, Patou recognized instantly that she personified the fashionable "new woman." In 1921 Lenglen appeared on court at Wimbledon wearing a white pleated silk skirt that skimmed her knees (and flew above them when she ran, revealing her knotted stockings), a sleeveless white sweater based on a man's cardigan, and a vivid orange headband—she was dressed head to toe by Patou. The audience gasped at Lenglen's audacity, but the women attending were soon to appropriate similar styles of dress for themselves. Lenglen may have been the first sports champion to endorse the look of a specific fashion designer.

By 1922 Patou had introduced sportswear styles for his fashionable clientele, who wanted to look sporty even if they did not undertake any form of exercise. The same year he introduced his "JP" monogram on his garments; he was the first fashion designer to exploit the cachet of a well-known name. He has also been credited as the originator of the triangular sports scarf worn knotted at one shoulder. In 1924 Patou opened additional branches of his house at the fashionable French seaside resorts of Deauville and Biarritz to sell his ready-made sportswear and accessories. The following year he opened a specialized sportswear boutique called "le coin des sports" within his couture house. This boutique consisted of a suite of rooms, each devoted to a different sport, including aviation, yachting, tennis, golf, riding, and fishing. Patou worked closely with the French textile manufacturers Bianchini-Ferrier and Rodier to develop functional sportswear fabrics.

Patou's fashions always appealed to the American market, and he brought himself plentiful publicity through his regular contributions to News Enterprise Association (N.E.A.), the nationwide syndication service. To highlight the fact that his designs were as well suited to the "American Diana" as the "Parisian Venus," the couturier brought six American models to Paris in 1924 (Chase, p. 163). Patou had placed an advertisement in which he advised aspiring applicants that they "must be

House of Patou, 1955. This two-piece ensemble worn by a French model is made from chalk white shantung, or orlon-acrylic fiber and silk. Its elegant yet simple lines are typical of early twentieth-century French couturier Jean Patou. © BETTMANN/CORBIS. REPRODUCED BY PERMISSION.

smart, slender, with well-shaped feet and ankles and refined of manner" (Chase, p. 164). Five hundred women responded, of which six were chosen by a committee consisting of society interior decorator Elsie de Wolfe; fashion photographer Edward Steichen; Edna Woolman Chase, the editor of American *Vogue; Condé Nast;* and Patou himself. The successful applicants were Josephine Armstrong, Dorothy Raynor, Carolyn Putnam, Edwina Prue, Rosalind Stair, and Lillian Farley. The French couture industry was fiercely nationalist, however, and Patou's action caused a furor.

Patou's perfumes. Patou developed his first perfumes in collaboration with Raymond Barbas. In 1925 he introduced three fruit-floral fragrances—Amour Amour, Que sais-je?, and Adieu Sagesse—each designed for a different feminine profile. Downstairs in his couture house he installed a cubist-style cocktail bar complete with a "bartender" who mixed special perfumes for his clients. Other fragrances that Patou introduced include Moment Suprême (1929), Le Sien and Cocktail (both 1930), Invitation (1932), Divine Folie (1933), Normandie (1935), and Vacances (1936). The most famous of all, however, was Joy (1930), which required 10,600 jasmine flowers and 336 roses to make just one ounce of perfume, and which was promoted even during the Great Depression as the costliest fragrance in the world.

The Later Twenties

For spring–summer 1927 Patou presented knitted sweaters in bois-de-rose wool and jersey with wide and narrow horizontal stripes, and a two-piece costume in palest green whose matching kasha coat was lined in very faint mauve and collared with lynx. All-black and all-white evening dresses were in vogue this season—Patou's collection included a white gown fashioned from crêpe Roma, with a graceful fluid cut, an uneven hemline, and rhinestone trimming running in diagonal lines across the front. This was also the year he introduced the first suntan oil, called Huile de Chaldée (which was relaunched in 1993).

By winter 1928 Patou was anticipating the silhouettes of the 1930s: his skirts were slightly fuller, there was an impression of length, and his garments were generally more body-conscious. *Vogue* described as "ideal for days on the Riviera" a three-piece ensemble with a coat and skirt with godet of black asperic (a lightweight wool) and a sweater of gray jersey with tiny black diamonds. An evening gown made in a rich caramel-beige crêpe featured a draped bodice that created a higher waistline, while winglike draperies provided extra length.

Edna Woolman Chase recalls an evening in 1929, when after staring across a room at a group of women clad in short dresses and suits designed by Chanel, Patou rushed to his workroom and started feverishly making frocks that swept the ground with natural waistelines. Fashion usually evolved gradually in the 1920s, so when one designer with international influence suddenly presented a new silhouette, it caused a sensation. Patou's sports costumes were worn four inches below the knee; woolen day dresses worn a little longer, and afternoon dresses a little longer still. His evening gowns—there were several in red with gold lamé—touched the floor on three sides and just skimmed the top of the wearer's feet at the front. Many items had lingerie details, and Patou's new color, "dark dahlia" (a red so deep that it was almost black), often replaced black for evening dresses. Other designers immediately followed suit.

The Thirties

Although Patou was to remain a leading couturier during the 1930s, he was no longer an innovator. A long white evening dress with a print of huge pink and gray flowers for spring–summer 1932, featuring a striking diagonal cut and fabric that trailed over the shoulders and down across the bare back, was perfectly in tune with current fashion trends, but was not instantly identifiable as a Patou model. Where the designer continued to make his mark was in sportswear. He showed a day dress for the same season in thin white woolen crêpe, with a cardigan in navy-blue jersey and a scarf in red, white, and blue

tussore. *Vogue* singled out the ensemble as perfect for summer life in the country, for tennis, boating, and spectator sports. Likewise a navy-blue flannel suit, consisting of a semi-fitted jacket with brass buttons, a straight-cut skirt, and a white crêpe blouse was considered correct for yachting, while looking equally proper on shore. In tune with the fashionable neoclassical styles of the mid-1930s, Patou presented asymmetric evening gowns in white romaine. For fall–winter 1935, dinner suits were important fashion news for semi-formal wear, and Patou offered them stylishly tailored, with one featuring a fantail.

Patou had been renowned for his dramatic openings and first-night parties, but his presentation of his spring–summer collection for 1936 was reported to be strictly businesslike. His new colors were tones situated between violet and pink as well as a clear lime green; several of his evening gowns featured fine shirring and tucking, and his stitched taffeta hoop hats with great bunches of flowers tumbling over one eye.

The 1936 presentation was Patou's final collection. Later the same year he died suddenly and unexpectedly. Various reasons were given for his death, including apoplexy, exhaustion from work and frenetic gambling, and the after-effects of a car wreck.

Recent History

Following Patou's death, Raymond Barbas became chairman of the House of Patou. Barbas had been particularly involved with the designer's perfumes since the mid-1920s, and the company went on to launch several new perfumes after 1936, including Colony (1938), L'Heure Attendue (1946), and Câline (1964). Designers for the House of Patou have included Marc Bohan and his assistant, Gérard Pipart (1953–1957); Karl Lagerfeld (1958–1963), Michel Goma and his assistant, Jean-Paul Gaultier (1963–1974); Angelo Tarlazzi (1973–1976); Gonzalés (1977–1981); and Christian Lacroix (1981–1987). The last fashion collection to be offered under the Patou label was shown for fall–winter 1987.

Since then the company has focused upon fragrances, continuing to produce new ones for both the American and European markets, and since 1984 on recreating a dozen of Patou's original fragrances under the direction of Jean Kerléo at the request of longstanding clients. As of 2004 Jean Patou was run by P&G Prestige Beauté, a division of Procter and Gamble.

See also **Chanel, Gabrielle (Coco); Gaultier, Jean-Paul; Haute Couture; Lacroix, Christian; Lagerfeld, Karl; Paris Fashion; Perfume; Sportswear; Swimwear; Vogue.**

BIBLIOGRAPHY

Chase, Edna Woolman, and Ilka Chase. *Always in Vogue.* London: Gollancz, 1954. Fashion memoirs of the editor of American *Vogue.* Includes accounts of the competition for editorial space between Chanel and Patou, rival houses that copied Patou's clothes, and the designer's recruitment of American models.

Etherington-Smith, Meredith. *Patou.* London: Hutchinson, 1983. Includes biographical details and major design achievements. Illustrated in black and white. Line drawings from *Vogue* magazine and the Patou archive are not attributed or dated.

Amy de la Haye

PATTERNS AND PATTERN MAKING

Clothing production was originally the responsibility of women. After the advent of form-fitting clothing in the thirteenth century, the responsibility expanded to include professional tailors and dressmakers. From the mid-fourteenth century, tailors authored published works on methods for cutting and constructing clothing. "How-To" books for the home dressmaker were published by the late eighteenth century and by the 1830s, small diagrams of pattern shapes appeared in various professional journals and women's magazines. Full-size patterns as free supplements with fashion periodicals emerged in the 1840s in Germany and France. In the United States, fashion periodicals introduced full-size pattern supplements by 1854. Unlike their European contemporaries, American pattern manufacturers produced patterns for the retail and mail-order market, thereby establishing the commercial pattern industry.

The earliest surviving tailors' patterns appeared in Juan de Alcega's *Libro de Geometria pratica y trac a para* (1580). Garasault's *Descriptions des arts et mètiers* (1769), and Diderot's *L'Encyclopédie Diderot et D'Alembert: arts de l'habillement* (1776), played a crucial role during the Enlightenment to disseminate practical knowledge (Kidwell, p. 4). Intended for the professional tailor, the pattern drafts were the first that were generally available to the public. A number of publications, such as the American *The Tailors' Instructor* by Queen and Lapsley (1809), and other journals specifically for the professional tailor proliferated in the nineteenth century. These included tailored garments for both sexes.

For the home dressmaker, manuals with full-size patterns and pattern drafts written for charitable ladies sewing for the poor included *Instructions for Cutting out Apparel for the Poor* (1789) and *The Lady's Economical Assistant* (1808). These featured full-size patterns for caps, baby linen, and men's shirts. *The Workwoman's Guide* (1838) contains pattern drafts, drawings of the finished piece, and pattern drafting instructions.

Small pattern diagrams became a popular method of promoting the latest women's and children's fashions. Appearing in *Godey's Lady's Book* and *Peterson's Magazine* in the early 1850s, these were unsized with no scale given for enlarging the diagram. Full-scale, foldout patterns were issued as supplements in periodicals as early as 1841 in France and Germany, and in England in *The World of Fashions* (1850).

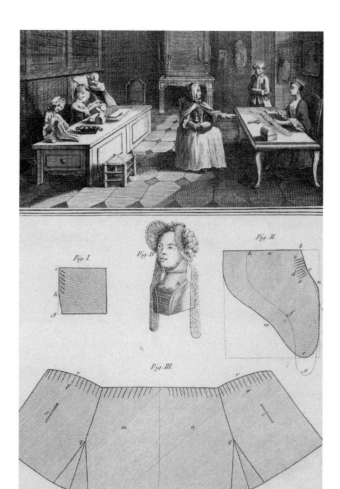

Dictionary of Sciences, **ca. 1770.** This image from the classical eighteenth-century French reference guide illustrates an embroidery workshop along with a contemporary dressmaking pattern. © HISTORICAL PICTURE ARCHIVE/CORBIS. REPRODUCED BY PERMISSION.

First Generation

In the United States, Godey's sold full-scale patterns by Mme Demorest through mail order in 1854. *Frank Leslie's Gazette of Fashions* included full-scale, foldout Demorest patterns in the monthly periodical as well as offering patterns by mail. The patterns were one size only. Because they were offered through retail or mail order, Demorest patterns were the first commercial patterns in the United States (Emery, p. 1999). They offered a wide range of ladies, children's, and men's tissue-paper patterns, either plain or trimmed.

Ebenezer Butterick began to make patterns for children's clothing and men's shirts in 1863. He expanded the line to include ladies' garments in 1866 and incorporated Butterick & Company in 1867. A former tailor, he was familiar with graded sizes and offered patterns in a range of sizes from the beginning. The competition expanded in 1873 when James McCall began to manufac-

A tailor traces a pattern. Patterns have been used in constructing garments for hundreds of years. The earliest surviving pattern was made in 1580. © ROYALTY-FREE/CORBIS. REPRODUCED BY PERMISSION.

ture McCall's Patterns, offering a range of sizes for all patterns.

Even though varying sizes had a strong appeal, two imports—German and French—were competing for the market. *Harper's Bazaar*, an American version of *Der Bazar* of Berlin, introduced a weekly periodical with a pull-out pattern supplement sheet with 24 or more patterns printed on two sides. The one-size-only patterns are defined by different line codes for each piece superimposed on each other. By 1871, *Harper's* was offering cut-paper patterns, although they continued the overlay pattern sheets until the early 1900s. From France, S. T. Taylor Company imported and marketed full-scale tissue patterns as supplements to each issue of *Le Bon Ton*, beginning in 1868. Taylor also offered made-to-measure patterns.

Two more companies joined the competition in 1873, Domestic and A. Burdette Smith. Domestic was a subsidiary of the Domestic Sewing Machine Company, and their patterns were available in a variety of sizes. Smith's patterns offered a cloth model to facilitate the fitting process.

Competition and Mergers

The success of the pattern industry encouraged new competitors. In 1887 Frank Keowing, a former Butterick employee, formed Standard Fashion Company and sold Standard Designer patterns through leading department stores. Between 1894 and 1900 several noteworthy pat-

tern companies were formed: New Idea (1894), Royal (1895), Elite (1897), Pictorial Review (1899), and Vogue (1899). Subsequently, these were joined by Ladies' Home Journal (1901), May Manton (1903), and Peerless (1904). Competition was keen, and each company touted the superiority of their patterns and the excellence of fit.

Demorest was the first to go out of business after Mme Demorest, née Ellen Curtis, retired in 1887. Domestic ceased pattern production in 1895; Smith in 1897, *Le Bon Ton* in 1907 and *Harper's* in 1913. Further realignment of the companies occurred through mergers. For example, Butterick acquired Standard Fashion in 1900 and New Idea in 1902, although each retained its identity until 1926. Royal merged with Vogue in 1924.

The New Generation

Joseph M. Shapiro formed the Simplicity Pattern Company in 1927. Depending on the pattern manufacturer, patterns in 1927 sold for 25¢ to $1.00. Shapiro's approach was to produce a less expensive pattern. Simplicity patterns sold for 15¢. In 1931 Simplicity formed a partnership with the F. W. Woolworth Company to produce DuBarry patterns, initially selling for 10¢. The company thrived and in 1936 acquired Pictorial Review and Excella, founded in 1922.

Condé Nast, publisher of Vogue patterns, introduced Hollywood patterns for 15¢ in 1932 to appeal to the mass market and the national fascination with the movies. Hollywood patterns ended production in 1947. Advance Pattern Company produced another 15¢ pattern. Established in 1932, evidence suggests Advance was affiliated with J.C. Penney Company (Emery 2001). Advance ceased production in 1964.

Syndicated pattern services such as Famous Features and Reader's Mail flourished in the 1920s. These companies produced inexpensive patterns for sale through newspapers. Mail-order patterns were a popular editorial feature, drawing the homemaker's attention to the paper's advertising pages. Patterns such as *Anne Adams, Sue Brunett,* and *Marion Martin* continued to be sold outright to the newspaper as a loss leader. Designs were targeted specifically for families in the middle-income and lower brackets.

Fashion Periodicals

Patterns were first advertised in existing periodicals such as *Godey's Lady's Book* and *Peterson's Magazine*. In 1860, Demorest introduced its own publication, *The Mirror of Fashion*. It was first offered as a quarterly and later was incorporated in *Demorest's Monthly Magazine*, which established publication practices for subsequent pattern manufactures. The history of U.S. fashion magazines is inextricably linked to the history of the U.S. pattern companies. The advantage of owning and publishing their own periodical was economically sound. Subscriptions were profitable. Extensive portions of the magazines of-

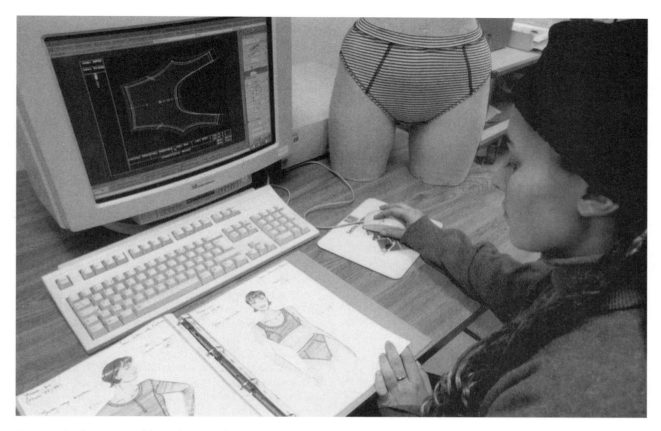

Computerized pattern-making. The use of computers in producing patterns has reduced the amount of time for a new pattern to be placed in stores. © ANNEBICQUE BERNARD/CORBIS SYGMA. REPRODUCED BY PERMISSION.

fered ample coverage of the patterns available as well as articles extolling the virtues of the pattern styles. Further in-house production of give-away flyers and pattern catalogs were cost-efficient.

Such periodicals as Butterick's *Delineator*, McCall's *Queen of Fashion*, and Standard's *Designer* were house organs to promote the patterns with additional editorial features, short stories, and essays on various women's issues. Other established periodicals such as *Ladies' Home Journal* and *Vogue* incorporated sections on their patterns when these lines were established. Pattern companies produced fashion periodicals until the 1930s. These were gradually phased out or purchased by other publishers and the companies concentrated on catalogs to promote their fashions.

Technology and Pattern Production
Four key factors supported the development of the pattern industry: the inch tape measure, c. 1820; the availability of the sewing machine by the 1850s; the expansion of the U.S. Postal Service in 1845; and availability of dress forms for the home sewer by the 1860s. These elements were essential components for the proliferation of pattern sales.

Making a Pattern
The pattern-making process is virtually unchanged from that developed by Demorest. Once approved, the designer's sketch is drafted to size by the pattern maker in muslin and fitted for an average size—usually size 36 for women. The line and fit of the mock-up is checked before being sent to the grading department for translation to various sizes and transferred to master pattern blocks. The blocks include darts, seams, notches, and other pertinent information. Until McCall introduced the printed pattern in 1921, tissue-paper patterns were made with a series of perforations cut into each piece. The perforation system was partially derived from tailor's markings. The process for making cut and punched patterns remained unchanged and was still practiced by Famous Features Pattern Company until 1996. When McCall's patent for all-printed patterns expired in 1938, other companies converted to printing, although Vogue retained perforated patterns until 1956. With the introduction of computerized-design systems, the time for a new pattern to reach the market has been reduced from 2.5 months to as little as four weeks (Chatzky, p. 154).

Early patterns had scant information on how to cut the garment and little instruction on how to make it.

Table 1: Typical Sizing

Years	Size 14	Size 18
1920s	Bust 32", Waist 27", Hip 35"	Bust 36", Waist 28", Hip 39"
1940s	Bust 32", Waist 26.5", Hip 35"	Bust 36", Waist 30", Hip 39"
Late 1950s	Bust 34", Waist 26", Hip 36"	Bust 38", Waist 30", Hip 40"
1967 (new sizing)	Bust 36", Waist 27", Hip 38"	Bust 38", Waist 31", Hip 42"
1970s	Bust 36", Waist 28", Hip 38"	Bust 38", Waist 32", Hip 42"
1980s-2000	Bust 36", Waist 28", Hip 38"	Bust 40", Waist 32", Hip 42"

Sizing Shift. Pattern companies use similar but not standard sizing systems, the proportions of which have shifted over time.

Initially patterns were folded and pinned together with an attached label to identify the garment and the number of its pieces. Demorest introduced pattern envelopes in 1872. By 1906, pattern layouts were included on the envelopes by many pattern companies. Instructions for making up the garment were introduced by Butterick in 1916. The instruction sheet was called the Deltor, named for the first and last three letters from Butterick's magazine, *The Delineator*. Both the pattern layouts and instruction sheets, which are now standard practice, were done by hand for each pattern style. Today layouts and instruction sheets are done on computer. For the latter, templates such as how to insert a zipper or set in a sleeve, are plugged into the instructions. Most illustrations, which were originally done by hand, are now done on computer, as are the paste-ups for counter catalogs and other promotional materials.

Fitting Everyone

Proportional systems based on bust or chest measurements combined with height for adults or age (girls and boys) are the foundation for sizing patterns. Developed by tailors, the systems assume that all human bodies are shaped according to common geometric or proportional rules. Thus the patterns are made for an idealized figure. Early pattern diagrams and full-size patterns such as Mme Demorest and Harper's Bazar in the 1850s and 1860s, and Vogue as late as 1905, were not available in a range of sizes. Women's patterns were usually made for an idealized figure of 5' 5" with a 36" bust. Fitting was done by pinning the pattern on the body or form to adjust it to the individual's proportions. Alternatively, the customer could send in detailed measurements to special order a pattern made-to-measure from the pattern company. (Butterick still offers this service.)

Current fashions and undergarments influence proportional systems. As explained in Butterick's *The Metropolitan* in 1871, a lady with a bust measure of 32" usually has a waist of 24", or 8" less than the bust; but a girl of 10 years usually has a bust measure of 27", with the waist usually 24". By 1905 when the flat-front corset was in vogue, the proportion for the 32" bust changed to a 22" waist.

Each company uses its own proportional system; they are similar but not standardized. By the 1920s, sizes for misses generally dropped the age reference and kept the sizes. Data compiled from the Commercial Pattern Archive digital database (CoPA) illustrate the shifts in typical sizing for size 14 and 18 from the 1920s through 2000 (see Table 1).

Each company continues to offer a wide range of sizes including misses, women's, half-size, petite, junior petite, maternity, toddler, girl/boy, child, men, and infant. Teenage fashions were introduced by Simplicity in the 1940s. In the 1980s Butterick instituted letter-coded sizes called *Today's Fit*, which are designed for the changing proportions of today's figure of about 5'5" with slightly larger waist and hips than misses' sizes. A full range of current size charts can be found in the catalogs and the Web sites of the pattern companies.

Realignment: 1960–2003

Four major companies currently produce patterns. Butterick acquired Vogue in 1961 producing patterns under both signatures. McCall acquired Butterick and Vogue in 2001 but is producing patterns under all three imprimaturs. Simplicity joined Conso Products Company in 1998.

Diversity is a major incentive. The companies have developed global markets, producing patterns in multiple languages. African American models were included in promotional materials in the 1960s. The style lines have been expanded to include more emphasis on crafts, patterns for period costumes, children's costumes, and vintage reproductions of previous eras.

Patterns are a valuable historical reference for everyday clothing, American ingenuity, entrepreneurship, and the democratization of fashion.

See also **Godey's Lady's Book; Sewing Machine; Tailoring.**

BIBLIOGRAPHY

Alcega, Juan de. *Tailor's Pattern Book, 1589.* Translated by Jean Pain and Cecilia Bainton. Bedford, U.K.: Ruth Bean, 1979.

Arnold, Janet. *Patterns of Fashion: 1560–1620.* London: Macmillan Publishing Company, 1985. One of three in the *Patterns of Fashion* series. Introductions in each contains an excellent overview of clothing production.

Burman, Barbara, ed. *The Culture of Sewing: Gender, Consumption and Home Dressmaking.* Oxford: Berg, 1999. Excellent series of essays covering a breadth of topics related to clothing production.

Chatzky, Jean Sherman. "Reaping from Sewing," *Forbes* 25 (May 1992): 154–158. Informative article for the pattern business in the early 1990s.

Emery, Joy S. "Development of the American Commercial Pattern Industry, 1850–1880." *Costume* 31 (1997): 78–91.

———. "Dress like a Star: Hollywood and the Pattern Industry." *Dress* 28 (2001): 92–99.

Kidwell, C. B. *Cutting a Fashionable Fit: Dressmakers Drafting Systems in the United States.* Washington D.C.: Smithsonian Institution Press, 1979. Concise introduction on the origins of clothing production.

Mott, Frank L. *A History of the American Magazines.* 5 vols. Cambridge: Harvard University Press, 1938–1968. Thorough coverage of fashion periodicals, especially volumes 3–5.

Ross, Ishbel. *Crusades and Crinolines: The Life and Times of Ellen Curtis Demorest and William Jennings Demorest.* New York: Harper and Row, 1963. The only full-length bibliography on Mme. Demorest.

Seligman, Kevin L. *Cutting for All!: The Sartorial Arts, Related Crafts and the Commercial Paper Pattern.* Carbondale, Ill.: Southern University Press, 1996. A comprehensive bibliographical reference related to clothing production.

Joy Spanabel Emery

PENIS SHEATH A penis sheath is a supplement to the male body enclosing the glans and penis, leaving the scrotum uncovered. Sometimes the term "phallocrypt" is used as a synonym, but Peter Ucko observes that "phallocrypt" refers to dress supplements that cover both the penis and scrotum, whereas the penis sheath conforms and is attached to the penis only. Archeological evidence suggests the practice of applying a penis sheath dates to the prehistoric Near East, Minoan Crete, archaic Greece, and Roman Italy. In the early 2000s, people living in small-scale tribal societies all around the world, including Africa, the Pacific Islands, North and South America, and the Himalayas, still used penis sheaths. Isolated examples have been documented in Japan and among the Inuit and Eskimo American Indians.

Penis sheaths are constructed of a wide variety of materials, including gourds, leaves, grass, raffia, bamboo, netting, basketry, shell, cocoons, ivory, horn, metal, leather, tapa cloth, and woven cotton trade cloth, depending on the culture. The sheath is attached to the body in a variety of ways depending on the style of sheath. The sheath can be shaped to cover and adhere to the penis; it can be attached directly to the glans; or it can be fastened to the end of the foreskin. Sometimes a cord or cloth wrap is used to hold the penis sheath on or at a particular angle. The sheath might be carved, painted, and/or tasseled. It can be as small as five or six centimeters or extend up to the ear of the wearer. The sheaths are not time consuming to make. Even a carved bamboo sheath will require only thirty to forty minutes to complete. The sheath is part of a whole ensemble of dress that can range from body painting and bead necklaces to shirt and trousers.

The function of the penis sheath in any society is the subject of some debate among scholars and requires more research. What tribal men report and what ethnographers interpret can differ. However, some anthropologically sound functions of the penis sheath can be identified, such as it acting as a carrying pouch, protection, display, or a marker of age, status, or tribal identity.

Informants report that the sheath protects their genitals from the natural environment, particularly bugs and insects when sitting on the ground. Since some sheaths are open at the end, do not cover the scrotum, and are not worn by all groups in the same geographic area, physical protection is not the only function. The penis sheath and its wrappings can serve as a place to store dry tinder and tobacco. Sheaths also act as spiritual protection from evil influences that can enter body orifices, particularly through the genitals. Some scholars suggest the penis sheath functioned as a threat or dominance display in battle. As threat displays became more symbolic than practical, some societies have developed penis sheaths for different occasions, from ceremonial use to everyday wear.

In the early days of anthropology, modesty was considered a function of the sheath. This idea has fallen to the wayside because human groups vary in their ideas of what is "naked" and "shameful." For many men, wearing the penis sheath is part of their definition of being dressed appropriately for interaction with others. A comparable example is the codpiece, which was fashionable in the sixteenth century, and part of the well-dressed European man's ensemble. In any case, one can see by looking at various examples of the penis sheath that it both conceals the penis and draws attention to the genital region. The codpiece and the twenty-first century men's Speedo or thong swimming-suit function the same way. The act of revealing while concealing appears to be a panhuman use of dress in general.

The age when a boy begins wearing a penis sheath varies from society to society. In some cultures, when the boy has his first semen emission, there is a ritual donning of his first sheath. In other cultures, the first sheathing is part of the process of coming of age from youth to adult. Throughout life, a change in style of sheath may mark achieved status from child to warrior to husband to elder. For example, in A. F. Gell's study of penis sheathing in a West Sepik village spanning the border of New Guinea and West Irian, there were both secular and ritual penis sheaths called *pedas* used across the lifespan, and the pattern of their use is cyclic in opposition to each other. Peter J. Ucko points out that in some groups the youth wear penis sheaths at a time in their lives when virility is alluring and the elders are freed from the responsibility of this signal. By contrast, in other groups the older men wear penis sheaths and the young do not, denoting changing times. Often, the morphology of the penis sheath will differ from place to place, so the individual can be visually identified as a member of one group or another. In Gell's study, we can see that in one part of the valley, egg-shaped penis sheaths were used in the north and elongated sheaths in the south.

Even though different groups may have a general style of penis sheath unique to them, there may be little standardization within the group, allowing the individual the opportunity for aesthetic expression. Similarly, absence of a penis sheath communicates state of mind. For some groups, not wearing a penis sheath means the man is an adulterer (implying one function of the penis sheath as contraception by inconvenience), feeble minded, or in mourning and temporarily withdrawing from social life.

With a handful of exceptions, the penis sheath is exclusively a masculine symbol. It is more than a covering or a display. It is a unique form of material culture that draws one in to an understanding of the physical, social, and aesthetic life of people.

See also **Cache-Sexe; Codpiece.**

BIBLIOGRAPHY
Gell, A. F. "Penis Sheathing and Ritual Status in a West Sepik Village." *Man* 6, no. 2 (June 1971): 165–181.

Heiser, Charles B., Jr. "The Penis Gourd of New Guinea." *Annals of the Association of American Geographers* 63, no. 3 (September 1973): 312–318.

Ucko, Peter J. "Penis Sheaths: A Comparative Study." *Proceedings of the Royal Anthropological Institute of Great Britain and Ireland* (1970): 24A–67.

Wickler, W. "Ursprung und biologische Deutung des Genitalpräsentierens männlicher Primaten." *Z Tierpsychol* 23: 422–437.

Sandra Lee Evenson

PENN, IRVING Irving Penn, who was born in 1917 in Plainfield, New Jersey, is considered one of the great American photographers of the mid-twentieth century, not solely one of its masters of fashion photography, in which he initially made his name. His reputation might equally have been secured by a command of portraiture and austere still life. In a career spanning six decades, he has had success too with botanical studies, the beauty photograph (most markedly for advertising purposes), ethnographical documents of cultural types, studies of voluptuous nudes, and with his book *Dancer* (2001), meditations on movement and the body. He disallows any of these disciplines from taking precedence in his oeuvre, but his name is inescapably synonymous with fashion photography. Since 1943 Penn's photographs have appeared regularly in *Vogue*, where his career was nurtured by Alexander Liberman, the magazine's art director from 1943 to 1962.

Beginnings at *Vogue*
Penn studied at the Philadelphia Museum School of Industrial Art (1934–1938). Alexey Brodovitch, art director of *Harper's Bazaar*, whose design seminars Penn attended, introduced him to fashion magazines; moreover, he hired Penn to be his assistant during two summers. Brodovitch published some of Penn's illustrations in 1937. In the same year, Penn undertook a series of street photographs of the shop signs and facades of New York, where he was laying the groundwork for a career in the fashion world by working as a freelance graphic designer and consultant art director for Saks Fifth Avenue.

By 1942, having spent a year painting in Mexico, Penn recognized that his future lay elsewhere. In 1943 Liberman hired him as a creative assistant in the art department of *Vogue*. Penn found *Vogue*'s photographers mostly ambivalent about his ideas for the magazine's cover artwork and instead put them into practice himself. His first *Vogue* cover, a still life composition of accessories, was published in October 1943. Over the next sixty years he photographed nearly 170 more. Shortly after his 1943 debut, he embarked on the photography of clothes. He followed this with a short-lived but inventive series, *Portraits with Symbols*, a stylish fusion of still life and portraiture in which well-known figures posed with objects that evoked aspects of their personalities.

Portraits
Between 1944 and 1950 Penn completed more than three hundred portrait sittings for *Vogue*, the subjects for which ranged from the Spanish artist Salvador Dalí to Senator Hubert Humphrey. He rarely photographed outside the formal confines of the studio during this period and approached these sessions as he did his still life studies that punctuated *Vogue*'s pages at this time: his models faced the lens in carefully arranged poses against the simplest of studio backdrops, where nothing was left to chance. His intention was to eschew artifice and flattery in favor of a timeless clarity. His celebrated "corner portraits" date from this period (1948–1949), too. Placing two studio flats at an acute angle to create a confining space for his sitters, Penn recalled that "the walls were a surface to lean on or push against. . . . [L]imiting the subjects' movement seemed to relieve me of part of the problem of holding on to them" (Penn, 1991, p. 50).

Apogee at *Vogue*
Penn's *Vogue* fashion photography reached its apogee with his coverage of the Paris collections of 1950. Stripped bare of props and artifice, the results appeared monumental in their simplicity, in the light of which the tableaux of Horst, Cecil Beaton, and Erwin Blumenfeld, his contemporaries in the pages of *Vogue*, suddenly seemed as overdressed as stage sets. Penn's uncluttered compositions against seamless gray paper, as taut and as concentrated as his portraits, remain unsurpassed as documents of haute couture at its zenith. For many of these

fashion photographs he collaborated with the model Lisa Fonssagrives (1911–1992), whom he married shortly after their completion. His most famous cover for *Vogue*, a monochromatic study of the model Jean Patchett in fashion by Larry Aldrich, dates from 1950 and marks the first occasion *Vogue* ran a black-and-white photographic cover.

Ethnographic Photography

Besides his important work for *Vogue* at mid-twentieth-century, Penn began pointing his camera in new directions. In 1949, while on a fashion story for *Vogue* in Peru, he found a nineteenth-century daylight studio in the town of Cuzco. There, over three days, he photographed the town's residents (wearing their exotic clothing) and visitors against a painted cloth backdrop, thereby initiating a regular series of portraits documenting different cultures. This pursuit led him far afield in later years, to such locales as Dahomey, Nepal, Cameroon, New Guinea, and Morocco. He brought the same spirit of wonderment to chronicling these exotic dresses as he brought to his photographs of ethnic types and his celebrated series of tradespeople in Paris, London, and New York, which he also initiated in 1950.

New Directions

Penn embarked on his nude studies in 1949, continuing to work on them intermittently between *Vogue* fashion assignments, to which they stand in stark contrast. His subjects were in his own words "soft and fleshy, some very heavy." But he required the same of them as he did his fashion models: it was "more important [that] they were comfortable with their bodies" (Penn, 1991, p. 66). *Vogue* commissions and other commercial work, mostly advertising, occupied Penn for the remainder of the 1950s. In 1960 he published his first book, *Moments Preserved*, which contained the best of his fashion photography of the previous decade. The following year, in tandem with his *Vogue* duties, he began a series of annual photographic essays for *Look* magazine (1961–1967).

In 1964 Penn began to experiment with printing in precious metals, most notably platinum, palladium, and iridium. He continued refining these processes for exhibition pieces, which have included fashion masterworks such as *Lisa in Harlequin Dress by Jerry Parnis* (1950) and *Sunny Harnett in Ben Reig Silk-Chiffon Blouse* (1951). Penn became increasingly disenchanted with fashion photography in the 1960s and from then on his photographs in *Vogue*'s fashion pages became something of a rarity. "Nowadays," he told one commentator, "all that is required is a banal photograph of a girl in a dress." From the mid-1970s Penn regarded original work for exhibitions and books as more creatively fulfilling than editorial commissions. However, his beauty and still life compositions, and occasionally fashion pictures, continue to be published by *Vogue* almost on a monthly basis; thus, with more than sixty years contributing to the magazine,

he is its longest-serving photographer. With an undeniable imprimatur on *Vogue*, he is one of the most influential fashion photographers of the twentieth century.

See also **Beaton, Cecil; Fashion Photography; Horst, Horst P.; Vogue.**

BIBLIOGRAPHY

Fielden, Jay, ed. *Grace: Thirty Years of Fashion at Vogue*. Paris: Edition 7L, 2002.

Fraser, Kennedy. *On the Edge: Images from 100 Years of Vogue*. New York: Random House, 1992.

Hall-Duncan, Nancy. *The History of Fashion Photography*. New York: Alpine Books, 1979.

Hambourg, Maria Morris. *Earthly Bodies: Irving Penn's Nudes, 1949–1950*. Boston: Little, Brown, 2002.

Harrison, Martin. *Appearances: Fashion Photography since 1945*. New York: Rizzoli, 1991.

———. *Lisa Fonssagrives: Three Decades of Classic Fashion Photography*. New York: St. Martin's Press, 1996.

Howell, Georgina. *In Vogue: Six Decades of Fashion*. London: Allen Lane, 1975.

Kazanjian, Dodie, and Calvin Tomkins. *Alex: The Life of Alexander Liberman*. New York: Alfred A. Knopf, 1993.

Liberman, Alexander. *The Art and Technique of Color Photography*. New York: Simon and Schuster, 1951.

Penn, Irving. *Moments Preserved: Eight Essays in Photographs and Words*. New York: Simon and Schuster, 1960.

———. *Worlds in a Small Room*. New York: Grossman, 1974.

———. *Inventive Paris Clothes 1909–1939: A Photographic Essay*. New York: Viking, 1977.

———. *Irving Penn: Photographs in Platinum Metals: Images 1947–1975*. New York: Marlborough Gallery, 1977. An exhibition catalog.

———. *Flowers: Photographs*. New York: Harmony Books, 1980.

———. *Recent Still Life: Negatives 1979–1980, Prints in Platinum Metals 1980–1982*. New York: Marlborough Gallery, 1982. An exhibition catalog.

———. *Issei Miyake*. New York: New York Graphic Society, 1988.

———. *Passage: A Work Record*, New York: Alfred A. Knopf, 1991.

———. *Irving Penn Photographs: A Donation in Memory of Lisa Fonssagrives-Penn*. Stockholm: Moderna Museet, 1995.

———. *Irving Penn Regards the Work of Issey Miyake: Photographs 1975–1988*. London: Jonathan Cape, 1999.

———. *Irving Penn*. New York: Pace/MacGill Gallery, 1999.

———. *Drawings*. New York: Apparition, 1999.

———. *The Astronomers Plan a Voyage to Earth*. New York: Apparition, 1999.

———. *Irving Penn: Objects for the Printed Page*. Essen, Germany: Museum Folkwang, 2001.

———. *Dancer*. Tucson, Ariz.: Nazraeli Press, 2001.

———. *Still Life: Photographs 1938–2000*. New York: Bulfinch Press, 2001.

Szarkowski, John. *Irving Penn*. New York: The Museum of Modern Art, 1984.

Westerbeck, Colin, ed. *Irving Penn: A Career in Photography.* Boston: The Art Institute of Chicago in association with Bulfinch Press/Little, Brown, 1997.

Robert Muir

PERFORMANCE FINISHES

PERFORMANCE FINISHES Performance, or functional, finishes are treatments that are applied to woven, knitted, or other textiles to modify their chemical or physical properties. Fabrics can be made to resist shrinking, fading, wrinkling, and soiling. Antimicrobial, antistatic, and water-repellent properties can be added and fabrics can be made more resistant to burning. Most fabrics (or in some cases garments) are treated after dyeing or printing, so that the finish will not interfere with the application of color.

Shrinkage Control

A textile property of significant consumer interest is the ability of fabrics to maintain their dimensions, whether the textile is used in apparel or home furnishings. Shrinkage is a reduction in fabric length or width; growth is a term used for an increase in a fabric dimension. A fabric that neither shrinks nor grows is said to be dimensionally stable. When one considers that a garment with a 25-inch waist will decrease by 1¼ inches if it shrinks only 5 percent, it is understandable that controlling shrinkage has been a goal of textile producers and finishers for many years. Such control has usually involved submitting the fabric to conditions such as moisture or heat that might induce shrinkage, before it is sewn into garments.

Fabrics most susceptible to shrinking during laundering are those that have high moisture absorbance. These include cotton, rayon, linen, and wool. Most synthetics (polyester, nylon, acrylic, and olefin) do not absorb water to a great extent and have higher dimensional stability. Manufacturing of woven or knitted fabrics imposes stresses in the materials as they are stretched and held taut. When the tension is removed and these fabrics are subjected to wetting during laundering, the yarns relax, moving closer together. The amount of relaxation depends on the degree of stretching the fibers underwent during manufacturing and the propensity of the fibers to absorb water and to stretch. Wool and rayon are more extensible than many other fibers and therefore shrink more. Wool has a further problem in that the fibers are covered with scales that can catch and lock together, entangling under conditions of moisture, mechanical action, and heat. This is called felting shrinkage and is the primary reason wool fabrics are not normally washable. These differences in fabrics and fibers point out not only the specification of laundering or dry-cleaning procedures for textiles, but also the need for development of shrinkage-control treatments that are fiber and fabric specific. Compressive shrinkage, the most general control method, is appropriate for 100-percent cotton, linen, or rayon fabrics. In the process, the fabric is dampened and placed on a thick woolen or felt blanket that travels around a small roller. The wet fabric is stretched as it moves around the contour of the roller and then compresses and squeezes as it enters a straight area. Heat is applied to set in the compressed structure. Sanforized and Sanfor-set are trade names for this type of shrinkage-control treatment.

Wool fabrics require special treatments to inhibit both relaxation and felting shrinkage. The former can be controlled by dampening or steaming the fabric and allowing it to dry in a relaxed state. In one variant of this, decating, the fabric is wound on a perforated cylinder and steam is injected. Cold air then sets the relaxed fabric structure. Preventing felting shrinkage allows wools to be laundered. These treatments involve altering the scales on the wool fibers so they do not catch on each other and become highly entangled. One such process degrades the outer scale layer, making the fibers smoother. A preferred method, which runs less risk of degrading the fiber itself, is to mask the scales by applying a thin polymer film.

Synthetic fibers, which are sensitive to heat, can shrink when heat is applied. This phenomenon is apparent when synthetic-fiber fabrics are ironed at too high a temperature. The tendency for heat shrinking can be controlled in finishing by heat setting the fabric at a temperature that allows the molecules in the fibers to relax somewhat. They are therefore less likely to relax further and shrink during the use and care of the textile product.

Wrinkle Resistance

Fabrics made from cotton, rayon, and linen wrinkle easily and will also retain these wrinkles. Cotton and cotton-blend fabrics particularly will often have wrinkle-resistance finishes applied to lessen the need for ironing. These finishes date back to 1929 when cotton fabrics were treated with a chemical compound of urea and formaldehyde to form a polymer resin inside the fiber. The chemical treatment stiffened the fabric, making it "crease resistant."

In the 1950s such treated fabrics, as well as those made from nylon and polyester, which have natural wrinkle resistance, were termed "wash-and-wear." This emphasized that they would not need to be ironed after laundering. Many of these wash-and-wear finishes did, however, require some touch-up ironing.

Further advances in the chemistry of formaldehyde containing finishes produced the permanent-press fabrics of the 1960s and 1970s. Today they are referred to as durable-press finishes in recognition of the fact that the finish is quite durable to laundering but is not permanent. The most frequently used durable-press finish is dimethyloldihydroxyethyleneurea (DMDHEU). The chemical is applied to the fabric and then cured (that is, heated in an oven to react with the cellulose molecules in the cotton or rayon). The reaction bonds the molecules together so that they cannot move around and allow wrinkles to set.

Treated fabrics are cured either before they are fashioned into garments or after. Precured fabrics have their flat shape set in and can be difficult to handle during manufacturing into final textile products. In an alternative postcuring process, the finish is applied to the fabric that is then made into apparel and the curing step occurs subsequently. This allows creases, pleats, hems, and other features to be durably set in the garments.

Soil and Stain Resistance
Soiling can be inhibited by preventing its deposition on the fabric or by facilitating its removal. The range of finishes that includes the patented Scotchgard are examples of the first category. The most effective ones contain fluoropolymers and work similarly to the finish on stick-resistant cookware in repelling stains and soils. The surface energy of the fluoropolymer finish is so much lower than that of liquids that may spill on the fabric that both water-borne and oily soils bead up and do not penetrate into the fibers. These stain- and soil-resistant finishes also provide a degree of water repellency to the treated fabrics. Another general class of stain-resistant finishes is based on silicones. Silicone finishes resist water-borne stains but do not repel oily liquids.

There are also finishes that aid in removing soils and stains that do become attached to fibers. These agents, generally referred to as soil-release finishes, were developed to address the tendency of polyester and durable-press fabrics to absorb and hold oil-borne stains. Water and detergent were not as readily able to penetrate these fabrics and lift out the stains, as had been the case with unfinished-cotton fabrics. The common mechanism of the variety of soil-release finishes is to make them more attractive to water-based detergent solutions. A secondary benefit of soil-release finishes is that, since they attract water, they reduce build-up of static electricity and therefore also serve as antistatic finishes.

Special fluorochemical finishes that confer both soil resistant and soil-release properties are available. These dual-acting finishes are long-chain polymers that have blocks containing fluorine to repel water, oil, and soil, and blocks that attract water. In air, the fluorochemical blocks come to the surface to resist stains. When the fabric is immersed in water, the other, water-loving, blocks are on the surface, enhancing the ability of the fibers to absorb water.

Flame Resistance
Providing some form of resistance to burning has been an objective of fabric finishers for centuries. Early finishes were temporary in that they were removed when the fabrics were laundered. Growing concern for safety in this century brought about federal regulations for required flame resistance for fabrics used in clothing. Local and state laws impose regulations on the flammability of textile materials in public buildings. As a result, durable flame-retardant finishes were developed.

In the literature in this area, a distinction is made between the terms "flame resistant" and "flame retardant." Flame resistant is more general, referring to the resistance of a material to burning. That property can be due to a fiber that is inherently resistant to ignition and/or propagation of flames or can be conferred by application of a finish. In the latter case, the finish is a flame-retardant chemical. Many synthetic fibers shrink from flames and therefore resist ignition. They will burn, however, upon ignition and can be treated to inhibit combustion. Modacrylic is naturally flame-resistant, as are some of the high-performance fibers used today in garments for firefighters and race-car drivers. Cotton and other cellulosic fibers such as rayon and linen will burn readily; they have the same chemical structure as paper. It is these fibers that normally require a retardant finish to make them flame-resistant.

Flame-retardant finishes work either by quenching the flame or by producing char that interferes with the combustion process. Finishes for nylon and polyester contain bromine that reduces the generation of flammable gases. Durable finishes for cotton and cotton-blend fabrics are phosphorus compounds which react chemically with the cellulose fibers and inhibit the production of compounds that fuel the flame.

Other Finishes
Other possible finishes include antimicrobial, light-resistant, mothproof, and temperature-regulating finishes.

Antimicrobial finishes. Clothing, particularly soiled clothing, is susceptible to growth of mold, mildew, and bacteria. Not only does the growth of these microbes on fabric present health problems, it also causes odors. Antimicrobial agents to protect against both can also be incorporated into manufactured fibers before they are spun or can be applied as finishes to fabrics. Antimicrobial finishes work either by setting up a barrier against the microbes, preventing them from attaching to the fibers, or alternatively by killing the offending organisms. Agents that kill fungi and bacteria are divided into two general classes; organic materials and compounds containing metals. Copper, zinc, and silver are biocidal metals that have been used on fabrics and clothing items such as socks and underwear. Ammonium salts and phenols are organic compounds that are applied. The active ingredient in Lysol antiseptic spray is a phenolic compound.

Light-resistant finishes. The ultraviolet (UV) rays in light can be harmful to clothing fabrics, as well as to the people wearing them. UV light breaks the polymer chains comprising fibers, ultimately weakening fabrics. Some fibers (cotton, rayon, silk, olefin) are more readily damaged than others. The light can also change the structure of dyes, causing fading of fabrics. Light-resistant finishes work either by preferentially absorbing UV radiation that would be harmful to fibers or dyes, or by reflecting such radiation so that the textile does not absorb it. Concerns over the harmful effects of UV light on skin have prompted development of finishes that enhance absorption or reflection. Apparel made from fabrics with these finishes is advertised as having UV or sun-protective qualities.

Mothproofing finishes. Wool fabrics are damaged by moth larvae, which consume the wool protein, leaving holes in the fabric. Traditionally, wools were stored in bags with mothballs, large pellets containing the ingredient naphthalene that killed the larvae. In the early 2000s, finishes were available for a durable application during fabric manufacturing or a renewable application when wool items are dry-cleaned.

Temperature-regulating finishes. Temperature-regulating fabrics are sensitive to the surrounding temperature or to body heat. They are generally referred to as phase changes materials because they change from one phase (solid to liquid or liquid to solid) in reaction to the surrounding temperature. The phase change consumes or releases heat. Polyethylene glycol exhibits this behavior when applied to fabrics. It absorbs and holds heat at high temperatures, cooling the wearer; it then releases this stored heat energy under cooler conditions. The finish has been applied to T-shirts, underwear, socks, and sportswear.

See also **Cotton; Rayon; Wool.**

BIBLIOGRAPHY

Mark, H., Norman S. Wooding, and Sheldon M. Atlas. *Chemical Aftertreatment of Textiles.* New York: Wiley-Interscience, 1971.

Slade, Philip E. *Handbook of Fiber Finish Technology.* New York: Marcel Dekker, 1997.

Billie J. Collier

PERFUME Perfume, from the Latin *per fumum*, meaning through smoke, has been a barometer of society and its mores throughout recorded history. Like fashion, it provides a road map to people's strivings for individuality, self-aggrandizement, social standing, and feelings of well-being.

Early Egyptians are credited as one of the first groups to improve their lives and deaths through the use of fragrance and fragrance ingredients, particularly blended for burning during religious services and burial. Historical references cite Ishmaelite traders who, in 2000 B.C.E., bore aromatic treasures to eager customers in Egypt via what was known as the Incense Road. Considered more precious than gold, flowers, herbs, and spices, perfumes were an expression of exaltation and admiration. The importance of perfumes gradually reached far beyond Egypt thanks to traders, crusaders, and shifting populations who took their precious fragrances with them. This was a fortuitous turn of events for the future of fragrance.

Perfume ingredients became indispensable in religious services, as medicants, to enhance personal environments, and to be applied to the skin for protection against the elements. Perfume was also used as an aphrodisiac. The famous and infamous embraced fragrance and made it their own. Cleopatra (60–30 B.C.E.) doused the sails of her ship to entice Mark Antony. The Queen of Sheba won the heart and devotion of King Solomon by bringing him gifts of rare spices all the way from Yemen. He particularly favored the fabled myrrh. It is said that each drop of Muhammad's sweat, as he ascended to heaven, morphed into the most precious of flowers—the rose.

It was the Egyptians who learned how to press the oils from flowers and leaves that they then smoothed on their sun-scorched skins. The Arabian doctor Avicenna is credited with developing the method of distillation, in the tenth century, which led to the creation of liquid perfume.

Little has changed in the gathering and processing of perfume ingredients. Flowers and plants are picked and gathered by hand, and distillation, in which steam separates the essential oils from the flowers and plants, remains one of the prime methods for extraction. (It is one of six methods: expression, maceration, enfluverage, extraction, and headspace technology.) In modern times, the greatest change has taken place in the fragrance laboratories where computer technology has become a basic tool, not only in establishing and maintaining quality standards, but also in allowing perfumers around the world to communicate with each other in developing unique new fragrance formulas.

Hand in Glove
Fragrance and fashion were linked for the first time in the thirteenth century. The setting was Grasse, France (located between Nice and Cannes) that at the time was the center of the glove-making industry. The problem these artisans faced, however, was the unbearable smell of the leather that was tanned with urine.

The fragrant flowers of Grasse, the province of the local perfumers, came to the rescue of the tanners and perfumed gloves became the rage throughout fashionable Europe. As a result, industrious glove-makers added the title of perfumer. They enjoyed great success until the early 1800s when they were taxed out of business and as a result moved away, leaving a talented coterie of flower growers and perfumers. Grasse flourished as the perfect source of flowers, especially lavender, jasmine, and tuberose that grew on the sun-drenched hills. In the twenty-first century, Grasse is a shadow of its former self, as real-estate developers usurped much of the land in the latter part of the twentieth century. It no longer is the prime source of flowers, roots, and herbs sought by the modern fragrance industry. The whole world serves the perfumers' fragrant needs.

Scents of Royalty
The desire to adorn the body with sweet smells and beautiful jewelry created a marriage of fashion and fragrance

that reached its heights in the early 1700s, particularly during the reign of Louis XIV. It was then that European royalty decided to have their fragrances at hand night and day no matter where they might be. Aromatic jewelry designed by master craftsmen was in great demand. In fact, royalty had their own private jewelers and perfumers to cater to their every whim. Chatelaines, rings, earrings, belts, and bracelets were considered indispensable. Wealthy men, women, and children all wore decorative aromatic accessories.

Courting Perfume

In 1533, when Catherine de Medici left Italy to marry Henry II, she took all of her personal perfumes and perfumers with her. It was not uncommon for royalty and wealthy citizens to employ their own perfumers and jewelers who were responsible for creating exquisite one-of-a-kind containers for each perfume. The marriage of Marie Antoinette to the future king of France, Louis XVI, united two intense devotees of perfume. Both reveled in environments heavy with scent. But it was Louis XIV who became known as "The Perfumed King" in the seventeenth and early eighteenth centuries. His retinue of perfumers created different scents for him and his court to wear morning, noon, and night. In his court, the wings of doves were drenched with fragrance to be released after a great banquet to fill the air with refreshing scents. Extravagance was the coin of the realm. Vessels were designed to allow incense to be sprinkled on carpets and in dresser drawers. Incense was also burned to fumigate clothes, living quarters, and to induce sleep.

Street Scents and Scenes

The growth of the urban environment in the eighteenth century gave meaning to fragrance for the masses. Overcrowding, lack of sanitation, and pollution made life unbearable. Fears of unknown diseases lurking in the water kept people from bathing. Perfumes emerged as the panacea for the great-unwashed populace. Crudely made perfumes and colognes could be bought on the street by roving self-appointed perfumers who hawked their fragrant wares from garments which looked like cook's aprons. Scent bottles filled the many pockets. The French Revolution put a stop to royalty's fragrant revelries and perfume didn't regain its popularity until the early nineteenth century, when Napoleon became emperor. There was no limit to his fragrance indulgences. He virtually bathed in *eau de cologne*, and never went into battle without a full supply of his favorites. His wife, Josephine, loved roses and musk, and she surrounded herself with them night and day. But, when Napoleon left her for Marie Louise, Josephine filled the rooms of Malmaison with the overpowering scent of musk, which she knew Napoleon disliked intensely. Visitors to Versailles report they smell it still.

The twentieth century saw the birth of fashion designer fragrances (primarily of French origin). They were

Chanel No. 5 advertisement. Chanel launched its No. 5 perfume in 1921. It was one of the first and most popular of the fashion designer perfumes that dominated the fragrance market of the twentieth century. THE ADVERTISING ARCHIVE LTD. REPRODUCED BY PERMISSION.

referred to as the invisible accessory by merchants and the media, to be worn on special occasions. Then, in 1921, the great couturier, Gabrielle Chanel, set the fashion world on fire when she launched her breakthrough creation, Chanel No. 5. It was the first aldehydic type that is characterized by its rich sparkling quality. It became an overnight sensation and established a new category for the perfume world.

Chanel was not the first designer to sniff the potential of scents, however. Credit must be given to Paul Poiret, whose exotic designs were inspired by the mysteries of the Far East and who achieved recognition and applause for his art deco costumes for theater and ballet. Fascinated by the imaginative and ephemeral, he adored fragrance and became a perfume entrepreneur in the early 1900s. He established his own laboratory and facilities for blowing glass and packaging his "small wonders." His company, Parfumes Rosine, was named for one of his daughters. Of the more than fifty perfumes (floral, spicy, and oriental types dominated) introduced between 1911 and 1924, several carried his daughter's name. La Rose de Rosine was presented to the public in the mid-twenties as was La Chemise de Rosine and Mon Choix de Rosine. In 1927, inspired by the flight of Charles Lindbergh, Poiret launched Spirit of St. Louis, which was one of his last fragrance creations.

Poiret's couture clients, artists, actresses, and the wealthy, in the U.S. and abroad, quickly became his fragrance customers as he encouraged them to consider fragrance one of his most important fashion accessories. They responded enthusiastically. After World War I, however, his fashion house floundered. His fragrances continued to enjoy popularity in the United States where they were reintroduced. Poiret closed his business in 1930.

Designers and Grand Dames
The fascination with fragrance did not lose its momentum thanks to Chanel and an unending parade of designers who became arbiters of styles in scents with innovations of their own: Worth (Dans La Nuit, 1922), Jeanne Lanvin (My Sin, 1925). The legendary Arpege wasn't introduced until 1927. What was described as the most expensive perfume in the world, Joy, was launched by Jean Patou in 1930. Elsa Schiaparelli startled twentieth century women with a sexy scent which she appropriately called Shocking. Women flocked to her salon to add the scent in its unique "torso" bottle to their dressing tables. The bottle was said to have been inspired by the measurements of the voluptuous American actress Mae West. It is considered one of the great collectibles in the twenty-first century.

Peacetime Scent-Sations
A fashion/fragrance explosion following World War II was led by Christian Dior who not only dropped skirts to the floor in 1947 with his New Look, but also intrigued his customers with the legendary Miss Dior perfume. Nina Ricci introduced her romantic perfume, L'Air du Temps, in l948 in its unforgettable "double doves" bottle. In 1951, the elegant Hubert Givenchy took his place in the perfume pantheon, with L'Interdit, inspired by his muse, Audrey Hepburn.

Hints of Globalization
In the second half of the twentieth century, the French couture world spawned a splendid group of designers including Yves Saint Laurent, Karl Lagerfeld, Guy Laroche, Pierre Cardin, and Paco Rabanne. Before long, all became perfume aficionados as fragrance and fashion became inextricably connected.

Fragrance in the United States, at the time was primarily French and considered a luxury to be worn only on special occasions. An interest in American fragrances began to accelerate when Estée Lauder introduced Youth Dew in 1953. The first perfume in an oil base (versus alcohol), it was particularly long lasting and became a nationwide success. The launch of Norell, however, catapulted America into the fashion/fragrance arena. Norell was the first American designer to lend his name to a perfume. Revlon introduced it in 1969. The sophisticated floral became the olfactory touchstone for executive women throughout the country. It suddenly became *de rigueur* for these career women to keep Norell perfume bottles in full view on their desks.

By the 1970s, American designer fragrances multiplied. Halston led the way with his first fragrance in 1975. Presented in the famed Elsa Peretti bean bottle, it was an immediate favorite. Ralph Lauren set new fragrance standards with Lauren and Polo in 1978. Calvin Klein rocked the fragrance world in 1985 with Obsession and its provocative, risqué advertising. He followed up in l994 with the first important unisex fragrance, CK-1. It created a sensation. America's designers Oscar de la Renta, Liz Claiborne, Bill Blass, and Donna Karan moved quickly to join the fragrance explosion.

Designing a Fragrant Future
France's commitment to fragrance and its formidable fashion designers also continued unabated. In the 1980s, new cutting-edge designers made their mark: The 1990s witnessed fragrance launches from Jean-Paul Gaultier and Issey Miyake. By the time the century was over, fashion designers from Italy (Armani, Moschino, and Dolce & Gabbana), Spain (Carolina Herrera and Paco Rabanne), and Germany (Jil Sander and Hugo Boss) were international fragrance stars.

In the twenty-first century, competition heated up with fragrance blockbusters from the newest fashion leaders in the United States and abroad: the namesake fragrances of Marc Jacobs, Michael Kors, and Vera Wang have joined John Galiano's Kingdom. The everwidening development of odor identical molecules and computer-generated techniques that extract and reproduce scents previously undetected or available has dramatically expanded the perfumer's palette. Amongst the original olfactory experiences that emerged are food, oceanic, and ozone notes. Researchers have explored scents emitted by coral growing in the Caribbean. Flowers have been sent into space to determine how the weightlessness impacts the flower's odor stability. Work has been undertaken to develop pleasing odor environments and delivery systems for future space stations. Research has revealed that humans are not comfortable living under odorless or negative odor conditions.

The key to the success of the designer scents has always depended on how well each designer interprets his or her fashion image in the packaging, name, advertising, and, of course, the fragrance. The appeal is especially powerful to the majority of consumers who could not afford the couture designs that appear alluringly in the pages of magazines, in store windows, and on popular TV shows. The perfumes have made it possible for almost everyone to experience the panache of the designers. As a result, designer fragrance successes have multiplied and captured the imagination and dedication of women everywhere.

There are eight basic fragrance categories: Green, single florals, floral bouquet, oriental blend, modern blend, fruity, spicy, and woodsy mossy. In recent years, fantasy formulations have grown increasingly popular. These are fragrances that defy description and are olfactory experiences based on the perfumers imagination.

In the twenty-first century, creating a fragrance demands scientific, technical, and artistic expertise. The time frame from start to finish can be as long as three years. Usually, a team of perfumers, assistants, and evaluators work against what the industry calls a "perfume profile." The profile identifies the type of fragrance (floral, spicy citrus, woodsy, green, or oriental), the characteristics of the type of woman who would wear the fragrance (sophisticated, conservative, sporty, adventurous), the pricing, the packaging, and among other factors, imagery. A number of perfumers from different supplier companies compete to win the assignment. Once the winning fragrance is selected, it is market-tested, which could take another six to eight months. During this period, the packaging, advertising, marketing, and sales promotion (including sampling) strategies are finalized.

There are only a handful of great perfumers and like all fine artists they are considered key to the success of creating a great luxury brand. They are in demand and remunerated accordingly. Because of the many elements involved in bringing a fragrance to market, there is no hard and fast rule for allocation of costs.

The future promises to expand the rarity and enjoyment of designer-inspired fragrances. New technologies and packaging concepts will make them available in a myriad of forms for personal wear and travel, as well as in the home and in public spaces. The olfactory adventure of the twenty-first century absolutely knows no bounds.

See also **Cosmetics, Nonwestern; Cosmetics, Western.**

BIBLIOGRAPHY

Ackerman, Diane. *A Natural History of the Senses.* New York: Random House, 1990.

Classen, Constance, ed. *Aroma: The Cultural History of Smell.* London and New York: Routledge, 1994.

Corbin, Alain, ed. *The Foul and the Fragrant: Odor and the French Social Imagination.* Cambridge, Mass.: Harvard University Press, 1986

Cunningham, Donna. *Flower Remedies Handbook: Emotional Healing and Growth: With Bach and Other Flower Essences.* New York: Sterling Publishing Company, 1992.

Dyett, Linda, and Annette Green. *Secrets of Aromatic Jewelry.* New York: Flammarion, 1998.

Le Guerer, Annick. *Scent: The Mysterious and Essential Powers of Smell.* Translation by Richard Miller. New York: Turtle Bay Books/Random House, 1992.

Murris, Edwin T. *The Story of Perfume from Cleopatra to Chanel.* New York: Charles Scribner's Sons, 1984.

White, Palmer. *Elsa Schiaparelli: Empress of Fashion.* New York: Rizzoli, 1986.

Annette Green

PERMANENT PRESS. *See* **Performance Finishes.**

PETTICOAT The petticoat is derived from the *jupe* or underskirt of the eighteenth century. As the skirts of women's robes were open at the front, the *jupe* had to be as highly decorative as the robe, and was often constructed of the same rich material. Around 1715 the petticoat became an undergarment that gave structure to the outer skirt by means of a series of whalebone hoops.

The Nineteenth Century

By the nineteenth century, petticoats had several functions. They were used as underlinen to provide warmth and protect outer clothing from an unclean body, to give a structure to the skirt depending on the fashionable silhouette of the time, and to disguise the shape of the legs to give a modest appearance to a woman. It formed part of an extensive range of underwear as worn by the Victorian woman, which was comprised of a chemise, drawers, corset, and several petticoats. Petticoats were generally in two forms until the end of the nineteenth century: a petticoat with a bodice attached or a separate waisted garment which was corded, that is, it had tucks with cords threaded through and drawn in to the waist to provide initial support for the crinoline skirt.

Made out of cotton, linen, cambric, and flannel for winter, several petticoats would be worn at once in the 1840s to provide a bell-shaped structure for the skirt and were stiffened with horsehair at the hem. With the invention of the cage crinoline, petticoats became less structural, and usually only one was worn under the crinoline cage for warmth and modesty as the cage had a habit of flying up when a wearer sat down too rapidly. Another petticoat was customarily worn over the crinoline to soften the steel rings of its outline and tended to have an ornately decorative hem, usually of *broderie anglaise* or crochet as it was likely to be exposed when the wearer was walking. The shape of the petticoat was very much determined by the fashionable shape of outerwear and thus changed over the century from the narrower shapes of the 1860s to the gored cuts of the 1870s and the overly frilled and flounced *froufrou* of the Edwardian Era. The slimmer cut of 1920s fashions and bias cut of the 1930s necessitated a different kind of underwear—usually French knickers and bias-cut slips derived from the petticoat and attached bodice of the nineteenth century.

Post–World War II

In 1947 Christian Dior's *Corolle Line*, later dubbed the New Look, heralded the revival of the bouffant skirt, a round crinoline shape with an understructure comprised of several petticoats. The look was incorporated into teenage culture in the 1950s as young women adopted the petticoat and wore several at once—usually of sugar-starched net and paper nylon, or (for evening) taffeta, at least one of which was stiffened with plastic hoops. The look was particularly associated with rock 'n' roll and jiving as the petticoats preserved the dancer's modesty when exhibiting twirls with her male partner. In the 1960s the petticoat disappeared in daywear and, in much the same way as the corset, became the preserve of fetishism. The allure of the petticoat can be explained by the way it exaggerates certain characteristics of the female body, by emphasizing the hips it highlights a fragile waist. It has thus earned a place in fetish culture as a signifier of femininity, and magazines such as *Petticoat Discipline* allude to the popular cross-dressing scenario of a little boy being forced to parade in front of his family and friends in petticoats as a punishment for some misdemeanor. The frisson of pleasure achieved through shame thus creates a fetishist.

British designer Vivienne Westwood revived the petticoat in the late 1970s and 1980s as a result of theatrical New Romantic dressing and the experiments with the mini-crini. The wedding of Lady Diana Spencer to Prince Charles in 1981 heralded a revival of the nineteenth-century silhouette in bridal design as a result of her crinoline-skirted wedding gown designed by David and Elizabeth Emmanuel. Thus, the contemporary petticoat is often used as an understructure in women's formal wear, in particular bridal gowns and in outfits worn by female country and western singers; Wynona Judd is associated with this look.

See also **Crinoline; Corset; Petticoat; Underwear.**

BIBLIOGRAPHY

Carter, Alison. *Underwear: The Fashion History.* London: Batsford, 1992.

Cunnington, C. Willet and Phillis. *The History of Underclothes.* London: Dover Publications, 1992.

Saint-Laurent, Cecil. *History of Women's Underwear.* London: Academy Editions, 1986.

Caroline Cox

PIMA COTTON. *See* **Cotton.**

PINA CLOTH. *See* **Fibers.**

PINAFORE. *See* **Aprons.**

PINS Pins range from the simplest devices used by humanity to some of the most elaborately decorated ornaments. Thorns, bones, and other plant and animal materials have been used for making and fastening garments since Neolithic times. Sumerians used iron and bone pins 5000 years ago. Wealthy Egyptians wore straight bronze pins with decorated heads; by Greek and Roman times the fashion had changed to a clasp or fibula. Medieval pins ranged from simple pieces of wood to ivory and silver, and measured 2.5 to 6 inches. Paris was the center of medieval pin manufacturing; by the seventeenth century, though, pin making was the leading industry of Gloucester, England. Less valuable than needles, metal pins were small luxuries in early modern Europe; pin money was originally a bonus given to a merchant on concluding a deal, for his wife's pins.

By the eighteenth century, pins were made with a division of labor that fascinated both Denis Diderot and Adam Smith because the specialization of workers was helping make a luxury affordable. Steel being too costly and difficult to work, brass wire was drawn at 60 feet per minute by a skilled specialist, then cut into lengths by other workers producing 4,200 pins an hour. Others then sharpened the points and made coiled brass into heads and affixed them, coated the pins with tin, and washed, dried, and polished them. A single worker going through all these stages would have been able to make only a handful of pins a day. Mechanized pin production began in Birmingham, England, in 1838. One of the most celebrated devices of antebellum America, John Howe's 1841 pin machine made a breakthrough in automation by performing the entire sequence of unwinding wire, cutting, grinding, and polishing in a single rotational sequence. It even formed heads by compressing one end of the wire.

Pins were one of the first articles so effectively automated that the challenge shifted from production to packing—especially inserting the pins rapidly and safely in crimped paper cards—and marketing. The card display, developed by Howe, assured customers of the quality of metal, points, and heads. In 1900 U.S. residents used 60 million common pins, or about 126 per capita; old obstacles to working with steel had been overcome. By 1980, a Cambridge University economist estimated that productivity per worker in the British pin industry had increased 167-fold in 200 years.

Perhaps the greatest impact of abundant, cheap, high-quality pins packed in closed cases was on the culture of sewing. Pins no longer had to be protected from theft, loss, and rust. Through peddlers, they were available to every country household, and their profusion helped pincushions reach a decorative peak in the Victorian era. By the early twenty-first century, pins had lost most of their industrial importance; only in luxury production and in-home sewing were they still used to attach patterns to fabric.

See also **Brooches and Pins; Needles; Safety Pins.**

BIBLIOGRAPHY

Andere, Mary. *Old Needlework Boxes and Tools.* New York: Drake Publications Ltd., 1971.

Gillispie, Charles C., ed. *A Diderot Pictorial Encyclopedia of Trades and Industry.* Volume 1. New York: Dover Publications, Inc., 1987. See plates 185–187.

Lubar, Steven. "Culture and Technological Design in the Nineteenth-century Pin Industry: John Howe and the Howe

Manufacturing Company." *Technology and Culture* 28, no. 2 (April 1987): 253–282.

Petroski, Henry. *The Evolution of Useful Things*. New York: Alfred A. Knopf, 1992.

Edward Tenner

PIQUE. *See* **Weave, Jacquard.**

PLAID Checked cloths were evident in many early cultures, however, the term plaid drives from Scottish Celtic culture of around the sixteenth and seventeenth centuries (Bonfante 1975; Barber 1991; Cheape 1995). The popularity of checked cloths in North America and the use of the word plaid to describe these cloths are almost certainly linked to the influence of Scottish immigrants from the late eighteenth century onward. The term is widely used in North America to describe a diverse range of checked cloths from heavy tartans and tweeds to fresh cotton ginghams. However, within Britain, plaid generally refers to either tartan or checked cloths similar to tartan. It also signifies a length of tartan cloth worn over the shoulder as part of the more elaborate forms of Highland Dress.

Origins in Celtic Culture
In the early Celtic culture of Scotland and Ireland, a type of shaped cloak known as a mantle was worn. In the sixteenth and seventeenth centuries, this developed into the simple, untailored length of cloth known as the plaid. Cheape further identifies that "plaids or plaiding were Scots terms used to describe the relatively coarse woven twilled cloth that might be used, for example, for bed coverings as well as garments" (p. 19). Indeed the Gaelic meaning for the word *plaide* is blanket, whereas the plaid as a garment tends to be referred to as a *breacan*, the belted

THE WOMEN OF EDINBURGH

Sir William Brereton, an English visitor to Edinburgh in 1636, described the dress of women as follows:

> Many wear (especially of the meaner sort) plaids, which is a garment of the same woollen stuff whereof saddle cloths in England are made, which is cast over their heads, and covers their faces on both sides, and would reach almost to the ground, but that they pluck them up, and wear them cast under their arms. (Cheape, p. 19)

Clair McCardell plaid playsuit. Scottish immigrants brought plaids to North America in the late eighteenth century, and the pattern has since become a popular one in modern design collections. [MODEL BIJOU BARRINGTON IN CLAIRE MCCARDELL "ROMPER"], HARPER'S BAZAAR, P46, 1942. PHOTOGRAPH BY LOUISE DAHL-WOLFE. © LOUISE DAHL-WOLFE ARCHIVE, CENTER FOR CREATIVE PHOTOGRAPHY, ARIZONA BOARD OF REGENTS. REPRODUCED BY PERMISSION.

plaid, which was commonly worn by men in Highland Scotland. Women throughout Scotland wore the plaid as a large tartan shawl, a style that was popular until the mid-eighteenth century (Dunbar 1981, p. 125; Cheape 1995, pp. 3–20).

Plaid in Fashion
By the early nineteenth century, plaids in their original form were scarcely worn, though; in that era plaid cloth gained an international profile as a fashion textile. American mail-order catalogs from the nineteenth century indicate that plaids were popular for men's work-wear and day wear, and for making women and children's dresses and blouses (Israel 1976; Kidwell and Christman 1974, p. 58). The colorful, geometric designs concerned have become embraced within modern, sporting, or "homely pioneer" notions of American sartorial identity. This is linked to the fact that plaid shirts and jackets form part of the image of American male stereotypes such as lumberjacks and frontiersmen. It is also connected to the influential work of American sportswear designers like Claire McCardell and Mildred Orrick, who frequently

used plaids in their designs of the mid-twentieth century (Milbank 1989; Yohannan and Nolf 1998). The embrace of plaid within American culture has influenced subsequent reinterpretations of it. For example, plaid has featured in cowboy, and work wear—inspired gay styles of the 1970s onward, as well as in the subcultural styles of skinheads, rockabillies, and punks. Plaid has also featured consistently in international designer collections, particularly since the 1970s.

See also **Scottish Dress; Tartan.**

BIBLIOGRAPHY

Barber, E. J. W. *Prehistoric Textiles: The Development of Cloth in the Neolithic and Bronze Ages, with Special Reference to the Aegean.* Princeton, N.J.: Princeton University Press, 1991.

Bonfante, Larissa. *Etruscan Dress.* Baltimore: Johns Hopkins University Press, 1976.

Cheape, Hugh. *Tartan: The Highland Habit.* Edinburgh: National Museums of Scotland, 1995.

Dunbar, J. Telfer. *The Costume of Scotland.* London: B.T. Batsford, Ltd., 1981.

Israel, Fred. *1897 Sears Roebuck Catalogue.* New York: Chelsea House Publishers, 1976.

Kidwell, C., and M. Christman, eds. *Suiting Everyone: The Democratization of Clothing in America.* Washington D.C.: Smithsonian Institution Press, 1974.

Milbank, Caroline Reynolds. *New York Fashion: The Evolution of American Style.* New York: Harry N. Abrams, 1989.

Yohannan, Kohle, and Nancy Nolf. *Claire McCardell: Redefining Modernism.* New York: Harry N. Abrams, 1998.

Fiona Anderson

PLASTIC AND COSMETIC SURGERY Cosmetic surgery began to be practiced in the last part of the nineteenth century as surgical intervention became increasingly possible because of the development of anesthesia and sterile techniques. One of the first cases to be reported in the last part of the nineteenth century had to do with correcting what was known as saddle nose, a deep depression in the middle of the nose. There are several causes of this condition, but one of them was syphilis. This association with syphilis made those with such noses particularly willing to try to get some surgical change. Large noses were also an issue and intranasal rhinoplasty (hiding the incisions inside the nose) was first done in the 1880s.

Public knowledge of the possibility of plastic surgery came during World War I (1914–1918) as surgeons treated patients in unprecedented number with bad facial and other visible scars. The "miracles" wrought by the surgeons brought plastic surgery out of the closet, and there were enough physicians engaged in it to found the American Association of Oral Surgeons in 1921, later called the American Association of Oral and Plastic Sur-

geons, and still later, the American Association of Plastic Surgeons.

These early-organized plastic surgeons were cautious about their reconstructive surgery, determined to use their skills to help the maimed but not to do frivolous surgery designed to make people more "beautiful." Not all would-be surgeons agreed with them, and a separate group popularly called "beauty surgeons" developed. These surgeons were looked down upon for their promises to improve the looks of their patients. They took shortcuts, avoiding some of the time-consuming operations involving bone and cartilage grafts. Instead, they relied upon the injection of paraffin, which for a time in the 1920s, was seen as a panacea for all soft-tissue defects. It was widely used to fill facial wrinkles. Unfortunately paraffin had a tendency to migrate to other areas, particularly if the patient spent time in the sun. That tended to disfigure the patient, who then had to go through the process again. One of the best known of these beauty surgeons was Charles C. Miller of Chicago, who wrote an early textbook entitled *Cosmetic Surgery: The Correction of Featural Imperfections.*

The attempt to distinguish between plastic surgery and beauty essentially failed. While surgery was still done for people whose bodily features had been altered by wounds or fires, increasingly it was used to meet personal beauty standards or to change identifiable ethnic features or to make someone appear younger by removing facial wrinkles or having eye tucks. Surgery was also done to change the contours of the body, particularly among women where breast augmentation or breast reduction became an important specialty. By 1988 breast enlargement surgery had become a $300 million business. Some urologists got into the business of penile augmentation, although this was far more controversial. One San Francisco urologist in the 1990s claimed to have done 3,500 such operations even though many urologists condemned the operations as unnecessary and potentially dangerous.

Silicone implants gave a big boost to the breast augmentation industry, and it became second only to liposuction (fat removal) as the most common cosmetic surgery. Some women complained that the silicone in their breast implants ruptured or leaked, causing them to have chronic fatigue, arthritis, and damage to the immune system. The result was a lawsuit that resulted in the largest fee ever negotiated in a class-action lawsuit. Dow Corning, Bristol-Myers Squibb Company, and others agreed to pay more $4 billion to 25,000 women. Breast-implant surgery grew even more prevalent, however, when the silicone was replaced by saline. Still the silicone worked better and research both before the lawsuit and after has tended to disprove the validity of the claims about the dangers of silicone. In 2003 there was an unsuccessful campaign to return to silicone as an option. The last word, however, has not been said on this issue.

While many women want to increase the size of their breasts, others want to lessen theirs, and breast reduction remains an important part of cosmetic surgery. By 1992, 40,000 women a year were having reduction surgery.

Probably the most radical of plastic or cosmetic surgery is that involved in transsexual surgery. Surgery to change males to female has changed drastically in the last 40 years, and skilled surgeons can use the penis and testicles to make functional labia and vaginas. The surgery for changing females to males is less well-developed since it has proved difficult to make a penis that can be used for both urination and sexual intercourse, but research is still continuing in the field.

See also **Body Building and Sculpting; Body Piercing; Branding; Implants; Scarification; Tattoos.**

BIBLIOGRAPHY

Haiken, Beth. "Plastic Surgery and American Beauty at 1921." *Bulletin of the History of Medicine* 68 (1994): 429–453.

Haiken, Elizabeth. *Venus Envy: A History of Cosmetic Surgery.* Baltimore, Md.: Johns Hopkins University Press, 1997.

Miller, Charles C. *Cosmetic Surgery: The Correction of Featural Imperfections.* Chicago: Oak Printing Company, 1907.

Yalom, Marilyn. *A History of the Breast.* New York: Alfred A. Knopf, 1998.

Vern L. Bullough

PLAITING. *See* **Braiding.**

PLEATHER. *See* **Techno–Textiles.**

PLUSH. *See* **Weave, Pile.**

POCKETS Pockets are a small but important component of western clothing. Despite their deceptive obscurity and utilitarian nature, pockets are sensitive to fashion changes and they can reveal a wealth of social and cultural information. Pockets are an alternative or supplement to bags, purses, and pouches in the carrying and securing of portable personal possessions, and historically it is often illuminating to consider them together. There has been a close gender-specific association between pockets and the bodily gestures and posture they facilitate. In the period before mass-produced clothing, first for men and then for women, there was scope for individual customers, or their tailors and dressmakers, to choose where pockets should be placed, and though there were common preferences and styles, pockets were by no means uniform; in the early twenty-first century, the same applies in expensive bespoke clothing. There has always

"...because I have no safer a store-house, these pockets do serve me for a roome to lay up my goods in, and though it be a straight prison, yet it is a store-house big enough for them, for I have many things more of value yet within..." (Bulwer, p. 77).

been a difference in the number and position of pockets customarily provided for men, women, and children.

Pockets in Men's Dress

For men, the most prominent pockets are those on the outside of their coats. In the seventeenth century, they had been close to the lower edge and then moved higher. In the eighteenth century, like pockets in waistcoats, they became marked out by flaps becoming deeper and often decorative, sometimes lavishly so in keeping with the color and embellishment of fashionable garments. The great coat, which was common before the railway age, provided a capacious range of pockets suitable for the needs of male travelers. Its demise may have contributed to the widespread adoption of the briefcase in the twentieth century by businessmen and commuters. In the voluminous trunk hose worn by men with doublets in the sixteenth and seventeenth centuries, very large pockets could be accessed from the side. Pockets in later styles of breeches and trousers have been situated in the side seams, but also at the back and front.

Smaller pockets, such as those for coins or hanging watches, were less visible, for example placed in the front of the waistband of breeches; chamois leather was sometimes used as lining. Watches became small enough at the start of the seventeenth century to be concealed in pockets made for the purpose. These remained common until the wristwatch became popular in the twentieth century. The inside top pocket is commonly found in many male garments past and present. Men's garments utilized integrated pockets and positioned them to achieve balance across the body generally before women's garments did so. The number of pockets for men has been substantial. Extant historical breeches and trousers show evidence of the cycle of patching made necessary by wear and tear caused to pocket linings by coins and keys, a problem that has continued.

Pockets in Women's Dress

Women's clothing was slower to adopt the integral pockets widely used by men. The old-established custom of hanging small utensils and tools from the belt has never entirely ceased. It enjoyed a renaissance amongst women in the second half of the nineteenth century when there

"At the present time men and women employ quite different systems, men carrying what is needful in their pockets, women in bags which are not attached in any way to their persons, but carried loosely in their hands. Both systems have serious disadvantages" (Flügel, p. 186).

was a vogue for antique-looking chatelaines. Throughout the eighteenth century, women commonly had slits in the sides of the skirts of their gowns and informal jackets to gain access to tie-on or hanging pockets worn beneath. These large pockets were made in pairs or singly, usually with vertical slit openings and worn on a tape around the waist, independent of the garments worn over them, and consisted of linen, cotton, silk, or materials recycled from older furnishings or patchwork. In the eighteenth century these were also often beautifully embroidered, but this practice seems to have ceased in the nineteenth century. Integral pockets then became more popular; bags and reticules of various kinds supplemented capacity for carrying small personal possessions, but tie-on pockets continued in use throughout the nineteenth century, when later they were often associated with children, or of rural or working-class women, and they disappeared altogether by the 1920s.

Integral pockets were distributed in various places in formal and informal dresses and suits, between skirt gores, even in folds over the bustle drapes. Patch pockets have been prominent on aprons, both the decorative ones fashionable amongst women of leisure in the eighteenth century, and the utilitarian aprons found in many situations throughout the period. In the twentieth century, the use of trousers and jeans by women has provided them with more pockets, but rarely have women's coats or jackets been made with the useful inside pocket so typical of menswear. In periods of history where women and girls have had little or no domestic privacy or financial independence, pockets (as well as stays) have provided them with one of the few available forms of security and privacy for letters, money, or other small possessions.

Social and Cultural Factors

Both men and women have faced the conflict of interest inherent in retaining fashionable, smooth outlines to their garments whilst carrying things in their pockets. Changes in the type and number of pockets for both sexes derive both from fashion and from the necessity to accommodate different kinds of things, ranging from a woman's snuffbox of the eighteenth century to car keys in more recent times. These goods are expressive of gender roles and social class. However, despite the wide range of types of pockets available, they have not been entirely effective for men or women. There have been frequent complaints over the last three centuries about their inadequacy or inaccessibility and, paradoxically, court records and newspapers over this time show the frequency with which pickpockets and pocket snatchers found them only too accessible. Tie-on pockets were sometimes lost, a loss suffered by Lucy Locket and described in a nursery rhyme:

> Lucy Locket lost her pocket,
> Kitty Fisher found it,
> Not a penny was there in it,
> Only ribbon round it. (Opie, p. 279)

Some small possessions have generated their own carrying devices worn separately, such as holsters for small arms, specialist aprons to carry small tools for skilled trades, and binocular cases. Latterly conventional pockets have been to some extent superseded by small bags, based on hiking gear, worn around the waist or on the back by both sexes, but innovation in pockets still continues. They are seen sited in unconventional positions, sometimes borrowed from combat clothing or used to accommodate new urban lifestyles and technological innovations such as mobile phones and computer games. This suggests that there is sufficient need for pockets not only to continue in use, but also to attract inventive new solutions.

See also **Handbags and Purses; Trousers; Watches.**

BIBLIOGRAPHY

Arnold, Janet. *Patterns of Fashion: Englishwomen's Dresses and Their Construction c. 1660–1860.* London: Macmillan, 1977.

———. *Patterns of Fashion: The Cut and Construction of Clothes for Men and Women c. 1560–1620.* London: Macmillan, 1985.

Baumgarten, Linda, and John Watson. *Costume Close-up: Clothing Construction and Pattern 1750–1790,* Williamsburg, Va.: Colonial Williamsburg Foundation with Quite Specific Media Group, 1999.

Bradfield, Nancy. *Costume in Detail, 1730–1930.* London: Harrap, 1968.

Bulwer, John. *Anthropometamorphosis: Man Transform'd* or *The Artificial Changling.* London: Printed by W. Hunt, 1653.

Burman, Barbara. "Pocketing the Difference: Pockets and Gender in Nineteenth-Century Britain." In *Material Strategies: Dress and Gender in Historical Perspective.* Edited by Barbara Burman and Carole Turbin. Oxford: Blackwell, 2003.

Flügel, J. C. *The Psychology of Clothes* New York: International Universities Press, 1969 (first published 1930), p. 186.

Opie, Iona, and Peter Opie, eds. *The Oxford Dictionary of Nursery Rhymes.* Oxford: Claredon Press.

Barbara Burman

POINTE SHOES Pointe shoes, also known as toe shoes, represent an essential part of the ballet dancer's costume. The aesthetic concept of ballet calls for a long line in the leg, which is further enhanced by the nearly conical shape of a pointe shoe.

The Birth of Pointe Shoes

In the early 1700s, ballet technique developed rapidly and incorporated a new emphasis on graceful foot technique. In 1726, Marie Camargo debuted at the Paris Opéra Ballet in a performance of *Les Caractères de la Danse*, dancing in slippers instead of heeled shoes. She had also shortened her stage skirt to show off the turnout of her legs and feet. After the French Revolution in 1789, emphasis was placed on the functional aspect of stage costumes in order to facilitate the fully extended pointing of the foot during turns and jumps. Accordingly, short-soled slippers with pleats under the toes became standard footwear for ballet dancers. At the beginning of the nineteenth century, an increasingly challenging ballet technique, *en demi pointe*, allowed dancers to carry out multiple pirouettes and jumps. While men were identified as playing a secondary role in the performance, from this point onward ballerinas rose to the toes and contributed to a new dance aesthetic. This overt emphasis on the lightness of dancers was reflected by Marie Taglioni, who appeared *sur les pointes* in the first performance of *La Sylphide* in 1832. Some early examples of pointe shoes from this period are exhibited in the Haydn Museum in Austria.

The introduction of pointe has related to the development of narrative ballets, allowing for and responding to ethereal elements, like the mystic sylphs in *La Sylphide* (1832), the suggestion of dramatic ethereality in *Giselle* (1841), and the enchanted swans in *Swan Lake* (1895). By the end of the nineteenth century, the pointe technique was highly developed. Being tied entirely to the growing challenge of pointe work, Pierina Legnani introduced thirty-two *fouettés* in a performance of *Swan Lake*. In 1905, toe dancing reached a new high point when Anna Pawlowa portrayed *The Dying Swan*—a three minute solo—constantly *en pointe bourrée*. Although Pawlowa is said to have used pointe shoes with wider platforms, which she was supposed to have covered up in photographs to look narrower, she brought a new dimension of pointe dance into the twentieth century.

Les Ballets Russes, which emerged from 1909 until 1929 under the direction of Sergei Diaghilev, developed ballet *en pointe* to a very high technical level. In 1931, Russian teenage ballerinas performed sixty-four *fouettés en pointe*, six unsupported pirouettes, thus setting an extremely high standard in classical ballet. Russian pointe shoes, which are said to be softer than their American or British counterparts, contributed to a growing demand for these shoes within other companies. After the end of World War I, when modern dance groups emerged, dance moved away from traditional ballet techniques and pointe work and modern dance gave rise to a new era of costuming and dance footwear, and in modern dance pointe shoes were completely abandoned.

The Making of Pointe Shoes

Traditionally, pointe shoes are sewn inside out. The shoe is only turned to the right side after the toe block has been constructed. The constructing of a pointe shoe requires a pre-cut piece of satin and lining (which will form the upper part of the shoe), and the insertion of a vamp section (which will form the sole of the shoe). Peach pink shades remain the traditional color for pointe shoes, implying the illusion of an extended leg. Pointe shoes have no right or left. The craftsman will use a special glue formula (based on a simple flour and water paste) to form the block. The shoes enter a hardening process in a hot-air oven. Finally, the excess cloth is trimmed and the insole is attached with glue. The dancer herself undertakes the last step: Four pieces of ribbon are sewn onto the insides of a pair of shoes. Pointe shoe dancers usually experiment with the right placement of the ribbons in order to give maximum hold. To extend the short life of a pointe shoe, the ballerina will bake them and apply resin, floor wax, or super glue before she "breaks-in" the shoes to make them feel like a second skin. The altering caused by "breaking-in" can often shorten the life of a shoe by 50 percent.

New Technology versus Old Traditions

In the last few decades of the twentieth century, the technical requirements of ballet rapidly increased. This resulted in a demand for more elaborate pointe shoes. A wide range of designs were on the market: from soft block shoes, which are designed for transition from soft shoes to pointe shoes, to extremely hard shoes, which give extra strength, to machine-manufactured rehearsal pointes for dance students operating on a smaller budget. About thirty-five ballet shoe manufacturers, such as Freed, Capezio, and Gaynor Minden, operate in the market, but as a result of a long history of traditional pointe shoe manufacturing with cardboard and simple flour and water paste glue, the innovative pointe shoe with unbreakable shanks produced by the U.S. ballet shoe manufacturer Gaynor Minden are ubiquitous. At the end of the twentieth century, the fashion industry picked up the idea of ribbons and look-alike pointe shoes, and designer brands such as Manolo Blahnik, Sonia Rykiel, Etro, and Blumarine have used the pointe shoe style to create "ballerina" fashion shoes.

See also **Ballet Costume; Shoes; Theatrical Costume.**

BIBLIOGRAPHY

Barringer, Janice and Schlesinger Sarah. *The Pointe Book: Shoes, Training & Technique.* Hightstown, N.J.: Princeton Book Company, 1990.

Bentley, Tony. *The Heart and Sole of a Ballerina's Art: Her Toe Shoes.* Washington, D.C.: Smithsonian Institution, 1984.

Cunningham, B. W. et al. "A Comparative Mechanical Analysis of the Pointe Shoe Toe Box." *American Journal of Sports Medicine* 26, no. 4 (1998): 555–561.

Terry, Walter. *On Pointe.* New York: Dodd Mead, 1962.

Trucco, Terry. "To the Pointe." *Ballet News* 3 (1982): 21.

Internet Resource

Brown, Ismene. "Arch Rivals." *Telegraph.* 8 March 2003. Available from <http://www.art.telegraph.co.uk>.

Thomas Hecht

POIRET, PAUL Before Paul Poiret (1879–1944), there was the couture: clothing whose raison d'être was beauty as well as the display of wealth and taste. Paul Poiret brought a new element of fashion to the couture; thanks to him fashion can be a mirror of the times, an art form, and a grand entertainment. Poiret, in the opinion of many, was fashion's first genius.

Paul Poiret, 1922. On a shipdeck in New York City, Paul Poiret stands with his arms spread wide open. Poiret, who infused fashion with art and broke down nineteenth-century conventional clothing styles, is considered by many to be fashion's first "genius." © UNDERWOOD & UNDERWOOD/CORBIS. REPRODUCED BY PERMISSION.

Born into a solidly bourgeois Parisian family (his father, Auguste Poiret, was a respectable cloth merchant), Poiret attended a Catholic *lycée*, finishing as was typical in his early teens. Following school came an apprenticeship to an umbrella maker, a métier that did not suit him. At the time, it was possible to begin a couture career by shopping around one's drawings of original fashion designs. Couture houses purchased these to use as inspiration. Poiret's first encouragement came when Mme. Chéruit, a good but minor couturière, bought a dozen of his designs. He was still a teenager when, in 1896, he began working for Jacques Doucet, one of Paris's most prominent couturiers.

Auspiciously, Doucet sold four hundred copies of one of Poiret's first designs, a simple red cape with gray lining and revers. And in four years there, the novice designer rose up in the ranks to become head of the tailoring department. His greatest coup was making an evening coat to be worn by the great actress Réjane in a play called *Zaza*. The biggest splash fashion could make in those days was on the stage, and Poiret made sure to design something attention-worthy: a mantle of black tulle over black taffeta painted with large-scale iris by a well-known fan painter. Next came the custom of more actresses, and then, while working on the play *L'Aiglon* starring Sarah Bernhardt, Poiret snuck into a dress rehearsal where his scathing critique of the sets and costumes were overheard by the playwright, costing him his job. (The remarks could not have alienated Madame Bernhardt, as he would dress her for several 1912 films.) He fulfilled his military service during the next year and then joined Worth, the top couture house as an assistant designer in 1901. There he was given a sous chef job of creating what Jean Worth (grandson of the founder) called the "fried potatoes," meaning the side dish to Worth's main course of lavish evening and reception gowns. Poiret was responsible for the kind of serviceable, simple clothes needed by women who took the bus as opposed to languishing in a carriage, and while he felt himself to be looked down on by his fellow workers, his designs were commercial successes.

In September 1903 he opened his own couture house on the avenue Auber (corner of the rue Scribe). There he quickly attracted the custom of such former clients as the actress Réjane. In 1905 he married Denise Boulet, the daughter of a textile manufacturer, whose waiflike figure and nonconventional looks would change the way he designed. In 1906 Poiret moved into 37, rue Pasquier, and by 1909 he was able to relocate to quite grand quarters: a large eighteenth-century *hôtel particulier* at 9 avenue d'Antin (perpendicular to the Faubourg Saint-Honoré and since World War II known as Avenue Franklin-Roosevelt). The architect Louis Süe oversaw the renovations; the spectacular open grounds included a parterre garden. Poiret also purchased two adjoining buildings on the Faubourg St. Honore, which he later established as Martine and Rosine.

THE POIRET ROSE

While there are some designers associated with specific flowers (Chanel and the camellia, Dior and the lily-of-the-valley) no one can claim the achievement of having reinvented a flower in such a way as to have it always identified with them. The Poiret rose (reduced to its simplest elements of overlapping curving lines) may have appeared for the first time in the form of a three-dimensional silk chiffon flower sewn to the empire bodice of Josephine, one of the 1907 dresses featured in the 1908 album *Les Robes de Paul Poiret.* Flat versions of the Poiret rose, embroidered in beads, appeared on the minaret tunic of the well-known dress Sorbet, 1913. Poiret's characteristically large and showy label also featured a rose.

Les Robes of Paul Poiret

Until the October 1908 publication of *Les Robes de Paul Poiret,* Poiret was merely an up-and-coming couturier, likely to assume a place in the hierarchy as secure as that of Doucet or Worth. However, the limited edition deluxe album of Poiret designs as envisioned and exquisitely rendered by new artist Paul Iribe would have far-reaching impact, placing Poiret in a new uncharted position, that of daringly inventive designer and arbiter of taste. Fashion presentation up to then had been quite straightforward: magazines showed clothes in a variety of media, based on what was possible technically: black-and-white sketches, hand-colored woodblock prints, or colored lithographs, and, in the case of the French magazine *Les Modes,* black-and-white photographs or pastel-tinted black-and-white photographs. The poses were typical photographer's studio ones, carefully posed models against a muted ground, vaguely landscape or interior in feeling.

Using the pochoir method of printing, resulting in brilliantly saturated areas of color, Paul Iribe juxtaposed Poiret's graphically striking clothes against stylishly arranged backgrounds including pieces of antique furniture, decorative works of art, and old master paintings. The dresses, depicted in color, popped out from the black-and-white backgrounds. This inventive approach was tremendously influential, not only affecting future fashion illustration and photography, but cementing the relationship between art and fashion and probably inspiring the launch of such exquisitely conceived publications as the *Gazette du Bon Ton.*

The dresses were no less newsworthy and influential. When Poiret introduced his lean, high-waisted silhouette of 1908, it was the first time (but hardly the last) that a radically new fashion would be based fairly literally on the past. The dresses, primarily for evening, feature narrow lines, high waists, covered arms, low décolletés. Their inspiration is both Directoire and medieval. In abandoning the bifurcated figure of the turn of the twentieth century, Poiret looked back to a time when revolutionary dress itself was referencing ancient times. Suddenly the hourglass silhouette was passé.

Poiret, Bakst, and Orientalism

Poiret had an affinity with all things Eastern, claiming to have been a Persian prince in a previous life. Significantly, the first Asian-inspired piece he ever designed, while still at Worth, was controversial. A simple Chinese-style cloak called Confucius, it offended the occidental sensibilities of an important client, a Russian princess. To her grand eyes it seemed shockingly simple, the kind of thing a peasant might wear; when Poiret opened his own establishment such mandarin-robe-style cloaks would be best-sellers.

The year 1910 was a watershed for orientalism in fashion and the arts. In June, the Ballet Russe performed *Scheherazade* at the Paris Opera, with sets and costumes by Leon Bakst. Its effect on the world of design was immediate. Those who saw the production or Bakst's watercolor sketches reproduced in such luxurious journals as *Art et Decoration* (in 1911) were dazzled by the daring color combinations and swirling profusion of patterns. Since the belle époque could be said to have been defined by the delicate, subtle tints of the impressionists, such a use of color would be seen as groundbreaking.

Although color and pattern were what people talked about, they serve to obscure the most daring aspect of the Ballet Russe costumes: the sheerness (not to mention scantiness) of the materials. Even in the drawings published in 1911, nipples can be seen through sheer silk bodices, and not just legs, but thighs in harem trousers. Midriffs, male and female, were bare altogether. Whether inspired or reinforced by Bakst, certain near-Eastern effects: the softly ballooning legs, turbans, and the surplice neckline and tunic effect became Poiret signatures.

The cover of *Les Modes* for April 1912 featured a Georges Barbier illustration of two Poiret enchantresses in a moonlit garden, one dressed in the sort of boldly patterned cocoon wraps for which Poiret would be known throughout his career, the other in a soft evening dress with high waist, below-the-knee-length overskirt, narrow trailing underskirt, the bodice sheer enough to reveal the nipples.

While Poiret's claim to have single-handedly banished the Edwardian palette of swooning mauves can be viewed as egotistical, given Bakst's tremendous influence, his assertions about doing away with the corset have more validity. In each of the numerous photographs of Denise Poiret she is dressed in a fluid slide of fabric; there is no evidence of the lumps ands bumps of corsets and other underpinnings. Corsetry and sheerness are hardly compatible and boning would interrupt Poiret's narrow lines.

The Jupe-Culotte

In the course of producing his (hugely successful) second album of designs *Les Choses de Paul Poiret* (1911), Poiret asked his latest discovery, the artist Georges Lepape, to come up with an idea for a new look. It was Mme. Lepape who sketched her idea of a modern costume and put it in her husband's pocket. When Poiret asked where the new idea was, Lepape had to be reminded to fish it out. The next time they met, Poiret surprised the couple with a mannequin wearing his version of their design: a long tunic with boat neck and high waist worn over dark pants gathered into cuffs at the ankle. And so, at the end of the album under the heading: Tomorrow's Fashions, there appeared several dress/trouser hybrids, which would become known as *jupe-culottes*.

The jupe-culotte caused an international sensation. The Victorian age had left the sexes cemented in rigid roles easily visible in their dress—men in the drab yet freeing uniform of business, and women in an almost literal gilded cage of whalebone and steel, brocade and lace. While Poiret's impulse seems to have been primarily aesthetic, the fact that it coincided with the crusade of suffragists taking up where Amelia Bloomer had left off, served to bring about a real change in how women dressed. For months anything relating to the jupe-culotte was major news. In its most common incarnation, a kind of high-waisted evening dress with tunic lines revealing soft chiffon harem pants, the jupe-culotte was wildly unmodern, requiring the help of a maid to get in and out of and utterly impractical for anything other than looking au courant. Poiret did design numerous more tailored versions, however, often featuring military details and his favorite checked or striped materials; these do look ahead (about fifty years) to the high-fashion trouser suit.

Martine

In the space of five years, Poiret had become a world-renown success. Now came another influential act. Martine, named after one of Poiret's daughters, opened 1 April 1911 as a school of decorative art. Poiret admitted to being inspired by his 1910 visit to the Wiener Werkstätte, but his idea for Martine entailed a place where imagination could flourish as opposed to being disciplined in a certain style. Young girls, who, in their early teens had finished their traditional schooling, became the pupils. Their assignment was to visit zoos, gardens, the aquarium, and markets and make rough sketches. Their sketches were then developed into decorative motifs. Once a wall full of studies had been completed, Poiret would invite artist colleagues and wallpaper, textile, or embroidery specialists for a kind of critique. The students were rewarded for selected designs, but also got to see their work turned into such Martine wares as rugs, china, pottery, wallpaper, textiles for interiors, and fashions. The Salon d'Automne of 1912 displayed many such items made after designs of the École Martine and Poiret opened a Martine store at 107, Faubourg Saint-Honoré.

Within a few years, a typical Martine style of interior had been developed, juxtaposing spare, simple shapes with large-scale native designs inspired in the main from nature. A 1914 bathroom featured micro-mosaic tiles turning the floor, sink case, and tub into a continuous smooth expanse punctuated by murals or tile panels patterned with stylized grapes on the vine. There were Martine departments in shops all over Europe; although more decorative than what would become known as art deco and art moderne, Martine deserves an early place in the chronology of modern furniture and interior design.

Also in 1911 Poiret inaugurated a perfume concern, naming it after another daughter, Rosine, and locating it at the same address as Martine. Poiret's visionary aesthetic was perfectly suited to the world of scents and he was involved in every aspect of the bottle design, packaging, and advertising, including the Rosine advertising fans. He was also interested in new developments of synthetic scents and in expanding the idea of what is a fragrance by adding lotions, cosmetics, and soaps. Fellow couturiers like Babani, the Callot Soeurs, Chanel, and Patou were among the first to follow suit; thanks to Poiret, perfumes continue to be an integral part of the image (and business) of a fashion house.

Poiret the Showman

At a time when the runway had yet to be invented and clothes were shown on models in intimate settings in couture houses, Poiret's 1911 and 1914 promotional tours of Europe with models wearing his latest designs made a tremendous splash.

On 24 June 1911 the renowned 1,002-night ball was held in the avenue d'Antin garden featuring Paul Poiret as sultan and Denise Poiret as the sultan's favorite in a combination of two of Poiret's greatest hits, a jupe-culotte with a minaret tunic. The invitations specified how the guests should dress: Dunoyer de Segonzac was told to come as Champagne, His Majesty's Valet and Raoul Dufy as The King's Fool. If one of the 300 guests showed up in Chinese (or, worse, conventional evening) dress, he or she was sent to a wardrobe room to be decked out in Persian taste. Although fancy dress balls had been all the rage for several decades, this one seems to have struck a chord; perhaps it was the first hugely luxurious (champagne, oysters, and other delicacies flowed freely) event staged by a creative person (in trade no less) rather than an aristocrat. Future fêtes, each with a carefully thought-out theme, failed to achieve the same level of excitement. After the war, Poiret's thoughts had turned toward increasingly zany moneymaking ventures. The nightclub was the latest diversion after World War I and Poiret turned his garden first into a nightspot, and then in 1921 it became an open-air theater, Oasis, with a retractable roof devised for him by the automobile manufacturer Voisin. This venture lasted six months.

His last truly notable bit of showmanship was his display at the 1925 Paris Exposition des Arts Décoratifs et

Industriels. Rather than set up a display in an approved location in an official building, Poiret installed three barges on the Seine. Decorated in patriotic French colors, Delices was a restaurant decorated with red anemones; Amours was decorated with blue Martine carnations; and Orgues was white featuring fourteen canvases by Dufy depicting regattas at Le Havre, Ile de France, Deauville; and races at Longchamps, showing some of Poiret's last dress designs under his own label. It was clear that his zest for ideas was being directed elsewhere other than fashion. Typically over the top, he also commissioned a merry-go-round on which one could ride figures of Parisian life, including him and his *midinettes*, or shopgirls.

The Poiret Milieu

Poiret's interest in the fine, contemporary arts of the day began while he was still quite young. His artist friends included Francis Picabia and André Derain, who painted his portrait when they were both serving in the French army in 1914. His sisters were Nicole Groult, married to Andre Groult, the modern furniture designer; and Mme. Boivin, the jeweler; another was a poet. Besides discovering Paul Iribe and Georges Barbier, he reinvigorated the career of Raoul Dufy by commissioning woodcut-based fabric designs from him and starting him off on a long career in textile design and giving new life to his paintings as well. Bernard Boutet de Monvel worked on numerous early projects for Poiret, including, curiously, writing catalog copy for his perfume brochures. While quite young, Erté saw (and sketched) Poiret's mannequins in Russia in 1911; after emigrating to Paris he worked as an assistant designer to Poiret from the beginning of 1913 to the outbreak of war in 1914. His illustrations accompanied articles about Poiret fashion in *Harper's Bazaar* and reveal a signature Erté style that might not have developed without the inspiration of Poiret. He also launched the careers of Madeleine Panizon, a Martine student who became a milliner, and discovered shoemaker Andre Perugia, whom he helped establish in business after World War I.

Poiret's Clientele

Not surprisingly, Poiret's clients were more than professional beauties, clotheshorses, or socialites. Besides the very top actresses of his time, Réjane and Sarah Bernhardt, the entertainer Josephine Baker, and the celebrated Liane de Pougy, one of the last of the grandes horizontales, there were: the Countess Grefulhe, muse of Marcel Proust, and Margot Asquith, wife of the English prime minister, who invited him to show his styles in London, creating a political furor for her (and her husband's) disloyalty to British designers. Nancy Cunard, ivory bracelet–clad icon of early twentieth-century style, recalled that she had been wearing a gold-panniered Poiret dress in 1922 at a ball where she was bored dancing with the Prince of Wales but thrilled to meet and chat with T. S. Eliot.

The international cosmetics entrepreneur Helena Rubinstein met Poiret while he was a young design assistant at Worth and followed him as he struck out on his own. She was photographed in one of his daring jupe-culottes in 1913 and wore a Poiret Egyptian style dress in her advertisements in 1924. The quintessentially French author Colette was a client. Boldini painted the Marchesa Casati in a chic swirl of Poiret and greyhounds. The American art patrons Peggy Guggenheim and Gertrude Whitney dressed in high bohemian Poiret and Natasha Hudnut Rambova, herself a designer and the exotic wife of the matinee idol Rudolf Valentino, went to Poiret for her trousseau.

Postwar Poiret

Poiret was involved for the duration of the war as a military tailor, and although he occasionally made news with a design or article, when he was demobilized in 1919 he had to relaunch his fashion, decorating, and perfume businesses. His first collection after the war, shown in the summer of 1919, was enthusiastically received and fashion magazines like *Harper's Bazaar* continued to regularly feature his luxurious creations, typically made in vivid colors, lush-patterned fabrics, and trimmed lavishly with fur. Poiret's work perfectly suited the first part of the 1920s. The dominant silhouette was tubular, and fairly long, and most coats were cut on the full side with kimono or dolman sleeves. Such silhouettes were perfect for displaying the marvelous Poiret decorations, either Martine-inspired or borrowed from native clothing around the world. He continued to occasionally show such previous greatest hits as jupe-culottes and dresses with minaret tunics. In 1924 he left his grand quarters in the avenue d'Antin, moving to the Rond Point in 1925. He would leave that business in 1929.

Obscurity

By 1925 Poiret had begun to sound like a curmudgeon, holding forth against chemise dresses, short skirts, flesh-colored hose, and thick ankles with the same kind of ranting tone once used by M. Worth to criticize Poiret's trouser skirt. Financially, he did poorly too, and he sold his business in 1929.

In 1931, *Women's Wear Daily* announced that Paul Poiret was reentering the couture, using as a business name his telephone number "Passy Ten Seventeen." Prevented from using his own name by a legal arrangement, he told the paper that he planned to print his photograph on his stationery, since presumably he still owned the rights to his face. This venture closed in 1932. After designing some for department stores such as Liberty in London in 1933, he turned his attention to an assortment of endeavors including writing (an autobiography called *King of Fashion*) and painting. He succumbed to Parkinson's disease on 28 April 1944.

While Gabrielle Chanel is credited with being the first woman to live the modern life of the twentieth century (designing accordingly), it is Poiret who created the contemporary idea of a couturier as wide-reaching arbiter. His specific fashion contributions aside, Poiret was the first to make fashion front-page news; to collaborate with fine artists; develop lines of fragrances; expand into interior decoration; and to be known for his lavish lifestyle. Poignantly he was also the first to lose the rights to his own name.

Poiret's earliest styles were radically simple; these would give way to increasingly lavish "artistic" designs and showman-like behavior. By 1913 *Harper's Bazaar* was already looking back at his notable achievements: originating the narrow silhouette, starting the fashion for the uncorseted figure, doing away with the petticoat, being the first to show the jupe-culotte and the minaret tunic. That the fashion world was already nostalgic about his achievements proved oddly prescient: his ability to transform how women dressed would pass with World War I.

See also **Doucet, Jacques; Fashion Designer; Orientalism; Paris Fashion; Worth, Charles Frederick.**

BIBLIOGRAPHY

Deslandres, Yvonne, with Dorothée Lalanne. *Poiret Paul Poiret 1879–1944.* New York: Rizzoli International, 1987.

Poiret, Paul. *King of Fashion: The Autobiography of Paul Poiret.* Philadelphia and London: J. B. Lippincott, 1931.

Remaury, Bruno, ed. *Dictionnaire de la Mode Au XXe Siecle.* Paris: Editions du Regard, 1994.

Sweeney, James Johnson. "Poiret Inspiration for Artists, Designers, and Women." *Vogue,* 1 September 1971, 186–196.

White, Palmer. *Poiret.* New York: Clarkson N. Potter Inc., 1973.

Caroline Rennolds Milbank

POLITICS AND FASHION Every large society and social group develops a system of social control or polity that is shared by the members of the group and relates in some way to their system of dress. The power to address diverse problems and needs of a society is invested in people who become specialists in delivery of the services of social control. Only those individuals so designated and recognized have the right to power and authority over group members. This system of control or government is reflected in the rules of the organization and evolves from the normative order and moral beliefs of the group. The moral ideas of a group both mold and reflect the group's beliefs concerning what is right or wrong behavior for members. Developing expectations for appearance, dress, and the extent to which one participates in fashion (defined here as the accepted way of behaving of the majority of individuals at a specific time and place) are social behaviors that are frequently subject to control by social organizations.

Control over dress and fashion participation is exercised both informally and formally through the political structure of an organization and its power. The governing body serves several functions, including: (a) developing, delineating, and assessing rules and regulations so that the beliefs of the organization are molded by and reflected in them; (b) establishing a framework regarding the rights and responsibilities of members of the group; and (c) developing a process for applying and enforcing the rules for all members. A process for adding new regulations and a method to dispute existing regulations can be developed along with penalties and sanctions for violations of these rules. The court system in Western societies is an example of a process used to manage power in interpreting and applying regulations, which may prohibit members from participation in some activities as well as prescribe participation in others. Government also has power over relations with other societies in matters that involve group interests including mobilizing legitimate use of force to defend the group against infringement of others. Government also involves relationships with other societies in the form of trade agreements and regulations. For example, when foreign manufacturers can produce apparel products at a lower cost than domestic manufacturers, the domestic industries are threatened. Governments may make regulations to control the flow of foreign-produced products into domestic markets to force consumers to purchase domestic products and maintain domestic industries.

Another area related to dress where the government uses power is in developing regulations for consumer protection. Laws can be developed to protect consumers from unsafe or unhealthy apparel products as well as protect the environment from human exploitation. An example of the former are the laws that prohibit the use of flammable fabrics in apparel. An example of the latter are endangered species laws that prohibit the use of skin and furs of specific animals in apparel.

Examples of power conveyed through dress are common in all societies. Topics frequently addressed through formal and informal regulations include body exposure and gender differences. Societies have regulations concerning under what circumstances, if any, different aspects of both male and female bodies can appear uncovered or covered. The amount or type of skin exposed tends to be interpreted as symbolic of certain sexual behaviors. General societal efforts to control sexual behavior may include regulations regarding appearing naked in public, exposure of genitals, appearing in clothing associated with the opposite sex (cross-dressing), or the separation of the sexes (such as government-mandated separate swimming pools or even separate cash register lines for men and women). These regulations may be formal, as in the case of health laws concerning body exposure and food service (no shoes, no shirt, no service), or informal, as in the case of amount of body exposure on public beaches. Informal regulations often vary depending on the situation. For example, a brassiere and briefs worn by a female can offer as much if not more body coverage than a swimsuit. However, a garment defined as a swimsuit is acceptable at locations like the beach or swimming pool, while a brassiere and briefs in the same place would be considered inappropriate.

Rules and regulations of social organizations vary in their degree of importance, in how they came into being, in the degree of emotional response that violating regulations might evoke, and the type of sanctions that might be applied to individuals who violate them. There are both positive and negative sanctions associated with engaging in or failing to participate in fashion. Positive sanctions such as praise or emulation reinforce behaviors perceived as correct. In contrast, a continuum in scope and intensity of negative sanctions can apply to individuals who fail to comply with the expectations of the group or group norms concerning dress and participation in fashion.

The type of negative sanction that results when individuals violate group norms for dress are tied to the degree of emotional response evoked. If the violation evoked a low degree of emotional response, concern is with violating a customary dress practice of the group. Violation of a customary practice generally does not create a great disturbance in the social organization of the group. If a sanction is applied by members of the group to influence the individual to change their behavior in keeping with the existing norm, the sanction may be in the form of gossip or teasing. In small organizations or societies where all members are known to each other, a negative sanction like gossip is probably all that is needed to force compliance with the expectations of group members. It is also possible that a mild sanction may result where a slight deviation from the group norm is tolerated if not accepted as only a minor deviation.

If the violation of the expectation for dress evokes a strong emotional response from group members, the violation is concerned with a moral standard of the group. Moral standards may be informally controlled, as is the case with customs concerning dress. Customs are associated with a history of practice, and violations may meet with negative sanctions from the group in the form of ridicule, avoidance, or ostracism. Moral standards concerning dress may also become codified into laws and formally controlled. Negative sanctions for violating laws concerning dress can include arrest, incarceration, or death.

Development of power through the rules of an organization or society do not guarantee that the rules equally reflect all members' interests. Whether the interests of men are favored over the interests of women was at issue in Terengganu, Malaysia, where the state government was said to have supported gender-based discrimination through dress codes as well as other practices. According to Endaya (2002), the government supported Islamic law as dress codes were developed that barred women from wearing bikinis and other clothing that exposed their bodies. Other dress codes that imposed

Middle East politics and fashion merge, Beirut, 2002. Saudi designer Yahya al-Bushairy debuts a dress featuring fake bloodstains, an Israeli tank, and the image of a young Palestinian boy killed by Israeli soldiers at the outbreak of the second Palestinian *intifada*. AP/WIDE WORLD PHOTOS. REPRODUCED WITH PERMISSION.

restrictions based on gender included a requirement for young Muslim women to cover their heads. Laws of this kind have become commonplace in the contemporary Islamic world. Another dress code exemplifying promotion of the interests of one group over another was a decree in 2002 made by King Mswati III of Swasiland, in southern Africa, who banned women from wearing trousers in the capital of Mbabane because the practice "violated the country's traditions" (Familara 2002, p 4).

Few laws exist in the United States that regulate appearance, dress, or fashion in the workplace or in schools. However, dress codes are used to regulate appearances in the workplace as well as in schools, and judicial decisions (case laws) have developed concerning dress. In general, most courts uphold an employer's right to set appearance standards through dress codes as long as the codes are related to a legitimate business interest, government interest, or for health and sanitation reasons (Rothstein et al,

Political fashion by Gattinoni, fall-winter 2000–2001 collection, Milan, Italy. A model displays a Gattinoni creation that criticizes the politics of right-wing Austrian politician Joerg Haider. AP/WIDE WORLD PHOTOS. REPRODUCED BY PERMISSION.

FREEDOM OF EXPRESSION IN DRESS

While the right to express a political opinion through dress may be protected by the constitution, customs concerning appropriate dress based upon gender may not be protected. In the United States, a reported case where clothing was disruptive of the learning process occurred when a young man was suspended from school for wearing a long peasant dress with a plunging neckline (Rabinovotz 1998). The issue was not only that the young man appeared in clothing customarily associated with young women, but that he stuffed tissue paper down the front. School officials noted that they did not want to create "a carnival-like atmosphere in the school" (p. B5).

1994). As a result, few complaints brought forward by employees have been upheld in the courts unless the dress code differs between men and women, the code is demeaning, or is more costly to one sex versus the other (Lennon, Schultz, and Johnson 1999).

The courts have also held that students retain their constitutional rights when they enter the school building, although student conduct, including their appearance, can be regulated. Dress codes in schools are generally considered valid if they promote safety or if they prevent disruption or distraction of peers (Alexander and Alexander 1984). Since dress is a form of communication, students in the United States have voiced the complaint that some school dress codes violate their constitutional right to freedom of speech, which is guaranteed by the First Amendment (Lennon, Schultz, and Johnson 1999). Lewin (2003) reported on a student that was sent home from school for wearing a T-shirt with a picture of President Bush and the words "international terrorist." The high school junior wore the T-shirt to express his antiwar sentiment and believed his right to express his political beliefs were violated when he was sent home from school. In this case, the school would have to prove that the stu-

dent's T-shirt was so different and disruptive that it detracted from the educational process.

The classic case concerning dress codes and students' freedom of speech in the United States is *Tinker* vs. *Des Moines Independent School District* (1969). The Tinker case involved a plan by students to wear black armbands to school to symbolize their opposition to the Vietnam War. Officials of the school learned of the students' decision two days before it happened and implemented a special dress code banning armbands in school. The U.S. Supreme Court held that wearing armbands constituted a form of speech protected by the constitution. The court held that for student activity to be prohibited, school officials must reasonably forecast disruption in the school and must have some evidence to support their forecast. The courts also ruled that the predicted disruption must be substantial, and judged to be physical and damaging to the learning environment at school (Alexander and Alexander 1984).

Regulations of an organization, such as dress codes, can shape the dress of its members. Dress can also serve as a platform for protest against such regulations. In 2001, King Mswati III of Swaziland also revived an old law requiring girls to wear chastity belts with tassels. The belts, according to the king, would not only preserve a young girl's virginity but also prevent HIV-AIDS. Subsequently, Swazi women protested and showed defiance against the law by dropping tassels in front of the royal palace (Familara 2002).

Interpersonal Social Power and Dress
While the government of a society is involved in regulations concerning dress, customs concerning dress often

involve the use of dress as a symbol to communicate interpersonal social power. Interpersonal social power is defined as the potential to have social influence (French and Raven 1959). Social influence refers to a change in the behavior or belief of a person as a result of the action or presence of another person (Raven 1992). A typology originally developed by French and Raven and subsequently refined by Raven (1992; 1993) outlines six sources of social power that an influencing agent can draw upon to affect change in another person: legitimate power, reward power, coercion power, expert power, referent power, and the power of information. These sources of social power can be either formal or informal and can be communicated through dress.

Legitimate power is influence that is based on a social position or rank within the organization. This is power that is assigned to a position by the group to enforce the rules of the group (described previously as government). Symbolic of legitimate power is the uniform of an officer in the military or the robes of a judge. Reward power is influence derived from the ability to provide social approval or some form of compensation. Fashion editors and other arbiters of taste may exercise reward power as they name individuals to best-dressed lists or feature individuals repeatedly on the cover of magazines. A woman's beauty may also yield reward power as many men consider physical attractiveness in women to be highly desirable (Buss 1989). A woman's attractiveness may be rewarding to a man who is seen with her. Coercive power is reflective of influence that is achieved as a result of threats of punishment or rejection. Symbolic of coercive power is the uniform of a police officer because of their power to deter, detain, and arrest citizens. Expert power is influence stemming from knowledge or experience. Symbolic of this type of influence are the cap and gown of the academic or the lab coats of scientists and physicians. These individuals offer recommendations that are followed because individuals' believe in their expertise. Referent power is influence derived from the desire to identify with someone. Fashion models and movie stars wield referent power when individuals copy their dress. Information power is influence that is based on a logical presentation of information by the influencing agent, which persuades the individual to comply. Lennon (1999) noted that to Catholics the white clothing of the pope might represent informational power as a result of the belief that the pope has direct communication with God. Fashion is shaped by each of these types of social power.

As noted, legitimate power over fashion is in evidence when societies develop regulations concerning dress. Sumptuary laws have been used to maintain class and gender distinctions by disallowing certain individuals to wear certain styles or colors of clothing as well as requiring certain individuals to wear specific forms of dress. When the communist party came into power in China, coercive power became evident. According to

Scott (1958), communists developed a standardization of dress that made no distinction between the sexes or on the basis of rank. The military uniform of the communists consisted of a high-collared tunic, trousers with puttees, and Chinese shoes or rubber boots. After troops occupied the cities, the industrial workers adopted dress styled more or less identical to the military uniform except the color differed. Soon afterward, students, clerical workers, and manual workers adopted the party uniform. According to Scott, no one issued directives but citizens tacitly understood that clothes other than the uniform seemed unpatriotic, and those not adopting the new style were publicly reprimanded or lectured.

The effect of reward power on fashion becomes evident through the practice of naming certain highly visible individuals to "best dressed" lists. Other individuals emulate the appearance of those named to the list and fuel fashion change in terms of speeding the diffusion of a style as well as providing an impetus for change. The impact of expert power and information power on the direction of fashion comes from numerous fashion magazines sharing perspectives on what styles comprise the fashion of a time or place. From all the styles made available by designers and manufacturers, fashion editors select and feature those styles they believe will appeal to the readers of their publications. In this way, they weld their knowledge and expertise and hence attempt to shape fashion. Newspapers feature advice columnists who answer questions about what is appropriate dress for specific social events, and subsequently impact their readers about what styles are acceptable for a given time and place (and what is the current fashion).

See also **Dress Codes; Military Style; Religion and Dress.**

BIBLIOGRAPHY

Alexander, K., and M. D. Alexander. *The Law of School, Students, and Teachers in a Nutshell.* St. Paul, Minn.: West Publishing Co., 1984.

Buss, D. M. "Sex Differences in Human Mate Preferences: Evolutionary Hypotheses Tested in 37 Cultures." *Behavioral and Brain Sciences* 12 (1989): 1–49.

French, J. R. P., and B. Raven. "The Bases of Social Power." In *Studies in Social Power.* Edited by D. Cartwright. Ann Arbor, Mich.: University of Michigan, 1958, pp. 150–167.

Lennon, S. J. "Sex, Dress and Power in the Workplace: Star Trek, the Next Generation." In *Appearance and Power*, pp. 103–126. Edited by K. Johnson and S. Lennon. Oxford: Berg, 1999.

Lennon, S. J., T. L. Schultz, and K. K. P. Johnson. "Forging Linkages Between Dress and the Law in the U.S., Part II: Dress Codes." *Clothing and Textiles Research Journal* 17, no. 3 (1999): 157–167.

Lewin, T. "High School Tells Student to Remove Antiwar Shirt." *New York Times* (23 February 2003): A12.

Raven, B. "A Power Interaction Model of Interpersonal Influence: French and Raven Thirty Years Later." *Journal of Social Behavior and Personality* 7 (1992): 217–244.

———. "The Bases of Power: Origins and Recent Developments." *Journal of Social Issues* 49 (1993): 227–254.

Rothstein, M., C. B. Craver, E. P. Schroeder, E. W. Shoben, and L. S. Vandervelde. *Employment Law*. St. Paul, Minn.: West Publishing Company, 1994.

Scott, A. C. *Chinese Costume in Transition*. New York: Theatre Arts, 1958.

Tinker v. Des Moines Independence Community School District, 393 U.S. 503, 1969.

Internet Resources

Endaya, I. "Malaysian Government Reinforces Gender Segregation." *We* 19 (2002): 5. Available from <http://straitstimes.asia1.com.sg/women/0,3320,00.html>.

Familara, A. "Women Can't Wear Trousers, Orders Swazi King." *We* 20 (2002): 4. Available from <http://news.bbc.co.uk/hi/english/world/africa/newsid_206000/2062320.stm>.

Kim K. P. Johnson

POLO SHIRT The polo shirt is a short-sleeved, open-necked white wool jersey pullover with turned-down collar, first worn by polo players from the United States and England. It is one of the first pieces of men's bona fide sports apparel to filter into mainstream fashion at all levels of the market.

Like most sportswear, the polo shirt was functional in origin, designed to allow players greater freedom of movement on the polo pitch. Originally (that is, around 1900), the polo shirt was usually made from cashmere or, sometimes, from a mix of silk and wool; the cloth was designed to be close knit and absorbent. Although it was designed specifically for the rigors of polo, during the late 1920s the polo shirt was given a stamp of approval by the fashionable. It could be seen on the French Riviera as well as on the influential Palm Beach set, many of whom were wearing them on the tennis courts.

By the 1930s the all-white polo shirt had become a classic, and brightly colored polo shirts had become very popular as golf wear. It was not until 1933, however, that tennis star Rene Lacoste adapted and redesigned the classic polo shirt specially to be worn for playing golf and tennis. He is understood to have said at the time: "Pour moi, pour jouer au tennis comme au golf, j'eus un jour l'idee de creer une chemise." (For myself, I had an idea one day to create a shirt for playing tennis as well as golf.) (Keers, p. 316). Lacoste's white cotton pique shirt featured a green crocodile logo, both on account of his nickname, "Le Crocodile," on the tennis court, and also as a trademark to help prevent imitations.

By 1935 the polo shirt was as popular off the sports fields as it was on them. A journalist sent to the Riviera pointed out: "Polo shirts have resulted in the oneness of the sexes and the equality of classes. Ties are gone. Personal touches, out. Individualism, abolished. Personality, extinct. The Riviera has produced a communism that would be the envy of the U.S.S.R." (Schoeffler, p. 578).

This popularity endured, and the polo shirt became a cult shirt later taken on as a style essential by label-conscious football terrace casuals and customized by B-boys and Fly-girls during the late 1970s and 1980s, and often worn with Lyle and Scott or Pringle Knits. Meanwhile a version by Fred Perry was the polo shirt of choice by skinheads in the 1970s, the gay crowd during the 1980s, and more recently certain exponents of Britpop and skate (as freedom of movement is still key).

Although Lacoste was there first, Ralph Lauren has built an empire in part on his version of the polo shirt. The pique shirt with the iconic polo player logo was the shirt for the status-conscious consumer to own during the 1980s. Aimed at a more exclusive segment of the market, the Polo, was cut longer and narrower than the French version and continued as a cult classic among the more affluent, the label-conscious, and vintage experts alike.

See also **Jersey; Sport Shirt; Sportswear; T-Shirt.**

BIBLIOGRAPHY

Amies, Hardy. *A, B, C of Men's Fashion*. London: Cahill and Company, Ltd., 1964.

Byrde, Penelope. *The Male Image: Men's Fashion in England 1300–1970*. London: B.T. Batsford, Ltd., 1979.

Chenoune, Farid. *A History of Men's Fashion*. Paris: Flammarion, 1993.

De Marley, Diana. *Fashion for Men: An Illustrated History*. London: B.T. Batsford, Ltd., 1985.

Keers, Paul. *A Gentleman's Wardrobe*. London: Weidenfield and Nicolson, 1987.

Schoeffler, O. E., and William Gale. *Esquire's Encyclopedia of 20th Century Fashions*. New York: McGraw-Hill, 1973.

Tom Greatrex

POLYESTER In 1929 Wallace Carothers, a researcher at DuPont, published an article describing his creation of polyester. DuPont obtained patents on this early form of polyester in 1931. Facing problems with this material, DuPont did not begin commercialization of it at that time, choosing instead to concentrate on the development of nylon. In the 1940s English researchers at Imperial Chemical Industries (ICI) developed the first practical version of polyester. It was made by combining ethylene glycol and terephthalic acid into polyethylene terephthalate (PET). DuPont bought the rights to PET in 1945 and began commercial production of Dacron polyester in 1953.

Polyester Defined

The Federal Trade Commission defines polyester as "a manufactured fiber in which the fiber-forming substance is any long-chain synthetic polymer composed of at least 85 percent by weight of an ester of a substituted aromatic carboxylic acid, including but not restricted to substituted terephthalic units, $_p(-R-O-CO-C_6H_4-CO-O-)_x$ and parasubstituted hydroxyl-benzoate units, $_p(-R-O-CO-C_6H_4-O-)_x$." (Collier and Tortor, p. 179). The polyester most commonly used for fibers is PET.

Properties of Polyester

To the average consumer, who is not a chemist, polyester is an extraordinary fiber with many desirable properties. Polyester is strong, both dry and wet. It is considered to be easy-care since it can be washed, dried quickly, and resists wrinkling. It holds up well in use because it has high resistance to stretching, shrinking, most chemicals, abrasion, mildew, and moths.

As with all fibers, polyester has some properties that are not desirable. While resistant to water-born stains, polyester is an oil scavenger. Due to its strength, polyester, particularly when cut into short staple lengths, does form pills (becomes rough with little balls). Polyester will burn with a strong odor and the molten residue can cause severe burns to the skin. Because polyester has low absorbency, it can become uncomfortable in hot weather. This problem has been addressed by making polyester fibers with multilobal cross sections (as opposed to round ones). Since the multilobal fibers cannot pack together as tightly as round ones, perspiration can be wicked (carried on the surface of the fibers) away from the body, thereby improving the wearer's comfort.

Care of Polyester

Polyester is often blended with other fibers that require different care procedures. For this reason care procedures may vary across fabrics.

For 100 percent polyester fabrics, oily stains should be removed before washing. Generally they can be machine washed on a warm or cold setting using a gentle cycle. They can be tumble dried on a low setting and should be removed from the dryer as soon as the cycle is completed. Garments should immediately be either hung on hangers or folded. When handled in this way, fabrics made from 100 percent polyester rarely need ironing. If a touch-up is needed, it should be done at a moderate temperature on the wrong side of the fabric.

Some garments made from polyester or polyester blends may require dry cleaning. Tailored garments with multiple components, such as suits, may need to be dry-cleaned. It is important to follow care instructions and not assume that dry cleaning is better than washing. Pigment prints on polyester should not be dry cleaned, as the solvent would dissolve the adhesive that holds the pigment on the surface of the fabric.

Uses of Polyester

Polyester could be called the tofu of manufactured fibers since its appearance takes on many forms. Depending upon the actual manufacturing process, polyester can resemble silk, cotton, linen, or wool. When blended with other fibers, polyester takes on even more forms, com-

POLYESTER'S IMAGE

When polyester first reached the market in the 1950s, it was hailed as a wonder fiber. Travelers could wash a garment, hang it up, and have it ready to wear in a couple of hours. It needed no ironing.

By the late 1960s, polyester's image was very different. Polyester leisure suits for men and polyester double knit pantsuits for women were embraced by the middle-aged and elderly. College students, on the other hand, hated polyester. In the 1970s they even referred to it as the "P" curse. They perceived it as cheap and certainly not "with it."

To combat this image, the Tennessee Eastman Company launched a "polyester" campaign to revive its image. The Man-Made Fiber Producers Association, which became the Manufactured Fiber Producers Association—Polyester Fashion Council, launched its own campaign.

Both groups focused on polyester's easy-care properties instead of its cheapness. In 1984 the Man-Made Fiber Producer's Association and the Council of Fashion Designers endorsed collections made almost exclusively of polyester or polyester blends. Well-known designers, like Oscar de la Renta, Perry Ellis, Calvin Klein, and Mary McFadden, participated. Such publicity helped a little.

Probably a more important contributor to the improved image of polyester has been the technological advances made by the producers. High-tech fibers made of polyester have revolutionized the active sportswear market. Polyester microfibers are used to make fabric that feels like silk. Recycled PET polyester from soda bottles is transformed into comfortable fleece, thereby appealing to those concerned with the environment.

bining the good qualities of each contributing fiber. Polyester is also the most-used manufactured fiber. The DuPont company estimates that the 17.7 million metric tons consumed worldwide in 1995 will rise to almost 40 million metric tons by 2005.

Apparel uses of polyester. Polyester is used for all kinds of apparel, by itself and in blends. It is found in every type of clothing, from loungewear to formal eveningwear. Some common blends include polyester and cotton for shirts and polyester, and wool for suits. Polyester contributes easy-care properties to both of those blends while cotton and wool provide comfort. Another use of polyester fiber is found inside some garments. A ski jacket with hollow polyester fibers used between the outer fabric and the lining provides warmth without weight.

Home furnishings uses of polyester. Polyester and polyester blends are used for curtains, draperies, upholstery, wall coverings, and carpets, as well as for bedding. Sheets and pillowcases made from polyester and cotton blends, do not need to be ironed, but they are not quite as comfortable as those made from 100 percent cotton. Carpets made from 100 percent polyester are less expensive than nylon, more apt to get packed down with wear, and allow considerable build-up of static electricity during the dry winter months.

Other uses of polyester. Polyester's low absorbency and high strength even when wet make it ideal for umbrellas, tents, and sleeping bags. Some industrial uses of polyester take advantage of the same characteristics. Hence, polyester is used for hoses, tire cords, belts, filter cloth, fishing nets, and ropes. Polyester is used for sewing thread, but thread made of 100 percent polyester tends to heat up and form knots when used in high-speed sewing. Cotton-covered polyester thread eliminates the problem.

See also **Microfibers; Recycled Textiles.**

BIBLIOGRAPHY

Collier, B. J., and P. G. Tortora. *Understanding Textiles.* 6th ed. Upper Saddle River, N.J. Prentice-Hall, Inc., 2001.

Humphries, M. *Fabric Reference.* 3rd ed. Upper Saddle River, N.J.: Pearson Education, Inc., 2004.

Internet Resource

Polyester Revival. 2004. Available from <http://schwartz.eng.auburn.edu/polyester/revival.html>.

Elizabeth D. Lowe

POLYESTER FIBER, RECYCLED. *See* **Recycled Textiles.**

POLYETHYLENE. *See* **Olefin Fibers.**

POLYOLEFIN. *See* **Olefin Fibers.**

POLYPROPYLENE. *See* **Olefin Fibers.**

PRADA Prada was founded in Milan in 1913 by Mario Prada as a luxury leather-goods firm, but it made little impact on the world of fashion until after Miuccia Prada took charge of her grandfather's company in 1978. Her first big success was a black nylon backpack with a triangular silver label. Soon her shoe and handbag designs became the focus of a veritable cult of fashionable consumers in Europe, America, and Japan. Miuccia Prada and her husband and business partner, Patrizio Bertelli, maintain close control over the company. They added a ready-to-wear line in 1989 and inaugurated the younger, slightly less expensive Miu Miu line in 1992, followed by Prada Sport, whose iconic red line is almost as recognized in certain circles as Nike's swoosh symbol. A string of shops and boutiques in Paris, New York, and San Francisco, designed in collaboration with the architect Rem Koolhaas, became

Miuccia Prada, Milan, Italy, 1998. Granddaughter of Prada's founder, Mario Prada, Miuccia took the Italian fashion design house to international heights of fame after taking over in 1978. AP/WIDE WORLD PHOTOS. REPRODUCED BY PERMISSION.

instantly famous. Prada also engaged in a series of complex ownership maneuvers in the late 1990s, buying and selling stakes in Gucci, Fendi, and other companies and forming a partnership with Azzedine Alaïa in 2000.

Prada clothes and accessories have been described as both classic and eccentric, frumpy but hip, marked by an ambiguous techno-retro sensibility. On the one hand, Prada's style is modern, drawing on northern Italian traditions of discreet elegance and fine craftsmanship. On the other hand, as Miuccia Prada said in 1995, "I make ugly clothes from ugly material. Simply bad taste. But they end up looking good anyway." She may have been referring to that season's "bad taste" collection, featuring such styles as a Formica check design, which evoked the look of 1970s polyester. Several years later she said, "I have always thought that Prada clothes looked kind of normal, but not quite normal. Maybe they have little twists that are disturbing, or something about them that's not quite acceptable. . . . Prada is not clothing for the bourgeoisie."

The eccentricity and intellectual purity of Miuccia Prada's clothes appeal to intellectuals and artists, while fashion editors are drawn to her constant experimentalism. Prada produced very strong collections in 2003 and 2004 that reaffirm her own aesthetic sensibilities and the stature of her company.

See also **Alaïa, Azzedine; Fendi; Gucci; Handbags and Purses; Retro Styles; Shoes.**

BIBLIOGRAPHY

Buxbaum, Gerda, ed. *Icons of Fashion: The Twentieth Century.* New York: Prestel, 1999.

John S. Major

PRISON DRESS Prison dress fluctuates historically and from country to country; from regimented "uniform" to the wearing of everyday clothes; and from work wear to nongendered jumpsuits as categorization of "criminality." Its implementation, design, and production varies according to current penal thinking, the degree of surveillance required by political regimes, types of crime committed, and according to the criminal institution— from young offenders' to women's prisons; from "top security" to local prisons or from federal to state penitentiaries.

In eighteenth-century America, Britain and Europe, regimes of "malign neglect" were prevalent, resulting in a disorder characterized by both men and women in rags, almost naked and the majority chained. Since crime was, and still is, for the most part, committed by the poor, privileges have been known to be exercised by inmates to procure their own clothing. Voltaire, arrested in France in 1727, demanded to wear his own clothes. In Ireland, in 1887, Home Rule dissenters were permitted to supplement prison issue coarse woolen (frieze) garments with overcoats.

Prison reforms in America and Europe in the early nineteenth century, influenced by the Enlightenment and early "normalization" penal theories, saw prison dress as integral to the philosophy of discipline, as a tool in the "curing" of deviant behavior. In America between 1820 and 1930, quasi-military regimes of "silence" and solitary confinement saw the introduction of black-and-white striped all-in-one prison uniforms in order to demean and identify prisoners, and to increase the likelihood of recapture should they escape.

In Europe and specifically France, in the 1830s, the wearing of striped pants and blue linen overalls augmented surveillance of prisoners in chain gangs. In Australia, convict work gangs wore arrowed uniforms, while in Britain broad-arrowed, all-in-one prison uniforms were introduced in the 1870s Prison Act, as both a shaming and branding device. The arrows were not abolished until the 1920s in conjunction with post–World War I penal reforms.

In addition to uniforms, prisoners wore hoods when moving from "useful" work to cells or when exercising, reinforcing nineteenth-century debates focusing on the convicted criminals reflecting on their criminal activities in isolation and silence.

Continuing into the twenty-first century, it is evident globally that there is often a direct correlation between the degree of social control of prison regimes and the disregard for prisoners' human rights in the wearing of regulation clothing.

International Prison reforms of the 1950s culminated in a UN declaration in 1955, stating that:

> Every prisoner who is not allowed to wear his own clothing shall be provided with an outfit of clothing suitable for the climate and adequate to keep him in good health. Such clothing should in no way be degrading or humiliating (Orland, p. 169).

Since the 1950s, variations in prison clothing have only approximated to the UN declaration and "'normalization" debates that consider confinement, itself, to be punishment enough, while prison conditions should apply civilian standards in relation to food, clothing, and education facilities.

In the United Kingdom, unconvicted prisoners are allowed to wear their personal clothes and each prison sets its own system of privileges, one of which may be the wearing of civilian clothes. However, women in Holloway prison, given the choice, tend to wear prison issue maroon or gray tracksuits, white T-shirts, and trainers, either to preserve their own clothes or to identify with their "total institution" selves as a survival mechanism. Convicted male prisoners are issued jeans, sweatshirts, blue-and-white-striped shirts, green work overalls and unbranded trainers. On arrival, they are often offered

Penetentiary workers. Prisoners of the Mississippi State Penetentiary walk to work on cotton fields in 1939. Black and white striped uniforms were designed to humiliate the prisoners as well as make them easy to spot should they escape. AP/WIDE WORLD PHOTOS. REPRODUCED BY PERMISSION.

clothes rejected by other prisoners, which as a result are demeaning in their lack of fit.

In the United States prison clothing is determined by type of institution and category of crime committed. In federal prisons white jumpsuits are worn inside the prison, while orange outfits are worn in transit. Women prisoners are allowed to wear their own clothes after 5 P.M. In both state and federal prisons some categories of prisoners are able to wear their own clothes or prison-issue jeans, T-shirts, branded trainers and loose prison-issue overalls as work wear. In Immigration Detention orange loose-fitting jumpsuits are issued to both men and women, which some women find demeaning because it is against their cultural norms to wear pants.

Both British and American prison dress is produced in prison workshops by inmates under strict controls as to design, regarding seam allowances, lack of pockets, sizing, fabric, and color.

Internationally, prison dress varies in relation to a country's penal policies, wealth, or prisoner categorization system. The degree to which prisoners are allowed to wear their own clothes at times demarcates "normalization" as rehabilitation, foreseeing the return of the prisoner to "normal" life after release, as in Sweden and Holland's 1997–1998 "model" prison systems, Switzerland's "open prisons," and Lithuania's 1997 "own clothes" policy, which was hailed by penal reformers as a victory for prisoners' rights. The issue of not wearing prison dress has been central to protests by political prisoners campaigning for the right to separate political status from convicted criminals, as in Irish prisoners' "blanket protests," 1976–1982, and in Peru, 1985–1989. In other circumstances the wearing of civilian clothing reflects a return to regimes of "malign neglect," as in Haiti's unsegregated men, women, and juveniles' prison in Port-au-Prince in the late 1990s.

Recent penal debates include the advantages and disadvantages of electronic tagging and, although not strictly a prison-dress issue, it raises concerns, as Foucault indicated, about the "recoding of existence" within prison walls, commensurate with social control or the rehabilitation of prisoners through the regulation of dress and identity.

See also **Dress Codes; Uniforms, Occupational.**

BIBLIOGRAPHY

Foucault, Michel. *Discipline and Punish: The Birth of the Prison.* London and New York: Penguin Books, 1991.

Goffman, Erving. *Asylums.* London: Penguin Books, 1968.

Mayhew, Henry, and John Binny. *Criminal Prisons of London.* London: Frank Cass and Company, Ltd., 1971.

Morris, Norval, and David Rothman, eds. *Oxford History of the Prison.* Oxford and New York: Oxford University Press, 1995.

Orland, Leonard. *Prisons: Houses of Darkness.* New York: Free Press; London: Macmillan, 1978.

Juliet Ash

PROFESSIONAL ASSOCIATIONS The fashion and clothing industries are notable for their interdependence, their sharing of information, and their support of each other within their specific areas. Their professional associations may be divided roughly into two categories: membership organizations with either individual or corporate members, and trade organizations whose purpose is to further the goals and enhance the image of a particular segment of the industry.

The oldest and most prestigious of the individual member organizations is the Fashion Group, founded in 1931. Its catalyst was *Vogue*'s editor-in-chief, Edna Woolman Chase, who, at the urging of one of her staff, gathered a small group of women who held positions of consequence in the fashion industry and related fields. Aiming to draw membership from several areas, they formed an advisory board consisting of: Dorothy Shaver, first woman to become president of a major department store, Lord and Taylor; Mrs. Stanley Resor, executive of the advertising agency J. Walter Thompson; Mrs. Ogden Reid of the *New York Herald Tribune* publishing family; and Mrs. Franklin D. Roosevelt, wife of the then governor of New York State, who, because of her labor activism, represented her interest in the garment industry and the International Ladies Garment Workers Union (ILGWU). Other early founding members eager to join this first nonprofit group were the cosmetic stars Elizabeth Arden and Helena Rubinstein, the designer Claire McCardell, the *Harper's Bazaar* editor Carmel Snow and as regional chapters opened, Edith Head in Los Angeles. They defined their mission as a forum in which to exchange information and a force to support women in their emerging role in a male-dominated industry. In the early

2000s, men were invited to membership, but it remained primarily a woman's group. It serves 6,000 members of the fashion communities of every major U.S. city and internationally from Paris to Tokyo, over 40 in all; and now known as FGI (Fashion Group International). The same goals still remain—sharing information by covering the seasonal trends from Europe and America and enhancing women's careers by providing informational seminars and networking opportunities. FGI also maintains an archive of its history, documents, and fashion images dating from 1931.

Women in the beauty, cosmetics, fragrance, and related industries created an organization in 1954 called Cosmetic Executive Women (CEW). Based in New York, it has associated organizations in France and the United Kingdom. At its founding, it was a social organization, remaining relatively small until 1975 when its mission was expanded to promote the contributions of women in the industry; in 1985 it again expanded to include education, philanthropy, and industry development. The establishment in 1993 of the CEW Foundation provided a philanthropic arm to fund charities dedicated to helping women better their lives.

Dominant on the international scene is the venerable Chambre Syndicale de la Couture Parisienne. Behind the rich and elaborate pageantry of Paris haute couture is the organization that sets the rules and regulations for fashion's most exclusive and expensive enterprise. The Chambre is the iron hand in fashion's velvet glove.

Established over a century ago, this governing force dictates which houses may distinguish themselves with the appellation "haute couture," which means high sewing or high fashion. There is a demanding regimen involved in becoming one of these privileged few. The Chambre's rules state that a design house meet these requirements: a house must employ at least twenty employees in its atelier; present a collection of at least seventy-five designs twice a year, and show them at least forty-five times annually in a special area of the house.

Headed by a president and a director of public relations, the Chambre organizes the calendar and venues for the biannual showings, provides public relations support, and requires that videos and portions of the collections are shown in New York, Tokyo, and the Middle East.

A house's jewel in the crown, haute couture is profitable only through licensees and fragrances, for example, but is the foundation for influence and prestige crucial to a designer's image. It is the laboratory for new ideas, the research and development of the fashion industry. The Chambre Syndicale, through its exacting standards, perpetuates the authority of these fashion laboratories.

Few of the organizations of the other fashion capitals are regarded with the same respect. Rather, they were created to function as their organizing, marketing, and public relations entities, involved with designer collection shows as well as trade shows, identified by titles such as

Collezione Milano and the London Fashion Council. But all serve an important purpose—the vital support of an international economic force and its creative energies.

American designers are invited to join the Council of Fashion Designers of America (CFDA), an organization founded in the 1960s by the publicist Eleanor Lambert and others, when they saw that most American designers were toiling in the back rooms, unrecognized; few had their names on their garments' labels and even fewer on the showroom's front door. The American fashion industry and its design talent were not achieving the recognition and publicity it deserved.

The Council achieved its mission of gaining worldwide credibility for the industry. In the early 2000s, its membership is made up of both apparel and accessory designers. Its most famous contributions to the industry have been "7th on Sixth," organizing the seasonal showings and relocating them from individual venues to tents in New York's Bryant Park, and their fund-raising efforts on behalf of AIDS. Seventh on Sixth has been acquired by the talent agency IMG and continues as a separate entity; the CFDA continues its original mission, the support for and recognition of American design talent, granting scholarships and presenting its annual awards, which have become the "Oscars" of the fashion industry.

See also **Fashion Advertising; Fashion Editors; Fashion Industry.**

BIBLIOGRAPHY
CEW, Cosmetic Executive Women Website. 2004. Available from <http://cew.org>.
Council of Fashion Designers of America. Website. 2004. Available from <www.cfda.com.flash.html>.
Fashion Group International. Website. 2004. Available from <www.fgi.org/home.html>.
International Association of Clothing Designers. Website. 2004. Available from <www.iacde.com>.
UNITE! Website. 2004. Available from <www.uniteunion.org>.

Lenore Benson

PROTECTIVE CLOTHING Clothing has been used for protection since the beginning of time, shielding the human body from physical, social, emotional, and spiritual threats, real and imagined. Today, the term, *protective clothing* is generally used to denote apparel and apparel accessories that focus on *physical* protection for the body.

Protective clothing may be as simple as a sun hat or as complex as a space suit. Defined broadly, it may include items that have not traditionally been thought of as clothing, such as flotation vests or football helmets. Watkins uses the term *portable environment* to describe protective clothing, defining it as "a unique environment that is carried everywhere with an individual, creating its own room within a room and its own climate within the larger climate of our surroundings" (1995, p. xv).

The array of physical threats from which clothing provides protection today is endless. Most people use clothing to protect themselves from cold, heat, rain, snow, sun, and other aspects of day-to-day weather. But protective clothing also allows the body to exist in hazardous environments such as the deep sea or outer space. It is worn to protect individuals from many different hazards in war zones or in the workplace—from falling debris to toxic chemicals to bullets to insect bites. It provides protection for sports and leisure activities as diverse as hockey, cycling, and skiing. Many individuals with injuries or handicaps use protective clothing to prevent further body damage or to substitute for loss of body functions.

The concept of protection has had many connotations for various cultures in different eras. There is evidence to suggest that the bodies of early peoples acclimated to extremes of heat and cold without the use of clothing and that the earliest garments were *not* worn for what we might now consider to be physical protection. Instead, it is believed that the first garment was a girdle worn around the hips to protect the genital region from magic (Renbourn and Rees 1972, p. 228). While some might consider these girdles to be merely a form of spiritual protection, their wearers surely believed that it kept them from physical harm. Throughout history, even the most sophisticated forms of physically protective clothing have had to meet the social, emotional, and spiritual needs of those who wore them, or they were rejected, regardless of the protection they offered.

Weather and War
Prior to the twentieth century, protective clothing generally served one of two functions: as shelter from climatic conditions or as protective armor. The materials used to make clothing a shelter were as varied as the regions in which people lived and the natural resources found in them. For the earliest protective garments, leaves were worn in the tropics and animal furs were used in more frigid climates. Garments used for shelter from the weather were greatly influenced by the fashions of the times. Social mores, societal beliefs, and traditions may have had even more influence on their design than the actual climatic conditions from which they were purported to provide protection.

To a certain extent, the same was true of the design of protective armor. The European suits of armor and the elaborate costumes of the Japanese samurai warrior both carried with them significant symbolic meaning. However, armor evolved through the ages in large part as a response to the evolution of weapons.

The first known armor, worn by the Egyptians in 1,500 B.C.E., consisted of an unwieldy shirt-like garment to which overlapping bronze plates were sewn. In the eighth century B.C.E., the Greeks made improvements on this garment by shaping metal plates to each body part. With the development of chain mail by the Celts in the third century B.C.E., a warrior's ability to function in battle was significantly improved. Mail was lighter than earlier armor and flexed with every body movement. Since it provided protection from arrows and knives and other weapons of the times, chain mail remained as the primary protective material used in battle for many centuries.

When crossbows were developed, chain mail could no longer provide sufficient protection. Full suits of metal armor, with overlapping metal plates sewn to a flexible leather backing, came into use at the end of the thirteenth century. A full suit of armor was considerably more effective against the weapons of the times and actually provided better mobility than the early Egyptian plated shirts since the metal was shaped and distributed more evenly over the whole body.

With the development of gunpowder and firearms, metal suits of armor became a thing of the past. Soldiers in World War I and gangsters in the 1920s continued to wear garments to which metal plates were attached. Metal and ceramic coverings provided protection for airmen during World War II, but these were much too heavy for the ground soldier. It took advanced-technology developments in the mid-twentieth century to lead designers to truly suitable responses to firearms. In the mid-1960s, when Kevlar aramid fibers were patented and made into fabrics, it finally became possible to design relatively thin, lightweight, flexible shields for bullets and explosive fragments. These designs made it possible for armor to function covertly as well. Thus, the new soft armor could be used not only in battle, but also by police and undercover professionals.

The Technological Boom

The whole concept of protective clothing expanded exponentially during the second half of the twentieth century. The explosion of technological advances during this time made possible forms of protective clothing that had previously existed only in the minds of writers of science fiction. As in the case of armor, new hazards inspired new protective clothing designs. And new designs often changed the behavior of their wearers.

For example, early firefighters stood at a distance from flames wearing their everyday clothing while throwing buckets of water on burning structures. Even in larger cities during the eighteenth and nineteenth centuries, where water was pumped through hoses, no real physical protection was provided by the ornate uniforms issued, and thus firefighters moved no closer to the fire. The rubber jackets and, later, the cotton duck bunker coats that were worn in the first half of the twentieth century kept firefighters dry and warm in the constant spray of water from hoses, but also moved them no closer to the fire.

Flame and high-heat resistant aramid fibers such as Nomex and Kevlar developed in the 1960s combined with portable breathing devices to allow firefighters to actually enter burning buildings. Aluminizing the surface of

Bio-safety level 4 hazmat suits. Two people wear hazardous materials (hazmat) protection suits, capable of protecting a human being from the most dangerous biological pathogens. Special gas masks filter out airborn germ particles. AP/WIDE WORLD PHOTOS. REPRODUCED BY PERMISSION.

these materials in fully enclosed ensembles called *proximity suits* made it possible for firefighters to move still closer to the flames. Further developments in protective materials resulted in *entry suits*, in which firefighters could actually walk into the flames.

Thus, there is a cycle in the evolution of protective clothing that is much like one in the medical world. As organisms develop a resistance to medicines designed to defeat them, they venture forward and new medicines need to be developed. As protective clothing removes each threat, individuals venture further into danger and require newer, more powerful forms of protection.

Protection from Multiple Hazards

While some items of protective clothing are designed to protect from only one hazard, many others must solve multiple problems. A list of the modern battle-ready soldier's requirements for protection illustrates the complexity of multiple physical threats. Military documents point to a daunting list of hazards from which clothing must provide protection: climate (heat, cold, rain, solar radiation, wind, sand, snow); weapons (ballistics, chemical, biological, flame, blast, nuclear flash, directed energy such as microwaves); detection (visual, infrared); mechanical (cuts, abrasions, crushing); sensory (damage to hearing, sight); and biting insects and animals.

The great dilemma in designing for protection from multiple hazards is that there rarely is a clear-cut hierarchy of threats. Designing always involves trade-offs. For example, to protect soldiers from chemical weapons, they must be fully isolated from the environment. This necessitates the provision of breathing air and a method of preventing heat build-up within protective clothing. However, the motors used to circulate air leave a signal that can be picked up by infrared detection devices, providing the enemy with a target. Since both heat exhaustion and exposure to chemical agents could be fatal, neither of these requirements can simply be ignored to satisfy the need for full camouflage. Multifunction protective clothing for outer space, deep-sea diving, chemical-spill cleanup, Arctic exploration, asbestos removal, bomb disposal, race-car driving, mountain-climbing expeditions, and many other activities and environments all involve protection from multiple hazards. Even clothing that has only one primary protective function involves challenging trade-offs between protection, mobility, thermal comfort, and use of the senses.

Litigation

The accelerated pace of technological development in the latter part of the twentieth century, combined with changes in society's attitudes toward lawsuits, had a significvant affect on the development of protective clothing. For centuries, many people had worked and played in hazardous conditions without physical protection. As technology made it increasingly possible to be protected from a wide array of hazards, many companies and organizations began to face lawsuits for not designing protective clothing properly or providing it when needed.

Improvements in sports equipment added another legal problem: The more fully equipment protected athletes, the more willing they were to take serious risks on the playing field and to use the equipment itself as a weapon. The litigation arising from serious football injuries in the 1960s spurred the formation of a number of regulatory groups to oversee the design and use of protective sports equipment. In 1978, the National Collegiate Athletic Association (NCAA) mandated that every football player in an NCAA game must wear a helmet that was certified to have met specific performance standards. In 1980, similar regulations were set for high school players.

Interest in consumer protection surged during this time as well, with the most notable development for protection in everyday clothing being the Flammable Fabrics Act: Children's Sleepwear, enacted in 1972.

The Occupational Safety and Health Administration (OSHA), formed in 1971, formalized government involvement in regulations to ensure health and safety in the workplace. Many places of work, even those in which protective clothing had never been worn, then became a target for litigation. Providing the wrong protective clothing was as risky as providing none at all. The resulting potential for financial liability spurred many companies to seek protection for their workers and led toward the development and refinement of many new protective materials and designs. As women began to enter more professions, equipment specifically geared toward a woman's size, shape, and specific protective needs also began to be developed.

Active Protection

Many future developments in protective clothing lie in the arena of active protection; that is, garments which interact with or change the environment of the wearer rather than passively insulating the body from it. High-tech materials and developments in the field of wearable computers make active rather than passive protection the wave of the future.

By the early twenty-first century, loggers wore pants that incorporated fibers that pull out of a protective fabric to clog the chains of a chain saw, stopping it immediately, should the saw accidentally drop onto the logger's leg. Epileptics wear vests that read muscle contractions and automatically inflate personal airbags around the head when a seizure is about to occur.

The U.S. Army envisions that full-body hard suits will one day "walk" injured or unconscious soldiers back to safety. Fabrics of the future may be self-cleaning, fibers rippling to move unwanted dirt away or emitting an agent to neutralize a toxin. Braddock and O'Mahoney describe a future garment as being "made of small cellular units connected to one another by screws" (1998, p. 141). These cells and screws would be directed by a computer link that could order minute automatic adjustments in the shape of any part of the garment or direct heat, cooling, massage, or medicines through tiny channels to isolated body areas when needed. The protective possibilities for future active clothing designs are endless.

See also **Aprons; Coat; Fashion, Health, and Disease; Space Suit.**

BIBLIOGRAPHY

Braddock, Sarah E., and Marie O'Mahoney. *TechnoTextiles: Revolutionary Fabrics for Fashion and Design.* New York: Thames and Hudson, Inc., 1998.

Hatch, Kathryn L. *Textile Science.* Minneapolis: West Publishing Company, 1993.

Renbourn, E.T., and W. H. Rees. *Materials and Clothing in Health and Disease.* London: H.K. Lewis and Company, 1972.

Watkins, Susan M. *Clothing: The Portable Environment.* Ames, Iowa: The Iowa State University Press, 1995.

Susan M. Watkins

PROUST, MARCEL Marcel Proust (1871–1922) is the author of the sixteen-volume *À la recherche du temps perdu* (known in English as *Remembrance of Things Past* [1922–1931]). The first volume was published in 1913, and the last after the writer's death. These novels reveal not only Proust's expert knowledge of dress—he researched very precise details of garment construction—but also the way in which his appreciation of fashion has far wider implications, both within his work and beyond.

Proust the Dandy

When Jacques-Émile Blanche completed his portrait of the young writer Proust in 1892, he captured on canvas Proust's image of himself, which has become our own. Possibly, he was first thought of as a dandy, a socialite, and a darling of the duchesses—moving between the different worlds of *fin-de-siècle* Paris with infinite ease—and last as a novelist. He was, in fact, born to wealthy middle-class parents. His father, a Catholic, was a surgeon, and his Jewish mother was the daughter of a stockbroker. Proust's entrée into society and his literary career began when he was still a schoolboy. At the Lycée Condorcet (1891–1893), his friends included the children of literary and artistic families, who invited him into their world and their salons; he and his friends edited and published two literary magazines.

By 1906, when Proust began to devote all his energies to his masterwork—after his legal studies at the École libre des Sciences-Politiques, a prestigious school which formed part of the Sorbonne, and the publication of various juvenilia, pastiches, gossip columns, and translations—he was less inclined to haunt the salons. He had been keenly affected by the "Dreyfus affair": In 1897 a Jewish army officer, Captain Alfred Dreyfus, was accused and convicted of passing government secrets to the Germans and was sentenced to deportation to Devil's Island. The controversy played out over the course of a decade, until a court of appeals exonerated Dreyfus and he was pardoned. As a Jew and a man of conscience, Proust was active and passionate in his defense of Dreyfus, while most of his former grand hostesses sided with the government and army. The deaths of both Proust's parents soon afterward and the increasing problems caused by his ill health strengthened his belief that he was wasting his time.

By 1913 his appearance had changed so radically that a young visitor to his flat, who glimpsed the Blanche portrait, did not recognize the slender young man pictured with a gray cravat and an orchid in his buttonhole. But that young man, who had gone to Cabourg, the "Balbec" of the novels, "armed with Liberty ties in all shades," as he wrote to a friend in 1894 (Painter, p. 174) had not entirely disappeared. The huge coat that Proust always wore in later years was lined with fur, and he was never without a hat, gloves, and a cane.

Proust and His Circle

Proust's socializing began in the artistic salons of the late 1880s, but his desire to scale the heights of the Faubourg Saint-Germain—the wealthy and aristocratic section of Paris—to meet duchesses as well as the *grandes cocottes* ("great courtesans") of the Belle Epoque was strong and speedily gratified. The models for his later characters were found in these different settings. The character

Marcel Proust, 1932. While generally not linked to the world of clothing design but rather to literature, Proust's writings reveal his intense interest in fashion. AP/WIDE WORLD PHOTOS. REPRODUCED BY PERMISSION.

Baron de Charlus, for example, was based on Robert de Montesquieu, aristocrat and would-be poet, whom Proust first met in 1893. In the portrait of Montesquieu by the society painter Giovanni Boldini, the baron is raising his ebony cane like a rapier; the blue porcelain handle matches his large cuff links. His long-waisted jacket with wide lapels edged with broad ribbon and his white shirt with high, soft collar and dark cravat are part of the recognizable dress code of the *fin-de-siècle* dandy. His unusually high-coiffed hair, handlebar moustache, and small imperial-style beard, along with his arresting and extraordinary pose, created the kind of extreme image that Proust feared most, given its perceived links to homosexuality and to the writer Oscar Wilde, whom Proust had met and whose trial for homosexual conduct was thoroughly covered in the French press. Yet the young Proust himself was photographed with two close friends in a similar, though muted, mode of self-presentation.

Elisabeth, Comtesse Greffulhe, one of the models for Duchesse de Guermantes, was a friend and cousin of Montesquieu. She posed for an unknown photographer at about the same time as Montesquieu sat for Boldini. She stands arranging flowers in a tall Greek vase, showing off the unusual back detailing of her dress, with its large white collar appliquéd with flowers and its pattern of light-colored flowers flowing down the dark dress, spreading out and underlining the shape of the skirt. Comtesse de Chevigné, another model for the duchess, wore cornflowers in her hat to emphasize her bright blue eyes, just like the Duchesse de Guermantes in the novel. She chose to be depicted, by another unknown photographer, in far more somber attire, as if to emphasize her intellectual credentials. This yoking of art and high society, which so fascinated Proust, caused André Gide, as a young publisher, to reject the first volume of the novel. In his later years Proust did not forgo the company of artists nor did he eschew high society completely. He became friendly with the writer Jean Cocteau and dined with the ballet producer Sergey Diaghilev and the dancer Vaslav Nijinsky, but his work took priority.

Fashion within the Novels
We are told, toward the end of *Swann's Way*, that the young narrator is glad of his Charvet tie and patent boots as he waits for the former courtesan Odette de Crécy in the Bois de Boulogne. She is now married to the rich and respectable Charles Swann. Earlier in the volume she has been described as one of the most stylish women in Paris, with "rich garb such as no other woman wore." Her toilettes are always depicted in great detail, and the narrator is fascinated by the Japanese-style gowns that she wears at home. She has an inordinate number in different fabrics—silk, crepe de chine, chiffon—and the colors vary from old rose and mauve to Tiepolo pink and gold, all described carefully and frequently in *Within a Budding Grove*. An intense focus on sensuous detail is one way in which dress operates within the novel's sequence.

Fashion is also vital as the way in which an individual constructs his or her personal identity while remaining mindful of the rules of social caste. Odette's outdoor clothes show small details in their trimmings or patterns, which hark back to her heyday as Second Empire courtesan. The craftsmanship and the overall design of her garments are stressed. The narrator follows Odette, enchanted, through the Bois de Boulogne, and Proust records the details of the linings of her jackets and the collars of her blouses, likening them to Gothic carvings. Such details may never be noticed by a casual observer but they are nevertheless vital.

The woman to whom Proust awards the accolade of the very best-dressed woman in Paris is also one of the most socially elevated—Oriane, Duchesse de Guermantes, who is always spectacular and distinctive in her toilette. In *The Guermantes Way*, the narrator tells us of her appearance at the opera with a single egret feather in her hair and a white spangled dress, designed to make her companion and cousin, the Princess, seem overdressed. It is she, as well as Odette, to whom the narrator turns in *The Captive* when he wants help with the selection of clothes for his mistress, Albertine. Indeed, it is Oriane's Fortuny gowns that Albertine is seen to covet.

Male elegance, too, is described—particularly that of Swann, whose leather-lined hat, in *Within a Budding Grove*, the Duchess of Guermantes notes, just as Swann comments on the tiny coral balls frosted with diamonds that she wears in her hair at the soirée described toward the end of *Swann's Way*, likening them to rose hips dusted with ice. Dress, fabric, texture, and detail are seen as vital factors in the evocation of memory so germane to the novel. In the very last pages the narrator speaks of discerning the different threads woven together in a fabric of which he can now perceive the overall design.

Proust's Legacy
Although other writers have been fascinated by fashion, Proust is among the first to mention designers by name and to award them equal stature with painters and composers. Perhaps no author before him described an outfit, jewels, or accessories in such careful, minute detail. More significant, perhaps, is his *roman-à-clef* technique; celebrities are thinly disguised and their valorization permeates his work. In the twenty-first century's celebrity-dominated culture, this seems peculiarly pertinent.

See also **Art and Fashion; Canes and Walking Sticks; Dandyism; Fashion and Homosexuality; Liberty & Co.; Social Class and Clothing; Wilde, Oscar.**

BIBLIOGRAPHY

Adams, William Howard. *A Proust Souvenir.* New York: Vendome Press, 1984.

Balsani, Leo. *Marcel Proust: The Fictions of Life and Art.* New York: Oxford University Press, 1965.

Bowie, Malcolm. *Proust among the Stars.* New York: Columbia University Press, 1998.

Carter, William C. *Marcel Proust: A Life.* New Haven, Conn.: Yale University Press, 2000.

Painter, George D. *Marcel Proust: A Biography.* New York: Random House, 1989.

Pringue, Gabriel-Louis. *Trente ans de dîners en ville.* Paris: Revue Adam, 1948.

Steele, Valerie. *Paris Fashion: A Cultural History.* Rev. ed. New York: Berg, 1998.

White, Edmund. *Marcel Proust.* London: Viking, 1999.

Pamela Church Gibson

PSYCHEDELIC FASHION Psychedelia—the range of sensations, epiphanies, and hallucinations induced by chemical stimulants—was an epochal cultural phenomenal of the 1960s; in retrospect, it seems not only a key component of the decade's sensibility, but an apt symbol of the 1960s reordering of social, political, and artistic structures. It was inevitable that fashion and psychedelic experience would go hand-in-hand since one of the effects of an LSD [lysergic acid diethylamide) "trip" was a heightened appreciation of color, texture, and line. Psychedelic fashion did more than evoke or pay tribute to the mind-alerting experience; it became a way to enhance participation. Given that the LSD—popularly called acid—experience involved erasing discreet boundaries, it was appropriate to dress in clothes that enhanced the ability of the communicant to merge into an experience that for many became nearly sacerdotal rite.

The Big Bang

Partaking of LSD was central to the hippie credo, and the outlandish clothes of the hippies disseminated the psychedelic sensibility. Flowing shapes seemed to relate to the unbinding of restrictions unloosed by the hallucinogenic experience. The prevalence of tactile fabrics in hippie fashions spoke to the sense-enhancing properties of the acid trip. Most visible were its innovations in palette and imagery: equally provocative vibrating patterns and colors. Certain traditional motifs—the amoebalike crawl of Indian paisley, for example—were appropriated as psychedelic imagery. The accoutrements included face painting in Day-glo neon colors that recreated the incandescence of acid chimeras. But the principal topos of psychedelic fashion were portraits of light as it was fractured, made mobile by the lens of the acid trip. The awakened kineticism of light made flat surfaces seem to churn and roil. Colors bled, emulsified, and merged kaleidoscopically.

LSD existed for thirty years before reaching the widespread cultural acceptance and curiosity it aroused during the 1960s. Similarly, slightly before the apogee of psychedelic fashion in the mid to late 1960s, fashion inspired by the oscillatory geometries of op art deployed a pleasurable hoodwinking of perceptual faculties. Psychedelic experience and psychedelic fashion's incongruous reshuffling of identifiable reference points recalled surrealistic art and Dada, which also were the progenitors to some extent of pop art. Pop art functioned in the 1960s as its own sometimes surreal rebuke to nonrepresentational abstract expressionism.

The Total Environment

Psychedelic fashion became a way for external reality to seemingly be transformed by the visions projected on the mind's internal screen. Psychedelic fashions existed within a cultural context that encompassed the radical lifestyles of the hippies, the transcendent "acid" experience as well as constructed environments that sought to simulate the acid experience. These encompassed communal affirmations such as the "be-in," and performance art "happenings." Psychedelic fashion became an indispensable component of the total environment created in discotheques or rock palaces; it allowed an integration of the reformed environment and the remade self. The *dereglement de tous les sens* that Artur Rimbaud had once propounded, was heightened orally by the fuzz box and "wah-wah" pedal distortions. Light shows at the rock concerts and at the discotheque hurled pulsating apparitions at the spectator. The blinking strobe light atomized the continuity, the gestalt of visual perception. It might be said that under the strobe light, all fashion became psychedelic.

Psychedelic fashion was a quintessential 1960s movement. Although it was eventually, and to some degree opportunistically, embraced by virtually every mainstream design and sector of the fashion industry, it would be hard to isolated a single designer or even a cluster of designers who could be credited for its invention or promotion. Nevertheless, the psychedelic preoccupation with light and the total environment reached a paradigm at the Manhattan boutique Paraphernalia in 1966, when electrical engineer Diana Dew devised a vinyl dress that turned-on at the command of the wearer. A miniaturized potentiometer fit on the belt of the dress and regulated the frequency of the blinking hearts or stars, which could be coordinated to the throbbing beat of the disco soundtrack. That same year, Yves Saint Laurent brought psychedelic light and color to pop art's disembodied trademarks with a bridal gown that flashed an incandescent flower, which enlivened the runway show's traditional finale.

Psychedelic sensibility was essential to the second phase of 1960s' fashion vocabulary, the move away from some of the sleeker and brusquer characteristics of mod fashion. It was consanguineous with the second phase's absorption of folk and tribal lexicon, the experimentation in role playing and persona construction made possible by the improvised costumes adopted by youth cultures and spilling out into the Western world's clothes-wearing population at large. The unprecedented outfits certainly owed something to the phantasmagoria of acid visions. Tribal and psychedelic converged with mottled patterns of African and Indonesian fabrics, the phosphorescent splotches and showers of tie-dye.

Psychedelic fashion was a grass-roots groundswell, a radically demotic movement that eventually generated a ubiquitous acknowledgment. In New York, for example, one could buy made-to-order tie-dye ensembles at both The Fur Balloon on West 4th Street in Greenwich Village and at Halston's salon on East 68th Street on the Upper East Side.

Cycles of renewal

Ultimately, the lexicon and the fashion became degraded. New adjectives introduced into colloquial language and the language of fashion, "psychedelic" and "trippy" among them, no longer retained their original referents but became generic adjectives of approval. Psychedelia not only offered the keys to the cosmos but became the latest marketing ploy. "Call it psychedelic and it will sell fast, some merchants say," was a page-one headline on *The Wall Street Journal* in 1968. Psychedelic fashion petered out in the early 1970s, partly from overkill and overexposure, and partly from the changing zeitgeist. Yet it remained popular with students until enjoying a full-scale revival in the mid-1980s, and has continued as a recurring motif.

See also **Art and Fashion; Paisley; Saint Laurent, Yves; Subcultures.**

BIBLIOGRAPHY

Lobenthal, Joel. *Radical Rags: Fashions of the Sixties.* New York: Abbeville Press, 1990.

Masters, Robert E. L., and Jean Houston. *Psychedelic Art.* New York: Grove Press, 1968.

Joel Lobenthal

PUCCI, EMILIO Emilio Pucci, the *marchese di Barsento a Cavallo*, was born in Naples on 20 November 1914. The scion of an illustrious family tracing its heritage to the thirteenth century, Pucci grew up in the Palazzo Pucci on the *via dei Pucci* in Florence.

Education and Early Career

Reared within a strict aristocratic environment, Pucci turned out to be a rebel both personally and professionally. He graduated from the Università di Firenze in 1941 with a doctorate in political science, after having attended the University of Georgia in Athens, Georgia, and Reed College in Portland, Oregon. His decision to study in the United States, however, introduced him to the American way of life.

Proficiency in skiing started Pucci's fashion career. He had been a member of the Italian Olympic skiing team in 1934 and had gone to Reed College on a skiing scholarship in 1937. In 1947 the photographer Toni Frissell took photographs of Pucci and his female companions in Zermatt, Switzerland, wearing form-fitting, colorful, but practical ski clothes that Pucci had designed. These photographs were shown to the head buyer for Lord and Taylor, Marjorie Griswold, and the fashion editor of *Harper's Bazaar*, the legendary Diana Vreeland. The pictures were published in the December 1948 issue of *Bazaar*, while several Pucci models were ordered for Lord and Taylor's New York store. This order was Pucci's first retail success in the United States.

Pucci, however, needed additional financial security after World War II. In 1949 he opened a boutique in Capri, Italy, where he sold the tapered pants that became known as Capri pants, as well as sexy silk shirts fitted to show off the female figure. With the return of peace, people were again traveling for pleasure. Pucci astutely surmised that his boutique, which he named Emilio of Capri, and his casual, colorful resort fashions would be popular with the new visitors. International sophisticates like Consuelo Crespi, Mona Harrison von Bismarck, and Maxime de la Falaise were frequent customers at Emilio of Capri. Diana Vreeland praised Pucci as "divinely Italian" (Kennedy, p. 57). Although it was extremely unusual

at that time for an aristocrat to be a shop owner and designer or dressmaker, Pucci enjoyed the creative process.

Post–World War II Innovations

The next phase of Pucci's career began at the first fashion show of Italian designers, which was organized by Giovanni Battista Giorgini in 1951 and held in the *Sala Bianca* at the Palazzo Pitti in Florence. Other designers who presented their work at the show included Simonetta, the Fontana sisters, Alberto Fabiani, and Emilio Schuberth. Major American stores like Neiman Marcus and Saks Fifth Avenue sent their buyers, who brought Italian, postwar, ready-to-wear fashion back across the Atlantic. Pucci's sleek, lightweight T-shirts, jersey dresses, silk shirts, and tapered pants made for an exciting new style.

Once the original and somewhat daring look of Pucci's designs appeared in the top U.S. stores, he was on the way to celebrity-designer status. Pucci won the coveted Neiman Marcus Award in 1954. He won the award a second time in 1967. Marcus, the head of the Dallas-based store, said, "Postwar fashion was hungry for a color explosion and [Pucci's] exotic, vivid color combinations were timed to perfection" (Kennedy, p. 67). Marjorie Griswold, Pucci's major retail supporter, had already suggested that he sign his name in script within the print design because the motifs themselves could be copied. Hence, the authenticity of a Pucci garment can be verified when the signature "Emilio" is visible throughout the print. Pucci used his first name rather than his family name because it was considered shocking for a member of the Italian nobility to work as a dressmaker or tradesman instead of a diplomat or politician. He said, "I am the first member of my family to work in a thousand years" (Kennedy, p. 42).

Pucci introduced a very lightweight, wrinkle-free, silk jersey that could be rolled up and packed easily—a feature appreciated by growing numbers of jet-set travelers. Technically advanced fabrics allowed him to fashion nonrestrictive clothes that were modern yet glamorous. Pucci also introduced an exciting array of colors, boldly mixing espresso and azure, tangerine and fuchsia, lime and turquoise, plum, and many other shades.

In addition to designing sleek silhouettes that allowed easy movement, using packable fabrics in an abundance of joyful colors, and insisting on top-quality workmanship, Pucci also designed his own prints. His prints included swirls, filigrees, arabesques, geometric figures, and kaleidoscopic or mosaic patterns. They were inspired by his far-flung travels to North and South America, Bali, Africa, the Middle East, Australia, and Asia. Pucci's finely-engineered prints also represented rich aspects of Italian history and cultural events as well as Mediterranean land- and seascapes. His prints from the 1950s, for example, featured motifs from Renaissance art, Florentine landmarks, the sunscapes and flowers of

Italian designer Emilio Pucci at a Berlin fashion show, 1972. Pucci stands on the runway with the models that presented his exotic silk and chiffon gowns. Bold, wild patterns adorn the sleek sheath dresses, reflecting Pucci's rebellious spirit. CHARISSA CRAIG, MODEL. REPRODUCED BY PERMISSION.

Capri, the mosaics of the Duomo di Monreale in Sicily, nightlife in Naples, and the flags from the famous annual Palio race in Siena. From the 1960s to the 1980s, his prints were inspired by his travels to Cuba, Bali, India, Hong Kong, and Tanzania. The American space program, underwater explorations, pop art, op art, rock music, and psychedelia also influenced his designs. One of Pucci's most famous prints, called Vivara, was inspired by the island Ischia; it became the name of his first fragrance in 1965. He even found time to sketch ideas for new print patterns during plane trips or sessions of the Italian Parliament, where he served from 1963 to 1972.

Designer Accessories

Emilio Pucci became one of the first designers with a recognizable high-status label and signature style. He was a leading pioneer of diversification and paved the way to widespread fashion licensing. He designed various products from perfumes to accessories, including handbags, scarves, sunglasses, tights, shoes, and lingerie—the last made by the American company Formfit Rogers. In 1977 Pucci even designed the interior of an automobile for a special edition of the Lincoln Continental Mark IV.

Pucci personally supervised the design of all his products. He designed colorful, sexy, and futuristic uniforms for the flight hostesses of Braniff Airways in 1965 and Quantas Airways in 1974. He also found time to design uniforms for the policewomen of Florence and clothes for Barbie dolls. Pucci took special pleasure in designing the mission patch for the Apollo 15 space mission in 1971.

Pucci married Christina Nannini and had two children, Laudomia and Alessandro. The family's elegant palazzo lifestyle was chronicled in fashion magazines. The "Prince of Prints" became as famous as the women who wore his designs—a list that included Marilyn Monroe (who was buried in a green Pucci dress), Elizabeth

Taylor, Audrey Hepburn, Sophia Loren, Gina Lollobrigida, Lauren Bacall, Jacqueline Kennedy, Grace Kelly, Barbara ("Babe") Paley, Gloria Guinness, Barbara Walters, Gloria Steinem, and many others. Helen Gurley Brown, the author and former editor of *Cosmopolitan*, said, "The dresses were spare, sexy, and liberating!" (Kennedy, p. 8). Not to be outdone by fashionable women, men also wore wild and colorful Pucci ties, bowties, jackets, and beach attire.

The Pucci Revival

The wave of enthusiasm for Pucci's clothes known as "Puccimania" reached its height in 1967. Pucci's dresses became less popular in the 1970s as fashion trends changed, but the early 1990s saw a resurgence of interest in current Pucci styles and a blossoming market for vintage fashion—especially Puccis from the 1960s. Pucci collectors of the early 2000s included Madonna, Jennifer Lopez, Nicole Kidman, Julia Roberts, Paloma Picasso, and Ivana Trump. Vintage Puccis were sold in specialty shops and at auction for as much as $500 in 2002, whereas as a Pucci silk jersey dress from Saks Fifth Avenue in New York had been priced at $150 to $200 in the mid-1960s. When Pucci died on 29 November 1992, the fashion editor Carrie Donovan wrote in the *New York Times*, "He personified a moment, rather a long one in history" (1 December 1992).

After Pucci's death, his company continued under the guidance of his daughter, Laudomia, and wife, Cristina. The rich archive of fabrics maintained in the Palazzo Pucci provided an ongoing source of fashions for the Pucci boutiques. As creative director, Laudomia Pucci hired talented designers to continue her father's concepts. In February 2000 LVMH, the French luxury goods conglomerate headed by Bernard Arnault, purchased 67 percent of the Emilio Pucci SRL company, with the Pucci family retaining the rest of the business. More Pucci boutiques were opened around the world, from Bangkok to Palm Beach.

Christian Lacroix, the contemporary French designer known for his fantastical, exuberant, and exotically colorful fashions, became artistic director of the Emilio Pucci collection in April 2002. He said in the December 2002 issue of *Vogue*, "Emilio Pucci's vision is still very modern.... It's a way of life" (p. 76).

See also **Brands and Labels; Fontana Sisters; Italian Fashion; Lacroix, Christian; Perfume; Ski Clothing; Vintage Fashion.**

BIBLIOGRAPHY

Biennale di Firenze. *Looking at Fashion, Emilio Pucci*. Milan: Skira Editore, 1996.

Collins, Amy Fine. "Pucci's Jet-Set Revolution." *Vanity Fair* (October 2000): 380–393.

Kennedy, Shirley. *Pucci: A Renaissance in Fashion*. New York: Abbeville Press, 1991.

Tally, Andre Leon. "Style Fax." *Vogue* (December 2002): 76.

Vergani, Guido. *The Sala Bianca: The Birth of Italian Fashion*. Milan: Electa, 1992.

Shirley Kennedy

PTFE. *See* **Techno-Textiles.**

PUNK Punk as dress cannot be discussed without at least some reference to its musical underpinnings. It has to be recognized that within the field of cultural studies, it both energized and produced a series of new responses to the theoretical construction of youth culture. Thus, it can be regarded as a formative movement in both its sartorial and visual presentation, and the consequent analysis of it as a subcultural style. It can be further argued that punk culture stands at a pivotal point in the relationship between youth cultural style and its commodification.

The United States

Punk had its roots in inner city America at the beginning of the 1970s. While its inspiration could be traced farther back, as a movement with a set of cohesive identities, New York appears to be its birthplace. But as befits its urban nature, punk cannot be said to have a singular geographic location. Detroit, Cleveland, and possibly Los Angeles are other sites that could also claim an emergent aesthetic and style identified as punk.

One of the many effects of the post–World War II consumer boom within the United States and Europe was an ever-expanding market for goods, particularly within a youth cultural market that led to an active struggle from young people to shape and realize their own identities through the consumption of music and fashion. This popularization of "youth" as "style" and "surface" was in part reflected in the breakdown of distinctions between high and low culture within the pop art movements—of Britain's Independent Group and its U.S. equivalent—of the 1950s and 1960s. In the latter grouping was Andy Warhol and the Factory. Symptomatic of pop, Warhol's work, its repetitive nature, and its insistence in articulating nothing more than the surface engaged with a youth cultural perspective of nihilism that revolved around the adage of "live fast, die young." As such, alongside Warhol's desire to surround himself with a coterie of the young, dangerous, and beautiful, the seeds of an avant-garde music scene began to be established.

Set around Warhol's Factory and the Lower East Side in a time of political and financial meltdown in New York, the music of these artists, in particular the Velvet Underground, reflected the repetitivity and surface of the Factory's output. Playing at seedy venues such as Max's Kansas City, CBGBs, and Mother's, the music of the Stooges, New York Dolls, MC5's, Wayne County, and Patti Smith took their influences from a variety of sources

Punk fashion, 1983. Standing around in London's Brockwell Park, punks show off wild hairstyles and metal-studded black leather clothing, typical of the later punk fashion. While earlier years saw various other styles within the movement, it was this look that became the iconic punk image. © RICHARD OLIVIER/CORBIS. REPRODUCED BY PERMISSION.

all intent in demolishing what was seen as the pompous, sterile sound of contemporary music in the guise of "progressive" and "stadium" rock. So a disillusionment with all things commercial and the be-suited executives at the record companies led to a desire to perform music that would shock people to their senses, bringing music back to the poverty/richness of the everyday. While this was going on in the United States, Britain was in the grip of glam rock, a pub rock sound characterized in part by the clothing of its performers that looked to the transgressive in their stage presence. Of these perhaps the most original was David Bowie. Under a string of different pseudonyms and increasingly bizarre record personalities, David Bowie proved influential in his effect on both music and clothing in Britain and the United States.

By 1975 the American "punk scene" had evolved into a subculture characterized by the music of Television, and perhaps most famously The Ramones who wore clothes that reflected their rent boy street personas. Given that many of the musicians had gravitated from a bohemian inner-city scene detailed in the writings of William Burroughs and Alexander Trocchi, it seemed like a natural continuation of this aesthetic. The black

leather jacket, T-shirt, straight jeans, and sneakers of the hustler proved the initial look of an American underground scene. While there were those such as the New York Dolls, who followed an English glam rock look of androgyny—made up with leather and knee-length boots, chest hair, and bleach—the majority pursued an understated street look. It was this musical explosion within the United States that brought a youngish Malcolm McLaren over to the United States to manage the New York Dolls where he fell into the punk scene and made clear his intentions to ship it back to the United Kingdom.

The United Kingdom
While it is obvious that Malcolm McLaren and his partner, Vivienne Westwood, are central to any definition of punk, especially in relation to its clothing, it is also clear that the self-aggrandizing machine which is Malcolm McClaren has skewed any historical understanding. In part this is justified, as McClaren and Westwood's string of shops on the Kings Road defined a particular look and McLaren's desire to exploit punk as a scene in the United Kingdom led directly to his management and dressing of the Sex Pistols, the most notorious of all punk bands.

Starting out on the Kings Road in 1972 as *Let It Rock* a shop that catered to a late working-class Teddy Boy revival, drape coats, and brothel creepers, Vivienne Westwood and Malcolm McLaren's shop then moved through a number of reincarnations, including *Too Fast to Live* and the fetish-orientated *Sex*, and later *Seditionaries*, and finally *World's End*. As in the United States, McLaren encouraged those who railed against society to hang around the shop. His and Westwood's antiestablishment aesthetic soon earned them a place in the London underground scene. However, we are not talking of the sophistication of New York, but a more rag-tag army of disillusioned teenagers. And it is from this group that the Sex Pistols were formed. Apart from the "rock" posturing of Glen Matlock, the rest of the band—Johnny Rotten, Sid Vicious, Steve Jones, and Paul Cook—were wholly working class and outside any artistic or intellectual clique. While many of the other emerging punk bands had members from an art school background, the *Sex Pistols* could claim to be the genuine thing: an authentic working-class group of kids celebrating the boredom of their socially proscribed position.

Theoretical Angles

It is this notion of authenticity and working class that, in part, has always demarcated a British and U.S. understanding of punk as a philosophy or cultural experience. Whereas in the United Kingdom youth counter cultures had generally been a central experience of working-class youth—an expression of dissent and isolation from their parents and a reaction against a dominant ideology that on the surface worked to repress their ambition, in the United States the readings had not taken on such class-bound strictures.

The result in the United Kingdom was the publication in 1977, the peak of punk in Britain, of Dick Hebdige's *Subculture: The Meaning of Style*. Using punk as its central example, Hebdige employed a series of methodologies from Marxism to Structuralism and Semiotics to chart a view of post–World War II British youth cultures that were constructed through their working-class credentials and a desire to react against the dominant powers that appeared to shape their lives. In this analysis, Hebdige applied the notion of "bricolage" as the stylistic combination of disparate coded objects to juxtapose and create fresh meaning to punk dress and style. The safety pin's original meaning as something to hold together a diaper and to prevent injury to the child was pierced through a nose or stuck onto ripped jeans and jackets. Its once certain assigned meaning through was contexually redefined through its wearing as a stylistic device.

Clothing

In Britain the spectacular nature of punk as a style surpassed that of the United States. Westwood's designs—from "Destroy" T-shirts, bum bags, tartan bondage trousers, safety-pinned and ripped muslin shirts, and sloganed clothing—were a visible affront to a population who, for the most part, regarded long hair on a man as a concern. While youth cultures had previously been vilified within the national press for violence and drug taking, punk directly challenged the dress aesthetic and morals of a conservative nation. Beyond the Kings Road in 1976, 1977, and 1978, the influence of McLaren and Westwood diminished rapidly. Though they may have attracted a contingent of followers in London and their home counties, punk was a nationwide phenomenon and as such developed a style that was perhaps more coherent and less showy than Westwood's ready-to-wear clothing.

This do-it–yourself (D.I.Y.) aesthetic consisted of Hebdige's "bricolage" as the throwing together of a series of looks based around a few staple elements, such as mohair sweaters, tight jeans, and "jelly shoes." There was also the widespread use of secondhand clothing from charity shops and rummage sales—suits with T-shirts and basketball boots, collarless granddad shirts, and peroxided hair—with or without the ubiquitous stenciling and letter art of favorite bands, anarchist slogans, or the Situationist politicizing of groups such as The Clash.

This aesthetic was perhaps more subdued than the Kings Road look, but is more representative of punk as a dress code within the United Kingdom both for individuals and bands such as The Buzzcocks, The Damned, The Adverts, 999, and out on a style limb The Undertones. By 1977 punk's popularity as a musical form had seen by then the infamous Grundy television interviews; the Sex Pistols single "God Save the Queen" reaching number one in the week of the Queen's Golden Jubilee; and the interest of record companies in signing up groups who claimed in any manner, shape, or form to espouse a punk belief.

Commercialization

By 1979 the first stage of punk in the United Kingdom was coming to an end. Its commercial status became assured, from advertisements in music papers such as *NME* and *Sounds* advertising punk clothing, badges, and T-shirts to the record companies' desires to promote a gentler, more public-friendly "new wave" and to the release of various compilations that promised to tell the whole punk story. However, punk itself as both a music and a style attempted to change in order to avoid its co-option/commercialization by hardcore bands such as The Exploited and political bands such as Crass. In terms of dress, there was a re-engagement with the motorcycle jacket, the use of Dr. Martin work-wear boots, and the introduction of a wide variety of commercial rainbow hair colorants, along with the ubiquitous Mohawk haircut, which, along with a penchant for black, crossed over into both Goth and the New Romantic movements of the early 1980s. It is this look that for many years characterized, and as such became the iconic image of, punk.

As a direct result of the energy of punk and the diffusion of a whole series of offshoots from punk with fanzines such as *Punk* in the United States and *Sniffin' Glue* in Britain, it became clear that there was a market for hard-edged youth journalism, which dealt specifically with an urban street scene. Punk fostered the emergence in 1980 of street-style magazines such as *The Face, iD,* and *Blitz.* Yet, as a consequence of these magazines trying to locate and expose scenes bubbling up from the streets, it became increasingly difficult for "subcultural" movements to resist commercialization through exposure. And it is this that is perhaps punk's greatest legacy to youth cultural style. While it would be inaccurate to suggest that youth cultures prior to punk were left to get on without the prying eyes of parents and large commercial operations intent on supplying, if not co-opting, youth culture toward their own ends, it is clear that punk stood at the crossroads of a contemporary "lifestyle" aesthetic. That youth culture in the early 2000s is so heavily mediated and prey to the intense gaze of commercial pressures is perhaps one of the less-appreciated consequences of punk as an historical event.

From the sounds of Seattle and grunge, through to a swathe of bands in 2004 that look more like The Ramones than The Ramones, punk has endured. For the fashion industry, its stylistic conceptualization as both "bricolage" and "rebellion" makes it the perfect vehicle to reappropriate the old in the spirit of the new, which gives rise to the interpretation of punk as a seasonal look on a cyclical basis. As such, its legacy is assured within both its musical and stylistic qualities. Yet whether its politics of change or its celebration of the bored and nihilistic attitude of teenagers can ever be faithfully played out again is another question.

See also **Fashion and Identity; Subcultures; Teenage Fashions; T-Shirt.**

BIBLIOGRAPHY

Anscombe, Isabelle. *Not Another Punk Book.* London: Aurum Press, 1978.

Colegrave, Stephen, and Chris Sullivan. *Punk.* New York: Thunder's Mouth Press, 2001.

Coon, Caroline. *1988: The New Wave Punk Rock Explosion.* London: Orbach and Chambers Ltd, 1977.

Hebdige, Dick. *Subculture: The Meaning of Style.* London: Methuen, 1979.

Heylin, Clinton. *From the Velvets to the Voidoids: A Pre-Punk History for a Post-Punk World.* New York: Penguin USA, 1993.

Laing, David, and Milton Keynes. *One Chord Wonders: Power and Meaning in Punk Rock.* Philadelphia: Open University Press, 1985.

Makos, Christopher. *White Trash.* London: Stonehill Publishing, 1977.

McNeil, Legs and Gillian McCain. *Please Kill Me: The Uncensored Oral History of Punk.* New York: Penguin USA, 1996.

Perry, Mark. *Sniffin' Glue: The Essential Punk Accessory.* London: Sanctuary Publishing, 2000.

Sabin, Roger, ed. *Punk Rock: So What?* London and New York: Routledge, 1999.

Savage, Jon. *England's Dreaming: Sex Pistols and Punk Rock.* London: Faber, 1991.

Frank Cartledge

PURIM COSTUME. *See* **Halloween Costume.**

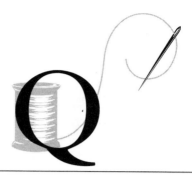

QIPAO The *qipao* is a Chinese dress for women. The style is also called *cheongsam* in Cantonese, and this term has come to be the more widely used one in English, though spelled in several different ways. The defining features of the dress are a fitted silhouette, a high collar, and side skirt slits. In its classic form, there is a front flap overlapping to the right, which fastens along the collarbone, under the arm, and down the right side. The details are subject to changing fashions within the limits of the basic form. It can be sleeveless, or have sleeves of any length. The hemline varies, but usually reaches somewhere between the knee and the ankle. The *qipao* can be made of almost any fabric, although it is mostly associated with silk. The dress material can have a printed or woven repeat pattern across its surface or, if the material is plain, a favorite way of tailoring the style is for the front panel of the dress to be pre-embroidered with a sweeping floral or dragon design, leaving the back of the garment unadorned. The entire dress is often edged in one or more strips of narrow binding, which is sometimes in plain-colored bias-cut satin, or else of lace or patterned ribbon. Although press-stud and zip fastenings are used, traditional knot buttons made from fabric are popular. These can be extravagantly shaped and are specially made to suit the pattern or color of the chosen dress material. To be a genuine *qipao*, the dress needs to be custom-made. Purchasing off the rack is not considered correct form.

Origins and development.
The *qipao* can be elegant rather than flashy. Although one of its hallmarks is a good fit, it does not need to fit tightly. In the first half of the twentieth century, there is no doubt that the *qipao* provided a cross-section of Chinese women with a style of dress, and consequently a mode of deportment and way of moving, that suited their increasingly public lives. But, bound up with the charges of decadence leveled at the dress, it became enmeshed in questions concerning nationalism. At the height of the style's popularity, China, having overthrown imperial rule in 1911, was trying to forge itself into a modern nation-state. For some, certain traits of the *qipao* were perceived as western and therefore tainted, especially when worn with high-heeled shoes and bobbed hair. For many others, however, the *qipao* seemed both modern and Chinese, and Song Meiling (1897–2003), the wife of the Chinese Nationalist leader Chiang Kai-shek (1888–1975), was rarely seen in any other style and used it to good effect to rally supporters to her husband's cause.

Survival
After 1949, the *qipao* survived outside China among overseas Chinese, in Hong Kong, a British colony until 1997, and also in Taiwan, where Chiang Kai-shek set up an opposing government after being defeated by Mao. However, in these places too, by the 1960s, a younger generation of women came to view the *qipao* as old-fashioned and adopted a more international style of dressing. Older women still favored it as formal wear and in Hong Kong, a big tourist destination, it became associated with the service industries as a type of uniform. With the loosening up of the strictures after the death of Mao, all kinds of dress regimes became possible in greater China and the *qipao* was just one of several styles that was revived and also re-worked by Chinese fashion designers. Hong Kong's return to the People's Republic of China heightened the profile of the dress and some saw it as a patriotic garment. *Qipao* are increasingly worn by students of Chinese origin at graduation ceremonies both in East Asia and in the United States. Weddings in Chinese communities across the globe provide arenas for lavish spending and the *qipao* has become an accepted part of the marriage ritual. Western women, too, have eagerly taken up the dress and it continues to provide inspiration for Euro-American couture designers.

See also **China, History of Dress; Orientalism.**

BIBLIOGRAPHY
Roberts, Claire, ed. *Evolution and Revolution: Chinese Dress, 1700s–1900s.* Sydney: Powerhouse Publishing, 1997.
Steele, Valerie, and John S. Major, eds. *China Chic: East Meets West.* Yale and London: Yale University Press, 1999.

Verity Wilson

QUANT, MARY Mary Quant was born in London on 11 February 1934. A self-taught designer, she cut up bedspreads to make clothes when she was only six; as a teenager, she restyled and shortened her gingham school dresses.

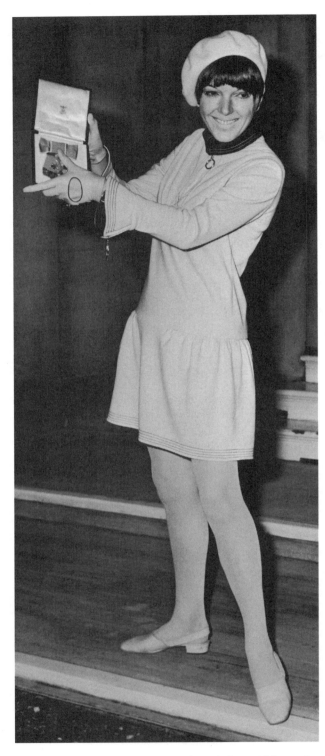

Mary Quant showing off her Order of the British Empire award. The self-taught Quant was the recipient of several awards for her innovative, progressive fashion designs. © BETTMAN/CORBIS. REPRODUCED BY PERMISSION.

She recalled admiring the appearance of a child at a tap-dancing class who wore a black "skinny" sweater, pleated skirt, and pantyhose with white ankle socks and black patent shoes (Quant: 1966, p. 16). From the mid-1950s she transformed styles like these into amusing and sexy clothes for young women, and paved the way for London to become a center of irreverent youth-oriented fashion.

Quant's parents would not accept her attending a school of fashion design, but compromised by allowing her to go to art school. She met Alexander Plunkett Greene while she was studying illustration at Goldsmith's College of the University of London. Plunkett Greene later became her business partner and husband. After leaving art school, Quant was apprenticed to Erik of Brook Street, a Danish milliner working in London. In 1955 Quant's husband purchased Markham House in London's King's Road to start a shop named Bazaar, and open a restaurant called Alexander's in the basement. Mary was responsible for buying the stock for Bazaar, Alexander for sales and marketing, while Archie McNair, an ex-solicitor who ran a photography business, handled the legal and commercial side of the business. Quant designed a black five-petaled daisy logo during this period; it eventually became her worldwide trademark.

Quant sourced innovative jewelry from art students and bought clothes from various wholesalers to stock the boutique. One of the items designed for Bazaar's opening was a pair of "mad" house-pajamas, which were featured in *Harper's Bazaar* and purchased by an American manufacturer to copy. Encouraged by her success as well as dissatisfied with the styles on the market, Quant decided to design her own stock. After attending a few evening classes on cutting, she adjusted some Butterick patterns to achieve the look she wanted. Quant was designing for Butterick by 1964; some of her pattern designs sold over 70,000 copies. Each day's sales at Bazaar paid for the cloth made up that evening into the next day's stock. As business took off, Quant employed a dressmaker to help her, and then another, and another, and so on.

Quant brought a groundbreaking approach to fashion retailing by providing an informal shopping experience. In contrast to traditional fashion retail outlets, which ranged from high-class couturiers through staid town-center department stores and chain stores such as C and A Modes to High Street dress shops, Bazaar set out to make shopping for clothes enjoyable: loud music played, wine flowed, and the boutique stayed open until late in the evening. Most importantly, the stock was constantly replenished with new and highly desirable designs. "The clothes were very simple. Basically tunic dresses, and very easy to wear, unlike the couturier clothes which were very structured. And put together with other things—tights and knickers in ginger and prune and a grapey colour, that people weren't used to" (Harris, 1994). Quant persuaded theatrical costume manufacturers to make the tights she sold, as there were no pantyhose in the color that Quant required on the market.

While Quant's prices were reasonable in comparison to those of the traditional fashion houses, her clothes were made to a high standard—many were silk-lined—and were not cheap.

Quant was probably the first designer to acknowledge the influence of youth subcultures, and she credits the Mods as an important source of inspiration. Mods were a sub-cultural youth group characterized by their immaculate dress—their 'sharp' tailoring and love of Italian sportswear, and the parka coat that they wore to protect their clothes whilst traveling by scooter. One of her most successful early designs was a white plastic collar to be added to a sweater or dress. One of Quant's trademark innovations was the mini skirt: by 1960 her hemlines were above the knee and crept up the leg to reach thigh level by the mid-1960s. She also derived inspiration from school uniforms and menswear, especially traditional country clothes—knickerbockers, Norfolk jackets, "granddaddy" tab-collared shirts, Liberty bodices or combinations (one-piece garments), and traditional children's underwear. Quant undertook much of her research at London's Victoria and Albert Museum. She bought her fabrics, notably Prince of Wales checks and herringbone weaves, from Harrod's, and persuaded knitwear manufacturers to make their men's cardigans 25 centimeters longer so that they could be worn as dresses. Whereas fashion designers had traditionally looked to Paris for stylistic guidance, Quant and her husband watched youth programs on television and attended fashionable London nightspots to identify new trends.

One example of Quant's work from 1956/57 was a dress in black-and-white checked wool cut in a sleeveless balloon style and teamed with a skinny-rib black sweater. For the winter of 1957/58 Quant designed an ensemble comprised of a rust-red Norfolk-style jacket, Harris tweed knickerbockers—she favored knickerbockers—, and a pinafore dress. Another pinafore of the same year, made of striped menswear suiting, featured two bold pockets at the bust. Her popular hipster pants were based on the styles that her husband had the fashionable tailor Dougie Hayward make for him. Quant was the first designer to use Polu-Vinyl-Chloride (PVC) in fashion; the first to introduce pantyhose in stunning colors to match her knitwear; and the first to introduce "fashion" lingerie—her seamless brassieres were called "booby traps," and her uplifting brassieres "bacon savers."

Quant also exerted a profound influence upon the representation of fashion by designing and commissioning young-looking animated mannequins and staging witty window displays. In her 1966 autobiography, she recalled one display in which "we had all the figures in bathing suits made of Banlon stretch fabric with madly wide coloured stripes like rugger sweat shirts. . . . The models were sprayed completely white with bald heads" (p. 8). In 1957 the trio (Mary, Alexander, and Archie) opened a second branch of Bazaar, designed by their friend Terence Conran, in London's Knightsbridge

Models wearing Quant designs. Quant's fashions were fun and irreverent, drawing heavily from the youth subcultures of London. One of her trademarks was updating traditional styles to make them more hip and trendy. AP/WIDE WORLD PHOTOS. REPRODUCED BY PERMISSION.

neighborhood. At the launch party, Quant's models danced to loud jazz music with glasses of champagne in their hands, "and floated around as if they had been to the wildest party or looking dreamily intellectual with a copy of Karl Marx or Engels in the other hand. . . . No one had ever used this style of showing. . . . At the end, the place just exploded!" (Quant, 1966, p. 95).

In 1962 Quant entered into a lucrative design contract with J. C. Penney, which had 1,700 retail outlets across the United States; and in 1963 she launched her own cheaper diffusion line, called the Ginger Group. Her talent was acknowledged that same year by the *Sunday Times*, which gave her its International Award for "jolting England out of its conventional attitude towards clothes" (Quant, 1966, p. 96). In 1966 she was awarded the Order of the British Empire and in 1967 she won the Annual Design Medal of the Royal Society of Arts. In the same year she opened her third shop, designed by Jon Bannenberg, in London's New Bond Street. Quant was awarded the Hall of Fame Award for Outstanding Contribution to British Fashion by the British Fashion Council in 1969.

Quant remained in fashion's vanguard throughout the first half of the 1970s. In 1971 she designed a spotted summer playsuit in cotton jersey called "Babygro," named after the ubiquitous babies' romper suits, and a long flared skirt printed with dots and daisies called

"Sauce," which was teamed with a matching "Radish" bra-top. Summer evening dresses with plunging necklines, puffed sleeves, and ruffled skirts were made in pretty Liberty floral prints—once again borrowed from childrenswear—and glamorous striped Lurex. Quant's sporty styles for 1975 included brightly colored and striped jumpsuits, many with drawstring waists and ankle ties, and sailor-inspired slit-sided tunic dresses worn over pants. In 1978 she introduced her own range of childrenswear. She has also designed furnishings and bed linens since the 1980s, and won numerous awards for her carpet designs.

Mary Quant always wanted to create a total fashion look—her own geometric hairstyle, cut by Vidal Sassoon, was widely copied. As an art student she had used Caran d'Ache crayons and a box of watercolors for her own makeup. In 1966 she startled the cosmetics industry by offering makeup in a staggering choice of wild colors as well as a more natural palette. The range was advertised using top model Penelope Tree, and photographed by Richard Avedon. Her book *Colour by Quant* was published in 1984, followed by *Quant on Make-Up* in 1986, and the *Classic Make-Up and Beauty Book* in 1996.

In 1990 Quant was awarded the British Council's Award for Contribution to British Industry, and in 1993 she became a Fellow of the Society of Industrial Artists and Designers. Her cosmetics business is thriving as of the early 2000s; she has over 200 shops in Japan as well as outlets in London, Paris, and New York City.

See also **Avedon, Richard; Children's Clothing; Cosmetics, Western; Fashion Marketing and Merchandising; London Fashion; Miniskirt; Retailing; Youthquake Fashions.**

BIBLIOGRAPHY

Harris, Martin, Interviewer. "Quantum Leap Back to the Street." *Daily Telegraph*, 22 June 1994.

Morris, Brian. *Mary Quant's London.* Museum of London, London, 1973. Extensively illustrated with an introduction by Ernestine Carter.

Quant, Mary. *Classic Make-Up and Beauty.* London: Dorling Kindersley, 1996.

——. *Quant by Quant.* London: Cassell and Company, Ltd., 1966. An entertaining and informative autobiographical insight into London's postwar youth scene and the rise of Quant's fashion empire.

——. *Make 'Up' by Mary Quant.* New York: Harper Collins, 1987.

Quant, Mary, and Felicity Green. *Colour by Quant.* London: Octopus Books, 1984.

Amy de la Haye

QUILTING Quilting is a technique whereby layers of fabric are sewn together, usually in order to make a warm bedcovering. Quilting can be performed in many ways,

but a quilt frame is often utilized to stabilize the layers while a quilter or group of quilters uses needle and thread to sew a running stitch through all the layers across the surface of the quilt. Hand-quilting was standard practice until the 1980s; by the twenty-first century, many quilters used sewing machines or long-arm quilting machines to sew the layers together. Sometimes the quilting stitches follow a decorative pattern; other times they are made in a basic grid format simply for their functional purpose of attachment.

Typically, a quilt consists of three layers. The top layer, often simply called the quilt top, is usually made up of fabrics sewn together to create a decorative design, either through the use of piecing (seaming fabric pieces together along their edges), or appliqué (attaching fabric pieces to a ground fabric). Whole cloth quilts are those whose tops are made up of a single piece of fabric (or pieces seamed together to imitate the appearance of a single piece) and which feature the quilting as their sole design element. The middle layer of a quilt is the batting, a sheet of loosely joined fibers, which provide loft and warmth. Traditionally, wool and cotton were used as batting; however, polyester also came to be used. The backing of a quilt, usually less decorative than the top, is usually made from plain muslin, a single printed fabric, or from old bed linens. Once all three layers have been attached with quilting stitches, the raw edges on all four sides are covered and joined with a long narrow piece of fabric called a binding.

Quilting in History

Quilting has been practiced all over the world for millennia. Quilting frequently was used in the past to construct warm or protective clothing. Evidence of quilted garments reaches as far back as pharaonic Egypt, as seen in a thirty-fifth century B.C.E. ivory carving (in the collections of the British Museum) depicting a pharaoh wearing a mantle or cloak that appears to be quilted.

In medieval Europe, quilted garments were used first as stand-alone armor and later as supplements to metal armor. Worn under metal armor, quilted garments protected the wearer from bruising and scratching by the heavy outer armor and absorbed some of the shock of weapon blows. Surviving kaftans and other garments in the collections of the Topkapi Saray Museum in Istanbul show that around the same time (sixteenth to seventeenth centuries), quilted clothing was also popular in Turkey.

By the eighteenth century, quilted clothing had become the height of fashion in Europe and colonial America. Although waistcoats and jackets were also sometimes quilted, quilted petticoats were especially popular. Dress styles eventually evolved to have an open panel in the front, extending outward and downward from the waist to the hem, in order to show off elaborately quilted petticoats.

By the late eighteenth century, quilting in Europe, the British Isles, and America was mainly used in the construction of bedcoverings. Although quilted bedding had been made for centuries in Europe (the earliest surviving pieces are from Sicily, c. 1395), quilts became more common as fabrics imported by the East India companies and domestic textile production increased the availability of materials. Most of the late eighteenth-century quilts were whole cloth quilts, sometimes constructed from recycled petticoats (which had largely gone out of fashion by 1775). Whole cloth quilts were sometimes plain, with quilting as the main decoration, and sometimes embroidered. Piecing and appliqué were not as common, although extant pieces, such as a dated 1718 patchwork coverlet in the collection of the Quilter's Guild of the British Isles, prove that these techniques were not unknown.

Appliqué and piecing became the predominant techniques for creating quilt tops in the nineteenth century. Appliqué was more common during the first half of the century, but was largely superceded by piecing during the second half. Some quilts from the first half of the century, such as those in the so-called *broderie perse*, or cut-out chintz appliqué, style are thought to have been made to imitate *palampores*, printed Indian bedspreads. Baltimore album quilts, made in the Baltimore, Maryland, area between 1840 and 1850, are often considered the peak of the appliqué style, featuring highly detailed scenes and motifs.

The invention of the sewing machine during the 1840s, and its widespread use following the American Civil War, made piecing a faster, and therefore more popular, technique for creating a quilt top. Log cabin quilts are often the most recognizable nineteenth-century pieced style. Others include nine patch, triple Irish chain, and Bethlehem star.

During the first part of the twentieth century, technological advances strongly influenced quiltmaking. Quilt kits made from die-cut fabrics in "Easter egg" colors produced with synthetic (rather than natural) dyes, are trademarks of 1920s to 1940s quilts. Amish quilts, first made during the last quarter of the nineteenth century, flourished in the first half of the twentieth century and became icons of American quiltmaking. Quilts made by Amish women often feature simple pieced designs and intricate quilting designs similar to those found on whole cloth quilts of the late nineteenth century, hearkening back to an earlier era of quilting.

Modern Quilting

After declining in popularity during the middle decades of the twentieth century, quilting has experienced a resurgence in the late twentieth and early twenty-first centuries. Sparked in the late 1960s and early 1970s by the women's movement and a few pivotal quilt exhibitions and conferences, quilting has enjoyed a revival that endured. In addition to the creation of quilts in the styles of earlier eras, studio artists are making quilts that push

Woman quilting. Until as recently as the 1980s, most quilts were made by hand. In proceeding decades, sewing or quilting machines were generally employed. © ROYALTY-FREE/CORBIS. REPRODUCED BY PERMISSION.

the boundaries of the traditional quilt aesthetic. Artists such as Michael James, Nancy Crow, and Faith Ringgold are creating pieces that prove that quilting continues to grow and thrive as a medium of expression.

See also **Appliqué; Sewing Machine.**

BIBLIOGRAPHY

Bassett, Lynne, and Jack Larkin. *Northern Comfort: New England's Early Quilts, 1789–1850.* Nashville: Rutledge Hill Press, 1998.

Berlo, Janet, and Patricia Crews, eds. *Wild by Design: Two Hundred Years of Innovation and Artistry in American Quilts.* Seattle: University of Washington Press, 2003.

Colby, Averil. *Quilting.* New York: Charles Scribner's Sons, 1971.

Holstein, Jonathan. *The Pieced Quilt: An American Design Tradition.* New York: Galahad Books, 1973.

Orlofsky, Patsy, and Myron Orlofsky. *Quilts in America.* New York: McGraw-Hill, 1974.

Rae, Janet. *Quilts of the British Isles.* New York: E. P. Dutton, 1987.

Smith, Tina F., and Dorothy Osler. "The 1718 Silk Patchwork Coverlet: Introduction." *Quilt Studies: The Journal of the British Quilt Study Group* 4/5 (2002/3): 24–30.

Tezcan, Hulye, and Selma Delibas. *The Topkapi Saray Museum: Costumes, Embroideries and Other Textiles.* Translated by J. M. Rogers. Boston: Little, Brown and Company, 1986.

Marin F. Hanson and Patricia Cox Crews

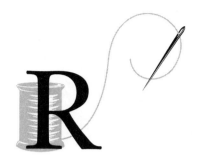

RABANNE, PACO Paco Rabanne (1934–) was born Francisco Rabaneda y Cuervo in Pasagès de San Pedro in the Basque region of Spain. His family fled to France in 1939 after his father was captured and executed by Francisco Franco's troops. Rabanne studied architecture at the École nationale supérieure des Beaux-arts in Paris from 1951 to 1963. In 1963 he won an award at the Biennale de Paris for an inhabitable garden sculpture, which was exhibited at the Musée d'art moderne de la ville de Paris.

Early Career

Rabanne's drawing skills made it possible for him to enter the world of fashion as early as 1955; indeed, to finance his architecture studies, he regularly supplied drawings of handbags for Roger Model and shoes for Charles Jourdan until 1963. In 1959 *Women's Wear Daily* published seven sketches of dresses signed "Franck Rabanne." Though this was the first time the designer's name appeared in public, he chose "Franck" because the number of letters in the first and last names totaled a lucky thirteen. (He did not begin using the name Paco professionally until 1965.) These dresses bore the imprint of the style of Balenciaga, whose work was familiar to the young Rabanne through his mother, a former chief seamstress in the master's workshop in San Sebastián in Spain.

Rabanne put his artistic gifts and the skills of his family to good use between 1962 and 1966: together they hand-produced unusual buttons and embroideries for the houses of haute couture. His clients at the time included Nina Ricci, Cristóbal Balenciaga, Maggy Rouff, Philippe Venet, Pierre Cardin, and Hubert de Givenchy.

In 1965, Rabanne's creation of oversized *rhodoïd* jewelry in various geometric forms and bright colors brought him his first major commercial and media success. It also established one of the principles of his style: the use of rigid divisible materials held together by metallic rings or rivets.

Paco Rabanne's first show took place on 1 February 1966 at the Hotel George V. This collection, which the designer called "Twelve Unwearable Dresses in Contemporary Materials," was worn by barefoot models parading to the sounds of Pierre Boulez's *Le marteau sans maître*, which Rabanne chose to reflect modernity and to shock the audience. It was a veritable fashion manifesto and helped to establish Rabanne's reputation as a revolutionary. On 21 April 1966, the dancers of the celebrated Parisian cabaret, the Crazy Horse Saloon, presented Rabanne's collection of beachwear made of rhodoïd disks or leather. The dancers modeled the unconventional clothes in the form of a strip tease, creating another scandal. Rabanne also set up his workshop in 1966 at 33, rue Bergère, with a black décor accented with industrial scaffolding and bicycle seats for chairs.

Experiments in Design

Following the example of contemporary artists who had given up the traditional media of paint and canvas, Paco Rabanne chose to base his fashion experiments on a systematic challenge to the art of cutting and sewing. His work was characterized from the beginning by a complete rejection of traditional couture techniques in favor of the exploration of unusual materials and methods of assemblage.

Rabanne followed up his experiments in rhodoïd with garments made of metal, making metal something of a distinctive signature. He used it from one collection to the next in all its forms: disks and rectangles normally used to make protective aprons for butchers, coats of mail, hammered plates, aluminum jerseys, or elements of jewelry or decoration used as modified ready-mades. This work led Coco Chanel to call him "the metal worker." Rabanne readily acknowledged that the recycling of ready-mades was very much in the tradition of the dadaists, such as his acknowledged master Marcel Duchamp.

He experimented with other materials, whether previously unknown to fashion or reimagined and redirected from their original purposes. Among Rabanne's most notable creations were: paper dresses, which were presented in his collections in 1967, 1988, and 1992; molded clothing known by the name of the patented Giffo process, in which all the individual parts, including the buttons and pockets, were molded in a single block (1968); designs made from knitted fur (1967); and several made entirely of buttons (1970), wood (1977), coconuts (1993), or laser discs (1988). Far from being incidental, these experiments were developed according to a rigorous artistic and ideological perspective. In the process, they helped to free

Paco Rabanne with several of his designs, 1977. Rabanne was famous for creating strikingly unusual clothing from unlikely materials such as plastic, paper, and various metals. © JAMES L. AMOS/CORBIS. REPRODUCED BY PERMISSION.

the art of clothing design from its strictly utilitarian context, and they inspired many other designers to adopt their current positions.

The innovative and nonconformist character of Rabanne's work was recognized in avant-garde artistic circles. The gallery owner Iris Clert exhibited Paco Rabanne's creations in 1966 among those of other artists she supported, like Lucio Fontana. Salvador Dalí referred to his young compatriot as the second Spanish genius for his Unwearable Dresses collection. Rabanne's clothes also appealed to such 1960s icons as Brigitte Bardot and Françoise Hardy. It was also in this period that the cinema made the most frequent use of his dresses, so singular in appearance and so photogenic.

Other Activities

In the 1960s and 1970s Rabanne was in great demand as a costume designer for theatrical productions and ballets as well as films. His many noteworthy contributions to the cinema include: *Two or Three Things I Know About Her*, directed by Jean-Luc Godard (1967); *The Adventurers (Les aventuriers)* also known as "The Last Adventure," directed by Robert Enrico (1967); *Two for the Road*, di-

rected by Stanley Donen (1967); *Casino Royale*, directed by John Huston (1967); and *Barbarella*, directed by Roger Vadim (1968).

In addition to Rabanne's work in costume design, he produced a series of sophisticated perfumes. Calandre, launched in 1969 by the Spanish company Puig (which bought out Paco Rabanne in 1986), has proven to be one of the most successful contemporary fragrances. Subsequent fragrances have sold well also. Rabanne's perfumes, as well as his numerous licenses for other products around the world, have made it possible for the designer to continue his fashion experiments without suffering unduly from the low profit margins of haute couture.

In 1999, Rabanne decided to put an end to haute couture activity, while the ready-to-wear sector that he had developed since 1990 experienced new growth, particularly with the arrival in 2000 of Rosemary Rodriguez as the head of Rabanne's creative studio. Rodriguez has developed several collections in harmony with the very particular stylistic grammar of Paco Rabanne.

On the occasion of Rabanne's thirtieth anniversary as a designer, the first retrospective exhibition of his fashions was presented in 1995 at the Musée de la Mode in Marseille, followed in 1996 by the bilingual publication of the first monograph devoted to his work.

Paco Rabanne has been involved since the late 1980s in several artistic projects beyond the confines of fashion, including the production of Mira Nair's film *Salaam, Bombay!* The film was awarded the Caméra d'Or at the Festival de Cannes in 1988.

In 1991 Rabanne published his first book, *Trajectoire.* He has since written several other works of reflection on mystical subjects and practices.

See also **Balenciaga, Cristóbal; Extreme Fashions; Givenchy, Hubert de; High-Tech Fashion; Paper Dresses; Paris Fashion; Perfume; Theatrical Costume.**

BIBLIOGRAPHY

Kamitsis, Lydia. *Paco Rabanne: les sens de la recherche.* Translated by Sylvia Carter. Paris: M. Lafon, 1996.

———. *Paco Rabanne.* Paris: Editions Assouline, 1997. Translated by Harriet Mason. London: Thames and Hudson, Inc., 1999.

Rabanne, Paco. *Trajectoire: d'une vie à l'autre.* Paris: M. Lafon, 1991.

Lydia Kamitsis

RAINCOAT A raincoat is a functional, lightweight single- or double-breasted waterproof coat, worn as protection from the rain. One of the most typically British of men's coats, it was created when Scottish chemist Charles Macintosh patented a waterproof fabric in 1823 and his name has become synonymous with the raincoat ever since. A raincoat, which is closely related to the riding mac in cut and color, should be cut large enough to fit over a suit, with a one-piece raglan sleeve (or with set-in sleeves and broad shoulders to accommodate wide-shouldered jackets), Prussian collar, and metal eyelets under the armpits to allow the arms to breathe.

History

Although not all outerwear needs to be waterproof, up to the turn of the nineteenth century the majority of outerwear on the market could not repel water unless specifically treated with oil. There had been many attempts to waterproof fabric effectively in the early part of the nineteenth century, but the actual method discovered by Charles Macintosh in the early 1820s was in fact intended for use for tarpaulin. He described his patented material as "'India rubber cloth," whereby the texture of hemp, flax, wool, cotton, and silk, and also leather, paper, and other substances may be rendered impervious to water and air. It was made as a "sandwich" of two pieces of material surrounding a core of rubber softened by naptha.

Macintosh warned tailors that the coats sewn from this material (without special precautions) would leak because of needle holes, but the "India rubber cloth" was deemed such a success that tailors hurried to try to use it nevertheless. After some time Macintosh was forced to open his own shops to make coats with properly waterproofed seams in order to protect his reputation. His tartan-lined rubber cloth coat with fully sealed seams remains the iconic raincoat. However, because temperature always rises in the rain and because rubberized cloth is nonporous, the raincoats were liable to make the body perspire when worn. London manufacturer George Spill discovered a solution to this by inserting metal eyelets under the armpits; such eyelets continue to be used in many raincoats.

During World War I, Thomas Burberry devised a weatherproof coat for the officers in the trenches, made of a fine-twilled cotton gabardine that was put through a chemical process to repel water while allowing the fabric to breathe. The "trench coat" was not totally waterproof, but was effectively water resistant under most weather conditions and the raglan sleeves, which allow for ease of movement, as well as the gabardine fabric used, became the norm for waterproof coats of later years.

Basic styles of raincoats have changed little since World War II, but raincoats for both men and women started being offered in a wide range of colors, in contrast to the older tans and grays that once were the only colors available. Advances in fiber and fabric technology, including surface treatments of fabrics, have made modern raincoats more water-repellent than ever before.

Although men and women in the early twenty-first century rely on cars, trains, and buses to protect them on the way to work—and the raincoat remains a business overcoat—the raincoat remains as popular a form of protection from the rain as it was when it was first conceived.

See also **Outerwear; Rainwear; Umbrellas and Parasols.**

BIBLIOGRAPHY

Amies, Hardy. *A, B, C of Men's Fashion.* London: Cahill and Co Ltd., 1964.

Byrde, Penelope. *The Male Image: Men's Fashion in England 1300–1970.* London: B. T. Batsford, Ltd., 1979.

Chenoune, Farid. *A History of Men's Fashion.* Paris: Flammarion, 1993.

De Marley, Diana. *Fashion for Men: An Illustrated History.* London: B. T. Batsford, Ltd., 1985.

Schoeffler, O. E., and William Gale. *Esquire's Encyclopedia of 20th Century Fashions.* New York: McGraw-Hill, 1973.

Wilkins, Christobel. *The Story of Occupational Costume.* Poole: Blandford Press, 1982.

Tom Greatrex

RAINWEAR The primary function of rainwear—outerwear including raincoats, trench coats, mackintosh coats, rain slickers, rain parkas, and even oilskin coats—is to protect the wearer from the cold, rain, and sleet while preventing penetration of moisture to whatever is being worn underneath.

Unlike most coats and jackets—which are usually appropriate for a particular occasion—rainwear manufacturers have to respond to the functional needs of the wearer: the classic case of form following function. But although fashion is often a secondary consideration when it comes to rainwear, most rainwear items nevertheless are also expressions of style.

History

The original mackintosh raincoats dating from the early 1820s were of a fairly crude construction and awkward appearance. The "India-rubber cloth" designed by the Scottish chemist Charles Mackintosh, consisting of two layers of cotton cemented with a layer of rubber, was not originally intended for outerwear at all, but instead was developed to waterproof tarpaulin.

The mackintosh concept was seized upon by tailors, even though problems arose as needle holes greatly decreased the material's ability to protect against the rain. Mackintosh eventually developed a process to seal the seams, and his name became synonymous with rainwear. Even as late as 1900 almost any raincoat was referred to as a mackintosh.

In the first decade of the twentieth century, many raincoats were still being made of rubber, and were cut long enough to reach a man's ankles and made in either single- or double-breasted styles.

World War I

The biggest development in the rainwear category came with the need to provide an all-weather coat to the officers serving in the trenches during Word War I. The London firm of Burberry owned the patent to a fabric of fine cotton gabardine that had been chemically processed to repel rain in order to protect shepherds and farm workers in wind-swept rural England. Although the Burberry cloth coat had been used by some officers during the Boer War (1899–1902), it was not until 1914 that the brand would receive the approval of the British war ministry.

More than 500,000 Burberry coats were produced for the war effort, and these "trench coats," as they would become known, very quickly became the official coat of Allied fighting men. Characterized by its shoulder tabs, a collar with storm flap, and D-shaped rings on the belt (to which pieces of a military kit, such as a water bottle or hand grenade, could be attached) the trench coat was produced by Burberry as well as by the London firm Aquascutum—each featuring its company's distinctive house-check lining.

Hundreds of thousands of trench coats have been sold in the early twenty-first century, but they are more likely to be worn by someone ready to do battle on New York's Wall Street or in London's Square Mile than on the muddy fields of the Somme or Ypres. Versions of the trench coat have graced the catwalks of Yves Saint Laurent, Giorgio Armani, Chloe, and Moschino. In 2004, the original trench coat was still an Aquascutum and Burberry staple item, one that seems to epitomize British style for many American and Japanese consumers. It thus has been highly successful as a piece of military attire as well as a stylish, practical, and iconic piece of clothing.

Post–World War I

By 1928, the rainwear of choice had become the French aviation coat. Similar to the trench coat, a French aviation coat was most frequently double-breasted with raglan sleeves, and was often cut in gabardine lined with oiled silk and lined with a plaid wool to ensure the coat was both warm and dry. Like the trench coat, the aviation coats also had belted waists as well as straps of gabardine at the ends of the sleeves and would become known as an all-weather coat.

During the 1930s, there was a trend toward a wider skirted, looser hanging style of coat. This was in fact excellent for keeping rain from the body, taking into account that the gabardine from which it was constructed was only water-repellent rather than waterproof. In 1934 *Men's Wear* explained: "A coat is like a tent. An ordinary tent of canvas will not leak in a driving shower, as long as you do not scrape the underside. Touch the underside and the water will begin to seep through instead of shedding off. The same principle applies to a loose fitting coat" (p. 27). Oiled silk and cotton raincoats and rubber ponchos also began to make an appearance at the time.

Not a great deal else changed in rainwear fashions, leaving aside color trends (it was fashionable to wear white raincoats in the 1930s, for example, and instead of blocks of color, different shades and tones were employed) and occasional changes in the typical length of a raincoat, until the 1953 introduction of a raincoat made from 50 percent cotton and 50 percent polyester. The London Fog, as this coat would become known, was the first on the market that was both water-repellent and washable. It was originally brought out as a single-breasted raglan and as a double-breasted trench coat, with a third style (a single-breasted belted trench coat with zippered sleeve pocket) added later.

The Peacock Revolution, born in Carnaby Street in the 1960s, would see many women's-wear designers cross over to the menswear realm, and inevitably their influence was noticed in rainwear. The Sherlock Holmes-esque raincoat with cape made a reappearance, as did houndstooth raglan coats. With the vogue for highly shaped suits, raincoats with wide Napoleon collars and flared lines soon appeared. At this time, and during the 1970s, the raincoat graduated from being a solely functional item to fashion "must have," something that has continued well into the twenty-first century with Burberry and Aquascutum raincoats and trench coats being fashion essentials almost 100 years after they were first conceived.

See also **Outerwear; Raincoat; Umbrellas and Parasols.**

BIBLIOGRAPHY

Amies, Hardy. *A, B, C of Men's Fashion*. London: Cahill and Co. Ltd, 1964.

Barnes, Richard. *Mods!* London: Plexus Publishing Limited, 1979.

Byrde, Penelope. *The Male Image: Men's Fashion in England 1300–1970*. London: B. T. Batsford, 1979.

Chenoune, Farid. *A History of Men's Fashion*. Paris: Flammarion, 1993.

De Marley, Diana. *Fashion for Men: An Illustrated History*. London: B. T. Batsford, 1985.

Keers, Paul. *A Gentleman's Wardrobe*. London: Weidenfield and Nicolson, 1987.

Roetzel, Bernhard. *Gentleman: A Timeless Fashion*. Cologne: Konemann, 1999.

Schoeffler, O. E., and William Gale. *Esquire's Encyclopedia of 20th Century Fashions*. New York: McGraw-Hill, 1973.

Wilkins, Christobel. *The Story of Occupational Costume*. Poole: Blandford Press, 1982.

Tom Greatrex

RAMIE Ramie (pronounced Ray-me), one of the oldest textile fibers, comes in two forms. Boehmeria nivea is also known as white ramie or China grass. It has been cultivated in China for thousands of years under the name *zhuma*. Boehmeria nivea (*var*. tenacissima) is also known as green ramie or rhea.

Properties of Ramie

Advantages. Ramie fibers come from the stems of the plant. They are harvested just before or right after the flowers bloom by cutting near the roots. The stems are processed in a manner similar to that used for transforming flax fibers into linen fabrics. The ramie stems go through the following steps to produce fibers suitable for spinning: (1) decortication—breaking up the hard outer bark to create long ribbons of bark and fiber; (2) degumming—immersing the fiber in caustic soda and heating in a closed container; and (3) washing and drying.

Producers of Ramie

The leading producers of ramie include China, Taiwan, Korea, the Philippines, and Brazil. Ramie is also produced in India, Thailand, Malaya, Queensland (Australia), Mauritius, the Cameroons, West Indies, Mexico, the southern states of the United States, and in south Europe.

Uses of Ramie

Ramie fibers were used for burial shrouds in ancient Egypt and ancient China. They have been used for centuries in Korea for the hanbok, Korea's traditional costume.

Ramie has for the most part been used in the country in which it was produced. In the 1970s a loophole in the Multifiber Arrangement (MFA) allowed ramie fiber to be exported without import restrictions as long as at least 50 percent of the fabric was made of ramie. This encouraged the use of ramie in blends and contributed to its popularity in the 1970s and 1980s. The MFA was modified in 1986, thereby closing the loophole.

In the twenty-first century, ramie, either in blends or alone, is used for a wide range of clothing: dresses, suits, sportswear, and underwear. Other uses include gas mantles for lanterns, ropes, nets, fire hoses, table linens, filter cloth, upholstery, straw hats, and sewing thread.

Care of Ramie Textiles

Since ramie used for apparel is most often blended with other fibers, the care of the fabric can vary. Fabric made from 100 percent ramie may be machine washed, machine dried, and ironed at high temperatures. Dry cleaning (if safe for the dyes and finishes used) is best at preserving the color, shape, and wrinkle-free appearance of fabrics made of ramie fibers.

See also **Fibers; Korean Dress and Adornment; Shroud.**

BIBLIOGRAPHY

Collier, Billie J., and Phyllis G. Tortora. *Understanding Textiles.* 6th ed. Upper Saddle River, N.J.: Prentice Hall, 2000.

Internet Resources

"Ramie." In *The 1911 Edition Encyclopedia.* Available from <http://18.1911encyclopedia.org/R/RA/RAMIE.htm>.

Korean Information Overseas Information Service. "Ramie Clothes." Available from <http://www.korea.net/learnaboutkorea/library/magazine/pictorial/199908/19990801.html>.

Scruggs, Barbara, and Joyce Smith. "Ramie: Old Fiber —New Image." Ohio State University Extension Fact Sheet (HYG —5501–90). Available from <http://ohioline.osu.edu/hyg-fact/5000/5501.html>.

Tondl, Rose Marie. "Ramie." Nebraska Cooperative Extension (NF 91–45). Available from <http://ianrpubs.unl.edu/textiles/nf45.htm>.

Wood, Ian. "16.2 Ramie: The Different Bast Fibre Crop." *The Australian New Crops Newsletter*, no. 11 (January 1999). Available from <http://www.newcrops.uq.edu.au/newslett/ncn11162.htm>.

Elizabeth D. Lowe

RATINE. *See* **Yarns.**

RAYON Rayon, acetate, and lyocell are all regenerated cellulose fibers. They originate from chemical treatment of natural materials. The materials most often used are cotton fibers too short to spin into yarns or wood chips. The Federal Trade Commission establishes generic categories of fibers for regulation and labeling purposes.

The generic classification "rayon" includes several variants. *Viscose rayon* is the most common form. A variation of viscose, *high-wet-modulus rayon* was produced in 1955 with trade names of Avril and Zantrel as a modification to generate high strength, reduce elongation, and improve washability of rayon. *Cuprammonium rayon* is subjected to slightly different processing. U.S. cuprammonium production ceased in 1975, but it is still produced in Japan (FiberSource Web site; Kadolph and Langford 2001).

Acetate has its own generic category, which also includes a variant, triacetate. Triacetate is a manufactured cellulosic that is similar to acetate but limited in production and usage. (Collier and Tortora 2000). Lyocell was given its own classification by the FTC for labeling purposes, but it was also designated as a sub-classification of rayon.

Rayon, the earliest manufactured fiber, was first patented in 1855 by the Swiss chemist Georges Audemars. It was called "artificial silk." Sir Joseph Swan, an English chemist, was inspired by Thomas Edison's incandescent electric lamp to experiment with extruding Audemars's cellulose solution through fine holes into a coagulating bath in order to create filaments for the electric light. His fibers were used in Edison's invention as well as for an 1885 exhibition of textiles his wife crocheted from his new fiber. "Artificial silk" was also exhibited at the Paris Exhibition in 1889 by the French chemist Count Hilaire de Chardonnet who is known as the "father of the rayon industry" because he built the first plant for commercial production of "Chardonnet silk" in Besancon, France.

The French chemist Louis-Henri Despeissis patented cuprammonium rayon producing what he called "Bemberg silk" as early as 1908. A British silk company, Samuel Courtaulds and Company, Ltd., began production of a rayon known as viscose rayon in 1905 and by 1911 helped start American Viscose Corporation in the United States (FiberSource Web site; Encyclopaedia Britannica 2003). Some researchers theorize that getting access to the science of producing rayon was such a benefit for the United States that it contributed to American involvement in World War I (Clairmonte and Cavanagh 1981).

The invention of acetate was rapidly followed by commercial production, as early as 1910. In Switzerland, Camille and Henry Dreyfus created acetate motion picture film and toilet articles and during World War I built a plant in England to help the war effort with cellulose acetate dope for airplane wings. The Dreyfus brothers were invited to build an acetate plant in Maryland to provide cellulose acetate dope for American airplanes. The Celanese Company began commercial production of acetate fiber in 1924. Both rayon and acetate garments were available to consumers by the 1920s. Confusion between the two fibers was partially due to the Federal Trade Commission designating both as rayon. This was not corrected until 1953 when rayon and acetate were given separate generic fiber classifications.

Cellulosic manufactured fibers reached peak production in the 1980s with a market share of 21 percent. Fiber was produced in North America, Europe, and Asia. By 2002, Asia had become the leading manufactured fiber producer with 65 percent of the market and cellulosics had dropped to 6 percent of fiber production (FiberSource Web site). Given that polyester production soared while cellulosics dropped, it seems that polyester became accepted as the most optimal "artificial silk."

Lyocell, developed as a "better" manufactured cellulosic, may be fundamental to reinventing enthusiasm for manufactured cellulosic fibers. Introduced to the U.S. market in the early 1990s, lyocell is sold under the trademark Tencel by Tencel, Inc., and by the Austrian producer Lenzing AG as Lyocell by Lenzing. Promoted as a designer level apparel textile that is more environmentally friendly than rayon, lyocell promotions tended to downplay association with rayon and focused on being a new textile with considerable potential for comfort and aesthetic appeal.

Producing rayon, acetate, and lyocell fibers. Although each manufacturing process has technical differences and variations in the steps, the basic procedure for the manufacture of rayon and lyocell begins with wood chips or cotton linters. These materials are treated with chemicals and subjected to various treatments, depending on the end product. Eventually these materials are reduced to a cellulosic solution. This solution passes through spinnerets, patterned after the small holes that silkworms use to extrude silk filament, and dries to become mostly pure cellulose filaments.

Wood pulp or cotton linters are also used in production of acetate, however, as a result of the chemical treatments, the fiber produced is no longer pure cellulose, but rather a form called cellulose acetate. As a result, the characteristics of acetate differ from those of the purely cellulose fibers. Acetate was the first thermoplastic fiber, a fiber that will soften and melt when exposed to high levels of heat (Kadolph and Langford 2001).

In the manufacture of lyocell, chemicals can be recovered and recycled, making lyocell one of the most environmentally friendly fibers to produce. Rayon and acetate involve considerable potential for hazardous chemical by-products. Efforts have been made to recycle chemicals and minimize environmental impacts, but the strict environmental pollution regulations in the United States have led many American manufacturers to discontinue rayon production.

Characteristics of rayon, acetate, and lyocell textiles. Rayon and lyocell have high absorbency, low heat retention, and soft, non-irritating surfaces that make them comfortable next to the skin in warm weather. Both can also be manipulated to emulate the aesthetic character of cotton, wool, silk, and linen. Additionally, lyocell has the capacity to simulate the aesthetics of silk, suede, and leather.

By contrast, acetate has more heat retention and less absorbency and is subject to static electricity build-up.

Viscose rayon and lyocell tend to be produced as staple (short) fibers and thereby have a textured surface that softens light reflectance. Acetate fibers are typically produced as filament fibers, and as a result acetate is more successful in simulating the luster and body of silk in such fabrics as taffeta and satin. Both rayon and lyocell dye easily although color will fade over time and with abrasion. Acetate was difficult to dye and subject to fading until synthetic solution dyes were developed to solve this problem. Acetate now is produced in a wide color range and color stability is good when fabrics are exposed to sunlight, perspiration, air pollution, and cleaning. Acetate is dissolved by fingernail polish remover containing acetone and is damaged by extended exposure to sunlight.

Unless it is the high wet modulus type, rayon has poor durability and resiliency. Rayon and acetate perform better if dry-cleaned than if laundered because they are weaker when wet. Acetate also has poor abrasion resistance and is sensitive to chemicals. While rayon may shrink or be distorted after laundering unless given special finishes, acetate is dimensionally stable. Lyocell is much stronger when wet than rayon or acetate and is considered to have good durability and dimensional stability. Resiliency is better than either rayon or acetate. Lyocell can be successfully washed by using the gentle cycle and can be pressed with a warm iron. Wrinkle-resistant treatments do not greatly affect strength. Lyocell has potential to fibrillate, which results in a fuzzy appearance on the surface. This is beneficial for a textured surface but makes the fabric subject to abrasion damage. New variations developed to lower fibrillation contribute to the versatility of this promising textile. Lyocell is often manufactured in microfiber (ultrafine) form to enhance the extremely soft feel and drape.

A major concern with acetate is its reaction to heat and to fire. While acetate wrinkles easily, it fuses and melts if ironed at high temperatures. Acetate also burns readily, as do all cellulosics, but spits molten pieces while burning that melt and fuse to the skin. Acetate is mildew and insect resistant. (FiberSource Web site; Kadolph and Langford 2001; Collier and Tortora 2000).

Rayon, acetate, and lyocell in fashion across time. Early in the twentieth century, rayon and acetate were both explored as an economical alternative to silk. The marketing of both fibers became confused as acetate was first sold as a form of rayon labeled "acetate rayon." Following World War I, which temporarily disrupted fiber development, consumers experienced problems with shrinkage and distortion of rayon and the thermoplasticity of acetate that had to be addressed. World War II disrupted access to silk fiber. Manufacturers in the United States used this opportunity to expand the market for rayon and acetate, allowing them to be accepted as new fibers rather than silk substitutes.

New fibers competed with rayon and acetate in the postwar period. While consumers enjoyed their low cost, unpredictability of performance was a deterrent. Use of manufactured cellulosics has declined. The large market share of polyester in the 2002 market leads one to assume that the aesthetic of silk is still important, but better performance than either rayon or acetate tend to provide has become a higher priority (FiberSource Web site).

Lyocell may be an exception to this downward trend. Manufacturers have been careful to differentiate lyocell from rayon. As a new fiber, it has a cachet of novelty and designer level taste that fits well with fashion. Recently, the versatility of Tencel lyocell is being expanded through new finishing processes that expand options for the aesthetic character of the final textile or garment (American Fiber Manufacturer's Association). Having the aesthetic of cellulosics with better performance and the aura of being good for the environment may help lyocell become the manufactured cellulosic of choice.

Common rayon, acetate, and lyocell textile uses. Rayon is used for a range of apparel as either 100 percent rayon or blended to create blouses, dresses, suiting, sport shirts, work clothes, slacks, and accessories. Interior products are also frequently blended and primarily include upholstery, draperies, slipcovers, bed coverings, and tablecloths. High wet modulus rayon tends to be used in knitwear and lingerie. Nonwoven applications for rayon are also extensive due to its high absorbency. These include cosmetic "cotton" balls, industrial wipes, reusable cleaning cloths, disposable diapers and sanitary products, and medical surgical materials. High tenacity rayon can be used for tire cords and other industrial products (Collier and Tortora 2000; Kadolph and Hollen 2001; FiberSource Web site).

Acetate fiber is primarily used for linings and also special occasion apparel, such as taffeta, satin, and brocade wedding and prom dresses. It is commonly found blended with rayon in interior textiles, such as antique satin or brocade draperies, textured upholstery, and bedspreads and quilts. Acetate is used for cigarette filters.

Because it is nearly twice the price of rayon, lyocell has been targeted primarily to upscale apparel, such as business wear, dresses, slacks, and coats. Recent innovations resulting from the Tencel Inc., Intellect research program has moved lyocell into more formal wear, such as men's suits. Lyocell is also being seen in lingerie, hosiery, and casual wear. Interior uses include upholstery and draperies. Lyocell can be blended with cotton, wool, linen, silk, nylon, and polyester, a broad range of possibilities for combining fiber characteristics. New modifications have made production of lyocell knitwear optimal.

BIBLIOGRAPHY
Clairmonte, Frederick, and John Cavanagh. *The World in Their Web: Dynamics of Textile Multinationals.* London: Zed Press; Westport, Conn.: L. Hill, 1981.

Collier, Billie, and Phyllis Tortora. *Understanding Textiles*. New York: Macmillan, 2000. Contains good illustrations.

Hatch, Kathryn. *Textile Science*. Minneapolis, Minn.: West Publishing, 1993. Contains good illustrations.

Kadolph, Sara, and Anna Langford. *Textiles*. 9th ed. New York: Prentice-Hall, 2002. Contains good illustrations.

Internet Resource

"A Short History of Manufactured Fibers." Available from <http://www.fibersource.com>.

Carol J. Salusso

READY-TO-WEAR The textile and apparel industry constitutes the largest global manufacturing employer with approximately 200 nations involved in production resulting in $313.5 billion in trade during 1996. Of this amount, $163.3 billion was derived from apparel, the tenth largest trade category in the world. The apparel industry comprises many small but interrelated firms. Making garments to sell as ready-to-wear is labor intensive but to initiate production requires less capital investment and less advanced technology than many other businesses. Women constitute the majority of the labor force worldwide and have found apparel a continuing source of employment throughout history. These factors have made the business of ready-to-wear clothing of particular importance to the economies of developing nations in the twentieth and early twenty-first centuries, and to entrepreneurs in many earlier eras.

The illustrated chart shows the relationships of the many associated firms involved in the production of all price levels of ready-to-wear. In the modern industry, these firms are located in many different parts of the world. Thus production emphasis is now placed on the coordination and logistics of each aspect of the process.

There are four aspects of ready-to-wear with historic antecedents that remain important businesses in the twenty-first century. The most common is the speculative production of fashionable garments to be sold at retail as described in the chart. Secondly, commissioned garment production, for example military uniforms, differs from speculative production in the nature of financial risk because there is no need to sell at retail. Thirdly, the used-clothing market has traditionally been a ready-made clothing source for the poor. However, the enormous growth of used clothing as a viable and expanding business in the late twentieth and early twenty-first centuries is notable for the breadth of its market, which reaches almost all socioeconomic levels through resale and thrift shops as well as auctions. Due in part to the relaxation of standards of dress, in part to popular culture and in part to affluence in the last quarter of the twentieth century, used clothing is an important sector of the current ready-to-wear market. Firms that provide services for international trade via shipping and logistics constitute a fourth important and profitable aspect, especially because of the decentralization of the modern industry.

Pre-Industrial Ready-to-Wear: Speculative Production

Speculative production began in antiquity with garments and accessories traded internationally. For example, ready-to-wear was part of ancient Babylonian business life as recorded on clay tablets dating from 1400 to 1200 B.C.E. A merchant there wrote to his associates to instruct them to open his warehouse, take out garments from his sealed chests and from the chests of garments returned to him by another merchant. He instructed them to "Write your tablets as follows: they have taken so-and-so many garments from the chest, so-and-so many from the regular deliveries have not been received, so-and-so many are from the garments returned to me—and send all the tablets to me" (Oppenheim, p. 85). These instructions are not unlike inventories taken in modern industry.

Speculative production requires capital investment and the ability to assume the risks inherent in recouping investment through the sale of merchandise at a profit. In the pre-industrial era such production included useful but semi-fitted garments. After 1350, as clothing became more fitted, shirts and accessories such as collars, hair nets, hats, and gloves became the primary kinds of products traded. In Renaissance Florence, embroidered detachable sleeves could be purchased ready-made and were also exported. London customs records for the second half of the sixteenth century show gloves from Belgium, Spain, and Italy imported by the gross; hair nets, straw hats, and caps from France by the dozen; as well as knitted nightcaps, gloves, stockings, and petticoats. Sixteenth-century London silkwomen, who processed imported raw silk from Italy into thread, could weave ribbons and other trimmings to make silk accessories which they sold in their own shops along with imported silk items, such as hair nets, netted neckwear, and netted sleeves. Elsewhere, women did most of the work of making small accessories, and such products were ordered and sold through men's trade guilds.

Pre-Industrial Ready-to-Wear: Commissions and Donations

Commissions were given for the provisioning of armies, household retainers, or charitable donations. In ancient Rome records indicate that garments were produced in factory-like settings with perhaps 100 workers, and that some early form of mass production outfitted the Roman legions. Commissions also feature in later European religious rituals and charitable donations. For example, in the annual Maundy Thursday foot-washing ceremony, Elizabeth I of England (1533–1603) provided a woolen gown, a pair of shoes, and a smock—mass produced at

New York tailors, circa 1890. Around the turn of the century, many arriving immigrants with tailoring skills found work producing clothing in New York City, the center of the American ready-to-wear industry. © HULTON-DEUTCH COLLECTION/CORBIS. REPRODUCED BY PERMISSION.

her expense—to as many women as equaled the years of the queen's age. In another sixteenth-century example, a wealthy citizen of Nuremberg, Germany, provided in his will of 1577 that each year on 31 October, 100 poor men would be provided with a coat, waistcoat, and trousers of black wool, a black hat, a white linen shirt, and a pair of shoes. This particular donation continued until 1809 and required two master tailors and their journeymen to use specific patterns, standard measures, and materials purchased from specified vendors, requirements similar to practices in twenty-first century ready-to-wear. Wealthy individuals might also provide in their wills for mourning clothes to be made and given to mourners at their funerals.

Pre-Industrial Ready-to-Wear: Used Clothing
By far the most widespread and common source of ready-to-wear clothing in the pre-industrial era was the used

clothing market. Throughout Europe records beginning in the Middle Ages document dealers in used clothing, often women, who supplied many in the lower socioeconomic levels for whom new clothing was too expensive. Used clothing dealers sometimes rented stalls in market areas designated for their trade, or simply sold their wares on the streets. A retail guild including dealers in second-hand clothing was organized in Florence, Italy, in 1266. The necessity for having used clothing available is apparent in the following examples from Nuremberg, Germany, in 1509 where a new coat given to a servant girl by her employer was equal to 56 percent of her annual income, and the fabric provided for a servant's coat and trousers was 148 percent of his annual wage. Some members of the upper classes also purchased used clothing, most of which was acquired by dealers at estate sales. During plague years, when there was fear of infection, used clothing markets were closed.

Model of Shannon Rodgers-designed dress, 1973. Rodgers would skillfully select an element of haute couture design and incorporate it into several ready-to-wear fashions. © CONDÉ NAST ARCHIVE/CORBIS. REPRODUCED BY PERMISSION.

Pre-Industrial Ready-to-Wear: International Trade

International trade in ready-to-wear garments and accessories increased as other regions of the world opened to European business in the sixteenth century. By the seventeenth century some larger ready-made garments, such as the *banyan* or *Indian gown* for men, and the *mantua* for women, were imported to Europe. Both were T-shaped garments similar to caftans, and were considered informal dress.

The first merchant ship to fly the flag of the United States, *The Empress of China*, sailed for the Orient in 1784. Its cargo of Virginia ginseng was traded at Canton, China, for porcelains and soft goods including ready-made umbrellas, 600 pairs of ladies' mitts; six pairs of ladies' satin shoes, more than 250 pairs of men's satin breeches, and a large number of textiles. On the second voyage in 1786, the ship returned with similar wares that included more than 600 pairs of satin breeches. These cargos were consigned to merchants who advertised the contents up and down the east coast of the United States.

Bristol, England, had more than 200 merchant houses trading internationally by the late eighteenth century, exporting felt hats, worsted caps, stockings, hosiery, footwear, and wearing apparel such as canvas frocks, trousers, shirts, jackets, and drawers. As part of the slave trade, this kind of ready-made clothing was traded in Africa to buy slaves and sold in America and the West Indies to provide clothing for slaves. Similar ill-fitting loose clothing was provided for sailors and was known as slops.

Early Industrialization of Ready-to-Wear in the United States

Merchant tailors, long prevented from making clothing on speculation because of guild restrictions and lack of capital, began to work in mass production during the nineteenth century. Systems of standardized and proportional measurements enabled them to make better fitting ready-to-wear at more affordable prices. The introduction by 1820 of a tape measure marked in inches made more standardization possible. Statistics kept for soldiers in the American Civil War helped determine how men's measurements could be better adapted for mass production. Ebeneezer Butterick's 1863 patent for the sized paper pattern provided increased standardization for women's garments. During the first half of the nineteenth century, mass produced ready-to-wear clothing was almost exclusively for men. Only mantles and cloaks with little fit were produced for women.

In the early years of industrialization, labor costs remained cheaper than fabric, with women and boys doing much of the sewing by hand at home while the pattern making, cutting, and inspection of finished goods were under the supervision of the tailor in his shop. At the end of the nineteenth century, immigrants met the growing need for labor. Many arriving with tailoring and dressmaking skills found work producing ready-to-wear in New York City, the center of the American ready-to-wear industry.

Early Industrialization: The Sewing Machine

The first technological innovation impacting industrial garment making directly was the sewing machine. Following developments by Elias Howe and Isaac Singer among others, Nathan Wheeler and Allen B. Wilson made and marketed a machine clothing manufacturers found efficient because it allowed fabric to feed evenly on curved seams. The sewing machine made possible the piecework concept of factory organization where each step was performed by a different person, eliminating the need for skilled workers.

Steam-powered sewing machines in factory workrooms were used from the early 1850s to produce men's shirts and collars, and were then adapted for the production of suits for men and boys. Overcoats of heavy cloth could be sewn by machine in three days instead of six by hand. The business of women's cloaks and mantles as well as crinolines and hooped petticoats was improved by the use of the sewing machine, and consequently these items became cheaper when ready-made. Women's fashions using braids and trimmings increased as machines made the application easier.

Improvements to the sewing machine continued, with 7,339 patents for sewing machines and accessories granted between 1842 and 1895. Technologies for cutting and pressing were the last fundamental industrial processes to be developed. The most successful mechanism for cutting multiple layers of cloth arrived in 1890, and the modern pressing machine was developed in the first years of the twentieth century.

Clothing Distribution after 1850

The nature of clothing distribution changed in the second half of the nineteenth century with the creation of department stores in large urban centers in Europe and North America. With these stores came greater variety for the consumer and the advent of advertising to influence choice. Department stores appeared in the early 1850s, and, by the end of the century had become enormous architectural wonders that encompassed many kinds of merchandise including ready-made garments for men, women, and children. Although these large stores offered products through illustrated catalogs, their focus was on the urban population.

In the United States, Aaron Montgomery Ward established a mail-order business in 1872 offering to furnish "Farmers and Mechanics throughout the Northwest with all kinds of Merchandise at Wholesale Prices." Sears, Roebuck and Company followed in 1893. By 1920, Ward's catalog had grown from a single sheet to 872 pages, and Sears' 1921 edition was 1,064 pages with the first 96 pages devoted to women's clothing, followed by 40 pages for men and boys. In addition to illustrated catalogs, women's magazines, first appearing in Europe at the end of the eighteenth century, proliferated throughout the nineteenth century. Initially limited fashion coverage focused on illustrations featuring the latest fashions, their materials and colors, and sometimes the providers. By the end of the nineteenth century, more pages were given over to product advertisements.

Speculative Production of Ready-To-Wear as a Mature Industry

By the 1920s mass production and mass merchandising were fully integrated into the ready-to-wear industry. The focus of advertising had shifted from declarations of quality to exhortations urging readers to keep up with fashion, and from an emphasis on men's wear to one on women's wear. This gave impetus to the modern industry's strategy of rapid fashion change. The women's ready-to-wear industry in the United States became concentrated in New York City between Sixth Avenue and Ninth Avenue from 35th Street to 41st Street, where 65 percent of the women's garment workers were employed by 1940. The proximity of manufacturers to labor and suppliers as well as associated businesses gave New York firms the flexibility to react quickly and efficiently to changing fashions. Employment in the domestic American apparel industry peaked in 1950 at 1.4 million.

Jerry Silverman, Inc., a manufacturer of women's better dresses, organized in 1959, provides an example of

Used goods sold in open-air market. People sort through used clothing at this outdoor market in Kenya in 2000. Because of the poor economy and resulting widespread poverty, this type of business forms an integral part of Kenya's informal economy. © AP/WIDE WORLD PHOTOS. REPRODUCED BY PERMISSION.

typical production processes. In 1970 Silverman sold dresses at wholesale from $39.75 to $89.75 to about 3,000 stores nationwide, where they cost the consumer from $70 to $175. Not including CMT (cut, make, trim) contractors, the firm employed about eighty people. Shannon Rodgers, the firm's designer, had his name on the label, an unusual acknowledgment when most designers working for manufacturers remain anonymous.

To develop a concept for his ready-to-wear line in a given season, Rodgers went to Europe to view collections. The industry in the United States usually depends on Parisian fashion ideas, especially for silhouette and color. However, the complex and detailed French haute couture (fine, luxurious made-to-order clothing) cannot be directly copied for ready-to-wear garments intended to fit thousands of consumers. Rodgers was skilled at taking single elements of a haute couture design, for example, a skirt detail, a neckline treatment, or a sleeve style,

Women sew clothes at a textile mill. Women constitute the majority of the labor force in the apparel industry throughout the world. © Brownie Harris/Corbis. Reproduced by permission.

and incorporating them into various garments, getting perhaps six ready-to-wear ideas from a single haute couture garment. These trips also gave Rodgers ideas for fabric choices that would give the finished garment the texture, volume, and movement he envisioned.

After sketches for the line were completed, fabrics and trimmings were purchased and a sample produced in company workrooms. Once the sample had been approved, it was sent to the pattern maker, graded into various sizes, and sent out to be duplicated for fashion show and showroom use. The Silverman fashion show for retail buyers and the fashion press usually featured about 100 different styles. Initial orders from buyers were confirmed after approval from the stores they represented. The success of the business depended on the quantity of confirmed orders and timely delivery—first of the fabrics and trimmings for production and then of the finished garments to the stores—as well as keeping production costs minimized.

Outside contractors cut the garments, bundled the pieces of each individual dress, and sent the bundles to machine operators for sewing. After sewing, the garments were finished, pressed, and returned to the Silverman Company for a final quality check and proper labeling. Labels included the firm's label, "Shannon Rodgers for Jerry Silverman," the union label, fiber content and cleaning instructions, style and size, and the store label and price tag.

Next came the firm's promotion and advertising to prepare customers for the new season. Once the finished garments had been shipped and received by the store, retail display, promotion, and advertising began. The salesperson and the customer at the point-of-sale completed the business process.

U.S. Ready-to-Wear Production in the Late Twentieth Century

By the early 1960s, manufacturers in the United States began to look for cheaper labor costs and production facilities off-shore. This resulted in a decrease in domestic apparel employment to 684,000 by 1999. It also resulted in a new focus on the logistics of coordinating off-shore production facilities where each part of an ensemble might be manufactured in a different country but is expected to reach the stores as a complete look. Modern communication and transportation make this kind of decentralized production process possible. Another significant change in late twentieth and early twenty-first century ready-to-wear is the importance of marketing strategies to product development.

Procedures associated with a retailer acting as manufacturer, or jobber, for merchandise bearing the store's private label, offer an instructive comparison with mid-twentieth century processes. In the 1990s, beginning at least 15 months in advance of the arrival of the garments in the store, the design director, color specialist, and product merchandisers would consult color and textile services and view collections in Europe and America. Fabric specialists and product merchandisers then shopped for yarns and textiles at major textile trade fairs. The initial line concept including color, mood, theme, silhouette, fabrics, and key components was presented to the product management team. The design team planned their internal strategy and refined the line concept before they joined the product merchandisers to make a final presentation to store committee members and management. Samples were reviewed and target prices agreed to before trips abroad to select contractors. Five months before the products were due to be shipped, the line was finalized and contracts signed. The products reached the stores six to eight weeks from the shipping date.

In order to track production at distant sites and cut costs even further, some mass-market firms use videoconferencing and other sophisticated technologies to send and receive information, thereby insuring product quality without the need to travel to the producer. As the time frame for fashion changes in ready-to-wear becomes more compressed, communication technology becomes more essential to success.

Conclusion

Innovations in transportation, communication, and technology have been major forces for change throughout the history of ready-to-wear clothing production. Additionally, rapid fashion changes have influenced the modern apparel industry by compressing the production timetable. However, the production of ready-to-wear apparel has been consistently labor intensive, leading modern manufacturers to seek lower labor costs by repeatedly moving production facilities. Challenges faced by the industry in

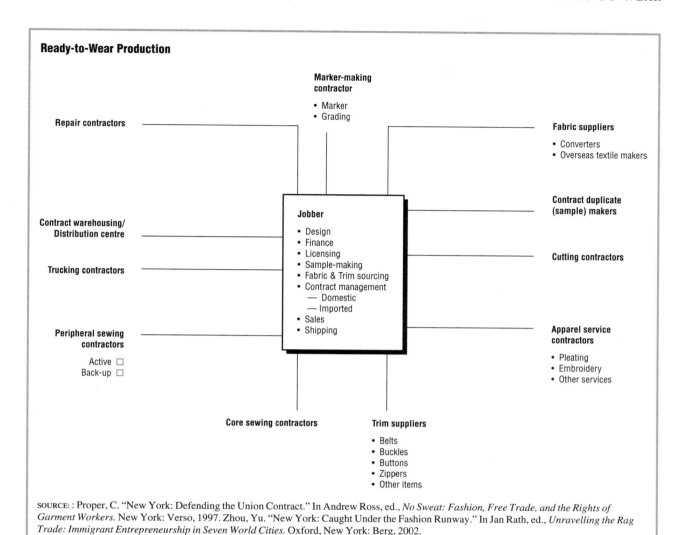

Ready-to-Wear Production

SOURCE: : Proper, C. "New York: Defending the Union Contract." In Andrew Ross, ed., *No Sweat: Fashion, Free Trade, and the Rights of Garment Workers.* New York: Verso, 1997. Zhou, Yu. "New York: Caught Under the Fashion Runway." In Jan Rath, ed., *Unravelling the Rag Trade: Immigrant Entrepreneurship in Seven World Cities.* Oxford, New York: Berg, 2002.

the early twenty-first century remain similar to those faced in earlier eras, particularly in the area of speculative production where the customer must be inclined to purchase at a price that yields a profit to the manufacturer.

See also **Fashion Industry; Seventh Avenue; Sewing Machine; Sweatshops.**

BIBLIOGRAPHY

Arnold, Janet. "Smocks, Shirts, Falling Bands and Mantuas: Evidence of Loosely-Fitting Garments and Neckwear Produced for the Ready-to-Wear Market, c. 1560–1700." In *Per una Storia della Moda Pronta, Problemi e Ricerche* (A History of Ready to Wear, Problems and Research). Proceedings of the Fifth International Conference of CISST (The Italian Center for the Study of the History of Textiles), Milan, 26–28 February, 1990. Firenze: EDIFIR, 1991.

CISST. *Per una Storia della Moda Pronta, Problemi e Ricerche* (A History of Ready to Wear, Problems and Research). Proceedings of the Fifth International Conference of CISST (The Italian Center for the Study of the History of Textiles), Milan, 26–28 February, 1990. Firenze: EDIFIR, 1991.

Dickerson, Kitty G. *Textiles and Apparel in the Global Economy.* 3rd ed. Upper Saddle River, N.J.: Prentice-Hall, Inc., 1999.

Druesedow, Jean L. "Designing for Off-shore Manufacture in the New York Ready-to-Wear Industry." In *Per una Storia della Moda Pronta, Problemi e Ricerche* (A History of Ready to Wear, Problems and Research). Proceedings of the Fifth International Conference of CISST (The Italian Center for the Study of the History of Textiles), Milan, 26–28 February 1990. Firenze: EDIFIR, 1991.

Frick, Carole Collier. *Dressing Renaissance Florence.* Baltimore: The Johns Hopkins University Press, 2002.

Kidwell, Claudia B., and Margaret C. Christman. *Suiting Everyone: The Democratization of Clothing in America.* Washington, D.C.: The Smithsonian Institution Press, 1974.

Levitt, Sarah. "Bristol Clothing Trades and Exports in the Georgian Period." In *Per una Storia della Moda Pronta, Problemi e Ricerche* (A History of Ready to Wear, Problems and Research). Proceedings of the Fifth International Conference of CISST (The Italian Center for the Study of the History of Textiles), Milan, 26–28 February 1990. Firenze, EDIFIR, 1991.

Oppenheim, A. Leo. *Letters from Mesopotamia: Official Business and Private Letters on Clay Tablets from Two Millennia.* Translated and with an introduction by A. Leo Oppenheim. Chicago: University of Chicago Press, 1967.

Rath, Jan, ed. *Unravelling the Rag Trade: Immigrant Entrepreneurship in Seven World Cities.* Oxford and New York: Berg, 2002.

Seidel, Jutta Zander, "Ready-to-Wear Clothing in Germany in the Sixteenth and Seventeenth Centuries: New Ready-Made Garments and Second-Hand Clothes Trade." In *Per una Storia della Moda Pronta, Problemi e Ricerche* (A History of Ready to Wear, Problems and Research). Proceedings of the Fifth International Conference of CISST (The Italian Center for the Study of the History of Textiles), Milan, 26–28 February, 1990. Firenze: EDIFIR, 1991.

Smith, Philip Chadwick Foster. *The Empress of China.* Philadelphia: The Philadelphia Maritime Museum, 1984.

Tortora, Phyllis G., and Keith Eubank. *A Survey of Historic Costume: A History of Western Dress.* 3rd ed. New York: Fairchild Publications, 1996.

Zhou, Yu. "New York: Caught under the Fashion Runway." In *Unravelling the Rag Trade: Immigrant Entrepreneurship in Seven World Cities.* Edited by Jan Rath. Oxford and New York: Berg, 2002.

Jean L. Druesedow

RECYCLED TEXTILES Textile recycling is one of the oldest and most established recycling industries in the world, yet, few people understand the industry and its myriad players. Textiles have been recycled since the eighteenth century when the Napoleonic War caused virgin wool shortages and required that wool fibers be garneted into new yarns. Even though the textile industry has been utilizing used fibers for at least 150 years, the markets for recycled textile fiber continue to evolve.

The textile recycling process functions as a multifaceted system that occurs along a pipeline of interrelated constituents that not only turns pre- and post-consumer waste back into fiber, but also is extracting new fiber from domestic waste. Specifically, PET (polyethylene terephthalate), the chemical substance from which some polyester is made, is reclaimed from plastic soda bottles. Although recycling is politically correct and ecologically friendly, 4–6 percent of landfills are comprised of recyclable textile products since discarded clothing and textile waste fail to reach the recycling pipeline, primarily because consumers do not understand the recycling process. The Council for Textile Recycling reports that the per capita consumption of fiber in the United States is 67.9 pounds with over 40 pounds (59 percent) per capita being discarded per year. Of countries where statistics are available, the United Kingdom deposits the highest percentages (90 percent) of textile waste to the landfill, compared to 65 percent from Germany, 30 percent from Denmark, and 20 percent from Switzerland.

A Global Problem

Western consumption patterns encourage excessiveness that leads to a negative impact on global sustainability. By implementing textile recycling, global sustainability increases. Two important issues regarding the global nature of textile recycling include: (1) textile waste is cre-

---

Recycled Textiles: Source, Usage, and Benefits

Source	Usage	Primary Benefit
Wearable post-consumer clothing	Export to less developed countries Disaster relief Vintage collectibles	Cost Charity Premium resale
Non-wearable post-consumer clothing	Wipers	Cost Ecological
Polyester/cotton manufacturing waste	Feedstock for engineered plastics	Energy savings Cost Relative weight Abundance of materials
Shoddy mungo	Insulating pads Bedding Blankets	Cost Durability
Linters	Cotton felts	Cost
Fiber waste	Paper pulp Hi-density composite Fibrous composites Laminated composites Particulate composites Concrete filler material	Low water absorption Does not release harmful chemicals
Recycled PET	Fleece outerwear Carpets	Thermal properties Environmental

---

GLOSSARY OF TECHNICAL TERMS

Clippings: Waste generated from a sewn-products cutting room.

Cream: Goods in like-new condition that have not been circulated in the consumer market.

Deadstock: A product that is not useable or saleable.

Garnet: To separate fabric into the fibers from which it is made by using a machine with needlike teeth that pull the fabric apart.

Mill Overruns: Anything made for first quality but not used, e.g. overproduction.

Mungo: Fibers extracted from woven garments. Fibers obtained by this method are very short and must be mixed with longer fibers to enable successful spinning.

Needlepunch wipers: Wipers manufactured from textile waste products.

PET: Thermoplastic polyester based on polyethylene terephthalate, i.e. recyclable plastics.

Post-Consumer Textile Waste: Textile waste from the home.

Pre-Consumer Textile Waste: Waste produced from manufacturing processes.

Rag Sorter: A company that grades post-consumer textile waste based on product, condition, or material content.

Reworkable waste: Waste from the manufacturing process that can be fed more or less directly back into the process.

Shoddy: Fibers produced from knitted garments

Soft waste: Waste from the manufacture of garments and yarns, mixed with new fiber by spinners to produce cheaper yarns.

Textile MRF: A facility that grades and sorts post-consumer waste.

Vintage Used Clothing: Reused clothing that has become fashionable or has collectible value.

Wipers: Squares cut from any cloth or material used to clean or polish.

Some of these glossary terms specific to the textile recycling industry have been adapted from the *Council for Textile Recycling Buyers Guide and Directory*, Bethesda, Md.: Council for Textile Recycling, 1995.

---

ated and disposed of on a global scale, and (2) much of the used-clothing market is located in developing countries where annual wages are sometimes less than the cost of one outfit in the United States. For many people in developing countries, it is necessary to be able to receive used clothing surplus from industrialized nations. Simpson (1996) reports that nearly 34,000 tons of used clothing is sent to Africa annually. Because not all countries allow the importation of used clothing, black markets have risen as goods move across borders to meet market demands.

The three primary areas for processing of reclaimed apparel are Prato, Italy; Dewsbury, United Kingdom; and, more recently, India. These processing centers obtain used apparel from all over the world, sort items based on color and fiber content, mechanically reduce the apparel back to a fiber state, then reprocess into new yarns and end products.

The Process of Recycling Textiles

The range of markets for used textile fiber varies from vintage collectibles; to used clothing exported to less de-

veloped countries, to industrial uses. Traditional sources of textile waste come from three different sources:

1. fiber, yarn, and fabric processing
2. sewn products manufacture
3. discard at the end of its useful life

Textile and cutting wastes at the manufacturing level are considered pre-consumer waste and are easier to recycle because the fibers, dyes, and finishes are known and in like-new condition. Post-consumer waste is of uncertain origin and has a wide variance in quality and condition, making it more difficult to recycle. Ongoing research and development focuses on the problem of processing used, mixed fibers.

Most post-consumer textiles are collected by charity organizations, but it is impossible for charities to utilize all of the collected clothing so they sell the balance to rag graders. Approximately 500 textile recycling companies in the United States are responsible for diverting 775,000 tons of post-consumer textile waste from the landfills. These "rag sorters" sort used clothes for export, wipers, and fiber and fabric manufacturers (Council for Textile Recycling 1997). Although textile-recycling processors

Women sorting recycled textiles. Textile recycling companies sort through clothing for fabrics that can be reclaimed for industrial use and those that can be sent to needy people in developing countries. PHOTOGRAPH TAKEN BY JANA M. HAWLEY, TAKEN IN PRATO, ITALY. REPRODUCED BY PERMISSION.

have historically purchased their inventory by weight from charity surplus, they have recently begun to expand their base of suppliers by helping municipalities develop curbside and drop-off textile collection programs. Almost half (45 percent) of the collected goods are recycled as secondhand clothing, typically sold to markets in developing countries. Thirty percent is used for the wiper industry and another 26 percent are converted to new raw materials used primarily as stuffing or insulation pads

See also **Polyester; Secondhand Clothes, Anthropology of; Secondhand Clothes, History of; Textiles and International Trade.**

BIBLIOGRAPHY

Council for Textile Recycling. "Don't Overlook Textiles!" Council for Textile Recycling, 1997.

Goodard, Robert, and Daly Herman. "Environmental Sustainability: Universal and Non-Negotiable." *Ecological Applications* 6, no. 4 (1996): 1002–1117.

Hawley, Jana M. "Textile Recycling as a System: The Micro-Macro Analysis." *Journal of Family and Consumer Sciences* 92, no. 4 (2001): 40–46.

Meis, M. "Consumption Patterns of the North: The Cause of Environmental Destruction and Poverty in the South: Women and Children First." Geneva, Switzerland: United Nations Commission on Environment and Development, 1991.

Platt, Brenda. "Weaving Textile Reuse into Waste Reduction." Washington, D.C.: Institute for Local Self Reliance, 1997.

Watson, Jacky. *Textiles and the Environment.* New York: The Economist Intelligence Unit, 1991.

Jana M. Hawley, Pauline Sullivan,
and Youn Kyung-Kim

REENACTORS Reenactors, referring to themselves sometimes as "living historians," are individuals who publicly recreate historical events and eras by donning historical dress and emulating period behavior. For most it is a hobby or pastime, occurring among all age groups and genders in varying locations around the world. People in the United States can be found reenacting the European medieval era, the American Revolutionary War, the early 1800s westward expansion, World War II, and other events. In the early 2000s the most popular era, judged by the frequency of reenactments and number of participants, is the American Civil War.

The best reenactors carefully craft the persona of individuals from the past. They refer to this activity as creating an "impression." To develop a credible impression reenactors must be authentic, which is indicated by the closeness to which a reenactor approaches exact replication of the "historical personage, place, scene, or event from the past" (Handler and Saxton, p. 243). Serious reenactors invest a great deal of time researching their historical impressions to ensure authenticity. In fact, achieving authenticity in reenacting is viewed as an "index of performance competence" (Turner, p. 127). Those who master authenticity are admired by their fellow reenactors, and those who do not are frequently ridiculed by their peers.

Replicating period material culture is an important necessity for achieving authenticity. In other words, dress and accessories must give every appearance of being from the past. For the sake of authenticity reenactors spend considerable time and money buying and/or creating costumes congruent with their historical personae. For example, a first-rate Civil War uniform, including trousers, jacket, shirt, underwear, shoes, and hat can cost several hundred dollars. In addition, accessories such as a musket, military leathers, and bedrolls can push the entire investment to well over one thousand dollars. Great care is taken to ensure that historical anomalies are not apparent in the reenactor's kit or ensemble. Some even go so far as to count the number of thread stitches per inch in a garment's construction. "The objects of reenactment become deeply treasured emblems of identity . . . The form these objects take is guided by a collective aesthetic . . . of painstaking detail and accuracy " (Turner, p. 126).

Why Do People Reenact?

Much of the scholarly literature on reenacting is focused on reenactor motivation. Allred regards reenacting as a postmodern "flight from an age of isolation and fragmentation into an age of community and shared ideals" (p. 7). Handler and Saxton also place reenacting in postmodern context, suggesting that "practitioners seek . . . an authentic world . . . to realize themselves through the simulation of historical worlds" (p. 243). Hall postulates that reenacting is a postmodern, nostalgic impulse in re-

American Civil War reenactors. Serious reenactors spend great amounts of time and care in assembling their costumes. Authenticity is the key, and often participants will pay hundreds of dollars to get every detail correct. © KEVIN FLEMING/CORBIS. REPRODUCED BY PERMISSION.

sponse to social, political, and economic turmoil of late capitalism. Turner sees reenacting as a public expression of self where the sense that reenactor's make of the past form "themes [for] self-examination" (p. 134). "For some [reenacting] is a political statement, for others an affirmation of cultural identity . . . individuals discover the themes that apply to themselves and their lives" (p. 130). For example, Belk and Costa find reenactors challenging a "number of American values such as reverence for nature, frontier as freedom, individualism, materialism, and statusless egalitarianism" (p. 32).

Confederate Civil War Reenacting

Most Civil War reenactments are local/regional affairs, taking place in park-like settings, attracting reenactors from the host state and surrounding region. Several hundred reenactors representing both Confederate and Federal armies typically participate together in an event. Throughout the year, a handful of national reenactments are also staged, where several thousand reenactors might convene. Most reenactments commemorate a specific Civil War battle; however, unlike the actual war, the events are generally conducted on weekends, with the arrival of the reenactors on a Friday evening. They quickly and efficiently establish separate Confederate and Union camps, characterized by an expanse of canvas tents and a multitude of cook fires. It is not unusual to see horses and cannons, representing cavalry and artillery. Separating the two military camps is usually a civilian camp, containing nonmilitary reenactors and sutlers who supply the reenactors with their "period" material needs. Saturday and Sunday activities entail military drills and staged battles. Other activities during the weekend might include a period religious service, recruiting rally, and military ball. By late Sunday afternoon, the reenactors break camp and return to their everyday lives.

There are many reasons why Confederate reenactors participate in the hobby. Strauss has identified several key motivations: a love of Civil War era history, an opportunity to play a role "larger than life," social bonding, and perhaps most disturbing, some reenactors express discontent with the outcome of the Civil War and the resultant erosion of white hegemony in the United States. Consider the reenactor from Michigan, whose eyes burned with intensity when he said, "I do this because I believe in what they believed in . . . my ancestors fought for the Confederacy" (Strauss 2001, p. 150).

Why would unhappy white hegemonists couch themselves within the hobby of Confederate reenacting? Because expressing whiteness, a subtle form of racism, publicly in a more overt manner can be problematic. In the United States overt racism is a stigmatic behavior, and to avoid stigma, Confederate reenactor expressions of whiteness are embedded within the pageantry of a widely accepted public pastime. In essence, Confederate reenactors are able to veil their protestations symbolically and keep them politically correct and publicly palatable.

Of all the elements used by Confederate reenactors to project themselves and their sense of whiteness, the importance of appearance in the form of dress cannot be overemphasized. Without the uniform, there would be no reenacting. The uniform is used to step into character and to drape history over the shoulders of the reenactor. Without the uniform, the stage upon which history is replayed evaporates, and without the reenactor's stage the projection of the white self in a publicly palatable manner becomes virtually impossible.

See also **Military Style.**

BIBLIOGRAPHY

Allred, Randal. "Catharsis, Revision, and Reenactment: Negotiating the Meaning of the American Civil War." *Journal of American Culture* 19, no. 4 (Winter 1996): 1–13.

Belk, Russell W., and Janeen Arnold Costa. "The Mountain Man Myth: A Contemporary Consuming Fantasy." *Journal of Consumer Research* 25, no. 3 (December 1998): 218–240.

Dobratz, Betty A., and Stephanie L. Shanks-Meile. *The White Separatist Movement in the United States: "White Power, White Pride!"* Baltimore: Johns Hopkins University Press, 1997.

Hall, Dennis. "Civil War Reenactors and the Postmodern Sense of History." *Journal of American Culture* 17, no. 3 (Fall 1994): 7–11.

Handler, Richard, and William Saxton. "Dyssimulation: Reflexivity, Narrative, and the Quest for Authenticity in 'Living History.'" *Cultural Anthropology* 3 (1998): 242–260.

Singer, Mark. "Never Surrender: The Sons of Confederate Veterans Have a Bad Day at the Mall." *The New Yorker* (14 May 2001): 52–56.

Strauss, Mitchell D. "A Framework for Assessing Military Dress Authenticity in Civil War Reenacting." *Clothing and Textiles Research Journal* 19, no. 4 (2001): 145–157.

———. "Identity Construction Among Confederate Civil War Reenactors: A Study of Dress, Stage Props, and Discourse." *Clothing and Textiles Research Journal* 21, no. 4 (2003): 149–161.

———. "Pattern Categorization of Male U.S. Civil War Reenactor Images." *Clothing and Textiles Research Journal* 29, no. 2 (2002): 99–109.

Turner, Rory. "Bloodless Battles: The Civil War Reenacted." *The Drama Review* 34, no. 4 (1990): 123–126.

Mitchell D. Strauss

RELIGION AND DRESS The interaction between religion, culture, and dress is fascinating. Dress can be a window into the social world, which is bound by a tacit set of rules, customs, conventions, and rituals that guide face-to-face interaction. To many religious organizations, clothing is an important symbol of religious identification. However, for most groups, the regulation of personal appearance goes beyond clothing. The term dress as it is used here includes clothing, grooming, and all forms of body adornment. Dress also includes behaviors related to the control of the body, such as dieting, plastic

Orthodox Jewish attire. An Orthodox Jewish man teaching children Hebrew. Orthodox Jews cultivate a distinctive appearance, including the hat and beard visible here, as a sign of their beliefs. © David Turnley/Corbis. Reproduced by permission.

surgery, and cosmetics. Holistically, then, dress functions as an effective means of nonverbal communication. Ideas, concepts, and categories fundamental to a group, such as age, gender, ethnicity, and religion, help to define a person's identity that is then expressed outwardly through a person's appearance. Both individual and group identity is projected through dress because people use self-presentation and self-promotion to visually present identity that is congruent with their belief systems.

The Sacred and the Secular

Where religion is concerned, clothing can be divided into two categories often referred to as the sacred and the secular (or profane). In some instances, what is treated as sacred is merely a garment that has important cultural implications with regard to gendered power. In patriarchal religions where the perception is that males are given the responsibility of seeing to the enforcement of religious rules, some garments become associated with the sacred primarily through the prescription and enforcement of a dress code. The most recent example of the conflation of gendered power and dress is the prescrip-

tion that women in Afghanistan in the early 2000s were required to wear the burqa (or *chadaree*).

While secular dress is not exclusively associated with religious activities, secular dress is used in ritual or is worn by certain religious practitioners such as the clergy. Dress used for religious ceremonies and rituals is referred to as ecclesiastical dress; modern dress for Roman Catholic priests resembles dress from the early days of the Christian church when the clergy were not distinguished from other male members of the church by their dress. However, in the sixth century as fashion changed, the clergy did not adopt the new fashions and continued to wear the older styles. Ecclesiastical dress has become a form of fossilized fashion, a phenomenon where the garments worn seem frozen in time and continues to be worn even as other forms of dress evolved.

A common theme with regard to liturgical garments worn by male clergy is the de-masculinization of sacred dress. For many religions, sacred dress for male clergy commonly avoids pants in favor of loose, flowing robes. Because hair is symbolic of sexuality, it is controlled in

Muslim men at prayer. A wide variety of clothing styles can be seen among these Muslim men. While some are in traditional dress, many are wearing western attire, both formal and informal. © Peter Turnley/Corbis. Reproduced by permission.

many religions. Some orders of priests, nuns, and monks shave their heads, remove a lock of hair, or cut their hair to symbolize their turning away from the pleasures of the world.

Interestingly, everyday dress for certain ethno-religious subcultures, such as Hasidic Jews, Amish, and conservative Mennonites, is considered sacred, especially in the symbolic separation of the ethno-religious subculture from a dominant culture. As religious groups encounter social change, dress often symbolically becomes important as certain items of a religious group's clothing may be classified as sacred in contrast to what is considered secular. Generally the most symbolic dress features of Amish and Mennonites (hats, beards, head coverings, bonnets, aprons) are considered sacred. Similarly, among conservative Muslim women, very fashionable clothing may be worn underneath the veils (sacred garments), known as *chador*, *chadaree*, or *burqa*, that are seen by outsiders. Sacred dress worn externally then becomes used intentionally to visually separate these religious groups from the larger culture. Often, the rules as to dress codes are imposed by male clergy on female members of the community, and in doing so, these patriarchal religious societies intentionally use dress codes to maintain a gendered imbalance of power.

Some religions have sacred garments that are not visible to outsiders. Mormons who have been to temple wear sacred undergarments beneath otherwise ordinary clothing. The sacred undergarments reinforce their commitment to their religion.

Religious Ideologies

Organized religion has used dress in two related ways: to maintain the customs and traditions of the organization, thereby establishing a visual identity for the religion; and to simultaneously control the individual identities of its members by symbolically denoting dress as in-need of control. Religions create dress codes to overtly define morality and modesty while covertly controlling sexuality. Fundamentally, dress codes are less about clothing than about the control of the body by the more powerful church members who enforce their groups' ideologies. Religious dress codes express group identity and simultaneously function as a means of reinforcing male patriarchal control.

When a religion uses dress to reinforce tradition, it will usually be seen in opposition to fashion, which by its very nature is dynamic. Religious dress will change slowly as organized religions often reject fashion as an attempt to focus on individuality rather than salvation.

To understand how dress is expressive of religious ideologies, it is helpful to understand how each of the world's major religions perceives the role of dress as a means of identity expression. In a later section, more detail will be given as to how particular religious groups use dress to establish sectarian identities.

Hinduism is a polytheistic religion encompassing a holistic view of life in which the inner self is highly valued, and life in the world is seen as temporary. Reincarnation is a belief at the base of both the caste system and religious expression. The individual works through levels of moral development that are indicated by caste. It is believed that the higher the person's caste, the closer the individual is to the spiritual world. Since the focus in Hinduism is on the inner self, dress, an expression of the external self, is less important. Dress is tradition bound, and slow to change by comparison to costume found in other religious groups. Dress and adornment in Hindu society does show a person's caste, level of piety, or the specific god to which the individual is devoted.

Islam is the newest of the major religions and its followers are commonly referred to as Muslims. This religion emphasizes the group over the individual, and Islamic ideology focuses on male power and the separation of the sexes through both physical and visual means. Dress codes for Muslims have great impact on daily life, which involves frequent religious expressions and rituals. Among Muslims, codes of modesty go beyond the covering of women's bodies to include restriction of women's behavior. The Koran requires women to dress modestly, but does not specifically state that they must wear veils. Dress codes regarding veiling vary among Islamic families and cultures; however, among the most conservative Islamic groups the requirements for women to wear veils are seriously enforced. In addition to their ostensible function to protect gender segregation, these rules also are intended to slow down assimilation that began after World War II when westernization started in Islamic societies. As western dress became common, the Islamic fundamentalist movement began pushing for a return to tradition. Modest dress and veils became symbolic of both the acceptance of patriarchal power and nationalism. Throughout the larger cities in Iran, posters announced the specifics of the dress code requiring women to dress in chadors that cover all but the face. In Afghanistan under Taliban control, women were killed if they did not wear the all-enveloping burqa or *chadaree*.

Judaism, the oldest of the major monotheistic religions, is based on the concept that people exist to glorify God; to be appropriately dressed, then, is a religious duty. Historically, the ancient Jews had customs that indicated dress was seen as symbolic. Since the upper body was seen as pure, but the lower body was perceived as impure, Jews wore girdles to make the division between pure and impure visibly clear. Morality was connected with dress early on; Moses forbade nudity. Similarly, he forbade Jews from wearing the clothing of non-Jews in

An Amish girl. In an example of fossilized fashion, the Amish continue to dress in the same style that was prevalent when they originated in the seventeenth century. This practice serves both to set the Amish apart from the rest of society and to demonstrate their beliefs and traditions. © DAVID TURNLEY/CORBIS. REPRODUCED BY PERMISSION.

an attempt to keep his people separate from influences that might lead to assimilation. In recent times, levels of Judaic conservatism are denoted by dress where the most assimilated Jews dress like non-Jews. However orthodox and Hasidic Jews wear specific garments to visibly show their religious conservatism.

Christianity is less clear about values pertaining to dress than is Judaism. Values in Christian theology relating to the body are conflicting; women's bodies are seen as the site of temptation, in that male sexual guilt is projected onto the female body. Adam's fall from grace is attributed to Eve's sexuality. Christian women are required to dress modestly, but this standard is not equally applied to Christian men. Modesty with regard to body exposure is an important value that is a key indicator of religious conservatism.

During the Protestant Reformation of the sixteenth century, early leaders used dress as a symbol of piety. Fashionable, colorful dress and adornment were equated with sensuality and pride, while somber dress showed the Christian's focus on salvation. For fundamentalist Christians (who evolved out of the Reformation) such as the Anabaptist groups (such as Amish, Mennonites, and Hutterites) who believe themselves to be uniquely separate from the larger society, dress is used to show that separation. In these groups, dress is often hyper-conservative or may even be a form of fossilized fashion.

Sectarian Dress

Some of America's sectarian ethno-religious groups use fossilized fashion to separate themselves from the outside world. Notable among these are the Shakers, Amish, Hasidic Jews, Hutterites, and several conservative Mennonite groups. Fossilized fashion has been explained as a sudden "freezing" of fashion whereby a group continues to wear certain clothing long after it has gone out of style for the general population. This phenomenon has been explained as expressing dignity and high social status or the group's religious, old-fashioned, sectarian identity. Within certain ethno-religious groups, fossilized fashion is used in contemporary settings as a visual symbol of traditional gender roles for women; this generally occurs in societies that find change to be a threat.

Most of the conservative ethno-religious groups who wear fossilized fashion continue to wear clothing styles that were in use for the general population during the time their sect originated. For instance, the Amish separated from the larger Mennonite movement in the beginning of the seventeenth century; their garments in the early 2000s include full-fall trousers for men, and for women, dresses, bonnets, capes, aprons, and head coverings like their forebearers. Like the Amish, Shakers and the most conservative Mennonites in the United States continue to wear long dresses with aprons that provide an additional covering of the bust and stomach, again, like their forebearers. Other Mennonites dress in styles that were popular when their sect broke off from the larger Mennonite movement. Hasidic Jews have retained a complex code of dress for men that indicates a man's level of religiosity; these garments include particular hats, shoes, socks, and coats that are identifiable by members of their community. For Hasidic Jewish women, wigs are worn to cover their natural hair.

Modesty and Female Sexuality in Dress

Among all of the major religions, modesty in women's dress is associated with gender norms; this is a major issue to religious groups. Gender issues are paramount in the dress codes of conservative religious groups since the control of female sexuality is often of great importance in patriarchal religious groups. The dress codes generally relate to modesty and require clothing to cover the contours of the female body. Additionally, some religious groups, particularly the most conservative Islamic, Anabaptist, and Jewish sects, also require that women's hair be covered as well.

As used by religious groups, the issue of modesty goes beyond the covering of the body in order to disguise female curves and secondary sexual characteristics; in the conservative strains of all of the major religions, dress codes also deal with the care and covering of women's hair as it is associated with women's sexuality (Scott, p. 33). Further complicating matters, dress codes are conflated with gender and power issues in religious groups. At the root of this issue is the control of female sexuality that is perceived to be necessary by some religious groups as a means to maintain social order.

An understanding of how dress works within religious groups calls attention to the complexity of meanings surrounding visible symbols such as dress, and sheds light on the ways that bodies can communicate social and religious values. The dress of religious groups can be used to facilitate social and ideological agendas. Clothing and personal adornment are used for establishing and maintaining personal and social identities, social hierarchies, definitions of deviance, and systems of control and power. As a consequence, then, dress within conservative religious groups is a symbol of the individual's commitment to the group while it also symbolizes the group's control over individual lives. For America's fundamentalist Christian groups, and the Anabaptist groups in particular, dress is particularly important with regard to its role in social control and in social change.

Dress and Social Control

Dress is an immediate and visible indicator of how a person fits into his/her religious system. As a marker of identity, dress can be used to gauge the person's commitment to the group and to the religious value system. In many conservative groups, suppression of individuality is expected, in obedience to the rules of the religious organization. Several religious groups are also ethnically homogenous; these are referred to as ethno-religious groups (In the United States, some of these groups are the Amish, Mennonites, Hutterites, Hasidic Jews, Sikhs, and certain Islamic groups.) The conservative branches of ethno-religious groups frequently use clothing to simultaneously express ethnicity, gender norms, and level of religious involvement (religiosity). Through conformance to a strict religious value system, the most conservative of the religious social bodies exert control over their members' physical bodies. Since strict conformity is often equated with religiosity, compliance to strict codes of behavior is demanded. The internal body is subject to control by the religious culture, especially with regard to food and sex. The external body, however, is much more visibly restrained. Strict dress codes are enforced because dress is considered symbolic of religiosity. Clothing becomes a symbol of social control as it controls the external body. While a person's level of religiosity cannot be objectively perceived, symbols such as clothing are used as evidence that the member of the religious group is on the "right and true path."

Normative social control begins with personal social control through self-regulation, followed by informal social control. The member wants to fit into the group, and expresses role commitment by following the social norms, visibly expressed in the group's dress code. When the individual begins to offend, for example by wearing a garment that is too revealing of body contours, peers may disapprove and use subtle methods of informal control to pressure the individual to conform to the group norms. Finally, the threat that an offender introduces to the social order is managed through formal social control measures, such as disciplinary measures and expulsion administered by specialized agents, including ministers, rabbis, and other moral arbiters. Thus, norms are managed through social control to inhibit deviation and insure conformity to social norms at even the most-minute level.

Through symbolic devices, the physical body exhibits the normative values of the social body. Symbols, such as dress, help delineate the social unit and visually define its boundaries because they give nonverbal information about the individual. Unique dress attached to specific religious and cultural groups, then, can function to insulate group members from outsiders, while bonding the members to each other. Normative behavior within the culture re-affirms loyalty to the group and can be evidenced by the wearing of a uniform type of attire.

Within American culture there are specific ethno-religious groups that intentionally separate themselves from the rest of society and attempt to re-establish the small, face-to-face community. Many originated in Europe and moved to America when religious freedom was promised to immigrants. Shakers (Scott, p. 54), Mennonites, Hutterites (Scott, p. 72), and Amish (Scott, p. 87) are such groups. These groups are often perceived by the outside world as quite unusual, but that derives more from their deviant behaviors, visually manifest in dress, than from their religious differences from mainstream Christianity. An essential factor in ethno-religious groups, social control is significant in terms of the survival prospects of the group. Among orthodox Jews (Scott, p. 57) in Williamsburg New York, social control was achieved in ways remarkably similar to those used by the Amish and conservative Mennonites. The most important features included isolation from the external society; emphasis on conformity with status related to religiosity, symbolized by clothing status markers; a powerful clergy and rigorous sanctions to insure conformity to norms.

Dress and Social Change

With changing social, political, and economic environments, even the most sectarian religious group has to contend with the impact of social change. Changes in dress often signal underlying changes in social roles as well as gender roles. Traditional gender roles can be marked by a particular form of dress where the roles are stable for long periods of time; when dress changes suddenly in these groups, we can expect to find a change in gender roles. A good example is that of the change in the dress of Roman Catholic priests and nuns following the changes instituted by Vatican II in the 1960s. The changes were more pronounced for nuns as their roles within the Church dramatically changed; so too did their dress. Additionally, when roles are restrictive, we can expect to see a restriction in women's dress, in the form of either dress codes or physically restrictive clothing.

With immigration and colonization, clothing figured into the power imbalance between people of different religious backgrounds. As American missionaries in the nineteenth century encountered indigenous people, clothing became an issue almost immediately. Christian missionaries advanced their own ethnocentric perceptions of appropriate behavior and dress and, often through subtle coercion, guided the acculturation of indigenous peoples. Missionaries have often taken on the role of introducing western clothing to indigenous people as a means of "civilizing the natives." In some cases the transformation to western-styled clothing was part of the need of a religious group to dominate an indigenous culture. In other cases, a religious group immigrating to another country might also voluntarily make changes to their dress to facilitate their assimilation into the new society. One such example is that of Hawaii where missionaries objected to the indigenous dress of *kapa* skirts with no covering of the breasts. The missionaries required Hawaiians to wear western dress when at the missions; a particular garment called the *holoku* was created for Hawaiian women to wear. As Christianized Hawaiians became missionaries to Oceania, they brought the *holoku* into the islands, but the garment was known by different names outside of Hawaii.

Occasionally a reciprocal relationship occured, in which the indigenous group more willingly took on the dress of the more powerful religious group. Strategic shifts from traditional dress to western dress among the Dakota tribes in Minnesota were somewhat voluntary. Similarly, the immigration of European Jews to America led to many Jews using dress as a means of blending into the larger society. On the other hand, Hasidic Jews chose to reflect their ethnicity by retaining fossilized fashion to intentionally separate them from the larger American culture. At the end of the twentieth century, some Christian and Roman Catholic churches began to incorporate indigenous textiles in their liturgical garments used in religious ceremonies. While this practice is seen primarily in missionary work of churches establishing missions in Africa and other locations such as the Philippines and South America. The use of ethnic textiles in African American churches has been a long-standing tradition that honors African heritage.

In conclusion, many religious groups have developed cultural norms with regard to dress. Dress codes, both formal and informal, exist as a means of showing group identity. Members of religious groups actively construct their own lives and use dress symbolically to express religious beliefs, adaptation to social change, and the conformity to social norms and religious authority.

See also **Ecclesiastical Dress; Islamic Dress, Contemporary Jewish Dress.**

BIBLIOGRAPHY

Arthur, Linda B. "Clothing Is a Window to the Soul: The Social Control of Women in a Holdeman Mennonite Community." *Journal of Mennonite Studies* 15 (1997): 11–29.

———, ed. *Religion, Dress and the Body.* Dress and the Body Series. Oxford: Berg, 1999.

———, ed. *Undressing Religion: Commitment and Conversion from a Cross-cultural Perspective.* Dress and Body Series. Oxford: Berg, 2000.

Damhorst, Mary Lynn, Kimberly Miller, and Susan Michelman. *Meanings of Dress.* New York: Fairchild Publications, 1999.

Goffman, Erving. *The Presentation of Self in Everyday Life.* Garden City, N.J.: Doubleday, 1959.

Hostetler, John. *Amish Society.* Baltimore: Johns Hopkins Press, 1989.

Poll, Soloman. *The Hasidic Community in Williamsburg.* New York: Glencoe Free Press, 1962.

Scott, Stephen. *Why Do They Dress That Way?* Intercourse, Pa.: Good Books, 1986.

Linda B. Arthur

RETAILING Retailing consists of the set of business activities involved in selling products and services to consumers for their personal, family, or household use. Traditionally, a retailer serves as the last distribution channel that links manufacturers and consumers; however, in order to have control and exclusivity with their merchandise, most large retailers, such as Wal-Mart and the Gap, are vertically integrated and perform more than one set of activities in the distribution channel, such as both wholesaling and retailing activities or both manufacturing and retailing activities.

Retailing is a significant portion of world commerce. The world's 200 largest retailers generated $2.14 trillion in sales during 2002 and captured 30 percent of worldwide sales. These firms represent a variety of nations and such categories as department stores, specialty stores, category killers, discount stores, mail order, and so forth. However, the top nine largest retailers are discount stores or category killers, indicating a consumer trend to demand low prices. With increasing globalization, 56 percent of the top 200 retailers operated in more than one country. Geographically, U.S. companies, including Wal-Mart, Home Depot, Kroger, and Target, represented 53 percent of the total sales from the top 200 global retailers. Wal-Mart was the world's largest retailer in terms of sales and number of stores in the world. It was more than three times the size of the second largest retailer, France's Carrefour.

Retailers are characterized by their retail mix, including the type of merchandise sold, the price of the merchandise, the variety and assortment of merchandise, and the level of customer service. Retailers are also categorized by a primary channel that they use to reach their customers such as store-based (specialty stores, department stores, discount stores) or nonstore (catalog, TV home shopping, Internet) retailers. However, successful retailers in the early 2000s are multichannel retailers that sell products or services through more than one channel. For example, retailers such as Wal-Mart (discount store) and Macy's (department store) use Internet and catalog channels, and utilize the unique feature provided by each channel.

Store-Based Retail Channel

Store-based retailers use brick-and-mortar stores as primary modes of operation. Major types of store-based retailers include department stores, specialty stores, category killers, discount stores, off-price stores, outlet stores, and boutiques.

Department stores. A department store is a large-scale retail unit that carries a wide and in-depth assortment of merchandise that is classified into section divisions by product type and brand name. While department stores originated in downtown areas of major cities in the nineteenth century, with the advent of car travel and suburban flight, they came to be located in regional malls and have a typical size of between 100,000 and 200,000 square feet (930–1860 square meters). Merchandise quality, pricing, and customer service (sales help, credit card, and delivery) range from average to quite high. Accordingly, department stores target consumers with household incomes that are at least average. Two types of department store are commonly noted: the full-line department store and the specialized department store. Full-line department stores such as Macy's and Marshall Field's carry both hard goods (such as furniture, housewares, and home electronics) and soft goods (apparel, accessories, and bedding). Except for Sears, most full-line department stores no longer offer major appliances. Specialized department stores or limited-line department stores restrict their inventories rather than carry full lines. For example, Saks Fifth Avenue, Neiman Marcus, and Nordstrom focus on apparel and wearable accessories and may not carry lines such as furniture and home electronics. Other merchants emphasize jewelry and home furnishings, such as Fortunoff.

In the early twenty-first century, the largest department stores in the United States in terms of sales include Sears ($41.4 billion), JCPenny ($32.3 billion), Federated Department Stores, which owns Macy's and Bloomingdale's among others ($15.4 billion), and the May company, which owns such entities as Filene's, Lord & Taylor, and Famous-Barr ($13.5 billion). With the fierce competition that arises from specialty stores and discount stores, department stores' market shares have fallen since the mid-1990s. This decline has resulted in the reduced perceived-value for merchandise and services, unproductive selling space, low turnover merchandise, and fuzzy store images. A vast majority of department-store merchants in the early 2000s place great emphasis on soft goods and accessories, and less emphasis on hard goods.

Specialty stores. Specialty stores, also called limited-line stores, focus on selling one line of merchandise (such as jewelry) or serving one particular market (for example, maternity apparel). Specialty stores offer a narrow but deep assortment in the chosen category and tailor selection of products to a defined market segment. Specialty stores also feature a high level of customer service with knowledgeable sales personnel and customer service policies and intimate store size and atmosphere. A typical size of specialty stores is less than 8,000 square feet. Some specialty stores target affluent consumers with high price and upscale merchandise, whereas others target price-conscious consumers with discount merchandise. Popular product categories of specialty stores include apparel, personal care, home furnishings, jewelry, and sporting goods. The largest U.S. specialty stores in sales include GAP brands, which includes Gap, Baby Gap, Banana Republic, Gap Kids, and Old Navy ($14.4 billion), and Limited brands, which includes The Limited, Henri Bendel, Intimate Brands, Lane Bryant, Lerner New York, Limited Too, Structure, and Express ($8.4 billion).

Category killers. Also known as category specialist, category killers combine attributes of both specialty stores and discount stores because they feature a great breadth of assortment in one classification of merchandise (e.g., toys, electronics) and low prices. Because of the large volume of merchandise they require from suppliers, category killers can use their buying power to negotiate for low prices. Category killers provide consumers a warehouse environment with a typical store size of 50,000 to 120,000 square feet. Few sales people are available for assistance, but some category killers such as Office Depot (office supply) make knowledgeable salespeople available throughout the store to answer questions and make suggestions. The largest U.S. category killers in sales are Home Depot ($58.2 billion), Lowe's ($26.5 billion) and Best Buy ($20.9 billion). Home Depot and Lowe's offer equipment and material used to make home improvements while Best Buy carries consumer electronics.

Discount stores. Discount stores offer customers broad assortments of merchandise, limited services, and low prices. Discount stores are also referred to full-line discount stores or discount department stores. For their commonly recognizable huge retail format, discount stores are also referred to as big box retailers. The biggest U.S. discount stores in terms of sales include Wal-Mart ($246.5 billion), Target ($42.7 billion), and Kmart ($30.8 billion). In discount stores, customers can expect a similar range of product lines as those offered by full-line department stores, such as electronics, furniture, appliances,

Gap store in New York City. Specialty stores such as the vertically-integrated Gap limit their line to one area of merchandise. © GAIL MOONEY/CORBIS. REPRODUCED BY PERMISSION.

auto accessories, housewares, apparel, and wearable accessories, but these product lines in discount stores are less fashion-oriented than the product lines in department stores. Discount stores usually sell on only one floor rather than in a multifloored building, as traditional department stores do. A typical size of a discount store is between 60,000 and 80,000 square feet, but a supercenter that combines a discount store with a supermarket ranges from 150,000 to 220,000 square feet. Wal-Mart, Kmart, and Target all operate supercenters.

The maintenance of low prices and lean gross margin contribute to the fast growing business of discount stores. Due to intense competition from category killers, the trends for discount stores are to create attractive shopping environments, to provide consumers branded merchandise (such as Levi Strauss in Wal-Mart) or to develop licensing agreements (for example, Isaac Mizrahi in Target).

Off-price stores. Off-price stores offer an inconsistent assortment of fashion-oriented and brand-name products at low prices and limited customer services. The leading

French retail supermarket. France's Carrefour is the second largest retailer in the world, but its yearly sales are less than a third of the top retailer, Wal-Mart. AP/WIDE WORLD PHOTOS. REPRODUCED BY PERMISSION.

U.S. off-price retailers are T.J. Maxx and Marshalls (both owned by TJX), Ross Stores, and Burlington Coat Factory. Most merchandise is purchased opportunistically from manufactures or from other retailers late in a selling season in exchange for low prices. This merchandise might be end-of-season excess inventory, unpopular styles and colors, returned merchandise, or irregulars. Due to this opportunistic buying practice, consumers cannot expect consistent offerings of merchandise. However, off-price stores appeal to budget and fashion-conscious consumers.

Outlet stores. Outlet stores are retailing units owned by manufacturers or by retailers that sell their leftover, low-quality, discontinued, irregular, out-of-season, or overstock merchandise at prices less than full retail prices of their regular stores. Manufacturer-owned outlet stores are frequently referred to as factory outlets. Outlet stores were traditionally located at or near the manufacturing plant. Contemporary outlet stores are typically clustered in outlet centers or malls and located far enough from key department stores or specialty stores to avoid jeopardizing sales at full retail prices. There are 14,000 U.S. outlet stores and many are located in one of the 260 outlet centers nationwide. These stores generated total sales of $14.3 billion in 1999. Stores are characterized by few services, low rents, limited displays, and plain store fixtures, which reduce operating costs of the stores. Outlet retailing has been a popular way of disposing of unwanted merchandise by manufacturers and retailers. Even popular designers such as DKNY, Ralph Lauren, Calvin Klein, and Gucci use outlet stores to dispose of leftover items. However, most outlets also have product made especially for them—which is not just unwanted merchandise but low-quality product produced specially for that market.

Boutiques. A boutique is a small store that concentrates on a specific and narrow market niche and features top-of-the-line merchandise. "Boutique" is a French term for little shop; the term was first used for small stores run by Paris couturiers. American boutique retailers include many top designers, such as Donna Karan, Calvin Klein, and Ralph Lauren. Boutiques offer high-priced, fashion-oriented merchandise and attract customers who want more sophisticated and individualized products than mass-produced goods. Boutiques cater to narrow, well-defined customer segments that usually consist of affluent men and women. Key to a boutique's attraction is its personal one-to-one service. Many designers are building flagship stores in their home country as well as in foreign markets.

Nonstore Retail Channels

Nonstore retailers utilize their retail mix in environments that are not store-based. U.S. nonstore retailers generated a total of $156 billion in 2001, accounting for roughly 5 percent of all U.S. retail sales. The major appeal of nonstore retailers is the convenience of shopping: shopping anytime and anywhere. Three major types of nonstore retailers include catalog retailers, electronic retailers (e-tailing), and television home-shopping retailers.

Catalog retailers. Catalog retailers promote products by mailing merchandise directly to a target market and process sales transactions using the mail, telephone, or fax, or Internet. Many catalog retailers embrace the Internet. When customers are mailed a catalog from the retailer, they either can order products by telephone or mail, or through the retailer's Web site. According to *Catalog Age* (2001), the most popular catalogers recognized by U.S consumers include J.C. Penny, Land's End, L.L. Bean, and Sears.

Television home-shopping retailers. Television home-shopping retailers use a program to promote and demonstrate their merchandise and process transaction over the telephone or Internet or through the mail. The two biggest home shopping retailers are QVC ("Quality, Value, Convenience") and HSN (Home Shopping Network). The best-selling merchandise of TV home shopping is inexpensive jewelry. Other categories include apparel, cosmetics, and exercise equipment.

E-tailers. The fastest-growing form of nonstore retailing is electronic retailing (e-tailing). Electronic retailers interact with customers and provide products or services for sale using the Internet. During the last five years of the 1990s, electronic retailing had a rapid growth with the creation of more than 10,000 entrepreneurial electronic retailing ventures. However, a large number of electronic retailers, especially electronic retailers that only used the Internet for selling products or services, have gone out of business since the Internet bubble burst in 2000. In 2001, U.S. electronic retailers generated about $50 billion in sales, accounting for 1.5 percent of total retail sales. The best-selling merchandise online includes computers and electronics, sporting goods, books and CDs, toys, and apparel. Due to continued consumer interest in shopping using the Internet, store-based and catalog retailers have also began to sell their merchandise using the Internet.

See also **Department Store; Fashion Marketing and Merchandising; Shopping.**

BIBLIOGRAPHY

Berman, Barry, and Joel R. Evans. *Retail Management.* 9th ed. Upper Saddle River, N.J.: Prentice Hall, 2004.

Levy, Michael, and Barton A. Weitz. *Retailing Management.* 5th ed. New York: McGraw-Hill/Irwin, 2004.

Internet Resources

"Catalog Age Top Ten." Catalog Age June 2001. Available from <http://catalogagemag.com/ar/marketing_catalog_age_top_2>.

"Research Data: Outlet Industry Data." Value Retail News (2003). Available from <http://www.valueretailnews.com/research/research_index.htm>.

"Top 100 retailers." Stores July 2003. Available from <http://www.stores.org/archives/TopRetailers.asp?year=2003>.

"2003 Global Power of Retailing." Stores January 2003. Available from <http://www.stores.org>.

Seung-Eun Lee

RETRO STYLES The fashion meaning of retro, first applied to clothes in the 1970s, refers to styles that are either copied or adapted from earlier periods. The retro reference was coined by London designers, and soon became a common coin throughout the fashion world. Thus the prefix for backward became a catchword for fashion in retrograde, fashion in retrogression—or retrospective fashion. While the word retro was "new" in the style context, the concept of born-again fashion was not.

Fashion has often taken the past as inspiration. In the 1910s, Paul Poiret's fashions were inspired by the Directoire, the style of French design in the mid-1790s, which itself used Greco-Roman forms and Egyptian motifs.

The Neoclassicism of the 1790s alluded to the political heritage of Greek democracy and the Roman Republic, while later Egyptian motifs memorialized Napoleon's conquest of Egypt. Poiret's Neoclassicism, however, seems to have had no political significance, although it certainly emphasized physical freedom. In the 1930s, French fashion surrealists were influenced by the second empire of Louis Napoleon (1852–1870).

The mannish styles of World War II gave way in 1947 to Christian Dior's New Look. His wasp-waisted, hip-padded, full-skirted silhouette represented a release from wartime austerity, and was in itself a homage to his mother and her *fin de siècle* finery. Dior's fitted jacked segued into the 1970s and 1980s, becoming a template for designers such as Claude Montana, Thierry Mugler, Azzedine Alaia, and Christian Lacroix, all of whom grew up in the Dior oeuvre. The full, petticoated skirts that marked the 1950s (which were in many respects a continuation of the New Look) reflected a societal return to pre–World War II gender stereotypes and Cold War social conservatism.

The 1960s relaunched aspects of the 1920s, the two decades sharing the same spirit of youth and anarchy—although sixties fashion originated on the streets of London (Mary Quant and the miniskirted Mods) instead of the salons of Paris. Perhaps because the 1960s symbolized the Youthquake and the mini, they have been resuscitated more than any other decade, most obviously every time designers show thigh-high miniskirts.

As the twenty-first century progresses, the 1970s, especially the mid-1970s, which were nostalgic for the 1930s, have been a favorite playback by designers in their forties. The shoulder-padded 1980s, which owe a big debt to the 1940s, were first returned to by designers in their thirties. And the minimalist, less-is-more 1990s are waiting to be rehashed when designers born in that decade reach their twenties. It seems that designers are inspired by the period when they first became interested in fashion—usually during their teens or twenties—or the period in which their design heroes lived. (One reason the 1960s have had so many sequels is that the designers of that decade were legends whose work was photographed, cataloged, and exhibited in museums as perhaps no other until that time.)

At the beginning of the twenty-first century, a new fashion amalgam appeared, one based on borrowing from other times, therefore retro, but one tweaked with "newness." This idea of taking bits of someone else's original work and either copying it or mixing it and then calling it one's own is also seen in other art forms. In the art world, it is called "appropriation." In music, it is "sampling." In the movies, it is sequels or "part twos." And in fashion, as in food, it is known as fusion. Another favorite expression for retro styles is called is referencing.

In fusion, the originality consisted in how the old was made "new." For example, the original space-age designs worn by Paris designer Andre Courrèges's moon maidens were worn with low-heeled, calf-high, white patent-leather boots. In the fused versions, Courrèges's A-line jumpers were subverted with high heels or combat boots, and some of the minis were layered over evening dresses or paired with leggings.

To this day, there are designers who plunder the past verbatim, seam-for-seam, stitch-for-stitch, line-for-line. Some credit the originals. To his credit, the late Bill Blass, in his book, *Bare Blass*, edited by the *New York Times*'s fashion critic Cathy Horyn, writes about First Lady Nancy Reagan wearing his gown to the Washington gala the night before Ronald Reagan's first inauguration: "…she wore a black velvet dress of mine. Which *Women's Wear* said was a knock-off of Saint Laurent's. Which indeed it was." Other designers cite no provenance. Those who do not are usually not called for copying for three reasons. First, few seem to care if a designer such as Nicolas Ghesquiere of Balenciaga calls a design by Kaisik Wong his own, even when confronted with visual proof. Appropriation is now considered not just acceptable, but expected. Second, few magazine editors can risk jeopardizing the loss of advertising pages if they offend the big-advertising designer by accusing him of stealing—whoops, appropriation. And third, there are not too many fashion journalists in the media mix of the early 2000s who would recognize a purloined design if they saw one.

One of the reasons retro styles became a fashion byword during the late twentieth and early twenty-first centuries can be attributed to the rage for vintage clothes. After almost a decade of simple, spare, less-is-more fashion, many women sought relief from the minimalist mode at swap meets, thrift shops, and vintage boutiques, where the old looked suddenly newer than the new.

It's the nature of the fashion beast to feed on the past. This apologia by TV host/designer Isaac Mizrahi hits the mark. He says that to complain about revivals of clothes from other decades is to complain about chicken. "A good classic recipe for *poulet* has existed for centuries, yet people still make chicken dishes. They may change some of the spices, but the basis is still chicken. In the same way, a classic dress from any period attained classic status because it is a good, time-tested design that is worthy of being modernized with new fabrics and new accessories. In other words, you just change the recipe to suit modern tastes."

See also **Fashion, Historical Studies of.**

Marylou Luther

RHODES, ZANDRA Zandra Lindsey Rhodes was born in 1940 in Kent, England. Her first fashion influence was her mother, who was a fitter at the House of Worth in Paris before she became a senior lecturer in fashion at Medway College of Art. Zandra Rhodes subsequently studied textile design at the same college for two years, before going on to the Royal College of Art to extend her studies. She graduated with first class honors in 1964 from the Royal College of Art at a time when design creativity was at a premium and London was the center of avant-garde fashion. After leaving college she designed for a print studio she had established with Alexander McIntyre, until teaming up with Sylvia Ayton, a fellow graduate, to produce a range of garments in which Rhodes was able to explore innovative ideas like her famous lipstick print. In 1968 the two decided to open their own boutique, the Fulham Road Clothes Shop, selling garments designed by Sylvia Ayton and made up in Zandra Rhodes's printed fabrics. Among their most innovative ideas were tattoo print transfers and paper dresses.

Freelance Designer
Although commercially successful, lack of financial acumen closed the business, and Rhodes went on become a freelance designer, producing her first solo collection in 1969. She was encouraged by a successful visit to New York, where she sold work to the department store Henri Bendel, but it was difficult to convince buyers from the big British department stores to stock avant-garde designers. Marit Allen, then editor of "Young Ideas" in *Vogue*, showed Rhodes's clothes in the pages of the magazine, even though they had no retail outlet at the time. The ploy persuaded retailers that there was a market for innovative design, and Allen introduced Rhodes's clothes to the London store Fortnum and Mason.

Evening Wear
Renowned primarily for her evening wear, Zandra Rhodes produced instantly identifiable garments that reflected the early 1970s preoccupation with a floating, unreconstructed silhouette. During this period printed textiles were an intrinsic element of fashion, and together with Celia Birtwell and Bernard Nevill, she was responsible for the multipatterned and colorful look that defined the era. Her inspiration is rooted in the use of autographic sketchbooks, where she researched primary sources such as organic matter and transformed the initial drawings into her signature style: abstract, loose, screen-printed, flowing forms that play with scale and vibrant color combinations, all handmade and often including her signature "squiggle." Prints occasionally include handwritten text; one of her pieces for the Fulham Road Clothes Shop was a blouse printed with the name of the shop on the collar and cuffs, an early use of the logo. Zandra Rhodes was one of the first designers to use the street-style punk look, reversing seams and using safety pins and tears for a dress in the 1977 Conceptual Chic collection. Her personal style has always reflected the flamboyant quality of her clothes. She accessorized her outfits with outsized jewelry and sported green, then pink hair, with emphatic eye makeup and multicolored face paint.

Construction and Features
The construction of Rhodes's garments is very much inspired by the cut and form of vernacular dress. She is attracted to the simplicity of the shapes that are both functional and also use the whole piece of fabric. She notes:

> I had come across the actual chronicle of costume, the definitive book by Max Tilke on *Costume Patterns and Designs*, its simple and detailed pages showing the cut and form of traditional clothing throughout the world. Details of armholes, wrapped trousers, em-

Zandra Rhodes. British fashion designer Zandra Rhodes reclines in a garden. She is wearing a print dress, a style she helped bring to prominence in the 1970s. © ERIC CRICHTON/CORBIS. REPRODUCED BY PERMISSION.

broidered waistcoats and flat, worked-out-kaftan and peasant shapes were all explained with the simplicity of a gardening book (Rhodes and Knight, p. 37).

These garment shapes maximize the effect of the print, relying on layers, gathers, smocking, and shirring and often featuring handkerchief points to create the silhouette. The clothes are engineered to accommodate the placement of the prints, rather than cut from continuous, repetitive yardage. For this reason Rhodes's garments remain outside the seasonal transitions of mainstream fashion.

Rhodes went on to design handmade, elaborate, feminine, evening dresses using her distinctive prints. Her clients included the late Princess of Wales and Princess Anne, who wore a Rhodes dress in her engagement portrait. During the minimalistic 1990s, her fantasy gowns, embellished with beads, sequins, and feathers, found less favor with the fashion press, but with the revival of vintage fashion in the early 2000s, her clothes are once again sought after.

Recognition

Zandra Rhodes has been the recipient of many academic and professional awards over the years, including honorary doctorates from the Royal College of Art and other universities in both Great Britain and the United States. She was made a Commander of the British Empire in 1997 in recognition of her services to the fashion and textile industry. Early in the twenty-first century, Rhodes was spending some of her time in San Diego, California, and it was here that she was invited to design the costumes for the San Diego Opera's production of *The Magic Flute* in 2001, garments that received great critical acclaim.

Diversification

Rhodes has diversified her design business into household linens and textiles, glassware, linens, cushions, throws, rugs, and screens. In collaboration with the artist David Humphries, she fashioned a number of terrazzo designs, such as the Global Plaza at Harbourside in Sydney, Australia, and the Del Mar House Terrazzo project in California, for which she was given an honor award by the National Terrazzo and Mosaic Association in 1998.

In 2003 Zandra Rhodes realized a long-held ambition to open a museum. The strikingly colored frontage of her Fashion and Textile Museum has become one of London's landmarks. Sited in Bermondsey on the south bank of the river Thames, it was designed by the Mexican architect Ricardo Legoreta. As a select showcase for contemporary and vintage fashion and textile design, the museum is intended to provide an accessible archive and resource center. It also seeks to generate discourse on design by providing a forum for debate and student activity. The inaugural exhibition, *My Favourite Dress*, included the work of seventy of the most internationally renowned contemporary designers, including John Galliano, Yohji Yamamoto, Julien MacDonald, Antonio Berardi, Roland Mouret, and Sophia Kokosalaki.

See also **Diana, Princess of Wales; Evening Dress; Fashion Museums and Collections.**

BIBLIOGRAPHY

Rhodes, Zandra, and Anne Knight. *The Art of Zandra Rhodes.* London: Cape, 1984.

Steele, Valerie. *Women of Fashion: Twentieth Century Designers.* New York: Rizzoli International, 1991.

Marnie Fogg

RIBBON The term "ribbon" refers to narrow loom-woven strips of cloth, often with a visible selvage on each side that helps them to maintain their form. Ribbons can be made of any fiber and are usually woven in satin, plain, gauze, twill, and velvet weaves. The origins of the term "ribbon" and its earlier forms, ruban or riband, are obscure, but they may be Teutonic and a compound of the word "band"—the ancestor of the modern day ribbon. As early as the Neolithic period, people wove very narrow, dense, often utilitarian strips of fabric on small portable looms. Impressions of warp-faced plain weave bands dating back to 6000 B.C.E. were excavated from the Turkish archaeological site of Çatal Hüyük. While their purpose was primarily functional, some evidence suggests that bands also could be used for more flirtatious and decora-

Naval ribbons and medals. In military institutions ribbons covering metal pins serve as indicators of award and rank. Ribbons are also used to attach medals to the uniforms of soldiers. © YOGI, INC./CORBIS. REPRODUCED BY PERMISSION.

tive purposes. Elizabeth Wayland Barber has suggested that dancers waved strips of fabric while performing beginning in the Middle Bronze Age. Evidence exists that in the Aegean cultures of 2000 thruogh 1200 B.C.E., specialized weavers used a warp-weighted vertical loom to weave decorative edgings and bands to ornament and trim garments.

In Europe, the weaving of lightweight ribbons as opposed to the sturdy, warp-faced bands of antiquity probably began as soon as the horizontal loom was introduced during the eleventh century. Lightweight ribbons were not unknown, however; archaeologists working in London uncovered several plain weave ribbons of unspun, undegummed silk, which were probably imported from the East.

References to ribbons occur with increasing frequency during the fourteenth and fifteenth centuries as more tailored clothing developed and ribbons with aiglets (metal points) at each end were used to lace garments together. Ribbons also trimmed garments as they had in the past, encircled waists as girdles, and were worn in the hair. London archaeologists excavated ribbons of spun silk (probably woven locally) found in digs dating to the

fourteenth and early fifteenth centuries. While ribbons continued to be an aspect of fashionable dress throughout the Middle Ages and Renaissance, they did not become a focus of fashion until the seventeenth century after a loom was invented that could weave more than one ribbon at a time. This new loom allowed multiple ribbons to be woven at once by providing a separate warp beam and shuttle for each ribbon. An Italian abbé, Lancellotti, was the first to write about such a loom, which he said was invented in Danzig around 1530. He also wrote that the loom so threatened traditional ribbon weavers that it was destroyed and the inventor secretly strangled or drowned. The new loom was not totally lost, for it appears again in Leiden by 1604 and in London by 1610. However, it was in France that the use of ribbons took hold when Louis XIV turned them into a fashion obsession.

The city of Paris was well known for its ribbons, as were the cities of Saint-Étienne and Saint-Chamond, where ribbons were woven as early as the beginning of the fourteenth century. Charles VII published the first statutes of the master tissutiers and Rubanniers of Paris in 1403. Statutes were again published in 1524 and in 1585, when the rubanniers were assigned their own guild. Ribbon weavers during this period worked on small looms that were light, compact, and sat on tabletops. Men, women, and even children easily wove on these looms, producing one ribbon at a time, and small workshops predominated. When the new ribbon loom was introduced during the seventeenth century, it revolutionized the trades and, as in Danzig, at first encountered resistance among the ribbon weavers of France.

Despite the reluctance of the French ribbon weavers to use the new loom, Louis XIV's finance minister Jean-Baptiste Colbert strongly encouraged its acceptance and, because the king adopted ribbons as an important element of fashionable dress, the trade flourished. Ribbons of silk and gold and silver thread were woven in many different structures, including plain weave taffetas, satin, and velvets. A wide range of brilliant dyes was employed to color the ribbons, including cerulean blue, yellow, and a variety of reds such as crimson, scarlet, cherry, and Louis XIV's favorite *couleur de feu,* or flame. Courtiers attached ribbons to hats, sword handles, shoes, sleeves, around the knees, and even to the lower bodice front, where yards of ribbon loops emphasized the wearer's masculinity. Diana de Marly writes in her book on fashion during the reign of Louis XIV that the Marquis de Louvois and the Marquis de Villeroi would shut themselves up in a chamber for days discussing the best placement for a ribbon on a suit.

By the end of the seventeenth century, ribbons began to lose their popularity with men as the more somber three-piece suit came into favor. Women continued to wear ribbons, but not to the extent that they were worn during the previous decade. By the middle of the eighteenth century, ribbons again came to the forefront of women's fashion when dresses were trimmed with silk-ribbon bows. Stomacher trims, known in French as the *echelle* and used to close the front of the dress, had horizontal rows of large bows down the front. Bows further decorated the elbows and were often worn around the neck. By the end of the eighteenth century, dressmakers and milliners began to use ribbons in increasing quantities as fashion's focus turned to the trimmings of dresses and hats.

Fashion's growing interest in ribbons increased during the early nineteenth century as the jacquard mechanism was adapted for use with ribbons looms. Weavers wove intricately patterned silk ribbons that became extremely fashionable during the nineteenth century. These ribbons trimmed the lavish and large bonnets of the 1820s and 1830s. The town of Saint-Étienne adapted itself to these new developments and became a leading center in the ribbon trade, specializing in weaving floral patterned ribbons. Saint-Étienne also specialized in weaving the ribbons that played an increasingly important role in national dress, especially the dress of French women from Brittany, Savoy, Alsace, and Provence. Ribbons ornamented bonnets, caps, aprons, blouses, and skirts, and their color could be used to indicate the religious beliefs of the wearer, as in Alsace, where a red ribbon indicated a Protestant background and black, a Catholic one.

Fashionable dressmakers and milliners continued to use ribbons in their work throughout the nineteenth and even twentieth centuries, although not as frequently as in the past. During some periods ribbons enjoyed more popularity than others, such as the mid-nineteenth century, when trimmings on dresses became increasingly fashionable and ribbons edged flounces and were folded and braided to create complex trims. Ribbons again took on importance during the years between 1910 and 1920, when they were formed into flowers and trimmed elaborate evening dresses, known as *robes de styles*. Couturiers such as Lucile and the Callot sisters were well known for these gowns. Ribbons played less of a role in fashionable dress during the rest of the twentieth century, but they did not escape the notice of several designers. Charles James, Karl Lagerfeld, and James Galanos all designed dresses composed entirely of ribbons stitched together to form a cloth.

While the jacquard was adapted to create ribbons patterned with complex floral designs for fashionable and national dress, novelty ribbons and pictures also were woven with extremely detailed imagery that resembled the work of etchers and engravers. The weavers showed many of these pictures and ribbons at international expositions, trumpeting the jacquard's technical achievements. The ribbons often were woven to commemorate special occasions or events, such as elections and political or historic anniversaries, and they point to another aspect of the use of ribbons, to honor and remember.

It is impossible to say when ribbons took on significance outside of their role in dress, but the *Oxford English Dictionary* indicates that as early as the sixteenth

Dress with a ribbon bodice. This 2002 Benjamin Cho dress features a bodice made entirely of ribbons. AP/WIDE WORLD PHOTOS. REPRODUCED WITH PERMISSION.

century they were given between men and women as favors and that by the seventeenth century wide blue ribbons were worn across the chest by members of the Order of the Garter, the highest honor bestowed by the British ruler. Ribbons were also used to attached medals to the chests of honored military men, and today small pins covered with ribbons patterned in a variety of stripes are worn on American military uniforms in place of the medals. The use of blue ribbons and red ribbons as first and second prizes in competition appears to have begun in the late nineteenth century.

Ribbons also served to commemorate the dead. Mourners wore black armbands and hatbands, while narrow black "ribbons of love" decorated the caps and blankets of babies. The use of ribbons as a token of remembrance took on particular significance in the later part of the twentieth century. In 1981, Americans bedecked their trees with yards of yellow ribbons as a sign of remembrance and to welcome home American hostages taken in Iran. While many believed the custom started during the Civil War as a way to welcome home returning soldiers, in reality, Penne Laingen, the wife of one of the Iran hostages who began the tradition in 1979, was inspired by the act of another woman. In 1975, Gail Magruder festooned her front porch with yellow ribbons to welcome home her husband, Jeb Stuart Magruder, who had recently been released from prison after his conviction during the Watergate investigations. The number one single of 1973, "Tie a Yellow Ribbon Round the Ole Oak Tree," sung by Tony Orlando and Dawn, inspired Gail Magruder's act. The song was in turn inspired by the legend of a man released from prison who told his wife to tie a yellow ribbon on an old oak tree if she welcomed him back. Yellow ribbons again appeared in Americans' front yards after the first Persian Gulf War of 1991 to greet returning soldiers.

The symbolic use of ribbons increased toward the end of the twentieth century, and the wearing of a small colored ribbon pinned to one's clothing came to indicate a sympathy toward one cause or another. In 1990, the art activism group Visual AIDS introduced the custom of wearing a small loop of red ribbon as an international symbol of AIDS awareness. A small pink bow is indicative of an awareness and support of breast cancer research.

While ribbons are still manufactured and can be found trimming hats and lingerie, they are no longer an important element of fashion. Their place as commemorative tokens and in the work of crafters has ensured the continued production of ribbons; however, manufacturing methods have evolved to make them cheaper to produce. Ribbons woven on a loom are more rarely produced today, and cut-edge or fused ribbons are more common. Thermoplastic fibers woven in satin or plain weave taffeta are slit in the desired width with a heated cutting tool that fuses and seals the edges of the ribbon—a far distant cousin to the luxurious silk, silver, and gold ribbons of the seventeenth century.

See also **Callot Sisters; Loom; Lucile; Politics and Fashion; Silk; Trimmings.**

BIBLIOGRAPHY

Barber, Elizabeth Wayland. *Prehistoric Textiles.* Princeton, N.J.: Princeton University Press, 1991.

de Marly, Diana. *Louis XIV & Versailles.* New York: Holmes and Meier, 1987.

Kerridge, Eric. *Textile Manufactures in Early Modern England.* Manchester, U.K., and Dover, N.H.: Manchester University Press, 1985.

Musée National des Arts et Traditions Populaires. *Rubans et Galons.* Paris: Musée National des Arts et Traditions Populaires, 1992.

Pamela A. Parmal

RINGS The circular form surrounding the finger without beginning or end was subject to numerous beliefs and superstitions. Even if the finger ring initially served a dec-

orative purpose, of all types of jewelry, it has possibly the most personal of meanings for the wearer. Finger rings were worn as a sign of wealth, power, and love and given for special occasions marking various stages of the wearer's life. Rarely can the wearer be identified, yet the choice of symbols, materials, or stones of a ring often identify the function or occasion to which a finger ring adorned the wearer's hand, and tells a personal story.

The ring is a very compact form of jewel, with its dimensions determined by the size of the finger and thus confining the maker to work in a miniature scale. Despite the rigidly restricted form based on the finger, the diversity of the designs throughout the millennia is proof of the wealth of artistic imagination. The small dimensions are also challenging for the jewelry historian, who is often confronted with only minute details to give a precise date to a piece. Unlike any other type of jewelry, the shape of the finger ring has never been dependent on any dress fashions, yet in every civilization their designs mirror the heritage and contemporary art styles of the period or region.

Pictorial images illustrating how rings were worn on the hand are rare in antiquity, either on mummies of Ancient Egypt or tomb sculptures of the Etruscan and Roman periods, more revealing though are portraits of men, women, and children in Western Art from the fifteenth century onward.

Finger rings may have existed since early humankind, yet many of the organic materials used in the prehistoric era, such as bones, shells and plants, would not have survived. Earliest known examples go back to the Sumerian civilization in Mesopotamia of the third millennium B.C.E. Decorative examples of gold with inlaid lapis-lazuli or carnelian are very rare; more common are the stamp and cylinder seals of the Ancient Near East, generally made of stone with gold caps and swivel hoops, from which the signet ring, the oldest form of finger ring originated. The early signets had a distinctive function, at a time when the art of writing was known to few; they served as a guarantee of authenticity or ownership, and were used for trade as well as for legal transactions. While wax seals are generally a thing of the past, as late as the 2000s the signet ring remains unchanged.

In the Middle Kingdom of Ancient Egypt in the second millennium B.C.E., the cylinder seal ring developed into a form that was to dominate Egyptian finger rings for many centuries, that of the scarab, the dung beetle carved in gemstones, such as lapis-lazuli, obsidian, jasper, faience or glass imitations, with a drill hole and either a cord or gold wire running through the beetle and encircling the finger. The hoops and settings became more elaborate in their design, yet the basic shape remained the same: the scarab could be swiveled on its mount to use the engraved underside for sealing, and the beetle was worn as a decorative ornament on the finger. A scarab with the engraved name of its owner, such as that of the pharaoh or priest, was worn for its magical qualities as a good-luck charm.

The scarab on the revolving bezel was a ring type copied by the Phoenicians, Etruscans, and Greeks, as well as the heavy gold stirrup rings of Ancient Egypt with cartouche-shaped bezels. These were refined in Ancient Greece, and the shapes became more varied and the decorations intricate. The bezel in either gold, silver, bronze, or set with a gemstone, illustrated mythological scenes or beasts transmitting the attributes of deities or the diligence and strength of the animals to the wearer. During the Hellenistic period, rings became fancy, the gold intricate, and settings for stones more elaborate, and the function tended to be decorative.

With the love for gemstones and their availability through newly opened trade routes, the art of cutting gems evolved in ancient Greece and later in ancient Rome, where a stone became an essential element of the ring. The motifs incised as intaglios or carved in relief showed apart from mythological figures, subjects from literature, theater, and everyday life to assist or mark momentous occasions or provide good luck. During the early Roman period, iron rings were common among all classes, and later were only worn by slaves and soldiers, and as betrothal rings. Even though the Greeks had love rings, the Romans appear to be the first to have introduced the betrothal ring given by the prospective husband as a warranty or pledge of marriage. The early examples were circles made of iron. In the second and third centuries C.E. with the ever-expanding Roman Empire and newly acquired wealth, social structures had changed, and this was very much reflected in the bold proportions and designs of heavy gold betrothal rings with devices such as Hercules knots (love knots), the *dextrarum iunctio* showing two right hands clasped together (both motifs continued into the nineteenth century), and other erotic symbols. The ring became a display of luxury and status, even remarked on in contemporary accounts. By the Roman period, jewelry was accessible to a wider range of social classes, but with the new wealth, restrictions were imposed as to who was allowed to wear gold or silver.

The early Christians used late Roman ring shapes, mainly in gilt bronze or silver, and replaced the pagan divinities and other heathen symbols with Christian motifs as a sign of their allegiance to the new faith; these included the Chi-Rho monogram of Christ, a fish, a dolphin and Agnus Dei. The Byzantines, in turn, adopted in silver and gold with niello, the Christian ring forms and symbols. The iconography, however, was expanded to include images of the Virgin and Child, numerous saints, crosses with coded personal monograms of the owners and scenes—such as the marriage ritual with the couple being blessed by Christ—and also sacred Greek inscriptions. Splendid gold rings from the Byzantine period, with high bezels in ornately pierced gold set with sapphires, garnets, and pearls, also exist. These decora-

tive specimens, which exemplify the goldsmithing art and the technique of inlaying stones of the Byzantines, influenced the numerous tribes crossing Europe during the early Middle Ages.

From the twelfth century onward, while the wearing of finger rings was not restricted to any social classes, the use of gold or certain gemstones was limited by each country according to its sumptuary laws. Many pieces have survived through hoards all over Europe. While it is fascinating to observe the international style of many medieval ring types, it is almost impossible to determine the place of manufacture without knowledge of the provenance. Design ideas often with high constructed bezels appear to have traveled with the trade of gemstones from the Orient. Diamonds, sapphires, rubies, spinels, and amethysts in cabochon cut were favored by the church clerics as a sign of rank. Devotional images, such as various cross forms, the Virgin Mary, and symbolic beasts such as the Pelican and her Piety, often complemented Greek and Latin inscriptions to be worn by the devout. Figures of saints or relics in rings were thought to have protective or curative powers against cramps, fevers, epilepsy, or illnesses of the eyes, kidneys, or whatever ailment the wearer had.

Rings with amorous symbols and messages of love, often in French as the international language of the courts, were popular during the medieval and Renaissance periods. They were worn as signs of affection in courtship and later in marriage. One of the most widespread is the *fede* ring (Italian for "trust") with two right hands in gold clasped to indicate the pledge of troth, known in Roman times and continued well into the nineteenth century. Rubies and diamonds in table-cut were traditionally symbolic of love and constancy and only affordable by the wealthy. Gimmel rings (*gemellus* is Latin for "twin") with twin bezels served as settings for this traditional combination, and to underline the significance, figures of lovers or hearts united were combined with inscriptions, such as "What God hath joined together, let man not put asunder" (Matthew 19:6) in Latin or the language of the country of origin. The exchange of marriage rings during the ceremony instead of giving a ring as a pledge of betrothal varied from country to country. The engagement ring, as is known today, was more of an invention of the nineteenth century with the diamond cluster rings.

Whether in gilt bronze, silver, or heavy gold, or even in the splendor of engraved rock crystal with colored foils beneath the heraldry, the signet became a status symbol for all. Even the merchant, gaining ever more influence from the fifteenth century onward, copied the aristocratic codes and practice, and wore a family coat of arms, merchant's mark, or guild rings, taking pride in his profession and position in society.

In the sixteenth and seventeenth centuries, signet rings occasionally had a double-sided bezel, which could be swiveled to include a *memento mori* motif—a death's head, miniature skeleton, or hourglass—and symbols of decay with creeping things, such as worms, reminding people of their transience and preparing them for death.

Mourning rings were popular from about the fifteenth to nineteenth centuries, in particular during the baroque period and eighteenth century. Memorial rings with commemorative inscriptions and portraits of the deceased became fashionable, and mourning rings were given at funerals as a token of remembrance; these were black or dark blue in combination with white enamel surrounding the name of the deceased person and their birth and death dates. In the late eighteenth century, memorial rings reached a peak together with the ritual of mourning. Large elaborate bezels illustrated death through symbols such as the broken column, the obelisk, with the most popular being the funerary urn derived from antiquity. These were often accompanied by weeping willows, cypresses, faithful dogs, and lamenting women in classical drapery, either diamond-studded or made of the hair of the deceased, against a dark blue enamel or glass over an engine-turned background.

In contrast to this, the eighteenth century showed an abundance of fancy rings, with hearts entwined in rubies and diamonds, billing doves, love knots, flowers tied with ribbons or filling a basket, and other themes of nature, masquerade or games in polychrome choice of stones. The decorative feature of the ring culminated in the multilayered bezels and clusters of stones in rose-cut and other fancy cuts that became stylish in the eighteenth century, which continues to be popular in the early twenty-first century.

In the nineteenth century, the ring was characterized by romantic iconography with symbols of sentiment and inscriptions: the language of flowers, such as forget-me-nots for memory; from the animal world, snakes as a sign of eternity, butterflies for vanity, or miniature envelopes and purses enclosing love declarations; and the language of stones, such as the turquoise serving as a token of friendship and affection.

As historical portraits of rulers or heroes show, rings were worn as a sign of political allegiance, but they also depicted scenes of historic political events such as the French Revolution or the Napoleonic Wars. Rings also signify allegiance to social groups and institutions.

A small, yet fascinating group of rings exist that are used for specific functions such as the archer's ring in antiquity, the rosary ring for saying prayers, the pipe-stopper ring, sundial or watch rings, squirt rings, vinaigrettes, or those with some scientific novelty such as a spy glass or miniature photograph.

Throughout the millennia of its history, the ring with bezel, shank, and hoop encircled the finger with a round, oval, or derivative shape. In the early twentieth century, the ring had undergone a radical change when, in the art nouveau period, the bezel together with the hoop became a freestanding piece of sculpture that challenged all traditional forms. The foundations were laid for the artist jeweler of the twentieth and twenty-first centuries who creates rings as free art forms. The materials and designs used for rings in the second half of the twentieth century broke all boundaries, and precious metals were combined with nonprecious materials of the period, such as plastics, paper, and everything hitherto unconventional.

See also **Bracelets; Brooches and Pins; Jewelry; Necklaces and Pendants.**

BIBLIOGRAPHY

Chadour, Anna Beatriz. *Rings: The Alice and Louis Koch Collection.* Leeds, England: Maney Publishing, 1994.

Cutsem, Anne van. *A World of Rings: Africa, Asia, America.* Milan: Skira Editore, 2000.

Dalton, O. M. *Catalogue of Finger Rings, Early Christian, Byzantine, Teutonic, Medieval and Later.* London: British Museum, 1912.

Kunz, George Frederick. *Rings for the Finger.* New York: Dover Publications, 1973. Reprint of original edition published in 1917.

Marshall, Frederick Henry. *Catalogue of Finger Rings: Greek, Etruscan and Roman in the Department of Antiquities, British Museum.* London: British Museum, 1968. Reprint of original edition published in 1907.

Oman, Charles C. *Victoria and Albert Museum, Catalogue of Rings.* Ipswich, U.K.: Anglia Publishing, 1993. Reprint of original edition published in 1930.

Scarisbrick, Diana. *Rings: Symbols of Wealth, Power, and Affection.* London and New York: Abrams, 1993.

Anna Beatriz Chadour-Sampson

RING-SPUN YARNS. *See* **Yarns.**

ROBE The word "robe" has an intriguing etymology, its stem coming from the verb "rob," whose original meaning was the spoils of war. Its primary definition in English specifies it as a garment worn in the European Middle Ages, its most salient features being a long, loose, billowing form and its use as a signifier of rank, office, or special position. "Robe" is often used interchangeably with the word "gown," though the original meaning of the latter denotes clothing styles particular to classical antiquity, such as the Roman toga. Common usage in the early twenty-first century expands these definitions further, to include a variety of garment forms ranging from informal bathrobes to women's formal evening wear and wedding gowns.

Loose-flowing outer garments in general have come to be known in the modern English-speaking world as markers of certain members of the clerisy, professoriate, or legal profession. Indeed, the words "robe" and "gown" are used as metonyms, shorthand terms that stand for each of these groups as a distinct social class. For example, "robe" or "black robe" can refer either to monks, especially missionaries, or to judges, while "gown" is the preferred term for representing scholars and professors, as seen in the phrase "town and gown." These particular professional garments are all in one way or another based originally on ecclesiastical vestments, though the ones worn by judges and professors have undergone major changes in usage. In the early 2000s, judicial robes and academic gowns are worn over everyday costume and only on formal occasions, and so are therefore made of lightweight fabrics.

Religious Robes

The plain, ankle-length robe of Christian monastic orders was anything but lightweight. Patterned after the long, wide-sleeved tunic of Roman times, it was necessarily made of coarse and humble material, usually wool. The monastic robe was an all-purpose garment worn by both men and women. There were slight variations of it over time among the different orders, but it kept to a single basic form that was meant to represent the Christian ideals of poverty and humility. Rules stipulated that the fabric should be the cheapest kind available in the local community and that the garment should be gathered and tied at the waist at all times. As for color, these robes tended to be neutral (subdued or understated), in dark or light tones. The overall effect was one of simplicity and timelessness.

Robes—as garments signifying special individuals or distinct social groups—are a worldwide phenomenon. Their visual features cannot be precisely defined. Robes of many shapes, sizes, designs, and cuts have been employed to represent certain religious or ethical principles, to designate members of religious orders, and, in some cases, to delineate levels of rank within them. One well-

Zen Buddhist robe. This sixteenth century statue depicts the bodhisatva Kishitigarbha wearing an ornate example of the robes that were traditional to Japanese Zen Buddhism at that time. SEATTLE ART MUSEUM, EUGENE FULLER MEMORIAL COLLECTION. PHOTO CREDIT: PAUL MACAPIN.

STYLE IN THE COURTROOM

U.S. Supreme Court Chief Justice William Rehnquist made news in January of 1995 by adding a striking feature to the traditionally plain, black robes that have been worn by the justices for two hundred years. He was inspired to make the change after attending a performance of the Gilbert and Sullivan operetta *Iolanthe*. In it, the character of Lord Chancellor, speaker of the House of Lords in Britain, was handsomely costumed in a robe adorned with vividly colored stripes. Rehnquist wanted the same, and had four gold stripes sewn onto each sleeve of his own judicial robe, giving it a rather sporty look. As of 2004 the other justices have stayed with their basic black. (Reske, p. 35)

documented example of the latter is the system of robes that developed among Zen Buddhist monasteries of Japan. Individual monks were restricted to three robes. One of them was worn as an everyday garment, another more formal robe was for special occasions within the monastery, and the best one, the "great robe," was reserved for ceremonies and duties outside the monastery. The color of the robe varied according to the individual's rank within the religious hierarchy and also according to where his community was placed in the rankings of particular monasteries. At one end of the spectrum were the ordinary provincial priests who wore black robes, while at the other end were the heads of the imperial monasteries in Kyoto, who were allowed the privilege of wearing yellow ones. Another robe, a *kesa*, was worn on top, draped over one or both shoulders. It was a rectangular patchwork stole made of silk brocade remnants, and followed a system of ranking based on the number of pieces sewn together.

An extraordinary mantle from an archaeological site in Paracas, Peru, offers us glimpses of religious robes that

Sokoto Caliphate robe. The Sokoto Caliphate encouraged the manufacture of robes, such as the late nineteenth or early twentieth century example displayed here, and bestowed them to notable citizens as a mark of honor or achievement. © NATIONAL MUSEUMS LIVERPOOL. REPRODUCED BY PERMISSION.

were in use there before the Incan Empire. Excavated from the tomb of an important and revered figure, most likely a priest, the rectangular cloth is made of cotton that is then painstakingly embellished with polychrome wool embroidery. What remains of its border consists of a frieze of ninety figures that are depicted in remarkable detail. Altogether they portray a vibrant pantheistic ideal that permeated these peoples' belief system. Human beings merge into animals and plant forms, suggesting that all of life was conceptualized as intimately and spiritually interconnected. The more elaborately dressed and equipped figures in the frieze wear mantles of varying length draped over the body, some of them with zoomorphic terminations. Interpreting the identities of these figures is problematic. Nevertheless, on the basis of their headdresses and the types of implements held in their hands, it appears very likely that the ceremonial robe or mantle was a prerogative shared by priests and war leaders.

Court Robes

Robes also became institutionalized in various parts of the world at different times as a major component in in-

vestiture ceremonies for political leaders. Such was the case in Christian Europe, where the coronation of kings and queens relied heavily on symbolic regalia, especially crowns, robes, and scepters. Coronation robes were often based on the vestments of bishops—tunic, chlamys, dalmatic—which were thought of and revered as ancient garb dating back to the kings and priests of Old Testament times. As such, these garments were deemed appropriate vehicles for articulating the transformation of a royal candidate into the holder of sacred office. Similarly, the robing ceremony itself paralleled the ritual of Christian baptism. One prominent example is the 1953 coronation of Elizabeth II of England. Held in Westminster Abbey, according to tradition, the ceremony began with the singing of a psalm dating back to the coronation of Charles I. Then came the entrance of the Queen, wearing her white coronation robe, an elegantly embroidered formal gown. Draped on her shoulders was a very long crimson cape, its train carried by six attendants. She was escorted by two bishops, resplendent in their brocaded ceremonial copes. The service consisted of four main segments: the recognition, when the queen was presented to her people; her swearing of the oath of office on the Bible; the anointing ritual, with the queen wearing a plain white robe; and, finally, the robing ceremony, during which the Mistress of the Robes helped her don the spectacular royal tunic and belt. A much more elaborate cape was draped on her shoulders for the final act, the crowning of the queen. Throughout, the term "robe" referred to the queen's garments—gown, cape, tunic—and the ceremonial changing of them to symbolize her ascension to the throne.

One of the most well-known examples of imperial robes is the Chinese "dragon robe" tradition. Although the emperor himself and his throne were symbolized by dragon imagery, this was not a garment reserved for him alone. The dragon robe proper meant a particular type of garment worn at court and by government officials, especially during the Qing Dynasty (1644–1911). Over time, the garment style varied from ample, flowing forms to trimmer, more tailored ones. In all cases, the dragon motif was central, either brocaded into the textile or embroidered onto it with silk and gold threads. Early versions of the dragon robe included design features deemed appropriate for certain ranks, such as the placement of dragon motifs, their scale, and how the dragon was depicted. After 1759, a set of laws were put in place in an attempt to systematize the imagery and regulate who was entitled to wear it. For example, only the emperor's robe could be brilliant yellow, with nine golden dragon motifs, while the robe of the heir apparent was a shade of orange-yellow. Background color and the number of claws on the dragon were features that distinguished rank among the imperial princes. Although these rules were not strictly followed, the visual elements remained relatively constant until the ending of the dynasty and its costume traditions in 1911. Dragon robes, along with kimonos and other similar garments, have served as inspiration for modern designers of elegant dressing gowns and housecoats for men and women.

Robes of Honor

Yet another kind of robe became an institution—the "robe of honor"—which was developed most fully in the Muslim world for designating and formalizing a variety of important relationships. It circulated in special ways, being ceremoniously awarded from one individual to another in order to confer authority, seal alliances, and publicly proclaim official ties and positions. Already in ancient times, rulers in parts of Asia had personally bestowed valuable garments on their followers as a sign of special favor. The prophet Muhammad reportedly did this as well, which set the precedent for the robe of honor—*khil'a*, in Islam. Muhammad's successors, caliphs of the Umayyad and Abbasid dynasties, wore robes of office that were identifiable by their embroidered borders. The *khil'a* was patterned after these official garments. During the Abbasid period, production and distribution of honorific robes expanded—especially under

the rule of Harun al-Rashid (786–809), when thousands of them flowed into and out of his treasury. A distinctive feature of the robe of honor was the type of imagery embroidered along its border, which included signs, symbols, or epigraphic inscriptions referring to the reigns of specific rulers. Such robes were ceremonially bestowed by many people in a variety of contexts—patron to client, scholar to student, merchant to merchant—thereby encouraging a sense of loyalty among individuals who otherwise might differ according to their ethnicity, religion, language, social class, profession, or family group. Circulating robes of honor became, therefore, an effective social and political tool for creating solidarity within the cosmopolitan cultures of Islam.

The example of the Sokoto caliphate (1804–1903, became northern Nigeria) shows that robes of honor were influential in other ways as well. Over the century of its existence, this Muslim state grew to be the largest polity in West Africa, and it impressed Europeans with the quality and volume of its cotton textile production. At least some of this achievement can be credited to the robe of honor tradition and how it was subsidized and encouraged by the caliphate's leaders and elites. Intent on bringing about an Islamic revival, they promoted, among other things, the manufacture and circulation of flowing robes with a distinctive pattern of motifs embroidered in silk along the neck and pocket. They were instantly recognizable as caliphate robes, and the imagery signified divine protection and good fortune. Favorable taxation policies encouraged merchants to set up spinning and weaving workshops, while officially supported Quranic scholars managed the work of hand embroidery. As in the Abbasid period of classical Islam, robes were brought into the central and emirate treasuries in large quantities as tribute and spoils of war. They were then redistributed, as a mark of military achievement or appointment to office, and as a gift to honorable allies, subordinates, and foreign visitors. In 2004, similar robes were made in Nigeria for sale in the market, though most of these were embroidered by sewing machine.

Many robes and robing traditions are no longer being made or practiced; fortunately, some have found their way into museum collections. As objects of study and exhibition display, they remain richly rewarding in their new role as documents of cultural and social history.

See also **Religion and Dress; Royal and Aristocratic Dress.**

BIBLIOGRAPHY

Brinker, Helmut, and Hiroshi Kanazawa. *Zen: Masters of Meditation in Images and Writings.* Zurich: Artibus Asiae Publishers, 1996. Masterful catalogue of the art and culture of Zen.

Cammann, Schuyler. *China's Dragon Robes.* New York: Ronald Press Company, 1952. Classic study of the history and variants of the dragon robe.

Country Life: Coronation Number. London, June 1953. Facsimile edition, June 2003.

D'Harcourt, Raoul. *Textiles of Ancient Peru and Their Techniques.* Seattle: University of Washington Press, 1974. Invaluable description and technical analysis of major Peruvian archaeological textiles.

Gordon, Stewart, ed. *Robes and Honor: The Medieval World of Investiture.* New York: Palgrave, 2001. Excellent edited volume containing cross-cultural case studies of robes and robing ceremonies.

Kriger, Colleen. "Robes of the Sokoto Caliphate." *African Arts* 21, no. 3 (May 1988): 52–57, 78–79, 85–86. Case study of the robe of honor in a nineteenth-century West African caliphate.

Pollack, David. *Zen Poems of the Five Mountains.* New York: American Academy of Religion, 1985.

Reske, Henry J. "Showing His Stripes." *ABA Journal* 81, no. 3 (March 1995): 35.

Stillman, Yedida Kalfon. *Arab Dress: From the Dawn of Islam to Modern Times. A Short History.* Leiden, The Netherlands: Brill, 2000. Excellent synthesis of research on Arab and Islamic dress.

Colleen E. Kriger

ROMA AND GYPSY Roma is the Romani word used to refer to Gypsies, a label that has pejorative connotations. Since many Roma use the term Gypsy with outsiders, and there are contexts in which Gypsy is the broader term, its use is still applicable in certain settings and certainly appears in literature as well as search engines. In Europe and the British Isles, terms such as Romanies, Travelers, or Tinkers are also used. Many different groups form the Roma population based on a common sense of belonging, although they may have very diverse characteristics and call themselves by different names.

Roma live in the United States, South America, Europe, Russia, Middle East, North Africa, and North and Central Asia. Some have migrated to Australia, Hawaii, and Alaska as well. The Roma migrated into Eastern and Western Europe in the fourteenth century through Persia en route from India, which they left approximately 1,000 years ago. Since leaving India, Roma have always lived within another culture or country as a minority and pariah group. They have been subjected to extreme discrimination and persecution throughout history, especially in Western and Central Europe where they were enslaved in the Middle Ages. Between 500,000 and 600,000 European Roma perished under the Nazis in World War II. In the nineteenth century they migrated to North and South America where they continue to be a nomadic or semi-nomadic group.

Roma in the United States are estimated to range between 100,000 and 300,000 members of various groups (such as Vlach Roma, Boyash, Irish Travelers, and Hungarian Roma) living in all parts of the country. Estimates of Roma in Europe are between 4 and 10 million, with the largest numbers concentrated in Central European and Balkan countries (as much as 5 percent of the population). Different groups have taken up various occupations, including music, metal work, buying and selling horses or cars, fortune-telling (primarily women), and selling craft items. Middle-class Roma have entered the professions, but in the early 2000s this was still a relatively small group.

Roma trace descent through both parents but take on patriline names and have a patrilocal marriage preference. Authority is based on age, with both older women and men enjoying a high status. Men are powerfully situated in the system of juridical authority, and women hold power through the complex system of religious, spiritual, and medical authority. Roma have no religious specialists other than older women, but they use clergy from local churches to conduct baptisms. In the United States their own religion is punctuated by certain rituals, including the baptism of a six-week-old child, marriage, the *pomana* (death ritual), *slava* (Saint's Day feast) and some American holidays, such as Easter and Thanksgiving.

In the United States, Roma generally live in urban areas, usually on main streets and in the poorer parts of towns. They are not as easily recognizable to the American population as they are in Europe, where they stand out more. They often prefer to represent themselves as a member of an ethnic group other than Roma since it abates the stereotyping and discrimination against them. One of their survival mechanisms is to keep to themselves and avoid contact with non-Roma except in work-related circumstances.

The Roma wear clothing that reflects their religion, customs, and ethics. Many Roma, both men and women (but not children), treat clothes worn on the upper body separately from clothes worn on the lower body. Upper and lower body clothes may be washed separately as the lower body is considered "impure," and it is desirable not to "pollute" the upper body. The head in particular is protected from impurity. Hats worn by men and scarves worn by married women are kept away from any surface (such as the seat of a chair) or other clothes that touch the lower body. In addition, men's clothes may be kept separate from women's clothes, and women's skirts are considered dangerously polluting to a man. Women must wear a skirt long enough to cover their legs at least to the mid-calf. Items (such as dish towels) that are used with food are also given particular attention to purity.

During ritual occasions, the Roma often purchase or make new clothes to wear. New clothes have never touched anyone's body and therefore are guaranteed to be pure. A Saint's Day feast, wedding, or pomana (death ritual) are occasions when special pure clothing is desirable. During the pomana, a living person representing the deceased is dressed in new clothes and is called "the wearer of the clothes." This person stands in for the spirit of the deceased who is thought to be watching the pomana to make sure the relatives are displaying the proper respect for the dead.

Roma men. A group of four young Roma men in Brasov, Romania. In Roma tradition, hats are kept away from any surface and must not touch any clothing on the lower body. © Wolfgang Kaehler/Corbis. Reproduced by permission.

The presentation of self through dress and fashion is very important to the Roma and part of their public performance as Roma. Roma fashions do change over time and place. Furthermore, fashions for men and women seem to be based on different criteria. Whereas men dress to present an image to the outside world that they associate with power and authority, women dress to present an image to the Roma that is associated with Roma ideas of the power of purity and pollution.

Men

In the United States Roma have adopted fashions that project a particular masculine stereotype, often gleaned from the movies. Their public and private appearance is a performance of a certain recognizable style that they associate with masculinity and authority. They are not concerned with being stylishly up-to-date, rather they are concerned with the images of power projected by the clothing. Examples of commonly seen styles include:

1. Urban cowboy—hat, cowboy shirt, bolo tie, jeans, and boots; sometimes a Western-style jacket.

2. 1930s Chicago gangster—loose pants, two toned shoes, wide splashy tie, and double breasted jacket.

3. Palm Springs golfer—white or loud color pants, red golf shirt, Irish hat.

4. Casual modern—polo shirts, white shirts, or Hawaiian shirts, long pants.

Young men who are not yet old enough to present an image of power may adopt a more youthful modern dress. For example: (1) Beatles attire—pencil thin tie, loud tight shirt, and stove pipe pants; (2) Spanish or Hungarian Gypsy musician—longish hair, red diklo at the neck, "Gypsy" shirt; or (3) Modern—shirt and baggy shorts.

Women

Women are interested in fashion that shows their sense of "shame" and their status as guardians of purity for the family. Because of this role, women are expected to cover their legs at least to the mid-calf. Married women traditionally cover their head with a scarf and tie their long hair up or braid it. There is no shame associated with showing a low-cut neckline; in fact, it is rare to see a woman who does not wear low-cut tops. Women may wear modern western clothing when they do not want to be recognized as Roma. Some, for example, wear "Hopi" Indian dress to "pass" as American Indians. Even within these limitations, women have a great deal of leeway to adopt different styles:

1. Traditional Serbian or Russian Roma—homemade, long, pleated, light chiffon, sari-like skirt; tight low-cut blouse with V-neck showing cleavage; bra that acts as a pocketbook and place for cigarettes; hair put up in a chignon or bun; pocket handkerchief or larger style scarf on the head; flat shoes.
2. 1970s fashion—store-bought suit with A-line maxi-skirt and fitted jacket; floppy straw Easter bonnet hat; high heels.
3. Eastern European Roma contemporary—flowered, bright calf-length skirt; short puffed-sleeved peasant blouse with gold coins around the neck; and scarf on head; barefoot or in flat shoes. (Located in Bulgaria, Romania, Hungary.)
4. Spanish Roma entertainment—flamenco dress that is calf-length; bright polka-dot material; sleeveless low-cut top.

Children

In general, children are considered pure until puberty and do not have to worry about being polluting or being polluted. Mostly they wear current store-bought American clothes. Very small children can wear shorts or tank tops. Boys wear jeans and a shirt, and on special occasions a suit. Girls wear dresses or pants, and on special occasions long dresses. They usually have long hair hanging down or a ponytail.

See also **Ethnic Dress; Fashion and Identity; Religion and Dress.**

BIBLIOGRAPHY

Gay y Blasco, Paloma. *Gypsies in Madrid: Sex, Gender and the Performance of Identity.* Oxford: Berg, 1999.

Sutherland, Anne. *Gypsies: The Hidden Americans.* Prospect Heights, Ill.: Waveland Press, 1986.

———. "Pollution, Boundaries and Beliefs," In *Dress and Identity,* pp. 436–444. Edited by Roach-Higgens, Mary Ellen, Joanne Eicher and Kim Johnson. New York: Fairchild Publications, 1995.

Anne Hartley Sutherland

ROYAL AND ARISTOCRATIC DRESS Rules governing ceremonial court and aristocratic dress not only reflected power ranking in the premodern world, but also were designed to reaffirm the legal status of royal and aristocratic privilege, and thus to secure the influence of the ruling class. Elisabeth Mikosch (1999, pp. 18–19) points out a dramatic example of how the wearing of royal clothes was taboo to others:

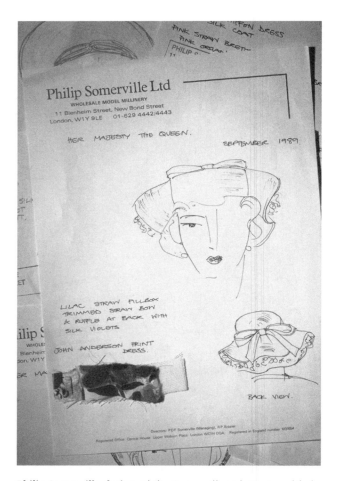

Philip Somerville design. Philip Somerville Ltd. Designed fashions for Britain's Queen Elizabeth II. © TIM GRAHAM/CORBIS SYGMA. REPRODUCED BY PERMISSION.

After her flight from Lochleven to Carlisle, Mary [Stuart of Scotland] was in dire need of clothes and asked [Queen] Elizabeth to send her some dresses. Elizabeth harshly denied her request, because Mary had not asked Elizabeth for just any kind of clothes, but for used dresses from Elizabeth's own wardrobe. As a reply, Elizabeth sent some lengths of black velvet, black satin and black taffeta. With this gift Elizabeth not only denied Mary royal dignity but also sent a sharp reprimand for Mary's personal behavior.

Ceremonial dress rules were also used by rulers to express their political opinions. In 1766 Emperor Joseph II decided to abolish the wearing of Spanish-style dress at the Viennese court, as the "Spanish cloak dress" was understood as a symbol for "an absolute ruler, who represented the entire state" (Mikosch 1999, pp. 49–50). Thus, it was inappropriate for the court of an Enlightenment monarch. The "Spanish cloak dress" was a fashionable predecessor of the uniform court dress or *justaucorps.* It was the obligatory court dress for gentlemen at the Vienna imperial court from the seventeenth

King Charles I and Queen Zita of Austria-Hungary. The elaborate ceremonial dress worn by royals prior to World War I was an indication of exclusive power and prestige. © UNDERWOOD & UNDERWOOD/CORBIS. REPRODUCED BY PERMISSION.

century until 1766. Court ceremonial required that one had to wear it whenever the emperor was in residence. Mikosch traces its antiquated form back to the fashion of the second half of the sixteenth century and describes it as follows:

> The dress consisted of a tightly fitted short doublet with a collar and cuffed sleeves as well as breeches and a circular wide cloak or cape [Spanish *cappa*] reaching to the knees and displaying a flat collar. A rich lace collar or a falling band of lace or fine linen, called a *rabat,* and a large hat decorated with ostrich plumes, completed the ceremonial male dress.

Comparing the state portraits of the emperors Leopold I, Joseph I, Charles VI, and Joseph II, one finds that the main features remained unchanged throughout their reigns, but certain details were altered to conform to changing fashions. For special occasions the clothes were made of silk fabrics richly woven with gold threads (*drap d'or*), lined with silver fabric (*drap d'argent*), and abundantly trimmed with gold lace.

Lady Mary Wortley Montagu notes that in Vienna in 1716 "I saw t'other day the gala for Count Altheim, the emperor's favourite, and never in my life saw so many fine clothes illfancied. They embroider the richest gold stuffs; and provided they can make their clothes expensive enough, that is all the taste they shew in them" (*Letters of Lady Montagu,* vol. 1. p. 249).

Austrian books of emblems or *impresa* from the beginning of the eighteenth century show ladies' Spanish court dresses. The cut of these resembled the pattern of the *grand habit* or *robe manteau,* modeled after late seventeenth-century French court dress from Louix XIV's new palace at Versailles. The ensemble consisted of a skirt with a train and a matching stiff bodice that was drawn into a long point toward the waist; it had short sleeves and a very décolleté neckline that displayed the shoulders and bosom. Rows of lace ruffles and *engageantes* of fine lace decorated the short sleeves. The wide skirt had a long train and it was generally open in the front and turned back to reveal a petticoat. The skirt was sup-

Roderick Random (1748), Tobias Smollett's (1721–1771) first novel, shows a boisterous and unprincipled hero who answers life's many misfortunes with a sledgehammer; but sometimes he does very well and then he acquires possessions like the following:

> "My wardrobe consisted of five fashionable coats full mounted, two of which were plain, one of cut velvet (velvet having the pile cut so as to form patterns), one trimmed with gold, and another with silver-lace; two frocks, one of white drab (sort of woollen cloth) with large plate buttons, the other of blue, with gold binding; one waistcoat of gold brocade; one of blue satin, embroidered with silver; one of green silk, trimmed with broad figured gold lace; one of black silk, with figures; one of white satin; one of black cloth, and one of scarlet; six pair of cloth breeches; one pair of crimson, and another of black velvet; twelve pair of white silk stockings, as many of black silk, and the same number of fine cotton; one hat, laced with gold *point d'Espagne* [kind of lace], another with silver-lace scalloped, a third with gold binding, and a fourth plain; three dozen of fine ruffled shirts, as many neckcloths; one dozen of cambrick handkerchiefs, and the like number of silk" (Smollett, p. 256).

ported by stays, and its shape, whether slender, round, or wide, depended on contemporary fashions. False or hanging sleeves were reminiscent to the original Spanish roots of the dress and called *"Adlerflügel"* (eagle's wings).

Lady Wortley Montagu observed of the Viennese court: "Their dress agrees with the French or English in no one article but wearing petticoats, and they have many fashions peculiar to themselves; as that it is indecent for a widow ever to wear green or rose colour, but all the other gayest colours at her own descretion" (*Letters of Lady Montagu*, 1866, vol. 1, p. 248; fine examples given by Bönsch 1990, 176/14 and 15). A letter from Johanna Theresia, countess of Harrach, to her husband, Ferdinand, on 9 December 1676, illustrates the importance of fashionable dress at court. The countess wrote that she had bought light-colored underwear for herself and their daughter from a merchant, "for when the Empress arrives, one has to have something to wear, for it is impossible to show up wearing nothing" (Bastl 2001, p. 365).

The impact of fashionable dress worn in elite circles, and the ability of rulers to make political statements through their dress can be seen in Charles Le Brun's tapestry series called *History of the King*. The scene illustrating the meeting between Louis XIV and Philip IV of Spain on 7 June 1660 shows that Le Brun gave precedence to the French king by placing him on the more

distinguished left side of the tapestry and by making him larger than the Spanish king. The fashionable clothes of Louis draw the attention of the spectator, while Philip's clothing looks modest and old-fashioned.

The French court was seen as the new cultural leader of Europe in fashion and court ceremony, and Louis XIV used sartorial rules as a means of exercising power. For example, in 1665 the king awarded to a select group of cavaliers who enjoyed special favors personally granted by the king, the right to wear a blue *justaucorps à brevet* (warrant coat), lined in red and richly embroidered with gold and silver thread according to a prescribed pattern. (Mikosch 1999, 65/57). Paintings of King Louis XIV and his aristocracy provide vivid visual evidence of the importance of fashion at the royal court.

Conspicuous consumption, which expressed social distinction through a lavish lifestyle, was an instrument of royal and aristocratic self-esteem in the eternal con-

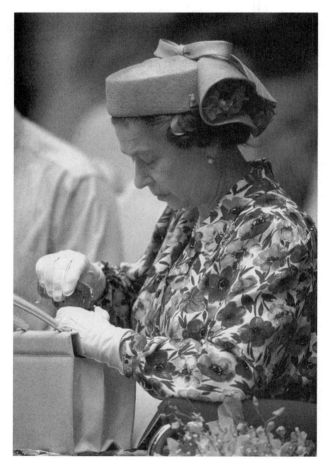

Queen Elizabeth II. By the early twentieth century, royal dress had ceased to be regulated and ceremonial, and—with some exceptions—the aristocracy were no longer considered fashion leaders. © Tim Graham/Corbis Sygma. Reproduced by permission.

test over rank and prestige. In general, expenditures for clothing correlate less with a person's wealth than with his or her wish to achieve distinction through dress, but in the case of the European aristocracy there was also considerable pressure to dress appropriately to one's status. Maria Magdalena, countess of Hardegg (1595–1657) complained to her father, Georg Friedrich Prüschenk, count of Hardegg (1568–1628, in Vienna), that others made fun of her because of her attire:

> I cannot describe to your Lordship how they make fun of me because of my attire; they say it is a shame that I am dressed thus, that my attire ruins a person's looks, and I laugh with them when they criticize my dress, which I would not change for anyone if it were not on your will and order. (Bastl 2001, p. 362)

Aristocratic country life in premodern Europe was relatively simple, even boring; the pace of life was determined by the seasons and by ordinary everyday events, punctuated by celebrations and festive occasions. Festivals appealed to the eye and used a vocabulary of peculiar attributes that are difficult to decipher nowadays, but that constituted a wordless but well understood language at court in early modern times. There was an inevitable tendency for nonmembers of the elite to engage in what is called "power dressing" in the twenty-first century by appropriating elements of elite dress. One sees in this behavior that dress is both intimate and potent as a means of expressing power; much dressing is power dressing, and power dressing is by its very nature political, in that it is public.

In this context the "big event" of a wedding became a celebration that, like everything else, needed to be regulated within the order of a hierarchical society. When Anna of Starhemberg (1513–1551) had to wed her niece Elizabeth to Marquart of Kuenring in 1536, she was in charge of putting together the bride's wardrobe. In one of her letters (15 November 1536) she writes to her husband Erasmus about Elizabeth's wedding dress:

> Since you wrote to me that Els [Elizabeth] needed a white beret for her white damask dress, I want to let you know that she is not going to wear a beret but a wreath, which she has to wear at her betrothal. Also, when you said that she is going to need a red beret, I don't think it is necessary because she has a pretty one with a pearl border although it is only black; give it to her, with the jewels on it. But if you want her to have a red one to go with her red velvet jacket, you can get one that has nothing on it so that we can sew the jewels on to it. (Bastl 2001, pp. 363–364)

This letter is revealing for various reasons: For one, it is an early documentation of a white wedding dress, which was already worn with a wreath at the engagement party, although the "beret" (Bönsch 1990, pp. 174–175) was also considered to be appropriate headwear at a wedding. Secondly, it is clear that the color red for garments also achieved similar, perhaps even greater, popularity with the nobility and was worn in matching shades for the dress and

BLACK AND WHITE

The color or rather the non-color, black was associated with the grave impersonality of authority. In Europe its oldest association is with death, with grief, and with the fear of death. As the color worn by mourners, its use is very old. It is sometimes suggested that the use of black for mourning was a medieval development: but its use at that time was a revival, not an invention. Roman mourners wore black togas (though the deceased body itself was wrapped in a white toga). And funeral processions in ancient Greece wore black. We are dealing in death with a reversal of the dress code, which converts elegant court attire "a bright red-colored precious dress with trim of silver lace of Spain"—to a funeral dress, or as Anna Maria Countess of Trauttmansdorff writes in her last will of 1704, "the black court gown: the clothing of my corpse in a dark taffeta nightgown." This is an ambivalent procedure in more ways than one: on the one hand, the clothing of the live body in garments that are considered to be beautiful and that maintain or promote status; on the other, the clothing of the dead body with garments that are ugly, and hence diminish or reduce status (Bastl 2001, p. 371).

the hat. Apparently velvet was also considered to be a fabric similar in value to damask, since they seem to have been interchangeable for wedding attire. Most generally, it is understood that clothing itself is a matter of intense concern for the family of the bride at an elite wedding.

Clothing was precious and expensive and was worn throughout a lifetime. In 1595 Helena of Schallenberg was a lady-in-waiting at the court of the duke of Bavaria, and she wrote to her brother:

> I am asking you with all my heart to ask our father for a martenskin—I cannot go without one. I have not had one made since I was a child. I have had a coat long enough—all my life—for which one cannot buy a lining at the market. I cannot wait any longer. We have to go to the Reichstag in appropriate dress and other necessary things; but I don't know how to go about it. (Bastl 2001, p. 365)

In the above-mentioned letters, Maria Magdalena of Hardegg wrote to her father in September 1616 that her late mother's lambskin has become too small for her and her little sister Sidonia might have her dressing gown, which she was not able to wear any more. The implication is that were she still able to fit into these clothes she would expect (and be expected) to continue wearing them, rather than replacing them with new clothing.

Aristocratic families must have had collections of clothes, for the tailor Hans Janoss found "an old tan-colored wool fabric dress, completely redone, sewn with fringes on it" in Regina Sybilla Countess Khevenhüller's trousseau in 1627. The same was true in sixteenth-century England, where Anne Basset had been criticized by Queen Jane Seymour and her ladies for her smocks and sleeves because they were "too coarse" and asked Lady Lisle to send finer material for new ones. Instead, "the Countess of Sussex had decided to have Anne's old gowns made into kirtles (skirts, or skirts and bodices) to save some expense" (Harris 2002, p. 229).

The discourse about court culture and aristocratic behavior and clothing in late nineteenth- and early twentieth-century Germany came to a curious conclusion. French *civilisation*, which implicated the art and artifice of fashion (expressed, for example, in the imperial court of Napoleon III), was dismissed as superficial, opposed philosophically in the emerging ideology of German nationalism by "deep" German *Kultur*, which was hostile to fashion (Duindam 2003, p. 295). At the same time, fashionable clothing was readily available to a much wider segment of the population than ever before; the court and its clothing no longer held a privileged position as the leader of fashion.

By the end of World War I, aristocratic titles survived in some European countries and were abolished in others, but royal and aristocratic dress lost its distinctiveness and exclusivity throughout European society. In the twentieth century, some royals were fashion leaders (Edward, Prince of Wales; Princess Grace of Monaco) and others were models of bourgeois respectability (Queen Beatrix of the Netherlands, Elizabeth II of England), but royals and aristocrats as a group no longer dressed in distinctive and regulated clothing, and were no longer society's principal leaders of fashion.

See also **Court Dress; Uniforms, Diplomatic.**

BIBLIOGRAPHY

Arnold, Janet. *English Women's Dresses and Their Construction c. 1660–1860.* London: Macmillan, 1964.

———. *Patterns of Fashion: The Cut and Construction of Clothes for Men and Women c.1560–1620.* London: Drama Publishers, 1985.

Bastl, Beatrix. "Das Österreichische Frauenzimmer. Zur Rolle der Frau im höfischen Fest- und Hofleben 15.–17. Jahrhundert." In *Slavnost ia zábavy na dvorech a v residenčních mestech raného novoveku.* Edited by Václav Buzek and Pavel Král, 79–105. České Budějovice, Czech Republic: 1996. Gives an overview about expenses for clothes for the lady-in-waiting Anna Josepha von Thürheim 1709–1711.

———. *Tugend, Liebe, Ehre. Die adelige Frau in der Frühen Neuzeit.* Wien, Köln, and Weimar, Germany: Böhlau, 2000.

———. "Das Österreichische Frauenzimmer. Zum Beruf der Hofdame in der Frühen Neuzeit." In *Residenzenforschung 11: Das Frauenzimmer.* Edited by Werner Paravicini, 355–375. Wiesbaden Germany: 2000. Edition of the *trousseau* for the court of Anna Maria Thurn 1559.

———. "Clothing the Living and the Dead: Memory, Social Identity and Aristocratic Habit in the Early Modern Habsburg Empire." *Fashion Theory* 5, no. 4 (2001): 1–32.

Bourdieu, Pierre. *Distinction. A Social Critique of the Judgement of Taste.* London: Routledge, 1999.

Duindam, Jeroen. *Vienna and Versailles. The Courts of Europe's Dynastic Rivals, 1550–1780.* Cambridge, U.K.: Cambridge University Press, 2003.

Elias, Norbert. *The Civilizing Process.* Oxford and Malden, U.K.: Blackwell, 2000.

Harris, Barbara J. *English Aristocratic Women 1450–1550: Marriage and Family, Property and Careers.* Oxford: Oxford University Press, 2002.

Hollander, Anne. *Seeing Through Clothes.* Berkeley, Los Angeles, and London: University of California Press, 1993.

The Letters and Works of Lady Mary Wortley Montagu, edited by her great grandson Lord Wharncliffe in two volumes. London, 1866.

Mikosch, Elisabeth. "Court Dress and Ceremony in the Age of the Baroque. The Royal/Imperial Wedding of 1719 in Dresden: A Case Study." Ph.D. diss., Institute of Fine Arts, New York University, 1999.

Pallmert, Sigrid. "Kleider machen Leute—Könige machen Mode. Ein Aspekt des sogenannten Allianzteppichs." *Zeitschrift für Schweizer Archäologie und Kunstgeschichte* 47 (1990): 49–54.

Roche, Daniel. *The Culture of Clothing. Dress and Fashion in the Ancient Regime.* Cambridge, U.K.: Cambridge University Press, 1994.

Smollett, Tobias. *The Adventures of Roderick Random.* Oxford: Oxford University Press, 1979.

Zander-Seidel, Jutta. *Textiler Hausrat. Kleidung und Haustextilien in Nürnberg von 1500–1650.* München: Deutscher Kunstverlag, 1990.

Beatrix Bastl

RUBBER AS FASHION FABRIC Natural rubber (*caoutchouc*) comes from latex, the milky secretions of tropical plants that coagulate on exposure to air. Prior to European discovery, the indigenous peoples of South and Central America used rubber to waterproof fabrics. The initial use of rubber in eighteenth century Europe was limited to elastic bands and erasers. Over time, various methods evolved to grind rubber so that fillers and other powders could be incorporated to stabilize thermal and chemical properties. In the United States, Charles Goodyear hit upon vulcanization (the process of treating rubber to give it useful properties, such as elasticity and strength) in 1839. In 1842 English inventor Thomas Hancock used his patented "masticator" on Goodyear's vulcanized rubber, and what had been a lab curiosity became an industrial commodity.

Successful vulcanization prompted Henry Wickham to smuggle rubber seeds out of Brazil in 1876. British botanical experiments resulted in hardier rubber plants that were exported to Malaysia, Ceylon, and Singapore where dense plantings increased rubber yield exponentially. During World War I, the Germans invented a synthetic rubber that was prohibitively expensive. When Allied forces were isolated from Asian rubber manufacturing centers during World War II, development of affordable synthetic rubber and rubber-recycling processes became part of the war effort. The reclaiming of cured rubber products was not commercially viable until 1991 when the Goodyear Company developed environmentally friendly devulcanization.

In 1823 Scotsman Charles Macintosh sandwiched rubber softened with naphtha between two thicknesses of woven wool. Macintosh remedied the problem of thermal instability in 1830 by adopting Thomas Hancock's vulcanization process. Draping and sewing rubberized wool proved to be a daunting task, so early floor-length coats were minimally designed. Over time the "mackintosh" came to feature trench coat details that made it more utilitarian and fashionable.

Rubber's elasticity, impermeability, stickiness, and electrical resistance make it extremely useful as an adhesive, protective coating, molding compound, and electrical insulator. Latex is cast, used as sheeting, combined with powder that produces gases to form foam rubber, or oxygenated to form sponge rubber.

By the twenty-first century high-tech fibers and laminates all but replaced rubber for waterproofing apparel. However, from early Sears and Roebuck "sweat" suits to twenty-first century haute couture, the surface qualities of rubber continue to appeal to fashion designers and fetishists alike. In the 1960s, John Sutcliffe's catsuits designed for the Emma Peel character on the TV series *The Avengers* caused rubber to come into vogue. In 2003, rubber wear combined with other fashion fabrics was prominently featured in collections by Julien Macdonald, Helmut Lang, Nicolas Ghesquiere for Balenciaga, and John Galliano for Christian Dior.

Garments constructed of rubberized cloth, rubber sheeting, or molded latex present specific design challenges. Rubberized cloth resists piercing and cannot be pressed; therefore facings and hems must be understitched, glued, or heat welded. Pinholes and tailor tacks will create permanent holes. Because it is difficult to create buttonholes, garments typically feature zipper, Velcro, and snap closures. Grommets are used to vent unbreathable membranes. Garments made of rubber sheeting are more likely to be constructed utilizing cement and heat or pressure welding. Seamless molded garments offer the most serviceable construction.

See also **Fetish Fashion; Rainwear.**

BIBLIOGRAPHY

Allen, Peter William. *Natural Rubber and the Synthetics.* London: C. Lockwood; New York: Wiley, 1972.

Morton, Maurice, ed. *Rubber Technology.* 3rd edition. New York: Van Nostrand Reinhold Co., 1987.

Norwich, William. "Rubber Maids." In *Fashions of the Times: 60th Anniversary Issue, The New York Times Magazine* (17 August 2003): pp. 76–78.

Michele Wesen Bryant

RUBBER FIBER. *See* **Elastomers.**

RUSSIA: HISTORY OF DRESS The systematic study of the history of dress in Russia began in 1832 with the publication of a book by the president of the Academy of Arts, Aleksei Nikolaevich Olenin (1763–1843). The occasion for the writing of this book was a decree of the Emperor Nicholas I, who expressed the desire to see a painting with many figures on the theme of the most important event in Russian history: the baptism of the Russian people by Prince Vladimir. The goal here would be to represent all the classes of Russian society in conditions and clothing that approximated as accurately as possible the actual conditions and clothing.

Actual specimens of Russian dress from early Russian history and even from the ninth to the thirteenth centuries had not been preserved. The only way to recreate what Russians looked like in that epoch was to examine all the possible sources: the archaeological data, all manner of written documents, as well as works of handicraft and decorative art. The most reliable information that we have concerning Russians dress of the pre-Christian period comes from our knowledge of the materials common to that period: hides and leather, bast, wool, flax, and hemp. The style of dress did not differ from that of the other Slavonic nations. This was determined by constant communication between these nations, by a similar manner of life, and by the climatic conditions. Women wore *rubakhi* (long shirts) down to their ankles and with long sleeves gathered up on the wrists; married women also wore the so-called *ponevu* (a kind of skirt consisting of a checked-pattern woolen fabric. Married women completely covered their hair by a *povoi* or *ubrus* in the form of a towel, while maidens wore a *venchik* (a narrow band of fabric or metal) on their foreheads. Maidens of the richer urban families had the resources to ornament themselves with a *koruna*, which differed from the *venchik* only by its more complex shape and finish. Men wore narrow *porty* (trousers) and tunic-like *sorochki* (shirts) of linen, down to their knees or their mid-calves. The footwear consisted in primitive shoes called *lapti* woven of bast, while the city-dwellers wore *lapti* made of raw leather. We also know that men of the upper classes wore boots of fine workmanship. According to the testimony of Akhmet (the ambassador of the Bagdal caliph Muktedir), at the beginning of the tenth century Slavonic men wore cloaks of dense fabrics that left one arm free.

The appearance on the territory of Eastern Europe of the first feudal Slavonic state, that of Kievan Russia,

Traditional Russian dress. A group of Russian women, dressed in an elaborate, old-fashioned, Russian style, wait to greet Boris Yeltsin during the 1996 Russian presidential election campaign. © PETER TURNLEY/CORBIS. REPRODUCED BY PERMISSION.

led not only to political and economic advancement, but also to increased trade and diplomatic contacts. At this stage of development, up to the Tatar-Mongol invasion in the thirteenth century, the dress of the upper classes of Russian society corresponded to general European tendencies in the domain of clothing, although it preserved certain native characteristics.

According to tradition, it was the magnificence and great solemnity of the Byzantine liturgy that led the Kievan prince Vladimir to baptize Russia in 988. Grandiosity and pomp, a magnificent manner of walking, become the accepted ideal of beauty in Russia until the period of the reforms of Peter the Great at the beginning of the eighteenth century. The short-flap male dress virtually disappeared from the Russian court under the Byzantine influence, although peasants continued to wear it for two more centuries. However, the size and length of the dress were substantially reduced compared with what was worn in Constantinople. There was a prohibition against taking many types of fabrics out of Constantinople, and for this reason the garments of the Russian princes and of those close to them were, for the most part, rougher and less colorful. They were made decorative by an abundance of finishing touches on the

collar, cuff, and hem. We know that when Prince Sviatoslav Igorevich (who died in 972) met the Byzantine Emperor John I Tzimisces, he was dressed with emphatic simplicity in a white shirt and *porty*. The sole luxurious object that he wore was a single golden earring with two pearls and a ruby. It was only by the middle of the eleventh century that dress of the Byzantine type took firm root in Russia. A ceremonial garment to be worn in the court was defined by which members of other classes were prohibited from wearing it. It consisted of a *korzno*, a small rectangular or round cloak, which was thrown onto the left shoulder and clasped on the right shoulder by a precious fibula. All that remained of the former dress was a round, fur-trimmed hat and various small details of cut and decoration. There was no difference between the woman's hat and that of the man, although the former was worn with a shawl or veil. Of very ancient origin were the *poliki* and *lastovitsy*—colored inserts on the shoulders and under the arms, which were both extremely functional and also served as a decoration on the linen shirts that peasants wore until the end of the nineteenth century. Members of the upper classes and rich city-dwellers wore such shirts at home. To garments simple in cut a decorative character was imparted by hanging ornaments: numerous bracelets, beads, finger rings, and small and large *kolty* (earrings) for women. The dress of this period did not reveal the shape of the body but had a bulky character. As a rule, the clothes were put on over the head and had a small decorative opening in front. Russian dress did not have any draping elements, either in the case of the upper classes or, especially, in the case of the peasantry. Common folk contented themselves with *rubakhi* of homemade cloth, while members of the upper classes wore a *sorochka* (second shirt) made of expensive imported fabrics.

One of the earliest images of the princely family is known from the "Collection of Sviatoslav" (1073), which gives an idea of the style of that epoch and which is clearly connected with the tendencies common in medieval Europe. The prince and his son are represented in fur-trimmed hats, which promoted the legend of the "hat of Monomakh." The Kievan prince Vladimir (1053–1125) received the name "Monomakh" because he was a grandson of the Byzantine emperor Constantine Monomakh, who supposedly sent the regalia and the hat-crown to the son of his daughter. However, it has been established with certainty that the first crown appeared in Moscow only at the beginning of the fourteenth century and was a sharp-pointed golden hat of eastern craftsmanship, with a cross and sable trim. The subsequent hat-crowns were made in the workshops of the Moscow Kremlin in imitation of this headdress (for example, the crown of Peter the Great, 1627).

The Tatar-Mongol invasion led to a break in the contacts with Western Europe, and the immediate proximity with Turkic-speaking peoples led to a change in the form of Russian dress. *Rashpatnyi* clothing with a slit in front from top to bottom appeared, and men wore broad trousers. One must say at once that, even after having borrowed the cut, terminology, and certain elements of this foreign dress, Russians never lost their own national identity when it came to clothing. A good example of this is the caftan, a type of wide-opening garment with a deep wrap-over, worn by both men and women. The old Russian word for this garment is derived from the Persian word. In those cases when, in its fabric and details of cut, the caftan did not differ from the garments of other Eastern nations, it was wrapped over on the right side and belted or buttoned with *klapyshi* (coral, silver, or bone stick-buttons, which, in the twentieth century, Russian artists began to use once again, this time for athletic dress), decorative braided fabric buttons (*uzelki*), or circular buttons. The Russian caftan, in contrast to all the foreign types of cut (Arkhaluk, Turkish), was sewn along the waist with straight gathers, and it could be wrapped over on either side. This feature could be observed in pictures of peasants and common folk up until the middle of the nineteenth century. N. S. Leskov, a celebrated Russian writer, characterized such a caftan as having "Christian folds on the leg."

The need to protect their national sovereignty compelled Russians to preserve their national dress by modifying imported types of dress. For example, caftans brought from the East or acquired from neighboring nations were decorated according to the local manner: they were adorned with lace, or a collar sewn with *ozherel'e* (stones) was attached to them.

Starting with the fourteenth century, trade between Muscovite Russia and Europe expanded. Brocade, velvet, and various kinds of silk and wool were brought to Moscow from England, Italy, and France. Russia served as the intermediary in the trade between Europe and Persia as well as Turkey. Clothing made of diverse patterned and bright-colored fabrics acquired an especially decorative character, and details consisting of gold (metallic) lace and precious stones made the garments particularly magnificent. It is well known that, during the reign of Tsar Ivan IV (Ivan the Terrible, 1530–1584), foreigners desiring to receive an audience in the Kremlin were required to put on Russian clothing as a way to recognize the magnificence of the Russian throne. In order to make a favorable impression, servants were temporarily given fine and expensive clothing from the tsar's storehouse.

It was only during the time of Patriarch Nikon (1605–1681) that foreigners were forbidden to wear Russian clothing, since the patriarch was made unhappy by the fact that, when they were in the presence of the head of the Russian church, foreign guests did not fall to their knees but, by remaining standing in Russian dress, disrupted the usual order of things and could exert a bad influence on the people. At the same time, Tsar Aleksei Mikhailovich (1629–1676) made more severe the punishment for Russians who wore European dress or imitated foreign hairstyles.

The boyars wore the richest and most decorative clothing. A distinctive feature of the boyar dress was the *gorlatnyi* or "neck" hat (a tall cylinder made of the neck furs of black foxes or other expensive fur). Boyars gave as gifts and rewards their sable furs, covered with gold brocade or patterned velvet, but they never parted with their hats, which were symbols of their power. At home, their hats were safeguarded on wooden stands with painted designs. The tsar's everyday dress did not differ from that of the nobles, and during his reception of ambassadors, he was obliged to wear the *platno* (a long, collarless brocade garment that had broad sleeves extending to the wrists). Instead of a collar, *barmy* garments covering the shoulders and decorated with precious stones and pearls, were worn. Only the tsar and priests had the right to wear a "breast" cross. During especially important ceremonies, the tsar had to wear a crown (the hat of Monomakh) and the *okladen'* (a gold chain of two-headed eagles).

The outer formal piece of clothing worn by a nobleman was the *feriaz'* (broad and with long sleeves) and the *okhaben'* (with narrow folded-back sleeves that could be tied at the back and with a large rectangular folded-back collar). Women and young girls of the nobility wore the *letnik* (a garment with very broad, short sleeves with detachable flaps made of expensive fabrics embroidered with stones and pearls). Because of the heavy fabrics and the abundance of precious stones and pearls, the dress of both men and women was very heavy, weighing as much as 44 pounds.

In the middle of the fourteenth century occurs the first mention of the *sarafanets* (male dress consisting of a long, narrow opened-out garment with sleeves), from which later the main part of the *sarafan*—a long, sleeveless garment which became the national costume of the Russian woman—got its name. This gender confusion is associated with the fact that the original Persian word meant "honorable dress" and referred to clothes made of imported fabric. Only in the seventeenth century did this term come to apply exclusively to women's clothing. The *sarafan* was worn over the *rubakha* (shirt), and became common in the central and northern regions of Russia. The south preferred the *paneva*, which necessarily was combined with the apron. The sarafans of rich city women were made of silk and velvet, whereas those of peasant women were made of painted domestic linen. The cut of the sarafan differed greatly depending on the place where it was made and on the material: it could be straight, or it could be composed of oblique wedges, *kumanchiki*, *kindiaki*, and so on. Over the sarafan was worn the *dushegreia* (a short, wide jacket).

The enormous extent of the territory, the diversity of the raw materials, and the conditions of life did not favor the creation of a single national costume in Russia. There existed many different kinds of clothing and headdresses, differing not only from region to region, but even from village to village. In the central and northern parts of the country, the chief decoration of the female headdress was river pearls, while in the south of Russia it was painted goose down, glass beads and buttons, and woolen embroidery. The names of the headdresses also differed: *soroka*, *kokoshnik*, *kika*. But one can say with certainty that all the versions of the national costume—from the most ancient combination with the *poneva* to the later combination with the sarafan—tended toward a general esthetic ideal: a massive, not-highly articulated form and a distinct and simple silhouette.

The men's national costume was more uniform and consisted everywhere of *rubakha*, *porty*, and belt.

The reforms of Peter the Great changed the dress only of the upper strata of society. The clothes worn by the common folk changed very slowly and were gradually displaced from the cities to the villages. From this time forth it became accepted to speak not of the national dress, but of the people's dress. The clothes worn by the urban poor and handicraftsmen combined traditional and fashionable elements. Even the rich merchant class did not part all at once with the earlier ideas of dignity. Mer-

chants' wives might have worn the most fashionable low-necked dresses, but on their heads they wore shawls tied in a special way, the *povoiniki*, and they kept wearing them until the middle of the nineteenth century.

Furniture and the configuration of home interiors changed under the influence of European fashion. Skirts worn on frames made it necessary to replace traditional benches with chairs and to acquire fans, gloves, feathers, and lace to decorate one's hairdo. Together with decrees, which changed the national dress, the tsar instituted measures to establish the national production of fabrics. Female lace-makers were invited from Flanders and taught weaving to nuns from nunnery workshops. If the efforts to establish a national industry came to fruition only at the end of the century, the dress reform was realized in and transformed both capitals (St. Petersburg and Moscow) very rapidly.

Over the course of his reign, Peter the Great (1672–1725; tsar from 1682, emperor from 1721) issued seventeen decrees in his name that laid down the rules governing the wearing of European-type dress, the types of fabrics, and the character of the trim for uniforms and festive attire. This attests that Peter the Great reserved a special role for clothing in the system of reforms he was instituting. Two decrees–*On the wearing of German dress and footwear by all ranks of people and on the use of German saddles in horseback riding* and *On the shaving of beards and whiskers by all ranks of men, except priests and deacons, on the taxing of those who do not obey this decree, and on the handing-out of tokens to those who pay the tax*—were viewed as disastrous for the sense of national identity in the nineteenth century polemic concerning the consequences of the Petrine reforms. However, here it was not taken into account that, in Peter's time, the word "German" referred not to the nation of Germany but to foreign lands in general; and what was implied was that Saxon, French, and other elements would be combined to create a European style of dress suitable for solving problems that the reformer-tsar set for himself. As far as the dress for the various military services was concerned, the superiority of the short-flap uniform in the European style was obvious and did not raise any questions. The prohibition against wearing the national dress extended only to the narrow circle of people close to the throne, especially the boyars. In order to institute his new policies, Peter needed new people, whom he enlisted for service to the throne without regard to which class they belonged. The national dress remained a precise indicator of class. Moreover, the consciousness that the peasant's son who wore the *armiak* (plain cloth coat) had of himself was, even if he was invested with the personal trust of the tsar, different from that of the boyars who wore the hereditary *gorlatnyi* hat and the brocade-covered sable fur. In forcibly changing the form in which class was manifested, Peter did not meet with any resistance. For the lower classes, the wearing of European clothing made it possible to change their lives, and they did this without regrets. But the boyars, who from ancient times prided themselves on the luxuriousness of their furs, their long beards, and the precious stones they wore in their rings—also were concerned more with preserving the proximity of their families to the throne than with their personal dignity.

In all things the new dress contradicted the traditional clothing. If a man's feet were uncovered, that was a sign that he had not yet reached marriage age; however, the new decree commanded the wearing of stockings and shoes. The former large multilayer garments gave people the appearance of great bulk and were handed down from generation to generation, but the new clothing was cut to the person's figure and was sewn from several pieces. The most troubling consequence of the introduction of the new dress was the change produced in the habitual gestures and behavior. People's manner of walking became less stately; and when the chin was shaved, the need to smooth out one's beard disappeared, and there was thus no pretext to speak more slowly or to be expressively silent. This was accompanied by the disappearance of the *kushak* (sash), which had customarily been worn beneath the waist; and there was now no place to stick one's hands. Nevertheless, the boyars offered virtually no resistance. Only single individuals, inspired by true religiosity and fidelity to tradition, offered any resistance.

The formative element of the European female dress that had been brought to Russia in the eighteenth century was the corset, and it contradicted the Russian ideal of beauty; however, more important for the female dress was a type of headdress—the *fontange*. The latter was successful in supplanting, if only in part, the traditional headdress of the married woman, which had to cover the hair fully. In combination with heavy silken fabrics, this considerably facilitated the assimilation of the new forms. A. S. Pushkin later wrote: "The aged grand ladies cleverly tried to combine the new form of dress with the persecuted past: their caps imitated the sable cap of the Empress Natal'a Kirillovna, and their hoop skirts and mantillas were reminiscent to some extent of the *sarafan* and *dushegreia*." The first to change their dress were the members of the tsar's family; and members of the court followed them. The Petrine period had already seen the appearance of the notions of "fashionable" and "unfashionable" with reference to European-style dress; and this signified that the reforms had borne their fruit.

Nearly until the end of the eighteenth century, European-style dress (as in the past, Byzantine-style dress) signified that one belonged to the powerful classes, whereas the remaining classes of society retained the traditional dress. The process of the assimilation of European fashions was incredibly rapid. The severe and heavy style of the beginning of the century was replaced fairly rapidly by the rococo style, since with the enthronement of Elizaveta Petrovna (1709–1761, empress from 1741), the quotidian culture and life were oriented toward French fashion.

Catherine the Great (1729–1796, empress from 1762), German by birth and having occupied the throne as the result of a conspiracy, considered it necessary to emphasize the national character of her reign by means of dress. She created her own fashion, including elements of traditional dress. She wore round dresses without a train and a wide-opening outer garment with folded-back sleeves; and in contrast to the French style, the coiffures in the Russian court were worn rather low. This was called fashion "in the manner of the Empress," and it was imitated at the court.

Tsar Nicholas I (1796–1855, emperor from 1825), from the first days of his reign, desired to see ladies at the court wearing Russian dress, and in 1834, a female court "uniform" was introduced by the law of 27 February. Contemporaries called this uniform a "Frenchified sarafan," since it combined the traditional headdress and folded-back sleeves with a tightly cinched waist and an enormous train. The gold or silver embroidery on the velvet dresses corresponded to the embroidery on the uniforms of the court officials. This dress continued to exist at the Russian court without modification until 1917. Even men of the nobility who were not engaged in military or civil service were required to wear the noble uniform, and interest in traditional male dress was viewed as ideological opposition to the existing order.

From 1829, industrial exhibitions were held in Russia. The first exhibition of Russian textile articles was held in Saint Petersburg and showed the indisputable successes of Russian manufacturers of textiles, accessories, and shawls. The manufacture of the latter is an important stage in the history of Russian textiles. This marked the first competitive production of fashionable European accessories. The first textile factory for shawls belonged to N. A. Merlina. In 1800, Merlina began to produce reticules (which became fashionable because of the absence of pockets in dresses of the traditional style) and *bordiury* (vertical and horizontal borders); and in 1804 she began to produce complete shawls. Then, in the province of Saratov, D. A. Kolokol'tsov opened his factory. The last to start operation, in 1813, was V. A. Eliseeva's *complete shawl factory*, which meant that it used native, not imported, raw materials. Instead of the wool of mountain goats, the owner used the fur of the saigak antelopes of the southern Russian steppe. Prince Iusupov was also engaged in the production of shawls; his factory in Kupavna, near Moscow, produced fashionable shawls for merchant women and city women, which indicates how ingrained the European fashions became in the everyday life of Russians.

By the end of the nineteenth century, Russian culture, having passed through its period of apprenticeship, had accumulated a vast creative potential, manifested in all spheres of art, including the art of clothing. The best artists of that time, M. Vrubel' (1856–1910), Ivan Bilibin (1876–1942), L. Bakst (1866–1924), and others, created not only costumes for the stage but also everyday clothing for their female relations and female acquaintances.

The *First International Exhibition of Historical and Contemporary Dress and Its Accessories* was held in Saint Petersburg in 1902 and 1903. In January 1903, the exhibition "Contemporary Art" opened, with an entire section being devoted to dress. The majority of the pieces were based on the sketches of V. von Meck (1877–1932). The interest in the applied arts and in dress in particular was exemplified in the most spectacular manner by the success of Russian stagecraft, justly appreciated by the international community, during the "Russian Seasons" program in Paris in 1908 and 1909, organized by Serge Diaghilev (1872–1929). The European spectator encountered an indisputable innovation in the art of stagecraft: a single artist was responsible for creating the decorations and the dress of all the characters, something unprecedented for either the Russian or the European stage prior to the group of Russian artists associated with the celebrated magazine *The World of Art*.

Alexander Benois (1870–1960), A. Golovin (1863–1930), and N. Goncharova (1881–1962) had an enormous influence on the Parisian public, and L. Bakst was invited to work with the Parisian fashion houses. The influence of Russian artists on the European fashions of the first decade of the twentieth century was indisputable. P. Poire repeatedly collaborated with Bakst.

Of the professional dressmakers the most celebrated was N. Lamanova, who started her own business in 1885, and in 1901 began her collaboration with the Moscow Art Theater. It was at Lamanova's invitation that Poire, with whom she frequently met in Paris, visited Moscow and Saint Petersburg in 1911. Lamanova continued to work in Moscow, and after 1917 she became one of the founders of Soviet dress: she participated in the publication of the magazine *Atel'e* (1923), devised programs for teaching the dressmaking craft, and continued her collaboration with the Moscow Art Theater and other Moscow theaters. In 1925, at the Paris world exhibition, Lamanova's collection was deemed worthy of the grand prize "for national originality in combination with a contemporary orientation in fashion." However, shortly after receiving this award, she lost the right to vote because she had used hired workers in her workshop.

Shortly after 1917, the group of constructivist artists who were associated with the magazine *Lef*—V. Stepanova (1894–1958), Alexander Rodchenko (1891–1956), L. Popova (1889–1924), as well as A. Exter (1884–1949)—distinguished themselves in the making of contemporary dress. Rejecting the previous forms of dress, the constructivists proclaimed "comfort and purposefulness" as their main principle. Clothes had to be comfortable to work in, easy to put on, and easy to move around in. The main orientation of their work was the so-called *prozodezhda*, production dress. The basic elements of this

clothing were simple geometrical shapes: squares, circles, and triangles. Particular attention was given to athletic dress; bright color combinations were used to distinguish the various competing teams. The fashion of those years was urban fashion, and the places of action were stadiums and squares, which were appropriate only for young and strong people. Private life, as well as the private person, disappeared. Individual taste was inappropriate. All resources were expended on the industrial production of clothing; here, complicated cuts and intricate ornaments hindered the unceasing operation of the machines.

In 1921, V. Stepanova and L. Popova were invited to the first cotton-print factory in Moscow. Both of them stopped working on machine painting and began to work with great enthusiasm on cotton specimens, preferring geometrical patterns and deliberately rejecting traditional vegetation motifs. The ornaments they created did not have analogues in the history of textiles, and with their bright colors they imparted a festive and fresh appearance to simple cotton fabrics.

The rigid ideological control of all spheres of life in the second half of the 1920s led to a situation in which the creative heritage of brilliant artists was not understood, not actualized, and was forgotten for a long period of time. The rulers considered it necessary to rewrite the recent history, expelling from everyday life all mention of the past and, first and foremost, the material incarnation of the revolutionary aesthetic ideal. The administrative system controlled consumption and encouraged the formation of new elites, offering them the possibility of acquiring clothing in special ateliers and stores. Clothes designers were being educated in the arts department of the Textile Institute, but this profession was not considered a creative one, with corresponding privileges. Furthermore, since there was no private enterprise, these designers could find work only at state-owned firms and institutions (design houses, large specialized studios), submitting to the state plan and worrying that they would be accused of being bourgeois degenerates.

All attempts to express one's individuality through dress, to separate oneself from the faceless gray crowd, were thwarted by administrative measures. In 1949, the word *stiliaga* entered the Russian language and was used to stigmatize lovers of colorful clothing. In each city there appeared a "Broadway" (usually the main thoroughfare of the city, named after the street in New York City); and a promenade on this street could result in expulsion from the Textile Institute or arrest for hooliganism.

The first to legalize the profession and to escape from the administrative captivity was Slava Zaitsev (b. 1938), who established the *Theater of Fashions* (1980), which later became his fashion house. By this time Russia had more than a few brilliant designers who were also recognized abroad. Irina Krutikova (b. 1936) became widely known as a designer of fur clothing and received the title "queen of fur." She resurrected many old traditions and created new methods for coloring and finishing fur. She opened her own studio in 1992.

The *perestroika* or great political change of the late 1980s made it possible to organize one's own business, to travel the globe, and to open boutiques of international brands in Moscow, Saint Petersburg, and other cities of the former Soviet Union. It also offered great opportunities for both creators and consumers of Russian fashion. This changed the appearance of cities and liberated people from having to expend enormous effort to acquire the necessities of life. Designers appeared who specialized in accessories. Irina Deineg (b. 1961) became known as a designer of both common and exclusive styles of hats. Viktoriia Andreianova, Viktor Zubets, Andrei Sharov, Andrei Bartenev, Valentin Iudashkin, and Iulia Ianina exhibit their collections every year, and at the same they are developing designs for private individuals as well as for mass production, filling corporate orders.

See also **Ethnic Dress; Royal and Aristocratic Dress; Traditional Dress.**

BIBLIOGRAPHY

Kirsaova, R. M. "*Kostium v russkoi khudozhestvennoi kul'ture 18—pervoi poloviny 20 vv. (Opyt entsiklopedii)*" [Dress in Russian Artistic Culture from the Eighteenth Century to the First Half of the Twentieth Century (An Attempt at an Encyclopedic Account)]. Moscow: The Large Russian Encyclopedia, 1995.

———. "*Obraz 'krasivogo cheloveka' v russkoi literature 1918–1930-kh godov*" [The Image of the "Beautiful Human Being" in Russian Literature from 1918 to 1930]. In *Znakomyi neznakomets. Sotsialisticheskii realism kak istoriko-kul'turnaia problema* [The Familiar Unfamiliar One. Socialist Realism as a Historical-Cultural Problem]. Moscow: Institute of Slavic Studies and Balkanology, 1995.

———. *Russkii kostium i byt XVII–XIX vekov* [Russian Dress and Everyday Life in the Seventeenth, Eighteenth, and Nineteenth Centuries]. Moscow: Slovo, 2002.

Lebina, N. B. *Povsednevnaia zhizn' sovetskogo goroda. 1920/1930 gody* [The Everyday Life of the Soviet City in the 1920s/1930s]. St. Petersburg: Kikimora, 1999.

Molotova, L. N and N. N. Sosnina. *Russkii narodnyi kostium. Iz sobraniia Gosudarstvennogo muzeia etnografii narodov SSSR* [Russian National Dress. From the Collection of the State Museum of the Ethnography of the Peoples of the USSR]. Leningrad: Khudozhnik RSFSR, 1984.

Olenin, A. N. *Opyt ob odezhde, oruzhii, nravakh, obychaiakh i stepeni prosveshcheniia slavian ot vremeni Traiana i russkikh do nashestviia tatar* [Essay on the Dress, Weapons, Mores, Customs, and Degree of Education of the Slavs from the Time of Trajan and the Russians to the Tatar Invasion]. St. Petersburg: Glazunov's Press, 1832.

Prokhorov, V. A. *Materialy po istorii russkikh odezhd i obstanovski zhizni narodnoi, izdavaemye V. Prokhorovym* [Materials on the History of Russian Dress and the Circumstances of the Peoples' Life, Published by V. Prokhorov]. St. Petersburg: V. Prokhorov, Issues 1-7, 1871–1884.

Sosnina, N. and I. Shangina, ed. *Russkii traditsionnyi kostium. Il-liustrirovannaia entsiklopediia* [Russian Traditional Dress. Illustrated Encyclopedia]. St. Petersburg: Iskusstvo-SPB, 1998.

Strizhenova, T. K. *Iz istorii sovetskogo kostiuma* [From the History of Soviet Dress]. Moscow: Sovetskii khudozhnik, 1972.

Tereshchenko, A. V. *Byt russkogo naroda* [The Everyday Life of the Russian People]. St. Petersburg: The Press of the Ministry of Internal Affairs, 1848. Reprint, Moscow: Russkaia kniga, 1997.

Zabreva, A. E. *Istoriia kostiuma. Bibliograficheskii ukazatel' knig i statei na russkom iazyke 1710–2001* [History of Dress. Bibliographic Index of Books and Articles in Russian, 1710–2001]. St. Petersburg: Professiia, 2002.

Raisa Kirsanova

RYKIEL, SONIA Sonia Rykiel was born Sonia Flis in Paris on 25 May 1930. She married Sam Rykiel in 1953, and was initially inspired to design clothes by her own desire for fashionable maternity wear when she was pregnant with her first child. The clothes she designed were then sold in her husband's boutique, Laura, which he

Sonia Rykiel. Acclaimed French fashion designer Sonia Rykiel in 2002. Rykiel spearheaded the boutique movement in France during the late 1960s. © STEPHANE CARDINALE/PEOPLE AVENUE/CORBIS. REPRODUCED BY PERMISSION.

started in 1962. With the opening of the designer's first Sonia Rykiel boutique on the Left Bank in 1968, she spearheaded the boutique movement of small shops selling avant-garde clothes in France at a time when women of fashion were rejecting the constricted styles of haute couture and seeking clothes that projected a more youthful and modern image. The early 1960s were a time of massive cultural upheaval when many social institutions underwent major changes, including haute couture. Along with Emmanuelle Khan, Yves Saint Laurent, and Dorothée Bis, Rykiel was responsible for a dramatic shift from status dressing to the youthful informality of the Rive Gauche. With her extraordinary mass of red hair, pale complexion, and trademark black clothes, she typified the look of Left Bank bohemia.

It soon became apparent that Rykiel's strength was in knitwear design, and she helped to transform a medium previously dismissed as old-fashioned into one associated with covetable items for the young. Offering her clothes in such fashionable New York stores as Henri Bendel and Bloomingdale's, Rykiel was nicknamed the "queen of knitwear" in 1964.

Rykiel created her signature silhouette by cutting the garment high in the armholes and close to the body, with narrow sleeves that elongated the torso. Using a distinctive palette of colored stripes against a backdrop of black, her designs for knitwear often involved such innovative details as lockstitched hems, reversed seams, and carefully placed pockets. All her clothes tended to be light-hearted with an element of wit, whether in the use of contrasting textures and shapes or in the detailing. In the early 1980s Rykiel began to add words to her clothes—for example, "Black Tie" spelled out in studs on a black leather jacket, or "Special Edition Evening Dreams" emblazoned in rhinestones on the belt of a black lace dress.

As the fashionable silhouette became looser during the 1980s, Rykiel emphasized relaxed tailoring and geometric layers. She diversified into household linens in 1975, with children's wear, men's wear, shoes, and fragrance following in 1993. Her flagship store on the boulevard Saint-Germain opened in 1990.

Rykiel has become a French institution. She received the medal of a Chevalier de la Légion d'Honneur in 1985. Her thirtieth-anniversary show was held in March 1998 at the Bibliothèque nationale de France.

See also **Boutique; Paris Fashion; Saint Laurent, Yves.**

BIBLIOGRAPHY

Rykiel, Sonia, Hélène Cixous, and Madeleine Chapsal. *Rykiel.* Paris: Herscher, 1985.

Marnie Fogg

SACK DRESS (OR SAQUE). *See* **Chemise Dress.**

SAFETY PINS The first clothing fasteners with the principle of a pin (metal) retained by a bow (generally organic) appeared in central Europe during the Middle Bronze Age in the second millennium B.C.E. From these a variant developed in the thirteenth or twelfth century B.C.E. that archaeologists have identified as the direct ancestor of the modern safety pin. It was a single piece of bronze wire coiled at one end as a spring, with a point that engaged a guard of sheet bronze. With many variants it spread rapidly around the Mediterranean, especially in Greek lands. For male and female wearers it is thought to have been a badge of both worldly and spiritual privilege. Around 500 B.C.E., new trends in clothing construction (especially the toga) ended its prestige in the Mediterranean, though it flourished north of the Alps until the third century C.E., when provincials were granted Roman citizenship with its right to the toga. In the Middle Ages, in the West, the luxury fibula resumed its role as an upper-class ornament.

The nineteenth-century safety pin may have been a conscious classical revival, influenced by increasing museum display of and publication of articles on ancient fibulae. The first U.S. patent for a coiled-wire pin of this type granted to Walter Hunt in 1849 is significantly entitled "Dress-Pin," even though other patents had been issued for "safety pins." The inventor claimed durability, beauty, convenience, and injury protection, in that order. Only beginning in the late 1870s did other inventors add the guard that protected the wearer fully. Crucially, they also developed machinery for automating the production of the pins. By 1914, American factories alone were making over 1.33 billion safety pins annually at a cost of $0.007 each, a stunning example of the industrial order's democratization of an ancient and medieval luxury product. The maverick economist Thorstein Veblen affixed his watch to his clothing with a safety pin to show his indifference to conspicuous consumption—a gesture of reverse snobbery later followed more drastically by the punk movement's use of safety pins as piercing jewelry from the 1970s onward.

The spread of disposable diapers with snap fasteners after World War II reduced the role of safety pins in the household, or rather redefined safety as protection from embarrassment by malfunctioning apparel. On the negative side, the fasteners' reassuring name conceals their real hazards to unsupervised children, who swallow them all too often. Extracting open safety pins requires special instruments first developed over one hundred years ago, and exceptional medical skill.

See also **Brooches and Pins; Fasteners; Pins.**

BIBLIOGRAPHY

Alexander, J. A. "The History of the Fibula." In *The Explanation of Culture Change: Models in Prehistory.* Edited by Colin Renfrew. Pittsburgh, Pa.: University of Pittsburgh Press, 1973.

Kaghan, Theodore. "Humanity's Hall of Fame: They Gave Us the Safety Pin." *Los Angeles Times,* 1 January 1939, H12.

Internet Resource

Hunt, Walter. 1849. Dress Pin. U.S. Patent 6,281. Available from <http://www.uspto.gov>.

Edward Tenner

SAINT LAURENT, YVES A direct heir of the couture tradition of Gabrielle (Coco) Chanel, Cristóbal Balenciaga, and Christian Dior, Yves Saint Laurent explored, discovered, and polished, in the course of a career lasting more than forty years, the infinite resources of his vocabulary. Taming the signs and codes of his age, he created the grammar of the contemporary wardrobe and imposed his language, which became the inescapable reference of the twentieth century. In search of a uniform for elegance, Saint Laurent combined the greatest rigor of production with extreme sophistication of form to create clothing of impeccable cut with harmonious proportions, where the aesthetic of the detail was transformed into an absolute necessity. "Fashion is like a party. Getting dressed is preparing to play a role. I am not a couturier, I am a craftsman, a maker of happiness" (Teboul 2002).

Yves Mathieu Saint Laurent was born on 1 August 1936 in the Algerian city of Oran, the oldest of the three

Yves Saint Laurent. Yves Saint Laurent stands next to Laeticia Casta as she models a wedding dress from his spring/summer 2000 high fashion collection. From the beginning of his career in the 1960s until his 2002 retirement, Saint Laurent was one of the world's most influential fashion designers. © REUTERS NEW-MEDIA, INC./ CORBIS. REPRODUCED BY PERMISSION.

children of Lucienne-Andrée and Charles Mathieu Saint Laurent. He said later: "As long as I live I will remember my childhood and adolescence in the marvelous country that Algeria was then. I don't think of myself as a *pied noir*. I think of myself as a Frenchman born in Algeria" (Teboul 2002). He entered the Collège du Sacré-Cœur in September 1948. Strongly influenced by the play *L'École à deux têtes* of Jean Cocteau, he designed his first dresses: stage costumes for paper puppets with which he performed for his sisters. "I had a terrible time in class, and when I got home at night I was completely free. I thought only of my puppets, my marionettes, which I dressed up in imitation of the plays I had seen" (Benaïm, p. 451).

Saint Laurent designed a good deal, imitating Jean Gabriel-Domergue, Christian Bérard, René Gruau, Christian Dior, Cristóbal Balenciaga, and Hubert de Givenchy. In February 1949 he created his first dresses, made for his mother and his two sisters. At the age of sixteen he attended a performance of Molière's *L'École des femmes*, performed and directed by Louis Jouvet. Bérard had designed both sets and costumes. Seeing this play inspired in Saint Laurent a passion that he never surren-

dered for the theater. In December 1953 he went with his mother to Paris to receive the third prize in the competition of the Secrétariat de la Laine. There he was introduced to Michel de Brunhoff, who was then editor of the French edition of the essential fashion magazine *Vogue*.

Back in Oran, he began a correspondence with de Brunhoff, sending him fashion and theater sketches. The following year, armed with his baccalaureat (earning second prize for the philosophy essay and a score of 20 out of 20 in drawing), Saint Laurent settled in Paris and attended the École de la Chambre Syndicale de la Haute Couture for three months. He won first prize for dresses in the Secrétariat de la Laine competition. It was at about this time that, struck by the similarity of Saint Laurent's designs to those of the fall–winter collection of Christian Dior, de Brunhoff decided to introduce him to Dior, who promptly hired him as an assistant. During the next two years—years of apprenticeship and intense collaboration—a lasting complicity was established between the two men. "I remember him above all…. The elegance of his feelings matched the elegance of his style" (Yves Saint Laurent, p. 31).

On 24 October 1957 Christian Dior died from a heart attack at the age of fifty-two. On 15 November Saint Laurent was designated his successor. At age twenty-one he became the youngest couturier in the world. He presented his first collection in January 1958 and had his first triumph with the Trapeze line, which propelled him onto the international scene with its enormous success. He was given the Neiman Marcus Award. That same year he met Pierre Bergé, who soon became his companion and business partner.

While designing six collections a year for the house of Dior, Saint Laurent satisfied his passion for the theater, and he designed his first stage costumes (*Cyrano de Bergerac*, Ballets de Paris de Roland Petit, 1959). Influenced by Chanel, the spring–summer collection had solid success and provoked a craze, but the autumn–winter collection saw the appearance of a more controversial style: turtleneck knits and the first black leather jackets. Singularly prophetic, Saint Laurent had taken his inspiration directly from the street. Drafted into the Algerian armed forces in 1960, he was replaced at Dior by Marc Bohan.

Saint Laurent was soon declared unfit for service and hospitalized for nervous depression, and it was thanks to Bergé that he was able to leave the army. "Victoire" Doutrouleau, one of Dior's star models and a "marvelous muse" for Saint Laurent, recalls: "He left the hospital anxious, dazed, and alone. Yves a soldier? You might as well try changing a swan into a crocodile!" (Benaïm, p. 108). In open conflict with the Dior fashion house, which he sued for breach of contract, Saint Laurent decided to establish his own couture house in 1961, in association with Bergé. The financial support came from an American businessman, J. Mack Robinson: "I was impressed by such great talent in such a young man. I knew nothing about fashion, and I didn't want to get involved. This was the realm of Yves, the creator, and I immediately saw that he was a genius" (Yves Saint Laurent, p. 16).

The house opened officially on 4 December 1961. Former employees of Christian Dior left Dior to work for Saint Laurent, and more than half the seamstresses came from the Dior workshops. The graphic designer Cassandre created the YSL logo. Saint Laurent designed his first dress—labeled 00001—for Mrs. Arturo Lopez Willshaw, followed by the famous white feather costume for the dancer Zizi Jeanmaire. In 1962, on rue Spontini in Paris, the house presented its first show, described by *Life* as "the best suitmaker since Chanel" (p. 49). Dino Buzzati, special correspondent for the *Corriere della sera*, wrote: "Closing the show, a wedding dress in goffered white piqué brought an ovation from the public. The pale face of the young couturier then appeared for a moment from backstage; only for a moment, because a swarm of admirers surrounded him, embraced him, devoured him." This collection was memorable for the Norman jacket, the smock, and the pea jacket, which became "foundations" of the Saint Laurent style.

Saint Laurent designed the sets and costumes for *Les chants de maldoror* and *Rapsodie espagnole*, staged by Roland Petit, and the dresses for Claudia Cardinale in Blake Edwards's film *The Pink Panther* (1964). In April 1963, accompanied by Pierre Bergé, who had become his Pygmalion, he made his first trip to Japan, where he presented shows in Osaka and Tokyo.

The year 1964 saw the launch of a perfume for women, called "Y." But Saint Laurent's new collection was showered with negative criticism. The press spoke only of the André Courrèges' bombshell collection. Saint Laurent explained: "I have never been able to work on a wooden mannequin; I play by unrolling the fabric on the model, walking around her, making her move. … The only collection that I made a mess of, a complete fiasco, the very year when Courrèges's came on the scene and succeeded, I did not have good models, and I was not inspired" (Vacher, p. 68). Still drawn to the theater, he designed the costumes for *Le mariage de Figaro* and *Il faut passer par les nuages* for the Renaud-Barrault company.

In 1965 he triumphed with the Mondrian collection (named for the modern artist Piet Mondrian), which was surprising for its strict cut and the play of colors. Showered with praise by the American fashion press, he had become, according to *Women's Wear Daily*, "the Young King Yves of Paris." It was at this time that he made his first trip to New York, accompanied by Bergé. Richard Salomon (of Charles of the Ritz) acquired all the stock of the Yves Saint Laurent design company. At this time, too, Saint Laurent began a long friendship with the dancer Rudolph Nureyev, for whom he designed stage costumes and street clothes. He also created the wardrobe that Sophia Loren wore in Stanley Donen's film *Arabesque* (1966), as well as the costumes for Roland Petit's *Notre-Dame de Paris*.

For his summer 1966 haute couture show Saint Laurent presented the first see-through garments, the "nude look," and the first dinner jacket: "If I had to choose a design among all those that I have presented, it would unquestionably be the tuxedo jacket…. And since then, it has been in every one of my collections. It is in a sense the 'label' of Yves Saint Laurent" (Vacher, p. 64). For his haute couture collection of winter 1966–1967 he introduced the Pop Art collection. He met Andy Warhol and Loulou de la Falaise, his future muse. On 26 September 1966 Saint Laurent opened his first ready-to-wear shop, Saint Laurent Rive Gauche, at 21, rue de Tournon, with Catherine Deneuve, for whom he had designed the costumes in Luis Buñuel's film *Belle de jour* (1967), as godmother.

With the designs of Saint Laurent, ready-to-wear fashion established its pedigree, for he himself supervised the creation, manufacture, and distribution of the clothing: "The ready-to-wear is not a poor substitute for couture. It is the future. We know that we are dressing younger, more receptive women. With them it is easy to be bolder" (Benaïm, p. 153). That same year he won the *Harper's Bazaar* Oscar award; published an illustrated book, *La vilaine Lulu*; and launched his so-called African dresses. It was at that time that Saint Laurent and Bergé discovered Marrakesh, where they bought a house. For the spring–summer 1968 show, he presented the first jacket for the safari look, more see-through garments, and the jumpsuit, which would be successfully repeated in 1975. The style "Il" or "He" was born, comprising mini evening dresses and men's suits: "I was deeply struck by a photograph of Marlene Dietrich wearing men's clothes. A tuxedo, a blazer, or a navel officer's uniform—any of them. A woman dressed as a man must be at the height of femininity to fight against a costume that isn't hers" (Buck, p. 301). In September, the first Saint Laurent Rive Gauche shop was opened in New York. In a television interview, Chanel identified Saint Laurent as her spiritual heir, while galleries in London and New York exhibited his theater drawings.

The autumn–winter 1969 collection was dominated by the tapestry coat, patchwork furs, and jeweled dresses created by his sculptor friends the Lalannes. He continued to work in the cinema, designing costumes for Catherine Deneuve in François Truffaut's *La sirène du Mississippi* (1969); then, with Bergé, he opened the first Saint Laurent Rive Gauche shop for men at 17, rue de Tournon. In 1971, inspired by the designer Paloma Picasso, who bought her clothes at flea markets, he created the Libération collection, also known as Quarante, which provoked a scandal with its "retro" style. Saint Laurent later said that this collection—featuring puffed sleeves, square shoulders, platform shoes, and his famous green fox short jacket—was a humorous reaction to new fashion tendencies. In its wake, he posed nude for the photographer Jean-loup Sieff to advertise his first eau de toilette for men, YSL pour Homme, provoking another scandal.

Beginning in 1972 great changes took place. Pierre Bergé, whose ultimate aim was to recover all the stock of Yves Saint Laurent, repurchased from Charles of the Ritz (which had become a subsidiary of the American pharmaceutical giant Squibb) its shares in the couture house, thereby taking control of the couture and ready-to-wear businesses. Bergé and Saint Laurent then developed a licensing policy; although it had existed earlier, it was strengthened and enforced. The designs presented in the spring of 1972 (embroidered cardigans, padded jackets, "Proust" dresses with taffeta frills) were greeted triumphantly by a press once again overflowing with praise: "the man is pure and simple, the greatest fashion designer in the world today," said *Harper's Bazaar* (March 1972, p. 93). To close the season with a flourish, Andy Warhol did a series of portraits of Saint Laurent.

The following years found Saint Laurent ever more in demand in the world of film and theater. He designed costumes in succession for Anny Duperey in Alain Resnais's film *Stavisky . . .*, for Ellen Burstyn in the same director's *Providence*, and for Helmut Berger in Joseph Losey's *The Romantic Englishwoman*. He created the costumes for the ballets *La rose malade* (1973) and *Schéhérazade* (1974) for Roland Petit; for *Harold and Maude* (1973), a play by Colin Higgins; and for Jeanne Moreau and Gérard Depardieu in *The Ride across Lake Constance* (1974) by Peter Handke. In 1974 an exhibition of his costume and stage set sketches was staged in the Proscenium gallery in Paris. In July of the same year, the couture house moved from its cramped quarters to a Second Empire mansion at 5, avenue Marceau.

In 1976 the Opéra-Ballets Russes collection (homage to the Russian ballet producer Sergey Diaghilev) enjoyed international success and was featured on the front page of the *New York Times*. Saint Laurent, who was celebrating his fortieth birthday, said: "I don't know if this is my best collection, but it is my most beautiful collection" (August 16, 1976, p. 39). At about this time, Saint Laurent suffered a severe depression, and beginning in 1977 rumors circulated about his impending death. He replied with major colorful collections with exotic themes: the Espagnoles, with dresses straight out of a painting by Diego Velázquez, and the Chinoises, celebrating the annals of imperial China. He also launched a new perfume, Opium, the advertising for which, orchestrated by the Mafia agency, created a scandal with the slogan "For those who are addicted to Yves Saint Laurent."

In 1978, having just designed the sets and costumes for Cocteau's *L'Aigle à deux têtes* and for Ingrid Caven's cabaret show and written the preface for Nancy Hall-Duncan's book *The History of Fashion Photography* (1979), Saint Laurent demonstrated with his spring-summer collections, "Broadway suits" that he was still in touch with the current climate. He said, "This collection is very elegant, provocative, and at the same time wildly modern, which might appear contradictory. I have sought for purity, but I have interjected unexpected accessories: pointed collars, little hats, shoes with pompons. With these kinds of winks, I wanted to bring a little humor to haute couture, … give it the same sense of freedom one feels in the street, the same provocative and arrogant appearance as, for example, punk fashion. All of that, of course, with dignity, luxury, and style" (Yves Saint Laurent, p. 23).

During the ensuing decade Saint Laurent carried on with his favorite themes—the now classic blazer, dinner jacket, smock, pea jacket, raincoat, pants suit, and safari jacket—while presenting his collections in the form of the homage to various artists and writers. Pablo Picasso, the surrealist poet Aragon, the French poet Guillaume Apollinaire, Cocteau, the French artist Henri Matisse, Shakespeare, the American painter David Hockney, the French artist Georges Braque, the French painter Pierre Bonnard, and the Dutch painter Vincent van Gogh were invoked in turn, inspiring strongly colored garments in which were inscribed the emblematic forms of the painters and the verses of the poets. His creations were "setting static things in motion on the body of a woman," he said in *Paris-Match* (12 Février 1988, p. 69). The press around the world never stopped singing his praises.

The 1980s were full and rich for Saint Laurent. In 1981 he designed the uniform for the writer Marguerite Yourcenar, the first woman elected to the Académie Française, and launched a men's perfume, Kouros. The year 1982 was the twentieth anniversary of the founding of his couture house; the occasion was celebrated at the Lido, where he received the International Fashion Award of the Council of Fashion Designers of America.

In 1983 he showed the Noire et Rose collection, introduced the perfume Paris, designed costumes for the play *Savannah Bay* by Marguerite Duras, and enjoyed the opening of the exhibition "Yves Saint Laurent, 25 Years of Design" at the Metropolitan Museum of New York, the largest retrospective ever devoted to a living couturier. One million visitors attended the exhibition, organized by Diana Vreeland. As Vreeland put it, "Saint Laurent has been built into the history of fashion now for a long time. Twenty-six years is proof that he can please most of the people most of the time four times a year. That's quite a reputation" (*Time*, December 12, 1983, p. 56). That same year he made his appearance in the *Larousse* dictionary.

President François Mitterrand awarded Saint Laurent the medal of Chevalier de la Légion d'Honneur in 1985, the same year the African Look collection debuted. Accompanied by Pierre Bergé, he traveled to China for the exhibition devoted to his work at the Fine Arts Museum of Beijing (which recorded 600,000 visitors) and received, at the Paris Opera, the award for Best Couturier for the body of his work. In 1986 he presented his fiftieth haute couture collection, and a retrospective of his work was given at the Musée des Arts de la Mode in Paris. Bergé and Saint Laurent, with the participation of Cerus, purchased Charles of the Ritz, owner of Yves Saint Laurent perfumes, for $630 million.

The next year retrospectives were mounted in the U.S.S.R. (Hermitage, Saint Petersburg) and in Australia (Art Gallery of New South Wales, Sydney). That season five hundred of his pieces sold, principally to a foreign clientele. In 1988, Saint Laurent became the first couturier to present a show for the French Communist Party, at the Fête de l'Humanité. Shares of the Saint Laurent group were introduced on the secondary market of the Paris Bourse in 1989, and the revenues of the house of Saint Laurent reached 3 million francs.

The decade of the 1990s began with an exhibition at the Sezon Museum of Art in Tokyo; the opening of the first shop for accessories, at 32, rue du Faubourg Saint-Honoré; and the presentation of the collection Hommages, considered a "farewell" by some of the press. Scandal arose, however, from an interview Saint Laurent gave to *Le figaro*, in which he spoke of detoxification, his homosexuality, his overuse of alcohol, and his fits of nervous depression. But in 1992, like the phoenix reborn from his ashes, he presented his 121st collection, Une Renaissance, and celebrated the thirtieth anniversary of the Saint Laurent fashion house by inviting 2,800 guests to the Opéra Bastille.

In May 1993 the Yves Saint Laurent group merged with the Elf-Sanofi company. With this acquisition, Elf-Sanofi became the third-largest international prestige perfume and cosmetic company, after L'Oréal and Estée Lauder. Saint Laurent then launched the perfume Champagne, "for happy, lighthearted women, who sparkle." On 21 July, he presented his 124th haute couture collection, with models parading to the melody of *The Merry Widow*. In a major spectacle at the Stade de France, for the opening of the 1998 World Cup of soccer Saint Laurent and Bergé paraded three hundred models before a packed stadium, while two billion spectators watched the event on television. In November of that year, in order to devote himself entirely to haute couture, Saint Laurent turned women's ready-to-wear over to Albert Elbaz and men's ready-to-wear to Hedi Slimane.

In 1999 François Pinault, owner of the department store Printemps, bought Saint Laurent from Elf for 1.12 billion euros and pumped in an additional 78 million euros to take control of all rights to the label, which he turned over to Tom Ford, the Texan designer for Gucci, a house also controlled by Pinault. Bergé announced the opening of the Centre de Documentation Yves Saint Laurent, in Paris, planned for January 2000.

After forty-four years of fashion designing, Saint Laurent announced the closing of his house at a press conference given on 7 January 2002. He took his leave of haute couture with these words: "I have always stood fast against the fantasies of some people who satisfy their egos through fashion. On the contrary, I wanted to put myself at the service of women. … I wanted to accompany them in the great movement of liberation that they went through in the last century. … I am naïve enough to believe that [my designs] can stand up to the attacks

of time and hold their place in the world of today. They have already proved it."

Saint Laurent fixed the ephemeral and constantly sought beauty, shifting between classicism and provocation. Favoring methodical work, recurrent themes, and improvisations in the form of homages, he referred to other artists as catalysts. Shakespeare, Velázquez, Picasso, Proust, and Mondrian each, in turn, served as an inspiration to him. By pushing to extremes the exoticism of the street and delving into forgotten folk traditions, he brought forth a new spirit that illuminated his palette, for example, in the African, Ballets Russes, and Chinoises collections. In an even more radical shift, he took on the male wardrobe, diverting and transposing the dinner jacket, pants suit, safari jacket, and pea jacket to bring masculine and feminine together in a single design. But, it is Pierre Bergé who best describes Yves Saint Laurent's contribution for Yves—and herein lies his uniqueness— each collection is a means of bringing dreams to life, expressing fantasies, encountering myths, and creating out of them a contemporary fashion" (Saint Laurent, p. 27).

See also **Art and Fashion; Ballet Costume; Fashion Shows; Film and Fashion; Haute Couture; Paris Fashion; Perfume; Ready-to-Wear; Retro Styles; Theatrical Costume.**

BIBLIOGRAPHY
Benaïm, Laurence. *Yves Saint Laurent*. Paris: Grasset, 1993.
Buck, Joan Juliet. "Yves Saint Laurent on Style, Passion, and Beauty." *Vogue* (December 1983): 301.
Saint Laurent, Yves, Diana Vreeland, et al. *Yves Saint Laurent*. New York: Clarkson N. Potter, Inc., 1983.
Teboul, David. *Yves Saint Laurent: 5, Avenue Marceau, 75116 Paris, France*. Paris: Martinière, 2002.
Vacher, Irène. "Lesgens." Paris Match, 4 décembre 1981, p. 68.
Yves Saint Laurent par Yves Saint Laurent, 28 ans de création. Paris: editions Herscher, 1986.

Pamela Golbin

SALWAR-KAMEEZ The *salwar-kameez*, or the Punjabi suit (referred to here simply as "the suit"), has traditionally been worn by women of North India and Pakistan and their sisters who have immigrated overseas. It consists of three separate parts: *kameez* (shirt), *salwar* (trousers, nearly always with *ponchay*, or cuffs, at the ankles), and a *chuni* or *dupatta* (scarf or stole). These three components have remained constant over time, though women might not wear the *chuni* on certain occasions. The *chuni* is nearly always worn inside temples to cover the head. The styles, lengths, and widths of these separate parts vary to suit the fashions of the times.

There has always been, however, a "classic suit" that maintains all the components and changes little over long periods of time. These classic suits are interpreted according to personal idiosyncrasies and tastes. For example, the "Patiala suit" (from the princely state of Patialia in the Punjab, which has old and highly developed traditions of arts and crafts) is worn by women in that area regardless of caste, class, and religion and has remained the same for many years. It consists of a knee-length kameez, a baggy salwar (much more voluminous than the average salwar), and a long *chuni*. This classic style is distinctive and a widely recognized marker of this region of the Punjab.

The salwar-kameez is also worn by men, especially by Muslim men, in both Pakistan and India, though the men's version is different from its female counterpart. It is possible that the suit's connotations of maleness have played a role in the adoption of the salwar-kameez by Indian women who might once have worn saris, as a result of women's entry into the waged-labor market. In the world of business and commerce, women are asserting their identities through this practical and comfortable outfit, which they consider to be the most suitable garment for the public realms of economic participation. But, of course, the suit has been worn in public domains for centuries by North Indian women, before this dramatic adoption of the suit in the recent past by wage-earning women throughout the subcontinent.

Another facet of the suit's popularity is a result of the professionalizing of its design, both on the subcontinent and in Europe, since the 1980s. Design professionals trained at fashion schools on the subcontinent or in Europe or America have created innovative new styles and silhouettes while relying upon, and helping to revive, old traditions of embroidery, dyeing, and other forms of embellishment. They have thus developed new techniques of making suits using existing craft skills. These new interpretations have led to a dramatic expansion of markets for the salwar-kameez, both on the subcontinent and in such cities as London, Durban (South Africa), Sydney, Los Angeles, New York, Dubai (United Arab Emirates), Nairobi (Kenya), and other centers of diaspora communities. In these markets, suits of all types and levels of quality are sold at a wide range of prices. Designer suits can cost upward of $9,000, and wedding suits as much as $20,000. Suits that bear "designer labels" might cost $300 to $500, while suits selling for as little as $30 can be found in street markets. The suit economy, in other words, has become quite elaborate.

The suit in the 1990s and the early part of the twenty-first century emerged as a mainstream high-fashion garment, popular both on the catwalk (in Paris and London) and on the street. In Great Britain it was front-page news when the salwar-kameez was worn by such fashion leaders as Diana, Princess of Wales, and Cheri Booth, wife of British Prime Minister Tony Blair. The suit thus has been reimagined and recontextualized as a "global chic" garment. In London diaspora communities, fashion entrepreneurs have been key agents in moving the suit beyond Indian and "ethnic" markets and into the mainstream. As Asian women residing and raised in London, they are attuned to local design trends, which they incorporate in the suits they create for their customers in a global city.

It is this improvisational sensibility—the modus vivendi of their diaspora—that gives them an edge over subcontinental fashion entrepreneurs. They have created new styles that encode their racial politics through their design sensibilities and retail skills. Along with older suit-wearing women, they have transformed what were formerly negatively coded "immigrant ethnic clothes," derided by the mainstream, into the most fashionable border-crossing clothes of our times. The suit is worn by women across ethnic and racial lines in many parts of the world. Black women in London were among the first to wear the suit, much before British women of the upper classes, fashion icons, and the white political elite.

Of course, these suit trends are part of the wider dynamics of the ethnicization and Asianization of Western culture as well as of images created by Asians living in the West, as seen in film, music, literature, and other media. The British Asian diasporic film director Gurinder Chadha's film *Bend It Like Beckham* (2003) has been a phenomenal international success. She is also an innovative hybridizing suit wearer, a savvy image maker with an influential suit style. In Britain, curry has replaced roast beef as the favorite food of the nation. For a younger set of Asians, *bhangra* dance music—a reworking of Punjabi harvest music as interpreted through jazz, reggae, hip-hop, and many other musical genres—was a strong influence in favor of adopting the salwar-kameez and also in introducing this generation to the Punjabi language and cultural scene.

In this complex and multifaceted suit economy, the real heroines are the older women, who wore their "classic suits" despite the cultural and racial odds and regardless of the sartorial terrain in the displaced contexts of the diaspora. These powerful and culturally confident women are the agents of sartorial transmission, who socialized their second-generation daughters to wear the suits on their own terms and according to their design codes. The diaspora daughters of these astute and assertive women have been the pathbreaking fashion entrepreneurs who have created the commercial markets for the suit in cities across the globe and have ushered the salwar-kameez into fashion's mainstream.

See also **Diana, Princess of Wales; Ethnic Dress; India: Clothing and Adornment; Sari.**

BIBLIOGRAPHY

Bhachu, Parminder. *Dangerous Designs: Asian Women Fashion the Diaspora Economies.* New York: Routledge, 2004.

Freeman, Carla. *High Tech and High Heels in the Global Economy: Women, Work, and Pink-Collar Identities in the Caribbean.* Durham, N.C.: Duke University Press, 2000.

Kondo, Dorinne. *About Face: Performing Race in Fashion and Theatre.* New York: Routledge, 1997.

Tarlo, Emma. *Clothing Matters: Questions of Dress and Identity in India.* London: Hurst, 1996.

Parminder Bhachu

SANDALS The sandal is the simplest form of foot covering, consisting of a sole held to the foot using a configuration of straps. Sandals can be utilitarian and bought from a street vendor in Bombay for a few rupees, or a work of art, designed by Manolo Blahnik and selling for several hundred dollars from a high-end boutique. Sandals have been made from every possible material—wood, leather, textile, straw, metal, and even stone, and have graced every echelon of society in almost every culture of the world.

Sandals are the oldest and most commonly found foot covering worldwide. Archaeological examples, uncovered from the Anasazi culture of the American Southwest, date back 8,000 years. These plaited and woven sandals provided a flexible protective sole and utilized a simple V-shaped strap.

Sandals are most commonly found amongst the peoples of hot climates where searing sands and rocky landscapes, inhabited with poisonous insects and thorny plants, necessitated the development of the most basic form of foot covering. Hot, dry climates generally precluded the use of a closed shoe or boot, something that would develop in colder, wetter climates. However, historically, sandals are not found exclusively among the peoples of hot climates.

In Japan, *geta*, wooden-soled sandals, are worn with fabric socks called *tabi* that keep out wetness and winter's chill. Similarly, natives of Eastern Siberia and Alaska wear fur boots that originated in antiquity as sandals tied over fur stockings. At some time in history, the fur stockings were sewn to the soles, creating a boot, but the sandals' straps remained, sewn into the sole seam and tied around the ankle.

While most sandals made for the global market of the early 2000s are usually manufactured of synthetic or recycled materials, such as tires, some indigenous materials are still employed for local markets. In India, water buffalo hide is commonly used for making sandals or *chappli* for the Indian marketplace. Metal and wood have also been used in India to produce *paduka*, the traditional toe-knob sandals of the Hindu: the soles were often stilted, limiting the surface area of the earth trod, protecting the tiniest and humblest of life forms. Similar stilted wooden-soled sandals can be found in Pakistan, Afghanistan, and as far west as Syria and Turkey, although the knobs are replaced with straps ranging from embroidered fabric to simple twisted fiber loops. Syrian wooden sandals, often inlaid with silver wire and mother-of-pearl, were dubbed *kab-kabs* after the sound they make when being walked in. Although the use of these styles is not influenced by Hinduism, their origins were most assuredly from the Hindu toe-knob sandal.

North African and Middle Eastern nomads developed various inventive sole shapes to allow for better movement in desert terrains. The sub-Saharan Hausa used sandals with large soles that extend well beyond the foot, while curved soles were utilized in Uganda, and rolled toes were developed in Arabia. In more humid climates, sandals were preferred for their cool breathability. Ancient Aztecs and Mayans of Central America adopted a thick-soled sandal with a protective legging attached at the heel, while the top of the foot and shin remained exposed.

The Ancient Sandal

Western culture traces the origins of the sandal from ancient Egyptian tombs, the earliest evidence dating from around the period of unification, about 5,100 years ago. A frieze in the Cairo museum depicts the Pharaoh Narmer followed by his sandal bearer, suggesting the sandals were a symbol of the pharaoh's sovereignty. This is underscored by the ancient Egyptian practice of placing the Pharaoh's sandals upon his throne in his absence. Sandals were status-oriented for the elite, beginning with the pharaoh and working down the ranks of society throughout the Egyptian dynastic period, so that by the period of Roman occupation around 30 B.C.E. all but the very lowest of society were permitted to wear footwear.

However, it appears that the wearing of sandals still remained an occasional one, reserved mostly for outdoor wear, especially while traveling. The vast majority of ancient Egyptians never wore footwear. Most Egyptians with status never wore footwear inside the home and in fact it appears that the Pharaoh himself did not regularly wear footwear indoors until the late dynasties, about 3,000 years ago. It is also evident that in the presence of a higher-ranking individual or deity, removing one's sandals exhibited deference.

Sandals were often metaphors for the journey into the afterlife—either real (those worn by the deceased in life) or models made especially for the tomb. The earliest examples dating back more than 4,000 years are most often life-size models made of hard wooden soles, suggesting that in death the objects were symbolic or made available to those who did not wear footwear in life. Newer tombs, aged 2,000–2,500 years, reveal everyday footwear, including styles with coil-woven soles similar to modern *espadrilles*.

When Alexander the Great united the Greeks in the fourth century B.C.E., the resulting society was one of great wealth and leisure that developed the arts, sciences, and sports under a democratic system. The Greeks also developed many different types of sandals and other styles of footwear, giving names to the various styles. Fortunately the Greeks kept thorough records, thereby giving accurate descriptions and references to the various styles of footwear and what those names were. This is indeed fortuitous as archaeological examples of Greek footwear are nonexistent, and historians must work from these descriptions and from those styles portrayed in surviving artwork. There were strict rules as to who could wear what, when, and for what purpose.

Sandals used during the early Roman Empire were very similar to the Greek styles and even followed the same precedents set for restricted use according to the citizen's rank in society. Like the Greeks, the Romans named the various styles, and in fact, "sandal" comes from its Latin name *sandalium*.

As the Roman Empire grew to include all the kingdoms held by Greece and Egypt, the Romans then continued their forays into northern Europe. The *caliga*, a military sandal with a thick-layered leather and hobnail-studded sole was named from the Greek *kalikioi*. The young Caius Caesar was nicknamed Caligula after this style of sandals which he wore as a boy when he would dress up as a soldier to stay in military encampments. The *caliga* protected the feet of Roman centurions on the long marches into northern Europe. However, the northern European climate, with its mud and snow, made it necessary for Roman invaders to adopt a more enclosed shoe style, beginning the decline of the sandal in the classical period.

As the Empire's strength diminished after the second century C.E., so did the quality of manufacture of footwear. Statuary, as this is more plentiful than actual extant examples of Roman footwear shows simple V-straps utilized on sandals. These are far less complex than the strap arrangements in use when the Empire was expanding and at its greatest.

In the seventh century the Christian Roman Empire, based in Constantinople, decreed that bare toes were immodest in mixed company. The sandal all but disappeared for the next 1,300 years, remaining in constant use only in cloistered monastic orders.

Although gone, sandals were not forgotten. Artists portrayed sandal-wearing classical figures in biblically themed frescoes during the Renaissance, and sandals were worn by actors portraying historical figures in theatrical presentations.

The Fashion Sandal

After the 1789 Revolution, the new French republic looked to ancient Greece and Rome for inspiration; along with classically draped garments, the sandal made a brief return to the feet of fashionable women. By the 1810s, a closed-shoe style, resembling a ballerina's slipper with crisscrossed silk ankle ties, became fashionable, and although no toes were exposed and technically the style was not a true sandal, the long ties did suggest a classical association, and the shoes were commonly referred to in period literature as "sandal-slippers."

The Empress Eugénie is depicted wearing toe-baring sandals in a photograph taken in the 1850s, but this was not to be a successful attempt at re-introducing the sandal as a staple into the fashionable woman's wardrobe. Propriety kept men's and women's toes hidden even on the beach, where bathing sandals consisting of cork-soled cotton closed-toe shoes with crisscrossed laces, first adopted

in the 1860s. Similarly another classical revival in fashions brought about the sandal-boot for women. This was a closed-boot style, but cutouts in the shaft exposed the stocking-clad leg beneath. This style of boot first appeared in the late 1860s and remained fashionable into the early years of the twentieth century.

It was back at the beach in the early twentieth century where bathing sandals and boots gradually bared more of the ankle and instep. During the late 1920s, women donned beach pajamas for the poolside or at the beach. These loose-fitting pantsuits were paired with low-heeled sandals made of wide leather or cotton straps. It was a short jump from poolside to the dance floor in the early 1930s, where under long evening gowns, high-heeled leather and silk sandals permitted feet to remain air-conditioned for long nights of fox-trots and rumbas. By the late 1930s, the sandal was a fully reinstated necessity in a fashionable shoe wardrobe and included styles for all times of day.

World War II inadvertently aided in the re-establishment of the sandal as certain materials, such as leather, were rationed for civilian usage. Sandal straps require less leather in their production than an enclosed pump, and summer sandals made up of twisted and woven fibers and other nonrationed materials were available without coupons on both sides of the Atlantic.

By the 1950s, many European men were wearing sandals for casual wear but most North American men considered them too effete. Women's evening sandals in the 1950s used the barest of straps to give the illusion of no footwear at all, as if the wearer was walking on tiptoe. The vamp strap-sandal style, also known as an open-toe mule, created a similar illusion, although quick steps proved impossible without losing a shoe in the process. American shoe designer Beth Levine solved this issue with the addition of an elastic web running the length of the insole. This innovation was called a *spring-o-later*.

In the late 1960s hippie anti-fashion introduced the most basic sandal style to American streets. Dubbed "Jesus" sandals, these simple leather toe ring or V-strap sandals were imported from Mexico and Asia, or made up locally by fledgling street artisans. Gender neutral, this sandal embraced naturalism, comfort, and ethnic-inspired style. This paved the way for the introduction of "health" sandals into the fashionable wardrobe, such as Birkenstocks in the 1970s. Contoured insoles and minimal curtailing of the foot were touted as perfect aids to foot health and comfort.

While high-fashion sandals have remained a staple in women's wardrobes since the 1930s, men's sandals have never achieved a place beyond the beach and casual wear. However, boundaries have been crossed in recent years. Sport sandals, introduced in the 1990s, transcended the sandal into a foot covering suitable for a variety of sports activities by including a synthetic rubber-treaded sole. And the simplest of colored rubber flip-flop thongs, intended for basic seaside foot covering, has even made it into the pages of *Vogue* and other au courante fashion publications, gracing the feet of well-dressed models in clothes deemed suitable for a day of shopping on Fifth Avenue or the Champs Élysées.

See also **Boots; High Heels; Shoes; Shoes, Children's; Shoes, Men's; Shoes, Women's.**

BIBLIOGRAPHY

Bondi, Federico, and Giovanni Mariacher. *If the Shoe Fits.* Venice, Italy: Cavallino Venezia, 1983

Durian-Ress, Saskia. *Schuhe: vom späten Mittelalter bis zur Gegenwart Hirmer.* Munich: Verlag, 1991.

Ferragamo, Salvatore. *The Art of the Shoe, 1927–1960.* Florence, Italy: Centro Di, 1992.

Rexford, Nancy E. *Women's Shoes in America, 1795-1930.* Kent, Ohio: Kent State University Press, 2000.

Swann, June. *Shoes.* London: B.T. Batsford, Ltd., 1982.

———. *Shoemaking.* Shire Album 155. Jersey City, N.J.: Parkwest Publications, 1986.

Walford, Jonathan. *The Gentle Step.* Toronto: Bata Shoe Museum, 1994.

Jonathan Walford

SAPEURS The words *sape* (*Société des Ambianceurs et des Personnes Élégantes*) and *sapeurs* are neologisms that were coined by Congolese diasporic youth living in Western metropolises, especially Paris and Brussels, to authenticate and validate their quest for a new social identity through high fashion. The *sape*'s history, however, dates back to the first years of the colonial encounter in the Congolese capital cities of Kinshasa and Brazzaville.

As early as 1910, the *sape* was in full bloom in Brazzaville, as several observers complainingly noted. In 1913, French Baron Jehan De Witte demurred at what he thought was "overdressing" among the Brazzaville locals: "[...] on Sunday, those that have several pairs of pants, several cardigans, put these clothes on one layer over the other, to flaunt their wealth. Many pride themselves on following Parisian fashion ..." (p. 164). In an article arguing that colonial subjects encountered European modernity first through fashion, Phyllis Martin notes that in 1920s Brazzaville "men wore suits and used accessories such as canes, monocles, gloves, and pocketwatches on chains. They formed clubs around their interest in fashion, gathering to drink aperitifs and dance to Cuban and European music played on the phonograph" (p. 407). Most of these young people who prided themselves on being unremitting consumers and fervent connoisseurs of Parisian fashion were domestic servants, civil servants, and musicians. They spent their meager wages to order, through catalogs, the latest fashions from France.

The 1950s witnessed the creation of several associations of urban youth, whose main interests seemed to have revolved around sartorial display. Bars had sprouted in every corner of the Congolese twin capitals, owing to the emergence in the 1940s of Congolese popular rumba. These venues provided a natural platform for the youth.

Sapeurs in the early 2000s represent at least the third generation of Congolese dandyism. But what sets them apart from their colonial counterparts is their migratory trajectory to European cities and their social dereliction in countries that adopt discriminatory policies toward Third World immigrants. For these young people, the *sape* therefore becomes a refuge and a vehicle through which to forge new identities away from their chaotic homeland. Before the 1990s, *sapeurs* living in Paris or elsewhere in Europe were conferred this status only by returning to Kinshasa or Brazzaville during their summer vacation to flaunt their wardrobe. With the two countries in the throes of civil war, and given that many of these youth live in Europe without proper and lawful immigrant documents, they are more reticent to go back home and thus are redefining their relationship to their homeland. The *sape* thus allows them to avoid the dreadful connivance of Scylla (sojourn) and Charibdis (return). Although confined to the bottom rung of society, these young people are loyal customers of the most prestigious fashion designers of Paris and sport Cerruti or Kenzo suits that can cost as much as $1,000 apiece. This said, it would be erroneous to define the *sape* solely as a paradoxical fashion statement. *Sapeurs* justify some of their deviant (such as loud talking in public places), sometimes delinquent (cheating public transportation) attitudes by arguing that they are making the French and the Belgians pay for colonization (the colonial debt). *Sapeurs* from Congo-Kinshasa could be said to have reacted against Mobutusese Seko's longtime ban on Western suits (and ties) by adopting a more exuberant form of *sape*. On the other hand, those from Congo-Brazzaville, predominantly southern Balaris, have used the *sape* to oppose the northerners (in power since 1969), whom they accuse of squandering the country's wealth by building lavish mansions and buying expensive cars. Indeed, these political attitudes remain inseparable from the hedonistic quest for perfection through fashion and speak to the ways African youth are attempting to negotiate and shape the marginal situation they have been confined to within the global village.

See also **Africa, Sub-Saharan: History of Dress; Paris Fashion.**

BIBLIOGRAPHY

Bazenguissa, Rémy. "'Belles maisons' contre S.A.P.E.: Pratiques de valorisation symbolique au Congo." In *État et société dans le Tiers-Monde: de la modernisation à la démocratisation.* Edited by Maxime Haubert et al. Paris: Publications de la Sorbonne, 1992, pp. 247–255.

———, and Janet MacGaffey. "Vivre et briller à Paris. Des jeunes Congolais et Zaïrois en marge de la légalité économique," *Politique africaine* 57 (March 1995): 124–133.

———, and Janet MacGaffey. *Congo-Paris: Transnational Traders on the Margins of the Law.* Bloomington: Indiana University Press, 2000.

Friedman, Jonathan. "The Political Economy of Elegance: An African Cult of Beauty." *Culture and History* 7 (1990): 101–125.

Gandoulou, Justin-Daniel. *Entre Bacongo et Paris.* Paris: Centre Georges Pompidou, 1984.

———. *Dandies à Bacongo. Le culte de l'élégance dans la société congolaise contemporaine.* Paris: L'Harmattan, 1989.

Gondola, Ch. Didier. "Popular Music, Urban Society, and Changing Gender Relations in Kinshasa, Zaire." In *Gendered Encounters: Challenging Cultural Boundaries and Social Hierarchies in Africa.* Edited by Maria Grosz-Ngaté and Omari H. Kokole. London and New York: Routledge, 1996, pp. 65–84.

———. "La contestation politique des jeunes à Kinshasa à travers l'exemple du mouvement 'Kindoubill' (1950–1959)." *Brood und Rozen, Tijdschrift voor de Geschiedenis van Sociale Bewegingen* 2 (January1999): 171–183.

———. "Dream and Drama: The Search for Elegance among Congolese Youth." *African Studies Review* 42 (April 1999): 23–48.

———. "La sape des *mikilistes*: théâtre de l'artifice et représentation onirique." *Cahiers d'études africaines* 153, no. 39-1 (1999): 13–47.

———. "La Sape: Migration, Fashion, and Resistance among Congolese Youth in Paris." *Elimu. Newsletter of the University of California, San Diego African and African-American Studies Research Project* 4 (Summer/Fall 2000): 4, 12.

Phyllis, Martin. "Contesting Clothes in Colonial Brazzaville." *Journal of African History* 35 (1994): 401–426.

———. *Leisure and Society in Colonial Brazzaville.* Cambridge, New York: Cambridge University Press, 1995.

Thomas, Dominic. "Fashion Matters: La Sape and Vestimentary Codes in Transnational Contexts and Urban Diasporas." *Francophone Studies: New Landscapes, Modern Language Notes* 118 (September 2003): 947–973.

Witte, Baron Jehan de. *Les deux Congo.* Paris: Plon, 1913.

Ch. Didier Gondola

SARI The word "sari" has come into general use to cover a generic category, including any draped untailored textile of about five meters in length, worn by the women of South Asia. In common parlance outside the region, the term "sari" refers to an increasingly standardized form of drape. More urban and cosmopolitan women have adapted the Nivi style, but this drape is a relatively new phenomenon. In India alone, around a hundred other forms of drapes continue to be worn. These vary from the eight-yard Koli drape of fisherwomen in Maharashtra to the thrice-wrapped drape of Bengal.

There is a general belief that the sari as a draped and seamless garment is the contemporary representative of the traditional female attire of Hindu South Asia that became diluted by the introduction from the North of tailored and stitched garments under the influence of Islam. Historical and archaeological sources do not support this reading, however. Representations on statues, wall paintings, and other sources suggests that for as far back as there are records, women in the South Asia area wore a wide variety of regional styles that included both stitched and unstitched garments, tailored and untailored. Indeed in the twenty-first century, a sari is as likely to be associated with Muslim women in the Bengal region as Hindus in the South of India. Furthermore, the seamless piece of cloth of the sari is increasingly worn along with two stitched garments, a full-length underskirt tied at the waist with a drawstring, and a fitted waist-length blouse done up at the front. The sari itself covers little of the body that is not already hidden by these accompanying garments, although conceptually a woman would see herself as unclothed without the final addition. Most women also wear underwear to make a third layer of clothing.

In the latter half of the twentieth century, the emergence of the Nivi style of draping the sari may be attributed to middle-class women entering the public sphere during the struggle for independence. It was considered more suitable to public appearances and greater mobility. This style consists of the sari being wrapped around the lower body with about a meter of cloth pleated and tucked into the waist at the center and the remainder used to cover the bosom and then falls over the left shoulder. The loose end of the sari that hangs from the shoulder is known as the *pallu.* Younger and less confident women or those wearing the sari as a uniform (such as nurses, policewomen, or receptionists) usually pin the *pallu* to their shoulder in carefully arranged pleats. As a result of the development of this pan-Indian cosmopolitan drape of the sari, the influence of local regional traditions of draping has declined in urban spaces and has become either confined to being worn within the home or in rural areas. The Nivi style of wearing the sari was further popularized through its increased association with other pan-Indian phenomena, such as the film industry and national politicians. As a result this has become the style that is symbolic of India as a state and women's sense of themselves as Indian (although it may also be found more widely in South Asia, in Bangladesh and Nepal). As a result of this development, women in areas of India where the sari was not traditional garb adopted the sari for specific formal occasions such as weddings and important public events.

Saris can be made of natural or synthetic fibers, and can be woven on hand looms or power looms. Natural fibers such as silk and cotton, which are also more fragile, are worn mostly by middle- and upper-class women. They are named after the regions in which they are made such as Kanchipuram, Sambhalpur, or Kota. Each style is associated with particular weaves, motifs, and even colors. Some saris can be very ornate and may include real gold wash on silver thread (*zari*) in their embroidery (though most *zari* work in the early 2000s is nonmetal).

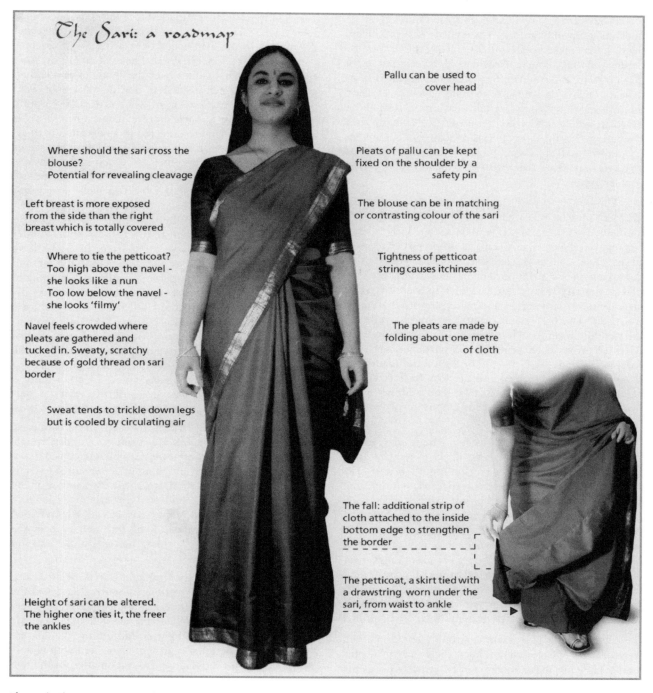

The sari. The sari is a versatile garment worn by women throughout South Asia. The *Nivi* style shown here is the most familiar to the rest of the world, but many other styles are in use. Courtesy of Dixie. Reproduced by permission.

Other varieties may include highly elaborate embroidery styles such as *chikan* work from Lucknow. These saris may cost hundreds of dollars and are often associated with the glamour attached to the Bollywood (the film industry based in India) and politicians such as Indira Gandhi who is famous for having chosen her wardrobe carefully to reflect aesthetic taste and populist appeal. Hand-loom saris are adopted by women not only for their traditional designs and beauty but also as a statement of support for the threatened cottage industry of weaving.

However, the vast majority of saris worn by working women in the early 2000s are made of synthetic materials.

While the yarn is largely spun in major mills, the large mills make up only around 4 percent of sari production (hand-looms make up around 9 percent); the rest are the product of a vast, largely unregulated, power-loom sector, that varies from a couple of machines in someone's home to factory units consisting of two hundred looms, to whom the mill sector subcontracts the weaving process. By far the main fashion influence in the early 2000s upon these synthetic saris is the rise of television soap operas and films. Typically a market or shop includes saris that have labels attached associating them with particular characters from popular culture.

The sari is not worn by young girls anywhere in India. Girls tend to wear what are locally called frocks. Traditionally, wearing the sari was associated with puberty, but many regions have specific clothing associated with adolescence, such as the half-sari or *salwaar-kameez*, and these have grown in importance as fewer girls are married at puberty. Many mothers of girls start to collect saris from an early age, building up toward a wedding trousseau. The high point of sari wearing is commonly the wedding itself, which is (given sufficient resources) a series of events each demanding a particular sari. The color of the sari worn by the bride for the main ceremony is strictly prescribed and can vary from red in the north and east to white in Kerala. The wedding is also the occasion for much sari gifting among relatives of the bride and groom.

The period immediately after the wedding is usually the time when women are most likely to wear a sari in exclusion to all other types of clothing. As a new bride she is expected to sport the most expensive, dazzling, and bright saris. Through her years as a married woman and mother, the bright colors of her sari are expected to reflect the fecundity of her life. With age, however, the widow or elderly woman is expected to wear mainly simple and less elaborate saris. There is a cosmological significance to this shift in which the fading of the sari stands for the gradual detachment from an interest in and engagement with material things in general and with the specificity of a particular person and their occupation.

The sari as a possession is strongly correlated with wealth. Most village women keep their saris in a small trunk. They may have only one or two working saris that they wear on a daily basis, with another two or three better-quality saris kept for special occasions, such as weddings or visits to town. Some have even less than this number and most village women obtain the bulk of their saris as gifts associated with particular occasions, such as festivals. Poorer women may hardly buy any saris themselves during their lives. By contrast, middle-class salaried women in the towns may possess two or three hundred saris, often kept in steel cupboards, which reflect a wide spectrum of colors and styles. Many of these may also be gifts and are associated with particular relationships and events.

A more intimate examination of the consequences of wearing the sari demonstrates that there may be profound differences in the experience of wearing a sari as compared to wearing western dress. The existence of the *pallu* as a loose-end that comes over the shoulder and is then available to be manipulated in a wide variety of ways means that the relationship of women to their clothing can often take on a much more dynamic form. For example, most women are expected to appear in a particularly modest, if not veiled, manner in relation to various contexts, such as the presence of certain male relatives. Covering one's head with the *pallu* is a common response. Urban women, who are not subject to such restrictions, may be seen using the *pallu* to constantly change their appearance, for example, by tucking it into the waist to express anger or allowing it to reveal the bosom in order to flirt. The *pallu* is also very important in establishing key relationships, such as those between mother and child. The *pallu* may be used as a cradle, as a support to the child in learning to walk, and as a kind of "transitional object" that helps the child to separate from the mother into an independent person. This ability to manipulate one's clothing during the day and not be constrained by choices made when getting dressed in the morning makes the sari more of a companion in playing out a number of different social roles. This flexibility is what makes the sari a perfect garment to inhabit the multiplicity of roles which modernity brings to women's lives.

In areas of India where the sari was ubiquitous, women of the early 2000s are turning to alternative attire, especially the *salwar-kameez*, which is considered a more informal garment and thought better suited to commuting and work. In rural areas, the association of the *salwar-kameez* with the educated girl has given it more progressive connotations and has led to an increased availability and acceptance of this garment even in the heartlands of sari-wearing areas, such as Tamil Nadu and West Bengal.

In summary, the significance of sari wearing as opposed to other available options in South Asia lies in the dynamism and ambiguity that is the defining characteristic of the garment. While this has left open a niche which is being increasingly colonized by the *salwar-kameez* as a "functional" garment associated with educational values and rationality, the combination of the two has in the early 2000s effectively prevented the adoption in South Asia of western dress, which is mainly worn by a small number of elite or by unmarried women.

See also **India: Clothing and Adornment; Textiles, South Asian.**

BIBLIOGRAPHY

Banerjee, Mukulika, and Daniel Miller. *The Sari.* Oxford: Berg, 2003.

Boulanger, Chantal. *Saris: An Illustrated Guide to the Indian Art of Draping.* New York: Shakti Press International, 1997.

Chishti, Rta Kapur, and Amba Sanyal. *Saris of India: Madhya Pradesh.* New Delhi: Wiley Eastern, 1989.

Ghurye, Govind Sadashiv. *Indian Costume.* Bombay: Popular Book Depot, 1951.

Lynton, Linda, and Sanjay K. Singh. *The Sari: Styles, Patterns, History, Techniques.* New York: Harry N. Abrams, 1995.

Mukulika Banerjee and Daniel Miller

SARONG The *sarong* is a wrapper sewn together into a tube. Both men and women in Indonesia and other parts of Southeast Asia wear it. In Indonesia the sarong is an item of everyday dress as well as an essential component of formalized ethnic dress. It is made in a variety of fabrics, including woven plaids, batik, warp ikats, songkets, or silk plaid and/or silk weft ikats. Hollywood's appropriation of the sarong has imbued it with exotic and erotic overtones and reinterpreted it as a wrapper rather than a tube. As a result, in the Western hemisphere the sarong has come to be defined in popular usage as a cloth wrapper, not as a tube.

The Southeast Asian sarong is typically made of mill-woven cloth and is about 100 centimeters high and up to 220 centimeters in circumference. The wearer steps into a sarong, secures it at the hip (or under the arms, a variant for women) either by lapping both ends to meet in the center or by pulling the sarong taut at one side of the body and lapping the remaining fabric to the front, and then rolling the top down and tucking it in or tying the ends in a knot. In this way, hip to ankle are covered.

As a multipurpose garment, the sarong is worn in other ways as well. For women it might be secured under the arms to sleep in or to walk to the river for a bath. Male laborers in T-shirts and shorts hike it at their hips or wear it over their shoulder like a sash when working, only to wear it about their legs on the return home. Enveloped about a person, the sarong serves as a blanket against cool nights.

Origin of the Sarong

The sarong was the dress of the seafaring peoples of the Malay Peninsula near Sumatra and Java; according to Gittinger, it was subsequently introduced on the island of Madura and along the north coast of Java. In the late nineteenth century, an observer recorded its absence in the Java interior. Early sea traders in these waters were Moslems from India, and Islam spread from the coastal areas, so it is thought that these early sarongs may have been woven plaids, which were associated with Moslem men.

What makes the cloth produced for sarongs unique is the decorative panel (*kepala*, head) that contrasts with the rest of the fabric (*badan*, body), seen at the front when lapped over and secured. In a plaid, this panel may vary in color and/or weave.

One of the earliest panel configurations in batik sarongs of the north coast of Java and Madura is two rows of triangles (*tumpal*) whose points face each other.

Traders brought chintzes from the Coromandel Coast of eastern India whose ends were rows of triangles. When sewn together, this created what is now the *kepala*, and eventually the two bands of triangles were positioned as a set at the end of the pre-sewn batik sarong. The *tumpal* motif is found on gold thread *songkets* of Sumatra and triangle end borders are seen in ikats, perhaps an influence from Indian chintzes.

In the clothing traditions of Java and adjacent western Indonesian islands, the sarong is an alternative to the *kain* (cloth wrapper). North coast batik sarongs are noted for their floral bouquet *kepala* and exuberant colors. At the turn of the twentieth century, Eurasian batik makers experimented with new chemical dyes and motifs, and the thigh-length jacket blouse (*kebaya*) worn with the sarong was shortened to hip length to better show off the *kepala* panel. The sarong is not as long as the *kain panjang* (long, cloth wrapper) batiks of court traditions of Yogyakarta and Surakarta in central Java. The *kain panjang* batiks are of an overall pattern, without a *kepala* panel; they are usually made with subdued colors such as browns, indigos, creams, and whites. When wrapped about the lower body, the end might be fan-folded in tight pleats, or with a loose drape.

The sarong varies in size and material. In all of Indonesia's twenty-six provinces, there are representative forms of ethnic dress in which sarongs, worn with a sleeved upper garment, figure prominently. In southern Sulawesi the Buginese silk sarong is extra wide. In Maluku sarongs are layered, the first one is long, and the second one is folded and worn at the hips, often revealing a *tumpal* motif. In Rote, the handwoven warp ikat sarong is narrow and tall; it is about twenty-five inches in circumference and would almost conceal the wearer's head. Here, the sarong is secured at the breasts and the excess folded over, and secured again at the waist with a belt. Another ikat (not a sarong) would be draped over the woman's shoulders. Generally speaking, the overall silhouette was tubular.

International Appropriation of Sarong

The sarong as appropriated by Hollywood bears little resemblance to the original. Hedy Lamarr in *White Cargo* (1942) and Dorothy Lamour in *Road to Bali* (1952) both wear wrappers (more like pareos), tied at the side in a way that emphasizes, rather than concealing, the curve of the hips. We know that what the actresses are wearing is a "sarong," because in *Road to Bali* Bob Hope specifically refers to Lamour's wrapper by that term. The draped, lapped frontal portion creates a diagonal line revealing the actress's entire leg. Both protagonists wear form-fitting tops baring midriff and shoulder, bangles, heavy necklaces and earrings. Lamarr and Lamour are seated in languorous poses to show off even more skin. The sarong here is a presentation of exotic femininity that is meant to titillate the western film audience. While *White Cargo* is set in Africa and *Road to Bali* is set in Indonesia on an unnamed island near Bali, the specifics of place and culture are immaterial. Tondelayo (Lamarr) and the Princess (Lamour) are not "natives," but rather a nebulous mixture of the Western and the "other." They conform to western ideals of beauty and allure, while the "ethnic" dress they wear is a fabrication of Hollywood costume designers, unrelated to anything attested in the anthropological record. What is depicted is the "East" as orientalized by the West.

According to Jones and Leshkowich, "Oriental" elements of clothing and decorative arts became part of the Western retail lifestyles markets in the 1990s at a time when Asian economic prowess was on the rise. The fashionable sarong as interpreted by Western fashion designers followed Hollywood's imagined version of the sarong as a knee- or thigh-length wrapper, tied at the side. Indonesian fashion designers, participating in self-orientalizing, also offered these Western-interpreted sarongs to cosmopolitan Indonesian women. Clearly, for these designers the sarong now referred to two kinds of dress, one local and one global, where the global one was an orientalizing of the local.

See also **Asia, Southeastern Islands and the Pacific: History of Dress; Ikat; Kain-kebaya.**

BIBLIOGRAPHY

Achjadi, Judi. *Pakaian Daerah Wanita Indonesia [Indonesian Women's Costumes]*. Jakarta, Indonesia: Djambatan, 1976.

Djumena, Nian S. *Batik dan Mitra [Batik and its Kind]*. Jakarta, Indonesia: Djambatan, 1990.

Elliot, Inger McCabe. *Batik: Fabled Cloth of Java*. New York: Clarkson N. Potter, Inc., 1984.

Gittinger, Mattiebelle. *Splendid Symbols: Textiles and Tradition in Indonesia*. Washington, D.C.: The Textile Museum, 1979.

Jones, Carla, and Ann Marie Leshkowich. "Introduction: Globalization of Asian Dress." In *Re-Orienting Fashion: The Globalization of Asian Dress*. Edited by Sandra Niessen, Ann Marie Leshkowich, and Carla Jones. Oxford: Berg Press, 2003.

Taylor, Jean G. "Costume and Gender in Colonial Java." In *Outward Appearances: Dressing State and Society in Indonesia*, edited by Henk Schulte Nordholt. Leiden: KITLV Press, 1997.

Heidi Boehlke

SATEEN. *See* **Weave, Satin.**

SAVILE ROW Savile Row is a typical central London street of fairly modest eighteenth- and nineteenth-century brick town houses mixed with late twentieth-century developments. It stretches from Vigo Street in the south to Conduit Street in the north, running parallel with Regent and New Bond Streets. Sitting at the heart of the city's West End luxury shopping district, the Row is particularly famous as the center of the British bespoke tailoring trade.

The Row traces its beginnings back to the late seventeenth century when Richard Boyle, the first Earl of Burlington, acquired a mansion on nearby Piccadilly (now Burlington House, home of the Royal Academy). Burlington protected the privacy of his estate by buying up the surrounding land, which was eventually developed by his descendant, the enlightened third Earl from the 1730s on. Savile Row was one of the resulting streets of genteel residences, which were generally rented by members of the nobility and affluent professionals who formed part of the new fashionable trend for living "in town" during the social season. The aristocratic atmosphere of the Row was an important component of its rise as a center of style. Its residents required expensive and well-made goods that befitted their rank, and thus attracted the attention of manufacturers and traders in luxury commodities. The high proportion of top-rank military and medical men living in the district also ensured that the provision of smart uniforms and civilian suits were prominent in this commercial expansion.

By the early nineteenth century, the Row had become synonymous with the London-based dandy craze, popularized by personalities such as Beau Brummel, and several ambitious tailors were establishing their reputations in nearby streets. Henry Creed and Meyer & Mortimer for example, were based in Conduit Street, with a rapidly expanding customer-base, thanks to the demand for uniforms initiated by the Napoleonic Wars. The first major incursion of tailoring into Savile Row itself was made by Henry Poole in the late 1840s. A few smaller tailors had opened workshops there in the 1820s, but Poole's were of a different order. They enjoyed the custom of high-profile clients, including royalty, statesmen, sporting stars, and literary and theatrical celebrities, and put unprecedented effort into the design of their showrooms and marketing ventures. Arguably it was Poole who established the international fame of the Row as a "Mecca" for men's fashion (though like most tailors he also fitted women with riding outfits and "tailor-mades").

Through the remainder of the Victorian age and into the twentieth-century, Savile Row shifted its character from that of a residential enclave to a thriving street of tailoring concerns. Distancing themselves from the sweated trades that were providing the mass-manufactured suits of the modern office worker, the tailors of the Row prided themselves on their mastery of traditional handcrafts, the quality of their textiles, and their attention to the individualized needs of their customers. Savile Row firms also came to be associated with a particularly English "look": restrained, narrow shouldered with a long waist; though each company pioneered a subtly differentiated version of the Savile Row staple. Huntsman, for example, was known for their heavy tweed sporting jackets while Gieves provided a sleek naval cut. By the mid-twentieth century, tailors such as Davies, Kilgour, and Anderson & Sheppard pioneered a more glamorous version of Savile Row style through their fitting-out of fashion leaders such as the

Duke of Windsor and Hollywood stars including Cary Grant and Fred Astaire. This greater attention to "fashion" was also marked by the presence of couturier Hardy Amies in the street from 1945. The Row had adapted following the decline of the British Empire from its role as Imperial outfitter to a new incarnation as the epitome of urbane sophistication.

The final decades of the twentieth century saw further flowerings of talent on Savile Row. Echoing the explosion of boutique culture on Carnaby Street and the King's Road in the 1960s, Tommy Nutter and Rupert Lycett Green of Blades introduced the Row to styles that were well suited to the culture of Swinging London, a phenomenon brought to the heart of the Row by the arrival of the Beatles's management company, Apple, at number 3 in 1968. And in the 1990s and 2000s, the association of the Row with "cool" was reinforced once more by the innovations of a new generation of tailor/retailers, including Ozwald Boateng, Richard James, and Spencer Hart who attracted a younger, less hide-bound clientele to their bright and airy emporia. Thus, it can be seen that Savile Row has been highly adaptable to the vagaries of styles in clothing and social trends, maintaining its reputation for traditional manufacturing methods while subtly embracing the challenges of novelty. It is still the premier street in the world for male fashion aficionados.

See also **Boutique; Dandyism; London Fashion; Tailoring.**

BIBLIOGRAPHY

Breward, Christopher. *The Hidden Consumer: Masculinities, Fashion and City Life 1860–1914.* Manchester, U.K.: Manchester University Press, 1999.

———. *Fashioning London: Clothing and the Modern Metropolis.* New York: Berg Publishers, 2004.

Chenoune, Farid. *A History of Men's Fashion.* Paris: Flammarion, 1992.

Walker, Richard. *The Savile Row: An Illustrated History.* New York: Rizzoli, 1989.

Christopher Breward

SCARF Scarves have been an enduring fashion accessory for hundreds of years, ranging from humble bandannas to luxurious silks. Worn by women around the neck or as a head cover, scarves protect modesty or promote attention. Using basic shapes of cloth, typically triangular, square, or rectangular, scarves lend themselves to a wide variety of ornamentation. Scarves are commonly printed, but the techniques of weaving, batik, painting, and embroidery are also used to create scarf designs. While the scarf's popularity has fluctuated throughout its history, in certain decades of the twentieth century scarves were essential fashion items, glamorized by dancers, movie stars, socialites, fashion illustrators, and photographers. Scarves accentuate an outfit, provide covering for the neck or head, and serve as a canvas for decorative patterns and designers' names.

In eighteenth-century Western fashions, bodices were cut revealingly low, requiring a piece of cloth, known as a fichu, to cover a woman's chest. Worn around the neck and crossed or tied at the bosom, fichus were either triangular or square in shape. Fichus were often made of white cotton or linen finely embroidered in whitework; others were of colored silks with rich embroidery. This style of scarf continued into the early nineteenth century, but as fashions shifted, chests were covered by bodices and large shawls predominated as accessories.

The scarf as a modern fashion accessory was defined in the early decades of the twentieth century. Flowing lengths of silk worn draped about the body had been made fashionable, in part, by dancers such as Isadora Duncan. That Duncan's death was caused by a long scarf wound around her neck becoming caught in the wheels of a Bugatti is one of the scarf's morbid associations. Throughout the 1920s and 1930s, the scarf was incorporated into the sleek, elongated fashions of these decades. As seen in numerous fashion illustrations and photographs of this period, the scarf served as both a sensuous wrap and a geometric design element.

In the course of the twentieth century, the scarf's viability as a blank canvas on which to present elaborate designs, advertising, humorous motifs, and artists' creations was used to advantage. The idea of printing scarves and handkerchiefs to commemorate heroes, political events, inventions, and other occasions began in the late eighteenth century and was popular throughout the nineteenth century. This use continued into the twentieth century, with scarves commemorating world's fairs, political campaigns, cities, tourist attractions, and numerous other themes. Fashion designers employed the signed scarf as a means to accessorize their clothing and promote their names. As licensing became an established part of the fashion industry, designers names on scarves became a lucrative sideline.

Various well-known firms and designers have contributed to producing chic and collectible scarves. Hermès began printing silk scarves with horse motifs in 1937; in the 1940s, the English textile firm of Ascher commissioned artists Henry Moore, Jean Cocteau, and others to create designs for scarves; during the heyday of scarf wearing in the 1950s, Americans Brooke Cadwallader and Vera and Tammis Keefe set the tone for decorative scarves with whimsical and playful motifs; and 1960s fashions were often accentuated with scarves by Emilio Pucci, Rudi Gernreich, and other designers of the period. While the wearing of scarves has diminished with the twenty-first century, the scarf remains a versatile accessory, its connotations ranging from the chic to the matronly depending on the scarf and the wearer's aplomb.

See also **Gernreich, Ruci; Pucci, Emilio.**

BIBLIOGRAPHY

Baseman, Andrew. *The Scarf.* New York: Stewart, Tabori and Chang, 1989.

Mackrell, Alice. *Shawls, Stoles and Scarves.* London: B. T. Batsford, Ltd., 1986.

Donna Ghelerter

SCARIFICATION Scarification, also known as cicatrisation, is a permanent body modification that transforms the texture and appearance of the surface of the skin (dermis). Although scarification operates as a controlled injury, it is not the result of an accident or health-related surgery. Branding, cutting, and some tattoo practices are types of scarification. In the practice of scarification the dermis and epidermis of the skin are cut, burned (see Branding), scratched, removed, or chemically altered according to the desired designs, symbols, or patterns. The result is a wound, which when healed creates raised scars or keloids that are formed on the skin's surface from increased amounts of collagen. Persons with darker skin tones have typically chosen scarification designs, because scars and keloids are more visible than tattoos.

Historic Scarification

The earliest evidence of scarification is the archaeological site at Ain Ghazal, in Jordan, where two headless figurines of Paleolithic (8000 B.C.E.) fertility goddess statues were found with thick scarification lines curving around the buttocks and abdomen. The Sahara rock painting (c. 7000 B.C.E.) at Tassili N'Ajjer at Tanzoumaitak, Algeria, also depicts scarification on the breasts, belly, thighs, shoulders, and calves of a Horned Goddess. Similar scarification designs as depicted on the figurines and paintings have been found on females from West and Central Africa.

The significance of the scarification process and resulting scars varies from culture to culture. Historically, scarification has been practiced in Africa, Australia, Papua New Guinea, South America, Central America, and North America. Among the cultural groups in these areas scarification has been used to emphasize the permanency of social and political roles; ritual and cultural values; rites of passage and age-grades; eroticizing the body; promoting sexual attraction and enhancing sexual pleasure; group and cultural identity; spiritual relationships; and aesthetic values. It has also been used as part of medicinal and healing rituals, as well as demonstrating the ability to endure pain. As a result of changing cultures and globalization, most of these scarification practices have been outlawed or banned by local governments.

Contemporary Scarification

In the twentieth and twenty-first centuries, Western microcultures, such as the modern primitives and punks, as well as fraternities and sororities, practice scarification. Scarification among these cultural groups varies in significance, such as group identity, personal identity, rite of passage, spiritual belief, and connection to tribal cultures. These microcultures utilize a variety of methods of scarification, such as cutting, packing, ink rubbings, skinning, abrasion, and chemical agents to acquire desired scarification patterns or designs.

Cutting. Cutting is a form of scarification that involves cutting the surface of the skin with a sharp instrument, such as a sharpened bone, small medical scalpel, or razor blade, called a scarifier. Contemporary cutting tools may be either single-piece disposable units or blades that can be mounted on an assortment of handles. Cuts are about one-sixteenth of an inch deep; deeper cuts increase the amount of scarring and the chances of complications, while shallow cuts may heal without scarring, negating the purpose of the modification.

Emphasizing scars. Maintaining an open wound by repeatedly re-cutting the healing skin will result in a more pronounced scar; it will also delay the healing process and may result in serious health-related complications. Packing also creates more pronounced scars by introducing inert substances, such as ashes or clay, into the open incisions or lifting cut areas of skin and allowing the scars to heal around or over it. While cicatrisation can refer to any scar, it is usually used in connection with more pronounced scars resulting from packing.

Ink rubbing is a cutting in which indelible tattoo ink or other pigment is rubbed into a fresh cut. The ink remains in the cut as it heals, resulting in a colored scar. Although the intensity varies from person to person, this method creates more visible scars for lighter skin tones.

Skinning. Skinning is a common method used to create large areas of scarification. An outline of the designated area to be scarred is cut. Then the scarifier or a lifting tool is placed under the surface of the skin to lift and remove it in manageable sections. An alternative skinning method, to increase the scarring, is to pack inert materials under the lifted skin and allow it to heal. The healing process is lengthy and complications may occur. This method creates large and more precise scarification areas.

Abrasion Scarification. Abrasion scarification is achieved by using friction to remove the dermis layers of skin to create scarring. Power tools equipped with sandpaper, steel wool, or grinding stones are a few of the instruments employed to create abrasion scarification. Abrasion scarification can also be achieved with manual pressure, but power tools expedite the process. This method creates subtle scars, unless excessive pressure is applied with the abrasion scarifier.

Chemical Scarification. Chemical scarification uses chemical compounds, such as liquid nitrogen, to damage and burn the skin, which results in scarring. Intricate designs are difficult to achieve with liquid chemical agents, otherwise the results are similar to other types of scarification. This method is relatively new and there is little research on it.

Scarification Risks. As with most permanent body modifications, scarification has been associated with aesthetic and health-related risks. The resulting appearances of the scars vary, because there are so many variables in the healing process. Scarification may take a year to completely heal, and longer if skinning or packing is involved. During the initial healing process diligent care is necessary in order to avoid infections.

Additional health-related risks include improper technique, such as cutting too deep, or acquiring bloodborne infections such as hepatitis B and C. Appropriate measures should be taken by scarification practitioners to assure the health and safety of their clients. Equipment and instruments that will be used for more than one client are sterilized in an autoclave, a high temperature steamer that kills blood-borne pathogens and bacterial agents. The area of skin to be scarred is disinfected and prepared by the scarification practitioner. During the scarification process, the skin is continually cleaned of excess blood and is disinfected.

See also **Body Piercing; Branding; Modern Primitives; Tattoos.**

BIBLIOGRAPHY

Beck, Peggy, Nia Francisco, and Anna Lee Walters, eds. *The Sacred: Ways of Knowledge, Sources of Life.* Tsaile, Ariz.: Navajo Community College Press, 1995.

Bohannon, Paul. "Beauty and Scarification among the Tiv." *Man* 51 (1956): 117–121.

Camphausen, Rufus C. *Return to the Tribal: A Celebration of Body Adornment.* Rochester, Vt.: Park Street Press, 1997.

Rubin, Arnold, ed. *Marks of Civilization: Artistic Transformation of the Human Body.* Los Angeles: Museum of Cultural History, University of California, 1988.

Vale, V. *Modern Primitives: An Investigation of Contemporary Adornment and Ritual.* San Francisco Re/Search Publications, 1989.

Theresa M. Winge

SCHIAPARELLI, ELSA The Italian-born Elsa Schiaparelli (1890–1973) was in many ways an outsider, yet one who successfully made her way to the heart of French haute couture in the interwar years, operating her business between 1927 and 1954. Born in Rome in 1890, the daughter of an orientalist scholar, she first left Italy in 1913. She traveled via Paris to London, where she married a theosophist named Wilhelm Went de Kerlor in 1914. During World War I, she and her husband moved in artistic and cosmopolitan circles between Europe and the United States. When Schiaparelli separated from her husband in the early 1920s, she returned to Paris with her young daughter. There she came to know Paul Poiret, who often loaned the impoverished young woman dresses to wear.

Early Career

With Poiret's encouragement, Schiaparelli began to design clothes and sell her designs on a freelance basis to small fashion houses. She briefly became the designer of a small house, Maison Lambal, in 1925 before setting up an atelier in her own name in 1927. Schiaparelli's first collection featured hand-knitted trompe l'oeil sweaters, including an extremely successful black-and-white "bow-knot" sweater that was illustrated in *Vogue* and immediately sold in the United States. Her subsequent collections extended beyond sweaters to include dresses and suits, swimsuits and beach pyjamas, ski costumes and sports jackets. In the early 1930s her "Mad Cap," a simple knitted hat with distinctive pointed ends that could be pulled into any shape, was a runaway success in the United States, where, like the "bow-know" sweater, it was widely copied by mass-market manufacturers. In 1928 she launched her first perfume, S.

In the late 1920s and early 1930s Schiaparelli was primarily a designer of sportswear whose geometric patterns and sleek lines were in keeping with the mood of the moment. Yet these early collections contained many hallmarks of her styles of the later 1930s: the innovative use of fabrics, often synthetic; striking color contrasts; such unusual fastenings as zippers; and such eccentric or amusing costume jewelry as a white porcelain "Aspirin" necklace designed by the writer Elsa Triolet.

Schiaparelli's designs proved popular with Parisians and New Yorkers alike. Despite the 1929 economic crash, which significantly depleted the fortunes of French haute couture, Schiaparelli was still able to work successfully with American manufacturers in the early 1930s, and to sell her models to exclusive importers like William H. Davidow and such stores as Saks Fifth Avenue in New York. Later she was to remark that the more outrageous her designs became, the better they sold to a conservative clientele. Despite Schiaparelli's reputation as an artistic designer, she was always commercially successful.

Throughout the 1930s the fashionable silhouette changed; from the early 1930s Schiaparelli developed the boxy padded shoulders that were to characterize her mature style. Notable designs from 1934 included a "tree-bark" dress—actually crinkled rayon—and a "glass" evening cape made from a new synthetic material called Rhodophane. Schiaparelli benefited from significant developments in textiles in the 1930s, but she was never purely technologically driven. Rather, her work was galvanized by the themes of masquerade, artifice, and play—themes that related closely to the changing status of women in the interwar years, as well as to the avant-garde discourse of the surrealist artists and their circles, some of whom she worked with in the 1930s.

The Later 1930s

Schiaparelli moved her boutique to the Place Vendôme in 1935, commissioning Jean-Michel Franck to decorate

Elsa Schiaparelli. One of the top designers of the 1920s through the 1940s, Elsa Schiaparelli is known for both her playful and elaborate fashions and her success in the marketplace. AP/WIDE WORLD PHOTOS. REPRODUCED BY PERMISSION.

her new premises. Their ever-changing décor incorporated, at various times, a stuffed bear that the artist Salvador Dalí had dyed shocking pink and fitted with drawers in its stomach, a life-size dummy of Mae West, and a gilded bamboo birdcage for the perfume boutique. In 1935 Schiaparelli inaugurated themed collections, starting with Stop, Look and Listen for summer 1935. "Schiaparelli collection enough to cause crisis in vocabulary," read a contemporary review of Stop, Look and Listen (Schiaparelli, p. 87). Following the Music Collection of 1937, Schiaparelli surpassed herself in 1938 and showed four collections in a single year: the Circus Collection for summer 1938, the Pagan Collection for autumn 1938, the Zodiac or Lucky Stars Collection for winter 1938–1939, and the Commedia dell'Arte Collection or A Modern Comedy for spring 1939. Her presentations were more like shows or plays than the conventional mannequin parade. Incorporating stunts, tricks, jokes, music, and light effects, they were dramatic

and lively, and entry to them was as much sought after as tickets to a new play.

In 1937 Schiaparelli launched the color of vivid pink that she named "shocking," alongside her perfume Shocking!, packaged in a bottle designed by the artist Leonor Fini and based on the shape of Mae West's torso. The same year saw the designer's Shoe Hat ensemble, a black suit with pockets embroidered with lips and an inverted high-heeled shoe for a hat. The hat came in two versions, one that was all black, and the other, black with a shocking pink heel. The 1938 Circus collection featured a black evening dress with a padded skeleton stitched on it, boleros heavily embroidered with circus themes, and an inkwell-shaped hat whose feather resembled a quill pen. The 1938 Zodiac collection featured more highly encrusted embroidery such as the mirror suit, in which inverted baroque mirrors were embroidered on the front panels of the jacket and incorporated pieces of real mirrored glass. Schiaparelli encouraged the embroidery firm Maison Lesage to revive techniques from both medieval ecclesiastical vestments and eighteenth-century military uniforms. The result was a series of highly wrought evening jackets and accessories in which the decoration of the garment became a carapace or form of female armor.

While Schiaparelli was clearly established commercially as a fashion designer, she also retained many links, both personal and professional, with surrealist artists. In New York during World War I she knew Francis Picabia and his then wife Gabrielle, who introduced her to the artistic photographer Man Ray and the painter/sculptor Marcel Duchamp. Schiaparelli was photographed by Man Ray in the early 1920s and then again in 1930. Man Ray regularly took photographs for fashion magazines, including *Vogue* and *Harper's Bazaar*; some of these photographs also appeared in the surrealist magazine *Minotaure*, which was published between 1933 and 1939. An essay of 1933 by the surrealist writer Tristan Tzara was illustrated by Man Ray's photographs of Schiaparelli's hats. She in turn employed many surrealist artists to design accessories for her. The writer Elsa Triolet made jewelry for Schiapiarelli and other couturiers, with her husband Louis Aragon acting as the salesman. Alberto Giacometti made brooches for Schiaparelli, while Meret Oppenheim produced fur-lined metal bracelets. Christian Bérard illustrated Schiaparelli's designs and many of the program covers for her openings or fashion shows. In 1937 the designer used drawings done for her by the artist Jean Cocteau as trompe l'oeil embroidery on two evening garments, a blue silk coat and a grey linen jacket.

Schiaparelli's collaboration with Salvador Dalí, however, which began in 1936, produced a series of the most striking designs: chest of drawer suits (with horizontal pockets that looked like drawers and buttons that resembled drawer handles) from 1936, an evening dress with lobster print and a shoe hat and suit from 1937, and an evening dress with a tear design from 1938.

Apart from these accredited collaborations Schiaparelli produced many surrealist designs of her own from the start of her career, some clearly in homage to her contemporaries, others apparently her own inspiration: black suede gloves appliquéd with red snakeskin fingernails inspired by Man Ray; a telephone-shaped handbag inspired by Dalí and a brain-shaped hat made of corrugated pink velvet; buttons in the shape of peanuts, padlocks, and paper clips; multicolored wigs coordinated with gowns; and the first fabric designed to mimic newsprint, printed with Schiaparelli's own reviews in several languages. Meanwhile, Schiaparelli maintained her contacts with fashion-related industries in both the United States and Britain, collaborating with textile and accessory designers on specific ranges as well as selling model gowns through exclusive importers. She also worked in both theater and the cinema as a costume designer, most notably dressing Mae West for the film *Every Day's a Holiday* (1937).

Throughout the 1930s Schiaparelli continued to travel, many times to the United States, and once in 1935 to a trade fair in the Soviet Union. Although based in Paris, she had opened a branch of her salon in London in 1933. Schiaparelli's international clientele included Lady Mendl, Wallis Simpson, and various titled Englishwomen; she frequently designed costumes for such elaborate costume balls of the decade as the honorable Mrs. Reginald Fellowes's Oriental Ball in 1935 and Lady Mendl's Circus Ball of 1938. The chic and distinctive Daisy Fellowes was Schiaparelli's unofficial mannequin; the designer dressed her for free and she in turn attracted international publicity in newspapers and magazines as one of the few women who wore Schiaparelli's more outré designs. If Daisy Fellowes personified the Schiaparelli look, the American Bettina Bergery, née Jones, personified the designer's spirit. Equally elegant and rakish in her own person, Bergery was the editor of French *Vogue* between 1935 and 1940 as well as Schiaparelli's assistant, responsible in the late 1930s for the witty and iconoclastic window displays in Schiaparelli's salon on the Place Vendôme.

The 1940s and 1950s

Schiaparelli, who had taken French citizenship in 1931, set out on an American lecture tour after the Germans occupied Paris in 1940. She chose to return to the occupied city in January 1941, but within a short period was forced to leave again for New York, where she spent the remainder of the war. Schiaparelli's Paris house remained open throughout the war and produced collections, although they were not designed by Schiaparelli herself. Her early wartime designs, made before she departed for the United States, often used military themes but in a playful way, such as a one-piece "air-raid shelter" trouser suit. She also pioneered many innovative pocket designs in her Cash and Carry collection for spring 1940. She returned to Paris immediately after the end of the occupation in 1945 and resumed designing, picking up where

she had left off in 1940, but focusing more on unusual cuttings and draping. Schiaparelli's designs from this period included a hat like a bird's nest with nesting birds; illusion bustle dresses; and inverted necklines that rose to cover the cleavage but dipped to reveal the breasts.

Throughout the late 1940s and early 1950s Schiaparelli continued to make merchandising and licensing deals with several American companies, but in terms of innovative design Cristóbal Balenciaga and Christian Dior took the lead in the 1950s. Dior's New Look of 1947 ushered in a new era in fashion. Schiaparelli's fortunes declined gradually after that; in 1954, the same year that Coco Chanel returned to Paris couture, Schiaparelli's Paris salon filed for bankruptcy. Thereafter the designer spent much of her time in Tunisia, where she had bought a house in 1950. Her autobiography, *Shocking Life*, was published in 1954. Schiaparelli died in Paris in 1973 at the age of 83, survived by her daughter Gogo and her granddaughters, the actresses Marisa Berenson and Berinthia ("Berry") Berenson Perkins.

Schiaparelli's fashion legacy was a vast body of endlessly inventive and original designs. She made elaborate visual jokes in garments that layered images deceptively on the body, to explore the themes of illusion, artifice, and masquerade. One of her couture clients, Nadia Georges Port, recalled: "For us 'Schiap' was much more than a natter of mere dresses: through clothes she expressed a defiance of aesthetic conventions in a period when couture was in danger of losing itself in anemic subtitles" (Musée de la mode, p. 125). Less well known, however, is the fact that, despite her apparently avante garde designs, she always maintained successful business relationships with American middle market manufacturers. In this respect she is a paradigm of the modern designer, marrying a fertile imagination and dramatic showmanship to a pragmatic and commercial base.

See also **Art and Fashion; Cardin, Pierre; Fashion Designer; Givenchy, Hubert de; Paris Fashion; Poiret, Paul; Vogue; Windsor, Duke and Duchess of.**

BIBLIOGRAPHY

Ballard, Bettina. *In My Fashion.* New York: David McKay and Co., Inc., 1960.

Blum, Dilys E. *Shocking! The Art and Fashion of Elsa Schiaparelli.* Philadelphia, New Haven, Conn., and London: Philadelphia Museum of Art in association with Yale University Press, 2003.

Evans, Caroline. "Masks, Mirrors and Mannequins: Elsa Schiaparelli and the Decentered Subject." *Fashion Theory* 3 (1999): 3–32.

Musée de la mode et du costume, Palais Galliera. *Hommage à Elsa Schiaparelli: exposition organisée au Pavillon des arts... Paris, 21 juin–30 août 1984.* Paris: Ville de Paris, Musée de la mode et du costume, 1984.

Schiaparelli, Elsa. *Shocking Life.* New York: E. P. Dutton and Co., 1954.

White, Palmer. *Elsa Schiaparelli: Empress of Paris Fashion.* London: Aurum Press, 1986.

———. *Haute Couture Embroidery: The Art of Lesage.* Paris: Vendôme Press, 1988; and Berkeley, Calif.: Lacis Publications, 1994.

Caroline Evans

SCOTCHGUARD. *See* **Performance Finishes.**

SCOTTISH DRESS The most renowned form of Scottish dress is Highland dress, which is internationally recognized as a symbol of Scottish identity. The predominant feature of the Scottish contribution to western fashionable dress is that of distinctive fashion textiles that have international appeal once made up into garments.

Portrait of Lord Mungo Murray (1668–1700) of Scotland. The combination of a long shirt, trews, and a plaid kilt is an example of the most renowned form of Scottish fashion, known as Highland dress. © SCOTTISH NATIONAL PORTRAIT GALLERY. REPRODUCED BY PERMISSION.

Highland Dress

Highland dress has been worn, interpreted, and mythologized in many different ways and its history is therefore fascinating and complex. From the early nineteenth century, Highland dress began to be seen as synonymous with Scotland as a whole. However, its origins relate to the specific culture that existed in the northerly Highland region of Scotland up until the late eighteenth century. Dress in the Highlands was initially closely linked to Irish Gaelic culture, consequently men's dress included long "saffron" shirts, trews (leg-coverings between trousers and stockings), and brown or multicolored mantles (a type of simple-shaped cloak). By 1600 men's dress had evolved to fit the following description:

> the habite of the Highland men … is stockings (which they call short hose) made of a warm stuff of divers colours, which they call tartane…a jerkin of the same stuff that their hose is of … with a plaid about their shoulders, which is a mantle of divers colours (Cheape: 15).

The plaid or *breacan* was worn by all sections of Highland society and by both genders. It was a versatile garment, comprising an untailored piece of cloth, usually tartan, that was draped around the body in various ways. Men commonly wore it as the *breacan an fheilidh* or belted plaid, where it was gathered in folds around the waist to form a short-skirted shape, and the remainder was draped over the shoulder and fastened with a brooch. The belted plaid formed the basis of the tailored *feileadh beag*, in English phillabeg or little kilt, which is the form the kilt takes in the early 2000s. This adaptation was initiated by the English industrialist Thomas Rawlinson between 1727 and 1734, when he found that workmen at his Invergarry furnace needed a more practical form of dress than the unwieldy belted plaid.

The defeat of the Jacobite army at the battle of Culloden in 1745 was followed by the Disarming Acts of 1746, which involved the proscription of all forms of Highland dress until 1782. The kilt survived this period largely owing to the British establishment's adoption of Highland dress as the uniform of its Highland regiments. The militarization of Highland dress was to play an important role in shaping the visual imagery of the British Empire. It also informed the design of the fanciful version of Highland dress worn by George IV on a state visit to Edinburgh in 1822. This period also involved the creation of popular, romanticized interpretations of Scotland's history by several authors, including Sir Walter Scott. From the 1840s Queen Victoria's passion for the Highlands was to further promote the fashionability of Highland dress. Victorian interpretations of it were often outlandish; however, this period also saw the establishment of the key elements of the style as it is worn in the early twenty-first century, namely, the combination of neatly pleated kilt, decorative sporran, knee-length hose with *sgian dubh* (black knife), tweed or other short tailored jacket, and sturdy brogue shoes.

Queen Victoria promoted the fashionability of Highland dress in her instructions to Edwin Landseer concerning the painting *Royal Sports on Hill and Loch,* 1874. "It is to be thus: I, stepping out of the boat at Loch Muich, Albert in his Highland dress, assisting me out. Bertie is on the deer pony with McDonald … standing behind, with rifles and plaids on his shoulder. In the water … are several of the men in their kilts." (Ormond, pp. 159–160)

Scottish Textiles as Fashion Garments

Tweed was transformed from a locally crafted product into a fashion textile sold to international markets by Scottish woolen manufacturers of the 1820s. Since that time tweed has played an important role in defining various clothing styles, from the Chanel suit, to men's sports jackets of the 1950s. The prominent Scottish tweed manufacturer J. & J. Crombie of Grandholm, founded in 1805, soon became renowned for their quality Elysian overcoatings, which subsequently led to the development of the Crombie coat style.

The distinctive design of the Paisley shawl originated in India in the fifteenth century. However, the garment derives its name from a town on the west coast of Scotland, which from about 1805 to the 1870s built a highly successful trade on the weaving of Paisley shawls.

Knitwear

Scottish knitwear patterns and yarns, derived from remote rural communities such as Fair Isle and Shetland, are well known internationally. In addition, companies such as Pringle, Johnstons of Elgin, and Ballantynes Cashmere, who sell to the international luxury knitwear market, design and make their products in Scotland. In the 1930s a designer who worked for Pringle, Otto Weisz, introduced the twinset style, which became hugely popular with Hollywood starlets and the wider market.

Scotland and the Fashion Industry

Scottish clothing manufacturers, designers, and retailers tend to be of international significance only when they are linked to the knitwear or textile industry. Notable exceptions to this include the retailer John Stephen, who initiated the Carnaby Street boutique phenomenon of the 1960s, and the designers Bill Gibb, Alastair Blair, Pam Hogg, and Jean Muir. In the twenty-first century anonymous Scottish-based knitwear and textile designers continue to make an important contribution to international fashion, supplying international brands such as Prada, Dolce & Gabbana, and Ralph Lauren. Many twentieth-century fashion designers have referenced Scottish dress

in some form in their collections. However, it is notable that it tends to be the more iconoclastic designers such as Vivienne Westwood, Jean-Paul Gaultier, John Galliano, and Alexander McQueen who repeatedly return to the use of either distinctively Scottish textiles, or the paraphernalia of Highland dress in their work. This demonstrates that despite the capacity of Highland dress and Scottish fashion textiles to encapsulate "authentic" reassuring connotations of history, they have also been endlessly reinvented to suit the changing character of fashion and popular notions of Scottish identity.

See also **Kilt; Paisley; Plaid; Shawls; Tartan; Tweed; Uniforms, Military.**

BIBLIOGRAPHY

Allan, John. *Crombies of Grandholm and Cothal 1805–1960: Records of an Aberdeenshire Enterprise.* Aberdeen: The Central Press, 1960.

Cheape, Hugh. *Tartan the Highland Habit.* Edinburgh: National Museums of Scotland, 1995.

Dunbar, John Telfer. *The Costume of Scotland.* London: B.T. Batsford, Ltd., 1981.

Gulvin, Clifford. *The Tweedmakers: A History of the Scottish Fancy Woollen Industry 1600–1914.* New York: Newton Abbott, David and Charles, 1973.

Haye, Amy de la. *The Cutting Edge: 50 Years of British Fashion 1947–1997.* London: V & A Publications, 1996.

Lochrie, Maureen. "The Paisley Shawl Industry." In *Scottish Textile History.* Edited by John Butt and Kenneth Ponting. Aberdeen, Scotland: Aberdeen University Press, 1987.

Ormond, Richard. *Sir Edwin Landseer.* London: Thames and Hudson, Inc. New York: Rizzoli International, 1981.

Trevor-Roper, Hugh. "The Invention of Tradition: The Highland Tradition of Scotland." In *The Invention of Tradition.* Edited by Eric Hobsbawn and Terence Ranger. Cambridge, U.K., and New York: Cambridge University Press, 1983.

Fiona Anderson

SEAMSTRESSES Seamstresses formed the main labor force, outside tailoring, which fueled the expansion of clothing production and related trades from the seventeenth century onward. This expansion was not dependent initially on technological developments or the introduction of a factory system, but on the pool of women workers. Their expendability and cheapness to their employers was effectively guaranteed by the sheer number of available women able and willing to use a needle, their general lack of alternative employment, and by the fact they then worked outside the control of guilds and latterly have been under-unionized. These seamstresses sewed goods for the increasing market for ready-made basic clothes such as shirts, breeches, waistcoats, shifts, and petticoats for working people, or slops as they were known (after the practice of sailors who stored their

"THE SONG OF THE SHIRT" BY THOMAS HOOD

With fingers weary and worn,
With eyelids heavy and red,
A Woman sat in unwomanly rags.
Plying her needle and thread—
Stitch! Stitch! Stitch!
In poverty, hunger, and dirt,
And still with a voice of dolorous pitch
Would that its tone could reach the Rich! —
She sang this 'Song of the shirt!'

Thomas Hood, "The Song of the Shirt," *Punch*, Christmas 1843. (Flint, p.105)

working clothes in slop chests). Their history is largely anonymous. However, social and economic historians with an interest in gender are now extending the knowledge of seamstresses' central role in the historical growth of clothing production and consumption.

At the cheaper end of the trade, the work of seamstresses did not involve complex cutting, fitting, or designing, though there were no hard and fast rules. "Seamstress" has always been a flexible term, with the work involved dependent on local conditions and the agency of individuals. Some elaboration and finishing was involved, such as tucking or buttonholes. While work done in this style continued, seamstresses were generally distinguished from dressmakers, milliners, mantua-makers, stay-makers, embroiderers, and tailoresses by their lower levels of craft and skill, but at the top-end of the market fine sewing was valued. Their existence was precarious and exacerbated by layoffs due to seasonal demand and unpredictable changes of fashion. In the Victorian period, widespread demand for mourning clothes, short notice given for elaborate evening dresses, and fickle customers were commonly cited as causes of distress through overwork.

"Riding an omnibus through … [London's commercial districts] at the turn of the century, one could hardly avoid noticing gaunt and harried women and children scurrying through the streets … carrying heavy bundles … passing along from workroom to workroom the shirts, suits, blouses, ties and shoes that soon would dress much of the world." (Schmiechen, p. 1)

There were large numbers of seamstresses in a wide range of situations. They frequently worked as outworkers, on per-piece pay, in small workshops or in their homes. Having learned their trade in waged work, many seamstresses continued to use their skills after marriage by taking in work, often making simple garments or restyling old ones in their own poor communities where they played an important role in the provision of cheap clothing outside the regular retail trade. Some seamstresses were employed in a temporary but regular visiting capacity in wealthier households where they supplemented existing domestic staff and worked by arrangement through an accumulation of sewing and mending tasks, in exchange for a day rate of pay and meals. This practice lingered until World War II in some areas of Britain.

The widespread use of the sewing machine from the 1860s increased the pace of production of clothing because it could stitch up to thirty times faster than a hand sewer, but it did not immediately result in centralized factories becoming the dominant means of production. Clothing production remained characterized by many small-scale businesses, often subcontracting work, and by the subdivision of the various tasks involved in the making of a garment, using many outworkers and home workers. This drove down prices and wages and produced the sweatshop system in which many seamstresses worked very long hours for low wages. Despite well-meant attempts to reform the trade, pay and conditions remained bad throughout the nineteenth century and well into the twentieth. It was said that a practiced observer could identify a seamstress in the street because of her stooped carriage. Seamstresses in outworking were vulnerable to employers who could withhold or delay payment if work was deemed substandard. It was common practice for seamstresses in this kind of work to have to pay for their own thread, needles, and candles, in addition to their heating and costs of collecting and returning the work. "My usual time of work is from five in the morning till nine at night—winter and summer…. But when there is a press of business, I work earlier and later…. I clears about 2s 6d a week…. I know it's so little I can't get a rag to my back" (London shirt maker talking to Henry Mayhew in 1849, cited in Yeo, p. 145). Despite enormous disadvantages, it was seamstresses who staged the first all-female strike in America, in New York in 1825. Apprenticeship provided one means, however, unreliable and open to abuse, for women to learn the better end of the trade. Some women found that the clothing trade presented opportunities for them to trade effectively as seamstresses on their own account or to work as middle women, putting out work. Health and safety legislation, greater unionization, and factory production have combined to improve the lot of women working in the late twentieth and early twenty-first centuries in the clothing trades; nevertheless, globally, it remains a fragmented industry with widespread homework and low wages.

Popular Debates and Imagery

Prints and paintings, often sympathetic if moralistic, frequently showed individual women bent over their sewing, in shabby interiors, sewing either to support themselves or their families. Middle-class women, fallen on hard times, were also depicted eking out a living in this way, a particular anxiety in Victorian Britain. Allegations of immorality, including prostitution, were frequently made, based on perceptions of the effects of poverty or, in better-class workrooms, the supposed temptations caused by familiarity of young seamstresses with fashion and luxury beyond their means. In Britain in 1843, Thomas Hood's poem *The Song of the Shirt* dramatized their plight and helped focus attention on potential reforms to wages and conditions, mostly without long-term effect. In 1853 Elizabeth Gaskell's novel *Ruth* expanded on the theme of exploitation of seamstresses and the suffering caused by extravagant demands of selfish or ignorant customers; the subject was treated in the United States in Charles Burdett's 1850 *The Elliott Family or the Trial of New York Seamstresses*.

See also **Sewing Machine; Sweatshops; Textile Workers.**

BIBLIOGRAPHY

Coffin, Judith. *The Politics of Women's Work: The Paris Garment Trades 1750–1915.* Princeton, N.J.: Princeton University Press, 1996.

Flint, Joy. *Thomas Hood: Selected Poems.* Manchester, U.K.: Carcanet, 1992.

Gamber, Wendy. *The Female Economy: The Millinery and Dressmaking Trades, 1860–1930.* Urbana: University of Illinois Press, 1997.

Green, Nancy. *Ready-to-Wear and Ready-to-Work: A Century of Industry and Immigrants in Paris and New York.* Durham, N.C.: Duke University Press, 1997.

Jenson, Joan M., and Davidson, Sue, eds. *A Needle, a Bobbin, a Strike: Women Needleworkers in America.* Philadelphia: Temple University Press, 1984.

Lemire, Beverly. *Dress, Culture and Commerce: The English Clothing Trade before the Factory, 1660–1800.* New York: St. Martin's Press, 1997.

Schmiechen, James A. *Sweated Industries and Sweated Labour: The London Clothing Trades 1860–1914.* Urbana: University of Illinois Press, 1984.

Stansell, Christine. *City of Women: Sex and Class in New York 1789–1860.* Urbana: University of Illinois Press, 1987.

Stewart, Margaret, and Hunter, Leslie. *The Needle Is Threaded: The History of an Industry.* London: Heinemann/Newman Neame, 1964.

Yeo, Eileen, and E. P. Thompson. *The Unknown Mayhew.* New York: Pantheon Books, 1971.

Walkley, Christina. *The Ghost in the Looking Glass: The Victorian Seamstress.* London: Peter Owen, 1981.

Barbara Burman

SECONDHAND CLOTHES, ANTHROPOLOGY OF

Well into the nineteenth century, secondhand garments constituted the clothing market for much of the population in Europe and North America except the very rich. In the post–World War II economic growth era, affordable mass-produced garments, broader income distribution, and growing purchasing power reduced the need for large segments of the population to purchase used clothing, although people with small means still frequent secondhand clothing stores. Throughout the West in the early 2000s, secondhand clothing by and large makes up fringe or niche markets for the purchase of retro, vintage, or special garments, while in many developing countries, secondhand clothing imported from the West is an important clothing source.

Secondhand clothing consumption is often described as consisting of two distinct worlds: one is the world of fashion and the other the world of thrift. These divisions are then mapped onto distinctions between industrialized and the developing nations, hiding the attraction of secondhand clothes to rich and poor dress-conscious consumers alike, regardless of their location.

Charitable organizations are the largest single source of the garments that fuel the international trade in secondhand clothing. Because consumers in the West donate much more clothing than the charitable organizations can possibly sell in their thrift stores, the charitable organizations resell their massive overstock at bulk prices to secondhand clothing dealers. These dealers are the textile recyclers/graders who sort, grade, and compress used clothes into bales for export. The United States is the world's largest exporter, and Africa the largest importing region in an international trade that has grown rapidly since the late 1980s. There are several Asian and Middle Eastern countries among the large importers of secondhand clothing. Sizeable imports go not only to developing countries but also to eastern Europe and Japan. Some countries restrict or ban the commercial import of secondhand clothes in efforts to protect domestic textile and garment industries.

The charitable connection attached to secondhand clothes vanishes at the point of resale when used garments enter the wardrobes of their new wearers to begin another stage of their lives. Past and present, the trade and consumption of secondhand clothing not only enabled its participants to support livelihoods but also to experience well-being and construct identities in a changing world. In the contemporary West, this process often involves the incorporation of accessories and specific garments into distinct dress styles. Secondhand clothes got a new cachet when shoppers for vintage couturier styles began turning to upscale used clothing stores that sell garments on consignment from the rich and famous. As vintage has become fashion, buyers for Urban Outfitters stores source clothes directly from secondhand dealers, then chop them up into raw materials that are redyed,

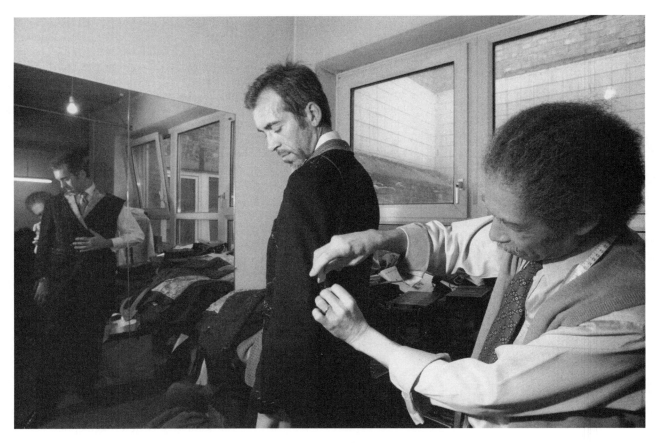

Secondhand suit. A man has a secondhand suit adjusted at a tailor shop in 1998. © Simonpetri Christian/Corbis Sygma. Reproduced by permission.

resewn, and resold as new garments. Buying secondhand clothes is an important choice for the young and trendy.

In twenty-first-century Germany, the 1960s style scene of movies, music, and material culture is popular with young people who dress in garments from the 1960s or in self-made clothes constructed from old patterns. This retro style attributes history and authenticity to garments that wearers experience as unique and personal.

Dress practices arising around the consumption of imported secondhand clothing in developing countries have frequently been noted in passing only to be dismissed offhandedly as faded and poor imitations of the West's fashions. Many economists would be inclined to view the growth of the secondhand clothing market in developing countries as a response to economic decline. Such accounts miss the opportunities this vast import offers consumers to construe themselves through dress.

In Zambia, a country in the southern part of Africa, consumers from all income levels turned eagerly to the secondhand clothing markets when import restrictions were lifted in the 1980s. Shipped for export by dealers in North America and Europe, containers loaded with bales of secondhand clothes arrive at ports in South Africa,

Mozambique, and Tanzania, reaching the warehouses of wholesalers in Zambia by truck. The market soon reached remote villages, enabling residents not only to clothe their bodies but also to present themselves with style. The attraction of secondhand clothes to dress-conscious Zambians goes far beyond the price factor and the good quality for the money that many of these garments offer. Finding the uniqueness they miss in much store-bought clothing, consumers turn to secondhand clothing markets for garments that are not common. The abundance and variety of secondhand clothing allows consumers to make their individual mark on the culturally accepted dress profile. Far from emulating the West's fashions, secondhand clothing practices implicate clothing-conscious consumers in efforts to change their lives for the better.

In Ifugao, the translocal trade circulates through channels rooted in local cultural scripts, guided by notions of personalized associations that women traders use in their business activities. In narratives about secondhand clothing, retailers, vendors, and consumers draw connections between people and clothes that constantly change. Such tales domesticate the logic of the market and the meaning of this global commodity in terms of local norms of status and values and in the process, they transform them. Combining secondhand garments into styles that display knowledge of wider clothing practice or subvert its received meanings, traders and consumers create new meanings around this imported commodity to serve their personal and community identities.

While India prohibits the import of secondhand clothing, it does permit the import of woolen fibers, among which are "mutilated hosiery," a trade term for wool garments shredded by machines in the West prior to export. These imported "mutilated" fabrics are sorted into color ranges, shredded, carded, and spun before they reappear as thread used for blankets, knitting yarn, and wool fabrics for local consumption and export. India also has a large domestic secondhand clothing market that is a product of shifts in wardrobes, dress changes over the course of a person's life cycle, and hand-me-downs to servants and relatives. This process gives rise to considerable domestic recycling of Indian clothing by barter, donations, and resale. Here, the materiality of cloth itself serves as a strategic resource for the unmaking and remaking of persons and identities.

See also **Recycled Textiles; Secondhand Clothes, History of; Vintage Fashion.**

BIBLIOGRAPHY

Hansen, Karen Tranberg. *Salaula: The World of Secondhand Clothing and Zambia.* Chicago: University of Chicago Press, 2000.

Jenss, Heike. "Sixties Dress Only! The Consumption of the Past in a Youth-cultural Retro-Scene." In *Old Clothes, New Looks: Second-Hand Fashion.* Edited by Alexandra Palmer and Hazel Clark. Oxford: Berg, 2004.

Milgram, Lynne B. "'Ukay-Ykay' Chic: Tales of Fashion and Trade in Secondhand Clothing in the Philippine Cordillera." In *Old Clothes, New Looks: Second-Hand Fashion.* Edited by Alexandra Palmer and Hazel Clark. Oxford, U.K.: Berg, 2004.

Norris, Lucy. "The Life Cycle of Clothing in Contemporary Urban India (Delhi)." In *Old Clothes, New Looks: Second-Hand Fashion.* Edited by Alexandra Palmer and Hazel Clark. Oxford, U.K.: Berg, 2004.

Karen Tranberg Hansen

SECONDHAND CLOTHES, HISTORY OF

The reappropriation of pre-worn clothes and accessories, historically reviewed, includes a range of practices, from straightforward methods of unhemming garments and reusing the raw material, perhaps turning it to the less worn side, as would have been practiced in medieval times, to the complex scaffold of trades in the nineteenth century. These industries recycled all manner of clothing, with machine-like economy, through specialist and discreet skills. Perhaps the most technologically advanced

was the production of "shoddy" cloth in the North of England from rags of wool, cotton, and indeed all fibers (except silk) which became the staple fabric for the ready-to-wear garment production in 1834.

An exploration of the formal and informal ways by which secondhand clothes reached the resale market should highlight that some apparently informal ways may indeed be considered formal, especially in the case of servants receiving their masters' "gifts" of clothing, which were actually considered a part of their remuneration.

In fact, the secondhand clothing trade could be said to have actually diminished in complexity over the last two centuries. It used to consist of many separate businesses employing various skills necessary for the economical recycling and remarketing of different categories of actual garments, as well as the raw material of cloth.

But the origins of the advanced complexity of the secondhand clothing industries of the nineteenth century can be discerned much earlier in records of the extensive exchanges of secondhand garments amongst the Western world's urban populations during the latter half of the seventeenth century.

A Seventeenth Century Londoner's Wardrobe

The Londoner Samuel Pepys' diary (1660–1669) tells of many transactions involving clothing, and perhaps many more where such gifts are offered and accepted. Scholars of the diary often note intimations of Pepys' vanity: he did indeed regularly employ his father's tailoring skills to restyle old garments, often to reflect London's fluctuating fashions. Thus many gifts from the wardrobes of Pepys' more affluent friends were adapted to better suit the needs of their new master. "Samuel Pepys, though vain, was not too proud to sport a second-hand accessory of quality which he could not afford to buy himself" (Stanlisland, p. 5).

At this time London's secondhand tradesmen were dealing in very large amounts of stock, both old clothing and new, in some cases bringing in thousands of pounds. Such traders were very profitably engaged in the provision of ready-made clothing for the seamen living and working aboard sailing fleets for months at a time, for which the clothes' dealers would be paid thousands of pounds in each transaction. The seventeenth-century Venetian experience contrasts with that of London in that the framework by which tradesmen were permitted to go about their business was strictly governed by regulatory bodies. For instance, the Venetian Guild of secondhand clothes dealers, *L'Arte degli Strazzaruoli*, in tandem with various civic bodies, including Venetian health officials, conspired to regulate every aspect of the trade, particularly during plague outbreaks as used cloth exchanges were suspected of transmitting disease. A particularly interesting feature of the Venetian trade is its close association with prostitution; Venetian courtesans procured clothing, by buying or renting, from such secondhand sources.

Secondhand clothes stand. Customers browse the offerings at a secondhand clothing stand in Liverpool, England, 1957. © HULTON-DEUTSCH COLLECTION/CORBIS. REPRODUCED BY PERMISSION.

The Eighteenth, Nineteenth, and Twentieth Centuries

During the eighteenth century, London's secondhand clothes industry was closely allied with its "slop" or ready-made clothing trade. Madeleine Ginsburg, a leading scholar in this field, identifies a considerable disparity between the provincial availability of used clothing in comparison to urban areas at this time. It is an equally important point that secondhand clothing not only furnished the affluent with more or less fashionable clothing, it was also an essential source of basic clothing provision for the poor. Focusing specifically on the Scottish city of Edinburgh, Elizabeth C. Sanderson has evaluated the role of the trade as a central part of the everyday life of most citizens. She makes the important point that during the eighteenth century the use of pre-worn clothing was an experience familiar to nearly all classes in society.

Considered perhaps the definitive account of the mid-nineteenth century increase in the trade, H. Mayhew's *London Labour and London's Poor* tells of the concentration of activity in London's East End. However,

the most consequential development at this time was the increasingly competitive pricing of cotton and wool fabrics, and accordingly, ready-to-wear garments, thus exponentially limiting the appeal of secondhand clothing, in home markets at least. In this way, used clothing exports, especially to Africa, became an ever more significant aspect of the trade. This is an angle explored particularly thoroughly by Karen Tranberg Hansen's research into Zambia's trade, whereas Ginsburg interprets charity, and the rise of the rummage sale, as the most important developments taking the industry into the twentieth century. Certainly the retail environment constituted by such sales, where purchasers rummage through large quantities of stock, could be considered conducive to the quick and efficient sale of used goods, particularly in urban areas.

World Wars I and II saw the increase of the profitable potential of secondhand clothing, especially for resale in Africa. At this time the supply and demand aspect could be strongly linked to the West's veritable accumulation of serviceable and wearable, but outmoded, clothing and the real needs for clothing in developing countries.

"Having my old black suit new-furbished, I was pretty neat in clothes today—and my boy [footboy], his old suit new-trimmed very handsome" (Stanisland, p. 46).

And it is here that one may perceive the beginnings of the nature that characterizes the trade in the early 2000s.

Interpreting Contemporary Trends

From the 1970s onward, fashion commentators have often noted a marked plurality of styles, compared to the former singularity of fashion houses' diktats; a development engendering fertile environments for alternative, niche fashions, and retrogressive styling. Thus secondhand clothing has come to be seen as offering potential for expressing individual and more autonomous style.

The early 2000s have seen widespread fashion trends reflecting early twentieth-century styles and the decades after World War II. In such a fashion zeitgeist, the cultural and economic capital of secondhand clothing, or vintage as it is latterly termed, has vastly increased. Secondhand clothes' stylistic appreciation has created new markets for its retail: for instance, in designated concessions of urban fashion multiples, within the high-fashion collections of designers including Martin Margiela, and on auction websites, such as Ebay.

The international recirculation of used clothing is not as straightforward as simply the export from richer to poorer nations: specific markets present more demand for particular items, for example Japan imports a considerable percentage of the world's trade in used designer denim jeans and sneakers. In these ways the state of the secondhand clothes trade could be understood as diversifying in economic potential and enjoying a favorable shift in its industrial, public, and cultural profiles.

See also **Recycled Textiles; Secondhand Clothes, Anthropology of; Vintage Fashion.**

BIBLIOGRAPHY

Allerston, Patricia. "Reconstructing the Second-Hand Clothes Trade in Sixteenth and Seventeenth Century Venice." *Costume* 33 (1999): 46–56.

Arnold, Rebecca. *Fashion, Desire and Anxiety.* I. B. Tauris and Co., 2001.

Ginsburg, Madeleine. "Rags to Riches: The Second-Hand Clothes Trade 1700–1978." *Costume* 14 (1980): 121–135. Often-quoted and very thorough.

Sanderson, C. Elizabeth. "Nearly New: The Second-Hand Clothing Trade in Eighteenth-Century Edinburgh." *Costume* 31 (1997): 38–48.

Stanisland, Kay. "Samuel Pepys and His Wardrobe" *Costume* 37 (1997): 41–50.

Transberg, Karen Hansen. "Other People's Clothes? The International Second-hand Clothing Trade and Dress Practises in Zambia." *Fashion Theory* 4, no. 3 (2000): 245–274. Excellent overview of international trade.

Lynda Fitzwater

SEQUINS. *See* **Spangles.**

SERGE. *See* **Denim.**

SEVENTH AVENUE When a famed street is both conceptual and geographic, as Seventh Avenue in New York City is, commenting on it becomes many-pronged. To David Wolfe, the creative director of the Doneger Group, a major buying office, Seventh Avenue is a state of the mind, the creative epicenter of American fashion. He believes that where it once was a vital apparel and distribution center, it now functions as a showcase for designers and manufacturers. To Wolfe, "It is more than a street or a neighborhood, it is the geographic symbol of the power of American style."

In the 1930s, the Garment Center, as this area was called—between 6th and 9th Avenues from 30th to 42nd Streets—was the city's largest industry, and the fourth largest in the country. Three-quarters of ready-made coats and dresses, and four out of five fur coats worn by American women, were made here.

Surprisingly, over the years, not that many books have been written about Seventh Avenue, the reality, but one author (and manufacturer) who tackled it was Murray Sices, who in 1953, could still write in his tome, not surprisingly, called *Seventh Avenue,* "Seventh Avenue in the city of New York, between 35th and 40th Street, is not merely a geographic location. It's a legend. It's the birthplace of miracles. It's the fast-beating heart of an industry whose bloodstreams course through America. … Here with almost 4,000 firms crowded into a few square blocks, you have a concentration of apparel manufacturers such as the world has never seen elsewhere."

That was then, this is now, and there have been many changes, most of them disastrous for Seventh Avenue and its environs. In 2000 alone, citywide garment-making jobs fell to 60,700 down from 70,100 in 1998. There were 3,260 apparel-making shops in 2000 as opposed to 3,591 in 1999, according to *Crain's New York Business Magazine.* The publication reported in 2001, "Voluntarily or not, garment workers in New York are mobbing the exits." Industry watchers were shocked at what was happening, especially those who thought the employment drop had bottomed out in the late 1990s. Historically, however, there has been a loss of manufacturing jobs going back more than thirty years. Gone are many wholesalers and textile companies as well as companies that supplied everything. Garment manufacturing has dropped along with everything else, from buttons to zippers and other necessities for a complete garment; even jobbers have disappeared and positions in showrooms also have evaporated.

Also there is the major question of rents that have reportedly increased in double or triple digits. Cheap imports, too, have become major culprits in the changing face of Seventh Avenue.

On the slightly brighter side, even though manufacturing of apparel is down from the 300,000 workers at its peak in the 1950s, clothing accounts for about one-fourth of the manufacturing jobs in the city, and it's still a most important entry into the business world for immigrants from everywhere. Seventh Avenue and its surrounding businesses probably will endure, because designers, even in the age of the computer, will still need workers nearby to whip up small runs of high-end clothing.

However, that segment of the business is also no longer so significant. At a time when conglomerates have swallowed up many of the major department stores, and specialty stores and discounters swamp shopping malls, the ability to ship quickly is no longer so vital. Bud Konheim, the head of Nicole Miller Inc., one of Seventh Avenue's stalwarts, still refers to himself as a "quick turnaround guy," and retains his belief in "Made in the U.S.A." through thick and thin.

In the early 2000s, *Crain's* reported that the New York Industrial Retention Network would release a study showing 60 percent of apparel leases in the garment district will expire momentarily, putting the entire local industry in a negative position.

Even though everything is changing, there is still plenty of excitement just walking Seventh Avenue and the adjacent Broadway buildings like 1410 Broadway or 550 Seventh Avenue. Models still run to do a day's work at a manufacturer's showroom during New York Fashion Week. The Tower of Babel voices from different cultures still are part of street life and lore. There are still plenty of small cafés doing takeout, or one can sit and have bagels or more exotic fare served fast and furiously.

Plenty of New Yorkers, including the mayor and other politicians, want to keep Seventh Avenue and its environs as vital as they have ever been. In 1993 the Fashion Center Business Improvement Center was inaugurated, its mission to promote garment manufacturing, but ten years later BID's concept had changed. The idea is to perhaps create for the district (running roughly from Fifth to Ninth Avenues and West 35th to 41st streets) a 24-hour seven-day-a-week place with diverse and residential units, including a fashion museum and more retail stores. BID's design center will add to the neighborhood's continuing unique personality, and allow it to remain, if not strictly a garment manufacturing area, a fashion district.

Gerald Scupp, the deputy director of the Fashion Center (which has its street of famous designers, called the Fashion Walk of Fame, similar to Grauman's Chinese Theatre in Hollywood which has its famous actors' hand- and footprints) notes many initiatives have failed, but he believes, and the report suggests, that abolishing special zoning that restricts non-manufacturing uses and keeps rents low for manufacturers could work. There will be those who will object, however.

Rent alone does not explain the declining job numbers, nor do cheap imports, for some manufacturers have defected to cheaper spaces in Brooklyn and Queens, but even this has not been entirely satisfactory. Another factor is the sub rosa conversion to office space with city officials looking the other way, rather than upholding the special district concept, according to Adam Friedman, the network's executive director. He notes the city stopped inspections in 1993.

Also taking a toll on legitimate design houses in New York City are manufacturers who violate the law by not paying overtime or taxes, so many of their workers do not show up on official job statistics. If all workers were truly accounted for, the number of city garment workers might double, according to Louis Vanegas, district director of the Wage and Hour Division of the U.S. Department of Labor. But even Vanegas agrees the uncounted jobs are declining and don't really account for the precipitous drop in manufacturing.

So, what will happen to Seventh Avenue and its environs if jobs decline at historic rates? According to the BID report in the early 2000s, only about 17,000 of the city's 50,000 apparel manufacturing positions will be around by 2010. However, as of early 2004, fashion-related businesses still make up the majority of the district—64 percent or 4,245—but more of these are showrooms or mixed uses. Other tenants range from printers, ad agencies, theaters, and an unknown number of illegal residential tenants who are tucked away in lofts and other spaces. Actually, the area is becoming more residential legally, and BID supports the idea. Many property owners would love to see zoning laws changed.

That the problems of Seventh Avenue remain is borne out by a *Woman's Wear Daily* article on June 10, 2003 headed "U.S. Makers Fading Away." The piece, by Scott Malone, notes, "The withering of the nation's production base has gotten to the point where even the makers of high-end apparel, who typically were able to digest the higher costs of domestic production because of their higher prices, have begun to break into camps on the question of whether making clothing in the U.S. will remain a viable strategy for the years to come."

The article maintains that the same economic pressures that pushed most mainstream apparel manufacturing out of the country are taking hold in the top-drawer designer market. "Eventually all that will be left in this country will be a small clique of sample makers."

But all is not lost for the Seventh Avenue of the early twenty-first century. The article makes clear there is still a shrinking group of high-end designers whose dresses carry three or even four-figure price tags who contend that domestic manufacturing in New York continues to make sense. These businessmen argue that being close to their factories allows a higher level of quality control and a faster rate of turnaround than is available overseas. Bud Konheim, "the quick turnaround guy" of Nicole Miller says, "The advantage of being domestic has nothing to do with cost." What keeps half of his company's manufacturing here are garment-district contractors. Konheim says, "You can get cheaper prices by going offshore, but then you've got a longer lead time; you have to make your decisions earlier, and you have to cut bigger quantities, so you have a lack of control. And, lack of control, in this marketplace, is very dangerous because some orders you take are not real orders. You have people canceling." He adds that domestic manufacturing is viable only if a brand's fashions are sufficiently distinctive so that retailers can't get a similar product elsewhere.

Another major manufacturer, who is also a highly prized designer, Oscar de la Renta, whose firm has long been on Seventh Avenue, still makes the majority of his line in the United States. For him also, quality concerns are a key reason for staying here. The firm's mixture of local and foreign sourcing has not changed since the early 1990s.

Famed handbag and accessories firm Judith Leiber continues to manufacture on West 33rd Street because so many of its workers have been with the company for a long time and their talents are specialized.

However, one of the problems of the apparel industry decline is that so many of the businesses that supported companies like trim suppliers or firms that stocked replacement parts died because of lack of customers. Konheim said his company has to contract many operations overseas including beading, embroidering, and hand knitting, because it no longer can find domestic companies doing that work. Ironically, at a time when going global has caused so many problems for unique Seventh Avenue and its environs, the cachet of a "Made in the U.S.A." label remains high in Asian markets as well as in the United States and throughout the world, so there is hope.

Nowhere where apparel and its appurtenances are created is there the excitement that was and is Seventh Avenue with its polyglot charisma, its smells and street noises, its buying and selling, its rushing and stopping, its garment racks flying down the street in competent hands. Clothing is manufactured around the world, but no one has a Seventh Avenue except New York, New York.

See also **Fashion Designer; Garments, International Trade in; Leiber, Judith; Ready-to-Wear.**

BIBLIOGRAPHY

Curan, Catherine. "More Fashionable Garment Area Plan." *Crain's New York Business* (10 March 2003).

Fredrickson, Tom. "Garment Area Jobs Stripped." *Crain's New York Business* (26 March 2001).

Malone, Scott. "U.S. Makers Fading Away." *Women's Wear Daily* (10 June 2003): 10.

Sices, Murray. *Seventh Avenue.* New York: Fairchild Publications, 1953. Outdated, but provides interesting earlier background information on Seventh Avenue.

Margot Siegel

SEWING MACHINE Just as the needle marked the beginning of humanity's first technological and aesthetic efflorescence, the sewing machine affected not just tailoring and dressmaking but manufacturing technology, intellectual property management, marketing, advertising, consumer finance, world commerce, and technological leadership. Even more fundamentally, and largely unexpectedly, the sewing machine became a new kind of product—it was both commercial and domestic, and, in appearance, both industrial and ornamental. The continuing development of machine sewing is in part the story of the changing balance between household and factory.

Like the personal computer over 125 years later, early commercially successful sewing machines combined a number of separate innovations into a new system for which an immense latent demand existed. In fact, the crucial single innovation, made by Elias Howe Jr. in his patent of 1846, was a system based on a radically new curved, grooved needle with an eye at the point end. Instead of making an easily unraveled chain stitch that emulated manual work, it engaged thread from the needle with another in a moving shuttle to create a stronger lock stitch. It was the first machine with a significant advantage in speed over hand sewing, but was limited to straight stitching and could complete only a limited length of material at a time. Another inventor, John Bachelder, remedied the Howe machine's drawbacks with an improved design patented in 1849, allowing continuous sewing of material with a needle moving up and down on a horizontal table. Isaac Merritt Singer made a series of other improvements in 1850 and 1851, making curved stitching possible and replacing the hand wheel with a treadle.

While no single inventor controlled all the patents needed to make commercially successful equipment, Singer and the others were able to settle the claims of Howe and to include his original patent in a pool. For a substantial fixed fee per machine, partly distributed by the corporation to its patent holders, any manufacturer could produce sewing machines without infringement.

The American setting was essential for the sewing machine's success in the 1850s. A French tailor, Barthélemy Thimonnier, had secured French government support in the 1830s for establishment of a firm using his wooden-framed sewing machines to produce military uniforms. A crowd of journeyman tailors had wrecked them as a threat to their livelihoods. In the United States of the 1850s there was no comparably powerful and politically active craft organization. To the contrary, America was already leading the world in production of ready-made garments; even before the Civil War, companies were using standardized measurements and patterns to remove the most skilled and best-paid parts of tailoring from the manufacturing process. Jacksonian Americans hoped ready-made clothing of mechanically spun and woven fabrics would limit visible class distinctions in public life, closing the gap between the custom tailoring of middle- and upper-class men and the rough workman's clothing called slops. In 1835, one New York firm was advertising for three hundred male and five hundred female tailors, and another for twelve hundred "plain sewers."

Such manufacturers embraced mechanical sewing rapidly, as it increased productivity by up to 500 percent. From 1853 to 1860 the number of machines sold in the United States rose from 1,609 to 31,105, reaching 353,592 by 1875. But domestic applications soon overtook industrial uses. Isaac Singer, a former actor, pioneered a national and international sales campaign to introduce his machine into the home. Singer's associate, the attorney Edward Clark, developed the first national sales organization and the first widely accepted hire-purchase plan, successful even among buyers who could have paid cash. Since women of all social classes were expected to sew and repair women's and children's clothing, it appeared to offer a great savings in time. Its high price actually helped make it a prestigious purchase, usually on prominent display—one of the first manifestations of an industrial aesthetic in the home. (The Singer machine contained over one hundred pounds of cast iron, among other materials.) Yet working-class women who could afford payments also saw it as a means of self-sufficiency; for young women it was an attractive alternative to domestic service.

Clark and Singer established luxurious sales rooms for displaying machines and their use, spent millions in advertising, and established global sales and service organizations, the first of their kind. Economic historians have suggested that the vigorous marketing by Singer and other firms spread information that, in turn, stimulated new improvements of the machine in a virtuous circle. They have also noted that the Singer Company continued to use conservative, European-style craft production systems after its rivals had adopted interchangeable parts, making the change only when sales volume demanded it. Despite this delay, the sewing machine industry became a new foundation of productive techniques that helped U.S. industry challenge Britain's dominance in mechanical engineering.

The sewing machine reached maturity relatively quickly. The 1865 Singer New Family machine was sold into the twentieth century, and some home sewers still swear by the robustness of related surviving models. After the original patents expired in 1877 and the combination of patent holders was dissolved, prices continued to drop. Sears, Roebuck and other new merchandisers aggressively promoted well-built and relatively inexpensive private-brand machines. While this strategy helped

maintain real-dollar sales and widespread home sewing machine use, it also hastened the decline of the sewing machine's status. Meanwhile technicians and inventors who worked in sewing machine production were turning design and production skills to new generations of devices, including typewriters (which offered similar challenges in precise alignment) and phonographs (which also used rotary motion and the needle).

Motor-powered machines began to appear in the 1910s, but until the 1930s many potential customers outside major cities still lacked home electricity. The great change in the early twentieth century was in attitudes toward home sewing and the machine. The increased availability, improved styling, and higher quality of ready-made women's clothing turned the sewing machine from a time-saver to a money-saver. Homemade clothing began to be stigmatized. In the 1920s, domestic management shifted from making to selecting things. Electrification of factory sewing machines reinforced this trend by increasing productivity and reducing the prices of ready-made clothing. And the expense of materials wasted by mistakes discouraged neophyte home sewers. Ironically, electrification was welcome in part because it made it easier to hide the machine on a closet shelf between uses.

Expanding career opportunities for women after World War II made the domestic sewing machine a niche appliance, sometimes used as a fallback during price inflation and for mending. With the rise of sold-state control, using programmable integrated circuits instead of or in addition to mechanical controls like cams and with the globalization of the apparel and footwear industries, sewing machine production moved in the later twentieth century first to Japan and then to China. The division of labor in industry encouraged the multiplication of special-purpose machines, of which Japanese firms in the 1990s offered over one thousand models. High-speed production is posing a new range of technical challenges; needles, threads, and fabrics must be designed to work with advanced equipment. (Some economists believe that stronger thread for machine sewing was one of the twentieth century's most productive innovations.)

In home sewing, computerization has encouraged not output but creative control, in that a new variety of stitches and functions are available. High-end home machines can exceed the cost of some industrial machines in price. The attraction is no longer saving time or money, but creating apparel and home furnishings with designs unavailable in the marketplace. In the global economy pioneered by the sewing machine, household and industrial sewing have parted ways again.

See also **Needles; Seamstresses.**

BIBLIOGRAPHY

Burman, Barbara, ed. *The Culture of Sewing: Gender, Consumption, and Home Dressmaking.* Oxford and New York: Berg, 1999.

Connolly, Marguerite. "The Disappearance of the Domestic Sewing Machine, 1890–1925." *Winterthur Portfolio* (1999): 31–48.

Cooper, Grace Rogers. *The Sewing Machine: Its Invention and Development.* Washington, D.C.: Smithsonian Press, 1976.

Godfrey, Frank P. *An International History of the Sewing Machine.* London: Robert Hale, 1982.

Hounshell, David. *From the American System to Mass Production, 1800–1932: The Development of Manufacturing Technology in the United States.* Baltimore: Johns Hopkins University Press, 1984.

Jensen, Joan M., and Sue Davidson. *A Needle, a Bobbin, a Strike: Women Needleworkers in America.* Philadelphia: Temple University Press, 1984.

Edward Tenner

SEYDOU, CHRIS Chris Seydou (1949–1994) was a pioneer in promoting African fashion designers on the international stage. He created clothing that drew on his roots in Mali, West Africa, yet his designs evaded neat categorization as African. Seydou was well known for his adaptation of African textiles, including Mali's bogolan fabric, to haute couture. Seydou's bell-bottom pants, motorcycle jackets, and tight miniskirts made of distinctively African fabrics caused a stir in Mali and drew attention to his work abroad. Seydou's designs have been published in numerous French, German, Ivoirian, and Senegalese as well as Malian fashion magazines. He showed his designs in Europe as well as Africa, and worked with internationally renowned designers, most notably Paco Rabanne.

The Designer's Roots

Chris Seydou was born Seydou Nourou Doumbia on 18 May 1949 in Kati, a small town centered around a military base forty kilometers north of Bamako, the capital of Mali. Because Seydou's mother worked as an embroiderer, he was familiar with the tools of the clothing trade from an early age. His mother had copies of European fashion magazines that greatly impressed Seydou; he was fascinated by the photographs of elegant women in beautiful clothes (Seydou 1993). He left school to pursue his interest in fashion at fifteen. In 1965, his family apprenticed him to a local tailor. In 1968 Seydou relocated to Ouagadougou in Burkina Faso (then called Upper Volta), and the following year he moved to the cosmopolitan city of Abidjan in Côte d'Ivoire. He changed his name when he embarked on his professional career, adopting the name "Chris" as a tribute to Christian Dior, whose work had been a great influence on his early development. He kept the name "Seydou" in order to preserve part of the name his family had given him, thus creating a professional name combining the European and African influences that are apparent in his work ("Interview: Chris Seydou," p. 10).

Abidjan was in the forefront of African fashion design in 1969, and Seydou found great success in the city, designing clothing for many of Abidjan's wealthy and influential women. Seydou then spent seven years in Paris beginning in 1972, where he studied European couture. He met other African artists and designers in Paris, with whom he organized the *Fédération Africaine de Prêt à Porter* (African Federation of Ready-to-Wear Designers), an association that seeks to promote African designers on the international market. Seydou was also one of the three founders of the *Fédération Internationale de la Mode Africaine* (International Federation of African Fashion), which continues to provide an important forum for African designers. Seydou found that his work appealed to African women who sought clothes made in "la mode occidentale" (Western style), and that European women appreciated his "exoticism" (Seydou; and "Chris Seydou: Le roman d'une vie," p. 34). As Seydou explained, these women did not buy his work because he was African, but because he "brought an African sensibility" to his designs (Seydou 1993).

Seydou returned to his country of birth in 1990. He came to Bamako in search of "the authors, the origins" of "the real African traditions" (Seydou 1993). He was particularly interested in bogolan or bogolanfini, a cotton textile traditionally made for ritual functions in rural Mali, and known as mudcloth in North American markets. Seydou had begun to use the cloth while he was working in Paris in 1975–1976. He described his return to Paris in 1973 or 1974 after a visit home and finding in his suitcase several pieces of bogolan he had received as gifts. He was already familiar with the material from his childhood in Kati, but there he had associated it with hunters and local ritual practices rather than with his own interest in fashion. In unfamiliar Paris the familiar cloth was transformed into a souvenir—a reminder of the place and the people of home (Seydou 1993).

Transforming Traditions

Seydou's work with bogolan and other indigenous textiles illustrates the balance between local tradition and global markets that characterizes the work of many non-Western designers. Seydou focused on making Malian fabrics relevant to contemporary fashion rather than preserving local traditions. Yet the cultural significance of the textiles shaped his methods, as illustrated by his work with bogolan. Seydou edited, modified, or discarded some aspects of the fabric while preserving others. "I am a contemporary designer who knows what I can do technically and how to do it. Bogolan can simply be a cultural base for my work" (Seydou 1993).

One of Seydou's primary modifications of bogolan concerned the density of its designs, for the fabric customarily incorporates a variety of distinct motifs. Cutting and assembling a garment from this cloth was extremely difficult for Seydou, for no two portions of a given piece of cloth are identical. Seydou adapted by commissioning

THE CHRIS SEYDOU PHENOMENON

Journalists in Africa and Europe recognized Seydou's role as an ambassador between African and Western fashion worlds.

He flouted every convention, showing bogolan made into mini-skirts or bustiers, as large berets or full-fitting coats and even as a fitted suit worn by the President's wife Adame Ba Konaré for the opening of a film festival in Marseilles in 1993. (Duponchel, p. 36)

À travers ses créations, le Mali s'est fait mieux connaître dans ses valeurs culturelles à travers le monde, jusqu'en Amérique où les Noirs américains font aujourd'hui du bogolan une source d'identification culturelle. (Through his creations, Mali became better known throughout the world for its cultural

treasures, all the way to America where black Americans today make bogolan into a source of cultural identity) (Diakité, p. 4).

Chris Seydou en fut le premier artisan, faisant naître une generation de stylists de premier niveau, tous visionnaires d'une Afrique renaissante… (Chris Seydou was the first…, breeding a generation of first class designers, visionaries of a born again Africa) (Pivin, p. 7–8 Trans Gail de Courcy-Ireland).

It all began with the unforgettable, incomparable Chris Seydou. More than anyone, he helped to give African men and women a new way of thinking, of looking at things, and inspired numerous designers and models to aim even higher. (Traoré, p. 8).

his own versions of bogolan, isolating a single pattern in a process he referred to as "decoding" the cloth. Seydou also expressed reluctance to cut and tailor material that was adorned with symbolic motifs, out of respect for the cloth's ritual significance in the context of rural Mali: "For me it was symbolic. For me, I didn't want to cut bogolan early on; it was difficult to put my scissors to it." (Seydou 1993). Among Seydou's most popular and influential bogolan-related projects was his 1990 collaboration with the Industrie Textile du Mali, a textile manufacturing company in Bamako, for which he designed a fabric inspired by bogolan that was printed and sold in 1990–1991. Seydou's death in 1994, at the age of 45, reverberated powerfully in the worlds of fashion, art, and popular culture throughout west Africa and beyond. He is considered by many to be the father of African fashion design.

See also **Afrocentric Fashion; Bogolan; Dior, Christian; Ethnic Style in Fashion; Rabanne, Paco; Textiles, African.**

BIBLIOGRAPHY

"Chris Seydou: Le roman d'une vie…." *Africa International* 271 (July–August 1994): 31–37.

Diakité, K. B. "Chris Seydou." *L'Essor* 12673 (8 March 1994): 4.

Domingo, Macy. "Ivory Scissors—Ciseaux d'Ivoire." *Revue noire* 2 (September 1991): 6–7.

Duponchel, Pauline. "Bogolan: From Symbolic Material to National Emblem." In *The Art of African Textiles: Technology, Tradition and Lurex.* Edited by John Picton. London: Barbican Art Gallery and Lund Humphries, 1995.

"Interview: Chris Seydou." *Grin-Grin: Magazine mensuel des jeunes* 9 (April–June 1989): 10.

Pivin, Jean-Loup. "Renaissance d'un style africain" (Rebirth of an African Style). Translated by Gail de Courcy-Ireland. *Revue noire* 27 (December 1997–January 1998): 7–8.

Rovine, Victoria. *Bogolan: Shaping Culture through Cloth in Contemporary Mali.* Washington, D. C.: Smithsonian Institution Press, 2001.

Seydou, Chris. Interview by author. Bamako, Mali. 6 March 1993.

Traoré, Aminata Dramane. "African Fashion: A Message." In *The Art of African Fashion.* Edited by Els van der Plas and Marlous Willemsen. The Hague, Netherlands: Prince Claus Fund; Asmara, Eritrea, and Trenton, N.J.: Africa World Press, 1998.

Victoria L. Rovine

SHATOOSH. *See* **Cashmere and Pashmina.**

SHAWLS The shawl as an item of female fashionable dress derives from the Indian *shal*, which is a male garment that consists of an unstructured length of material with woven or embroidered patterning. The first shawls worn by Europeans in India or elsewhere, were worn by men, although this practice mainly involved those connected to colonial trade. Britain had strong trading links with India from the late seventeenth century, and after 1757 the British East India Company "was inextricably involved in effective colonization" (Morgan, p. 460). These historic developments generated a huge fascination with Indian culture in Britain, which was expressed partly by an enthusiasm to consume new "exotic" luxuries such as the *shal* (Morgan, p. 460).

Female Fashionable Dress

The emergence of neoclassical dress as informal wear in the 1760s greatly contributed to the embrace of the shawl within fashionable dress. Female neoclassical dress was made from flimsy, lightweight materials and it referred

For a long time English fashions have formed part of those of France. The shawls, a type of unusually ample handkerchief, hail from India, where they replace mantles. Adopted by the English, they have come to France and go rather well with fashionable undress. (*Journal de la Mode et du Gout*, pp. 1–3)

back to the draped elegance of ancient Greek and Roman dress. Therefore, it was perfectly complemented by the warm and gracefully draped shawl. The shawl was adopted in Britain from the 1760s through the 1770s and by the 1790s it was also highly fashionable in France. Initially the Indian shawls were only worn by the upper classes, as they were very expensive, so much so that they were often treated as family heirlooms. However, the fact that they were highly desirable luxuries meant that by the 1820s cheaper copies were made widely available to middle-class consumers. Good-quality shawls were prized possessions and they were often used as gifts linked to weddings and baptisms. As the nineteenth century progressed, increases in the range of designs and prices available, meant that the associations of wealth, class, and respectability linked to a particular shawl and how it was worn became more complex. Retailers catered to this diversity; for example, the firm J. & J. Holmes, of London, offered a wide range of designs and prices from 1 guinea to 100 guineas. Efforts by manufacturers to create still cheaper shawls meant that they were worn by working-class women, and even the very poor wore second-hand or coarse woolen versions.

Materials, Production, and Patterns
Genuine cashmere shawls were made from the fine, silky underfleece of the Himalayan mountain goat, which was a rare and expensive fiber. British and French manufacturers who aimed to copy the Indian shawls attempted to imitate this fiber in various ways—for example, by using different combinations of wool and silk. Methods of manufacture also created distinctive differences between Indian- and European-made shawls. As Sarah Pauly notes, "European shawls, whether woven on the drawloom or the Jacquard loom, were always machine-woven, while the Indian product was always made by hand-manipulated weaving (when not embroidered)" (p. 20). The result of this was that the design and construction of European shawls was limited by machine capabilities. From 1824, the introduction of the Jacquard loom enabled more sophisticated designs to be produced than previously possible on the drawloom. However, no machine could match the immensely complex and time-consuming double-interlocking twill-tapestry technique used by the Kashmiri weavers, which was only possible by hand.

Another singular feature of the Indian shawls was the pine or cone pattern, which was a stylized interpretation of a flowering plant, known as a *buta*. This design was also linked to Arab culture, as many of the Kashmiri weavers came from Persia. In the nineteenth century the pine became the distinctive motif of the Paisley shawl, a pattern that became even more stylized after the introduction of the Jacquard loom. Three other early shawl designs that remained popular until the 1870s were the spade center, the blue-style, and the zebra. Despite the dominance of Indian-inspired patterns, the ubiquity of the shawl from the 1820s meant that many different fancy designs were also worn.

Important Shawl Manufacturing Centers
The most notable British centers for the weaving of shawls in the period discussed were Paisley, Norwich, and Edinburgh. Norwich and Edinburgh manufacturers experimented in the 1790s with producing good, cheaper imitations of the Indian shawls. Despite their relative success in producing high-quality copies, these efforts were soon overshadowed by Paisley in Scotland, which became a thriving international center for the production of shawls from about 1805 to the early 1870s. Leading Paisley manufacturers, such as John Morgan & Co., Forbes and Hutcheson, and J. J. Robertson, were successful in bringing the shawl to a mass market of consumers, largely because they were cheaper than their rivals. Despite its Indian derivation, the stylized pine design has since become internationally known as the Paisley pattern.

In France, manufacturers in Lyons, Paris, Jouy, and Nimes also began making shawls from the early nineteenth century. French shawls tended to be of high quality of both design and manufacture; they were renowned as being second only to the Kashmir shawls of India.

1870 to the Early 2000s
The shawl ceased to be a ubiquitous fashion item from the 1870s, owing to the introduction of the fitted bustle style. It regained popularity in the twentieth century as an element of formal evening dress; however, in general it has had a minimal presence within the fashionable female wardrobe. The mid to late-1990s witnessed a brief period of fashionability for the pashmina, a cashmere shawl usually made in attractive, plain colors.

See also **Sari; Scarf.**

BIBLIOGRAPHY

Alfrey, Penelope. "The Social Background to the Shawl." In *The Norwich Shawl*. Edited by Pamela Clabburn. London: HMSO, 1995.

Clabburn, Pamela, ed. *The Norwich Shawl*. London: HMSO, 1995.

Journal de la Mode et du Gout. No. 11 (5 June 1790): 1–3.

Lochrie, Maureen. "The Paisley Shawl Industry." In *Scottish Textile History*. Edited by John Butt and Kenneth Ponting. Aberdeen, Scotland: Aberdeen University Press, 1987.

Mackrell, Alice. *Shawls, Stoles and Scarves.* London: B. T. Batsford Ltd., 1986.

Morgan, Kenneth O. *The Oxford History of Britain.* Oxford and New York: Oxford University Press, 1992, 2001.

Pauly, Sarah. *The Kashmir Shawl.* New Haven, Conn.: Yale University Art Gallery, 1975.

Perrot, Philippe. *Fashioning the Bourgeoisie: A History of Clothing in the Nineteenth Century.* Princeton, N.J.: Princeton University Press, 1994.

Fiona Anderson

SHIBORI. *See* **Tie-Dyeing.**

SHIRT A shirt is a garment worn on the upper part of the body, usually consisting of a buttoned front, a collar, and long or short sleeves. Possibly the most important item in the male wardrobe after the suit, the shirt has always been considered the symbol of a gentleman. The finest shirts are single-stitched, pleated at the cuff, and feature a split shoulder yoke to allow for different heights of each shoulder.

History

Shirts appeared first in European dress in the seventeenth century as a kind of underwear, designed to protect expensive waistcoats and frock coats from sweat and soil. By the early eighteenth century, shirts had assumed importance as garments in their own right. The emphasis placed by Beau Brummel and other dandies on wearing clean, perfectly styled linen brought the shirt into increased prominence as an essential male garment. Before the middle of the nineteenth century, only those considered to be gentlemen could afford to wear white shirts, as only they had the means to buy, change, and wash them regularly. Because shirts soiled so easily, men involved in manual labor found it completely impractical to wear them. The development of improved laundry techniques after the mid-nineteenth century expanded the market for shirts, but they remained emblematic of upper-class, or at least "white-collar" middle-class men.

At first, shirts were put on by being pulled over the head. Shirts that opened all the way down the front were unknown before 1871, when Brown, Davis & Co. of Aldermanbury registered the first "coat style" of shirt. Striped shirts became fashionable in the late nineteenth century, but some viewed them with the suspicion that the color was hiding dirt.

In the early twenty-first century, a similar style of shirt to those originally produced by Brown, Davis & Co. is available in either plain or placket front. The placket is used to give the shirt extra strength and consists of an extra fold of fabric where the shirt is buttoned. Other essential requirements for a shirt of the highest quality include gussets for reinforcement between the breast and the back of the shirt, mother-of-pearl buttons, and re-movable collar bones (preferably made from brass) to prevent the collar tips from curling upwards. On the other hand, a good shirt will never feature a breast pocket as these only appeared much later with the demise of the waistcoat. Use of a shirt breast pocket to carry pens, cigarettes, and other paraphernalia can spoil the lines of the shirt. By the turn of the twentieth century, the traditional stand-up collar was supplanted by the turndown collar—a development that coincided with the demise of the cravat in favor of the necktie. Although there are as many as twenty different styles of collar (both attached or detachable), the most formal remains the broad turndown. With the rise of the Windsor tie knot (invented in the 1920s, and revived periodically), the cutaway collar has become the collar of choice for younger shirt wearers.

Although the word "shirt" has been expanded to include a number of men's and women's garments, with dress shirt, sports shirt, sweatshirt, T-shirt, and shirtwaist counted among them, a plain white shirt cut from the softest sea-island cotton is a sartorial must for any man. The tailored shirtwaister or shirtwaist blouse with starched and coat-style front is the women's version that evolved from a man's shirt, beginning in the late nineteenth century and enjoying great popularity beginning in the 1930s. Many formerly exclusively male shirt styles have been adopted essentially unchanged for women's wear in the late twentieth century.

See also **Neckties and Neckwear; Shirtwaist; Suit, Business; Tailored Suit; T-Shirt; Waistcoat.**

BIBLIOGRAPHY

Amies, Hardy. *A, B, C's of Men's Fashion.* London: Cahill and Co. Ltd, 1964.

Byrde, Penelope. *The Male Image: Men's Fashion in England 1300–1970.* London: B. T. Batsford, Ltd., 1979.

Chenoune, Farid. *A History of Men's Fashion.* Paris: Flammarion, 1993.

De Marley, Diana. *Fashion for Men: An Illustrated History.* London: B.T. Batsford, Ltd., 1985.

Keers, Paul. *A Gentleman's Wardrobe.* London: Weidenfield and Nicolson, 1987.

Roetzel, Bernhard. *Gentleman: A Timeless Fashion.* Cologne: Konemann, 1999.

Schoeffler, O. E., and William Gale. *Esquire's Encyclopedia of 20th Century Fashions.* New York: McGraw-Hill, 1973.

Tom Greatrex

SHIRTWAIST The shirtwaist dress, also known as the shirtmaker or simply the shirtdress, is one of the most American of all fashions. It has endured throughout the entire twentieth century into the early twenty-first. It owes its origins to the shirtwaist blouse, that very early product of the American ready-to-wear industry that emerged as part of the uniform of the New Woman in the 1890s. Its styling is based on a man's tailored shirt

Advertisement for McMullen shirt frocks. The shirtwaist has been known by many names since its development in the late twentieth century. The McMullen Company helped popularize the style when it introduced its "shirt frocks" in 1935, in an attempt to overcome declining sales in men's dress shirts. Courtesy of The Chapman Historical Museum. REPRODUCED BY PERMISSION.

with a skirt added, either as a one-piece dress or as separates. If separate, the skirt and shirt are usually made from the same material.

It began as a practical, washable nurse's uniform, usually cotton, sometime around the turn of the twentieth century and continued in this mode into World War I, where it became the uniform for the Red Cross and other organizations needing practical, washable clothing for their women workers.

Trim and becoming, the shirtwaist's practicality lent itself to the postwar enthusiasm for active sports, and by the 1920s, occasional "sports dresses" based on it but not using the name were adopted for golf and tennis. Caroline Millbank notes that by 1926, Best & Co. promoted what they called their "shirtmaker frocks" for sports, made of cotton and ready to be monogrammed. As a fashion, it hit its stride in the 1930s, in large part because of the upscale men's shirt manufacturer, the McMullen Company of Glens Falls, N.Y. who, in its attempt to overcome the falling market in fine men's shirts during the Depression, introduced to the retail industry a line for women, the "shirt frock," in 1935. These were two-piece cotton, linen, or lightweight wool dresses, with choices of either skirts or culottes that looked like skirts.

The term "shirtwaist," derived from "waist," the nineteenth-century term for what we would now call a blouse (in itself so-called because it bloused over the waistband as it was tucked into the skirt), was commonplace by the 1890s. However, the name as applied to sports dresses was not generally used until considerably later. Women's magazines from the 1930s and into the 1940s referred to it rather clumsily as "the button-down-the-front style" or, more vaguely, the "sports dress" even as they acknowledged that it had become a classic of American style. In a very early version, Simplicity Patterns offered a "shirtmaker" in 1937, but *The Ladies' Home Journal* did not consistently use the name in their articles and advertising until sometime around 1941, and even Best & Co. called its dress a "golfer" that same year. However, a major article in *Life* (9 May) on "Summer Sports Style" devoted two full pages showing 18 illustrations of various "classic shirtwaists," in all price points and in both day and evening wear. By so doing, perhaps they helped to codify the name that has stuck. Full-skirted versions following the New Look's dictates became the outfits of choice for the American housewife of the 1950s and early 1960s. Later in the century, in the late 1970s and 1980s, Geoffrey Beene and Bill Blass took it to a new and elegant high, introducing the classic shirtmaker in luxurious and unusual fabric combinations for evening wear. It continues to remain staple of American style in the twenty-first century, by now a conservative classic whose practicality and versatility make it a necessary part of many women's wardrobes.

See also **Beene, Geoffrey; Blass, Bill; Blouse; New Look; Shirt; Ready-to-Wear; Uniforms, Sports.**

BIBLIOGRAPHY

Ladies Home Journal, February 1938, p. 63.

Millbank, Caroline Rennolds. *New York Fashion: The Evolution of American Style.* New York: Harry N. Abrams, 1996.

Payne, Winakor, and Jane Farrell-Beck. *The History of Costume.* 2nd edition. New York: HarperCollins Publishers, 1992.

Patricia Campbell Warner

SHOEMAKING Shoemaking continues to be the work of a family member in many cultures of the early 2000s. Inuit and other circumpolar peoples continue the tradition of footwear production by the mother of the family—the craft learned from her mother and passed on to her daughters, as it has always been.

The earliest professional shoemakers can only be supposed from Egyptian friezes where laborers are depicted making sandals, using tools not dissimilar to tools still used by hand shoemakers. However, leatherworkers also used the same tools as the shoemaker, and so it is impossible to define the period in which shoemaking as a singular profession developed.

During the Roman Empire shoemaking progressed from artisans working alone in small settlements to congregating in streets near the town's center or marketplace, where guilds became established. Guilds protected and regulated the shoemakers, their suppliers, and their clients from unfair business practices and pricing, and ensured quality products. Apollo was chosen patron deity of Roman shoemakers, with images and statues of him gracing the entrance to streets reserved for members of that profession.

Similarly, images of the Christian patron saints of shoemakers adorned the churches and guildhalls of medieval Europe. During the third century, noble Roman brothers Crispin and Crispinian were converted to Christianity and went to Gaul to preach the gospel, working as shoemakers at night. They were eventually tortured for their faith and put to death. Although the legend is unreliable and Saints Crispin and Crispinian have lost their status of sainthood, they have remained the patron saints of shoemakers since the fifteenth century, and their feast day, October 25, is still celebrated as a holiday for the shoe industry in France.

There is evidence that by the fourteenth century, shoemakers were already making footwear for speculative sale, essentially "ready to wear." This was aided by the adoption of standardized measurement. In England in 1324, measurements for distance were standardized under King Edward II. Consistent in size, three barleycorns laid end-to-end equaled one inch and the foot-long "ruler" became the foot measurement of King Edward, the ruler of England. The other standard of measurement was the hand, used since biblical times, and used to this day for measuring the height of horses. A hand equals $4\frac{1}{3}$ inches or 13 barleycorns. When a standardized mea-

Jimmy Choo. Fashion clothing and footwear designer Jimmy Choo in his London workshop, 1997. © Tim Graham/Corbis. Reproduced by permission.

surement for shoe sizing began in the late seventeenth century, children's sizes were deemed to be less than the measurement of a hand and adult sizes were those over a hand. Adult sizes began with the deduction of $4\frac{1}{3}$ inches, so an adult woman's size 4 shoe means it is made for a foot $8\frac{1}{3}$ inches long. Under Louis XIV the Paris Point system was standardized as $\frac{2}{3}$ centimeter, and became the standard for most of Europe, but Germany continued to follow the English measuring system.

By 1400 most large European cities had shoemakers' guilds. This did not include cobblers, who were shoe repairers and not part of the shoemakers' guild. Shoemakers are capable of doing repairs but this is considered inferior work. In England shoemakers were more properly known as *cordwainers*, and in France as *cordonniers*, after the fine Cordwain leather tanned in Cordoba, Spain, and imported in great quantities. Their very name suggested the quality of their goods.

Shoemaking 1600 to 1850

In the late sixteenth century, welted shoe construction became standard whereby the upper was sewn to a welt with a second row of stitches made through the welt into the outer sole. From this development until the intro-

duction of machinery in the mid-nineteenth century there is very little change in the tools or methods used for shoemaking. And for hand shoemakers, changes in this tradition have been minimal. The tools to achieve this construction consisted of a knife, last, dogs, hammer, awl, and shoulder stick.

The first and most important step in making a shoe is to measure the foot accurately, translating these measurements to a corresponding wooden last. The word *last* comes from the old English word for foot and is the wooden form used as a mold for making the shoe. The last is made to the same shape and size as the client's foot, or a standard last is adjusted adding built-up layers of leather to attain the same measurements. The last is frequently made up of at least two pieces, so that it can be more easily removed from the finished shoe.

After measuring the foot and translating those calculations onto a pattern, cutting out, or *clicking*, the leather is the first step in constructing a pair of shoes. The round, or moon knife is an early tool that can be seen as far back as ancient Egypt. Used by most workers in leather until the nineteenth century, the skill to use it to its full advantage was acquired during apprenticeship. Straight knives were also used but it was only with the

An eighteenth-century shoemaker's shop. This diagram from the *Dictionary of Sciences* (1770) depicts the shoemaking technology and tools of the day. Standardized measurements helped ensure a good fit for length in shoes, and pre-made footwear may have already been in production by the late 1700s. © HISTORICAL PICTURE ARCHIVE/CORBIS. REPRODUCED BY PERMISSION.

mass entry of workers into the shoe factories of the nineteenth century that straight knives and scissors were preferred by the less-skilled labor force, resulting in the extinction of the moon knife.

Lasting pincers or *dogs* are used for pulling the top of the shoe, or upper, tight around the last so that it may be secured with tacks to the underside. Most dogs have serrated teeth that help to pull the upper taut and often have a hammer's peen on the other side to set the tacks so that the welted shoe can then be sewn. A hammer is rarely used to set the tacks into the last but rather is used for *peening* the leather. Once soaked, leather is hammered to flatten the fibrous tissues creating a surface that is more resilient to wear and dampness.

Shoes are traditionally not sewn with a needle, but rather holes are created using awls through which a waxed linen thread is inserted with a pig's bristle. The shapes of awl blades vary according to their intended use. A stitching awl has a straight blade and is used for making holes through multiple layers of leather. The closing awl has a curved blade and is used for joining the sole to the upper.

The shoulder stick, made of wood, burnished the welt and edge of the sole after the shoe was sewn, trimmed, and waxed. The shoulder stick was displaced in the nineteenth century with the use of heated irons, which did the same job but more quickly.

Heels began to be added to footwear beginning in the 1590s. Lasts are required to obtain the correct slope of the sole to accommodate the lift of the heel and as it is too expensive to have a huge inventory of lasts representing the various heel heights as well as for each foot, so most footwear would now be made without left or right definition. This practice of making shoes with straight soles would remain for the next two hundred years, gradually falling from favor throughout the nineteenth century and only finally disappearing in the 1880s. Many surviving examples of lightweight leather and textile footwear from this period show evidence of wear on the uppers where the widths of feet have splayed the upper onto the ground where the sole was insufficiently narrow. However, sturdy leather footwear, like riding boots, continued to be made to order with left and right foot definition for fit and comfort.

With standardized shoe measurements well established and the ease of production for shoemakers of straight soles, it became profitable for shoemakers to pre-make quantities of footwear. No doubt when the shoemaker was not employed by client's orders, he created shoes for speculative sale. Extant shoes dating as early as the 1740s and increasingly toward the end of the eighteenth century display sizes written on linings, suggesting pre-made footwear, as well as shoemaker's names printed on paper labels, usually with their address, suggesting an attempt by shoemakers to encourage repeat business. Footwear had become the first ready-to-wear clothing article sold through shoemaker shops, and also haberdashers and "cheap shoe" warehouses, another name for off-the-rack retailers. Standardized measurements ensured a good fit for length, but it would not be until the 1880s that American shoe manufacturers introduced width sizing.

Shortages of military footwear, and in fact all leather footwear, were a problem in the late eighteenth and early nineteenth centuries. According to period journals, boots and shoes from fallen soldiers were usually taken for reuse at the battle's end. All sides suffered from a lack of product, and methods to bypass the long years of apprenticeship to make a proficient shoemaker were sought. Improvements in the pantograph allowed for mirror images of lasts to be made proficiently, allowing for sturdy leather footwear to be made economically on speculation. The English developed a sole-riveting machine for military footwear in 1810 and also devised a press for cutting out leather around the same time. The French improved quotas by streamlining elements of construction, using a factory method for cottage production. Americans devised soles attached with wooden pegs rather than stitching, a process that had been used since the sixteenth century for attaching heels and repairing soles. And in 1823, the metal eyelet was introduced, eventually displacing the more time-consuming task of hand stitching lace holes.

Shoemaking 1850 to the Present

By 1830, exports of women's footwear from France and men's footwear from England dominated the fashionable marketplace. Shoemaking centers were now firmly established in Paris and Northampton, but the United States, whose shoe industry was centered in and around Lynn, Massachusetts, was about to change everything. Factory-style mass production using semi-skilled workers could undercut imported goods and with the American perfection of the lock-stitch sewing machine by 1860, shoes could be made as quickly as the machine-sewn uppers could be attached to the soles.

The invention of the sewing machine was primarily initiated by the need for sewing leather, not cloth, more proficiently. Chain-stitching machines were introduced in early French shoemaking factories in the 1830s, resulting in Luddite-like revolts by workers who smashed the machines in fear of losing their jobs to technology. However, chain stitching was found to be more suitable for decorative work than seam construction. It was the American Isaac Singer's patented lock-stitch sewing machine for leather in 1856 that was to begin a series of major changes to the shoemaking industry over the next thirty years.

In 1858 the McKay Closing Machine was perfected that sewed the sole to the upper efficiently without the need of a trained shoemaker. The Goodyear welting machine, developed in 1875 by Charles Goodyear Jr., the son of the man who invented the process of vulcanizing rubber, imitated the difficult stitching of a leather shoe through an upper, welt, and sole. Unlike the McKay closing machine, a Goodyear welting machine did not puncture the bottom of the sole, resulting in a suitable walking shoe for outdoor wear. The Lasting machine, invented in 1883 by Jan Matzelinger, copied the multiple motions of pulling leather around a last and tacking it into position—a time-consuming job.

These machines, all invented in the United States, secured the American ability to mass-produce footwear,

as shoes could now be made at great speed and little cost. By the end of the nineteenth century, American shoes were flooding every market. Even the American idea of shoe boxes allowed for more efficient stock management and exporting of goods to Europe and the rest of the world. The European tradition of hand shoemaking was all but ruined.

Some European shoemakers survived the onslaught of cheaper American footwear by catering to the elite, creating footwear of exceptional quality and beauty. However, this worked for only a few small shoemakers. In order to survive, many European shoe companies modernized their factories, fitting them out with the latest machinery to compete with American goods, and many were successful, such as Clarks in England, Bally in Switzerland, Pelikan in Germany, and Bata in Czechoslovakia.

Through a changing workforce and insecure economy due to World War I, postwar recession, and the Great Depression, many shoe companies found it difficult to survive. However, a new process for cemented, or glued, soles in the mid-1930s brought production costs down and eliminated the need for many of the American machines. The 1930s put a focus on women's shoes in the wardrobe, now fully visible under shorter hemlines and thus a necessity for the fashion conscious. The importance of style, color, and decoration enabled European manufacturers the chance to regain supremacy. Companies such as I. Miller and Delman in the United States now saw competition from manufacturers such as Charles Jourdan in France, Rayne in England, and Ferragamo in Italy, who catered to a fashion-conscious clientele.

World War II changed the focus from style to durability. Shoe manufacturers did not suffer, because they were kept busy producing military footwear and other goods under military contract, but fashion footwear was limited by availability of materials.

As part of their postwar recovery, the Italian state aided indigenous shoe companies that were less wieldy than the huge American shoe manufacturers. Undercutting production costs, Italian shoe manufacturers quickly found a niche in the high-fashion footwear industry. By the 1960s French designers were going to Italy to have their shoes made, bypassing their own shoe-manufacturing nationals. Similar sized and modeled companies in Spain and South America with access to cheap and plentiful hides also found success in the 1970s and 1980s, at the cost of American, English, German, and French shoe manufacturers.

But the death knell for many American and European shoe manufacturers came in the development of Southeast Asian shoe industries in the late 1950s and 1960s. Cheaper labor costs for traditionally sewn footwear combined with the new slush molded plastic footwear, which could be produced by machine alone, resulted in the most profitable center in the world for the production of sports shoes—the most popular shoe style since the late 1960s.

While hand shoemakers still exist in London, Venice, and other locales, their numbers are limited and their clients few. High-fashion footwear is produced with a modicum of skilled labor in the finishing; workers whose greatest skill is computer programming make most of the shoes of the early 2000s. Cost, durability, and branding are what drive footwear production in the twenty-first century.

See also **Inuit and Arctic Footwear; Ready-to-Wear; Sewing Machine; Shoes; Shoes, Children's Shoes, Men's; Shoes, Women's.**

BIBLIOGRAPHY

Bondi, Federico, and Giovanni Mariacher. *If the Shoe Fits.* Venice, Italy: Cavallino Venezia, 1983

Durian-Ress, Saskia. *Schuhe: vom späten Mittelalter bis zur Gegenwart Hirmer.* Munich: Verlag, 1991.

Ferragamo, Salvatore. *The Art of the Shoe, 1927–1960.* Florence, Italy: Centro Di, 1992,

Rexford, Nancy E. *Women's Shoes in America, 1795–1930.* Kent, Ohio: Kent State University Press, 2000.

Swann, June. *Shoes.* London: B.T. Batsford, Ltd., 1982.

———. *Shoemaking.* Shire Album 155. Jersey City, N.J.: Parkwest Publications, 1986.

Walford, Jonathan. *The Gentle Step.* Toronto: Bata Shoe Museum, 1994.

Jonathan Walford

SHOES Neil Armstrong uttered, "One small step for man—one giant leap for mankind" upon his first step on the moon on 20 July 1969. In Teflon-coated nylon and rubber boots, Armstrong became the first man to come into contact with an unknown, hostile extraterrestrial environment. Ten thousand years earlier, dwellers of caves in the Pyrenees emerged from the Ice Age also wearing footwear, made from the hides of the animals they hunted, to protect them from the elements and environment.

Footwear's primary purpose is to protect, but in 10,000 years of history, footwear has taken nearly every form possible to service and compliment human bodies, influenced by environment, morality, practicality, economy, and beauty. Footwear is literally the foundation of fashion. It is the only article of clothing required to come into regular contact with the earth, taking the punishment of hundreds of pounds per square inch with every step. At the same time, it is usually expected to resist dampness, comfort the foot, last a long time, and also look attractive.

Footwear has been the subject of literature and folklore. From Cinderella and Dutch clogs laid out for Sinter Claus, to tying shoes to a newlywed's car bumper, and fetish boots—footwear is steeped in tradition and cultural meaning. From biblical times, the sandal or slipper has been used as a symbol. The Assyrians and Hebrews gave a sandal as a token of good faith and to signify the trans-fer of property. In Jewish ritual, the shoe represents wealth as when a loved one dies, the grieving family goes shoeless during the shivah as a sign of poverty, for without the deceased they are poor.

Five Basic Styles

Hot, dry climates generally saw the development of the sandal. Believed to be the world's first crafted foot covering, the sandal was a basic footwear style of the ancient Egyptians of the Nile valley and the Anasazi of the ancient American Southwest. Sandals have been the dominant footwear of Africa, Asia, and Central and South America. Their firm soles protect the feet from scorching surfaces, while the minimal uppers allow air to circulate. Sandals can be made of almost any material that is readily at hand, from woven grasses and leather to wood and even metal.

The moccasin, an Algonquian Native American word for footwear, is essentially a shoe made up of one piece of hide drawn up around the foot and sewn with no seams on the lower part. Moccasin-like foot coverings, gathered on top of the foot with a drawstring were the style of ancient northern Europeans. A descendant of this style survives in folk dress from the Balkans to the Baltic, most often referred to by its Croatian name—the *opanke*.

The shoe may have been the result of a union between the Roman *sandallium* and the *opanke* of northern Europe, essentially being a closed sandal. However, it is most aptly traced to the Christian Copts who developed the turnshoe in the first century. The turnshoe was made, as the names suggests, inside out and turned, with a seam along the edge of the hard sole attaching to the upper. Improvements to this style developed in Europe during the twelfth century when a welt was sewn in the seam to aid the shoe in keeping out water.

Similar in construction, boots provide protection to not only the foot, but also the lower leg. It is conjectured that boots originated in arctic Asia and over time spread across the circumpolar region. Certainly, boots are the dominant traditional footwear for natives of the coldest regions on earth, but ancient examples from Mesopotamia, among many hot climate cultures, prove that boots can also offer protection from desert heat and scrubby brushlands, as well as insect and snakebites. Boots also developed in nomadic cultures where riders of horses or camels wore them to protect their legs from chafing.

Clogs most likely originated from the wooden-soled footwear discovered by the Romans to be worn in Gaul (ancient France). Their wooden-soled footwear was made for inclement weather, which is the origin of the modern word "galosh." Similar overshoes were made throughout the medieval period in Europe to protect good footwear from the filth of the streets. By the fourteenth century a shoe carved from one piece of wood became common for many northern European peasants who required waterproof, warm, inexpensive, and long-wearing footwear.

All footwear is based on these five historic styles. Created for different ranks, rituals, occupations, and uses, footwear can take on many looks when made of different materials and ornamentation. And the main cause for change in footwear is fashion.

From the tenth to twelfth centuries, Europe emerged from the dark ages by uniting itself into nations and developing a mercantile capitalist economy. Crusaders, sent to free the Holy land from Islamic occupation, brought back technical knowledge and fineries from the Arabs, which whetted the appetites of nobles who craved more novelty. By the fourteenth century, quality cloth and fine leathers were being fashioned into shoes that were conspicuous displays of style and elegance, worn with the purpose of expressing personal status.

During the fourteenth century, a fashion for pointed toes spread across Europe. The style originated in Poland, as it became known as the *poulaine* or *cracow*. Edicts were proclaimed limiting its use according to the wealth and social standing of its wearer. When the style fell from fashion at the end of the fifteenth century, it was replaced by wide-toe fashions, known variously as the *hornbill*, *cowmouth*, or *bearpaw*.

A curious woman's fashion, which was at its height of popularity during the 1590s, was the *chopine*—a platform-soled mule that raised the wearer sometimes as high as 39 inches (one meter) off the ground. By the time this fashion had subsided in the early seventeenth century, heels had emerged as a standard addition to both men's and women's footwear.

As Europe positioned itself into nations of power and wealth, the elite distinguished themselves from the masses through conspicuous refinement and extravagant ornamentation. Through the Rococo and Baroque arts, a noble's status was visible in everything he or she did and wore. High-heeled footwear made of expensive silks expressed the idle lifestyles and accumulated wealth of the well heeled. Buckles became a fashionable way of closing shoes during the 1660s, and a century later these large and showy objects had become the feature of the shoe.

By the late eighteenth century, the industrial revolution had brought wealth to the middle classes and the French Revolution ended the divine right of the ruling monarchy. These events empowered the middle classes who would now become the brokers of taste. As everyone was now born on the same level, heels disappeared, fancy buckles were elitist and were replaced by shoelaces, and expensive silk footwear was displaced by more affordable and better-wearing leather footwear. The industrial production of shoes, beginning in the nineteenth century, made attractive, good-quality footwear affordable to almost everyone.

Fashion footwear became a commodity available to all levels of society. Its style was now disseminated through the new communicator—the fashion magazine. Elitism still existed by the quality of the shoe's construction and decoration but what became the real elitist separator was the ability to remain "au courante." Styles, materials, colors, and ornaments changed noticeably enough each season to keep the unfashionable out of the game.

See also **Boots; High Heels; Inuit and Arctic Footwear; Sandals; Shoes, Children's; Shoes, Men's; Shoes, Women's; Sneakers; Sport Shoes.**

BIBLIOGRAPHY

Bondi, Federico, and Giovanni Mariacher. *If the Shoe Fits.* Venice, Italy: Cavallino Venezia, 1983

Durian-Ress, Saskia. *Schuhe: vom späten Mittelalter bis zur Gegenwart Hirmer.* Munich: Verlag, 1991.

Ferragamo, Salvatore. *The Art of the Shoe, 1927–1960.* Florence, Italy: Centro Di, 1992,

Rexford, Nancy E. *Women's Shoes in America, 1795–1930.* Kent, Ohio: Kent State University Press, 2000.

Swann, June. *Shoes.* London: B.T. Batsford, Ltd., 1982.

———. *Shoemaking.* Shire Album 155. Jersey City, N.J.: Parkwest Publications, 1986.

Walford, Jonathan. *The Gentle Step.* Toronto: Bata Shoe Museum, 1994.

Jonathan Walford

SHOES, CHILDREN'S Until recent times, footwear made for children generally mimicked the idiosyncratic styles of the adults of their time and place (taking into account the special characteristics of the feet of infants and young children). It was not until the twentieth century that footwear highly divergent from the dominant adult prototype evolved specifically for children. However, in premodern times there were some circumstances concerning children's footwear that are of historical interest.

In ancient Greece, sandals and slipper-like shoes predominated for both children and adults. Boys were "sandaled" around the age of seven when they first left their homes for school, a rite of passage similar to a boy's receiving his first pair of breeches in later eras. Young girls making their first departure from home, which took place with the girl's marriage shortly after reaching biological adulthood, also went to the shoemaker's for their first pair of sandals. A survey of Tanagra terra-cotta figures from the first half of the third century B.C.E. suggests that young children, perhaps specifically girls, wore slippers before their official departure from family life. There is much debate surrounding the question when and if children in ancient times were shod.

Swaddling, the practice of tightly wrapping the limbs of newborn infants, was widespread in Europe prior to the middle of the eighteenth century. However, when Jean-Jacques Rousseau published *Émile*, his polemic on "natural" methods of child rearing in 1762, swaddling was already on the wane. There was disagreement about whether children should wear shoes. Thomas Delaney, a

Adidas shoes advertisement. An advertisement for Adidas introduces a line of sneakers for children that are much like its adult models, but in colors and branding that appeal to children. THE ADVERTISING ARCHIVE LTD. REPRODUCED BY PERMISSION.

shoe advocate with a vested interest in shoe-wearing, suggested in his 1597–1600 book *The Gentle Craft* that shoes for the newborn should be part of the midwife's kit. On the other hand, Dr. William Cadogan in *Essay on Nursing* (1748) rails against the practice of swaddling but also contends that "Shoes and stockings are very needless Incumbrances" for the young (Cunnington, pp. 24, 33).

Archaeological artifacts from in and around medieval London (1100–1450) show how children's footwear reflected the dominant adult forms, but with slight differences. It appears that children's shoe styling lagged about fifty years behind the fashions of adults. The closures for children's shoes were designed more for practicality than for fashion, being usually on the center front vamp rather than style-consciously on the side. Fashion extremes, such as the *Poulaine* shoe with a long pointed toe, were more modest for children (Grew and De Neergaard). A case study showing that more than one style of footwear for children existed simultaneously can be found in seventeenth-century Boston, Massachusetts, specifically around the year 1670. Five portraits of young Bostonians circa 1670 are extant: the portrait of the Mason children at the De Young Museum in San Francisco and Alice Mason at the National Park Service

Adams Historic Site in Quincy, Massachusetts, and three portraits of the Gibbs children, Henry and Margaret Gibbs in private collections and Robert Gibbs at the Museum of Fine Arts, Boston. All of the portraits may have been painted by the same artist. Of the discernible footwear styles, the rounded toe and the square folded toe with setback sole can be differentiated. Archaeological evidence from the Nanny Privy Site in Boston from roughly the same date also reveals the possibility of multiple styles, a rounded toe, a square toe setback sole, and a possible variation of the square setback toe with equidistant triangular openings on either side of the toe (Butterworth, pp. 66, 67).

In *Emile*, Jean-Jacques Rousseau encouraged baring the child's feet. "Let Emile run about barefoot all the year round, upstairs, downstairs, and in the garden. Far from scolding him, I shall follow his example; only I shall be careful to remove any broken glass." But raising a child "ála Jean-Jacques" sometimes had unwelcome results: "[T]heir hair straggles in a hideous and disgusting way ...They are longer checked, but clamber on to you with their muddy feet."

In the nineteenth century as the making of shoes became more systematic, particularly in New England, evidence emerges of the development of particular styles of shoes for children. The Reverend Richard Manning Chipman noted, for example, that "cack" was a specific term developed in Massachusetts around the year 1820 for a baby's soft leather-soled heelless shoe. On the other hand, the *Oxford English Dictionary* discloses that the word "bootee" or "bootie" did not occur in popular English usage as a description of infant's shoes until its appearance in a Sears, Roebuck and Co. catalog in 1929.

Throughout the nineteenth century, periodicals encouraged women to try their hands at creating shoes for their young children. Patterns appeared in *Godey's Ladies' Book* (1830–1898), and *Peterson's Magazine* (begun 1842). In the anonymously written *The Workwoman's Guide* (1838), the author gives patterns and sewing directions for baby's first and second pair of shoes, as well as a pair made of ticking material (A Lady, pp. 173, 174). One hundred and fifty years after Monsieur Rousseau encouraged the possibility of childlike-children, footwear began to be developed specifically for them, albeit in the form of variations on already existing adult shoes. In 1890, George Warren Brown opened the Brown Shoe Company in St. Louis, Missouri, but it was not until the 1904 World's Fair that his variation on the Oxford tie for boys came into its own. In that year a young executive from Brown's company met artist Richard F. Outcault and the "Buster Brown" shoe was born. Of equal importance is Buster's sister "Mary Jane" who gave her name to the ubiquitous girl's low-strapped shoes.

Children's increasing participation in sports was an important twentieth-century development for their shoes. Keds, originally produced by the U. S. Rubber Company and acquired by Stride Rite in 1979. They "were the first shoe mass marketed as a canvas-top *sneaker*" a word coined by Henry Nelson McKinney because "all other shoes, with the exception of moccasins, made noise when you walked." In the early 1920s, the Converse Shoe Company hired Chuck Taylor away from a basketball team to conduct basketball clinics and in 1923 the *All Star Chuck Taylor* Converse rubber shoe was introduced. The Bata Shoe Company marketed a similar shoe internationally.

"Jellies," the translucent plastic (polyvinyl chloride) shoes, were developed due to leather shortages resulting from World War II. They were created by Mr. Jean Dauphant and family at Plastic-Auvergne and are a continuing international success.

The twentieth century increasingly saw shoe manufacturers appealing directly to children through such techniques as tie-ins with television shows such as *Howdy Doody*, *The Lone Ranger*, various cartoons, and *Sesame Street*. The 1980s saw catalog and department store giant Sears, Roebuck and Co. introduce Grranimals, a line of children's clothing with accompanying footwear that had strategically placed emblems that aided children in creating coordinated outfits on their own.

On the basis of an examination of recent children's footwear styles, it could be argued that after thousands of years of the subjugation of children to the vagaries of adult shoe styling, it is now children's shoes that are influencing adult shoes, particularly in the area of slip-ons and Velcro-closures. The history of children's shoes is a relatively underdeveloped field that offers many possibilities for fruitful further study.

See also **Shoes; Shoes, Men's; Shoes, Women's; Sneakers.**

BIBLIOGRAPHY

Butterworth, Jeffrey A. "Gentle Souls: Shoemakers in Seventeenth Century Boston." Master's thesis, University of Rhode Island, 1998.

Cunnington, Phillis, and Catherine Lucas. *Costume for Births, Marriages and Deaths.* London: Adam and Charles Black, 1972.

Grew, Francis, and Margrethe De Neergaard. *Shoes and Pattens.* London: Museum of London, 1988, 2001.

A Lady. *The Workwoman's Guide.* Reprint. Guilford, Conn.: Opus Publications, 1986. Originally published in 1838.

Neils, Jennifer, and John H. Oakley. *Coming of Age in Ancient Greece: Images of Childhood from the Classical Past.* New Haven, Conn.: Yale University Press, 2003.

Jeffrey Butterworth

SHOES, MEN'S In the medieval period new shoes were available only to a tiny elite of aristocrats and wealthy merchants. However, it appears that in Britain almost all of the poor wore some kind of footwear, which was made possible through the widespread practice of re-

A pair of black leather winkle-picker shoes. Developed as a men's shoe style in the 1950s, the pointed toes of the winkle-pickers led to their name being derived from a sharply-pointed tool. COLLECTION: POWERHOUSE MUSEUM, SYDNEY, AUSTRALIA. PHOTO: SUE STAFFORD. REPRODUCED BY PERMISSION.

making and repairing old shoes. Medieval shoes were made from leather, silk, and other cloths and up to the end of the sixteenth century, all men's footwear tended to be flat. The most extreme style of the fourteenth and fifteenth centuries was the "poulaine," or "pike," which featured extremely pointed toes, sometimes up to four inches (10 centimeters) in length.

Shoes with an arched sole and heel emerged at the end of the sixteenth century, a novelty that was to become a predominant feature of men's shoes in the seventeenth and eighteenth centuries. During the reign of James I (1603–1625), masculine court fashions became particularly flamboyant and stockings and shoes became a key focus of attention. The shoes of the wealthy began to be decorated with large bows, rosettes, or "roses." These styles were superseded in the reign of Charles I (1625–1649), when political instability and war in Britain and Europe encouraged the popularity of military-inspired, knee-high, leather boots. These were fashionable from the 1620s to the 1690s and despite their practical origins as riding wear, they were often elegant and decorative.

"A sewing machine for leather was in use by the 1850s … and by the end of the century most shoes were made in large factories. The personal relationship between shoemaker and wearer disappeared except at the most expensive end of the market" (Mitchell, p. 34).

Early Modern Period

The rise of France as an international fashion center under Louis XIV (1643–1715) promoted the popularity of French court styles. Shoes were adorned with decorative buckles, a style that remained highly fashionable until the 1780s. Buckles were bought as separate items and by the late eighteenth century they were available for all tastes and pockets, from sparkling precious stones for the wealthy, to plain steel, brass, and pinchbeck for the lower orders.

New shoes became more accessible to the middle classes in the eighteenth century, owing to relative increases in incomes and new manufacturing methods. The development of large workshops, which produced ready-made shoes by hand helped to make shoes more affordable.

Modernity and Men's Footwear

The Enlightenment and the French Revolution (1789–1799) stimulated tastes for the plain, English, country mode of dress, which dominated international fashion from the 1780s. An important element of this style was the jockey or top boot, which featured a top of lighter colored leather. Popular men's wear styles of the early nineteenth century included laced-up walking shoes, flat leather evening pumps, and boots of various styles including top boots, Wellington, Hessian, and Blucher boots. The latter three illustrate the tendency for boot styles of the era to be named after significant military figures or developments.

By the mid-nineteenth century, ankle boots, such as the Balmoral, became the most common type of footwear for men and popular shoe styles included the Oxford and the Derby. These shoe types along with the brogue were widely worn in the twentieth century and are still common in the twenty-first century.

Shoe production was increasingly mechanized in the mid-nineteenth century and by 1900 most people wore shoes made in factories and sold by shoe retailers, rather than patronizing shoemakers. By the 1890s, relative increases in wealth, increased participation in sport and leisure activities such as tennis, golf, and cycling, and improvements in mass-manufacturing techniques led to middle-class consumption of an increasingly diverse range of styles, suitable for various contexts and activities. Despite these transformations in the production and consumption of shoes, leading bespoke shoemakers from this era such as John Lobb Ltd., London, and New & Lingwood, London, have survived into the twenty-first century.

Men's Shoes Post-1945

The predominant features of men's shoes in the post-1945 period have been an expanding diversity of styles and price levels and a more rapid turnover of fashionable designs. The manufacture of ready-made shoes became global after 1945, with low-cost production now concentrated in Asian countries and more exclusive shoes being made in Italy. From the 1950s the rise of youth fashion generated a greater degree of experimentation in men's footwear, with the emergence of designs such as brothel creepers, winklepickers, Chelsea boots, and Doctor Martens boots.

Since the mid-1970s, the trainer or sneaker has come to be ubiquitous footwear for men of all ages and tastes. This has partly been owing to a general move toward informality in male appearances, but is also linked to the influence of black street fashion and the aggressive marketing efforts of global sportswear companies like Nike, Puma, and Adidas.

The 1970s saw the appropriation of men's shoe styles such as Dr. Martens by women, a trend that was linked to the influence of feminist ideas and the punk subculture. Unisex or androgynous footwear has continued as a feature of mainstream dress in the early twenty-first century. However, despite these developments, there remain significant differences between men's and women's shoes. High heels are still seen as exclusively feminine and men's businesswear remains focused around variations on the Derby and Oxford styles.

See also **Boots; Inuit and Arctic Footwear; Sandals; Shoemaking; Shoes; Shoes, Women's; Sneakers; Sport Shoes.**

BIBLIOGRAPHY

Baynes, Ken, and Kate Baynes. *The Shoe Show: British Shoes since 1790.* London: The Crafts Council, 1979.

Boydell, Christine. "The Training Shoe: 'Pump Up the Power.'" In *The Gendered Object.* Edited by Pat Kirham. Manchester, U.K.: Manchester University Press, 1996.

Cohn, Nik. *Today There Are No Gentlemen.* London: Weidenfeld and Nicolson, 1971.

de la Haye, Amy. *The Cutting Edge: 50 Years of British Fashion 1947–1997.* London: V & A Publications, 1996.

Mitchell, Louise. *Stepping Out: Three Centuries of Shoes.* Sydney: Powerhouse Publishing, 1997.

Woolley, Linda, and Lucy Pratt. *Shoes.* London: V & A Publications, 1999.

Fiona Anderson

SHOES, WOMEN'S In cultures where bare feet are customary or only simple sandals are worn, little interest exists in the female foot as a sensual appendage. However, hidden away in tight, decorative shoes and boots, the female foot has been revered as a powerful sexual stimulus in many cultures. Smaller and narrower than a man's foot, the attributes of a woman's comparatively delicate foot has been appreciated and accentuated throughout much of history. This is most apparent in the extreme practice of Chinese foot binding.

For a thousand years in China it was considered refined and sexually attractive for a woman to have bound feet. Outside of weekly washing and perfuming, the feet were kept bound tightly at all times. Several attempts over the years to outlaw the practice by the ruling Manchurians failed and even the Republic made an attempt at stopping the tradition in 1912 when it came to power. The tradition slowly discontinued over time, being finally eliminated in 1949 under the communists. This is by far the most extreme example of sexual differentiation in footwear history. Most cultures cover the female foot differently than the male foot, but in a far less dramatic manner.

Amongst the traditional Inuit of central Northern Canada inlaid furred sealskin boots are designed with vertical patterns for men and horizontal patterns for women. In some cultures it is a matter of who wears the boots. Native Southwestern American Zuni women wear tall white skin boots, while the men wear shorter boots or shoes. Greenlander women's traditional costume includes thigh-high blood-red sealskin boots with decorative appliqués while men wear shorter, darker colored boots.

Fashion Footwear to 1600

In Western culture, it is women who generally wear more architecturally significant or decorous foot coverings. With few exceptions, until the Renaissance, women's footwear was generally less interesting for the simple reason that it was less visible under the longer garments worn, and it was men who were the peacocks in the footwear department.

In ancient Egypt, Greece, and Rome, women wore sandals consisting of fewer straps and less decoration than men's sandals, baring more toe cleavage. During the late Roman or Byzantine Empire, Christianity brought about radical change from the ancient classical ways. Christian morality considered it sinful to expose the body. St. Clement of Alexandria, in the third century, was already preaching humility for women, commanding them not to bare their toes. Byzantine footwear was designed to cover the feet, and shoes replaced sandals. Roman-style sandals remained the privilege of high-ranking church officials, and abundant decoration was seen as too worldly for the people to wear, appropriate only for the Pope and other prelates.

The largest threat to the Byzantine Empire came with the expansion of Islam that, by 750, had grown to include most of the old Roman territory including Egypt and its Christian Copt population. By the eighth century, Coptic steles (gravestones) depict the deceased wearing shoes and mules, sometimes decorated with gilded figures and etched linear designs, often in sacred imagery. The shoe had evolved to include a pointed toe and peaked throat and was often made of red kid. Called *mulleus* in Latin, referring to the red color, it is from this connection that the modern term "mule"— for a backless shoe— originates. This style can still be found in parts of the Middle and Far East.

Christianity reinforced the alliance of what was once Rome's domain. During the Carolingian age of Charlemagne (768–814) a close relationship between the various kings and the pope secured the Church in much of Europe unifying the European kingdoms.

Europe began to emerge from the Dark Ages in about 1000 C.E. Christian Europe was uniting into nations, headed by monarchies. These European states began crusades into the Holy Land, bringing themselves into contact with Islamic thought and products. The crusaders brought back silk, embroidery, and the button, whetting the appetites of nobles who craved finery and novelty. The textile arts flourished with the production of quality weavings, embroideries, leather goods, and felts. At the same time, merchants became wealthy importing and exporting these goods, making enough money to dress like nobles. Fashion was now a commodity that expressed the status of its wearer. Elitism could be expressed through a sumptuous display of fashion excess.

The first footwear fashion excess was the elongated pointed toe, said to have originated in the late 1100s. The style was popular in the late 1100s but subsided from fashion, and when reintroduced from Poland in the early 1300s it had become known as a *poulaine* or *crakow*, reflecting its supposed Polish origin.

Expensive materials and excessive styles were royalty's way of staying ahead of the moneyed bourgeoisie. If the sheer cost of dressing well did not create enough of a gap between the well-to-do and the have-nots, then edicts were placed upon materials, styles, and decorations restricting their use to persons of appropriate status. The church also set restrictions against obscene or excessive fashions. Together, these governing bodies attempted to keep the classes in their place, making each identifiable by their dress.

In England, in 1363, Edward III proclaimed a sumptuary law that limited the length of the toe to the wearer's income and social standing; commoners earning less than 40 *livres* per year were forbidden the use of long toes; those who made more than 40 *livres* annually could wear a toe no longer than six inches; a gentleman no more than twelve inches; a nobleman no more than 24 inches; and a prince was unlimited in the length he chose.

Northern Europe continued to don the style until the end of the fifteenth century, even though Italy, southern France, and Spain essentially stopped wearing the protrusive toe, choosing instead to have less pointed footwear made of the finest kid leather or silk.

When length finally became old fashioned, width became the next fashion excess. Popular in the English Tudor court and other northern European states of the sixteenth century, shoes with widths that extended well beyond the foot were known variously as the *hornbill, cow-mouth,* or *bearpaw.* This new dimension suffered the same excesses as the long toe. Under England's Queen Mary, another sumptuary law was passed, and although its wording is lost, it can be assumed that the width of the toe was similarly limited according to social status and wealth of its wearer.

The last dimension was now to be explored—height. The ancient Greeks first put platform sandals on the feet of their actors to give them distinction, suggesting the performer was playing an important person. Ancient Greek women adopted cork-soled versions, called *Cothurnus.* Fifteenth-century aristocratic Venetian women donned stilted mules or shoes, called *chopines,* to reflect their high social status. Fashioned in velvet with tack-work or white alum tanned kid with punch-work brogueing, *chopines* not only added height, but also décor to the silhouette. Although called "depraved" and "dissolute" by the church, the style traveled across Europe where by 1600 even Shakespeare wrote in Hamlet "Your Ladyship is nearer to heaven than when I saw you last by the altitude of a *chopine.*" Maidservants were required to steady the wearers of some of the tallest *chopines* that could reach a height of up to 39 inches (one meter). *Chopines* fell from fashion when prostitutes donned them, ruining their status for women of breeding. Heels, introduced in the 1590s, eventually displaced the platform mules, although some extant examples of *chopines* date as late as 1620.

Seventeenth and Eighteenth Centuries

When heels were first added to shoes in the 1590s they were only about an inch in height. Women's heels took on greater elevations during the reign of Louis XIV (1643–1715) in France. Heels towered two to three inches, although "well-heeled" women's skirts made their shoes virtually invisible. The heel expressed the status of the wearer as they were quite literally at a higher level than the hordes of common folk. Under Louis XIV, red heels were worn strictly at court. Although this law existed only in France, by restriction the color came to represent the power and status of the aristocratic elite across Europe.

Three different heel types developed in Europe during the eighteenth century. The Italian heel was tall and spiked, like a stiletto. The French heel was of mid-height and curvaceous and later became known as the Louis heel; and the English heel was thicker and generally low to mid-

height. Fashionable continental European women were more inclined to be at court or at home in an urban setting, so their heels could generally be more delicate, while English women of breeding tended to live at their country estates for most of the year, so a thicker heel was necessary for the more natural terrain they traversed.

When the skirts of French gowns inched toward the ankles in the mid-eighteenth century, suddenly there seemed to be an erotic interest in the high-heeled shoe, as it made the foot appear smaller and narrower, and gave the ankle a delicate shape. In the meantime, due to practicality, men were now solidly planted on the ground with heels of less than an inch. It was appropriate for a gentleman to walk upon a muddy, cobbled street that required a low-heeled shoe or boot. A lady of quality, however, did not walk the streets and likely traveled by coach or other means, so a high heel was appropriate for most occasions she would encounter.

Throughout the seventeenth and eighteenth centuries an increasing fondness for luxurious fabrics and decorative trimmings ensued. European-made damask and brocaded silks had been produced in Italy and France until the emigration of Protestant French Huguenots in the last quarter of the seventeenth century. They brought with them the knowledge of silk production when they resettled throughout Protestant Europe, from Spitalfields, England, to Krefeld, Germany. The costly development of this new industry, however, kept domestically produced silks at a higher price than imported Chinese silks.

Chinese silks were usually brocaded patterns of abstract geometric designs, made specifically for the western market. To support the development of a domestic silk industry, England banned the wearing of Chinese silk in 1699; other countries proclaimed similar edicts. Silks produced in Europe followed the Oriental taste of abstract patterns and became known as "bizarres," remaining in fashion until the 1730s when tastes changed and grand floral designs came into vogue.

The decoration of shoes used many techniques: silk embroidery, applied cord *passementerie,* and silver and gold thread embroidery that was made by professional male embroiderers who belonged to embroidery guilds.

Originally, buckles came into fashion because of their utility. Samuel Pepys refers to putting on buckles for the first time in 1660. By the end of the seventeenth century, buckles overtook the standard of ribbon laces. Both men and women increasingly suffered from buckle mania throughout the eighteenth century. Buckles grew in size and became more elaborate, set with showy paste and semiprecious stones. Men's buckles were larger but both sexes displayed their shoe jewelry during a bow and curtsy with extended foot—the appropriate method of introduction of the day.

By the end of the eighteenth century mercantile and industrial wealth had created a strong, affluent, educated,

Illustration of woman wearing chopines. In the fifteenth century, aristocratic Venetian women began wearing platform shoes as a symbol of status, and the style quickly spread across Europe. THE GRANGER COLLECTION LTD. REPRODUCED BY PERMISSION.

yet politically under-represented middle class who were set between an ever-deepening rift of the noble elite and the working poor. The American and French revolutions exploded out of this imbalance, and, in the end, demographics won. The middle classes rose to power and would become the brokers of taste.

In the early months of the French Revolution, the French National Assembly demanded that all deputies give up their valuable shoe buckles for the benefit of the treasury. The legislative session of 22 November 1789 opened with le Marechal de Maille making the patriotic gift of his gold buckles.

The Nineteenth Century

Following the French Revolution, plain leather footwear became the mode. Durable and affordable, it was considered more democratic than the fussily embroidered and expensive silk shoes previously preferred by the elite.

Heels also fell from use after the French Revolution, in keeping with the new democratic philosophy that all people are born equal. The new French and American republics looked to classical models of democracy for inspiration and excavations at Pompeii and from Napoleon's military campaigns in Egypt brought renewed interest in the ancient world and provided inspiration for neoclassical designs.

Women's fashion took on the silhouette of a Greek column. Neutrals of white and tan were complimented by dark tones of the classical world: Pompeiin red, crocodile green, and rich gold. The sandal was revived during the neoclassical period, although not with great success, especially in the colder northern European climates where instead, shoes were fashioned with cutouts lined with colored underlays or painted with stripes to emulate sandals. During the Napoleonic wars an inconsistent fashion image existed. In shoes, the use of heels

Physical Culture women's shoes advertisement, 1938. By the 1930s, the color, shape, and decoration of shoes had expanded to offer numerous options for fashionable women. © LAKE COUNTY MUSEUM/CORBIS. REPRODUCED BY PERMISSION.

and the shapes of toes varied, with no one style predominating. The square toe, introduced as early as the 1790s, did not become the main style until the late 1820s but would remain so for the next half century.

As factories disfigured the horizon, many longed for the picturesque qualities of an unspoiled landscape. A naturalism movement brought long country promenades into fashion; ladies began to wear "spatterdashes," leggings adapted from men's military dress that protected stockings from spatters and dashes of mud. Walking became a fad called "pedestrianism" and a prescribed activity for women. Boots were worn for this activity as a sensible alternative to fashion shoes. Ankle boots, referred to as demi-boots or half boots, found international appeal in this period.

By the time Queen Victoria ascended the throne in 1837 a sentimental, romanticized movement had swept popular thought. Women became expressions of virtue and femininity, their conservative costume and demure decorum reflected conscious gentility. Fine slippers of kid and silk were made in great quantities in Paris and exported around the world. Soles, which had been made without left or right definition for more than 200 years, were exceptionally narrow now and the delicate uppers

tended not to last long as they were pulled under the sole at the ball of the foot, deteriorating with one wearing. Colored footwear found favor during the 1830s with ankle-length skirts, but fell from use for the next two decades. The long, full skirts of the mid-nineteenth century hid the feet from view, with perhaps the occasional peep at a vamp when the woman walked or waltzed across a floor. By the mid-1850s, black or white footwear was deemed by fashion delineators to be the most elegant and tasteful choice, a standard that would last for many years.

However, after the mid-1850s, with the introduction of wire frame "crinoline" skirt supports, skirts tended to tip and swing, exposing the foot and ankle. This brought about interest in the decoration of shoe vamps. Machine chain-stitched designs with colorful silk underlays, dubbed "chameleons," became fashionable for home and evening wear. For daytime, however, boots became modest essentials underneath the wire-frame supported skirts. Side-laced boots called "Adelaides" in England, after William IV's consort, were made for most outdoor occasions until improvements in the elasticity of rubber resulted in the development of elastic thread which, woven into webbing, was used for ankle-boot gussets. Elastic-sided boots were referred to as "Garibaldi" boots in Europe after the Italian statesman who united Italy during the 1860s, and as "Congress" boots in the United States after the American Congress. Front-laced boots came back into fashion by 1860. Called "Balmorals," after Queen Victoria's Scottish home, the style was deemed suitable for informal daywear and sporting occasions at first, but by the 1870s had become the more common closure of all boots. Button boots were introduced in the 1850s, but were generally not favored until the 1880s when their tight fit and elegant closure flattered the slim ankle and foot more than laced styles.

Heels were re-introduced on ladies' footwear during the late 1850s, but did not find universal appeal until the late 1870s. Historicism was an important movement of the mid-nineteenth century; Rococo and Baroque styling was evident on shoes in the 1860s with a return to buckles and bows. Large, multiple loop bows were called "Fenelon," after the seventeenth-century French writer. Mules, too, came back into fashion as part of the historical revival of the *ancien regime*.

Exoticism was another important movement of the nineteenth century. Via the Crimean war, Turkish embroideries were exported for the production of shoe uppers in the late 1850s and when Japan opened its doors to foreign trade in 1867, a taste for all-things Oriental made a strong comeback. Chinese embroidered silks or European embroidered silks in the taste of Chinese and Japanese textiles were in fashion and a Japanese-influenced palette of colors resulted in brown leather footwear coming into vogue, which would become a fashion staple.

By the late 1880s the square toe had finally fallen from fashion, replaced by rounded and even almond-shaped toes and all shoes were now being made with right and left sole definitions. Business began to decline for hand shoemakers as mass manufacturers standardized sizes and provided widths for customer fit. Improvements in American manufacturing methods and machinery, as well as cheaper production costs positioned the Americans as the leading footwear manufacturers for the next fifty years.

The Twentieth Century

Black, brown, and white footwear predominated until the 1920s. Colored footwear was made almost entirely for evening dress, as it was seen as inappropriately gaudy for street or daywear. After the start of World War I in 1914, hemlines began a steady climb up the leg, so that by armistice the sensuous curves of the instep and ankle were exposed. The climbing hemline made the gap between the top of the boot and bottom of the hemline an unsightly distraction. The boot was generally abandoned from fashion, although a "Cossack" boot, or pull-on style was introduced and found some success in the late 1920s.

The impact of the shoe on the complete silhouette now had to be calculated to find a complimentary style. During the 1920s, short and curvy heels grew taller and straighter, which tightened the calf muscle, slimming the appearance of the ankle and foreshortening the foot making it appear smaller. Even the vamp was cut lower to expose more of the instep.

By the 1930s, shoemakers had become shoe designers. Color, shape, and decoration literally exploded at the feet of fashion. A wide variety of spectators, oxfords, pumps, sandals, brogues, and other styles filled the shoe stores. Salvatore Ferragamo revived the *chopine* in 1937, using cork to create platform soles. Internationally, the style found limited success, but with the beginning of World War II (1939–1945) the style grew in popularity. The war resulted in a shortage of leather for civilian footwear; thick wood or cork soles and substitute leather uppers made of raffia, hemp, or textile substituted. In the United States, where rationing was less severe than in Europe, platform shoes were more often made of leather, but women were rationed to two pairs of shoes per year.

The tall tapered heel remained in fashion from the late 1920s to the mid-1950s with only subtle changes in form until the Italian heel, renamed the "stiletto," became the fashion in the late 1950s. Tall and very slender with a metal core, the heel was named after the weapon for a reason. The narrow heel created pressure of hundreds of pounds per square inch with every step, pockmarking linoleum and wooden floors. Visitors to the Louvre were required to don plastic heel caps to protect the ancient floors. The stiletto heel, paired with a sharp pointed toe, was the most aesthetically complimentary shoe style ever designed. The pointed toe visually narrowed the foot and the high heel tightened the calf muscle, slimming the ankle. Medically, it was the worst

combination ever created. Many women turned their ankles on the metal spikes, catching the tips in manholes, subway grates, or even cracks in the sidewalk; the high heel forced the foot forward into the pointed toe, which curtailed the toes, causing bunions and hammertoes.

In reaction, a low-heeled, square boot came back into fashion in the mid-1960s. Paired with miniskirts, the boot highlighted the leg and gave a youthful élan to the fashions of the day. Boots came on the fashion scene at the same time as the popular "go-go" dances of the day and quickly became known as go-go boots—usually white ankle boots.

The early 1970s saw the return of the platform that accomplished two feats at once. Women's liberation was reflected in the elevated soles that put women on an equal footing to men. At the same time, platforms were complimentary to the length of the leg, made apparent in hot pants, miniskirts, and long-legged pants.

Since the early 1970s fashion footwear has been eclipsed by the sports-shoe phenomenon. More runners, joggers, cross-trainers, and basketball shoes have been sold than high-fashion shoes on an annual basis. Scientific advances in fit and comfort has been paired with conscious design and celebrity marketing, creating a mad frenzy for every new design released. Fashion experts may scoff at sports shoes as fashion, but many designers have paid homage to the style in upscale versions over the past thirty years.

High-fashion footwear of the last quarter of the twentieth century consisted almost entirely of revivals. The stiletto-heeled, pointed-toe shoe of the late 1950s and early 1960s was the mainstream high-fashion style of the late 1980s and early 1990s. Every time the platform shoe has come back into fashion it has been heavily inspired by its previous incarnation. The platform shoes of the 1990s were many times perfect re-creations of their 1970s predecessors, to the point where it was nearly impossible to tell the difference between the retro and the true vintage versions.

Subtle tweaking of heel shapes, toe shapes, decorations, colors, and materials, and the combinations in which they are used are the only elements that define the past thirty years of fashion footwear from previous styles. Multiplicity is key to the fashion footwear of the early 2000s: stilettos, platforms, chunky heels, low heels, pointed toes, square toes, boots, shoes, and ballerina flats. Virtually all styles are available at the same time, and all of them are at the height of fashion.

See also **Boots; Footbinding; High Heels; Inuit and Arctic Dress; Sandals; Shoes; Shoes, Men's; Sneakers; Sports Shoes.**

BIBLIOGRAPHY
Bondi, Federico, and Giovanni Mariacher. *If the Shoe Fits.* Venice, Italy: Cavallino Venezia, 1983.

Durian-Ress, Saskia. *Schuhe: vom späten Mittelalter bis zur Gegenwart Hirmer*. Munich: Verlag, 1991.

Ferragamo, Salvatore. *The Art of the Shoe, 1927–1960*. Florence, Italy: Centro Di, 1992.

Rexford, Nancy E. *Women's Shoes in America, 1795–1930*. Kent, Ohio: Kent State University Press, 2000.

Swann, June. *Shoes*. London: B.T. Batsford, Ltd., 1982.

———. *Shoemaking*. Shire Album 155. Jersey City, N.J.: Parkwest Publications, 1986.

Walford, Jonathan. *The Gentle Step*. Toronto: Bata Shoe Museum, 1994.

Jonathan Walford

SHOPPING Early histories of shopping comprised celebratory histories of individual shops, and chronological accounts of retail progress (Adburgham). Recent studies have come from social, economic, and increasingly cultural history. They balance empirical and focused studies of shops and shopping with the more thematic agenda offered by consumption studies. A significant proportion of studies is devoted to shopping for clothes and related fashionable goods. This kind of shopping was associated with a particular set of shopping and retail practices.

The popularity of shopping as a subject for research is linked to the meteoric rise of the topic of consumption within a multitude of different disciplines, including history, sociology, anthropology, cultural studies, psychology, and geography. This phenomenon has been connected to an increasing dissatisfaction with Marxist production-led explanations for historical trends. The way people shop has since been identified as a defining characteristic of historical and contemporary societies (Miller et al.). Early work in the field connected the birth of modern consumer culture with the new availability of mass-produced goods in the late eighteenth century (McKendrick et al.). Subsequent studies have given more significance to changes in shopping practices. The arrival of the department store in the late nineteenth century has been seen as a marker of modern consumer cultures (Bowlby, Rappaport), and postwar supermarkets and malls have been closely tied to understandings of contemporary consumer society (Bowlby, Campbell in Miller).

The Shopper

The identification and definition of consumer identities has been an increasingly central component of shopping studies. Drawing on the semiotic theories of postmodernists such as Jean Baudrillard, consumer identities, and shopping types have often been appropriated for source material by a range of disciplines. These figures have been seen as the embodiment of contemporary attitudes to, and anxieties about, consumption, gender, class, ethnicity, modernity, and the urbanites. This approach has been criticized for obscuring the meaning of shopping itself within these identities, as Miller et al. express, "the shopper … nearly always figures as a sign for something else." Within this work, shopping has been shown to be an important part of identity construction and performance, leading to the suggestion that within modern and post-modern consumer society, the self *was* the sum of consumption practices and goods bought. This idea of self-construction through shopping has been consistently promoted through store advertising, women's magazines, and other institutions of consumer culture. However, more specific studies have allowed shopping cultures and consumer identity to be mutually constitutive, ascribing more agency to the individual shopper, and the ability to negotiate different identities.

There has been a particular emphasis on identity within studies of Victorian consumption. For example, the Victorian London's shopping district has been revealed as home to newly confident female shoppers who used shopping to stake a claim to the city (Rappaport). This focus signals the advent of modern consumer culture, in which shopping was recognized as a meaningful practice and the consumer the key protagonist. From this point on, shops can be seen to sell "image" in addition to actual commodities, an image that was bound up with modern consumer identities. During the twentieth century, the centrality of the shopper within retail theory and its histories grew, reflecting a heightened understanding of how consumer psychology could be applied to marketing. By the late twentieth century, the consumer was acknowledged as a primary economic and cultural force in society.

The study of the female shopper has dominated the field. This relates to the conceptualization of shopping as a strongly gendered practice by contemporaries as well as by many subsequent theorists. It has been presented as an essential component of the female domestic role, interpreted as a masculine seduction of the feminine through strategies of temptation and spectacle, and more recently as a more empowering, but essentially feminine, means of engaging with urban life. Bowlby summarizes this position: "The history of shopping is largely a history of women, who have overwhelmingly been the principal shoppers both in reality and in the multifarious representations of shopping" (Bowlby, p. 7). This gender imbalance has begun to be seriously addressed in the early twenty-first century. For example, Breward has identified significant groups of male shoppers in Victorian and Edwardian London, for whom shopping for clothes was an essential component of their fashionable urban identities.

Past studies of the shopper have often overlooked the centrality of the fashionable commodities themselves, which newer work has sought to address. It is the focus of consumers' attention on the goods in the window, and on the activity of shopping, that distinguishes them from other actors in the urban scene; the *flaneur*, the tourist, the prostitute. This approach allows an understanding of the role of shopping within the identity of clothes. It acknowledges the significance of garments' nature as "searched for" and "bought."

A Typography of Shops

Specificity of time and place are important to an understanding of shopping. Particular retail formats, each with their characteristic architecture, planning, and shopping practices, have been considered emblematic of social trends within studies of consumption. Miller et al. relate how during the late 1980s and early 1990s the story of modern consumption coincided with a particular genealogy of the shop; "an accepted natural history of consumption took shape which, identifying consumption as a key characteristic of modernity, described an arc from the arcades and department stores of Paris through to the shopping malls of the United States."

Of course, shopping for clothes did not begin with the birth of modern consumer cultures. There is an older tradition of shopping, which includes drapers, tailors, and markets. The beginnings of a new approach to shop design and shopping, which emphasized luxury, spectacle, and leisure, have been identified in the seventeenth- and eighteenth-century shopping gallery, for example London's Westminster Hall, and the nineteenth-century arcade, such as the Burlington Arcade adjoining Piccadilly (Walsh in Benson and Ugolini).

The huge department stores of the late nineteenth century exploited these characteristics to the full. Drawing on the model of the Parisian Bon Marché, they styled themselves as "universal providers" and offered a range of additional services from hairdressing to libraries, but drapery and ready-made garments formed a central part of their trade. The department store has been associated with the advent of modern consumer cultures, the democratization of "luxury" consumer goods, and the prominence of display. It has also been linked to the broader themes of the growth of the middle classes, urbanization, and shifts in gender definitions (Bowlby, Rappaport).

The first half of the twentieth century witnessed the development of "multiples" or chain stores, which catered especially to the growing group of lower-middle-class consumers. In Britain, Marks & Spencer, C&A, and the Co-op were especially important for women's and children's wear, while multiple tailors, such as Montague Burton, targeted men (Winship in Jackson et al.). There were also more exclusive multiples such as Austin Reed menswear and Russell and Bromley shoes. The shops constituted clearly identifiable brands, through their architecture, interior design, advertising, as well as merchandise. While frequently establishing a flagship on the principal urban thoroughfares, multiples have largely been associated with the suburban and provincial high street.

The story of postwar shopping has been dominated by the development of the "shopping center" and mall, burgeoning in the interwar United States, and spreading to Europe during the 1960s (Longstreth). They have

Burlington Arcade, London, England. A doorman stands in London's Burlington Arcade, which was founded in the nineteenth century and emphasized luxury, spectacle, and leisure. © BO ZAUNDRES/CORBIS. REPRODUCED BY PERMISSION.

been studied intensively, and have often been interpreted as an articulation of postmodern society (Campbell in Miller). The new format was purpose-built and often privately regulated, usually enveloping both shops and a shopping street for pedestrians within a single building. Some have been located within city and town centers, replicating some of the characteristics of the department store. But they have been mainly associated with the urban fringe, dependent for business on increased levels of car ownership. A typical example in the United Kingdom is Meadow Hall, near Sheffield. Although very successful, these new shopping environments did not destroy the cultural and economic importance of the traditional high street.

An associated late twentieth-century development is the retail park: a series of shopping warehouses located out of town. This period additionally saw the expansion of the big supermarkets into clothing. Their marketing has emphasized value, with the controversial provision of cut-price designer jeans, and attempts have been made to secure the services of established designers, for example George at Asda in the United Kingdom. This era has also been characterized by the internationalization of retailing. On one hand, powerful controlling interests such as Wal-Mart have developed as a result of construction of new stores. On the other, multiples such as the Gap have opened outlets in shopping thoroughfares throughout the world.

Other Ways of Shopping

Alongside these sites of consumption, secondhand clothing continued to be an important part of shopping practices. Its retail venues shifted format and location within shopping networks over time, and were historically associated with a succession of different immigrant communities, working from street markets. From the latter part of the twentieth century, buying secondhand has flourished within the charity shop, retro-clothing specialists, market stalls, and flea markets.

However, shopping has not exclusively been tied to physically located retail sites. Mail order allowed shopping to take place from the home. Sears, Roebuck and Co. spearheaded mail order in the United States, with companies such as Freemans and Kays important in the United Kingdom.

It proved consistently popular throughout the nineteenth and twentieth centuries, often linked to credit schemes and to companies with associated retail outlets, such as the United Kingdom's "Next Directory." From the end of the twentieth century, the potential of mail-order shopping expanded exponentially with the arrival of Internet shopping, potentially posing a more serious challenge to the future viability of the traditional shop, although retail clothing stores has been less seriously affected than other sectors.

There has been an unwillingness to study shopping cultures, which were not essentially novel, however, a more integrated understanding of shopping can be gained by studying the established and declining models alongside new ones. This approach better reflects the landscape of different shops, configured in particular ways within a single main street, a shopping route, or an individual's shopping trip. It also relates more closely to the clothing bought by shoppers; within a single wardrobe a chain-store shirt hangs next to a secondhand jacket quite unproblematically, although their owner remains aware of the provenance of each.

See also **Boutique; Department Store; Mannequins; Window Displays.**

BIBLIOGRAPHY

Adburgham, Alison. *Shops and Shopping.* London: Allen and Unwin, 1964.

Benson, John, and Laura Ugolini, eds. *A Nation of Shopkeepers: Five Centuries of British Retailing.* London: I. B. Taurus, 2003.

Bowlby, Rachel. *Carried Away: The Invention of Modern Shopping.* London: Faber and Faber, 2000.

Breward, Christopher. *The Hidden Consumer: Masculinities, Fashion and City Life, 1860–1914.* Manchester and New York: Manchester University Press, 1999.

Crossick, Geoffrey and Serge Jaumain, eds. *Cathedrals of Consumption: The European Department Store.* Aldershot, U.K.: Ashgate, 1999.

Jackson, Peter, Michelle Lowe, Daniel Miller, and Frank Mort. *Commercial Cultures: Economies, Practices, Spaces.* Oxford and New York: Berg, 2000.

Longstreth, Richard. *City Center to Regional Mall: Architecture, the Automobile, and Retailing in Los Angeles, 1920–1950.* Cambridge, Mass.: MIT, 1997.

McKendrick, N., J. Brewer, and J. H. Plumb. *The Birth of Consumer Society.* London: Europa, 1982.

Miller, Daniel, ed. *Acknowledging Consumption: A Review of New Studies.* London: Routledge, 1995.

Miller, Daniel, et al. *Shopping, Place and Identity.* London: Routledge, 1998.

Poster, Mark, ed. *Jean Baudrillard: Selected Writings.* Oxford: Polity Press, 1988.

Rappaport, Erika. *Shopping for Pleasure: Women and the Making of London's West End.* Princeton, N.J.: Princeton University Press, 2000.

Somake, Ellis E. and Rolf Hellberg. *Shops and Stores Today: Their Design, Planning and Organisation.* London: B. T. Batsford, Ltd., 1956.

Bronwen Edwards

SHROUD The word "shroud" originated in fourteenth century England to describe the clothing used to dress or wrap a corpse prior to burial, derived from older words *scrud* meaning garment and *screade*—a piece or strip of fabric. It has since become widely used to refer to garments or coverings specifically made to dress the dead body prior to its final disposal, whether by burial or cremation. Its form generally ranges from a length of cloth to basic loose-fitting purpose-made garments. Although the word shroud can be traced back to a specific place in history, it should not be regarded as the point when burial clothing for the corpse first became used. Contemporary descriptions, archaeological accounts, and artistic depictions occasionally provide evidence of shrouds from earlier periods of history and other cultures, although examples of actual garments rarely survive intact, usually decaying along with the body they were used to dress. An early reference to shrouding can be found in biblical accounts—the New Testament describes Jesus' body wrapped in a linen sheet for burial.

Early English Shrouds

The early shroud fulfilled the function of containing the decaying corpse, while modestly covering the body. During the eleventh century, ordinary people would have clothed their dead in a loose shirt before wrapping them in a sheet, often colored rather than white, and sometimes swaddled or wound tightly with extra bands of cloth. The sixteenth-century shroud, also referred to as a winding sheet, was usually a length of linen, which was wound around the body and secured by knotting the fabric at the head and feet. Containment and ease of transporting the shrouded body was important as most people were buried without a coffin at this time. Cunnington and Lucas (1972) and Litten (1991) both provide detailed descriptions of variations of English shrouds before the twentieth century, including alternative grave clothes used for the aristocracy and royalty.

Shrouds increasingly became indicators of social status, reflected in changing designs. A Parliamentary Act was passed in 1678 to enforce burial in woolen shrouds, to promote the ailing English wool trade. A legal document had to be signed at each burial certifying that the corpse had been buried only in wool. The wealthy disregarded this, preferring to pay a fine rather than bury their dead in wool, choosing instead more expensive fabrics and trimmings made from linen, silk, lace, gold, and silver which seemed more appropriate to their social status.

Funeral Industry

Early shrouds were made specifically for each corpse, often by a family member. The growth of the new undertaking profession from the early eighteenth century onward, coupled with changes in textile and garment manufacture, led to an expanding range of ready-to-wear shrouds in a variety of styles, fabrics, and prices. A typical woolen shroud set at this time might have consisted of a long flannel shirt with a front opening edged in woolen lace or black thread, long sleeves with gathered wrists, a pair of gloves, a cravat, a cap or headdress, and a small square piece of cloth to cover the face.

Victorian shrouds resembled long one-piece nightgowns, white with back opening and long sleeves. The range of fabrics had expanded to include calico, cashmere, linen, muslin, poplin, satin, and silk, trimmed with ruffles, lace, or pin-tucks depending on personal choice and the gender of the corpse.

Designs available increased throughout the twentieth century, also becoming more gender-specific. Within the Western funeral industry, particularly in the United Kingdom and the United States, male shrouds became described as robes, resembling dressing gowns in darker shades of paisley, satin, or suiting. Some give the appearance of a formal suit but are constructed as a one-piece garment. Ladies shrouds have become gowns, frequently styled like nightgowns in pastel shades of satin, taffeta, or printed cotton and trimmed with lace or ruffles. All are full-length, long-sleeved, and open-backed to assist the funeral director in dressing the corpse.

Religious Ritual

Religious belief frequently provides traditional guidelines for clothing the dead, using specific garments with their own significance. Shrouding the body (*kafan*) plays a cen-

Funeral effigy of John Donne. This effigy of John Donne shows the famous poet and priest wrapped in a funeral shroud. The word "shroud" refers to material used to dress a dead body prior to its final disposal. © ANGELO HORNAK/CORBIS. REPRODUCED BY PERMISISON.

tral part in Islamic burial ritual, using plain white lengths of cotton for everyone, regardless of social status or wealth, although variations may occur. After washing the body, it is systematically wrapped in several unstitched pieces of cloth, three for men and five for women. One piece has a hole cut out for the head, resembling a long basic shirt, which covers the whole body.

Shrouds form a similarly crucial part in Jewish burial ritual. Simple white burial garments (*tachrichim*) are used to clothe the body regardless of gender, avoiding ostentation and emphasizing equality after death. Garments include a head covering, shirt, pants, belt, and finally a linen sheet. Fabrics generally used for the garments are white linen, cotton, or muslin and traditionally hand-sewn, although machine-made sets are now available.

Contemporary Alternatives

Contemporary Western society exhibits a diversity of styles in clothing for the corpse, dependent on age, gender, religious beliefs, and broader cultural background. Anecdotal evidence from within the funeral industry suggests that the use of everyday clothes is increasingly replacing shrouds, especially in the absence of cultural traditions specifying particular garments. The choice of a final outfit for the deceased becomes a meaningful act for the bereaved family or friends and presents an appropriate last memory, particularly if viewing the body. To be dressed in their own clothes signifies a heightened sense of the individual before death, illustrating aspects of personal taste and character and forming an increasingly important part of personalized funeral ceremonies from the late twentieth century onward.

A growing awareness of the environmental impact of contemporary Western burial and cremation practice is also producing alternative shrouds to those manufactured by the mainstream funeral industry. Simple biodegradable shrouds can be found within the green burial movement made from lengths of silk, wool, unbleached cotton, or linen, large enough to envelop the body.

Despite variations in shrouds both historically and cross-culturally, clothing the corpse remains a significant part of the final rite of passage in all human societies for whom clothing is important during life.

See also **Ceremonial and Festival Costumes; Mourning Dress.**

BIBLIOGRAPHY

Cunnington, Phillis, and Catherine Lucas. *Costume for Births, Marriages and Deaths.* London: Adam and Charles Black, 1972.

Litten, Julian. *The English Way of Death.* London: Robert Hale, 1991.

Claire Barratt

SILK Among the oldest known textiles, silk was produced in China as early as the mid-third millennium B.C.E. The discovery that silk filament produced by silkworms could be spun into yarns and woven into textiles was later attributed to a legendary Chinese empress who was worshipped as the Patron Diety of Weaving. This account of silk's origins is purely mythical, but it perhaps demonstrates an awareness of both the antiquity of silk production and its importance to Chinese culture. Sericulture, the term used to refer to all aspects of silk production from the raising of silkworms to the spinning of yarn and weaving of cloth, was subject to state control for many centuries, and it was forbidden to export silkworms or reveal the secrets of sericulture outside China. Bolts of silk textiles, produced to standard width and length, were used in ancient China as official trade goods, and were accepted in payment of taxes. Gradually a trade also developed in silk produced for private use and commerce.

The Silk Road, along which silk fabrics were conveyed from China to elsewhere in the ancient world, holds a special place in history. Silk fabrics were sold in such places as Greece and Rome for fabulous prices. The secret of sericulture continued to be carefully protected by the Chinese authorities, but ultimately silk production spread to other places. Rulers of countries beyond China's borders often aspired to marry Chinese princesses, in part to gain access to their knowledge of sericulture. Silk production was found in Korea as early as 200 B.C.E. and in India and Japan by C.E. 300. (Wild silk was also produced as an indigenous product in India beginning in ancient times.)

According to legend, in C.E. 553, some Nestorian Christian monks returned from China to Byzantium with silkworm eggs and a knowledge of silk production; whether this story is precisely true or not, the silk industry that was transplanted to Western Asia around that time became a major contributor to the wealth of the Byzantine Empire and a source of its leadership in the production of royal and ecclesiastical garments and furnishings. By the eighth century, sericulture had spread to northern Africa, Spain, and Sicily. Spain and Sicily became famous for weaving exquisite silks in what would later become known as jacquard designs. In the early Renaissance, silk production became well established across Italy with Lucca and Florence as major centers. Lyons, France, also became the center of a major silk-producing region. Attempts to create an industry in England struggled, however.

An attempt to establish sericulture in the American colonies in the early to mid-nineteenth century failed, in part because of technical difficulties (such as diseases afflicting silkworms), and partly due to competition from cotton. Cotton was by then a major crop and cotton spinning and weaving were important industries, better suited than silk to the climate and industrial base of the United States. Over time, silk fiber production also failed or became uneconomical everywhere in Europe, leaving China, Japan, India and Thailand as the major sources of silk fiber in the world. Italy and France continue to produce high-quality silk textiles from imported fibers. Silk textiles are also produced in commercial quantities in China, Thailand, India, and some other Asian countries. While silk accounts for only .2 percent of the global textile fiber market, raw silk is valued at about 20 times the unit price of raw cotton. Demand remains strong, and the value of this historically luxury fiber remains high, though the price varies with supply and demand, as with all commodities. Environmental stresses may be a limiting factor in silk production in the future, which would reduce supply and increase price.

Sericulture

Like wool, silk is a natural protein fiber. The larvae of the *Bombyx mori* moth, commonly known as silkworms, extrude silk fibers to form their cocoons and simultaneously secrete a gummy coating known as sericin. There are basically two kinds of silk: wild silk and cultivated silk. In both cases, silk is produced when silk moths lay eggs that hatch into caterpillars that eat either mulberry or oak leaves and then spin their cocoons, resulting in silk fibers. Spinning the cocoon takes about a month of the larva's life and yields about a mile of silk fiber, which can be spun into as much as 1,000 yards of silk yarn. Wild silkworms feed on oak leaves. Wild silk is harvested by picking cocoons left behind when the moths break free. This can result in a short and uneven staple fiber often labeled Tussah silk. Raw and Tussah silks are used in fabrics that have a more textured appearance than typical cultivated silk.

The majority of silk comes from a more controlled production process, known as sericulture, that extends over all stages of production, from the moths selected to lay eggs, to identification of the healthiest silkworms, to harvesting and processing of the best quality cocoons. Domestic silkworms are fed mulberry leaves. A selection of moths deemed the best breeding stock are allowed to break through the cocoons and become part of the next cycle of silk production. A majority of larvae are killed with dry heat to prevent the moth from breaking open the cocoons and thus retain the long natural filament characteristic of silk.

After soaking whole, unbroken cocoons in warm water to soften the gummy sericin secretion on the silk, a hand operation known as *reeling* combines the filaments from approximately four cocoons into one uniform filament yarn that is wound onto a reel. Reeled filaments are twisted together in a process known as *throwing*. Outer layers often yield broken yarns that are diverted to production of spun silk, also known as silk noil. If silk is left as raw silk (silk-in-the-gum), the sericin is not removed. However, most cultivated silk is *degummed* through use of a soap solution that dissolves the sericin and produces very smooth, uniform yarns. *Scouring* and *bleaching* may be necessary to get silk white enough for white or pale colors. This causes loss of weight. *Weighting* with metallic salts such as tin may be used to replace the weight. This practice has been found to diminish the strength and durability of silk fabrics and is required to be disclosed on the label. *Dyeing* is done at the yarn or at the fabric level. Some noteworthy aesthetic finishes demonstrate ways silk can be modified. *Sandwashing* silks produces a more faded, casual fabric that is washable. *Sueded silk* is a further processing of washable silks with alkali to pit the surface and raise a slight nap. *Moiré calendaring* creates a watermarked effect on silk taffeta and faille fabrics. The process combines an etched roller, heat and pressure to flatten ribs into the watermarked pattern called moiré.

Characteristics of Silk Textiles

Most silk cloth is made from cultivated and degummed smooth filament and therefore displays the smooth, lustrous qualities associated with the concept "silky." Silk textiles vary from very soft and fluid satins and crepes to extremely stiff and bouffant taffetas and organzas and sumptuous silk velvet. Interior furnishing textiles often produced in silk include ottoman, bengaline, repp, and tapestry.

Duppioni silk is made from the fibers of twinned cocoons growing together; the resulting thick and thin yarns are used to best advantage in a textured, linen-like

Silkworm cocoons. A Japanese girl examines silkworm cocoons with the help of an illuminated table. © HORACE BRISTOL/CORBIS. REPRODUCED BY PERMISSION.

fabric called shantung. Wild silk and silk noil are spun yarns that often have sericin left in the fiber, resulting in fabrics with the appearance of a rough linen and a soft, somewhat gummy feel.

Examined microscopically, cultivated silk fibers have a triangular cross-sectional shape that contributes to a soft, deep, luster and smooth feel typical of silk. Silk has long been considered the ultimate in luxurious feel on the skin. Many synthetic fibers are engineered to emulate the look and feel of silk. Raw silk fibers are more ribbon-like, with a nearly rectangular cross-sectional shape so textiles are not as lustrous or as smooth. With removal of sericin, cultivated silk is almost white while raw and wild silk range from tan to light brown.

As a protein fiber, silk is somewhat warm and very absorbent. Silk can absorb 30 percent of its weight, and dries quickly. Since it is fairly lightweight and typically smooth, silk is often more comfortable than wool for next-to-the-skin apparel or furnishings. Like wool, silk bonds with dyes and supports a wide range of long-lasting colors. In filament form, silk is the strongest natural fiber with greater durability than cotton and fine wools. Silk has a natural elasticity that allows 20 percent elongation. Since silk is subject to water spotting and perspiration stains, silk is often dry-cleaned to avoid potential detergent and bleach damage. Silk resists dirt but can be damaged by perspiration if not cleaned often enough. Silk can also be damaged by prolonged exposure to sunlight. Filament silks wrinkle less than spun silks; both must be ironed with moderate, moist heat to avoid damage. Though resistant to fire, mildew, and moths, silk is eaten by carpet beetles.

Silk lounging robe. Actress Anna May Wong in an embroidered Chinese lounging robe made of silk satin. Silk was first cultivated in China and continues to be associated with that country. © CONDÉ NAST ARCHIVE/CORBIS. REPRODUCED BY PERMISSION.

Silk in Fashion

Silk has historically been a prestige fiber associated with high status. In ancient China it was proverbial that members of the upper classes wore silk, while commoners wore garments of hempen cloth. With the advent of silk exportation, there was such demand in Damascus and Rome that only the very wealthy could afford it. Silk was reserved for special events such as festivals, weddings, and other celebrations, and silk wall hangings and carpet were symbols of great wealth and privilege. In the eighteenth century, the clothing of the rich was often made of silk, and as fashion designers in the nineteenth and twentieth centuries continued to produce garments for a wealthy clientele, fashion tended to perpetrate silk's aura of luxury and prestige. More recently, businesspeople "dressing for success" have considered silk shirts, blouses, dresses, and raw silk suiting to be classic indicators of prestige.

By the 1930s, synthetic fibers were developed to give the look of silk at an affordable price. With the wartime decline of the silk industries in China and Japan, nylon took over most of the market for silk stockings, and "nylons" became commonly available. Acetate was routinely substituted for silk in prom dresses and wedding attire. Polyester, particularly microfiber, has been the most suc-

cessful artificial fiber in emulating the look and sometimes almost the feel of silk at an affordable price.

By the 1990s fashion embraced silk as a fiber that should be available to most people. Silk was reinterpreted as a textile appropriate not only for special events but also for casual, everyday wear. Very important to this expansion in silk was the creation of washable silks with a somewhat faded look and sueded silks that were closer to the aesthetic of cotton. Washable silk was also discovered in home textiles for fabulous sheets, bed coverings, table coverings, and upholstery. Silk even became adopted in sportswear as people discovered that silk underwear was warm and non-itching. Raw silk also became popular for linen-like summer attire. Silk was rediscovered not only for its beautiful fabrics, but for its great comfort and affordable price (as increased production of fiber and improved processing techniques have lowered the cost of silk). Meanwhile, the growth of the craft movement and interest in wearable art has put another kind of focus on silk as a fiber that easily lends itself to creating art that is also apparel.

Common Silk Textile Uses

Silk is used primarily in apparel and interiors. The range of apparel extends from special occasion costumes to casual T-shirts and silk underwear. Considerable demand for silk for use in wearable art and craft designs has fostered development of catalog and web sourcing for silk, a textile that has become hard to find at the retail level as specialty, high-quality fabric stores have become less common throughout the country. Interior textiles are primarily upholstery, wall hangings, carpets, hand-made rugs, and sometimes wild silk wall coverings treasured for their texture. Silk flowers and plants hold a special place among interior accessories. Recently, there has been a growing demand for silk liners for sleeping bags, silk blankets and sheets. Silk is found in medical products such as dental floss, braces, and surgical sutures, prosthetic arteries, and bandages. Often wigs are made of silk. Silk is also used to make tennis racket strings, fishing lines, parachutes, and hot-air balloons. Remarkably, silk has a number of industrial uses as well, including as crosshairs in optical instruments, as a component of electrical insulation, and even as an ingredients in facial power and cream. Silk was even used in the nose cone of the Concorde jet. Nevertheless, the primary contemporary use for silk is as a fashion textile, continuing a tradition that has lasted for thousands of years.

See also **Fibers; Textiles, Chinese; Wool.**

BIBLIOGRAPHY

Collier, Billie J., and Phyllis G. Tortora. *Understanding Textiles.* Upper Saddle River, N.J.: Prentice Hall, 2000.

Hatch, Kathryn L. *Textile Science.* Minneapolis: West Publishing, 1993.

Kadolph, Sara J., and Anna L. Langford. *Textiles.* 9th ed. Upper Saddle River, N.J.: Prentice-Hall, 2001.

Parker, Julie. *All about Silk: A Fabric Dictionary and Swatchbook.* Seattle, Wash.: Rain City Publishing, 1991.

Carol J. Salusso

SIMMEL, GEORG The German sociologist and philosopher Georg Simmel was born in Berlin on 1 March 1858 to assimilated Jewish parents. Between 1876 and 1881 Simmel studied history and philosophy in Berlin. His doctoral thesis (1881) and post-doctoral dissertation (1885) both dealt with Immanual Kant. His rhetorical gift proved to be successful with academic and nonacademic audiences alike, and his lectures became social events. In 1890 he married the writer Gertrud Kinel. A year later they had their only son, Hans. In 1894 he published the essay "The Problem of Sociology," which inaugurated a separate social science. Simmel and his wife were at the center of cultural circles in Berlin; their friends included the poets Rainer Maria Rilke and Stefan George as well as the sculptor Auguste Rodin. In 1903 his essay "The Metropolis and Mental Life" constituted an early study of urban modernity. Latent anti-Semitism, reservations about the academic validity of sociological studies, and envy of Simmel's social popularity hindered his professional progress in Berlin, and in 1914 he accepted a call to the university in Strasbourg, where he died on 26 September 1918.

Simmel's discussion of fashion, significant for its early date within academic discourse, its conceptual rigor, as well as its metaphysical breadth are defined by his simultaneous adherence to philosophical tradition and the formation of a sociological methodology. Accordingly, he viewed fashion both as an abstract concept that generates and influences cultural perception and as a defining factor in social and interpersonal relations. Simmel's beginnings as a neo-Kantian philosopher prepared his view of cognition as a biological process of adaptation by human beings to their environment, a view which is not only situated in a scientific (neo-Darwinian) discourse but also extended to culture—intellectual as well as sensory—within a contemporary (modern and urban) environment. Simmel defined the truth within expressions of reality pragmatically through its appropriateness for living practice. This led him to the emerging discipline of sociology, which developed the ground for direct application of such concepts to sociopolitical existence. His precursors herein were Auguste Comte, Herbert Spencer, and Gabriel Tarde, and among his contemporaries were Ferdinand Tönnies, Werner Sombart, Émile Durkheim, and Marcel Mauss.

Early Investigations

The methodological mix of metaphysics, economics, and social theory generated for Simmel an interest in fashion, which he viewed as a theoretical and material field of investigation that offered space for emphatic, almost literary, evocations of clothing but also for a formal description of (dress) codes as visual and structural primers for social groups and settings. He began to investigate the topic in an 1895 essay titled "Zur Psychologie der Mode" (On the psychology of fashion). In this essay, Kantian heritage accounts for a philosophical focus on the subject-object relation. Simmel asks where cognition is founded, in the objects of cognition or in the cognitive subject itself. He applies the question to fashion: Is cognition founded in the clothes we choose to wear, or is it the human mind that chooses the clothes? In this, his first essay about fashion, cognition and self-awareness are regarded as creative achievements of the subject, aided by guidelines extracted from the conglomerate of experience.

In his book *The Philosophy of Money*, Simmel returned to the progressive division of subject and object in modernity, this time applying socioeconomic criteria. In this work Simmel devotes a telling passage to fashion, describing how "the radical opposition between subject and object has been reconciled in theory by making the object part of the subject's perception," partly through a practice that produces the object by a single subject for a single subject. In modernity, mass production—with its division of labor—renders such reconciliation impossible. The analogy that Simmel draws here is "the difference … between the modern clothing store, geared towards utmost specialisation, and the work of the tailor whom one used to invite into one's home" (Simmel, p. 457). The example is indicative of Simmel's approach. Not only does the object of fashion—more than any other object of consumption that must remain at a distance from the body—allow for an introduction of sensuality and haptic experience within theory, but it also applies abstract concepts directly to corporeality. In discussing the production and consumption of fashion, Simmel leads the reader directly back to his or her own experience as a wearer of clothes and as a modern consumer, thus generating an important link to personal experience that coined contemporary philosophy (Simmel's subsequent term *Lebensphilosophie* [metaphysics of existence] would follow French philosopher Henri-Louis Bergson's *élan vital*, or nature's creative impulse).

In 1904–1905 two extended essays by Simmel were published—one in English under the simple heading "Fashion" and one in German titled "Philosophie der Mode" (Philosophy of fashion). They share a similar structure, but the former set an empiricist or rationalist tone that would determine Simmel's reception in Anglo-Saxon social sciences as a formal sociologist and precursor to the Chicago school of empiricist, urban sociology.

Akin to set theory, Simmel describes in his sociology the developmental process of social differentiation as a confluence of the homogeneous segments of heterogeneous circles. In modern (especially urban) culture both psychological and social differentiation are geared to minimizing physical friction and channeling the energy of personal collisions into dynamic movement as an economic principle (e.g., competition). Fashion exemplifies this process acutely. The complex mix within modern dressing between invention and imitation, between socially sanctioned conformity for societal survival and necessary independence for personal gratification and the formation of the self (even cognition), is found in all clothing rituals and codification. The abstract and generalized tone with which fashion is debated makes Simmel's analyses still pertinent in the twenty-first century, because he eschewed historicity, romanticism, or concreteness vis-à-vis sartorial styles.

Key Observations about Fashion

Two sets of his observations, in particular, render fashion a generic model both for the recognition of societal procedures and a phenomenology of modernity itself. The first is the import of fashion by strangers from outside a given set or circle. Here the term "role-playing," which would become so significant for modern sociology, is prefigured. In his essays Simmel analyzes how a style or appearance of dress undergoes a developmental process of rejection to acceptance. "Because of their external origin," he wrote in 1904, "these imported fashions create a special and significant form of socialization, which arises through mutual relation to a point without the circle. It sometimes appears as though social elements, just like the axes of vision, converge best at a point that is not too near.... Paris modes are frequently created with the sole intention of setting a fashion elsewhere" (Simmel; 1904, p. 136). The methodological move from anthropology to economics here is characteristic for the formation of early social theory. Also, the strong interest in temporal structures (partly influenced through Bergson's *durée*, the natural milieu of a person's "deep self, or the true foundation of one's spiritual identity") and accelerated rhythm of modernity leads Simmel to a contemplation of sartorial transitoriness.

In the last of his four essays on fashion, "Die Mode" (Fashion, 1911), he explains how wider acceptance and distribution of a fashion herald its demise, since a widely accepted dress code no longer poses to the individual a challenge that is associated with the constitutive process of fractious assimilation. Accordingly, a novel form or style of clothing needs to be introduced to generate anew the dualities of innovation and imitation, social separation and inclusion. As soon as fashion manages to determine the totality of a group's appearance—which has to be its ultimate creative and economic aim—fashion will, owing to the logical contradiction inherent in its characteristics, die and become replaced. And the more subjective and individualized a style of clothing is, the quicker it perishes. For Simmel, this transitory character of fashion remains its essence and elevates its material objects to transhistorical significance. "The question of fashion is not 'to be or not to be'," he concluded in 1911, "... but it always

stands on the watershed between past and future" (Simmel: 1911, p. 41).

See also **Benjamin, Walter; Fashion, Theories of.**

BIBLIOGRAPHY

Böhringer, Hannes, and Karlfried Gründer, eds. *Ästhetik und Soziologie um die Jahrhundertwende: Georg Simmel.* Frankfurt am Main, Germany: Vittorio Klostermann Verlag, 1976.

Dahme, Heinz-Jürgen, and Otthein Rammstedt, eds. *Georg Simmel und die Moderne.* Frankfurt am Main, Germany: Suhrkamp, 1984.

Frisby, David. *Fragments of Modernity: Theories of Modernity in the Work of Simmel, Kracauer, and Benjamin.* Cambridge, U.K.: Polity Press, 1985.

———. *Sociological Impressionism: A Reassessment of Georg Simmel's Social Theory.* 2nd ed. London: Routledge, 1992.

Kaern, Michael, Bernard S. Phillips, and Robert S. Cohen, eds. *Georg Simmel and Contemporary Sociology.* Dordrecht, Germany: Kluwer Academic Publishers, 1990.

Lehmann, Ulrich. *Tigersprung: Fashion in Modernity.* Cambridge, Mass.: MIT Press, 2000.

Lichtblau, Klaus. *Kulturkrise und Soziologie um die Jahrhundertwende.* Frankfurt am Main, Germany: Suhrkamp, 1996.

Rammstedt, Otthein, ed. *Simmel und die frühen Soziologen: Nähe und Distanz zu Durkheim, Tönnies, und Max Weber.* Frankfurt am Main, Germany: Suhrkamp, 1988.

Remy, Jean, ed. *Georg Simmel: Ville et modernité.* Paris: Éditions L'Harmattan, 1995.

Simmel, Georg. *On Individuality and Social Forms: Selected Writings.* Edited by Donald N. Levine. Chicago: University of Chicago Press, 1971.

———. *Georg Simmel on Women, Sexuality, and Love.* New Haven, Conn.: Yale University Press, 1984.

———. *Gesamtausgabe.* Edited by Ottheim Rammstedt. Frankfurt am Main, Germany: Suhrkamp, 1989–2002.

Wolff, Kurt H., ed. *The Sociology of Georg Simmel.* Glencoe, Ill.: Free Press, 1950.

Ulrich Lehmann

SKATING DRESS Although skating is an activity that takes many forms—each with its unique clothing requirements—ice-skating, and specifically figure skating, provides the most prominent image of the skating dress. Figure skating is an athletic and expressive sport. Whether skating recreationally on a frozen-over outdoor pond or as a competitor with a rigorous daily training schedule on an indoor rink, clothing plays a major role in enhancing the experience.

The movements involved in figure skating engage the entire body. The motion and flow across the ice requires smooth actions of the arms and legs along with powerful gliding strokes, quick turns and rotations, explosive jumps, and fast footwork. The clothing that the skater wears can enhance these movements while at the same time allowing the skater to maintain a comfortable temperature while moving efficiently and without distraction. This blend of aesthetic and functional possibilities of dress mix in action to become almost one with the skater, the result being a total athletic and artistic expression.

Beginning with the functional requirements, the regulation of body temperature is primary. Skaters start a workout by wearing layers, shedding sweaters or jackets as they warm up, and donning them again as they cool down. The ability to move freely is key to performance. Therefore, outfits are close to the body, allowing for movement without the garments getting in the way of action. Women typically wear tights or snug pants that protect the legs from abrasions during falls. Many wear short skirts or dresses, and long-sleeved tops with plenty of stretch. Men wear close-fitting pants and shirts. The skates (boots and blades) are usually white for women and black for men. Laces keep the boot securely fitted to the foot and the ankle supported, yet allowing for bend and movement. Accessories are minimally worn so as to not interfere with fast moves or get caught or tangled in hair or garments. Gloves provide extra warmth and protection, and hats or headbands warm the head and secure the hair.

The aesthetic component of skating dress at best enhances the sensation of movement, while connecting the overall visual effect to the music and theme of the skater's performance. Competition clothing is much dressier and showier than everyday practice dress. The possibilities are almost endless, given the intended expressive results. Sequins, rhinestones, jewels, and shiny textures reflect light and add excitement and elegance. Flowing, lightweight fabrics lift and float as they move across the ice with the skater. The placement of embellishments actively draws the eye to various locations on the body, whether centered in predictable neckline and skirt edging or along sleeves or pants to enhance arm and leg extensions. Sometimes the visual activity in a costume can overtake the overall impression, almost negating the skater, and at other times, subtle highlights in dress put the skater's body as the primary point of attraction. The most exquisite outcome occurs when the skater's body and the dress work together to form action and visual effect, one enhancing the other within the context of the performance.

Behind aesthetic and performance possibilities are major advances in fabric technology. The functional requirements of movement and comfort have been greatly enhanced by the development of fabrics with stretch. Prior to the development of elastine fibers, particularly Lycra, skaters' ensembles were limited to nonstretch fabrics, or bulky knits with limited range and recovery. This meant that movement potential was designed into garments by placing gussets (small patches of fabric joining garment sections, such as at the armpit) so that the arm could move above the shoulder without the sleeve lifting the rest of the garment.

Figure skater Oksana Baiul. Gold-medal winner Oksana Baiul, of Ukraine, during the figure skating competition at the 1994 Winter Olympics in Lillehammer, France. The outfits of competitive skaters like Baiul are designed for freedom of movement and artistic effect. GETTY IMAGES. REPRODUCED BY PERMISSION.

As more fiber combinations became possible, skaters were no longer limited to pleats, gores, drape, and gathers to provide shape and fullness. Layers of lightweight novelty fabrics rich with embellishments can create theatrical aesthetic effects without the heavy structural constraint of days past. Adding to the design possibilities is a sheer mesh fabric that can "bare" the skin and support sparkles and trims. Now skating costumes can be created to cover the body strategically, and still stay on and function with extreme movement demands. The possibilities are unlimited.

Skating dress has evolved to reflect the spirit of the times as well as dress regulations of everyday fashion. In the early twentieth century, skirts were worn to the top of the skate, reflecting the modesty practice of women not showing their legs despite the movement restrictions. As women's status advanced and their place in sport widened, skirts became shorter and necklines lower. Although this is a simplified observation, along with other forms of athletic apparel (for gymnasts and dancers), skating dress evolved to allow the body to be more primary in viewing and in action potential. Dress now supports and enhances women as athletes. Men had traditionally been in the background, relative to skating dress. Instead of a "flashy" presence in competitions, men mostly wore outfits that resembled suits that had limited decoration. As with women's dress, men's dress has since evolved along with attitudes toward gender roles. Now male skaters often wear costumes that are every bit as showy and elaborate as women's dress.

Because skating is a popular spectator sport, skaters in the spotlight have been behind many fashion trends. Dorothy Hamill and her bobbed hair is an example of this. The elegance and excitement of skating dress in major competitions is awaited by some people with the same anticipation commonly seen on Oscar night in Hollywood. Although the form of the dress is unique to skating, the colors, textures, and surface embellishments, often inspire and follow fashions in other environments

Skating dress is at best a synergy of artistry, comfort, and movement. It is a part of a total experience, reflecting athleticism and cultural expression.

See also **Activewear; Sportswear.**

BIBLIOGRAPHY
Stephenson, Lois and Richard. *A History and Annotated Bibliography of Skating Costume.* Meriden, Conn.: Bayberry Hill Press, 1970.

Janet Hethorn

SKI CLOTHING During the nineteenth century, enthusiasts and explorers helped transform skiing from a practical activity into a sophisticated sport. Along with its growing popularity came progress in equipment and clothing to protect the body from mountain extremes. Experienced skiers realized the importance of layering, which enabled them to take off or put on clothing as required, tailoring what they were wearing to the activity level. The layers comprised lightweight long underwear and stockings, sweater, socks, gloves, and a weatherproof coat and breeches. Long skirts were inappropriate for the rigors of skiing, so by 1910, the only difference between male and female skiwear was a knee-length skirt worn over knickerbockers. Burberry gabardine was recognized as the most suitable fabric for jackets and breeches as its proofed cotton threads, dense weave, and smooth surface

"The ski outfit that one puts on in the morning is the same as that which one wears until dinner. One of the most surprising aspects of St. Moritz is this contrast between the . . . luxury of hotels and the casual appearance which the winter sports costume gives to the guests."

Vogue, 1 December 1926 (Paris: Editions Condé Nast): 9.

provided a barrier to the wind and snow. Unlike earlier rubberized and waxed jackets it was also breathable.

Uniforms worn during World War I had an impact on skiwear. By 1920 outfits based on tunics and breeches worn by the British Land Girls (a volunteer corps of agricultural workers known as the "Women's Land Army" that substituted for men who had enlisted during the war) began to appear. More relaxed attitudes toward fashion made it easier for women to wear this type of clothing without fear of criticism. Sportswear manufacturing companies also incorporated practical elements from male military uniform into their designs, such as buttoned top pockets. During the 1920s trousers rapidly became an accepted form of clothing, and the women's skiing outfit signalled a dress equality less evident back home, where trousers were still taboo for most activities.

Development

The growth of ski tourism and the first winter Olympics in 1924 encouraged manufacturers to specialize in skiwear and create weatherproof yet fashionable outfits. Companies such as Drecoll, Burberry, Lillywhites, and Aquascutum and fashion designers including Patou, Lanvin, and Regny produced trouser suits in a wide range of colors, combining practicality with elegance. The main technical advances were in design features such as zip fastenings, which were more effective at sealing openings on trousers, jackets and pockets than buttons or laces. By the early 1930s, short jackets inspired by pilots' uniforms, and full "Norwegian" trousers were fashionable for men and women. These loose-fitting garments allowed greater freedom of movement and a more casual style to prevail.

During the 1930s the mechanization of the ski industry in the form of rope tows and ski lifts started to impact the design of ski outfits. The shift from mountain touring to downhill skiing demanded a different design of clothing. Fashion gradually shifted away from baggy styles to shaped trousers that followed the streamlined look of ski racers and were better suited to the new skiing techniques.

Equipping the forces during World War II led to the manufacture of high quality outdoor clothing, including skiwear. Developments in synthetic fibers and polymers for the mountaineering troops brought about improvements in materials for ski clothing. Nylon was used in the outer shell of stylish parkas and synthetic quilted linings were added for extra warmth. Stretch nylon pants suited the streamlined look of 1950s' skiwear perfectly, emphasizing the fashionable curve of the hips and a narrow waist. They could be teamed up with colorful mohair sweaters for after skiing or worn as slacks at home. Specialist manufacturers and a new generation of fashion designers such as Balmain and Pucci capitalized on these styles, creating fashionable yet functional clothing.

In 1959 the arrival of spandex heralded another revolution in ski clothing. This elastomeric fiber was combined with other synthetic fibers or wool to allow greater stretch than nylon plus instant recovery. Skiwear could now stretch with the wearer and retain its shape. Spandex was ideal for ski racing outfits, allowing greater freedom of movement and aerodynamic qualities. Inspired by events such as the Olympic games, Pucci, Hermès, and Dior featured tight stretch ski pants and curvaceous all-in-one suits in their 1960s' collections. Experts, however, advised looser versions for recreational skiing that, when combined with turtlenecks, functioned for social occasions and other outdoor activities.

Technology

In the 1970s growing numbers of companies such as Killy, Lange, and Berghaus started to provide specialist clothing, and a kaleidoscope of designs evolved to suit all tastes and levels of skier. Wider-legged, over-the-boot pants created a more relaxed look in tune with mainstream fashion and quilted down-filled jackets were versatile additions to the skiing wardrobe. V. de V. and de Castelbajac created flamboyant designs in authentic ski clothing while warm-up suits worn by ski racers were translated into fashionable styles. Novelty fabrics such as fake fur, vinyls, and metallics were used for parkas, and ski outfits in psychedelic color combinations had a safety as well as aesthetic appeal. Ponchos and capes were popular for après-ski and "space-age" moon boots walked their way into the fashion scene.

There were also significant developments in technology. In 1969, plastic molded boots replaced the traditional leather footwear, giving the skier greater control over the skis. Plastic coatings were introduced onto ski garments to keep out moisture, but although waterproof, they led to a buildup of condensation inside. Introduced in 1976, Gore-Tex fabric revolutionized outdoor wear by allowing perspiration to escape while keeping water out. It was developed for ski clothing in collaboration with Berghaus, and soon other companies were promoting their own versions. The development of circular knit brushed fleece in the late 1970s also transformed skiwear. Made of lightweight, warm, and quick-drying polyester filaments, it made layering garments as a means to keep warm easy and became a staple in casual outerwear.

Innovation

As the latest technologies were incorporated into skiwear, leading brands faced fierce competition to market a new wonder fiber or design feature. During the 1980s branding with logos became increasingly common, and the choice of clothing was almost bewildering. Fashion was also of prime importance and manufacturers such as Killy, Luhta, Head, Elho, and Ocean Pacific styled their outfits to complement the latest trends. Fluorescent colors, soft pastel shades, and striking abstract and animal designs were all featured. A casual "winter surf" look emerged among young winter sports enthusiasts. One-piece suits were often zipped at the waist for more ver-

Two women model ski clothing, 1929. During the 1920s, trousers became a rapidly accepted form of women's ski clothing, an equality in clothing that was not reflected in attire outside of the sport. PUBLIC DOMAIN.

satility, and bib pants (known as salopettes in the United Kingdom) became an increasingly important component of the jacket-and-pants combination. The popularity of sportswear for leisurewear also meant that ski pants and quilted jackets made their way into the high street.

In the new millennium, the booming snowboarding industry and rise of extreme winter sports have encouraged skiwear manufacturers to emphasize innovation. Fabrics with ever increasing property and performance tolerances such as "soft shell" constructions with welded waterproof zips, jackets with inflatable insulating air pockets, and seam-free underwear promise to transform the skiing experience. The increasing use of helmets and the incorporation of body armor into skiwear, including back protectors and built-in lumbar supports, have improved safety on the slopes. Competition has also encouraged manufacturers to diversify, focusing on specific "looks" for different styles of skiing and ensuring that more components of the outfit than ever before can be worn on or off the slopes.

See also **Sportswear.**

BIBLIOGRAPHY

A–Z Ski Fashion and Equipment Guide. London: Hill, 1988.

Loring, Maggie. *Skiing.* Camden, Me., and London: Ragged Mountain Press/McGraw-Hill, 2000.

Lunn, Sir Arnold. *A History of Skiing.* London: Humphrey Milford, 1927.

Scharff, Robert. *SKI Magazine's Encyclopedia of Skiing.* New York and London: Harper and Row, 1976.

Skiing International Yearbook. New York: Periodical Publications, 1965.

Lucy Johnston

SKIRT The skirt, the lower part of a gown or robe that covers the wearer from waist downward, has been called "the simplest and most obvious of garments" by John Flügel (p. 35). He theorized that "tropical" skirts, which developed as a class of clothing distinct from "arctic" bifurcated forms, had certain advantages: "Instead of being supported on just two legs with nothing but thin air between them, a skirted human being assumes much more ample and voluminous proportions . . . often with great increase of dignity" (p. 35).

In Western culture, both genders long exploited the skirt's inherent characteristics, but since the sixteenth century a true skirt has not been a feature of standard masculine dress (if, with Anne Hollander [1994], one excepts the male kilt as a survival of drapery). The skirt separated from the dress bodice in the early sixteenth century; shortly thereafter "skirt" became synonymous with a woman, at first as standard English and then as slang in the nineteenth century. The skirt had become the defining female garment.

For several centuries feminine skirts were often very full, worn over petticoats, and sometimes supported by understructures and lengthened with trains. According to Hollander, shrouded legs visually confused rather than explained the structure of the female body. An inherent dichotomy was imagined between women's mysterious skirted forms—that included no type of bifurcated garment, not even as underwear—and tightly garbed trousered males, as illustrated by the furor over the Bloomer fashion of the 1850s.

While expansive and expensive skirts of previous eras may have demonstrated women's abstinence from productive employment, the slimmer line of the early twentieth century was restrictive in other ways, culminating in the "hobble skirt" of about 1910. Mobility, however, triumphed in the 1920s as skirts shortened to reveal women's legs. A new statement in the continuous dialogue between modesty and sexual attractiveness, the shortened skirt was, Hollander believes, "the most original modern contribution to feminine fashion accomplished without recourse to the standard male vocabulary" (p. 146).

For much of the rest of the twentieth century, hemlines served as the primary indicator of fashionability, alternating higher and lower, from extravagantly long New Look skirts to scanty miniskirts and "micro-minis." To explain seemingly quixotic hemlines, inventive (if unsubstantiated) theories linked short skirts with high stock prices. By the 1970s pants increasingly comprised an accepted part of women's wardrobes. In *The Woman's Dress for Success Book*, however, John T. Molloy, advised businesswomen to avoid what he called the "imitation man look," by wearing skirted suits with the hem length fixed at slightly below the knee, thus "taking a major step toward liberation from the fashion industry" (p. 51). Since that time, however, the array of feminine skirts has only gotten more eclectic—slit, tight, see-through, or full in any length from floor to crotch. Short skirts remain a way to attract attention, whether admiring or outraged. Flaunting legs under an abbreviated skirt has been interpreted as a form of feminine empowerment.

Wearing a skirt has become a choice for women, and since the 1990s even a rare and provocative masculine sub-fashion. Yet the tenacity of this garment as a female signifier is evidenced by standardized international gender symbols: with no innate anatomical basis for the skirt of one figure, cultural conditioning makes her femininity instantly indisputable.

See also **Bloomer Costume; Crinoline; Miniskirt.**

BIBLIOGRAPHY

Bolton, Andrew. *Bravehearts: Men in Skirts.* London: Victoria and Albert Museum, distributed by Harry N. Abrams, Inc., 2003.

Flügel, John Carl. *The Psychology of Clothes.* London: Hogarth Press, 1930.

Hollander, Anne. *Sex and Suits: The Evolution of Modern Dress.* New York: Alfred A. Knopf, Inc., 1994.

Molloy, John T. *The Woman's Dress for Success Book.* New York: Warner Brooks; Chicago: Follet Publishing Co., 1977.

Tarrant, Naomi. *The Development of Costume.* Edinburgh: National Museums of Scotland, 1994.

H. Kristina Haugland

SKIRT SUPPORTS The skirt, for centuries the defining feminine garment in Western fashion, can be expanded to increase the wearer's apparent size and thereby her importance and dignity. Skirts are often given volume by cloth petticoats, but stiffer structures are more effective and may be lighter and more comfortable; when exaggerated, however, these supports can become amazingly encumbering. Skirts have been supported at the back by bustles, while extended skirt circumferences have been produced by farthingales in the sixteenth and early seventeenth centuries, *paniers* in the eighteenth century, and crinolines or hoop skirts in the mid-nineteenth century.

Around 1470, fashionable Spanish women began to hold their skirts out with bands of heavy cord or rope in casings on the outside of their skirts. From this, a separate hooped underskirt developed that abstracted a woman's legs into a seemingly motionless cone shape. By the 1540s this fashion had spread to other countries, including England, where it was known as the verdingale or farthingale, derived from the Spanish *verdugo*, a type of flexible twig also used as hoops for skirts. This conical skirt, called the Spanish farthingale, stiffened with whalebone, wire, or other material, became very wide in the early 1580s. About his time, women's hips began to be augmented by padded rolls, altering the skirt silhouette into a shape termed the French farthingale. By the 1590s, French farthingales could take the form of a wheel or drum that held the skirt out from the waist at right angles. Exclusive to the upper classes, these supports magnificently displayed rich, heavy skirt fabric, which, as authority Janet Arnold shows, was fit in place by a servant who pinned in a horizontal fold to form a ruff-like flounce at the top of the skirt. Farthingales began to go out of fashion in England in the late 1610s, but the style lasted somewhat longer in France, and as Spanish court dress it continued into the 1660s.

The wish to distend the skirt returned in the early eighteenth century. By about 1710, fashionable skirts were supported by devices called hoop-petticoats or hoops in England and *paniers* (baskets) in France. These structures were at first dome-shaped, but by mid-century were usually flattened front to back into an oval or took the form of separate side or "pocket" hoops; they were typically of stiff fabric reinforced by hoops of whalebone, wood, or cane, but could be open frameworks of metal or other material. Hoops were usually modestly sized for informal wear, but often reached over six feet from side to side for formal occasions, necessitating some skillful maneuvering such as going sideways through doors. While large hoops were labeled monstrous by some, others believed they gave women elegance and grace, and ensured each was physically distinct. Extreme hoop-petticoats also distinguished the elite who wore them, functioning, according to Henry Fielding, as an "Article of Distinction" between classes.

Although they were going out of style by the 1770s, large *paniers* continued to be *de rigueur* at the French court until the revolution of 1789. Just as the earlier farthingale had fossilized as Spanish court dress, side hoops were retained until 1820 at the English court, worn anachronistically with high-waisted neo-classical dresses. Skirt supports may have been intended to bestow dignity and grace, but the result was sometimes antithetical: in *The Art of Dress* (p. 123), Aileen Ribeiro cites an early nineteenth century observation that a behooped lady stuffed into a sedan chair "does not ill resemble a foetus of a hippopotamus in its brandy bottle."

See also **Bustle; Crinoline; Skirt.**

BIBLIOGRAPHY

Arnold, Janet. *Patterns of Fashion: The Cut and Construction of Clothes for Men and Women, c1560–1620.* London: Macmillan, 1985.

———. *Queen Elizabeth's Wardrobe Unlock'd* Leeds, U.K.: W. S. Maney, 1988.

Cunnington, C. Willett and Phillis. *The History of Underclothes.* London: Michael Joseph Ltd, 1951 (new edition revised by A. D. Mansfield and Valerie Mansfield published in London by Faber and Faber, 1981).

Ewing, Elizabeth. *Dress and Undress : A History of Women's Underwear.* London: Bibliophile, 1978.

Ribeiro, Aileen. *The Art of Dress: Fashion in England and France, 1750–1820* New Haven, Conn., and London: Yale University Press, 1995.

———. *Dress in Eighteenth Century Europe, 1715–1789.* London: B. T. Batsford, 1984.

Waugh, Norah. *Corsets and Crinolines.* New York: Theatre Arts Books, 1954.

H. Kristina Haugland

SLIP Petticoats or underskirts have been used for centuries to support the various shapes of the skirt, add warmth, and protect outer garments. Since the seventeenth century the word slip was occasionally used for certain garments worn under sheer dresses, but the forerunner of the modern slip originated in the late nineteenth century, when the petticoat was combined with a chemise or corset cover to form a one-piece, fitted, sleeveless undergarment. Because this garment used a princess cut, which shaped the bodice and skirt by vertical seaming, it was called a "princess petticoat" or "princess slip." In the early twentieth century, it came to be called a costume slip, and then merely a slip.

As an underdress or underskirt, a slip provides a middle layer that mediates between underwear and outerwear. Among its functions, a slip can make transparent garments more modest and eliminate rubbing and unsightly clinging. Originally slips were of daintily trimmed cotton or occasionally of silk, although by the 1920s rayon was widely used. The straight-cut tubes of that period gave way to more fitted slips that accentuated the figure. In the mid-twentieth century, newly invented nylon was preferred since it was washable, drip dry, required no ironing, and was also inexpensive and colorfast. Advertisements stressed that slips were durable, shadowproof, and cut to never embarrassingly ride up. Good taste demanded that a slip be long enough—ideally exactly one inch shorter than the outer garment—but *never* show at the hem. For all their opaque respectability, slips were molded to the contour of the body, often daintily decorated, and ordinarily hidden from view, giving them a certain eroticism. Films and publicity photographs of stars and starlets of the time exploited the allure of the slip, most famously on Elizabeth Taylor in the 1958 film version of Tennessee Williams's *Cat on a Hot Tin Roof.*

With the general reduction of underwear in the 1960s some full slips incorporated bras while half-slips, bright colors, and patterns became increasingly popular.

As skirt hems rose, slip lengths shortened, but they remained provocative garments. In 1962 Helen Gurley Brown's *Sex and the Single Girl* advised would-be flirts that showing a bit of lovely lingerie is sexy, citing a girl whose "beautiful half-slips (she has them in ten colors) always peek-a-boo a bit beneath her short sheath skirts when she sits down" (p. 78). Nevertheless, in the following decades slips came to be associated with prudish and frumpy older women. A candid photograph from 1980 caught Lady Diana Spencer, the shy young fiancée of the Prince of Wales, in a lightweight skirt against the sun, revealing the outline of her legs and her relinquishment of this once mandatory undergarment.

The slip, however, was reborn as a result of the "underwear as outerwear" phenomenon of the early 1990s. The "slip dress" became a nostalgic yet daring fashion favorite, edgily imbued with the frisson of lingerie. Its revealing cut, lightweight fabric, and spaghetti straps precluded supportive undergarments, requiring a toned body and a confident attitude. As slip dresses became more popular, they were made more practical by women and even designers who layered them over white T-shirts, completing the slip's transmutation from undergarment to outergarment.

See also **Lingerie; Nylon; Petticoat.**

BIBLIOGRAPHY
Brown, Helen Gurley. *Sex and the Single Girl*. New York: B. Geis Associates, 1962. Reprint, Fort Lee, N.J.: Barricade Books, 2003.
Cunnington, C. Willett, and Phillis Cunnington. *The History of Underclothes*. London: Michael Joseph Ltd., 1951. Reprint, London: Faber and Faber, 1981.
Ewing, Elizabeth. *Dress and Undress: A History of Women's Underwear*. London: Bibliophile, 1978.

H. Kristina Haugland

SMITH, PAUL Paul Smith is renowned for classic garments that also demonstrate a discreet eccentricity that is essentially as British as his name. Committed to the idea of creative independence, he is Britain's most commercially successful designer, with a turnover of £230 million and retail outlets in forty-two countries.

Born in the city of Nottingham in 1946, he left school at age fifteen and began his career running errands in a fashion warehouse. When he was only seventeen, he was instrumental in the success of a local boutique, running the men's wear department and sourcing labels that were previously unavailable outside of London. In 1970 he opened his first shop, a three-meter-square room at the back of a tailor's space, together with a basement that he turned into a gallery, where he sold limited edition lithographs by Warhol and Hockney. He recalled,

I had … [m]odern classics you couldn't get anywhere else. I knew that … if I started selling clothes that I didn't like, but that lots of people did want, then the job would have changed me. I called the boutique Paul Smith as a reaction to the silly names … [of] the time (Fogg, p. 130).

Smith began manufacturing and retailing shirts, trousers, and jackets under his own label, and in 1976 he showed for the first time in Paris. The opening of the first Paul Smith store in London's Covent Garden in 1979 coincided with a resurgence in the money markets of the city and subsequent changes in social attitudes. His suits for men became standard wear for the 1980s young urban professional, the "yuppie." "Young people were willing to wear suits and were not embarrassed about saying that they had money. That was what the 1980s were all about and my clothes reflected the times" (Smith p. 148). Smith's amalgamation of traditional tailoring skills with a witty and subversive eye for detail, together with his quirky use of color and texture, allowed his customers the reassurance that it was permissible to be fashion conscious without being outrageous. It was this particular brand of Britishness that appealed to the Japanese market, where Smith has a £212 million retail business of more than 240 shops. As the Paul Smith style infiltrated mainstream retail chains on the High Street, his company developed a stronger fashion emphasis, and in 1993 he introduced a women's wear collection.

An important element of Smith's shops has always been his ability to source quirky and idiosyncratic objects to sell alongside the clothes. With the opening of the Westbourne Grove shop in London's Notting Hill Gate in 1998, he introduced another retail concept, that of the shop as home, and he has diversified into home furnishings. Smith has always been concerned that each shop is individual and reflects the unique quality of the city in which it is placed, rather than presenting a homogeneous ideal that is brand- and marketing-led. In the year 2000 Queen Elizabeth II knighted him for his services to the British fashion industry.

See also **Suit, Business; Tailored Suit; Tailoring.**

BIBLIOGRAPHY
Fogg, Marnie. *Boutique: A '60s Cultural Phenomenon*. London: Mitchell Beazley, 2003.
Smith, Paul. *You Can Find Inspiration in Anything: (And If You Can't, Look Again!)*. London: Violette Editions, 2001.

Marnie Fogg

SMITH, WILLI Born Willi Donnell Smith in Philadelphia on 29 February 1948, Smith studied fashion illustration at the Philadelphia Museum College of Art from 1962 to 1965 and continued his studies in fashion design at the Parsons School of Design in New York

City from 1965 to 1967. He died at age thirty-nine on 17 April 1987. According to Liz Rittersporn of the *New York Daily News*, he was the most successful black designer in fashion history.

On leaving college, Smith worked as a fashion illustrator with Arnold Scaasi for several years. From 1967 to 1976 he also worked as a freelance designer for companies such as Bobbi Brooks and Digits Inc. He specialized in sportswear, injecting an element of playfulness into functional garments such as the jump suit that he cut out of silver-coated cloth. In 1976 he and Laurie Mallet, who subsequently became president of the company, established the successful label WilliWear Limited, which captured the spirit of pragmatic leisurewear. Together they launched a collection of clothes consisting of thirteen silhouettes in soft cotton, manufactured in India and sold in New York. Such was the demand for the relaxed styling and affordable clothes of the label that the company's revenue grew from $30,000 in its first year to $25 million in 1986.

In 1978 Smith added a men's wear collection, and in 1986 he designed the navy, linen, double-breasted suit worn by Edwin Schlossberg for his marriage to Caroline Kennedy, together with the violet linen blazers and white trousers worn by the groom's party. He was, however, primarily a designer of women's wear. From its origins in a single New York store, the company went on to open offices in London (a boutique in St. Christopher's Place), Paris, and Los Angeles, as well as more than a thousand outlets in stores throughout the United States. The Paris store—his first eponymous store—opened posthumously in 1987. Just before his untimely death that year, he expressed his desire to Deny Filmer of *Fashion Weekly* to see all WilliWear products housed under one roof. "I want my stores to be a little funkier, like, wilder and fun to go into. You know that wonderful feeling when you go into an army surplus store, they have an unpretentious atmosphere. I don't want to push a lifestyle" (p. 7).

Smith's attitude toward fashion was democratic and the antithesis of the ostentatious 1980s. His main concern was that his clothes should be comfortable and affordable. He was dismissive of the edict "dress for success," identifying with the youth cults he saw on the streets of New York and drawing much of his inspiration from them. To this end he provided comfortable, functional clothes in soft fabrics that did not restrict the body in any way. He very often chose Indian textiles for their suppleness, diffused colors, and attractively distressed quality. His clothes were moderately priced, loose-fitting, occasionally oversized separates. Skirts were full and long and jackets oversized, in natural fabrics that wore well and were easy to maintain.

He disliked the pretentiousness of haute couture. "I would love to have a salon and design couture collections, but it's so expensive ... and I hate the theory of 'We the rich can dress up and have fun, and the rest can dress in blazers and slacks.' Fashion is a people thing, and designers should remember that" (Filmer, p. 9).

Smith's obituary in the *Village Voice* (28 April 1987) by Hilton Als read,

> As both designer and person, Willi embodied all that was the brightest, best and most youthful in spirit in his field. ... That a WilliWear garment was simple to care for italicised the designer's democratic urge: to clothe people as simply, beautifully, and inexpensively as possible.

For a brief period after his death, the company continued to function, and it opened its own store on lower Fifth Avenue in New York. In 1996 WilliWear was relaunched, designed by Michael Shulman, and available in T.J. Maxx stores.

Although never an innovator, Willi Smith represented a paradigm of casual American style, creating affordable classic separates. Their functionality and informality was not reliant on overt sexuality or on the status implied by high fashion, and they appealed to a broad spectrum of people. Smith received the Coty American Fashion Critics Award in 1983, and New York City designated 23 February as "Willi Smith Day." He was also honored by the Fashion Walk of Fame.

See also **Fashion and Identity.**

BIBLIOGRAPHY

Filmer, Deny. "Just William." *Fashion Weekly* (London). (12 February 1987).

Milbank, Caroline Rennolds. *New York Fashion: The Evolution of American Style.* New York: Harry N. Abrams, 1989.

Rittersporn, Liz. "Designer Willi Smith Is Dead." *New York Daily News* (19 April 1987).

Marnie Fogg

SNEAKERS The first athletic shoes were created thousands of years ago to protect the foot from rough terrain when hunting and participating in combat games (Cheskin 1987, pp. 2–3). In Mesopotamia (c. 1600–1200 B.C.E.) soft shoes were worn by the mountain people who lived on the border of Iran. These shoes were constructed with crude tools such as bone needles and stone knives; and made of indigenous materials like leaves, bark, hide, and twine. With the available manufacturing processes and materials, primitive shoes were only constructed as sandals or wraparound moccasins. In a sandal construction the foot is attached to a platform with straps, bands, or loops. A moccasin construction entails a piece of material wrapped under and over the top of the foot then anchored with a drawstring. As sports became more competitive throughout history, athletic shoes needed to perform better and be sport-specific. Functional attributes like weight, flexibility, cushioning, and traction became key features to making successful athletic shoes.

Folklore

According to some historians, King Henry VIII of England expressed ideas related to an athletic sneaker-type construction in the 1500s. According to folklore, the king was getting a bit overweight, and he decided playing tennis would be a good way to get in shape. But he was not happy with the shoes he had. He ordered his servant to get "syxe paire of shooys with feltys, to pleye in at tennis" (six pairs of shoes with felt bottoms to play tennis in), from the local cobbler (Paquin 1990). Although the king was not exactly ordering sneakers, as we technically know them, he had the right idea—to make lightweight shoes with a separate functional outsole to play tennis better.

What Is a Sneaker?

The word "sneaker" was a marketing term coined in the United States many years after the actual shoe construction was created. "Sneaker" is one of many names given to a shoe that consists of a canvas upper attached to a vulcanized rubber outsole. A shoe made any differently (e.g., a shoe with a foam midsole and a stability shank) is not technically a sneaker.

The first shoes constructed with canvas uppers and vulcanized rubber outsoles were called "Sand Shoes." These shoes were an evolution of a former sand shoe design that had a cotton canvas upper and outsole made from flat leather or jute rope. In the 1830s an English company called Liverpool Rubber evolved the original sand shoe, by bonding canvas to rubber, making the outsole more durable. The name "sand shoe" came from the fact that they were worn on the beach, by the Victorian middle class (Kippen 2004). Sand shoes were revolutionary as they replaced heavy and more expensive leatherwork boots. Around the 1860s, a croquet shoe was created that had a rubber outsole with a canvas upper fastened with cotton laces. Sand shoes were different than the croquet shoe as they had a T-strap upper construction fastened with a metal buckle. Sand shoes were also the basis for traditional English school sandals, sometimes called "Sandies" (Wagner 1999).

In the 1870s, a more robust sand shoe was created; it was called a "Plimsoll" (also spelled Plimsol or Plimsole). The name came from Samuel Plimsoll (1824–1898), a British merchant and shipping reformer who designated the "Plimsoll Mark"—a mark on the hull of cargo ships that designated the waterline when it was at full capacity (*Britannica Student Encyclopedia* 2004). The term Plimsoll was adopted by the shoe industry because the point where the canvas upper and vulcanized rubber outsole bonded together looked similar to a ship's Plimsoll line. This line aesthetically made the shoe look more expensive than previous models and became adopted by all social classes for a variety of athletic activities.

Around the same time the Plimsoll was popular in England, the term "sneaker" was coined in the United States. There are several cited origins and dates of the term. Some say the word is merely an Americanism, made from the word "sneak" (1870), because the shoe was noiseless (Coye 1986, pp. 366–369). There is also a reference that the noise-less rubber shoes were preferred by "sneak thieves" (1891) hence the name sneakers (Vanderbuilt 1998, p. 9). There is even a source that mentions the shoe got its name from "sneaky" (1895) baseball players who liked stealing bases in them (Hendrickson 2000). Many sources reference Henry Nelson McKinney (1917), an advertising agent for N. W. Ayer & Son. He came up with the name "sneaker," because the rubber outsole allowed the shoe to be quiet or "sneaky" (Bellis 2004)

No matter how the name was born, shoes with a canvas upper and a vulcanized rubber outsole evolved into many forms. These evolutions allowed people to enhance their athletic skills and provided an aesthetic opportunity for casual shoe design. In the 1880s, vulcanized rubber was added to the toe box to stop the big toenail from breaking through the canvas. It also provided abrasion resistance in sports where the forefoot was dragged to provide balance (e.g., tennis). Functional outsole patterns (e.g., herringbone) were also created to add traction, facilitate player movements, and cushion the load when jumping. Similar types of shoes became useful for sailing and yachting, since they provided traction on the wet deck. The military also used them, and had them colored according to rank. Schools recommended them to students for gym class. Athletes wore them at the first modern Olympics in Paris (1900), and Robert Falcon Scott wore them on his Antarctic expedition (1901–1904) (Kippen 2004).

Names

Since the creation of the sand shoe, there have been numerous names used globally to describe a shoe with a canvas upper and vulcanized rubber outsole. In the beginning, plimsoll and sneaker were popular names. Over time, a variety of other names have been created. Some are based on function, while others are based on materials, people, and even street slang. A few of the names include: Bobos, Bumper Boots, Chuck's, Creepers, Daps, Felonies, Fish Heads, Go Fasters, Grips, Gym Shoes, Gymmers, Joggers, Jumps, Kicks, Outing Shoes, Pumps, Runners, Sabogs, Skiffs, Sneaks, Tackies, Tennies, Trainers, and Treads (Perrin 2004).

Materials and Construction

Although athletes have been wearing performance-related footwear for thousands of years, the "sneaker" is only a recent creation based upon serendipity and adaptations of several industrial revolution inventions.

The most recognized feature of a sneaker is its vulcanized rubber outsole. Natural or India rubber, a byproduct of trees, has been cultivated since 1600 B.C.E. (by the Mayans). However, natural rubber "as is," is not really appropriate for shoes. In hot and sticky weather it melts; in cold weather it becomes brittle and hard. In 1839, Charles Goodyear from the United States serendipitously created the modern form of rubber used for sneakers when he was trying to come up with a waterproof mailbag material for the U.S. government. Goodyear's recipe, later named "vulcanization" was discovered when he accidentally dropped a mixture of rubber, lead, and sulfur onto a hot stove. His accident resulted in a substance that was not affected by the weather, and would snap back to its original shape when stretched (Goodyear 2003). The same type of rubber was reinvented and patented in England (1843), by a rubber pioneer named Thomas Hancock, who analyzed and copied samples from Goodyear. A friend of Hancock's coined the term "vulcanization" after Vulcan, the Roman god of fire (Goodyear 2003).

Sewing Machine

Cotton canvas was around for a long time before the creation of the first sneaker-type construction; however, sewing small pieces of canvas into a three-dimensional shape that conforms to the foot is quite tedious by hand. The lockstitch sewing machine was invented and patented in 1845 by Elias Howe, which allowed fabrics of all weights and constructions to be quickly and neatly stitched together. In 1851, Isaac Merrit Singer improved upon Howe's invention (and also infringed on Howe's patent), and started his own sewing machine business that still prospers among home sewers and clothing factories (Bellis 2004). Singer's sewing machine was further evolved for the shoe industry by one of his own employees: Lyman Reed Blake. In 1856, Blake became a partner in a shoemaking company and was dedicated to inventing machines that helped automate the shoe-manufacturing process. In 1858, he received a patent for a machine that could stitch shoe uppers to outsoles. He sold his patent to Gordon McKay in 1859, and worked for McKay from 1861 until his retirement in 1874. The shoes made on this machine were known as "McKays" (United Shoe Machinery Corporation 2004).

Lasting Machine

The sewing machine was helpful in automating the shoe-making process, but it was not the ultimate solution of joining an upper to an outsole. A typical sewing machine cannot manipulate around small, curvy parts that exist in a shoe design, and it takes great skill to bend, shape, and hold the upper while it is stitched to the outsole. American immigrant Jan Matzeliger (from Dutch Guiana) helped revolutionize the shoe industry by developing a shoe lasting machine that could attach an outsole to an upper in one minute. His shoe lasting machine was able to adjust an upper snugly over a last (a foot form used for shoemaking), arrange the upper under the outsole and pin it in place with nails while the outsole is stitched to

SHOELACES

Before shoelaces, shoes were typically fastened with metal buckles. The shoelace (lace and shoe holes) was invented in England (1790). An aglet is the small plastic or metal tube that binds the end of a shoelace to prevent it from fraying. It also allows the lace to pass easily through the shoe's eyelets or other openings (e.g., webbing/leather loops). The term "aglet" comes from the Latin word for "needle" (Bellis).

the upper. On March 20, 1883, the United States Patent Office awarded Matzeliger patent number 274,207 for his do-it-all shoe lasting machine (Tenner 2000, p. 37). The lasting machine revolutionized the shoe-making process as it could make hundreds of pairs of shoes a day and enabled the mass production of affordable shoes.

Early Sneaker Marketing

There are hundreds of companies that produce sneakers for the global marketplace. The first sneakers were manufactured and marketed by rubber companies, as they were the major producers of vulcanized rubber.

Dunlop Green Flash. The Dunlop rubber company in England can trace their first marketed sneaker (plimsoll) back to the 1870s. In 1933, their Green Flash collection was launched and proved to be very popular. It had a higher quality canvas upper and a better outsole (with a herringbone pattern) to provide good traction on grass tennis courts. Dunlop's Green Flash was worn by Fred Perry to win three Wimbledon titles (Heard 2003, pp. 290–291).

U.S. Rubber Keds. Keds was the first mass-marketed sneaker brand in the United States (1917), by U.S. Rubber. Much debate took place around naming U.S. Rubber's sneaker, as the initial favorite was Peds meaning, "foot" in Latin. Unfortunately another company trademarked the name, so U.S. Rubber narrowed the name down to two other possibilities—"Veds or Keds." Keds was chosen because the company felt that "K" was the strongest letter in the alphabet (Paquin). Another story says that the letter "K" represents the word "Kids," and that Keds is rhyming slang for Peds—the name that U.S. Rubber originally wanted to use for their sneaker (Vanderbuilt 1998, p. 22).

Converse Chuck Taylor. In 1908, Marquis M. Converse from Massachusetts was producing rubber galoshes and decided that he would like a more exciting career. In 1917, he introduced the Converse All-Star, a high-top sneaker designed especially for basketball. At the same time, Charles H. Taylor, a basketball player for the Akron Firestones, believed so much in Converse's shoe that he joined the sales force in 1921 and traveled across the United States promoting the All-Star Sneaker. He was so successful in promoting, selling, and making important changes to the original design that in 1923 his signature "Chuck Taylor" appeared on the ankle patch and the shoes were known as "Chucks" (Heard 2003, pp. 278–279). Converse's Chuck Taylor design is still popular around the world.

Modern Sneaker Marketing

Once the basic processes were established to make and market sneakers, companies other than rubber manufacturers were founded. These companies evolved technologies and created competition in the marketplace. Some of the most influential companies are reviewed chronologically.

Reebok. In the 1890s, Joseph William Foster from Bolton, England made some of the world's first known track spikes. Although track spikes are technically different than sneakers, Foster was interested in making athletes run faster by evolving shoe technologies. By 1895, he was in business making spikes for an international circle of distinguished runners. In 1924, J. W. Foster and Sons made the spikes worn in Summer Olympic Games by the athletes celebrated in the film *Chariots of Fire* (Vanderbuilt 1998, p. 11). In 1958, two of Fosters' grandsons started a companion company named Reebok (which went on to make sneakers), after the African gazelle. Reebok has grown to be one of the world's largest athletic shoe manufacturers, producing products for many sports like tennis, basketball, and cross-training.

New Balance. Location was another commonality between the first sneaker manufacturers, as talent and machinery were important in keeping manufacturers in business. Most came from England or the New England region of the United States, particularly Massachusetts. New Balance was one of those companies, and was established in 1906, by William J. Riley from Watertown, Massachusetts. Riley was a 33-year-old English immigrant who committed to help people with troubled feet by making personal arch supports and prescription footwear to improve shoe fit. Arch supports and prescription footwear remained the core of New Balance's business until 1961, when they manufactured the "Trackster," a performance running shoe (weighing 96 grams) that was made with a rippled rubber outsole and came in multiple widths (Heard 2003, pp. 48–49). The Trackster was the preferred shoe of college running coaches and YMCA fitness directors. Since the 1960s, New Balance's reputation for manufacturing performance footwear in multiple widths has grown through word of mouth and "grassroots" marketing programs for which they are still known.

Adidas. The first major non-English or American sneaker manufacturers were the Dassler brothers, Adolf (nicknamed Adi) and Rudolf (nicknamed Rudi) who set-up business in Herzogenaurach, Germany (1926). Their first sneakers cost two German Reich marks, and followed three guiding principles: to be the best shoes for the requirements of the sport, to protect athletes from injury, and to be durable. The Dasslers developed many firsts in the athletic shoe industry. Some of them included shoes with spikes and studs for soccer, track, and field. They also looked at constructing shoes with materials other than leather and canvas to reduce weight. By 1936, the Dasslers' shoes were internationally known, and were worn by many great athletes like Jesse Owens. In the Berlin 1936 Olympics, Owens won in almost every track and field event he competed in, earning four gold medals while wearing the Dasslers' shoes (Cheskin 1987, p. 11). Due to irreconcilable differences, Adi Dassler parted from his brother Rudi (1948), and they formed two separate shoe companies (Vanderbuilt 1998, p. 29). Rudi's company was called Puma, named after the powerful wild cat. Adi's company was called Adidas, where he took the first two syllables of his first and last name to create the famous name for his product line. To give support to the runner's midfoot, Adi created the three side stripes trademark in 1949 which is still used in almost every Adidas athletic shoe design (Heard 2003, pp. 90–93).

Onitsuka Tiger (ASICS). Although most sneakers in the early 2000s are manufactured in Asia, Onitsuka Tiger (later named ASICS) was the first Asian brand to make a statement in the sneaker market. Established in Kobe, Japan (1949), by Kihachiro Onitsuka, the company's philosophy was based on "bringing-up sound youth through sports." Onitsuka believed that playing sports was a solution to keeping kids out of prison, especially after World War II. The company's first shoes were made in Onitsuka's living room and resembled the Converse All-Star. Another philosophy of Onitsuka's was "harmony between human and science." In an interview with Onitsuka, he said: "We try to analyze all phenomena which affect a human body during sports and to make shoes which will meet the needs of the users is our principle toward the shoe making" (ASICS 2004). The company's name evolved to ASICS in 1977 based on the Latin phrase "Anima Sana In Corpore Sano," which translates to "A Sound Mind in a Sound Body." Although ASICS is a smaller company compared to the others mentioned, it is important to note, as it inspired the creation of Nike. Nike's founders, Bill Bowerman and Phil Knight, started their careers in the sneaker business working for ASICS, where they designed, developed, and sold their products.

Nike. Of all the major sneaker companies, Nike is the youngest, yet the largest globally. Nike was a business venture between the track coach Bill Bowerman from the University of Oregon and Phil Knight (who ran for Bowerman). Bowerman always had a desire for better-quality running shoes and was always tinkering with new ideas. He even made customized shoes for his own athletes. Bowerman was very inspirational to Knight, and while studying for his MBA at Stanford University in the early 1960s, he devised a small business plan for making quality running shoes, producing them in Japan, and shipping to the United States for distribution. After graduation, Knight traveled in 1963 to Japan to seek a way to live his dream. Representing Blue Ribbon Sports (BRS), he met with the president of Tiger ASICS (Onitsuka Company) and they agreed to go into business. Knight traveled throughout the West Coast of the United States and sold ASICS out of his car. Even Bowerman got involved and evolved some of the designs. Eventually the partners decided to split from the Onitsuka Company and create their own company. In 1971, Jeff Johnson (the first Nike employee) coined the name "Nike," and the Swoosh was created. The name originates from the Greek goddess of victory, and the famous Swoosh design was the creation of student Caroline Davidson, who was paid only $35 (Nike 2004). The first Nike shoe to feature the Swoosh was the Cortez in 1972. Product innovation and marketing has been key to Nike's success. By the end of the twentieth century, technologies like the waffle outsole, AIR, SHOX and legacies like Michael Jordan and Tiger Woods were just a few things that contributed to making Nike the largest sneaker company in the world.

Trainers. Technically, a sneaker is a shoe made of a canvas upper and a soft rubber outsole. What some refer to as a sneaker is much different and a more correct term to use is "trainer or "athletic shoe." Since the creation of the first sneaker-type construction, technology, fashion, and the desire for athletes to perform more efficiently and accurately have led to design evolution. The most typical types of sneakers are: running, cross-training, walking, basketball, and tennis. Technologies in materials have allowed sneakers to be made of synthetic leathers and 3D knits that are lightweight, breathable, and waterproof. A modern-day trainer could be as complicated as a shoe with an upper, midsole, insole, outsole, and shank. Within those parts, there are often subparts that better define each particular technology and give it its own specific performance advantage to others in the marketplace.

See also **Shoemaking; Shoes.**

BIBLIOGRAPHY

Cheskin, Melvyn P. *The Complete Handbook of Athletic Footwear.* New York: Fairchild Publications, 1987.

Coye, Dale. "The Sneakers/Tennis Shoes Boundary." *American Speech* 61 (1986): 366–369.

Heard, Neal. *Sneakers: Over 300 Classics from Rare Vintage to the Latest Designs.* London: Carlton Books, 2003.

Hendrickson, Robert. *Facts on File Encyclopedia of Word and Phrase Origins.* New York: Facts on File Inc., 2000.

Tenner, Edward. "Lasting Impressions: An Ancient Craft's Surprising Legacy in Harvard's Museums and Laboratories." *Harvard Magazine* 103, no. 1 (September–October 2000): 37.

Vanderbuilt, Tom. *The Sneaker Book: Anatomy of an Industry and an Icon.* New York: The New Press, 1998.

Internet Resources

ASICS. "Special Interview: The Reasons Why I Keep Making Sports Shoes." ASICS Shoe History: Epochs of 1949–2000. Available from <http://asics.cyplus.com/index_e.html>.

Bellis, Mary. "Footware and Shoes: What You Need to Know About." Available from <http://inventors.about.com/library/inventors/blshoe.htm>.

Goodyear. "Charles Goodyear and the Strange Story of Rubber." Goodyear. Available from <http://www.goodyear.com/corporate/strange.html>.

"The History of Your Shoes." Shoe Info Net. Available from <http://www.shoeinfonet.com>.

Kippen, Cameron. "History of Sport Shoes." Curtin University of Technology: Department of Podiatry. Available from <http://podiatry.curtin.edu.au/sport.html#science>.

Nike Inc. "Niketimeline: From Humbling Beginnings to a Promising Future." Nikebiz.com, The Inside Story. Available from <http://www.nike.com/nikebiz>.

Paquin, Ethel. "From Creepers to High-tops: A Brief History of the Sneaker." Lands' End Catalog. Available from <http://www.landsend.com>.

Perrin, Charles L. "Athletic Shoes: Many Types, Many Nicknames." Charlie's Sneaker Pages. Available from <http://sneakers.pair.com>.

"Plimsoll Line." *Britannica Student Encyclopedia.* Encyclopedia Britannica Premium Service. Available from <http://www.britannica.com>.

Wagner, Christopher. "School Sandals." Historical Boys Clothing (HBC). Available from <http://histclo.hispeed.com/index3.html>.

Susan L. Sokolowski

SOCIAL CLASS AND CLOTHING Display of wealth through dress became customary in Europe in the late thirteenth century. Therefore, a person's class affiliation could be assessed with relative ease. Because dress was recognized as an expressive and a potent means of social distinction, it was often exploited in class warfare to gain leverage. Dress was capable of signifying one's culture, propriety, moral standards, economic status, and social power, and so it became a powerful tool to negotiate and structure social relations as well as to enforce class differences.

For example, the sumptuary laws in Europe in the Middle Ages emerged as a way to monitor and maintain social hierarchy and order through clothes. People's visual representation was prescriptive, standardized, and regulated to the minutest detail. The types of dress, the length and width of the garment, the use of particular materials, the colors and decorative elements, and the number of layers in the garment, for instance, were confined to specific class categories. However, after society's lower-class groups relentlessly challenged the class structure and evaded the sumptuary laws' strictures, the laws were finally removed from statute books in the second half of the eighteenth century.

The sartorial expression of difference in social rank is also historically cross-cultural. For example, in China, a robe in yellow, which stood for the center and the earth, was to be used only by the emperor. In Africa among the Hausa community, members of the ruling aristocracy wore large turbans and layers of several gowns made of expensive imported cloth to increase their body size and thus set them apart from the rest of the society. In Japan, the colors of the kimono, its weave, the way it was worn, the size and stiffness of the obi (sash), and accoutrements gave away the wearer's social rank and gentility.

The History and Substance of Social Class System

Social class is a system of multilayered hierarchy among people. Historically, social stratification emerged as the consequence of surplus production. This surplus created the basis for economic inequality, and in turn prompted a ceaseless striving for upward mobility among people in the lower strata of society.

Those who possess or have access to scarce resources tend to form the higher social class. In every society this elite has more power, authority, prestige, and privileges than those in the lower echelons. Therefore, society's values and rules are usually dictated by the upper classes.

Social Class Theories

Philosopher and economist Karl Marx argued that class membership is defined by one's relationship to the means of production. According to Marx, society can be divided into two main groups: people who own the means of production and those who do not. These groups are in a perpetual, antagonistic relationship with one another, attempting either to keep up or reverse the status quo. Sociologist Max Weber extended Marx's ideas by contending that social class refers to a group of people who occupy similar positions of power, prestige, and privileges and share a life style that is a result of their economic rank in society.

Social class theories are problematic for a number of reasons. They often conceptualize all classes as homogenous entities and do not adequately account for the disparities among different strata within a particular social class. These theories also tend to gloss over geographic variants of class manifestations, such as urban and rural areas. A host of other factors, such as gender, race, ethnicity, religion, nationality, and even age or sexuality, further complicate the theories.

Social Class in the Twenty-First Century

In the twenty-first century, assessing one's social class is no longer a straightforward task because categories have become blurred and the boundaries are no longer well defined or fixed. Now one's social class would be decided by one's life-style choices, consumption practices, time spent on leisure, patterns of social interaction, occupation, political leanings, personal values, educational level, and/or health and nutritional standards.

Since, in global capitalism, inter- and intra-class mobility is not only socially acceptable but encouraged, people do not develop a singular class-consciousness or distinct class culture. Instead, they make an effort to achieve self-representation and vie for the acceptance of their chosen peer group. The progress of technology has also helped provide access to comparable and often identical status symbols to people of different class backgrounds across the globe. At the same time, however, as sociologist Pierre Bourdieu argues in his treatise *Distinction* (1984), the dominant social classes tend to possess not only wealth but "cultural capital" as well. In matters of dress, this capital manifests itself in the possession of refined taste and sensibilities that are passed down from generation to generation or are acquired in educational establishments.

Conspicuous Leisure, Consumption, and Waste

According to economist and social commentator Thorstein Veblen, the drive for social mobility moves fashion. In his seminal work, *The Theory of the Leisure Class* (1899), Veblen claims that the wealthy class exercised fashion leadership through sartorial display of conspicuous leisure, consumption, and waste. The dress of people in this group indicated that they did not carry out strenuous manual work, that they had enough disposable income to spend on an extensive wardrobe, and that they were able to wear a garment only a few times before deeming it obsolete.

Imitation and differentiation: Trickle-down, bubble-up, and trickle-across theories. Although sociologist Georg Simmel is not the sole author of the "trickle-down" theory, the general public still attributes it to him. In his article, *Fashion* (1904), Simmel argued that upper-class members of society introduce fashion changes. The middle and lower classes express their changing relationship to the upper classes and their social claims by imitating the styles set by the upper classes. However, as soon as they complete this emulation, the elite changes its style to reinforce social hierarchy. But as Michael Carter's research in *Fashion Classics* (2003) demonstrates, imitation and differentiation does not occur necessarily one after the other in a neat fashion. Instead, there is an ongoing, dynamic interaction between the two. Besides, within each class as well as among the different classes, there is an internal drive to express and assert one's unique individuality.

By the 1960s, the fashion industry had begun to produce and distribute more than enough products for everyone to be able to dress fashionably. This democratization of fashion means that by the twenty-first century anyone across the world could imitate a new style instantaneously. The direction of fashion change is no longer unilinear—it traverses geographical places, and flows from both the traditional centers of style as well as "the periphery." Through global media and popular culture, members of the lower classes, and subcultural and marginal groups, have been able to influence fashion as much as those in the upper classes. Therefore, it has become more appropriate to talk about a "bubble-up" or "trickle-across" theory.

Although social class is no longer a significant category of social analysis, one remains cognizant of it. The display of one's social standing through dress has become more subtle, eclectic, and nonprescriptive. The key to assessment in the early 2000s is often in the details. Higher status is indicated by a perfectly cut and fitted garment, the use of natural and expensive fabrics, and brand-name wear. One's class affiliation is often given away only by the choice of accessories, such as eyeglasses, watches, or shoes. A stylish haircut, perfect and even teeth, and especially a slender body often have become more of a class signifier than dress itself.

See also **Gender, Dress, and Fashion.**

BIBLIOGRAPHY

Bourdieu, Pierre. *Distinction.* Cambridge, Mass.: Harvard University Press, 1984.

Carter, Michael. *Fashion Classics from Carlyle to Barthes.* New York: Berg, 2003.

Crane Diana. *Fashion and Its Social Agendas.* Chicago: University of Chicago Press, 2000.

Damhorst, Mary Lynn, Kimberley A. Miller, and Susan O. Michelman, eds. *The Meanings of Dress.* New York: Fairchild Publications, 1999.

Davis, Fred. *Fashion, Culture, and Identity.* Chicago: University of Chicago Press, 1992.

Kaiser, Susan. *The Social Psychology of Clothing.* New York: Macmillan Publishing Company, 1990.

Simmel, Georg. "Fashion." *International Quarterly* 10: 130–155.

Veblen, Thorstein. *The Theory of the Leisure Class.* New York: Macmillan, 1899.

Katalin Medvedev

SPACE AGE STYLES Humans did not walk on the moon until 1969, but their imminent arrival was slotted on the world's calendar from the very beginning of the decade. Space exploration's grip on the popular consciousness during the 1960s contributed to a new fashion philosophy, becoming a pool of design inspiration; an analog to speculation about a radically transformed future that preoccupied the sensibilities of the decade. In

Space age outfit. A woman models an outfit from Andre Courrèges's 1994 spring/summer collection. In the 1960s, Courrèges was instrumental in developing the sleek, shiny, aerodynamic look called space age. © PHOTO B.D.V./CORBIS. REPRODUCED BY PERMISSION.

the April 1965 issue of *Harper's Bazaar,* Richard Avedon photographed British fashion model Jean Shrimpton wearing an astronaut's helmet and flight uniform. But it was hardly necessary to don an actual flight suit to be part of the styles that came to be known as "space age." Sleek as a fuselage, space age fashion emulated the aerodynamic simplicity and severity of a space capsule. Frills and flounces were eschewed in favor of a new, hard-edged and streamlined silhouette that also incorporated industrial materials. Space age fashion created a brusque and frequently shocking brave new universe within the 1960s fashion cosmos.

Blast off. As a design movement, space age fashion was above all a French phenomenon, promulgated mostly by men in their thirties who had been trained in the old-guard Paris couture, but saw the need to refute some of their pedigree. André Courrèges was perhaps the most creative. Courrèges was a member of Balenciaga's couture house for ten years before beginning his own business in 1961 in partnership with his wife Coqueline, who had also worked for Balenciaga. It took him but a couple of years to find his own feet, and when he did he kicked out the props from under establishment couture. "Things have never been the same since Courrèges had his explosion," Yves Saint Laurent said in a 1966 *Women's Wear Daily* (9 December, p. 1).

Before turning to fashion, Courrèges had dallied in both architecture and engineering, and this was reflected in his clothes. His dresses, suits, and trouser suits might be fitted, semi-fitted, or tubular, but they presented a bold and graphic silhouette, delineated as interlocking geometries by welt seaming and strategic piping. He preferred a restricted palette of monochromes and pastels, and was partial to aggressive checks and stripes. Courrèges used white a great deal, exploiting its myriad and contradictory connotations of sterility and/or purity as well as all-inclusive spectrum-spanning synergy.

Courrèges's work surely owed a debt to London ready-to-wear, but ever present in his work was the active, constructing hand of the couturier. His fabrics were flat, tailored wools, more intractable than what ready-to-wear was espousing. In a Courrèges suit a woman herself became a Brancusi-like distillation, an avatar of streamlined strength. Courrèges inveighed against the traditional appurtenances of femininity and foreswore the curvilinear. Reaching his meridian in 1964 and 1965, he advocated very short skirts as well as pants for all occasions, at the time a highly controversial proposition.

Women of the future. "Working women have always interested me the most," Courrèges said in *Life Magazine* in 1965. "They belong to the present, the future" (21 May, p. 57). Yet what he produced could not be easily transferred to the workplace, although his clothes and mass-manufactured imitations were seen on streets around the world. He offered what might be considered fashion manifestos. For him, high heels were as absurd as the bound feet of Asian women. He outfitted his models, instead, in flat Mary Jane slippers, or white boots that enhanced the graphic rectangularity of his silhouette.

After six years working for Balenciaga, Emanuel Ungaro assisted Courrèges for one year before opening his own doors in 1965. He also promised a radical departure from couture business-as-usual, pledging that there would be no evening clothes in this first collection, since he did not believe in them. He was certainly Courrèges's disciple during these years but his suits and dresses in childlike flaring shapes were gentle and more ingratiating. Essential to the success of the young house as unique fabrics designed exclusively for him by his partner Sonia Knapp. Knapp worked as closely with Ungaro as Coqueline Courrèges did with her husband.

A decade older than Courrèges or Ungaro, Pierre Cardin began his own business in 1957 after apprenticeships at several couture houses. During the epoch of space age, Cardin offered some of the couture's most

outré designs, offered like so much during the 1960s as provocative hypothesis rather than empirical prototype. His shapes might resemble floral abstractions that devoured conventional clothing dimensions. His enormous collars and frequent use of vinyl evoked outer-space gear. Cardin was a Renaissance man whose many endeavors included his own theater. Both Courrèges and Ungaro established ready-to-wear and licensing franchises, but Cardin's endeavors were waged on an exponential scale. His empire included a highly successful men's wear line—"Cardin's cosmonauts" presented a complementary vision of men's apparel.

Like much of Cardin's ideas, Paco Rabanne pushed space age fashion toward wearable art. He too trained as an architect, then designed accessories, before the young designer created a sensation in 1966 with ready-to-wear sheaths of plastic squares and discs attached to fabric backing. They were *le dernier cri* of Paris fashion, memorably commemorated in William Klein's film of the same year, *Qui Etes Vous Polly McGoo*. For him the new and ultimate frontier of fashion had become "the finding of new materials." His investigation of plastics and other hardware as possible human carapaces proclaimed a new epoch in Paris's wonted tradition of clothes so intricately constructed that they could stand on their own.

Space age fashion was gestated in a salon environment that was just as stark and unadorned as the clothes. New-style fashion shows went hand in hand with the fashion experiments they showcased. They were hectic rather than stately, built around mysterious theatrical effects rather than the old-style hauteur.

Splashdown. In the early 2000s, space age styles seem a paradigm of the teleological mentality of the 1960s, a last glorification of industrialization before the realization of its downside. Hard-edged fashion stayed influential all through the 1960s, eventually being vanquished by the unconstructed fashion that prevailed during the first half of the 1970s. The leaders of space age fashion have all remained in vogue, and from time to time pay homage to their bellwether work of the 1960s.

See also **Extreme Fashions; Futurist Fashion, Italian.**

BIBLIOGRAPHY

Lobenthal, Joel. *Radical Rags: Fashions of the Sixties*. New York: Abbeville Press, 1990.

Ryan, Ann, and Serena Sinclair. "Space Age Fashion." In *Couture*. Garden City, N.Y.: Doubleday, 1972.

Joel Lobenthal

SPACE SUIT While there have been many different ensembles of clothing worn by astronauts, the term "space suit" generally refers to the total life-support system for Extra-Vehicular Activity (EVA) that takes place outside the shelter of the spacecraft. The extreme conditions of

***Apollo 12* astronauts.** Astronaut Alan Bean holds up a sample of lunar soil during the *Apollo 12* mission. Commander Charles Conrad can be seen reflected in Bean's visor. The space suits used by the *Apollo* astronauts were custom-made for each astronaut and were the first suits capable of operating with a portable life support system, freeing astronauts from physical connection to a space ship. © BETTMANN/CORBIS. REPRODUCED BY PERMISSION.

outer space demand ensembles for EVA that are among the most complex clothing items ever designed.

Hazards of Outer Space

There are a variety of environmental conditions in outer space that humans cannot survive. Temperatures on the moon, for example, range from +250° F. to −250° F. (+121° C. to −157° C.). These temperature extremes are experienced instantly, as one moves from sunlight into shade. Astronauts are exposed to cosmic rays and charged particles from the sun. There is little filtration of ultraviolet light, so they must also have significant protection for their eyes.

The absence of atmosphere means that there is neither oxygen for breathing nor atmospheric pressure to keep body tissues intact. Without at least a portion of the pressure of the Earth's atmosphere on the body, its flu-

ids begin to boil and migrate outward. When unprotected a person becomes unconscious in 15 seconds, with death quickly following.

Finally, micrometeoroids are small particle-like grains of sand that travel at great rates of speed. These pose the threat of suit puncture and the risk of loss of pressure.

Early Space Suits

Most space suits comprise many layers of fabric, grouped to serve three basic functions: (1) application of pressure, (2) thermal and impact protection from the environment, and (3) thermal and general comfort. Accessories add breathing air, abrasion protection, vision protection, and communications tools.

The precursors to the space suit, the pressure suits worn by high-altitude pilots, focused almost exclusively on one function: application of pressure. In 1934, Wiley

Post developed the first pressure suit as a practical alternative to pressurizing his plane. His suit was pressurized with pure oxygen, which also provided him with breathing air, and was shaped to his position in the cockpit. As with several generations of suits that followed, it was almost impossible to move in Post's suit once it was inflated.

The first true space suits, worn by astronauts in the Mercury program in 1961, provided air for breathing and cooling and allowed for emergency inflation in case the pressurization of the spacecraft failed. Using inflation only as an emergency measure solved the movement problems created by Post's suit. The Mercury suits also had an outer layer of aluminized Mylar for thermal protection.

When a walk outside the spacecraft was planned for the Gemini program in 1962, it became clear that a new suit design was needed. Astronauts would need more mobility and greatly increased thermal and micrometeoroid protection. A specially constructed "link-net" fabric covered the suit's "bladder" layer, the inflated neoprene suit used for pressure to keep the suit from ballooning. This made it easier for astronauts to move. For thermal and micrometeoroid protection, the Gemini suits relied on high-temperature nylons and nonflammable metals, with the outermost layer of the Gemini IX pants being made of a woven stainless steel. Gemini suits were air-cooled using umbilical cords that tethered astronauts to the spacecraft. The astronauts complained that these suits were too warm and reported that the air fogged their helmet visors.

The Apollo Suits

The EVA ensemble for the Apollo moonwalk in 1969 included a number of new features: gloves with rubberized fingertips; overboots for abrasion protection; and extra visors for eye protection. To increase thermal comfort, a Liquid Cooling and Ventilation Garment (LCVG) was used. It consisted of a stretchable bodysuit with cooled water circulating in tubing covering a major portion of the body. Excess body heat was conducted to the water in the tubing, then cooled and recirculated. A backpack, the Portable Life Support System (PLSS), enabled the astronaut to travel in outer space entirely without connection to the spacecraft.

The Thermal Micrometeoroid Garment (TMG), which covered the Apollo suit, provided protection from puncture and temperature extremes. It incorporated multiple layers of fabrics, many of them aluminized with spacers (noncollapsible structures that incorporated many protected air spaces) in between them. The outer layer was made of Teflon-coated Beta Fiberglas, which was resistant to ignition and melting.

Molded rubber constant-volume bellows joints at the shoulders, elbows, hips, and knees greatly improved mobility over earlier suits. The entire EVA ensemble weighed 180 pounds (82 kg) on Earth, but only 30 pounds (14 kg) in the moon's gravity. This basic Apollo spacesuit was also used for space walking during the Skylab missions.

Designs for the Future

The unique goals for the Shuttle missions were reflected in the Shuttle space suit, the Extravehicular Mobility Unit (EMU). The EMU was not custom-made or designed to be used on a single mission, as were previous suits. The upper torso, lower torso, arms, and gloves were manufactured in different sizes that could be assembled to fit almost any body size and shape. Suits were designed to last for fifteen years and many missions. The EMU weighed almost twice as much as the Apollo EVA suits, but this was acceptable since they would be used in microgravity rather than within the gravitational pull of a planet. The outer layer of the Shuttle suits was an *ortho* fabric—a blend of Teflon, Nomex, and Kevlar fibers in a unique weave. This covered seven layers of aluminized materials in the TMG rather than the fourteen used for Apollo suits.

Another new feature of the Shuttle EMU was its Hard Upper Torso Assembly (HUT), a rigid fiberglass shell on which the backpack was mounted. Fabric arm and lower torso coverings and a rigid helmet were joined to the HUT with rigid bearing joints. Similar rigid structures are seen in designs for future space missions, such as one to Mars, for which completely rigid hard suits, much like deep-sea diving suits, have been developed. These suits are purported to allow greater ease of movement, and be more durable, lighter-weight, and easier to don than previous space suits.

See also **Techno-Textiles.**

BIBLIOGRAPHY

Harris, Gary L., ed. *The Origins and Technology of the Advanced Extra-Vehicular Space Suit.* American Astronautical Society History Series, Vol. 24. San Diego: Univelt, Inc., 2001.

Joels, Kerry M., and Gregory P. Kennedy. *The Space Shuttle Operator's Manual.* New York: Ballantine Books, 1982.

Kozloski, Lillian D. *U.S. Space Gear: Outfitting the American Astronaut.* Washington, D.C: Smithsonian Institution Press, 2000.

Mohler, Stanley R., and Bobby H. Johnson. *Wiley Post, His Winnie Mae and the World's First Pressure Suit.* Washington, D.C: Smithsonian Institution Press, 1971.

Watkins, Susan M. *Clothing: The Portable Environment.* Ames: Iowa State University Press, 1995.

Susan M. Watkins

SPANDEX. *See* **Elastomers.**

SPANGLES Spangles, also known as sequins or *paillettes*, are small, flat, circular ornaments usually made of metal, metallicized plastic, or other light-reflecting materials. Their primary use is to embellish apparel and accessories. Whereas beads are three-dimensional, spangles are essentially two-dimensional and can be overlapped to produce linear patterns.

The word "sequin" derives from the name of a small gold coin, the *zecchino*, which it resembles. The *zecchino* was introduced in Venice in 1284. *Chequeen*, a variant of the word, appeared in the English language in the late 1500s. By the nineteenth century, the word "sequin" was preferred to "spangle."

Historically, spangles, (which were once also known as "oes," because of their shape) were made by twisting gold or silver wire around a thin metal rod. The metal rings were cut off and hammered flat, resulting in a circular object with a central hole used to stitch it in place. In the 1920s, sequins were sometimes made of gelatin. In the twenty-first century, they are stamped out from plastic sheeting.

Spangles were a popular form of embellishment for the clothing of the aristocracy from the sixteenth through the eighteenth century. A host of sumptuary laws governing the dress of all classes of society prevented their being worn by anyone not of the nobility. In the seventeenth century, spangles were used to decorate men's and women's bodices, gloves, and shoes, as well as embroidered boxes and other decorative household items. In the eighteenth century, they appeared on muffs, shoes, women's gowns, and on men's coats and waistcoats. In the nineteenth century, sequins were still seen on court dress but they were also available to the general population. In the twentieth century, a craze for sequined "flapper" dresses emerged briefly during the 1920s. In the twenty-first century, sequins use in the apparel industry is primarily confined to womenswear and to the entertainment industry.

While other contemporary light-reflecting materials such as Lurex offer competition, designers including Norman Norell, Bob Mackie, and Carolina Herrera have used, and continue to use, sequins to produce eye-catching, shimmering evening wear.

See also **Mackie, Bob; Norell, Norman.**

BIBLIOGRAPHY
Campbell, R. *The London Tradesman*. London: T. Gardiner, 1747. Reprint, Newton Abbot, England: David and Charles, 1969.
Rivers, Victoria Z. *The Shining Cloth: Dress and Adornment that Glitters*. London and New York: Thames and Hudson, Inc., 1999.

Whitney Blausen

SPANISH DRESS A reliable overview of the history of Spanish dress from the Middle Ages to the twenty-first century, including its borrowings from and impact on the dress of other cultures, remains to be written. The subject is complex because of the internal make-up of the country, the multicultural society that spawned and epitomized the great Spanish empire of the early modern pe-

riod, and constant shifts in Spain's political and economic relationship with the rest of the world. A large if sparsely inhabited country, located on the most southwestern periphery of Europe, Spain embraces a variety of regional identities that owe much to differences in climate, geography, and language, and to a rich historical legacy. Spain has been a country of contrasts: partially occupied by the Moors for more than 700 years, it experienced the cohabitation (*convivencia*) of different faiths (Jewish, Muslim, and Christian) until 1492; from that date it became the consistent, vociferous and sometimes intolerant champion of Catholicism, a nation state that experienced its Golden Age in the sixteenth and seventeenth centuries. Its massive empire, acquired through inheritance of lands in the southern Netherlands and Italy and the forceful occupation of colonies in the Americas, Asia, and Africa, brought great wealth and power in world affairs until the early seventeenth century. As both gradually dwindled, Spain turned into "marginal Europe," modernizing only from the 1960s onward during the dictatorship of General Francisco Franco (1939–1975), and selling its cultural products, notably film and fashion, beyond its own frontiers and former colonies on an unprecedented scale since the 1980s.

The Spanish climate has lent itself to the cultivation of a wide range of raw materials for textile production, and skills in craft production have long been nurtured. Industrialization, having begun early, lagged behind that of northern Europe, and mass-production of clothing only took off gradually during the twentieth century. In the Middle Ages wool from the plains of Castile was much prized domestically and exported widely; flax (for fine and not-so-fine linens) grew plenteously in the damp climate of Galicia, and the Moors enriched Andalusia and Valencia by introducing sericulture and silk weaving. First of the peninsula, from the sixteenth century onward, the Spanish colonies supplied exotic dyestuffs, which delivered brilliant reds and the deepest blacks, colors that still inform the Spanish palette in ecclesiastical, regional, and fashionable dress. Weaving was well established by the Middle Ages, while knitting arrived by the thirteenth century, possibly introduced to Europe by the Moors via Andalusia. Spain became mechanized during the nineteenth century, while skills such as embroidery and leatherwork survived as prized handicrafts up to the present day.

Dress with a Difference
In the Middle Ages, Spain divided into Christian and Muslim zones, and hosted a variety of dress styles whose terminology and cut from the tenth century onward reveal a debt to Arab materials and garb—even in the Christian kingdoms. The contents of the tombs of the thirteenth- and early fourteenth-century kings of Castile in Burgos, for example, include mantles, surcoats, and tunics made of silks brocaded in northern taste with heraldic devices, such as the lions and castles of Léon and Castile, while the coffins are lined with silks with

COMMENTARY BY FOREIGNERS VISITING SPAIN

Mid-Sixteenth Century

"The women generally wear black, as do the men, and around the face they wear a veil like nuns, using the whole shawl (*manto*) over the head. And when they do not wear the veil over the face, they wear high collars with huge ruffs; and they use [excessive] makeup...."
  Camilo Borghese in 1594 on a visit to Madrid, (cited in *Garcia Mercadal*, p. 112)

Mid-Eighteenth Century

"Women of all ranks wear their rosaries in their hands whenever they go to church, and always in such manner that every body may see them. They are a part of their church-dress. I am told that it is customary, amongst the lower ranks, for the young men to present fine rosaries to their sweethearts. Women

of whatever condition never go to church but with the *basquiña* and the *mantilla* on. The *basquiña* is a black petticoat, commonly of silk, which covers their gowns from the waist down, and the *mantilla* is a muslin or cambrick veil that hides their heads and the upper part of their bodies. If they do not turn up their veils, as some of them will do both at church and in the streets, it is difficult, if not impossible, even for husbands to know their wives" (Bareti, p. 421).

Mid-Twentieth Century

"... striking ... are the differences in regional costumes. Except for the familiar Andalusian costume of high comb, mantilla, sleeveless bodice, and wide flounced skirts with large white spots, it is safe to say that nearly all Spanish regional costumes clearly reveal Moorish influence" (Bush, p. 69).

Islamic patterns—stylized vegetation, geometric motifs, stars, zigzags, and inscriptions in Arabic script. By the eleventh century the pilgrimage route across the north of Spain to Santiago de Compostela connected Spain with neighboring Europeans consistently and by the middle of the fourteenth century, the Spanish aristocracy and urban elite were wealthy enough to change styles in clothing regularly, enriching their wardrobes with fashions from Burgundy and Italy. The accession of Charles I (son of Philip of Burgundy) to the Spanish throne in 1516 sealed Spain's intimate relationship with both states and introduced the austere black and white dress so familiar from portraits of Spain's Golden Age: this formal dress (*gala negra*) was accessorized with lavish gold chains, buttons, and jewelry wrought from the precious metals from the Spanish-American colonies. The Spanish monopoly on logwood, a black dyestuff also imported from the new colonies, may well have had some bearing on this urban predilection for the color, as well as the devout Catholicism of subsequent monarchs (especially Philip II, III, and IV and Charles II) who, to some extent, eschewed overbearing ostentation. Nonetheless, descriptions of festivities throughout the sixteenth and seventeenth centuries show that on holidays, those who could afford to do so often wore brightly colored garments of silk that were embroidered, brocaded, or trimmed in silver or gold. Spanish sumptuary laws made serious attempts to limit excess in the consumption of luxuries and to codify the distinctions between noble and bourgeois in the interests of protecting the Spanish economy and Spanish morals. References to the appropriate dress for Christian and non-Christian, promulgated in

the first laws from 1252 onward, ceased after the expulsion of Jews at the end of the fifteenth century and Moors at the beginning of the seventeenth century. Throughout this period, such laws were of little relevance to the poor and marginalized who wore inexpensive undyed cloth in tones of brown, gray, or off-white. They thus earned the epithet "people of brown clothes" (*gente de ropa parda*), which instantly differentiated them from their social superiors (*gente de ropa negra*).

The Golden Age

Significantly, during this Golden Age, when Spain was wealthy and powerful, and the literary and plastic arts flourished, the king's censors approved the publication of the first Spanish manuals devoted to disseminating superior skills in tailoring. The first book, published in 1580 and reprinted in 1589, came from the plume of a Basque tailor, the second in 1617 from a Frenchman turned Valencian, the third in 1640 from a father and son from Madrid—in other words, representatives of all major regions. These books convey the shifts in Spanish fashions and allegiances over the period, and the requirements of the upper and educated echelons of society. Consisting of patterns for men's and women's fashionable garments, mourning dress, clerical garb, robes for the military orders of Santiago and Calatrava, horses' caparisons and military banners, they reveal that most garments were Spanish in origin. The late sixteenth-century examples of Moorish and Italian gowns encountered Hungarian and French suits in the later work of Anduxar (1640)—a sign of royal alliance through marriage to Hungary and of the rise of French fashions, slimmer in silhouette than their

Spanish counterparts. Change in cut demonstrated the gradual isolation of Spanish noblemen from their European peers as their highly influential dress composed of doublets, jerkins, trunk hose, and cloaks of various lengths gave way to the rather singular padded breeches (*calzones*) that made Spaniards look broad and solid in comparison with their northern peers. At around the same time, Spaniards' crinkly white ruffs (*lechuguillas*) ceded pride of place at men's necks to the *golilla*, a plain white semicircular collar built on a base of cardboard. Both forms of neckwear performed much the same function, as did their matching cuffs, preventing hard manual labor and in the case of the former keeping heads high and haughty. Women of the upper classes were similarly constricted: decked out in impressive jewelry, they wore richly patterned gowns with bell-shaped skirts over the Spanish farthingale (*verdugado*), a cage-like underskirt constructed of bands of willow. This item of clothing appeared in the 1470s and underwent several changes in shape thereafter, reaching enormous proportions between the late 1630s and 1670s. In its early manifestation it found its way into the fashions of neighboring states, while later it merely demonstrated Spanish distance from the mainstream.

Other aspects of Spanish dress that were constants in the urban landscape were the robes of clergy and members of religious orders, the voluminous mantles worn by women in the streets to cover themselves up (a sign of modesty evidently inherited from Moorish dress), and the addiction to all-enveloping mourning garments. Not only was black the color of formal court dress, but many of these items also had religious and moral connotations even into the third quarter of the twentieth century: the clergy and the bereaved were a particularly potent provincial and urban presence, especially among the white, sun-lit villages of the south.

Dominance of Foreign Fashions

From about 1700 until the mid-twentieth century, the Spanish cognoscenti depended on Parisian (and sometimes British) modes. In the eighteenth century, under the ruling Bourbon dynasty, Spain received fashion news consistently from Paris via Spanish and French intermediaries—the powerful shopkeepers of the *Cinco Gremios Mayores*, ambassadors and well-traveled aristocrats, manufacturers' agents, the burgeoning French fashion press, and French emigrant dressmakers who set up businesses in the Spanish capital (as in other European cities). From the second half of the nineteenth century, wealthy female consumers and the most prestigious Spanish dressmakers made the annual or biannual pilgrimage to Paris to attend the haute couture shows, from which they acquired models for themselves or to adapt for their middle-class Spanish clients. In the major fashionable shopping centers of Madrid (center of government), Barcelona (heart of cotton and woolen production), and San Sebastián/Donostia (summer retreat of the court), by

the beginning of the twentieth century there was a host of major dressmaking establishments whose reputation did not transcend national boundaries (such as Carolina Montagne, María Molist, El Dique Flotante, Santa Eulalia, Pedro Rodriguez, and Carmen Mir). In men's dress, reliance on Spanish tailors continued although the wave of Anglomania that hit France in the late eighteenth century extended to Spain. This legacy may even have carried over into the twentieth century: the first Spanish dictator, José Primo de Rivera, ordered clothes from Savile Row prior to his espousal of a politically sensitized form of dress; Cristóbal Balenciaga, a skilled tailor, chose England in 1935 as his first destination before moving to Paris; and Spain's only department store, founded in 1935 as a tailoring outlet with a line in ready-made children's clothes, still carries the name *El Corte Inglés* (English cut).

The fashion press played its part in disseminating fashionable styles. While those who could afford high-class fashions probably read French publications, printed matter in Spanish was available from the early nineteenth century. It owed much to its French or northern European models: fashion plates remained the same while captions were translated into Spanish (in the early nineteenth century Rudolph Ackerman's *Repository for the Arts* received this treatment; in the 1830s and from the 1880s respectively, the *Semanario Pintoresco Español* and *El Salón de la Moda* followed a similar procedure). In the twentieth century, *El Hoga y Moda* from 1909, the *Boletín de la Moda* from 1952, and *Telva* from 1963 represented national production. These journals dispersed styles to local, small-scale professional dressmakers and their amateur counterparts (home-dressmakers). Indeed, sewing and knitting skills probably thrived longer in Spain than in wealthier, industrialized European states where ready-made clothing was widespread and traditional roles for women were called into question earlier. The continued presence of the church as patron and educator of needlework skills and morals probably contributed to keeping these traditions alive until the end of the twentieth century.

Regional Dress

Despite the dominance of mainstream European fashions in the eighteenth and nineteenth centuries, and a noticeable rejection of traditional mores from the 1960s as large numbers of young Spaniards moved from rural areas into the cities, regional dress survived, often preserved carefully for use at national or local fiestas (religious holidays) and rites of passage such as marriage. It is still commissioned and made in the early 2000s for special occasions. Such dress has always varied by region, its materials and form relating to local textile supplies, agricultural activities, and calendar. Anthropologists have identified three main types by zone—north and Cantabrian, central, and Andalusian-Mediterranean—but they are still far from completing a comprehensive study. In the north and center, woolens and linens dominate festive dress; sometimes decorated with bands of silk or embroidery, the colors are often deep (brown, black, and red or green), and heavy jewelry is common. In the south and east, gloriously colored silks, cottons, and linens flourish in the sun, accessorized with lace or transparent veiling often with a flash of metallic thread, a heady reminder of the legacy of the Moors. Such dress, although not immune to change over the centuries, is a fossilized version of earlier fashionable, festive, or working dress. While many of its features have their roots in the eighteenth century, some go much further back, and others date to more recent times. In Valencia, silks with eighteenth-century designs are still woven to satisfy the demand for festive dress comprising full, ankle-length skirts, worn with a tight-fitting bodice over a chemise and below a neckerchief and lace mantilla. Bullfighters' suits of lights (*trajes de luces*) fall into this category, their most obvious roots in popular Andalusian *majo* attire of the eighteenth century, worn at the time that the sport commercialized. The short jacket with braiding covering its seams harks back to seventeenth-century practices in tailoring, while the knitted net hairpiece (*redecilla*) so familiar from Francisco Goya's paintings located its wearers among the popular classes. The tight-fitting breeches or pantaloons belong to late eighteenth- or early nineteenth-century fashionable men's dress.

The exchange between fashionable and regional dress works both ways: at the end of the eighteenth century, certain aristocrats and Queen María Luisa herself adopted a version of Andalusian *maja* dress, the black lace mantilla and overdress, secured by bold red or pink sash; in the work of twentieth century and contemporary Hispanic fashion designers regional variations are often a leitmotiv. Cristóbal Balenciaga (1895–1972) and Antonio Canovas del Castillo (1913–1984), who made their reputations outside Spain through austere modernist designs, provided bursts of Spanish drama in their many flamenco-inspired dresses, even once they were resident in Paris. The picturesque qualities of such gowns were no doubt familiar (and possibly desirable) by then to the many foreign tourists who visited the Costa Brava, Costa Blanca, and Costa del Sol in growing numbers from the 1950s onward. Regional dress, sentimentalized as a symbol of a lost golden age with superior values since the nineteenth century, has also served an overtly political function: following the Civil War (1936–1939), the right-wing Falangist party encouraged the celebration of regional festivities and the wearing of regional dress in the interests of promoting national cohesion and identity (much as the Nazis did in Germany and the Vichy government in France).

A New Golden Age?

Spanish dress may inadvertently have reached beyond Spanish frontiers before the 1980s via the acquisitions of tourists at the establishments advertised in tourist guides to Spain, via the creations of those Spanish couturiers who sought a propitious environment for their creativity in Paris, and via limited coverage in high-class fashion magazines such as *Vogue*. It is only since the mid-1980s or so, however, that Spanish designers and clothing companies have marketed their wares abroad on a significant scale. Spanish government initiatives probably played some role in this drive although the industry is still relatively undercapitalized and undeveloped. In the early 1980s the socialists began with the revitalization of the textile industries, and by the middle of the decade turned their attention to the clothing sector. In 1985 they established the Center for the Promotion of Design and Fashion (CPDM) under the auspices of the Ministry of Labor and Energy, and in 1987, the Cristóbal Balenciaga prize that recognizes annually the achievement of the best Spanish designer, the best international designer, the best textile design company, and the best new designer. Subsequently, exhibitions of Spanish fashion brought design into the public eye: in 1988, *Spain: Fifty Years of Fashion* held in Barcelona; in 1990 *Spanish Designers* held in Murcia; and the projected opening of a fashion museum and research center in Guetaria received government backing of $3.2 million in 2000. An elite group of fashion designers has emerged: they are known on the international catwalk as well as at the equivalent national events (Gaudí in Barcelona and Cibeles in Madrid), and they have outlets worldwide (such as Sibylla, Adolfo Domínguez, Pedro del Hierro, Antonio Miró, Purifiación García, and Roberto Verino, to name a few). Even more impressive is the forceful, expanding ready-to-wear sector, notably the retailers Cortefiel and Loewe (both established in the late nineteenth century), Pronovias (the first company to provide ready-to-wear wedding dresses in Spain from the 1960s), and Mango and Zara, notorious internationally for its rapid reproduction of catwalk fashions. The expansion of their shops worldwide demonstrates the growth of these young empires: between 1964 and 2003, Pronovias opened 100 shops under its own name in Spain, one in Paris, with one in New York in the pipeline. It also distributes its goods through 1,000 multibrand shops in more than 40 countries, having diversified into cocktail wear and accessories. Zara, the original firm from which the Galician Inditex group grew, opened its first store in A Coruña in 1975, its first stores outside Spain (in Portugal, United States, and France) in the late 1980s, by 2000 had 375 stores worldwide, and only one year later more than 600. Barcelona-based Mango entered the arena in 1984 in Spain, expanded gradually in the following decade, and exponentially from the 1990s onward, boasting a total of 630 shops in 70 countries by 2002. The manufacturing base of these firms is located in the traditional textile manufacturing areas of Galicia and Catalonia.

Although these empires have grown quickly and, significantly, have flourished since the late 1980s, it is difficult to measure their impact on Spanish consumers who have access to all the top international brands in their major city centers and probably mix and match such brands with the Spanish newcomers, as fashion magazines recommend (indigenous *Dunia* between 1978 and 1998, and *Telva* since 1963 and Spanish language editions of *Cosmopolitan, Elle, Vogue, GQ* since 1976, 1986, 1988, and 1993 respectively). It is not always possible to detect overtly Spanish features in products intended to sell in the global market and Spanish consumers are anxious to espouse a broadly fashionable appearance, like their counterparts in neighboring France and Italy. The kind of personal expression typified by the sub-cultural styles of northern Europe seems absent from Spanish streets. Increasing wealth and new professional opportunities and lifestyles for women may have boosted demand for fashion. In 1989, the CPDM published a survey on the changing habits of Spanish consumers since the mid 1980s. The findings suggested that there was an acute awareness of and pride in Spanish fashion, whose variety of styles and different price ranges competed with other European goods—even young consumers who aspired to American styles could create them through buying Spanish. Designer clothes were no longer reserved for special occasions but were now worn for everyday wear. Eleven years later, a Galician sociologist noted the correlation between lifestyle, social class, and choice of dress: the professional and educated classes in Spain aspired to follow seasonal fashion and conform to a recognizable "correct" appearance; they shopped in city center designer stores. The classic suit remained the main preference for both sexes. The epitome of this awareness of and national pride in domestic designer products must surely be the addition to the credits at the end of the Spanish national news on television of the name of the designer of the presenter's clothes—all too often, it is Adolfo Domínguez, the doyen of classic, unstructured tailoring and a color palette of black, gray, and aubergine. This second Golden Age of Spanish fashion has surely inherited features from its august forebear.

See also **Ethnic Style and Fashion; Europe and America: History of Dress in (400–1900 C.E.).**

BIBLIOGRAPHY

Alçega, Juan de. *Tailor's Pattern Book 1589.* Facsimile, with translation by J. Pain and C. Bainton. Introduction and notes by J. L. Nevinson. Bedford, U.K.: Ruth Bean, 1979. A translation accompanies this facsimile edition of the second edition of the first Spanish publication on tailoring, as does an excellent introduction on the context for tailoring in sixteenth-century Spain.

Anderson, Ruth Matilda. *Spanish Costume: Extremadura.* New York: Hispanic Society of America, 1951. Fieldwork undertaken in this region of Spain allowed Anderson to document the state of regional dress in this area in the late 1940s.

———.*Hispanic costume, 1480–1530.* New York: Hispanic Society of America, 1979. The most comprehensive and well-illustrated account of Spanish dress of this period, it follows the format of Bernis's writing, identifying particular garments in paintings, and providing a useful explanation of terminology.

Baretti, J. *A Journey from London to Genoa through England, Portugal, Spain, and, France.* Vol. 1, Letter 56. Madrid, 9 Oct. 1760.

Berges, Manuel, et al. *Moda en Sombras.* Madrid: Museo Nacional del Pueblo Español, 1991. This catalogue accompanied an exhibition of the museum's collection of regional and fashionable dress dating from the eighteenth to twentieth centuries. Seven excellent introductory essays are devoted to different aspects of regional and fashionable dress and its production and consumption in Spain over that period.

Bernis Madrazo, Carmen. *Indumentaria medieval española.* Serie Artes y Artistas. Madrid: Instituto Diego Velázquez del Consejo Superior de Investigaciones Científicas, 1955.

———. *Indumentaria española en tiempos de Carlos V.* Madrid:Instituto Diego Velázquez del Consejo Superior de Investigaciones Científicas, 1962.

———. *Trajes y Modas en las España de los Reyes Católicos.* Serie Artes y Artistas. Madrid:Instituto Diego Velázquez del Consejo Superior de Investigaciones Científicas, 1978.

———. *Trajes y tipos en el Quijote.* Madrid: El Viso, 2001. These seminal accounts of the characteristics of dress in Spain from the Middle Ages to the early seventeenth century, offer a brief historical background to changing styles, identify the terminology in use, and the garments to which it applies through details from different works of art, from manuscripts to paintings and sculpture, and in the most recent volume concentrates on a single literary source.

Bush, Jocelyn. *Spain and Portugal.* Fodor's Modern Guides. London: Newman Neame Limited, London, 1955.

Carbonel, Danièle, after text by Pedro Soler. *Oro Plata: Embroidered Costumes of the Bullfight.* Paris: Assouline, 1997. A visually stunning insight into the production of suits of lights today, via the workshops of Fermín, a Spanish specialist. Superlative black-and-white and color illustrations show a variety of suits on and off their owners, as well as some interesting shots of bullfighters off duty.

Carretero Pérez, Andrés. *José Ortiz Echagüe en las colecciones del Museo Nacional de Antropología.* Madrid: Museo de Antropología, 2002. Catalog of exhibition held on the work of the photographer José Ortiz Echagüe who actively recorded traditional costume and custom across Spain from the 1920s to the 1960s. The introductory text is a useful evaluation of the visual recording and attitudes to isolated communities.

Clapés, Mercedes, and Rosa María Martín i Ros. *España: 50 años de moda.* Barcelona: Ajuntament de Barcelona & Centro de Promoción de Diseño y Moda, 1987. This catalog accompanied an exhibition of fifty years of Spanish fashion held at the Palau de la Virreina in Barcelona in 1987. Beginning with Balenciaga and haute couture, it offers succinct biographies of major Spanish dressmakers and fashion designers, illustrated by a photograph of each designer and several of their creations via the fashion press. A few examples of surviving dress in museum collections are included. There are also brief sections on fashion photographers, fashion as art, and a catalog of the exhibited garments.

Datatèxtil. Semi-annual magazine published by the Centre de Documentació i Museu Tèxtil de Terrassa. This popular magazine often contains useful articles on Spanish dress and textiles, deriving from exhibitions, collections, and from academic theses. Early issues were in Castilian and Catalan, but since 2001, Castilian and English are the two languages in use. In addition, the Centre consistently publishes excellent catalogs that accompany its exhibitions that often delve into local or national aspects of a particular theme.

Dent Coad, Emma. *Spanish Design and Architecture.* London: Studio Vista, 1990. Beginning with a rapid overview of Spanish fashion since 1492, this chapter introduces regional dress, but concentrates on the fashion industry of the 1980s as represented by official government sources.

Diaz-Plaja, Fernando. *La vida cotidiana en La España de la Ilustración.* Madrid: EDAF, 1997. An overview of fashion and its use in eighteenth century Spain, drawing attention to the difference between the distinctiveness of Spanish dress of the seventeenth century and the fashionable Spanish assimilation of French styles in the eighteenth century under the ruling Bourbon dynasty.

Franco Rubio, Gloria A. *La vida cotidiana en tiempos de Carlos III.* Madrid: Ediciones Libertarias, 2001. An overview of clothing and its uses in eighteenth-century Spain which draws attention to the tension between the adoption of an overtly French form of fashionable dress and the retention or reinvention of a native Spanish style.

Garcia Mercadal, José. *Viajes por España.* Madrid: Alianza Editorial, 1972.

Herrero Carretero, Concha. *Museo de Telas Medievales. Monasterio de Santa María de Huelgas.* Madrid: Patrimonio Nacional, 1988. Catalog of the museum of medieval textiles in Burgos in which a detailed description of each of the garments found in the thirteenth- and early fourteenth-century tombs of the kings of Castile and Léon are described, as well as the jewelry and textiles found therein. Fine color illustrations show the textiles before and after conservation.

Morral i Romeu, Eulalia, and Anton Segura i Mas. *La seda en España: Llegenda, poder i realitat.* Barcelona: Lunweg Editores, 1991. Catalog of an exhibition on silk in Spain, this is a useful introduction to the silk route, sericulture, and silk weaving in Spain, with excellent illustrations of surviving artifacts.

Morral i Romeu, Eulalia, et al. *Mil anys de disseny en punt.* Tarasa: Centre de Documentació i Museu Tèxtil, 1997. Catalog in Castilian and Catalan from a pioneering exhibition on knitting over the last one thousand years with introductory essays by historians, curators, and designers, this book demonstrates the amount of research that needs to be dedicated to this important area as well as the current state of scholarship. The color illustrations of important knitted objects and graphic material are a useful starting point for any number of projects. They are not limited to Spain.

Reade, Brian. *The Dominance of Spain, 1550–1660.* London: Harrap, 1951. An overview of the fashions of Spain in this period, with a good range of supporting visual evidence mainly drawn from portraits of the period.

Ribeiro, Aileen. "Fashioning the Feminine: Dress in Goya's Portraits of Women." In *Goya: Images of Women.* Edited by Janis A. Tomlinson. Washington, D.C.: National Gallery of Art, 2002. This article reveals the eighteenth-century Spanish predilection for French fashions and the adoption of Andalusian models, drawing on an unpublished doctoral thesis by S. Worth, "Andalusian Dress and the Image of Spain 1759–1936." Ph.D. diss. Ohio State University, 1990.

Rocamora, Manuel. *Museo de Indumentaria: Colección Rocamora.* Barcelona: Gráficas Europeas, 1970. A catalog of the major private collection that forms the basis of the national museum of dress in Barcelona with brief descriptions for each inventoried garment, and a few black-and-white and color illustrations that reveal the strengths of the collection.

Smith, Paul Julian. "Analysis of Contemporary Spanish Fashion, Written from the Perspective of Cultural Studies." In *Contemporary Spanish Culture: TV, Fashion, Art, and Film.* Malden, Mass.: Polity Press, 2003. Covering contemporary Spanish fashion and written from the perspective of cultural studies, chapter 2 offers an analysis of the factors that typify the consumption and production of fashionable dress in Spain, with particular reference to the work and brand of the designer Adolfo Domínguez.

Internet Resources

Cortefiel. Available from <http://www.cortefiel.com>.

El Corte Inglés. Available from <http://www.elcorteingles.es>.

Inditex. Available from <http://www.inditex.com>.

Loewe. Available from <http://www.loewe.com>.

Mango. Available from <http://www.mango.com>.

Pronovias. Available from <http://www.provonias.com>.

Lesley Ellis Miller

SPECTACLES. *See* **Eyeglasses.**

SPINNING The origins of hand spinning, or twisting fiber to make yarn or thread, perhaps date back to the Paleolithic period. An ivory figurine found in France has been carbon-dated to 25,000 B.C.E. The figure is shown wearing a loincloth made of strands which were probably formed by hand-twisting since the earliest known hand spindles are from the later Neolithic period.

Hand Spindles

A hand spindle is any implement which can be rotated or twisted by hand to spin yarn or thread. In its most primitive form, a hand spindle can be a branch pulled from a tree or a rock picked up from the ground. In its most common form, it is somewhat like a top. It has a straight shaft with a weight attached to give added momentum. Along with primitive weapons, such as the axe and the knife, it is one of the oldest and most widely used tools of the human race.

The oldest hand-spun weaving fragment found was unearthed at the archaeological excavation of Catal Huyuk in south-central Turkey, and has been carbon-dated to more than 8,000 years old. It appears to be a bast fiber carefully prepared and spun into a very smooth yarn. It was woven at 30 threads per inch in one direction and 38 in the other direction.

Spindle whorls have been found in recent Middle Eastern excavations which date back to 8,000 B.C.E. The date generally accorded to the invention of the wheel is 3,500 B.C.E. Thus, it is possible that understanding the principle of rotation as it was applied in a spindle whorl subsequently led to the invention of the wheel.

Development of Styles

Hand spindles developed into an astonishing array of styles designed for different types of fibers and yarns and various methods of spinning. Some are designed to revolve freely, suspended from the yarn. Others rotate with the weight of the spindle supported on a surface. Whorls can be positioned at the top, center, or bottom of the spindle shaft. A range of sizes developed, from little needle-like slivers of bamboo weighted with tiny beads of clay to yard-long wooden shafts with large plate-like wooden whorls.

The spindle style most widely used throughout history has been the small bead whorl type. It was the basic spinning tool in India, Africa, Southeast Asia, much of China, and throughout Meso-America.

By 2,500 B.C.E., the Egyptians were spinning linen so fine it could be woven at 540 threads per inch. The Peruvians were able to spin alpaca yarn at 191 miles per pound. The famous Dhaka muslins spun in India measured 253 miles per pound. Using the Tex System of measuring yarns gravimetrically, we can determine that they reached the highest level of skill that it is possible to achieve by hand or machine.

Simple spindles produced all the thread, yarn, and cordage for household use, for commerce, and for war. They met all these needs: clothing, household fabrics, blankets, tents, uniforms for armies, cloth wrapping, and cordage for packages, trappings for animals, rugs and tapestries, sails for ships, and vestments for church and the nobility.

Since spindles are small enough to be carried easily, they were used while walking, shopping in markets, watching flocks, visiting neighbors, and caring for children.

Spindles continued to be used long after spinning wheels appeared. They are still in use in many parts of the world. One can watch them being used in Southeast Asia, the Middle East, North Africa, and Latin America.

Spinning Wheels

Spinning wheels evolved from the hand spindle. They first appeared in India about 750 C.E. From India they spread to Persia by 1257. They reached China by 1270. The first evidence of spinning wheels being used in Europe occurs in the guild laws of Speyer, Germany, in 1298.

The spinning wheels in Asia did not have legs. The base rested on the floor or ground and the spinners sat on the ground while spinning. In Europe, the base rested on legs. In the simplest design, a spindle with a grooved whorl

Line art drawing of spindles used throughout the world. The spindles are used for handspinning, or the process of twisting fiber to make yarn or thread. BETTE HOCHBERG. REPRODUCED BY PERMISISON.

was mounted horizontally between two vertical posts at one end of the base. A large wheel was placed at the other end of the base. A single cord encircled the groove in the whorl and the large wheel. Each time the large wheel revolved one time, the little whorl revolved many times.

The spinner turned the large wheel with one hand, and drafted the fiber as it was spun into yarn with the other hand. The yarn was then wound onto the shaft of the spindle.

The Great Wheel

As time passed, spinning wheels evolved into what is called the great wheel or walking wheel. The diameter of the wheel grew to three or four feet. Legs were added to the base. The spinner gave a quick turn to the wheel and walked back from the wheel as the yarn twisted, and walked forward to the spindle to wind on the yarn. This style of wheel was usually used for spinning short staple wool and cotton.

Lack of space in small cottages limited its use. Great wheels were about two feet wide and six feet long. They were widely used in northern Europe and were still in use on some American farms in the early twentieth century.

The Flyer Spinning Wheel

The earliest evidence of a spinning wheel with a flyer is a woodcut illustration in the "Waldburg Hausbuch" in Speyer, Germany, dated 1480. The flyer eliminated the need for the spinner to pause and wind each length of yarn as it was spun.

The flyer holds a bobbin on its shaft. A drive cord is doubled to encircle the large drive wheel and both the whorl on the metal shaft of the flyer and the bobbin, which turns freely on the shaft. Since the groove on the bobbin is deeper than the groove on the flyer, it rotates faster and continuously winds on the yarn as it is spun.

Adding a Treadle

The Chinese were probably the first people to add foot treadles to spinning wheels. The addition of a treadle meant the spinner could sit comfortably and no longer had to turn the wheel by hand. The design of the spinning wheel as we think of it today was now complete.

Distaffs

Spinners using either hand spindles or spinning wheels usually used a distaff to hold a ready supply of fibers as they spun. Distaffs could be held in the hand or belt, mounted on a spinning wheel or free standing. They were used throughout Britain, Scandinavia, Russia, Greece, the Middle East, and many parts of Latin America.

They varied from simple sticks to elaborately carved and painted artifacts. Small distaffs designed to be held in the hand or worn on the wrist were used to hold short fibers. Long or tall distaffs were used with long wools, flax, and hemp.

Preparation of Fibers

Better yarn or thread can be spun from most fibers if they are carded or combed before spinning. To card wool, early people used the dried heads of the teasel plant, which are covered with firm, fine, hooked bristles. This helped to remove debris and align the fibers.

Thorns set into a leatherback were found in a prehistoric lake village in Glastonbury, England. They were used to card animal fibers. Similar carders are still made with wire teeth. Carding removes debris, disentangles the fibers, and more or less aligns them. Combing aligns the fibers and removes the short fibers. Seeds had to be pulled from cotton bolls by hand. Then the cotton was beaten with wandlike sticks to loosen and fluff the fiber before spinning. The most important bast fibers, which are taken from the center stalk of the plant, are linen, jute, and hemp. After drying and retting, they underwent breaking and hackling. This freed the fibers from the stalk.

Working at Home

Before the industrial revolution, families worked together at home. They raised their own sheep, which provided wool for spinning. Sheep also provided milk, cheese, meat, leather, tallow for candles, and parchment for writing. These could be used by the family and village, or sold to traders. Farmers had economic independence and the freedom it provided.

Families could spin as they watched over the children and farm animals and while walking to town to shop or trade. At night, groups of neighbors gathered together to spin by firelight. They gossiped, told stories, and sang. By working together, families and communities could provide for all of their needs. Skills were passed down from generation to generation. The first sign of change was the "putting out" system. Merchants began to deliver fibers to farms and villages to be spun in homes. This eliminated the cost of maintaining factories, but could not supply sufficient yarn.

The Industrial Revolution

The population of England doubled in the seventeenth century. There were more people than the farm and village economy could employ. England's leading companies had created enough capital for the industrialization necessary to spin and weave great quantities of fabric cheaply.

The industrial revolution really began with a revolution in the way cloth was spun and woven. All of the conditions necessary to change the family and village-based culture and economy into the factory system occurred in the eighteenth century.

In 1733, John Kay invented the fly shuttle loom, which increased weaving speed and thus the need for more yarn. By 1767, James Hargreaves devised the spinning jenny, which could only spin weft yarn. To supply the need for higher-twist warp yarn, Richard Arkwright invented the water frame, and by 1782 his mill employed 5,000 workers. The cotton mule, invented by Samuel Crompton in 1779, required only one worker to watch over 1,000 spindles. By the 1780s, Edmund Cartwright devised a way to connect the machines to power supplies.

People from villages, which had bred farmers, craftsmen, and merchants for centuries, now flocked to the cities to find work. Home production could no longer compete in speed and price. Some villages were decimated, with only the old, the infirm, and babies left to fend for themselves. Conditions in most of the early textile mills were deplorable. Children as young as five or six worked long hours. Workers were fined for arriving late, being ill, or breaking any rules. When people could not find work, they turned to drink or begging.

Hand Spinning and the American Revolution

During this period, economics was guided by mercantilist philosophy. Mother countries expected their colonies to supply them with raw materials at low prices. They would then manufacture great quantities of goods and sell them to the colonies at high prices. British restrictions on American production and trade were major causes of the American war for independence.

American colonists were forbidden to export textiles. It was illegal to transport yarns or yardage from one colony to another. The British decreed the death penalty for anyone attempting to take plans or information or textile machinery to the colonies.

In 1768, Washington commanded his militia to wear hand-spun uniforms, and the Harvard graduating class wore hand-spun suits to protest British restrictions. During the American Revolution, 13,000 hand-spun, hand-woven coats were made for the Continental Army. During the Civil War, most of the Confederate soldiers wore hand-spun uniforms.

The use of cotton in the United States surged forward with Eli Whitney's invention in 1793 of the cotton gin, which made cotton the most widely used fiber in America. By 1816, power looms began to be installed in the United States. At that time, 95 percent of American cloth was still being made with hand-spun yarn.

Contemporary Hand Spinning

It would be wrong to assume that technological improvements were destined to replace traditional methods all over the world. Hand spinning is still done with all styles of spindles and spinning wheels in many part of Southeast and Central Asia, the Near East, Africa, and Latin America.

In industrially developed countries, hand spinning has become an enjoyable pastime. Excellent spindles, spinning wheels, and looms, and a wide selection of fibers, are available. Many industrialized countries have guilds of spinners and weavers, which meet to share skills and information.

Many art museums have collections of old textiles in which one can see quality that equals or surpasses anything produced by twenty-first century industry. There are excellent art history books in which one can study clothing in paintings of the sixteenth through the eighteenth centuries. Magnificent gilded cut velvets, satins, brocades, and laces are depicted in pictures that were painted on hand-spun, hand-woven canvas.

See also **Loom.**

BIBLIOGRAPHY

Ciba Reviews, numbers 14, 20, 27, 28, 48, and 64. Basel, 1939–1948.

Encyclopedia of Textiles. Englewood Cliffs, N.J.: Prentice Hall, 1972.

Hochberg, Bette. *Handspindles.* Santa Cruz, Calif.: B and B Hochberg, 1977.

———. *Spin Span Spun.* Santa Cruz, Calif.: B and B Hochberg, 1998.

Montell, Gosta. *Spinning Tools and Spinning Methods in Asia.* Stockholm: Tryckeri Aktiebolaget Thule, 1941.

Singer, Charles, E. J. Holmyard, and A. R. Hall. *History of Technology.* Oxford: Clarendon Press, 1954.

Weir, Shelagh. *Spinning and Weaving in Palestine.* London: The British Museum, 1970.

Wild, J. P. *Textile Manufacture in the Northern Roman Provinces.* Cambridge, U.K.: Cambridge University Press, 1970.

Wilson, Kax. *A History of Textiles.* Boulder, Colo.: Westview Press, 1979.

Bette Hochberg

SPINNING MACHINERY The machinery for spinning threads and yarns has evolved from hand spinning flax into linen using a spindle in Egypt as long ago as 4,500 B.C.E. to computer-controlled open-end spinning in 2000 C.E. The evolution of textile processing has been a major contributor to technical development in general. The Romans founded colleges, essentially the first agricultural experiment stations, at which enhancements of the methods for flax and wool production were developed and disseminated throughout their empire. Yarn spinning is needed to impart strength and continuity to collections of fibers, particularly if they are discontinuous. Fibers as short as one inch (2.5 cm) can be formed into continuous yarns by twisting them around each other and, if the fibers have a natural twist, such as cotton, the limit can be as short as 3/8 inch (1 cm).

By around 3,500 B.C.E. the Egyptians started using cotton as a fiber and a parallel development occurred in Peru around 3,000 B.C.E. Since the cotton fibers are round while growing but flatten and become ribbonlike when dry, the shorter fibers can be twisted into a yarn using a supported spindle. However, since cotton was difficult to spin prior to the development of more mechanized spinning techniques, it was not used extensively in Europe until the industrial revolution.

An important early mechanical innovation for spinning was to attach a whorl, or flywheel, at the lower end of the spindle in order to facilitate rapid rotation, which resulted in an increase in the production rate. In India around 750 C.E. the Charkha, or Jersey Wheel, was developed by mounting the spindle on a frame, and rotated by connection to a wheel, with a treadle being added by the Chinese. Still, the spinning process was discontinuous because the drafting, that is drawing out of the fibers, and twisting were carried out in separate steps. Leonardo da Vinci contributed the flyer, which allows the twisting and winding to be carried out continuously and simultaneously, leading to development in the sixteenth century of an efficient way of spinning that was used for a long time. Subsequently the feeding and drafting of the fibers became the rate-limiting steps in the spinning process, until significant improvements occurred in the eighteenth century: John Wyatt introduced the concept of drafting rollers in 1733, being incorporated by Richard Arkwright into the Water Frame spinning machine. In 1770 James Hargreaves invented a spinning machine named the Spinning Jenny in which the stretching and twisting were mechanized. In 1779 Samuel Crompton combined the concepts of incorporating the drafting rollers, stretching, and twisting into an enhanced spinning machine—which he dubbed the Mule—but it was still a discontinuous process. Charles Danforth's throstle and John Thorpe's frame and traveler are the precursors of the modern continuous ring spinning machines, which revolutionized textile machinery. As a result the spinning speed was limited only by the maximum traveler speed, determined by heat generated due to friction in ring frame.

Until the development of the break spinning, or open-end spinning, drafting and twisting took place concurrently. In open-end spinning, drafting, twisting, and winding are completely separated. The drafting stage ends up with the creation of a stream of individual or single fibers at a point on the spinning line where the air velocity is at its maximum. Subsequently, twisting begins in the "condensation stage," where the velocity is decreased enabling the assembly and twisting of multiple fibers to form yarns, of which fineness depends on the drafting ratio. The most important advantage of open-end spinning is its very high productivity, the package size depending on the winder and not on the spinning device, as is the case with ring spinning.

There are many ways to perform open-end spinning, but rotor spinning seems to be one of the best air-mechanical ways to enhance the technology. As of the early 2000s high performance rotor spinning units can run at speeds up to 150,000 revolutions per minute, delivering yarn are the rate of 235 meters per minute. They produce large packages of yarn in contrast to ring spinning bobbins that are limited by the size of the spindle.

A critical aspect of yarn spinning from the early spindles to the modern ring spinning and open-end methods is imparting twist to the fibers making up the yarn to provide cohesion and strength. In all cases, that is imparted by taking up the yarn on a rotating device with the collection of fibers being fed either parallel to the long axis of the rotating device or at an angle less than 90 degrees to it. If the fibers were fed perpendicular to the axis of the rotating device, no twist would be imposed. This twisting is accomplished with a spindle by having the fibers fed almost parallel to the long axis of the spindle. For the early spinning wheel this was accomplished by feeding the fibers at an angle onto a mule (a rotating rod), so that they would move toward the opposite end of the take up. In ring spinning the traveler is a guide that spins around the take up guiding the lay down of the fibers (sometimes under computer control) and the traveler is fed nearly parallel to the long axis of the take up. In open-end spinning the fibers are deposited on the inside of a rotating drum after being fed into one end of the drum.

See also **Yarns.**

BIBLIOGRAPHY

Baines, Patricia. *Spinning Wheels: Spinners and Spinning.* New York: Charles Scribner's Sons, 1977.

Benson, Anna P. *Textile Machines.* Aylesbury, U.K.: Shire Publications, 1983. Shire Album 103.

Catling, Harold. *The Spinning Mule.* Newton Abbot, U.K.: David and Charles, 1970.

Dyson, Eric, ed. *Rotor Spinning: Technical and Economic Aspects.* Stockport, U.K.: The Textile Trade Press, 1975.

English, Walter. *The Textile Industry.* London: Longmans, 1969.

Lord, P. R., ed. *Spinning in the '70s.* Watford, U.K.: Merrow Publishing Company, Ltd., 1970.

Wilson, Kax. *A History of Textiles.* Boulder, Colo.: Westview Press, 1979.

John R. Collier and Simioan Petrovan

SPORT SHIRT The term "sport shirt" describes any of several styles of shirt originally designed and worn for sporting pursuits, but in the early 2000s are incorporated into the broader category of informal or leisure wear. Examples include polo shirts, rugby shirts, and short-sleeved shirts cut similarly to business shirts but in less formal fabrics and colors, and with collars designed to be worn open.

It is almost impossible to discuss a man's wardrobe without mentioning the importance of sportswear in providing some of its key silhouettes throughout recent history. With the decline (and in some places the actual demise) of the suit in the workplace, and by default the shirt and tie, and the rise of "dress down," or business casual, men have looked to the clothing they wear in their leisure time as the basis for both adherence to sartorial standards and the display of individual taste. For many, regardless of sporting intention or not, these items tend to have either a sporting association (possibly by celebrity endorsement) or have a dual purpose as sports and casual dress item. Sport shirts play a vital role in the dress-down wardrobe. They are readily available, accessible price-wise, and require little thought when being coordinated with other items.

The polo shirt is a classic example of sportswear filtering through to the mainstream as a fashion staple. Designed for the rigours of the polo pitch during the nineteenth century, the polo shirt was later adapted for the tennis court. The tennis version designed during the 1930s by René Lacoste was welcomed with enthusiasm by the rich and famous on the French Riviera.

With the rise of the leisure-wear market during the 1970s (when many men broke with the tradition of wearing a shirt and tie both during the week as well as on the weekend), the polo shirt was adopted into the working wardrobe and was also worn with jeans or unstructured slacks for leisure time. This marked the advent of an era when men and women began to put comfort first as a criterion for choosing their clothing.

Although Lacoste pioneered the sports-shirt look, Adidas, Fred Perry, Ben Sherman, and (in particular) Ralph Lauren championed the look from the 1980s onward. During this period, its popularity coincided with rise of style tribes such as the mods, casuals, B-boys, and skins. Each group incorporated a particular manufacturer's version to create its individual look.

During the same period, the generally small and inconspicuous monograms that had been tastefully embroidered on many of these shirts (Lacoste's crocodile, Lauren's polo player) were imitated and enlarged by rival companies (Henry Cotton used a fly fisherman, Fiorucci a triangle). Logos and branding came to be an integral part of the look of some polo shirts, rugby shirts, and other leisure wear. The look would be picked up and exploited by many designers and brands, including Tommy Hilfiger, Chipie, Nike, Benetton, and Diesel.

The rugby shirt, like the polo shirt, originated in a jersey garment worn for a particular sport. The standard rugby shirt, with a knit collar and broad stripes (originally in team colors) moved off the playing field and into the leisure wardrobe in the mid-twentieth century and has remained a staple item of male casual dress.

The American men's outfitter Brooks Brothers was instrumental in developing sports shirts derived from the white shirt that had become standard business wear in the early twentieth century. The company introduced madras cotton shirts (in bright stripes and plaids) in the 1920s, cut similarly to business shirts (though looser-fitting) but intended to be worn without a necktie. And at least according to legend, John Brooks, president of Brooks Brothers, noticed at a polo match in England that the players had their collars pinned down in order to stop them flapping in the wind. Taking this idea back to America, he developed it into the Brooks trademark button-down collar shirt. Originally intended to be worn, like the polo shirt, as a sports shirt (that is, without a tie and with its top button unbuttoned), the button-down collared shirt was adopted in the 1950s as part of the Ivy League look, worn with a tie, sports jacket, and casual slacks; it is a look that has endured.

See also **Polo Shirt; Sports Jacket.**

BIBLIOGRAPHY
Barnes, Richard. *Mods!* London: Plexus Publishing Limited, 1979.

Byrde, Penelope. *The Male Image: Men's Fashion in England 1300–1970.* London: B. T. Batsford, Ltd., 1979.

Chenoune, Farid. *A History of Men's Fashion.* Paris: Flammarion, 1993.

De Marley, Diana. *Fashion for Men: An Illustrated History.* London: B. T. Batsford, Ltd., 1985.

Schoeffler, O. E., and William Gale. *Esquire's Encyclopedia of 20th Century Fashions.* New York: McGraw-Hill, 1973.

Tom Greatrex

SPORT SHOES Athletic footwear has become ubiquitous since the mid-1950s, and it is easy to forget that sport shoes were initially designed for a specific purpose—for functionality, comfort, and to maximize athletic performance. As diverse as traditional footwear itself, athletic shoes fall into the following categories: running/training/walking, court sports, field sports, winter sports, outdoor sports, track and field, and specialty shoes (i.e. gymnastics, weight lifting, water, etc.).

Shoe development dates back 10,000 years, stemming from the need for protection from rough terrain. Egyptians used sandals for ball games as far back as 2050 B.C.E. Ancient Roman spiked military shoes called "caliga" were used as weapons against opponents. Greek athletes in the ancient Olympics preferred running barefoot before adopting sandals in the eighth century B.C.E.

Until 1860, more attention was given to style and fashion rather than to functionality—particularly for women. Sport shoes, if worn at all, did not differentiate much from each other and imitated the handmade styles and leather construction of traditional footwear. Skating boots, for example, were merely adaptations of high-cut Victorian style street boots with blades. Leather bars were sometimes placed across the soles of soccer shoes for traction. Football and baseball players wore identical high-cut leather shoes before cleats were introduced in 1890 and fashion determined the height of the boot.

Early twentieth-century sport shoes. Sport shoes began to appear in the late 1800s, as increased time for leisure led to the rising popularity of sports in general. © Sandro Vannini/Corbis. Reproduced by permission.

The popularity of recreational sports, previously restricted to the wealthy upper class, developed in the late nineteenth century as a response to increased amounts of leisure time by the general public. Public interest in sports coincided with the marathon era and the beginning of the modern Olympics. Of significant importance was the advent of the canvas sport shoe—adopting the term "sneaker" in 1873—that followed Charles Goodyear's 1839 development of vulcanized rubber. From croquet to running, boating, tennis, and bicycling, this multipurpose shoe influenced street fashion with its variations of sateen, canvas, or buckskin uppers and black or brown leather bands.

It was not until the beginning of the twentieth century that mass production of shoes made athletic footwear readily available to the general public. The first great athletic shoemakers, including Joseph W. Foster for Reebok, the Dassler brothers, Marquis Converse, and Leon Leonwood Bean (L.L. Bean) arose at this time. Increased competition in sports accelerated the quest for developing more comfortable, better-performing, flat-soled

shoes. As amateur athletes became professional, they influenced the maturity of sports and athletic shoes became more specialized.

By the 1930s, athletic shoe companies J. E. Sullivan and G. L. Pearce of the Spalding Company, the Dassler brothers (who later split into Adidas, Inc. and Puma, Inc.), Richings of the Riley Company (later renamed New Balance), Chuck Taylor of Converse, and J. Law of England became internationally recognized. Vulcanized rubber sole tennis and basketball shoes, traditionally in black and white shades, were now offered in a variety of colors. Skating boots with Nordic pin binding, previously in black and brown, became available for ladies in white. Interchangeable cleats and nailed-on studs were used for field and winter sports, and track shoes became lighter and more functional.

Out of sheer necessity, protection and function were major factors in the design of many sport shoes. In 1935, inspired by near-fatal accidents involving footwear, Vitale Bramani invented a multipurpose-soled mountain boot and Paul Sperry created a non-slip sole for boating.

L.L. Bean launched his company in 1911 with leather and rubber galoshes that served as a solution to chronically wet feet during his hunting expeditions.

As competition increased on the Olympic track fields and collegiate basketball courts following World War II, better-performing, lighter-weight athletic shoes were highly sought after. Keds and the Converse "sneaker" basketball shoe led the American athletic market while simultaneously becoming an American postwar youth symbol when worn with blue jeans on the streets. Onitsuka Tiger, formed in 1949 and forerunner to the brand Asics, introduced new materials such as nylon uppers and blown rubber wedges and midsoles on their shoes for long-distance runners. New Balance also catered to this group by introducing width fittings and engineering shoes with rippled soles for traction and heel wedges for shock absorption. Bob Lange's mono-bloc polyurethane injected downhill ski boot invented in 1957 was voted the most innovative shoe construction of the century a decade later.

European manufacturers Adidas and Puma dominated the athletic footwear market in the international sports of soccer, tennis, and track, as they aligned themselves with winning collegiate and professional teams to promote the performance image of their shoes. Adidas's leather basketball stitched-shell shoe construction, for example, was launched, outfitting half the UCLA and Houston players in their national championship competition. Along with Tiger in Japan, they gave birth to centralized sport-shoe marketing and early biomechanical shoe designing.

By the end of the 1970s, the U.S. sports scene evolved into a more general pursuit of individual fitness. American sport shoe pioneers Bill Bowerman, Jeff Johnson, and Phil Knight (founders of Nike, Inc.) introduced major innovations ranging from nylon uppers and full-length cushioned midsoles to running shoes, the waffle sole, air cushioning, and a variable width lacing system. Meanwhile, traditional U.S. sport shoe companies also began to compete internationally with Europeans and Japanese with "pseudo-athletic" styles to cater to this new market. Reebok, catering to the trend toward fitness activities at the time, created a soft napa leather athletic shoe aimed specifically at the female consumer in 1982.

Spearheaded by the running boom in the United States, sport shoe design went beyond material composition to encompass biomechanical ergonomic footwear design. Biomechanical, electronic, and computer testing were added to the old practice of wear testing. Ratings of running shoes in the magazine *Runner's World* (established in 1975) also intensified product development improvements. Advanced technological and biomechanical research has made athletic shoes more specialized, more functional, more technical, and more expensive.

Sport shoe companies, once a humble and modest specialized segment seeking practical solutions to footwear problems, developed into trendsetting multibillion-dollar lifestyle brands since the 1950s. Professionalism through

Golf shoes. By the end of the twentieth century, specialized sport shoes, such as these golf shoes and spikes, were available for a wide variety of athletic activities, as well as for everyday wear. © ROYALTY-FREE/CORBIS. REPRODUCED BY PERMISSION.

televised sporting events and sports star endorsements has dramatically increased the public's interest in sports. Advanced science, athletic professionalism, and an increasing population seeking more comfortable lifestyles in the second half of the twentieth century, has provided an environment that allows sport shoes to become even more pervasive in the future of fashion and apparel.

See also **Sneakers; Sportswear.**

BIBLIOGRAPHY

Cavanagh, Peter R. *The Running Shoe Book.* Mountain View, Calif.: Anderson World, 1980.

Cheskin, Melvyn P. *The Complete Handbook of Athletic Footwear.* New York: Fairchild Publications, 1987. Provides an in-depth analysis of sport shoes, including their history, their technical construction, and contemporary approaches in marketing and advertising.

Farrelly, Liz, ed. *The Sneaker Book.* London: Booth-Clibborn Editions, 1998. A global collection of opinions covering trendsetting sneakers as social phenomenon.

Heard, Neal. *Sneakers.* London: Carlton Books Limited, 2003. American collector's manual of classic athletic footwear in the twentieth century.

Rexford, Nancy E. *Women's Shoes in America, 1795–1930.* Kent, Ohio, and London: The Kent State University Press, 2000.

Includes a chapter on women's sport shoes and the relationship between shoe styles and gender roles in American culture.

Angel Chang

SPORTS JACKET A sports jacket is a short single-breasted coat, originally men's wear but in the early 2000s worn by both men and women. Similar to a suit jacket in fit, detailing, and fabrication, it is usually less shaped than a suit jacket. Originally intended to be worn in the country for sporting pursuits, the sports jacket is often seen in many other contexts as well. Its nineteenth-century ancestor, the original Norfolk jacket, was made of tweed, checked, or herringbone woolen cloth, and was cut quite differently from the sports jacket of the early twenty-first century. The Norfolk jacket was not simply the jacket of a country suit, but a suit jacket designed with a particular purpose in mind; it was intended for, and could only be afforded by, the rich for leisure pursuits.

History

At its inception, in the 1860s, the sports jacket was part of the hunting attire worn by the Duke of Norfolk. The Norfolk jacket was buttoned high to the neck, had a box pleat centered on its back, and two box pleats in the front. Because of its structure, the jacket was ideal for shooting, with flapped pockets used to store ammunition and provisions; its belted waist allowed for full mobility of the hunter's arm while he was taking aim with his gun. These sports jackets would often be worn with knickerbockers and deerstalker hats or sometimes, less frequently, with bowler hats.

Cut from heavy wool or tweed in autumnal and rural tones such as mustard, ginger, green, and brown (very different from the business stripes and plain colors worn in the city), the sports jacket was rarely worn with another piece of outerwear as it was itself specifically designed for the outdoors.

The Twentieth Century

By the early twentieth century, the Norfolk jacket, still associated with the rural life enjoyed by the landed gentry and the rich alike, had been modified from its original design. The signature belt and box pleats were removed, and it began to be worn for other country activities, including as garb for spectators at sporting events, and also as an alternative to the traditional suit jacket. The shoulders were fuller, sleeves wider, and the armholes larger. The sports jacket gave men the opportunity to dress differently after work or on the weekends. Just as the lounge suit was beginning to replace formal suiting worn to the office, the tweed jacket became an acceptable part of casual dress.

This new sports jacket, as worn by urban consumers, was cut in a style more akin to that designed for horse riding and was usually worn with flannel trousers. The New Look sports jackets were typified by angled waisted pockets, a breast pocket, and, often, leather buttons as well as a swelled edge instead of the customary plain buff edge associated with suiting. Further features were developed such as leather patching at the cuff or even on the elbow.

The desire to maintain a clear difference between the attire worn at work and in one's leisure time has clearly driven the sales of the sports jacket. However, many creative professions, such as advertising during the 1960s, began to allow their staff to wear the sports jacket as business clothing. For many, it became an expression of freedom and individualism. The informality of the look gave men the opportunity to be more creative in their choice of fabrics and patterns than they ever could with a formal suit. Even the late Duke of Windsor commented that the brighter a pattern on a sports jacket, the better he liked it.

Twenty-first Century Sports Jackets

In the early 2000s, sports jackets are available in wide choice of patterns and colors. As the idea of the separate jacket has spread throughout the world, other materials have been employed to allow for climatic variations. Seersucker has become a favorite in the southern United States. Deriving its name from the Persian *shlr-o-shakkar* (literally, milk and sugar), the blue-and-white-striped jacket in this lightweight fabric has become an American classic. The Italians are also noted for making up exceptional lightweight sports jackets in soft fabrics. However, for many, traditional sports jackets cut either on London's Savile Row or bought from a tweed expert such as Cordings of Piccadilly remain classic staples. In these versions, buttons should be made of natural materials, especially horn; the lining should be sewn into the jacket by hand; and should feature working cuffs (that is, with buttons that fasten into buttonholes rather than being sewn on simply as decorations).

As with many other articles of clothing that once were exclusively men's wear, sports jackets have been modified in cut and style for women. The women's sports jacket, worn with trousers or a woolen skirt, forms the foundation of a distinctive style that is simultaneously dressy and relaxed.

For men, the older rule that a sports jacket should be worn with knickers or with a pair of gray flannel trousers has been relaxed. It is fully acceptable to wear a jacket with a smart pair of moleskin, corduroy, cavalry twill trousers, a simple pair of plain woolen trousers, or even jeans. With the increased popularity of casual wear, for many men in the United States and Europe, the combination of a sports jacket and slacks is deemed a somewhat formal look.

See also **Sports Shoes; Sportswear.**

BIBLIOGRAPHY

Amies, Hardy. *A, B, C's of Men's Fashion*. London: Cahill and Co. Ltd., 1964.

Byrde, Penelope. *The Male Image: Men's Fashion in England 1300–1970*. London: B. T. Batsford, Ltd., 1979.

Chenoune, Farid. *A History of Men's Fashion*. Paris: Flammarion, 1993.

De Marley, Diana. *Fashion for Men: An Illustrated History*. London: B. T. Batsford, Ltd., 1985.

Keers, Paul. *A Gentleman's Wardrobe*. London: Weidenfield and Nicolson, 1987.

Roetzel, Bernhard. *Gentleman: A Timeless Fashion*. Cologne, Germany: Konemann, 1999.

Schoeffler, O. E., and William Gale. *Esquire's Encyclopedia of 20th Century Fashions*. New York: McGraw-Hill, 1973.

Tom Greatrex

SPORTSWEAR

At the beginning of the twenty-first century, "sportswear" describes a broad category of fashion-oriented comfortable attire based loosely on clothing developed for participation in sports. "Active sportswear" is the term used to cover the clothing worn specifically for sport and exercise activities. Now generally accepted as the most American of all categories of dress, sportswear has become, from the second half of the twentieth century, the clothing of the world. It consists of separate pieces that may be "mixed and matched," a merchandising term meaning that articles of clothing are designed to be coordinated in different combinations: trousers or shorts or skirts with shirts (either woven or knit, with or without collars, long-sleeved or short) and sweaters (either pullovers or cardigans) or jackets of a variety of sorts.

Pre-Twentieth Century

The origins of sportswear, so intimately tied to the rise of sports, are complex, arising from pervasive social change and cultural developments in the mid-nineteenth century. Previously, sport had been the domain of the landed well-to-do, revolving mostly around horses, shooting, and the hunt. Clothing generally was modified fashion wear, but distinctions between the clothing of the country and of town had appeared as early as the eighteenth century. Men, especially young men, wore the new collared, sometimes double-breasted, skirtless but tailed frock for shooting or country wear, itself probably adapted from the military uniform of the early eighteenth century. This coat was quickly adopted into fashionable dress for young gentlemen. Fox or stag hunting called for skirted coats and high boots to protect the legs, and for trim tailoring that would not hamper the rider maneuvering rough terrain and the new fences that were an outcome of the British Enclosure Acts (1760–1840). These acts, by transferring common grazing lands to private holdings, resulted in fences never needed before, thereby adding new challenges to cross-country riding and revolutionizing the sport of hunting.

Ralph Lauren sportswear. Two models show outfits from Ralph Lauren's spring/summer 1994 pret-a-porter collection. Elegant sportswear is a hallmark of Lauren's designs. © Brooke Randy/ Corbis Sygma. Reproduced by permission.

The long, straight, narrow, severely tailored riding coats that emerged toward the end of eighteenth-century England traveled to France as the *redingote*, to become a high-fashion garment for both men and women for the next several decades, through the 1820s. Eventually, red coats became the acceptable color for the hunt, possibly for the obvious reason of making the riders more easily visible. As early as the eighteenth-century, women also adopted severely tailored riding coats based directly on men's styles, creating a standard that still characterizes women's sportswear in the early twenty-first century. Americans, both men and women, followed the English lead in sporting activity. These upper-class choices set the tone and provided the models for the future, but it took democratization to effect change overall. That came with the industrial revolution and the rise of leisure activity among even the poorer classes.

With the movement of the population away from its agrarian past into the cities, reformers realized that the working classes had no real outlets other than drinking

Active sports ensemble. A model displays a 1952 Claire Mc-Cardell sportswear design. McCardell was one of several American designers who popularized sportswear for women after World War II (1939–1945). The comfort and versatility of sportswear helped it to quickly become a staple of American leisure clothing. © BETTMANN/CORBIS. REPRODUCED BY PERMISSION.

for what little leisure time they had. In an era of revivalist fervor that preached temperance, the concerned middle classes sought other, safer avenues of activity for the poorer classes. Both active and spectator sport and games helped fill that gap. European immigrants to the United States, particularly those from Germany and the Scandinavian countries, brought a variety of outdoor sports and games for men with them, and an accompanying culture of health and exercise that they nurtured in their private clubs. Clothing for these activities was more relaxed than the street clothes of the time, and consisted often of a shirt and trouser combination. Native-born Americans also had had a long history of team games, early versions of various ball games that continued to be played once the population moved to the cities. However, it was baseball, with its singular attire, that most influenced men's clothing for sport. Baseball had emerged as a popular team game with new rules after the first meeting of the elite New York Knickerbocker Base Ball Club with the New York Nines at Elysian Fields in Hoboken, New Jersey, on 19 June 1846. By the 1850s, many other more democratic clubs of workers played the game as well, quickly turning it into America's favorite sport. In 1868,

the Cincinnati Redstockings were the first major team to adopt a uniform of bloused shirt, baggy knee breeches, and sturdy knee socks. The unusual pants, so different from the long stove-pipe trousers of the time, were named after Washington Irving's seventeenth-century character, Dietrich Knickerbocker—not coincidentally the same surname the first baseball team in America had adopted as its own. These became the accepted trouser for active sports in general, and were dubbed "knicker-bockers" after the original team. Knickerbockers's success may be seen in their appearance for the next century for shooting, bicycling, hiking, and golf. By the 1920s, they were even worn by women.

Active sports uniforms and clothing grew out of necessity. Players needed protection from bodily harm in contact sports like football and hockey; they also needed to let the body breathe and enable it to move as easily and freely as possible while performing the sport. The entire history of active sports clothing is tied to higher education, the increasingly rapid developments in textile technology, and the Olympics. For example, football, a new and favorite game in men's colleges in the late nineteenth century, adopted a padded leather knickerbocker, pairing it with another innovation, the knitted wool jersey pullover. Lightweight wool jersey, an English invention of the 1880s, was perfect for men's sporting pullovers (which soon were referred to as "jerseys"). Perhaps the most enduring of these has been the rugby shirt—striped, collared, and ubiquitous. It had its beginnings as the uniform for the "new" nineteenth-century game begun at the venerable British school, Rugby, but proved so enduring that it is still worn in the early 2000s, by men, women and children who never thought of playing the game. Jersey was equally adopted into women's dress for sport as well. The new lawn tennis of the 1870s was ripe for a flexible fabric that allowed greater movement, and jersey filled that need by the 1880s. In that same decade, students in the new women's colleges left behind their corsets, petticoats, and bustles for simpler gathered dirndl-style skirts and jersey tops taken directly from men's styles in order to participate in sports like crew and baseball. At the same time, men's schools added a heavier outer layer of wool knit to keep the body warm, and since athletic activity brought on healthy sweating, "sweater" clearly described its role. When a high roll collar was added, the "turtleneck," still a staple of sportswear, was born. The college environment was important because it allowed a looser, less rigid, more casual kind of clothing on campuses frequently isolated from the formality of fashionable urban attire. Soon after the introduction of these pieces of specific clothing for sports in collegiate settings, women borrowed them, wearing them for their own sports and leisurewear from the end of the nineteenth century and on.

The modern Olympic Games introduced new generations of active sportswear. From the first meet in 1896, men appeared in very brief clothing to compete in track and field and swimming events: singlets, or tank tops, with above-the-knee shorts, and knit—sometimes fine wool and sometimes silk—skin-baring one-piece suits for swim competition. More surprising than these were the bikini-like liners that men wore under the sheer silk suits, without the tops, as typical practice garb. These items became the clothing for sport for men as the century progressed; even the briefs under the suits found their way into swimwear for men and women some half-century or so after their introduction.

Twentieth Century

Fabrics have played an important role in the development of active sportswear. As with sheer knits at the turn of the twentieth century, so too did stretch fabrics form a second skin shaving seconds off time in competition. From the introduction of Lastex in the 1930s to the spandex of the twenty-first century, clothing for active sports has reflected the attention to sleek bodies, to speed. Speedo, the Australian swimwear company, first introduced its one-piece stretchy suit in the 1950s. From that time on, swimwear became sleeker, tighter but more comfortable because of the manufactured stretch fibers. The concept proved irresistible for men and women in all active sports: new stretch textiles produced ski pants in the 1930s fashioned with stirrups to anchor the sleek lines, bicycle shorts in the 1970s, all-in-one cat suits for skiing, sledding, sailing, speed skating, even running in the 1980s and 1990s. With the biannual Olympic publicity, the new active suits, shorts, and tops found their way into active sportswear and onto athletic bodies everywhere. Even the nonathlete wanted the look, pressing fashion-wear manufacturers to adopt the tight-fitting yet comfortable clothing that technology had made possible.

Sportswear, as opposed to active sportswear, fulfills an entirely different role. Though their roots are the same, sportwear concerns the fashionable aspect of clothing for sport rather than the athletic. Individual items such as jerseys, sweaters, and turtlenecks came directly out of active sports. Certain jackets also became linked with sports and therefore sportswear. The most notable of these, still a staple of modern dress, is the blazer. This standard straight-cut lounge jacket of the late nineteenth century was adapted both by colleges and early sports clubs, the new tennis, golf, or country clubs that emerged in the 1870s and 1880s, who used their own club colors for these jackets, often fashioning them in stripes called "blazes." Hence, blazers. Striped blazers, popular through the 1920s, have had revivals since, most notably in the late 1950s and 1960s. Generally, however, they gave way to single-colored blazers in the 1930s. The best recognized of these is the bright green Masters jacket of golf.

For women's leisure wear (and it must be noted that women never wore this casual, "new" clothing in any other setting), women adopted men's clothing, as they had earlier. This had been noticeable in the 1890s with the clothes of the New Woman, with her blazer, shirt-

Tiger Woods. Golfer Tiger Woods after winning the 2002 U.S. Masters tournament. Woods wears the green blazer that is traditionally given to the tournament's winner. © Simon Bruty/SI/ NewSport/Corbis. Reproduced by permission.

waist, and easy skirt, or even, on occasion (though not as routinely as is now believed) with divided skirts for such activities as bicycling. By the turn of the twentieth century, young women wore jerseys, turtleneck sweaters, and cardigans, borrowed directly from their brothers. In addition, many chose to leave off their corsets when participating in active activities, opting instead for lighter, unboned "sporting waists." This last move was perhaps the most forward-thinking of all in affecting change in women's dress. Magazines of the day picked up the new "daring" fashions, with illustrations, to spread them across the country. Early movies, even those prior to the 1920s, also helped distribute and popularize the new styles, showing beautiful young women dressed for all sorts of activities: swimming, golf, tennis and, as time went on, simply for leisure. So the foundations had been laid in the nineteenth century, but the phenomenon of sportswear for women really began in the 1920s with the post–World War I emergence of mass production in women's wear.

The new loose, unfitted styles of the 1920s allowed a much freer approach to women's dress for play and

Rugby players. A group of rugby players, wearing the striped shirts after which their sport is named. © Duomo/Corbis. Reproduced by permission.

leisure. Although women still clung to skirts, the dresses for such sports as golf and tennis were so admired (to say nothing of the sports figures who wore them, like Suzanne Lenglen, a French tennis champion, and later, Babe Didrickson) that they became day dresses for women whose lifestyles and pocketbooks allowed variety in their clothing. These golf and tennis dresses, with their pleated skirts and tailored tops, sometimes two-piece and sometimes one, comfortable and washable, became the prototypes for the most American of all clothing, the shirtwaist dress. So welcome were tennis dresses that in the 2000s they still prevail over shorts for competition tennis and, as early as the 1940s, offered a new, short skirt length that eventually became accepted into fashion wear.

Trousers for women were another matter. The struggle for their acceptance was a long one, dating from the early nineteenth century when, as baggy "Turkish trowsers," they were introduced for water cures and exercise, then later adopted as dress reform. It was sport, however, that provided the reason for their acceptance, as long as they were kept within strictly sex-segregated environments like the emerging women's colleges or all-

women gyms. The heavy serge bifurcated bloomers worn for the new game of basketball were the first acceptable pants for women, and worn with turtlenecked sweaters in the early part of the twentieth century, became an outfit for magazine pinups. The bloomers slimmed down by the 1920s, becoming the popular knickers of that decade, and the introduction of beach pajamas for leisurewear at the same time led to further acceptance, even if not worn in town settings.

The movies helped to sell the image of women in trousers, especially in the 1930s with actresses like Katharine Hepburn and Marlene Dietrich. Even then, women did not wear pants for fashion wear. World War II changed their image, when trousers became the norm for factory workers, but still, pants were not acceptable for the average woman except when she was on vacation or in the country. Indeed, trousers were not accepted for professional working women until the end of the 1970s or early 1980s. But since that time, trousers have become the norm for women everywhere, professionals and vacationers alike, proving once again that women borrow their most comfortable clothing from men's wear.

220

Mass manufacturing made the simple items of ready-to-wear sportswear inexpensive and practical for everyone. The notion of designing separates to go together in coordinated fashion, a key concept of sportswear, began in New York in the mid-1920s when Berthe Holley introduced a line of separates that could be interchanged to suggest a larger wardrobe. The concept of easy separates for leisurewear in resort or casual surroundings, if not for more formal wear, grew in the 1930s and finally took hold for more general wear in the 1940s, during World War II. American designers such as Claire Mc-Cardell, Clare Potter, and Bonnie Cashin turned to designing ready-made American sportswear, using inexpensive fabrics and following the easy, comfortable styles that made it so popular in the United States. Companies such as B. H. Wragge in the 1940s marketed well-designed separates, particularly to the college-aged crowd, at inexpensive prices that they could afford. After the war, with manufacturing back to prewar norms and the introduction of the more formal New Look from France, the distinction between American and Parisian clothing became even more evident. American designers more and more turned to the casual expressions in fashion that American women loved. By midcentury, the great designers who captured the essence of American style, Bill Blass and Geoffrey Beene, had begun to be recognized, and were turning their attention to ready-to-wear sportswear. Eventually they even brought sportswear ideas into eveningwear, directly translating the shirts, sweaters, and skirts women were so attached to into elegance for evening. Finally, toward the later twentieth century, Ralph Lauren took what had become the staples of sportswear—jackets, sweaters, shirts, pants, and skirts—and gave them a distinctly upper-class edge by reviving the elegance of the club-based sports clothing of the 1930s and 1940s. These later twentieth-century designers captured the American Look and made it their own, turning the higher end of sportswear back to its origins by appealing to the upper classes. But by then, the style of dress known as sportswear was open to all, in all classes and levels of society, through mass manufacturing and mass marketing. A truly American style, sportwear has spread throughout the world, representing a first in clothing history.

See also **Activewear; Blazer; Lauren, Ralph; Sport Shirt; Sweater; Swimwear.**

BIBLIOGRAPHY

Armitage, John. *Man at Play: Nine Centuries of Pleasure Making.* London and New York: Frederick Warne and Co., 1977.

Mackay-Smith, Alexander, et al. *Man and the Horse.* New York: The Metropolitan Museum of Art and Simon and Schuster, 1984.

Milbank, Caroline Rennolds. *New York Fashion: The Evolution of American Style.* New York: Harry N. Abrams, 1996.

Schreier, Barbara A. "Sporting Wear." In *Men and Women: Dressing the Part.* Edited by Claudia Brush Kidwell and Valerie Steele. Washington, D.C.: Smithsonian Institution, 1989, pp. 102–103.

Warner, Patricia Campbell. "The Gym Suit: Freedom at Last." In *Dress in American Culture.* Edited by Patricia A. Cunningham and Susan Voso Lab. Bowling Green, Ohio: Popular Press, Bowling Green State University, 1992, pp. 140–179.

Patricia Campbell Warner

STEELE, LAWRENCE

STEELE, LAWRENCE Lawrence Dion Steele has been known since 1994 for his feminine and unapologetically sexy designs, produced in Milan, Italy. Lawrence Steele was the second of four children, born in 1963 to an Air Force family in Hampton, Virginia. Although Steele was raised in Rantoul, Illinois, he traveled extensively with his family. Working for a jeans company helped finance his education at the School of the Art Institute of Chicago. He graduated from the school with honors and a bachelor of fine arts degree in 1985.

After graduation Steele worked in Japan as an anonymous designer during the 1980s. He always knew, however, that he wanted to establish a business in Milan. Consequently he directed his attention toward Italy's fashion capital, where he lived and worked in the early 2000s.

Early Career

Steele began his career in Italy by assisting the design team of Jan and Carlos, known for minimalist design and fine machine-made knitwear. As manager of several collections for designer Franco Moschino from 1985 through 1990, Steele gained valuable experience translating the designer's riotous and radical ideas into actual designs. He was present when Patrizio Bertelli and Miuccia Prada expanded their vision of adding a ready-to-wear line to the Prada luxury leather goods company between 1990 and 1994. Steele recognized the value of their formidable personalities through collaborating with them.

Steele began defining his own fashion philosophy in the early 1990s. In 1994 he launched the Lawrence Steele label with the descriptive title of Platinum s.r.l., produced by Casor SpA in Bologna. The fashion press and industry gave Steele's first collection of 120 garments a particularly favorable response. This initial collection, however, did not reflect the minimalist construction and attention to details that became the hallmarks of his later style. Instead he paraded interpretations of Russian and Eskimo dress down the runway.

Beginning in 1998, Lawrence Steele's knitwear was produced by Miss Deanna SpA in Reggio Emilia. The most outstanding models of the early twenty-first century displayed his 1999 collection, "exalting feminine dress" (Lenoir, p. 27) in New York City. In the same year, Steele introduced LSD as a collection of urban active wear for men and women, made with innovative technical fabrics and produced by Alberto Aspesi and Company SpA. A Platinum s.r.l. spokesman announced an agreement with the Legnano-based manufacturer to produce and represent the Lawrence Steele label.

Fashion Innovations

The Lawrence Steele label was available in designer salons in department stores and high-end boutiques around the world in the early 2000s. During his association with Casor, Steele motivated the Bolognese factory to implement new and unusual methods for treating materials. To accommodate their exacting client, Casor's staff perfected gold-leaf finishing on baby alpaca, stretch cashmere, oil-slick neoprene, gold suede, sequin detailing on silk, and multiple zippers on satin. Steele also created ensembles of leather with Lycra at the request of the DuPont Corporation. This exclusive product gives exceptional elasticity to natural leather.

Steele collaborated with the artist Vanessa Beecroft, known for her living compositions and photographic documentation, in a public event in July 2001. Steele identified the event as an aesthetic presentation as opposed to a political protest. Thirty black female models stood motionless for several hours in the Palazzo Ducale of Genoa. The women had been made uniform in color with body paint and identical wigs, and were dressed in black two-piece bathing suits detailed with clear plastic straps. Designer Manolo Blahnik produced the models' spike-heeled footwear according to Steele's suggestions.

Characteristic Styles

While Steele's demeanor in interviews was calm and sweet, his intensity and ambition radiated through his descriptions of his clothing. "I make the clothes modern women will find utterly desirable; my vision is glamorous, sensuous and a little dangerous and it includes breasts!" (Specter, p. 98).

The on-screen glamor of Diana Ross in the film *Mahogany* dazzled Steele as a boy; as an African American, he proudly acknowledged her as his muse. His ideal female of the early 2000s had a long neck, even longer legs, and a slim, vibrant body. Marlene Dietrich, Marilyn Monroe, and Josephine Baker were the film sirens who appeared on his inspiration boards. Copies of line drawings by Madeleine Vionnet, Cristóbal Balenciaga, Coco Chanel, and Charles James were tacked to the walls of his atelier above random stacks of international periodicals.

Steele's memorable runway presentations attracted the interest of such stylish celebrities as Jennifer Aniston, Naomi Campbell, Erin O'Conner, Lauryn Hill, Meg Ryan, Oprah Winfrey, and Julia Roberts. The atmosphere at his shows compared with the electric excitement of a rock concert. Steele designed a "red carpet" gown in layers of black chiffon with a plunging back and twisted halter detail displaying the shoulder area, which he considered an erogenous zone. He watched Aniston walk down the aisle wearing the gown he designed for her wedding in 2001—hand-stitched and seed-pearl-encrusted with a 28-yard skirt of silk tulle. "I wanted the effect of a cloud around her feet" (Alexander, p. 29).

Designs and Artistic Hallmarks

Steele's sophisticated signature was evident throughout his collections of adaptable, supercharged, and sensuous clothing. He combined non-extreme styling, figure-flattering cuts of industrial luxe (such as metal-based fabric), and studied, monochromatic color schemes. He built thematic groups, ranging from "techno" to "viva-glam" (stretch cashmere) (Singer 1998, p. 352), all produced in shiny PVC, fiber-optic nylon, angora, marabou, perforated rubber, glossed chiffon, raffia spikes, netted Swarovski crystals, and slashed leather—examples of his unusual choices of material.

During the development of a Steele collection, swatches of sequined animal prints and paillette-strewn sheer fabrics may be arranged for inspection on the workroom floors of an uncluttered but busy atelier. Press releases described Steele's pieces as modular and precise, insulating and industro-luxe in such colors as metal, bark, and dust. Textures were described in terms of weightless quilting and padded taffeta. Themes derived from popular culture inspired bomber jackets molded in mink and track suits edged in gold braid. Program notes listed such directions as Refined versus Primitive. One collection contained references to "straight forward," "clean," and "necessary."

The designer's philosophy of modern minimalist design was embodied in such themes such as Smoking in Bed, Hand Finished, and New Volume. He mixed tuxedo detailing with lingerie that included oversized crepe pants and camisoles. Steele's floral patterns capitalized on the recognition of computer-generated patterns. Steele persisted in editing and refining his ideas, beginning with the concept of "elegance as refusal" (Singer 1998, p. 358).

See also **Blahnik, Manolo; Celebrities; Elastomers; High-Tech Fashion; Moschino, Franco; Prada; Techno-textiles.**

BIBLIOGRAPHY

Alexander, Hilary. "Secret Weapon." *Telegraph Magazine* 25 (November 2000): 28–30.

Lenoir, Lisa. "Steele in the Spotlight." *Chicago Sun Times— Showcase Arts and Leisure* (16 September 1999): 37.

McDowell, Colin. "Milan's Golden Boy." *The Sunday Times* [London], 5 March 2000.

Singer, Sally. "Our Man in Milan." *Elle* [USA], September 1998, p. 98.

———. "The New Guard." *Vogue*, (July 2000): 131–140.

Specter, Michael. "Designer on the Verge." *The New Yorker* (22 March 1999): 96–103.

Gillion Carrara

STOCKINGS, WOMEN'S

STOCKINGS, WOMEN'S The stocking has an established place in the contemporary lexicon of erotic imagery. Elmer Batters, an American photographer, dedicated his life's work to documenting thousands of women in their stockinged feet. Stockinged women offer one of the most powerful images of modern female glamour and provide for the marketing of sexual allure.

Origins

The stocking was not always considered a sexual symbol. The earliest known example of a knitted sock, flat-cut and seamed at the back, was found in Egypt, where both knitting and weaving are thought to have originated. There is some debate as to whether hand-knitting was introduced to Europe by Christian missionaries, sea traders, or Arabs who, after conquering Egypt in 641 C.E., made their way to Spain. What is known is that it was widely established throughout Europe as a domestic skill by the thirteenth century. The majority of stockings were made from wool, although silk was commonplace for the aristocratic and landed gentry, and were viewed as a covering for the legs that was particularly practical for the climate.

Mechanical Production

It was the development of the first knitting frame, by Reverend William Lee in Nottingham in 1589, that heralded an era of mechanical production that, along with Marc Isambard Brunel's circular-knitting machine (developed in 1816), was to transform the stocking from practical covering to erotic emblem. Lee's knitting frame took production out of the home, improved and standardized quality, and stimulated a demand for stockings that were an extension of the fashionable consumer's wardrobe.

The introduction of rayon in 1884, a cellulose-fiber material invented in France, changed production in a radical way. Rayon dominated the market for substitute silk stockings, facilitating widespread availability at an affordable price, until the invention of nylon, a more realistic alternative patented by DuPont in 1937. The first nylons were introduced in the United States in May 1940; four million pairs were sold in the first four days.

By the 1960s, the fully-fashioned, "one-size-fits-all" stocking began to outpace the flat-cut, classic seamed stocking, propelled by the introduction in 1958 of stretch Lycra. In addition, Lycra almost completely dispensed with the suspender belt as "roll-ons," early versions of tights, were developed. A British company, Bear Brand, first experimented with tights; by the arrival of the miniskirt in the early 1960s, tights were popular and widely available. Only the introduction of the "hold-up," a stocking with elasticized tops, breathed some life into the stocking market in the mid-1980s.

Fashion from 1400 to 1900

Men were the principal innovators in stocking fashions during the first few centuries of their introduction to Eu-

Christian Dior with woman modeling stockings. Christian Dior kneels at right, working on a new design in 1948. © BETTMAN/CORBIS. REPRODUCED BY PERMISSION.

rope, bright colors accentuating the calves, with cross-garters tied at the knee and ankles embellished with embroidered "clocks" or motifs. In the early Georgian period, women's stockings were woven in complex patterns with intricate embroidery. By 1740, formal dress dictated a plainer white stocking that dominated fashionable evening wear until the 1880s.

In the 1860s, hemlines began to rise and the white stocking was covered in candy-colored riots of spots and stripes; even tartan prints were used to honor Queen Victoria's passion for Scotland. By 1880, they were emblazoned with swallows, butterflies, flowers, and snakes and dyed in rich reds and pale yellows, although the end of the century saw color give way to practical black as women increasingly joined the workplace.

"What are the qualities essential to feminine allure? What is it that attracts and holds the eye of the male? Let me give you a hint. It begins at the tip of the toes and runs to the top of the hose … legs and feet" (Batters, p. 10).

Women line up for nylons. Nylon stockings were first introduced in 1940, and were in short supply during World War II (1939–1945). In 1946, with the war over and shortages easing, these women lined up at Selfridges and Company in London, waiting for a chance to purchase nylons. © HULTON-DEUTSCH COLLECTION/CORBIS. REPRODUCED BY PERMISSION.

Fashion and Retailing from 1900 to 2003

Women's magazines and mail-order catalogs provided manufacturers with new opportunities to introduce an ever-increasing array of stockings to an interested public. Thousands of small haberdashers were joined by department stores in major cities boasting dedicated hosiery sections. Positive magazine editorial became increasingly important in the aggressive marketing of hosiery products, as women's consumer power continued to grow.

The advent of the cinema heightened the appeal, and facilitated the marketing of stockings. Film stars like Betty Grable propelled the sleek, stockinged leg to iconic status—and it was an attainable glamour. In tandem, packaging design took on all the qualities of gift-wrapped candy—lined paper boxes tied with a bow made stockings a desirable gift. Brands such as Aristoc, launched in the 1920s, Wolford (1946), and Pretty Polly (1950s), are still major players in the hosiery market in the twenty-first century, principally by playing on the glamorous associations of their product—and the idea of womanhood as object of masculine desire, a sensual package waiting to be unwrapped.

The sleek, seamed black stocking was synonymous with postwar fashion, and a focal point for Christian Dior's "New Look" in Paris in 1947. It was another de-

signer, Mary Quant, who revolutionized hosiery fashions a decade later—and signaled the downfall of the stocking as a standard mass-market product. Targeting the new teen, Quant commissioned lacy and patterned tights, emblazoned with her daisy logo, that flattered the miniskirt she made famous in 1963 and expressed the feelings of vibrancy and emancipation that characterized the times. In contrast, by 1971 stockings, now stigmatized as a masculine fetish, held only 5 percent of the market.

As women of all ages turned toward the comfort of tights, lingerie designers who marketed the suspender and stocking did so increasingly as an erotic statement. Of these, the best known is Janet Reger in the United Kingdom and La Perla in Italy. Launching her business at the same time as Quant, Janet Reger appealed to women's desire to look and feel sexy.

Eroticism

For Elmer Batters (and many others), the eroticism of the stocking and suspender belt lies in the lines they create, framing the female body, and the consideration in dressing that they imply. The stocking's eroticism is, however, a relatively recent development in its history. Women's stockings were not publicly seen until the reign of Charles II, and, as practical coverings, held few erotic connotations until well into the eighteenth century.

It was in performance that the stocking took on an erotic charge; the art of striptease pivoted on the deliberate, prolonged undressing of the female form. Not coincidentally, the "Naughty Nineties" (1890–1900)—the decade of the cancan and the Moulin Rouge—defined the stocking as an erotic symbol. The rustle of petticoats against silk stockings came to signify the repressed sexual energy of the times. For respectable ladies, it was dances like the waltz and the polka, the Charleston and the tango that allowed them to flash gentlemen a glimpse of a silk-clad ankle.

During World War II, American GI's with a secure supply of nylon stockings frequently deployed them as part of their courtship rituals. The cinema and the pin-up did most to uphold the allure of stockinged feet in the 1950s (Betty Page is one of the most iconic figures of the period), continuing into the 1970s and 1980s. It was another performer, Madonna, who was to alter the stocking's erotic connotations, liberating it as a symbol of masculine desire as the stocking "acquired the force of a manifesto … no longer a symbol of slavery,… it announced the liberation of the dominatrix" (Néret, p. 18). It was a trend, begun by Reger in the 1960s, and perpetuated by British lingerie brand Agent Provocateur in the 1990s, toward lingerie, and in particular the stocking and suspender belt, as a positive, feminine choice. In the twenty-first century, the stocking has come to symbolize "a superior kind of woman, bold enough to exploit her assets … a new concept which has made the notion of the 'woman as sex object' obsolete" (Néret, p. 18).

BIBLIOGRAPHY

Batters, Elmer, and Eric Kroll, eds. *From the Tip of the Toes to the Top of the Hose.* Cologne, Germany: Taschen, 1995. An excellent overview of the photographer's work.

Corré, Joseph, and Serena Rees. *Agent Provocateur: A Celebration of Femininity.* London: Carlton, 1999. An interesting insight into the philosophy of one of Britain's most successful lingerie brands.

Deutch, Yvonne. *A Glimpse of Stocking: A Short History of Stockings.* London: Michael O'Mara Books Ltd., 2002. A brief overview of the subject.

Hawthorne, Rosemary. *Stockings and Suspenders: A Quick Flash.* London: Souvenir Press, 1993. An excellent, detailed insight into the origins and history of stockings.

Néret, Gilles. *1000 Dessous: A History of Lingerie.* Cologne, Germany: Taschen, 1998. A comprehensive guide to the retailing and representation of the stocking as an erotic force.

Alice Cicolini

STONEWASHING. *See* **Distressing.**

STREET STYLE Street style has always existed. It is, however, only since the mid-1950s that its significance has been recognized, valued, and emulated.

Why this change? Arguably the most profound and distinctive development of the twentieth century was this era's shift from high culture to popular culture—the slow but steady recognition that innovation in matters of art, music, and dress can derive from all social strata rather than, as previously, only from the upper classes. As much as, for example, the twentieth century's accreditation of jazz, blues, folk, and tango as respected musical forms, the re-evaluation of street style as a key source of innovation in dress and appearance—in the early 2000s, a principle engine of the clothing industry—demonstrates this democratization of aesthetics and culture.

With the development of that system of perpetual style change that is called "fashion" (in the Renaissance), most new designs "trickled down" the socioeconomic ladder to be copied by anyone who could afford to do so. This system was still the order of the day in 1947 when Christian Dior launched his "New Look": first available only to a tiny, wealthy elite, the tight-waisted and full, voluminous hem of this design rapidly became available in department stores (and via patterns for home sewing) throughout the West. (Interestingly, one of the first prominent British street style "tribes," the Teddy Boys, might be seen as another example of the "trickle down" principle in that the distinctive styling of their extra-long jackets—and even their name—was copied from the "edwardian" style fashionable amongst some upper-class British men.)

Yet even as the "New Look" demonstrates the extent to which—in the middle of the twentieth century—the high-fashion world remained largely impervious to influences from outside the tight sphere of elite designers and their wealthy customers, a broader perspective on dress reveals a growing appreciation of styles and fabrics with distinct, explicit working or lower-class roots and connotations. Denim is a good example of this: originally worn only by male manual workers, the 1947 and 1948 Sears & Roebuck catalogs both feature casual wear for women and children made from this material. While the designs and catalog presentation of these garments promotes the symbolic context of cowboys and the "Wild West" rather than urban manual labor, it could be argued that the cowboy was the first "working-class hero." At around the same time, the flamboyant, extrovert, and extravagant zoot-suited "hipster" styles of black jazz musicians and (at the other extreme stylistically) the rough and ready look of the Bikers (models for Brando in *The Wild One*) were increasingly influencing the dress style of the sort of middle-class male who previously had looked only to upper-class style (and upper-class sports) for sartorial inspiration. Thus, even before the end of the first half of the twentieth century, one finds significant examples of "bubble up" replacing the previously all-pervasive "trickle down" process; of the upper class loosening its stranglehold on "good taste" in matters of dress and, therefore, the emergence of street style as a potent and energizing force.

A "Teddy Boy." The distinctive look of London's Teddy Boys in the 1950s is among the earliest prominent street styles. HUL-TON ARCHIVE/GETTY IMAGES. REPRODUCED BY PERMISSION.

A Positive View of Street Style

The dramatic increase in the standardization of life after World War II (suburbanization, mass marketing, the franchising of restaurant and retail chains, the spread of television, and so on) may have increased the appeal of "alternative" lifestyles for individuals in search of "authenticity." The clothing styles of both the "outlaw" and those "from the wrong side of the tracks" became attractive as symbolic totems of escape from the bland (un)reality of what many cultural theorists have termed "late capitalism."

Important also was the astounding demographic blip of the "baby boomers" born just after World War II. As this generation grew up in the late 1950s and early 1960s, they came to represent a new sociocultural category—the "teenager"—who, by sheer dint of numbers and the fact that, by and large, they had money to spend, became a significant focus of the economic and cultural worlds. Slow off the mark in its embrace of "youth culture" (and still determinedly upper class and elitist), high fashion had little to offer the average baby-boom teenager who saw street style as a hipper, more authentic, and relevant source of stylistic inspiration. Every street "look" (beat, mod, rockabilly, biker, etc.) brought with it an entire lifestyle package of values and beliefs, a philosophy and, it was often hoped, a new, alternative, community.

This admiration of street style was especially true of young males. Fashionable male dress reached a crescendo of blandness in the 1950s with the typical, middle-class Western male reduced to near sartorial invisibility. It comes as no surprise, therefore, that street style in the twentieth century was as biased toward men (hipsters, beats, teddy boys, bikers, mods, hippies, psychedelics, skinheads, glam rockers, punks, new romantics, goths, casuals, b-boys, etc.) as fashion has been biased toward women. The rise of street style represents the return of the peacock male from near extinction and this undoubtedly plays a key part in its rising popularity and importance.

Finally, mention should be made of the importance of street style as a facilitator of group identity and subcultural cohesion. Since the close of World War II, Western culture has seen a dramatic decline in the significance of the traditional sociocultural divisions such as class, race, religion, ethnicity, regionalism, nationalism, and so on in defining and limiting personal identity. While liberating and egalitarian, this diminishing of the importance of such traditional sociocultural groupings created a huge amorphous, undifferentiated, homogenous mass within which a sense of community—"People Like Us"—became more problematic. The "tribelike" groupings of, for example, bikers, beats, and teddy boys in the 1950s; mods, hippies, and skinheads in the 1960s; headbangers, punks, and b-boys in the 1970s; and goths, new age travelers and ravers in the 1980s, offered a much needed sense of community—especially for teenagers who, beginning to separate from the parental family but not yet having created their own family unit, feel this need most acutely. Significantly, while throughout human history sociocultural groups have always used dress and body decoration styles to signal and reinforce their group identities and their shared culture, now, for the first time, one's appearance and style became a sociocultural glue which, it was hoped, would bind together disparate strangers—most of whom would never meet but all of whom shared a culture encrypted in a particular style of dress and music.

From the 1940s through the 1980s street style coalesced into dozens if not hundreds of alternative "tribes"—each with its own complex, integrated subcultural system of style, values, and beliefs. Many of these evolved, distinguishing one from the other (hipsters to beats to hippies) while others developed in an antagonistic process energized by opposition (mods/rockers, hippies/punks). In the process, a complex family tree of "styletribes" has spanned (and in many ways defined) several generations.

An Advertisement of Self

Street style "tribes" offered (and, for many, seem to have provided) that sense of community and shared identity that is so difficult to find in contemporary society. But while significant remnants of many of these subcultures remain scattered around the globe, such commitment and group identity have become less typical of the twenty-first cen-

Skateboarders. A group of teenage skateboarders pose for a picture in Manhattan. Many teenagers reject conventional fashions, instead developing their own street styles to better reflect their identities. © ROSE HARTMAN/CORBIS. REPRODUCED BY PERMISSION.

tury. Such looks are now, typically, plucked off the shelf of the post-modern "supermarket of style," tried out, promiscuously mixed with other looks, and then discarded.

However, while street style may now have entered a post-tribal phase, this is not to suggest that its importance has diminished, since fashion, in its strict, traditional sense, no longer structures and empowers most of the clothing industry. As the supreme expression of modernism, fashion's orderly, lineal production of new, "New Looks" and the consensus in the form of a singular, progressive "direction" that it demanded, is ill-suited to the complexity and pluralism of the postmodern age within which the possibility of progress, the value of uniformity, and the desirability of transience are increasingly questioned.

Originally attractive because of its perceived "authenticity," its offer of "alternative" choice and its capacity to "say" something significant about those who wear it, street style has moved into a key position within the clothing industry in a postmodern age characterized by a crises of identity, truth, and meaning. This is to say, not only has the "fashion industry" come to increasingly

and persistently look to "the street" for design inspiration, but, more significantly, that how clothing functions in the early 2000s from the perspective of the consumer—how it is purchased, worn, and valued—is more rooted in the history of street style than in the history of high fashion. Consumers have, in other words, moved a very long way indeed from the world of Dior's "New Look" in 1947 and the direction of this movement is commensurate with that approach to dress and appearance that has come to be known as "street style."

The "bubbling up" of stylistic inspiration (often, modeled by up-and-coming pop musicians) has become widespread within every segment of the clothing industry including "High Fashion." Moreover, street style's delight in "timeless classics" and its disdain for the ephemeral (Hell's Angels never coveted "This Season's New Biker Look") is seen in a widespread resistance to throwing out everything in one's wardrobe just because some fashion journalist might claim that "brown is the new black." While once the consumer sought out a "total look" from a particular designer, it is increasingly

Motorcycle gang from *The Wild One.* Johnny Strabler (Marlon Brando, center) and his motorcycle gang from the 1953 film *The Wild One,* which helped to popularize the tough, leather-clad look of bikers, is an early example of a street style influencing fashion. © JOHN SPRINGER COLLECTION/CORBIS. REPRODUCED BY PERMISSION.

thought that only a pathetic "fashion victim" takes such a passive approach. Thus, the construction of a presentation of self is increasingly seen as the work of the creative individual.

To this end, in a process that can be traced directly back to the Punks, the twenty-first century consumer—using garments and accessories from different designers, brands, or charity shops as "adjectives"—samples and mixes an eclectic (often even contradictory) range of looks into a personal style statement. This emphasis on what a look has to "say" also largely derives from street style. While pure fashion articulated only "This is new and I am therefore fashionable," street style was always deeply resonate with more complex personal (even philosophical and political) meanings—a choice of cut or color or fabric calculated to convey a precise summary of attitude and lifestyle. Street style obliged the individual to wear his or her values and beliefs on the sleeve—in a way that

more often than not required commitment and courage. Arguably, it is this capacity to give visual expression to where one is "at"—to articulate personal differences and, therefore, to create the possibility of interpersonal connection between like-minded individuals—which, in an age of too much communication and too little meaning, is street style's most valuable legacy.

See also **Hippie Style; Punk; Subcultures; Teenage Fashions; Zoot Suit.**

BIBLIOGRAPHY

Chenoune, Farid. *A History of Men's Fashion.* Paris: Flammarion, 1993.

Hebdige, Dick. *Subculture: The Meaning of Style.* London: Methuen and Co., 1979. A key text in the development of subcultural theory.

MacInnes, Colin. *Absolute Beginners.* London: Allison and Busby, 1992. A novel that was originally published in 1959.

McRobbie, Angela, ed. *Zoot Suits and Second-hand Dresses: An Anthology of Fashion and Music.* London: Macmillan, 1989.

Melly, George. *Revolt into Style: The Pop Arts in the 50s and 60s.* Oxford: Oxford University Press, 1989. A classic text; originally published in 1970.

Muggleton, David. *Inside Subculture: The Post-Modern Meaning of Style.* Oxford: Berg, 2000.

Muggleton, David, and Rupert Weinzierl, eds. *The Post-Subcultures Reader.* New York: New York University Press, 2003.

Olian, JoAnne. *Everyday Fashions of the Forties: As Pictured in Sears Catalogs.* New York: Dover Publications, Inc., 1992.

Polhemus, Ted. *Streetstyle: From Sidewalk to Catwalk.* London: Thames and Hudson, Inc., 1994. A summary of all significant "styletribes" from 1940s to 1990s; includes book, music, and film references for all groups in "Further Information."

———. *Style Surfing: What to Wear in the 3rd Millennium.* London: Thames and Hudson, Inc., 1996.

Redhead, Steve. *Subculture to Clubcultures: An Introduction to Popular Cultural Studies.* Oxford: Blackwell Publishers, 1997.

———, ed. *The Clubcultures Reader: Readings in Popular Cultural Studies.* Oxford: Blackwell Publishers, 1998.

Ted Polhemus

STRIPED CLOTH The term "striped cloth" describes any textile woven, knitted, or printed in such a way that bands of different colors, evenly or unevenly spaced, appear on the surface of the fabric. Striped cloth is usually warp-faced cloth (that is, cloth in which the warp yarns lie on the cloth's surface) in which the warp yarns are laid out in bands of different colors, but striped cloth can also be weft-faced, or knitted, or printed to emulate woven stripes. Fabrics in which bands of different colors appear in both the warp and the weft (or are printed in such a pattern) are known variously as checks, gingham, tartan, and plaid.

Origins

Striped cloth is found among the some of the earliest extant examples of woven textiles and must have arisen as a natural consequence of the color variability of yarns, particularly woolen yarns. Randomly distributed warp yarns of different colors or shades would have spontaneously produced a sort of asymmetrical striped cloth; it would then have been a very small step for the weaver to stretch her warp in such a way as to space out at even intervals the varying colors of yarn, producing true striped cloth. The use of yarns dyed in different colors must have been the next, equally obvious, step in the process of producing striped cloth. By early historic times, striped cloth was a normal part of the weaver's repertoire in cultures around the world, although it does not appear that the wearing of striped cloth predominated in any of the societies of antiquity.

The Devil's Cloth

As the French social historian Michel Pastoureau has pointed out, in the European Middle Ages striped cloth took on strong connotations of deviance and abasement. Servants and court jesters wore striped cloth; so did prostitutes, madmen, and criminals, not voluntarily but by official orders. The bold, broad, contrasting stripes of their garments seemed to stand for neither-this-nor-that, ambivalence, ambiguity, and a realm of unclear and violated boundaries. This connotation of striped cloth is with us still; a jumpsuit or a tunic-and-trousers combination garment made of broadly striped cloth, in either horizontal or vertical stripes, instantly carries the association of prisoners, convicted criminals, or, in a tragic variation, inmates of concentration camps. A loose, lightweight pajama-like union suit of brightly striped cloth, with a broad collar and cuffs, is the iconic outfit of the clown, a figure whose humor derives from his license to transgress the boundaries of orderly society.

The wearing of stripes was not always a sign of social deviance, but even as a fashion statement, stripes had connotations of boldness and daring, a willingness to test the boundaries of social tolerance. The broadly striped hose worn by young men in the Italian Renaissance, familiar from countless paintings and tapestries, gave them a swaggering air that must have seemed impudent and shocking to their more soberly dressed elders.

Striped cloth also had a role to play in heraldry, as overjackets, streamers, and banners of colored stripes could be used to display the colors of knights in combat or in the simulated combat of the tournament. The heraldic use of striped cloth survives in the practice of suspending medals signifying civil and military honors from striped grosgrain ribbon, with the color, width, and placement of stripes specified exactly by the rules of the decoration. In some cases the honor also includes the right to wear a wide sash of striped ribbon in the same colors as the ribbon of the medal itself. Ribbon in the tricolor pattern of red, white, and blue, often folded into a rosette worn as a hat decoration, became a potent symbol of the French Revolution.

Stripes in Fashion

Although striped cloth never entirely lost its connotations of danger and deviance, it acquired other associations, so that by the eighteenth century striped cloth entered the repertoire of ordinary European fashionable clothing. In particular, striped clothing acquired sporting or leisure connotations; Victorian paintings of seaside scenes frequently show women strolling in long summer dresses of black-and-white or blue-and-white striped fabric. As this association with the seaside suggests, stripes also called to mind nautical images. Woolen sweaters knitted with horizontal stripes of blue and white became standard gear for sailors, from Venetian gondoliers to crew members of private yachts.

The almost infinite number of possible combinations of colors and widths in which striped cloth could be produced led to a continued symbolic use of striped garments in a way that distantly recalled the old rules of heraldry. Boating clubs and cricket teams at English universities frequently sported boldly striped blazers in club colors. Neckties in stripes of prescribed colors and widths (with the cloth cut on the bias to produce diagonal stripes) similarly were used to identify members of military regiments, alumni of university colleges, clubs, and similar affinity groups.

The associations of striped cloth with leisure and sporting pursuits also made sturdy striped canvas popular for the upholstery of outdoor furniture, the canopies of beach umbrellas and cabanas, and the like. In the early twentieth century, before the invention of air-conditioning, buildings in Western cities were festooned in summertime with brightly striped awnings to keep sunshine and rain from entering open windows.

Striped Cloth in the Twenty-First Century

Since World War II, striped cloth has occasionally been fashionable for women's attire, and almost any year's ready-to-wear collections will include some striped dresses, skirts, and shirts. Horizontally striped sweaters remain sportswear standards for both men and women. But the major uses of striped cloth today are so understated as to escape immediate notice; striped cloth is primarily used now for men's suiting materials and for men's dress (business) shirts and ties. Partly in the hope that vertical stripes produce an illusion of a slimmer and taller body, many men wear dark suits with very thin stripes (pinstripes) or slightly fuzzy stripes (chalk stripes) of white or some other light color. Shirting materials, too, are frequently woven in white or light colors with dark pinstripes, or in stripes of even width (often of blue and white). In some years bright, multicolored stripes come into fashion; these are often made up into shirts with white collars and cuffs. And plain shirts are often worn with "regimental" striped ties (which, in America at least, seldom have or retain their specific symbolic associations). Sober business attire is the last bastion of a type of cloth that once had a far wider and more exciting range of meanings.

See also **Nautical Style; Neckties and Neckwear; Prison Dress; Ties; Uniforms, Sports.**

BIBLIOGRAPHY

Köhler, Karl. *A History of Costume*. Reprint, New York: Dover Publications, 1963.

Molloy, John. *Dress for Success*. New York: Peter H. Wyden, 1975.

Pastoureau, Michel. *The Devil's Cloth: A History of Stripes and Striped Fabric*. Translated by Jody Gladding. New York: Columbia University Press, 2001.

John S. Major

STRIPTEASE Publicists coined the word striptease in the late 1920s. It is still an evocative word, bringing to mind the lurid image of a busty, 1950s performer bumping and grinding in tasseled pasties and a sequined g-string. This icon of overtly commercial sexuality had its heyday in the 1950s, but the history of the striptease reaches as far back as the nineteenth century.

Starting in the 1850s, what is often referred to as the "scandal of tights" swept through America. Flesh-colored stockings were worn on the stage by comediennes, chorines, and cancan dancers revealing limbs that had been all but eliminated from the fashionable silhouette. The costume shocked audiences, but was allowed by censors since it had originated on ostensibly respectable stages in Europe, such as the Gaiety in London and the Folies Bergère in Paris. These nineteenth-century performers never actually disrobed, but they were harassed, fined, and occasionally jailed for pulling up their skirts, flashing their underwear, and swiveling their hips in a way that evoked the throes of passion. In 1893, the American purveyors of the tights-clad leg show, found mainly in burlesque and vaudeville theaters, shed even more clothes in order to adapt the "exotic" dance of the Chicago World's Fair's Little Egypt (whose performance launched the first and longest-lived euphemism for the stripteaser: exotic dancer).

The element of bare flesh was introduced around the turn of the century at the tea parties of socialite ladies. Early modern dancers like Isadora Duncan, Ruth St. Denis, and Maud Allan scandalized moralists with the degree of physical exposure in the costumes for their dances that were launched through the patronage of wealthy women interested in Orientalist art and culture. Duncan performed at ladies' matinees in bare feet and without tights, dressed only in a classical gown (made at first of her mother's muslin curtains). St. Denis adopted the exotic dance of the World's Fairs and dressed in ultra-sheer and bejeweled net garments. Allan developed a Dance of the Seven Veils based on the biblical story of Salome that was so popular that prominent women were inspired to hold a costume party of Salome-style dress. Through the popularity of modern dancers, a formula was filtered into American popular theater where numerous young women reduced their stage costumes to gauzy skirts, beaded bras, and bared midriffs in an effort to interpret foreign cultures, real and imagined, through the art of dance.

By the 1910s, the first accounts of striptease appeared on the heels of the advent of modern dance. Vaudeville historian Joe Laurie, Jr. claimed that vaudeville headliner Eva Tanguay let the veils drop in her version of the Salome dance in 1912. Morton Minsky claimed that burlesque performer Mae Dix invented it when she removed the detachable collar and cuffs of her costume in full view of the audience in order to save on her cleaning bill. Former stripteaser Ann Corio credited Hinda Wassau with inventing the act when forced to shimmy out of a chorus costume that had caught on the beads of the ensemble worn beneath for purposes of a quick change. The "Glorified Girls" featured in the mainstream Broadway revue of Florenz Ziegfeld, Jr. also made nudity more and more acceptable on the stage with opulent *tableaux* such as "Lady Godiva's Ride" in the *Follies of 1919*.

The acceptance of nudity necessitated bawdy entertainment to up the ante further in order to secure their lucratively raunchy reputations. The result was striptease. The precedent of nudity established by modern dancers implied artistic motives. The striptease represented a return to the flash-and-tickle approach of populist vaudeville dancers. That was infinitely more appealing to male audiences and it was achieved not through nudity, but through an undressing that mimicked the disrobing which preceded a sexual encounter. The formula was simple: the slow parade of a beautiful girl in a beautiful gown; the removal of stockings, gloves, hairpins; the slow shimmy out of the clinging, formal dress; and the briefest wriggle in only a g-string. Nudity made artistic became artistry made erotic.

Four burlesque producer brothers named Minsky became inextricably connected with striptease in the 1920s. Their publicists, George Alabama Florida and Mike Goldreyer, came up with the name for it and promoted its finest practitioners. These included Margie Hart, Georgia Southern, Ann Corio, and the incomparable Gypsy Rose Lee. When the Great Depression came, the Minskys were able to lease a theater on Broadway. Gypsy Rose Lee thrived in Minsky shows during this era and set the tone for high-style striptease as an extremely beautiful woman who was also an engaging comedienne and natural-born celebrity. The Minskys were so successful that theater producers and real-estate interests (along with some conservative religious organizations) banded together to get the act of striptease itself banned in New York City. They succeeded in 1937 when the word burlesque and the name Minsky were banned in New York City, and all the theaters that featured striptease were shut down. Similar bans followed in other cities across the nation.

Throughout the 1940s, a few burlesque houses survived and Minsky strippers used their fame to headline shows on carnival midways. In the years following the crackdown on striptease, some concessions were made to avoid trouble with the law. The use of pasties to cover the aureolas was the most noticeable change, but the addition of sequins, rhinestones, and tassels changed pasties from a handicap to an innovation. As nightclubs entered a boom following World War II, striptease came back in style again. A 1954 *Newsweek* article reported that the number of stripteasers had quadrupled since the 1930s and that 50 nightclubs in New York City featured striptease. The article gleefully recounts the props in the shows (snakes, monkeys, macaws, doves, parakeets, stuffed horses, swimming tanks, and bubble baths); the cost of the costumes

Dance of the Seven Veils. Lyn Seymour rehearses for a production of Oscar Wilde's 1891 play, *Salome*. Although tame by modern standards, the "Dance of the Seven Veils" perfomed in the play helped begin a trend towards the seductive, near-nude dancing known as striptease. © HULTON-DEUTSCH COLLECTION/CORBIS. REPRODUCED BY PERMISSION.

($850 to $1,000 for Lili St. Cyr's Vegas act); and the stage names in use (Carita La Dove—the Cuban Bombshell, Evelyn West—the $50,000 Treasure Chest Girl). The star performers of this era employed all the over-the-top shtick of 50 years of vaudeville in their acts. Blaze Starr had a red settee, which she had tricked out with a fan, canned smoke, and a piece of bright silk that would appear to go up in flames. Lili St. Cyr did interpretive striptease based on *Salome, Carmen, The Picture of Dorian Gray*, and *Sadie Thompson*. Tempest Storm promoted herself relentlessly, dating celebrities and accepting a mock award from Dean Martin and Jerry Lewis for having the two biggest props in Hollywood. These acts were so popular that in 1951 Frenchman Alain Bernadin opened the Crazy Horse Saloon in Paris to bring American-style striptease to European cabaret audiences. Another garish heyday for striptease had arrived. But by the 1960s, that heyday had come and gone.

In the decades that followed, striptease was rejected in favor of the direct appeal of already bare flesh. The topless trend kicked off in the mid-1960s when a go-go dancer at a San Francisco strip club performed in Rudi Gernreich's topless bathing suit without getting arrested. Topless lunches, topless shoeshines, and other mundane acts improved by toplessness were featured in the clubs that had showcased striptease. Bottomlessness logically followed. By the 1970s, the hugely profitable pornography industry almost eclipsed live nude girls altogether. Crackdowns on the pornography industry in the 1980s encouraged a resurgence of striptease, but much of the glamour and humorous shtick of 1950s striptease was excised in favor of the intimacy of the lap dance for an audience of one and as a result, the theatrically-inclined tassel-twirling stripteaser was replaced by the more readily accessible silicone-enhanced bottle blond with one leg wrapped around a metal pole.

BIBLIOGRAPHY

Alexander, H. M. *Strip Tease: The Vanished Art of Burlesque*. New York: Knight Publishers, 1938.

Allen, Robert C. *Horrible Prettiness: Burlesque and American Culture*. Chapel Hill: University of North Carolina Press, 1991.

Cherniasky, Felix. *The Salome Dancer: The Life and Times of Maud Allan*. Toronto, Ontario: McClelland and Stewart, Inc., 1991.

Corio, Ann with Joseph DiMona. *This Was Burlesque*. New York: Madison Square Press/Grosset and Dunlap, 1968.

Derval, Paul. *Folies-Bergere*. New York: E. P. Dutton and Co., Inc., 1955.

Fields, Armond, and L. Marc Fields. *From the Bowery to Broadway: Lew Fields and the Roots of American Popular Theater*. New York and Oxford, U.K.: Oxford University Press, 1993.

Jarret, Lucinda. *Stripping in Time: A History of Erotic Dancing*. London: Pandora-Harper, 1977.

Laurie, Joe, Jr. *Vaudeville: From the Honky-Tonks to the Palace*. New York: Henry Holt and Company, 1953.

Lee, Gypsy Rose. *Gypsy*. Berkeley, Calif: Frog, Ltd., 1957.

Macdougall, Allan Ross. *Isadora: A Revolutionary in Art and Love*. New York: Thomas Nelson and Sons, 1960.

Mariel, Pierre and Jean Trocher. *Paris Cancan*. Translated by Stephanie and Richard Sutton. London: Charles Skilton Ltd., 1961.

Minsky, Morton. *Minsky's Burlesque*. New York: Arbor, 1986.

Parker, Derek and Julia Parker. *The Natural History of the Chorus Girl*. Indianapolis, Ind., and New York: Bobbs-Merrill, 1975.

Shelton, Suzanne. *Divine Dancer: A Biography of Ruth St. Denis*. New York: Doubleday, 1981.

Sobel, Bernard. *Burleycue: An Underground History of Burlesque Days*. New York: Farrar and Rinehart, Inc., 1931.

——. *A Pictorial History of Burlesque*. New York: Bonanza Books, 1956.

Starr, Blaze and Huey Perry. *Blaze Starr: My Life as Told to Huey Perry*. Warner Paperback Library Edition. New York: Praeger Publishers, Inc., 1975.

Stencell, A. W. *Girl Show: Into the Canvas World of Bump and Grind*. Toronto, Ontario, Canada: ECW Press, 1999.

Storm, Tempest. *The Lady Is a Vamp*. Atlanta, Ga.: Peachtree Publishers, Ltd., 1987.

Zeidman, Irving. *The American Burlesque Show*. New York: Hawthorn Books, Inc., 1967.

Ziegfeld, Richard and Paulette. *The Ziegfeld Touch: The Life and Times of Florenz Ziegfeld, Jr*. New York: Harry N. Abrams, 1993.

Jessica Glasscock

SUBCULTURES A point on which many costume historians have concurred is that fashion, as it is currently understood—the propensity for continual change in clothing designs, colors, and tastes—is a relatively recent phenomenon in the history of humankind, virtually unknown before the fourteenth century and occurring only with the emergence of mercantile capitalism, the concomitant growth in global trade, and the rise of the medieval city. (Among the few exceptions are Tang Dynasty China and Heian Period Japan.) Other scholars have analyzed fashion as an aspect of a distinctively modern and Western consumer culture that first gained impetus in the eighteenth century, concurrent with the onset of the industrial revolution. Either way, to be "fashionable" in this sense of the term must not be understood as a natural, universal, or biologically given aspect of human behavior, but as a socially and historically specific condition. Fashion is, in other words, a cultural construction. Its very existence, form, and direction are dependent on the complex interplay of quite specific economic, political, and ideological forces.

If fashion is cultural then fashion subcultures are groups organized around or based upon certain features of costume, appearance, and adornment that render them distinctive enough to be recognized or defined as a subset of the wider culture. Depending on the group in question, subcultures may be loosely or tightly bounded; their collective identification may be self-attributed or imputed to them by outsiders. A particular gender, age span, social class, or ethnic identity may dominate membership. Subcultures often create their own distinctiveness by defining themselves in opposition to the "mainstream"—the accepted, prescribed, or prevailing fashion of the period. They may be either radical and forward-looking or reactionary and conservative in relation to the dominant mode of dressing: in either case, they aim toward exclusivity. Thus, while these subcultures may depend upon fashion for their very existence, their members may dispute the relevance of fashion (as both phenomenon and terminology) to their own identity, perhaps preferring to orient themselves around the idea of "style" or "anti-fashion." "Anti-fashion is that 'true chic' which used to be defined as the elegance that never draws attention to itself, the simplicity that is 'understated'… Anti-fashion attempts a timeless style, tries to get the essential element of change out of fashion altogether" (Wilson, pp. 183–184).

Early Examples

Elizabeth Wilson's *Adorned in Dreams* includes a useful introductory discussion of certain forms of early, European fashion subcultures that favored rebellious, or oppositional, dress. Along with the "great masculine renunciation" of the early nineteenth century, in which men forsook foppish perfumed effeminacy for classic understated sobriety, came the figure of the Regency dandy. Although English in origin, dandyism soon found a resonance in post-revolutionary France, where it was adopted by the avant-garde youth subculture, the Incroyables. The typical dandy was undoubtedly motivated by a narcissistic obsession with image, display, and the presentation of the self through dress; yet his overriding concern was with sheer quality of fabric, fit, and form, not overbearing or ostentatious ornamentation. This coterie of young gentlemen was thus characterized by an ethos of stoical heroism, a disciplined quest for refinement, elegance, and excellence, the diverse historical legacy of which can be seen in male Edwardian dress, the 1960s mod subculture, and the character of John Steed in the cult TV show, *The Avengers*.

The fastidiousness of the dandy can be contrasted with the flamboyance of the bohemian, who also emerged in the early nineteenth century, but as a romantic reaction against the perceived de-humanizing utilitarianism and rationalism of the industrial revolution. Although often solidly upper-middle class in origin, the romantic rebel—as artist, visionary, or intellectual—was fundamentally anti-bourgeois in tastes and outlook, their moral quest for self-renewal through art synonymous with a desire to escape the inhibitions of conventional lifestyles and appearances. Bohemian countercultures have been a feature of many major Western urban centers of creativity—Paris, London, New York, Berlin, San Francisco—at regular intervals over the past two hundred years. From the casual neckties, romantic robes, and ethnic exoticism of the early French bohemians, via the existentially-inspired black uniform and pale complexions of the 1950s beatniks, to the natural fibers, Eastern-influenced designs, and psychedelic aesthetic of the 1960s hippies, Wilson's book provides descriptions of their many and varied forms of sartorial dissent.

Because calls to free the physical self from the strictures imposed by social conventions of dress can imply a need for either increased functionality of design or a relaxation of hitherto too rigid forms, oppositional fashions and attempts at reformist dress can display both puritan rational and aesthetic romantic elements. Artistic or aesthetic dress of the nineteenth century called for the natural and free-flowing draping of the female body at a time when the tightly corseted, narrow-waisted, and heavily bustled female was the height of popular fashion; yet it is interesting that a movement founded in 1881 to free women from precisely these restrictions and impediments of conventional Victorian dress should be called "The Rational Dress Society." In the Soviet Union of the 1920s,

Hell's Angels. A member of the Hell's Angels Motorcycle Club, in Los Angeles, California, 2000. American motorcycle gangs cultivate a distinctive appearance that sets them apart from mainstream fashion, helps them to identify other members of the biker subculture, and identifies their place within that subculture. © TED SOQUI/CORBIS. REPRODUCED BY PERMISSION.

the rational aspects of dress design were underpinned by the scientific tenets of Marxist-Leninism. Constructivist artists such as Vladimir Tatlin, Liubov' Popova, and Varvara Stepanova combined geometric Modernist motifs with the principle that form follows function to address the utilitarian clothing needs of urban industrial workers. The resulting revolutionary garments, intended for mass production, were destined, however, to remain—like aesthetic dress—a minority taste—the artistic expression of an avant-garde subculture.

Youth Subcultural Styles

The British context. Despite assumptions to the contrary, working-class youth subcultures, based around distinctive, dissenting styles, were not confined to the period after World War II. Geoffrey Pearson, for example, in a study of the "history of respectable fears," notes the presence in late-nineteenth-century Britain of the troublesome teenage "hooligan" (an Australian equivalent of the same period was known as the "larrikin"). Notwithstanding some regional variations in style between the

Rastafarian family in Jamaica. The distinctive clothing and hairstyles of Rastafarians constitute a fashion subculture. © DAVID CUMMING; EYE UBIQUITOUS/CORBIS. REPRODUCED BY PERMISSION.

different hooligan groups—the Manchester "Scuttlers" and the Birmingham "Peaky Blinders," for example— there was adopted a quite distinct uniform of large boots, bell-bottomed trousers, a loosely worn muffler or scarf, and a peaked cap worn over a donkey-fringe haircut. The whole peculiar ensemble was set off with a broad, buckled, leather belt.

There were six or more intervening decades between the demise of the original "hooligans" and the emergence of the more familiar and clearly documented British youth subcultures of the post-1945 era—the teddy boys, mods, rockers, hippies, skinheads, and punks. Yet Pearson sees no fundamental difference between the way the Victorian gangs constructed clearly recognizable styles by appropriating elements from the range of fashionable sources available to them and the attempts by the more recent "spectacular" youth subcultures to create new, oppositional meanings through the recontextualization of raw commodities from the market—a process that the Centre for Contemporary Cultural Studies (CCCS) at the University of Birmingham, England, termed "bricolage." Hence, the working-class teddy boys of the early 1950s appropriated the long lapeled neo-Edwardian drape suit from exclusive London tailors who aimed to bring back the pre-1914 look for upper-class young men. But the teds combined this item with bootlace ties (from Western movies), greased-back haircuts, drainpipe trousers, and thick creped-soled shoes.

CCCS writers such as John Clarke and Dick Hebdige had adopted an analysis whereby subcultural styles were "decoded" or read as a text for their hidden meanings. Hence, the fastidious and narcissistic neatness of the mods, with their two-tone mohair suits, button-down collared shirts, and short, lacquered hair, could be interpreted as an attempt by young working-class people in menial and routine employment to live out on a symbolic level the affluent, consumerist, and classless aspirations of the early 1960s. By contrast, the skinheads who emerged later in the same decade typically sported very close-cropped hair or shaven heads, Ben Sherman shirts and suspenders, and short, tight jeans or sta-press trousers with Dr. Martens boots—a combination of elements that signified a "magical" desire to return to the puritan masculinity of a rapidly disappearing traditional proletarian lifestyle. By the end of the 1970s subcultural fashions had become less easy to decipher in this way. Hebdige, analyzing punk style in his classic text *Subculture*, was driven to assert that the punks' "cut-up" wardrobe of bondage trousers, school ties, safety pins, bin liners, and spiky hair signified meaningfully only in terms of its very meaninglessness, as a visual illustration of chaos.

American and Australian examples. In Britain during the early 1960s, the natural enemy of the cool, clean-looking, scooter-riding mods were the leather- and denim-clad, insignia-decorated, greasy-haired rockers, or motorbike boys as Paul Willis called them, renowned for their macho, rock 'n' roll image and "ton-up" speeding runs on heavy-duty Triumph Bonnevilles. Yet the reputation of the British rockers was tame by comparison with the notoriety of the American "outlaw" biker gangs of the postwar era, the most famous of which were—and still are—the Hell's Angels. Organized territorially in "chapters," and espousing an ideology of personal freedom and conservative patriotism, the "Angels" rode their collective "runs" on "chopped hogs"—customized Harley-Davidson bikes. Their famous Death-Head emblem or logo, as described by Hunter Thompson, is a cloth patch embroidered with a biker helmet atop a winged skull, and a band inscribed with the words Hell's Angels and the local chapter name. These "colors," as they are known, are typically sewn to the back of a sleeveless denim shirt.

Heavy Metal is a rock music genre that has given rise to a virtually global fashion, arguably derived from a crossover of elements from biker, glam, and hippie culture. Headbangers or metalers, as they are known, are characterized by their typical dress of black T-shirt, often bearing a heavy metal band name, faded denim jeans, and a leather or denim jacket, perhaps decorated with various badges, patches, and band insignia. For both men

The New Avengers. The stars of the 1970s British television series *The New Avengers,* (from left to right) Gareth Hunt, Joanna Lumley, and Patrick McNee. McNee's character, John Steed, epitomized the style of the later-day Edwardian dandy. © HULTON-DEUTSH COLLECTION/CORBIS. REPRODUCED BY PERMISSION.

and women, hair is usually long, the body or arms are often tattooed, and jewelry may be worn. The music itself has fragmented into various subgenres such as thrash-, death- and sleaze-metal, each with its own variant on the general metaler look. Jeffrey Arnett views young American metalheads (as they are named in the title of his book) as particularly prone to the alienation, anomie, and hyper-individualism that, from his point of view, characterize contemporary American youth more generally.

Because of the immense power of its market, and the dependence of subcultural fashions upon commodity production and consumption, styles originally developed or popularized in America have rapidly spread to other cultural contexts. In a chapter in Rob White's edited book on the Australian experience of youth subcultures, Stratton discusses the case of the 1950s bodgies and widgies —terms used to denote male and female members respectively. The style of the bodgie and widgies was originally jazz- and jive-oriented and loosely derived from the zoot suit (discussed below) worn by young black and Hispanic Americans in the 1940s. Later, however, this Aus-

tralian subculture became influenced by American biker culture and also began to incorporate elements from rock 'n' roll. Boys wore leather jackets or drapes with thin ties, drainpipe trousers, and winkle-picker shoes; girls had pencil skirts, stilettos or pedal-pusher shoes, and beehive or ponytail hairstyles.

Neglected Dimensions and New Developments

Gender and ethnicity. In a chapter in *Resistance through Rituals,* Angela McRobbie and Jenny Garber noted that most of the subcultures and styles examined by the CCCS appeared overwhelmingly male in both composition and orientation. They concluded that girls *had* actually been present in such subcultures, but were rendered marginalized and invisible by the masculinist bias of the writers. It was only with the publication nearly a quarter of a century later of *Pretty in Punk,* Lauren Leblanc's noteworthy text on Canadian female punk rockers, that females in a male-dominated style subculture were studied comprehensively, in their own right and on their own terms. Leblanc's sample displayed a range of punk signifiers, including hair brightly dyed and worn in a Mohawk style, facial piercings, tattoos, and the "street-" or gutter-punk look—dark, baggy T-shirts and trousers with black boots. Leblanc concludes that women's presence in a largely male punk subculture can be explained by the way their membership enables them to resist certain normative and stylistic aspects of fashionable (i.e. mainstream) femininity.

Although ethnicity, like gender, has been a relatively neglected dimension in the writings of subcultural style, the American "zooties" of the 1940s are one of the better-documented examples of black and Hispanic rebellious fashion. Derived from black, hipster jazz culture, the zoot suit comprised an oversized, draped and pleated jacket with hugely padded shoulders, worn with high-waisted, baggy-kneed and ankle-taped pants, often set off with a wide-brimmed hat worn over a ducktail hairstyle. During a period of wartime rationing of material, the wearing of such an extravagant, luxurious, and ostentatious style led to rising tensions between the young black and Hispanic male zooties and white U.S. servicemen, sparking off full-scale riots in a number of U.S. cities.

Within the British literature on subcultures, the ethnic dimension has been more typically viewed in terms of the effects of postwar British "race relations" and black style on the formation of indigenous rebellious youth fashions. A noted example of such an approach is Dick Hebdige's discussion of the Jamaican rude boy and Rastafarian subcultures. Elements from the first of these styles—the cool look, shades, porkpie hat, and slim trousers with cropped legs —fed first into 1960s mod and then the Two-Tone movement of the late 1970s. Rastafarians, to symbolize their oppression by white society (Babylon) and their prophesied return to Zion (Africa), have adopted knitted caps (called "tams"), scarves, and jerseys in red, gold, and green, the colors of the Ethiopian flag. It is, though, the Rasta's dreadlock hairstyle that has most significantly been taken up by certain groups of white youth, particularly new-age hippies and anarcho-punks, to show subcultural disaffection toward the dominant social order.

Post-Modernism and Post-Subculture

The practice of borrowing ethnic signifiers has reached extreme proportions in the contemporary, transatlantic example of the Modern Primitive subculture. The chapter by Winge, in David Muggleton and Rupert Weinzierl's *The Post-Subcultures Reader*, details how this subculture with its largely white membership adopts aspects of so-called "primitive" tribal cultures, such as black-work tattoos, brandings, keloids, and septum piercings. While subcultural styles have typically been constructed by a borrowing of elements from other sources, this relocation of traditional elements in a modern, urban setting could be seen as a prime example of a tendency toward a more complex cross-fertilization of time-compressed stylistic symbols in an increasingly global context. It is further argued that the identities fashioned from these diverse sources are themselves ever more eclectic, hybrid, and fragmented. Such a position has led some writers to proclaim that subculture—traditionally used to denote a coherent, stable, and specific group identification—is no longer a useful concept by which to comprehend these so-called "post-modern" or "post-subcultural" characteristics of contemporary styles.

That attempts at re-conceptualizing the term subculture, such as "neo-tribe," or "post-subculture," have proceeded on the terrain of post-modernism owes much to the American anthropologist Ted Polhemus. His *Streetstyle* is particularly worth singling out here, most obviously for its vividly illustrated genealogy of late-twentieth-century subcultures, from the 1940s zoot-suiters to the 1990s new-age travelers, but also for its attempt in the final chapters to conceptualize a new stage of development in the history of popular street fashion—"the supermarket of style." "Those who frequent the Supermarket of Style display…a stylistic promiscuity which is breathtaking in its casualness. 'Punks' one day, 'Hippies' the next, they fleeting leap across ideological divides—converting the history of street style into a vast theme park. All of which fits very neatly within postmodern theory" (Polhemus, p. 131).

Muggleton's *Inside Subculture* represents the first attempt to test such theoretical propositions about post-modern fashions. Using data from interviews with members from a range of subcultures, Muggleton generally agrees with post-modern claims concerning the fluidity, fragmentation, and radical individuality of dissident youth styles. He describes, for example, those such as the respondent with a Chinese hairstyle, baggy skateboarder shorts, leather biker jacket, and boots, whose eclecticism arguably leads them to disavow any affiliation to a group identity. Paul Hodkinson's *Goth* is a qualitative study of self-identifying members of the gothic subculture. Both male and female goths are noted for their dark and macabre appearance, typical features being black clothes, whitened faces, long, dyed black hair, plus dark eyeliner and lipstick. *Goth* differs somewhat from *Inside Subculture* in its stress on the continuing cultural coherence and stylistic substance of the British subcultural scene. Yet the potential reader is advised to seek out these two texts for their complimentary rather than conflicting assessments of the contemporary fashion subculture situation.

See also **Extreme Fashions; Punk; Retro Styles; Zoot Suit.**

BIBLIOGRAPHY

Arnett, Jeffrey. *Metalheads: Heavy Metal Music and Adolescent Alienation.* Boulder, Colo.: Westview, 1996.

Hall, Stuart, and Tony Jefferson, eds. *Resistance Through Rituals: Youth Subcultures in Post-War Britain.* London: Hutchinson, 1976.

Hebdige, Dick. *Subculture: The Meaning of Style*. London: Methuen, 1979.

Hodkinson, Paul. *Goth: Identity, Style and Subculture*. Oxford: Berg, 2002.

Leblanc, Lauren. *Pretty in Punk: Girls' Gender Resistance in a Boys' Subculture*. New Brunswick, N.J., and London: Rutgers University Press, 2002.

Muggleton, David. *Inside Subculture: The Postmodern Meaning of Style*. Oxford: Berg, 2000.

———, and Rupert Weinzierl, eds. *The Post-Subcultures Reader*. Oxford: Berg, 2003.

Pearson, Geoffrey. *Hooligan: A History of Respectable Fears*. London: Macmillan, 1983.

Polhemus, Ted. *Streetstyle: From Sidewalk to Catwalk*. London: Thames and Hudson, Inc., 1994.

Thompson, Hunter. *Hell's Angels*. New York: Random House, 1966.

White, Rob, ed. *Youth Subcultures: Theory, History and the Australian Experience*. Hobart: National Clearinghouse for Youth Studies, 1993.

Willis, Paul. *Profane Culture*. London: Routledge and Kegan Paul, 1978.

Wilson, Elizabeth. *Adorned in Dreams: Fashion and Modernity*. London: Virago, 1985.

David Muggleton

SUIT, BUSINESS The man's business suit is an emblem of official power and professional identity, suggesting a life free from physical toil. The three-piece suit, allowing for differences of cut and fabric, has been the basis of the male wardrobe since the last quarter of the seventeenth century. King Charles II, on the restoration of the British throne in 1660, set the style for a new way of dressing. He appeared in a knee-length coat, vest (waistcoat), and breeches. As diarist Samuel Pepys recorded, "Oct 15th 1666. This day the king begins to put on his vest. It being a long cassock close to the body, of black cloth, and pinked with white silk under it, and a coat over it" (p. 324).

The loosely cut knee-length coat, embellished with elaborately worked buttonholes and deep turned-back cuffs, and embroidered waistcoat remained the staple of the British court style until the mid-1720s. As the British nobility spent much of their time on their country estates, the boundaries between the clothing of the landed gentry and the middle classes became eroded. Clothes that had originally been made for riding became upgraded into acceptable day wear and even for more formal occasions.

The influence of sporting dress increased an appreciation of the solid virtues of fit and finish. Throughout the eighteenth century, the comfortable and practical coat, waistcoat, and breeches, made mostly of wool, underwent little alteration. Abstaining from overt display was a requirement of the prevailing nonconformist reli-

gion, and together with the need for equestrian practicality this resulted in a movement away from baroque splendor to greater simplicity. By the 1780s this style of dress was correct for all but the most formal of occasions and obligatory court appearances. During the next twenty years, the coat became more streamlined and the turned-back cuffs, full coat-skirts, and pocket flaps began to be refined, with the waistcoat cut straight across the waistline. Legs were clad in knitted pantaloons, to provide a long, lean line in keeping with the desire to ape the natural masculine ideal of classical revivalism that was a significant aspect of dress at the beginning of the nineteenth century. This look was exemplified by George Bryan "Beau" Brummell, born in 1778, who established himself as a paradigm of sartorial exactness and simplicity. A close friend of the Prince of Wales, who became Regent in 1811 and later George IV, Brummell created a vogue for bespoke tailoring. He took his patronage to the Burlington estate where fashionable tailors had begun to congregate in the late eighteenth century.

By 1806 the first tailor was established in Savile Row. By 1810 tailoring techniques were capable of producing an unembellished coat of exquisite fit with emphasis on sculptural seaming and construction. The coat now had a collar that curved around the neck and formed flat lying lapels across the chest, the most distinctive element of the modern-day suit. The perfect fit was also due to the use of woolen cloth, which is both pliable and responsive to steam pressing, unlike the taut weave of silk. Wool was also easily available, a staple cloth of England's sheep farmers. Ready-made clothes were available from the 1820s, and with the development of the railroads and the opening of department stores they came to dominate the market, though bespoke tailoring remained standard wear for the middle and upper classes. Secondhand merchants provided clothes for the poor, and hawkers redistributed redyed patched clothing at markets.

In 1815 trousers, very often looped under the foot, replaced pantaloons and were worn with the frock coat, which owed its origins to the military greatcoat. First appearing in 1816, it was the most usual coat for daywear, typifying middle-class respectability as it was worn by the professions and by businessmen. Buttoned from neck to knee it was decorated across the chest with frogging. By 1850 the morning coat was preferred. Based on the riding coat, (riding was a popular morning activity) it began to be worn on formal occasions, replacing the frock coat, and by 1900 it was the established norm for business and professional activities.

The nineteenth century saw an increasing division between the public and private roles for men and women. The psychologist J. C. Flügel identified the early nineteenth century as era of "The Great Masculine Renunciation," when men became more concerned with propriety than with the pleasures of adornment. This supposition that men gave up their right to a choice of elaborate clothing, leaving the pleasures of ornamentation only to women, can be countered by the many different masculine styles that developed at that time. For example, the Paletot was introduced in the 1830s. This was a jacket, cut loose and without a waist seam; it came to denote a certain bohemianism. Refined by the 1850s into the lounge jacket, and worn with matching waistcoat and trousers, it became the lounge suit and was initially worn after lunch and only in private, never on formal occasions or in the city. However, city workers were wearing ready-to-wear versions in darker colors, and by 1920 it assumed respectability and was subsequently worn for all business events. It became the all-purpose male costume of the twentieth century.

Advances in technology made possible the production of men's suits in large quantities, standard sizes, and a wide range of price points, thus helping to ensure the suit's continuing popularity over a long span of time. During the middle decades of the twentieth century, suiting materials became lighter in weight, reflecting the widespread use of central heating in homes and workplaces.

After World War II, men's wear became more casual and youthful in appearance; in America, the collegiate "Ivy League Look" became dominant. Also influential was the Italian streamlined silhouette developed by tailors in Rome and Milan. Italian and American suits influenced British tailoring in the 1950s and 1960s, just as London was becoming the center of youth fashion. John Stephen opened the first of his men's wear shops in Carnaby Street, purveying styles that were colorful, cheap, and fun. The clothes presaged the look of the hippie era in the use of richly textured and colored materials and exploitation of historical revivalism. The response of traditional male outfitters was to attempt to offer suits with some of the eccentricities of Carnaby Street but allied to something suitable for business wear. In 1965 men's outfitter Austin Reed filled the gap between Carnaby Street and traditional tailoring, providing contemporary suits for the young executive. Male-orientated publishing ventures such as *Man About Town*, which was first published in 1961, (subsequently called *About Town* and then simply *Town*) placed shopping for fashion firmly in the context of a leisure activity. The bespoke end of the market was not immune to change. Tommy Nutter, defined by the style press as a "designer tailor," took over premises on Savile Row and combined traditional qualities of craftsmanship with excessive detailing.

The 1970s and 1980s saw the rise of Italian luxury ready-to-wear. Giorgio Armani, in particular, became known for his unstructured suits, which combined ease and elegance, thus linking the freedom of the 1960s with the drive for financial success that typified much of 1980s culture. The revival of the suit heralded a new seriousness about being successful, epitomized by the aspirational "yuppie." The burgeoning style press and the advertising industry emphasized the importance of a lifestyle that included not only clothes but also iconic accessories such as the Rolex watch and the Mont Blanc fountain pen. The newly important role of the merchandiser, rather than the buyer or designer, underpinned the emphasis on lifestyle marketing. Men's shops took on the appearance of a gentleman's club. Retailers such as Ralph Lauren and Paul Smith sold the "English look" amidst the accoutrements of an Edwardian gentlemen's club such as sofas, leather-bound books, and sports paraphernalia, all evoking an era of leisured gentility.

When women entered the marketplace in substantial numbers in the 1980s, they began to adopt elements of male dress, wearing an approximation of the male suit. As they achieved more confidence they exaggerated the tailored qualities of the suit with ever widening shoulders and flying lapels, subverting its formality with short skirts and stiletto heels, a look known as "power dressing."

Despite a long-term trend toward more casual dressing, the suit remains an icon of authority. However its details might vary, it remains fundamentally the same. The business suit implicitly evokes the virtues of assertiveness with self-control, diffidence in success, and just enough socially acceptable narcissism to be attractive.

See also **Armani, Giorgio; Flügel, J. C.; Lauren, Ralph; Tailored Suit; Trousers.**

BIBLIOGRAPHY

Breward, Christopher. *The Hidden Consumer: Masculinity, Fashion, and City Life.* Manchester: Manchester University Press, 1995.

Chenoune, Farid. *A History of Men's Fashion.* Paris: Flammarion, 1993.

Hollander, Anne. *Sex and Suits.* New York, Tokyo, and London: Kodansha International, 1994.

Kuchta, David. *The Three-Piece Suit and Modern Masculinity: England, 1550–1850.* Berkeley, Los Angeles, and London: University of California Press, 2002.

Latham, R., and W. Matthews, eds. *The Diary of Samuel Pepys,* Vol. 7. New York: Harper Collins, 1995.

Marnie Fogg

SUMPTUARY LAWS Sumptuary laws can be dated to at least the fourth century B.C.E., and while they have largely disappeared in name, they have by no means disappeared in fact. By definition, they are intended to control behavior, specifically the excessive consumption of anything from foodstuffs to household goods. By convention, they have come to be largely associated with the regulation of apparel, their most frequent target. Typically, those issued by executive or legislative entities—and that are thus laws in the legal sense—have lasted no more than a few decades before being repealed or annulled. Infinitely more enduring have been extra-legal pronouncements that codify social or religious precepts, such as the injunction against garments woven of wool and linen proclaimed in Leviticus 19:19 and still obeyed by Orthodox

Jews. (The longevity of restrictions on women's dress issued by modern theocracies remains to be seen, now that these have passed from custom into law.)

Types

Sumptuary regulation is of two general types: prescriptive and proscriptive. The first defines what people must purchase, wear, or use, the second what they may not. Although both approaches limit choice, proscriptive laws can be seen as less onerous in so far as individual freedom is concerned since they imply acceptance of anything not expressly forbidden.

Goals and Outcomes

Personal liberty is never a factor in such legislation; however, actual statutes are written to address any of a number of sociocultural objectives deemed important by the issuing authority. Rulings in effect between 1337 and 1604 in medieval and renaissance England, for example, reflect multiple (and by no means mutually exclusive) goals: resisting new fashions, protecting public morals, preserving the public peace, maintaining social distinctions, and—extremely important to this commercial nation—defending the domestic economy and promoting home industries. Across the Channel, particularly in Protestant countries, sumptuary laws were more likely to assume the deity to be as offended by sartorial choices as was the government. Here, one might compare an English statute of 1483, which banned without explanation the stylishly short gowns that failed to mask "privy Members and Buttocks" (*Statues of the Realm*, p. 22) with a Bavarian injunction that prohibited uncovered codpieces because these were offensive to God. After the conclusion of the Thirty Years War in 1648, however, the sumptuary laws of the German states began to resemble those of England in their emphasis on economic issues.

One of the intended outcomes of much sumptuary law is that of separation, the division of people into explicit categories. Modern examples tend to differentiate by religion, whether by choice (the Amish cap) or by coercion (the yellow star). In earlier times, a populace was more likely to be divided by class than by creed; and in hierarchical societies in which ritualized honors were due those of superior rank, status had to be readily recognizable if people were neither to insult their betters (by failing to offer the proper marks of respect) nor embarrass themselves (by extending undeserved courtesies to those beneath them).

Parameters

The desire for upward mobility may be both innate and unquenchable; however, much of sumptuary legislation is concerned with defining the degrees of rank and wealth that govern the wearing of metals, textiles, colors, decorative techniques, furs, and jewels. Limitations on gold, silks, purples, lace, embroidery, sable, and precious stones are, thus, recurring elements, as are injunctions against

certain fashions (including short robes, long-toed shoes or *poulaines*, and great hose) considered unacceptable for moral, patriotic, or economic reasons. Improving economies raised not only the earnings but also the aspirations of, especially, the merchant classes, however, and England was not unusual in its continuing reformulation of vestimentary prohibitions relative to disposable income. While the threshold most commonly cited in English law is £40, in 1337 Edward III limited the wearing of furs to those with a disposable income of at least £100, and in 1554 Queen Mary lowered the minimum for silk to £20 (although she also insisted on a net worth of £200, an amount reiterated in a Massachusetts law of 1651).

Penalties

Most sumptuary legislation provides penalties for lawbreakers that could include confiscation of the offending garment, fines (up to £200 in England), tax auditing, the pillory, or even jail. That legislators were themselves subject to (and breakers of) these statutes may help to explain both their lax enforcement and their frequent repeal. In England, at least, lack of compliance was so general that in 1406 Henry IV vainly requested that violators be excommunicated. In 1670, women who used dress and cosmetics to "betray into matrimony any of his majesty's subjects" (Geocities.com Web site) were to be punished as witches.

Women

As might be expected, the attention paid to women in sumptuary law varies with time and country, and does so in ways that reflect their place in society. Generally speaking, early modern sumptuary legislation treats women in one of four ways: it exempts them specifically or ignores them completely (implying that women were of no consequence); or, conversely, it subjects them either to the same requirements as men or to parallel requirements (implying that women were not to be disregarded). There are of course exceptions. A few statutes imply fear of gender confusion. In the third century C.E., for example, the emperor Aurelian barred men from wearing shoes of yellow, green, white, or red since these colors were reserved for women. Others were aimed at keeping women in the home, as did an edict enacted in Rome in the second century B.C.E., that forbade their riding in a carriage in or near populated areas. More (both written and unwritten) were intended to keep them modest—Hebrews, Romans, early Christians, and early Americans alike mandated simplicity in feminine hairstyles, clothing, and accessories. Perhaps not surprisingly, prostitutes received special attention, as did courtesans, who, finding their consorts among the nobility, rather naturally rivaled wellborn women in their dress. From at least the thirteenth century onward, European prostitutes were commonly enjoined to wear some form of distinctive clothing, whether striped hoods, striped stockings, colored patches, or bells (interestingly, such markers were prescribed for other social outcasts, among them lepers and Jews).

Summary

Collectively, sumptuary laws reflect a need for permanence that is shared by governments, religions, and smaller societal groups alike. That so many have been written and so few endure speaks to the fundamental dissonance between the institutional need for stability and the personal desire for independence.

See also **Colonialism and Imperialism; Europe and America: History of Dress (400–1900 C.E.)**

BIBLIOGRAPHY

Baldwin, Frances Elizabeth. *Sumptuary Legislation and Personal Regulation in England.* Vol. 44: *Johns Hopkins University Studies in Historical and Political Science.* Baltimore: The Johns Hopkins Press, 1926.

Benhamou, Reed. "The Restraint of Excessive Apparel: England 1337–1604." *Dress* 15 (1989), 27–37.

Great Britain. *Statutes of the Realm.* London: 1890. Reprint, London: Dawson, 1963.

Vincent, John Martin. *Costume and Conduct in the Laws of Basel, Bern, and Zurich 1370–1800.* New York: Greenwood, 1969. Original edition published in 1935.

Internet Resource

Geocities.com. "Platform Shoes of the 1600s." Available from <http://www.geocities.com/FashionAvenue/1495/1600. html>.

Reed Benhamou

SUNGLASSES Sunglasses, spectacles with tinted lenses, were originally a purely practical safety device, designed to protect the eyes from excess sun and glare. In the twentieth century, however, they became an important fashion accessory, whose use and meaning continues to evolve.

Sun Glasses to Sunglasses

Tinted spectacles were made in Europe as early as the seventeenth century, but were used because they were thought to be beneficial to the eyes, or to conceal the eyes of the blind, and were not "sunglasses" in the modern sense. The need for eyewear to protect the eyes against sun and glare first became apparent in the mid-nineteenth century, when early polar explorers and high-altitude mountaineers experienced snow-blindness, and spectacles and goggles with tinted lenses were developed, some with side shields of glass or leather. (The Inuit used slit snow-goggles of wood or bone, which covered the eyes.) As increasing numbers of Europeans and Americans were exposed to the strong sun of tropical and equatorial colonies and territories, dark glasses began to be worn there as well.

Sunglasses became more widely available in the 1880s, when bathing and holidays by the sea became popular with the general public; by 1900, inexpensive tinted glasses (now known as "sun glasses") were sold by seaside vendors, and worn by English tourists in Egypt to reduce the desert glare. The invention of the automobile, and the popularity of motoring as a fashionable leisure activity, also brought protective eyewear into common use, and tinted motoring goggles were available by the 1910s.

Hollywood Style and Glare Control

In the 1920s, sunglasses were occasionally worn for active outdoor sports such as golf and tennis, and for the newly fashionable activity of sunbathing. They did not truly enter the fashion sphere, however, until the early 1930s, when Hollywood stars such as Bette Davis and Marlene Dietrich were photographed wearing them between takes on the set, attending tennis matches and horse races, or trying to appear in public incognito. Sunglasses began to symbolize the glamour of life in Hollywood, but there was little variation in style at first; most 1930s sunglasses, for both men and women, had round, flat glass lenses, with narrow celluloid frames. The only fashion decision lay in choosing the color of the frames; these were usually translucent and in colors close to tortoiseshell, but opaque white frames were also considered chic.

Toward the end of the decade, the demand for sunglasses, and the variety of available styles, increased dramatically; in 1938 the number of pairs sold went almost overnight from the tens of thousands into the millions, and manufacturers rushed to come up with new colors and styles. Sunglasses began to be shown with street clothes, in addition to ski and beach wear, and *Vogue* suggested styles, such as the white pair featured on the cover of the 1 August 1939 issue, with "wide rims and earpieces, giving the approved 'goggly' appearance" (p. 81). Sunglasses, being less expensive than prescription eyewear, and associated with vacation and leisure activities, were quickly embraced as a "fun" fashion accessory, and even bizarre novelty styles soon found a market.

The quality of sunglasses also improved in the 1930s, and both of the major U.S. optical companies introduced lines of sunglasses with optical glass lenses (ground and polished like prescription eyeglasses). Taking advantage of the public appeal of daring aviators such as Charles Lindbergh and Amelia Earhart, Bausch & Lomb introduced the metal-framed "Anti-Glare Aviator" sunglasses in 1936, and the following year gave them the more appealing brand name "Ray-Ban" (to emphasize protection from harmful infra-red and ultraviolet rays). American Optical teamed up with the Polaroid Corporation in 1938 to produce the first polarized sunglasses, with glass lenses incorporating a polarizing film. World War II brought new popularity to military-style sunglasses, especially Ray-Ban Aviators (worn by Navy pilots and General Douglas MacArthur), and lent them the air of toughness and competence that has kept the style popular ever since.

To See and Be Seen

After the war, the craze for sunglasses quickly resumed in full force. Advertisements began to emphasize smart styling over eye protection, and distinct men's and women's styles were developed. Sunglasses could now be purchased in drug, variety, and department stores, at prices from 25 cents to 25 dollars. With growing competition, established manufacturers increased their advertising and diversified; American Optical launched the "Cool-Ray" trademark, and in 1948 introduced inexpensive Polaroid plastic lenses. It became fashionable to have multiple pairs for sport, everyday, and even evening wear, and in colors to match particular outfits. Eyeglass wearers could have sunglasses made with their prescription, or choose from a variety of clip-on styles.

In the 1950s, to boost sales, sunglass manufacturers began coming out with new models every year, following the lead of the automobile industry. As with eyeglasses, the harlequin, or "cat-eye," shape was the dominant style for women, but sunglasses took the style to much more fanciful extremes. Sunglasses were made with carved, laminated frames shaped like flames, flowers, and butterflies, studded with rhinestones, imitating unlikely materials like bamboo, or trimmed with false "eyelashes" of raffia. Even relatively conservative frames were produced in bold and unusual shapes, colors, and patterns, and were given model names such as "Torrid," "Vivacious," and "Peekini." For men, new styles with clean lines and heavy plastic frames were popular, the most famous being the Ray-Ban "Wayfarer," introduced in 1952.

Whatever the frame style, sunglasses were also worn because of the air of mystery they imparted to the wearer. One could still hope to be mistaken for a celebrity such as Grace Kelly or Rita Hayworth, but sunglasses also offered, as a 1948 ad for the first mirrored sunglasses put it, "the wonderful fun of looking out at a world that can't see you" (Saks 34th St. advertisement for "Mirro-Lens" sunglasses, *New York Times*, 28 March 1948, p. 30). Dark "shades" contributed considerably to the "cool" of bebop jazz musicians and beatniks, who wore them even in dark nightclubs. Once the fad for wearing sunglasses at night caught on, however, it became harder to tell the "hip" from the "square"; as one observer told the *New York Times* in 1964, "If you're really 'in' you wouldn't be caught dead wearing them indoors or at night because you'd look like someone who is 'out' but is trying to look 'in'" (Warren, p. 66).

By the early 1960s, sunglasses were more popular than ever, with an estimated 50 million pairs per year sold in the United States by 1963. They were also available in more styles than ever before; Ray-Ban advertised "the see and be-seen sunglasses, [in] all kinds of designs—bold, shy, classic, crazy, round, oval, square, oriental" (Evans, p. 17). President Kennedy often appeared in public wearing sunglasses, and Jacqueline Kennedy started a fad for wraparound sunglasses when she began wearing them in 1962. Similar sleek, futuristic styles from Europe inspired Polaroid to launch the French-sounding C'Bon brand,

Women model the latest fashions in sunglasses in California, 1941. Sunglasses first became popular as a fashion accessory in the 1930s. By the 1940s they were beginning to be offered in a variety of styles, some of them quite fanciful, such as the sunflower-shaped frames at the bottom right. © BETTMANN/CORBIS. REPRODUCED BY PERMISSION.

featuring "the St. Tropez look." Sunglass advertising was also taken to new and imaginative heights; the famous "Who's that behind those Foster Grants?" campaign of the mid-1960s, in which celebrities such as Vanessa Redgrave and Peter Sellers were shown transformed into a series of exotic characters by Foster Grant sunglasses, were highly successful in promoting the power of sunglasses to "subtly alter the personality," (Foster Grant advertisement, 1964, available from www.fostergrant.com) and release the wearer's inner tycoon or femme fatale.

In 1965, André Courrèges's sunglasses with solid white lenses and viewing slits were the first designer sunglasses to receive wide attention. They soon inspired other space-age designs such as Sea-and-Ski's "Boy-watcher," a seamless slit goggle that could also be worn as a headband, and a variety of alien-looking "bug-eye" styles, with frames in day-glo colors or shiny chrome. So-called "granny glasses" were also popular, as were large round wire-rims with lenses in pale psychedelic tints. Enormous round dark glasses, such as those designed by Emilio Pucci, were another style favored by celebrities late in the decade.

In the 1970s, the trend toward oversized designer frames continued. In keeping with the fashionable "natural" look, lenses became paler, with gradient tints in the same rosy shades fashionable for eye makeup. The eyes were now visible, and in the April 1977 issue of *Vogue* sunglasses were declared "the new cosmetic" (p. 146). As the decade progressed, expensive sunglasses by designers such as Pierre Cardin and Givenchy became sought-after status symbols, and were frequently worn on top of the head like a headband when not in use. Sporty mirrored styles were also popular, especially for men.

New Optical Identities

In the early 1980s, the trend to harder-edged styles in black and bright colors coincided with the revival of Ray-Ban's Wayfarer style, which was given a high profile by the Blues Brothers, the 1983 film *Risky Business*, and the TV series *Miami Vice*. Heavy black sunglasses with conspicuous designer logos harmonized with the era's penchant for "power dressing," and similar flashy styles were reproduced for every price range. Oddly shaped, futuristic "new wave" styles were another trend, and the mirrored aviator style was revived once again by the 1986 film *Top Gun*. High-tech "performance" styles designed specifically for outdoor sports, by makers such as Vuarnet and Revo, first became popular in the 1980s, and started a craze for iridescent mirrored lenses.

In the late 1980s and 1990s, in sunglasses as in eyeglasses, minimalism, industrial design, and revivals of earlier styles were the dominant themes. Designer logos fell out of favor early in the decade, and pared-down fashion and hairstyles required clean-lined, sleek frames with meticulous detailing. New sports styles by Oakley, so close-fitting that they seemed to merge with the face, were popularized by athletes such as Michael Jordan and Olympic speed-skater Bonnie Blair. These high-tech glasses, using novel materials such as magnesium alloy and gold iridium, were highly influential, and began to blur the line between sports and fashion eyewear.

At the turn of the century, sunglasses are more important than ever as an individual fashion statement, but there is no dominant style, unless it is "freedom of choice." After a series of "retro" revivals, and trends started by musical celebrities, avant-garde designers, athletes such as Lance Armstrong, the NASCAR circuit, and films such as *The Matrix*, the sunglass market has fractured into many specialized niches. An unprecedented variety of designer collections is available to choose from in the early 2000s, and larger makers such as Ray-Ban feature several smaller "themed" collections, each with its own distinct aesthetic. Over the course of the twentieth century, sunglasses have become an essential part of the fashion and image-making vocabulary, and they seem likely to continue to fill this role in the future.

See also **Eyeglasses.**

BIBLIOGRAPHY

Baker, Russell. "Observer—New Upward Movement in Clothing." *New York Times* (16 June 1964): 38.

Evans, Mike, ed. *Sunglasses.* New York: Universe, 1996. Brief, popular introduction.

Warren, Virginia Lee. "Dark Glasses After Dark: For the Eyes or Ego?" *New York Times* (10 Dec. 1964): 66.

Internet Resources

Foster Grant. "Foster Grant History." Available from <http://www.fostergrant.com/history.html>.

Ray-Ban. "Ray-Ban History." Available from <http://www.rayban.com>.

Whitman, Anne. "Retro-Specs." *Eyecare Business.* December 1999. Available from <http://www.eyecarebiz.com>.

Susan Ward

SUPERMODELS "Supermodel" ranks with "genius" and "original" as one of the most-abused terms in the fashion lexicon. Indeed, it has been so overused that by the late 1990s, when the Supermodel phenomenon (personified by larger-than-life mannequins such as Cindy Crawford, Claudia Schiffer, Naomi Campbell, and Christy Turlington) had long-since peaked and passed, the word had lost almost all meaning, becoming a generic gossip-column descriptive promiscuously pinned on almost any fashion model with, or in some cases, merely wanting, a public profile.

Though many claimed to have coined the term, notably the 1970s model Janice Dickinson, the first recorded use of the word was in a 1948 book, *So You Want to Be a Model!* by a small-time model agent named Clyde Matthew Dessner. It came into more general usage in 1981, when *New York* magazine published "The Spoiled Supermodels," in which Anthony Haden-Guest, the incisive British journalist, chronicled the myriad misbehaviors of highly paid models and photographers in the cocaine-clouded world of post-Studio-54 New York City.

In pure terms, there had been supermodels long before that—at least, if supermodels are defined, as they properly should be, as mannequins whose renown and activities stretch beyond the bubble-world of fashion.

Supermodels don't just look the part—they have to live it. The earliest one was probably Anita Colby, who began her career in the 1930s as a model with the Conover Agency in New York, but was soon lured to Hollywood where, in 1944, she served as ringleader of a gang of models who co-starred with Rita Hayworth in the big-budget film, *Cover Girl*. Colby's success in publicizing the film—she arranged an average three magazine cover stories per cover girl—won her a job as image consultant for the great producer, David O. Selznick, an appearance on the cover of *Time* magazine, a recurring spot on the *Today Show* (where a young Barbara Walters

Designer Gianni Versace and supermodels. Fashion designer Gianni Versace stands amidst models (*From left:* Unknown, Unknown, Shalom Harlow, Linda Evangelista, Kate Moss, Naomi Campbell, Amber Valletta) for his autumn-winter 1996–1997 haute-couture collection. © Photo B.D.V./Corbis. Reproduced by permission.

wrote her scripts), and marriage proposals from Clark Gable and James Stewart.

The 1940s and 1950s were dominated by the supermodel sisters Dorian Leigh and Suzy Parker. Leigh, the older sister, lived large; she had affairs with Harry Belafonte, Irving Penn, and the Marquis de Portago, and a two-day marriage to drummer Buddy Rich; she founded two modeling agencies, and gave Martha Stewart her first job when she owned a catering business. Sister Suzy Parker, best known as photographer Richard Avedon's muse, was also a gossip column staple and a Hollywood star before she settled into domesticity as the wife of actor Bradford Dillman.

The next generation of supermodels was led by Britons Jean Shrimpton and Twiggy. Shrimpton had the good fortune to hook up with David Bailey, the best of a batch of trendsetting British photographers known as the Terrible Trio, just as the 1960s were getting started. She was a pouty-lipped, saucer-eyed, eighteen-year-old modeling school graduate; he was a twenty-three-year-old East End rake-in-the-making. Together, they kicked off the Youthquake before he went on to marry actress Catherine Deneuve, and she to an affair with actor Terence Stamp and an appearance on the cover of *Newsweek*.

A year later, The Shrimp was replaced by a Twig, or rather Leslie Hornby, a.k.a Twiggy, who catapulted to worldwide fame (and another *Newsweek* cover) with the help of a hairdresser at Vidal Sassoon who called himself Justin de Villeneuve. Twiggy was the first model to gain a profile outside fashion before making the jump into film. But she was also a comet—by 1968, she'd burned out. In 1971, she made a comeback as an actress, but despite some success, never again saw super-stardom. "I used to be a thing," she said in 1993. "I am a person now" (Gross, p. 183).

By then, of course, many other women had donned the rainments of the supermodel, only to be disrobed by a public eager for the next new…thing. Thanks to a lift from *Sports Illustrated*'s swimsuit issue, Cheryl Tiegs revived the poster girl, and the supermodel phenomenon, when she crossed over from fashion into the worlds of the pinup and then the eponymous product marketer—a trajectory many wanna-be "supes" would follow thereafter. Hers wasn't the only path to stardom. Janice Dickinson made it by doffing her clothes at every opportunity, Iman by hooking up with the socialite photographer Peter Beard, who billed her as fresh out of the African bush, even though she was the educated daughter of a diplomat.

Supermodels. Naomi Campbell, Elle MacPherson, and Claudia Schiffer (left to right) pose for a picture at the opening of New York's Fashion Café in 1995. These women, and a few other top models, are known as supermodels on account of their celebrity status. © MITCHELL GERBER/CORBIS. REPRODUCED BY PERMISSION.

marchelier, Peter Lindberg, and Steven Meisel, and the Parisian model agent Gerald Marie. All of their behind-the-scenes machinations helped create the supermodel moment.

Each, in his own way, had seen a window of opportunity open in 1987, when fashion's excesses of the preceding ten years, followed hard by a stock-market crash on Wall Street, and a worldwide recession, put an end to the designer decade that had been launched along with Calvin Klein jeans back in the pre-super 1970s. When the pouf dress—symbol of those heady days—went pop, the air went out of fashion and designers lost their way, just at the moment when the mass market seemed to have discovered them. The supermodels were used as a placeholder, a distraction, a way to keep the attention of the audience focused on fashion, while behind the scenes, the designers scurried around looking for a new message better suited to their times and their greatly expanded audience. Only problem was the supes soon became the tail that wagged the dog of fashion.

But truth be told, they couldn't sustain their "suzerainity." By 1995, the public had tired of the supes and were ready for something, anything, else. The fashion business was tired of them, too. They were too demanding, too expensive (Evangelista had famously remarked that she wouldn't get out of bed for less than $10,000; by 1995, that price had risen to $25,000), too overexposed. The shelf life of models is generally seven years. The supermodels were pert nose up against their use-by date. "I won't use her," as designer Todd Oldham said of Campbell, then the worst behaved of the lot (Gross, p. 438).

In 1996, just in time, a new model movement came along. The small, unassuming girls who were newly in favor were called waifs, and they dressed in a style with the un-appealing name, grunge. Unfortunately, although it did take to Kate Moss, the last of the era's supermodels, the public didn't go along with the rest of the trend, and soon enough a new crop of larger-than-life models appeared. But fashion had been downsized—and they were too. Amber Valletta and Shalom Harlow made a run for the top but fell short. In their wake came other girls (for that's what the business calls them, even though they are its representation of womanhood), but few supes. Had you asked a boy tossing a football in Indiana to name the supermodels of 2003, he would probably say Gisele Bundchen and Heidi Klum (both stars of the ad campaigns run by Victoria's Secret, which replaced *Sports Illustrated*'s bathing suit issue as the source of all fashion knowledge for American men)…and then he would pause, searching for more names but not finding them.

Which means that as surely as long hems follow short ones, the time is probably nigh for the return of the supermodel.

See also **Fashion Models; Grunge; Twiggy.**

Christie Brinkley parlayed her moment into several decades, and in the early 2000s is a star-billed political activist. Patti Hansen and Jerry Hall married Rolling Stones and became celebrities through sexual association. But that path to staying power didn't always lead to the same destination. After Elaine Irwin married rocker John Mellencamp, she fell from view, apparently content to be a wife and mother.

Irwin was one of ten supermodels photographed for *Harper's Bazaar* by Patrick Demarchelier in 1992, the peak of Supermodeldom. With her in the picture were Christy Turlington, Cindy Crawford, Naomi Campbell, Linda Evangelista, Yasmeen Ghauri, Karen Mulder, Claudia Schiffer, Niki Taylor, and Tatjana Patitz. Along with Helena Christensen, Stephanie Seymour, and later, Kate Moss, this baker's dozen formed the core of the real Supermodel Corps, aided and abetted by image-conscious designers such as Karl Lagerfeld, Calvin Klein, and Gianni Versace, photographers such as Patrick De-

BIBLIOGRAPHY

Conover, Carole. *Cover Girls: The Story of Harry Conover.* Englewood Cliffs, N.J.: Prentice-Hall, 1978.

Gross, Michael. *Model: The Ugly Business of Beautiful Women.* New York: William Morrow, 1995.

Leigh, Dorian, with Laura Hobe. *The Girl Who Had Everything: The Story of "The Fire and Ice Girl."* Garden City, N.Y.: Doubleday, 1980.

Moncur, Susan. *They Still Shoot Models My Age.* London: Serpent's Tail, 1991.

Sims, Naomi. *How To Be A Top Model.* New York: Doubleday, 1989.

Michael Gross

This is the famous Schiaparelli sweater

Schiaparelli sweater. The sweater is a versatile garment that has been adapted for a wide variety of fashions. Elsa Schiaparelli's "bow-knot" sweater was a hit in 1920s America and stands as one of her most famous designs. FROM "SHOCKING LIFE" BY ELSA SCHIAPARELLI, COPYRIGHT 1954 BY ELSA SCHIAPARELLI. USED BY PERMISSION OF DUTTON, A DIVISION OF PENGUIN GROUP (USA) INC.

SWEATER The knitted sweater is a staple garment of everyday clothing, being functional, versatile, and fashionable. The hand-knitted "shirts" and "waistcoats," worn as underclothing by both rich and poor from the seventeenth century, can be linked to the "gansey" or "jersey" worn by fishermen and sailors of the British Isles and Scandinavia from the mid-nineteenth century. With the emergence of machine production, the functional, fitted woolen sweater was adopted for sailors' uniforms in 1881, and continues as standard issue for navy and army personnel into the early 2000s.

By the end of the nineteenth century, fashionable clothing had become more relaxed as outdoor and leisure pursuits grew in popularity, cumbersome multiple layers reduced, and knitted underwear transformed into outerwear. Fashionable young men increasingly took up sports activities, and the masculine "sweater" (a close-fitting, knitted undergarment for absorbing sweat generated by exercise) was soon adopted by women.

The growing emancipation of women saw their participation in sports such as golf, tennis, and cycling, and, together with the bifurcated "bloomer," the fitted sweater formed an outfit which gave unprecedented freedom of movement. The publication of instruction booklets for knitting designs fostered the rapid spread of new sweater fashions.

The evolving forms of the sweater have become symbolic of their time. During the 1920s and 1930s, key events influenced the sweater in fashionable dress: Coco Chanel's use of knitted jersey fabric (inspired by men's sweaters) for relaxed but sophisticated style; the Fair Isle patterned pullover worn by the Prince of Wales; Elsa Schiaparelli's famous trompe l'oeil hand-knitted sweaters; and the jazz age of F. Scott Fitzgerald and *The Great Gatsby.* The jumper-knitting craze that followed World War I's "knitting for victory" inspired several popular songs. Long lean "jazz jumpers" (both homemade and store bought) helped to define the softer, boyish silhouette of the "flapper" era.

The intricate tailored hand knits of wartime thrift; the glamorous styles and provocative image of the Hollywood "sweater girls" of the 1940s; golfing argyle-patterned sweaters, and the twin set of classic sophistication, (produced, for example, by Pringle of Scotland), have all become standards. The black polo-neck sweater of the avant-garde and the beatnik's "sloppy Joe" mohair sweater of the 1950s; the growth of Italian style and casual wear in the 1960s, and the ravaged punk sweater of the 1970s, have also become iconic.

Pioneered by British designers such as Patricia Roberts, Artwork, and Joseph, the craft revival of the 1970s and 1980s transformed the hand-knitted sweater with multiple colors, pictorial or graphic patterning, and intricate stitchery. "Designer knitting" strongly influenced the development of technology for more complex mass-produced sweaters. In Europe, Missoni and Kenzo applied new color, texture, and proportion to high-fashion sweater dressing, exploiting jacquard technology to the fullest. Krizia created a popular range of animal-patterned sweaters that became a signature in each successive collection. Sonia Rykiel, Vivienne Westwood, and later Clements Ribeiro recolored traditional sweaters in stripes and argyle pattern variations. By the mid 1990s, the knitwear designs of Missoni and Rykiel were again popular as revival fashion reinterpreted earlier periods. At the more commercial end of the fashion spectrum, Benetton focused on color and universal appeal for its low-priced knitwear, which, through global branding and retailing, made basic knitwear accessible, fashionable, and fun. In the twenty-first century, a wide range of machine-made sweaters regularly feature in high-fashion collections of such as Prada, Armani, and Donna Karan. Oversized, dramatic, and elaborate hand-knitted sweaters are a focus of Dior, Gaultier, and Alexander McQueen couture collections. As knitting technology advances, the sweater remains integral to fashion and a basic garment capable of infinite variation.

See also **Casual Dress; Knitting.**

BIBLIOGRAPHY

Black, Sandy. *Knitwear in Fashion.* London: Thames and Hudson, Inc., 2002. A comprehensive and well-illustrated overview of design developments in contemporary fashion knitwear from the 1970s to 2002. Also included: knitting in accessories, interiors, artworks, and performance. Reference section includes technology of knitting and designer biographies.

Macdonald, Anne L. *No Idle Hands. The Social History of American Knitting.* New York: Ballantine Books, 1988. A detailed social history reflecting the role of women in American history from colonial times to the 1980s. The relationship of women in society is expressed through the craft of knitting and traced through changing times and fashions.

Rutt, Richard. *A History of Hand Knitting.* London: B. T. Batsford, Ltd., 1987; Loveland, Colo.: Interweave Press, 2003. An excellent guide to the history and development of hand knitting as a domestic craft, from the sixteenth century. It begins with definitions and techniques, with a unique chronology of the publication of knitting patterns. British knitting is covered comprehensively, with American and Eastern traditions included.

Wright, Mary. *Cornish Guernseys and Knit-Frocks.* London: Ethnographica, 1979. A well-researched account of traditional work wear in Cornwall with a collection of knitting patterns.

Sandy Black

SWEATSHIRT According to Merriam-Webster's dictionary, the word "sweatshirt" materialized in 1925. It denoted a collarless, long-sleeved, oversize pullover made of thick fleecy cotton. The earliest sweatshirts were gray utilitarian gear that athletes wore while training for traditional sports. Sweatshirts not only provided warmth, but as their name revealed, they also possessed the functional ability to induce and absorb sweat during exercise.

The design of the sweatshirt evolved to include the zipper front "hoodie"—first marketed by Champion Athletic wear for football players to use on the sidelines. Sweatshirts with matching pants ("sweat pants") created an ensemble known as the jog suit, track suit, or sweatsuit, and they became widely popular in the 1970s along with the craze for jogging. Contemporary derivatives ranging from short-sleeved or sleeveless sweatshirts to "sweatskirts" and the development of high-tech materials with better insulation and increased comfort offer proof of the sweatshirt's continuous ability to adapt to the needs of the wearer.

Sweatshirt as a Sign

The sweatshirt's potential as a portable advertising tool was discovered in the 1960s when U.S. universities began printing their names on the medium. For students and parents alike, university names on sweats became the preferred casual attire for exhibiting school pride. The sweatshirt, along with the T-shirt, provided a cheap and effective way of disseminating information on a mass scale. The T-shirt slogan fad of the seventies inevitably translated to sweatshirts. Recognizing the relative simplicity of customization and the power of clever graphics combined with catchphrases, sweatshirts became a vehicle for personal expression for both the designer and the person wearing them.

Subcultural Appropriation

The rise of extreme sports in the 1980s, such as surfing and skateboarding, and the simultaneous establishment of hip-hop as a cultural phenomenon, reinjected a whole new level of cool into the sweatshirt. For surfers, the sweatshirt became a practical component of beachwear. The sweatshirt provided the obvious solution to quick warmth upon exiting the ocean, and facilitated drying off by absorbing excess water. As surfing gained a strong following, the sport's popularity was harnessed by various labels, the most successful perhaps being Stüssy and Quicksilver of the 1990s. Favorites of young adults and teens, the brands produced a lucrative globally-marketed clothing line that included, of course, the sweatshirt.

As skateboarders took to the streets translating the vertical movements of surfing to flatland, they too adopted the sweatshirt in part for its functionality—the heavy cotton was an extra layer of cushion between the skin and the concrete pavement. In the early 1980s *Thrasher Magazine* and *Transworld Skateboarding* both began publication and informed skaters of techniques and tricks through short articles and sequences of vivid photographs. The consequence of such a visual resource was the subtext of skate style. Scores of suburban youth, unable to emulate the moves, could now at least imitate the look. This look typically included a T-shirt, baggy cargo shorts/pants, a hooded sweatshirt, and a pair of trainers made for skateboarding. Like their surfing counterparts, skate labels increasingly catered to a wider audience hungry to appropriate the skater look.

Another revolution brewed in the late 1970s, that time on the east coast of the United States. In the South Bronx of New York, hip-hop culture was born out of a rebellion to disco and as an alternative to gang life. Rap, DJing, breakdance, graffiti, and fashion combined to produce an artistic phenomenon that would reach across global boundaries to become a billion-dollar industry.

Early components of hip-hop fashion, otherwise known as "old school," included sweatsuits, Adidas or Puma trainers, Kangol hats, and big, gold jewelry. Colorful sweat ensembles were not only everywhere and cost effective, but they reflected the vibrancy of graffiti murals and proved functional when performing breakdance moves. As groups such as the Sugar Hill Gang, and later Run DMC, began to garner recognition, the old-school look became representative of hip-hop style. The countless hip-hop fashion labels of the early 2000s continue to promote the legacy of the sweatsuit by maintaining it as a central focus in both their men's wear and women's wear lines.

Intersection with Fashion

From humble beginnings as athletic wear, the sweatshirt has achieved mass-market domination, re-propelled by the birth of logomania in the 1980s. Designers wishing to cash in on branding, utilized the sweatshirt in part to do so. From Vivienne Westwood's "Anglomania" sailor sweatshirts to Calvin Klein's ubiquitous "CK" example, sweatshirts with designer logos became the affordable version of designer wear for the masses.

The sweatshirt's commercial success is a direct result of its connotations of comfort, sportiness, and practicality. In the early 1980s, designer Norma Kamali sought to create a collection for the working woman that epitomized those aforementioned ideals. Her answer was the well-received Spring–Summer 1980 "Sweatshirt Collection" in which Kamali designed an entire wardrobe from sweatshirt fabric.

Subsequent designers have also utilized sweats—evidenced by sport's influence on both men's and women's Fall 2003 collections. Dolce & Gabbana literally referenced hip-hop on hooded sweatshirts that read "l'Hip-Hop C'est Chic" while Bernhard Willhelm's much anticipated menswear debut produced skateboarder inspired skull 'n' crossbone hoodies, Harlequin tracksuiting, and U.S. flag print sweats with confetti overprint. Jean Paul Gaultier's women's wear line put a sporty spin on the classic pinstriped suit with a hooded sweatshirt worn underneath the jacket, and Michael Kors's modern take on the sweatsuit included pairing it with a fur vest. The ultimate marriage, however, between fashion and athletic wear is Y-3, the collaborative by-product of Yohji Yamamoto and Adidas. Here, sportswear is reclassified as high fashion through the introduction of luxury detailing to classic athletic staples like the jog suit.

The sweatshirt's ability to transcend its athletic origins by becoming both an influential component of sportswear and an element of various subcultural dress, testifies to its importance in fashion; furthermore, the fashion system's innate ability to recycle pre-existing motifs guarantees that the sweatshirt will evolve for years to come.

See also **Casual Dress; T-Shirt.**

BIBLIOGRAPHY

"Norma Kamali." In *The Fashion Book.* London: Phaidon Press Ltd., 1998.

"Radical Footing." *Crash* no. 25 (Printemps) 2003.

Trebay, Guy. "Taking Hip-Hop Seriously. Seriously." *The New York Times* (20 May 2003): 11B.

Vuckovich, Miki. "Denim Wars." *Transworld Skateboarding Magazine* (3 March 2000).

WWD The Magazine (Fall 2003).

Internet Resource

Bennet, Eric. "Hip-Hop." Available from <http://www.africana.com>.

Jennifer Park

SWEATSHOPS Sweatshops are workplaces run by unscrupulous employers who pay low wages to workers for long hours under unsafe and unhealthy conditions. For example, in a clothing sweatshop in California in the early 2000s, Asian women sewed for ten to twelve hours per day, six or seven days per week, in a dim and unventilated factory loft where the windows were sealed and the emergency doors locked. The workers had no pension or health-care benefits and were paid at a piece rate that fell far below the legal minimum wage. When the company went bankrupt, the owner sold off the inventory, locked out the workers without paying them, moved his machines in the middle of the night to another factory, and reopened under a different name.

The term "sweatshop" is derived from the "sweating system" of production and its use of "sweated labor." At the heart of the sweating system are the contractors. A large company distributes its production to small contractors who profit from the difference between what they charge the company and what they spend on production. The work is low skilled and labor intensive, so the contractors do best when their workers are paid the least. Workers employed under these conditions are said to be doing sweated labor.

Sweatshops are often used in the clothing industry because it is easy to separate higher and lower skilled jobs and contract out the lower skilled ones. Clothing companies can do their own designing, marketing, and cutting, and contract out sewing and finishing work. New contractors can start up easily; all they need is a few sewing machines in a rented apartment or factory loft located in a neighborhood where workers can be recruited.

Sweatshops make the most fashion-oriented clothing—women's and girls'—because production has to be flexible, change quickly, and done in small batches. In less style-sensitive sectors—men's and boys' wear, hosiery, and knit products—there is less change and longer production runs, and clothing can be made competitively in large factories using advanced technology.

Since their earliest days, sweatshops have relied on immigrant labor, usually women, who were desperate for work under any pay and conditions. Sweatshops in New York City, for example, opened in Chinatown, the mostly Jewish Lower East Side, and Hispanic neighborhoods in the boroughs. Sweatshops in Seattle are near neighborhoods of Asian immigrants.

New York City sweatshop. A scene from a sweatshop on New York City's Lower East Side, 1908, as photographed by Lewis Hines. The workers here are probably recent Jewish immigrants. Modern-day American sweatshops continue to exist and continue to rely on recent immigrants willing to work long hours for very low pay. © CORBIS. REPRODUCED BY PERMISSION.

The evolution of sweatshops in London and Paris—two early and major centers of the garment industry—followed the pattern in New York City. First, garment manufacturing was localized in a few districts: the *Sentier* of Paris and the Hackney, Haringey, Islington, the Tower Hamlets, and Westminster boroughs of London. Second, the sweatshops employed mostly immigrants, at first men but then primarily women, who had few job alternatives. The source of immigrant workers changed over time. During the late nineteenth and twentieth century, most workers in the garment sweatshops of Paris were Germans and Belgians, then Polish and Russian Jews and, into the 2000s, Yugoslavs, Turks, Southeast Asians, Chinese and North African Jews. Eastern European Jews initially worked in London sweatshops, but most of these workers were replaced by Cypriots and Bengali immigrants. Also, sweatshop conditions in the two cities were the result of roughly similar forces; in the nineteenth century, production shifted to lower-grade, ready-made clothing that could be made by less skilled workers; skill requirements further declined with the in-

troduction of the sewing machine and the separation of cutting and less skilled sewing work; frequent style changes, particularly in ready-made women's wear, led to production in small lots and lower entry barriers to new entrepreneurs who sought contracts for sewing; and, as contractors competed among themselves, they tried to lower labor costs by reducing workers' pay, increasing hours, and allowing working conditions to deteriorate.

In developing countries, clothing sweatshops tend to be widely dispersed geographically rather than concentrated in a few districts of major cities, and they often operate alongside sweatshops, some of which are very large, that produce toys, shoes (primarily athletic shoes), carpets, and athletic equipment (particularly baseballs and soccer balls), among other goods. Sweatshops of all types tend to have child labor, forced unpaid overtime, and widespread violations of workers' freedom of association (i.e., the right to unionize). The underlying cause of sweatshops in developing nations—whether in China, Southeast Asia, the Caribbean or India and Bangladesh—is the intense cost-cutting done by contractors who compete among themselves for orders from larger contractors, major manufacturers, and retailers.

Clothing was not always produced with the sweating system. Throughout much of the nineteenth century, seamstresses made clothing by working long hours at home for low pay. They sewed precut fabric to make inexpensive clothes. Around the 1880s, clothing work shifted to contract shops that opened in the apartments of the recently arrived immigrants or in small, unsafe factories.

The spread of sweatshops was reversed in the United States in the years following a horrific fire in 1911 that destroyed the Triangle Shirtwaist Company, a women's blouse manufacturer near Washington Square in New York City. The company employed five hundred workers in notoriously poor conditions. One hundred and forty-six workers, mostly young Jewish and Italian women, perished in the fire; many jumped out windows to their deaths because the building's emergency exits were locked. The Triangle fire made the public acutely aware of conditions in the clothing industry and led to pressure for closer regulation. The number of sweatshops gradually declined as unions organized and negotiated improved wages and conditions and as government regulations were stiffened (particularly under the 1938 Fair Labor Standards Act, which imposed a minimum wage and required overtime pay for work of more than forty hours per week).

Unionization and government regulation never completely eliminated clothing sweatshops, and many continued on the edges of the industry; small sweatshops were difficult to locate and could easily close and move to avoid union organizers and government inspectors. In the 1960s, sweatshops began to reappear in large numbers among the growing labor force of immigrants, and by the 1980s sweatshops were again "business as usual." In the 1990s, atrocious conditions at a sweatshop once again shocked the public.

In 1995, police raided a clandestine sweatshop in El Monte, California (outside Los Angeles), where seventy-two illegal Thai immigrants were sewing clothing in near slavery in a locked and gated apartment complex. They sewed for up to seventeen hours per day and earned about sixty cents per hour. When they were not working, they slept ten to a room. The El Monte raid showed an unsuspecting public that sweatshop owners continued to prey on vulnerable immigrants and were ignoring the toughened workplace regulations. Under intense public pressure, the federal government worked with unions, industry representatives, and human rights organizations to attack the sweatshop problem. Large companies pledged to learn more about their contractors and avoid sweatshops. Congress proposed legislation that would make clothing manufacturers responsible for the conditions at their contractors. College students formed coalitions with labor unions and human rights organizations to organize consumer boycotts against clothing made in sweatshops. Despite these efforts, the old sweatshops continued and many new ones were opened.

In the early twenty-first century, about a third of garment manufacturers in the United States operate without licenses, keep no records, pay in cash, and pay no overtime. In New York City, about half of the garment manufacturers could be considered sweatshops because they repeatedly violate pay and workplace regulations. In Los Angeles, the nation's new sweatshop center, around three-quarters of the clothing contractors pay less than the minimum wage and regularly violate health regulations.

The resurgence of sweatshops in the United States is a byproduct of globalization—the lowering of trade barriers throughout the world—and the widespread use of sweatshops to make garments in developing countries. American clothing companies must compete against producers elsewhere that can hire from a nearly endless supply of cheap labor.

In the clothing industry, one sees a classic case of the "race to the bottom" that can come with unrestrained globalization. As trade barriers are reduced, clothing retailers face intensive competitive pressure and, squeezed for profits, they demand cheaper goods from manufacturers. The manufacturers respond by paying less to contractors, and the contractors lower their piece rates and spend less money maintaining working conditions. Quite often, the contractors move abroad because the "race to the bottom" also happens worldwide. Developing countries outbid each other with concessions (for example, wages are set below the legal minimum, child labor and unhealthy work conditions are overlooked) to attract foreign investors.

The fight against sweatshops is never a simple matter; there are mixed motives and unexpected outcomes. For example, unions object to sweatshops because they are genuinely concerned about the welfare of sweated labor, but they also want to protect their own members' jobs from low-wage competition even if this means ending the jobs of the working poor in other countries.

Also, sweatshops can be evaluated from moral and economic perspectives. Morally, it is easy to declare sweatshops unacceptable because they exploit and endanger workers. But from an economic perspective, many now argue that without sweatshops developing countries might not be able to compete with industrialized countries and achieve export growth. Working in a sweatshop may be the only alternative to subsistence farming, casual labor, prostitution, and unemployment. At least most sweatshops in other countries, it is argued, pay their workers above the poverty level and provide jobs for women who are otherwise shut out of manufacturing. And American consumers have greater purchasing power and a higher standard of living because of the availability of inexpensive imports.

The intense low-cost competition spurred by the opening of world markets is creating a resurgence of sweatshops in the United States. The response has been a large and energetic anti-sweatshop movement aimed at greater unionization, better government regulation, and consumer boycotts against goods produced by sweated labor. But despite the historical rise and fall and rise again of sweatshops in the clothing industry, their fundamental cause remains the same. The sweating system continues because contractors can profit by offering low wages and harsh conditions to workers in the United States and abroad who have no alternatives.

See also **Globalization.**

BIBLIOGRAPHY

Piore, Michael. "The Economics of the Sweatshop." In *No Sweat: Fashion, Free Trade, and the Rights of Garment Workers.* Edited by Andrew Ross. New York: Verso, 1997, pp. 135–142. A brief, well-written review of the economic factors behind the operation of sweatshops in the garment industry.

Rath, Jan, ed. *Unraveling the Rag Trade: Immigrant Entrepreneurship in Seven World Cities.* New York: Berg, 2002. A collection of articles about immigrant workers and entrepreneurs in the emerging garment industries of seven major production centers including New York, Paris, and London.

Rosen, Ellen Israel. *Making Sweatshops: The Globalization of the U.S. Apparel Industry.* Berkeley: University of California Press, 2002. A comprehensive study of the impact of globalization on sweatshops in the American garment industry, with detailed analyses of their historical development and present condition.

Stein, Leon, ed. *Out of the Sweatshop: The Struggle for Industrial Democracy.* New York: Quadrangle, 1977. A collection of classic essays, news stories, and workers' firsthand accounts of sweatshops with particularly strong sections on immigrants, early sweatshops, and union organizing and strikes.

Von Drehle, David. *Triangle: The Fire that Changed America.* New York: Atlantic Monthly Press, 2003. A vivid and informative account of the 1911 Triangle fire—the deadliest workplace fire in American history and an early turning point in the evolution of sweatshops and the government regulation of work.

Gary Chaison

SWIMWEAR Clothing for swimming, bathing, and seaside wear has been an important and influential area of fashionable dress since the late nineteenth century. The evolution of swimming and bathing costumes has been closely associated with trends in mainstream fashion and advancements in textile technology, but has also reflected broader societal attitudes about personal hygiene, body exposure, and modesty, and whether or not it was appropriate for women to participate in active sports.

Bathing Costumes

Swimming and bathing were common activities in the ancient world, and the Romans built public baths in even the most remote parts of their empire. After declining during the Middle Ages, bathing was revived in the seventeenth century, when it became popular as a medicinal treatment. At spas such as Bath and Baden, where bathers sought out the warm mineral waters for their therapeutic effects, linen bathing garments—knee-length drawers and waistcoats for men, and long-sleeved linen smocks or chemises for women—were in use by the late seventeenth century. These garments were worn for modesty rather than appearance, and could be hired from the baths by those who did not wish to purchase their own.

In the eighteenth century, medical authorities began to prescribe salt-water bathing, and seaside towns, along with large floating baths in most major cities, began to cater to large numbers of health-conscious visitors. Bathing usually consisted of a quick dip, often in the early morning, and was considered more a duty than a pleasure. Until the mid-nineteenth century, male and female bathers were almost always segregated from each other, either through the provision of separate bathhouses or stretches of beach, or by using the same area at different assigned times. Modesty was also preserved by the use of "bathing machines"—small buildings mounted on wheels, in which the bather would change from street clothes into a bathing costume while a horse and driver pulled the machine into the sea. The steps by which the bather would descend into the water were often covered with an awning to ensure that he or she would not be seen until mostly underwater. Thus protected from the eyes of the opposite sex, men generally bathed nude, or in simple trunks with a drawstring waist; women's bathing gowns were cut much like the chemise (undergarment) of the period, but were often made of stiffer material so as not to cling to the figure, and sometimes incorporated weights in the hem to keep the gown from floating. The only purpose of bathing garments at this time was to keep the bather warm and sufficiently covered up, and little thought was given to their appearance.

In the early nineteenth century, bathing began to be considered a recreational as well as beneficial activity, and seaside holidays grew in popularity. Each locality had its own standards for appropriate attire, and the costumes worn varied widely from place to place. In general, however, as women began to be more active in the water, rather than simply immersing themselves, their bathing dresses became slightly shorter, and were gathered or fitted around the waist. At the same time, ankle-length drawers or pantaloons, similar to the drawers worn as underwear by ladies in the 1840s, began to be worn underneath.

From the mid-century on, mixed bathing became more acceptable, and as stationary beach huts began to replace bathing machines, bathing costumes were more visible, and attention began to be paid to making them

BATHING BEAUTIES

Beautiful aquatic women have been important fantasy figures since ancient times, when sirens, mermaids, and water nymphs led heroes of mythology astray. The modern-day bathing beauty, however, did not appear until the late nineteenth century, when bathing dresses were first seen in public. As these were the most revealing costumes allowed for women at the time, images of pretty bathing girls, both in wholesome advertisements and on naughty postcards, soon proliferated. Around 1914, the comedies of silent film producer Mack Sennett began to feature a bevy of young women in exaggerated and revealing bathing dress, whom he called his Bathing Beauties. Their popularity inspired beach resorts such as Venice Beach, California, and Galveston, Texas, to stage annual bathing girl parades and beauty contests; the Miss America pageant started as one such bathing girl contest, held in Atlantic City, New Jersey in 1920 to encourage late-season tourism. Over the years this and other beauty pageants, with their parades of women in bathing suits and high heels featured in newsreels and television broadcasts, have been instrumental in associating swimwear with feminine beauty in the popular imagination. (This connection was not lost on Catalina Swimwear, a major pageant sponsor, which started the Miss USA and Miss Universe pageants after the 1951 Miss America refused to pose in a swimsuit during her reign.)

The Hollywood bathing beauty came of age in the 1930s, when photographs of stars and starlets posing in fashionable swimwear began appearing in large numbers. These images had an impact on fashions, as women sought to emulate the look of their favorite stars, and achieved iconic status during World War II, when pin-ups of Betty Grable and Rita Hayworth came to symbolize "what we're fighting for" to many American servicemen. Another, more active kind of bathing beauty was showcased in the aquatic ballets of Billy Rose's Aquacades at the 1939–1940 World's Fair, in the water-skiing spectaculars at Cypress Gardens in Florida, and, most memorably, in the lavish MGM films featuring Esther Williams, the first of which was the 1944 *Bathing Beauty*. Miss Williams, a 1939 national swimming champion, was a top box-office draw through the mid-1950s, and her film costumes, together with her ability to look glamorous before, during, and after swimming, did much to inspire the desired poolside look of the era.

Since its debut in 1964, *Sports Illustrated*'s annual swimsuit issue has probably been the most relevant modern incarnation of the bathing beauty tradition, and has come to symbolize its contradictions. Widely credited with popularizing the active, healthy California look in the 1960s, and thus encouraging women to be more athletic, the swimsuit issue has also been criticized for displaying women as sex objects for the enjoyment of a predominantly male audience. Seen as empowering, exploitative, or both, the bathing beauties seen in *Sports Illustrated* continue to influence swimwear fashion, and to act as a kind of barometer for changing cultural attitudes and standards of beauty.

---

more attractive. Bathing styles began to be covered by popular magazines, which both standardized bathing costumes and brought them into the realm of fashion, with new styles introduced each season. Women's costumes began to follow the silhouette of street fashions more closely in this period, but also developed their own fashion vocabulary; they were usually made of wool flannel or serge, in dark colors (which were less revealing of the figure when wet), and enlivened by jaunty details such as sailor collars and braid trim in contrasting colors. Bathing costumes also now required many fashionable accessories. Hats, rubberized and oilcloth caps, and a variety of turban-like head-wraps kept hair neat and protected from salt water. Full-length dark stockings kept the legs modestly covered, and flat-soled bathing shoes, often with ribbon ties crossing up the leg, protected the feet and set off the ankles. As wool bathing dresses became quite heavy when wet, and clung to the figure in a way that was considered unattractive and immodest, bathing capes and mantles were also considered necessary for the walk from the water to the changing room.

Later in the century, bathing dresses (the term "bathing suit" also came into use at this time) became more practical, with both skirt and pantaloons gradually shortened, necklines lowered, and sleeves shortened or even eliminated. In the United States, where it took longer for these styles to catch on, the one-piece (or "princess-style") costume became a popular alternative in the 1890s; this consisted of an attached blouse and knee-length drawers, with a separate knee-length or shorter skirt that could be removed for swimming. Even so, most bathing costumes were essentially variations of street fashions, intended largely for promenading by the sea and wading or frolicking in the surf; many required the wearing of a corset underneath, and were made of materials that would be ruined if they ever got wet. In the early

Models in jersey swimwear. As seen in this 1929 photo, swimwear in the 1920s was styled similarly for men and women. It had only recently become acceptable for women's swimwear to show bare legs. © CONDÉ NAST ARCHIVE/CORBIS. REPRODUCED BY PERMISSION.

twentieth century, the term "bathing dress" came to mean this kind of fashionable, skirted costume, as opposed to the utilitarian "swimming suit." Chemise-style silk bathing dresses with bloomers or tights continued to be worn by some women into the 1920s, but by the 1930s they were obsolete, and the terms "bathing suit" and "swimsuit" had become interchangeable.

Swimming Suits

Until the mid-nineteenth century, swimming was an activity almost entirely limited to men. While men and women were segregated at baths and beaches, men were free to practice swimming unencumbered by clothes. As mixed bathing became more popular, however, they were forced to find a suitable costume, and by the 1850s men generally wore one-piece knit suits very similar to contemporary one-piece underwear (called union suits), but usually with short sleeves and legs cut off at the knees. Later in the century, there was also a two-piece version available, consisting of a short-sleeved or sleeve-

less tunic over knee-length drawers. To avoid any hint of impropriety caused by appearing in garments so similar to underwear, men's bathing suits were usually dark in color, sometimes with contrasting bands at the edges; striped suits were also popular, especially in France. This practical knit costume remained basically unchanged until the 1930s.

Women who wished to swim, however, found it much more difficult to find a suitable costume. Beginning in the 1860s, women were encouraged to take up swimming for exercise, and by the 1870s many women were learning to swim at pools and bathhouses, which had separate times designated for male and female bathers. In these sex-segregated situations, and for swimming competitions and demonstrations, female swimmers adopted simple "princess-style" one-piece suits, knitted garments similar to men's suits, or suits with long tights similar to those worn by circus performers. However, these garments were still not acceptable in mixed company, or for public wear out of the water, until the early twentieth century. The Australian swimmer Annette Kellerman became famous early in the century for her long-distance swimming feats and exhibitions of fancy diving, for which she wore sleeveless, form-fitting one-piece suits of black wool knit, sometimes with full-length stockings attached. She was an outspoken advocate for practical swimwear for women, and when she was arrested for indecent exposure for wearing a one-piece suit to a public beach in Boston in 1907, the resulting trial and publicity helped to change public attitudes on the subject. In 1912, the Olympic Games in Stockholm were the first to include women's swimming events, and by the beginning of World War I, one-piece knit suits had gained wide acceptance. In many places, however, local authorities passed strict bathing suit regulations, and the battle over the alleged indecency of abbreviated suits, particularly when worn without stockings, continued in many places into the 1920s.

The Modern Swimsuit

After World War I, several factors combined to produce a radical change in swimwear. Women had achieved new levels of independence during the war, and fashions began to allow them more freedom of movement. Interest in active sports of all kinds increased during the 1920s, and sportswear achieved new importance in fashion. Swimming also gained in popularity due to an increase in the number of municipal swimming pools, and the publicity given to such celebrities as Gertrude Ederle, who in 1926 became the first woman to swim the English Channel. Form-fitting knitted wool tank suits, almost identical to those worn by men, were promoted as active swimwear for the modern woman, and soon became the dominant style. At the same time, beach resorts on the Riviera or at Palm Beach became an important part of the fashionable calendar, and beach fashions assumed new significance in society wardrobes. Paris couturiers such as Jean Patou, Jeanne Lanvin, and Elsa Schiaparelli used crisply detailed knit suits—both two-piece suits of tunic and trunks and one-piece suits (known as maillots)—as a canvas for geometric designs in bold, contrasting colors. Spending long leisurely days at the beach also required an extensive on-shore wardrobe, including sunsuits and sunbathing dresses, beach coats and capes, bathing shoes and sandals, close-fitting hats for swimming and wide-brimmed hats for shade, colorful beach umbrellas, beach pajamas (very popular in the late 1920s) and, to hold it all, large canvas beach bags.

By the early 1930s, the growing popularity of sun-bathing inspired suits with very low-cut "evening-gown" backs, suits with removable straps for sunning, and suits with large cutouts at the sides and back. The one-piece maillot, with or without a vestigial skirt or skirt front (called a "modesty panel"), was still the most common style, but two-piece suits, consisting of a high-waisted skirt or trunks and a brassiere or halter top, were introduced early in the decade. These sometimes coordinated with matching separates to convert into sundresses or playsuits, which succeeded beach pajamas as the most fashionable form of on-shore beachwear. So-called dress-maker suits were another popular style; these were skirted suits with attached trunks, cut like dresses and usually made of printed or textured woven fabrics (sometimes with an elastic liner).

The Swimwear Industry

In the years following World War I, American manu-facturers of ready-made swimwear, most of them based on the West Coast, played a major role in setting fash-ion trends, and in creating a mass market for fashionable swimwear. The first Jantzen swimming suits, introduced in the late 1910s, were knit in a double-sided rib stitch, which added elasticity and made knitted suits much more practical. The company's innovative advertising cam-paigns in the 1920s, often featuring Olympic champion swimmers such as Johnny Weissmuller, helped to popu-larize swimming as well as Jantzen bathing suits, and by 1930 Jantzen was the largest swimwear manufacturer in the world. Catalina and Cole of California, which became major competitors to Jantzen in the late 1920s, empha-sized appearance and styling in their suits and advertise-ments; Catalina became associated with the Miss America pageant, and Cole with Hollywood glamour. Competi-tion between these manufacturers, joined by B.V.D. in 1929, drove changes in swimwear styles and technology through much of the twentieth century.

When feminine curves returned to fashion around 1930, manufacturers began to find ways of shaping the body within the suit, using darts, seaming, and strategi-cally placed elastic to uplift and emphasize the bust. The most important innovation, however, was Lastex, an elas-tic yarn consisting of an extruded rubber core covered in cotton, rayon, silk, acetate, or wool, which was introduced

Bikini bras in production. Treated fabric, having been stretched over a plastic mold, is about to be baked in order to set its shape and create bikini brassieres. These bras were manufac-tured in 1949, but it was not until the 1960s that bikinis caught on in the United States. © HULTON-DEUTSCH COLLECTION/CORBIS. RE-PRODUCED BY PERMISSION.

in 1931 and soon revolutionized the industry. It could be used in both knitted and woven fabrics, gave improved fit and figure control, and allowed designers to add sup-porting layers, such as brassieres and tummy-control pan-els, without adding bulk to the silhouette. Lastex-based fabrics, some also incorporating new synthetic yarns, were soon available in a variety of textures and surface treat-ments, including stretch satins, velvets, shirred cottons, and novelty knits. All-rubber suits, made of embossed rub-ber sheeting, were introduced in 1932, and were an inex-pensive option throughout the decade, though they were easily torn, and sometimes peeled away from the body in pounding surf. Rubber found more practical application in bathing caps, which now fit close to the head to keep the hair dry, and in bathing shoes, many of which were molded rubber facsimiles of street footwear.

The 1930s were also when swimwear manufacturers first turned to Hollywood for style ideas and promotional tie-ins. Jantzen, Catalina, and B.V.D. began to use Hol-lywood stars in their advertising campaigns, and formed alliances with movie studios and studio designers, lend-ing mass-produced suits an air of Hollywood glamour. Bathing suits worn by stars in films and publicity photos became a major source of swimwear fashion. For exam-ple, the strapless sarong-like costumes worn by Dorothy

Esther Williams poses in a bathing suit in 1945. Esther Williams achieved stardom and box office success with a number of "swimming movies" in the 1940s and 1950s, musicals that featured elaborate aquatic dances and that showcased her swimming talents. © BETTMANN/CORBIS. REPRODUCED BY PERMISSION.

Lamour, first seen in the 1936 film *Jungle Princess*, immediately inspired manufacturers to include sarong suits in their lines, and helped set a fashion for tropical prints in swimwear.

New Styles for Men

While the detailing of men's suits had been somewhat updated by the late 1920s, and their construction and performance had been improved, decency regulations in many places still required men to wear suits thst covered the chest up to the level of the armpits. As sunbathing became more popular, manufacturers tried to work around these regulations, producing suits with side and back cutouts to permit more sun exposure. Pressure to reduce the amount of fabric in suits also came from competitive swimmers, who quickly adopted the silk knit racer-back suits (with low-cut sides and a single back strap to reduce drag) introduced by the Australian company Speedo in 1928. By the early 1930s, public opinion on the decency of the male chest had begun to shift, and American manufacturers developed convertible suits, with tops that could be zipped off where shirtless bathing was allowed. Swimming trunks, although sold with matching shirts in

more conservative markets, began selling well in 1934, and by 1937 had almost completely supplanted the one-piece tank suit. The more abbreviated and close-fitting styles of Lastex with built-in athletic supporters were given outerwear details, such as belts, pockets, and fly fronts, to distinguish them from underwear. Around 1940, the looser boxer-short style, usually boldly patterned, became another popular alternative, with matching short-sleeved sports shirts worn as cover-ups.

Postwar Styles

By the early 1940s, women could choose from a wide variety of styles and fabrics, and were encouraged to have a wardrobe of suits appropriate for different activities and occasions. The bust was increasingly emphasized in both one- and two-piece suits, through strategically placed cutouts, ruffles, and bra sections ruched or tied at the center to form a sweetheart neckline. Dressmaker suits made of woven fabrics were popular, in part because Lastex was in short supply during World War II; these included a new category of dressier suits, meant largely for lounging by the pool, with details borrowed from evening wear and an emphasis on firm figure control. Figure control became even more important after the war, as swimwear adopted the dramatic corseted silhouette made fashionable by Christian Dior's 1947 "New Look" collection. Lastex was once more available, and new synthetic fibers such as nylon were quickly adopted for use in swimwear. Suits began to be constructed like foundation garments, with boning, underwires, interfacing, and padding producing the desired high, pointed breasts, tiny waist, and jiggle-free figure.

Though the first bikini was introduced in 1946, the reaction in America was to move toward more covered-up suits, exemplified by the ladylike designs of Rose Marie Reid. In the 1950s, amid growing prosperity and increasing amounts of leisure time, and as more Americans had access to resort vacations and backyard pools, swimwear became more than ever a vehicle for display and fantasy. Swimwear manufacturers found design inspiration in exotic locales such as Mexico and Polynesia, and tropical print and batik ensembles, worn with printed cotton cover-ups and rustic accessories of straw, wood, and raffia, were popular throughout the decade. Exotic animals, especially felines, were another popular theme, as exemplified by the seductive leopard-spotted suits of Cole of California's "Female Animal" collection. Some glamorous poolside ensembles were made of waterproof taffeta and lamé, cut like strapless evening gowns, and decorated with beading and sequins to evoke ancient Egypt or the Arabian Nights. A wide variety of sunsuits, terry-cloth robes, footwear, bathing caps, and sunglasses, along with waterproof makeup, allowed women to maintain a polished appearance, both in and out of the water.

While most 1950s suits were designed to mold the figure to an artificial ideal, a few American designers, including Claire McCardell, Carolyn Schnurer, and Tina Leser, took a different approach. Beginning in the 1940s, they designed unpretentious swimwear and playsuits, usually of wool jersey or printed cotton, which emphasized practicality and freedom of movement over static display. McCardell's ingeniously draped and wrapped jersey suits were praised by the fashion media, but her body-conscious approach had little impact on mainstream styles until the mid-1950s, when swimwear in a similar spirit by designer Rudi Gernreich began to receive attention. Gernreich's sleek wool knit suits, inspired by dancewear, offered a stylish alternative to structured suits, and embodied the casual spirit of California, the source of many lifestyle trends in the late 1950s.

The 1960s to the Present

By the early 1960s, changing attitudes toward body exposure, together with the growing influence of the youth market, brought a new mood to swimwear. The new ideal of a youthful, tanned, and healthy look, with girls in bikinis and boys in cut-off blue jeans or baggy trunks (known as "jams"), was disseminated by beach party movies and the surf music craze. As the decade progressed, swimwear became briefer and more daring, with tiny bikinis, cutouts, mesh and transparent panels, and Rudi Gernreich's famous topless suit. Designs were drawn from an eclectic variety of sources, including pop art, scuba-diving gear, science fiction, and tribal costumes from around the world. The most important swimwear development, however, was the availability of spandex, a lightweight synthetic polyurethane fiber much stronger and more elastic than rubber, which was introduced for use in foundation garments in 1958. Spandex expanded the range of novelty fabrics available to designers, and that meant suits could now be made to fit like a second skin without heavy linings and supporting layers.

In the 1970s and 1980s, a fit, sculpted, and toned body became the new ideal. Rather than shaping the body, fashionable swimwear and beachwear was now designed to frame and reveal it, and difficult-to-tone areas such as the buttocks and upper thighs became the new erogenous zones. Athletic styles, such as racer-back tank suits and the Speedo briefs worn by Mark Spitz at the 1972 Olympics, were a major influence. One-piece suits returned to fashion, though many of them were essentially complex networks of crossed and wrapped straps joining small areas of fabric, and offered little more coverage than contemporary thongs and string bikinis. Stretch fabrics could be made lighter than ever, and bright, solid colors and metallic finishes were used for sleek maillots with thin spaghetti straps, which with the addition of a wrap skirt could double as disco wear.

Since the 1980s, despite warnings about the dangers of ultraviolet radiation, swimwear and beachwear have remained an important part of most wardrobes. Swimwear has been in what might be called its postmodern phase, with a wide variety of styles and influences operating simultaneously. Retro styles first appeared in the early 1980s, when designers such as Norma Kamali revived the glamorous shirred and skirted styles of the 1940s, and designs recalling every decade of the twentieth century have since appeared. Other recurring themes have been underwear-as-outerwear styles, with visible boning and underwires; minimalism; and streamlined athletic styles, emphasizing high-tech fabrics and finishes. Men have also been able to choose from a range of retro looks and amounts of coverage, from skimpy bikini briefs to baggy knee-length surfer styles; extremely baggy shorts with low-rise waists are a popular look in the early 2000s. Two late-1990s innovations were the tankini, a two-piece suit with the coverage and figure control of a one-piece, and the concept of mix-and-match swim separates, with a variety of bra styles, trunks, and skirted bottoms recalling the versatile playsuits of the 1930s and 1940s, and offering consumers unprecedented freedom of choice.

See also **Bikini; Gernreich, Rudi; Kamali, Norma; McCardell, Claire; Patou, Jean.**

BIBLIOGRAPHY

Cunningham, Patricia. "Swimwear in the Thirties: The B.V.D. Company in a Decade of Innovation." *Dress* 12 (1986): 11–27.

Johns, Maxine James, and Jane Farrell-Beck. "Cut Out the Sleeves: Nineteenth-Century U.S. Women Swimmers and Their Attire." *Dress* 28 (2001): 53–63.

Kidwell, Claudia. *Women's Bathing and Swimming Costume in the United States.* Washington, D.C.: Smithsonian Institution Press, 1968.

Lansdell, Avril. *Seaside Fashions 1860–1939.* Princes Risborough, U.K.: Shire Publications, 1990.

Lenček, Lena, and Gideon Bosker. *Making Waves: Swimsuits and the Undressing of America.* San Francisco: Chronicle Books, 1989.

Martin, Richard, and Harold Koda. *Splash!: A History of Swimwear.* New York: Rizzoli International, 1990.

Probert, Christina. *Swimwear in Vogue.* New York: Abbeville Press, 1981.

Internet Resource

Miss America Organization. "Miss America History." Available from <http://www.missamerica.org/meet/history/default .asp>.

Susan Ward

SY, OUMOU Oumou Sy (1952–) was born in Podor, Senegal. An autodidact, she is an internationally renowned and unique creative force who works at the intersection of art, spectacle, and social space. While her imaginative talent has been honed on costume design and manufacture since the early 1980s, her contribution is marked by her collaborations with other African artists in multiple media, including cinema, theater, music, and dance. This theatrical predilection provides a signature to her designs of costumes, haute couture, jewelry, and accessories, while her recent prêt-à-porter lines rely more on local conventions of dress.

Cultural Imperatives

Sy's work and life raise the arts of cloth, clothing, and body adornment to parity with the fine arts, literature, and cinema, in all of which the Senegalese excel. In the context of Dakar's Francophilic cultural elite, Sy openly and fiercely declares that she chooses not to write or read French. She often reminds listeners that she was raised in a conservative Toucouleur Muslim family in St. Louis, an old trading and colonial city of coastal Senegal. Yet, her articulate spoken voice in French lends an unusual intelligence and authority to her presence and designs. When she puts on her colonial officer's hat and says she is here to conquer, she means it. Her spectacular fashion shows are therefore not only visual and sensory feasts but also a platform for the articulation of an African pride that mines the past and present to produce a future that is in constant dialogue with origins. In effect, she places the cherished, rich Senegambian heritage of artisanship and body adornment into dialogue with the transnational terrain of the contemporary arts. Centuries of transregional trade with Europe and the Middle East and its former status as a French colonial capital have bred a fertile terrain for African and diasporic cultural production in Dakar. Sy is a bold, creative talent and figure for the arts in Dakar who innovates, even more than her creative cohort of African designers, with the materials, forms, and images of both African heritage and modernity. In 1996 Sy and her husband, Michel Mavros, a French filmmaker, founded Metissacana, a Web site, cyber café, and cultural center in downtown Dakar, Senegal. *Metissacana* is a Bambara French creole word meaning "the mixing of races and cultures (*metissage*) has arrived." This center spearheaded an emergent infrastructure for African fashion until its closure in 2002.

Launch of a Career

The complex place of gender in Sy's personal and creative narratives involves self-affirmation, transgression, and play. In her own life, Sy speaks of her mother's loyalty when she used profits from weaving commissions to buy her talented teenage daughter a sewing machine. Refusing her family's choice of suitors, Sy rebelled and married a mixed-race, Roman Catholic, Cape Verdean. The marriage ended in divorce, however, and at that point she moved around the country, finally settling in the old African district of colonial Dakar, the Medina, with her children. With the help of Dakar artists like Kalidou Sy, director of the School of Fine Arts, she launched her career in Dakar. Sy conceals her struggle in her playful figures of womanhood, especially perfume woman, cy-

berwoman, and calabash woman. The costumes worn by these characters present a subversive, mocking femininity in which icons used to polarize Africa and the West as primitive and civilized societies, respectively, are employed as decoration. She said in an interview for France's TV5, "Europeans think Africa is just too much, excess, and that's what calabash woman is about." She also commented in an interview at the Prince Claus Fund award ceremony, "Women of the future will be complete, outfit, accessories, everything" by looking to origins and reconstructing themselves aesthetically.

Since 1989 Sy has produced costumes, sets, hairstyles, and makeup for seventeen films, thirteen staged shows, and for musicians such as Baaba Maal and Youssou N'dour. This has brought her prizes from major festival contests and a much broader audience than fashion shows would allow. In the film *Hyenas* (1992), splendor adorns not royalty but the slaves of an old woman who was cast out from her home village as a young, pregnant girl and comes back to exact revenge. Obsessed with raw power, she uses her slaves to exhibit her beauty, power, and wealth. While Sy's designs for this woman and her entourage create spectacles in some scenes, their neutral tones fuse with the desert scenery to create visual effects of severity.

Design Characteristics

Sy constructs silhouettes of power expressed through volume and density. Refined artisanship provides the foundation of the costume's primary elements of cloth, and careful adornment of both the cloth and the body complete the effect. Inspired by the aristocratic traditions of the Wolof and Toucouleur—the major ethnic groups in Senegal—as well as the Islamic grand boubou, a six meter flowing, embroidered robe (called *mbubb* in Wolof), her garment forms are characterized by simple stitching of long swathes of cloth that are layered and wrapped. Like many other African designers, she innovates cloth traditions through production technology or the use of "African" cloth (such as cotton prints, woven strips, handdyed fabric) in Western styles. She designs tie-dye motifs and weaving for the broadloom, which she uses to weave cloth strips from two- to four-feet long, thereby producing large strips of cloth and reducing the number of seams required to stitch a garment; she also employs expert artisans who often experiment with mixtures of thread or dyes. Sy makes frequent use of embroidery in her costumes and fashion lines. Moreover, in these lines, she gives these traditional garments a Westernized form with belts, sashes, or tailored waistlines that lend contours to the body. African heritage is also the basis for her ornate accessories, jewelry, hairstyles, and makeup.

More than a collection based upon a design concept, Sy's costumes present tableaux of historical epochs. For example, the *Rois et Reines* series (Kings and Queens), dates from the mid-1990s and is inspired by the few historical images available of precolonial Wolof and Toucouleur royal finery. Heavy woven wrappers made of stitched strips of cloth are worn with simple tunic tops of the same cloth. Stoles, heavy amber jewelry, hair jewelry, woolen wigs, and makeup complete the adornment. Dark hues define the natural cloth dyes and the black facial makeup on tattooed lips and lined eyes. Silver and gold decorations on arms and in woolen wigs lend a luxurious feeling to the wearer.

Like the most innovative of designers, Sy's usage of primary materials is distinctive, for she does not limit herself to textiles. Her work is deeply modern, ironic, and humorous and uses an excess of materials from all sources. These media range from the urban garbage of perfume bottles to compact discs, calabashes, baskets, and feathers. The cyberwoman wears a taffeta pastel ball gown with CDs adorning the gown's neck and front surface as if embroidering a boubou. Perfume woman is adorned in a slinky, purple silk, wrap skirt and halter top with small perfume bottles—the cheap, sweet kind from Mecca—sewn on as if they were beadwork. Her face is framed with colored glass wands. Calabash woman wears a tight evening dress with a slit right up her leg and gourds springing from her headdress. These designs have often been photographed in the city streets of Dakar amid garbage, wrecked cars, and minivans. These icons of Africa and the West become signposts in the urban landscape for the tragicomedy of modernity, invoking an historical epoch through a series of garments.

Awards and Legacy

Sy has won prestigious prizes such as the Prince Claus Fund's 1998 prize, given to African fashion and shared with Alphadi of Niger and Adzedou of Ghana; the same fund gave her an honorary mention as an urban hero for her work with Metissacana (2000). She has also garnered honors for her representation of African fashion at the World Expo of Hanover (2000) and has won the prize of the festival of Wurzburg, Germany (2002); a special prize of the city of Rome (2003); and woman of the millennium (Guinea, 2003). Additionally, her costumes have won awards at the Pan-African Film Festival (1993) and those of Milan (1993) and Johannesburg (1995). She was commissioned by the French government to design costumes for the Dakar celebration of the French revolution's bicentennial (1989). She won the Radio France International Net Africa Prize for founding Metissacana, the first cybercafe in West Africa (2001). Her work has also been exhibited at several museums in Germany, and her couture is sold in boutiques in Paris and New York as well as in Dakar.

As an institution builder in culture and the arts, Sy has founded schools of modeling (Macsy) and couture (Leydi) that have produced prizewinning students. Since 1997 she has organized annual international African fashion weeks (SIMOD) that bring together African designers and models for display and networking in a collaborative, noncompetitive environment. In the 1990s she organized the Carnaval of Dakar, a revival of the traditional Fanal parade from her hometown, St. Louis. The event parades models in the costumes and fashions described above through the streets of Dakar's popular neighborhoods. The Metissacana Web site provided links to and information about cultural events and designers as well as an online store for distributing Sy's own clothing and jewelry line. More than this, the site was intended to spearhead national Internet culture in urban and rural Senegal, but it was closed in 2002 due to financial constraints and privatization of national telecommunications systems.

Sy's work of translation across historical epochs, social strata, and cultures make her art, spectacle, and social spaces so appealing to so many. In sum, the broad scope of Sy's creative and institutional interventions in Senegalese culture demonstrates not only her individual genius but also the way that cloth and fashion are embedded in so many aspects of Senegalese society and culture from elite consumption to popular festivity.

See also **Colonialism and Imperialism; Ethnic Dress; Ethnic Style in Fashion; Textiles, African; Tie-Dyeing.**

BIBLIOGRAPHY

There is very little written on Oumou Sy. An Internet search on her name would yield press reports, images, and some interviews from fashion shows in Europe. Two Internet sites with documentation are <www.metissacana.sn> and <www.perso.wanadoo.fr/afro.art.cybergallery/fashion/prince-claus-fond>. On the Senegalese fashion context generally, see the following sources.

FROM *LA VIE A DE LONGUES JAMBES*

La beauté, c'est une chose à l'intérieur. La beauté du corps, ce n'est pas très important. Tous les corps sont beaux. Mais la vraie beauté, la vraie valeur de la beauté, c'est à l'intérieur qu'il faut la chercher. C'est là qu'elle a sa vraie valeur, et c'est là qu'elle est rare. Voilà la réponse à ta question. La beauté à l'intérieur, c'est ce qui devrait être notre but à tous.

[Beauty, it is an interior matter. Bodily beauty is not very important. All bodies are beautiful. But true beauty, the true value of beauty, it's in the interior that one must search. It is there that there is true value and it's there that is rare. That's the answer to your question. Interior beauty should be the goal of us all.]

Oumou Sy and Jean-Michel Bruyere, *La Vie a de Longues Jambes* [Life has long legs], 1995; translated by Hudita Mustafa.

Mustafa, Hudita. "The African Place: Oumou Sy, Dakar, Senegal." *Archis: A Journal of Architecture, City, Visual Culture* 12 (2000): 48–51.

———. "Ruins and Spectacles: Fashion and City Life in Contemporary Senegal." *Nka: A Journal of Contemporary African Art* 15 (2002): 47–53.

Plas, Els van der, and Marlous Willemsen, eds. *The Art of African Fashion.* The Hague, Netherlands: Prince Claus Fund for Culture and Develoment and Africa World Press, 1998. General resource with essays and color images.

Revue Noire 27 (March 1998). Special issue on African fashion that reviews important contemporary African designers, including Sy.

Hudita Mustafa

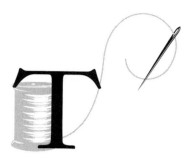

TAILORED SUIT The tailored suit is a garment for women consisting of a jacket and a skirt, most often made of the same fabric. This name for the garment appeared in the fashion press around 1885. It owes its name to the particular manner in which it is made. Produced for women by tailors who specialized in the making of men's garments, it came to prominence at a time when the norm was to differentiate men's and women's clothing by means of very specific techniques, forms, fabrics, colors, and designs. The fashion spread almost everywhere in Europe and the United States thanks to the fame of the English company Redfern, whose style was made popular by famous women, notably Queen Victoria. The Parisian branch of the company, established on the rue de Rivoli at the end of the nineteenth century, contributed to this success.

The emergence of this practical and functional garment within a previously uncomfortable and ostentatious female wardrobe shows the transformation in attitudes by Western society in the late nineteenth century. Women in search of new garments better adapted to ways of life connected to the industrial revolution and its resultant social transformations found the ideal garment in the tailored suit. Since the suit fit the requirements of such new forms of behavior as sport and travel, as well as the progress of hygiene, upper-class women played a role in its adoption by the general population. The affirmation of the suit by the urban middle class—primarily its emancipated women who took up professional careers—was the principal force behind its acceptance.

The tailored suit had a veritable genealogy, however, and was not created ex nihilo. In particular, women's riding costumes became fashionable in aristocratic circles in the late seventeenth century. The costume of English Amazons, made up of a fitted coat and a short skirt, in favor in the late eighteenth century, was already close in style to what would become the tailored suit. Although dresses made up the bulk of women's wardrobes, jackets and skirts, often matched, had been worn since the late sixteenth century by the urban working class.

This fashion spread in Enlightenment circles concerned with egalitarianism in clothing. Many details borrowed from men's clothing—buttons, pockets, colors, fabrics, and sometimes even pants—went along with the jackets and asserted equality between the sexes, suggesting the future of the tailored suit. Throughout the nineteenth century, jackets matched with skirts or pants were worn as a kind of manifesto for the emancipation of women, and the costume thereby acquired a nefarious reputation. A few major female representatives of nonconformism and radicalism, such as George Sand, Flora Tristan, Amelia Bloomer, and Emmeline Pankhurst, gave it an almost political character.

Around 1850, the walking suit appealed to an urban society fascinated by nature and open space. This outfit made up of a jacket and a skirt that did not cover the ankles, in the age of crinolines and corsets, was the last avatar before the emergence and the success of the tailored suit.

The first suits that can truly be given the name were marked by the English influence that predominated in the late nineteenth century. British women, who launched the craze for sports, travel, and tourism, were the first to adopt them. London society, where feminists were influential, adopted the style, which incidentally corresponded to the sobriety admired by countries with a Protestant culture. These first tailored suits had jackets whose cut and details were borrowed from men's clothing, but their forms were adjusted to match the curves of the corset. Skirts, particularly for traveling, were slit or made with wide pleats in order to facilitate walking. Suits were worn most often with accessories influenced by men's clothing, such as vests, shirts with wing collars, and men's hats. From 1890 to 1914, under the influence of sports, their form became more flexible: skirts flared, and less fitted jackets were freed from masculine criteria and standards. The swift adoption of the tailored suit led to its presentation in a variety of forms, with short or long jackets, for summer or winter, and for holidays or urban life. Sober and practical, its use was nonetheless coded. The garment was worn during the day for occasions on which no convention was required (shopping, walking, visiting).

In the early twentieth century, the popularity of the tailored suit tended to make it the uniform of the middle classes. Young women employed in new professions, such as office workers and elementary schoolteachers, adopted it as a professional uniform.

Solid and protective, like a coat, the tailored suit was mass produced, and its price thus made it accessible to a broad clientele. Department stores made it into a sale item. World War I accelerated changes. The tailored suit spread, becoming the war uniform of committed women wishing thereby to show their patriotism. The fashion press galvanized its use, thereby bringing together male and female wardrobes as well as blurring class distinctions.

Haute Couture Becomes Interested

Couturiers expressed mistrust toward the tailored suit. The sober and comfortable appearance of the garment broke with the tradition of the ostentatious elegance of the Parisian houses. Similarly, the Anglo-Saxon influence was treated by the French fashion press with a certain contempt. The unquestionable superiority of London tailors in men's fashion was recognized, but there was firm opposition to any intrusion on their part into the universe of women's clothing. The first couturiers to introduce tailored suits in their collections in the early twentieth century were Jacques Doucet, Jeanne Paquin, and Paul Poiret, all creators who contributed to radical transformations in women's fashion. Jackets had a Directoire cut, a reminiscence of the eccentric elegance of the Incroyables. Coats, single-breasted and fitted, were high-waisted and usually made of fabric with broad stripes. However, when Paul Poiret launched the fashion for pencil skirts around 1911, after having liberated the torso from the corset, he imposed a new constraint, contrasting with the functional use of the suit.

Under the influence of the younger generation, from 1910 to 1925, the tailored suit became one of the favored garments of Parisian couture. Jeanne Lanvin, Gabrielle Chanel, and Jean Patou were the most ardent advocates of the new garment. The style of the Parisian suit set the tone for the rest of the world throughout the twentieth century.

Around 1910, the designs of Jeanne Lanvin blended the sporty informality of new men's fashion with youthful and refined elegance. The jacket was now worn open, revealing a simple blouse embellished with lace inserts, with a soft collar and no tie. Chanel, a beginner at the time, presented outfits made of soft jersey with an unfitted waist, large armholes, and short slit skirts facilitating walking. This very avant-garde version, which she had adopted from sports clothing, came together with the style imposed by the war in 1916. For her first advertisement, she chose three flowing suits with very short and flared skirts to show in *Vogue*.

The Garçonne in the Tailored Suit

The sobriety of dress prescribed by the state of war became the rule in the 1920s. The modern democratic suit was worn night and day. The woolen suit, in masculine style, adopted the new straight and short line. The jersey outfit was extremely popular. Made of knitted wool, silk, or cotton, it was worn with a sweater taken from sporty

and American fashions. The boldest of suits of the time was no doubt the pants suit. After a timid appearance around 1890 for riding bicycles, in the form of culottes or bloomers, in the 1920s it was worn as broad trousers with a navy blue jacket, exaggerating the masculine silhouette that was fashionable in the jazz age. Softer, made of silk or printed cotton, the beach pajama was an addition to the summer wardrobe. On the ski slopes, elegant women displayed, with a degree of insolence, outfits of jackets, tunics, and pants in mountain style, the most fashionable made by Hermès. The use of this androgynous outfit, however, remained confined to emancipated and eccentric circles, typical of California or French Riviera lifestyles. Outfits made of flowing silk, dressier, decorated with geometric or exotic designs in rainbow colors, provided a new and more feminine version of the suit. Similarly, the evening suit, lamé, embroidered, and glittering, indicated an unbounded love of partying after years of privation. Jean Patou was the most representative designer of the period; his style, influenced by American lifestyles, gave his suits, which had a masculine and sporty spirit, a singularity that appealed to *garçonnes* and was gradually more widely imitated. The strict, straight, almost geometric appearance of these suits achieved sophistication through the use of very refined accessories. The images of the American actress Louise Brooks wearing his suits in films and photographs perpetrate the influence of the modernist style of Jean Patou.

The Tailored Suit Advances

By the 1930s, the tailored suit had definitively entered the wardrobe of Western women, on many occasions replacing the dress as the garment of the bourgeoisie. Its sober appearance was reassuring, and it attenuated social, cultural, and even national differences. However, the cost of the garment made it hardly accessible to the working classes. It became the symbol of a degree of success for the middle class, worn by women at work as well as those who stayed at home. Often very subtle details, in terms of the quality of fabric, of cut, or of accessories, revealed the economic and social status of the woman who was wearing it.

Because of the economic crisis of 1929 and its political consequences in Europe, the rise of conservative and reactionary movements radically changed the image and the perception of the tailored suit. It lost its androgynous character for a newfound femininity.

The use of sporty suits, notably those made of jersey in favor in the 1920s, was limited to leisure activities. Beginning in 1931, the woolen suit worn in town emphasized feminine curves: it outlined the breast, emphasized the waist, and flared in widened basques on the hips. Skirts were longer and adopted a narrower line, created by pleats, darts, and complicated cuts. Suits often had a severe and feminine line, exaggerated by the adoption of shoulder pads. This almost martial style experienced its apogee in the success it achieved in the authoritarian and totalitarian regimes of the period. Parisian couturiers, seized by the fad for neo-romanticism, decorated jackets in a manner increasingly distant from the original masculine cut, with lace, guipure, flowered-patterned linings, smocked shirtfronts, and jeweled buttons. The actress Marlene Dietrich stood out in contrast to this vogue, in which glamour and femininity went together, by appearing in films and in her life in men's suits made by the celebrated Austrian tailor Knize. In the 1930s and during the war, women in pants caused discomfort. The evening jacket, in a variant with a long dress, very fashionable in elegant circles, was the only exception to this general tendency. The suits made by Elsa Schiaparelli, influenced by the surrealist movement, with evening jackets richly embroidered with baroque and unexpected motifs, contributed notes of humor, derision, and refinement in a period that was conservative and conventional in taste.

In the postwar period, the style of Dior did not challenge this orientation. The New Look suits, with very feminine lines, were the continuation of a form of attachment to the past. The stiff jacket with broad shoulders, a fitted waist, and oversized basques was worn over wide pleated skirts, recalling the silhouettes of the eighteenth century and the Second Empire.

A Classic of Fashion

From 1955 to 1965, Parisian couturiers made the tailored suit their showpiece. They gave it a second wind by adapting it to the transformations of the consumer society. Balenciaga was the first couturier to dare to break with Dior's New Look. His single-breasted, full, and flowing jackets once again underemphasized the breasts and the waist, recalling the style of the 1920s. Similarly, Chanel suits, in tweed and colored woolens, were a modern version of the first styles that had made the house's name. In the early 1960s, the tailored suit became an absolute must, immortalized by Jacqueline Kennedy. Despite the boldness of mini-suits by Courrèges and the very colorful versions by Cardin, young women, in open rebellion, had little taste for the garment, preferring an explicitly rebellious wardrobe: leather jacket, mess jacket, cardigan, and work jacket, which they mixed and matched, rejecting anything that could in any way evoke a bourgeois uniform. For young women, the tailored suit embodied a fashion that resembled a yoke. Only the pants suit, whose ambiguous and androgynous character corresponded to the prevailing nonconformism, found favor in the eyes of young women who had made the liberation of mores a veritable battle cry. The denim or corduroy version was for those who wore it a symbol of political commitment. Yves Saint Laurent was able to echo this movement of rebellion in his collections: car coats, safari jackets, Mao jackets, and dinner jackets were modern versions of the tailored suit.

The 1980s saw a revival of the fashion for the tailored suit, associating a certain taste for the classic with a representation of the consecration of women in the world of work. Armani's suits were hugely successful among executive women; those of Chanel enjoyed renewed favor as symbols of relaxed luxury and elegance; and suits by Thierry Mugler and Christian Lacroix were baroque and festive. This rebirth was only an apparent one because the tailored suit was gradually losing its raison d'être and being replaced by other garments. The uniform no longer appealed to women at a time when fashion was governed by the cult of youth; the jacket had become a free element, and it alone continued to develop. Pants suits, like those of Jean Paul Gaultier, can still express, in a society where clothing taboos have largely faded, a way for women to emphasize their difference and their particularity.

See also **Chanel, Gabrielle (Coco); Doucet, Jacques; Paquin, Jeanne; Patou, Jean; Tailoring.**

BIBLIOGRAPHY

Breward, Christopher. *Fashion.* Oxford and New York: Oxford University Press, 2003.

Chenoune, Farid. *A History of Men's Fashion.* Translated by Deke Dusinberre. Paris: Flammarion, 1993.

Steele, Valerie. *Fifty Years of Fashion: New Look to Now.* New Haven, Conn.: Yale University Press, 2000.

Waugh, Norah. *The Cut of Women's Clothes 1600–1930.* London: Faber, 1968.

Xavier Chaumette

TAILORING Tailoring is the art of designing, cutting, fitting, and finishing clothes. The word tailor comes from the French *tailler*, to cut, and appears in the English language during the fourteenth century. In Latin, the word for tailor was *sartor*, meaning patcher or mender, hence the English "sartorial," or relating to the tailor, tailoring, or tailored clothing. The term bespoke, or custom, tailoring describes garments made to measure for a specific client. Bespoke tailoring signals that these items are already "spoken for" rather than made on speculation.

As a craft, tailoring dates back to the early Middle Ages, when tailors' guilds were established in major European towns. Tailoring had its beginnings in the trade of linen armorers, who skillfully fitted men with padded linen undergarments to protect their bodies against the chafing of chain mail and later plate armor. Men's clothing at the time consisted of a loosely fitted tunic and hose. In 1100 Henry I confirmed the royal rights and privileges to the Taylors of Oxford. In London, the Guild of Taylors and Linen Armorers were granted arms in 1299. They became a Company in 1466 and were incorporated into the company of Merchant Taylors in 1503. In France, the tailors of Paris (*Tailleurs de Robes*) received a charter in 1293, but there were separate guilds for Linen Armorers and Hose-Makers. In 1588, various guilds for French tailors were united as the powerful *Maitres Tailleurs d'Habits*. Tailoring has traditionally been and remains a hierarchical and male-dominated trade, though some women tailoresses have learned the trade.

Products

In the sixteenth and seventeenth centuries, tailors were responsible for making a variety of outer garments including capes, cloaks, coats, doublets, and breeches. They gave shape to them by using coarse, stiff linen and canvas for interlining, horsehair cloth and even cardboard stiffened with whalebone for structural elements. Imperfect or asymmetrical body shapes could be evened out with wool or cotton padding. Luxury garments were often lined with satins or furs to keep their wearers warm. Tailors were the structural engineers for women's fashions and made whalebone stays or corsets until the nineteenth century. Women largely made relatively unshaped undergarments and shirts for men, women, and children. The nineteenth-century tailor added trousers, fancy waistcoats, and sporting clothing of all sorts to his repertoire. The tailor was particularly adept at working woolen fabrics, which he shaped and sculpted using steam and heavy irons. Menswear had long used wool as a staple fabric. In Britain wool connoted masculinity, sobriety, and patriotism but in the early nineteenth century, it became extremely fashionable, almost completely replacing the silks and velvets used in the previous century. At the same time, men began to wear trousers rather than breeches and by the 1820s, tightly cut trousers or pantaloons could be worn as evening wear. Though they no longer made corsets, women's sidesaddle riding habits and walking suits remained the province of the tailor and were cut and fashioned from the same fabrics as male garments.

Early Tailoring Manuals

Because tailoring was taught by traditional apprenticeships, skills were passed on from master to apprentice without the need for written manuals. The most skilled aspect of the trade was cutting out garments from the bolt of cloth. In G. B. Moroni's painting *The Tailor* (c. 1570), the fashionably dressed artisan prepares to use his shears on a length of cloth marked with tailor's chalk. These markings would probably have been based on a master pattern. The earliest tailors used cloth patterns because paper and parchment were too expensive at this period. Paper patterns became widespread and commercially available in the nineteenth century.

The earliest known tailoring manuals are Spanish. These are Juaan de Alcega's *Libro de Geometric Practica y Traca* of 1589 and La Rocha Burguen's *Geometrica y Traca* of 1618. These books illustrate ways of drawing patterns to use fabric in the most economical manner, but have no information on technique. Later manuals, such as the important *L'Art du Tailleur* by de Garsault (1769) have more detailed instructions as to measurement, cutting, fit, and construction. The typical workshop had a master tailor, who dealt directly with the client and cut out garments. There might be several cutters in a large es-

tablishment and they were at the top of the tailoring hierarchy, for cutting out was the most skilled part of the trade. Under them other journeymen tailors were responsible for a variety of activities, including padding and sewing in interlinings, pockets, and the difficult task of assembling the sleeve and turning the collar, as well as manipulating the heavy shaping iron called a goose. Apprentices were usually responsible for running errands and sweeping up scraps of fabric before being taught basic sewing skills. When sewing machines were introduced, machinists, who might be women, were also added to the workshop floor. The tailors who sewed the garment together sat on a workbench near natural light with legs crossed, hunched over their work. To sit cross-legged in French is still to be *assis en tailleur*, or sitting in the tailor's pose.

The first manual in the English language is the anonymous *The Taylor's Complete Guide*, published in 1796. After this publication, there were many important manuals produced during the nineteenth century, including Compaing and Devere's *Tailor's Guide* (1855) and most importantly, E. B. Giles's *History of the Art of Cutting* (1889) which has been reprinted and provides great insight into the nineteenth-century techniques from a master tailor who knew many of its practitioners personally.

A spirit of competition and enterprise marked the first half of the nineteenth century, when tailors patented a multitude of inventions, manuals, systems of measurement, and fashion journals aimed at the man-about-town and his tailor. Some of the most important of these were the *Tailor and Cutter* and *West-End Gazette*. The endless cycles and revivals of women's fashions seemed illogical and capricious compared to the more rational, linear, and technologically innovative development of men's dress. The finest tailoring combined the principles of science and art to produce clothing that was both engineered and sculptural.

Measurement

Systems of measurement changed radically during the history of tailoring. Tailors have always had the difficult task of creating three-dimensional garments for asymmetrical and highly varied body shapes. Unlike static sculpture, garments also had to allow the wearer to move freely and gracefully during their daily pursuits. Early tailors developed complex systems for measuring the bodies of their clients. However, as most manuals observe, no system could replace the observant eye and hand of the tailor, who noted the more subtle nuances of his client's posture and anatomy and could make allowances for a slight hunch, uneven shoulders, or a protruding stomach. In his tailoring manual of 1769, de Garsault illustrated the strip of paper he used for taking measure. His system involved cutting notches in the strip to measure the breadth of the back and the length of the arm to the elbow. Each client was measured against shifts in his own body's size and shape.

The modern tape measure was introduced in about 1800. In Britain, cloth had been accurately measured in ells (short for elbows), but the body was not quantified in units. In post-revolutionary France the metric system was used to measure the body, whereas British tailors favored inches. The tape measure was soon joined by a compass, ruler, and tracing paper to produce elaborate geometric systems used throughout the nineteenth century. These mathematical patterns could be produced in scaled sizes and were designed around the more abstract idea of a bodily norm or average. In their most elaborate forms these systems used machines like Delas's somatometer or body meter of 1839, which was an adjustable metal cage for measuring the bodies of clients. Entrepreneurs who used them to produce ready-made clothing in standardized sizes gratefully appropriated systems designed to ensure a more accurate fit. Reporting on the inroads made by ready-made tailoring exhibited at the 1867 World's Fair in Paris, Auguste Luchet wrote that the age of the sculptural tailors was over: "There are no more measurements, there are sizes ... Meters and centimeters. One is no longer a *client*, one is a *size eighty*! A hundred vestimentary factories are leading us toward the absolute and indifferent uniform." Though loosely fitting, ready-made clothing for the lower classes had existed since the seventeenth century, the nineteenth century saw the introduction of high-quality, fitted tailored garments sold off the rack.

Shop Displays

The fully equipped tailor's establishment of the nineteenth and twentieth centuries could be sparsely or luxuriously fitted. The basic requirements of the trade included shelving for the display of cloth bales, a counter where swatches could be consulted, a space where the client could be measured, a fitting room with mirrors, a sturdy table for cutting out, and possibly blocks for saddles to fit riding clothes properly. Fashion prints were also hung as decoration or shown to clients as models. The shop might or might not include a space for workshops. More prestigious firms made garments on the premises while "jobbing" tailors sent bundles of pieces to outworkers, often women, who would assemble the garments at home or in sweatshops. At the top end of the scale, establishments like Henry Poole on Savile Row at the turn of the twentieth century combined more functional elements with the thick carpets, mahogany fittings, satin upholstery and gilded mirrors of the palace or exclusive gentlemen's club. In the twentieth century many tailors kept traditional interiors, though some, like Simpsons of Piccadilly and Austin Reed innovated with modern, Art Deco, or Bauhaus styles and included amenities such as barbershops. In the middle of the nineteenth century, the tailor was joined by hosiers, who specialized in high-end accessories and outfitters, whose trade was based on made-to-measure shirts, but who also sold suits, coats, hats, boots, and all manner of accessories. Their shop window displays tended to emphasize orderliness and neatness to appeal to the male customer.

Tailoring in the Twentieth Century

Bond Street, Savile Row, and St James's Street in the fashionable West End of London have been the center for elite, traditional tailoring since the turn of the eighteenth century. However, tailoring spanned the whole class spectrum, from tailors with royal warrants to immigrants working in the warehouses of the East End.

One of the most important shifts in Savile Row tailoring was the transition from a more traditional client base of British gentry and aristocracy to a more international, clientele including American financiers and eventually Hollywood celebrities. Though Savile Row rose to prominence in the late eighteenth century, dressing such figures as the Prince Regent and dandy Beau Brummel, in the twentieth it created the movie wardrobes of Fred Astaire, Cary Grant, and Roger Moore. Though many American stars sought the cachet of Savile Row, there were very talented tailors in the United States. In Harlem, the exaggerated shapes and bright colors of the zoot suit were launched by stylish young black men in the mid-1930s. When the War Production Board tried to curtail this "antipatriotic" tailoring because of wool rationing in 1942, race riots ensued. In Britain, there was a brief revival in elegant Edwardian tailoring after World War II, when so-called Teddy Boys—working-class men who spent large sums on their wardrobes—adopted it. In 1960s London, fashionable men's goods were democratized in the "Peacock Revolution," which saw the center of fashion gravitate toward Carnaby Street and the King's Road—along with Cecil Gee, John Stephen, John Michael, John Pears, Michael Rainey, and Rupert Lycett Green. One of the most important figures in the rejuvenation of menswear was the celebrity tailor Tommy Nutter. He created unique suits for both men and women, including suits for the Beatles, Mick and Bianca Jagger, and Twiggy.

In the 1980s, Italian tailoring began to receive more attention on the international fashion scene. With their "unstructured" suits, designers such as Giorgio Armani catered to a desire for more informal, lighter weight garments for both men and women. At the turn of the millennium, the Italian tailoring firm Brioni dressed the British movie icon James Bond, played by the actor Pierce Brosnan. In Britain, a new generation of designers combine the flawless cut and construction of traditional tailoring with the flair of haute couture. Ozwald Boateng is an Anglo-Ghanian whose work displays a dazzling sense of color and who prefers to describe his work as "bespoke couture." Alexander McQueen, who trained for a short two years on Savile Row, also incorporates tailoring's emphasis on structure and materials into his couture womenswear.

Though it represents a very small part of the contemporary menswear market, custom tailoring still has pride of place in the wardrobe of the sharply dressed man. Whether it applies to computer software or kitchens, the expression "tailor-made" still carries positive connotations of individualized, customized service. In the clothing trade, as long as the suit remains the classic form of formal attire, tailors will elegantly dress their clients. These may include men whose bodies may not fit the norms of the ready-made clothing industry, as well as royalty, businesspeople, or celebrities who turn to the tailor for a classic or innovative suit of clothing made to their precise measure.

See also **Armani, Giorgio; Cutting; Savile Row; Sewing Machine; Suit, Business.**

BIBLIOGRAPHY

Breward, Chris. *The Hidden Consumer: Masculinities, Fashion and City Life 1860–1914.* New York and Manchester, U.K.: Manchester University Press, 1999.

———, ed. *Fashion Theory* 4, no. 4 (December 2000). Special issue focusing on "masculinities."

Chenoune, Farid. *A History of Men's Fashion.* Paris: Flammarion, 1993.

Garsault, M. de. *L'Art du Tailleur* [The art of the tailor]. Paris: Académie Royale des Sciences, 1769.

Giles, E. B. *The History of the Art of Cutting in England.* London: F. T. Prewett, 1887.

Luchet, Auguste. *L'Art Industriel à l'exposition universelle de 1867* [Industrial art at the 1867 World's Fair]. Paris: Librairie Internationale, 1868.

Walker, Richard. *The Savile Row Story.* London: Prion, 1988.

Waugh, Norah. *The Cut of Men's Clothes, 1600–1900.* London: Faber and Faber, 1964.

Alison Matthews David

TANNING OF LEATHER It would not be an exaggeration to call leather the first human industry, since the wearing of animal skins goes back to the beginning of human existence. Before early humans mastered the art of weaving, skins from animals slain for food (with and without the fur) were utilized for garments, footwear, headgear, and protective clothing, as well as a host of practical applications, and were linked to warmth and to humans' very survival.

Before domestication of cattle and pigs, skins of deer and wild animals, as well as wild sheep and goats were dressed. Paleolithic cave paintings depict figures wearing skins and furs, and excavations at these sites have revealed an active leather industry. Flint instruments, including knives, scrapers, and awls used for removing flesh, have been found in addition to wooden poles and beams used for beating and draping hides. Later Neolithic and Bronze Age sites have yielded leather dagger sheaths, scabbards, shields, footwear, and jerkins of a sophistication that indicates that leather manufacture was mastered early in human history.

As humans learned to domesticate cattle, horses, sheep, goats, and pigs, the availability of raw materials for leather production swelled. Uses of leather by ancient peoples included all types of clothing, belts, thongs, footwear, headwear, gloves, ties, bags and vessels, armor, sheaths, packs, seat covers, saddles, animal trappings, tents, and even sails for ships. Excavations of Sumerian peoples at Ur of the Chaldees brought to light extraordinary leather tires used on wooden wagons. In the early 2000s, the Masai women of Africa were clad in cloaks and petticoats of leather, which harkened back to the earliest years.

Traditional Tanning Methods

Prehistoric humans quickly discovered that raw skins removed from the animal needed to be treated before they could be useful. Indeed, leather is a manufactured product that requires many steps. The series of chemical processes by which natural skins are converted to leather is known as tanning. The object of tanning is to render natural skins impervious to putrescence while imbuing them with greater pliability, suppleness, and durability. Early tanning methods employed natural substances, in contrast to modern manufactured chemicals.

However, before tanning can occur, the skins must be clean. Hides are washed of blood and dung and the hair removed. This process is not actually tanning, but a necessary preliminary step done by early peoples in a variety of ways. Some utilized alkaline substances to loosen hair, such as lime found in ash; others utilized urine to accelerate putrefaction and hair loosening; while still others such as the native Inuit peoples employed the enzymes in saliva via the chewing of skins. All cultures have employed stages of stretching and scraping of skins to remove flesh and hair prior to the actual tanning process.

The three historical methods of making leather are vegetable, oil, and mineral tanning. Oil tanning is considered to be the oldest process, probably employed in combination with smoke curing. Neolithic excavations have revealed elk and deerskins dressed with oil and smoked. Traditional oil tannage methods employ fish oils (of which cod oil is the most important) or animal fats worked ("stuffed") into the hides to bring about oxidation, transforming skin into leather. Variations of oil tannage include the milk and butter used by nomads of Central Asia (Kyrgyz) and egg yolk tannage by peoples of northern China. Native Americans of North America are known to have tanned leather with a mixture of brains and oil. Smoke curing in pits has a long tradition in China.

Vegetable tanning, a 4,000-year-old process, was developed widely across the world by ancient peoples utilizing their own local flora. Plants containing tannins (compounds of gallic acid) infused in water were discovered as early as the Paleolithic period to affix to skins forming an impenetrable substance. Egyptians preferred using the mimosa plant for tanning purposes, while peoples of the ancient Mediterranean employed sumach leaves. Oak (and pine) bark, nuts, and galls have been the most important sources for tanning compounds in Europe, practically until the advent of chemical processes in the nineteenth century.

Mineral tanning, until the modern age, meant alum. Ancient peoples mined alum for tanning skins in a process that became known as tawing. Tawed leather produced a supple, distinctive white leather and developed into a specialized guild in medieval Europe. Alum-tanned leather was developed to a particularly high standard in the Near East. The Moors, who conquered Spain in the eighth century, brought with them their expertise in this process; and the precious leather goods they produced, referred to as cordovan or cordwan, were indelibly associated with the city of Cordova, Spain, giving rise to the name of the leather shoemakers in England, known as cordwainers. Combination tanning, utilizing more than one method, was also exploited in making leather.

The importance of leather goods in all aspects of daily life made it a highly desirable trade item. Primitive peoples who needed leather for clothing, weapons, and other applications bartered goods for leather products. Leather became so vital to the flourishing of communities that it progressed into a form of currency. It has been used as money continuously throughout history. The historian Seneca noted that Romans used stamped leather money in 2 C.E.; so did the ancient Chinese early in the second century B.C.E. Even in sixteenth century Russia, leather pieces stamped with Czar Ivan IV's symbol were being used until metal currency took hold during the reign of Peter the Great.

Decorating Leather

While leathers were often left with their simple tanned finish, the urge to color and embellish tanned leather has an equally early history. Coloring leathers was achieved through animal, but predominantly vegetable, dyes in combination with metal salts. Tawed leather accepts dye well and was a skill refined by ancient Phoenicians and Egyptians as indicated by the find of a 4,000-year-old fragment of leather dyed with kermes. Egyptians also employed safflower to stain leather. Indigo, woad, buckthorn, and hollyhocks were at various times utilized to dye leather in combination with mineral mordants. In addition to coloring, leather has also been decorated by peoples around the globe in various ways, including tooling, painting, embossing, pleating, perforating, plaiting, and embroidering to suit their tastes.

Modern Tanning Methods

Interestingly, the tanning of leather was one of the last industries to lift itself out of medieval conditions in the nineteenth century. Before then, methods had endured for centuries. Modernization since the late nineteenth century, however, has been swift and complete, and what used to be a craftsman's art has become increasingly a science handled by technicians. Mechanization has brought significant changes in speed and efficiency. Prior to specialized drum machinery, liming the skins, tanning, and dyeing was manipulated by hand. A wider range of tanning materials has also been introduced. Mineral tanning through chromium salt, which produces a supple, versatile leather, is by far the most widely used method of tanning in the early twenty-first century.

Even more significant are the myriad new methods of dyeing and finishing that have revolutionized the modern leather industry. Since their invention in 1856, aniline (synthetic) dyes have become universally standard in dyeing leather, producing an enormous range of colors and shades. This had a major impact on leather fashions in the twentieth century, bringing about innovative new looks hitherto unknown in natural leathers. Like dyes, finishing methods have revolutionized leather fashion. In the early 2000s, imperfect skins of any type—cow, pig, sheep, and goat—can be made to look identical to any other skin through sophisticated finishing processes such as sanding, plating, embossing, dyeing, and spraying. Pigskin, traditionally tough and used for shoe leather, has become an important and versatile garment leather through the modern finishing treatments, which represents a huge export product for China. Bulk industrial tanning is done less and less in Western Europe and America, having been shifted to India and the Far East, for economic reasons.

Some of the finest leather continues to be tanned by traditional methods, although it represents a tiny fraction of leather produced in the early 2000s. Among the most superior fashion and upholstery leathers are those processed by traditional vegetable tanning, piece-dyed by hand, and rubbed with oils to achieve a rich finish. Much of this luxury leather is produced in France and Italy, although a new industry is emerging in South America aimed at the high-end garment and fashion accessory market.

See also **Leather and Suede.**

BIBLIOGRAPHY

Gansser, A. "The Early History of Tanning." *Ciba Review* 81 (1950): 2938–2960.

Hamilton, William L. "The Private Life of Club Chairs." *New York Times* (22 January 1998): F1.

Issenman, Betty Kobayashi. *Sinews of Survival: The Living Legacy of Inuit Clothing.* Vancouver: UBC Press, 1997.

Kaufman, Leslie, and Craig S. Smith. "Chinese Pigs Feed a Western Fashion Boom." *New York Times* (24 December 2000).

Reed, Richard. *Ancient Skins, Parchments, and Leathers.* London: Seminar Press, 1972.

Waterer, John William. *Leather in Life, Art, and Industry.* London: Faber and Faber, 1946.

Lauren Whitley

TAPA. *See* **Bark Cloth.**

TAPESTRY Since early medieval European times tapestry's major purpose has been well-established as the making of large pictorial wall hangings. This use of a 3000-year-old textile structure has been held as standard, particularly in western society, right through to the twentieth and twenty-first centuries.

Out of central Asia and over many centuries the kilim rug, using the same woven structure, has established a highly respected role as a religious, decorative or a simply functional floor covering, and domestic application abounds in the modern world. One should recognize, too, tapestry as an upholstery fabric for chairs and sofas, not an inconsiderable application in the eighteenth, nineteenth, and into the twentieth century.

However, as recently as the late 1990s, the discovery of woven garments in burial sites in a remote area of central Asia—garments with extensive use of woven tapestry as part of their construction—further identifies what can be argued as tapestry's widest application over world history: tapestry as clothing. These particular garments date from between 200 B.C.E. and 200 C.E. and were unearthed from sites in the remote town of Shanpula, once part of the ancient southern silk route. They are woolen skirts and have graphic pictorial bands as inserts, set horizontally around the entire circumference and range between 2 to 8 inches (5 to 20 cms) high. When considered alongside the use of tapestry in the woven tunics of Coptic Egypt, in the application of diverse items of clothing in pre-Columbian Peru and the knowledge of Chinese Kessi or silken tapestry robes, there is reason to believe that this medium had a wide purpose beyond that of creating wall hangings. This is not in any way to diminish the richest of history of the mural tapestry; rather, it is to recognize that the evidence we have of dry desert-like conditions (Egypt, coastal Peru and the Mongolian region) having preserved such clothing, this application could have been even more widespread in less protective climates.

In Egypt, roughly between 300 to 800 C.E., the Copts, a Christian sect in that country, are known for the application tapestry to clothing. This process was employed particularly in the construction of linen cloth garments where passages of colored wool and undyed linen tapestry were woven as an integral part of the plain all linen cloth in the form of roundels, rectangles and vertical bands. Such garments, simple rectangular sleeved tunics, were clearly in regular use. As wear took place on more vulnerable areas of the plain linen cloth, the tapestry passages, with their highly evolved, sophisticated and complex imagery, would be cut out and patched onto entirely new plain woven tunics. That they were subsequently used as burial garments after frequent daily use suggests that such tunics were of significant value to the wearer. There is also strong argument to suggest that this developed skill of woven tapestry, which was also employed in complex wall hangings in religious and ceremonial architecture in Egypt, has direct links to the emergence of the large mural tapestries in northern and western early medieval Europe. However there is little or no evidence to suggest that tapestry as clothing made this northern journey.

In South America, particularly in the coastal and western Andes region that is now Peru, and during the period between 200 B.C.E. and 1600 C.E., tapestry vestments were clearly widespread in use. These were short, square, sleeveless tunics of a seemingly military, almost heraldic appearance. They were often of an entirely tapestry construction, sometimes of simple contrasting checkers or of an extremely evolved figurative iconography which could be seen as complex pattern to the less experienced viewer. The range of application was for domestic, ceremonial, regal, military or symbolic use, for identifying groups of individuals and as burial clothing. They were used as tunics, mantles, masks, hats, belts, shrouds, shoes, even gloves. And the technical skills employed in the weaving were of the highest order, of great inventiveness and on a level that is hardly understood, let alone practiced in the early twenty-first century.

Given the extensive history here described, it is surprising that in the early twenty-first century and particularly in the world of high fashion, tapestry has virtually no presence. There may have been brief individual experiments that never emerged to sufficient degree except to hint at a potentially rich vein of expression. One example may have been a gentleman's tapestry vest (waistcoat) worn by the designer that was made of complex pattern in black, gray, white and much silver metal. It was quite stunning but most often concealed behind a nondescript button jacket. In London two of the ancient guilds, that of the wax chandlers and the cappers and felter, in the 1960s and 1970s made ceremonial robes for their chief office bearers. Both garments were full length silk with quite extensive tapestry woven insets. The main dignitaries of London's Royal College of Art wore black silken robes. The collar, which is some 16 inches (40 cms) square and hangs down the wearer's back, depicts a stylized phoenix bird in sparkling gold metals, (the college symbol), while the robe's front facings fall all the way to the floor. These are wide, flame-like golden bands, even having extensions to fit the height of different dignitaries.

Perhaps the nearest approach to tapestry as clothing in the western world emerged at the peak of medieval tapestry. Great skill and design was employed in illustrating the nature of the complex vestments of the individuals illustrated in that period. By the use of wool, linen, and silk the cloaks, robes, tunics, hats and hose imitated all fabrics and fashions of the relevant period. This practice was employed to such a degree that, if not otherwise known, the precise dates of the making of these tapestries can be established. The extremely labor intensive nature of this ancient craft—tapestry—makes it very costly cloth for the smallest areas.

See also **Africa, North: History of Dress; America, South: History of Dress; Textiles, Byzantine; Textiles, Chinese.**

BIBLIOGRAPHY

Kybalova, Ludmila. *Coptic Textiles.* London: Paul Hamlyn, 1967.

L. L. Editores. *The Textile Art of Peru.* Lima, Peru: Jiron A Miro Quesada Lima.

Archie Brennan

TARTAN This cloth has powerful connections with often-romanticized notions of Scottish identity and history. Tartan has also been widely used as a fashion textile owing to the appealing and distinctive nature of its various patterns, which are known as *setts*.

Origins and Development

The precise origins of tartan are not known; however, a fragment found in Falkirk, which dates from the third century C.E., suggests that simple woolen checked cloths existed in Scotland at an early period. Complex patterning of the type now associated with tartan did not exist in Scotland until the sixteenth century. Hugh Cheape discusses the origins of the name tartan as follows:

> The word "tartan," probably French (from the word *tiretaine*), was in use early in the sixteenth century.... It seems likely that in some way that we can't now trace, this word came to describe the fabric we now call tartan. (p. 3)

Contrary to contemporary popular belief, tartan patterns have no traceable historical links with specific Scottish families or clans. These associations developed from the early nineteenth century, when they were actively promoted by historians and writers, as well as woolen manufacturers and tailors. Tartan, however, was by 1600

In 1746 the following law was passed:

> [N]o man or boy within . . . Scotland, shall, on any pretext whatever, wear or put on the clothes commonly called Highland clothes (that is to say) the Plaid, Philabeg, or little Kilt, Trowse, Shoulderbelts, or any part whatever of what peculiarly belongs to the Highland Garb; and that no tartan or party-colored plaid or stuff shall be used for Great Coats or upper coats, and if any such person shall presume after the said first day of August, to wear or put on the aforesaid garments or any part of them, every such person so offending . . . shall be liable to be transported to any of His Majesty's plantations beyond the seas, there to remain for the space of seven years. (Disarming Act of 1746)

Sir James MacDonald of Sleat and Sir Alexander MacDonald in tartan pattern. Tartan is a distinctive, patterned cloth that, by 1600, had come to represent Scottish Highland fashion. © THE SCOTTISH NATIONAL PORTRAIT GALLERY. REPRODUCED BY PERMISSION.

established as part of the culture of the Highlands of Scotland. It was widely worn by all levels of that society and it formed a distinctive element of Highland dress, which was largely based around the plaid or *breacan*. Men wore the plaid belted, and women adopted it as a large shawl. Up until the late eighteenth century, the *setts* worn were largely determined by the locality and the tastes of the weaver and purchaser.

Culloden and After

The battle of Culloden in 1745 was the last stand in the campaign by supporters of the Catholic Prince Charles Edward Stuart, to form a challenge to the ruling Hanovarian King, George II. Owing to his family's Scottish origins and the support he had from the largely Catholic Highlanders, the "Young Pretender" promoted Highland dress as the uniform of his Jacobite army. This led to tartan being associated with political rebellion and sedition and to its proscription under the Disarming Act of 1746. Under this act, the wearing of tartan was forbidden, with the penalty of possible transportation for seven years. In addition to the brutal repression that followed Culloden, these measures, which lasted until 1782, began to put an end to the distinctive Highland way of life.

The fact that tartan survived this period of dramatic social and political change was also linked to the actions of the British government. After Culloden, a systematic effort was made to divert Highlanders away from Jacobite adventure and toward the cause of British imperial war. The Highland regiments formed at this period were exempt from the ban on Highland dress, and the British establishment decided to make use of tartan in their uniforms to encourage martial kinship amongst their recruits. The Highland regiments' involvement in British imperialist expansion, and the fact that their role was somewhat over-represented in imagery, helped to spread the popularity of tartan internationally. New military *setts* were designed by tartan manufacturers beginning in 1739 with the original "government tartan," a design of green, blue, and black, usually known as the Black Watch.

From the early nineteenth century tartan began to be internationally recognized as representative of Scottish, rather than merely Highland Scottish, identity. Its popularity was linked to romanticized notions of Scottish history put forward by writers such as the poet James MacPherson in his dubious translations of the work of the Gaelic bard Ossian. The more credible literary works of Sir Walter Scott also increasingly captured the public imagination. Scott played a significant role in orchestrating the well-publicized visit of King George IV to Edinburgh in 1822, during which the monarch appeared in a version of full Highland dress. This royal endorsement of tartan was continued from the 1840s by Queen Victoria, and was a great stimulus to its fashionability in Britain, France, and elsewhere.

Manufacture and Design

From the mid-eighteenth century, tartan design and manufacture began to be carried out within large-scale commercial enterprises, rather than primarily being the concern of local weavers. The firm Wilson's of Bannockburn was the most prominent tartan manufacturer from the mid-eighteenth to the mid-nineteenth centuries and Cheape claims that they "were mainly responsible for creating tartan as we know it today" (Cheape, p. 52). Their archive indicates that they catered to a fashionable market eager to consume new patterns named either after ancient clans or popular Scottish figures such as Sir Walter Scott. In addition to their prodigious innovation in tartan design, they also contributed to the modernization of tartan manufacture by "regularizing the sett, colors, and thread count" involved with each design (Rawson, Burnett, and Quye, p. 20).

Throughout the twentieth century tartan retained its role as both an internationally recognized symbol of "Scottishness" and as an attractive fashion textile. Tartan is currently widely worn by Scots as Highland dress on formal occasions and also to sporting events. Since the 1970s tartan has featured in the subcultural dress of skinheads, rockabillies, and punks, as well as being prominent in the work of international designers such as Vivienne Westwood, Jean Paul Gaultier, and Alexander McQueen.

See also **Kilt; Scottish Dress.**

BIBLIOGRAPHY

Cheape, Hugh. *Tartan, the Highland Habit.* 2nd ed. Edinburgh: National Museums of Scotland, 1995.

MacKillop, Andrew. *"More Fruitful than the Soil": Army, Empire and the Scottish Highlands, 1715–1815.* East Linton, U.K.: Tuckwell Press, 2000.

Morgan, Kenneth O. *The Oxford History of Britain.* Oxford: Oxford University Press, 2001.

Rawson, Helen, John Burnett, and Anita Quye. "The Import of Textile Dyes to Scotland: The Case of William Wilson and Son, Tartan Weavers of Bannockburn, 1780–1820." *Review of Scottish Culture* 13 (2000–2001): 18–29.

Scarlett, James D. "Tartan: The Highland Cloth and Highland Art Form." In *Scottish Textile History.* Edited by John Butt and Kenneth Ponting. Aberdeen, U.K.: Aberdeen University Press, 1987.

———. *Tartan: The Highland Textile.* London: Shepeard Walwyn, 1990.

Fiona Anderson

TATTOOS Tattooing is a process of creating a permanent or semipermanent body modification that transforms the skin. The word tattoo comes from the Tahitian *tatau,* which means "to mark something"; it is also hypothesized that the term comes from the sound the tatau sticks make when clicking together to mark the skin with ink. Tattooing is a process of puncturing the skin and depositing pigments, usually indelible ink, by a variety of methods beneath the skin to create a desired design or pattern. Tattoos range from "blackwork," large areas of heavy black ink in designs, to fine details and elaborate color schemes including fluorescent inks.

Historic Tattoos

The earliest evidence of tattooing includes tattooing tools and tattooed mummies. At 10,000-year-old sites in Tanzoumaitak, Algeria, tattooing instruments used for puncturing the skin were found with the female tattooed mummy of Tassili N'Ajje. In 1991, Ötzi, a Stone Age male mummy, was found in the Ötztal Alps, bordering Austria and Italy. This mummy had numerous tattoos, which were hypothesized as being used for medicinal cures, spiritual ceremonies, or indicating social status. Two well-preserved Egyptian mummies from 4160 B.C.E., a priestess and a temple dancer for the fertility goddess Hathor, bear random dot and dash tattoo patterns on the lower abdomen, thighs, arms, and chest. In 1993, a fifth-century B.C.E. Ukok priestess mummy, nicknamed the Siberian Ice Maiden, was found on the steppes of eastern Russia. She had several tattoos believed to have had medicinal, spiritual, and social significance. Most of the 4,000-year-old adult mummies from Xinjiang, China, had tattoos that related to their gender or social position.

A Japanese artist tattoos a pattern to a customer's back, 1955. These elaborate and symbolic Japanese tattoos became a popular fashion during the late eighteenth to nineteenth century. © BETTMANN/CORBIS. REPRODUCED BY PERMISSION.

Classical authors have written about tattoos used by the Thracians, Greeks, Romans, ancient Germans, ancient Celts, and ancient Britons. Tattooing has been practiced in most parts of the world, although it is rare among people with darker skins, such as those of Africa, who more often practice scarification and cicatrisation. Scholars hypothesize that tattooing was a permanent version of the desired aesthetic of body painting. Motivations, meanings, and exact techniques relating to tattoos vary from culture to culture. Tattoos have emphasized social and political roles; indicated cultural values and created an identity for the individual; reinforced aesthetic ideals; encouraged sexual attraction; eroticized the body; served medicinal and healing roles; communicated group affiliation or membership, and emphasized ritual and spiritual roles and customs of a culture.

Polynesia. In 1787, a French expedition led by Jan Francoise de la Perouse landed on Samoa and reported the men's thighs were heavily painted or tattooed, which gave the appearance of wearing pants. Samoan tattoos were applied with ink, tattoo combs, and hammer. Male tattoos had larger black areas than females, who had lighter, more filigreed lines.

Borneo. In the nineteenth century, Americans with tattoos were sailors and naval personnel, who wrote about their tattoo experiences in ships' logs, letters, and journals. During World Wars I and II, some U.S. soldiers and sailors decorated their bodies with tattoos. Usually these tattoos were from a set of stereotypical symbols—courage, patriotism, and defiance of death—later referred to as "flash." In the early 2000s, flash includes a wide variety of stock art used for tattoos.

Central America. In the nineteenth century most of Europe did not allow tattooing because the Catholic Church admonished it. However, tattooing flourished in England, due primarily to the tradition of tattooing in the British Navy. Many British sailors returned home with tattoos that commemorated their travels, and by the eighteenth century most British ports had at least one tattoo practitioner in residence.

In 1862, Prince Edward of Wales had a Jerusalem cross tattooed on his arm to commemorate his visit to the Holy Land. Later, as King Edward VII, he acquired additional tattoos, and even instructed his sons, the Duke of Clarence and the Duke of York (King George V), to obtain tattoos to commemorate their visit to Japan.

In 1941, the Nazis registered all prisoners entering the Auschwitz concentration camp who were not ethnic Germans with a tattooed serial number. This tattoo was first placed on the left side of the chest; later, the location was moved to the inner forearm.

Contemporary Tattoos

During the latter part of the twentieth century, tattoos were primarily utilized by microcultures, such as motorcycle gangs, street gangs, and punks. In the twenty-first century, tattoos have gained popularity in Western culture and become commonplace and even fashion statements.

At the same time, some microcultures, such as the Modern Primitives, have sought alternative and perhaps more extreme tattooing methods and designs. Often these methods and designs have been borrowed from anthropological texts about ancient cultures and related tattooing practices. There are tattoo practitioners who specialize in "tribal tattoos" and "primitive technologies." "Tribal tattoos" are typically heavy black ink and focus on designs that resemble Polynesian designs, ancient Celtic knotwork, or archaic languages. "Primitive technologies" include a wide variety of manual tattoo application methods, such as sharpened bones and ink; bone combs, hammer and ink; and tatau sticks and soot-based ink. These methods require lengthy tattooing sessions even for the smallest tattoos.

Electric Tattooing Practices

In 1891, the first electric tattooing implement was patented in the United States. In the early twenty-first century, many tattoos are applied in tattoo parlors using hand-held electric tattooing machines controlled by a foot pedal. These machines have a needle bar that holds from one to fourteen needles. The type or specific area of the tattoo design being worked on determines the number of needles. A single needle is used to make fine, delicate lines and shading. Additional needles are used for dense lines and filling with color. Even with the use of all fourteen needles, large or heavily detailed tattoos could take several months to complete.

Each needle extends a couple of millimeters beyond its own ink reservoir, which is loaded with a small amount of ink. Only one color is applied at a time. The tattoo practitioner holds the machine steady and guides the dye-loaded needles across the skin to create the desired pattern or design. A small motor moves the needles up and down to penetrate and deposit ink in the superficial (epidermis) and middle (dermis) layers of the skin.

Tattoo Health-Related Risks

Licensed tattoo establishments are required by law to take measures to ensure the health and safety of their clients. Since puncturing the skin and inserting the inks cause inflammation and bleeding, precautions are taken to prevent the possible spread of blood-borne infections, such as hepatitis B and C. Rooms used in the tattooing process are disinfected before and after each client. An autoclave, a regulated high-temperature steamer that kills blood-borne pathogens and bacterial agents, is used to sterilize the needle bar and reservoirs before each tattoo session. Sterile needles are removed from individual packaging in front of the client. The area of skin to be tattooed is shaved and disinfected by the tattoo practitioner. During the tattooing process, the skin is continually cleaned of excess ink and blood that seep from punctures with absorbent sanitary tissues.

Tattoo Removal

Tattoos have become part of fashion trends, resulting in the need for effective tattoo removal. Past methods of removing tattoos have often left scars. Tattoo removal with laser technology has become the most effective method used and has a minimal risk of scarring. Despite advances in laser technology, many tattoos cannot be completely removed, due to the unique nature of each tattoo. Successful tattoo removal depends on the tattoo's age, size, color, and type, as well as the patient's skin color and the depth of the pigment.

Semipermanent and Temporary Tattoos

Cosmetic tattoos are semipermanent makeup, such as eyeliner and lip color, tattooed on the face. These tattoos use plant-derived inks that are deposited in the superficial skin layer, resulting in a tattoo that lasts up to five years. Temporary tattoos come in a wide variety of designs and patterns. Unlike permanent and semipermanent tattoos, most temporary tattoos can be applied and removed by the wearer. These tattoos are burnished onto the skin and secured with an adhesive. Most temporary tattoos can be removed with soap and water or acetone, depending on the adhesive. Another type of temporary tattoo is henna or *mehndi*, which is a shrublike plant that grows in hot, dry climates, mostly in India, North African countries, and Middle Eastern countries. The leaves are dried, ground into a powder, and made into a paste, which is applied in desired designs to the skin. After several hours of drying, a reddish-brown stain temporarily tattoos the skin. This tattoo begins to fade as the skin exfoliates and renews itself.

See also **Body Piercing; Scarification.**

BIBLIOGRAPHY

Beck, Peggy, Nia Francisco, and Anna Lee Walters, eds. *The Sacred: Ways of Knowledge, Sources of Life*. Tsaile, Ariz.: Navajo Community College Press, 1995.

Camphausen, Rufus C. *Return to the Tribal: A Celebration of Body Adornment*. Rochester, Vt.: Park Street Press, 1997.

Demello, Margo. *Bodies of Inscription: A Cultural History of the Modern Tattoo Community*. Durham, N.C.: Duke University Press, 2000.

Gilbert, Steve. *Tattoo History: A Source Book*. New York: Juno Books, 2001.

Hadingham, Evan. "The Mummies of Xinjiang." *Discover* 15, no. 4 (April 1994): 68–77.

Polosmak, Natalya. "A Mummy Unearthed from the Pastures of Heaven." *National Geographic* 186, no. 4 (October 1994): 80–103.

Simmons, David R. *Ta Moko: The Art of Maori Tattoo*. Auckland: Reed Methuen Publishers, Ltd., 1986.

Tanaka, Shelley. *Discovering the Iceman: What Was It Like to Find a 5,300-Year-Old Mummy?* Toronto: The Madison Press, Ltd., 1996.

Theresa M. Winge

TEA GOWN The tea gown is an interior gown that emerged in England and France in the 1870s at a time when increased urbanization affected social behavior. The growing number of etiquette manuals and lady's periodicals produced at this time contributed to the revival of teatime by the middle classes and to the adoption of a whimsical type of gown worn by hostesses in their homes at five o'clock tea. Marked by Victorian eclecticism, this unique gown often incorporated elements of fashionable European dress from previous centuries, with exotic fabrics and stylistic components of foreign dress. The tea gown provided respectable women with an outlet for fantasy and innovation within the codified system of nineteenth-century dress and behavioral codes.

The nature and origin of teatime had considerable impact on the development of tea gowns. As tea was worth its weight in gold at the time of its introduction in Europe in the early seventeenth century, its consumption was reserved for the elite. Although this exotic beverage had become widely accessible in Europe and America by the mid-eighteenth century, tea drinking had been established as a class-conscious social event through which a network of selected individuals attained group membership. A sign of hospitality and politeness, serving tea to one's friends and relations retained an air of gentility and exclusivity that appealed to the rising middle classes. This mode of refined social entertainment entailed distinct refreshments, equipment, and rituals and would foster the emergence of a distinctive form of dress.

Specialization was also perceptible in interior spaces and manners, and gave rise to the development of the dining room and parlor. Both have significance in the tea gown's rise in popularity. The emergence of the dining room and the refinement of table etiquette in the mid-nineteenth century led to increased cost and formality when hosting dinners to repay social obligations and entertain friends. In comparison, teatime was far less costly and formal and could host a greater number of individuals, as custom required that guests stay between fifteen minutes and half an hour. With increased urbanization, social circles expanded rapidly and teatime became a more accommodating and feasible event in a system of reciprocity that was often daunting, and where hosting anxieties were on the rise. The parlor was in nature more flexible and became a stage for public display where teatime was held. As socializing was frequently conducted in private residences, home was also a public stage, and many late nineteenth-century parlors aimed to convey to visitors the owners' artistic sensibilities. This contributed to the popularity of the tea gown, which was considered to be the appropriate form of dress for artistic and exotic features. Many such gowns were aesthetically coordinated with their surroundings. This also influenced artist James Abbott McNeil Whistler and architect Henry van de Velde to design tea gowns for sitters or clients.

As teatime had long been conducted in private residences, the type of gown worn for the occasion was derived from interior gowns, which fit into the category of "undress." Nineteenth-century dress code was mainly divided in three categories: "undress," "half dress," and "full dress." Although this classification suggests a crescendo from least to most formal, elevated levels of formality existed within each category. As both men and women participated in social tea-drinking, and because teatime could be attended by distant acquaintances, tea gowns worn by hostesses did not stray far from Victorian propriety and became very formal interior gowns that were fit for public exposure. The state of "undress" could thus include gowns that were loose or semi-fitted to those, like the tea gown, that could be as fitted as other day and evening dresses. However, artistic elements such as Watteau pleats (wide pleats emerging from the center back neckline borrowed from eighteenth-century gowns) and draped front panels were among the features often added to a fitted understructure that gave the impression of looseness. These elements gave way to very elaborate interior gowns that were not labeled as "tea gowns" until the late 1870s.

The earliest labeled tea gowns discovered to date appeared in the 1878 British periodical, *The Queen, The Lady's Newspaper*. These one-piece gowns with long sleeves, high necklines, and back trains were made to give the impression of being closely fitted open robes with under dresses. One had the Watteau pleats and was named "The Louis XV Tea Gown." This is of interest as it names its source of inspiration and reinforces the eighteenth-century salon connection that was mentioned by writers of the period, and helped to intellectualize and elevate the status of teatime. Such tea gowns co-exist with numerous other elaborate interior gowns of the same style, which, until the turn of the century, were as likely to be named with the new term "tea gown" as they were to be labeled by the variant French term, *robe de chambre*. The words *robe* and *toilette* were also used interchangeably, as were *chambre* and *intérieur*. Terminology is thus a problem because tea gowns were derived from interior gowns, but not all interior gowns were fit to be worn in mixed company at teatime.

Nineteenth-century tea gowns seen in fashion plates followed the bustled styles of their times, and descriptions mentioned elaborate fashion fabrics and trims. This serves to differentiate these gowns further from other interior gowns. Although loose and artistic features were acceptable in tea gowns, their public use mandated the adoption of the fashionable and highly-fitted silhouette.

As wearing underpinnings such as bustles without a corset was not a Victorian practice, the contrived fashionable silhouette present in tea gowns observed in fashion plates and in surviving specimens in museum collections suggests that corsets were worn under some of theses gowns.

From the late 1870s to the mid-1910s, tea gowns were immensely popular. Their magnificence was on the rise and leading designers joined in with fanciful creations that could easily have been mistaken for fancy dresses.

As Edwardian dress gave rise to a love of different colors and fabrics and introduced Empire revival features in high fashion, a progressive blurring occurred. The appropriateness of historically inspired gowns with looser and exotic elements was no longer confined to teatime. This also expanded the tea gown's use to other day and evening events. As the revivalist Empire silhouette gained ground and exoticism became the rage, it became hard to differentiate tea gowns from other types of gowns. Changes also occurred in the physical settings of teatime, which migrated to newly-popular tea pavilions and helped the *thés dansants* of the 1910s supersede teatime in the home as the fashionable thing to do.

See also **Empire Style; Europe and America: History of Dress (400–1900 C.E.); Robe.**

BIBLIOGRAPHY

Kasson, John F. *Rudeness and Civility: Manners in Nineteenth-Century Urban America.* New York: Hill and Wang, 1990.

Roth, Rodris. "Tea-Drinking in Eighteenth-Century America: Its Etiquette and Equipage." In *Material Life in America, 1600–1860.* Edited by Robert Blair St. George. Boston: Northeastern University Press, 1988, pp. 439–462.

Montgomery, Maureen E. *Displaying Women: Spectacles of Leisure in Edith Wharton's New York.* New York: Routledge, 1998.

Anne Bissonnette

TECHNO-TEXTILES Techno-textiles are fabrics that incorporate new technologies and new functionality into a traditional textile material. Sometimes called "tech-textiles" or "technical fabrics," most techno-textiles have their roots in industrial or military applications. Techno-textiles are employed in many different applications, ranging across biomedical devices, aircraft, automobiles, electronics, and more, including clothing and home furnishing.

Textiles are products basically constructed of fibers. These fibers are frequently twisted together (thousands at a time) to create yarns, and the yarns can be woven, knitted, or braided to make fabrics. When looking at a fabric, it is easy to forget that fabric is really made of thousands or millions of small fibers. However, the fibers are the most important component of the textile. The choice of fibers and yarns can change the behavior of the textile material. Most techno-textiles are developed at the fiber level. By modifying materials thinner than a human hair, the performance of a fabric can change dramatically.

Since the dawn of synthetic plastics, techno-textiles have been marketed. One of the earliest examples of fibers made for high-tech application is nylon. As the air force was developing as a significant component of the armed forces, parachutes became more and more important. Parachutes were made from woven silk fabric. Researchers were interested in developing a synthetic substitute for silk to control quality, source, and improve strength. Nylon was an ideal source and rapidly developed to satisfy this market.

Recognizing nylon as a silk substitute, however, quickly led people to consider other products made from silk as candidates for nylon. Stockings, which were extremely popular and rather expensive at the time, were identified as a likely market. The success was so great that the public started calling stockings "nylons" within a few years. The increased strength and durability of the nylon compared to silk made this a tremendous success.

By the early 2000s, nylon was no longer considered a techno-textile, but rather a commodity fiber. This continues to happen: as new technologies become commonplace and accepted, they cease to be considered high-tech. What at first seem like fantastic applications will likely, within years or decades, become commonplace.

Comfort through Technology

One of the most popular applications of techno-textiles is to provide comfort in a garment. Generally speaking, there are two aspects of comfort that clothing can address: perspiration and temperature. A comfortable garment will take moisture away from the body and maintain a good temperature level.

Moisture control. Expanded polytetraflouroethylene (ePTFE) has transitioned from the laboratory to apparel. PTFE is the same chemical structure as Teflon, but when it is expanded, some unique properties can be realized. Gore popularized this technology as the Gore-Tex membrane. The basic idea is that the membrane has very small holes in it. These holes permit water vapor to pass, but are too small to allow a water droplet through. Thus, if a person wearing this garment is perspiring, the water vapor can move through the membrane. However, if it is raining, the droplets cannot pass through to make the person wet.

Temperature control. Phase change materials are becoming quite popular as a way to control temperature in a garment. Basically, microencapsulated waxes are embedded into the fabric. When the wax melts, it absorbs thermal energy, effectively cooling the material when it is heated. Conversely, when the molten wax solidifies, it releases heat while the overall system is cooling. The result of this is a material that tries to maintain a certain temperature, effectively taking the peaks of heat and cold away.

There are methods to actively change the temperature of clothing as well. Astronauts, aircraft test pilots, and racecar drivers have been using refrigerated clothing for some time. Tubes of coolant are embedded in the clothing and a small pump pushes the cool liquid throughout the garment. Thermal-electrical devices are also being considered.

E-Textiles

Some of the more exciting possibilities for techno-textiles come from using modern electronics and computer technologies in clothing. The key elements are the use of electrically conductive fibers or yarns so that signals can be sent throughout the garment, flexible power sources, flexible computer equipment, and flexible display systems.

Conductive materials in fibrous form, such as metals or carbon, or even conductive polymers such as polyanyline, can be used as wiring within a piece of fabric. These wires can carry electricity to various components, such as sensors, actuators, or computer chips, that are embedded in the garment. Wireless communication devices can communicate information to and from the clothing.

For example, Infineon Technologies, AG, is developing a method to incorporate motion detection devices into carpeting. This can be used for a variety of purposes, including controlling lighting to turn on when someone enters the room, or to detect intruders. In addition to detecting motion, the chip can measure temperature, which could lead to applications such as automatic floor lighting in the event of a fire, showing the occupants a path to safety.

The motion detection module is woven into the carpet backing. Red wires supply voltage, green wires carry data, and blue wires are ground for Infineon's demonstrator smart carpet motion-detection module. A capacitive sensor in the module detects when a green wire is touched, which lights the red LED.

Optical fibers can be incorporated into fabric structures in such a way as to create light patterns on the surface of the fabric. By proper control, the fabric can effectively become a television or computer screen. France Télécom demonstrated such a technology—a fabric display screen. Eventually this technology could be incorporated into everyday clothing or home furnishings. Imagine a simple, businesslike shirt that can be converted into a dynamic flashing nightclub outfit with the flip of a switch. Draperies and wallpaper could become display units so that the pattern or color scheme can be changed to the owner's instantaneous desire.

Maggie Orth has developed Electric Plaid for this purpose. Electric Plaid doesn't work by controlling fiber optics, but rather by controlling temperature-sensitive dyes—another techno-textile application. Temperature-sensitive dyes can change color depending on how cold or hot the fabric becomes. Electric Plaid has heating and cooling filaments embedded in the fabric. By changing the degree of heating and cooling at different places in the fabric, Orth has created a fabric that changes color and pattern slowly throughout the day.

Embedded sensors. Sensors to determine such disparate phenomenon as temperature or oxygen content can be created in a fibrous form. Typically these are fiber optics that have Bragg diffraction gratings that can measure small changes in the environment. Because they are produced as fiber optics, they can be incorporated into clothing. A number of companies, such as Big Light and SensaTex, have embedded these sensors into underwear so that the fibers are touching or close to the human body.

The information received by these sensors can be transmitted to another location. Some of the life-critical applications for these include infant garments to provide early warning against SIDS (Sudden Infant Death Syndrome), and for soldiers. In either case, information can be sent back to the parents or commander to provide details about the health and well being of the wearer. Should a problem arise, quick response can prevent serious difficulties. If the infant's breathing becomes irregular, the control system will notify the parent who will rush to assistance. If the soldier is wounded, the change in body temperature and heart rate will create a warning for the medics to come to his aid. Not only will the medics know there is a problem, but also a location system on the soldier will allow the medic to find the soldier quickly.

This kind of technology is also being transmitted to the world of sports. One of the obvious applications is for training purposes. Both the athlete and the trainer can observe changes in vital signs and determine the degree and efficiency of the workout. At Tampere University of Technology (Finland), researchers have made a snowmobile suit that includes a location sensor and transmitter as well as accelerometers to detect crashes. If a crash should occur, the suit will send a distress call that includes the location of the athlete as well as vital signs.

Sources of power. As exciting new applications of electronics in textiles develop, there is a need to provide electrical power to these devices. There are several interesting approaches in development that will see future applications.

A few companies have produced very thin and flexible batteries that are about as intrusive as a label. Although these don't provide very much power, they can be sufficient to handle electrochromic devices or even small fiber optics.

There are some interesting variations being developed other than batteries. One is a generator that is attached to shoes. A generator creates electrical energy by spinning a magnet through a coil of wire. This is the opposite of making a magnet by wrapping a wire around a nail and running electricity through the wire. The basic idea is to make the heel of the shoe able to move up and down so that with each step the wearer pushes the heel up, which moves magnets through a coil and electricity is generated. Then the shoe is simply connected to the garment to provide electricity. There are a few problems with this idea, such as the wires required to connect the shoe to the clothes, and the fact that the heel of the shoe might be larger than normal.

Electricity can also be converted from thermal energy through a process known as the Seebeck effect. In the Seebeck effect, two different conducting materials are joined, and when the temperature between them is different, an electric current is produced. This can be great for cold weather environments, where one conductor is on the outside of a coat, so it is cold, and the other conductor is on the inside by the wearer where it is warm. This difference in temperature can create electricity that can be used for various things, such as charging a cell phone or MP3 player, or finding one's coordinates through a global positioning system.

The opposite of the Seebeck effect is the Peltier effect, wherein electricity can be used to create temperature, but not like a heater, rather like a cooler. By proper choice of the conducting materials, the Peltier device can become cooler than the environment, allowing a flexible cooling system. Such devices can be embedded in fabrics.

Various companies have developed flexible solar cells. Solar cells convert light into electricity. The recent possibility to make them flexible allows them to be used in clothing and accessories. Recently a student of the author of this article, Lauren Sabia, developed a shoulder bag that incorporates flexible solar cells in the strap and has conducting wires that run to a cell phone holder allowing the solar cells to charge a cell phone when not in use.

The Future

It is not known what the future holds for high-tech textiles. There may exist far-out concepts such as a tie made from fibers that are semiconductors allowing the garment to double as a memory storage device for a computer.

Perhaps yarns will be developed that have muscle-like behavior that allows them to contract, making the sleeves of a shirt give the wearer extra strength or speed. What is known, though, is that most technological advances eventually make their way into textile products because just about everybody wears clothing.

See also **Future of Fashion; High-Tech Fashion.**

BIBLIOGRAPHY

Bolton, Andrew. *The Supermodern Wardrobe*. London: Victoria and Albert Museum, 2002.

Braddock, Sarah E., and Marie O'Mahony. *Techno Textiles: Revolutionary Fabrics for Fashion and Design*. London and New York: Thames and Hudson, Inc., 1999.

———. *Sportstech: Revolutionary Fabrics, Fashion, and Design*. London and New York: Thames and Hudson, Inc., 2002.

Christopher M. Pastore

TEENAGE FASHION Since World War II, clothing styles adopted by young people have been a powerful influence on the development of fashion in North America and Europe. The postwar growth of young people's spending power ensured that the youth market became a crucial sector of the fashion business. The styles adopted by young people, moreover, also became an important influence on wider fashion trends. Indeed, by the 1990s the "youth" market had expanded to embrace not only teenagers, but also consumers in their twenties, thirties, and older.

"B'hoys" and "Scuttlers"

Distinctive fashions for young people were not unique to the twentieth century. During the Victorian era a gradual increase in young workers' leisure time and disposable income laid the basis for an embryonic youth market, with cities in America and Europe seeing the development of mass-produced goods, entertainments, and fashions targeted at the young.

Young people also used fashion to mark out individual and collective identities. During the 1890s, for example, many working girls in urban America rejected conservative modes of feminine dress in favor of gaudy colors, fancy accessories, and skirts and dresses cut to accentuate their hips and thighs. Young working men also adopted distinctive styles. In the mid-nineteenth century, for instance, the Bowery area of New York City was home to dandified street toughs known as "B'hoys." According to the socialite Abraham Dayton, "These 'B'hoys' … were the most consummate dandies of the day," and paraded the streets with lavishly greased front locks, broad-brimmed hats, turned-down shirt collars, black frock-coats with skirts below the knee, embroidered shirts, and "a profusion of jewelry as varied and costly as the b'hoy could procure" (Dayton, pp. 217–218).

Comparable fashions also appeared in Europe. For instance, in his autobiographical account of life in the British town of Salford, Robert Roberts recalled the gangs of young toughs known as "scuttlers" who, at the turn of the century, sported a trademark style of "union shirt, bell-bottomed trousers, heavy leather belt picked out in fancy designs with a large steel buckle, and thick, iron-shod clogs" (Roberts, p. 155).

Flappers and Campus Culture

The 1920s and 1930s saw the youth market expand further. In Britain, despite a general economic downturn, young workers' disposable incomes gradually rose, and they were courted by a growing range of consumer industries. In the United States, the economic boom of the 1920s also ensured a budding youth market, while distinctive styles became increasingly associated with the young. The image of the young, female "flapper" was especially prominent. With her sleek fashions, short bobbed hair, and energetic leisure pursuits, the archetypal flapper featured in many advertising campaigns as the embodiment of chic modernity.

Clothing styles geared to young men also became more distinctive. From the 1890s sportswear became popular for casual attire. Shirt styles previously worn for sports replaced more formal garb as a new, leisure-oriented aesthetic surfaced within young men's fashion. Indicative was the appearance of the "Arrow Man," who became a fixture of advertisements for Arrow shirts from 1905 onward. A model of well-groomed and chisel-jawed masculinity, the "Arrow Man" was a youthful and stylish masculine archetype whose virile muscularity guaranteed a fashionability untainted by suspicions of effeminacy. With the expansion of American colleges and universities during the 1920s, an identifiable "collegiate" or "Ivy League" style of dress also took shape. Clothing firms such as Campus Leisure-wear (founded in 1922), together with the movie, magazine, and advertising industries, gave coherence to this smart-but-casual combination of button-down shirts, chino slacks, letter sweaters, cardigans, and loafers.

Bobby Soxers and Teenagers

During the 1940s the economic pressures of wartime drew significant numbers of young people into the American workforce. As a consequence, youth enjoyed a greater measure of disposable income, with U.S. youngsters wielding a spending power of around $750 million by 1944. This economic muscle prompted a further expansion of the consumer industries geared to youth. Young women emerged as a particularly important market, and during the 1940s the epithet "bobby-soxer" was coined to denote adolescent girls who sported a new style of sweaters, full skirts, and saddle shoes, and who jitterbugged to the sounds of big-band swing or swooned over show-business stars such as Mickey Rooney and Frank Sinatra.

The "teenager" was also a creation of the 1940s. Since the 1600s it had been common to refer to an adolescent as being someone in their "teens," yet it was only during the 1940s that the term "teenager" entered the popular vocabulary. The U.S. advertising and marketing industries were crucial in popularizing the concept. American marketers used the term "teenager" to denote what they saw as a new market of affluent, young consumers associated with leisure-oriented lifestyles. Eugene Gilbert made a particularly notable contribution. Gilbert launched his career as a specialist in youth marketing in 1945, and by 1947 his market research firm, Youth Marketing Co., was flourishing. Gilbert was acknowledged as an authority on the teenage market, and during the 1950s his book, *Advertising and Marketing to Young People* (1957), became a manual for teen merchandising.

The success of *Seventeen* magazine also testified to the growth of the American "teen" market. Conceived as a magazine for college girls, *Seventeen* was launched in 1944. By 1949 its monthly circulation had reached two and a half million, the magazine's features and advertising helping to disseminate "teenage" tastes throughout America.

The Teenage Market Explodes

During the 1950s the scope and scale of the U.S. youth market grew further. This was partly a consequence of demographic trends. A wartime increase in births and a postwar "baby boom" saw the American teen population grow from 10 million to 15 million during the 1950s, eventually hitting a peak of 20 million by 1970. A postwar expansion of education, meanwhile, further accentuated notions of youth as a distinct social group, with the proportion of American teenagers attending high school rising from 60 percent in the 1930s, to virtually 100 percent during the 1960s. The vital stimulus behind the growth of the youth market, however, was economic. Peacetime saw a decline in full-time youth employment, but a rise in youth spending was sustained by a combination of part-time work and parental allowances, some estimates suggesting that teenage Americans' average weekly income rose from just over $2 in 1944 to around $10 by 1958 (Macdonald, p. 60).

During the 1950s, teen spending was concentrated in America's affluent, white suburbs. In contrast, embedded racism and economic inequality ensured that African American and working-class youngsters were relatively marginal to the commercial youth market. Nevertheless, African American, Mexican American, and working-class youths generated their own styles that were a crucial influence on the wider universe of youth culture. During the 1930s, for example, young African Americans developed the zoot suit style of broad, draped jackets and pegged trousers that gradually filtered into mainstream fashion. During the 1950s, meanwhile, African American rhythm and blues records began to pick up a young, white audience. Reconfigured as "rock 'n' roll" by major record companies, the music was pitched to a mainstream market and became the soundtrack to 1950s youth culture.

The 1950s also saw work wear incorporated within youth style. Denim jeans, especially, became a stock item of teen fashion. During the 1860s Levi Strauss had patented the idea of putting rivets on the stress points of workmen's waist-high overalls commonly known as "jeans." By the 1940s jeans were considered leisure wear, but during the 1950s their specific association with youth culture was cemented after they were worn by young film stars such as James Dean and Marlon Brando, and by pop stars such as Elvis Presley. Levi Strauss remained a leading jeans manufacturer, but firms such as Lee Cooper and Wrangler also became famous for their own distinctive styles.

Global Circulation of Teenage Fashion

The growth of the mass media was a crucial factor in the dissemination of teenage fashion. The proliferation of teen magazines, films, and TV music shows such as *American Bandstand* (syndicated on the ABC network from 1957), ensured that shifts in teen styles spread quickly throughout the United States. The global circulation of U.S. media also allowed the fashions of teenage America to spread worldwide. In Britain, for example, the zoot suit was adopted by London youths during the 1940s, the style subsequently evolving into the long, "draped" jackets that were the badge of 1950s toughs known as "Teddy boys." Behind the "iron curtain," too, youngsters were influenced by American fashion. In the Soviet Union, for example, the 1950s saw a style known as "*stil*" develop as a Russian interpretation of American teenage fashion.

As in the U.S., demographic shifts underpinned the growth of the European teen market. In Britain, for example, a postwar baby boom saw the number of people aged under twenty grow from three million in 1951 to over four million by 1966. An expansion of education also reinforced notions of young people as a discreet social group. As in America, economic trends were also vital. In Britain, for instance, buoyant levels of youth employment enhanced youth's disposable income, and market researchers such as Mark Abrams identified the rise of "distinctive teenage spending for distinctive teenage ends in a distinctive teenage world" (Abrams, p. 10). The teen market that emerged in postwar Britain, however, was more working-class in character than its American equivalent. In Britain increases in youth spending were concentrated among young workers, and Abrams estimated that "not far short of 90 percent of all teenage spending" was "conditioned by working class taste and values" (Abrams, p. 13).

European youth style fed back into the development of U.S. youth culture. During the mid-1960s, for example, America was captivated by a British pop music "invasion" spearheaded by the Beatles and the Rolling Stones. American women's fashion, meanwhile, was transformed by British exports such as the miniskirt and Mary Quant's chic modernist designs. British menswear was also influential. Surveying the fashion scene in "Swinging London," for example, *Time* magazine was impressed by "the new, way-out fashion in young men's clothes" (*Time*, 15 April 1966). In autumn 1966 a flurry of media excitement also surrounded the arrival in America of British "Mod" style—a fusion of fitted shirts, sharply cut jackets, and tapered trousers, which was itself inspired by the smoothly tailored lines of Italian fashion.

Counterculture, Race, and Teenage Style

The counterculture of the late 1960s and early 1970s had a major impact on international youth style. A loose coalition of young bohemians, students, and political radicals, the counterculture shared an interest in self-exploration, creativity, and alternative lifestyles. The counterculture's spiritual home was the Haight-Ashbury neighborhood of San Francisco, but films, magazines, and television, together with the success of rock bands such as Jefferson Airplane and the Grateful Dead, disseminated countercultural styles throughout the world. The nonconformity and exoticism of the counterculture leaked into mainstream youth style, and hip boutiques abounded with countercultural influences in the form of ethnic designs, psychedelic patterns, faded denim, and tie-dye.

The 1960s and 1970s also saw African American youngsters become a more prominent consumer group. A combination of civil rights activism and greater employment opportunities improved living standards for many African Americans and, as a consequence, black teenagers gradually emerged as a significant market. This was reflected in the soul music boom of the 1960s and the success of record labels such as Berry Gordy's Tamala-Motown empire. Soul also picked up a significant white audience, and the influence of African-American style on the wider universe of youth culture continued throughout the 1970s—first with the funk sounds pioneered by James Brown and George Clinton, and then with the eruption of the vibrant disco scene.

The late 1970s also saw the emergence of rap music and hip-hop culture (which combined graffiti, dance, and fashion). Hip-hop first took shape in New York's South Bronx, where performers such as Afrika Bambaataa and Grandmaster Flash combined pulsating soundscapes with deft wordplay. Hip-hop style was characterized by a passion for brand-name sportswear—trainers, tracksuits, and accessories produced by firms such as Adidas, Reebok, and Nike. Rap trio Run-DMC even paid homage to their favorite sports brand in their anthem "My Adidas." During the 1990s rap impresarios even launched their own hip-hop fashion labels. For example, in 1992 Russell Simmons (head of the Def Jam corporation) launched the Phat Farm sportswear range, while in 1998 Sean "Puffy" Combs (head of Bad Boy Records) launched the Sean John clothing line.

The 1990s and Beyond

During the 1980s and 1990s, a rise in youth unemployment, coupled with the declining size of the Western youth population, threatened to undermine the growth of teen spending. By the beginning of the twenty-first century, however, demographic shifts and economic trends indicated that youth would continue to be a lucrative commercial market. Despite a long-term decline in Western birth rates, the youth population was set to increase during the new millennium as the "echo" of the "baby boom" worked its way through the demographic profiles of America and Europe. On both sides of the Atlantic, moreover, market research indicated that teenagers' spending power was still growing.

Teenage fashions also increasingly appealed to other age groups. For example, manufacturers, retailers, and advertisers increasingly targeted teenage fashions at pre-teens (especially girls), who were encouraged to buy products ostensibly geared to older consumers. Teenage fashions also crept up the age scale. By the end of the 1990s, many consumers aged from their twenties to their forties and above were favoring tastes and lifestyles associated with youth culture. "Teenage fashion" therefore, was no longer the preserve of teenagers, but had won a much broader cultural appeal.

See also **Street Style; Subcultures.**

BIBLIOGRAPHY

Abrams, Mark. *The Teenage Consumer*. London: Press Exchange, 1959.

Austin, Joe, and Michael Willard, eds. *Generations of Youth: Youth Cultures and History in Twentieth-Century America*. New York: New York University Press, 1998.

Dayton, Abraham. *The Last Days of Knickerbocker Life in New York*. New York: G. P. Putnam's Sons, 1897.

Fass, Paula. *The Damned and the Beautiful: American Youth in the 1920s*. Oxford: Oxford University Press, 1978.

Frank, Thomas. *The Conquest of Cool: Business Culture, Counterculture, and the Rise of Hip Consumerism*. Chicago: University of Chicago Press, 1997.

Fowler, David. *The First Teenagers: The Lifestyle of Young Wage-Earners in Interwar Britain*. London: Woburn, 1995.

Gilbert, Eugene. *Advertising and Marketing to Young People*. New York: Printer's Ink, 1957.

Hollander, Stanley C., and Richard Germain. *Was There a Pepsi Generation Before Pepsi Discovered It? Youth-Based Segmentation in Marketing*. Chicago: American Marketing Association, 1993.

Macdonald, Dwight. "A Caste, a Culture, a Market." *New Yorker* (22 November 1958).

Osgerby, Bill. *Youth in Britain Since 1945*. Oxford: Blackwell, 1998.

Palladino, Grace. *Teenagers: An American History*. New York: Basic Books, 1996.

Pilkington, Hilary. *Russia's Youth and Its Culture: A Nation's Constructors and Constructed*. London: Routledge, 1994.

Roberts, Robert. *The Classic Slum: Salford Life in the First Quarter Century*. Harmondsworth: Pelican, 1973.

Rollin, Lucy. *Twentieth Century Teen Culture by the Decades: A Reference Guide*. Westport, Conn.: Greenwood Press, 1999.

Bill Osgerby

TENCEL. *See* **Rayon.**

TENNIS COSTUMES The game of tennis or *Jeu de Paume* originated in France in the thirteenth century. It was played on an indoor court and became known as Real Tennis in Britain, Court Tennis in the United States, and Royal Tennis in Australia. No special clothes were worn by the nobility who played this game, although King Henry VIII, who was a keen player, preferred playing in a linen shirt and breeches. By the seventeenth century, a player is mentioned "cloathed all in white" (Cunnington and Mansfield, p. 86), the first reference to what was to become the standard color for the newer game of long, open, or lawn tennis, which was played outside.

Bunny Austin with J. Asboth at Wimbeldon. During the 1930s, male tennis players faced a debate over whether it was appropriate for them to wear tennis shorts. Male players have seldom faced the controversy over attire that has at times embroiled their female counterparts. HULTON ARCHIVE/GETTY IMAGES. REPRODUCED BY PERMISSION.

Venus Williams. Sporting an outfit designed by Diane von Furstenburg, Venus Williams is not the first to wear designer attire on the tennis court. In 1949, Gussy Moran created controversy with an outfit she wore by designer Teddy Tinling. AP/WIDE WORLD PHOTOS. REPRODUCED BY PERMISSION.

Lawn Tennis

There was a lull in the popularity of the game in the eighteenth century, but by the 1860s, lawn tennis was firmly established as a favorite sporting activity, particularly in Britain. In 1877, the All England Croquet and Lawn Tennis Club (AECLTC), the ruling body for the Wimbledon Championships, established the first Championship match, a Gentleman's Singles Event. There were no formal dress codes. Instead, the AECLTC relied on the unwritten rules of middle-class decorum. Men traditionally wore white flannels with long-sleeved white cotton shirts. However, for women, the fashions of the time made it difficult to find a practical alternative to the restrictive clothes of the period. "Lawn tennis shoes, black with India rubber soles" (Cunnington and Mansfield, p. 88) were helpful, but long narrow skirts with trains,

even those that could be tied back, hindered women from fully participating in the sport in an athletic way.

Shorts and Skirts

By the beginning of the twentieth century, women were still playing in corsets with shirts buttoned to the neck and long ankle-length skirts. The arrival at Wimbledon in 1919 of Suzanne Lenglen from France changed forever the way women dressed on the tennis court. Lenglen wore a short-sleeved, calf-length, loose white cotton frock with white stockings and a floppy linen hat that she later replaced with her trademark bandeau. This style of dress, often made from white cotton pique but occasionally silk, influenced not just serious tennis players but was copied by young girls across the United Kingdom. However, as day-dress lengths grew longer in the 1930s, the divided skirt and then shorts became the norm for female players across the Western world taking the lead from American players. Men were also wearing shorts and short-sleeved shirts in the United States and France by the 1930s. Champion French player Rene Lacoste designed the first "polo" shirt in 1925 with his signature "crocodile" emblem chosen for his tenacity of play. Within a year, similar versions were available in London, made by Izod's of London's West End, who claimed they developed from golf shirts. British men were reluctant to wear shorts for competition tennis until after 1945. "Bunny" Austin was the only man to wear shorts on Wimbledon's Center Court in the 1930s. Although white was always the favored color, there were no regulations at Wimbledon about color until a 1948 restriction to discourage the increased use of colored trimmings on women's outfits. By 1963, the only items allowed to be not purely white at Wimbledon were a cardigan, pullover, or headwear. With the advent of sports manufacturers' sponsorship deals with top players, in 1995, Wimbledon restricted logos so that outfits were "almost entirely white" (Little, p. 305). Even away from Wimbledon, white remains the favored color.

Naughty Knickers

In 1949, American Gussy Moran caused an uproar by wearing visibly lace-trimmed panties at Wimbledon under her short white tennis skirt. They had been designed for "Gorgeous" Gussy by British ex-tennis player turned designer Teddy Tinling for $17 from an experimental rayon fabric. Tinling remained the key name in women's tennis-wear design for the next twenty years, styling dresses for most of the famous female names in tennis. Throughout the 1950s and 1960s, frilly panties were popular for female tennis players. But Moran was not the first to flash her panties on court:

> Dainty garments trimmed with lace do not look quite appropriate for a strenuous game, and in these days when the game is played really hard, lady's undergarments often do not leave much to the imagination, therefore knickers made of silk stockingette seem to be quite the thing. (*Woman's Life*, 31 July 1924, p. 12)

Male modesty ruled on court in the 1930s, as evidenced in this quote from New Health:

> Try even to wear "shorts" for tennis ... and every "right-minded" male on the courts will react with a resentful leer. The implication is that they would look like a lot of funny little boys. Yet ... no one feels like jeering when eleven hefty footballers run on to the field in "shorts." (New Health, May 1930)

British player and former Wimbledon champion Fred Perry developed a leading line of men's sportswear from the 1950s, focusing on the traditional tailored shorts and short-sleeved shirts for men. New fabric technologies, in particular breathable fabrics, have slowly revolutionized sportswear in general. One of the oldest, Aertex, was developed in the late nineteenth century by two British doctors, mainly for underwear. From the 1920s, it was being used to make men's tennis shirts. By the 1960s, synthetic fibers such as quick-drying polyester were replacing cotton. In the 1970s, the fashion of long hair for men meant that many copied their idol Bjorn Borg's signature headband, reminiscent of Suzanne Lenglen's bandeau. The 1980s was a decade of traditional styling for both men and women, with close-fitting short shorts being worn by men and wraparound skirts popular for female players. An exception was U.S. player Anne White who, in 1985, caused a sensation at Wimbledon by wearing a white catsuit. It was not a fashion that caught on. By the 1990s, men's tennis shorts became longer and looser, and shirts baggier. For women, however, the introduction of Lycra into tennis wear drew the focus away from their playing skills. Players with sponsorship deals, such as Serena Williams with sportswear firm Puma and Anna Kournikova with Adidas, promoted a body-clinging style light-years away from the corseted players of a hundred years before.

See also **Uniforms, Sports.**

BIBLIOGRAPHY

Cunnington, Phillis, and Alan Mansfield. *English Costume for Sports and Outdoor Recreation from the 16th to the 19th Centuries.* London: Adam and Charles Black, 1969. Fascinating for the early period.

Horwood, Catherine. "Dressing like a Champion: Women's Tennis Wear in Interwar England." In *The Englishness of English Dress.* Edited by Christopher Breward, Becky Conekin, and Caroline Cox. Oxford: Berg, 2002. Concentrates on the period up to 1939.

———. "'Anyone for Tennis?': Male Modesty on the Tennis Courts of Interwar Britain." *Costume* 38 (2004): 101–106.

Lee-Potter, Charlie. *Sportswear in Vogue Since 1910.* London: Thames and Hudson, Inc., 1984. Useful illustrations.

Little, Alan. *Wimbledon Compendium 1999.* London: The All England Lawn Tennis and Croquet Club, 1999. Detailed listings.

Schreier, Barbara A. "Sporting Wear." In *Men and Women: Dressing the Part.* Edited by Claudia Brush Kidwell and Va-

lerie Steele. Washington, D.C.: Smithsonian Institution Press, 1989. Section on tennis, pp. 112–116.

Catherine Horwood

TERRYCLOTH. *See* **Weave, Slack Tension.**

TEXTILES, AFRICAN For more than a thousand years, West Africa has been one of the world's great textile-producing regions. The yarn available locally for spinning was cotton, which grew in at least two colors, white and pale brown. In some places a wild silk was also spun, while raffia and bast fibers were available in addition, as were imported textiles and fibers from trans-Saharan and coastal trade networks, the latter from the late fifteenth century onward. Only in the inland Niger delta region of Mali were the wool fibers of local sheep of sufficient length to permit spinning, whereas north of the Sahara wool was the major source of spun yarn. Fragments of bast-fiber textile were recovered from the ninth-century site of Igbo-Ukwu in Nigeria, and cotton and woolen cloth from eleventh-century deposits in Mali, suggest traditions already well established. (Earlier archaeological textiles from Egypt and the Mahgreb are beyond the scope of this essay.) Elsewhere in the sub-Saharan region, in the forests of central Africa, raffia was the only available fiber, and in the savannas of east and southern Africa cotton was spun, at least as far south as Great Zimbabwe.

Throughout West Africa the most widely used dye was a locally produced indigo, also exported for use north of the Sahara, though in both regions other colors were available from vegetable and mineral sources. These dyestuffs might be used on the yarns prior to weaving, sometimes tie-dyed to form simple ikat-like patterns, and they were used in the coloring and patterning of woven cloth. In some areas woven textiles and tailored garments were embroidered, especially in the region from Lake Chad westward to the inland Niger delta of Mali. There was also some occurrence of patchwork, appliqué, and quilting; and one tradition of handprinted cloth. Handprinted cloth was also found in Zanzibar, brought from India. In the raffia-weaving region of central Africa, cut-pile embroidery was well developed together with appliqué and patchwork. In eastern and southern Africa, local textile traditions seem to have depended on the weaving process for patterning. From the late nineteenth century onward, local textile industries in sub-Saharan Africa have had to compete with factory-printed cotton cloth, sometimes successfully, though in eastern and southern Africa the local production of woven cloth was supplanted in the early twentieth century. The felting of vegetable fibers to produce bark cloth (strictly speaking not a textile) has survived in Ghana and Uganda, though it was at one time more widespread.

The mechanical basis for the interlacing of warps and wefts throughout pre-industrial handloom production in Africa takes one of two forms. The most widespread system consists in leashing one set of warps to a single heddle-rod, which is manipulated with the aid of a shed stick. This is the basis of the upright fixed heddle loom used by Berber women in north Africa for weaving the fabrics used in their clothing, and of the loom laid out on the ground through the Sahara and in northern Sudan for weaving tent cloth. In Nigeria and Cameroon, women used an upright version of it, manipulating both heddle and shed stick to weave cotton and other yarns. Except in the southern Igbo town of Akwete, however, it has recently largely given way to the double-heddle loom, yet to be described. In the Cross River region in southeast Nigeria, as throughout the central African forests, male weavers used a more-or-less upright single-heddle loom to weave raffia. In parts of northeast Nigeria, and seemingly across the savannas to east Africa and south to Zimbabwe, a horizontal version of this loom type, raised off the ground but with a fixed heddle, was used in weaving cotton textiles.

Throughout West Africa, from Senegal to Chad and from the sahel to the coastal region, the more commonplace loom type has both sets of warps leashed, each to one or other of a pair of heddles linked by means of a pulley suspended above the loom and with pedals worked by the feet below. The advantage is, of course, that both hands and feet are employed, enabling cloth to be woven with greater speed and efficiency than is possible using single-heddle equipment. This loom type is also used in Ethiopia and by Arab weavers in North Africa. However, in West Africa the loom itself, with which this double-heddle system is used, has two features particular to the region: the first is the dragstone with which the warp elements are held taut. The second is the narrowness of the web; for it continues to be both normal and commonplace for cloth to be woven in a long, narrow strip often no more than about 4 inches (10 cms) wide, although in some traditions the web may be broader, perhaps up to about 12 to 14 inches (30–35 cms) and cloth as narrow as a .5 inches (1.5 cms) is known. Once the desired length is complete, it will be cut into pieces and sewn together edge-to-edge. It is only then that any visual effects intended by the weaver can be seen, manifesting a specific arithmetic in the precise counting of warps and wefts, as well as in the geometry in the layout of pattern that weavers must learn, and learn how to develop, if a given tradition is to flourish.

The patterning obtained through the process of weaving in West Africa is most commonly of three or four kinds. The first is warp striping, achieved simply by laying the warps as close as possible in the preparation of the loom and using different colors. The same pattern of stripes can be repeated across the face of the cloth, or two or more sequences of stripes can be placed in sequence, and the visual effects can sometimes dazzle the eyes as if the colors were dancing. The second means of patterning depends upon spreading the warp elements apart as the loom is set up so that, in the woven cloth, the warps are hidden by the weft. For in allowing the weft to be seen, it becomes possible to create blocks of color that can be aligned across the cloth, or alternated to produce a chessboard-type effect, or so placed as to create a seemingly random scattering of color. A third type of woven pattern involves an additional or supplementary weft that floats across the warps. This is either floated across each face, or is woven in with the ground weft when not required for the design.

In West Africa, particular ethnic and/or regional traditions are characterized by specific ways of using these techniques. Warp stripes are still the most commonplace throughout the region, sometimes with supplementary floating weft patterns. One of the best examples of this is the Yoruba cloth known as *aso oke*, literally "top-of-the-hill cloth," the hill identified as the location of the tradition received from one's ancestors, and woven in the major weaving households of Nigerian cities such as Ilorin, Oyo Iseyin, and Ibadan. Yoruba weavers also weave openwork. Since the 1970s young women in Yoruba weaving households have taken up the double-heddle technology and have established themselves as independent weaving masters with great success in places where hitherto the upright loom was the sole apparatus, with the further result of inducing its obsolescence. Weft-faced patterns are especially located in Sierra Leone and in Mali, where it has sometimes been used as a picture-making process. In both countries warp-faced and weft-faced traditions flourish side by side. Only two traditions, Asante and Ewe, both in Ghana, bring all three weave structures together in one strip of fabric, thereby creating forms that are impossible to replicate exactly on a European broadloom. (It has been tried.) The narrower loom facilitates these design processes by allowing very different patterns to be placed beside each other in the one cloth. This may in the end be the justification for the continuing flourishing of these traditions. The use of supplementary warps is rare, but is beginning to be popular with some Ewe weavers. Asante and Ewe weaving is popularly known as *kente*, and while not a word with any obvious etymological significance, it may be derived from the Ewe verbs that refer to the processes of opening up the warp and beating in the weft.

Most North African weaving, whichever type of loom is used, tends to be weft-faced, and one can see this in textiles for clothing and in carpets. Tent cloths, however, are mostly warp-striped. In Somalia, locally woven cloth is generally a balanced plain weave that encourages plaid-like patterning, with stripes in both warp and weft. Weft-float patterns are a feature of some Ethiopian weaving, together with tablet-woven patterns of extraordinary complexity. In the raffia traditions of central Africa, cut-pile is the best-known means of patterning a cloth, but this is not part of the weaving process. In the cotton-weaving traditions of east and southern Africa, the few surviving examples suggest that patterning was no more than stripes making use of the naturally different colors of local cotton.

Africa is a complex social and historical entity. There are many histories in which the traditions of a given locality have become engaged with forms and fabrics introduced from elsewhere in the formation of local modernities now taken for granted. This occurred in the Middle East, Europe, and Africa; there is more on this to follow. There are continuities of form, practice, and ideas from one place to another, especially seen in the delight in breaking up an otherwise plain surface. In principle, there is nothing specifically African about this, of course, but there are specifically African forms of its manifestation. It also happens that some of these specificities depend upon a particular inheritance of the technical means available locally for the manufacture of a piece of cloth. The delight in breaking up an otherwise plain surface manifested in hand-woven patterns, in a thousand different ways, especially in West Africa, is also seen in the techniques of resist-dyeing. In the western Yoruba city of Abeokuta founded in the 1830s, two forms of the indigo-dyed cloths known as *adire* developed with the advent of factory-woven cotton shirting. In one, raffia fiber was used to stitch or tie a pattern across the whole length and breadth of the cloth, while the other was made by pasting starch in a repeat pattern through cut-metal stencils. The raffia and the starch, each in its own way, would resist the dye to create the patterned surface. The manner in which the patterns developed was conditioned by the quality of the factory-woven fabric which was finer in texture than a textile locally woven of hand-spun cotton. Moreover, although indigo-dyed yarn was a commonplace element in weaving, locally woven cloths would normally only have been resist-dyed if they were old and worn and in need of toughening up for continued use. Then a few sticks or stones might have been stitched into the cloth, providing the original basis of the raffia-tied *adire*. The starch-pasted method almost certainly was adapted from European packaging; the zinc linings of colonial tea chests provided the original source of the metal for the stencils. In another Yoruba city, Ibadan, also founded in the 1830s, rather than use cut-metal stencils, comparable designs were painted freehand, again using the starch. There is also now some suggestion that while the imperative to pattern, and the raffia-resist method, has its origins in local sensibilities and practices, at least some aspects of these developments were influenced by ideas and/or practices brought to Nigeria by freed slaves repatriated from Sierra Leone. In any case, much of the early imagery of the starch-resist designs can be derived from topical events in colonial history.

Long-running trade and family contacts between Lagos and Freetown may also have provided the route whereby a new set of resist-dyeing techniques arrived in Nigeria in the late 1960s. They quickly became known as *kampala*, so named after a well-reported peace conference in that Ugandan city. *Kampala* techniques include folding and tying, and stitching, the use of melted candle wax as a resist agent, and the use of factory-made dyes. These and other techniques are indeed found in Freetown, but also in Bamako in Mali, St. Louis in Senegal, and indeed all over West Africa. Meanwhile, the popularity of Kampala signaled the decline of *adire* in Nigeria. There has been a limited revival, mainly through the work of textiles artist Nike Olaniyi at her art center in Oshogbo; but otherwise the resist-dyed patterning using the technology identified in Nigeria as *kampala* flourishes throughout West Africa, even as Yoruba *adire* remains at best obsolescent. Mali is also the location of the Bamana technique known as *bogolan*. This is a method of dyeing the cloth yellow, painting designs in iron-rich earth to darken the dye, and bleaching out the yellow in the unpainted areas. Originally for the magical protection of young women as they are initiated into adult status, and of hunters, this technique has evolved in recent years to provide a modern fashion fabric in Mali and widely available and imitated in Europe and the United States, and also a means of current picture making.

With so much variety in local traditions, we might ask why traders found a ready market for the cloths they brought with them; and yet we know that from the very first records of trans-Saharan trade, textiles were proceeding in both directions. The desirability of cloth, locally made and imported from elsewhere, was thus a well-established West African preference long before coastal trade with Europe, and the merchants must have known this from information available to them via North African sources. European traders from the outset of coastal trade had always included linen and woolen cloth amongst their goods. Some, in particular the Portuguese, traded local textiles from one part of the West African coast to another. They also captured slaves who were weavers and put them to work on the Cape Verde Islands making cloth with North Africa designs for the coastal trade. On the other hand, Danish merchants in the early eighteenth century were surprised to discover that Asante weavers unraveled the silk cloths they had obtained from them in order to reweave the yarn to local design specifications. Their shininess and well-saturated colors, though quite different to anything available locally, were perceived as effective within a local aesthetic. The local wild silk produced a less shiny grayish yarn, that was prestigious in some traditions but not in others. With local cotton and indigo together with other dyes, various shades of blue, yellow, green, brown, black, and a weak purplish pink were produced. A well-saturated red was not available, however; and yet red was almost everywhere a color of ritual value, though the precise content of that value was always locally specific. The color might have to do with transition from one condition of social existence to another, it could denote the volatile nature of a deity, or have wide-ranging connotations from success in childbirth to bloodshed in war. As soon as red woolen cloth and cotton yarn were available they were in demand. Similarly in the nineteenth century, the waste from Italian magenta-dyed silk weaving was traded across the Sahara to be re-spun for local weaving.

In the late nineteenth century, silk was replaced by rayon and in due course by other artificial fibers, while ready-dyed cotton yarn assumed a substantial place in colonial trading accounts. The greater intensity and variety of color with modern dyes was one advantage, while the finer quality of machine-spun yarn was another. In a part of the world where conspicuous consumption was particularly manifested in the cloth you wore, in a context of increased demand given the democratization of systems of authority in colonial and post-colonial histories, the fact that machine-spun yarn could be woven faster than hand-spun cotton gave it an obvious advantage. The catalog of available textures was thus impressive: hand-spun cotton, machine-spun cotton, wild silk, imported silk (and its successors); and from the 1970s onward a laminated plastic fiber with a metallic core in all colors of the rainbow and more.

We can see this same design aesthetic in the bright, almost blatant, African-print fabrics now so ubiquitous throughout Africa, Europe, and the Americas. Indeed, this is a proposition that is supported by what we know of their history. In the course of the nineteenth century, Dutch textile manufacturers wanted to find a way of replicating the Indonesian wax batik process, to produce the textiles at a cheaper price, thereby undercutting Indonesian production. In due course, they developed a duplex roller system that printed hot resin on both faces of the cloth in the manner of the wax used in Indonesia (hence the term "waxprint"). The resin resisted the indigo, and once cleaned off, allowed for the hand-blocking of additional colors. However, two unintended developments in this process rendered the designs unacceptable in Indonesia: an inability to clean all the resin off, leaving spots that continued to resist the additional colors, together with the way these additional colors were not an exact fit but overlapped with adjacent parts of the design. These essentially technical problems imparted to the cloths a variegated quality that Indonesians did not like; and yet, when, by chance, Dutch merchants, probably in Elmina (the precise details remain unknown), tried these fabrics on their customers they proved to be extremely popular. Once the sights of the designers in the Netherlands were trained upon this region of West Africa, they quickly learned that the visualization of local proverbs added to the local interest in these fabrics. The earliest dated example, is located in the archive of the ABC (Arnold Brunnschweiler and Co.) factory at Hyde, Cheshire, though it was produced by the Haarlem Cotton Company, is 1895. It shows the palm of the hand with the twelve pennies of the English shilling: "the palm of the hand is sweeter than the back of the hand," the point being that as the palm holds the money so we hope to receive good fortune.

In the preindustrial technologies of Africa, printed textiles were unknown but for the two examples of *adinkra* and *kanga*. The former is an Asante cotton cloth produced at Ntonso, north of Kumasi, in which graphic signs are printed in black, using stamps made from carved calabash (gourd). Almost all of the individual patterns have an associated proverb, but this has not prevented the appearance of novel patterns based on the Mercedes-Benz logo, or making use of writing. These cloths do not convey precise messages, but evoke a tradition of knowledge about the social world. When the designs are printed on red, black, brown, or purple, *adinkra* is worn at funerals, whereas on white it has celebratory implications. In Zanzibar and related centers of East African Swahili-speaking coastal visual practice the tradition of the *kanga*, developed from a hand-block-printing tradition brought from India. A length of cloth about one by two yards was printed in a variegated pattern with a differently patterned border that became identified by the Swahili word for guinea fowl due to its speckled plumage. Once these fabrics began to be factory-printed in India and East Africa, Swahili proverbs and political slogans found their way into these cloths with the development of designs that visualized the printed words. In both East and West Africa, variegated design and the visualization of proverbs seem to have been the keys to the success of cloths now designed and printed in substantial quantities in local factories.

See also **Adinkra; Adire; Bark Cloth; Bogolan; Indigo; Kanga; Kente; Loom.**

BIBLIOGRAPHY

Barbican Art Gallery [John Picton et al]. *The Art of African Textiles: Technology, Tradition and Lurex.* London: Lund Humphries, 1995.

Bolland, Rita. *Tellem Textiles: Archaeological Finds from Burial Caves in Mali's Bandiagara Cliff.* Leiden, Netherlands: Rijksmuseum voor Volkenkunde, 1991.

Byfield, Judith. *The Bluest Hands, A Social and Economic History of Women Dyers in Abeokuta.* Oxford: James Currey, 2002.

Clarke, Duncan. *The Art of African Textiles.* London: Grange Books, 1997.

Gardi, Bernhard. *Le Boubou—C'est Chic.* Basel: Museum der Kulturen, 2000.

Idiens Dale, and K. G. Ponting, eds. *Textiles of Africa.* Bath, U.K.: Pasold Institute, 1980.

Kreamer, Christine Mullen, and Sarah Fee. *Objects as Envoys: Cloth Imagery and Diplomacy in Madagascar.* Seattle and London: National Museum of African Art, University of Washington Press, 2002.

Lamb, Venice. *West African Weaving.* London: Duckworth, 1975.

Lamb, Venice, and Judy Holmes. *Nigerian Weaving.* Hertingfordbury, U.K.: Roxford Books, 1980.

Lamb, Venice, and Alastair Lamb. *Au Cameroun: Weaving—Tissage.* Hertingfordbury: Roxford Books, 1981.

Woman in "Chinese" slacks and a jacket. Stylistic conventions from diverse cultures spanning the Asian continent have been a source of inspiration for fashion designers since the seventeenth century. (*See* Orientalism) John S. Major. Reproduced by permission.

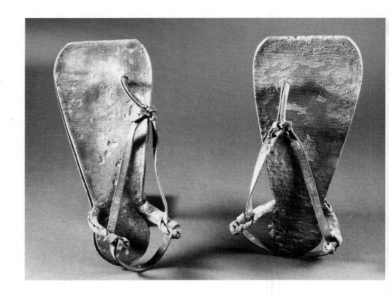

Top: **Ancient sandals.** Sandals are the oldest form of footwear. These leather sandals from Egypt date from the fourth millenium B.C.E. (*See* Sandals) © Gianni Dagli Orti/Corbis.

Middle: **Eighteenth-century shoe with clog.** By the eighteenth century, shoes of varying heels were in use. The English heel, as pictured in this example from 1750–1760, was thicker and low to mid-height. (*See* Shoes, Women's) Courtesy of the Bata Shoe Museum, Toronto. Reproduced by permission.

Bottom: **Art Deco style shoe, 1922–1925.** By the 1920s, heels grew taller and colored footwear began to appear, though it was seen as inappropriate for anything other than evening wear. (*See* Shoes, Women's) Courtesy of the Bata Shoe Museum, Toronto. Reproduced by permission.

Carved printing blocks. Intricately carved printing blocks are used to decorate textiles. In the twentieth century, modern textiles replaced much of this traditional production. (*See* Textiles, Middle Eastern) © Arthur Thevenart/Corbis.

Top: **Embroidered silk robe.** Ever since the domestication of the silkworm around the third millennium B.C.E., silk has been the favored fabric of the Chinese upper class. (*See* Textiles, Chinese; China: History of Dress) © Christie's Images/Corbis.

Middle: **Coptic textile fragments.** An estimated 150,000 of these archeological fabrics were found in Egyptian burial sites, representing the fashions and furnishings of Egypt's Coptic period, dating from the late third- to mid-seventh centuries. (*See* Textiles, Coptic) Henry Art Gallery, University of Washington, Seattle, Helen Stager Poulsen Collection, 83.7–56, 93.7–57, 83.7–58. Photo credit: Richard Nicol. Reproduced by permission.

Bottom: **Iranian fabric printer.** This artisan is using a wooden printing block to print fabric by hand. With its fine details and complex coloring, Iranian designs have been considered to be among the finest in the Middle East. (*See* Textiles, Middle Eastern) © Corbis.

Top left: **Chinese wedding costumes.** Both the bride and groom in traditional Chinese ceremonies wear elaborate headdresses. (*See* Wedding Costume) © Royalty-Free/Corbis.

Top right: **Nigerian bride and groom.** Despite the prevalence in many societies to incorporate Western wedding fashion into their marriage ceremonies, many people continue to value national and local traditions. (*See* Wedding Costume) © Kerstin Geier/Corbis.

Bottom: **Bridal fashions from *Godey's Lady's Book,* 1868.** The traditional white wedding gown known in the twentieth and twenty-first centuries was less common in the nineteenth century, when women often wore one of their few "good" gowns at their marriage ceremony. These gowns were often black. (*See* Wedding Costume) © Cynthia Hart Designer/Corbis.

A Hindu bride and groom. A Hindu bride and groom are seated for their traditional marriage ceremony. The bride wears an elaborate red *sari,* while the groom is dressed in a white *sherwani.* (*See* Wedding Costume) © Bob Krist/Corbis.

Kid Creole performs in the musical *Oh! What a Night,* **at London's Apollo Theatre.** The zoot suit projected a sophisticated and daring image for its wearer, associated as it was with hipsters, drugs, and sex. (*See* Zoot Suit) © Robbie Jack/Corbis.

———. *Sierra Leone Weaving*. Hertingfordbury: Roxford Books, 1984.

Menzel, Brigitte. *Textilien aus Westafrika*. 3 vols. Berlin: Museums fur Volkerkunde, 1972.

Picton, John, and John Mack. *African Textiles*, 2nd ed. London: British Museum, 1989.

Prince Claus Fund, 1998: *The Art of African Fashion*, Prince Claus Fund, The Hague, and Africa World Press, Asmara and Trenton, N.J. Note especially Hudita Nura Mustafa's "Sartorial ecumenes: African styles in a social and economic context," pp. 15–45.

Renne, Elisha. *Cloth that Does Not Die: The Meaning of Cloth in Bunu Social Life*. Seattle and London: University of Washington Press, 1995.

Ross, Doran. *Wrapped in Pride*. Los Angeles: University of California, 1998.

Rovine, Victoria. *Bogolan: Shaping Culture through Cloth in Contemporary Mali*. Washington, D.C.: Smithsonian Institution Press, 2001.

Sieber, Roy, John Picton, Rita Bolland, et al. *History, Design, and Craft in West African Strip-Woven Cloth*. Washington, D.C.: Smithsonian Institute, 1992.

Spring, Christopher, and Julie Hudson. *North African Textiles*, British Museum, 1995.

Tulloch, Carol, ed. *Black Style*. London: Victoria and Albert Museum, 2004. Note especially John Picton's "What to wear in West Africa," pp. 18–46.

John Picton

TEXTILES, ANDEAN

TEXTILES, ANDEAN Perhaps no other society in history poured as much cultural energy into textiles as indigenous Andean civilization. Galvanized by inhospitable terrain—soaring mountain ranges, impenetrable jungles, dry deserts, and cold oceans—Andean people achieved great technological accomplishment, economic prosperity, and political cohesion without written language. Textiles developed as the primary material focus of civilization, serving to embody wealth, communicate complex ideas, and conceptualize abstractions, as well as more familiar roles of personal identity in a fashion system. For Andean societies, the textile medium paralleled uses of gold, writing, mathematics, and painted art in European history. Meaning was conveyed not just in color, pattern, and style, but also through complex processes of weaving and fabric structures. The centrality of fiber art to the Andean mind resulted in a remarkable development of skills, design, and technique unmatched anywhere.

Clothing in the Ancient Andes

Andean textile art flowered long before the sixteenth-century European invasion. Dry coastal deserts were home to third-millennium B.C.E. cotton traditions based on ingenious structural elaboration rather than color to achieve design. At the same time, mountain societies developed traditions of working colorful dyed camelid fibers. Climate conditions leave few examples of highland wool traditions until brightly colored yarns appear on the coast during the first millennium B.C.E. The fusion of the two traditions established the character and brilliance of the Andean textile tradition that has persisted into the twenty-first-century.

Andean textile evidence comes from tombs in the coastal deserts with ideal preservation conditions. While opulent tombs may yield spectacular textiles, reconstruction of ordinary costume from grave goods demands care. Garments buried with important persons may reveal technical and design sophistication but not represent daily clothing. Less elaborate tombs, miniatures, and human images in tapestry or painted pottery show that a basic Andean costume existed by at least the first millennium B.C.E. and persisted until the arrival of Europeans two thousand years later. Constructed of short warp fabrics with little or no tailoring, the costume varied in pattern, layout, color, and structure to reflect cultural identity.

Across most of the Andean area, men wore a breechclout and a pullover shirt. The shirt extended nearly to the knee in some cultures but in others stopped at the waist, making the breechclout visible. Shirts might have a fringe at the bottom and arm openings, ornamental bindings, or other elaborate decoration that indicated social roles. A Nazca culture shirt of the late first millennium B.C.E. might be plain-woven natural-colored cotton embellished by complex wool embroidery at the neck slit, arm openings, and hem. The Middle Horizon Wari culture (500–1100 C.E.) made fine-spun alpaca tapestry shirts as symbols of rank and authority that conveyed complex patterned meanings. Men wore a mantle as an overgarment, carried a shoulder bag, and used a headdress to express cultural identity. Headdresses included hats, turbans, and braided cords wound around the heads. Elaborate tapestry shirts of Wari men were complimented by a four-sided pile or knotted hat that expressed mythological themes.

FABULOUS TOMBS

The dry deserts of coastal Peru hold elaborate tombs filled with fabric treasures demonstrating technical and design control over the textile medium, but not necessarily reflecting daily costume. Mummy bundles from Paracas (first millennium B.C.E.) contain huge wrapping cloths, fine decorated bands, and embroideries proving a keen understanding of mathematics as well as design. Patterns on cloth found in these bundles chronicle a rich spiritual life filled with mythical beings and elaborate rituals in a highly-stratified society.

The basic women's garment in pre-Colombian societies was a square cloth wrapped around the body below the arms and pinned or stitched above the shoulders. The dress reached below the knee and may have had plain color or more elaborate patterned stripes worn horizontally. Many cultures added a patterned belt. For cultures like Nazca, large shoulder pins were part of the fashion statement. Over the dress, Andean women wore a square or rectangular shawl around the shoulders and pinned at the breast. Highly visible shawls often had complex patterning in tapestry, embroidery, or warp-faced techniques. Like men, women wore culturally specific headdresses, such as woven headbands or head cloths that fell down the shoulders and back. Hair, generally worn long and loose, or in multibraided styles, also figured in statements of fashion and identity.

The Inca Period

At the time of the sixteenth-century European invasion, the Inca Empire spanned highland and coastal Andes from present-day Colombia to Chile and united many ethnic and language groups into a single political and economic structure. Local costume from the basic Andean style of shirts and mantles, dresses and shawls, was preserved as an indicator of ethnic identity, useful in administration of the sprawling Inca enterprise. Evidence for Inca costume includes burials, figurines, and painted images found in earlier times, but also writings, line drawings, and portraits by early European visitors. Inca use of cloth may provide a good model for understanding costume and fashion in earlier Andean cultures.

Two modes of production characterized Inca textiles. *Qompi* was fine camelid cloth, mostly of tapestry, produced with state support by cloistered women or men. They worked on an unusual frame loom at least twice as wide as it was tall. The fabrics were folded in the middle to become men's shirts that were distributed by the government as uniforms or rewards for state service. Large checkerboard patterns and other repeating designs indicated social or military roles, while more elaborate registered patterns called *tokapu* may have functioned within a still obscure system of communication. *Tokapu* blocks are also found on belts used by both Inca men and women. *Awasqa*, a second mode of textile production made in the rural villages, was warp-faced cloth with complex patterns made from two oppositely colored warps in a technique known as complimentary warp weaving. Some *Awasqa* was tax payment to the state, but most local style cloth stayed within the village-specific fashion system.

People of all ranks within the Inca Empire probably wore the same essential costume of shirts, breechclouts, and mantles for men and wraparound dresses and shawls for women, with marked differences in quality to indicate class or identity. Finely spun and brightly colored cloth reserved for the Inca nobility was called silk by the Spanish because such smooth, lustrous, and fine-to-the-

touch fabric was only known in Europe from Chinese cloth. These fabrics became shirts that reached to the knee and were sometimes belted over a breechclout with a relatively plain mantle as outergarment. Inca men wore very short hair, and the upper classes used large earplugs that stretched the lobes. Men's headdress was rigidly controlled; higher classes wrapped ornate braided strands around their heads. Inca-period women's dress often had broad horizontal stripes and reached the ground, held at the waist with a highly patterned belt. The shawl pinned in front usually had more elaborate patterning in bands of complementary warp or weft weaves. Women's hair was loose or in two braids, and held by a patterned headband or covered with a cloth. Wrapped in striped and patterned cloth, Inca nobility must have made a very colorful sight indeed. People of lower status wore the same garment types, but they were constructed of coarser natural-colored yarns with less patterning laid out in village-specific formats.

The Colonial Period

The European invasion of the sixteenth century altered costume drastically, and introduced new materials such as sheep's wool and silk, as well as new ideas and forms. In less than a hundred years, Andean men adopted European breeches, hose, and felt hats. The Inca tapestry shirt became ritual costume used to claim royal descent, and specific meaning of patterns was lost. Portraits of Inca noblewomen show fuller, ground-length Inca-style dresses. Decorated belts define the waist, and highly patterned shawls cover the shoulders. Common people of the Andes continued to use much of the basic costume but added pants for men and hats in the new European technique of knitting.

Spanish Peru, a closed colony until the eighteenth century, developed a unique Creole costume from European, Islamic, and indigenous sources. In addition to the long full skirts and lace trim familiar in Europe, Spanish Creole women added the *manta*, a small hood that could cover the face in the manner of the Islamic Moors, and the *saya*, a long straight overskirt from indigenous Andean models. The *Limeña Tapada* (Covered Woman of Lima) of the seventeenth century wore long skirts to obscure the feet, while tight bodices went so far as to reveal the breasts in public.

The eighteenth-century advent of the Bourbon Kings in Spain and political ferment in Peru led to profound changes in the clothing and fashion. With the colony opened to trade, Creole costume fell into step with European fashion. Meanwhile, leaders claiming Inca royal descent revitalized indigenous costume as part of rebellion against Spanish authorities. Insurrections led to prohibition against indigenous costume and to sumptuary laws requiring Andeans to adopt a new costume derived from that of Iberian commoners. This set of clothes included vests, jackets, and knee-length breeches for men and full skirts for women. Both genders adopted a saucer-shaped hat

GLOSSARY OF TECHNICAL TERMS

Bayeta: Fabric originally manufactured in Spain that was widely used in South America in the Colonial period. Made from cotton or wool fiber, it was loosely woven from softly twisted yarns that were brushed up on the surface. In order to make the fabric more compact and dense it was subjected to a special finishing process.

Complementary warp pattern: A pattern in which an additional set of lengthwise (warp) yarns is used in the same way as the primary set of warp yarns. Emery

(The Primary Structures of Fabrics, 1980) describes such warps as "co-equal."

Warp: Lengthwise yarns in a woven fabric.

Warp-faced: Fabric in which the lengthwise (warp) yarns predominate on the surface of the fabric.

Weft: Crosswise yarns in a woven fabric. Synonyms include filling and woof.

Weft-faced: Fabric in which the crosswise (weft) yarns predominate on the surface of the fabric.

---

made of felt over an armature of coiled basketry. Widespread throughout the Peruvian Andes by the beginning of the nineteenth century, these costumes were precursors of the twenty-first century's traditional Andean costume.

The Late Twentieth and Early Twenty-First Centuries

The multicultural Andes in 2004 encompasses parts of Ecuador, Peru, Bolivia, Chile, and Argentina, where nearly 30 million people speak indigenous languages. Millions more without language identity still live fundamentally Andean lives, with cultural identities reflected through widely-differing costume. Many use style flexibly, changing costume to express different aspects of the multiple identities that are their heritage.

The most elaborately-patterned handwoven Andean cloth is made in rural villages from Cuzco south through Bolivia. Each village has a distinctive costume derived from fusion of Iberian and indigenous Andean models. Many village women wear full skirts of balanced, plain-weave, woolen cloth known as *bayeta*, white cotton blouses and vests with machine embroidery, and felt or *bayeta* jackets. Village-specific felt-covered basket hats and decorated warp-faced shawls indicate identity. Some Bolivian women use a patterned straight *aksu* overskirt derived from the original Andean dress.

The distinctive costumes of women who leave village identity behind to live in major highland cities, use manufactured goods to declare participation in the money economy and class, rather than village identity. Knee-length pleated skirts with machine-made sweaters and blouses mimic but are not confused with rural costume. Women wear shoes and hose rolled at the knee, and cover their shoulders with machine-made shawls. High-crowned white straw hats are the most distinctive feature of the area-wide costume worn by women of commerce.

Highland men may own village-specific clothes for special occasions, but usually wear an area-wide costume to indicate class rather than village identity. Most costume elements are store bought, such as pants and shirts, although men use a poncho handmade by women in their lives. In the twentieth century throughout most of Peru and Bolivia, this poncho was walnut-dyed brown without pattern, but red ponchos with supplementary warp-woven patterns have more recently become popular with university-educated men. Brown ponchos are usually worn with a felt fedora, while red-poncho men prefer to go hatless with a neck scarf in very cold conditions.

The northern Andes of Ecuador has very different costumes, mostly made by specialists from machine-made cloth. Women wear dark wraparound skirts at the knee or below and cotton lace blouses topped with voluminous bead necklaces. Felt fedoras crown the head. Men wear shirts and pants of white cotton covered with a machine-made or handmade poncho that may be reversible or even have a collar but has little patterning. The belt that both sexes wrap around the waist may be the last remaining handwoven costume item.

The arrival of the money economy, tourism, and the information age has brought great change to traditional Andean costume. While some villages adhere to traditional productive patterns and costume norms, even rural people adopt conventional store-bought clothes as they enter the money economy. Many discover the warmth and convenience of down coats and other garments left by hikers and tourists. With even the most remote villages now within reach of television, many women abandon braided hairstyles of previous generations and adopt jogging suits and other casual dress. For thousands of years, technology of cloth production and use has been both a visible fashion statement and the primary mode of intellectual exploration. Recent changes challenge the fundamental identity of Andean people, whose culture was built on cloth.

See also **America, South: History of Dress.**

BIBLIOGRAPHY

Adelson, Laurie and Bruce Takami. *Weaving Traditions of Highland Bolivia.* Los Angeles: Craft and Folk Art Museum, 1979. Excellent photos of village specific cloth and costume from Bolivia.

Guaman Poma de Ayala, Felipe. *Nueva Corónica y Buen Gobierno.* Paris: Université de Paris, Travaux et Mémoires de l'Institut d'Ethnologie XXIII, 1936. Over a thousand drawings of Inca life, costume, and history sent to the King of Spain in 1615.

Murra, John V. "Cloth and Its Function in the Inca State." *American Anthropologist* 64, no. 4 (August 1962): 710–728. A fundamental account of the expanded use of cloth by Andean society.

Paul, Anne. *Paracas Ritual Attire.* Norman: University of Oklahoma Press, 1990. An excellent analysis of textiles and costume found in sumptuous burials from the Paracas peninsula.

Rowe, Ann Pollard, ed. "Nazca Figurines and Costume." *Textile Museum Journal* 29 and 30 (1991): 93–128. An excellent reconstruction of costume in ancient Peru.

———. "Inca Weaving and Costume." *Textile Museum Journal* 34 and 35 (1996): 5–53. An authoritative account of what people looked like during the Inca period.

———. *Costume and Identity in Highland Ecuador.* Seattle: University of Washington Press, 1998. An excellent and comprehensive examination of the costume used in the many cultural areas of Ecuador at the end of the twentieth century.

Rowe, Ann Pollard, and John Cohen. *Hidden Threads of Peru: Q'ero Textiles.* London: Merrell, 2002. An exceptional view of cloth and culture in a contemporary Andean community.

Ed Franquemont

TEXTILES, BYZANTINE

TEXTILES, BYZANTINE Constantine the Great (r. 324–337) reunified the Roman Empire as its sole ruler in 324 and promptly began the expansion of the little harbor city of Byzantium on the Bosporus, renaming it Constantinople. Replacing Rome as the imperial capital, the city reflected the emperor's new Christian faith in the central cathedral complex, while Hellenistic and Eastern schemes were used in the city's public areas. The Byzantine Empire's vast, all-Mediterranean territory was greatly reduced after Justinian (527–565). It was beset by many reverses and crises throughout the flowering of the Macedonian dynasty (867–1056) and suffered its most brutal shock during the Sack of Constantinople by the Crusaders in 1204. Throughout the period Constantinople exerted a cultural, a spiritual, and at times, a military authority on its western and eastern neighbors, an influence that was reestablished during the Palaiologan dynasty (1261–1453). Byzantine art and architecture survived the empire's fall in 1453 to the Ottoman Turks by continuing in the Eastern Orthodox heritage.

The Textile Context

A Spanish rabbi and traveler, Benjamin of Tudela (1127–1173), reported on a visit to Constantinople that, "All the people look like princes. The Second Rome is a glittering city of miracles. Everybody is dressed in silk, purple and gold" (Geijer, p. 129). Such awe was a frequent reaction in Western visitors when encountering the splendor of the capital; they were also hopeful to be on the receiving end for imperial favors. These might take the form of superb Byzantine textiles, exceptional gifts of prestige and diplomacy for select secular or ecclesiastical rulers. Many of these silken achievements of superior loom technology and dyeing excellence survive in the early 2000s, often reduced to tiny fragments in church treasuries and museums. Patterned and figured, monochrome or multihued, these silks were made into vestments for powerful bishops and abbots, served as wrappers or purses for relics, and were draped, as large *pallia*, over the remains of saints in shrines and tombs. Rare imperial inscribed silks are known to have been stored in the west for decades or centuries before being used as funerary textiles. Silks from the imperial workshops and city guilds also came west in the trousseaus of Byzantine princesses. Yet others were silks of lesser quality, some made in the Islamic East, and purchased by Western visitors to Constantinople.

Europeans were probably unaware that an important reason for the strict ceremony of the imperial court in Constantinople was a long-standing game of one-upmanship vis-à-vis the equally elaborate etiquette in the courts of Middle East, and, from the late seventh century, Islamic rulers. Intricate court ceremony had a long history in ideas of divine kingship. Prior to Islam's introduction, the Byzantines had established relationships of reciprocity in peacetime as well as war with the Sassanian dynasty (224–651), by sharing designs, motifs, and figures. The first Islamic rulers of the Umayyad Caliphate (661–750) attempted to match the opulence of Byzantium in the architecture and decoration of their desert palaces. The Abbasid Caliphs (763–1258), settling in Baghdad, provided further rivalry to Constantinople in conspicuous consumption; late eighth-century texts describe how Syria's merchant fleet supplied luxury items to the Byzantine court. These interdependencies explain the numerous shared features in the art and architecture of the Mediterranean cultures, as well as the staying power of certain recurring motifs. After 1453, Byzantine style survived and continued, especially in embroidered panels used in the sacred and secular life of Greece, Armenia, Bulgaria, and in the monasteries of Kievan Rus.

Silk Manufacture and Importation

The 912 *Book of Ceremonies* of Constantine VII (d. 959) sets out the elaborate, ranked dress requirements for courtiers and administrators of the empire. To meet these prodigious needs, textile production was prioritized and put under imperial control. The first generation of skilled weavers had been brought during the sixth century from the Mediterranean or Persia, where the draw-loom pattern device had developed since the third century. This technology allowed figured motifs to be mechanically replicated. The weavers' privileged position was hereditary to begin with, but later the conditions worsened as the state attempted to maintain control of the market forces. Texts such as the *Book of the Prefect* (*Eparchikon Biblion*), in which the regulations for the city's five private guilds were codified, details the organization of textile manufacture in Constantinople. There were merchants (*metaxoprates*, raw-silk dealers; *bestioprates*, silk-cloth vendors; and *prandioprates*, Syrian silk sellers) and manufacturers (*katartarii*, silk-thread producers; and *serikarii*, weavers).

Specialized trades of dyers of purple, weavers, and tailors worked in the imperial workshops, but information about the actual operations or types of equipment can only be inferred from the few surviving examples that can be securely identified. One striking feature of the finest silk *pallia* with their large-scale designs and multiple colors is the loom width. Some were more than 6 feet (2 meters) wide, requiring extraordinary technical capability in loom construction and accomplished levels of collaboration during the weaving. Silks from production centers outside the Empire do not match these dimensions; the widest from Zandaneh, near Bukhara, measured 47 inches (120 centimeters).

The Abbasid silk fabrics, imported in significant quantities to Constantinople by Syrian traders, indicate a range in weaving quality—the Byzantine wealthy may well have been dressed in imported Syrian silks, while true *panni imperialis* were reserved for the court. A surviving group of red-ground textiles, the so-called Samson silks, shows a standing man wrestling a lion framed by undulating borders; it is proof of the merchants' ability to provide an efficient supply chain for various markets. Details in the drawing of the figure and the execution vary from one example to the next, giving a range of quality for a popular theme from fine and perfectly woven to coarse and replete with weaving errors.

Rabbi Benjamin mentioned in his eleventh-century report that 2,500 Jews worked as dyers in Byzantine Pera, and 2,000 more in Thebes on Peleponnesos, evidence of the degree and scope of specialization in the trades. The rare Tyrian, or Murex, purple dye was of ideological importance especially to the Macedonian dynasty that designated its heirs as *Porphyrogennetos* (i.e., born in the palace's purple marble room). Analyses of the dye content in the surviving corpus of Byzantine textiles reveal that a small minority contains the fabled and prohibitively expensive true shellfish purple; most are combinations of indigo-blue dye, cross-dyed with madder or kermes red. Murex purple has been confirmed in the silk yarns weaving the clothing of the Virgin Mary in the famous *Sancta Sanctorum* silks, and in certain of the imperial eagle silks.

Types of Textiles

The imperial production centers prioritized pattern-woven silks in mechanically repeated designs, produced with relative speed and ease on the draw-loom. Other types of textiles, such as plain woolens and linens, certainly coexisted with the prodigious output of the Constantinopolitan looms, but their survival rate is scant by comparison.

Silk weaves. Structurally, the great majority of the surviving patterned silks use compound twill (*samit, samitum*), in one or more colors. Plain weave (*tabby*) is represented; some display supplemental or compound patterning. A novel compound weave, *lampas*, appears in its fully developed version in which different weave structures are combined (such as plain weave and twill or satin), first in Baghdad, and presumably soon thereafter reaching Islamic Spain and Constantinople circa 1100.

Tapestry. Early Byzantine textiles rendered in tapestry technique with Greek inscriptions have survived in Egypt's dry sands in considerable numbers. Usually termed "Coptic," although some have been shown to be Syrian, they are made of linen and colored wool thread for making clothing components, *clavi*, and for decorative curtains and wall hangings. A later, rare and large eleventh-century example in silk, circa 2 meters square, was found in the tomb of Bishop Gunther (d. 1065); it depicts a mounted, triumphant emperor.

Embroidery. In classical texts, Greek women's needlework skills are celebrated, and establish traditions that lived on in Byzantine women's quarters, *gynacea*. Groups of fourth- to seventh-century woolen embroidered panels for clothing and interior decoration with late antique themes and Greek inscriptions have been found in excavations in Egypt. The figures in the border of Empress Theodora's mantle in the famous Ravenna mosaic, for example, are thought to be embroideries. Needlework in the Palaiologan style survives in splendid works created for Russian monasteries from the fifteenth century.

Design Motifs, Iconography

The meta-language of power and divine privilege in ancient Middle Eastern royal motifs and compositional schemes was assimilated in the cultures around the Mediterranean. Weavers in Tang Dynasty China (618–906) also adopted it for silk designs produced for trade. The animal motifs include lions, elephants, eagles, and fantasy hybrids such as the senmurv and griffin, often incorporating a tree-of-life, and nearly always framed by the ubiquitous decorated roundel, a long-lived style that only waned by the thirteenth century. Small floral and geometric motifs, also based on Sassanian models, include heart- and spade-shaped foliate motifs in horizontal or offset registers. During the periods of Iconoclasm (726–787, 814–843) when no figurative depictions of Christian divinities and persons were allowed, Constantinopolitan workshops favored motifs that evoked the heritage of the late antique, depicting charioteers and hunt scenes.

See also **Textiles, Coptic.**

BIBLIOGRAPHY
There are still only a few monographs on Byzantine textiles. Most works cited below treat the topic in considerable detail, however, and in context.

Benjamin of Tudela. *The Itinerary of Rabbi Benjamin of Tudela.* Translated and edited by A. Asher. London and Berlin: A. Asher and Company, 1840.

Boak, A. E. R. "Notes and Documents: The Book of the Prefect." *Journal of Economic and Business History* 1 (1929): 597–618.

Falke, Otto von. *Kunstgeschichte der Seidenweberei.* Berlin: Verlag Ernst Wasmuth, 1921. Standard text, superseded in some respects by recent findings, still required reading. Exists in English translation.

Flury-Lemberg, Mechtild. *Textile Conservation and Research.* Bern: Abegg-Stiftung, 1988. Meticulously researched, comprehensive case studies.

Geijer, Agnes. *A History of Textile Art: A Selective Account.* Stockholm and London: Pasold Research Fund, 1979. Lucid and concise, a gold-standard survey.

Kalavrezou, Ioli. "Luxury Objects." In *The Glory of Byzantium: Art and Culture of the Middle Byzantine Era A.D. 843–1261.* Edited by Helen C. Evans and William D. Wixom. New York: The Metropolitan Museum of Art (1997): 218–253. Good survey in important, recent exhibition catalog.

Kislinger, E. "Jüdische Gewerbetreibende in Byzanz." In *Die Juden in ihrer mittelalterlichen Umwelt.* Weimar, 1991. Source for primary texts on pivotal role Jews played in trade and manufacture of textiles.

Martiniani-Reber, Marielle. *Soieries sassanides, coptes et Byzantines Ve-Xie siècles.* Lyon: Musée historique des tissus; Paris: Editions de la Réunion des muses nationaux, 1986. Fine, detailed catalog of this museum's textiles collections.

Mathews, Thomas F. *Byzantium from Antiquity to the Renaissance.* New York: Harry N. Abrams, 1998. Refreshing and synthesizing examination of the Empire and its aftermath.

Muthesius, Anna. *Byzantine Silk Weaving A.D. 400 to A.D. 1200.* Vienna: Verlag Fassbaender, 1997. A valiant and welcome attempt to catalog all surviving Byzantine silk examples; unfortunately, not all are illustrated. Indispensable for further fieldwork.

Petrova, Yevgenia, ed. *Russian Monasteries: Art and Tradition.* St. Petersburg: The State Russian Museum, 1997. A catalog of monastic art, including important embroideries.

Sandberg, Gösta. *The Red Dyes: Cochineal, Madder, and Murex Purple.* Asheville, N.C.: Lark Books, 1994. A richly illustrated guide to the history and technology of red dyes.

Schorta, Regula. "Zur Entwicklung der Lampastechnik." In *Islamische Textilkunst des Mittelalters: Aktuelle Probleme. Riggisberger Berichte 5.* Riggisberg, Switzerland: Abbeggstiftung, 1997. One of the foremost textile-structure specialists accounts for the development of lampas.

Soucek, Priscilla P. "Artistic Exchange in the Mediterranean Context." In *The Meeting of Two Worlds: The Crusades and the Mediterranean Context.* Edited by Clifton Olds. Ann Arbor, Mich.: The University of Michigan Museum of Art, 1981. An early contribution to the accepted notion of the shared Mediterranean heritage in art and architecture.

———. "Byzantium and the Islamic East." In *The Glory of Byzantium: Art and Culture of the Middle Byzantine Era, A.D. 843–1261.* Edited by Helen C. Evans and William D. Wixom. New York: The Metropolitan Museum of Art, 1997. A lucid and definitive contribution on the cultural interactions between Byzantium and Islam.

Vogt, A. *Constantin VII porphyrogénète: Le Livre des cérémonies.* Paris, 1935–1939. Primary source text.

Volbach, W. Fritz. *Early Decorative Textiles.* London: Paul Hamlyn, 1969. A discursive standby, with a focus on the Byzantine material.

Zagorsk Museum Collection. *Early Russian Embroidery in the Zagorsk Museum* Moscow: Collection Sovietskaya Russia Publishers, 1983. Ample black-and-white illustrations add to this important Russian collection.

Désirée Koslin

TEXTILES, CENTRAL ASIAN Central Asia consists of a great sweep of landmass running from the Pacific Ocean, off the coast of Siberia, to the plains of central Europe, with high mountain chains edged with tundra and desert. The foothills, plateaus, and valleys are often luxuriant, supporting villages and towns. In the vast deserts, rivers nurture the isolated oasis cities. The great cultural centers of Asia—India, China, and Iran—lie beyond the mountains. These cultural centers both influenced and were influenced by Central Asian tradition. At the center of this landmass are the Pamir Mountains. The Tien Shan range runs up through Tajikistan, Uzbekistan, Kyrgyzstan, and Xinjiang to circle the Tarim Basin (Tarim Pendi) and the Taklimakan Desert. Beyond, the Altai Mountains separate Mongolia from the steppes of Kazakhstan.

Two major ethnic groups populated the area during prehistoric times. The people of Indo-European descent, who had an agrarian background, moved eastward and were responsible for the oasis settlements, while the nomadic Turkic tribes, belonging to a number of Mongoloid people, moved westward from the steppes.

The fertile ravine and upland areas, running in an arc from Iran to China, have a network of autonomous kingdoms; the oasis cities of the Silk Road were linked by trade and religious beliefs. From the first century B.C.E. to the Arab conquests of the eighth century C.E. the main kingdoms, known as khanates, were Chorasmia, largely Turkmenistan, Bactria, northern Afghanistan, and Soghdia (in the area of Uzbekistan) lying between two main rivers Amu and Syr Darya. Fergana included Uzbekistan and Tajikistan and ran up to the Osh area of Kyrgyzstan, with the cities of Nisa, Merv, Samarkand, Piandjikent, and Bamyan.

The vast open areas were home to a number of tribes whose way of life was nomadic. They moved over the vast steep lands with their herds of sheep and camels, as well as their horses, which gave them the mobility to strike at powerful enemies and subdue them. The horse was in a way their lifeline, as they could travel long distances living on the mare's milk and the fermented kumis. The Greek historian Heroditus (484–425 B.C.E.) wrote about the tribes, describing their mobile homes (yurta) and the seasonal movement over vast areas. The description would still fit the way of life of some Kazaks, who inhabit the remote area of Noi in Uzbekistan, and the Torkomans of remote parts of Turkmenistan and the extreme northern part of Iran.

The nomadic way of life led to the development of a range of textiles for fabrics used for their homes as protection from the harsh elements, and also as woven, felted, and embroidered objects. These made up furniture, containers, habitat, clothing, objects that marked the rites of passage, and exchange that built social ties. The woven designs signified their identity; many motifs had an esoteric meaning, helping them to control the evil spirits that governed the unknown.

The fleece of the sheep provided wool for felting, creating the yurta, caps, shoes, and coats. Wool was also spun, crocheted, knitted, and woven into fabrics. Excavations have revealed felted fibers indicating that this art was known from Neolithic times. The frozen Pazyryk burials (400 B.C.E.) of the Scythians have led to the discovery of extraordinary felts with complex patterns, woven carpets of great fineness, and embroidered silks, which reveal the sophistication of the culture of these people, who were termed "barbarians."

Trade was carried out by the tribes from very early onward with the Chinese to the east, as well as with the Greeks to the west. The Silk Road may have existed from an earlier time, according to some scholars, than the historic date associated with Emperor Wu-ti (145–187 B.C.E.). The fact that Emperor Wu-ti negotiated with the King of Fergana for brood mares and stallions indicates that he wanted to play an important role in the exchange of commodities.

The excavations at Loulan and Niya by Sir Auriel Stein revealed rich colored figured textiles, felt, carpets, tapestry weaves, and remnants of wool garments and other fibers for wrapping bodies for burial. The rich tradition of textiles shared by the area indicates close links with China. The trade contacts also brought influences from India, as well as the near east. Pliny (41–45 C.E.) mentions trading with Central Asia since ancient times. Some of the finest historical textiles after the discovery of the Scythian burial sites are the Sogdian textiles woven from the seventh to the ninth centuries. The weft-faced complex twill woven in silk has patterns enclosed in roundels with juxtaposed animals and birds similar to the Scythian traditions. A common motif is paired ducks facing each other with a tree of life between them, and juxtaposed lions enclosed in circular beaded enclosures—a device very com-

mon among Sassanian textiles. However, the delineation of the hunt is powerful and shows a remarkable linear strength and mastery over the technique.

Under the Mongol leader Ghenghis Khan, a large number of Turko-Mongol tribes—the Sakas, Scythians, Sarmatians, and others—were united and controlled the entire area. Khan brought many masters of craft traditions, which enriched the Central Asian traditions and added to the cultural heritage. Upon Khan's death, Central Asia was divided amongst his sons. Uzbek Khan, (1312–1340) a descendant of Ghenghis Khan's son, ruled a large area, converted to Islam, and along with his followers became prominent in the area as their faith unified the people. At the end of fifteenth century, the Uzbek army conquered much of Central Asian territory, mixed with the settled population, and created a dominant group, enhancing the area, which is now known as Uzbekistan.

The Timurid Empire, from the mid-fourteenth century to the end of the sixteenth century, was a period of abundant cultural development of the urban settlements of Central Asia. Emperor Timur Lang followed the precept of his ancestor Genghis Khan and brought many of the masters of arts and crafts to his capital, and Samarkand began to produce woven textiles, which could compare to the very best.

The nomadic tradition continued throughout the period, maintaining many of the woven techniques and woven patterns that reflected their identity and way of life. For instance, the hearth rug was central to the Torkomans' yurta and had deep significance as well as distinctive patterns. The subjugation of the tribe would mean the introduction of the pattern of the dominant tribe in the hearth rug.

Textile Materials

Wool was the most important fabric used, not only by the nomadic people but also by the settled population. Their flocks provided them with material, with men shearing and the women cleaning, sorting, and carding for spinning. Men, women, and children all spun the wool as they moved with their animals. Amongst the nomadic people, the women used local plants as the base and minerals as mordants and generally did dyeing. In the large urban centers such as Bokhara, Samarkand, and Fergana expert dyers were known for their skills. Two different groups of dyers were known in Bokhara, those who worked with cold dyes and those who used hot dyes. The cold dyes were the domain of the Jews in the area, while the hot dyes were the specialty of Tajiks and Chalas, who dyed mostly silk or cotton. Dyeing was considered to have mystic qualities. Its practice was kept a secret even from the daughters of the household, and a number of ceremonies and taboos were related to the practice.

Silk was obtained early from China, and there are Han records of 81 B.C.E. that talk of the importance of trade with the Hsiung-nu (tribal people) for large quantities of gold, which reduced their resources and weakened the enemy. Silk was the dress of the elite and is still referred to as *padshahoki*, the king's cloth. Only those allowed to wear silk by the local ruler could use it, or else they could face imprisonment and even death.

Until the coming of the Soviet system of collectivization, sericulture was practiced as an individual activity in the rural areas or confined to small workshops in the towns. The process was quite primitive, and after the closure of the silk reeling factories in 1992, they returned to the old methods of processing.

Cotton was grown in the oasis from ancient times, and the women processed the cotton, ginning it by using traditional wooden hand rollers (*chirik*). It was then separated, rolled, and made ready for spinning with the use of a spinning wheel (*charakh*). The weaving of plain cotton (*carbos*) was done by the weavers. Very fine-spun thread was woven along with silk to produce the mixed silk and cotton fabric known as *adras* for which the area was famous and which was also in demand for exporting. Gold thread and silk embroidery was sought after for the rich garments worn by the elite and for the production of *khilats*, royal robes of honor presented to distinguished guests or for esteemed members of their own clan. Bokhara was known for its expert gold embroiderers.

Felting and Weaving Techniques

The techniques can be divided into nomadic and urban, though the distinction cannot be rigid. Among the nomadic people the women for their own use did weaving, while in the urban centers it was the work of men, though in some cases there were looms in the home, which were used by the women.

Felting was essentially a nomadic tradition and was carried out with pure wool. Two types of felts were created: the plain single natural color of the wool used for the making of apparel or for the yurta, and the patterned ones known as *alakhiz*. The patterns were integrated into the felt by laying the designs on a canvas with use of long slivers of loosely twisted dyed wool and then covering the pattern with finely carded single colored wool. The finest *namads* (Iranian artisan felt rugs) of inlay designs were made by the Torkomans and also by the Kyrghyz women, a tradition that was found in the Pazryz burial mounds. Sprinkling the fibers with water mixed with a soap solution and rolling them with the feet and hands would result in a thick felt. Shaped caps, coats, jackets, mittens, and shoes were also made and decorated with embroidery. Another popular form of patterned felt was the *shirdak* created by cutting dyed felt pieces and creating myriad patterns, which was a specialty of the Kyrgyzi.

Weaving of plain and twill weave woolen cloth for apparel was common and similar to the type found in ancient burial sites. The fine woolen weaving was for creation of shawls, which were used by men and women, as well as fine cloth for the long gowns—*abas*—worn by the priests, as wool was considered pure. Very fine quality lengths were woven for the *imame* worn as turbans in earlier times. The shawls were woven with motifs on the border with silken dyed threads.

The mastery of the woolen technique was in the weaving of flat weaves for rugs and for hangings. Noncontinuous weft weaving was used for *soamak* weaves with intricate multicolored woven patterns. Another technique with noncontinuous weft was the method of interlocking tapestry. Both of these techniques later evolved into highly specialized weaving traditions, the *termeh*, which is associated with the Persian shawl weaving, and *kesi*, an intricate form of silk tapestry with interlocking weave. Recent research has revealed examples of *kesi*, which appear to have all the characteristics of Soghdian textiles with a liveliness of the flow of the patterns and brilliant use of color. An interesting *kesi* of the thirteenth century in the Metropolitan Museum has floating leaves, buds, and flowers, with ducks swimming among them. It has the spontaneity of the Soghdian textile repertoire. The earliest *kesi* to be found is in Turfan, which dates to the sixth century C.E.

Soghdian brocades of silk were used for creating apparel, as well as for funerary cloth. Woven in weft-faced compound twill, its technique is quite distinct from the Chinese style of silk patterned brocade.

The settlement of Muslim weavers in Central Asia by Ghengis Khan, of which two settlements are mentioned in the records of the period, contributed greatly to the stylistic development of designs and techniques. Khan also brought weavers from China and settled them in Samarkand, leading to a blending of styles and technical skills. The greatest contribution is their expertise in weaving cloth of gold known as *nasij*.

Another important silk technique was the warp ikat known as *abr*. While the word means cloud, it here refers to the ikat technique and *khan atlas* for the pure silk of very fine patterns often woven with seven colors. Bokhara, Samarkand, and Fergana were the centers for these very dramatic fabrics with rich colors and bold patterns. Research being carried out by the newly opened Department of Cultural History in Uzbekistan has located Sukhandarya as a place where ikat silk was also woven. Known locally as *abrabandi*, the technique is generally seen as having been introduced rather late, in the eighteenth century, but it is likely that this technique was used much earlier. The degummed washed silk warp threads were marked by the *nishanzan* or the designers, who chose a range of patterns derived from the diverse repertoire of patterns of Central Asia. They include ram's horns, tulips, pomegranates, *kora-karga*, black ravens, the *badam*, almonds, peacocks, cloud motifs, *shonagul*, comb design, as well as bold *oi*, the circular moon motif in blue and the red sun motifs combined with a stylized dragon. During the Soviet era, they created *Ulag Oktyabr*, October Revolution, and Kremlin patterns. The most prized and complex patterns in the ikat technique were the *bakhmal*, the ikat velvet, which was highly valued and was reserved for the royalty.

The mixed cotton weft and silk warp-faced ikats known as *adras* were very popular as most households could wear these. Pure cotton striped ikat, *yalong doveran*, was also woven and was in great demand as only the royal household and those permitted by them were allowed to wear pure silk, while cotton could be worn by everyone. Often these were given to the *kudunggars*, the glossing workshop where the material was glazed with egg white and polished.

A range of cotton fabrics was woven. *Alacha* and *kalami* were fine striped cotton. One of the most popular striped materials was known as *mashku-zafar* and was woven with black and saffron-yellow. Textured cottons woven with threads of different counts created a rich effect and were known as *Salori bular*.

Central Asia has a tradition of printing on cotton and silk. It appears to have been practiced from ancient times, which is confirmed by the discovery of a fragment in an excavation carried out near Termez in Sukhandarya region of Uzbekistan. A fragment was also found in the fourteenth century C.E. grave of Bibi Kanum, wife of Tamerlane. The direct printing with the use of wooden blocks, *qalib*, was prepared in Bokhara, Samarkand, Fergana, Qorcom, Tashkent, as well as in Tajikistan bordering the Ferghan Valley. It is interesting that the word for printing is *chint*, which is also used in India. The printer is *chintsar*. *Chintsaz* is the word used in Isfahan, Iran, as well as in India. The carver of the blocks is known as *kolkbhar*. Some scholars are of the opinion that possibly printing came from India. Research in India has, however, revealed that *chipa* for the printer and *chint* for printed cloth are not Sanskrit words.

The silk gauzelike cloth was printed with resist-printing near Bokhara in a town known as Chidgaron, which was known for its printing. Between 1840 and 1849, 2,500,000 printed cloth pieces of each were exported to Russia and Bokhara. Unfortunately the silk-resist printed scarves are no longer being produced.

Silk embroidery known as *suzan dozi* was practiced throughout Central Asia. The style of embroidery, however, was quite distinct even within the same tribe. Uzbekistan has the richest variation, the *suzani* of Nouratta has great delicacy and is quite distinct from that of Bokhara, Samarkand, and Sukhandarya. Some settled people use satin stitch, while stem stitch is used for the more delicate motifs. Chain stitch with the use of the needle or the awl is used specially for bolder work and that prepared on leather, suede, or felt. *Basma* is a form of couching used for either gold embroidery or for bolder work covering large areas, as for the *suzanis* used as tent hangings. One of the most interesting embroideries is the Lakai embroidery, which often uses wool for the embroidery and

has a bold primitive appearance and asymmetrical motifs. The embroidery of the Torkomans is very bold and done on silk with silken threads.

Gold embroidery often worked on velvet dresses was an essential part of the embellishment carried out on robes used by the royalty, their families, and court, and the robe of honor was often worked in rich gold thread. Bokhara was the most important center for this work, and many workshops specialized in this.

A range of techniques was prevalent and enriched the dress of the people of Central Asia. Their love of brilliant colors and bold patterns created a richness in the rather arid conditions of Central Asia.

See also **Dyeing, Resist; Felt; Ikat.**

BIBLIOGRAPHY

Abdullaev, T., et al. *A Song in Metal: Folk Art of Uzbekistan.* Tashkent, Uzbekistan: Gafura Guliama, 1986.

Asian Costumes and Textiles from the Bosphorus to Fujiyama. Milan, Italy: Skira, 2001.

Beresneva, L. *The Decorative and Applied Art of the Turkmen.* Leningrad, Russia: Aurora Art Pub., 1976.

Block Printing in Uzbekistan: Past and Present. Tashkent, Uzbekistan: UNDP, 1979.

Burkett, Mary E. *The Art of the Felt Maker.* Kendal, U.K.: Abbot Hall Art Gallery, 1979.

Grube, Ernst J. *Keshte: Central Asian Embroideries.* New York: Marshall and Marilyn Wolf, 2003.

Kirghyz Arcok es Himzesek. Neprajzi Museum, 1995.

The Kirghyz Pattern. Kyrgyzstan, 1986.

Morozova, A. S. *Folk Art of Uzbekistan.* Tashkent, Uzbekistan, 1979.

Pope, A. V., and P. Ackerman. *A Survey of Persian Art.* New York: Oxford University Press, 1939.

Undeland, Charles. *The Central Asian Republics: Fragments of Empire, Magnets of Wealth.* New York: The Asia Society, 1994.

Vollmer, John E., E. J. Keal, and E. Nagai-Berthrong. *Silk Roads, China Ships.* Toronto: Royal Ontario Museum, 1983.

Watt James, C. Y., and Anne E. Wardwell. *When Silk Was Gold: Central Asian and Chinese Textiles.* Abrahams, New York, 1997.

Zhao Feng. *Treasures of Silk: An Illustrated History of Chinese Textiles.* Hong Kong: ISAT/Costume Squad, 1999.

Jasleen Dhamija

TEXTILES, CHINESE Silk production, characteristic of China's earliest civilization, has been an enduring feature of Chinese tradition and a distinctive aspect of China's interaction with other cultures. From China's Neolithic era, hemp and ramie were cultivated and woven into textiles for clothing and other uses. Wool textiles played a minor role, associated with border peoples of the north and west. Cotton cultivation began at least by the eighth century. By the Ming dynasty (1368–1644),

SILK AND DIPLOMACY

The value of silks for diplomatic gifts was recognized early. Confucian texts of the third century B.C.E. mention the practice. During the Song dynasty (960–1279), some diplomatic gifts to border peoples included 200,000 bolts of silk.

In the first century C.E., Pliny the Elder wrote in his *Natural History* (Book XII, translation by H. Rackham, 1952, p.3): "This inspires us with ever greater . . . wonder that starting from these beginnings man has come to quarry the mountains for marbles, to go as far as China for raiment, and to explore the depths of the Red Sea for the pear."

In 1912 Sir Aurel Stein (1862–1943) described the textiles found in the "walled up temple library," at Dunhuang, including a large embroidery of a Buddha with bodhisattvas, an embroidered cushion cover with scrolling floral motifs, "a number of triangular headpieces . . . detached from their painted banners . . . composed either in their body or in their broad borders of pieces of fine silk damask," and "a silk cover . . . intended for a manuscript roll" (Stein, pp. 207–210). The objects collected by Stein are now in the British Museum and the Museum of Central Asian Antiquities in New Delhi, India. Textiles were also collected at Dunhuang by the French archaeologist Paul Pelliot (1878–1945), now preserved in the Musée Guimet and the Bibliothèque Nationale, Paris. Another group of Dunhuang materials is in St. Petersburg, and more recent finds are kept in Chinese collections.

needlework, and yet the spirit of the phrase was preserved. As late as the seventeenth century, the state collected taxes in silk as well as in grain, underscoring the essential value of this human endeavor. Ultimately, the uses of silk expanded to include textiles made for appreciation as art as well as for clothing and furnishings.

Elaborate techniques were developed for producing complex designs, both in the woven cloth itself and in embellishments worked onto the surface. Brocades, weaves with supplementary weft yarns creating complex patterns, were employed in many variations, including the complex lampas weave with its extra binding warps. *Kesi*, a tapestry weave, perhaps originally developed by Central Asians with wool yarn, came to be highly refined in the works of Chinese weavers of the Song dynasty (960–1279) and later. Embroidery, a means of embellishing a woven fabric with stitches made using a threaded needle, flourished throughout the history of silk textiles in China.

Historical and Archaeological Evidence

Needles have been found in some of China's earliest inhabited sites. Abundant evidence of the making of fabrics from hemp and ramie has been found in sites of the fifth millennium B.C.E. Spindle whorls of stone or pottery found in these sites confirm the spinning of hemp or ramie fibers into threads for weaving and sewing. Components of what may have been a backstrap loom have also been identified. Impressions of woven materials on the bases of pottery vessels, such as those found at Banpo, Shaanxi province, suggest the varied uses of coarse cloth or matting, in this case to create a simple turntable for pottery making. Remains at sites of the Liangzhu culture of the Lower Yangtze River region confirm the initiation of sericulture by the third millen-

it had become an industry to rival silk production. Though silk retained its role as a luxury fabric and a symbol of Chinese culture, cotton cloth ultimately became a widespread material and an economic staple.

From the Han dynasty (206 B.C.E.–220 C.E.), silk manufacture comprised a major state-controlled industry. For thousands of years, along land routes through Central Asia and sea routes along the coasts of East and Southeast Asia, silk was both a major commodity and at times a standard medium of exchange. In China's diplomacy, silk played a stabilizing role, bringing large areas of Inner Asia into the Chinese sphere of influence. At home, silk production was viewed as a moral imperative as well as a practical necessity. The Confucian adage, "men till, women weave," expresses the essential role of the women in a household in preparing silk yarn and cloth. Later, an increase in industrial specialization encouraged a shift of women's efforts from weaving to

THE MANILA GALLEON

The fall of Constantinople in 1453 disrupted trade and led Europeans to find their own sea routes to Asia. Chinese silk textiles were included in the earliest voyages of the Manila galleon in 1573. According to the inventory by Antonio de Morga, president of the *audiencia* at Manila, Spanish traders bought:

> raw silk in bundles, . . . fine untwisted silk, white and of all colors, . . . quantities of velvets . . . others with body of gold and embroidered with gold; woven stuffs and brocades, of gold and silver upon silk . . . gold and silver thread . . . damasks, satins, taffetas, . . . linen . . . cotton. (Schurz, p. 73)

nium B.C.E. Here can be found the earliest confirmed evidence of the development of the complex process of raising silkworms (*Bombyx mori*), harvesting the filaments from their cocoons and then reeling the silk and weaving it into cloth.

Shang (c. 1550 B.C.E.–1045 B.C.E.) and Zhou (c. 1045 B.C.E.–221 B.C.E.) Dynasties

Tombs of China's Bronze Age provide evidence that silk, like bronze and jade, was a luxury commodity, important for ritual use. The royal tombs at Anyang, Henan province, reveal that ritual bronze objects and also ritual jades were wrapped in silk before being buried as grave goods. In the tomb of Lady Fu Hao (twelfth century B.C.E.), more than fifty ritual bronzes are known to have been wrapped in silk cloth. Anyang silks included various weaves, damasks as well as plain (tabby) weave, and some examples were embroidered with patterns in chain stitch.

Spectacular finds of Zhou dynasty silks from the Warring States period (453–221 B.C.E.) are identified with the distinctive Zhou culture centered in China's middle Yangtze River valley. A tomb at Mashan, Hubei province (datable to the fourth century B.C.E.), yielded the following silks: a coffin cover, a silk painting, bags of utensils, costumes on wooden tomb figures, and nineteen layers of clothing and quilts around the corpse itself. Plain silks, brocades, and plain and patterned gauzes were included as well as embroidery in cross-stitch and counted stitch. Analysis of the complex and densely woven Mashan silks has led scholars to suggest that an early form of the drawloom must have been used to produce them.

Other well-known finds from the Zhou culture confirm the early use of silk as a ground for painting, specifically in two third-century B.C.E. pictorial banners used in funerary rituals and then buried with the deceased. A work known as the "Zhou Silk Manuscript," dated to circa 300 B.C.E., documents the tradition that early Chinese texts were written on silk cloth and bamboo as well as cast in bronze or carved on stone. Examples of shop marks have been found on silks of this period, including a brocade with an impressed seal, suggesting a growing respect for distinctive workshop products and the commercial value of textiles.

Archaeological finds outside China's traditional borders confirm the scattered early references to China's export of silk to neighboring lands. In the Scythian tombs at Pazyryk in the Altai mountains of Siberia (excavated in 1929 and 1947–1949) silks datable to 500–400 B.C.E. were found together with textiles of Near Eastern origin. This evidence gives credence to the belief that the Greeks had imported Chinese silk by the fifth or fourth century B.C.E.

Qin (221–206 B.C.E.) and Han (206 B.C.E.–220 C.E.) Dynasties

Having built the first empire of China, Qin Shi Huangdi (best known in the early 2000s for the 1974 discovery of his "terra-cotta army") built a great palace. Among its remains have been found silks, including brocade, damask, plain silk, and embroidered silk. After the reconsolidation of the empire under Han imperial rule, silk production became a primary industry, with state-supervised factories employing thousands of workers who produced silks and imperial costumes. Officials were sometimes paid or rewarded with silk textiles. As stability declined at the end of the period, textiles and grain replaced coinage as a recognized medium of exchange.

The legacy of the former state of Zhou continued to flourish, as shown by the rich treasures found at the noble tombs at Mawangdui, Hunan province (second century B.C.E.). Here was preserved silk clothing in fully intact robes. In addition there were manuscripts, maps, and paintings on silk, including elaborate funerary banners showing a portrait of the deceased entering an afterworld of cosmic symbols and signs of immortality. Embroidered silks follow patterns seen in the earlier Mashan silks, using chain stitch worked in cloud-scroll patterns. Printed silks found at Mawangdui correspond to a relief stamp found in the tomb of the Second King of Nan Yue (in Guangzhou, datable to before 122 B.C.E.), providing confirmation that techniques and styles had spread throughout the empire.

Han tombs have yielded a variety of silks, including plain weave, gauze weave, both plain and patterned, and pile-loop brocade similar to velvet. More than twenty dyed colors have been identified. Embellishment of woven fabrics included new techniques of embroidery incorporating gold or feathers, as well as block-printing, stenciling, and painting on silk. Later Han silks include a striking number of woven patterns with texts, usually several characters with auspicious meanings. From pictorial representations, scholars have deduced that Han weavers used treadle looms.

Finds in remote areas have added to our understanding of production and commerce relating to silk textiles. Sir Aurel Stein found in Western China a strip of undyed silk inscribed by hand stating the origin, dimensions, weight, and price. A seal impression designates its origin in Shandong province in Northeast China. Other finds established the standard selvage-to-selvage width of Han silk, at between $17\frac{1}{2}$ and $19\frac{1}{2}$ inches (from 45 to 50 centimeters). At Loulan, in the Tarim Basin in the far Northwest of modern China (Xinjiang province), excavated by Stein (1906–1908 and 1913–1914), Han figured silk textile fragments (datable to the third century C.E. or earlier) were found together with an early example of slit tapestry woven in wool. The latter may be a precursor of the later *kesi* slit tapestry in silk. Finds at Noin-Ula, in northern Mongolia, dated second century C.E., give further evidence of the widespread exchange of silks throughout Asia. Although details of the trade are yet to be fully understood, comments by early writers make clear the admiration for Chinese silks in the Roman world.

The Birds and the Flower, National Palace Museum, Taiwan. In the Song Dynasty, textile production was fine-tuned with such artistry as the weaving of *kesi* tapestries and the development of needle-loop embroidery. THE ART ARCHIVE/NATIONAL PALACE MUSEUM TAIWAN/HARPER COLLINS PUBLISHERS. REPRODUCED BY PERMISSION.

Six Dynasties Period (220–589) and the Tang Dynasty (618–907)

Political disunity during the third to sixth centuries brought close interaction with Central Asia, leading to new styles and techniques relating to textile production. Tang silks reflect these closer contacts established during the previous centuries. The Tang maintained an open capital with foreigners among its merchants and varied ethnic and religious groups among its populace. A general shift in weaving techniques distinguishes Tang silk from that of the Han dynasty. While Han patterns were warp-patterned, the weavings of Tang came to be weft-patterned.

Some of the best Tang textiles survive in temples in Japan, where Chinese fabrics have been carefully preserved in Buddhist temples since before the eighth century. The most important of these holdings is that of the Shōsō-in (a storehouse dedicated at Tōdai-ji, Nara, in 756, for the donated collection of Emperor Shōmu), which contains various garments and other textiles believed to have been brought back to Japan by Buddhist monks returning from China.

Investigation of Chinese textiles was stimulated by stunning discoveries of well-preserved ancient textiles in Central Asian sites, including Sir Aurel Stein's expeditions in northwest China and inner Asia (in 1900, 1906–1908, 1913–1916 and 1930). Discoveries at Dunhuang's Buddhist cave temples yielded a new range of textiles for study, and brought about an early appreciation of the importance of textiles in Buddhist ritual. Such textiles were probably pious offerings made by Buddhists from Central Asia, especially Sogdiana, as well as from China. Many of the silks were sewn into banners or other adornments for Buddhist chapels, or into wrappers for sacred texts (sutra scrolls). A mantle (*kashaya*) for a Buddhist priest, its patchwork symbolizing the vow of poverty, was also found. Many of the silk textiles have bright patterns, woven or embroidered, while others were adorned after weaving by painting, printing, stenciling, or by dyeing using resist techniques including clamp-resist, wax-resist and tie-dyeing. The weaving techniques documented in these finds include silk tapestry (*kesi*), gauze, and damasks, as well as compound weft-faced and warp-faced weaves that were probably woven on a drawloom. These finds confirm that patronage of Buddhism encouraged creation of pictorial textiles either woven in the *kesi* technique or embroidered with highly refined use of stitches (often satin stitch) to create representational effects.

Important examples of Tang silks have been found at Famen Temple, Shaanxi province. Here, a ritual offering datable to C.E. 874 included about 700 textiles including brocades (many with metallic threads), twill, gauze, pongee, embroidery, and printed silk. Among them was a set of miniature Buddhist vestments including a model of a *kashaya*, an apron (or altar frontal), and clothing, all couched with gold-wrapped threads on a silk gauze ground in patterns of lotus blossoms and clouds.

Song Dynasty (960–1279)

Song weavers brought refinement to textile technology, especially the weaving of satin and of *kesi* tapestries. Generally the use of gold and silver increased both in embroidery and in woven brocades. Needle-loop embroidery, a detached looping stitch sometimes combined with appliqué of gilt paper, came into use. In Song times as in the Tang, embroidery and tapestry were used for devotional Buddhist images, but now the techniques were also employed to create items for aesthetic appreciation, like paintings, in the form of scrolls or album leaves.

Jin (1115–1234) and Yuan (1279–1368) Dynasties

Silk played a major role in trade, diplomacy, and court life under the Jin dynasty, founded by the Jurchen, a Tatar people, and the Yuan, founded by the Mongols, both non-Chinese ruling houses. Jin and Yuan brocades, notable for rich patterning with gilt wefts of leather or paper substrate, have been a focus of recent exhibitions. Due to the open trade connections encouraged by the Mongol conquests, these silks spread widely. Examples reached the pope through trade and diplomatic gifts. Thus, the cloth of gold favored by Mongol leaders had its counterpart in the *panno tartarico* of fourteenth-century Europe.

Ming Dynasty (1368–1644)

By Ming times, weavers employed elaborate drawlooms using up to forty different colored wefts and incorporating flat gold (gilt paper) strips, gold-wrapped threads as well as iridescent peacock feathers to produce their brocades. The Yongle reign (1403–1424) saw a tremendous dedication of resources to the production of diplomatic gifts including textiles for Buddhist purposes, a practice carried over into the Xuande reign period (1426–1435). Excavations at the tomb of the Ming emperor Wanli (reigned 1572–1620) yielded two complete sets of uncut woven silk for dragon robes, as well as silk brocades and patterned gauzes marked as products of the imperial workshops in Nanjing and Suzhou.

By the late sixteenth century, cotton cultivation, which had been encouraged under the Yuan dynasty and expanded further under the Ming, became a major part of the Chinese economy. From at least Tang dynasty times, cotton had been used to make clothing for the lower classes (Cahill [p. 113] observes that "cotton-clad" meant a commoner in medieval Chinese poetry). In subsequent centuries, cotton cloth was associated with the virtues of humility. Ginned cotton was transported south from Henan and Shandong provinces, or shipped north from Fujian and Guangdong, to the Jiangnan region where it would be made into thread and woven into cloth. Cotton thread is noted among Chinese exports to Japan, and white cotton cloth as well as cotton garments of blue or white are recorded among the items exported on the Manila galleon.

Domestically, cotton found wide use in undergarments and in linings for silk (such as in silk garments for ceremonial use), and it also came to be dyed in bright colors and calendered to an attractively polished surface. The most distinctive artistic developments in Chinese cotton textiles are those that survive primarily in rural traditions and folk art relating to minority groups, including the Miao of Guizhou and Yunnan provinces. The primary techniques, resist dyeing (using stencils to apply a paste that would retain white undyed areas), and batik (using wax to reserve undyed areas), had been known in China, along with block printing, tie-dyeing, and clamp-resist, since the Han dynasty, and are found in silk examples preserved from the Tang period. The characteristic blue from indigo, typical of dyed cotton, also reflects an ancient tradition, recorded in detail in Ming dynasty texts.

Anthropologists and historians have noted a shift in importance among China's women from activities in weaving to embroidery in the seventeenth century. Increasing specialization meant that finished yarn and finished cloth could be purchased routinely. This spurred a rising interest in embroidery among the gentry, and a re-

lated rise in the status of embroidery to verge upon that of the fine arts of painting and calligraphy. The Gu family of Shanghai, for example, came to prominence for their distinctive pictorial embroidery style. A manual of embroidery designs compiled by the scholar-calligrapher Shen Linqi (1602–1664), published in woodblock-printed form, set out themes and patterns that inspired embroiderers for centuries.

Qing Dynasty (1644–1911)

Study of Qing textiles has focused on the court collections, now in Beijing's Palace Museum and in the National Palace Museum, Taipei, including wall decorations, curtains, desk frontals and upholstery fabrics, ceremonial and informal costumes, and works of art. When the Qianlong emperor, inspired by scholar-collectors of the late Ming as well as by the precedent of the Song Emperor Huizong (reigned 1101–1125), commissioned scholar-officials to catalog his art collections (producing the *Bidian Zhulin* and the *Shiqu Baoji*, published in 1744–1745, 1793, and 1816) these catalogs included examples of *kesi* and embroidery alongside painting and calligraphy. Qianlong himself may have selected works to be "reproduced" in *kesi*, including his own painting and poetry and works in his collection of painting and calligraphy.

The Qing emperors were Manchus whose homeland was in the far Northeast beyond China's traditional borders. When they conquered China, they were quick to adopt the Chinese practice of using gifts of silk, particularly cloth for dragon robes, as a means to bring the powerful leaders of vassal states into their own military bureaucracy. The Qing forebears had been on the receiving end of this practice during the late Ming period. Silk had long been used to pacify border peoples; Song examples are striking, but the practice began before the Han dynasty. Most visible among textiles surviving up to the twenty-first century are the lavish silk brocades bestowed upon Tibetan nobles and preserved in Tibet's dry climate until recent years.

Collecting and Study of Textile

Until recently, the study of Chinese textiles revolved around Beijing's imperial palaces, a focal point for interest in Chinese culture after the end of Qing dynasty rule in 1911. In the years before the formal establishment of the Palace Museum within the former Forbidden City in 1925, many court costumes and other textiles were dispersed into collections worldwide. Western scholars took a keen interest in Chinese textiles as they came to know them through these court robes and interior furnishings. In recent years, collections have been technically analyzed and historically documented in studies carried out at the Association pour l'Étude et la Documentation des Textiles d'Asie (AEDTA), Paris; the Royal Ontario Museum, Toronto; Hong Kong Museum of Art; the Metropolitan Museum of Art, New York; the Cleveland Museum of Art; Los Angeles County Museum of Art; the Phoenix

Art Museum; the Chicago Art Institute; and the Minneapolis Institute of Arts.

See also **China: History of Dress; Silk.**

BIBLIOGRAPHY

Arnold, Lauren. *Princely Gifts and Papal Treasures: The Franciscan Mission to China and Its Influence on the Art of the West, 1250–1350.* San Francisco: Desiderata Press, 1999.

Bray, Francesca. *Technology and Gender: Fabrics of Power in Late Imperial China.* Berkeley: University of California Press, 1997.

Brook, Timothy. *The Confusions of Pleasure: Commerce and Culture in Ming China.* Berkeley: University of California Press, 1998.

Brown, Claudia, et al. *Weaving China's Past: The Amy S. Clague Collection of Chinese Textiles.* Exhibit catalog. Phoenix: Phoenix Art Museum, 2000.

Cahill, Suzanne. "'Our Women Are Acting Like Foreigners' Wives!': Western Influences on Tang Dynasty Women's Fashion." In *China Chic: East Meets West.* Edited by Valerie Steele and John S. Major. New Haven, Conn.: Yale University Press, 1999.

Feng, Zhao. *Zhixiu zhenpin: Tushuo Zhongguo sizhou yishu shi/ Treasures in Silk: An Illustrated History of Chinese Textiles.* Hong Kong: ISAT/Costume Squad Ltd., 1999. In Chinese and English.

Hanyu, Gao. *Chinese Textile Designs.* Translated by Rosemary Scott and Susan Whitfield. London: Viking, 1992.

Jacobsen, Robert D. *Imperial Silks: Ch'ing Dynasty Textiles in the Minneapolis Institute of Arts.* Chicago: Art Media Resources Ltd., 2000.

Komaroff, Linda, and Stefano Carboni, eds. *The Legacy of Genghis Khan: Courtly Art and Culture in Western Asia, 1256–1353.* Exhibition catalog. New York: The Metropolitan Museum of Art, 2002.

Kuhn, Dieter. "The Silk Workshops of the Shang Dynasty (16th–11th century B.C.E.)." *Explorations in the History of Science and Technology in China: A Special Number of the "Collections of Essays on Chinese Literature and History."* Edited by Li Guohao et al., 367–408. Shanghai: Chinese Classics Publications House, 1982.

Ledderose, Lothar. *Ten Thousand Things: Module and Mass Production in Chinese Art.* Princeton, N.J.: Princeton University Press, 2000.

Nai, Xia. *Jade and Silk of Han China.* Edited and Translated by Chu-tsing Li. Lawrence, Kans.: Spencer Museum of Art, 1983.

Nengfu, Huang, ed. *Yin ran zhi xiu* (Printing, dyeing, weaving, and embroidery). In *Zhongguo meishu quanji: Part 3—Gongyi meishu bian* (The great treasury of Chinese fine arts: Part 3—Arts and crafts). Vols. 6 and 7. Beijing: Wenwu chu ban she, 1985 and 1987. In Chinese.

Pu, Lu. *Designs of Chinese Indigo Batik.* Beijing: Beijing New World Press, 1981.

Riboud, Krishna. "The Silks of Dunhuang." In *The Arts of Central Asia: The Pelliot Collection in the Musée Guimet.* Edited by Jacques Giès, 115–120, 155–164. Paris: Serindia Publications, 1996.

Schurz, William. *The Manila Galleon.* New York: E. P. Dutton, 1939.

Steele, Valerie, and John S. Major. *China Chic: East Meets West.* New Haven, Conn.: Yale University Press, 1999.

Stein, Sir Marc Aurel. *Ruins of Desert Cathay: Personal Narrative of Explorations in Central Asian and Westernmost China.* London: Macmillan and Company, 1912. Reprint, New York: B. Blom, 1968.

Urban Council, Hong Kong, and the Oriental Ceramic Society of Hong Kong in association with the Liaoning Provincial Museum. *Jinxiu luoyi qiao tiangong / Heavens' Embroidered Cloths: One-Thousand Years of Chinese Textiles.* Exhibition catalog. Hong Kong: Hong Kong Museum of Art, 1995. In Chinese and English.

Vollmer, John, et al. *Clothed to Rule the Universe: Ming and Qing Dynasty Textiles at the Art Institute of Chicago.* Exhibition catalog. The Art Institute of Chicago. Seattle: University of Washington Press, 2000.

Watt, James C. Y., and Anne E. Wardwell, with an essay by Morris Rossabi. *When Silk Was Gold: Central Asian and Chinese Textiles.* Exhibition catalog. New York: The Metropolitan Museum of Art, 1997.

Wilson, Verity. *Chinese Dress.* London: Victoria and Albert Museum, 1987.

Claudia Brown

TEXTILES, COPTIC An estimated 150,000 textiles were found in Egyptian burial sites that date from the late third to mid-seventh century C.E., Egypt's Coptic Period. Most of these grave goods were fragments of clothing and domestic textiles, but some were nearly complete costumes. These archaeological fabrics represent the fashions and furnishings of that distant time and place.

The Coptic Period

Egypt was conquered by Alexander the Great in 332 B.C.E., then colonized and ruled by Greek pharaohs, the Ptolemies. After 30 B.C.E. Egypt was ruled from Rome, later from Byzantium, and briefly from Persia prior to the Islamic conquest of 641 C.E. Christianity became the dominant religion during the Coptic Period. A "Copt" in early usage identified an indigenous Egyptian, but in modern usage only a Christian Egyptian is a Copt. After 451 C.E. the Coptic Church separated from the Roman Catholic Church. There are six million Copts in 2004. Christian burial practices were adopted after the prohibition of mummification in the fourth century C.E. The deceased were dressed in their garments, swaddled with other cloth, and buried in sandy, shallow graves; or, in some instances, in small brick-covered vaults. The dry desert clime preserved the textiles.

The Discovery of Coptic Textiles

Some Coptic textiles were discovered as early as the seventeenth century and others during Napoleon's expedi-

PHASES OF COPTIC TEXTILE ART

The conquest and colonization of one country by another creates a rich cultural brew that transforms indigenous art. Though Coptic scholars use different descriptive terms, they generally agree that the style of the tapestries and other pictorial textiles can be sorted into these broad categories:

Pre-Coptic

The Pre-Coptic category (first to late third centuries C.E.) includes only a few painterly examples.

Early Coptic

The Early Coptic, Proto-Coptic, or Late Roman-Egyptian category (late third century to fourth century C.E.) is dominated by Greco-Roman influence with themes drawn from nature and mythology. Subtle modeling with blended colors can be seen in the polychrome textiles and fluency of line is evident in the monochrome faces and figure drawn with the ecru linen wefts. Monochrome interlace and endless knot motifs are also popular and enduring.

Middle Coptic

The Middle Coptic, High Coptic, or Early Byzantine (fifth to mid-seventh century C.E.) is categorized by the abstraction of naturalistic elements. Color areas, no longer blended, are separated by heavy outlines or juxtaposed. Faces and figures are distorted. Christian saints and symbols begin to replace the pagan iconography.

Late Coptic

The Late Coptic (mid-seventh to twelfth century C.E.) category extends into the Islamic period in which geometric patterns and calligraphic motifs supersede figurative art.

Polychrome and monochrome palettes were used throughout all phases and some popular themes, especially dancing figures and interlace patterns persisted. While there was continuity throughout the Coptic period in the construction, composition, content, and palette of the tapestries there were profound changes in the iconography. The naturalistic style of rendering faces, figures, and narrative vignettes was altered by abstraction, and familiar Greco-Roman motifs and themes were imbued with Christian messages.

---

tion to Egypt. Nineteenth and early-twentieth-century excavations at Saqqâra, Akhmîm, Hawarah, Karanis, and other sites by Theodor Graf, Wladimir Bock, Gaston Maspero, Sir Flinders Petrie, and other Egyptologists contributed to the textile collections of European museums. However, the impact of Coptic textiles on the history of clothing, fashion, art, and archaeology can best be understood by examining the career of the charismatic, but controversial, French Egyptologist Albert Gayet (1856–1916). He collected tens of thousands of textiles between 1895 and 1910, primarily from Antinoé (ancient Antinoöpolis), but also from Akhmim, Sheikh-Shata, Deir-el-Dyk, and Dronkah. Gayet believed he had discovered at Antinoé " . . . an efflorescent civilization to rival Pompeii."

Gayet became known as "The Archaeologist of Antinoé." Antinoé was founded in 130 C.E. by Emperor Hadrian. Drawings of Antinoé made during Napoleon's 1804 expedition to Egypt reveal the grandeur of this Greco-Roman city with its broad avenues, impressive triumphal arches, temples, theaters, and baths. The city was colonized by cultured, literate citizens of Greco-Egyptian ancestry who called themselves the *New Hellenes*. Antinoé slowly declined after the seventh-century Islamic conquest of Egypt. Eventually, even the architectural remnants of the city disappeared. By the time of Gayet's excavations there was only a small mud-brick village called Sheik Abada at the site.

After each winter's expedition to Egypt, the fabrics and artifacts—even mummies—were brought back to Paris for exhibitions by Gayet. His displays in Paris featured tunics, mantles, shawls, head coverings, leggings, shoes, socks, cushion covers, curtains, wall hangings, strips of precious silk, coats of cashmere, mummy portraits on linen, and woolen tapestry fragments decorated with flora, fauna, figures, geometric motifs, and narrative vignettes in polychrome and monochrome palettes. He presented lectures with dancers dressed in faux Coptic garments. During the Paris Exposition Universelle de 1900, Gayet displayed textiles at the Palais du Costume in "sensational tableaux." The costume exhibit was for the "glorification of feminine fashion from the nineteenth century back through history to the Late Antique world." In 1901 Gayet became a celebrity for his discovery of the mummy of Thaïs, a legendary fourth-century converted courtesan and popular heroine of Anatole France's 1890 novel and Jules Massenet's 1894 opera. Gayet estimated that he had uncovered forty thousand graves by 1902.

Eventually the Gayet acquisitions were doled out to the Musée du Louvre and other museums in France. Gayet collections are also in museums in Italy, Belgium, and Switzerland. Many Gayet textiles, sold to public and private collections, are now scattered around the world. Often early Islamic textiles are included in Coptic collections. No radical difference in the way cloth was made resulted from the political change, however, the iconography slowly segued toward the Islamic taste for non-representational art. Few of these early excavators preserved archaeological context or recorded sufficient documentation to accurately date the fabrics: clues in the cloth and design are all that remain.

Coptic Fabrics

The dominant fiber of Egypt's ancient and late antique fabrics is flax. The common Coptic linen yarn is an s-spun single (yarn spun in a clockwise direction), but z-spun yarns (yarn spun in a counter-clockwise direction), single or plied, are used with certain tapestry styles considered late and perhaps Near Eastern. The typical woolen yarn used during the Coptic period is an s-spun single. Occasionally z-spun yarns, and—in rare instances—plied yarns of two colored strands spun together are found. Silk, imported as fiber or fabric, was a rarity in Egypt. Soft weft (crosswise yarns) fibers of cashmere are found on some imported garments. Cotton and ramie are reported in Coptic and early Islamic fabrics. Precious gold thread can be documented on two separate pieces in French collections.

Linen, which does not readily accept dyeing, is typically undyed: wool readily accepts dyestuffs. Every color of the rainbow can be found in Coptic cloth. Blues were from indigo and woad; yellows from saffron, pomegranate, suntberry, weld, broom, iron buff, and safflower; reds from alkanet root, madder root, kermes, henna, and lac-dye; and purples from lichens and from the glands of shellfish of the Purpuridae family. The accepted theory among Coptic scholars is that wools were dyed in the fleece prior to spinning.

Horizontal ground-staked looms and upright vertical looms were in use in New Kingdom Egypt. The Alexandrian conquest brought warp-weighted looms to Egypt, but they were not extensively used. Pit-looms and upright Roman looms may have been used. There are tablet-woven textiles and sets of tablets that were discovered in Antinoé. Some type of loom with a pattern-making device, a precursor of the drawloom, was in use during the Coptic Period. The one-piece tunics so common in Coptic Egypt must have been woven on looms eight or nine feet wide.

Many types of fabrics were found in Coptic burial grounds: tabby or plain weaves, plaid tabby weaves, tapestries, tabby-tapestries, extended tabby or basket weaves, weft-loop weaves, warp-loop weaves, brocades, tapestries, taquetés (weft-faced compound tabbies), and samitums (weft-faced compound twills), resist-dyed textiles, warp-faced tablet weaves, sprang, knits, and some embroideries. Weaving was a guild or government controlled industry, but also always a cottage craft. The technical skills and artistry ranged from the rustic to the sophisticated and sublime.

There came into fashion in the late Augustinian age a "smooth cloth with woolen decorations." This is the quintessential cloth of Coptic Egypt, a combination tabby-tapestry (inserted tapestry) weave used for tunics, shawls, curtains, cushion covers, and large wall hangings. The basic fabric is a slightly warp-dominant tabby of linen warp and weft with an average sett of 56 ends per inch. The tapestry decorations are woven on the same linen warp with dyed woolen and ecru linen wefts. The transition from tabby to tapestry is typically achieved by grouping the warp in sets of two of more. This changes the average sett to 28/2 ends per inch and allows the weft yarns to pack down and completely cover the warp. Tapestry at this sett has a soft and wearable handle, not like the heavy, dense fabric of kilim rugs or medieval wall hangings.

Scholars believe that tapestry weaving came to Egypt with the Greek colonists. The tapestries of Coptic Egypt range in size from mere shreds of warp and weft to wall hangings nine yards long with nearly life-size figures. There are all wool tapestries as well as those of linen and wool. Weavers knew traditional methods of dealing with slits and joins. Early polychrome tapestries shade and blend color areas, while later pieces have separate segments of bold color. Some special techniques were used on the monochrome tapestries. Silhouette-style figures in white linen or dark wool yarn were woven on a mid-value background with a supplementary sketching-weft defining features on the tapestry faces and figures and patterns on a tapestry field.

Coptic Costume

The common costume of Coptic Egypt—as ubiquitous as blue jeans are in the early 2000s—was a tunic with tapestry embellishment. The one-piece tunic of tabby-tapestry was woven from cuff-to-cuff on a hem-to-hem loom width with a slit for the neck opening. To finish the garment the fabric is folded at the shoulder line and seamed up the sides. Some tunics were woven in sections on a narrow loom and then pieced together. Tapestry cuff bands, shoulder or knee medallions, yoke panels, hem bands, and clavi (weft-wise bands) decorate the tunics. The clavi, which become the vertical strips of tapestry running down the front and back of the tunic, can be recognized as an early twenty-first century priestly stole. Men's decorations were typically monochrome, while the women's were often polychrome. Though there are variations in the size and arrangement of tapestry embellishments, the tunic stays in style for nearly a thousand years. Precious tapestry remnants were recycled and appliquéd on other tunics. Brocaded bands, tablet-woven bands, scraps of patterned taqueté or samitum, and some separately woven tapestry bands were sewn to tunics. All wool tunics, decorated with tapestry and some with hoods, were also found. In frescoes, mosaics, and both secular and sacred manuscript illustrations from the early medieval world one can identify the same type of cloth and costume found in the necropolis of Coptic Egypt.

The *Antinoé Riding Coat* is an elegant knee-length coat nipped in at the waist with long flaring sleeves. Though found in Antinoé, they are considered Near Eastern. The coats of wool or cashmere were dyed a luscious red or blue-green. Scraps of delicately patterned silk samitums—the first draw-loom fabrics found in the western world—were used as facings and trim on these garments.

Shawls of linen tabby-tapestry textiles decorated with lavishly colored flowers, dyed woolen shawls, and perhaps silk scarves for the wealthy were worn over tunics. Patterned taqueté woolens, that Gayet found used as duvet covers, were probably reused mantle fabrics. Tapestry leggings, knit socks, leather mules embossed with gilt, and leather sandals with perforated straps were all found in Coptic graves. Hairnets of sprang, as well as bags, made of linen or linen and wool were a fashion item of the day. A *bourrelet de chenille* is an unusual women's head ornament worn to frame the face. A *bourrelet* is a roll of material and *chenille* is French for caterpillar—an apt description for this fuzzy roll of multicolored, long woolen weft-loops on a linen fabric. Thaïs is illustrated in Gayet's book wearing a *bourrelet de chenille*.

Gayet's many exhibits of Antinoé textiles—especially the one he created for the Palais du Costume at the Paris exposition of 1900—inspired costumes for opera, theater, silent films, and even a haute couture gown by Mariano Fortuny. Embroiderers could find Coptic patterns in three booklets published by Dollfus-Meig Company. Rodin collected Coptic textiles. Matisse and other Fauve artists, fascinated by Coptic tapestry art, discovered a new way of interpreting color, shape, and archaic scenes. The impact of Coptic textiles continues with new excavations, exhibitions, and publications.

Gayet believed that the exploration of Antinoé was ". . . the resurrection of a lost world" and the artifacts ". . . of inestimable value for the history of art." His dream of an Antinoé museum was never realized, but the textiles discovered by Gayet—once quotidian cloth—grace modern galleries of museums around the globe. The diverse textile themes, techniques, and technology reflect influences from the languishing classical, flourishing Christian, and emerging Islamic world.

See also **Dyes, Natural; Loom; Textiles, Byzantine; Weave Types.**

BIBLIOGRAPHY

Du Bourguet, Pierre. *Musée National du Louvre Catalogue des etoffes coptes.* Paris: Editions des Musée Nationaux, Ministere d'Etat-Affaires Culturelles, 1964.

Hoskins, Nancy Arthur. *The Coptic Tapestry Albums and the Archaeologist of Antinoé, Albert Gayet.* Eugene, Ore.: Skein Publications in association with the University of Washington Press, 2003.

Lorquin, Alexandra. *Étoffes égyptiennes de l'Antiquité tardive du musée Georges-Labit.* Toulouse: Somogy Editions d'Art, 1999.

Martiniani-Reber, Marielle. *Soieries sassanides, coptes et byzantines V–XI Siècles.* Paris: Editions de la Reunion des Musées Nationaux, 1986.

Rutschowscaya, M. H. *Coptic Fabrics.* Paris: Musée du Louvre, 1990.

Santrot, Marie-Hélène, M. H. Rutschowscaya, Dominique Bénazeth, and Cécile Giroire. *Au Fíl du Níl: couleurs de l'Egypte chrétienne.* Paris: Somogy Éditions D'Art, 2001.

Trilling, James. *The Roman Heritage, Textiles from Egypt and the Eastern Mediterranean 300 to 600 A.D.* Washington, D.C.: The Textile Museum, 1982.

Nancy Arthur Hoskins

TEXTILES, JAPANESE Textiles have long played an important role in Japanese life. Japanese weavers and dyers used silk, hemp, ramie, cotton and other fibers, and a range of weaves and decorative treatments, to produce textiles of distinctive design and exceptional aesthetic merit. These textiles were put to many different uses: for clothing of both commoners and elites; for banners, hangings, and other materials produced for use in temples; for theatrical costumes; and for cushion covers, curtains, and other domestic uses. As with many other Japanese arts, Japanese textiles historically have developed through an interaction of external influences and indigenous techniques and design choices, and a tendency to develop both technology and aesthetics to a high degree of refinement.

Historical Overview

The original inhabitants of Japan (people of the Jômon Culture) wove cloth of plant fiber. Invaders from the northeast Asian mainland established the Yayoi Culture in Japan beginning around 300 B.C.E., introducing more sophisticated materials (including ramie and silk) and techniques. But a recognizably Japanese textile culture can be said to have begun in the Yamato Period (c. 300–710 C.E.), when aristocratic clans and the emergent monarchy led to a greatly increased demand for fine fabrics, especially of silk. The introduction of Buddhism in the mid-sixth century swelled the demand for fine textiles for ecclesiastical use. Some of these textiles were imported from mainland Asia, but increasing amounts were produced in Japan. Weavers, dyers and other textile workers from Korea and China were encouraged to settle in Japan under court patronage; the production of textiles was both patronized and regulated by the state, and the best textiles were produced in imperial workshops.

Silk fabrics in both plain and twill weave were often dyed in solid colors or in patterns produced by stamped wax-resist dyeing. Brocades were produced for both aristocratic and temple use. Other techniques included appliqué, embroidery, and braiding.

The explosive growth in the number, wealth, and power of Buddhist temples in the Nara Period (710–785) led to an intensified development of textile arts, as well as the importation of mainland textiles on a massive scale. The ensuing Heian Period (795–1185) saw a greater emphasis on domestic production, partly in imperial workshops and partly in private ones. This period saw the continued importance of brocade and embroidery, along with increased use of pattern-woven cloth as a ground for patterned dyeing, whether done by wax- or paste-resist methods or various techniques of shaped-resist dyeing. As the harmonious use of colors in multiple layers of clothing was one of the chief aesthetic principles of dress in this era, great efforts were made to expand and perfect dyeing methods.

The Kamakura (1185–1233) and Muromachi (1338–1477) periods saw the establishment of military rule under the auspices of the samurai (warrior) class. International trade increased again during this period, bringing a wealth of new materials, techniques and design motifs to Japan. Cotton was introduced at this time, largely supplanting the use of hemp fiber in textiles used by commoners. The development of the Nôh theater under the patronage of the military aristocracy during the Muromachi Period, with its attendant demand for luxurious and brilliantly beautiful costumes, stimulated textile production and innovation. The introduction of multi-harness looms and improved drawlooms led to an increase in production of complex silk fabrics such as damask and satin, which often were used as background fabrics for patterned dyeing (damask) and for embroidery (satin).

After more than a century of civil warfare (1477–1601), the establishment of the Tokugawa Shogunate (1601–1868) brought an era of renewed peace and prosperity to Japan. By the sixteenth century the *kosode* had become established as the basic garment of Japanese dress; the rapid growth of cities, and of well-to-do urban populations, made this and ensuing forms of the kimono a focus for textile arts. Sumptuary laws designed to prevent commoners from wearing brocades and other complex textiles simply stimulated weavers and dyers to produce surface-decorated fabrics of exceptional beauty and variety that stayed within the letter of the law. The growth of urban pleasure quarters inhabited by courtesans who sometimes could command gifts of great value stimulated the brocade-weaving and tapestry-weaving industries, as demand grew for elaborate and luxurious sashes (*obi*) with which women fastened their kimonos. Meanwhile, in the countryside, peasants were establishing or maintaining their own techniques for weaving and dyeing cotton fabrics, often in distinctive regional styles.

The abolition of military government and the restoration of imperial rule in 1868 led to a period of rapid modernization in Japan. There was a significant vogue in the late 19th century for Western clothing for both men and women; in the early twentieth century, however, many women returned to wearing kimonos much of the time. Following World War II, kimono wearing declined again, becoming limited by the 1960s almost entirely to festival and special-occasion dress, or occupational dress for women in the hospitality industries. The traditional textile arts had already entered a long period of decline by the late nineteenth century, when Japan turned to the industrial production of textiles as an early step toward economic development and modernization. Cheap machine-made fabrics cut deeply into the peasant production of handwoven and hand dyed cotton cloth. Conscious efforts to maintain or revive old textile traditions has kept many techniques from disappearing entirely, but the hand production of textiles in Japan now belongs almost entirely to the world of art and craft.

Woven Textiles

The weave types most commonly encountered in Japanese textiles, regardless of the fiber used, are plain (tabby) weave, twill weave, satin, damask and other patterned weaves, and brocade.

Silk fabrics intended for use in kimono in which the principal decorative elements are batch-dyed or resist-dyed rather than woven or embroidered are usually made in plain weave or damask weave. Colored damasks (*donsu*) employing dyed silk warp threads and weft threads in contrasting colors were used without further dyeing or embellishment; colored damasks were particularly favored for decorative purposes, such as mounting fabric for scroll paintings, and in cloths employed in the tea ceremony. Floating-weft or floating-warp satin (*shusu*) is often used for silk garment fabrics in which the main decorative elements will be applied by embroidery. Patterned twill (*aya*) and twisted-warp gauze (*ra*), often in lightweight, semi-transparent fabrics, have been used for garments since the Nara period, and in later times were especially favored for the wide, loose trousers (*hakama*) and stiff jackets (*kamishimo*) worn by samurai on formal occasions. Twill is frequently also used as the ground weave for a multicolored, brocade-like, drawloom-woven fabric called *nishiki*.

Brocades and tapestry weaves of various kinds were used in ancient times for Buddhist ecclesiastical garments and temple decorations. As garment fabrics they are used especially in obi sashes, which are often tied in very elaborate and decorative ways that display to good effect the luxurious textiles of which they are made. Both obi and kimono, the latter particularly as costumes for Nôh dance-drama, are often made of *kara-ori* ("Chinese weave," i.e. weft-float brocade), a stiff, heavy fabric in which supplementary weft threads on bobbins are float-woven by hand over a plain or twill background fabric.

Fingernail tapestry (*tsuzure*), as the name suggests, is a bobbin-woven tapestry, capable of producing patterns of extreme complexity, and often used for obi.

Plain weave is by far the commonest weave for cotton fabrics. Rural, or faux-rustic, cotton textiles in stripes and plaids of indigo and other vegetable-dye colors, were extremely popular during the Tokugawa period for informal kimono; such fabrics were also used for domestic décor such as covers for sleeping mats and sitting cushions. Plain-woven textiles of plain white cotton were used as the ground for a wide range of dyeing techniques, described below.

Dyeing

Much of the distinctive beauty of Japanese textiles rests on the use of highly developed techniques of dyeing, including paste-resist, shaped-resist, and ikat, as well as composite techniques employing two or more of these methods in concert.

Wax-resist dyeing (batik) was known in ancient Japan, but was abandoned by the end of the Heian Period in favor of paste-resist methods, employing a thick paste of rice flour instead of wax. Paste-resist methods include stencil dyeing and freehand dyeing.

Stencil dyeing (*katazome*) employs stencils made of mulberry bark paper, laminated in several layers with persimmon juice and toughened and waterproofed by smoking. Patterns are cut into these stencils using special knives. Paste is forced through the openwork of the stencil onto the cloth, where it then resists taking the dye when the cloth is immersed in a dyebath. The paste is washed from the cloth after dyeing. Simple stencil dyeing is most commonly found in folk-art indigo-dyed cotton textiles, used for domestic furnishings as well as for clothing. The most common contemporary application of paste-resist dyed indigo-and-white cotton cloth is for *yukata*, cotton kimono used as sleepwear and for informal streetwear, especially at hot spring resorts. Stencil dyeing can also be done in two or more stages to produce a multi-colored result.

Freehand paste-resist dyeing (*tsutsugaki*) uses a waterproof paper cone to apply paste to the fabric; this technique is often employed to create large, bold patterns such as are found on shop curtains (*noren*) and package-carrying cloths (*furoshiki*).

Shaped-resist dyeing techniques are generically known as *shibori* in Japanese; the word is commonly translated "tie-dyed," but that does not convey the very wide range of techniques involved in *shibori* dyeing. *Shibori* includes resists created by sewing portions of cloth in tight gathers; or by twisting cloth, often in complicated ways; or by folding cloth and then compressing it between boards or in wooden or paper tubes; and similar techniques. In every case the aim is to compress portions of cloth so that they will be unaffected by the dye when the whole cloth is placed in a dyebath. Although expert prac-

titioners can achieve a high degree of control over the process, *shibori* dyeing always also includes some element of accident or uncertainty, which adds to its aesthetic appeal. Undyed areas of *shibori* textiles can be embellished in various ways, including hand-application of dyes using brushes, embroidery, or by using paste to apply gold or silver foil to the fabric.

Ikat, known as *kasuri* in Japanese, is a technique in which warp yarns, weft yarns, or both are bound in thread in pre-arranged patterns and dyed. The yarns are then assembled into a warp and/or woven as weft in the proper sequence, the pattern emerging as the weaving progresses. Kasuri textiles are produced in silk, in a wide range of colors; in ramie; in cotton, typically indigo-dyed; and in Okinawa in banana fiber, often with several colors produced by successive wrappings and dyeings of the yarn.

Yuzen, invented around 1700, is probably the most famous of Japanese dyeing techniques. It is produced by a combination of either freehand or stenciled paste-resist work and hand-application of dyes. With the cloth (either silk or cotton) stretched on a frame, a pattern is applied with a fine brush using a non-permanent blue vegetable dye, and then covered freehand with paste; or else the paste is applied directly with a stencil. A thin soybean extract is then brushed over the entire cloth. The cloth is then moistened with water, and dye is applied by hand with brushes; the dye spreads on the damp cloth to produce the color-shaded effect characteristic of *yuzen*. *Yuzen* is capable of achieving color effects of astonishing subtlety and complexity, and is used to produce the finest and most prized of all kimono fabrics.

The Okinawan art of *bingata* stencil dyeing can be thought of as a paste-resist version of batik. It uses multiple steps of stencil-applied paste and dyeing (either by vat dyeing or by hand application of dyes), with dyed areas covered with paste resist in subsequent stages of work. *Bingata* is typically produced in bright colors and with pictorial motifs of birds, flowers, and landscapes.

Embroidery

Like brocade and tapestry weaving, embroidery arrived in Japan in ancient times in connection with Buddhism, and was often used to produce pictorial hangings for use in temples. Japanese embroidery uses a fairly small repertoire of stitches, including French knots, chain stitch, satin stitch, and couched satin stitch. In garments, particularly kimono, embroidery is applied to vat-dyed plain weave silk textiles, to silk satin, and as an embellishment to textiles decorated with various dye techniques, including *shibori* and *katazome*.

Decorative Stitching

Japanese farm women developed a technique for salvaging worn cotton textiles for re-use by stitching them together in layers for use in jackets, aprons, and other protective garments. The technique, akin to quilting, is known as *sashiko*, and developed from a practical way of using cloth to a unique craft of decorative stitching. *Sashiko* is almost always done with white cotton thread on indigo-dyed cotton cloth. Stitches may run parallel to the warp, or to the weft, or both; patterns are usually geometric, and often elaborately lacy.

Ainu Textiles

The Ainu are the aboriginal inhabitants of Hokkaido, the northernmost main island of Japan; their ancestors were among the original occupants of Japan, prior to the arrival of the Yayoi people. Ainu culture is closer to that of Sakhalin Island and other parts of northeastern Siberia than it is to Japanese culture. The Ainu are known for preserving old techniques of making jackets and other items of clothing decorated with appliqué and embroidery in bold, curvilinear designs, often in light colors on a dark background.

Contemporary Japanese Textiles

The status of textiles in contemporary Japan can be considered in four categories. *Commercial textiles* are a declining industry in Japan. Textile production, particularly of man-made fiber textiles such as rayon and polyester, played an important role in Japan's postwar economic recovery, but has been in decline in recent decades as production has moved to countries with lower labor costs. Some silk is produced in Japan by the country's heavily subsidized agricultural sector.

Traditional textiles continue to flourish. The Japanese government encourages the preservation of traditional arts and crafts through subsidies to "Holders of Important Intangible Cultural Properties," colloquially known as "Living National Treasures." These master practitioners of their arts provide leadership to thousands of other full-time craft workers. Of approximately 100 Living National Treasures at any time, about one-third are in the field of textile arts. Notable examples include brocade weaver Kitagawa Hyôji, the late stencil paste-resist dyer Serizawa Keisuke, and *yuzen* dyer Yamada Mitsugi.

Fashion textiles have received significant support from some of Japan's internationally famous fashion designers, notably Issey Miyake, whose innovative use of such material as tube-knitted jersey has bolstered Japan's fine textile industry.

Art textiles, or fiber arts more broadly, are a thriving field of Japan's contemporary art scene, and have achieved international recognition through such exhibitions as "Structure and Surface" (New York, 1999) and "Through the Surface" (London, 2004). A number of individual fiber artists have won international reputations, including Arai Junichi, known for his innovative use of techno-textiles; Sudo Reiko, known for her sculptural woven fabrics; and Tomita Jun, who uses traditional dyeing techniques to produce contemporary textile art.

See also **Dyeing; Embroidery; Ikat; Kimono; Yukata.**

BIBLIOGRAPHY

Dusenbury, Mary. "Textiles." In *The Kodansha Encyclopedia of Japan.* 9 vols. Tokyo: Kodansha International, 1983.

McCarthy, Cara, and Matilda McQuaid. *Structure and Surface: Contemporary Japanese Textiles.* New York: Museum of Modern Art, 1999.

Yang, Sunny, and Rochelle Narasin. *Textile Art of Japan.* Tokyo: Shufunotomo, 2000.

John S. Major

TEXTILES, MIDDLE EASTERN Even before the Islamic period, the Middle East was a nexus of Eurasian textile production and trade. The complex of trade routes commonly referred to as the Silk Road reached their western end at the ports of the eastern Mediterranean. Inevitably these markets were also centers of textile production. The spread of Islamic rule in the seventh and eighth centuries encompassed and incorporated the previous textile industries of the Byzantine and Sassanian Empires. In the early Islamic period textile design was derived from that of their predecessors, but Islamic cultures soon evolved their own forms of expression. During the Middle Ages, the textiles of the Middle East were highly prized goods that in due course stimulated the development of indigenous European production. The connection between Islamic and European cloth can be seen in the extensive textile terminology that is derived from Persian, Arabic, or Turkish, including terms such as damask, taffeta, cotton, muslin, seersucker, and mohair.

In the Islamic world, textiles were highly valued goods, accepted as tribute in lieu of taxes in some periods. Gifts of textiles and garments were presented to honor officials or visiting ambassadors. In a part of the world where much of the population could claim nomadic antecedents, interiors were primarily furnished with textiles, used to cover floors, walls, cushions, and to create beds and storage of all kinds. Gifts were presented in a textile wrapper, and the more elaborate the workmanship of the wrapper the greater the honor intended. Textiles were also held to have the power to protect or harm, and so inscriptions and symbols were frequently incorporated into them to this end. In the century following the death of Muhammad, representation of living creatures were banned, particularly in the Sunnī tradition. Islamic design developed its own metaphorical language, utilizing geometry, calligraphy, vegetal, and architectural forms. However, it should be pointed out that in some Islamic textiles human and animal figures do appear, particularly in Persian and Central Asian silks and carpets.

Silk

Elaborately patterned silk textiles were produced throughout the Islamic world in various complex weaves, including compound twills, lampas, and brocades, as well as double and triple cloth. Motifs were stylized and varied greatly depending on the period and region. Simpler textiles including *tafta* and satin weaves were also important and numerous, as were a variety of very lightweight silks. In addition, there were textiles in which silk warp and cotton weft were combined, frequently striped. In the rep weave known as *alaca* the silk warp (yarns stretched on the loom) covered the cotton weft (yarns interlaced with the warp) to produce an economical silk textile. In the satin weave known as *kutnu* the silk warp shows on the face of the fabric, but the back shows the cotton weft. This textile was widely favored because according to Islamic tradition men were forbidden to wear silk against the skin. Tapestry technique was another important category of silk weaving.

One of the most characteristic early Islamic silk textiles was *tiraz*, which was particularly important from the tenth to fourteenth centuries. It was a product of royal workshops. *Tiraz* textiles were embellished with borders containing inscriptions, usually embroidered or tapestry woven in gold thread. Baghdad was the best-known source of *tiraz*, but it was produced in workshops sponsored by many rulers in many locations from Egypt and Yemen to Syria and Moorish Spain. These borders appear most commonly as bands on the upper sleeve, but were also used on the edges or in the body of the garment. They were also found on burial shrouds and ceremonial textiles. The inscriptions usually included the name of the current ruler as well as religious quotations. *Tiraz* embellished garments were worn by high-court officials and presented as honorific robes. Linen or cotton textiles might also have *tiraz* bands.

The Moorish conquest of Spain beginning in the eighth century led to the introduction of *tiraz* workshops, as well as workshops for the production of compound-weave silk textiles. These silks might resemble the textiles of late Byzantine or Sassanian workshops, but soon Spanish workshops were producing distinctly Islamic motifs, including elaborate geometric designs as well as stylized floral designs. Spanish textiles were varied, but strongly contrasting colors and geometric motifs were common.

Bursa was the most important center for silk production in the Ottoman Empire from the fifteenth century on, although not the only producer of high-quality silk textiles. Ottoman silks were richly colored, and frequently featured large-scale patterns. Although in the fifteenth century Ottoman textiles could be said to have influenced Italian silk design, thereafter Italian design influenced some Ottoman silks. However, many designs were distinctively Turkish, showing an affinity with Ottoman miniature painting and tile design. These featured stylized flowers, foliage, and vines. A common motif was a cluster of three circles in combination with wavy lines. The Ottoman repertoire included voided velvet as well as other compound weaves. Fine silk embroidery, done on silk, velvet, linen, or cotton, was another important category of Ottoman textile work.

Safavid Iran produced exquisite silks that were considered to be among the finest in the Islamic world. Yazd in the fifteenth century and Isfahan and Kashan in the sixteenth and seventeenth centuries were among its most important centers of production. Elaborate voided velvets and a wide array of intricate compound weaves, as well as fine embroidery were characteristics of Persian silks. Persian designs were finely detailed with complex coloring. A distinctive group of Persian textiles used human and animal figures, done in the style of miniature painting. The most elaborate of these woven textiles included scenes from Persian literature. Silk embroidery was also an important category of Persian textiles. The fine quality of Persian silk fibers contributed to the high quality, and made Persian raw silk highly sought after by foreign merchants. Persian textiles also influenced Moghul India.

Cotton and Linen

A variety of types of flax were raised in the Islamic world, as well as other types of bast fibers, including hemp. Both cotton and linen textiles were widely used throughout the region. These textiles ranged from the heavy cotton canvas produced for sailing ships to extremely fine muslins and gauzes. Although India is best known for fine cottons, all of the countries of the Levant also developed their own fine cotton weaving industries. However, trade with India for textiles was important for the entire Muslim world.

Textile printing was known in pre-Islamic Egypt, but dating and provenance of early Islamic printed textiles is generally not clear. Printing blocks have been identified from the Fatimid period, and a number of examples found in Mamluk Egypt are believed to have been produced there. By the sixteenth century a printing industry existed in Syria, and in the seventeenth and eighteenth century this industry expanded into Anatolia, stimulated by the expanding European demand for Indian printed textiles being transported through the Eastern Mediterranean ports.

Mohair, Wool and Other Animal Fibers

Mohair and camel hair, as well as the goat hair referred to variously as cashmere or pashmina, were used to weave soft and beautifully patterned shawls in many locations throughout the Islamic world. These shawls became very popular in the west in the nineteenth century, but had long been a feature of dress in Muslim northern India, Persia, and Ottoman Turkey. The patterns were woven in twill tapestry or a variety of compound weaves, but in either case featured elaborately patterned and colored designs. Some of these were patterned stripes. Many were complex vegetal designs, the most well-known example of which is the *boteh*. The *boteh* is also referred to by other names depending on the language of the weaver. In the west this design came to be known as the paisley motif, named after Paisley, Scotland, where textile mills produced copies of the Indian shawls in the latter nineteenth century.

GLOSSARY OF TECHNICAL TERMS

Compound (twill, weave): An adjective applied to any fabric or weave in which there are two or more sets of yarns in the lengthwise, the crosswise, or in both directions.

Lampas: Fabric with a woven figure in which crosswise yarns form the design and a second warp yarn holds the crosswise design-forming yarns in place.

Tafta: A fabric made from tightly twisted silk ply yarns in a plain weave.

Rep weave: Plain weave fabric in which crosswise yarns are larger than lengthwise yarns, thereby forming a pronounced crosswise rib.

Tapestry weaving: A handweaving technique in which crosswise (weft) yarns create a solid color patterned effect in selected areas (1) by being so closely packed that they completely hide the lengthwise (warp) yarns and (2) by not crossing the entire width of the fabric, but instead moving back and forth in the area of the design. In this way patterns of great complexity and size can be made.

Voided velvet: Velvet fabric in which the pile (standing fibers or loops) is limited to selected areas in order to form a design.

Although wool was widely used to produce a variety of apparel textiles, the best known Islamic wool textiles are the pile and flat woven textiles made as rugs, bags, bands, wall coverings, cushions, and other household equipment. Knotted pile weaving seems to have originated in Central Asia well before the date of the oldest known example, which was made about 2,500 years ago. The oldest examples of Islamic carpet weaving that have survived are the ninth century "Fostat" carpet fragment found in Cairo, and a group of thirteenth-century Seljuk Turkish fragments found in Konya in Central Anatolia. Sixteenth-century examples from Mamluk Egypt and Safavid Persia both attest to a sophisticated and long-established tradition. Carpet design can be divided into three categories that reflect their visual style, origins, and degree of technical excellence. The tribal carpets were produced by nomadic or village households primarily for their own use. The designs reflect tribal and regional affiliations, and tend to be relatively geometric in design. Although some are quite finely woven, many are relatively coarse. Court carpets were commissioned in court ateliers according to designs created by the finest artists of the day. These designs, which often bear a close relation to those of tile work, manuscript illumination, and silk textiles, are technically the most finely knotted, and visually the most intricate. Urban manufactory carpets constitute the third category. These carpets, produced under the direction of merchant entrepreneurs, may be technically very fine, but are characterized by somewhat more repetitive and less intricate designs as compared to court carpets.

Flat weaves include a variety of techniques, the best known of which include *kilim* (slit tapestry), *jajim* (compound discontinuous brocade), and *soumak* (warp wrapping). Card-weaving is a widespread method of making bands that appears to have a long history of use throughout the Islamic world. These techniques and others are used to create floor and wall coverings, storage bags, tent bands, and door panels, as well as animal trappings. Generally flat woven wool textiles were produced primarily for local use and are characterized by distinctive tribal or regional designs and color palettes. Modern production, however, is increasingly tailored to the color and design preferences of western markets.

Dyeing and Finishing

In the early twenty-first century much of this traditional production has been lost as modern textiles replace traditional ones. Where traditional textile production continues, the products are being transformed as the weavers seek to adapt to modern taste and lifestyles.

See also **Iran, History of Pre-Islamic Dress; Islamic Dress, Contemporary.**

BIBLIOGRAPHY

Baker, Patricia L. *Islamic Textiles.* London: British Museum Press, 1995.

Eiland, Murray L. *Oriental Carpets: A Complete Guide.* Boston: Bulfinch Press, 1998.

Fleet, Kate. *European and Islamic Trade in the Early Ottoman State: The Merchants of Genoa and Turkey.* Cambridge: Cambridge University Press, 1999.

Kahlenberg, Mary Hunt. *Asian Costumes and Textiles from the Bosphorus to Fujiyama.* Milan: Skira, 2001.

Harris, Jennifer, ed. *Textiles, 5000 Years: An International History and Illustrated Survey.* New York: Harry N. Abrams, 1993.

Hull, Alastair, and Jose Wyhowska. *Kilim, The Complete Guide: History, Pattern, Technique, Identification.* New York: Chronicle Books, 2000.

Miller, Charlotte Jirousek. "Dyes in Rugs from the Milas Area." *Hali* 4, no. 3 (1982): 258–261.

Tezcan, Hülye. *The Topkapi Saray Museum: Costumes, Embroideries, and Other Textiles.* New York: Little, Brown and Company, 1986.

Charlotte Jirousek

TEXTILES, PREHISTORIC Textiles require long, pliable string-like elements. The earliest current evidence for human awareness and manufacture of string comes (as impressions on clay) from Pavlov, a Palaeolithic site of about 25,000 B.C.E. in the Czech Republic. Thin, breakable filaments of plant-bast fiber were twisted into longer, stronger threads yarns that were then twined as weft (crosswise yarns) around the warp (lengthwise yarns) and around each other to make net-like fabrics. These fabrics are sophisticated enough that this cannot be the very beginning of either thread-, yarn-, or net-making. Other slightly later finds, plus the fact that all human cultures know the art of making string, confirm that this technology began in the Palaeolithic and spread everywhere with the human race. Indeed, string-making probably made it possible for humans to spread into difficult eco-niches, since it improves hunting/fishing capabilities and enables food-packaging.

Interestingly, a few of the so-called Venus figures (hand-sized carvings of women, usually plump, dating to about 20,000 B.C.E. and found from France to Russia) wear garments clearly fashioned of string: string skirts, bandeaux, or netted caps. These garments seem to signal information about marital status.

The first proof of true weaving occurs circa 7000 B.C.E. at the start of the Neolithic, with impressions of plain-weave and basket-weave on clay at Jarmo (northeast Iraq) and a pseudomorph (minerals having outward characteristics of organic materials) of a plain-weave textile on a bone at Çayönü Tepesi (southern Turkey). Again, these fabrics are too well done to be the start of weaving. Over the next millennium, fragments and impressions of mats, baskets, and twined textiles are found scattered through Iraq, western Iran, Turkey, and the Levant. Sizable pieces of linen actually survived in a desert cave at Nahal Hemar, Israel, circa 6500 B.C.E.; one needle-netted piece adorned with stone buttons is apparently a ritual hat.

Around 6000 B.C.E., at Çatal Hüyük in central Turkey, there was such a preponderance of plain-weave over twining, among the many fragments of linens used to wrap ancestral bones, that one can conclude the heddle (mounted loop) that forms a harness to separate warp yarns in a loom had been invented. (True-weave fabrics ravel easily, unlike twined ones, so the only advantage to

GLOSSARY OF TECHNICAL TERMS

Bast fiber: Fiber that is obtained from the stem of a plant. Examples include linen from the flax plant, ramie, and hemp.

Heddle: Device on a loom through which each lengthwise yarn (warp yarn) is threaded that allows warps to be raised and lowered during weaving.

Kemp: Straight, short, stiff, silvery white fibers in wool fleece that do not spin or dye well.

Kermes: Natural red dye used since ancient times that is made from the eggs obtained by crushing the bodies of a tiny female insect parasite found on oak trees.

Overshot: A type of weaving in which an additional set of crosswise yarns extend across two or more lengthwise yarns in a plain background weave to form a pattern or design. Pile fabric surface on which fibers, yarns, or raised loops that may be cut or uncut or stand up on the surface of a background fabric.

Pseudomorph: When used in reference to textile evidence found in archeological sites, a mineralized imprint of textile yarns or fabrics.

Selvage: The lengthwise edge of a woven fabric that is often made with heavier yarns and woven more tightly than the rest of the fabric in order to make this area strong and secure.

Shed bar: Rod or stick on a primitive loom that is used to separate one set of lengthwise (warp) yarns from another set so a space (called the shed) is made that allows the passage of the crosswise (weft) yarns.

Supplementary weft: An extra crosswise yarn, in addition to the primary crosswise yarn.

Warp/warp yarn: Lengthwise yarns in a woven fabric.

Weft/weft yarn: Crosswise yarns in a woven fabric.

Woad: Natural blue dye obtained by fermenting the leaves of the woad plant, *Isatis Tinctoria*.

to about 8000 B.C.E. But true weave does not appear until nearly 2000 B.C.E., radiating from an area of northwest South America containing both archaeological and linguistic evidence that some Asiatic foreigners had somehow arrived. That suggests that the heddle was invented only once, in either the northwestern Near East or southeastern Europe, some time before 7000 B.C.E., and spread worldwide from there.

Despite the subsistence-level economy of the Swiss pile-dwellers and their neighbors, central and western Europe is the one area where there is evidence of decorative patterning in Neolithic textiles: supplementary weft and occasionally warp patterns (both overshot and brocaded), beading (with seeds), an example of the Log Cabin (color-and-weave) pattern, and what may be embroidery (the originals were lost in one of the wars—only drawings survived). All these textiles were too blackened to show color, but the investigator of the most ornate claimed that it would not have been made that way unless the weaver were juggling at least three colors. A Neolithic site in France produced evidence of dyeing thread yarn with both kermes (red) and woad (blue), both colorfast dyes. Other evidence for patterning comes from clay figurines of women found in the Balkans and Ukraine: Many are naked and some wear string skirts, but others wear simple wraparound skirts with a square or checked pattern.

Up to 4000 B.C.E., the only readily available fibers came from plant stems (bast fibers: flax around the Mediterranean; hemp farther north across Eurasia, including China; yucca, maguey, among others in the western hemisphere). Sheep (Ovis orientalis) had been domesticated in the Near East around 8000 B.C.E., but for meat—their coats consisted primarily of bristly kemp, with only a short undercoat of ultra-fine wool (5 microns) for insulation. "Nice" modern wool runs 15 to 30 microns in diameter, but the wild kemp runs about 300 microns and has no torsional strength, so it cannot be twisted into yarn. It appears to have taken 4000 years of inbreeding to develop sheep with usable amounts of wool in their coats (genetic changes gradually eliminated the kemp, while the wool grew longer and heavier). Once woolly sheep were available, however, everyone wanted them and soon they were taken to Europe and the Eurasian grasslands. Unlike bast, moreover, the wool of even a single sheep typically includes several shades of color, which can be sorted for patterning one's cloth. This helped fuel the explosion of textile technology in the next era.

Bronze Age

It is only as people began experimenting with metals, shortly before 3000 B.C.E., that they seem to have begun using cloth widely, and in particular to differentiate themselves with clothing. Since metals had to be obtained through trade or distant mining expeditions, people began moving around much more, causing new concentrations of wealth and greatly increased movement of ideas.

Egyptian textile workers depicted in funerary model. Though only women are seen here, ancient Egypt differed from other early civilizations in that both men and women wove the favored white linen. THE METROPOLITAN MUSEUM OF ART, PHOTOGRAPH BY EGYPTIAN EXPEDITION. 1919–1920. REPRODUCED BY PERMISSION.

true weave is that the process, unlike twining, can be mechanized with shed bars and heddles. So once the heddle—a conceptually difficult invention—is available, weaving ousts twining thanks to the speed of manufacture.) This corpus includes tied fringes, reinforced selvages (closed edges of a fabric that prevent unraveling), rolled and whipped hems, weft twining and warp-wrapped twining, as well as coarse, fine, tightly- and loosely-woven fabrics.

With the heddle invented and domestic flax available, large-scale weaving began to spread in all directions. In Europe have been found remains of vertical warp-weighted looms in villages around the central Danube by 5500 B.C.E., a tradition reaching the Swiss pile-dwellings by 3000 B.C.E. as it spread west and north. By 5000 B.C.E. crude linen-weaving spread south to Egypt, where someone painted the first known depiction of a loom circa 4200 B.C.E. Weaving with heddles also spread eastward across Eurasia, apparently reaching Tibet and China circa 5000 B.C.E.

Inhabitants of the western hemisphere probably invented twined fabrics on their own (unless, like string, this technology entered with them); the earliest finds date

A tall stone vase from Uruk (the Mesopotamian city in which writing first appeared about this time) shows the key domesticates—grain and sheep—in the bottom registers, with lines of naked workers bringing in the harvest above them, while in the top register we see the fancily dressed elite presenting gifts of food to a fully clothed goddess or priestess. As in the Palaeolithic, clothing developed—as seen here—primarily to send social messages, becoming ever more elaborate in both the Near East and Europe.

Neither textiles nor paintings survive well in the Near East, but cuneiform texts attest to the importance of textiles. We see this particularly in the dowry lists of young women, with their chests of clothing (and numerous hats), in the high prices fetched by some textiles, and also in some women's letters (about 1800 B.C.E.) concerning textile manufacture. In one group, two queens, good friends, discuss their woes in overseeing the palace manufacture (by slave women) of fancy cloth and clothing that their husbands expect to use as important diplomatic gifts. In another set, a group of merchant-class women in Assyria, who were in business for themselves making and selling textiles, discuss and argue with their far-faraway husbands (who sold the textiles abroad) about types of cloth to make, prompt payment, tax-dodging, opportunistic purchases, and problems with the caravan-drivers who transported the goods. Textile manufacture, in fact, was basically women's work in early times, as shown by the representations (which generally show women doing the spinning and weaving) and the location of textile tools in women's graves, not men's. Men, however, often helped with fiber production, felting or fulling, dyeing, and final sale (although much cloth was made for the family itself).

In Egypt, however, many matters differed. Traditionally women spun thread and wove it into cloth, but men also spun, making the string and rope needed in the fields; and mat-weaving was men's work. In the murals, we see children learning to spin beside their mothers in the textile workshops. Men also did the laundry, which had to be done in the Nile where crocodile attacks were a problem. Archaeologists have found linens of all grades, from coarse sailcloth to pieces as fine as silk handkerchiefs (200 threads per inch). Unlike their northern neighbors, the Egyptians wore mostly only white linen, since they preferred to have clean, bleached clothes every day (Egypt is very dusty and linen is wonderfully wash-and-wear, unlike wool); for color they used beads and other jewelry, instead of patterned cloth. Since textiles are preserved far better in Egypt than most other places, people tend to think everyone "back then" wore only white cloth, which is not true.

The glory of Bronze Age weaving designs is most visible in the frescoes of Minoan Crete, where we see women in particular arrayed in sophisticated polychrome patterns, especially running spirals, three- and four-petaled interlocks, and small all-over patterns closely reminiscent of twill and rosepath designs. The men wore simple loincloths with fancy woven edgings, but the women wore long flounced skirts and tight-fitting short-sleeved bodices and sashes sewn up from these elaborately patterned cloths. For a millennium (c. 2100–1200 B.C.E.), Aegean weavers even exported large, brightly patterned cloths to the Egyptians, who apparently coveted them for making ostentatious canopies. For actual color, some Bronze Age textiles of Central Asia have preserved stunning reds, blues, and yellows.

As the Bronze Age progressed, the Mesopotamians, Minoans, and Egyptians all began importing ornate textiles from Syria, which seems from its texts to have been an important center of the industry. (Textiles themselves do not survive there.) Around 1475 B.C.E., Egypt even imported both tapestry technique and the "tapestry loom" (vertical two-beam loom) from Syria, where both seem to have begun a millennium earlier. By 1200 B.C.E., Egyptians depict Syrian and Aegean captives as wearing extremely ornate clothing characterized by friezes of animals. This tradition of friezed textiles seems to have survived in Greece through the period of destructive attacks that ended the Bronze Age around 1200 B.C.E., resurfacing there about 800 B.C.E., where, in being copied onto Iron Age Geometric and Wild Goat styles of pottery, it jump-started Greek art.

Other Areas

In India, cotton was domesticated before 3000 B.C.E., but it reached the Mediterranean only after 1000 B.C.E. Cotton is easy to dye, and the Bronze Age city-dwellers of the Indus valley apparently exploited this trait, judging by the dye-installations and occasional depictions. In northern China, people discovered silk by 2000 B.C.E., developing its production, dyeing, and weaving into a high art—and a royal monopoly—during the great Shang dynasty (1500–1100 B.C.E.). Unfortunately, little but pseudomorphs has survived from periods before the mid-first millennium B.C.E.

True weaving was well developed in the Andes and in Central America before Europeans arrived. The Andean people had available not only cotton (native to both New and Old Worlds) but also the wool from alpacas, which occurs in a wide variety of shades from white through soft browns to black. Many superbly crafted pieces of tapestry and embroidery have survived, thanks to the cold, dry climate of the high Andes. Mayan and Aztec textiles have seldom survived, although we know from accounts and images that they were sometimes quite ornate. North of the "four-corners" area of the western United States, the heddle was still unknown. The one famous type of ornamented cloth from prehistoric North America, the Chilkat blanket, was laboriously twined onto a hanging but unweighted warp. (The Navajo did not start to weave their colorful blankets until the late nineteenth century.) The feathered garments of the

Hawaiian royalty, too, were made by twining, using the twist of the plant-fiber weft to bind in the brightly colored feathers.

See also **Dyes, Natural; Linen; Loom; Wool.**

BIBLIOGRAPHY

Adovasio, J. M., Olga Soffer, and B. Klima. "Palaeolithic Fiber Technology: Data from Pavlov I, ca. 26,000 B.P." *Antiquity* 70 (1996): 526–534. Earliest preserved textile remains yet found.

Barber, Elizabeth Wayland. *Prehistoric Textiles.* Princeton: Princeton University Press, 1991. Compendium of archaeological textile data from 20,000 B.C.E. to about 400 B.C.E., from Iran to Britain; technical history of early textiles. Massive index and bibliography.

——. *Women's Work: The First 20,000 Years.* New York: W. W. Norton and Company, 1994. Social and economic history of early cloth and clothing.

——. *The Mummies of Ürümchi.* New York: W. W. Norton and Company, 1999. Superbly preserved textile finds from prehistoric Central Asia.

Burnham, Harold B. "Çatal Hüyük: The Textiles and Twined Fabrics." *Anatolian Studies* 15 (1965): 169–174. Preserved textiles from 6000 B.C.E.

Cotte, J., and Ch. Cotte. "Le Kermès dans l'antiquité." *Revue archéologique* 7 (1918): 92–112. Neolithic fiber-dyes.

Dalley, Stephanie. "Old Babylonian Dowries." *Iraq* 42 (1980): 53–74. What women wore in Mesopotamia 4,000 years ago.

——. *Mari and Karana.* London: Longman, 1984. Letters (often about textile work) of two Mesopotamian queens.

Schick, Tamar. "Perishable Remains from the Nahal Hamar Cave." *Journal of the Israel Prehistoric Society* 19 (1986): 84–86 and 95–97. Preserved textiles from 6500 B.C.E.

Schlabow, Karl. "Beitrage zur Erforschung der jungsteinzeitlichen und bronzezeitlichen Gewebetechnik." *Jahresschrift für mitteldeutsche Vorgeschichte* 43 (1959): 101–120. Patterned Neolithic textiles from Germany.

Veenhof, Klaas R. *Aspects of Old Assyrian Trade and Its Terminology.* Leiden, Netherlands: E. J. Brill, 1972. Old Assyrian textile trade, including letters of women weavers.

Vogt, Emil. *Geflechte und Gewebe der Steinzeit.* Basel: Verlag E. Birkhäuser, 1937. Full analysis of Neolithic Swiss lake-bed textiles, circa 3000 B.C.E.

Welters, Linda, ed. *Folk Dress in Europe and Anatolia: Beliefs about Protection and Fertility.* Oxford and New York: Berg, 1999. Analysis of rural survivals of important (message-bearing) prehistoric designs in women's cloth and clothing.

E. J. W. Barber

TEXTILES, SOUTH ASIAN

TEXTILES, SOUTH ASIAN The large geographic region of South Asia consists of many diverse nations, each distinguished by their varied religions, geographic and climatic conditions, peoples, and diverse cultural, economic, and political and social dynamics. The countries that constitute South Asia are: Bangladesh, Bhutan, India, Maldives, Nepal, Pakistan, and Sri Lanka. (Tibet, administratively an "autonomous region" of China, is also usually included.)

Throughout recorded history, textiles have played an important role in the social, cultural, and economic life of South Asia. Cotton, as well as many dye plants, is native to the Indian subcontinent, facilitating the development of many textile techniques. Distinctive dress forms evolved from lengths of unstitched cloth. Furthermore, much of this region lies along or occupies great historic sea and land trade routes whereby textile products were disseminated along with great cultural exchange and the spread of Buddhism, Hinduism, and Islam.

Bangladesh

Bangladesh historically occupied an important position linking trade between South and Southeast Asia. Its cottons were traded throughout Asia, Persia, and Africa. Once largely Buddhist and Hindu, beginning in the thirteenth century, the country became predominantly Muslim. Bengal (the region now divided between Bangladesh and India's West Bengal Province) was affected politically and economically by the arrival of the British East India Company in the eighteenth century, which led to increased religious, economic, and political polarization and class conflicts. East Bengal became independent (as East Pakistan) in 1947, and broke away to become the independent state of Bangladesh in 1971.

Bangladesh has long been famous for its high-quality woven cottons, silks, and jute production. Especially famous were the ultra-fine muslins of Dahka (or Dacca). Plain, striped, checked, and figured saris woven of fine muslin threads were often given poetic names to describe their cobweb-like lightness and softness. *Jamdanis* are figured cloths, where small images are woven or inlaid in an embroidery-like weaving technique called discontinuous supplementary weft. Equally famous silk brocade saris have also been woven in present-day Bangladesh.

In rural areas, there were varieties of tribal backstrap weavings formed into clothing. Two-piece clothing worn by women, consisted of the *mekhala*, or saronglike lower-body wrap, and the *riah*, or upper-body breast cloth. Women also wove and wore chaddar, or head cover/shawls. Men wore the dhoti, or loin cloth, a shoulder wrap and occasionally a simple untailored jacket stitched from several pieces of hand-loomed fabric.

The *kantha* is a famous embroidered textile from Bangladesh and Bengal. Made from layers of worn saris and dhotis, these thin blankets were embroidered with figures and scenes of everyday and religious life, then quilted in tiny white stitches. Although *kantha* vary in style and color scheme by region, a characteristic feature is a central lotus medallion.

Pakistan

Pakistan is an ancient land with a fascinating multicultural history. Remains of woven and dyed cottons have been found among the third millennium B.C.E. Indus Valley settlements located in present-day Punjab and Sind regions.

Many ethnic and tribal groups of Pakistan wear slightly varying garments of vastly different names. There are numerous names for head covers, upper body garments, and lower. From the Sind area, a woman's embroidered headcloth is named *bochini* or *abocchnai;* in Punjab all-over embroidered headcloths in geometric patterns were *phulkari bagh* or *chope,* while the figured embroidered ones were called *sainchi.* Women generally wear three-piece sets consisting of drawstring-waisted *salwar* (sometimes spelled *shalwar*), long over-tunics variously called *kameez, pushk,* or *cholo,* and head covers. A long embroidered wedding blouse is called *guj* or *chola,* depending on the region and community. Men formerly wore the kurta, a collarless long-sleeved upper body garment over *salwar* drawstring trousers, or over the *lunghi,* a sarong-style lower-body garment. In the twenty-first century, men typically wear Western-style trousers. The *malir,* or *bhet* or *bukhano* (depending on the community) was an important male wedding cloth that could be worn over the shoulder or as a turban. In cooler regions of both India and Pakistan, men wear an outer coat called *choga.*

India

This vast landmass is home to numerous languages, religions, tribal groups, and diverse communities. Cotton is native to India, as are many dye plants including indigo and madder, and the cultures of India have produced exceptional skills and creativity in textile arts. Due to India's religions, social customs, textile skills and products, hereditary castes of crafts workers, and the role of women in producing dowry textiles, the textile arts and diverse forms of Indian dress are distinctive, impressive, numerous, and ancient. Specific forms of dress, employing characteristic textiles, were intricately intertwined with and dictated by factors such as region, urban or rural setting, caste and social station, ceremony or religious activity, and historical time period.

Trade, invasions, and imperialism brought many changes to Indian culture, including textiles and dress. The introduction of Islam beginning in the thirteenth century, and the establishment of the Delhi-based Mughal Empire in the sixteenth century, brought new types of fabric and new garments. Rich dress and splendid outward appearance was preferred, and the Mughals rewarded their administrators and loyal military staff with lavish dress. Simultaneously, in the fifteenth century, Europeans opened sea routes that challenged the longstanding routes of Arab traders who had heretofore monopolized the trade between Asia and Europe. The Portuguese established themselves in south India and made Goa the seat of their power and trade. The Dutch Netherlands East India Company understood the intrinsic aesthetic and symbolic value of Indian textiles and utilized them in exchange for spices with present-day Indonesia. Textiles played an important ritual role in

many of the diverse cultures of the East Indies islands, and so Indian trade textiles (for example, the silk ikat known as patola cloth) were in strong demand there. The British East India Company traded largely between India and England, and eventually established British domination of the subcontinent, exerting power in part through subservient local rulers. *Maharajas* (kings), *maharanis* (queens), and their Islamic counterparts, the *Nawabs,* demanded elaborate courtly dress to declare their elite status. These courts generated large demands for woven silks, gold and silver brocades, embroideries, and jewels. Wealthy merchants and traders also dressed in similar splendid style.

British rule in India, and its economic effects, had a profound impact on Indian-made cotton, textiles and clothing. Homespun thread and yarn was displaced by imported British factory-spun thread, while foreign markets for traditional Indian cotton trade goods, such as muslin and chintz, were also undercut by British manufacturing might and discriminatory trade rules. One tactic of Indian nationalist opposition to British rule in the early twentieth century sought to counter the domination of British mill-woven goods in favor of self-reliance through making and buying Indian *khaddar* (handspun, hand-loomed cottons) and other hand-made goods. Factors intrinsic to local culture also led to the preservation of many textile types and techniques.

In both India and Pakistan, marriages are occasions for the production of ceremonial and decorative textiles and special dress. In northwest India and twenty-first-century eastern Pakistan, textiles and dress are important items in the dowry that a bride brings to her new home. Brides' families prepared decorative textiles such as *torans* (doorway hangings), *chaklas* (decorative squares), *dhraniyo* (quilt covers), and quilts called *rilli* as part of the dowry. New clothing sets were also made, including the garments to be worn for the marriage ceremony.

Early records show that textiles were closely linked with ritual and purity, and early texts describe unisex upper- and lower-body garments of hand-loomed, wrapped cloth, as well as tailored garments. Woven cotton, wool and silk were commonly mentioned for clothing and trade. Ways of dressing by wrapping cloth is seen in ancient sculptures as well. The *dhoti,* or male lower garment, and loin cloth have been tied in similar fashion for thousands of years. In ancient India, the fibers, quality of a fabric, and the ornamentation materials and methods constituted a well-understood visual language to convey the status of the wearer. Garments woven with gold thread were referred to as *zari,* and if particularly heavily woven, they were called *kinkhab.* Tie dyed-garments were referred to as *bandanna* and diagonally tie-dyed clothing was called *laheria* for the specific designs resulting from the process.

Dress in traditional India varied greatly by climate and region, religious group, and community, and also by fiber, method of construction, and type of imagery or ornamentation. Saris continue to be identified by regions of production and outstanding visual characteristics. An Indian woman can name countless regional weaves and describe the main characteristics of saris by their names, such as Baluchari Buttidar, Varanasi (heavily brocaded weaving, also called *benarasi;* common designs include the mango, moon, vines, and small flowers), Himroo, (brocaded weaves from the central Deccan area), and Patola (double ikat silk woven in Patan, Gujarat; designs consisting of repeated geometric grid-like patters and striped borders), to name a few.

Forms of dress have evolved dramatically in India to reflect the dynamic social shifts that have occurred, as well as external influences, changing styles and influences of globalization through new styles, materials, economic development and attitudinal changes. Where urban women throughout India once wore the sari, by the 1970s many had adopted the Muslim and Punjabi style of dress consisting of *salwar* and *kameez* worn with a *dupatta,* a long head cover/shawl. In the mid-1980s, a movement called the "ethnic style" reflected a new interest in the aesthetics of rural embroideries, by applying commoditized embroidery elements to the bodice of the *kameez.* Combinations of embroideries from diverse groups with Indian-made fabrics like block print, recycled saris, or hand-loomed fabrics were sometimes styled into dress echoing contemporary Western styles. The dress of men in rural areas changed from wrapped lengths of cloth called the *dhoti,* or *lunghi,* to the wearing of trousers, and from loose upper body garments to more traditional western shirts. Many rural women shifted to wearing synthetic-fiber saris, which were cheaper and easier to care for and had a more contemporary association. By the 1990s, many urban women abandoned wearing saris and *salwar-kameez,* adopting instead casual, Western sportswear and wearing more traditional *salwar-kameez* or saris on special occasions.

Sri Lanka

Sri Lanka, formerly known as Ceylon, is located in the Indian Ocean, southeast of the subcontinent of India. The textile arts of Sri Lanka are very similar to those of southern India. Rulers from the south brought artisans and established handicrafts production around 300 B.C.E. Indigenous weavers made primarily cotton goods, while the higher caste weavers of south Indian origin wove cloths with gold thread.

The indigenous population of the greater part of Sri Lanka is Sinhalese. Historically, Sinhalese women bared their breasts and wore white, or red or white with red-striped cotton lower garments that were draped like a dhoti, pleated and tied with a knot at the waist. When working, women bound their breasts with the *thanapatiya,* or breast bandage. Buddhist monks and nuns wear yellow, brownish, and maroon *kasaya,* or robes.

The Tamils of northeastern and eastern Sri Lanka dress in saris and Western dress, as do the people of Tamil Nadu in India. Sinhalese men are frequently barechested and wear checked cotton or synthetic sarongs. On formal occasions, men wear white shirts and European-style jackets. Contemporary women's dress was greatly influenced by the Dutch as well, with the wearing of Javanese batiks and prints wrapped sarong-style and topped with long-sleeved, low-necked blouses.

Maldives

The Maldives is a chain of small islands lying in the Indian Ocean off the southwestern coast of India. The earliest settlers of these lands immigrated from India and Sri Lanka perhaps more than 2,500 years ago. The Maldivians have long been fishers and traders. Maldivian cowry shells (which were widely used as currency in ancient times), coir fiber from coconuts, and fine cottons attracted trade with Arabs who first introduced the Islamic faith in the twelfth century. In the hot, humid climate of the Maldive Islands, people traditionally were bare-breasted but wore lower body wrappers of very fine cotton. Men wore light-colored *lunghis* and women wore the saronglike garment called *feyli,* which was started below the navel and fell to the ankles.

In the seventeenth century, a devoutly Islamic sultan imposed regulations that women cover their breasts and wear *burugaa,* the Dhivehi word for burqa, Hijab, or veil. After several sultans' rule, the women's Islamic dress code disappeared and did not reemerge until the mid-1980s. Since this time, many Maldivian women have felt pressure to don the *burugaa,* and the issue of whether or not to wear Middle Eastern-style Islamic dress is hotly contested. On the main island of Malé, men wear Western-style clothing and many women wear dresses topped by shiny synthetic fabric overcoats and head scarves. For festive occasions, modern Maldivian "national dress" for men consists of a white shirt and light-colored check or plaid *lunghi,* and for women, a solid-colored dress trimmed with white accent bands at the skirt bottom.

Nepal

Nepal is a Himalayan kingdom that unites numerous formerly independent principalities. The population is roughly divided into Tibeto-Burmans in the mountainous north, and Indo-Aryans in the southern lowlands; these populations are further divided into numerous ethnic groups, with many different cultures, languages, and religious beliefs. Nepal's diverse climate and geography also yields diverse fibers ranging from yak hair in the north to sheep's wool, silk, nettle, hemp fiber, and cotton in the tropical areas. While at one time people produced their own fibers and garments, barter trade with India and Tibet led to new sources of textile materials and ready-made clothes. In the early twenty-first century, hand-loomed fabrics have largely been replaced by ready-made garments and mill-woven goods.

Distinctive textiles of Nepal include *dhaka*, an inlaid tapestry-woven cloth used to make caps, or *topis*, and *rari*, thick, rain-proof woolen blankets made from several lengths of hand-loomed fabric. Although most traditional Nepalese textiles have been or are in danger of being displaced by manufactured imported fabrics, the demand for hand-loomed *dhaka* fabric, created on jacquard looms, remains high. There is also increasing interest in the hemp fiber clothing.

Tibet

Tibet, the northernmost of the South Asian countries, occupies the northern slopes of the Himalayas and the high Tibetan plateau. Historically, Tibet has been largely isolated from foreign influences, but traded with China (as well as with India, via trans-Himalayan caravan routes). Consequently, numerous aspects of Chinese culture are visible through the silk weaves, images, symbols, and some basic garment forms throughout much of Tibet's textiles and dress. Generally Tibetan people wear long, side-closing robes called *phyu-pa* for the sleeveless type and *chupa* for the long-sleeved robes, long sleeveless vests, jackets, sashes, aprons, and hats, with long fleece coats and high boots in cold weather. Types and qualities of materials were dictated by (and proclaimed) the wearer's status in Tibet's once highly stratified society. Garments are made of brocaded silk, wool, cotton and fleeced-lined hide.

Pastoralists of both genders wear leather robes, with the fleece side against the skin. In hot weather, men pull the robes back over one or both shoulders and tie the sleeves at the waist. Sewn by men, these hide garments are called *lokbar*. Women's *lokbar* are frequently trimmed with colored cloth bands at hem and cuffs. Buddhist personnel wear garments with distinctive details to indicate hierarchy and roles. The shape of the hat distinguishes monastic orders. The Buddhist monk's common garment is called *kasaya*. The inner *kasaya* is yellow and the outer one is deep red/maroon. Worn in pairs, the large rectangular *kasaya* are topped with a cloak in the winter. High-ranking lamas wear yellow silk, often lotus flower–brocaded robes, embroidered vests, tall brocade boots, and golden hats appropriate to their station when traveling. Religious festivals, performances and ceremonies call for special dress, masks, and headgear.

Among the most distinctive Tibetan fabrics are those used in women's aprons, called *bangdian*, which consist of three or four parts stitched together. Rectangular and trapezoidal, these aprons are usually made of hand-woven cotton with contrasting color stripes.

Due to increased Chinese immigration into Tibet and sweeping social changes, the ancient hierarchical rules that once dictated rigid Tibetan forms of dress have disappeared. Globalization in the form of more readily available Chinese garments and mill-woven and brightly printed cottons has led to changes in dress. Frequently, women in the early 2000s wear printed blouses under their *chuba* or *lokbar*, and urbanites generally prefer more subtle color schemes and streamlined silhouettes. In response to the flood of Chinese goods, many Tibetans are making efforts to not lose their traditional dress and weaving skills.

Bhutan

Bhutan is a Himalayan Buddhist kingdom that historically has been linked through religion to its neighboring countries of India and Tibet and through trade to China. It has been and remains relatively isolated from the rest of the world. The population is diverse, including ethnic groups of Tibetan, Assamese, Burmese, and Nepalese affinities and significant numbers of Tibetan refugees and Nepalese immigrants. The dress of these groups varies, reflecting their distinctive cultural origins.

In Bhutan, textiles are symbolic of wealth. They serve functional and decorative purposes in the home, in religion and ritual, are given as offerings or gifts, and are made for dress. Women weave hand-woven textiles that often have complex striped warps, brocade weaves, and inlaid (or supplementary) weft patterns, while men tailor and embroider. Some of the supplementary weft patterns seen in Bhutanese weavings are similar to motifs also seen in Southeast Asian textiles. The chief fibers are silk, cotton, and wool, with synthetic fibers and colors now readily available. At one time, wealthy families produced their own spun and dyed fibers, but synthetic colors and mass-produced fibers have contributed to more colorful and rapidly changing fashion subtleties.

Although Bhutan is composed of many diverse populations with their own forms of dress, a national dress has been established to visually communicate unity. Bhutanese national dress for women is the *kira*, while the *gho*, or *go*, is the national dress for men. The *kira* is a large, hand-loomed rectangular cloth that is wrapped about the body and held in place with a *kera*, or belt and pins at the shoulders. A *khenja*, blouse, and a slip, are worn under the *kira*, and the dress set is accompanied by a jacket and ceremonial shoulder cloth called *adha*. The blouse cuffs are folded over the jacket cuffs. Patterns and styles abound, each with specific descriptive names. *Gho* (or *go*), the male dress, is similar to the Tibetan *chuba* in that it is a tailored, long-sleeved, asymmetrical closing robe. However, the *gho* has large turned-back contrasting sleeve cuffs and is raised from the ground to just below the knees and held in place with a *kera*. Men wear knee-high socks and a *tego*, or shirt, under the *gho*. The folded-up portion at the waist of the *gho* serves as a multipurpose pouch. On special occasions, over the *gho* men wear a swag-like, ceremonial shoulder cloth called *kumney*. Other garments include three-panel woolen cloaks called *charkab* and *pangkheb*, or carrying cloths. Additionally, many forms of archaic dress survive for use in religious dances and festivals.

See also **Textiles, Southeast Asian Islands; Textiles, Southeast Asian Mainland.**

BIBLIOGRAPHY

Askari, Nasreen, and Rosemary Crill. *Colours of the Indus.* London: V & A Publications, 1997.

Barker, David K. *Designs of Bhutan.* Bangkok: White Lotus, 1985.

Bartholomew, Mark. *Thunder Dragon Textiles from Bhutan.* Kyoto: Shikosha, 1985.

Bhushan, Jamila Brij. *The Costumes and Textiles of India.* Bombay: Taraporevala, 1958.

Dar, S. N. *Costumes of India and Pakistan.* Bombay: Taraporevala, 1969.

Dhamija, Jasleen, and Jyotindra Jain. *Handwoven Fabrics of India.* Ahmedabad, India: Mapin, 1989.

Dunsmore, Susi. *Nepalese Textiles.* London: British Museum Press, 1993.

Goldstein, Melvin, and Cynthia M. Beall. *Nomads of Western Tibet.* Berkeley: University of California Press, 1990.

Goswamy, B. N. *Indian Costumes in the Collection of the Calico Museum of Textiles.* Ahmedabad, India: The Calico Museum, 1993.

Lynton, Linda. *The Sari.* New York: Harry N. Abrams, 1995.

Maloney, Clarence. *People of the Maldive Islands.* Madras: Orient Longman, 1980.

Myers, Diana K. *From the Land of the Thunder Dragon.* Salem, Mass.: Peabody Essex Museum, 1994.

Nabholz-Kartaschoff, Marie-Louise. *Golden Sprays and Scarlet Flowers.* Kyoto: Shikosha, 1986.

Yacopino, Feliccia. *Threadlines Pakistan.* Karachi, Pakistan: Ministry of Industries, 1977.

Internet Resources

Ciolek, Dr. T. Matthew. "Tibetan Studies WWW Virtual Library." Available from <http://www.ciolek.com/wwwvl-TibetanStudies.html>.

Craft Revival Trust: Indian Handicrafts, Textiles, Artisans, Craftspersons. Available from <http://www.craftrevival.org>.

Fernando, Romesh. "A Time of Toplessness." Available from <http://livingheritage.org/toplessness.htm>.

Hettiarachchi, Rohan. "Virtual Library of Sri Lanka." Available from <http://www.lankalibrary.com>.

InfoLanka: Gateway to Sri Lanka. Available from <http://www.infolanka.com>.

"Kingdom of Bhutan Country." Far Flung Places LLC and Bhutan Tourism Corporation Ltd. Available from <http://www.kingdomofbhutan.com/kingdom.html>.

Maldives Culture Magazine. Available from <http://www.maldivesculture.com/main.html>.

"Tibetan Costume and Ornaments." China Tibet Information Center. Available from <http://www.tibet.cn/tibetzt-en/tcao/3robes/3jianjie.htm>.

Tibet Online. Available from <http://www.Tibet.org>.

"Nepal Information: People and Culture." Travel Information Network. Available from <http://www.visitnepal.com/Nepal_information/people.htm>.

Victoria Z. Rivers

TEXTILES, SOUTHEAST ASIAN ISLANDS

The textile traditions of insular Southeast Asia, an area from Sumatra, the westernmost island of Indonesia, to the northernmost region of Luzon in the Philippine Islands, covers an equally wide variety of types, styles, and traditions. These insular people are related by language and customs from former waves of migrations and by methods of textile manufacture as well as design elements and patterns. Trade through the region influenced styles with those in direct contact adapting new techniques of weaving while peoples farthest from these influences retained older traditions the longest. The following essay examines textiles in insular Southeast Asia from the broad perspective, seeking commonalities that link groups and regions together.

Reception of New Forms

Very early on plant products (bark, leaves, and vines) were processed to use as coverings for parts of the body. In the warm tropics minimal covering was necessary; what was worn was mainly to protect certain parts of the body, the genitals and the head. Other pieces of clothing made of plant products were more decorative than functional (capes, caps, shawls, or shoulder cloths) or fabrics are made as furniture (floor mats, wall dividers, hangings, coverings) for ceremonies and festivals. The end use and function dictated the size and shape of the pieces as well as the materials employed. Thus, large woven mats were used as coverings for the ground, as wall partitions, as sleeping surfaces, or to wrap the bodies of the deceased; bark cloth, a more pliable material, served as skirts, breast coverings, headcloths, loincloths, capes, and caps or hoods.

Woven materials existed long before the adoption of loom weaving in the area. An examination of the variety of twining and net making from neighboring peoples in New Guinea reveals older customs that may have existed prior to the adoption of weaving in Southeast Asia. Mats and baskets woven of reeds, vines, and grasses are an ancient craft form in insular Southeast Asia. Functional pieces such as containers and mats were quite light, which made them easily transported. Designs were easily woven into basketry. Complex patterns from mats and baskets of some tribal groups (Iban of Borneo and Kalimantan) were readily transferred to cloth weaving. The technology employed in weaving fine mats from fibers as thin as thread was in use in the Philippines. Such plaiting can withstand folding without breaking the fibers, unlike coarser materials used in mat weaving. Twining using bast fibers may have been an intermediary step between loom weaving and basketry. Here the process of spinning strands to produce a continuous thread was known, but the loom frame necessary for maintaining tension on the threads to produce a tight weave was yet to be discovered or adopted.

Origins: First Cloth

Cloth from the bark of trees was used to make practical items of clothing such as loincloths or G-strings for men and narrow hip wraps for women. Scarves would have protected the head from sun or rain. To produce bark cloth, the inner layer of certain kinds of trees was removed, then beaten to produce a soft, flexible material that could be worn next to the skin without chafing it. Clothing that was cut and sewn together and pieces that were elaborately decorated were probably reserved for individuals of high status and wealth or for communal ceremonies. Old photographs and early museum pieces stand as records of early examples of bark cloth from Southeast Asian peoples.

In Indonesia some of the finest examples of bark cloth clothing are found among the Toraja (from the highlands of central Sulawesi), where women's blouselike tops with sleeves were decorated with painted designs. The Kayan people of Borneo created vestlike jackets with painted motifs. Rectangular cloths in Bali were painted with stories or calendars of the Balinese year. Decorative bark cloth was used to cover the deceased; square cloths to cover the head. In Palu, North Sulawesi women wore full-tiered skirts. Toraja women wore dark-colored cowl-like hoods to signify widowhood. The T'Boli of the Southern Philippines cut and sewed shirts and trousers of bark cloth, shapes that were repeated later on in woven fabric. Examples of bark cloth are preserved in some cultures because they are still a part of certain sacred ceremonies (Bali calendars). However, in most areas bark cloth has been replaced by woven cloth; skills necessary for production have been lost, and this type of fabric has become extinct.

Loom Weaving

While the origin of loom weaving is unknown, it is assumed to have been introduced in ancient times. Its antiquity can be inferred by the fact that some cultures possess legends about weaving. The Bagobo, Mandaya, and Bilaan have origin myths that mention the weaving and dyeing of bast fibers. (In many of these cultures, spirits are invoked to ensure skill and accuracy during the weaving process. Certain weaving implements are considered sacred.) For the Sundanese, in West Java, the introduction of weaving is attributed to the rice goddess, Sang Hyang Dewi Sri. There are Javanese stories of types of *lurik* (a plain-weave cloth) that enable a goddess to fly. Among the Batak, a distinctive cloth used in rituals, the *ulos*, was said to have been the first weaving given to humankind. Possibly early woven pieces were the reserve of the wealthy and worn only for ceremonial purposes or used in rituals. As looms and the technique of weaving

became common, cloth quickly became the fiber of choice as a covering for the body and for use in rituals.

Wearing of Cloth

A common theme about cloth that links insular Southeast Asian cultures (as well as mainland Southeast Asia) is that woven cloth is rarely cut to the shape of the body but rather draped or folded. In the warm, humid climate draping allowed air to circulate around the body. More importantly, the respect for the design on the cloth may have led to this preferred method of dress. A typical rectangular piece about two and a half meters in length with open ends (*kain*) is wrapped around the waist and tucked in or cinched by a belt. Two identical pieces sewn in the middle allow the wearer to start the cloth above the breasts with enough width to cover the ankles (most Indonesian cultures). Among the mountain tribes of Luzon, the width covered the female body from the waist to the knees. The result of this draped fabric was that the intricate designs woven into the cloth were not compromised and were visible over the entire front of the body.

Another style for the lower half of the body is a rectangle sewn at the ends to form a tube (*sarong*), which becomes a skirt, worn by a man or a woman. Other uses for various sizes of cloth are as follows: a long, narrow strip of cloth serving as a loincloth with end flaps in front and back; a breast covering (Bali, Java royalty, Eastern Indonesia); and a decorative sash worn over the shoulders by a man or a woman (Eastern Indonesia, Sumatra, northern Philippines cultures, for example). A rectangle tied at the shoulders serves as a baby carrier or sling to carry goods. A square folded in many different ways becomes a hat or head scarf (for example, the Batak fashioned a two-pronged head covering that imitates the horns of the water buffalo). A plain two-meter length serves as a sheet or covering for the shoulders when it is cool. Clothing had no pockets, so woven knapsacks or bags served as containers. In some cultures, layers of cloth draped on the body, one on top of the other, symbolized wealth and position (Central Javanese royalty, Timor cultures). On the practical side, uncut cloth lengths were more easily folded for storage.

Cloth that was cut generally was not woven with the elaborate designs that uncut cloth possessed. This cloth followed the shape of the weave; thus, a sleeveless shirt was made by cutting an opening in the middle of the cloth for the head; the selvages were sewn together leaving only holes for the arms (Gayo of Sumatra, Toraja of Sulawesi, Bagobo, Bliaan and Mandaya of Mindanao). Jackets with sleeves also followed the form of the weave with the sleeves (end pieces of the fabric cut and sewn onto the selvages at the ends (Kauer of Sumatra, Iban of Borneo, Bagobo, Mandaya and Bilaan of Mindanao, and peoples of Northern Luzon). These were usually richly decorated with anthropomorphic or zoomorphic forms and geometric designs. Patterns were created in embroidery, and with beads, seeds, or shells at the neck and front slit and along the edges of the sleeve; more often the entire front and back was richly embroidered.

Division of Labor

Women were the weavers for home use and in the small cottage industry. Girls from an early age participated in steps of the process, starting with processing the fiber and spinning. Young girls first learned basic weaves; in their late teens they were taught the complex process of weaving patterns using supplementary weft or warp threads and working with fine fibers such as silk. Dyeing was generally a task left for the older women. Some women, usually an older woman, were specialists in certain types of dyes, such as indigo; these women were considered to have special powers over these dyes. In their late teens young women were entrusted with the treasured patterns. In some areas girls wove their own wedding cloths, some of which were given during the nuptial celebration by the bride's family to the groom's family. In Java, *lurik*, a relatively plain cloth worn by participants in ceremonies, is given by the groom's family to the bride's.

Patterns were the reserve of women of the family in some areas (Eastern Sumba), handed down from generation to generation. The patterns were preserved as examples so that each generation could copy them. If there were no more female weavers in the family, the patterns were buried with the last known weaver rather than risk having these revealed to someone outside the line of descent.

Some patterns were the preserve of descent groups, and the patterns worn by the members (women and men) identified them with a particular descent group (Savu Island people). In Rote, patterns identified a person with a particular kingdom. In some areas, such as East Sumba, bright colors and certain patterns were reserved for royalty; the commoners were relegated to one or two colors and little patterning. Generally subdued patterns or plain cloth was worn for daily use; the intricate, highly patterned, and colorful textiles were reserved for ceremonies. In Java, even in the early 2000s, *lurik* was said to ward off bad luck. Participants wore *lurik* in ceremonies after a marriage proposal, for the bathing ritual of a pregnant woman in her seventh month, and for the first haircutting of a child. The fact that this fabric has been used by people of all social classes for specific ritual is a good indicator that *lurik* was well established in ritual life of the Javanese long before batik was introduced. For status among the Javanese some batik patterns were reserved for royalty, other patterns for wedding cloth, others associated with the retainers at court, and still others used by commoners.

Types of Looms

The back-strap loom, a conveniently portable weaving mechanism, was the earliest form of loom. To this day, some cultures in areas away from major population centers continue to produce textiles by this means. The most ancient form of weaving involved a continuous warp with patterns created on the warp threads. Through trade new fibers (silk) and techniques were adopted. Weft patterning replaced warp patterning in coastal areas that were directly in contact with trade from India. The adoption of the frame loom in lowland areas enabled wider and longer fabrics to be woven. Complexity of pattern, however, does not go hand in hand with the larger stationary loom. The simple backstrap loom has produced some of the most complex types of weaves in Southeast Asia—for instance, supplementary weft or warp patterns and long tapestry woven fringes that are part of the men's warrior apron in East Timor.

Types of Fibers

The leaf fibers such as *abaca* (a variety of banana plant), and ramie and hemp, bast or stem fibers, were probably used very early on in twining as well as in the first weaving. The Philippines is noted for its use of these fibers in combination with cotton or silk as warp or weft threads. *Abaca* and hemp are the main fibers for clothing of Mindanao cultural groups. A leaf fiber that developed quite late in the Philippines is *piña* or pineapple fiber. It is unusual in that it is knotted rather than twisted to make thread. Probably more widespread throughout the Philippines and Indonesia, it is now produced solely in Aklan province.

Cotton, however, is the main material used in the production of textiles throughout insular Southeast Asia. It is used in combination with leaf or bast fibers as well as with silk. Cotton plants are easily processed for home consumption, thus making this fiber the egalitarian material. Most village people can produce enough cotton to serve their own cloth-making needs. Thus, the skill in weaving technique rather than the high cost of the materials determines the status of the weaver and wearer. Most mountain groups still produce most cloth from cotton, although now they generally purchase the thread rather than produce it themselves.

Silk, a late arrival, probably from China, became a popular cloth for the wealthy. The ability of silk thread to absorb dyes, producing vibrant colors, was one of its main attractions. As silk production developed in insular Southeast Asia, its use became more widespread. To cut costs and for ease in weaving, silk is mixed with cotton or other plant fibers. The Philippines in particular create a fabric, *sinamay*, that combines *piña* or a hemp warp with a silk or fine *abaca* weft for a type of men's shirt, the *barong Tagolog*.

Piña, like silk, is time consuming to process and was used in special garments for the wealthy. *Piña* fiber clothing imitated the Spanish-style dress. Wealthy Spanish, mestizos, and Philippine women wore blouses (*camisa*) and kerchiefs (*pañuelos*) over Spanish-style collars with long voluminous silk skirts; the men wore long-sleeved shirts over trousers. *Piña* fiber clothing and cloths were heavily embroidered with patterns borrowed from Spanish motifs—flowers, vine, or religious symbols—along with some native plants. Its popularity went beyond the Philippines. Finely embroidered handkerchiefs and collars were imported to Spain and the United States in the late nineteenth century. Many fine examples of pieces of clothing exist in collections but only a few sacred cloths used as vestments or altar cloths exist.

Production Techniques

A division can be made between those cultures that continued to produce warp-patterned weaving (a more ancient tradition) and those that switched to weft-patterned weaving. Silk is generally associated with weft-patterned weaving and is a fabric most often found in lowland cultures (Bali, Java, Sunda, Mindanao) that were associating with traders from India and China. Sumptuous supplementary weft patterns in gold thread were added to the silk cloth and were worn by high-status persons at weddings or other ritual occasions. In the Lampung area metallic thread and mirrors were embroidered on plain cottons to produce a luxurious cloth. Wealth was woven into cloth as it was received in trade. In Java and Bali gold leaf or paint was applied to plain fabric or batik designs to create a sumptuous-looking cloth, which was especially effective in a performance context. Theater was a means of attracting and ensuring the support of the masses, and the glitter of metallic threads and mirrors on cloth was a visible means of marking the status of the elite and creating a sense of pageantry for these emerging polities.

In inland cultures, which were less affected by trade, cloth was more closely linked to cohesion of the group. Designs and colors were the reserve of the high-status person in the village, but to some extent the distinctions between commoner and high status was less than it was in the large-scale societies of Java, Bali, and lowland Philippines. Status was linked to skills, such as prowess for the warrior class. Skills in head-hunting were acknowledged by special sashes, designs in weaves, or other articles of clothing worn by the successful hunter (Iban, Mindanao cultural groups, Nusatenggara region). Skull trees figure on Sumba cloths that once were associated with this practice. In Mindanao cloth that was predominantly red in color was symbolic of the success of a headhunter, and the Iban, too, used red for cloth in rituals for head-hunting.

Conclusion

The textile traditions of insular Southeast Asia identify a cultural group by their design, colors, and style. Their beauty has attracted much devotion of research at a time when their function in these cultures is waning. Change is not uniform. Some cultures quickly adopt change (the Achenese now wear a Persian-style tunic and favor gold couched embroidery in plant patterns or Arabic writing for their clothing and religious articles). As in the past when woven cotton cloth replaced bark cloth, so, too, new materials and styles are replacing the traditional pieces that are so admired. Status that was marked by the use of textiles has been replaced by other objects that are highly valued—a car, a TV, radio, name-brand jeans, and so forth. Instead of a pile of textiles as a gift of exchange in marriage, a Western bed and microwave might be given. One can lament the loss of the former rich tradition of textile weaving, yet its value was woven into its role in the society. As symbols of status and wealth change, its role is reduced. However, for critical communal ceremonies, change occurs more slowly. The ritual cloths of old will emerge from storage chests to ensure that the spirits are remembered and appeased to guarantee good health, a long life, and happiness in birth or marriage, or a peaceful existence in death.

See also **Asia, Southeastern Islands and the Pacific: History of Dress.**

BIBLIOGRAPHY

Fraser-Lu, Sylvia. *Handwoven Textiles of South-East Asia.* Singapore: Oxford University Press, 1988.

Gittinger, Mattiebelle. *Splendid Symbols: Textiles and Tradition in Indonesia.* Washington, D.C.: The Textile Museum, 1979.

Haddon, A. C., and L. E. Start. *Iban or Sea Dayak Fabrics and their Patterns.* Cambridge, U.K.: Cambridge University Press, 1936.

Hamilton, Roy W., ed. *From the Rainbow's Varied Hue: Textiles of the Southern Philippines.* Los Angeles: UCLA Fowler Museum of Cultural History, 1998.

Maxwell, Robyn. *Textiles of Southeast Asia: Tradition, Trade, and Transformation.* Rev. Ed. Hong Kong: Periplus Editions Ltd., 2003.

Roces, Marian Pastor. *Sinaunang Habi: Philippine Ancestral Weave.* Manila, the Philippines: The Nikki Coseteng Filipiniana Series, 1991.

Ann Wright-Parsons

TEXTILES, SOUTHEAST ASIAN MAINLAND

The textiles of mainland Southeast Asia share much of their production technology, design repertoires, and consumption patterns with other regions of Asia to the north (China) and west (South Asia, India), as well as insular Southeast Asia. The student of mainland Southeast Asian textiles must be as concerned with Indian, Bhutanese, and Northeast Indian textiles, and those of Southwestern and southern China, including Hainan Island and aboriginal Taiwan, as with the more traditional areas of the mainland, included in the current political entities of Vietnam, Laos, Cambodia, Thailand, Burma (Myanmar), and peninsular Malaysia. Exploration of continuities and discontinuities between "traditional" Southeast Asia and the peoples, cultures, and textiles of these "peripheral" regions pays great dividends. The migrations of many Southeast Asian cultures began in southern China, and mainland Southeast Asia's major religion, Theravada Buddhism, and its textiles came from

South Asia; also, South Asia and China provided royal textiles which became models emulated even in rural Southeast Asia.

The region's "traditional" textiles include tube skirts, shawls, blankets, and other items that have as their probable model weaving on back-tensioned looms with circular warps. These can be elaborated in a variety of ways, using resist tie-dyed warp or weft elements, intricate supplementary weft or warp floats, tapestry weaves, appliqués, embroideries, and other methods. Additionally, Southeast Asian textiles include Buddhist monk's robes, developed by the Buddha to contrast with the uncut textile tradition of South Asia, as well as tailored coats, pants, and robes derived from Chinese forms.

Early Southeast Asian Textiles

While it is often asserted that the preservation and recovery of Southeast Asian textiles is hindered by the region's tropical and semi-tropical climate, recent creative archaeological research has filled in some gaps. Fragments of textiles adhering to bone caused by bronze deposition have been discovered in Ban Chiang (Northeast Thai) sites. Innovative archaeological recovery techniques from burials have shown that asbestos was used to make cloth. Finally, Green's (2000) work on Khmer bas-reliefs used to decorate Angkorean temples shows that these consisted of designs found on Indian block-printed and ikat-motifed cloth also found in Fustat, Egypt. This innovative work shows that earlier eras of textile production and consumption may not be lost.

Historical Southeast Asian Textiles

With European contact one begins to gain a more holistic sense of the complex world of mainland Southeast Asian textiles. Unfortunately, most early information is concerned with textile display and consumption within the worlds of Southeast Asian monarchies. Louis XIV's French ambassadors' discussions of their 1685 reception at Ayutthaya (then capital of Siam) show that the extensive use of textiles reflected their reception's significance, as well as designated the ranks of the various people involved in these ceremonies. Many of the textiles sent in return by King Narai were noted as coming from Persia, Hindustan, Japan, and China. This evidenced the cosmopolitan connections of Southeast Asian kingship. Non-Southeast Asian pieces using block-prints and metallic interweave, quite beautiful and sumptuous, served as markers of god-king status and as gifts to subjects to secure their status, roles, and allegiances to the monarchy. The goal of European adventurers and trading companies was to imitate and insert themselves into this lucrative, royally controlled South Asian trade as part of their monopolistic takeover of world trading patterns.

However, because of the rigors of Southeast Asian environments, cloth's intensive uses, and the difficulties of production before industrial manufacture, little is known of nonelite textiles prior to the mid-1800s. It is

assumed that local production of silk and cotton yarn and trade in this yarn and textiles was a part of local life. Early European explorers venturing into mainland, especially upland, northern Southeast Asia were impressed with the amount of trade with southwestern China in cotton and silk yarn: cotton was traded north, silk came south. Additionally, explorers visiting the royal families of the northern principalities were impressed by the use of Chinese textiles in the repertory, partially to replace textiles traded or granted by kings to the south.

Members of the Mekong expedition of 1866–1868 were awed by the willingness of local women to trade homemade textiles for European goods. Finally, in addition to having use as clothing, textiles acted as currency. Careful studies of tax receipts flowing into Bangkok from upcountry dependencies during the early reigns of the Chakri dynasty (1782–c. 1830) show that white cotton cloth was a major tribute item. In part, this cloth was requisitioned for royal funerals; in many Southeast Asian cultures, white cloth is required for wrapping the deceased. For royal funerals, even more was needed to dignify the cremation bier and for participant dress (Lefferts, 1994). Some upland Lao cultures use magnificent lengths of tie-dyed weft silk cloth to adorn coffins.

Rural production of Southeast Asian textiles takes place at the household level. It is women's work; women are responsible for growing cotton, raising mulberry trees and silkworms, controlling the production technology, weaving, and, finally, distributing the cloth. However, as the evidence of cloth for tribute indicates, this does not mean that women could engage in this production without elite interference. Bowie has documented that, under rigorous royal control, severe constraints could be placed on local production. In the late nineteenth and early twentieth centuries, it was quite common for northern Thai villagers to wear rags and patched clothing. However, in many other locations, elite control of textile production was probably less severe, laying the foundation for the fluorescence of wondrously woven textiles that came to light in the late twentieth century.

Twentieth-Century Textiles

Industrially produced textiles, initially from the looms of England and France, but, later production, from pre–World War II Shanghai, South Asian, and American factories, coupled with the intrusion of European tailored clothes, wrought major changes in rural Southeast Asian textile production and urban and rural consumption.

Domestic production of white cloth declined dramatically. Rather than remaining a major consumer of a woman's production, white cloth became a residual meant for donation and personal use. In addition to funerals, a major use was in monk's robes. Cheap, factory-made white cloth, smooth (in contrast with rough home-spun and home-woven pieces), cut, sewn, and dyed the appropriate saffron color, seems to have quickly replaced much of the demand for white cloth produced by rural women. At the same time, white cloth tribute ceased, replaced by government levies for cash to run expanding bureaucracies. Finally, the first chemical indigo dyes produced in Euro-American factories, rapidly followed by the development of other artificial colors, replaced locally produced natural dyes. Brilliant chemical dyes proved a boon to Southeast Asian weavers and consumers who wanted sharp colors that contrasted with the dull dyes they had endured for generations.

While there is no secure data, it seems that the period leading up to and through World War II and the following one to two decades resulted in the production of an extraordinary range of indigenous village textiles of complicated designs and patterns, a creative explosion by many accomplished women. These textiles, many used but even more saved for future use, flooded the textile markets of Southeast Asia following the end of the cold war and the opening of transportation and consumption across the whole broad sweep of northern mainland Southeast Asia and southern China. It is fair to say that these textiles represented a culmination of Southeast Asian women's artistic and technological prowess. This was especially the case in the cloth women wove for their own garments, both skirts and sashes. Beautiful tie-dyed patterns dominated in some areas, while in others complicated brocades produced by a loom with a multistrand vertical pattern heddle became common. Finally, in some areas, complicated tapestry weaves and double-warp cloth with supplementary weft became standard.

Euro-American and Japanese connoisseurs became aware of Southeast Asian textiles through the dispersal of Southeast Asian refugees fleeing the American-Indochinese War. These groups included highlanders, some of whom, such as the Hmong (Miao, Meo), were relatively recent migrants into Southeast Asia from China; others, such as the Thai Dam and Thai Khaaw (Black and White Thai) and ethnic Lao of Laos, had been wet-rice cultivators resident in their areas for several generations. All were displaced by war and arrived in refugee camps and countries of final settlement with their traditions, homemade textiles, and demands to reinstitute their culture. The evolution of indigenously produced textiles into articles of consumption by neighbors becoming aware of these refugees, such as the "story quilts" of the Hmong and other changes to their design repertory, has been documented by Cohen. Other weaving traditions, such as that of Lao women in the U.S. and France, have also survived. Several mainland Southeast Asian textile producers have been awarded personal recognition, as, for instance, through the U.S. National Endowment for the Arts National Heritage Fellowship program.

Mainland Southeast Asian Textiles Production

Detailed studies of the production technologies of mainland Southeast Asian textiles are now bearing fruit. The relation between the woman producer and her material and equipment is a more holistic one than for the typical Euro-American loom. Usually, the loom itself and much of its equipment is made by a man and gifted to the woman as a mark of respect or an inducement to undertake production, considering that textiles are one of the important ways by which a household may gain supplementary income and prestige.

Among some populations, cloth production is magically potent; men are forbidden from touching the loom. A weaver may be viewed as producing a changeable substance, resulting in something of a different quality from that with which she began. Thus, textile production may metaphorically represent a girl's maturation to womanly status, with the ability to bring new humans into the world.

In mainland as well as insular Southeast Asia, the means of textile production as well as knowledge of its technology is controlled by women. Women in many Southeast Asian cultures derive symbolic and cultural capital from their control of weaving and the disposition of production.

Women's textile production may make substantial contributions to household income. While textile production may vary through the year depending on the requirements and opportunities of other employment, textile production used to be, and, for many women remains, an important skill. At minimum, women can produce cloth for which the household would have to spend precious cash. Most weaving takes place using long warps containing several pieces to be cut off as needed. The weaver can give pieces to various individuals, keep others for future giving, or sell some or all of them as opportunities appear. The opportunity cost of time, coupled with the defrayed expenditures for purchasing textiles and the possibility of income production, thus may make a woman's weaving an essential part of household survival.

Modern Southeast Asian Textiles

The global reach of market forces into upland mainland Southeast Asia in the early 1990s resulted in the export of massive numbers of technologically important and aesthetically beautiful indigenous textiles. Most of these left the region without proper provenance or notes as to the uses to which they could be put. Moreover, this export robbed future weavers of pattern cloths of models for future designs and techniques.

However, even as commercialization and globalization have conspired to obliterate the indigenous, home-based production of mainland Southeast Asian textiles, countervailing forces have arisen to preserve and record it. Research by Western weavers and by scholars in mainland Southeast Asian textiles is relatively recent, beginning in earnest in the late 1980s. This effort has resulted in detailed studies of textile contexts, meanings, and uses. Importantly, accomplished foreign weavers have become interested in detailed studies of the intricacies of mainland Southeast Asian production technology. Because textile production is a process, these studies must include numerous still photographs or, even better, detailed, focused video. Fortunately, this work is underway and important studies are now appearing.

Finally, efforts are underway to conserve some of these traditions. Her Majesty, Queen Sirikit of Thailand, through her royally sponsored Support Foundation (the French acronym for Foundation for the Promotion of Supplementary Occupations and Related Techniques), has, for many years, supported local craftspeople who are expert in modes of production and design. For her pioneering and continuing efforts, Queen Sirikit won an ATA (Aid to Artisans) 2004 Award for Preservation of Craft. In Laos, the Lao Women's Union and private entrepreneur Carol Cassidy are engaged in preserving and expanding the repertoire of Lao weaving and bringing it international recognition. Similarly, in the early 1990s in devastated Cambodia, UNESCO began a massive effort not only to reestablish textile production, but also to reinstitute the cultivation of mulberry trees and silk yarn production to support it. In the early 2000s, some of the glory of Khmer silk weaving is returning. All of these efforts depend on working with local people, usually women, who remember what they accomplished so easily many years earlier, letting them know that their knowledge is of value and encouraging them to share it with others. Most of all, these and other efforts return income to villagers who have begun to see themselves as only poor and without meaningful resources.

See also **Textiles, South Asian; Textiles, Southeast Asian Islands.**

BIBLIOGRAPHY

Bowie, Katherine A. "Labor Organization and Textile Trade in Northern Thailand in the Nineteenth Century." In *Textiles in Trade, Proceedings of The Textile Society of America Biennial Symposium.* Washington, D.C., 14–16 September 1990, pp. 204–215. Analysis of royal control of pre-modern textile production.

Cohen, Eric. *The Commercialized Crafts of Thailand: Hill Tribes and Lowland Villages, Collected Articles.* Honolulu: University of Hawaii Press, 2000. Extensive selection of articles on Hmong textile adaptations to globalization and commercialization.

Conway, Susan. *Silken Threads and Lacquer Thrones: Lanna Court Textiles.* Bangkok: River Press, 2002. Comprehensive discussion of northern Thai royal textile traditions.

Gittinger, Mattiebelle, and Leedom Lefferts. *Textiles and the Tai Experience in Southeast Asia.* Washington, D.C.: The Textile Museum, 1992. Gittinger's chapter 1, "An Examination of Tai Textile Forms," provides a statement concerning the evolution of many mainstream Southeast Asian textiles; her chapter 4, "Textiles in the Service of Kings," provides an excellent summary of royal relations with external textile producers. Lefferts's chapter 2, "Contexts and Meanings in Tai Textiles," focuses on the symbolic significance of women's control of textile production and gifting.

Green, Gill. "Angkor: Textiles at the Khmer Court, Origins and Innovations." *Arts of Asia* 30, no. 4 (2000): 82–92.

Howard, Michael C., and Kim Be Howard. *Textiles of the Daic Peoples of Vietnam; Textiles of the Central Highlands of Vietnam*; and *Textiles of the Highland Peoples of Northern Vietnam: Mon-Khmer, Hmong-Mien, and Tibeto Burman.* Bangkok: White Lotus. Numbers 2, 3, and 4 in the series *Studies in the Material Cultures of Southeast Asia.* Comprehensive surveys of little-understood areas.

Lefferts, Leedom. "The Ritual Importance of the Mundane: White Cloth among the Tai of Southeast Asia." *Expedition* 38, no. 1 (1996): 37–50.

McClintock, Deborah. *The Ladies of Laos.* Greenville, Del.: Privately issued. CD-ROM; excellent investigation with slides and video of total textile production process.

Leedom Lefferts

TEXTILES AND INTERNATIONAL TRADE

Wars have been fought, ships sunk, and broader trade wars initiated over trade in textiles. No other industry comes close to matching the significant role the textile sector has held in the history of trade. Inventories of early sailing ships listed textiles as a vital part of the cargo. Critical to the economic development of country after country, the textile industry has provided both products and jobs needed by humans around the world. In the early 2000s, almost every country in the world produces textile goods, resulting in highly competitive global market conditions.

Historical Perspective

In the late 1600s, British capitalists, inspired by fine cotton fabrics from India, sought ways to produce domestic goods beyond the existing household industry. Thus, England banned Indian fabrics and developed mechanized means of weaving and spinning, launching the Industrial Revolution. Having led the way in changing how goods could be produced, the textile industry provided the groundwork for the transformation of the Western world into a true international economy.

Developments in the United States

British authorities tried to block the development of a textile industry in the colonies by refusing to share new technology and prohibiting trade with other nations. However, soon after America achieved independence, Eli Whitney's cotton gin and Samuel Slater's inventions transformed the budding industry. In years that followed, the sector led the way in many major industrial and social developments, including the emergence of factories, mill towns, employment of women outside the home, and early industrial reform. Later, it became a leader in international trade and trade problems.

Ironically, as soon as the industry began to develop in the states, they applied restrictive measures on imports, similar to the British restrictions they despised. By the late 1700s, Congress imposed tariffs and embargoes on foreign cotton to protect American cotton production. These early barriers on textile imports were a hint of later trade policies for the sector.

Global Textile Industry

Following industrialization of the textile sector in Europe and the United States, the industry also began to spread to Asia and other parts of the less-developed world. In country after country, the textile and apparel industries became the first sector for nations as each moved beyond an agrarian society. The nineteenth century was a period of tremendous growth for the U.S. cotton industry, emerging as the country's leading manufacturing industry prior to the Civil War. New England textile mills developed and prospered. Trade in general among nations expanded greatly, and a sense of international economic interdependence developed. Expansion in the twentieth century bridged the gaps between continents, creating the global textile and apparel markets that exist in the twenty-first century.

The Complexities of Textile Trade

In virtually every developing nation, the textile/apparel industry has been the springboard for economic development, relying on textile and apparel exports to gain much-needed income. Consequently, intense competition grew, as most countries produced textile and apparel goods for the same markets in more affluent countries. In both the United States and Western Europe, the combined textile/apparel/fiber industries were the top manufacturing employers and vital contributors to the economy in every case. Worried about loss of home markets to imports, domestic producers pressured their governments to enact measures to restrict textile and apparel imports. Political leaders could hardly afford to ignore this pressure because these large industries represented large, powerful voting blocs. As a result, complex trade policies emerged at both the international and national levels to manage textile trade.

A trade-policy dilemma. Applying restrictions on textile imports from other countries was a sensitive matter for the U.S. government, because this country had been one of the leaders in bringing countries together in 1947 to form the General Agreement on Tariffs and Trade (GATT). Of significance, the purpose of GATT was *to reduce and eliminate* restrictive barriers on trade from other countries. Restrictions on textile imports would seriously violate this principle.

With pressure from the United States and Europe, a multilateral system emerged that provided the protection the industry sought. Trade policies for textiles and apparel from the early 1960s on were no longer subject

Chinese worker operating a rotor spinning machine. The textile sector in Asia began to develop shortly after textile industrialization in Europe and the United States. © CLARO CORTES IV/REUTERS/CORBIS. REPRODUCED BY PERMISSION.

to the general rules of GATT that governed trade for all other sectors. Instead, the textile/apparel trade had its own set of rules that violated many of the basic aims of GATT by allowing restrictions on textile and apparel imports and by permitting discrimination among trading partners.

In the 1960s, policies limited cotton imports. As manufactured fibers emerged, new rules were needed to cover those. Under the resulting 1974 Multifiber Arrangement (MFA), trading partners negotiated agreements that set quota limits on the volume of textile and apparel products allowed into the more-developed countries. Always a controversial measure, less-developed nations felt the MFA quota system stifled exports in one of their leading sectors. In contrast, domestic producers in more-developed countries considered the MFA inadequate in stemming the tide of imports, while retailers and importers in those nations felt it limited their global buying. Additionally, scholars and economists considered the MFA an outrageous violation of GATT principles.

A New Era

Developing nations had long protested the barriers on their textile and apparel goods and succeeded in bringing an end to the quota system. As part of the GATT-sponsored Uruguay Round of trade talks, GATT became the World Trade Organization (WTO), and the MFA was replaced by the Agreement on Textiles and Clothing (ATC). The ATC was basically a ten-year phase-out plan that eliminated the quota system in three stages. At the end of the ten years, quotas were removed on textile and apparel products, and tariffs were reduced. On 1 January 2005, all products in this sector came under the general WTO rules for all trade and no longer received the special protection in place for forty years.

A new global trade era emerged for the sector, and major shifts in production sites are expected to occur. Developing countries, whose economic future is tied to this sector, will undoubtedly expand exports; however, some will suffer from competition from major players such as China—no longer having the guaranteed market access that quotas provided. More developed countries are likely to see a continuing shift of textile and apparel production going to low-wage countries. Retailers have free rein to shop global markets. And, finally, consumers reap benefits from the intense global competition that provides variety and competitive prices for textile and apparel goods.

See also **Garments, International Trade in.**

BIBLIOGRAPHY

Aggarwal, Vinod. *Liberal Protectionism: The International Politics of Organized Textile Trade.* Berkeley: University of California Press, 1985.

Cline, William. *The Future of World Trade in Textiles and Apparel.* Washington: Institute for International Economics, 1987.

Dickerson, Kitty. *Textiles and Apparel in the Global Economy,* 3rd ed. Upper Saddle River, N.J.: Prentice Hall, 1999.

Ellsworth, P. T., and J. Clark Leith. *The International Economy,* 6th ed. New York: Macmillan, 1984.

Kitty G. Dickerson

TEXTILE WORKERS Prior to the mid-eighteenth century, textile products were a main household manufacture, both for domestic use and on a commercial basis. Spun yarn, woven cloth, knitted stockings, and lace were the main products (Abbott 1910). Cotton, wool, flax, and hemp were the raw materials used by the women and girls in the household to make products to meet family needs; commercial weaving was often done at home by men.

Transition from the household to the shop system was slow, occurring at different times in different countries and regions. Tryon (1917) describes an "itinerant-supplementary stage" that preceded the shop system. During this stage, an itinerant worker (for example, a

weaver), could be hired to help complete the weaving process in the home. Supplementary businesses provided operations that were too difficult to do in the home. These included operations executed on the raw materials or semifinished products of the household, such as fulling, carding, dyeing, and bleaching.

During the latter part of the eighteenth century, spinning and weaving began to be mechanized, beginning in England, and "manufactories" began to take the place of household production. Mechanical spinning was much more efficient than spinning with a spinning wheel, and so factory production quickly predominated. Weaving still was often done at home, with materials being furnished by a factor or agent and the finished products returned to the manufactory. Workers were paid for each piece they had completed.

Employment and Wage Work

In the United States, mechanized spinning quickly caught on in New England, which had excellent sources of waterpower for the purpose. Power looms for weaving were introduced in 1814 in Waltham, Massachusetts. This was the first factory in America to integrate spinning and weaving under one roof. The displacement of household manufacture brought women and children into the factory to execute tasks they had always done at home, but with different equipment and on a much larger scale.

By 1850, there were 59,136 female "hands" employed in cotton manufactures and 33,150 males throughout the country, with the largest number of females employed in Massachusetts (19,437). Employment in woolen manufacturing was dominated by male "hands," with 22,678 men to 16,574 females. Average wages in both sectors were higher for men than for women in all states reporting (DeBow, 1854). According to Hooks, "by 1870, 104,080 women textile operatives and laborers were recorded in the census" (p. 103). During the 1900 census year, there were 298,867 men and 292,286 women, 16 years and over, employed in the different textile industries and more than 70,000 children under 16 years, with the largest number in cotton and silk manufactures (Twelfth Census, p. 12).

Effect of Relocation on Workers

The textile industry began relocation from the North to the South after the Civil War. The move was to take advantage of a large pool of low-cost and unorganized labor. The ethnic composition of the labor force in the North was primarily native- or foreign-born whites, unskilled and recruited from the farm population. In the South, operatives were recruited mainly from among native-born whites (Bureau of the Census, 1907). In both the North and the South, the employment of blacks in the textile industry was negligible until the 1960s and the passage of the Civil Rights Act of 1964 (Minchin, 1999; Rowan, 1970).

By 1950, the total number of males employed in the textile industry (708,000) outnumbered the females (523,000). Data for 1983 shows that 49.3 percent of 742,000 workers were women, 21.3 percent were black, and 4.4 percent of Hispanic origin. By 1987, 48.1 percent of 713,000 workers were female, with 24.8 percent black and 6.6 percent of Hispanic origin (United States Department of Labor, 1988). By 2002, of the 429,000 textile workers, there were 326,000 males (76%), 88,000 blacks (20.5%), and 62,000 Hispanics (14%).

Globalization and Free Trade Practices

While the number of textile employees declined between 1950 and 2002, the percentage of women and blacks also declined, while the percentage of Hispanics increased. The overall decrease in the number of workers has been accompanied by a decline in the American production of textiles in the post–World War II period, due to foreign competition and an influx of imports, particularly from Asian countries. Textile production and employment in the countries of Western Europe has seen similar declines.

Textile production and distribution is no longer a process of a single nation, but of a world economy. Increased foreign competition and trade exist among many textile-producing nations. To increase production and to remain competitive, textile manufacturers have invested in new machinery and techniques of production that increase the productivity of labor. This means that fewer workers are needed to "tend" to a larger number of machines. Corporations have merged, joint ventures with foreign companies have occurred, new plants have been constructed in foreign countries, and American-owned companies have increasingly shifted operations to offshore manufacturing. All of this means fewer jobs domestically, but increased employment abroad. This process is a continuation of the shift of textile jobs from high-wage to low-wage environments that was seen already in the movement of textile production from New England to the American South in the middle decades of the twentieth century.

Textile production has shifted to a number of developing countries, including China, India, Pakistan, Bulgaria, and Turkey. Because women are lower cost employees worldwide than men, textile manufacturers in these countries typically employ more than 50 percent females in textile production. Some Asian countries, including Japan and Korea, that once offered low-wage employment in the textile industry, have also seen a flight of textile production to countries with even lower wages overseas. In 2004 leading low-wage countries include Sri Lanka, Indonesia, and Bangladesh (Industrial United Nations Development Organization, 2003).

Although textile manufacturers argue that free-trade practices (such as the abandonment of trade quotas to restrain imports into the United States from China and the North American Free Trade Agreement) have been the cause of mill bankruptcies and closings and job losses in the United States (Nesbitt, 2003), many economists point out that tariffs, quotas, and other protectionist measures are generally ineffective in maintaining employment in declining industries, and result in higher prices for consumers. Only factories offering some specific comparative advantage (for example, techno-textile production, on-demand specialty textile production, extremely high labor productivity) are likely to survive in high-wage environments in the era of globalization. The portability of the textile industry (whole factories can be dismantled in one country and reassembled in another, lower-wage one) and the relatively unskilled nature of textile work means that production of basic textiles will continue to flow to low-wage environments. An important contemporary challenge is to protect textile workers (largely female, poor, young, and vulnerable) from exploitation, industrial hazards, and other negative effects of employment in an industry that has seldom seen worker protection as a high priority.

See also **Cotton; Dyeing; Fulling; Hemp; Lace; Wool; Yarns.**

BIBLIOGRAPHY

Abbott, Edith. *Women in Industry: A Study in American Economic History.* New York and London: D. Appleton, 1910. Reprint, New York: Arno, 1967.

Bureau of the Census, Department of Commerce and Labor. *Statistics of Women at Work.* Washington, D.C.: Government Printing Office, 1907.

DeBow, J. D. B. *Statistical View of the United States: A Compendium of the Seventh Census,* Volume 15: 1854. Reprint. New York: Norman Ross, 1970.

Dickerson, Kitty G. *Textiles and Apparel in the Global Economy,* 3rd ed. Upper Saddle River, N.J.: Prentice-Hall, 1999.

Dublin, Thomas. *Women at Work: The Transformation of Work and Community in Lowell, Massachusetts, 1826–1860.* New York: Columbia University Press.

Hooks, Janet M. *Women's Occupations through Seven Decades.* United States Department of Labor, Women's Bureau Bulletin no. 218. Washington, D.C.: Government Printing Office, 1947.

Janofsky, Michael. "In South Carolina, Job Losses May Erode Support for Bush." *New York Times,* 18 August 2003: A1, A12.

Minchin, Timothy J. "Federal Policy and the Racial Integration of Southern Industry, 1961–1980." *Journal of Policy History* 11, no. 2 (1999).

Nesbitt, Jim. "Trade Policy Blamed for Textile Fall." *Augusta Chronicle* (7 August 2003): B2.

Rowan, Richard L. *The Negro in the Textile Industry.* Wharton School of Finance and Commerce, Report No. 20. Philadelphia: University of Pennsylvania Press, 1970.

Sumner, Helen. *History of Women in Industry in the United States.* Report on Condition of Women and Child Wage-Earners in the United States, Volume 9. Washington, D.C.: Government Printing Office, 1910. Reprint, New York: Arno Press, 1974.

Truchil, Barry E. *Capital-Labor Relations in the United States Textile Industry.* New York: Praeger, 1988.

Tryon, Rolla. *Household Manufactures in the United States, 1640–1860: A Study in Industrial History.* Chicago: University of Chicago Press, 1917.

Twelfth Census of the United States. *1900 Manufactures, Part III, Selected Reports on Selected Industries.* Washington, D.C.: United States Census Office, 1902.

Uchitelle, Louis. "Blacks Lose Jobs Faster as Middle-Class Work Drops." *New York Times* (12 July 2003): B1, B4.

United Nations Industrial Development Organization. *International Yearbook of Industrial Statistics, 2003.* Vienna: UNIDO, 2003.

Internet Resource

Bureau of Labor Statistics, Current Population Survey. 2003. Unpublished detailed occupation and industry tables. Available from <http://www.dol.gov>.

Gloria M. Williams

THEATRICAL COSTUME Western theater tradition has its foundations in the Greek celebrations performed in the sixth century B.C.E., honoring Dionysus, the god of wine and revelry. The revels (dances, songs, and choral responses) evolved into spoken drama in 535 B.C.E., when the playwright Thespis introduced an actor to respond to the chorus leader. The result was dialogue.

Another playwright, Aeschylus (525–456 B.C.E.), is credited with establishing what became the traditional costume for Greek tragedy. It consisted of a long, sleeved, patterned tunic, a stylized mask for instant character recognition, and a pair of high-soled shoes called corthunae. All of these garments were exclusively for theatrical use. One cannot act the hero in everyday wear.

Actors in Greek comedies also wore masks to indicate which characters they portrayed. Additionally, they would often add exaggerated body parts, padded bottoms or stomachs, and oversize phalluses to heighten the comic effect. Short tunics, much like those worn by ordinary citizens, were thought appropriate to comedy.

Although the Romans added their own twists, the costume conventions established by the Greeks essentially remained the same until the fall of the Roman Empire, when Western theater virtually disappeared for eight hundred years.

The Middle Ages and the Renaissance

When theater re-emerged, it did so, ironically, in the context of the church. The Christian church was the sworn enemy of the drama (perceiving it to be both immodest and akin to devil-worshiping). But, since services were performed in Latin, which fewer and fewer parishioners could understand, priests had to devise a way to dramatize the liturgy.

From the fifth century C.E. forward, mystery plays, dramatizing events in the scriptures, and miracle plays, which depicted the lives of the saints, were increasingly performed both inside the church and on church grounds. As they became more elaborate, they moved into the market square.

Costumes worn in the early religious dramas were ecclesiastical garments. As the scripts became more secular, often involving townspeople in addition to the clergy, lay performers assumed responsibility for any costume pieces not owned by the church. Contemporary religious art provided inspiration for such characters as Daniel, Herod, the Virgin Mary, and assorted devils.

It was during the Renaissance that production elements, both scenery and costume, came to be even more important than the text. Throughout Europe, the nobility staged lavish court masques and pageants to entertain their guests. Costumes depicted gods, animals, and mythological creatures, as well as such emotions as hope and joy. Designers for these festivities included Leonardo da Vinci and Inigo Jones.

The Commedia Dell'arte

Commedia dell'arte, a form of popular street comedy, emerged in Italy during the sixteenth century. Groups of itinerant actors presented largely improvised plays throughout Italy and Europe.

Like the Greek comedies (to which commedia is thought to be linked), commedia actors portrayed stock characters identifiable by their masks and by their traditional costumes. Pantaloon, the archetypal doddering old man, was often dressed in the wide trousers that now bear his name. The wily servant Brighella had a coat of horizontal green stripes, the forerunner of nineteenth-century British livery. Other comic characters include Arlecchino, or Harlequin, Il Dottore, a pedantic academic always dressed in black, and Il Capitano, a cowardly Spaniard. The serious characters in commedia, two pair of lovers and a servant girl, wore contemporary clothing.

The works of William Shakespeare, Jean-Baptiste Moliere, and Jean-Antoine Watteau all show evidence of the influence of this important popular art form.

The Sixteenth through the Eighteenth Century

Costumes for Shakespeare's plays were a mixture of various periods that audiences accepted as the standard convention. Most parts were performed in contemporary dress either owned by the actor (all were men) or provided by the theater's patron. On occasion, a helmet or breastplate might indicate a soldier. Fairies and nymphs might wear classical draperies.

The same principle applies to costume in the seventeenth and eighteen centuries. Most actors and especially actresses dressed as fashionably as possible. A turban indicated an Eastern character. A plumed helmet signified a soldier. Performers provided their own wardrobe with the exception of specialty items provided by the theater.

The Nineteenth and Early Twentieth Centuries

The period between the 1770s and the 1870s saw a drive toward historical accuracy in costume design. As travel became relatively easier, reports, both written and visual, increased people's knowledge of other cultures. International exhibitions such as the Crystal Palace Exhibition in London in 1851 brought the material culture of exotic places to the public. They wanted what they saw and read about to be reflected on the stage.

In the German principality of Saxe-Meiningen, Duke George II established his own theatrical troupe called the Meiningers. The Duke used every available resource to create authentic costumes for his actors.

The Meiningers toured the continent widely, and the style of their productions greatly influenced such bastions of nineteenth century realism as the Théâtre Libre in Paris, and the Moscow Art Theater in Russia. In the United States, the productions of impresario David Belasco reflected his admiration for this new, realistic style.

An inevitable backlash followed. In Russia, to cite just one example, constructivist artists designed highly conceptual costumes whose only relationship to clothing was that they were worn by human beings.

Eventually both styles were recognized as valid, leading to the mixture of historically accurate or concept driven productions that continues in the twenty-first century.

Current Practice

Theatrical costumes are designed to support the script. If realism or historicism is central to the text, the costumes will accurately reflect the clothing appropriate to the period or to the environment. Examples include Henrik Ibsen's *The Master Builder*, which requires clothing of the early 1890s, or David Storey's *The Changing Room*, which calls for uniforms and street wear appropriate for a group of rugby players in the North of England.

Other scripts require a more fanciful approach. Shakespeare's *The Tempest* must be set on an island, but that island can be anywhere in the world. Prospero and Miranda can inhabit any time period agreed upon by the director and the design team.

Costume's Influence on Fashionable Dress

While film costume often influences fashionable clothing, theatrical costume almost never does. A film is seen by millions of people across the country in the first week of its release. By contrast, the average Broadway theater can accommodate only eight thousand people in the same one-week period.

Moreover, there is typically an interval of a year or more between the end of shooting and the film's release. In this interval fashion magazines and other periodicals can run spreads showcasing the costumes, creating customer demand. Historically, film studios, manufacturers, department stores, and dressmaker pattern companies en-

tered into partnerships to promote both the film and the ready-to-wear (or ready-to-sew) garments which the film inspired.

A classic example is the "Letty Lynton" dress worn by Joan Crawford in the 1932 film of the same name. More than 500,000 copies of Adrian's design were reputedly sold at every price point as soon as the film opened. In 1967, Theodora von Runkle's costumes for *Bonnie and Clyde* sparked the trend for 1930s revival styles that were so popular in the late 1960s. Ruth Morley's costumes for Diane Keaton produced *Annie Hall* look-alikes throughout the United States and Europe in the late 1970s.

Another reason why there can be little relationship between theatrical clothing and street wear is scale. A costume is designed to be seen from a distance of thirty or forty feet. Details are exaggerated to make them visible. Film, in contrast, is largely about close-ups. Movie costumes have to be "real" in a way that successful theatrical costumes cannot be.

A few exceptions exist, but they are rare. A red suit designed by Patricia Zipprodt for the 1969 Broadway production of Neil Simon's *Plaza Suite* was subsequently manufactured for Bergdorf Goodman. In 2002, Bloomingdale's introduced a collection of plus-size garments based on William Ivey Long's designs for the musical *Hairspray*.

The audience for a theatrical event is so small relative to the number of people who attend films that it makes little economic sense to use the theater as a design source. Contemporary clothing for the stage may reflect fashionable dress, but it does not influence it.

Special Requirements

Above everything, a theatrical costume is designed for movement. Armholes are cut higher than they are in mass-produced clothing to permit the actor to raise his arms without the whole garment following. Crotches are cut higher to allow for kicks without splitting a seam.

Costumes must be constructed to be strong enough to withstand eight wearings a week for months or even years, with infrequent cleaning or laundering. If the script calls for a "quick change," meaning that the performer makes a complete change of clothing in under a minute, the costume will be constructed to facilitate the change. To change a shirt quickly, for example, the buttons are sewn on top of the buttonholes. The shirt is held closed by snaps or hook and loop tape so that it can literally be ripped off the performer.

Dancers shoes must have soles thin enough to allow the dancer to flex and point her foot. When custom-made, elk skin is the material of choice.

Trends and Developments

Theatrical costumes rely heavily on natural fibers (cotton, linen, silk, and wool). Synthetics do not handle or drape like natural fibers. That said, however, the development of new materials has had a tremendous effect on the industry.

Before the late 1950s, for example, dancer's tights were made from elasticized cotton, given to sags and bags, or they were knitted and prone to runs. The invention of Lycra, spandex, and other two-way stretch fabrics eliminated such problems. Braided nylon horsehair can be used to make ruffs that simulate the starched linen originals but which hold their shape when laundered.

No firm manufactures textiles exclusively for use in costumes. The market is far too small. Costumers, however, are extremely creative in discovering theatrical uses for products designed for other purposes. Veri-form, a brand name for a type of thermoplastic sheeting, for example, is an open weave, plastic mesh fabric used by orthopedic surgeons for lightweight casts. It makes excellent armor and masks, is nontoxic and easy to work with.

The plastic netting used to ventilate baseball caps makes indestructible and inexpensive crinolines. Air conditioning and other types of foam can be cut and sculpted to form the understructure of lightweight mascot or other costumes that are taller and broader than the actor inside them. Birdseed, encased in a body suit, is excellent to simulate the movement of sagging breasts.

The most significant development in the field in the last twenty years has undoubtedly been a heightened awareness of health and safety issues. As late as the 1970s both designers and costume makers routinely treated fabrics with highly toxic paints, solvents, and glues with no understanding of the risks involved. In the twenty-first century, not only are less toxic products available, but material safety data sheets, respirators, spray booths, and other protective devices are the norm.

While materials continue to evolve, and styles of costume design go in and out of fashion, the principle remains constant. As Robert Edmond Jones wrote in 1941, "A stage costume is a creation of the theater. Its quality is purely theatrical and taken outside the theater it loses its magic at once. It dies as a plant dies when uprooted" (p. 91).

See also **Actors and Actresses, Impact on Fashion; Art and Fashion; Ballet Costume; Theatrical Makeup.**

BIBLIOGRAPHY

Bieber, Margaret. *The History of the Greek and Roman Theater.* Princeton, N.J.: Princeton University Press, 1961.

Cheney, Sheldon. *The Theatre: Three Thousand Years of Drama, Acting and Stagecraft.* New York, London, and Toronto: Longmans, Green and Co., 1952.

Gascoine, Bamber. *World Theater: An Illustrated History.* Boston and Toronto: Little, Brown and Co., 1968.

Jones, Robert Edmond. *The Dramatic Imagination.* New York: Theatre Arts, 1941.

Laver, James. *Costume in the Theatre.* New York: Hill and Wang, 1965.

Molinari, Cesare. *Theater through the Ages.* New York: McGraw Hill Book Company, 1975.

Whitney Blausen

THEATRICAL MAKEUP Thousands of years ago, people in many parts of the world discovered that powdered pigments mixed into a base of wax or grease could be used to create striking effects of personal adornment and transformation. The survival of that practice is reflected in a common term for theatrical makeup, "greasepaint." Select types or styles of makeup were often used for special occasions, which could include going to war, celebrating stages of life, and religious festivals. The latter often included performative aspects, such as dance and re-enactments of mythical events. Modern theatrical makeup therefore is heir to a very ancient performance tradition.

Some ancient theatrical traditions have relied on masks for the creation of visual characters; others have relied on makeup for the same purpose. In Asia, for example, one can point to the masked theater of Java and the elaborately made-up Kathakali dance theater of southwestern India, or the masked religious dances of Tibet and the strikingly masklike makeup of the Peking Opera and related theatrical forms in China. In Japan, the Noh drama is masked, while Kabuki drama employs extravagant makeup.

Ancient Greek theater was masked, but later European theater usually used stage makeup to create characters, heighten facial features, and compensate for the effects of stage lighting. (The Italian Commedia del'Arte, which continued to employ masks, was an important exception.) Until well into the twentieth century, performers were expected to do their own makeup, as they were expected to supply their own stage costumes. The professional theatrical makeup artist is a modern phenomenon, as is the theatrical costume designer.

Theatrical makeup is inseparable from the act of performance itself. The aim of theatrical makeup is to delineate and enhance the role of a character and to give performers an additional tool for conveying the characters being performed. Stage makeup is often used to create visual stereotypes or clichés that will be readily understood by the audience. Stage makeup is usually much more colorful and graphic than ordinary cosmetic makeup. When viewed closely, it can seem excessive and exaggerated, but it works when the performer is on stage being seen at a distance by the audience. Theatrical makeup itself is also heavier, more dense, and more strongly colored than ordinary cosmetics, and it is often produced in the form of lipstick-like waxy crayons or pencils. For many performers, the act of putting on makeup is an important part of the ritual of preparing for a performance; it allows the performer to move psychologically into the role of the character as the makeup is being applied.

of a performed role. Baz Luhrmann's successful films of *Romeo and Juliet* and *Moulin Rouge,* and his stage production of *La Bohême,* owed a significant part of their theatricality and audience appeal to his production team's careful use of makeup techniques that evoked a period style. As these examples indicate, by the early twenty-first century makeup in different theatrical and fashion genres began to cross previously rigid barriers. The world of film, especially in special effects, has had a profound impact on the development of new techniques of stage makeup, and today theatrical makeup shows up regularly on fashion catwalks as well. Recent fashion shows by Dior and Givenchy, for example, have been notable for their strong sense of theater. Fashion makeup artists have begun to borrow liberally from traditional stage makeup techniques to create striking new designs that help to showcase the fashions on display. Meanwhile, theatrical makeup is enriched by new developments in film, fashion photography, and other media.

See also **Makeup Artists.**

BIBLIOGRAPHY

Corson, Richard. *Fashions in Makeup: From Ancient to Modern Times.* London: Peter Owen Ltd., 1972.

Delamar, Penny. *The Complete Make-up Artist: Working in Film, Television, and Theater.* 2nd edition. Evanston, Ill.: Northwestern University Press, 2002.

Kehoe, Vincent. *The Technique of the Professional Make-up Artist.* New York: Focal Press, 1995.

Elizabeth McLafferty

Kabuki actor paints on theatrical makeup. Many ancient forms of theater, such as Kabuki, use makeup in order to enhance the characterizations of the actors. © ROYALTY-FREE/CORBIS. REPRODUCED BY PERMISSION.

Makeup artists are employed today in a variety of roles, and they often specialize in, for example, theatrical makeup, cinema makeup, fashion photography and runway makeup, or special effects. Regardless of specialty, they typically require years of training and practice to perfect their skills. Special effects makeup is particularly prominent in the world of film, but has also played an important role in the success of many popular Broadway productions, such as *Jekyll and Hyde* and *Beauty and the Beast.* In the film trilogy *The Lord of the Rings,* the prosthetic feet worn by the hobbits were made by a team of special effects makeup artists. Hundreds of pairs were made, as a new pair had to be worn daily by each actor in a hobbit role. In executing such assignments, makeup artists have to draw on skills in sculpture and other plastic arts as well as in the use of cosmetics.

Whether in the dramatic makeup of a horror film or the powerful aesthetic appeal of the unique makeup employed by the Cirque du Soleil, makeup plays an important part in establishing the characterization and impact

THONGS. *See* **Sandals; G-string and Thong.**

TIE-DYEING Tie-dyeing is one of the post-weaving physical resist-dyeing techniques using binding and compression to create patterning in textiles. This basic hand process involves binding or tying a raised portion of whole cloth with thread, string, twine, raffia, rubber bands, rope, or other linear materials to "reserve" or protect areas from receiving dye penetration during a vat-immersion or dip-dye process. Although dyeing is considered a "surface" technique, through this method the dyer can create random or controlled patterning and color manipulations that are fully integrated into the fibers of the cloth. According to Jack Lenor Larsen, leading textile authority and designer, "The marriage of thirsty cloth and liquid color produces ornament not on cloth, but *in* it" (p. 9). After dyeing, when the ties or resists are removed, the resulting pattern is created from the original color of the cloth, usually some version of white or light color that was bound off, contrasted with the dyed portions. The entire process may be repeated, and layers of color from over-dyeing or selective topical

GLOSSARY OF TECHNICAL TERMS

Techniques Related to Tie-Dyeing

arashi shibori: Japanese technique in which the cloth is compressed and tightly pleated as it is wrapped around a long pole, tied in place and dyed, giving an irregular, diagonally striped pattern to the fabric. The term *arashi* literally translated means "storm," as the pattern simulates the linear pattern of rain (Wada, page 34).

clamp resist or "itajime" (board-clamped dyeing): A type of compression resist in which the cloth is folded and tightly clamped using C-clamps between a pair of two identical shapes cut from wood, plexiglas, or other dye-resistant material. The resulting reserved shape is repeated throughout the cloth based on the number of layers folded and clamped together while the surrounding area has received dye.

dip dyeing: Wet cloth is dipped into a series of dye baths containing increasingly darker values of the same or related color or along the edges of a folded bundle of cloth.

fold dyeing: The cloth is folded into small pleats so compactly that it resists the dye and is bound together with string at intervals. A variation includes twisting the folded bundle, further giving an irregular repeat design to the fabric.

knot dyeing: The simplest form of physical resist involves tying the rectangle of cloth on itself in knots in the corners and center before dyeing to produce bold, turbulent patterns.

plaited or braid dyeing: Three strips of fabric are folded lengthwise and plaited together in a threefold braid and secured by string at the bottom before immersion in a dye bath. After dyeing they are unbraided and machine-stitched together with other braid-dyed strips side by side to form a wider cloth. The resulting pattern is an offset repeat of the exposed areas with a fringe-like edge where the ends were tied off; practiced in West Africa.

tritik: Javanese word for a resist-dye process in which outline patterns are stitched into a double-layered cloth using small running stitches and tightly gathered to prevent substantial penetration of dye. This creates a "mirror image," or double rows of parallel lines of undyed dots.

Resist Processes Related to Tie-Dyeing

batik: "A resist-dye process in which the resist, usually wax, is applied to the cloth surface; when dyed, patterns are reserved in the colors of the foundation material. Sequences of waxing and dyeing result in multiple color pattern" (Gittinger, p. 240). Other resists include cassava-based paste used in Africa and rice-paste resists used in Japan.

ikat (from Indonesia): "[A] resist-dye process in which patterns are created in the warp or weft by tying off small bundles of yarns with a dye-resistant material prior to weaving. Resists are cut away and/or new ones added for each color. When all are removed the yarns are patterned, ready for weaving" (Gittinger, p. 240). Yarns can also be executed as a "double-ikat" in which both the warp and the weft are resist-dyed prior to weaving. The same technique is called *kasuri* in Japan;   in Central America.

---

spot-dyeing increase the possibilities for complexity of imagery and patterning. Furthermore, the inherent crimped and puckered textures created by the compression contribute to the tactile and aesthetic appeal of the textile.

Origins and Evolution

The origins and evolution of traditional tie-dye methods are based upon the almost universal observation that areas of any foundation material protected from exposure to liquids, gases, heat, sun, or other substances, are left untouched in their original color or state. As a result of this protection or "resistance" to the flow of dye, the potential for controlled mark-making and patterning was discovered and subsequently explored and exploited. Typically the most basic patterns—circles, dots, squares, and diamond shapes—are repeated in varying sizes and scale.

It is believed that tie-dyeing developed in conjunction with indigo cultivation and has been widely practiced by peoples throughout the world for centuries to decorate their clothing, including in India and Indonesia, Japan, Central Asia, West Africa, Europe, Mesoamerica, and South America, notably in pre-Columbian Peru. It was introduced to Europe in the seventeenth century by cotton calico fabrics that were usually made by resist printing. Silk-printed squares from India used as neck cloths or snuff handkerchiefs, the bandanna, with characteristic dot patterning, is derived from Hindu *bandhnu* (to bind or tie). This technique is also called *plangi* among Malay-Indonesian peoples and *shibori* in Japan. Most recently, tie-dye was revived during the twentieth century as a major part of the 1960s "hippie" aesthetic thought to capture psychedelic phenomenon.

Specific countries and cultural areas have developed highly sophisticated and complex tie-dyeing traditions that are unique to their cultures. Historically, there is evidence of ancient Chinese silks from the ruins of Astana (418–683), one of a number of towns along the Silk Road, the great trade route that connected East Asia with the centers of western civilization, that used tie-dye methods to create patterned textiles, as well as in ancient Persia and the Middle East. Parts of rural China continue to use tie-dye, as do areas of Japan. Similarly, India developed *plangi*, in which tiny dots of tie-dyed cloth create larger patterns and motifs as well as rich, puckered textures. Rural areas of India still embellish their saris, veils, and turbans for both daily and festive wear using tie-dye patterning.

Japanese *Shibori*

Textile artisans, probably before recorded history in Japan, began to develop an elaborate array of highly controlled techniques for resist-dyed cloth, termed *shibori*, that was associated with particular geographical regions and became the "intellectual property" of specific villages and family groups. Most of the early patterns were based upon drawing up a portion of the cloth with the fingers and binding it around and around with thread before immersing it in the dye. The resulting patterns resemble rings, squares, or "spiderwebs," called *kumo shibori* (Wada, p. 17). A variation of the tie-dye process, usually known to textile historians by the Indonesian (Javanese) term *tritik*, or stitch-resist, is a technique in which the outline of the design is delineated with stitches and the stitching thread is drawn up, making it possible to protect ground areas from the dye. In Japanese textiles this technique reached its perfection in the sixteenth century. Rural peoples concentrated on indigo-dyed cotton cloth used for kimonos or short jackets, called *hippari*, while silk court robes and obi sashes utilized a vast array of colorful dyes. Traditional imagery was given specific names, such as, *yanagi shibori* (willow) or *mokume shibori* (wood grain), and can be re-created with recently recorded and published methods.

Africa

West and North Africa have specialized in indigo tie-dyed cloth, which was originally introduced through the Jewish dyers and merchants within the Muslim world. The combination of folded and bound resists with the special nature of indigo dye that requires oxidation to produce the blue color allows the textile artist to repeatedly expose the cloth very briefly to the dye bath through dipping instead of, or in addition to, immersed saturation, thereby controlling the degree and depth of penetration. In some cases seeds, pebbles, or other nonabsorbent articles are tied into the cloth to establish a uniform module for the resisted patterning. The folded or stitched areas of these

Musician John Sebastian in a tie-dyed jacket and pants. While the techniques of tie-dying date back to as early as the sixth century, tie-dyed clothing gained popularity in the 1960s with the "hippie" generation. PHOTO BY HENRY DILTZ. REPRODUCED BY PERMISSION.

primarily cotton cloths are used to create boldly striped or radiating patterns for robes, shirts, and tunics; large turbulent swirling motifs for *bou-bous* and caftans; or repeated, linear symbolic imagery for wrappers that serve as dresses and skirts. In Nigeria, the term *adire* means, quite literally, "to take, to tie and dye." Raffia is traditionally used as the binding or stitching material in African work that also includes stitched *tritik* and embroidered resists.

Because tie-dye is based on hand-dyeing that was often practiced as a domestic household industry, the process and its resulting visual qualities fell out of fashion during the mass-industrialization of textile printing during the nineteenth and early twentieth centuries. Rather, the hard-edged block, stencil, silk-screen, and roller-based printing processes were preferred. However, with the revaluing of the individual craftsman as hands-on producer during the 1960s, the characteristically blurred visual qualities produced by dye penetrating fiber regained favor because of the visual spontaneity and rich, uneven effects. The ubiquitous tie-dyed T-shirt became the symbol of the hippie generation. Since that revolutionary decade, many contemporary textile artist-craftsmen have explored and expanded upon a rich variety of tie-dye methods, resulting in a renaissance of these techniques during the late twentieth century. Foremost among contemporary practitioners is American Ana Lisa Hedstrom of California, whose innovative exploration of *arashi shibori* dyed-silk textiles for wearable art garments, has become trendsetting.

See also **Dyeing; Dyeing, Resist; Hippie Style; Indigo.**

BIBLIOGRAPHY

Gittinger, Mattibelle, ed. *To Speak with Cloth: Studies in Indonesian Textiles.* Los Angeles: Museum of Cultural History, University of California, 1989. Excellent articles on various Indonesian textile processes in their cultural context.

Larsen, Jack Lenor, with Alfred Buhler, Bronwen Solyom, and Garrett Solyom. *The Dyer's Art: Ikat, Batik, Plangi.* New York: Van Nostrand Reinhold, 1976. The classic authoritative source on worldwide resist-dyed textiles; superb visuals.

Picton, John, and John Mack. *African Textiles: Looms, Weaving and Design.* London: British Museum Publications, Ltd., 1979. Thorough discussion of resist-dyed textiles; excellent photographs.

Schoeser, Mary. *World Textiles: A Concise History.* World of Art Series. London: Thames and Hudson, Inc., 2003. Concise overview of textile processes, cultural interrelationships, and historical evolution.

Wada, Yoshiko, Mary Kellogg Rice, and Jane Barton. *Shibori: The Inventive Art of Japanese Shaped Resist Dyeing: Tradition, Techniques, Innovation.* Tokyo: Kodansha International, 1983. Pioneer source with outstanding overview of traditional techniques with detailed diagrams and contemporary examples.

Jo Ann C. Stabb

TIGHT-LACING The term "tight-lacing" refers to the laces that tighten a corset. There is no generally accepted definition of what constitutes tight-lacing since it could be argued that any corset that is not loose is tight. Furthermore, there is no agreement as to how tightly corsets were usually laced. Some nineteenth-century writers argued that any use of the corset was dangerously unhealthy, whereas others tolerated or praised "moderate" corsetry, reserving their criticism for tight-lacing, however this might be defined. When they mentioned measurements at all, they variously defined tight-lacing as a reduction of the waist by anywhere from three to ten inches. That is, depending on the definition, a natural waist of, say, 27 inches might be reduced to a circumference of anywhere between 24 inches and 17 inches.

John Collet's caricature *Tight Lacing, or Fashion Before Ease* (1770–1775) depicts a fashionable woman clutching a bedpost, while several people tug strenuously at her stay laces. Anyone who has seen the movie *Gone with the Wind* (1939) can picture Scarlett O'Hara in a similar situation, exclaiming that if she cannot be laced down to 18 inches, she will not be able to fit into any of her dresses.

Published accounts of extreme tight-lacing in Victorian periodicals, such as *The Englishwoman's Domestic Magazine* (EDM), describe young women reducing their waists to sixteen inches or less. For example, a letter signed Nora was published in the *EDM* in May 1867, claiming to have attended "a fashionable school in London" where "it was the custom for the waists of the pupils to be reduced one inch per month. When I left school . . . my waist measured only thirteen inches." Another letter signed Walter appeared in November 1867: "I was early sent to school in Austria, where lacing is not considered ridiculous in a gentleman . . . and I objected in a thoroughly English way when the doctor's wife required me to be laced. A sturdy *mädchen* was stoically deaf to my remonstrances, and speedily laced me up tightly . . . The daily lacing tighter and tighter produced inconvenience and absolute pain. In a few months, however, I was . . . anxious . . . to have my corsets laced as tightly as a pair of strong arms could draw them."

Between 1867 and 1874 *EDM* printed dozens of letters on tight-lacing, as well as on topics such as flagellation, high heels, and spurs for lady riders. Later in the century, other periodicals, such as *The Family Doctor*, published letters and articles on tight-lacing. The notorious "corset correspondence" has been cited by some writers, such as David Kunzle, as evidence of extreme tight-lacing during the Victorian era.

However, most scholars in the early 2000s believe that these accounts represent fantasies. Indeed, by the end of the century, the tight-lacing literature becomes increasingly pornographic, as fetishist themes overlap with sadomasochistic and transvestite scenarios. Such accounts may well indicate the existence in the later nineteenth century of sexual subcultures where corset fetishists (most of whom were probably men) enacted their fantasies in settings such as specialized brothels, where they paid prostitutes to role-play as sadistic governesses. Yet this is a far cry from the use of corsets in ordinary women's lives.

The popular belief that many Victorian women had 16-inch waists is almost certainly false. Corset advertisements in the second half of the nineteenth century usually give waist measurements of 18 to 30 inches, and larger sizes were also available. Within museum costume collections, it is rare to find a corset measuring less than 20 inches around the waist. Moreover, as the author of *The Dress Reform Problem* (1886) noted, "A distinction should be made between actual and corset measurements, because stays as ordinarily worn, do not meet at the back. Young girls, especially, derive intense satisfaction from proclaiming the diminutive size of their corset. Many purchase 18- and 19-inch stays, who must leave them open two, three, and four inches. 15, 16, and 17 inch waists are glibly chattered about . . . [yet] we question whether it is a physical possibility for women to reduce their natural waist measure below 17 or 18 inches."

This is not to say that women did not use corsets to reduce their waists. Writing in 1866, the English author Arnold Cooley claimed that, "The waist of healthy women . . . is found to measure 28 to 29 inches in circumference. Yet most women do not permit themselves to exceed 24 inches round the waist, whilst tens of thousands lace themselves down to 22 inches, and many deluded victims of fashion and vanity to 21 and even to 20 inches."

The discourse on tight-lacing needs to be analyzed in ways that move beyond simple measurements. Because the practice of tight-lacing was so ill-defined and yet was perceived as being so ubiquitous in the nineteenth century, it became the focus of widespread social anxieties about women.

Tight-lacing disappeared as a social issue with the decline of the corset as a fashionable garment in the early twentieth century. However, there still existed individuals who wore tightly laced corsets. In the mid-twentieth century, Ethel Granger was listed in the *Guinness Book of World Records* for having "the world's smallest waist," which measured 13 inches. In the early twenty-first century, the most famous tight-lacer is probably the corsetier Mr. Pearl, who claims to have a 19-inch waist. His friend Cathie J. boasts of having reduced her waist to 15 inches.

See also **Corset; Fetish Fashion.**

BIBLIOGRAPHY

Kunzle, David. *Fashion and Fetishism.* Totowa, N.J.: Rowman and Littlefield, 1982.

Steele, Valerie. *Fetish: Fashion, Sex and Power.* New York: Oxford University Press, 1996.

———. *The Corset: A Cultural History.* New Haven and London: Yale University Press, 2001.

Summers, Leigh. *Bound to Please.* Oxford: Berg, 2001.

Ward, E. *The Dress Reform Problem: A Chapter for Women.* London: Hamilton, Adams, 1886.

Valerie Steele

TOGA The toga was a wrapped outer garment worn in ancient Rome. Its origin is probably to be found in the *tebenna*, a semicircular mantle worn by the Etruscans, a people who lived on the Italian peninsula in an area close to that occupied by the Romans. Several Roman kings were Etruscan and many elements of Etruscan culture were taken over by the Romans. The toga may have been one of these elements.

The toga was a highly symbolic garment for the Romans. It had numerous forms, but the *toga pura* or *toga virilis* was the most significant. In its earliest form the toga pura was a semicircle of white wool.

Statue of Emperor Augustus in a toga. The toga, a garment wrapped around the body and over the shoulder, was worn by all ancient Roman men, though larger and longer togas were generally reserved for Romans with status and wealth. © ARALDO DE LUCA/CORBIS. REPRODUCED BY PERMISSION.

At the time of the Roman Republic (509 B.C.E. to 27 B.C.E.) and after, only free male citizens of Rome who were at least sixteen years of age could wear this toga. It was the symbol of Roman citizenship and was required dress for official activities. Men wore togas to audiences with the Emperor and to the games played in the Roman arena.

The toga was worn outermost, over a tunic. (A tunic was a T-shaped woven garment, similar in form to a long, modern T-shirt.) The toga wrapped around the body. The straight edge was placed at the center of the body, perpendicular to the floor. The bulk of the fabric was carried over the left shoulder, across the back and under the right arm, after which it was draped across the chest and over the left shoulder.

By the time of the Roman Empire, the earlier half-circle toga had changed its form and had an extended section added to the semicircle at the straight edge. The system of draping remained the same, however the extended section was first folded down. The overfold section fell at the front of the body and formed a pocketlike pouch, called the *sinus*, into which the wearer could place objects such as a scroll of paper. As the toga became still more elaborate and larger, the sinus eventually was too open and loose for holding things, so a knot of fabric was pulled up from underneath to form an area called the *umbo*, and this being smaller and more compact became the "pocket" area. The umbo may also have helped to hold the toga in place.

Individuals of some significant status wore special togas. Although both men and women had worn togas in early Roman times, by the time of the Republic only men wore togas. However, a vestige of the earlier practice remained. Sons and daughters of Roman citizens wore the *toga praetexta*, a toga with a purple border about two or three inches wide. Boys wore this toga until age fourteen to sixteen when they assumed the *toga pura*, while girls gave up the garment around the age of puberty. Certain priests and magistrates also wore the *toga praetexta*.

Political candidates wore a *toga candida* that was bleached very white. The English word "candidate" derives from the name of this garment.

A *toga picta* was purple with gold embroidery. Victorious generals and others who had been singled out for special honors were awarded the opportunity to wear this toga. A *toga pulla* appears to have been worn for mourning, and was dark or black in color. The *toga trabea* seems to have been worn by religious augurs or important officials.

The toga was an awkward garment. Roman writers speak of the difficulties in keeping the toga properly arranged. Apparently it was acceptable for men to wear longer or shorter togas. A poor man might wear a shorter toga in order to save money, while one seeking to impress others might wear an especially large and long toga. In order to keep this garment clean, it had to be washed often, which caused it to wear out frequently. Replacing a worn toga was an expense that is commented on by some Roman satirists.

By the time of the Roman Republic and after, respectable adult women did not wear togas. Prostitutes were said to wear togas, as were women who had been divorced for adultery. The connotation of a woman wearing a toga implied disapproval.

The form of the toga continued to change. It seems as if men were constantly searaching for variations that made the toga easier to keep in place. In one version dating from circa 118–119 C.E. and after, the umbo was eliminated by wrapping the section under the right arm at a higher point and twisting that upper section to form a sort of band. This band was called a *balteus*. In the third century it was an easy step from this to "the toga with the folded bands."

In the toga with the folded bands, the twisted balteus became an overfold that was folded and refolded over itself in order to form a flat, layered band of fabric that may have been fastened in place by either pinning or sewing. As the toga wrapped around the body, the bands lay flat, fitting smoothly in a diagonal band across the front of the body.

In the latter years of the Roman Empire, discipline in following prescribed forms of dress grew somewhat lax, and men preferred to wear the *pallium* instead of the toga. The pallium itself was an evolved form of a Greek wrapped garment, the himation, which draped much the same way as the toga. The pallium was a rectangular panel of fabric that, like the toga, ran perpendicular to the floor, around the left shoulder, under the right arm, and across the body, draping over the arm. It was a sort of skeletal form of the toga, retaining its draping but losing its semicircular form and most of its bulk.

Although the toga in its exact Roman form has not been revived in contemporary fashion, the name "toga" is often loosely applied to fashions that feature one covered and one uncovered shoulder. Examples include the "toga dress" defined by Calasibetta (2003) as an "Asymmetric dress or at-home robe styled with one shoulder bare, the other covered" or the "toga nightgown," which could be "styled with one shoulder." Both were styles introduced in the 1960s (Calasibetta 2003).

See also **Ancient World: History of Dress.**

BIBLIOGRAPHY

Calasibetta, C. M., and P. Tortora. *The Fairchild Dictionary of Fashion.* New York: Fairchild Publications, 2003.

Croom, A. T. *Roman Clothing and Fashion.* Charleston, S.C.: Tempus Publishing Inc., 2000.

Goldman, N. "Reconstructing Roman Clothing." In *The World of Roman Costume.* Edited by J. L. Sebesta and L. Bonfante, pp. 213–237 Madison: University of Wisconsin Press, 1994.

Houston, M. G. *Ancient Greek, Roman, and Byzantine Costume.* London: Adam and Charles Black, 1966.

Rudd, N., trans. *The Satires of Horace and Persius.* Baltimore, Md.: Penguin Books, 1973.

Stone, S. "The Toga: From National to Ceremonial Costume." In *The World of Roman Costume.* Edited by J. L. Sebesta, and L. Bonfante, pp. 13–45. Madison: University of Wisconsin Press, 1994.

Tortora, P., and K. Eubank. *Survey of Historic Costume.* New York: Fairchild Publications, 1998.

Wilson, L. M. *The Roman Toga.* Baltimore, Md.: Johns Hopkins Press, 1924.

Phyllis Tortora

TOLEDO, ISABEL AND RUBEN Ruben and Isabel Toledo are a husband-and-wife team who work closely together in several fields of fashion. She is a fashion designer known for producing clothing that combines sophisticated simplicity and meticulous craftsmanship. He is a fashion artist whose distinctive drawings have appeared in many fashion publications and whose work extends to designing mannequins and painting murals for fashionable restaurants; Isabel is his muse and almost invariably his model. He also is responsible for managing the business side of her clothing business. Theirs is a true creative partnership; it is impossible to delineate the boundaries of the contribution of each to the work of the other.

Born in Cuba in 1961, Isabel learned to sew as a child, when she was fascinated by her grandmother's sewing machine. She describes Cuban culture as one in which mastering the techniques of fine sewing was an admired accomplishment for women. When she first began designing clothes, she adopted the technique, associated with such great couturieres as Mmes. Grès and Madeleine Vionnet, of working directly with fabric by draping and cutting, designing in three dimensions. Like Claire McCardell, she works in simple materials such as denim, cotton jersey, and cotton flannel. She describes her garments as forward-looking and optimistic.

Ruben Toledo was born in Cuba in 1960; he and Isabel met in school as members of the large Cuban expatriate community of northern New Jersey. They quickly recognized one another as kindred spirits and began collaborating in art and design. They were married in 1984.

Isabel showed her first collection in 1985 and was immediately acclaimed as an important new talent on the New York fashion scene. Her clothes—architectural, slightly severe, with black or shades of gray dominating her palette—became highly prized by wearers of fashion-forward, "downtown" styles and were praised in such publications as the *Village Voice, Paper,* and *Visionaire.* Acquiring a cult following in New York, Paris, and Tokyo, Isabel nevertheless has had difficulties finding sufficient long-term financial backing to break out of niche markets to reach more widespread recognition.

The Toledos had a major exhibition, *Toledo/Toledo: A Marriage of Art and Fashion,* at the museum at the Fashion Institute of Technology (FIT) in 1999. Ruben's illustrations reached a wide audience in his witty book, *Style Dictionary* (1997). In one of his iconoclastic fashion illustrations, entitled "Fashion history goes on strike," Ruben portrayed dresses from the past, from New Look to Mod, parading across the page in a militant demonstration, carrying placards reading, "Let us rest in peace! No more retro! Look forward, not backward!" Both of the Toledos remain on the cutting edge of style, moving fashion forward.

See also **Art and Fashion.**

BIBLIOGRAPHY

Hastreiter, Kim. "Isabel Toledo." *Paper* (Fall 1998).

Mason, Christopher. "A Pair of Muses, above It All." *New York Times* (27 February 1997).

Toledo, Isabel and Ruben. *Toledo/Toledo: A Marriage of Art and Fashion.* Kyoto, Japan: Korinsha Press, 1998. An exhibition catalog.

Toledo, Ruben. *Style Dictionary: A Visualization, Exploration, Transformation, Mutation, Documentation, Investigation, Classification, Free-association, Interpretation and Exact Quotations of Fashion Terms and a Collection of Past Works.* New York: Abbeville, 1997.

Valerie Steele

TOOSH. *See* **Cashmere and Pashmina.**

TRADITIONAL DRESS Traditional dress may be defined as the ensemble of garments, jewelry, and accessories rooted in the past that is worn by an identifiable group of people. Though slight changes over time in color, form, and material are acknowledged, the assemblage seems to be handed down unchanged from the past. Traditional dress or costume is a phrase used widely both by the general public and writers on dress. It conjures up images of rural people dressed in colorful, layered, exotic clothing from an idealized past in some faraway place. This notion of traditional dress has been scrutinized and found inadequate by many researchers and scholars, but its uncritical use continues into the twenty-first century. The phrase traditional dress or costume is often used interchangeably with the terms ethnic, regional, and folk dress. For a concise discussion of this terminology see Welters and for a fascinating look at how the term is used try a Web search on the words "traditional costume."

In Webster's Third International Dictionary, tradition is defined as "an inherited or established way of thinking, feeling or doing: a cultural feature *preserved or evolved* from the past" (1993, p. 2422; italics by author). The concept of traditional dress as a static form carried over from the past is usually contrasted with the rapidly changing fashion of "the West." Ethnographers and travelers documenting actual dress practices provided the original data for later interpretation by other researchers. Early social psychologists were primarily concerned with understanding the human element of fashion change, not with the continuity of a particular dress tradition, thus the reference to tradition or custom was usually brief. General studies of folk or traditional costume were geared toward showing the diversity and splendor of peoples of the world while more recent, specific studies tend toward more historical and cultural analysis. Tarrant asks the pertinent questions, "What tradition?" and "How old is tradition?" (p. 153), questions that are essential for studying and analyzing the cultural and historic aspects of dress.

Evolution and Traditional Dress

Changing customs in Navajo women's dress shows clearly how dress traditions adapt to changing circumstances over time. Navajo myth tells of the people clothed in garments of shredded cedar bark or pounded yucca leaf. When they moved into New Mexico in the fifteenth century the Navajo wore garments of animal skin. They began to weave with wool after the Pueblo Revolt of 1680, when many Pueblo Indians, already weavers, took refuge with Navajo neighbors and taught them to weave. A dress made from two rectangular pieces of wool fabric, fastened at the shoulders, remained in use until the 1880s.

During four years (1864–1868) of confinement at Fort Sumner, the people were reduced to wearing cast-offs and garments made from flour sacks and whatever fabric they could find. With the advent of the railroad in New Mexico and the establishment of trading posts, Navajo women began to sell their wool and the blankets they made, trading for cotton cloth which they sewed into skirts and blouses. The use of a velvet blouse began in 1890, when a trader brought velvet or velveteen to a post. Only at this point did the ensemble of gathered skirt, close-fitting velvet blouse, and silver and turquoise jewelry worn in the early 2000s by elderly women and by young women on ceremonial occasions become traditional.

Materials

Often made in the family for personal use, traditional dress uses materials commonly available where the maker lives. These materials and styles are often assumed to have evolved in response to environments—wool in cold climates, cotton in warm. But traditional dress often also incorporates imported materials obtained by trade. Exotic fabrics or notions can be incorporated into a people's dress and become "traditional," as Indian madras has for the Kalabari Ijo of the Niger Delta. Although no one knows where it originated, a print cloth called *ondoba*, said to have arrived with the Portuguese in the fifteenth century, "belongs" to the Nembe Ijo of the Niger Delta.

Over time, factory-made materials are commonly substituted for those once produced by hand in the home. Hand embroidery is reproduced by machine. It is also of note that men often adopt cosmopolitan styles while women, as carriers of culture, seem more inclined to retain aspects of traditional dress.

Traditional Dress in the Early 2000s

Although immortalized in the world eye by romantic photos and tourist-oriented advertising, what is known as traditional dress is not commonly worn everyday anywhere in the world; elements of traditional styles are reg-

ularly seen. Education, access to international media, contact with outsiders, and the desire and ability to participate in global consumer culture have all contributed to changes in this form of material culture. Weddings, religious rituals, festivals, folkloric dance performances, and historical re-enactments are occasions for donning the dress of the past in parts of the world where virtually no elements of traditional dress are found in contemporary use.

In other places, traditional dress is one option in a person's wardrobe—there are times when it is expected and necessary but other times when cosmopolitan styles are appropriate. A young woman in South India, where the sari is considered traditional, can wear a North Indian *salwar-kameez* outfit one day, jeans and T-shirt the next, an "ethnic" skirt and blouse from Rajasthan another day, but put on a sari when attending a wedding. After marriage, the same woman might wear a sari more frequently, acknowledging her change in social status as a wife and mother.

Everyone in the world follows some dress traditions in varying degree. Although Americans often don't recognize it, there is a strong element of the past in ritual dress such as that for weddings and funerals. One would not be formally sanctioned for wearing bright colors to a funeral. However, there is a cultural tradition of black or somber dress that would be violated.

Unexamined, the phrase "traditional dress" implies a group of people living an integrated, rural life where group identity is paramount and community values are widely shared and important relative to individual expression. This romantic ideal of a meaningful community life contrasts with the perception of contemporary urban life lived in colorless anonymity. Linked with the common idea that globalized urban life is spiritually and culturally empty, this romantic ideal of traditional dress is kept alive in the minds of those who are furthest from it.

What is called traditional dress might in the early twenty-first century be more correctly called ethnic dress, donned to express diverse identities and affiliations such as cultural pride, nationalist or ethnic group politics, or to make a statement about personal, aesthetic, and cultural values.

See also **Ethnic Dress.**

BIBLIOGRAPHY

Baizerman, Suzanne, Joanne B. Eicher, and Cathleen Cerny. "Eurocentrism in the Study of Ethnic Dress." *Dress* 20 (1993): 19–32.

Blumer, Herbert. "Collective Behavior." In *An Outline of the Principles of Sociology.* Edited by Robert Park. New York: Barnes and Noble, 1939.

Boas, Franz. "The Social Organization and the Secret Societies of the Kwakiutl Indians." Report of the U.S. National Museum for 1895. Washington, D.C.: U.S. National Museum, 1897.

Ellwood, Charles. *An Introduction to Social Psychology.* New York: D. Appleton and Co., 1918.

Frater, Judy. "Rabari Dress." In *Mud, Mirror, and Thread: Folk Traditions in Rural India.* Edited by Nora Fisher. Santa Fe: Museum of New Mexico Pres; Ahmedabad: Mapin, 1993.

Freeman, Richard. *Travels and Life in Ashanti and Jaman.* New York: Frederick A. Stokes Co., 1898.

Harrold, Robert, and Phylidda Legg. *Folk Costumes of the World.* London: Cassell Academic Press, 1999.

Hendrikson, Carol. *Weaving Identities: Construction of Dress and Self in a Highland Guatemala Town.* Austin: University of Texas, 1995.

Kennett, Frances. *Ethnic Dress.* New York: Facts on File, 1995.

Lentz, Carola. "Ethnic Conflict and Changing Dress Codes: A Case Study of an Indian Migrant Village in Highland Ecuador." In *Dress and Ethnicity.* Edited by Joanne B. Eicher. Oxford: Berg, 1995.

Mera, H. P. *Navajo Women's Dresses.* General Series Bulletin No. 15. Santa Fe, N.M.: Laboratory of Anthropology, 1944.

Sapir, Edward. "Fashion." In *Encyclopedia of the Social Sciences.* Vol. 6. New York: Macmillan, 1931.

Sumberg, Barbara. "Dress and Ethnic Differentiation in the Niger Delta." In *Dress and Ethnicity.* Edited by Joanne Eicher. Oxford: Berg, 1995.

Tarrant, Naomi. *The Development of Costume.* London: Routledge, 1994.

Underhill, Ruth. *The Navajos.* Norman: University of Oklahoma, 1956.

Weir, Shelagh. *Palestinian Costume.* Austin: University of Texas, 1989.

Welters, Linda. "Introduction." In *Folk Dress in Europe and Anatolia.* Edited by Linda Welters. Oxford: Berg, 1999.

Westermarck, Edward. *Marriage Ceremonies in Morocco.* London: Macmillan and Co., Ltd., 1914.

Wilcox, R. Turner. *Folk and Festival Costume of the World.* New York: Charles Scribner's Sons, 1965.

Barbara Sumberg

TRAINERS. *See* **Sneakers.**

TRANSVESTISM. *See* **Cross-Dressing.**

TRAVEL CLOTHING Travel clothing hardly existed as a separate category of dress until the nineteenth century, when new forms of travel beyond horse, carriage, and sailing ship were developed, and when the Industrial Revolution permitted mass production of fabrics, enabling more classes to afford garments that were designed for specialized and infrequent use.

Prior to that, both urban and rural poor and middle-class people did little traveling and relied on whatever outer garments they possessed to protect them from dirt, dust, and the elements. Boots, cloaks, coats with extra shoulder capes, and wide-brimmed hats were available to men riding on horseback or in uncovered vehicles. Upper-class men traveling by horseback relied on the same garments. When traveling in carriages, women in the seventeenth and eighteenth centuries could wear a wool riding habit, more easily cleaned than fashionable silks. The cane-framed calash, a high, folding bonnet, introduced in the late eighteenth century, protected women's high hairstyles from the dust of travel; women's iron pattens worn over shoes also protected from dirt and mud.

Generally, however, the condition of roads, and the lack of leisure time for most people, prevented much travel except among the gentry classes. After 1800, more people could afford travel, with the development of public conveyances like canal boats and stagecoaches (old forms, but increasingly used in America) and new inventions, steamships and trains. Travelers were concerned not only with protection from dirt (soot and sparks from coal engines on trains and steamships, dust and mud on carriages), but about appearing in public among strangers—particularly a concern for middle-class women.

Canal travel was not particularly dirty, but its shared sleeping, bathing, and dressing quarters required its users to pack carefully so that propriety and modesty could be respected. Canal boats offered ladies' bathing and dressing rooms not necessarily connected to their sleeping quarters, so women were advised to pack a full-length, modest dressing gown. Men were expected to sleep in their shirt, trousers, and shoes, removing coat, waistcoat, collar, and cravat.

Railway travel had similar concerns and solutions. With limited room for luggage, a smaller holdall was needed for the duration of the journey. The "shawl strap" was a recommended and seemingly popular solution: a change of clothes and undergarments was spread on a large square of sturdy linen or wool, the edges folded over the clothes, and the whole rolled up and bound with two leather straps.

Steamship travel for leisure was not extensive until the last quarter of the century. The combined effects of seawater and soot from the smokestacks were ruinous to clothes, and during most parts of the year, decks could be chilly. Accordingly, warm, enveloping overcoats were recommended, particularly Ulsters , and fine clothes discouraged. Some guidebooks advised wearing old clothes that could be discarded after the journey. Others addressed seasickness, suggesting women wear dresses that could be donned with minimum effort. Shared bathrooms accessed by a walk down a corridor required, as had canal boats and railway cars, modest wrappers.

Small cabins required packing a minimum of clothes for the journey, allowing the remainder of the luggage to stay in the hold. Steamer trunks, unlike the vast trunks designed to hold the many bulky items in a women's wardrobe for an extensive foreign journey, were only twelve inches high and fit under the cabin's berth. The "shawl strap," beloved of railroad journeys, was often suggested as ideal for the transatlantic trip.

Travel clothing, when referring to extensive foreign travel, takes on two categories: what to wear on the voyage, and what to pack to last for the rest of the trip. Once the rigors of the steamship were over, travelers could resume normal dress, but guidebooks offered comprehensive packing lists, unanimously advising traveling light. Women were advised to bring a few sturdy undergarments without delicate trim to withstand hotel laundries, and a minimum of outfits—the black silk dress and wool tailored suits being top recommendations. Even when travel became more luxurious, women were advised to wear outfits uncluttered by trims and flounces, which were difficult to keep tidy and clean. The tailored outfits that entered women's fashions in the 1870s were ideal for travel.

Travel to tropical climates required specialized equipment such as pith helmets to protect from the sun (with veiling for women) and khaki-colored linen and cotton being logical fabrics and colors in dusty, sandy places. Green-lined parasols—green was thought to protect the eyes—and green sunglasses were also necessary accoutrements.

By about 1900, travel by both sea and rail had become less dirty. Fashion advice for travelers addressed matters of etiquette more than practical issues. Travel costume merely had to fit within pre-existing codes of dress: "The boat is the country, and the train [is] town in the morning," *Vogue* had only to declare in June of 1925, and its readers knew precisely what was proper (p. 58).

Travel by automobile was, in its early years, more of a sport than a mode of travel, and as such its specialized clothing need not be discussed at length here. Open cars required long linen dusters and goggles for both sexes as protection from dust, and ladies wore veils over their hats for some protection from sun, wind, and dust. A uniform emerged for chauffeurs, and long "car coats" kept passengers warm; later in the century, the "car coat" was by definition short, for convenient movement by the driver.

Choosing clothes for airplane travel was also largely a matter of etiquette. While choosing fabrics less likely to wrinkle and show dirt was always a concern, flying in an enclosed cabin did not require specialized clothing. However, luggage design had to adapt to the weight restrictions of airplane travel, and aluminum and smaller suitcases quickly replaced the heavy steamer and other trunks used in railway and steamship travel. Lately, travelers' desire to forgo checked luggage has led to the design of wheeled bags conforming to size restrictions for overhead or under-seat stowing. Additionally, the democratization of travel led to a decline in use of porters, further incentive for designing lightweight, convenient bags.

The later twentieth century saw innovations in synthetic fibers and fabrics useful to travelers seeking clothes that resist wrinkling when packed or worn, take little space in a suitcase, and can be washed in a hotel sink and hung to dry, avoiding costly and time-consuming laundering by a hotel—or easily done in less luxurious locales, as modern travelers venture into locations beyond the traditional centers of culture that were the destinations of nineteenth-century voyagers. Travelers can also purchase garments and gadgets to ease both their airplane journey and the rest of their travels, including specialized toiletry bags and packing organizers; reversible, wrinkle-proof, drip-dry, less bulky dresses and skirts; and garments suited to hot climates.

See also **Outerwear.**

BIBLIOGRAPHY

Cooper-Hewitt Museum. *Bon Voyage: Design for Travel.* New York, 1986. Exhibition Catalogue.

Dunbar, Seymour. *A History of Travel in America.* Indianapolis, Ind.: Bobbs Merrill, 1915.

Knox, Tomas W. *How to Travel: Hints, Advice, and Suggestions to Travelers by Land and Sea.* New York: G. P. Putnam's Sons, 1887.

Ledoux, Kate Reed. *Ocean Notes and Foreign Travel for Ladies.* New York: Cook, Son, and Jenkins, 1878.

Luce, Robert. *Going Abroad? Some Advice.* Boston: Clipping Bureau Press, 1897.

O'Brien, Alden. *Don't Leave Home without It: Travel Clothing in America, 1840–1940.* Unpublished Master's Thesis, Fashion Institute of Technology, New York, 1989.

Alden O'Brien

TREACY, PHILIP Born in rural Ireland in 1967, Philip Treacy was the second youngest of eight children of a baker in the Galway village of Ahascragh. He initially studied at the National College of Art and Design in Dublin in 1985 before moving to London to study millinery at the Royal College of Art. His acclaimed graduate show in 1990 resulted in offers to collaborate with international designers such as Valentino, Versace, and Karl Lagerfeld at Chanel, with whom he worked for ten years. The first hat he designed for Chanel was the twisted birdcage, photographed by Patrick Demarchelier for the cover of *British Vogue.* The same year he established his own company, Philip Treacy Limited, and went on to win the title of Accessory Designer of the Year at the British Fashion Awards in 1991, 1992, and 1993 and again in 1996 and 1997.

The dramatic power of his designs has meant that they appeal to extraordinary, iconic women such as Isabella Blow and Grace Jones. Renowned for her ability to spot and nurture talent, Isabella Blow is probably the most extreme showcase for his work. She first encountered his hats when working with the fashion editor Michael Roberts at *Tatler* magazine, and on Treacy's graduation invited him to set up a workshop in the basement of her house on Elizabeth Street, Belgravia, London. In 1994 he opened his own shop at 69 Elizabeth Street. Among Blow's other protégés was Alexander McQueen, with whom Philip Treacy collaborated in 1999 on his haute couture collection for Givenchy, which included hats constructed from gilded rams' horns.

Philip Treacy identified 1993 as the year that signaled a new attitude to millinery, resulting from the production of his first annual catwalk show at London Fashion Week. The showcasing of millinery as a design item independent of garments has led to a revival of interest in the wearing of hats. According to Isabella Blow (2003), "In the old days, people were frightened by my hats. But in the last year, or maybe two, Philip has single-handedly broken through the barriers."

Treacy has transformed the hat into an art form. His signature style of playful surrealism allied with complete mastery of the craft skills inherent in millinery has resulted in a unique reputation. Drawing on diverse subjects, from orchids to Andy Warhol, Philip Treacy continues to receive universal acclaim from both fashion press and buyers. Although his couture designs may be extreme in concept and not suitable for everyday wear, Treacy also designs a ready-to-wear line which retails through department stores, and in 1997 he launched an accessory collection that includes hair ornaments, scarves, bags, and gloves.

In 2000 he was invited by the Chambre Syndicale de la couture, the governing body of French fashion, to participate in the haute couture show, the first millinery designer to do so in seventy years. Evidence of the broad appeal of his aesthetic, Treacy exhibited at the Florence Biennale in 1996, and in 2001 he collaborated with artist Vanessa Beecroft on an installation at the Venice Biennale. In 2002 the Royal College of Art awarded him an honorary doctorate.

See also **Extreme Fashions; Hats, Women's; Milliners.**

BIBLIOGRAPHY

Blow, Isabella. "Tasmin Blanchard 'Blow by Blow.'" *The Observer* (23 June 2003).

Blow, Isabella, Philip Treacy, and Hamish Bowles. *Philip Treacy: When Philip Met Isabella*. New York. Assouline Publishing, 2002. An exhibition catalog.

Marnie Fogg

TRENDSETTERS Functionally, clothes provide warmth and protection. Socially, clothes express status and identity. The first trendsetters were members of the ruling class, particularly monarchs and aristocrats. Queen Elizabeth I, for example, adorned herself as if her person were the state, creating an unassailable image for herself as Britain's monarch. Similarly, Louis XIV of France dressed to impress, and also set rules regulating what members of the court aristocracy were to wear. By the eighteenth century, however, trends were increasingly set by individuals in urban centers, such as Paris and London, rather than at court.

In the mid-nineteenth century, the wife of Napoleon III, working with the couturier Charles Frederick Worth, set fashions for an eclectic array of nouveaux riches, social climbers, old aristocrats, and members of the demimonde. Women of the demimonde were often entertainers, actresses, and dancers, as well as courtesans. In some ways, they were precursors of modern stars.

By the beginning of the twentieth century, theatrical stars such as Sarah Bernhardt were joined by film stars such as Clara Bow, Marlene Dietrich, and Greta Garbo in setting sartorial trends. For example, the ballroom dancer Irene Castle helped to popularize the post–World War I trend for short hair when she cut her own hair in a "Castle bob." By the early 2000s, actresses remained among the most important trendsetters, joined by pop singers such as Madonna, arguably the most trendsetting woman of the twentieth century.

Fashion magazines—notably *Vogue*—have also played an important part in launching "the Beautiful People" as celebrity trendsetters. Among them were girls of good family, dressed and posed and photographed by fashion editors and photographers. The 1957 film *Funny Face* starred the gamine Audrey Hepburn, whose character lived out the transformation from duckling to swan.

What is a trendsetter? A woman put on a pedestal, an icon that others want to follow. In magazines, they fall into a few categories: the society girl (Gloria Guinness, sometimes known as "the swan," and Babe Paley); the model girl (Jean Shrimpton, Veruschka, Kate Moss); the entertainer (Katharine Hepburn, Sarah Jessica Parker). Gabrielle (Coco) Chanel is a rare case of the designer as trendsetter, since she was the best model of her own clothes.

The qualities these women possess include beauty, status, and larger-than-life personas. In the late twentieth century, models gave way to the phenomenon of supermodels, who commodified trendiness through brand association. Actresses also became associated with particular styles and designers. Trendsetters have become figures thrown into the light by the flare of the paparazzo's flash. Whereas yesterday's social elite had money and status, and actresses and models had beauty, contemporary trendsetters possess a lifestyle (encompassing fashion) that whets the appetite of a global public.

See also **Actors and Actresses, Impact on Fashion; Celebrities; Supermodels.**

BIBLIOGRAPHY

Howell, Georgina. *Vogue Women.* New York and London: Pavilion Books Ltd., 2000.

Keenan, Brigid. *The Women We Wanted to Look Like.* New York: St. Martin's Press, 1978.

Shakar, Alex. *The Savage Girl.* New York: HarperCollins, 2001.

Laird Borrelli

TRICKLE-DOWN The "trickle-down" theory offers a straightforward way of predicting fashion diffusion: a hierarchical process whereby individuals with high status establish fashion trends, only to be imitated by lower-status individuals wearing cheaper versions of the styles. Subsequently, high-status individuals become motivated to differentiate themselves by moving on to a new trend. Initially based upon an explanation of social-class dynamics within western modernity, the theory has since been applied to gender and age relations.

The origin of the theory is generally attributed to sociologist Georg Simmel, although he was actually only one of several writers (e.g., Spencer, Grosse, Veblen) who sought to explain fashion through class structure and social mobility in the late nineteenth century. Through a contemporary lens, Simmel (like others of his day) placed an inordinate emphasis on social class in his explanation of fashion (see Blumer; Davis; Crane). However, in many ways Simmel's analysis was especially nuanced in its blend of psychology and philosophy; it can be read as elaborating a fundamental blend of imitation and differentiation that surpasses social class alone (Lehmann; Carter).

Carter (2003) suggests that a modern scientific goal of assigning order to a seemingly disorderly phenomenon (fashion) led to the restricted (economic-based) naming and life of the trickle-down theory. The historical evidence of such an orderly trickling-down fashion is not very convincing (see Breward; Crane). By the late 1960s, the theory had come under attack, as class-based explanations could not explain the number of styles that bubbled or percolated up from working-class youth or diverse ethnicities (Blumer; King). Furthermore, the speed with which fashion could be "knocked off" in cheaper versions had accelerated to the point that any trickling that occurred was blurry. Indeed, in the twenty-first century's global economy, counterfeit versions of high-fashion handbags appear almost simultaneously with "original" handbags, on the sidewalks outside designer stores in major cities around the world.

McCracken (1985) attempted to rehabilitate the trickle-down theory by relating it to gender. He noted a process whereby women imitate men's fashions in order to obtain more status, only to be usurped by further changes in men's attire. Although McCracken has been critiqued for not demonstrating the differentiation function (on the part of men) adequately, if one goes back to Simmel's analysis, it is possible to establish how the di-alectical process of fashion simultaneously articulates twin opposites in a single "masculine" or "feminine" look.

More recently, Huun and Kaiser (2000) demonstrated how the basic elements of imitation and differentiation can explain changing infants' and young children's fashions—in terms of age, as well as gender. And, Cook and Kaiser (2004) reinterpreted the trickle-down theory to explain the recent "downsizing" of teen and adult fashion into children's and "tweens'" styles. Although the hierarchical (class-based) flow of the trickle-down theory may be challenged in many ways, the basic dynamic underlying Simmel's analysis of imitation and differentiation remains a critical part of fashion theory.

See also **Veblen, Thorstein.**

BIBLIOGRAPHY

Blumer, Herbert. "Fashion: From Class Differentiation to Collective Selection." *Sociological Quarterly* 10 (Summer 1969): 275–291.

Breward, Christopher. *The Culture of Fashion.* Manchester, U.K.: Manchester University Press, 1995.

Carter, Michael. *Fashion Classics: From Carlyle to Barthes.* Oxford, U.K., and New York: Berg Press, 2003.

Cook, Daniel, and Susan B. Kaiser. "Be Twixt and Be Tween: Age Ambiguity and the Sexualization of the Female Consuming Subject." *Journal of Consumer Culture* 4, no. 2 (2004): 203–227.

Crane, Diana. *Fashion and Its Social Agendas: Class Gender, and Identity in Clothing.* Chicago: University of Chicago Press, 2000.

Davis, Fred. *Fashion, Culture, and Identity.* Chicago: University of Chicago Press, 2002.

Huun, Kathleen, and Susan B. Kaiser. "The Emergence of Modern Infantwear, 1896–1962: Traditional White Dresses Succumb to Fashion's Gender Obsession." *Clothing and Textiles Research Journal* 19, no. 3 (2001): 103–119.

King, Charles W. "Fashion Adoption: A Rebuttal to the 'Trickle-Down' Theory." In *Toward Scientific Marketing.* Edited by S. A. Greyser. Chicago: American Marketing Association, 1963, pp. 108–125.

Lehmann, Ulrich. *Tigersprung: Fashion in Modernity.* Cambridge, Mass.: MIT Press, 2000.

McCracken, Grant. "The Trickle-Down Theory Rehabilitated." In *The Psychology of Fashion.* Edited by Michael R. Solomon. Lexington, Mass.: Heath, 1985.

Simmel, Georg. "Fashion." *American Journal of Sociology* 62 (May 1957): 541–558.

Susan B. Kaiser

TRIGÈRE, PAULINE Born in Paris in 1908 to Russian-Jewish émigrés, Pauline Trigère grew up behind the shop where her mother and father, former tailors of military uniforms for the Russian aristocracy, worked in the clothing trade. By age ten she was helping her mother with dressmaking tasks. Trigère was apprenticed at age fifteen to the couture house Martial et Armand on the place Vendôme, where she quickly showed her aptitude for tailoring and a mastery of the bias cut. In 1929 she married Lazar Radley, a Russian immigrant tailor; the couple had two sons. In 1935 she opened a small wholesale business specializing in tailored suits and dresses. Concerned about the Nazi threat, the Radleys left Paris in 1937, stopping in New York on their way to Chile. At the urging of the designer Adele Simpson, Trigère decided to stay in New York, and was hired first by Ben Gershel, then as Travis Banton's assistant by Hattie Carengie. In 1941 the Radleys opened a tailoring business with her brother, Robert, that closed when Lazar Radley left his wife and sons.

In January 1942 Pauline and Robert opened another business with a collection of eleven pieces. Robert sold them from a suitcase across the country, receiving orders from many important retail stores. In order to buy fabrics for that first New York collection, Pauline borrowed $1500 and sold some diamond jewelry for $800. Within three years her name was widely known. During nearly sixty years in business, she garnered many honors: three Coty Awards, inclusion in the Coty Hall of Fame, the Neiman Marcus and Filene's awards, the City of Paris silver and vermeil medals, and the French Legion of Honor. In addition, she was inducted into the Hall of Fame of the Shannon Rodgers and Jerry Silverman School of Fashion Design and Merchandising at Kent State University (1990); was given a retrospective fashion show to honor her fifty years in business at the Fashion Institute of Technology in New York (1992); received the Council of Fashion Designers of America's Lifetime Achievement Award (1993); and had a retrospective exhibition (1994) at the Kent State University Museum, the repository of several of her earliest garments and sketchbooks that chronicle each of her collections. Also in 1994 she closed her ready-to-wear business and formed a new company, P. T. Concepts, to market her scarves, jewelry, and other accessories. She died in 2002.

Trigère provided her own witty commentary during her fashion shows. She did not design by sketching, but rather cut and draped fabric directly on a model. The finished garment was later sketched as a record. She was noted especially for her elegant tailoring, innovative cut, frequent use of the bias, and sensitivity to fabric, line, and movement. Fur-trimmed evening dresses became a signature look. She was also the first major designer to use an African American model. Known as an intellectual "designer's designer," Trigère shaped her career as surely as she shaped her creations: with a strong sense of personal style. "Fashion is what people tell you to wear" she said (Epstein, p. 19). "Style is what comes from your own inner thing" (Nemy, p. C14).

See also **Fashion Designer; Russia: History of Dress; Tailoring.**

Pauline Trigère. Renowned for her attention to line, tailoring, and cut, fashion designer Pauline Trigère created her designs by using fabric and a model rather than by first drafting sketches. © MITCHELL GERBER/CORBIS. REPRODUCED BY PERMISSION.

BIBLIOGRAPHY

Epstein, Eleni Sakes. "Trigère." In *American Fashion: The Life and Lines of Adrian, Mainbocher, McCardell, Norell, and Trigère.* Edited by Sarah Tomerlin Lee. New York: Quadrangle/New York Times Book Company, 1975.

Milbank, Caroline Rennolds. *New York Fashion: The Evolution of American Style.* New York: Harry N. Abrams, Inc., 1989.

Nemy, Enid. "Pauline Trigère, 93, Exemplar of American Style, Dies." *New York Times* (15 February 2002): C14.

Jean L. Druesedow

TRIMMINGS A band of colorful ribbon, a silken tassel, a row of buttons, a flash of sequins—trimmings can add texture, color, drama, and visual interest to clothing and accessories.

Prior to the Industrial Revolution, garment trimmings were generally available only to the elite, who flaunted costly dress accents such as gemstones, fine lace, or egret plumes to signify their high social status. In the early 2000s, trimmings of all kinds are manufactured worldwide, from South America to Southeast Asia, and

LIBERACE: TRIMMED TO THE NINES

For his final performance at Radio City Music Hall in 1986, the famed showman Liberace (1919–1987) appeared in a series of elaborate ensembles completely encrusted with pearls, sequins, bugle beads, rhinestones, and ostrich feathers.

are available to all. They constitute a substantial portion of the total international fabric industry's sales, and are used in quantity by makers of evening wear, bridal wear, childrenswear, youth fashions, uniforms, costumes, and millinery.

It's All in the Details

Fabric trimmings such as lace, braid, cord, piping, embroidery trim, and fringe are most frequently used literally to "trim" a garment by attaching them along the edge of the sleeves, hem, collar, or bodice. Trimmings in this category can be made from natural fibers such as cotton, linen, silk, wool, rayon, or raffia, as well as from polyester, nylon, and other manufactured fibers.

Lace is a delicate openwork fabric made of yarn or thread in a weblike pattern. In the sixteenth and seventeenth centuries, the great demand for handmade linen and silk lace for apparel as well as domestic and church use gave rise to major lace-making centers in Antwerp, Brussels, Chantilly, Valenciennes, Venice, and elsewhere. A machine for making lace came into wide use by the 1840s, and the production of most lace today is done by machine, with modern varieties like eyelet lace and stretch lace available.

Braid, cord, and piping can be made from solid colored or metallic thread, or from groups of different-colored threads braided or twined together. They are a salient trimming on military, parade, and police uniforms, especially for dress occasions. Embroidery trim (as distinguished from embroidery done directly on a garment) is sold in bands of machine-embroidered floral or geometric motifs, popular for childrenswear. Another form of embroidery trim is a ribbon-banded style called a "jacquard," a notable detail on Tyrolean clothing. Fringe, which is also sold in bands, is a favorite trim on cowboy-style Western wear and garments affecting a rustic look.

Glitter and Glamour

Spangles, sequins, and rhinestones are often used to trim evening wear and theatrical or holiday costumes. Spangles and sequins—factory-made, small, shiny metal or plastic disks (or other shapes)—can be sewn over the en-

tire surface of a garment, or added to limited areas to add sparkle and color. The show-stopping gowns by designer Bob Mackie (1940–), who has been called the "sultan of sequins," stand out for their exuberant surface application of sequins, rhinestones, and other glittering elements.

The imitation gemstones called rhinestones are made of glass, paste, gem quartz, or crystal that has been cut and polished to provide high reflectiveness. Rhinestones can be attached to a garment by sewing or ironing on individual stones, or stitching on pre-made bands or patches. The Austrian company Swarovski is especially noted for its lustrous, faceted lead-crystal rhinestones in bold colors.

The Milliner's Art

Ribbons and bows are perhaps the most common hat trimmings, though they can be used to trim clothing as well. Contemporary ribbon styles are available in grosgrain, satin, silk, velvet, beaded, wire-edged, floral, pleated, polka dots, stripes, and more.

Individual items that lend themselves to hat trimming include feathers, artificial flowers, pom-poms, and tassels. In nineteenth- and early twentieth-century England and America, a cottage industry of hat trimmers kept workers busy, since no self-respecting woman would appear in public without an artfully trimmed hat. Indeed, some hat styles would not be complete without their particular trim: the pom-pom on the tam-o'-shanter, or the tassel on the fez, for example.

The decorative use of bird feathers was practiced in Pre-Columbian America and Polynesia, as seen in elaborate feather work headdresses and capes from Mexico, Hawaii, and New Zealand. In eighteenth-century Europe, tall plumed headdresses called "aigrettes" enjoyed a vogue among society women. In the twenty-first century, pheasant, turkey, rooster, and ostrich feathers are often used in millinery design, though concerns about the exploitation of rare birds have curbed the resale of imported feathers.

Artificial flowers have been a favorite trimming for millinery and haute couture since the nineteenth century. To create fake flowers, manufacturers treat silk, organza, cotton, chiffon, or velvet with a stiffening agent, dry the fabric, die-cut the petals and leaves in a press, and then paint or dye them for final assembly. Of note are the exquisitely lifelike blossoms made for four generations by Guillet of Paris, whose high-end clients include Lanvin, Emanuel Ungaro, and Christian Lacroix.

Buttons and Beads

Since antiquity, buttons have been made from a variety of materials including bone, metal, stone, wood, and shell. Besides being utilitarian fasteners, buttons can be sewn to a garment as a pure surface ornament. At the annual Pearly Kings and Queens harvest festival in London, buttons-as-trimmings take the spotlight as "royal" revelers sport elaborate costumes covered from head to toe with mother-of-pearl buttons.

Beads of clay, stone, and glass have a long history, used as a clothing or hair decoration in diverse cultures for centuries, from the Copts in Egypt, to the Benin and Yoruba tribes in Africa, to the Plains Indians of North America. Hand-beading in the contemporary garment industry is often the domain of couture houses, where lavish beaded creations by designers such as John Galliano (1960–) require long hours of careful stitching. Beading is also a major element in bridal wear, especially in the use of white seed pearls to decorate wedding gowns and headpieces. Affordable mass-produced forms of beaded trim include bands, patches, and fringe.

See also **Beads; Braiding; Buttons; Feathers; Knotting; Lace; Ribbon; Spangles.**

BIBLIOGRAPHY

Ashelford, Jane. *The Art of Dress: Clothes and Society, 1500–1914.* New York: Harry N. Abrams, 1996.

Fleming, John, and Hugh Honour. *The Penguin Dictionary of Decorative Arts.* London: Viking, 1989.

Geoffrey-Schneiter, Berenice. *Ethnic Style: History and Fashion.* Paris: Assouline, 2001.

Martin, Richard, ed. *Contemporary Fashion.* New York: St. James Press, 1995.

Specter, Michael. "The Fantasist: How John Galliano Changed Fashion." *The New Yorker* 22 September 2003.

Thrush, Elizabeth. "Made in Paris: Flower Child." *France Magazine* Fall 2003.

Kathleen Paton

TROUSERS Bifurcated lower-body garments made from textiles, fabric, or leather have existed since ancient times, and trousers rank among the most fundamental pieces of clothing. Ankle to calf-length trousers, wide or narrow, with seamed or wrapped legs were part of the costume of the ancient Chinese, Mongols, Sythians, Phrygians, and Persians. The Sarmatians, the Dakerians, and the Lydians presumably adopted them, after 700 B.C.E., from the Persians. Trouser-clad equestrians seem to have played an important role in their diffusion; even attempts at accurate fitting can be traced back to riding. Depictions of the stocking-like leg coverings, featuring stripes, dots, checks, or zigzag lines, of Asia Minor's soldiers and male and female riders, can be found on ancient Grecian ceramics. The Celts, Germanic peoples, and the Sarmatians were the first to wear the *truss*, a sort of linen undergarment, in the late Bronze and Iron Ages. Thigh-high and ankle-length trousers, sometimes luxuriously woven and artistically sewn out of fabric and leather, are documented as being worn by men and occasionally women of northern tribes.

The Greeks and Romans of the Classical period thought of trousers as the "garb of the Barbarians," from

Models display gray trouser suits. The trouser suit has remained the standard outfit of business for men and, by the early twenty-first century, was widely accepted attire for women in business as well. AP/WIDE WORLD PHOTOS. REPRODUCED BY PERMISSION.

whom they vehemently strove to distinguish themselves. When, in the second and third centuries C.E., Roman soldiers, and later, common people, began to adopt trousers for practical purposes, it was forbidden to wear them on pain of punishment in Rome. However, after the fall of the Western Roman Empire (fifth century C.E.), Roman dress no longer set the standards for all of Europe. *Beinlinge* (separate, unattached coverings for each leg) with *trusses* (a kind of short undergarment) became common throughout Europe. In the early and high Middle Ages, leg coverings—woolen, fastened to the belt of the *truss*, under long clothes or short tunics—served as protection from cold and as functional clothing. Women as well wore leg coverings in cold weather or when traveling.

After 1350, the demand for male leg coverings altered dramatically: as a result of the change in knights' armor from chain mail to plate armor; leg coverings had to fit the contours of the body more closely. The leggings became a second skin and—in response to the style of extremely short men's doublets—were made into a sin-

Movie stars model trousers, 1933. Actresses Marlene Dietrich (at left) and Bebe Daniels broke the fashion rule that women should not wear trousers. Trousers were not widely accepted as conventional women's wear until the 1970s. © Bettmann/Corbis. Reproduced by permission.

gle garment by attaching wedge-shaped inserts or fly flaps. The stocking-like hose of the fifteenth century, with its attached feet and heraldic patterns, may be regarded as the first veritable men's trouser fashion. It is, moreover, the first fashion where men and women went their separate ways, men adopting short tunics and hose, and women keeping to their long skirts.

This conspicuous marking of gender, through skirt and trousers respectively, continued in Western culture until quite recently. The identification of man and trousers became universal to such a degree, that trousers, in images and figures of speech, have evolved into symbols for man and manly strength. (See for example numerous prints and caricatures on the theme of the "battle of the trousers.") From the fifteenth century until the late nineteenth century, women very rarely donned men's trousers.

The stylish man's bifurcated garment changed its appearance countless times. At first, Italian sheath hose, with their limited freedom of movement, were widened with a slit; in 1500 the garment was separated into knee breeches, laced at the waist, with stockings attached to the breeches. From these developed, in the early sixteenth century, extremely broad, heavily slashed wide breeches lined with colorful fabrics and worn by the mercenary soldier. Despite all regulations (sumptuary laws), and public mockery (pamphlets, satirical drawings), extra wide, heavily slashed and flashily decorated breeches with fantastically padded codpieces remained the fashion during the sixteenth century. In Spain, after 1550, fashionable men began to overstuff their wide breeches, which in turn shortened them greatly, creating two balloon-like legs. Spanish trousers, so-called "military bass-drum pants," were worn in national variants throughout Europe, without codpieces after 1600. During the Thirty Years War (1616–1648), knee-length, extremely wide pantaloons, with decorative side buttons and ribbons, were introduced by the French; these developed, after peace was declared, into the skirtlike, heavily decorated Rheingrave, or petticoat, pantaloons (1655–1680). This extreme form of the 1670s was eventually replaced by the simple *culotte*, worn as part of Louis XIV's court attire. The *culotte* was the obligatory part of men's suits until the French Revolution. During the Revolution the *culotte* or breeches were replaced by the long pantaloons or trousers of working-class men.

Simple knee breeches, fastened at first under the knee with ribbons and then later with buckles or buttons, were worn by most upper-class men in the eighteenth century until they began to be replaced during the French Revolution by the long work pants of working-class revolutionaries (the *sans culottes*—"without breeches," so-called because they wore trousers instead). The trousers of the first half of the nineteenth century had varying styles; some were extremely tight, others were broadly pleated trousers (Russian or Cossack pants), and sharply flared, below-the-knee *matelot* trousers. In the 1830s, trousers were long, close fitting, and equipped with straps that fit under the soles of the feet. In the 1850s, pants legs were looser, and the old trouser fly was replaced by a concealed, buttoned middle slit. The former relatively colorful palette grew increasingly sober from the 1860s on, as dark colors and plain materials became usual in everyday and evening clothing. At the beginning of the twentieth century, pleats and cuffs completed the development of the daytime and evening trouser. At the same time, men's sports and leisure clothing became a field for experimentation with the development of knickerbockers, jeans, Bermuda shorts, chinos, and other styles.

The 1880s represent the first considerable public presence for women's trousers. In the 1840s a minority of women, such as Amelia Bloomer, had demanded a "right to trousers" which had been briskly denied. By the 1880s, however, women bicycle riders in pantaloons, bloomers, or trouser-skirts had become visible in many cities in Europe and North America. By the early twentieth century, trousers for women existed for various leisure activities. The couturier Paul Poiret, for example, launched trousers as fashionable dress for women and caused a great scandal. After World War I, however, when people got used to women in trousers, society accepted fashionable pants as beach-wear or exclusive evening suits.

And yet trousers for women still instigated scandals. Marlene Dietrich, for example, caused an uproar by wearing trousers in Hollywood and Europe. It was only in the 1970s that trousers finally won a secure place in the spectrum of women's clothing. Since then, trousers have become acceptable as women's business, recreation, and evening clothing. In cultures outside Europe, one may trace entirely different fashion traditions. Thus in cold climates, such as Siberia, the indigenous inhabitants developed an "arctic" garment, made of a combination long-sleeved jacket and long trousers of leather or fur, which is virtually identical for both men and women. The "tropical" clothing type, featuring wraparound skirts, also recognizes few gender differences, although sarongs and other wrapped garments tend to be tied differently for men and women. In the traditional dress of many Asian peoples, trousers are often seen on women and dresses are seen on men. Arab, Persian, Syrian, and Turkish women wear traditional leg-coverings, as do Cossaks, and Tatars. In Scotland, on the other hand, the kilt is an emphatically masculine garment.

In the context of spreading globalization, long trousers are gradually coming to replace the traditional masculine dress of cultures outside of the European context. The business suit, a standard in European and American fashion since the nineteenth century, is presently becoming a worldwide norm, and women in most of the world can wear trousers without being accused of being masculine.

BIBLIOGRAPHY

Benaim, Laurence. *Pants, Trousers: A Walking History.* Paris: Vilo Publishing, 2001,

Martin, Richard, and Harold Koda, eds. *Jocks and Nerds: Men's Style in the Twentieth Century.* New York: Rizzoli, 1989.

Polhemus, Ted. *Street Style From Sidewalk to Catwalk.* London: Thames and Hudson, Inc., 1994.

Wolter, Gundula. *Die Verpackung des männlichen Geschlechts. Eine illustrierte Kulturgeschichte der Hose.* Marburg: Jonas Verlag, 1991. A history of men's trousers.

——. *Hosen, weiblich. Kulturgeschichte der Frauenhose.* Marburg: Jonas Verlag, 1994. A cultural history of women's trousers.

Gundula Wolter

T-SHIRT From its origins as men's underwear to its complex role in modern fashion, the T-shirt is today one of the most universally worn items of clothing. Cheap, hygienic, and comfortable, the T-shirt has become an essential basic wardrobe item worn by people of all social classes and ages. Technically, the T-shirt evolved and proliferated at an astonishing rate, aided by the increased availability of American cotton and the invention of the circular knitting machine in the mid-nineteenth century. Its current shape and style developed during the 1930s and it became universally worn as an outer-garment after World War II. In 2004 over two billion were sold worldwide. Contemporary versions range from inexpensive multi-packaged units to haute couture editions to high-tech fiber versions used in sports and health industries.

Shirts of T-shaped construction were worn as early as the medieval times to protect the body from chafing by heavy, metal armor. Civilians adopted the shirt as a protective and hygienic barrier between the body and costly garments. Made of cotton or linen, the shirt was more easily washable than silk or woolen outer garments with complex ornamentation. These shirts were made with long tails that wrapped around the body serving as underpants. The shirt was still always worn with a waistcoat or vest and jacket over the shirt. Wearing a clean, laundered shirt showed off a gentleman's wealth and gentility. Shirts changed very little in shape from their introduction in medieval times through the mid-nineteenth century. They were loose fitting, made of a woven fabric, and constructed with rectangular pieces that formed a T shape.

In the late nineteenth century when health-oriented concerns became prevalent, doctors and physicians advised wearing warm undershirts to protect from colds and rheumatism. Dr. Jaeger lauded the healthful benefits of wearing knitted underwear made of wool and manufactured his own line of knit undershirts. The circular knitting machine patented in 1863 made it possible to mass-produce knit jersey undershirts and hosiery for wide distribution. This technology created a greater range of types and refinement in undergarments. Its closer fit looked more like the modern T-shirt than earlier loose-fitting, woven shirts.

Sailors in the nineteenth century wore white flannel undershirts under their woolen pullovers. These shirts were worn alone on deck for work that required freedom of movement. The white cotton knit T-shirt was adopted as official underwear for the U.S. Navy in 1913. Fast drying, quick, and easy to put on, sailors responded positively to the new garment. The U.S. Army adopted it in 1942, in its classic form. Nicknamed skivvies, each soldier's name was stenciled on. In 1944 the army colored the shirt khaki to camouflage with the extreme tropical environment of the South Pacific. The vast media coverage of World War II popularized the T-shirt as a symbol of victorious, modern America and glorified it as a masculine, military icon. Returning soldiers retained the style after the war because of its comfort, practicality, and image. A Sears, Roebuck and Co. catalog slogan in the 1940s took advantage of the heroic image that had developed during the war, "You needn't be a soldier to have your own personal T-shirt." Since that time it has been used in every war and has been appropriated by paramilitary factions. Like the trench coat it has also become an integral part of civilian dress from street fashion to haute couture.

Fruit of the Loom was the manufacturer who began marketing T-shirts on a large scale in the 1910s, first supplying the U.S. Navy and then universities with white T-shirts. The company manages its own cotton fields and yarn production. Each shirt undergoes 60 inspections before it is packaged. From the rebels of the 1950s to preppies who paired them with pearl necklaces in the 1980s, the company remained a number one producer of T-shirts through the 1990s and is still a competitive brand. The P. H. Hanes Knitting Company, founded in 1901, introduced a new style of men's two-piece underwear. They have been a major supplier of T-shirts to the military and to the Olympics in addition to vast civilian distribution.

An increase in sports and leisure activities gave rise to new forms of clothing in the latter part of the nineteenth century. Close-fitting knitted woolen swimsuits made in the tank-shaped style of undershirts accustomed the eye to seeing more skin and one's body shape in a public place. By the 1930s T-shirts were standard sporting wear at colleges and universities. The earliest shirts printed with school logos served as uniforms for school sport teams. These sport uniforms encouraged a new casualness in dress among the middle classes that was important to the T-shirt's general acceptance. The cotton T-shirt has remained a mainstay of sports activities because it is absorbent, quick-drying, and allows free range of movement. The T-shirts' role in sports has moved beyond team identification and practical function; it is crucial to the marketing, promotion, and profitability of the sports industry.

In post–World War II years, the T-shirt was primarily worn for athletics, informally at home, or by blue-collar workers for physical labor. Marlon Brando's portrayal of Stanley Kowalski in *A Streetcar Named Desire* (1951), wearing a visibly sweaty T-shirt clinging to his musculature, captured an erotic power of the shirt. The strong associations of masculinity developed earlier in patriotic form in military images, now had an amplified sexual expression. The silver-screen images of Marlon Brando in *The Wild Ones* (1953) and James Dean in *Rebel Without a Cause* (1955) embodied the spirit of American youth in the 1950s. The impact of these movies was profoundly influential on society in solidifying a language and image of rebellion. Through these movies the white T-shirt, blue jeans, and black leather motorcycle jacket became the uniform of nonconformists searching for meaning in conservative postwar consumerist society. Other important musicals, films, and television programs from *West Side Story* (1961) to *Happy Days* (1974) to *American Graffiti* (1973) repeated and confirmed the rebellious meanings. Young people recognized this style as a new American fashion. Administrators prohibited wearing the T-shirt to school in an era when most people still wore shirts with collars. Not only was it rejected because of its informality, but the knit quality of the T-shirt is more clinging than a shirt or blouse. The Underwear Institute declared in 1961 that the T-shirt had become a dual-purpose garment that was acceptable as both outerwear and underwear. In the early 1960s, a female image was promoted in the pivotal French film, *Breathless* (1960). Jean Seberg was featured as a young American selling the *Herald Tribune*, wearing a white T-shirt silkscreened with the newspaper logo that showed off her curvaceous figure and at the same time embodied a new, youthful androgynous style of seduction and feminine power. This film did much to introduce the style into female fashion. The erotic aspect of the T-shirt has been exploited in wet T-shirt contests that not only make use of the clinging quality of the fabric, but also its semi-transparency when wet.

Since the late 1960s and 1970s, the T-shirt has evolved and proliferated at a rapid rate. Decorative techniques used to create expressive statements on T-shirts became popular from the 1960s onward. Graphic designs, novelty patterns, and written words lionize rock 'n' roll bands, promote products and places, and express political and community-minded causes. Rapidly made and inexpensive, imprinted T-shirts can respond quickly to popular and political events. The first political use was in 1948 when the Republican candidate Thomas Dewey distributed T-shirts that read "Dew it with Dewey." The graphics for one of the most printed and widely copied designs, "I Love New York," was created in 1976 by graphic artist Milton Glaser.

Technological advancements in inks used for silkscreen printing in the early 1960s made this ancient technique easy, inexpensive, and fast. Underground artists who were decorating surfboards and skateboards on a cottage-industry level were some of the first to put designs on T-shirts. The shirts were an inexpensive canvas for expression. The hot iron transfer technique introduced in 1963 was even easier and faster to use. The fast-heat pressure-press widely available in the 1970s gave consumers the ability to choose the color of the shirt and its image or wording, and have it custom prepared in the store within minutes. In a 1976 *Time* magazine article, a Gimbels department store executive claimed that the Manhattan store sold over 1,000 imprinted shirts a week. Current digital processes allow for the printing of complex images with a professional appearance. Flocking, bubble coating, and embroidery are all used to create textured designs. With these two techniques the design area is coated with glue and then dusted with fibers that are attracted by electrostatic means that affix them perpendicularly to the surface of the fabric leaving a velvety surface. Embroidered designs, whether done mechanically or manually, can be enhanced with beads, sequins, feathers, and other materials.

Community-minded causes were print designs that were most popular in the 1960s and 1970s. Images and messages about the Vietnam War, Civil Rights, peace and love, and feminist movements were prevalent. "Make Love Not War" and "Save the Whales" were two of the most popular messages. British designer Katherine Hamnett created a revival in T-shirts bearing political written messages in 1984 when she wore an oversized T-shirt bearing the message "98% of people don't want Pershings" in a public meeting with British Prime Minister Margaret Thatcher at the height of the Falklands War.

More than a passing fad, imprinted T-shirts have become an integral part of brand marketing, whether distributed as promotional gifts or to generate revenue. In 1939, Metro-Goldwyn-Mayer used the T-shirt to promote one of the first color movies made in Hollywood, *The Wizard of Oz*. Budweiser started stamping its logo on shirts in 1965 but it was the following decade that the idea was spread to all types of brands, from Bic to Xerox. In the case of the Hard Rock Café, collecting logoed T-shirts from its locations around the world has become a significant portion of the draw to the restaurant.

In 1983 the *New Yorker* reported that the industry sold 32 million dozen items in 1982. Although there are fads for different styles and colors, the imprinted T-shirt is unique in that men, women, and children of all ages, shapes, and social standings universally wear it.

Pop artists Andy Warhol, Keith Haring, and Jenny Holzer pioneered the use of the T-shirt as a work of art. In the 1980s contemporary fashion's inclusion in museum exhibitions considered the many designer versions. Also in the 1980s, with the explosion of marketing of museums, masterworks of art were reproduced on T-shirts and sold in their gift stores.

High fashion adopted the T-shirt as early as 1948. A model appeared on the cover of *Life* magazine and ran a story that featured T-shirts by American designers Claire McCardell, Ceil Chapman, and Valentina. The article demonstrated how the sports shirt was now a street and evening style. The 1960s saw it go from street fashion to silk haute couture versions in the collections of such designers as Pierre Balmain and Christian Dior. From Woodstock to Yves Saint Laurent Rive Gauche to Vivienne Westwood, by the 1970s the T-shirt was part of all sectors of dress. Logoed shirts by Lacoste and Polo Ralph Lauren of the 1980s and 1990s were popular indicators of status. The black T-shirt became the uniform of the trendy and hip in the 1980s. Bruce Weber's photos of models wearing Calvin Klein's T-shirts became an icon of 1990s sexuality and minimalism. Designers such as Donna Karan, Giorgio Armani, Tom Ford, Jean Paul Gaultier, and Helmet Lang have worn the T-shirt as their own identifying uniform. Designer shirts are usually made from a high-quality cotton, have an elegant neckline, and well-cut and sewn sleeves. Japanese designers Issey Miyake and Yohji Yammamoto have led new ways of thinking about the T-shirt in their deconstructionist work through cutting, slashing, and knotting. Miyake's vision has ranged from his Janice Joplin and Jimi Hendrix T-shirt of the 1970s to his piece of cloth shirts by the yard of 1999. The T-shirt has been pivotal to the revolution in lifestyles and attitudes that formed the second half of the twentieth century and its impact on fashion continues.

See also **Politics and Fashion; Sportswear; Underwear.**

BIBLIOGRAPHY

Bayer, Ann. "What's the Message on Your T-Shirt?" *Seventeen* (April 1981): 186–187.

———. "1951 T-Shirt." *Life* (16 July 1951): 73–76.

———. "T-Shirts: Sports Standby is Now a Street and Evening Style." *Life* (7 June 1948): 103–106.

———. "Imprinted Sportswear." *New Yorker* (11 April 1983): 33.

Brunel, Charlotte. *The T-Shirt Book.* New York: Assouline, 2002.

Harris, Alice. *The White T.* New York: HarperCollins, 1996.

———. "The T-Shirt: A Startling Evolution." *Time* (1 March 1976): 48–50.

Russell, Mary. "The Top on Top." *Vogue* (March 1983): 316–317.

Dennita Sewell

TURBAN The turban is essentially a headgear that uses fabric of varying width and length, which is twisted and turned around the head. The wrapped folds derived produce a "fitted effect" akin to a stitched or an engineered head covering. Though length, style, color, and fabric may vary as geographical locations change, the basic concept and construction of the turban remains unaltered. This is probably the widest and most flexible definition of this garment considering the many forms in which it exists.

Little is conclusively known of the origins of the turban. The earliest evidence of a turban-like garment is from Mesopotamia in a royal sculpture dating from 2350 B.C.E. Thus, it is known that the turban was in use before the advent of Islam and Christianity, therefore the origin of the turban cannot be ascribed to religious reasons alone. It is also mentioned in the Old Testament and Vedic literature from India. Sculpture from Central India (100 B.C.E.) provides detailed visual evidence of the use of turbans. These headdresses were originally worn by royalty and spiritual leaders and used to commute power, often being adorned with jewels and accessories to display wealth and grandeur.

In some form or another, the turban has been important in many cultures and religions. It is still in use in rural areas in Persia, the Middle East, Turkey, parts of Africa, and the Indian subcontinent where wrapped, as opposed to stitched headgear, continues to be preferred. Historically, draped clothing has always had a special significance in eastern culture. Watson notes that "certain strict Hindus still do not wear cut or stitched cloth as for them a garment composed of several pieces sewn together is an abomination and defilement" (p.11). Though turbans are worn primarily by men, literary evidence reveals that they were used by women on rare occasions in the past. "In Vedic literature Indrani, wife of Indra, wears a headdress known as usnisa" (Ghuyre, p. 68). Some of the earliest terms for the turban in English are *turbant, tolibanl,* and *turband.* These represent the

French adaptation of the Turkish *tulbend*, a vulgarism for the term *dulbend* from Persia, *didband*, a scarf or sash wound around the neck.

In India this headdress is known by many different names locally. *Potia, usnisa, pag, pagri, safa,* and *veshtani* are some of the names used for the turban. The Sikhs, a community that dictates its followers to wear the turban, call it *dastaar*, while the Muslim religious leaders refer to it as the *kalansuwa*. In the earliest times, cotton was the fabric most commonly used as turban material. This is because it was affordable and abundant, apart from being the most comfortable fabric to use in tropical or temperate climates where it was most worn. Fabrics such as silk and satin saw limited usage among the more affluent and powerful class. Though there are innumerable variations in the turban, they can easily be divided into two broad types—long turbans and square turban pieces. The long piece is seven to ten meters long with the width varying from twenty-five to one hundred centimeters. The square pieces could vary in size between one to three meters per side, with one to one-and-a-half meters constituting the most useful size. There are an amazingly wide variety of turbans across different cultures and religions. Distinctions are made on the basis of size, shape, material, color, ornamentation, and method of wrapping. In the Muslim world, religious elders often wear a turban wrapped around a cap known in Arabic as a *kalansuwa*. The shape of these caps can be spherical or conical and this produces variations in the turban shape. In Iran, leaders wear black or white turbans wrapped in the flat, circular style. In the Indian state of Rajasthan the style of turban may vary even within the distance of a few miles. The Rajput turbans are remarkably different from the kind worn in any other region in India. There are specialists called *pagribands* whose skill is in the art of tying the turban and were employed by the erstwhile royalty for their services. Some famous styles from Rajasthan are the *Jaipur pagri* and the *Gaj Shahi* turban, the fabric of which is dyed in five distinctive colors and was developed by Maharaja Gaj Singh II from the Jodhpur royal family.

The turban as a headdress is not merely a fashion statement or cultural paraphernalia; it has symbolic meaning beyond the obvious. It serves to identify the wearer as a member of a particular group, tribe, or community, and serves as an introduction to their cultural, religious, political, and social orientations. Sikh men commonly wear a peaked turban, that serves partly as a covering for their hair, which is never cut out of respect for God's creation. The turban has significant associations with the concepts of respect and honor. A man's turban is supposed to signify his honor and the honor of his people. The exchange of turbans is considered a sign of everlasting friendship, while presenting someone with a turban is considered a great token of esteem. An exchange of turbans also signifies a long relationship and forges relationships between families. Thus, the turban is an intrinsic part of all ceremonies from birth until death.

Conversely, it is considered a grave insult to step over or pick up another man's turban. It is linked intrinsically to the "ego" of a person. To remove a turban and lay it at another's feet symbolizes submission and an expression of humbleness. The turban at a glance conveys the social and economic status of the wearer, the season, festival, community, and the region. It is also distinctive by the style of wrapping—each fold telling its own story. The tightness of the drape of the headgear, the lengths of the hanging end, the types of bands which are created on the surface, all say something about its wearer.

The colors of turbans vary in different cultures and are imbued with complex connotations, emotional context, and rich association. They are used to convey mood, religious values, customs, and ceremonial occasions. In India, ocher is the color of the saint, saffron denotes chivalry, and prosperity. White turbans, considered by some Muslims to be the holiest color, are used for mourning and by older men, whereas dark blue is reserved for a condolence visit. Among Sikhs of north India, blue and white cotton turbans are essentially religious in nature. In the Middle East, green turbans, thought to be the color of paradise, are worn by men who claim descent from the prophet Muhammad. Shape and size of the turban are determined by many conditions. Chief among these are the climate, status, and occupation of a person. Turbans are big and loose without hanging tails in the hot desert and thus serve a protective function. Merchants involved in more sedentary activities would wear ornamental turbans with long hanging tails.

The turban was introduced into fashionable European dress in the early fifteenth century and its usage continued until the sixteenth century. It has been revived many times in women's fashion at intervals since the sixteenth century. The turban has acquired a more contemporary form in the twenty-first century. Though it continues to exist in various parts of the world in its more traditional form, of late various fashion designers and couturiers have adapted the turban to give it a more fashionable and chic look, making it a popular fashion accessory. Even though in its more contemporary form the turban may not retain the same symbolism that is attached to its more traditional form, it nevertheless reinforces the importance of this garment.

See also **Headdress.**

BIBLIOGRAPHY

Bhandari, Vandana. *Women's Costume in Rajasthan.* Ph.D. diss., Delhi University, 1995.

———. "Mystical folds: The Turban in India." *Fashion and Beyond* (October 2001): 22–25.

Boucher, Francois. *A History of Costume in the West.* London: Thames and Hudson, Inc., 1987.

Ghurye, Govind Sadashiv. *Indian Costumes.* Bombay: Popular Book Depot, 1951.

Mathur, U. B. *Folkways in Rajasthan.* Jaipur: The Folklorists, 1986.

Nagar, Mahender Singh. *Rajasthan ki pag pagriyan*. Jodhpur: Mehranarh Museum Trust, 1994.

Singh, C. et al. *The Costumes of Royal India*. New Delhi: Festival of India in Japan, 1988.

Watson, John Forbes. *The Textile Manufacturers and the Costumes of the People of India*. Varanasi, India: Indological Book House, 1982. Originally published in London in 1866.

Yarwood, Doreen. *The Encyclopaedia of World Costume*. London: B. T. Batsford, Ltd., 1988.

Vandana Bhandari

TUXEDO Throughout the twentieth century, the tuxedo was emblematic of occasions when men were requested to dress formally after dark, whether for drinks, dinner, or some other gathering. The garment developed at a time in the late nineteenth century when men in the upper levels of society began to demand that their clothes be cut to accommodate the increasingly casual nature of leisure time. As with many fashion innovations, credit for the new style of jacket intended to be worn by men in the evening was claimed by many individuals. In fact the tuxedo jacket arose from sartorial innovations in both America and England. It succeeded in ushering in a new level of formality, intermediate between full white-tie formal wear and the lounge suit, that is only now showing signs of fading from usage.

The term tuxedo derives from Tuxedo Park, a residential club colony of rustic mansions in the outer suburbs of New York, founded in 1886 by the wealthy Lorillard family and some of their friends. The Tuxedo Club's annual Autumn Ball was an important event in the New York social calendar; the dress code for the ball would normally have been white-tie and tails. However, in 1885 James Brown Potter, a charter member of the Tuxedo Club and friend of the Lorillard family, had been introduced to the idea of the dinner jacket by the Prince of Wales, who was later to become Edward VII. The Prince had recently created a new evening jacket to be worn at his country estate at Sandringham; it was a black jacket without tails, inspired by the smoking jackets that men would wear when retiring to the smoking room after a meal. A year later, Pierre Lorillard and his son Griswold had their tailor design similar dinner jackets with satin lapels, with a cut similar to the equestrian jackets worn for fox hunting. These "Tuxedo jackets" soon caught on as the customary attire for semiformal evening events in New York society.

In a separate development, the French responded to the need for a lighter semiformal jacket for warm Mediterranean evenings by creating the Monte Carlo. Although all of these developments show the influence of sporting, hunting, and leisure dress as a means of modernizing a garment by the simplification of its attributes and by the easing of bodily restriction in its cut and construction, it is from the American sense of casualness in formality that the tuxedo derives most of its meaning.

As an alternative to the black tailcoat, the tuxedo was differentiated from the lounge jacket through a fairly strict definition of what constituted it and what it could be worn with. Principally in black, the jacket could bear peak lapels or a shawl collar faced in either silk or grosgrain, and was matched to a pair of trousers with a plain silk stripe running down the side of each leg, without turned-up cuffs. The obligatory furnishings of a black bow tie and cummerbund (when worn without a waistcoat) did not become fully established until the 1920s. At that time, too, the Duke of Windsor refined the narcissistic possibility of the tuxedo by having a dinner jacket made in midnight blue. Ever conscious of his own appearance, the Duke had noted that under artificial light, midnight blue seemed blacker than black. Better still, it also registered darker in photographic terms on newsprint giving the garment the weight of royal authority executed as a self-conscious exercise in style.

The co-option of the tuxedo by women from the late 1960s on indicates a performative sense of playfulness, transgressing the costume's once rigid gender implications. Yves Saint Laurent's *le smoking* (named after the French term for the tuxedo) was launched in spring 1967 as the singular concept for his entire couture collection. Saint Laurent's technique was to soften the tailoring while retaining the angularity of the cut which, when accessorized with stiletto heels and dramatic makeup, formed a contradictory image of femininity without compromise. This proposition is most clearly articulated in a photograph by Helmut Newton where a woman, unaccompanied in a street at night, pauses to light a cigarette. As a statement of style it is unsurpassed. All designers who have followed on from this deviation, including Ralph Lauren's form-following tuxedo suits, Giorgio Armani's textured interpretations, and Viktor and Rolf's historical pastiches, underline the singular importance of this sartorial appropriation in women's dress as expressive of modernity.

The modulations in the details of the tuxedo across the postwar period are reflected in the sartorial taste of the literary and filmic figure James Bond. More than any other figurehead, Bond has been the model that most men have looked to when considering a style of tuxedo when occasion demands. Sean Connery's depiction of Bond in early films such as *Dr. No* (1962) and *Diamonds Are Forever* (1971) crystallized an early 1960s sensibility of a black "tux" with lean lapels, satin cuffbacks, covered buttons, and a folded white handkerchief in the top pocket. The clipped and minimal detailing was suggestive of both acumen and agility in a louche world to which many men aspired. The contradiction is that Bond is better known in the public imagination for the white rather than the black tuxedo jacket, necessitated by the range of tropical settings and number of casinos that the character frequented.

The other institution that upholds the suitability of the tuxedo for special-occasion dress is the Oscar ceremony.

As a necessary foil to the elaborate costumes worn by the invited actresses, the tuxedo lends a certain formal gravity to support the very unstable nature of dress designs that appear on the red carpet on a yearly basis. In the vogue for women to reveal the actuality of their bodies in the dresses they wear, the tuxedo becomes the monochromatic means for men to encase the actuality of their own bodies in a formal armor that reveals very little of the true self.

Originating as a relaxed alternative to formal wear, the tuxedo has become emblematic of celebration and special occasions and a potent sartorial symbol of ceremony. When worn well, it conjures up a ritualistic sense of propriety and the debonair expression of a lost era.

See also **Formal Wear, Men's.**

BIBLIOGRAPHY
Curtis, Bryan, and John Bridges. *A Gentleman Gets Dressed Up: Knowing What to Wear, How to Wear It, and When to Wear It.* New York: Rutledge Hill Press, 2003.

Flusser, Alan. *Dressing the Man: Mastering the Art of Permanent Fashion.* New York: HarperCollins, 2002.

Hollander, Anne. *Sex and Suits: The Evolution of Modern Dress.* Tokyo and New York: Kodansha International, 1995.

Internet Resource

"The History of the Tuxedo." Village of Tuxedo Park official website. Available from <http://www.votuxpk.com>.

Alistair O'Neill

TWEED Tweed, made from wool and wool mixtures, comes in a phenomenal range of color and weave effects. Originally tweed was made only in the twill weave or variations of that structure. It is debatable whether the name tweed originated from a misreading of an order for *tweel* (Scottish for twill), or whether the cloth is named after the Tweed river in the Borders region of Scotland. However, it is certain that tweed originated in the Scottish woolen industry of the early nineteenth century, where locally crafted woolens were transformed into fashion textiles woven in a factory and sold to national and international markets. This shift of the late 1820s was partly precipitated by the adoption of the black-and-white shepherd's check as a fashionable cloth for men's trousers in the late 1820s.

Trade journals of the period, such as *Textile Manufacturer*, indicate the reputation of Scotch tweed for high aesthetic appeal and quality of manufacture. Interestingly for a branch of the nineteenth-century textile industry renowned for the production of constant novelty and variety in design, the bulk of their cloth was designed for menswear. The origins of the Scottish tweed industry and its success from the 1830s were largely driven by the consumption of cloth for sporting and leisure wear. However, the range of cloths produced including Saxonies,

"The products of Scottish woolen looms after 1830 were identifiable by three design characteristics—skillful use of color, employment of pure virgin wools, and uniqueness of texture. These factors, combined in a carded cloth, gave tweed its quality and distinctive appearance." (Clifford, p. 75)

Cheviots, and homespun tweeds and the increasing tendency towards informality in male dress meant that by 1900 tweed was also widely worn within a variety of urban contexts, mainly as overcoatings, trouserings and suitings. Saxony tweeds are fine and densely woven and have a soft, smooth handle. They are made from merino wools and the finest versions are indistinguishable from worsted cloths. Cheviot tweeds have a rougher appearance and more open texture than saxonies, although the lighter-weight versions were widely used as suiting and trousering cloths in the late nineteenth century. The popularity of tweed as a fashionable menswear cloth continued into the twentieth century; however, along with tailoring, it went into relative decline from the 1970s onward.

Important Tweed Patterns
Late nineteenth-century tweed patterns include two that are among the few seminal textile designs that have been repeatedly used in both men's- and women's wear since the mid-nineteenth century. The first of these is the Glen Urquhart, a black-and-white check that originated in the early 1840s and which, with the addition of a red or blue over-check, has widely and erroneously been known as the Prince of Wales check. In the United States, the term Glen plaid was used to describe this sporty but elegant cloth, particularly popular from the 1930s to 1960s for men's suitings. The Coigach, which Johnstons of Elgin trace in their records back to 1846, also became widely known throughout the trade. This black-and-brown check, a variation on the simple shepherd's check, was subsequently adopted in the 1870s by a gun club in America, which led to its being universally known as the gun-club check.

Expansion and Imitation
The international reputation for design of the Scottish mainland tweed industry led by the late nineteenth century to many imitators and competitors. These included those based in Yorkshire, Ireland (Donegal tweed), and the islands of Harris and Lewis in the Outer Hebrides of Scotland. The Yorkshire woolen manufacturers were among the first to use Scotch-tweed designs as a basis for making cheaper novelty cloths aimed at the mass market. Yorkshire tweeds thus tend to be defined by their place

The weaving of Harris tweed. Weavers of Harris and Lewis Islands, in the Scottish Outer Hebrides, started producing this coarse, homespun tweed in the 1880s. Designer Vivienne Westwood included this tweed in her fashions during the twentieth century. © DAVE BARTRUFF/CORBIS. REPRODUCED BY PERMISSION.

of manufacture, rather than by any distinctive visual characteristics. The Harris-tweed industry was established from the 1880s on the islands of Harris and Lewis, through coordination of the efforts of local hand weavers. This coarse-textured, homespun tweed has survived many difficult periods to be championed in the late twentieth century by the designer Vivienne Westwood, whose logo is closely related to the Harris-Tweed Orb label. Donegal tweed also developed in the late nineteenth century and again principally involved hand-woven cloths. Its characteristic salt-and-pepper effect initially came simply from the use of natural undyed wool, until cooperation with the Harris-tweed dyers generated more complex designs.

Tweed in Women's Wear

From at least the early 1860s, women adopted tweed for outer garments such as jackets, cloaks, paletots, and coats, despite the fact that tweed was predominantly a men's wear cloth. The increasing participation of women in sports, such as countryside walking, shooting, and, later, cycling, led in the 1870s to the development of the tailored costume. This featured a matching jacket and long skirt that were generally made from some form of tweed. By 1900, the tailored costume had become accepted as informal or sporting wear for women of all classes, despite its earlier connotations of "mannishness" and feminism. The tweed industry, however, did little at this period to adapt its designs for women, other than to make them in lighter weights of cloth.

In the early twentieth century, British couturiers, such as Digby Morton, Hardy Amies, and Charles Creed, helped to stimulate international markets for superbly tailored tweed suits. The French couturier Coco Chanel was also inspired to include it in her collections after traveling to Scotland on a fishing trip with the Duke of Westminster in the 1920s. Her desire to include tweed in her exclusive designs was such that the Duke subsequently bought her a Scottish tweed mill. Linton Tweeds of Carlisle in Northern England has maintained an exclusive relationship with the House of Chanel since 1928. Tweed has since become an integral element of the signature suits that are endlessly reinvented by the House of Chanel.

Contemporary tweed manufacturers aim to maximize the potential of international markets for "traditional

347

British style" and also to promote their links with the more volatile consumers of radical, innovative fashion. Tweed retains traces of its earlier history in the present, on the one hand as remaining representative of British class and conservatism. However, it also exists as an ephemeral fashion textile that contributes to the rapidly changing visions of designers such as John Galliano at Dior, Alexander McQueen, and Vivienne Westwood.

See also **Chanel, Gabrielle (Coco); Galliano, John; McQueen, Alexander; Scottish Dress; Westwood, Vivienne.**

BIBLIOGRAPHY

De la Haye, Amy, and Tobin Shelley. *Chanel: The Couturiere at Work.* London: V & A Publications, 1994.

Gulvin, Clifford. *The Tweedmakers: A History of the Scottish Fancy Woollen Industry, 1600–1914.* Newton Abbot, U.K.: David and Charles, 1973.

Harrison, E. P. *Scottish Estate Tweeds.* Elgin, Scotland: Johnstons of Elgin, 1995.

Henry Ballantyne & Sons Ltd. London: Biographical Publishing Company, 1929.

Hoad, Judith. *This is Donegal Tweed Co.* Donegal, Ireland: Shoestring Publications, 1987.

Ponting, Kenneth. "The Scottish Contribution to Wool Textile Design in the Nineteenth Century." In *Scottish Textile History.* Edited by John Butt and Kenneth Ponting. Aberdeen, Scotland: Aberdeen University Press, 1987.

Taylor, Lou. "Wool Cloth and Gender: The Use of Woollen Cloth in Women's Dress in Britain, 1865–85." In *Defining Dress: Dress as Object, Meaning and Identity.* Edited by Amy de la Haye and Elizabeth Wilson. Manchester, U.K.: Manchester University Press, 1999.

Textile Manufacturer 15 (January 1878): 2.

Fiona Anderson

TWENTIETH-CENTURY FASHION Women's fashion at the beginning of the twentieth century was largely a matter of status. The stylish silhouette was defined by the narrow *sans-ventre* corset, which squeezed away the belly and gave the body an S-shaped line; by the long, sweeping skirt lengths; and by high rigid collars. Textile designs took the lead from art nouveau plant ornamentation. Parisian couturiers, such as Jean-Philippe and Gaston Worth (sons of the first celebrated grand couturier Charles Frederick Worth), the Callot sisters, Jacques Doucet, and Jeanne Paquin, were at the forefront in such society dresses.

This style was diametrically opposed by the "health dress," propagated by advocates of women's rights, artistic women, and doctors. This design hung loosely without a corset. Its sack cut was rejected by most style-conscious women, despite the designs of art-nouveau artists like Henry van de Velde.

The suit began to establish itself as a multi-faceted garment, becoming a symbol, eventually, of democratic fashion. The businesswoman used it in her career and the society lady as a travel and recreation outfit. The jacket was mostly styled in a masculine cut with lapels and cuffs; the frock coat was occasionally shortened above the ankle. Suits were offered by manufacturers as well as posh tailors such as John Redfern and Henry Creed. With the advent of the suit, the blouse became the central style element, featuring both luxuriously decorated and simple models. Comfortable kimono blouses, with cut-out sleeves, could be worn over skirts. Top coats, or paletots, taken from men's fashion, and carcoats or dusters, satisfied the desire for functional clothing. Around 1908, the Parisian couturier Paul Poiret created a new style called *la vague.* Inspired by the *Ballets Russes,* he combined the body-liberating "health dress" with elements of Asian dress. Paul Poiret had ties with the world-famous Vienna Workshops, which operated their own fashion department.

Originating in England, the Edwardian style (named after King Edward VII) was the leader in international men's fashion. Men's fashion was regulated by exact rules, which were published by prominent tailors, as to when and under what circumstances each suit was to be worn.

Business attire included the sports jacket (sack coat) and the more elegant suit jacket. Daytime suites incorporated the frock coat (Prince Albert). The cut-away was considered suitable for more private and prestigious occasions. The smoking jacket fulfilled the role of comfortable, casual evening attire. There also existed specialized sporty ensembles. It was important always to choose the correct hat: soft felt, bowler, homburg, canotier, panama, or top hat. There were also many different coats to choose from, such as paletots, chesterfields, raglans, and ulsters.

Fashion 1910–1919
International fashion until 1914 was heavily influenced by the avant-garde French couturier Paul Poiret. He helped initiate the Art Deco style and inspired other designers such as Erté and Mariano Fortuny, whose delphos gowns of the finest pleated silk were also world famous. In 1910 Poiret publicized the hobble skirt, which was, despite its uncomfortable cut, quite fashionable for a short time. It fell loosely, straight to the top of the calf, but was narrowed, from below the knee to its ankle-length hem, with such a narrow yoke that a lady could only hobble. Poiret also proposed a long pants-dress, but few women dared to be seen on the streets in the new *jupes culottes.* For eveningwear, Poiret even suggested broad harem pants worn under a long tunic with a wire-stiffened, upturned hem.

From 1912 until the outbreak of World War I, evening clothes were marked by the new social dance craze, the Argentine tango. Poiret's creations seemed custom-made for the new popular dance: closely wrapped skirts with high slits in the front, gold-embroidered tunics, and turbans with upright feathers. Men wore the cutaway and the fashionable frock coat, sometimes in strong colors like dark red, or featuring checkered trim. Accompanying hats were oversized.

During World War I (1914–1918), clothing tended to be as simple as possible: moderately wide skirts, not quite reaching the foot, and hip-length jackets. In 1915–1916, war crinolines—ankle length and fluffed with two or three skirt layers—were *en vogue*; a year later, however, these fell victim to the more economical use of fabric provided by the sack cut. The fashion in 1918 was livened up by large side pockets and skirts that narrowed towards the hem, creating the barrel look of 1919. Most of the fashion salons in Paris had closed. But some wealthy women bought comfortable jersey suits with hip-length jumpers and simple skirts from Gabrielle Chanel in Deauville, thereby establishing her fame. In the United States, especially in New York, clothing manufacturers were active.

The most important novelty of twentieth century women's clothing occurred outside of the fashion world. Long trousers for women were inaugurated, neither by haute couture nor by every-day fashion, but by women's work clothing, which was still mostly borrowed from men. Directly following the war, people worked with what was available, altering uniforms and army tarps or other leftovers, to create civilian clothes.

During the war, the uniform replaced all other suit types, and most tailors—if they stayed in business at all—specialized in its manufacture. After the war, tailors resorted to alterations of uniforms and the reworking of recycled—sometimes fragile—materials into suits which had to be reinforced with buckram, thus creating the so-called starched suit. Men's trousers had very narrow legs all the way to the hem. The trench coat appeared, courtesy of the transition from military into civilian clothes.

The 1920s

During the 1920s the length of a skirt's hem became, for the first time, a serious fashion question. While the clothes of 1920–1921 were still calf length, and (around 1923) even ankle length for a short time, after 1924 women favored skirts that hardly covered the knee. In 1922–1923, fashion was influenced by the discovery of the grave of the Egyptian pharaoh Tutankhamen. Anyone who could afford it, bought a djellaba for a house dress or had their evening dresses decorated with Egyptian ornaments. Otherwise, loose-hanging dresses were characteristic for the time. Mostly they had drop waists and sometimes a pleated hem or *godet* folds which provided freedom of movement. Daytime clothes had high closings, dressed up with baby-doll or men's collars.

Evening clothes and elaborate society toilettes corresponded in cut to daytime clothes. Evening clothes, however, featured generous front and back décolletage, the front décolletage underlayed with a flesh-colored slip. It was not modern to show one's bosom, and breasts were pressed flat with fabric bands. The simple cut of the evening dress was compensated for by expensive fabrics of lace, gold or silver lamé, loose hanging pearl necklaces, the use of monkey-fur fringe, and extensive embroidery. In 1927, the tendency to lengthen the evening gown's hem set in and the waist returned to its natural place. By 1928 the evening gown was already calf length, while the daytime dress remained knee length until about 1930.

In haute couture, Gabrielle Chanel made her reputation with dresses, jersey suits, and knit jumpers. In 1926 she announced the "little black dress," a black evening dress impressive for its simple elegance. Like Chanel, Jean Patou favored clear lines and extremely simple elegance, beginning with his own collection for the United States. Jeanne Lanvin, in contrast, presented a decidedly feminine, romantic line. Her *robes de style* (based on historical styles), with their wide paniers, became world famous. Lanvin was also known for her mother-child creations.

Short skirts brought the legs, and thereby rayon stockings, into the picture. Bobs and page-boy haircuts were as typical of the time as were simple, form-fitting toques and cloche hats. Sports became a fashion trend: tennis in a short skirt without stockings, skiing in a Norwegian suit with long knickers, swimming in a one-piece bathing suit without whale-bone reinforcements. The 1920s metropolitan fashion spectrum included the *garçonne* (female boy) in a pants suit with man's hat and even an Eton crop. In the evenings, the *gamin* style featured a smoking (tuxedo jacket), or complete smoking suit, and a monocle. And the *garçonne* also appropriated men's pajamas for household and nighttime wear.

The Exposition International des Arts Décoratifs et Industrials Moderne, held in Paris in 1925, was an epoch making event which later gave the name Art Deco to the period. Among the seventy-two fashion designers, Sonia Delauney created the biggest sensation with her suits and coats in patterns of "simultaneous color contrast."

After 1924, men's suits had a slightly tapered waist, and the trousers widened slightly. Dandys were recognizable by their extremely broad trousers, known as "Oxford bags," and by their exaggeratedly pointed winkle pickers or shimmy shoes. For golf, hiking, or hunting, men wore Norfolk jackets and plus fours.

The 1930s

At the beginning of the 1930s, clothing was cut to be form-fitting again, with the waist at its natural place. Bodices, with rubber and stretch reinforcements, hugged the body's curves. Shoulder pads and wide lapels, off-the-shoulder collars with flounces, as well as tight belts, all aimed to make the waist appear slimmer. The hem was lengthened with *godet* folds and pleats from the knee to the calf, providing freedom of movement. Evening gowns were preferably of shimmering satin, and reached to the floor, often with a small "mermaid" train. It was *en vogue* to have plunging back décolletage, with wide crisscrossing straps, and a waterfall or sweetheart collar. The success of the new body-conscious line can be traced back to the Parisian designer Madeleine Vionnet and her "invention" of the bias cut, whereby material, cut diagonally to the weave, clung to the body and flared out towards the hem like a bell.

Elsa Schiaparelli was not to be outdone on the idea front. In her collections, she worked with *trompe l'oeil* effects as well as allusions to surrealistic artists. Schiaparelli's wide pagoda shoulders, invented in 1933, had a major influence on everyday fashion. Suits, jackets, and dresses after 1933 were unthinkable without padded shoulders.

In the fascist countries (Italy, Spain, and Germany), women's fashion became a matter of political agitation, as exemplified by the introduction of the German Girls Club (BDM, *Bund Deutscher Mädchen*) uniform. Alpine costumes also suited the tastes of National Socialist Germany. The world-famous Berlin manufacturers, which had been over 80 percent in Jewish hands, were, for the most part, ruined (i.e., liquidated) due to the "Aryan cleansing."

The year 1936 was one of the most innovative in men's fashion. The double-breasted suit, with four buttons instead of six, created a furor, as did patterned shirts worn with gray flannel suits. Shirts also featured the new kent collars and somewhat wider cravattes, tied into windsor knots. In daywear, three-button gabardine suit and oxford shirts with button-down collars were common.

The 1940s

During World War II (1939–1945) and the first years following, fashion was dictated by the need for practical, simple clothes and the rationing of resources and materials. In England the government encouraged "utility clothing." In Paris, during the German occupation, only very few haute couture houses remained open. In all countries, special magazines and brochures dispensed advice on re-modeling old clothes or how to make new clothes from combining pieces of old ones. Skirts and coats became shorter, suits took on the character of uniforms, and wide shoulders dominated more than ever. Hats and shoes were often hand-made and wool stockings and socks replaced silk. In the United States, Claire McCardell created a furor with her "pop-over" dresses, leotards, and sea-side "diaper suits."

A new epoch in fashion was marked on February 12, 1947, with the opening of Christian Dior's house. He called his first haute couture collection "Ligne Corolle" (calyx line), but the fashion press called it the "New Look," because almost everything about it was new. The simple suit jacket, the small lapels, the narrow wasp waist, which emphasized the hips, and, above all, the narrow shoulders. For the first time in over a decade, there were no shoulder pads. Just as new were the extremely wide calf-length skirt, flat broad-rimmed hats (wagon wheels), high-heeled pumps and long gloves, which lent this daytime wear an impressively elegant flair.

At first, due to the lack of necessary materials, the new style could only be produced slowly, but soon countless private seamstresses were busy fulfilling the dream of the "New Look." In the spring of 1948, Dior's "Ligne Envol" (pencil line) followed, introducing narrow skirts with the famous Dior slit, underlayed with material for walking ease. Nylon stockings were in high demand, leaving shiny rayon and woolen stockings forever in the past.

After the war, a new fashion invention created a lasting impression. On July 5th, in Paris, the French mechanical engineer Louis Réard presented his two-piece bathing suit which he called the bikini. Although there had already been two-piece bathing suits since 1928, Réard's bikini stood out because of its extremely skimpy cut. The bikini, however, was not generally accepted until the late 1960s.

Men's clothing played a rather limited role; uniforms dominated. Trench coats and duffle coats (montys) were all-around coats. The American jazz scene's zoot suit, with its long frock coat and wide trousers, was considered modern.

The 1950s

In the 1950s Paris regained its position as the capital of fashion. Christian Dior dictated the lines—every season he was ready with another: the H-Line of 1954, for example, which rejected the narrow waist for the first time, and the famous A-Line of 1955. Hardly less influential, however, were the designers Pierre Balmain, Jacques Fath, Hubert de Givenchy, Cristobel Balenciaga, and in Italy, Emilio Schuberth and Emilio Pucci. In 1954, Chanel reopened her salon and advertised an instantly famous suit with a loose jacket and slightly flared skirt in direct contrast to Dior's stiffer, more tailored style. In 1957, with Christian Dior's death, Yves Saint Laurent followed in his footsteps. His trapeze, or tent line, wherein he dared to negate the female figure, was a sensational, if controversial, debut success.

Naturally, women had other concerns besides Dior's fashion dictates, but many private seamstresses took cues from one or another haute couture line. The fashion magazines too adapted elite fashions for the average consumer.

The fashion picture at home and abroad was defined by two basic points: the narrow line with its strong body-consciousness and the attention drawn to the hip line by a gathered waistband, and the broad swinging, youthful petticoat. Both tried to create a dreamy wasp waist, magically narrowed by a corset—the *guepière*—or girdle. In addition to suits and jackets, the shirt dress, with its casual, sporty cut, shirt collar, and cuffed sleeves, was a garment suitable for all occasions.

In cocktail dresses, women favored extreme designs like Dior's cupola or Givenchy's balloon look, whose broad skirt was drawn in sharply at the hem. New synthetic materials like nylon, perlon, dralon, trevira, terylene, elastic, and imitation leather fulfilled the dream of fashion for all. "Drip dry" and "wash and wear" were the magic words of advertising, relegating the iron to the past. For teenage leisure time, there were jeans, capri pants, and ballerina shoes. The childishly-cut short night gown with bloomers, called the baby doll, was new. Aggressively intellectual teenagers were attracted to French existentialism and wore black turtlenecks, tight black leather clothes, and black stockings instead of transparent nylons.

Carefully coordinated accessories were a part of stylish every day wear. Shoes with rounded tips and square heels evolved in 1955–1956 to their famously pointy shape and stiletto heels.

German winter sports fashion became an international model. Maria Bogner's ski pants, "the Bogner's," became a household word in the United States, as did the first one-pieced elastic ski overall, invented by Bogner in 1955.

After 1953, Italy, with its body-conscious suits, began to compete with traditional English tailoring. On the whole, men's fashions were conservative: nylon shirts were snow white and ties narrow. The Hawaiian shirt was a popular leisure garment. The English Teddy Boys, a teenage fringe group, wore frock coat-like jackets and extremely narrow pants; their hair was styled back over their foreheads in a wave with lotion. The toughs, on the other hand, were known by their black leather outfits.

The 1960s

The years from 1959 to 1963 were a transition period from the decidedly lady-like style of the 1950s to the teenage style of the ensuing years. Teenagers favored wide-swinging petticoats while the mature woman chose narrow sheath dresses and, as an afternoon or cocktail dress, an extravagantly layered look, with a tight-fitting skirt layered under a shorter tulip skirt. The real 1960s fashion began in 1964. "Swinging London" became the fashion metropolis of the youth. Mary Quant and her little-girlish thigh-length smock dresses made headlines. Her mini-style was not intended to be elitist, but popular; thus she marketed her own fashion stockings, without which the mini was hardly wearable. The sharply-angled Vidal Sassoon hair style was also new. The counterpart to the Mary Quant look was Barbara Hulanicki's exotic Biba look from London. Twiggy became the most famous mannequin and the "most expensive beanstalk in the world." Thinness became, from this point on, a requirement of beauty. In 1964, Rudi Gernreich introduced his topless bathing suit, which corresponded to the tendency towards sexual liberation. He also invented the "no bra" brassiere.

Parisian designers participated in youthful unconventionality and ready-to-wear (prêt-à-porter) only reluctantly. Yves Saint Laurent presented clothes with large appliquéd pop-art images in shocking pink, a Mondrian collection with contrasting lines and surfaces, and, in

1966, the transparent look. Paco Rabanne created an uproar with mini sheath dresses of plastic and metal discs and Pierre Cardin's creations featured round holes, "cutouts," as well as molded structures. André Courrège's fashions were the last word in space-age euphoria. His moon maids with silver sequined stretch pants, white synthetic boots, and white sunglasses with slits for seeing, represented pure futurism. His Courrèges-suit, with its geometrically cut jacket and angled cut-out collar, was all the rage. For all opponents of the mini-skirt, trousers were popular in all imaginable forms and lengths, but jeans above all. Pants suits took the place of the traditional suit. Often a super short mini dress would be worn as a tunic over pants. The width of the trouser leg below the knee grew progressively wider. The wider the "bell," the more stylish.

For a moment in 1965 it appeared as if the younger generation had said goodbye to the mini skirt, as fashion imitated the film "Dr. Zhivago," with long coats and Russian caps. The hippie and beatnik looks, protesting consumerism, stood in ideological and stylistic opposition to mainstream fashion, and mixed and matched international peasant costumes, like ponchos, Peruvian hats, Eskimo boots, Indian blouses, and Afghani sheepskin jackets. Young people sewed flowers on jeans, wore floppy hats, or showed their naked bodies, painted only with flowers. Creativity was given free reign, under the motto "hand-made is chic": T-shirts were batiked or painted, jeans embroidered, caps sewn, leather-fringed belts braided, silver jewelry twined, vests crocheted, pullovers knit, but the hippie style was swiftly co-opted by the market.

Pierre Cardin's high-necked suits without lapels or collars or with small mandarin collars (or "Nehru") created a furor and were adopted by the Beatles. More radical were the English mods, for whom parkas and Clark shoes were typical. The Beatles' "mop top" hair-do became a generational conflict. After 1965, men favored the colorful ethnic hippie look. The turtle neck sweater and later the T-shirt substituted for the shirt.

The 1970s

"Do as you will," was the fashion motto of the early 1970s. The ideal of the hippies, "we are all equal," set the tone for unisex and folklore looks. Hand-made was in, from batik shirts, knitted shawls, and crocheted caps, to pullover sweaters of hand-spun sheep's wool. Understatement was cool and second-hand duds were no longer for the needy alone. The brassiere itself fell victim to the general liberation from all restraints. Feminists spoke of the "liberated bosom." Directions from high fashion were lacking; even the Parisian designers found themselves in a crisis. Fashion had to be multifarious, uncomplicated, original, and individual, and the hem length varied between mini, midi, and maxi according to whim and mood. Modern romanticism—the nostalgia wave—lent minidresses (still fashionable up to 1973), wraparound tops, wing and flounce sleeves, and bell skirts. Hair was long and softly waved or rolled into corkscrew curls. False eyelashes or painted-on lines magically conjured star-eyes.

Hardly any other fashion created as big a sensation as hot pants in 1971–1972. They were not only worn as super short summer shorts, but also intended for winter with thick wool socks. Hot pants were offset by the beloved maxi coats and high platform shoes. Pants of all kinds provided a relief from the length disputes. There were tight knee-length caddy pants, broad gauchos, knickers, culottes, harem pants, ankle-length drain-pipe trousers, wide Marlene Dietrich trousers, and—still up to 1974—wide bell bottoms. Jeans became the universal clothing, crossing all class and age boundaries. Jackets, pullovers, vests, and T-shirts clung tightly to the body. Pullover sweaters featured witty motifs like trees, houses, or cars. Maxi length party clothes (evening clothes were out) had bold patterns such as Vasarely graphics, pop-art, or Hundertwasser images.

After 1974, a series of looks followed without constituting a single unified style. In 1975 there were caftans and the Chinese look with short quilted jackets. In 1976 the Middle Eastern look dominated, with tunics over harem pants, and, later, the layered look. A master of the folklore mixture was the Japanese designer Kenzo (Takada), whose Parisian boutique "Jungle Jap," had a decided influence. Mainstream fashion, on the other hand, was rather conservative, featuring the umbrella-pleated (or gored) skirt, which came to just below the knee.

In 1976 the fashion press euphorically reported on Yves Saint Laurent's collection "Ballets Russes–Opéra." It was an elegant peasant look with long, wide skirts of shimmering silk and bolero jackets in unexpected color combinations like red, lilac, orange, and pink, delicate sheer blouses with wide sleeves, and golden turbans.

Beginning in 1977, punk clothing exerted a strong influence on fashion for the next few years. The anti-bourgeois, "no-future" generation shocked with their brutal look: safety pins through cheeks and ear lobes, dog collars and razor blades as necklaces, diabolically made-up eyes, black lips, ripped jeans and T-shirts, torn fishnet stockings, and tough Doc Marten's boots. Their hair, in contrast to their gray and black get-ups, differentiated itself from the mainstream "normals" by its green and red highlights and its spiked (mohawk) styling. Insiders met at Vivienne Westwood and Malcolm McLaren's shop on King's Road, called "Sex" in 1974 and then, later, "Seditionaries" in 1978.

In 1978, the Parisian prêt-à-porter designers, above all Claude Montana, brought the military and punk look onto the runway. Broad "power" shoulders and oversized garments initiated a new fashion silhouette which would become the characteristic style of the 1980s.

The 1975 American book, *Dress for Success* by John T. Molloy, gave the exile from hippie culture tips on how to market himself with the right clothes, on the power of the white shirt, on how to interpret the codes of tie patterns, and how make it in "big business." Two years later, in 1977, Molloy's sequel followed, *The Woman's Dress for Success Book.*

The 1980s

The fashion silhouette of the 1980s was defined by oversized, voluminous gigot (leg of mutton) sleeves and wide padded shoulders which coincided with the fight for women's equal rights. Even eveningwear, which emphasized low-cut necklines and narrow waists, had to have padded shoulders. Hemlines were no longer an issue. Teenagers wore loose mini dresses, but in general skirts extended from below the knee to calf-length. Women wore masculine jackets, short bell-hop jackets or broad-shouldered, box jackets with pants. At the same time, fashion became a sign of prestige and a status symbol, best represented by brand-name labels, and a preference for leather, fur, and gold-colored accessories.

The Japanese avant-garde designers, who attracted a good deal of attention in Europe during the 1980s, stood in sharp contrast to this trend. In the tradition of Japanese clothing, Yohji Yamamoto draped skeins of fabric loosely around the body. In 1981, Rei Kawakubo's fashion company "Comme des Garçons," called the entire Western fashion aesthetic into question. She shredded skirts into fluttering strips, tore material, knotted it together, and layered it crosswise. Black and gray dominated. Issey Miyake was known for his highly experimental use of materials and methods, demonstrated by his rattan bodices inspired by Samurai practice armor in 1982, and his first "Pleats Please" collection of 1989.

In 1983, Karl Lagerfeld became the designer for the haute couture house of Chanel. He reworked the legendary Chanel suit to be new and uncomplicated, and added leather skirts and pants suits. Parisian designers offered a new body consciousness as an alternative to the oversized craze. Thierry Mugler sparkled with corset suits and siren clothes, Jean-Paul Gaultier with skin-tight velvet and grenade bosoms, and Azzedine Alaïa with clinging lace-up clothes.

The American designer style became synonymous with sportswear and clean chic. Ralph Lauren gave tradition a modern face lift with his "country-style" concept. Donna Karan was treasured for her functional "all-day fashion" with jersey bodysuits instead of blouses. Calvin Klein was considered the inventor of designer jeans.

The music scene provided more and more style models. Pop icon Madonna was fascinating as a contemporary Marilyn Monroe. Her appearance in a corset was the impetus of the underwear-as-outerwear craze, featuring bustiers and corsets.

The fitness craze exerted the greatest influence on everyday fashion in the late 1980s. The ballet dancer's leg warmers, the aerobic fan's leggings, and the bicycle racer's pants appeared in everyday fashion. Leggings available in the wildest patterns, the most garish colors, and the shiniest stretchy fabrics, were worn with blazers or long pullover sweaters.

Towards the end of the decade, the long blazer with straight, knee-length skirt and black opaque stockings became the classic women's business outfit. Evening fashion, and the revival of the cocktail dress, was, in contrast, emphatically feminine. Christian Lacroix, whose first haute couture show in 1987 brought a frenzy of color, became the master of cocktail dresses with jaunty, short tutus and balloon skirts.

In response to massive animal rights' campaigns, the wearing of fur became a "question of conscience," making colorful fake furs and quilted down coats fashionable.

Yohji Yamamoto's new men's fashion, with its flowing, collarless jackets, proffered an alternative to the yuppie's conventional shoulder-padded business suit. Giorgio Armani led the rise of Milan menswear, and the German manufacturer, Boss, achieved international recognition for its men's fashions.

In 1982 Calvin Klein revolutionized men's underwear, making simple ribbed men's briefs a designer item by printing his name in the elastic waistband. In 1985, androgyny became a provocative fashion statement; Jean-Paul Gaultier created skirts for the body-conscious man.

The 1990s

Fashion became a question of "which designer?" with extremely varied styles. In the early 1990s, the Belgian designers Anne Demeulemeester and Martin Margiela started a new style direction with the advent of the grunge and poor-boy look, making Antwerp, which housed designers Dries Van Noten, Dirk Bikkembergs, and Walter Van Beirendock as well, the new fashion center. The English designer Vivianne Westwood finally received international recognition for her daring reinterpretations of historical styles. London newcomers John Galliano and Alexander McQueen established themselves as chief designers at, respectively, Christian Dior and Givenchy in Paris. Jean-Paul Gaultier continued to be very successful with his underwear fashions, particularly with Madonna at its center. The fashion palette of the Italian designer Gianni Versace spanned from neo-baroque patterns to bondage style, while the house of Gucci, under the direction of the Texan Tom Ford, combined purism and eroticism. Miuccia Prada caught on, with her "bad taste" style, and a successful re-launching of past styles. Giorgio Armani remained the master of purism, while Dolce & Gabbana celebrated women's eroticism with black lingerie and animal prints. Jill Sanders, of Hamburg, perfected her minimalism to international acclaim. The Austrian designer Helmut Lang established himself in New York; his transparent layer look and his minimalistic lines gave new stimulus to fashion. Alongside the designers, supermodels, like Claudia Schiffer, Naomi Campbell, Linda Evangelista, and Cindy Crawford, were central to all fashion events.

In everyday fashion, leggings, in all colors and patterns, dominated at the beginning of the decade. Worn under stylishly transparent, calf-length skirts and long blazers in multi-colored blockings, leggings covered the legs discretely. The transparent look appeared somewhat in mainstream fashion, layered over lace bodysuits, bustiers, and bras. Towards the end of the decade, crinkled shirts, ragged hems, and inside-out seams were accepted. The baguette bag, publicized by Fendi, brought the handbag, after two decades of backpacks, into fashion's center stage.

The marketing of brand names became increasingly important: adults favoring Louis Vuitton, Hermes, or Escada, and teenagers of both sexes favoring sportswear brands like Diesel, Chiemsee, Burton, Nike, Adidas, or Levis. The Italian fashion manufacturer Benetton stimulated heated controversies over its advertising.

Men's fashion was also increasingly determined by designers with clearly differentiated styles, ranging from Giorgio Armani's loosely cut suits to Hemut Lang's body-conscious, relatively high-necked suits and narrow trousers with a satin band on their outward-facing leg seams. Baggy pants and extra-large shirts remained popular with the younger generation. Cargo pants were introduced in 1999 as sportswear.

See also **Armani, Giorgio; Art Noveau and Art Deco; Cardin, Pierre; Chanel, Gabrielle (Coco); Corset; Dior, Christian; Europe and America: History of Dress (400–1900 C.E.); Gaultier, Jean-Paul; Haute Couture; Lagerfeld, Karl; Lang, Helmut; Patou, Jean; Poiret, Paul; Quant, Mary; Saint Laurent, Yves; Suit, Business; Youthquake Fashions.**

BIBLIOGRAPHY

Baudot, Francois. *Fashion of the Century.* New York: Universe Publishing, 1999.

Buxbaum, Gerda, ed. *Icons of Fashion: The 20th Century.* New York: Prestal, 1999.

Fukai, Akiko. *Fashion. Collection of the Kyoto Costume Institute. A History of the 18th to the 20th Century.* Tokyo: Taschen, 2002.

Loschek, Ingrid. *Fashion in the 20th Century. A Cultural History of Our Time.* Munich: Letzter Preis, 1995.

———. *Fashion of the Century. Fashion Chronicle from 1900 to Today.* Munich: Letzter Preis, 2001.

McDowell, Colin. *Forties Fashion and the New Look.* London: Bloomsbury, 1997.

Remaury, Bruno, ed. *Dictionary of 20th Century Fashion.* Paris, 1994.

Seeling, Charlotte. *Fashion 1900-1999.* London-Cologne: Konemann, 2000.

Steele, Valerie. *Fifty Years of Fashion: New Look to Now.* New Haven, Conn.: Yale University Press, 2000.

Vergani, Guido, ed. *Dictionary of Fashion.* Milan: Baldini and Castoldi, 1999.

Ingrid Loschek

TWIGGY In 1949 Lesley Hornby, later rechristened "Twiggy," was born in Neasden, an unfashionable suburb in North London, where she grew up. Only sixteen when she began modeling in 1966, she introduced the cult of the "celebrity model" and left an indelible legacy in other, more significant ways. Models in the 1950s, in both America and Britain, were styled and made up to look mature, sophisticated, and "ladylike," to complement the fashionable clothes of the time. In England many were young women from respectable families who had followed a modeling course at Lucie Clayton's Mod-

eling and Grooming School in Mayfair. In America, such top models as Suzy Parker were also well-groomed girls from middle-class backgrounds. New photographic techniques allowed mass-circulation newspapers and magazines to print high-fashion images, and the models' names soon became familiar to the public.

The social and demographic changes that followed created need for new designs and new models. Mary Quant's clothes for *Bazaar* were aimed at a young clientele, while the early 1960s saw the opening of innumerable boutiques in London, which, unlike Quant's shop,

Twiggy. Unlike the feminine and sophisticated looks of models in the 1950s, Twiggy became the celebrity model who typified the new, young, and boyish style of the 1960s. © HULTON-DEUTSCH COLLECTION/CORBIS. REPRODUCED BY PERMISSION.

were intended for girls of far more limited means. The first model whose image reflected this climate was Jean Shrimpton. Although she had attended Miss Clayton's school, her success was a result of the partnership she had formed with the working-class photographer David Bailey. The early pictures, which made them both famous, showed off her youth and her tomboy persona.

Lesley Hornby was working as a hairdresser in a salon near her home when an older man recognized the way in which she might personify the new London. Nigel Davies, a former boxer and stallholder, who called himself "Justin de Villeneuve," changed her name and transformed her appearance; it was at his suggestion that she painted on eyelashes under her eyes so as to resemble a porcelain doll and had her hair cut short. The photographer Barry Lategan took a picture for the salon, and, by chance, the fashion editor Deirdre McSharry saw it. In the February 1966 issue of the *Daily Express*, she used a center spread to portray this "Cockney Kid" as "the Face of '66." One of the shots showed Twiggy wearing homemade trousers and sweater, which accentuated both her androgynous appearance and her democratic appeal.

She was smaller than most models and invariably posed so as to emphasize her childlike qualities. In 1967 she was photographed for British *Vogue* by Ronald Traeger, who portrayed her riding a miniature bike in knee-high socks. Cecil Beaton sat her on a high shelf, and Helmut Newton asked her to jump toward the camera with arms outstretched. There followed a shoot with Richard Avedon and a cover for American *Vogue* in August of that year. At one point she was on twelve covers simultaneously; as a model, she was used by both traditional "glossies" and new, youth-oriented publications.

Although the syndication of her name to dresses, dolls, and other merchandise meant that she could retire from modeling by 1969 to pursue a career as actress and singer, she had permanently changed magazine culture. Now, to the deification of youth was added the idea of instant fame, the notion that class barriers that could be painlessly transcended, and the problematic pursuit of a pre-pubescent ideal of beauty.

See also **Fashion Photography; Fashion Magazines; London Fashion; Quant, Mary.**

BIBLIOGRAPHY

Aitken, Jonathan. *The Young Meteors.* New York: Atheneum, 1967.

Green, Jonathon. *All Dressed Up: The Sixties and the Counter-culture.* London: Jonathan Cape, 1998.

Levy, Shawn. *Ready, Steady, Go! The Smashing Rise and Giddy Fall of Swinging London.* New York: Doubleday, 2002.

Melly, George. *Revolt into Style: The Pop Arts in Britain.* London: Allen Lane, 1970.

Twiggy. *Twiggy: An Autobiography.* London: Hart-Davis, MacGibbon, 1975.

Pamela Church Gibson

ULTRASUEDE. *See* **Nonwoven Textiles; Flocking.**

UMBRELLAS AND PARASOLS The origins of the word "umbrella" lie in the Latin *umbra*, meaning shade, while "parasol" comes from the Latin *sol*, meaning sun, and the two words were used interchangeably up until the middle of the eighteenth century (Farrell 1985). Since then, "parasol" has come to denote specifically a shade that protects against the sun, while "umbrella" indicates an item that provides protection from the rain.

Most umbrellas and parasols consist of a central stick to which a number of ribs are attached. The ribs support the cover or canopy and, in turn, they are supported by stretchers from the center of their length to the tubular runner that slides up and down the stick (Farrell 1985). Historians indicate that while umbrellas were always designed to fold, some parasols were made rigid, with the cover consisting of a single circular piece of waxed cloth or taffeta supported on cane ribs.

Umbrellas date from over 3,000 years ago, and according to Crawford (1970), from early times they had religious and mythological symbolism. Most histories of the umbrella and parasol cite Egypt, China, and India as being important geographical locations in the pre-European history of the umbrellas.

In all such cultures where it has had a presence, the umbrella appears to have been associated with high status. Moreover, Stacey notes that: "The Oxford English Dictionary does in fact date the use of the word umbrella from 1653 as 'an Oriental or African symbol of dignity'" (1991, p. 114).

Many Asian countries have used the parasol in symbolic relation to their dignitaries, and Sangster notes: "In all eastern countries, with the exception of China and Turkey, the Parasol was reserved exclusively for the great men of the land." (1855, p. 18). According to Crawford (1970), Burma and Siam are two Asian countries that have the most regard for the umbrella as a symbol of sovereignty, and subsequently reports that the ruler of the ancient capital of the Burmese empire had the title of "King of the White Elephants and Lord of the Twenty-Four Umbrellas." The use of the umbrella as a symbol of respect appears to have continued into the twentieth century as Jacqueline Kennedy, widow of the American President John Kennedy, was accorded the privilege of the ceremonial umbrella when she visited Burma in 1967 (Crawford 1970).

In China, too, umbrellas have been used to denote status from as early as the eleventh century B.C.E. Frames at that time were made of cane or sandalwood and the covers of leather or feathers, for wet and dry days (Stacey 1991). During the period of the Ming dynasty (1368–1644), Crawford (1970) notes that ordinary people were not allowed to use umbrellas covered with cloth or silk: they had to use less prestigious items constructed from stout paper. Cheaper East Asian umbrellas are still made of paper manufactured from cotton rags, although better models use paper made from the bark bast of mulberry, which is much stronger. Covers are painted or lacquered and may be decorated with pictorial motifs or auspicious phrases (Crawford 1970).

Evidence of early European use of umbrellas is mentioned by Sangster: "We find frequent reference to the Umbrella in the Roman Classics, and it appears that it was, probably, a post of honour among maid-servants to bear it over their mistresses" (1855, p. 15). However, most historians indicate that the first European umbrellas were probably ceremonial items associated with the pope. There are extant depictions of the Emperor Constantine presenting Pope Sylvester I—who was in office from C.E. 314 to 335—with a brown and white striped umbrella (Crawford 1970) and Pope Eugenius IV (1431–1447) incorporated an *ombrellino* into his coat of arms. Although the emblem is no longer used by the pope himself, it still appears on certain institutions and seminaries (Stacey 1991).

It is likely that trading activity in Asian colonies from the sixteenth century onward ultimately brought the umbrella to wider European attention. Portuguese women in India in the sixteenth century, for instance, would not venture out without an escort of slaves, one of whom bore a shade over his mistress to protect her from the sun and to emphasize her prestige, Crawford (1970) writes. The umbrella subsequently became a custom that returned with the Portuguese to Europe.

The umbrella or parasol started to appear elsewhere in Europe around this time and the French king, Louis

Asian woman decorating an umbrella. In many Asian cultures, umbrellas, often painted with decorations, are associated with status and dignity. © Bohemian Nomad Picturemakers/Corbis. Reproduced by permission.

XIII, is reported to have owned a good number of umbrellas. Between 1619 and 1637 he enlarged his collection to include eleven sunshades made of taffeta and three umbrellas made of oiled cloth trimmed with gold and silver lace (Crawford 1970).

However, the umbrella had no significant presence in Britain until the eighteenth century. Although there are records of some eighteenth century "church umbrellas" designed specifically for use by members of the clergy, the traveler and philanthropist Jonas Hanway is generally credited with introducing the umbrella to London (Stacey 1991). Born in 1712, he traveled extensively to the British colonies and to Europe. On returning to London to carry out his philanthropic work, he was reportedly ridiculed by sedan chair carriers for his use of the umbrella, possibly because they perceived it as a threat to their business (Stacey 1991). Hanway's now infamous umbrella is most likely to have been French in origin (Farrell 1985).

But it took time for the waterproof umbrella to attain popularity in Britain, perhaps because to be seen with one was regarded as indicative of insufficient funds for a carriage (Farrell 1985). Moreover, Sangster writes that: "The earliest English Umbrellas . . . were made of oiled

silk, very clumsy and difficult to open when wet; the stick and furniture were heavy and inconvenient, and the article very expensive" (1855, p. 31). The ribs of umbrellas at this time were made of whalebone—which lost its elasticity when wet—and the oiled silk or cotton cover would quickly become saturated and leaky. Furthermore, walking-stick umbrellas were uncommon in England in the eighteenth century (although they were being marketed in France), so they generally had to be carried under the arm or slung across the back (Crawford 1970).

In terms of production, Stacey (1991) notes that the first patent was taken out on an umbrella in 1786, and there was subsequently a proliferation of developments with over 121 patents filed in the 1850s alone. But as Sangster points out, "The most important improvement dates from the introduction of steel instead of whalebone." (Sangster 1855, p. 58). The most successful umbrella designs involving metal ribs were those patented by Henry Holland of Birmingham in 1840, and later by Samuel Fox in 1852 (Farrell 1985).

By the middle of the nineteenth century, there was a thriving umbrella and parasol industry in Britain, and Sangster notes that these items were well represented in the great exhibition of 1851. In particular, the elaborate umbrella belonging to the Maharajah of Najpoor captured the imagination of visitors and drew attention from visitors: "The ribs and stretchers, sixteen in number, divided the Umbrella into as many segments, covered with silk, exquisitely embroidered with gold and silver ornaments" (1855, p. 63). There is, perhaps, just a hint of umbrella envy in his subsequent statement that "we were glad to find that the visitors turned away from this display of barbaric pomp to the plainer, but more valuable productions of our own land" (1855, p. 63). It was at this exhibition that two of the Sangster brothers, who were themselves umbrella manufacturers, won a prize medal for their alpaca-covered umbrellas. Inferior to silk, but far cheaper and sturdier, alpaca became a highly popular textile for umbrellas in Britain in the 1850s (Crawford 1970).

By the end of the nineteenth century, umbrellas had become less of a novelty and more of an item of convenience. Best quality umbrellas had covers made of silk, cheaper ones of cotton, and green was the most popular color although blue, red, and brown umbrellas were also available. Handles were made of horn, ivory, antler, or wood, and were often decorated with bands of gold or silver (Farrell 1985). By the close of the nineteenth century, *The Tailor and Cutter* reported that "fashionable men are wedded to them" (Stacey 1991, p. 27).

Throughout the eighteenth and nineteenth centuries, manufacturers of quality umbrellas and parasols had their own outlets, while cheaper products were sold in the streets by itinerant vendors (Crawford 1970). Many retailers would offer a repair service as well as new products, and by the nineteenth century there was a healthy trade in refurbished umbrellas (Farrell 1985).

Compared to umbrellas, parasols were light and elegant, and throughout the early nineteenth century a wide range of styles and color were available. They were frequently referred to in magazines and newspapers of the time (Crawford 1970), although parasols were not generally carried by men (Farrell 1985).

Covers were made of chiffon, silk, taffeta, or satin and were often decorated with fringes, lace details, and embroidery. Long wooden bone or ivory handles were elaborately carved to feature animals and insects, porcelain handles were painted with delicate floral designs and some parasol handles even featured gimmicks such as inlaid watches (Bordignon Elestici 1990). Around the mid-1800s, the *en-tout-cas* became popular, as it fulfilled the function of protecting against both the sun and the rain (Farrell 1985), but one of the most remarkable parasols documented belonged to Queen Victoria, which she had lined with chain mail following an attempt to assassinate her (Stacey 1991).

The introduction of the automobile in the early years of the twentieth century initially encouraged the development of driving-specific parasols and umbrellas (Farrell 1985), but the new vehicles probably precipitated the decline of umbrella use, as people were less often on foot when out of doors (Crawford 1970). However, even during the interwar years (1918–1939), an umbrella was still regarded as "part of the unofficial uniform of a gentleman in London" (Farrell 1985, p. 79).

Although parasols, particularly those that emulated the style of flat, oriental sunshades, were popular up until the 1920s, the growing fashion for tanned skin effectively put an end to widespread use of the parasol by the 1930s. Looking to North America, Stacey notes that "neither the umbrella nor the parasol gained quick acceptance in America (1991, p. 59) and although Sidney Fisher's *Men, Woman and Manners of Colonial Days*, published in 1898, recorded sightings of umbrellas and parasols in Philadelphia in 1771, as a means of keeping off the sun they were reportedly regarded as a "ridiculous effeminacy" (Stacey 1991, p. 59). By the 1950s, however, Americans had championed the "unisex" umbrella, a distinct shift away from the gender-specific umbrella styles of Europeans (Stacey 1991).

The British umbrella trade had flourished in the last quarter of the eighteenth century, as the colonies could be relied on to supply raw materials including canes, whalebone, horn, and ivory, and a thriving textile industry provided fabrics such as silk and cotton gingham for making covers. As a result, by 1851 London had about 1,330 workers in the trade, a third of whom were in the Stepney area of East London. But following the collapse of the parasol market in the 1930s and the domination of the umbrella market by cheap imports from the 1940s onward, the British umbrella industry effectively disappeared (Crawford 1970).

Farrell (1985) indicates that over time, each part of the umbrella and parasol has been the object of improvement, including the innovation of the cranked stick, which allowed the open umbrellas to be centered over the head rather than to one side, and the cycloidal umbrella, which had the stick placed off-center. Since the nineteenth century, however, the only significant structural development has been Hans Haupt's telescopic umbrella in 1930, and improvements to allow automatic opening, but patents continue to be filed at the rate of about twenty a year (Stacey 1991). Use of nylon covers since the 1950s was the only other notable development in umbrella design in the twentieth century (Farrell 1985).

Europe's oldest and biggest umbrella shop continues, in the early 2000s, to trade under the name of James Smith & Sons (Umbrellas) Ltd., which was established in 1830. According to the London and Home Counties Survey (1957), "at one period umbrellas were actually manufactured inside the shop in a space four feet wide, and stock had to be stored in the window," and the company was one of the first to use "Fox Frames" in their umbrellas. In addition to conventional umbrellas, the firm has also specialized in the production of ceremonial umbrellas for traditional rulers in Africa.

Despite its pan-global origins, the umbrella has come to be regarded, in literature at least, as a quintessentially English item, perhaps due to the inclement weather for which Britain is famous. Stacey notes that Max Beerbohm said: "What is an Englishman without his umbrella? . . . It is the umbrella which has made Englishmen what they are, and its material is the stuff of which Englishmen are made" (cited in Stacey 1991, p. 7). In the twenty-first century, however, cheap and poorly made folding umbrellas have become disposable items, displacing durable, high-quality umbrellas in most parts of the world.

See also **Protective Clothing; Raincoat; Rainwear.**

BIBLIOGRAPHY
Bordignon Elestici, Letizia. *Gli Ombrelli* [Umbrellas]. Milan: BE-MA Editrice, 1990.

Crawford, T. S. *A History of the Umbrella.* New York: Taplinger Publishing Company, 1970.

Farrell, Jeremy. *Umbrellas and Parasols.* London: B. T. Batsford, Ltd., 1985.

"Histories of Famous Firms." London and Home Counties Survey (part 4), 1957.

Sangster, William. *Umbrellas and Their History.* London: Effingham Wilson, Royal Exchange, 1855.

Stacey, Brenda. *The Ups and Downs of Umbrellas.* Stroud, U.K.: Alan Sutton Publishing, 1991.

Anna König

UNDERWEAR The idea of items of clothing being private or public or that a body can be in an appropriately clothed or unclothed state is a relative concept that differs over time and from culture to culture. No tribal society, unless it has been infiltrated by concepts of western dress, appears to have garments that could be considered as underwear: items of clothing that act as a layer of insulation between the skin of the body and its outer garments.

The anthropologist Ted Polhemus uses the example of the loincloth, which is a garment at once in direct contact with the wearer's genitals but at the same time open to the public gaze. He postulates that this intimacy is allowable in small established communities where everything is known of the participants, unlike the rituals followed in larger, more industrialized, and thus anonymous societies. It is only when the cultural notion of privacy is apparent that underwear can perform its ritualistic function of shielding the body from the open scrutiny of others.

It was in ancient Egypt that the concept of having a second layer of clothing between the skin and the outer, more decoratively embellished layer of dress was devised. At that time the inner layer was worn more as a status symbol than for any erotic or practical reasons.

In Europe and North America underwear appears to have developed in range and complexity as the sight of a naked body moves from being an everyday public occurrence to a social taboo, and codes of acceptable social etiquette and civility deem the naked body private. Strategies come into play to make the body respectable, and underwear thus achieves its primary role, to shield the sexual zones of the body from the gaze of others.

Up to the nineteenth century underwear in Europe and North America had two main functions: to protect expensive outer garments from the dirt of the body beneath, as bathing for most was an expensive and time-consuming luxury, and to add an extra layer of insulation. The first items of underwear were unisex and classless linen shifts with no particular erotic connotations. By the nineteenth century, however, the notion of underwear began to change as fashion became more inherently gendered.

Underwear remained practical and functional for men, with cotton being the staple material, but for women it became an erotic exoskeleton helping to achieve the fashionable silhouette by constraining the body and coding certain parts as sexual. The corset, for instance, derived from the *cotte* of the 1300s, a rigid laced tunic of linen, became a device used to compress the waist while simultaneously drawing attention to the breasts and hips. This leads to the inherent tension in the nature of underwear: it conceals but simultaneously reveals the erogenous zones of the body. Adam and Eve may have modestly covered their genitals with fig leaves, but by doing so, they drew attention to the sexual parts of their bodies.

The bra, for instance, supports the breasts but at the same time creates a cleavage, an entirely invented erogenous zone that exists only as a result of the underwear that creates it. Underwear also exists to disguise the messy reality of the functions of the body. On the one hand observers are fascinated by layers of clothing being stripped away but are repulsed when confronted with the traces of the body left behind. As the popular saying goes, "We should never wash our dirty linen in public."

Polhemus sees underwear as preventing what he dubs "erotic seepage" (p. 114) in public encounters, as in the case of men, whose penises are not always subject to voluntary control. Thus the tightly laced corset worn by women (and children up to the late eighteenth century, when the philosopher Jean-Jacques Rousseau advocated their abolition for children) was not just a whim of fashion, it was also believed to lend support to the fragile bodies of women and to constrain their sexuality; women could be "strait-laced" but also "loose."

The corset is also an example of how certain forms of underwear have moved in and out of fashion and have been reworked into different garments that retain the primary function of shaping the body into the fashionable ideal. The couturier Paul Poiret may have declared the corset dead by the 1920s, but it merely went on to assume other forms such as the dancing corset, girdle, and the roll-on of the 1950s.

By the 1980s the corset had moved to outerwear through the work of British designer Vivienne Westwood who in her seminal Portrait Collection of 1990 featured photographically printed corsets using the work of eighteenth-century artist François Boucher (1703–1770). She subverted the whole notion of the corset as a physically restricting item of underwear by using lycra rather than the original whalebone or steel stays of the nineteenth-century version. The elasticized sides of Westwood's design meant an end to laces at the front or back. The corset could now be pulled over the head in one easy movement.

By the nineteenth century the range of underwear available for women had become elaborate and its use proscribed by ideas of sexual etiquette to the extent that the accidental revealing of underwear was considered as mortifying as the naked body itself. In 1930 J. C. Flügel in *The Psychology of Clothes* attempted an explanation: "Garments which, through their lack of ornamentation are clearly not intended to be seen (such as women's corsets and suspenders, the coarser forms of underwear) when accidentally viewed produce an embarrassing sense of intrusion upon privacy that often verges on the indecent. It is like looking 'behind the scenes' and thus exposing an illusion" (p. 194). Vestiges of this idea can be seen in contemporary culture, such as the acutely embarrassing state of a man being seen with his trouser zipper down, even if all he will be revealing is his underwear.

In the nineteenth and early twentieth centuries underwear, in some instances, could not be referred to directly in polite conversation, with "unmentionables" being a favored phrase. The twentieth century brought changes, however, including a gradually more relaxed attitude toward both sexuality and underwear.

A key item of women's underwear was developed in 1913 when New York debutante Mary Phelps Jacob, under the name Caresse Crosby, designed one of first modern bras, although the notion of supporting the breasts dates back to the Roman Empire when women wore scarves or *strophium* to mark themselves out from the "barbarous" unfettered breasts of slaves. Jacob's bra was boneless and kept the midriff free, while suspending the breasts from above rather than pushing them upwards from beneath as was the nature of the corset.

Cantilevering was added to bras in the 1950s by firms such as Warner's, who had bought Jacob's original patent, and Triumph, whose cone-shaped, circular-stitched bra in nylon or cotton batiste was worn by the popular Hollywood incarnation of the Sweater Girl as exemplified by stars such as Jayne Mansfield and Mamie van Doren.

In America the union suit held sway for men until the 1930s, when the first shorts with buttons on the yoke, originally developed for soldiers during World War I, became more freely available. The union suit, fashioned out of knitted fabric that reached from the wrists to the ankles, was one of the first industrially produced items of underwear, and emphasized warmth rather than comfort or convenience. It made no direct reference to the penis—unlike the codpiece, which was less about sexuality and more about rank and status.

However, a massive cultural change occurred in the 1930s when Cooper Inc introduced its Jockey Y-front design with overlapping fly for ease of urination. In the same decade the boxer short, originally issued to infantrymen for summer wear in America during World War I, began its acceptability in men's underwear fashion. The 1960s saw a vogue for brightly colored underwear in nylon and polyester for both men and women, which continued through the 1970s. By the 1980s manufacturers responded to what appeared to be a newly fashion literate male consumer, popularly referred to as the New Man, who was taking a more active interest in his grooming and, concomitantly, his underwear.

Calvin Klein helped in a reworking of masculinity as erotic at the end of the twentieth century with his advertising campaign by photographer Herb Ritts in 1993, using pop-star-turned-actor Mark Wahlberg. Wahlberg was portrayed in Calvin Klein underwear as a powerfully sexual figure, overturning the traditional language of advertising and its representation of male bodies. Wahlberg displayed his semi-clad worked-out body in a mainstream advertising campaign that appealed to both a male and female gaze. A man's body could be sexualized outside the pages of gay erotic imagery, and women could find pleasure in looking. The social and physical power of masculinity was no longer expressed solely through the world of work, but through a semi-nude body clad in designer underwear.

While male underwear was playing with the idea of the erotic as well as the practical, women's underwear began to make reference to athletics, reflecting an increasing interest and participation in exercise and the world of physical culture. From the early twentieth century, as cultural attitudes toward women and sport have changed and an athletic rather than reproductive function has been acknowledged, manufacturers have responded with more practical underwear. One important development was Dupont's invention of nylon in 1938, which helped in the creation of ranges of easy-care, drip-dry underwear. Lycra followed made in 1950, a new material of a knit of two yarns: a synthetic polyester or polyamide, and elastic fiber or spandex.

Underwear that made direct reference to athletics was to reach a height in the 1980s when aerobic exercise and the newly toned and muscled body that ensued became the cultural ideal for women. The runner Hinda Miller invented the sports bra, which became a classic of women's underwear design, made of stretch fabric with no fasteners so as to be pulled over the head with ease—a direct response to the needs of sportswomen that has entered mainstream fashion. The sports bra has become a signifier of a healthy lifestyle rather than a garment simply worn by women athletes. By the early twenty-first century many items of underwear had body control as their primary function. The taboos around the intake of food and keeping the inner workings of the body pure through organic food and practices such as colonic irrigation have influenced underwear design, which evokes a "naturalness" and a "simplicity" to match the twenty-first century obsession with body engineering. Ironically, this supposedly "natural" look runs concurrently with an emphasis on the artificial in the guise of the Wonderbra and other forms of more erotic and body shaping underwear.

Underwear is no longer unmentionable, and the world's leading fashion designers and celebrities are prepared to lend their names to or launch ranges of directional underwear design—from Australian model Elle Macpherson and pop star Kylie Minogue to brands such as Tommy Hilfiger and Chanel. Designer label underwear carries such cachet for the young consumer that it is pulled up the body so as to be displayed openly over the waistbands of jeans, following a look originally associated with the protagonists of hip-hop culture from the South Bronx of New York in the 1980s.

See also **Corset; Jockey Shorts; Lingerie; Slip.**

BIBLIOGRAPHY

Carter, Alison. *Underwear: The Fashion History*. London: B. T. Batsford Ltd., 1992.

Flügel, J. C. *The Psychology of Clothes*. London: Hogarth Press, 1930.

Polhemus, Ted. *Bodystyles*. London: Lennard Publishing, 1988.

Caroline Cox

UNIFORMS, DIPLOMATIC Diplomatic uniforms are civilian uniforms worn by ambassadorial and consular officers at public occasions. These uniforms appeared around 1800 when European countries began to reform their administrations and assign uniforms to many of their public officials. Previously, diplomats, who usually belonged to the highest nobility, had worn their own splendid clothes at solemn occasions. Only the colors and badges of their livery servants' clothing indicated the ambassador's own court and the court of the ruler he represented (*Nach Rang und Stand*, pp. 85–93, 252–255).

History

In the second half of the eighteenth century, several European countries began to consider uniforms for their envoys to foreign countries. As early as 1768, France ordered that her consuls in charge of trade and shipping traffic in the Near East wear uniforms of the navy's commissioners and under-commissioners. By 1781, the French consuls received their own uniforms of blue cloth with red lining, red waistcoat, and breeches, decorated with buttons featuring the king's coat of arms and trimmed with gold braids denoting respective rank. One of the reasons for the introduction of diplomatic uniforms can be found in a letter sent by Netherlands consuls in Spain to their home country in 1776. They asked for uniforms in order to save money and claimed that uniforms would relieve them from buying expensive fashionable clothes needed for representing their country (Kramers, p. 23).

For patriotic reasons and in order to promote abroad the ideas of a national republican state, the First French Republic required that its representatives at foreign courts dress in the uniform of the French *Garde Nationale*. However, these early regulations were obviously not yet strictly followed, as an official portrait of Guillemardet, the French ambassador in Spain at that time, shows him wearing his private clothes together with a tricolor sash wound around his waist (Delpierre, p. 31).

Diplomatic uniforms became part of general administrative reforms issued by most European countries around 1800 as a response to the French Revolution and the Napoleonic wars. When in the past the ambassador's impressive appearance depended on his personality and his own individual means, now uniforms made the person stand back behind the office he represented (Lüttenberg, p. 86–87). In several countries, diplomatic uniforms were among the first civilian uniforms to be issued because they represented the new reformed state to the outside world. When Count Maximilian von Montgelas, minister and head of the new reforms in Bavaria, ordered uniforms for the Bavarian state officers in 1799, he began his campaign with the office of foreign affairs. His regulations, published in 1807, were basically kept until as late as 1918. In fact, in most European countries, the design of the diplomatic uniforms changed very little in contrast to other civilian uniforms.

Design

The design of the diplomatic uniforms preserved the court fashion of the early nineteenth century, which was marked by richly embroidered tailcoats with standing collar, breeches or pantaloons depending on the formal event, and completed by a sword and a two-cornered plumed hat. With their lavish gold embroidery, the diplomatic uniforms were always among the richest of civil uniforms and resembled those of distinguished court officials. This was considered appropriate because members of the diplomatic corps usually belonged to the highest court circles and represented their country at the most official events at court. While most Bavarian state employees were clad in blue uniforms, Barvarian diplomats dressed in red ones similar to the uniforms worn by high officials of the Bavarian royal court. In most countries, diplomats had to acquire at least two uniforms: a richly embroidered full dress uniform for formal events and a simpler uniform for everyday use. English and

Bavarian diplomats needed three kinds of uniforms: full dress, levée dress, and frock dress.

While military uniforms signal rank mainly by stars and badges, civilian uniforms distinguish rank by the amount and quality of the embroidery. By 1847, the Lord Chamberlain's office divided the British diplomatic corps into five ranks and laid down rules for their respective uniforms precisely specifying the amount and width of the gold embroidery allowed for each rank. Ambassadors, who belonged to the first class, enjoyed the privilege of wearing the richest full dress uniform at grand state occasions. Sparkling gold embroidery of oak and palm leafs covered large areas of the tailcoat's chest, collar, cuffs, pocket flaps, and back skirts, as well as the seams. Gilt buttons showing the royal arms buttoned down the chest. White breeches, a sword, sword knot and belt, gloves, and a two-cornered hat with white ostrich feathers completed the full dress uniform. For less grand occasions, the English ambassadors donned the so-called levée dress uniform. Being less opulent its gold embroidery was restricted to the collar, cuffs, pocket flaps, and between the buttons on the rear waist. Long trousers belonged to the levée dress because they were considered less formal than short breeches. The embroidery on the full dress and levée dress uniform diminished in amount and width as the rank descended. (At informal dinners and evening parties, all members of the English diplomatic corps wore plain black frockcoat). Signaling a lower status within the foreign services, the uniforms of the English consular staff were decorated with embroidery of silver instead of gold (Tendrell, 35–42).

Most European diplomatic uniforms were quite similar in shape but varied in color, design of embroidery, and of course in the design of the buttons showing the coat of arms or initials of the ambassador's ruler. Austrian diplomats dressed in dark green tail coats with cuffs and collars of black velvet covered with gold oak leaf embroidery. After 1817, Prussian diplomats wore dark blue tail coats with cuffs and a standing collar of black velvet, decorated with gold embroidery showing neoclassical oak leaf scrolls. Whereas during the course of the nineteenth century most uniforms of governmental officials became modernized along with the military uniforms, the ornate diplomatic uniforms tended to keep their traditional shape. In 1888, when the German government revived the *altbrandenburgische waffenrock* as the full state uniform to be used by most governmental officers of upper rank, the diplomats were at first excluded. Only later, after having launched several requests, did the German diplomats receive permission to wear the richly embroidered long coat, which revived elements of uniforms worn by Prussian military officers during the eighteenth century (Lüttenberg, p. 90).

Later and Non-European Developments

Although the majority of the European countries gave up uniforms for most of their governmental officers at the

Diplomats discuss the Treaty of Ghent, 1814. Early nineteenth-century, European diplomatic uniform boasted tailcoats with standing collar, breeches, and gold embroidery. A sword and two-cornered plumed hat, not pictured, completed the ensemble. THE GRANGER COLLECTION, NEW YORK. REPRODUCED BY PERMISSION.

end of World War I, several countries decided to keep diplomatic uniforms. Germany, for example, had already abandoned its richly embroidered diplomatic uniforms during the Weimar Republic, although the Nazis' fondness of impressive uniforms brought back the diplomatic uniform for a short while. The stage designer Benno von Arent recreated a new diplomatic uniform with the help of Mrs. von Ribbentrop, wife of the German foreign minister. Its full dress uniform consisted of a dark blue tailcoat with silver oak leaf embroidery covering the coat's modern lapels. A silver sash, silver aiguillette, and a small dagger completed the startling uniform. Even by the twenty-first century, some European ambassadors still appeared in full dress uniforms at special occasions. A photo taken of the New Year's reception at the Vatican in 2001 shows from left to right the ambassadors of Monaco, the Netherlands, Thailand, Great Britain, Spain, France, and Belgium, all clad in splendid diplomatic uniforms.

The embroidered full dress uniform of European diplomats impressed several non-European courts. Formal portrait photos taken during the nineteenth century depict Indonesian princes wearing jackets richly embroidered with gold thread in the style of Western diplomatic state uniforms together with multicolored native sarongs and pajamas. A most striking adaptation of Western state uniforms took place in Japan in 1872, when two centuries of isolation had come to an end and the Japanese emperor Meiji decided that all members of his military, court, and government (including the diplomatic corps), abandon traditional Japanese dress and adopt European uniforms.

Quite in contrast to monarchic countries, the republican United States renounced civil uniforms for its diplomats, and their use was even prohibited by Congress. Of Civil War veterans only those of the Northern states were allowed to wear their military uniforms. Consequently, during the nineteenth century, American diplomats frequently ran into trouble when trying to attend formal events at European courts, which would only admit men in uniform. Thus, Theodore Roosevelt attracted considerable attention when he attended the funeral of the English king Edward VII in 1910 and was the only foreign representative who did not appear in uniform.

See also **Fashion and Identity; Uniforms, Military.**

BIBLIOGRAPHY

Delpierre, Madeleine. "Fonctions diplomatiques." *Uniformes civils français cérémonial circonstances 1750–1980.* Paris: Musée de la mode et du costume, 1982. pp. 31–32.

Hackspiel-Mikosch, Elisabeth, ed. *Nach Rang und Stand: Deutsche Ziviluniformen* im 19. Jahrhundert. Deutsches Textilmuseum: Krefeld, 2002.

Kramers, C. J. M. "Iets over de ambtscostuums van de Buitenlandse Dienst." *BZ, Maanblaad vor de medewerkers van het Ministerie van Buitenlandse Zaken* 50 no. 6 (1988): 23–27.

Kugler, Georg J., and Monica Kurzel Runtscheiner *Des Kaisers teure Kleider, Festroben und Ornate, Hofuniformen und Livreen vom frühen 18. Jahrhundert bis 1918.* Vienna 2000: 135. Catalog nos. 67–72.

Lüttenberg, Thomas. "Der gestickte Rock—Deutsche Diplomatenuniformen im 19. Jahrhundert." *Nach Rang und Stand—Deutsche Ziviluniformen im 19. Jahrhundert.* Edited by Elisabeth Hackspiel-Mikosch. Deutsches Textilmuseum Krefeld 2002. pp. 85–93.

Schmidtl, Erwin A. "Tropen- und Sommeruniformen der k.u.k. Konsular und diplomatischen Beamten 1913–1918." *Mitteilungen des Österreichischen Staatsarchivs* 40 (1988): 302–319.

Trendell, Herbert A. P. *Dress Worn at his Majesty's Court. Issued with the authority of the Lord Chamberlain.* London, 1908. pp. 35–42.

Elisabeth Hackspiel-Mikosch

UNIFORMS, MILITARY Distinctive attire for pursuing the business of battle has been part of armed conflict everywhere in the world since humanity invented war. The very carrying of arms, both offensive and defensive (spears, clubs, shields, helmets, etc.), gives the warrior a different appearance from someone engaged in more pacific tasks. However, the idea of a military uniform, clothing all members of a unit in similar dress, is a relatively late development in the long history of human conflict.

In various parts of the world, minor or major potentates and warlords used part of their wealth to clothe a corps of guards in uniform dress in the same manner that other palace servants might wear some sort of personal livery. This sort of early uniform survives in the ceremonial dress of the contemporary Papal Guards in Rome (according to legend, designed by Michelangelo) and London's Yeomen of the Guard, whose uniform is similar to that worn in the courts of the Tudors. True military uniforms, however, only came into use with social and political developments in Europe that have come to be known as the "military revolution."

The military revolution came about in the late sixteenth and early seventeenth centuries, as musketry fire from mass formations became decisive on Europe's battlefields. While the individual musket was an ineffective weapon, when used by well-drilled and well-disciplined troops, the musket allowed infantry so armed to dominate any battle. This change in weaponry led to the crystallization of military organization into professional armies consisting of relatively highly trained rank and file soldiers arranged in permanent organizations. At first these units were raised by individuals who sold their services to the highest bidder. The unit commander then provided clothing for his troops; the interests of economy as well as building *esprit de corps* led to uniformity of clothing within these units.

An important aspect of combat is the ability to distinguish friend from foe. Prior to the domination of the battlefield by gunpowder this could be accomplished through the use of standards or flags (such as the eagle of the Roman Legion) or temporary identification devices (scarves or armbands) allowing one side to recognize its allies. However, the possibility for fatal errors in unit identification was great on seventeenth- and early eighteenth-century battlefields enshrouded in smoke from the volleys fired from black-powder weapons. Even flags were of little help as these were often emblazoned with the badge of the unit's commander rather than a national symbol.

This led to a spread of uniformity of dress beyond the battalion level to that of most of the military forces of a kingdom or state. As permanent military establishments were developed in Europe, the practicality of uniform regulation for all troops in the service of the state became recognized. By the mid-eighteenth century colors of clothing had become associated with national armies. Britain largely clothed its army in red, France in pale gray or white, Prussia in dark blue, Bavaria in sky blue, Austria in white, Russia in dark green, etc. There were exceptions; foreign regiments in the service of French monarchs, for example, often wore red or blue. Following the events of 1789 the new French republic changed the color of the uniform of the French infantry to blue.

Sometimes a uniform color had significance that crossed national boundaries. Both Britain and France dressed their artillery in blue. German and British rifle regiments were clothed in a very dark green. Naval uni-

The Texas A&M Drill Team in full dress uniform. Though military uniforms in the twentieth century adopted styles more functional for combat, some ceremonial uniforms continued to display elements of military pagaentry. © PHILIP GOULD/CORBIS. REPRODUCED BY PERMISSION.

forms throughout the globe have been of navy blue (white in the summer) and more recently the world's air forces have worn a dress uniform of light blue.

Principles Underlying Military Dress

James Laver has seen three competing principles that determine the form of military uniforms. He named these the hierarchical principle, the seduction principle, and the utility principle. The hierarchical principle manifests itself in differentiating ranks within a military organization and differentiating elite from ordinary soldiers. Hence, since 1831, the regiments of foot guards in the British army have worn the bearskin headdress that distinguishes them from line-infantry regiments. This also represents the seduction principle, since the headdress increases the height of its wearer, hence making him more masculine and attractive. Laver argues that both the hierarchical principle and the seduction principle manifest themselves in times of peace; however, both produce a form of dress often impractical in the face of the rigors of campaign. In times of war, badges of rank may be dispensed with because they draw enemy fire, illustrating the victory of the utility principle over the hierarchal

principle. Similarly, the seduction principle yields to utility as tight-fitting, "smart" uniforms of the parade ground are replaced by looser dress allowing the ease of movement necessary in combat.

While the hierarchical principle dictates that elite units differentiate their dress from ordinary military units, there is also the fact that it seems to be nearly universal that others if given the opportunity will appropriate the symbols of elite status. The jump boots of American paratroops in World War II were once a proud symbol of their elite status, but later in the war they came to be devalued as a status symbol as other soldiers, even those in noncombatant roles, acquired them.

It is also true that an army of one nation will adopt the dress of the army of that state which is perceived to be a superior military power. Throughout history one country or another has dominated military style, with others copying their uniforms. French military style dominated the uniforms of much of the world's military until its defeat in the Franco-Prussian war; then armies throughout the world replaced their French kepis with German spiked helmets. Also, units aspiring to similar elite status will ape dress of other elites. In many of the world's armies the green beret has come to be associated with elite commando formations, the red beret with airborne troops, and the black beret with armored troops. In World War II, the British commander Bernard Montgomery and the men of the Royal Tank Corps wore black berets, as did the Germans in the Panzers they fought in the North African desert. In earlier centuries light cavalry worldwide adopted the heavily laced jacket of the Hungarian hussar or the square-shaped *czapka* headdress of the Polish lancer.

The Evolution of Military Uniform

In cut and general form, military uniforms reflect the style of civilian fashion of their time, although distinctive elements, such as epaulets and headgear, are added that clearly mark the wearer as a soldier. After body armor largely fell into disuse in the mid-seventeenth century, the soldier dressed like his civilian cousin, although the colors of his clothing would reflect his unit and increasingly the state or monarch he served. The necessity to carry arms with belts capable of holding ammunition pouches, bayonets, swords and the like did give the soldier a distinctive appearance.

Even at this early point in the evolution of military uniforms a purely military form of headdress, the grenadier cap, came into being. During the late seventeenth century, the grenade was a significant factor in infantry tactics. It was an iron sphere filled with gunpowder that was ignited by a fuse. Specialist troops were trained to light these fuses from a hand-held match and then throw the grenades into the ranks of the enemy. Since two hands were required for this, grenadiers had to sling their muskets on their backs, an operation difficult to accomplish when wearing the broad-brimmed hats of the era. Thus grenadiers were given a sort of stocking cap. Some military tailor concluded that these grenadiers, already selected for their size and strength, would look even more impressive if the cap were stiffened to increase the apparent height of its wearer (Laver's seduction principle). The grenadier cap became a symbol of an elite soldier (Laver's hierarchical principle). Since elite troops were useful for assaulting or defending key positions on a battlefield, European armies continued to designate units as "grenadiers," and these wore grenadier caps long after grenades had become obsolete (hand grenades were reintroduced in warfare in the trenches of World War I). The grenadier cap was sometimes given a metal front (such as that worn by the Russian Life Guard Pavlovski Regiment in full dress until 1914) or made of fur. The fur headdress worn by the Brigade of Guards at Buckingham Palace in London is in fact a grenadier cap.

The horsed soldier was sometimes distinguished from mounted civilians by wearing the cuirass. This body armor continued to be utilized by heavy cavalry long after the infantry had abandoned it. The civilian hat was worn for a long period, despite its proclivity to be blown from the head when engaged in a charge. This tendency

eventually led to the cocked hat being replaced by helmets of various forms in the late eighteenth century. The crest on these helmets served both the seduction principle and the utility principle, for in addition to making the horseman more imposing, it provided some additional protection from sword cuts.

It was the recruiting of light cavalry from the eastern frontiers of Europe that provided a novel and exotic appearance for a large portion of the cavalry in eighteenth- and nineteenth-century European armies. Austria first recruited Hungarian horsemen to serve as light horse in its military establishment. The dress of these Hungarian hussars had a great influence on military style, both for mounted troops and soldiers. Many armies copied the appearance of the Hungarian jacket fastened by many rows of cords and toggles across the chest. A second, fur-lined jacket (the pelisse) slung over the left shoulder was also widely adopted in the dress of light cavalry, as was the sabretache, a leather pouch or envelope that was suspended from the sword belt.

It is Hungarian headgear that probably had the greatest impact on the appearance of the military. These horsemen wore either a stocking cap edged in fur or a cylindrical felt cap. Through time the fur on the stocking cap was expanded, making the fur cylinder with a bag falling to one side from the top, a form of headdress known as the busby. The cylindrical felt cap was the inspiration for the shako. The shako was widely adopted in all branches of the military during the Napoleonic Wars. Britain dressed its infantry in shakos in 1800; it was not until 1806 that the line infantry of Napoleonic France adopted this headdress. The shako continued as the most common form of military headgear until the defeat of France by Prussia in 1870 and continues to be worn by some units (as, for example, in the full dress of the Corps of Cadets of the U.S. Military Academy).

Just as Hungary provided the pattern for the dress of hussars in armies around the globe, Poland provided the model for the dress of lancers, particularly after Poles played a prominent role in the multiethnic armies of Napoleon. The square-topped *czapka* and plastron-fronted jacket or tunic with piping along its seams was worn by substantial segments of cavalry in Europe and even had an impact on the uniforms of colonial India.

In considering the pressure for elaboration of military uniform and the counter pressure for utility, one can contrast the European experience of the Napoleonic Wars and the long era of peace that followed that conflict. While in theory the armies that fought in the Napoleonic Wars had colorful and elaborate uniforms, in practice they presented a much more drab appearance. Uniforms faded in the sun or wore out on long campaigns and were replaced by clothing obtained locally. The rigors of winter campaigning forced troops to march in gray or brown overcoats rather than full-dress coatees. Plumes would be stowed in knapsacks, while shakos or bearskin

Early twentieth century West Point military academy cadets. The shako, a hat worn by the cadets shown here, held the allure of adding apparent height to the wearer. ANNE S.K. BROWN MILITARY COLLECTION, BROWN UNIVERSITY LIBRARY. REPRODUCED BY PERMISSION.

bonnets would be protected from the weather by oilskin covers. Loose trousers replaced the tight breeches and long buttoned spatterdashes or gaiters of the parade ground. With the coming of the long period of peace following Napoleon's defeat, the appearance on the parade ground moved to the forefront and uniforms reached a degree of fantastic elaboration not seen before or since. The realities of war returned in the late nineteenth and early twentieth centuries to banish such sartorial splendor from military life.

Reflecting changes in civilian fashion, by the mid-nineteenth century the tight-fitting waist-length coatee, widely worn for nearly fifty years, was replaced in the world's military by the tunic or frock coat with skirts that at least partially covered the thigh. Russia and Prussia also adopted leather helmets with brass spikes, while for the most part the rest of the world continued to wear the shako or kepi. At this same time there were developments in firearms technology that led to a revolution in military uniforms.

For almost three centuries the smooth-bore musket had dominated the battlefield. The effective range of this weapon was so short (one hundred yards or less) that troops were drilled not to fire until they could see the whites of the eyes of their enemy. Hence, the color of a uniform was unimportant as long as one could be recognized by one's allies and not be taken for the enemy. While there was some use in battle of firearms with rifled barrels that were effective at far greater distances, these early rifles were cumbersome to load. The invention shortly before the American Civil War of a rifle, which could be loaded as rapidly as the old smooth-bore musket, was soon followed by the invention of a breech-loading rifle. A further innovation was the magazine rifle allowing an infantryman to fire several shots after a single act of loading his weapon. Smokeless powder eliminated the huge clouds of acrid smoke that obscured vision on the black-powder battlefield. All of these factors led to the adoption of uniforms whose purpose was to inhibit the recognition of troops at the great distances at which they were now vulnerable to rifle fire.

Khaki was first used in India, originally in the Corps of Guides raised by Lieutenant Harry B. Lumsden in 1846. A decade later, during the Indian Mutiny, a number of British regiments dyed their white summer uniforms khaki to be less visible on the battlefield. While Britain experimented with other drab colors, notably gray, khaki was worn in India, becoming official dress for that station in 1885 and for all foreign stations in 1896. In 1902 Britain adopted a khaki service dress. Other nations followed Britain's example; the first three to adopt a khaki service dress were the United States, Japan, and Imperial Russia. Both France and Germany used khaki for their colonial troops, but Germany in 1910 chose a light gray for its regular army and France, while it began the Great War still in dark blue uniforms, switched to horizon blue early in 1915.

The trench warfare of 1914 to 1918 led to the universal adoption of steel helmets. The threat of gas attacks meant gas masks had to be easily accessible. Trenches, barbed wire, and the machine gun reduced the cavalry to no role at all. Increasing mechanization meant the auto mechanic replaced the farrier in keeping the supply lines functioning, and at least one critic of modern trends in uniforms has lamented that the dress of the soldier now mimics that of an employee of a service station. The war changed the view of the proper soldiers from that of impressively and colorfully dressed units executing precision drill on the parade ground to massive armies engaged in savage warfare under the appalling conditions of the modern battlefield. The pomp and splendor of military pageantry and glory of full dress observable before the war (as late as 1913 the German army was executing maneuvers in a version of full dress) was gone forever.

Wars subsequent to the watershed years of 1914 to 1918 have seen the combat uniform increasingly, and with greater sophistication, being designed to prevent the soldier from being seen rather than allowing an imposing appearance to frighten or cow the enemy. Khaki and olive drab have been replaced by "disruptive pattern" clothing to conceal even more effectively the fighting man or woman. Uniforms have come to be designed even to conceal the soldier from the night-vision equipment finding increasing use on battlefields. The small flashes of color, the division patches that identified the soldier's unit in World War II, have been reduced in the American army to black on olive drab. The increased emphasis on concealment has exacted a price, however, as "friendly fire" has at times proved as hazardous to troops engaged in military operations as the fire from a dispirited enemy overwhelmed by a long period of bombardment from aircraft and missiles.

There has also been an emphasis on attempting to protect the soldier in combat. Modern technology has produced lightweight body armor, "flak jackets," to protect the torso. Some nations have suits, yet untried in a combat situation, to enable the soldier to fight on a battlefield contaminated by nuclear or biochemical weapons.

Modern Ceremonial Dress

Ceremony still plays a role in the relation of the military to the state, and dress appropriate for this ceremonial role is still significant in most military establishments. Although in a few cases, as with the British Brigade of Guards and the U.S. Marine Corps, uniforms virtually unchanged from the pre-1914 full dress are utilized, most of the world's military carries out ceremonial duties in much more drab clothing. Although economy is often cited as the reason for this abandonment of the full-dress uniforms, major portions of most armies utilize an order of dress for parade that could easily reflect earlier full-dress uniforms. It is modern fashion that dictates that the modern soldier parade in khaki or a similar shade. Yet in most military organizations there remains pressure to present a "smart" appearance on parade. In some cases, contemporary combat dress is utilized with the addition of ceremonial elements of uniform. The French Foreign Legion parades in camouflage combat attire with the addition of spotless (and plastic) white belts and the traditional green and red epaulets and the white kepi that date to the nineteenth century. There is still more than simple utility in the creation of the dress of the soldier.

See also **Armor; Camouflage Cloth.**

BIBLIOGRAPHY

Abler, Thomas S. *Hinterland Warriors and Military Dress: European Empires and Exotic Uniforms.* Oxford: Berg, 1999.

Carman, William Young. *A Dictionary of Military Uniform.* London: B.T. Batsford, Ltd., 1977.

Joseph, Nathan. *Uniforms and Nonuniforms: Communication through Clothing.* New York: Greenwood, 1986.

Knötel, Richard, Herbert Knötel, Jr., and Herbert Sieg. *Uniforms of the World: A Compendium of Army, Navy, and Air Force Uniforms, 1700–1937.* Translated by Ronald G. Ball. New York: Scribners, 1980. Originally published as *Handbuch der Uniformkunde.* Hamburg: H. G. Schulz, 1937.

Laver, James. "Fashion and Class Distinction." *Pilot Papers* 1 (1945): 63–74.

———. *British Military Uniforms.* London: Penguin, 1948.

Lawson, Cecil C. P. *A History of the Uniforms of the British Army.* 5 vols. London: Kaye and Ward, 1940–1967.

Mollo, John. *Military Fashion: A Comparative History of the Uniforms of the Great Armies from the 17th Century to the First World War.* New York: G. P. Putnam's Sons, 1972.

Parker, Geoffrey. *The Military Revolution: Military Innovation and the Rise of the West, 1500–1800.* Cambridge and New York: Cambridge University Press, 1996.

Windrow, Martin, and Gerry Embleton. *Military Dress of North America, 1665–1970.* London: Ian Allan, 1973.

Thomas S. Abler

UNIFORMS, OCCUPATIONAL

Occupational uniforms are nonmilitary civilian uniforms worn by members of certain professional groups during work or at official occasions. Specified and usually handed out by the employer, the uniform is designed in certain colors and carries signs and badges which signal the employee's function and rank within a professional organization.

Court Liveries

The first examples of occupational uniforms are liveries (from the French word *livrer*, meaning to deliver), which were uniform garments handed out to servants at European courts during the early modern period. Uniform in color, form, and decorations, liveries represented the household for which a servant was working. The coat of arms or initials of his master appeared on the liveries' buttons, trimmings, or badges. Already during earlier periods, princes, such as the Burgundian dukes, had their court members and servants dress in a single color at festive events in order to present a unified court. The livery proper began to spread during the seventeenth century, when the social status of a prince depended more and more on the splendid appearance of his court and his servants. These early liveries corresponded closely to military uniforms, which developed at the same time and which in the beginning were also called livery (in France, *livrée*; in Germany, *liberey* or *montur*). The colors of the

Airline pilot in uniform. In the twenty-first century, commercial pilot uniforms were designed in accordance with the desired marketing image of the airline. © ROYALTY-FREE/CORBIS. REPRODUCED BY PERMISSION.

military uniforms were usually identical to the liveries belonging to the household of the regiment's chief who, prior to the establishment of national armies, often owned the regiment.

Just like military uniforms during the seventeenth and eighteenth centuries, most servant liveries were cut according to contemporary fashion. Their striking colors, heightened by lining and trimmings in contrasting hues corresponded to the colors of the noble household to which the servants belonged but were not necessarily identical with its heraldic colors.

Like military uniforms, the liveries also functioned as signs of rank and distinction. Most important, the servant's livery presented the social rank, ambitions, and financial means of the master. For this reason the American economic theorist Thorstein Veblen regarded servant liveries as a prime example for his seminal theory of conspicuous and vicarious consumption. The livery also indicated the servant's rank within a household. For example, the dress of pages, who themselves were members of noble families, were more richly decorated and made of more costly materials than the liveries of other servants. The servant's nearness to the master also determined the preciousness of his outfit. Since footmen accompanied their master very closely during travels, their dress had to be made of particularly fine materials, even though the footmen's small salary reflected a low position at court (Mikosch, p. 295). The livery always signaled the rank of the occasion: the more official the occasion, the richer the livery had to be; therefore, most courts provided simple liveries for everyday use and costly ones for festive events.

During the second half of the nineteenth century, when class distinctions became increasingly complex and

Depiction of nineteenth-century Austrian postman. In 1785, Prussian postmaster von Werder was an early proponent of obligatory uniforms for postal workers, arguing that the uniforms would not only distinguish postmen but also save them money. © SCHEUFLER COLLECTION/CORBIS. REPRODUCED BY PERMISSION.

nobility lost more and more of its privileges, servant clothes had to make up for the loss of status. Some late courts, like the one of the prince of Thurn and Taxis, put on a particularly rich display of servants fitted out with numerous liveries. The servants of Thurn and Taxis had to change clothes several times during the course of the day, even as late as the 1980s (Kliegel, p. 107). In order to project the image of a long aristocratic tradition, the design of the servant liveries tended to be antiquated. The tightly fitted *justeaucorps*, fashionable during the eighteenth century and decorated with rich gold braids, continued to be employed for formal occasions and tailcoats for less formal events or everyday use.

Early Professional Uniforms
Besides livery servants, postmen and miners were the earliest professional groups clad in uniforms. In the beginning, only certain signs, badges, or accessories symbolized their profession. During the sixteenth century,

messengers were not yet dressed in uniforms but in regular traveling coats. They carried a badge on their chest or cap with the coat of arms of the city or noble court they served. Records of the seventeenth century already identify the horn as the sign of postal servants. The first time postal servants and officers were dressed in complete uniform clothes was early in the eighteenth century during celebrations at the Prussian (1703) and Saxon courts (1719). When the Saxon Elector Frederick Augustus and Polish King Augustus I, called Augustus the Strong, married his son Frederick Augustus to the imperial daughter Maria Josepha in 1719, he organized lavish wedding celebrations in Dresden and ordered his postal service and Saxon miners to take part in large numbers. For this occasion uniforms were designed that distinguished between the ranks and functions within a profession for the first time (Mikosch, pp. 315–332). Augustus, who was the head of the postal services and of the mining industries in Saxony, used the uniforms in order to present the image of a modern prosperous country. Consequently, these early occupational uniforms were actually splendid state uniforms mainly used for parading during court festivals. Lacking the necessary funds and the administrative structure, neither the Prussian nor the Saxon ruler succeeded in establishing regular occupational uniforms for their entire country at this time.

Civil Uniforms for State Employees
One of the first serious campaigns that tried to introduce an obligatory everyday uniform for members of one profession can be traced back to Germany in 1785 when the Prussian king Frederick II followed the suggestions of his general postmaster von Werder and decreed that all postal servants had to wear uniforms. He ordered state uniforms and uniforms for daily use. They consisted basically of blue coats with orange-colored collars and cuffs. Accessories, such as epaulets, aiguillettes, hat decorations, and swords distinguished between the ranks of the postmaster, postal secretary, postal attendants, and postilions. Von Werder's arguments anticipate the coming years when civil uniforms for state employees became more prevalent. He suggested that postal uniforms would help the servants save money, prevent them from wasting money for extravagant outfits, and ensure they dressed in respectable clothes. At the same time the uniforms would make the postal servants more easily recognizable to the general public.

Around 1800, many European countries introduced occupational uniforms for state employees as an important part of extensive administrative reforms that most countries issued as a response to the French Revolution and Napoleonic wars. The new reforms broke down the privileges of the aristocracy and the church, and prepared the ground for the development of a modern bourgeois society. The governmental officers' uniforms were intended to serve as symbols for the new ideal of a nation state run by an efficient and just administration. Inspired by those of the military, the uniforms' shape, colors, and decorations signified the function and rank of the officer. The uniforms were intended to work on two levels. From within, they enhanced the new bureaucratic structure and lent new confidence and pride to the state employees. From without, the uniforms were intended to evoke acceptance of the new state and its regulations as well as elicit new respect for its employees as the executors and representatives of the new state. The uniforms' shape underlined this message. Forcing an upright position the uniforms' particularly tight cut enhanced the proud and masculine impression of the man in uniform. Gradually most employees of governmental departments were clad in uniforms, no matter if they worked in public or not. This included, among others, the police services, fire departments, postal services, state-run mining and metalworking industries, forestry and transportation departments, as well as the departments of finance, interior, justice, and foreign affairs.

The general form of the occupational uniforms for state employees varied little during the nineteenth century and followed the form of military uniforms, beginning with tailcoats early in the century and adding the more practical, buttoned-down military tunic after the mid-nineteenth century. Most departments demanded state uniforms embroidered with gold and silver thread to be worn by officers at special occasions and simpler ones for everyday use. Smaller states, such as the dukedom of Brunswick, wanted to enhance their political importance by affording a luxurious array of uniforms in different colors and embroidery designs for each department. The large states of Prussia and Bavaria emphasized unity and efficiency by restricting their uniforms to one color. Prussia chose a dark blue ("Prussian blue"), and Bavaria ordered uniforms in a medium blue. Certain trimmings and signs identified different departments and ranks. The Prussian postal services wore their blue uniforms with orange-colored collars, cuffs, and pocket flaps. Bavarian uniforms had small symbols embroidered in silver thread on the tail: small horns stood for the postal service and winged wheels for the department of transportation. Each country had its own buttons showing either the coat of arms of the state or the initials of the ruler. The richness and width of embroidery on the chest, collar, cuff, and pocket flaps were meticulously prescribed and varied according to the rank of the officer within the administrative hierarchy (Hackspiel-Mikosch, pp. 221–287).

If the civil uniform symbolized the new administrational structures of modern states early in the nineteenth century, by the end of the century the civil uniform was regarded as a sign of stultifying and overexpanding bureaucracies supporting conservative governments, which, as in the case of Germany, became increasingly militaristic. At the end of World War I, when the German empire and its local monarchies were abolished, most civil uniforms for state employees disappeared. The Weimar Republic regarded the civil uniforms as a symbol of an

Royal English footmen in traditional uniform. Due to their proximity to their masters during travel, footmen traditionally wore uniforms of quality and decoration well above their court standing. © TIM GRAHAM/CORBIS. REPRODUCED BY PERMISSION.

outdated authoritarian state. Although, a few decades later, the German Nazi regime indulged in impressive uniforms, it did not revive civil uniforms for state employees. Instead, mass organizations such as the labor service were established. These organizations were structured like military institutions, and employees dressed in uniforms closely reflecting military hierarchies.

After the two world wars, only law-enforcement sections of the government (police, immigration, or prison wards) as well as certain public services (postal services, railways, fire fighters, or foresters) continued to wear uniforms. In Germany, the devastating experience of two world wars that had been supported by widespread militarism triggered a pacifistic countermovement during the 1960s and 1970s that regarded state authority and its uniformed representatives with strong skepticism. Responding to a signature campaign initiated by a young policeman who wanted less military-like and identical modern uniforms for all of Germany, in 1973 the German fashion designer Heinz Oestergaard created a new green-beige police uniform, which, with certain changes, is still worn today. The modern design and friendly colors of Oestergaard's more casual-looking uniforms were intended to communicate a modern and democratic image of Germany.

Some traditional civil uniforms continue to be worn today. Servants clad in sparkling livery still attend at European courts during important public occasions. Some European diplomats go on dressing in traditional richly embroidered state uniforms at formal occasions, such as New Year's receptions given by a head of state. Members of the Institut de France, the most elevated academic institution in France, still wear uniforms that were originally introduced in 1801 and are richly embroidered with olive branches in shades of green silk on black cloth. The academician's uniform is completed with a plumed two-cornered hat and a sword. Each generation tends to adapt the uniform's basic tailcoat to contemporary fashion. In 1981 Yves Saint-Laurent designed a modern version for Marguerite Yourcenar, who became a member that year.

Modern Occupational Uniforms
Since the second half of the twentieth century, the character of occupational uniforms has changed significantly. Reflecting the democratization of Western society, the uniforms' military elements, which symbolized the rank and function within a hierarchical organization, have stepped more and more into the background. Instead, professional uniforms have become part of modern concepts of corporate identity and corporate culture. Called corporate wear or corporate fashion, uniform dress at work is designed to communicate the philosophy of an organization or company and thereby is an increasingly important tool of marketing strategies. Investigations show that corporate fashion can significantly raise the image of a company and thereby elevate its stock-market value. Within a company, uniform dress, which is comfortable, fashionable, and clean, has been shown to improve working performance of employees by increasing their motivation and their identification with their company and fellow workers. A good-looking professional uniform attracts new customers and produces the image of trustworthiness and economic achievement. In his study of the ubiquitous civilian uniform in Japan, Brian McVeigh has revealed how much uniforms discipline the mind and body of Japanese office workers and, at the same time, express a particular economic nationalism in Japan.

The style of corporate uniforms changes according to the message a company wants to convey. The new uniforms for the German airline Lufthansa, introduced in January 2002, for example, are rather conservative. According to the company's public release, Lufthansa wanted their new uniform to convey the values of traditionalism, respectability, service competence, and timeless elegance. Uniforms of national airlines vary in style and are often understood as the business card of an entire nation. In contrast to Lufthansa, the German Railway decided on more innovative and fashionable uniforms intended to create the impression of a modern inventive company. When the German postal services introduced new uniforms in 2002, they kept the traditional blue and yellow colors but chose a more casual design, emphasizing comfort, function, and a young sportive style. The uniform of the American postal services is less concerned with fashionable change. The uniforms of their letter carriers are designed to adjust to the different extreme climates of the United States and to be instantly recognizable by their particular colors. Fast food companies, such as McDonald's, which cater mainly to young people, frequently dress their employees in cheerful colorful and casual-looking uniforms that correspond to the tastes and lifestyles of children and teenagers.

Production
During the nineteenth century, officers who could afford to had their uniforms made-to-order by tailors who followed the uniforms regulations published by the government. Some prominent uniform suppliers published their own summaries of the regulations and added illustrations and pattern drawings. The widespread need for uniforms during the nineteenth century led to the development of factories that produced ready-to-wear as well as made-to-measure uniforms. Eventually, large department stores offered a whole range of civil uniforms, including very richly embroidered ones.

By the end of the twentieth and the beginning of the twenty-first century, an increasing section of the fashion industry was specializing in the production of corporate wear. According to Public Broadcasting Service (PBS), the National Association of Uniform Manufacturers and Distributors estimates that the American "career apparel" industry is worth at least $6 billion. International companies as large as McDonald's potentially spend as much as $60 million a year on their uniform programs (Fast Food Fashion).

Today the industry offers a wide variety of clothes ranging from simple standard items, such as T-shirts and sweaters individualized by embroideries and corporate colors, to complete corporate fashion lines. When a large organization decides to introduce new uniforms it usually follows a long procedure. Well-known designers are hired to work very closely with the executive management in order to develop a unique design that communicates the company's corporate image. Before ordering new uniforms, prudent companies find out their employees' wishes and expectations and have them test sample garments to determine whether the uniforms can fulfill the requirements of practical function, quality, and comfort.

In times of economic instability the importance of corporate fashion grows as the image of a company can determine its failure or success in an increasingly competitive market. As a result, the British marketing company Up &

Down Marketing and Management Consultancy forecasts considerable growth for the corporate wear market, climbing from 168.6 million garments in 2000 to nearly 200 million garments in 2010 in Europe. At the same time, corporate fashion is spreading to more types of companies. Besides airlines, railways, and postal services, which continue a long tradition, a wide variety of service industries make increasing use of corporate wear, such as grocery stores, shopping malls, department stores, entertainment parks, restaurants, hotels, hospitals, and cleaning companies.

The definition of the occupational uniform should not be confused with certain traditional professional garments. The white coats of doctors, and the caps or berets and long gowns of professors, judges, or priests are typical for their profession in some countries. Although these items of clothing communicate symbolic messages and emphasize the special social status and profession of the person, they do not function as uniforms because their shape usually is not precisely prescribed by the employer, nor do the garments necessarily carry badges indicating function or hierarchical status within a larger organization.

See also **Uniforms, Diplomatic; Uniforms, Military.**

BIBLIOGRAPHY

Antonoff, Roman. "Berufsbekleidung im Firmenstil." In *Kleidung im Beruf.* 2nd ed. Informationskreis "Kleidung im Beruf." Königswinter, 1996.

Chowdhary, Usha. *Clothing for Special Needs: An Annotated Bibliography.* 3rd ed. Mount Pleasant, Mich.: U. Chowdhary, 2002.

De Marly, Diana. *Working Dress: A History of Occupational Clothing.* London: B.T. Batsford, Ltd., 1986.

Delpierre, Madeleine. *Uniformes civils français cérémonial circonstances 1750–1980.* Musée de la mode et du costume. Paris, 1983.

"Des Kranichs neue Kleider: Neue Uniformen für 25.000 Lufthanseaten. Die Dienstkleidung, geht auf Strecke." In *Lufthansa Nachricht.* Deutsche Lufthansa AG Konzernkommunikation, Frankfurt, 17 January 2002.

Expedition der Europäischen Modenzeitung ed. *Lexikon des Kleidermachers.* vol. 1: forestry; no. 1 vol 2: liveries; vol 3: uniforms of the German Imperial and Prussian Royal state- and court officers around 1900; vol. 3: uniforms of the German Imperial postal services and railway, Royal Prussian Police etc. Dresden, 1895–1898, (reprint Osnabrück 1993).

Fasti della burocrazia: uniformi civili e di corte dei secoli XVIII-XIX. *Genua 1984.*

Fussell, Paul. *Uniforms: Why We Are What We Wear.* Boston: Houghton Mifflin, 2002.

Hackspiel-Mikosch, Elisabeth, ed. *Nach Rang und Stand: Deutsche Ziviluniformen in 19. Jahrhundert.* Krefeld: German Textile Museum, 2002. Exhibition catalog.

Kliegel, Marieluise. *Des Dieners alte Kleider. Livreen und Livreeкnöpfe - Ausgewählte Beispiele deutscher Adelshöfe des 19. Jahrhunderts.* Münster, 1999.

Lister, Margiot. *Costume of Everday Life. An Illustrated History of Working Clothes from 900 to 1910.* London: Barrie and Jenkins, 1977.

McVeigh, Brian. *Wearing Ideology: State, Schooling and Self-Presentation in Japan.* Oxford and New York: Berg, 2000.

Mikosch, Elisabeth. "Court livery and other professional uniforms made for the wedding celebrations of 1719." In "Court Dress and Ceremony in the Age of the Baroque. The Royal/Imperial Wedding of 1719 in Dresden: A Case Study." Ph.D. diss., New York University, 1999.

Shepelev, L. E. *Chinovnyi mir Rossii: XVIII – nachalo XXv.* (The Civil Service in Russia, 18th to the beginning of the 20th century) St. Petersberg 1999 (in Russian).

Sluzbeno odelo u 19. i. 20. veku. (Official dress in Serbia in the 19th and 20th century). ed. By Cedomir Vasic, Belgrade 2001. (Serbo-croatian language with English summary, numerous color illustrations)

Solomon, Michael. "Standard Issue: Many Organizations Believe Employees in Uniform Are More Obedient, Responsive and Reassuring Than Those in Mufti." *Psychology Today* Dec. 1987 vol. 21, no. 12, p. 30.

Turnau, Irena. *European Occupational Dress from the Fourteenth to the Eighteenth Century.* Institute of the Archaeology and Ethnology, Polish Academy of Sciences. Warsaw, 1994.

Williams-Mitchell, Christobal. *Dressed for the Job: The Story of Occupational Costume.* Poole and New York: Distributed by Sterling Pub., Co., 1982.

Internet Resources

"European Corporate Wear in the 21st Century" Up & Down Marketing and Management Consultancy, London 2003. Available from <http://www.upanddown.co.uk/CONS_Details.cfm?articleID=72, 8 August 2003>.

"Fast Food Fashion." PBS: Newshour, 2004. Available from <http://www.pbs.org/newshour/infocus/fashion/uniforms.html>.

Elisabeth Hackspiel-Mikosch

UNIFORMS, SCHOOL School uniforms have their historical antecedents in very old traditions. If understood broadly, "students" have donned special garments to set themselves apart for religious (monastic and priestly training) and economic purposes (apprentices wearing guild attire) for centuries. However, school uniforms as understood in their modern sense are a particular manifestation of a more general uniformization of populations apparent from about the early nineteenth century. This regulation of appearance is more specifically understood as "standardizing" and "disciplining" workers and citizens to meet the requirements of industrialization, capitalism, and national loyalty. Though historically some schools mandated uniforms for religious reasons or to maintain their "tradition," by and large school uniforms have been ideologically inspired by a notion that bodily control and regulated appearance beget social order, within the school and in society at large.

PRACTICAL CONSIDERATIONS AND FUNCTIONAL CRITERIA FOR SCHOOL UNIFORMS

Though the debate about the actual merits of student uniforms continues in the United States, advocates of school uniforms believe there are key elements to the successful uniformizing of a student body. These include: determining the style of uniforms should involve teachers, school administrators, parents, and students; uniforms should be affordable and available in all sizes; seasonal options should be available; the wearing of uniforms should be mandatory while allowing for special exemptions; recycling programs are suggested, as are the selling or trading of used uniforms; and uniforms should be introduced in the early grades first so students become accustomed to them as they progress through the higher grades.

School authorities might consider mandating age or grade-specific uniforms. Additionally, school authorities and educational administrators ideally should offer a variety of uniforms that are appropriate to gender and local weather conditions.

As for the materials used, important considerations include: durability (how many years it can be worn); dirt-resistant colors; colors that suit most complexions (for example, many suggest that bright red is discouraged since it does not flatter many people's natural coloring); fits all shapes and figure types; washability (preferably, materials should require little—or even no—ironing or dry cleaning); small two-way patterns for economical use of fabric.

Special climatic conditions should be assessed. For example, in Australia and New Zealand, there are criteria for "sun-safe" school uniforms. Or in other places, winter uniforms must be loose-fitting enough for individuals to layer clothes underneath the uniform.

Other practical considerations include degree of adjustability; comfort (enough so that students are not inhibited from engaging in typical school activities); how available mandated uniforms are at local outlets; if uniforms are within the price range of all students; and choosing an appropriate seller and supplier of uniforms.

Obviously, with so many students, selling school uniforms can be extremely profitable, and any in-depth analysis must explore the agenda of apparel manufacturers in advocating the use of school uniforms. Besides clothes manufacturers, giant retail chains such as JCPenney, Sears, Macy's, Target, Wal-Mart, and Kids "R" Us sell school uniforms.

Uniformity versus Individuality

School uniforms may be thought of as representing in material-cultural form the point in which the forces of two great upheavals, epitomized by the industrial and French revolutions, converge. However, despite encouraging the uniformizing of students (as well as workers and citizens), these two momentous transformations often work at cross-purposes. The industrial revolution was an economic project that eventually required formal schooling to learn radically new habits for rationalized labor. School uniforms came to symbolize the person as interchangeable and modular. Meanwhile, a more political project, the French Revolution (and other similar revolts of the same period), encouraged self-determinism and individuality, ideals that were often contravened by dress uniformity (in addition to demanding uniformed students—that is, workers-in-training—the industrial revolution immeasurably facilitated the spread of student uniforms through mechanical standardization and mass production). The tension between economic production and political liberation continues to shape debates about school uniforms: Some argue that school uniforms increase social order while others contend they run the danger of violating a person's right of self-expression. To what degree school uniforms actually do the latter, along with threatening a student's autonomy, self-worth, and dignity is, of course, debatable. In any case, contemporary discussions about school uniforms also reveal deeper concerns about student performance, school safety, the maintenance of social order, and the relation between the individual student (citizen-in-training) and the state.

From a more abstract perspective, one way to view the role of uniforms is by considering the person vis-à-vis uniformed dress. In regards to appearance and bodily regulation, one's person is either *impressed upon* (by societal rules) or it *gives off impressions* (by subjective intention). There are, then, two angles from which self-presentation practices associated with uniforms can be approached. The first is "person as a mannequin": one's body is inert, a passive object with clothes hung on it by others. The self is under control; one dresses for others. Roles and social status are imposed. The second angle is "self-governing": one's body is animate, something active, a self-regulating entity. The self is in control; one dresses, as it were, for one's self. Personal style and individuality are expressed. Arguably, one's appearance is a mixture of both these forms of self-presentation, but it is worth highlighting the self-governing perspective in order to illustrate the role of individual agency. Such a maneuver is necessary to account for what might be termed "resistance" (though not necessarily of a well-thought-out, explicit kind). For example, Japanese schools are known for enforcing uniform regulations, and yet many students routinely flaunt the rules by affecting a slovenly look, donning nonregulation articles, and even altering uniforms. Such dress practices are not political statements about the state, capitalism, and "the system," but rather personal expressions of insolence aimed at teachers, parents, and what is perceived to be the old-fashioned style of the older generation.

Here the difference between dress codes and uniforms needs clarification. If "uniformity" is a crucial component of any definition of uniforms, it is prudent to envision a continuum of dress codes, dress uniformity, and uniforms. In many places, there is debate about how much uniformity is desirable, and regulations vary widely. Some school policies are very liberal, requiring that students follow a dress code that does not require uniforms, while others ask students to don uniforms, and still others mandate that all students wear uniforms (though students are allowed to opt out for religious or personal reasons). Policies can even go further; in Japan, some schools are notorious for strictly enforcing, in military-fashion, every component of dress, including skirt length, hair style and color, and book bags.

Recent Historical Origins

Many British schools have a long history of school uniforms that have influenced school dress codes elsewhere (although the styles generally regarded as British school uniforms made their appearance in the late nineteenth century). By the early nineteenth century in Britain, the ensemble of student uniforms had more or less stabilized. At schools such as Eton and Harrow, a student uniform would include a short round jacket with deep lapels made of checkered woolen or strong cotton materials. By the 1920s, a typical boys' uniform for middle and upper-class schools might consist of a gray flannel suit (or blazer) with breast pockets, "Eton collar," school cap (or straw boater), and necktie with school colors. School badges or insignia would be affixed to the uniform. A typical girls' uniform might consist of a low-waisted dress in navy wool, pleated skirt, white collar with navy silk bow, navy blazer, black stockings and shoes, and a panama hat. Popular colors were navy blue, black, brown, or dark green. In the late nineteenth century, the introduction of sports, games, and gymnastics into the curriculum resulted in the modification of girls' uniforms.

Examples of dress uniformity among youth outside the school walls indicate broader cultural trends and attempts to acquaint children with the imperatives of formality, self-discipline, social order, and patriotism, as well as attempting to suppress working-class anomie and militancy. The uniforms of youth movements (such as Boy and Girl Scouts) illustrate these attempts. Another example is "sailor suits," which relied on a generalized "military metaphor"—children will be "recruited into society" through uniformization. The popularity of sailor suits, originally introduced in schools that trained boys for Britain's navy, spread to other countries (including Japan, where their influence can still be seen in girls' uniforms) among both boys and girls of all ages during the late nineteenth and early twentieth centuries. Such continued popularity is arguably an illustration of how uniforms generally preserve older, even obsolete, styles (for instance, boys' uniforms in Japan are modeled on Prussian officer uniforms).

School Uniforms in the United States

In the United States, dress codes were commonly enforced in schools in the 1950s (girls, prohibited from wearing pants, had to wear skirts or dresses). During the 1960s, blue jeans, black leather jackets, and other accoutrements associated with gangs were prohibited among boys (and, of course, girls as well). By the 1980s, problems with gang violence led to dress codes that attempted to do away with gang colors. Dress codes have routinely been used to prohibit clothes with threatening language, insulting racial slurs, and alcohol or drug-related messages. They have also been used to ban miniskirts, tube tops, halter tops, and see-through clothing (such restrictions raise an interesting gender issue; some note that they unfairly discriminate against women since male students supposedly face less bodily regulation). Uniform policies began to spread in the late 1980s and then steadily increased throughout the 1990s. Though parochial and private schools have a long history of mandating school uniforms, the first public-school system to require uniforms, California's Long Beach Unified School District, has become a model for uniform policies in other places. Begun in 1994, this program involves about 60,000 elementary and middle school students.

An important symbolic push for school uniforms came in January 1996, when President Clinton endorsed their use during his State of the Union Address. One month later, the National Association of Secondary School Principals also endorsed them. Then, shortly after the presidential endorsement, the U.S. Department of Education sent a manual, "School Uniforms: Where They Are and Why They Work," to all 16,000 school districts. The manual listed examples of model programs and explained what are perceived to be the benefits of school uniforms, such as improved discipline and a decrease in violence and gang activity.

By 2000, thirty-seven states had passed laws empowering local school districts to establish their own uniform policies, while numerous local authorities have instituted their own policies. Definite figures are hard to come by, but estimates of public schools that have adopted uniform policies range from 8 to 15 percent of American schools. Other estimates are even larger, and claim that nearly half of the large urban school systems in the U.S. have adopted school uniform policies for some or even all of their schools.

Arguments for School Uniforms

Advocates of school uniforms possess a large array of arguments about why they are beneficial. Such arguments can be categorized into three types:

Education-socialization benefits. Supporters of school uniforms commonly cite improved discipline, increased

Hong Kong boys in school blazers. Elements of the typical British school boy's uniform, such as a flannel blazer with breast pockets adorned with the school emblem, can often be seen in the school uniforms of other countries. © James Marshall/Corbis. Reproduced by permission.

self-esteem, and more school pride. Learning, rather than being distracted by "fashion wars," becomes the focus of schooling (though some schools have adopted more casual styles for uniforms, which might include blue jeans). Peer pressure is reduced. Embarrassment from not being fashionable, teasing, and bullying is mitigated. Moreover, any pedagogical practice that encourages students to find their sense of self-worth in something other than outward appearance is highly welcomed by parents.

Administrative benefits. Some teachers and administrators claim they have witnessed a decline in disciplinary problems while they have seen an increase in solidarity and camaraderie in schools since everyone appears to be on the same "team." Additionally, uniforms make it easier for school staff to identify who belongs on campus, thereby enhancing safety.

Social engineering. School uniforms act as "social equalizers," hiding the differences between the "haves" and "have-nots." Moreover, because parents do not have to contend with purchasing new clothes to keep up with constantly changing fads, educational expenses are kept down.

Arguments Against School Uniforms

Reasons against uniforms are fewer than those for, and usually include arguments about how uniforms dampen

freedom of expression and inhibit individuality. Some complain that, at schools with a uniform policy, teachers are burdened with being "fashion police." There are also legal issues: Opponents contend that dress codes violate the constitutional right of freedom of expression (though court decisions have generally upheld the constitutionality of dress codes). Others argue that the push for uniforms is a superficial response to serious problems and distracts from more pressing educational needs, such as lack of adequate school funding, dilapidated facilities, and drug use.

There are significant legal implications between dress codes and uniforms that involve students' rights and freedom of expression. A dress code usually stipulates what cannot be worn (proscription), while a uniform policy stipulates what must be worn (prescription). In the United States, the courts have viewed the former more positively. However, mandating the wearing of school uniforms faces more of a constitutional challenge (see DeMitchell, Fossey and Cobb; Starr).

Some policy-makers in support of school uniforms report dramatic declines in suspensions, fighting, substance abuse, robbery, and assault on teachers in schools in which uniforms have been adopted. Despite these success stories, research on the results of school uniforms is still inconclusive. Indeed, several studies have argued that there is no empirical evidence that uniforms have a positive effect on student behavior or academic achievement. More sophisticated studies are needed that factor in sociological variables such as type of school, composition of student body, class size, and socioeconomic level of school districts.

School Uniforms in Japan

Major themes emerged from a study of the views of Japanese student on uniforms.

Unity, integration, and solidarity. The most common terms that came up in discussions about student uniforms were "integration," "unit life" (*shûdan seikatsu*), and "solidarity." McVeigh relates that students commented on the feeling of unity, *esprit des corps*, school identity, and, later corporate identity enhanced by uniforms.

Social control and order. Notions of social control and order were evident in how some students explained that uniforms make it easy to identify one's social role and to which unit one is affiliated. Additionally, students learn to follow rules, a benefit for when they enter society.

Suppression of individuality. On the negative side, McVeigh notes that a number of students tapped into the debate about how a dress code infringes upon their "human rights" and "freedom," denying them "expression of personality" and diminution of individuality.

Institutional face. Many students made a strong association between uniforms and a school's "image." Being a student means wearing the "institutional face" of a

Girls in school uniforms. School uniforms based on sailor suits, such as these, have retained popularity since their first use by schools that trained for the British navy. BRIAN J. McVEIGH. REPRODUCED BY PERMISSION.

school off-campus. Others explained that uniforms made them proud of their school and that a uniform is the "school's face."

Being observed and monitored. Some students reported that uniforms gave them a "consciousness of rules" and being under control (person as mannequin). Uniforms allow teachers to keep an eye on students who can thus be more easily monitored in public.

Class distinctions and discrimination. Not a few students felt that uniforms were important not for only instilling a sense of solidarity, but also for hiding class differences that might lead to jealousy. One student reported liking to wear uniforms in middle school, "But when I entered high school, I noticed that low- and high-ranked high schools all had their uniforms. If one attended a lower-ranked school, people had a biased view of you. So I think high schools shouldn't have uniforms" (McVeigh 2000).

Ethnonational identity. Though it is very difficult to gauge to what degree uniforms construct ethnonational

identity, it is worth at least noting the linkages. McVeigh relates that one student explained how wearing a uniform made her "proud of being Japanese" while another said "uniforms protect Japanese culture." Some students linked uniforms to supposedly Japanese "virtues" and "tradition" such as harmony, unity, and politeness.

The "Consumerist Revolution"

The "who" and "why" of clothing guidelines changes the debate about uniformization. Militaries have used uniforms since ancient times, and policing and security forces have been more recently uniformed, while those subject to extreme control or sanction, such as criminals, paupers, and the mentally incapacitated, have been increasingly regulated during the last two centuries. Such practices of bodily regimentation are more or less uncontroversial. However, debates and discussions about the uniformization of youth are more contentious and will not soon disappear.

From a more scholarly perspective, student uniforms are significant because they implicate a number of concerns that still require investigation. These include how to disentangle—or link up—socialization, power, personhood, and self-presentation. Such topics deserve attention since they come together in what may be termed the "consumerist revolution." This is the emergence since the nineteenth century of what seem to be two contradictory trends that nevertheless mutually reinforce each other: (1) the desire or right to have choices over one's consumerist practices (wearing or not wearing certain articles of clothing; person as self-governing agent); and (2) the imperative to signal one's allegiance using clothing to the politico-economic machinery that produces these very choices (person as mannequin). As an instance of material culture, school uniforms offer a visible, concrete manifestation of this paradoxical historical development. Herein lies their significance.

See also **Academic Dress.**

BIBLIOGRAPHY

Brunsma, David L., and Kerry A. Rockquemore. "Effects of Student Uniforms on Attendance, Behavior Problems, Substance Abuse, and Academic Achievement." *Journal of Educational Research* 92, no. 1 (September/October 1998): 53–62.

Cunnington, Phillis, and Anne Buck. *Children's Costume in England.* London: Adam and Charles Black, 1965.

DeMitchell, Todd A., Richard Fossey, and Casey Cobb. "Dress Codes in the Public Schools: Principals, Policies, and Precepts." *Journal of Law and Education* 29 (January 2000): 31–50.

Joseph, Nathan. *Uniforms and Nonuniforms: Communication through Clothing.* New York: Greenwood Press, 1986.

McVeigh, Brian J. *Wearing Ideology: State, Schooling, and Self-Presentation in Japan.* Oxford: Berg, 2000.

Nunn, Joan. *Fashion in Costume, 1200–1980.* London: The Herbert Press, 1984.

Starr, Jennifer. "School Violence and Its Effect on the Constitutionality of Public School Uniform Policies." *Journal of Law & Education* 29, no. 1 (January 2000): 113–118.

Tanioka, Ichiro, and Daniel Glaser. "School Uniforms, Routine Activities, and the Social Control of Delinquency in Japan." *Youth and Society* 23, no. 1 (January 1991): 50–75.

Wade, Kiley K., and Mary E. Stafford. "Public School Uniforms: Effect on Perceptions of Gang Presence, School Climate, and Student Self-Perceptions." *Education and Urban Sociology* 35, no. 4 (August 2000): 399–420.

Internet Resource

"School Uniforms: Where They Are and Why They Work." U.S. Department of Education. Available from <http://www.ed.gov/updates/uniforms.html>.

Brian J. McVeigh

UNIFORMS, SPORTS Since the time when humans were able to stand upright, running has been an activity conducted for survival, in order to hunt for food and escape danger. In terms of competitive-running (track and field) events, the Ancient Olympics (776 B.C.E.), in Olympia, Greece, probably best document the history of running. The Olympics are typically associated with feats of superior athleticism and hundreds of sporting events, but the first Olympics were one-day religious festivals to celebrate the gods (specifically Zeus) that the Hellenic society worshiped. The "single foot race" (which covered one length of the stadium) was the only sporting competition until the fifteenth Olympiad. As the Olympic festival expanded, other sports like chariot racing, boxing, and pentathlon were added. Married women, who were forbidden to look at other men, were banned from the festival and were killed if they were caught attending. Virginal women were allowed to attend the Olympics so they could see what the ideal man looked like, and they had their own sports competition called the Heraean festival (after the goddess of Hera), where javelin throwing was a popular competition. All of the athletes participated in the nude (for ease of movement) and wore no foot protection. The branch of a wild olive tree was the official prize for an Olympic winner (Hickok Sports 2004).

The modern Olympics were revived in April 1896 and in the early 2000s they include twenty major track and field events (not including separate events for men and women). At the first modern events, the track and field dress consisted of woven shorts and knitted tank tops with colored athletic striping to identify athletes by country. Athletes wore leather track spikes that were constructed much like a traditional men's dress shoe with nails on the sole for traction. Twenty-first-century track and field athletes wear uniforms that are very lightweight, breathable, and aerodynamic. There are two trends. One is that the athlete wears as little as possible, so that the body is almost nude—reflecting the dress of the original Olympic athletes. Men who follow this philosophy wear body-conscious polyester and spandex knit shorts and a tank top. Women wear body-conscious polyester and spandex knit briefs and a sports bra top. The other trend is to cover the entire body (including the head) in aerodynamic body-conscious polyester and spandex knit "skin" where the athlete is theoretically making the body more "fluid," so that it has less resistance (drag) from the racing environment. This particular uniform technology is also seen in swimming, ski racing, and speed skating. For most of the running events, lightweight track spikes are worn to help propel the athlete over the running surface. In longer running events like the marathon, a lightweight racing flat is worn, which is constructed more like a modern day sneaker. For the field events, like discus and javelin, the athletes wear sport-specific footwear or ones that have been customized.

Football (Soccer)

Football or soccer is another sport that has a long history. Some historians credit the Chinese with the earliest form of football in 255–206 B.C.E. The sport was called Tsu Chu, and it was used to train soldiers as part

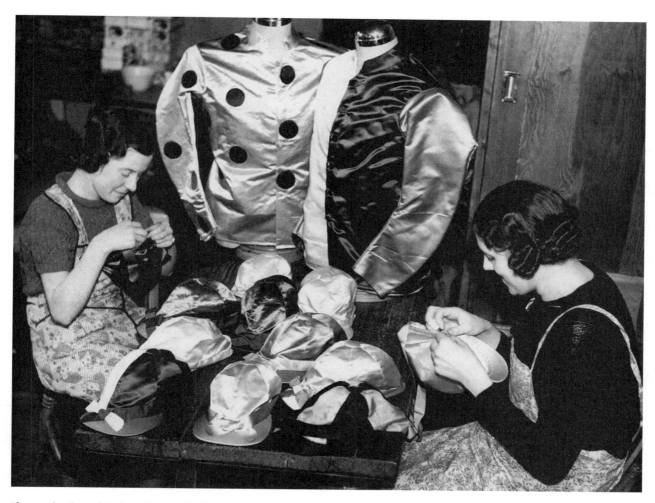

The production of jockeys' hats and shirts. Like the bright colors worn by a jockey, many sports' uniforms serve the purpose of enabling easier differentiation between players. © HULTON-DEUTSCH COLLECTION/CORBIS. REPRODUCED BY PERMISSION.

of their physical education program. Many societies including the Ancient Greeks, Aztecs, Romans, Japanese, and Egyptians have claimed to be the creators of football too, as any sport where a ball is kicked is seen as a predecessor to the modern sport (Miers and Trifari 1994 p. 26; Langton 1996, p. 15–27). The object of modern-day football is to move a single ball, by passing it between players, and kicking it into an opponent's goal. At the end of a ninety-minute game, the team that has the most goals wins the game. Hands cannot be used to pass the ball, as seen in rugby or American football. The sport is played between two teams, with eleven athletes on each team. Football as we know it in the early 2000s is based upon rules and regulations formed in London, England, in October 1863 by delegates from the Association of Football (Miers and Trifari 1994, p. 36–37).

The first modern day uniforms (1860s to 1880s) consisted of wool or cotton knickers, a woven or knitted pullover (typically with a buttoned welt opening), knee-length socks, a cap, and leather-work boots with leather or metal cleats. Some teams utilized colored stripes as a way to identify their team and because they were easy to incorporate into a woven or knitted material. Other teams had badges that were sewn onto their jersey (usually on the left side of the chest) for further identification. The sport was played with a round, leather ball that was inflated with a pig's bladder. Shin guards were not widely used during this time. In the latter part of the 1800s, woven shorts became popular, as they provided better freedom of movement. The use of woven materials for jerseys became less and less visible as the game evolved into the early 1900s. The use of wool declined, and synthetic fibers were more relevant (for laundering, durability, and comfort). Shin guards were more and more visible on players, but not mandatory until 1984. The original guards were made of leather and boning with horsehair stuffing, where twenty-first-century guards are made of synthetic plastics and high-performance foams. Football jerseys, shorts, and socks are made of high-wicking fibers and are designed to allow the athlete to move with efficiency and accuracy. The uniforms contain very little or no seaming and accessory pieces (buttons and zippers). The football "boot" is really a shoe-type construction with cleats or studs that is streamlined in design to help the player control the ball and run fast. Ball technology has changed the game most. The lighter the ball becomes, the faster the game becomes. Goalkeepers prior to the 1970s never wore goalkeeper gloves. But with players and ball technology, the ball can be kicked at speeds around 100 mph and the goalkeeper needs his or her hands protected with foam gloves. Uniform styles also include player numbers, names of the player on the back of the jersey, sponsorship, and club badge. There are also home and away uniforms. Many sport brands and football clubs have their own game-day and lifestyle collections that enable fans to wear their favorite team or player's colors as a supporter outside the stadium and as a fashion statement.

Cricket

Shepherds from the southeast of England are recognized as the creators of cricket in the 1300s. They played a game on the short grass pastures where it was possible to bowl a ball of wool or rags at a target. The target was usually the wicket gate of the sheep pasture, which was defended with a bat in the form of a shepherd's crooked staff. Records show that King Edward II was a fan of the game, as well as Oliver Cromwell. It was a sport adopted and appreciated by the upper class, and there are gambling records from 1751 showing bets made on matches exceeding £ 20,000 (Lords 2004). In an effort to formalize how the sport was played, rules and regulations were formed in 1787, at the Marylebone Cricket Club (Farmer 1979).

The objective of cricket is quite complicated, as it is based upon a multitude of rules and regulations. To simplify,

> cricket is a team sport for two teams of eleven players each. Although the game play and rules are very different, the basic concept of cricket is similar to that of baseball. Teams bat in successive innings and attempt to score runs, while the opposing team fields and attempts to bring an end to the batting team's innings. After each team has batted an equal number of innings (either one or two, depending on conditions chosen before the game), the team with the most runs wins. (Mar)

The traditional dress (sometimes referenced as "creams") worn for cricket is cream or white in color, symbolizing cleanliness, confidence, and keenness (Dunn et al. 1975). All players typically wear cotton/polyester trousers and a buttoned-down cotton/polyester shirt. Some will wear a cable or heavy rib-knitted V-neck vest or sweater (also in cream or white). White shoes or "boots" for cricket are worn, which look like golf shoes and serve a similar purpose of providing traction. Protective batting gloves, thigh pads (worn on the inside of the trousers), and combination thigh, knee, and shin pads

(worn on the outside of the trousers) are worn to protect the player from ball impact. Each batter has a wooden bat that is shaped long like a baseball bat, but has a flat surface for hitting. In the past caps were worn more than helmets and sometimes players did not cover their heads at all. Helmets are worn for impact protection, but even in the late 1970s many players thought they were not "manly." One reference states: "If a senior player feels sufficiently unnerved by the speed of a fast bowler then there is nothing in the rules to prevent him placing one on his head. But avoid the indignity if you can" (Farmer 1979, p. 10). Some international matches are played in football (soccer)-styled uniforms with colorful jerseys and trousers. Some traditionalists feel that these uniforms disrespect the heritage and eliteness of the sport, as football was traditionally a sport for the working class.

Rugby

Rugby is a version of football (soccer) where players are allowed to carry the ball with their hands. The sport originated at the Rugby School in England with a sixteen- year-old student named William Webb Ellis who picked up and carried the ball during a football (soccer) game in 1823. Some say that Ellis was inspired by the Irish-native game called Caid (where Ellis's father was stationed with the Third Dragoons guards). The sport was adopted in the 1860s by other schools and universities in England, and by 1871 the English Rugby Union was formed to standardize the rules (Trueman). The basic objective of the sport is that two teams, of fifteen players carry, pass, kick, or ground a ball to score as many points as possible. The team with the most points at the end of a match wins. Rugby became associated with the British upper class, whereas football (soccer) was the sport of choice for the working class, because of its origin at private schools and universities. This is quite ironic, since the game of rugby requires enormous physical strength, extensive physical contact, and is often played in the mud (created by inclement weather).

The original game was played with a round leather ball that had a pig's bladder. Since rugby was originally a schoolboy's sport, the school uniform was typically worn to play in. In the 1800s the upper-class school uniform consisted of a top hat, white trousers, braces (suspenders), black jacket, white shirt, and a tie. Black leather shoes or boots complemented the outfit. Everything except the top hat and jacket were worn to play rugby. Boys even tried to take the "newness" out of their school uniforms by getting them extra dirty while playing. At the end of the 1800s, knicker-length trousers in darker colors became popular for their ease of movement and ability to hide dirt. Caps were worn on the head in team colors, often with badges. Collarless jerseys (sometimes with a leather yoke) with numbers were seen in the early 1900s. The advent of synthetic fibers and knitted materials allowed for more comfortable uniforms in the 1900s. The rugby game in the early 2000s is played with an oval ball, a bit blunter in shape than the modern American football. This shape allows the ball to be easily bounced and drop-kicked. Cleats similar to the ones worn for football (soccer) are also worn to help the player run fast and establish traction with the ground, especially if it is muddy. Players who are larger and play defense wear a higher-cut version for ankle stability. A horizontally striped polo shirt design (with long sleeves), with three to four rubber buttons down a center front welt became known as the "rugby shirt" and was worn by players with traditional athletic shorts. Sporty teens and college students adopted this design in the 1970s, and again in the early 1990s. At the 2003 Rugby World Cup, teams were seen wearing body leotards that prohibited the opponent from grabbing and tugging down players during a match. Many players still do not wear any impact protection. The players who do, wear lightweight helmets, rib, and shoulder pads. Gloves are also worn to protect the hands and provide extra grip, while some players still choose to only tape their wrists and fingers. Some players tape their ears to prevent cauliflower ear.

Baseball

Like football (soccer) many ancient societies had some sort of game that could be linked to the sport of baseball. Most historians believe baseball is based on the English stick and ball game of rounders. In the early 1800s the sport became very popular in America and it was known by numerous names including townball, base, or baseball. Many small towns formed teams, and baseball clubs were formed in larger cities. By 1845 Alexander Cartwright formalized the rules of baseball, and in 1846 he organized the first recorded baseball contest (between the Cartwright Knickerbockers and the New York Baseball Club) at Elysian Field in Hoboken, New Jersey (Bowman and Zoss 1986, p. 10–11). The basic idea of baseball is to hit a ball that is pitched by an opposing team's pitcher with a wooden bat and get around three field bases to make a run (score) without getting caught. After nine innings, the team with the most runs wins the game.

The baseball uniform has a very rich history. The Knickerbockers adopted the original uniform in 1849, and it consisted of a white flannel collared shirt, woolen trousers, a straw hat, and leather shoes. Like other sports in the late 1800s, knickers were adopted (for more comfort) and leagues soon used color and patterns (like stripes and checks) to identify players, positions, and teams. At the turn of the twentieth century, team badges and names were on almost every player's shirt. The baseball shoe became a high top with cleats for better ankle stability and traction. The straw cap was now made of wool. The shirt collar was removed for more comfort and numbers were added on the sleeve for further player identification. In the 1940s, the All-American Girls Softball League was formed, and women wore uniforms featuring belted short-sleeved tunic dresses with caps. Player names were

added in the 1960s to the back of the jerseys (along with numbers) (National Baseball Hall of Fame). In the twenty-first century, the uniform is reminiscent of the original uniform in that it consists of a shirt or jersey and trousers, but they are constructed with nylon or polyester fibers and are often knitted, which allows them to fit very close to the body. Trousers typically have stirrups, which allude to the look of the old-fashioned knickers. Jerseys are still closed up the center front and are either short sleeved or sleeveless to allow a cotton T-shirt to be worn underneath for heat management. Players still wear caps (typically they are made of cotton and polyester fibers), and helmets are now used for impact protection when batting.

Basketball

Dr. James Naismith, a Canadian Presbyterian minister, invented the sport of "Basket Ball" on 21 December 1891 at a Springfield, Massachusetts, YMCA Training School in response to a work assignment that required him to create a sport that could be played indoors during the winter (Naismith Memorial Basketball Hall of Fame, Inc.). Naismith's idea was to utilize athletic skill instead of strength like in American football or rugby. With thirteen rules, the basic object of Naismith's new sport was to put a ball in an opponent's "basket." At the end of the game, the team with the most baskets wins. The first game of basketball was played with eighteen players (nine to a team) and used a football (soccer ball), and two peach baskets as the goals (Wolff 1991, p. 7–13). Women were involved in the game almost immediately, and Smith College in Northampton, Massachusetts, was the site of the first collegiate women's basketball game in 1893. Although there have been some major changes to the game since it was first invented, it is still one of the most popular games played. Over 300 million people play basketball in the early 2000s (Naismith Memorial Basketball Hall of Fame, Inc.).

The original basketball uniform consisted of everyday clothing that boys would wear to school, like a pair of full-length trousers, a buttoned-down shirt, and leather shoes. Over a period of twenty years, specific team uniforms were created for men to identify team names and colors. The first uniforms were composed of a knitted pullover with appliquéd team letters or names, knicker-length woven trousers, knitted striped knee socks, and leather shoes. The uniform soon reduced itself to a pair of woven short-shorts, a knitted tank top, leather kneepads, knee socks, and basketball sneakers like the Converse All-Star. For women, the first basketball uniforms consisted of large belted black bloomers that extended below the knees with stockings and white middy shirt. In the twenty-first century, basketball uniforms for men and women are almost identical, less complicated, and protective. They use nylon and polyester and material constructions to provide thermal comfort on the court. A typical uniform consists of a sleeveless knitted jersey tank, shorts that are almost knee-length, ankle-length socks, and basketball sneakers. Furthermore, each player's uniform typically has a number on the front and back of the jersey for identification on TV and for spectators. Sometimes the player's surname is printed on the back of the shirt for further identification. Basketball sneakers are built to provide traction on the wood court floor and ankle stability from medial-to-lateral movements.

American Football

The sport of American football derived from rugby. Football (soccer) has also been noted as a cousin to American football. The sport came to America in the mid-1800s and was played by many northeastern colleges, like Harvard, Yale, Princeton, and Columbia. In 1876, Harvard and Yale Universities met together in Massachusetts to formalize the rules of American football. The object of the game was to move an oblong-shaped ball across a goal line by kicking, throwing, or running with it. The team that can get the most points in four quarters wins. The game is played between two teams, each with eleven players. In American football, the teams can be rotated in and out of the game, which is different than football (soccer) and rugby.

In the beginning of the Professional Football League in the 1920s, there were no rules regarding the equipment players wore. Teams only provided players with long-sleeve knitted wool jerseys, and socks in team colors and logos. Many players used the equipment that they acquired at university (if they went). To protect the head from contact, players wore soft, pliable leather "head helmets" with nose guards, while some players felt that long hair was good enough. Pants were knicker-length and were made of brown cotton canvas (reminiscent of the original Levi's). Players also wore cleats to enhance traction when running, especially in the mud (McDonough et al. 1994, p. 31,). Throughout the 1900s elaborate equipment was developed for the player, including pads made with high-density plastics and foams for the neck, thighs, hips, groin, ribs, knees, shoulders, and sometimes the forearms. Over the protection, the player usually wears a knitted jersey, knee-length pants, and socks, in team colors and made of synthetic fibers that provide durability and thermal comfort. Like in many other sports, jerseys contained the name and number of the player and team logo for on-field identification. Many of the equipment developments during the last century were created by players themselves or by equipment managers. Players in the early 2000s wear proper, durable helmets with face and mouth guards (McDonough et al. 1994, p. 110). Lightweight cleats are worn for different field environments like grass or synthetic turf. Gloves are sometimes worn for warmth and to provide a better grip on the ball. Even the ball has gone through a series of changes, making it more durable, aerodynamic, and easier to handle.

See also **Sneakers.**

BIBLIOGRAPHY

Bowman, John, and Joel Zoss. *The Pictorial History of Baseball.* New York: Gallery Books, 1986.

Dunn, John, et al. *How to Play Cricket: Australian Style.* Hong Kong: Souvenir Press, 1975.

Farmer, Bob. *How to Play Cricket.* New York: Hamlyn, 1979.

Langton, Harry. *1000 Years of Football: FIFA Museum Collection.* Berlin: Edition Q, 1996.

McDonough, et al. *75 Seasons: The Complete Story of the National Football League 1920–1995.* Atlanta, Ga.: Turner Publishing, 1994.

Miers, Charles, and Elio Trifari. *Soccer! The Game and World Cup.* New York: Rizzoli International, 1994.

Wolff, Alexander. *100 Years of Hoops: A Fond Look Back at the Sport of Basketball.* New York: Bishop Books, 1991.

Internet Resources

Hickok Sports. 2004. *Sports History: The Ancient Olympic Games.* Available from <http://www.hickoksports.com/history/olancien.shtml>.

Mar, David. *An Explanation of Cricket: Rules and Game Play Described for Novices.* Available from <http://www.cricinfo.com/db/about_cricket/explanation/explanation_of_cricket.html>.

Naismith Memorial Basketball Hall of Fame, Inc. *Naismith Memorial Basketball Hall of Fame: History.* Available from <http://www.hoophall.com>.

National Baseball Hall of Fame. *Dressed to the Nines: A History of the Baseball Uniform.* Available from <http://www.baseballhalloffame.org/exhibits/online_exhibits/dressed_to_the_nines.htm>.

Trueman, N. *Rugby Football History: Timeline.* Available from <http://www.rugbyfootballhistory.com>.

Susan L. Sokolowski

UNISEX CLOTHING The term "unisex" as applied to dress was coined in the late sixties to denote clothing suitable or designed specifically for both males and females. Prior to this, fashion most traditionally contextualized stood for the clear demarcation of the sexes through the reaffirmation of gender identity. Simply put: women wore skirts, and men wore pants. Although historically there were of course experiments in appropriation, the decade that produced the Youthquake solidified the idea of universal dress.

Denim jeans and T-shirts, popularized in the 1950s by Hollywood cinema, inaugurated the democratization of clothing. Up until that point, they had served as working-class garments that signified a particular niveau in society. For the burgeoning younger generation, the seductive charm of young actors like Marlon Brando and James Dean, combined with the powerful vehicle of motion pictures, transformed jeans and T-shirts not only into fashion phenomena, but perhaps the first truly accepted unisex articles of clothing.

The seeds of youth revolution, planted in the 1950s, fully blossomed the following decade. The 1960s were a period of extraordinary change—one in which conventional notions of age, gender, and class were completely redefined. In an environment conducive to experimentation, the era pushed designers to incorporate new definitions of youth and universality into their work. The idea of unisex, in particular, gained currency precisely for its implications of multifaceted freedom. In the obvious sense, unisex meant liberation from gender, but more importantly, its association with the future in its disavowal of traditional hierarchies and old-fashioned attitudes made it a major driving force for fashion.

Key Designers

The 1960s not only brought the Youthquake, but it was also the age of space exploration. All aspects of society were affected by it—including fashion, which was directly reflective of the times. Placing a big importance on minimalist design, geometric construction, the use of synthetic materials, and the idea of unisex, designer Pierre Cardin revolutionized fashion by creating futuristic clothing fit for the space age. He produced single-breasted, round-necked jackets, stretch jersey tunics, and leggings for both sexes and dressed men and women alike in unitards and jumpsuits accessorized with rounded helmets and flat plastic eye shields.

Like his contemporary Cardin, Rudi Gernreich flourished in a time when political and social unrest called for the re-mapping of gender identity. Often labeled the "inventor" of unisex fashion, Gernreich explored male and female representation in society by playing with established ideals. His unisex project erased the line dividing the sexes through de-emphasizing the importance placed on sexual attributes and rendering them banal. The centerpiece of the unisex project was the monokini—a one-piece topless bathing suit intended to be worn by men or women who had shaved off all head and body hair.

Impact of Unisex

The concept of unisex has far-reaching implications because it disturbs society on such a basic level. Fashion becomes a powerful tool in subverting sexual identity through connotations of dress. Throughout history and with varying degrees of success, designers have challenged conventional dress codes. In the 1920s, Chanel envisioned a new femininity in fashion that incorporated trousers—the symbol of masculine power. However, it was not until the Women's Liberation movement of the 1970s that pants were universally accepted as female attire. From this point forward, the impact of unisex expands more broadly to encompass various themes in fashion including androgyny, mass-market retail, and conceptual clothing.

Androgyny. Androgynous habits of cross-gender impersonation date back to the privileged classes of seventeenth- and eighteenth-century England and France; however, after the industrial revolution and the subsequent rise of capitalist societies, a fairly structured dress code dividing men and women re-emerged. The next great revolution in fashion—the Youthquake of the 1960s—would shatter those gender ideals. The sixties' premium on youth led the way for fashion that was neither specifically feminine nor masculine. From space age to hippie, the idea of dressing was less about being boyish or girly than it was about an overall frenzy of youth fascination.

The 1970s continued with the exploration of gender both underground and in the mainstream. In fashion proper, Yves Saint Laurent advocated the masculine look for women while the subcultural movements of punk and glam rock established, at least visually, an identity through androgynous dress. Further, in the 1980s, Jean-Paul Gaultier sent men and women down the same catwalk in similar-style sarongs and pant-skirts inspired by the Orient. Simultaneously, the new-wave movement fused punk and glam-rock influences to create the next generation of unisex fashion.

In the contemporary moment, the styles of the 1970s and 1980s live on through countless retro revivals, but the pioneer of a new type of androgyny, one reborn in luxury lines, is Hedi Slimane, designer of Dior Homme. Slimane reworks men's classic tailoring through subtle detailing, and his collections have become coveted internationally by both chic men and women. As he himself states, "I think it's all a state of mind. Who cares whether a guy or a girl wears the garments? This masculine/feminine dialectic doesn't interest me—in my head, we're all a little bit of both" (eLuxury.com May 2003).

Mass-market retail. Retailers such as The Gap (incidentally born in revolutionary 1969) have produced wildly successful globally marketed clothing lines founded on a basic range of simple unisex separates: T-shirts, jeans, trousers, sweaters, and jackets. Their domination of the clothing market stems from their affordability, accessibility, and their capacity to transcend age, gender, and perhaps most importantly, trends. The Gap's consistency in design and marketing guarantees the firm's continual growth and success in a climate where the average consumer seeks more and more to dress in affordable, comfortable, casual wear that will stand the test of time.

Conceptual mode. The avant-garde in fashion has historically generated design based on a framework of conceptual ideas, converting theories into architecture for the body independent of gender. Ernesto Thayaht worked with fashion under the Futurist conviction that society could only be revolutionized through aesthetics. Fashion bridged the divide between the avant-garde and the masses. In the early 1920s Thayaht created the unisex garment known as the *tuta* that was similar in design to Russian Constructivist uniforms. The *tuta* was monotone, varied in fabric depending on the season, and was worn without an undershirt for all occasions.

The legacy of such experiments in fashion was rediscovered in various contexts from the 1980s onward. In contrast to the glitz and glamour of western fashion in the eighties, Japanese designers Rei Kawakubo and Yohji Yamamoto created collections the press dubbed as the "post-Hiroshima look." In a reaction to the hyper-feminized sexuality ubiquitous in European and American fashion, Kawakubo and Yamamoto designed genderless, loose, asymmetric and irregular clothing in black that placed a primacy on garment construction.

Conceptual fashion evolved the following decade with Belgian deconstructionists, most notably Ann Demeulemeester and Martin Margiela. Deconstruction revealed the process of tailoring, shape, and construction through surpassing gender codes and questioning body proportion. While traditional fashion physically reinforces sexual codification, these movements took the notion of gender identity away from clothing and reinserted the importance of garment fabrication and the conceptual origins of creation.

See also **Futurist Fashion, Italian; Space Age Styles.**

BIBLIOGRAPHY

Davis, Fred. *Fashion, Culture, and Identity.* Chicago and London: The University of Chicago Press, 1992.

Derycke, Luc, and Sandra Van De Veire, eds. *Belgian Fashion Design.* Bruges: DieKeure, 1999.

Hebdige, Dick. *Subculture: The Meaning of Style.* London and New York: Routledge, 1987.

McDowell, Colin. *Fashion Today.* London: Phaidon Press Ltd., 2000.

Steele, Valerie. *Fifty Years of Fashion: New Look to Now.* New Haven, Conn.: Yale University Press, 1997.

Vinken, Barbara. "Transvesty-Travesty: Fashion and Gender." *Fashion Theory* 3, no. 1 (1999).

Jennifer Park

UZANNE, OCTAVE Octave Uzanne (1852–1931) was a French writer and bibliophile, or book lover. Editor of several journals, such as *Le livre* (The Book), and founder of bibliophile societies that published illustrated books, he was also a prolific author who specialized in the art of making beautiful books. As of the early 2000s Uzanne is an obscure literary figure, remembered if at all as the author of a short story called "The End of Books" (1895), which foresaw how new technologies might result in such inventions as the audiobook. Yet he also produced a rich, albeit still neglected, body of work that helped to provoke discussion of fashion and femininity in fin-de-siècle France.

Uzanne was obsessed with women's fashions, which he described with ardent, even fetishistic attention to detail. Fashion, he insisted, was woman's only "literature," and he himself the only true "historian" of women's fashions. It is characteristic of Uzanne's work to regard fashion and femininity as inextricably linked. He revived the term *féminie* to describe everything that fell within the domain of woman—beauty, love, and fashion—and his reputation as a fashion authority was closely associated with his supposed expertise in female psychology. The famous dandy Jules Barbey d'Aurevilly, who wrote the preface to Uzanne's second book, *Le bric-à-brac de l'amour* (1879), told him, "Monsieur, you have *le sentiment de la femme.* You have what no one has anymore in our frigid era: You have an amorous imagination."

Uzanne's first and perhaps most famous book in the fashion genre was *L'éventail* (The Fan); (1882), a charming illustrated history of the fan. He admitted that his book was "not by any means a work of mighty wisdom and erudition," but merely the first of a projected series of "little books for the boudoir." Totally ignoring the use of the fan by East Asian men, Uzanne preferred to see it as the quintessential feminine accessory, "the scepter of a beautiful woman." His next book, *L'ombrelle, le gant, le manchon* (The Sunshade, the Glove, and the Muff); (1883), was also illustrated in rococo style by Paul Avril. Uzanne's tone continued to be playfully erotic. "The muff!" he exclaimed. "Its name alone has something adorable, downy, and voluptuous about it." Regrettably, he never wrote his promised book on shoes and stockings, although he later published *Les ornements de la femme* (Woman's Ornaments), which reproduced in one volume the combined texts of *The Fan* and *The Sunshade, the Glove, and the Muff,* both of which were also translated into English and published in London.

Son Altesse la femme (Her Highness, Woman); (1885) was an even more luxuriously produced book, with full-color illustrations by contemporary artists. Its subject, Uzanne wrote, was "the psychological history of the Frenchwoman from the Middle Ages to the present day." Her psychology, Uzanne implied, was quite sexual and therefore dangerous to mere men. Félicien Rops, best-known for his erotica, illustrated Uzanne's chapter on the medieval woman with a picture of a nude sorceress. One of Uzanne's favorite periods, the eighteenth century, was interpreted as a time of erotic dalliance, when upper-class Frenchwomen changed lovers as easily as they changed dresses.

La Française du siècle (The Frenchwoman of the Century; 1886) focused on the years since the beginning of the French Revolution in 1789. Uzanne drew on a host of memoirs of the period to create a dramatic picture of changing modes and manners. For example, his chapter on the latter part of the French Revolution, known as the Directoire or Directory, included descriptions of such events as the *bal des victimes.* These bals were parties attended only by people who had at least one relative who had been guillotined during the Reign of Terror. Women cut their hair short, as though they too were about to be guillotined; some even wore a ribbon of red satin around their necks.

Uzanne later republished what was essentially the same book under at least two different titles: *La Femme et la mode. Métamorphoses de la parisienne de 1792 à 1892* (Woman and Fashion: Metamorphoses of the Parisienne, 1792–1892); (1892) and *Les Modes de Paris. Variations du goût et de l'esthétique de la femme, 1797–1897* (literally *Fashions in Paris*, but translated into English as Fashion in Paris. The Various Phases of Feminine Taste and Aesthetics, 1797–1897]; (1897)). As these various titles indicate, women and fashion were virtually interchangeable concepts for Uzanne, at least with respect to Frenchwomen, or Parisiennes, whom he chauvinistically regarded as the most feminine of all women. Significantly, he also emphasized the importance of the specific venues within which fashion-oriented behavior occurred, such as the promenades in the Bois de Boulogne and the annual painting exhibitions at the musée du Louvre.

In the meantime, Uzanne wrote *La Femme à Paris*, translated into English as The Modern Parisienne; (1894), one of his most significant books. In this work, he moved beyond the restricted world of fashion to explore the lives of women at all levels of French society. Many working women in Paris were employed in some branch of the fashion industry, and Uzanne did considerable research into the lives of dressmakers and saleswomen as well as female artists, actresses, bourgeois housewives, and, of course, sex workers—from common prostitutes to expensive courtesans. In 1910 he republished *La Femme à Paris* in a cheap edition under the title *Parisiennes de ce temps*.

Many of Uzanne's books were masterpieces of the art of bookmaking, lavishly produced in numbered edi-

tions for collectors. He was solicitous of every detail from the typography to the paper and the design of the cover. His book *Féminies* (1896), for example, was a deluxe publication featuring numerous striking color illustrations by Félicien Rops. As previously mentioned, Uzanne revived the word *féminie* to refer to everything in the domain of women (beauty, love, fashion), claiming that it was now necessary to use the plural since there existed so many "gynecological republics." The cover illustration of *Féminies*, influenced by symbolist art, depicted a woman piercing a rose with a dagger.

By the early twentieth century, Uzanne was reduced to publishing small and inexpensive editions of his books. *L' Art et les artifices de la beauté* (The Art and Artifices of Beauty; 1902), for example, contained only black-and-white illustrations. In a series of chapters on such subjects as cosmetics, hairstyles, corsets, jewelry, and underwear, however, Uzanne continued to explore the ways in which fashion and artifice constructed feminine beauty.

See also **Dandyism; Fashion, Historical Studies of; Fashion, Theories of; Paris Fashion.**

BIBLIOGRAPHY

The books by Uzanne mentioned in this essay are all out of print and generally available only in large research libraries. No book-length study of Uzanne has been published as of early 2004. For Uzanne's era, however, the reader may consult the following works:

Steele, Valerie. *Paris Fashion: A Cultural History.* 2nd ed. Oxford, New York, and Tokyo: Berg/Oxford International Publishers, Ltd., 1998.

Weber, Eugen. *France, Fin de Siècle.* Cambridge, Mass.: Harvard University Press, 1986.

Valerie Steele

VALENTINA Working in New York City from the mid-1920s until 1957, Valentina Sanina Nicholaevna Schlée (known professionally as Valentina) was one of a very small, select coterie of mid-century female designers who achieved commercial success and maintained influential careers during the formative years of American fashion.

Working for a carefully chosen, exclusive clientele, Valentina turned out exquisitely cut and constructed evening, cocktail, and day ensembles that were commissioned and crafted in the manner of the French haute couture; every Valentina creation was made to order and was subject to multiple meticulous fittings and hand-finishing until the designer deemed the resulting garment worthy of her label. Known for her floor-gracing, draped, silk jersey gowns; body-skimming evening dresses with low-cut backs; deep décolleté; and bolero evening ensembles, Valentina also designed pared-down day dresses, linens, and undecorated cocktail dresses—all of which exuded a frank, forward-looking minimalist aesthetic.

Early Life and Marriage
Born in 1904 in the Kiev region of Russia, Valentina escaped the revolution in the late teens with her new husband and soon-to-be business manager, George Schlée, arriving in America in 1923 after several years spent in Paris, Athens, and various other European cities. Much like the French designer Coco Chanel, who offered as many versions of her colorful past as her admirers cared to indulge, Valentina was prone to invent and embroider her early life as it suited her. As a result, Valentina's origins are shrouded in mystery. But as one delves further, it becomes increasingly clear that this mystery is largely of her own making.

While U.S. immigration records indicate that she and her husband were affiliated with a traveling dance troupe known as the Revue Russe, Valentina was not above stretching that period to "her time in Paris with [dance impresario] Diaghilev." One account of her life after escaping Russia finds her dancing as part of a cabaret act with the Chauve Souris theater group in Paris. And while the Chauve Souris and the Revue Russe were hardly Diaghilev, one thing is certain: Valentina's early training as a performing artist played a critical role in the forma-tion of her talent for costuming actors as well as her uniquely dramatic personal style. Graced with an undeniably compelling natural beauty, and enhanced by a theatrical presence, Valentina became as famous for the disciplined elegance and reductive simplicity of her clothing as she was for her meticulously crafted public persona. Self-created in virtually every aspect of her existence, Valentina offered an exotic beauty and charmingly mangled English that played to her favor in America, adding a veil of dazzlingly misleading allure to an already intriguing personality.

Formation of Valentina Gowns
In operation from 1928 to 1956, Valentina Gowns, Inc., was preceded by two early businesses, one the mid-1920s operating under the spelling "Valentena," and another venture called "Valentina & Sonia." Both of these concerns had folded by 1928 when Valentina Gowns was formed on more solid ground—this time backed by the Wall Street lawyer and financier Eustace Seligman. With George Schlée as business manager and Schlée's extended family employed in the workrooms, what became the most exclusive and most expensive American house of couture actually began as a rather simple, family-run business under the shrewd and watchful eye of the firm's only designer, Valentina.

Providing a formidable livelihood for the entire Schlée family, Valentina and George lived with great flair and panache on the swelling coffers of an almost immediate success. Within the first decade of business, Valentina's client list read like a who's who of blue-book society. With customers ranging from Park Avenue matrons to stars of the stage and silver screen, Valentina soon claimed Millicent Rogers, Lillian Gish, Gloria Swanson, Katharine Hepburn, Jennifer Jones, and even White House wives among her loyal following. Eleanor Lambert, the pioneer fashion publicist who represented Valentina for more than twenty-two years, claimed that Valentina was the dominant fashion designer of the 1930s and 1940s.

Designs for Stage and Screen
From the early 1930s on, Valentina designed costumes for Broadway productions, operas, and (by the early 1940s) Hollywood films. Drawing on her experience in

theater, she was keenly aware of the character-specific, problem-solving needs of performers. Not surprisingly, Valentina's costume design quickly gained renown for helping to define a character's role without challenging an actor's stage presence. Aptly summing up Valentina's contribution to theater design, the drama critic Brooks Atkinson noted that "Valentina has designed clothes that act before ever a line is spoken." From Lily Pons to Rosa Ponselle to Gladys Swarthout, Valentina dressed and accessorized the world's most sought-after opera divas of the mid-twentieth century. Her stage and screen credits include longstanding working relations with Alfred Lunt and Lynn Fontanne, Norma Shearer, Paulette Goddard, Ginger Rogers, and Jennifer Jones, to name but a few. Her designs for and association with the reclusive film star Greta Garbo (who lived in the same Upper East Side apartment house as the Schlées) inspired endless sensationalistic journalism, but perhaps Valentina's most influential and highly publicized work was for Katharine Hepburn, whom she dressed in 1939 for Hepburn's starring role in the stage version of *The Philadelphia Story*. The white crepe, corselet-tied gown Hepburn wore was widely copied by designers at every price point across the nation for years.

In many ways, Valentina's work influenced fashion well beyond the scope of her limited elite clientele. In the 1940s, fashion editors coined the phrase "a poorman's Valentina" to describe an affordable, simple, well-cut black dress devoid of any decoration. One of the first designers to promote monochromatic dressing, opaque and black stockings, and simple, short dresses for formal eveningwear, Valentina launched fashion trends that immediately trickled down to the masses. If Valentina's most recognizable calling card was simplicity, it should be remembered that hers was a carefully studied, highly disciplined simplicity. Her signature fragrance, "My Own," which was in production by the 1950s, was remembered by one ardent admirer as "Just like Valentina. Deceptively simple. But wildly complex." This carefully measured restraint during a time when floral appliqué, sequins, and pussycat bows were the ubiquitous choice of American dressmakers lent Valentina's designs a cool, modernist edge and earned her the respect and patronage of many of the most celebrated names in art, theater, and society. Wary of obvious fads and proudly declaring herself an American designer, Valentina insisted that true style and well-designed clothing were, in their ideal form, timeless, and she duly advised women to "Fit the century. Forget the year!"

In 1957, Valentina Gowns closed its doors—an event that coincided with the end of Valentina's marriage to George Schlée. The business was jointly owned and run, and it was George's role to manage the business while Valentina created—a two-person performance that simply could not be accomplished by Valentina on her own. In retrospect, however, it appears that Valentina's career might have run its course. By the late 1950s, both in the press and on the streets, the sophisticated ladies of café society were reluctantly giving way to the youth-driven and fast-approaching 1960s, which would witness the imperious and haughty glamour of the preceding era slowly fading away like the lingering scent of a once ravishing perfume. From the very beginning of her career, up until her very last days, Valentina had remained at the very top of the most competitive, most exclusive, and perhaps least understood area of twentieth-century fashion history—American couture. She died in New York City in 1989 at the age of ninety.

See also **Film and Fashion; Hollywood Style; Theatrical Costume.**

BIBLIOGRAPHY

Milbank, Caroline Rennolds. *New York Fashion: The Evolution of American Style.* New York: Harry N. Abrams, 1989.

Steele, Valerie. *Women of Fashion: Twentieth-Century Designers.* New York: Rizzoli International, 1991.

Watt, Melinda. *Valentina: American Coutouriere.* Thesis New York University catalog holdings, n.d.

Kohle Yohannan

VALENTINO Valentino Garavani (1932–) was born in Voghera, a city in Lombardy, on 11 May. Even as a young man he was fascinated by fashion and decided to study design in Milan. When he was seventeen he discovered the extraordinary shade of red that would remain a design element throughout his career at a premiere of the Barcelona Opera.

Early Career

In 1950 Valentino went to Paris, where he studied design at the schools of the Chambre Syndicale de la Couture Parisienne. He obtained his first position as a designer with Jean Dessès. In 1957 Valentino went to work in Guy Laroche's new atelier, where he remained for two years. His training in France provided him with both technical skill and a sense of taste. In 1959 he decided to return to Italy and opened his own fashion house on the via Condotti in Rome with financial assistance from his family. In November he made his debut with his first couture collection, displaying 120 luxurious outfits notable for their stoles and draped panels that emphasized the shoulders. The *Sunday Times* of London was quick to take note of the new designer, singling him out for the refined lines of his tailoring and the sophistication of his garments.

In 1960 Valentino met Giancarlo Giammetti, who became his business administrator. At this time he moved his fashion house to via Gregoriana, 54. Valentino quickly became the favorite designer of the movie stars who were often found at Cinecittà, known as the new Hollywood during the years of Italy's economic boom. One of the first stars who wore Valentino's clothes was Elizabeth

Taylor, who was in Rome for the filming of *Cleopatra*. In 1960 Valentino signed an agreement with a British firm, Debenham and Freebody, to reproduce some of his couture designs. That same year he designed costumes for Monica Vitti in Michelangelo Antonioni's film *La Notte*. In 1963 Valentino's summer line was photographed on the set of Federico Fellini's film *8 1/2*.

Valentino's collection for fall–winter 1961–1962 featured twelve white outfits inspired by Jacqueline Kennedy. But what secured Valentino's fame was the success of his first fashion show on the runway of the Sala Bianca in the Palazzo Pitti in Florence in July 1962. For the first time French *Vogue* dedicated its cover to an Italian designer.

International Success

Valentino's fall–winter collection for 1963–1964 was inspired by wild animals. American *Vogue* published a photograph of the contessa Consuelo Crespi wearing one of his zebra-patterned models, which anticipated his op art and pop art-inspired collection of spring–summer 1966. The 1966 collection has become famous for its prints and geometric designs, its stylized animals, and its large dots. That same year Valentino started a lingerie line and stunned his audience with a winter show that included pink and violet furs. Ethel Kennedy chose a Valentino dress for her meeting with Pope Paul VI in June 1966.

In 1967 Valentino received the Neiman Marcus Award in Dallas, which spurred him to further develop his creative ideas. The award was the direct impetus for his first men's collection, Valentino Uomo. The designer's accessories, especially his handbags with a gold "V," became essential items for the elegant women of the jet set. In 1968 Valentino introduced his famous Collezione Bianca, a spring–summer line of white and off-white garments that included suits, wraps, coats, and legwear in white lace. The show took place at a critical moment in international fashion and helped alleviate the crisis in haute couture—a crises due to changes in international society in 1968 when people started looking at less exclusive models. In March of that year Valentino opened a store in Paris, followed by one in Milan in 1969. In October 1968 he designed Jacqueline Kennedy's dress for her wedding to Aristotle Onassis. He was the most acclaimed designer of the moment and expanded his circle of clients to include Paola di Liegi, Princess Margaret of England, Farah Diba, the Begum Aga Khan, Marella Agnelli, Princess Grace of Monaco, Sophia Loren, and many other well-known women.

Valentino lengthened hemlines and introduced folk and gypsy motifs in the early 1970s. He started his first boutique line in 1969. It was originally produced by Mendes, although ready-to-wear production was turned over to Gruppo Finanziario Tessile (GFT) in 1979. Valentino also opened a prêt-à-porter shop in the center of Rome in 1972. Throughout the 1970s his designs alternated between slender suits and harem pants coupled with maxi coats. These designs often evoked a Liberty and art deco atmosphere, as in his 1973 collection inspired by the art of Gustav Klimt and the Ballets Russes. In 1974 he opened new stores in London, Paris, New York, and Tokyo (in the early 2000s there are twenty-five stores throughout the world). In 1976 he decided to show his boutique line in Paris, while keeping his couture line in Rome. Valentino launched his first perfume, named Valentino, in 1978. The following year he introduced a line of blue jeans at a famous discothèque, Studio 54 in New York City, which was publicized through an advertising campaign photographed by Bruce Weber.

The collections of the 1980s were characterized by sarong skirts gathered on the hip, draped garments, ruched fabrics, breathtaking necklines, and dramatic slits in a range of colors that emphasized the famous Valentino red, together with black and white. In 1982 the designer presented his fall–winter collection at the Metropolitan Museum of Art. In 1986 he introduced Oliver, a more youthful line named after his faithful dog, which he used as a logo. Three years later, Valentino decided to show his couture line in Paris, a series of garments inspired by ancient and modern art.

Valentino's collections of the 1990s integrated the themes of revival and self-reference—flounces, embroidery, and dots—partly as a way of emphasizing his thirty years in fashion, which were celebrated in several short films, exhibitions, and books. In January 1998, after a difficult period, Valentino sold his brand to the Holding di Partecipazioni Industriali SpA (HdP) group run by Maurizio Romiti, although Valentino remained the creative director. In 2002 HdP sold the fashion house to Gruppo Marzotto.

Elements of Style

Valentino has paid his own personal tribute to contemporary fashion, inventing a recognizable look, modern yet sophisticated, which balances tradition and innovation through the image of an iconic femininity that is both classic and chic. Valentino's designs have as a common denominator the technical precision of fine tailoring, which he applies not so much for the sake of innovation but rather to provide a sense of stylistic continuity. Bows, ruching, and draping are distinctive features of many of his designs, together with the famous Valentino red. All these features are used strategically, serving to give the brand its mythic quality. Valentino's fabrics are printed with flowers, dots, and his own initial, which has doubled as a logo since the 1960s, highlighting the interplay between ornamental texture and effective communication.

A forceful interpreter of the lines and ambiance of the nineteenth century, with references ranging from the neoclassical with its fine drapery through the Second Empire with its crinolines, Valentino plays with the idea that his garments serve as a kind of aesthetic memory, a modern reference to a different time. Because of the designer's ability to work with tradition, he has found a unique, although elitist, stylistic solution that has satisfied sophisticated women throughout the world.

See also **Celebrities; Italian Fashion; Vogue.**

BIBLIOGRAPHY

Bianchino, Gloria, and Arturo Carlo Quintavalle. *Moda: Dalla fiaba al design.* Novara, Italy: De Agostini, 1989.

Cosi, Marina. *Valentino che veste di nuovo.* Milan: Camunia Editrice, 1984.

Morris, Bernadine. *Valentino.* Florence: Octavo, 1997.

Pellé, Marie-Paule. *Valentino's Magic.* Milan: Leonardo Arte Editore, 1998.

Sozzani, Franca. *Valentino's Red Book.* Milan: Rizzoli International, 2000.

Valentino. *Trent'anni di magia. Le opere. Le immagini.* Milan: Bompiani Editore, 1991.

Aurora Fiorentini

VEBLEN, THORSTEIN A North American economist and sociologist, Thorstein Veblen (1857–1929) was an unrelenting critic of late nineteenth-century industrial society and in particular of the hierarchy of values asso-

Portrait of Thorstein B. Veblen. In scrutinizing the leisure class, economist Veblen studied fashion trends and their relationship with the desire to display wealth. © BETTMANN/CORBIS. REPRODUCED BY PERMISSION.

ciated with its dominant group, which Veblen named the *leisure class.* Clothing and fashion, he argued, were important as a way in which this group competed among themselves for prestige and social status.

Veblen sought to understand the aims and ambitions of the leisure class by uncovering the economic motives that were at the center of their actions and values. In his classic text, *The Theory of the Leisure Class: An Economic Study in the Evolution of Institutions* (1899), he concluded that the economic activity of the leisure class is driven by a way of life given over to either the maintenance or the acquisition of "honorable repute." The key to gaining status, argued Veblen, is for the households within the leisure class to dispose publicly of their wealth according to the principles of conspicuous consumption and conspicuous leisure. Adherence to these principles shows that a household and its members are able to consume without participating in the "demeaning and unworthy" activities attached to the "the industrial process."

Although Veblen scrutinized a wide range of expenditures—including houses, food, gardens, and household pets—he singled out clothing for special consideration. As he observed, "no line of consumption affords a more apt illustration than expenditure on dress" (p. 123). This is because clothing is a social necessity and to be in public is, by necessity, to be clothed. By being on show, clothing becomes a prime indicator of its wearer's "pecuniary repute" (p. 123), and since, in modern industrial society, clothing is a universal item of consumption, it is difficult for anyone to ignore the pressures of competitive emulation. Dress, therefore, is ideally placed as a vehicle with which to assert superior status in relation to one's peers within the leisure class, as well as collectively displaying the superiority of this class over all others. Veblen concluded that dress has only a tentative connection to protection and bodily comfort, observing that "it is by no means an uncommon occurrence, in an inclement climate, for people to go ill clad in order to appear well dressed" (p. 124).

Dress and Conspicuous Consumption

Veblen argued that a prime function of dress within the leisure class is to display the wearer's wealth by their consumption "of valuable goods in excess of what is required for physical comfort" (p. 125). According to Veblen the most immediate form of conspicuous consumption is *quantity,* or the possession of items of clothing (for instance shoes or suits) far beyond the requirements of reasonable daily wear. However, dress in the leisure class is also subject to considerations of *quality.* Ability to pay can also be demonstrated by the ownership of garments distinguished by the expensiveness of their materials, such as the goat hair used to weave pashmina shawls. Time-consuming methods of garment construction, and therefore expense, can, Veblen argued, insinuate itself into the esteem in which its wearer will be held. The comparison between a handmade garment and a machine-made one is almost always in favor of the former. Finally, the *scarcity* of a garment can also be a factor in adding to the repute of its wearer. An original item from the studio of a famous designer, or a garment bearing the label of a chic fashion house, carries more prestige than an undistinguished item of clothing.

One final way that members of the leisure class exhibit pecuniary strength is always to appear in fashionable, up-to-date clothing. Veblen observed that "if each garment is permitted to serve for but a brief term, and if none of last season's apparel is carried over and made further use of during the present season, the wasteful expenditure on dress is greatly increased" (p. 127).

Conspicuous Leisure

Veblen's exploration of the dress of the leisure class extends beyond the ways in which individuals consume items of clothing and engages with the very forms and styles assumed by these garments. As he wrote, "Dress must not only be conspicuously expensive; it must also be 'inconvenient'" (p. 127). This is because, within the competitive logic of the leisure class, overt displays of wealth can be supplemented by wearing clothes that show the person in question "is not engaged in any kind of productive labour" (p. 125). Veblen uses this idea of conspicuous leisure to great effect in explaining the enormous differences in the form taken by men's and women's clothing at the end of the nineteenth century.

In scrutinizing contemporary men's clothing for evidence of the principle of conspicuous leisure, Veblen argued that there should be an absence on the male garments of any evidence of manual labor such as stains, shiny elbows, or creasing. Rather, elegant men's dress must exhibit signs that the wearer is a man of leisure. As he states, "Much of the charm that invests the patent-leather shoe, the stainless linen, the lustrous cylindrical hat, and the walking stick … comes of their pointedly suggesting that the wearer cannot when so attired bear a hand in any employment that is directly and immediately of any human use" (p. 126).

The dress of the women of the leisure class, while embodying the salient principles of conspicuous consumption and conspicuous leisure, is also influenced by the inferior social position they occupy within the leisure-class household. It is the job of the woman, argued Veblen, "to consume for the [male] head of the household; and her apparel is contrived with this object in view" (p. 132). By wearing garments that are both expensive and inconvenient, such as ornate dresses, corsets, and complicated hats, women show that they do not need to work and so increase the "pecuniary repute" in which the head of the family is held. Veblen was one of the first modern thinkers to relate the appearance of women to their weak social and economic position.

Although Veblen's analysis of dress and fashion has proved fruitful in social and historical contexts beyond what he originally envisaged, he always considered his study to be an explanation applicable primarily to what took place within the leisure class, not as a universal theory of dress. Strongly influenced by Charles Darwin's theory of evolution, Veblen believed that in the future men and women would progress beyond the restless changes of dress styles encouraged by "pecuniary culture." In their place would emerge a set of relatively stable costumes similar to those Veblen imagined had existed in ancient Greece and Rome, China, and Japan.

See also **Fashion, Theories of; Fashion and Identity.**

BIBLIOGRAPHY

Bell, Quentin. *On Human Finery*. London: Hogarth Press, 1976. An extended interpretation of Veblen's ideas on dress and fashion.

Carter, Michael. *Fashion Classics from Carlyle to Barthes*. Oxford and New York: Berg, 2003. See chapter 3, "Thorstein Veblen's Leisure Class."

Dorfman, Joseph. *Thorstein Veblen and His America*. New York: Viking Press, 1934. The standard biography of Veblen. Contains fascinating details of his personal taste in clothing.

Riesman, David. *Thorstein Veblen: A Critical Interpretation*. New York and London: Charles Scribner's Sons, 1953. See chapter 8 for a discussion of Veblen's analysis of the corset.

Veblen, Thorstein. "The Economic Theory of Women's Dress." In *Essays in Our Changing Order*. Edited by Leon Ardzrooni. New York: Viking Press, 1964. This is Veblen's account of the historical and economic origins of women's dress.

———. *The Theory of the Leisure Class*. New York: The Modern Library, Random House, 2001.

Michael Carter

VEILS *Veils*, *veiled*, and *veiling* emphasize different aspects of related "English" terms. As a noun, a veil is a piece of fabric draped as a head and upper or full body covering that functions as an item of dress. Whether an item of clothing or adornment, veils are physically used to cover and conceal, yet simultaneously draw attention to some visual aspect of the wearer. As a verb, "to veil" refers to the act of veiling or covering and concealing some visual or social aspect of the wearer, yet possibly, still inadvertently, revealing their identity. As an adjective, veiled, differentiates between the identity of the wearer who dons a veil or head covering or veils and covers and others who don't in the a variety of social contexts.

Derivative terms for veils, veiled, and veiling and their meanings exist in other European languages such as in French (*voile*) and Latin (*vela* and *velum*). And elsewhere comparable terms are used for items of dress that function in a similar manner, that is, as a piece of fabric draped as a head and upper or full body covering, that covers and conceals, yet reveals the identity of the wearer

Woman in wedding dress with veil. In many religions such as Christianity and Judaism, veils are frequently worn as part of a bride's wedding ensemble. AP/WIDE WORLD PHOTOS. REPRODUCED BY PERMISSION.

and that differentiates between those individuals that choose to cover and those that do not.

Historical Overview

The historical precedence for head coverings is vast, and references to veils, veiled, and veiling are complex. As El Guindi (1999) reviews, "veiling is a rich and nuanced phenomenon, a language that communicates social and cultural messages, a practice that has been present in tangible form since ancient times, a symbol ideologically fundamental to the Christian, and particularly, the Catholic, vision of womanhood and piety, and a vehicle for resistance in Islamic societies, and is currently the center of scholarly debate on gender and women in the Islamic east. In movements of Islamic activism, the veil occupies center stage as symbol of both identity and resistance."

Consequently, the use of the terms veils, veiled, and veiling and their comparables in other languages and cultures suggests many connotations. However, an understanding of the function and meaning of head coverings worn as veils is highly dependent on personal, social, and cultural perspectives. Frequently these views carry many ethnocentric and misogynistic representations and interpretations. Regardless of the linguistic terms used, generalizations are generational and there exist gender associations, varied social contextual variables, and cultural differentiations in veils, and veiling practices. The following descriptive and interpretive examples provide some insights in the range of people who veil or cover and are veiled or covered and the customs and cultures that govern veiling and covering practices.

Personal Identity

Historically, the terms *veils*, *veiled*, and *veiling* are associated with gendered and generational status. Though not the exclusive domain of women, as an article of dress, veils are associated with "being" female. They are typically draped fabric or head and/or body coverings that are generally the clothing or adornment form worn to differentiate female gender identity from males. Whether self-imposed or otherwise, customs associated with being female vary across cultures. For example, women in "western" cultures seldom wear veils while men rarely will wear them. In contrast, in the Middle East, men and women may frequently wear similarly draped garments that cover their heads, upper and lower bodies, but women may distinguish themselves by covering a portion of their face to conceal their identity in more public spaces. The *abaya* is one such example that is worn in many Arabic-speaking countries. Other examples, more culturally specific in historically Persian cultures are the *chador* worn in Iran and the *chaadar* worn in Afghanistan.

Age-related use of veils, veiled, and veiling practices across cultures frequently defines the transitions between stages of the female life cycle that reference physiological development and change as it relates to social status. One critical period is between youth and puberty. Veils, veiled, and veiling are often synonymous with the notion of symbolic space and specific rites of passage such as during puberty and coming of age ceremonies. Young Afghan girls begin wearing *chaadars*, veils, or head coverings to signal their change in status from a young nonmenstruating girl to a menstruating young woman, a young woman who is now of marriageable age. They may even wear them "prematurely" to appear more mature than their physiological development or chronological age.

The *dupatta* worn by Pakistani and Indian women also are gendered and generational examples of head coverings worn by young women on the Asian subcontinent. Few women would venture in public without one, and when traveling abroad the dupatta is still worn with either indigenous or local dress. The dupatta in these instances may be shawl- or scarf-like, a draped two-dimensional form.

Somali women wear a variety of head coverings or veils that differentiate the gender and age of the wearer. A *khaamar*, a scarf-like item, is worn singularly or in combination with a shawl-like garment or *gaarbo saar*. A more religious head covering is *hijab*, and the most religious form is the *nikaab*, which completely conceals the entire face except for the eyes.

In direct contrast to Arab custom, Tuareg men from Algeria, rather than women, wear veils. However, they often leave their face uncovered when they travel or are with their family.

Social Constructions

In addition to personal statements of gender and generational identity found geographically, closely linked social constructions are nearly inseparable from familial and marital status, geographic location, religious affiliation, memberships, and special associations.

Wearing a veil and following local customs that govern female space in both the domestic and public environment may express familial status as well as female position within a family. In a Gujarati village in India, veils, or *sadlo*, are worn, and the custom of veiling or *ghughut* is practiced. As Tarlo describes, "ghughut is a form of deference and respect performed by women largely to men" (1997; 160). The local term for many variations of veiling is *laj* or "doing shame." Laj variations, the way and degree in which the face, head, and body are covered, communicate a female's relationship to the males in the family but also the status of the family in the community.

Veils, veiled, and veiling may also suggest a change in marital status. During a Christian wedding ceremony a bride wears a veil. The bride's father "gives her away" wearing a veil that covers her face as part of her bridal ensemble. The bride and groom recite vows then the groom uncovers the bride's face. Also at times of death, widows, in the nineteenth and early twentieth century wore a black shroud, veils or head coverings, that covered their face, and honored a deceased husband.

In a Jewish marriage ceremony, the tradition of veiling the bride is traced back to the reference to Rebecca in Genesis "Rebecca took her veil and covered herself" upon first meeting Isaac. Popular legend attributes the custom to the Biblical story of Jacob and his wives. After working for seven years for permission to marry Rachel, Jacob was tricked on his wedding day into marrying Leah, Rachel's sister (she was wearing a veil) instead. To avoid such a mishap, according to legend, the groom "checks" to be sure that it is, indeed, his bride, before her veil is lowered over her face.

These examples of familial and marital status portray veils and veiling practices as a means to control personal symbolic space such as modesty or *haya*—an Arabic term that encompasses many concepts, including self-respect and scruples, in addition to modesty. This is especially evident in faith-based markers of female identity. For example, during calls to prayer, Muslim women wear hijab, head and upper body coverings, as they pray either in the private domestic sphere or when praying in more public, yet segregated, mosque settings. In contrast, dur-

ing confirmation ceremonies, young Christian girls dress modestly wearing white veils expressing their purity as they recite their acceptance of faith in church. In a similar fashion, religious women or nuns have worn various styles of veils or head coverings as part of their ensemble or habit, communicating purity, modesty, and devotion.

Veils, veiled, and veiling may also convey the geographic differences of the wearer. Traditionally, though not exclusive to Middle Eastern and Eastern cultures, urban and rural differences were evident in the use of veils, veiled, and veiling practices. In rural areas veils, veiled, and veiling were less evident among known kin groups but as travel permitted, women in more urban settings tended to veil, cover, and conceal themselves wearing *chaadarees* or *burqas* to "protect" themselves, their virtue, modesty, and purity, and their families from unknown or unrelated males (Daly 2000).

Socioeconomic distinctions highlight the aesthetic choices of veils, veiled, and veiling practices. The Pakistani woman's dupatta elaborately decorated with beads, sequins, and embroidery is a sign of social status, wealth, and prestige when worn.

Contemporary Examples

Early twenty-first century examples of veils, veiled, and veiling practices focus on Muslim women and their appearance. Throughout the twentieth century, veils, veiled, and veiling practices vacillated between issues resulting from personal, social, and cultural constructions of identity. Several examples are worth noting because of reform movements and the politicization of gender, religion, and nationality. At the beginning of the twentieth century, political leaders in Turkey and Afghanistan struggled to define women's national identity through control of their appearance in public contexts. Conservative leaders struggled to maintain customary practices that reinforced Islamic Sharia codes of conduct, while other progressive leaders initiated political reforms that not only permitted, but also encouraged Muslim women to eliminate head coverings as a sign of modernity. For the duration of the century and with each new regime, religious and political leaders alike revisited "the woman question."

By the end of the twentieth century, veils, veiled, and veiling practices resurfaced as a source of contention in the geopolitical and national realm. Now the woman question became aligned with sophisticated discrimination and human rights issues in diaspora immigrant communities where Muslim women live and also in their countries of origin. In addition, Islamists fought for women's inability to choose, while feminists fought for the same women's ability to choose whether or not to wear a veil. The Taliban in Afghanistan became the most strident example of female control, forcing both Islamic and Pushtunwali strict codes of conduct regardless of religious affiliation. In the United States, female Muslim refugees struggled to maintain gender, religious, and national head covering practices in the wake of anti-Islamic dress codes. Other countries such as France, Iran, and Pakistan lobbied to self define their own head and body covering practices.

See also **Burqa; Chador; Hijab; Wedding Costume.**

BIBLIOGRAPHY

Arthur, Linda, ed. *Religion, Dress and the Body.* Oxford: Berg, 1999.

———. *Undressing Religion: Commitment and Conversion from a Cross-Cultural Perspective.* Oxford: Berg, 2000.

Bailey, David A., and Gilane Tawadros, eds. *Veil, Veiling, Representation and Contemporary Art.* Cambridge, Mass.: The MIT Press, 2003.

Daly, M. Catherine. "The Paarda Expression of Hejaab among Afghan Women in a Non-Muslim Community." In *Religion, Dress, and the Body.* Edited by Linda Arthur. Oxford: Berg, 1999.

———. "The Afghan Woman's Chaadaree: An Evocative Religious Expression?" In *Undressing Religion: Commitment and Conversion from a Cross-Cultural Perspective.* Edited by Linda Arthur. Oxford: Berg, 2000.

El Guindi, Fadwa. *Veil: Modesty, Privacy and Resistance.* Oxford: Berg, 1999.

Lindisfarne-Tapper, Nancy and Bruce Ingham, eds. *Languages of Dress in the Middle East.* Surrey: Curzon Press, 1997.

Shirazi, Fegheh. *The Veil Unveiled: The Hijab in Modern Culture.* Gainesville: University Press of Florida, 2001.

Stimpfl, Joseph. "Veiling and Unveiling: Reconstructing Malay Female Identity in Singapore." In *Undressing Religion: Commitment and Conversion from a Cross-Cultural Perspective.* Edited by Linda Arthur. Oxford: Berg, 2000.

Tarlo, Emma. *Clothing Matters: Dress and Identity in India.* Chicago: University of Chicago Press, 1996.

M. Catherine Daly

VELCRO. *See* **Closures, Hook-and-Loop.**

VELVET Velvet is a pile fabric in which an extra warp (lengthwise) yarn creates a raised uncut loop or cut tuft on the fabric surface. Velvet is first encountered in low, uncut pile examples in Chinese silk *qirong jin* or *rongquan jin* that date to Warring States (403–221 B.C.E.), Qin (221–206 B.C.E.), and Western Han (206 B.C.E.–23 C.E.) dynasties. More consistent with velvet's allure of tactile seductiveness are the resplendent, late-medieval cut-pile velvets of Italy and Spain made possible by the rapid development of draw loom technology supported by discerning patrons. Parallel achievements were seen in Ottoman Turkey, Persia, and later in Mughal India.

The prodigious repeat sizes and lavish use of precious materials—fine and dense silk, and, for the most sumptuous versions, added gilt-silver wefts (yarn running crosswise) worked flat or in loops—are pervasive in fifteenth-century European depictions portraying sacred and secular elites dressed in vestments, gowns, and mantles of giant, serpentine pomegranate and artichoke designs. The velvets of Bursa and Istanbul made for fifteenth-century caftans, cushions, and tent panels for the sultans display similar splendor. In Persia, by contrast, where cut velvet seems to have originated, the long reign of the Safavid dynasty favored narrative designs of hunt scenes and literary genre figures, the rich coloristic effects made possible by intricate pile-warp substitutions.

The European capital-intensive velvet industry was closely allied with merchant banks and the courts, and flourished first in Italy (Florence, Genoa, Venice, and Milan), then elsewhere, particularly in France (Tours, and above all Lyon). Closely controlled velvet qualities developed, and were assigned dozens of specialized French terms to distinguish the types—some are still current. They ranged from plain velvets, sometimes given added value by stamped designs and other finishes, to patterned ones by varying pile heights and introducing two or more pile warp colors.

In the early modern period, wealthy patrons continued commissioning large-scale custom designs for special occasion outfits, while stock styles of smaller repeat patterns were used in standard dress velvets. A number of them were woven for Western customers in China, where interest in the structure had reawakened, and spread to Japan. Great numbers of these small-scale designs survive in art and textile fragments and show floral sprig, bird, and animal motifs subordinated into lattice-type patterns.

From the middle of the eighteenth century and into the next, silk velvet appeared in men's apparel (especially waistcoats) and luxury carriage interiors, but women's fashion abandoned stately velvet in favor of lighter fabrics. Through the nineteenth century, Lyon in particular, produced elaborate, fine velvets woven by hand on Jacquard looms, designed to win prizes at world fairs, and promoted in fashions of the emerging Parisian couture houses.

Plain, patterned, and printed silk velvets and the longer-piled relation, plush, were featured in glamorous opera coats during the early twentieth century. Cotton and rayon frequently substituted for scarce and expensive silk, and most plain velvets are now woven double on power looms, creating two fabrics sharing a pile warp, subsequently separated by horizontal cutting blades. In the late twentieth century, China exported quantities of inexpensive silk velvets, and innovative textile designers eagerly applied new looks with earlier methods, such as burn-out and resist dyeing for fashion accessories.

See also **China: History of Dress.**

BIBLIOGRAPHY

Becker, John. *Pattern and Loom: A Practical Study of the Development of Weaving Techniques in China, Western Asia and*

Europe. Copenhagen: Rhodos International Publishers, 1987. Meticulous descriptions of early textile structures and their possible loom technologies.

Burnham, Harold B. *Chinese Velvets: A Technical Study.* Occasional Papers 2. Art and Archeological Division, Royal Ontario Museum. Toronto: University of Toronto Press, 1959. An in-depth analysis of seventeenth-century velvets of East Asia.

Fauque, Claude, ed. *Le Velours ou la force de la douceur.* Paris: Syros, 1994. A cross-disciplinary survey touching on history, technology, ideologies and design that includes, in the French understanding of the term *velours,* weft-pile structures as well.

Geijer, Agnes. *A History of Textile Art: A Selective Account.* London: Pasold Research Fund, 1979. The indispensable reference for historic textiles, their trade, cultural exchanges, and context.

Hardoiun-Fugier, Elisabet, Bernard Berthod, and Martine Chevent-Fusaro, eds. *Les ftoffes: Dictionnaire historique.* Paris: Les editions de l'Amateur, 1994. Richly illustrated reference work, with comprehensive listings of velvet terms.

History of Textile Technology of Ancient China. New York: Science Press, 1992. Fundamental text on Chinese textiles and their materials although technical terms are at times at variance with Western accepted standards.

Janssen, Elsje. *Richesse de Velours* Brussels: Musee du Cinquantenaire, 1995. An exhibition catalog covering early examples to contemporary Belgian velvets.

King, Monique and Donald King. *European textiles in the Keir Collection 400 B.C. to 1800 A.D.* London and Boston: Faber and Faber, 1990. A catalog establishing important developments in design and interactions between cultures.

Mackie, Louise. *The Splendor of Turkish Weaving: An Exhibition of Silks and Carpets of the 13 Centuries.* Washington, D.C.: The Textile Museum, 1973. A fine hand list of the TMO's Turkish velvets.

Santangelo, Antonino. *A Treasury of Great Italian Textiles.* New York: Harry N. Abrams, 1964. A still useful standard in the literature on textiles.

Sonday, Milton. "Pattern and Weaves: Safavid Lampas and Velvet." In *Woven from the Soul, Spun from the Heart: Textile Arts of Safavid and Qajar Iran 16th–19th Centuries.* Edited by Carol Bier. Washington, D.C.: The Textile Museum, 1987. Detailed structural study and diagrams of Persian velvets.

Stack, Lotus. *The Pile Thread: Carpets, Velvets, and Variations.* Minneapolis: The Minneapolis Institute of Art, 1991. A succinct and comprehensive guide, with good illustrations of the technology, design, and context of velvet.

Désirée Koslin

VELVETEEN. *See* **Weave, Double; Weave, Pile.**

VERSACE, GIANNI AND DONATELLA Gianni Versace (1946–1997) was a defining figure in the world of design in the 1980s and 1990s. He dressed the inde-

Gianni Versace, with models Claudia Schiffer and Naomi Campbell. In the 1980s and 1990s, designer Gianni Versace dressed celebrities in his well-renowned, daring, and bold fashions. AP/WIDE WORLD PHOTOS. REPRODUCED BY PERMISSION.

pendent spirits, celebrities, and the rich, young, and fearless. His exclusive clique personified his ideals of men's and women's ready-to-wear and couture clothing. He also created accessories, linens, and a collection for the home inspired by his preference for the baroque style. Versace's knowledge was encyclopedic and his sense of history prophetic; his genius was the successful linkage of fashion and culture.

Following Versace's tragic death in July 1997, his sister Donatella was catapulted into the international limelight. Only three months later, no longer her brother's muse and collaborator, she assumed creative direction over the development of a dozen highly demanding collections. An earlier agreement between brother and sister had established that she would be the one to carry on his work if it were ever necessary. As a result the signature Versace Atelier collection was presented as usual in Paris in 1998.

Donatella Versace was born in Reggio Calabria, in southern Italy in 1955. She was one of four children born to a businessman and an accomplished seamstress. During Donatella's childhood, Gianni designed clothing for his younger sister, who became the embodiment of his standards. After she completed her studies in Italian literature at the Università di Firenze to supplement her sense of culture, she followed Gianni to Milan, where he had established his career. Initially he sketched his first ready-to-wear collections for the manufacturing firms of Genny, Complice, and Callaghan.

Donatella arrived with the intention of shaping her brother's public image through deft management of his public relations. When he established his signature company in 1978, she became his spirited muse-in-residence. Santo Versace, an older sibling, assisted in the organization of the business, which he continues to direct.

As the house's driving creative force since 1997, Donatella has forged on to energize her international team of fashion designers. Her entrance-making gowns, as well as practical, elegant ready-to-wear clothes and men's wear maintained a high profile in her design studios and corporate offices in the center of Milan. The Versace family estates are located in nearby Como, within an hour's drive from the Milan corporate headquarters.

Business Innovations

Donatella's larger-than-life approach to creating fashion mirrored her brother's maxim that fashion must fuse with the media, the performing arts, celebrity, vitality, and sexuality. Donatella staged the audacious, high-powered Versace runway shows after Gianni's death, enlisting the friendship and devotion of many of the supermodels. Her brother had initiated successful advertising campaigns with photographers and artists beginning in the late 1970s: Richard Avedon and Andy Warhol, among others, shared his flamboyant taste for self-promotion. Donatella continued in this vein, preferring to work with such photographers as Steven Meisel and Bruce Weber. The company continued to unleash dynamic, sexually charged media campaigns in the early 2000s as it expanded its share of the luxury trades.

Gianni Versace's penchant for extreme styling and unconventional choices of sumptuous and radiant fabrics combined themes from his studies in art history with new technology. The Versace label was more focused on the modern career woman in the early twenty-first century, a change reflected in the variety of garments it produced. Donatella's hallmarks included flashy materials fluidly draped. She presented herself on the international stage as the model of an invincible woman. Donatella also launched the fragrance Versace Woman in 2001.

Personal Image

During their adolescence and early adult years, brother and sister remained loyal to each other. Gianni created vibrant garments for Donatella that embodied his personal rationale of expression. The freedom to dare, to make personal choices, was one of the Versace duo's resonant manifestos. During their nineteen years of collaboration, Versace consulted his younger sibling in all important decisions. Her bravura and dedication made her an integral part of the company as it developed. In early 2000 she epitomized the liberation he sought as a designer. Gianni paid tribute to Donatella when he named his 1995 perfume Blonde to honor her trademark long, platinum locks. Surrounded by revelers, her frequent tours of nightspots provided her with access to the younger generation. In due course, Donatella became chief designer for Versace's Versus collection, where she further empowered her success with their dual vision of bold patterns and high glamour infused with sex appeal, designed for a younger clientele. While Donatella was independent in her thinking, she was also committed to her brother's enduring legacy. She continued to style flashy and extreme ready-to-wear clothing as well as a couture line, as she did during her apprenticeship with Gianni and in her position as an accessory designer and creator of a line of children's clothing in 1993.

Donatella's camaraderie with celebrities, including Elton John, Elizabeth Hurley, and Courtney Love, reflected her belief in the significance of uncompromising friendships. Madonna, Jon Bon Jovi, Sting, and Trudy Skyler were among her closest confidantes. Like her older brother, she combined music with the media and the spectacle of contemporary urban life. Donatella's designs affirmed sensuality, employing short skirts and plunging necklines as devices of freedom. "Fashion can be freedom or it can be a way to live with no freedom," she avowed in *Interview*.

Donatella married the former model Paul Beck, with whom she had two children—Allegra, her uncle's beneficiary, born in 1986, and Daniel, born in 1991.

Donatella Versace reveled in the attention she received in fashion and popular lifestyle magazines. She pursued visibility at all levels of society and was always ready to convey the glamorous extravagance that identified her company. Her fashion edicts remained consistent: "If I want to be blonde, I am not going to be a medium blonde. I am going to be totally blonde. If I am going to wear heels, they are not going to be two inches high. They are going to be much higher than that. It's the freedom of extremes that I love" (*Interview*). Her confident design ethic mirrored that of her late brother, who became a creative genius in high-end apparel and of bold gestures in the media.

See also **Avedon, Richard; Celebrities; Fashion Photography; Italian Fashion; Madonna; Meisel, Steven; Supermodels.**

BIBLIOGRAPHY

"Friendship is Freedom." *Interview* 30, no. 3 (March 2000): 212.

Martin, Richard. *Versace.* New York: Universe/Vendome, 1997.

———. *Gianni Versace.* New York: The Metropolitan Museum of Art and Harry N. Abrams, Inc., 1998.

Spindler, Amy M. "Style: The Great Gianni." *New York Times* (18 February 2001).

Gillion Carrara

VICTORIAN FASHION. *See* **Europe and America: History of Dress (400–1900 C.E.).**

VICUNA. *See* **Alpaca.**

VIKTOR & ROLF The Dutch saying, *Doe normaal, dan ben je al gek genoeg* (literally, Just be normal, then you are crazy enough) sheds light on the work of design team Viktor & Rolf. Viktor Horsting (b. 1969) and Rolf Snoeren (b. 1969) met while they were students at the Arnhem Academy of Art, the Netherlands, in 1988. They both sought to escape the boredom they experienced while growing up in small, quiet, suburban towns in southern Holland. "We had nothing to relate to, never saw glamour except for fashion magazines, and longed to escape to those dream worlds," Horsting once said to an interviewer. By pushing the boundaries of what defines fashion, Viktor & Rolf inspired a new generation of Dutch fashion designers and helped to expose the international fashion media to a country known more for wooden clogs than high fashion.

Viktor & Rolf are characterized in Stephen Gan's *Visionaire 2000* (1997) as "fashion's biggest fans and its toughest critics." While their works celebrate the detailed craftsmanship of tailoring and consistently reference classic silhouettes from the legendary couturiers Cristóbal Balenciaga, Coco Chanel, Christian Dior, and Yves Saint Laurent, they also critique the twentieth- and twenty-first century's fashion industry, tackle the stereotypes of fashion, and expose its vulnerabilities to a runway audience.

The Early Experiments
Viktor & Rolf's first collection won the grand prize at the *Salon européen des jeunes stylists* (1993), a fashion festival in the southern French city of Hyères. When deconstruction was the trend, Viktor & Rolf reconstructed by piling layers of men's button-down shirts to form ball gowns. The following year they suspended flashy gold garments adorned with oversized ribbons and excessive decorations from the ceiling in their installation *L'Apparence du vide* (1994) at the Galerie Patricia Dorfman, Paris, which sought to critique the aura and hype surrounding fashion. In another experiment, sleek marketing for *Viktor & Rolf, le parfum* (1996) served to critique the superficial, banal beauty of fragrance advertising. The neatly packaged, limited-edition (2,500) perfume bottles were deliberately designed so that they could not be opened. The bottles sold out at the Parisian boutique Colette. In *Launch* (1996), presented at the Torch Gallery in Amsterdam, Viktor & Rolf's dream world of the fashion process was realized on a small scale. They explained that, with a doll-sized runway, sketch and draping session, and photo shoot setup, "we created the ultimate goals we wanted to achieve in fashion (but felt unable to). These miniatures represented some of the most emblematic situations in fashion we wanted to become re-

Viktor Horsting (left) and Rolf Snoeren. The Dutch fashion duo are well known for their innovative, unusual clothing designs and inventive runway performances. MARTIN BUREAU/AFP/GETTY IMAGES. REPRODUCED BY PERMISSION.

ality" (Personal interview, 23 December 1999). Their dream was realized soon thereafter in the form of an haute couture collection.

The Haute Couture Collections
Viktor & Rolf brought an intellectual approach to the fashion process via art. They pursued haute couture because they found it to be "the most sublime" aspect of fashion. With Dutch government support and the Groninger Museum, the Netherlands, as their sole client, Viktor & Rolf were able to develop creatively without the pressure of maintaining profitability that most young designers experience. In their second spring/summer 1998 collection at the Thaddeus Ropac Gallery in Paris, Viktor & Rolf created their signature "atomic bomb silhouette"—exaggerated on top and pencil-skinny on the bottom. The clothes were dedicated to the millennium (fit either for the biggest celebration ever or apocalyptic destruction) and were deformed with silk balloons, streamers, and other brightly colored party elements. The Viktor & Rolf label was recognized by the Federation de la couture, the umbrella organization that oversees the Parisian haute couture houses and their events. This prestigious invitation for inclusion occurred even though Viktor & Rolf did not conform to the organization's rules and guidelines. Viktor & Rolf presented their entire fall/winter 1999–2000 collection on the shoulders of one model, Maggie Rizer. As she stood on a revolving platform, Viktor & Rolf layered, in nine successive stages à la Russian-doll style, precisely-engineered jute dresses decorated with Swarovski crystals. Through this mechanism they attempted to showcase their feelings about haute couture as a precious and unattainable jewel.

A model poses in an outfit by Viktor and Rolf. Critical of the twentieth- and twenty-first century's fashion industry, Dutch designers Viktor Horsting and Rolf Snoeren tackle the stereotypes of fashion. © REUTERS/CORBIS. REPRODUCED BY PERMISSION.

rimmed glasses, closely trimmed dark hair, and a serious demeanor despite the humor in their shows. They performed a tap-dance finale with tuxedos, top hats, and canes to "Putting on the Ritz" and "Singin' in the Rain" for their spring/summer 2001 collection. Additionally, they used themselves as models for the launch of their fall/winter 2003–2004 men's wear collection, Monsieur, as they synchronized changes into looks depicting clichés of traditional men's wear.

Viktor & Rolf continue to push the boundaries of fashion in ready-to-wear by using the catwalk as a stage for performance art. Models were cast as walking shadows, for example, in their "Black Hole" collection (fall/winter 2001–2002) when they were covered head-to-toe in black silhouettes and black makeup. Two years later (fall/winter 2003–2004) their models appeared as fair-skinned, red-haired clones of the actress Tilda Swinton.

Through their shows Viktor & Rolf try to bring fantasy, beauty, and magic back to fashion as they forge a path for the viewer to enter their dream. "For us," explains Rolf Snoeren, "it's always about escaping reality, so in that sense the clothes are meant to show beauty first. Beauty and hope. Because cynicism, you know, kills everything."

See also **Fashion Designer; Fashion Shows.**

BIBLIOGRAPHY

Alonso, Roman, and Lisa Eisner. "Double Dutch." *New York Times* (8 December 2002): 109. This in-depth interview reveals the personalities and fantasy worlds of Horsting and Snoeren.

Horsting, Viktor, and Artimo. *Viktor & Rolf.* Breda, Netherlands: Artimo Foundation, 1999. This artist's book covers Viktor & Rolf's early work, 1993–1999.

Lowthorpe, Rebecca. "The Gilbert & George of Fashion." *The Independent on Sunday* (30 September 2001): 35–38.

Martin, Richard. "A Note: Art & Fashion, Viktor & Rolf." *Fashion Theory: The Journal of Dress, Body & Culture* 3 (1999). Martin analyzes Viktor & Rolf's early works and emphasizes their importance in crossing the boundaries of fashion with art.

Spindler, Amy. *Viktor & Rolf Haute Couture Book.* Groningen, Netherlands: Groninger Museum, 2001. A retrospective exhibition catalog featuring the haute couture collections at the Groninger Museum.

Angel Chang

Viktor & Rolf in the Twenty-first Century

The fashion media's attraction to their exaggerated silhouettes and noteworthy runway performances has always played an integral role in the shaping of the Viktor & Rolf brand identity. With no advertising campaigns, no self-standing boutiques, and no mass-produced clothes to sell, their early relationship with the public depended heavily on the generous amounts of press coverage they received each season. (Close collaborations with photography teams Inez van Lamsweerde and Vinoodh Matadin, as well as Anouschka Blommers and Niels Schumm, also helped further their vision.) The media's acknowledgment of Viktor & Rolf as a leading avantgarde haute couture label was instrumental to the commercial success of their ready-to-wear line. Their first collection sold immediately to sixty stores worldwide during its launch in February 2000.

Viktor Horsting and Rolf Snoeren understand that a fashion designer's public image is nearly as important as the clothes that are created. Oftentimes referred to as "the Gilbert & George of fashion," the two present themselves as mirror images of each other: matching dark-

VINTAGE FASHION The trend for "vintage" clothing as fashion exploded in the 1960s. Prior to this, the trading and wearing of old clothing had different connotations. All levels of trade in old clothing were well supported by the increasing speed of fashion change from the fifteenth and sixteenth centuries, and the growth in consumer availability of these trends. As the commercial constituency for fashion increased, the growth in trade of old clothing was incremental as the quantity of these goods increased. The original ragpickers collected items that others had disposed of and returned them back to the economic cycle. Consequently, the ragpicker was allied with other outsiders, or members of the underclass. Karl Marx was later to define the philosophy of artistic bohemianism by its links to this social underclass. Bohemians, he believed, were vagabonds whose position was characterized by economic necessity *or* (crucially) romantic interpretation. This ambivalence between necessity and choice is essential to an understanding of vintage clothing.

The link between fashion and old clothing made the clothing a definitive indication of one's social status—the line and fabric of a jacket from a period too recent to be fashionable *or* classic immediately indicated that the wearer was drawn from the lower classes. It was a stigma that people were painfully aware of. The ethos of "make-do-and-mend" allowed the lower classes to position the wearing of old clothing as thrifty and, during wartime, patriotic. However, it was very specifically old clothing that was passed down through families. It was, most certainly, rarely purchased. Consumers of old clothing were, then, considered to be those seeking to give an impression of higher social status, the destitute, or actors, and consequently were treated, in some ways, as suspiciously as those who sold them the garments.

Prior to the mid-1960s old clothing had not been widely positioned within traditional retailing environments, its traders preferring the market stall, auction, or pawnbrokers as a venue for selling. The retailing of old clothing has been viewed in diametrically opposed lights—as a criminal activity for laundering money, as good business practice, and, from the advent of charity shops, as an altruistic pastime. Most cities in the United Kingdom had large warehouses that distributed secondhand clothes, and despite the falloff in trade in the late twentieth century, many still have significant export markets. As trade in old clothing fell, the practice of wearing old clothing rose and became known as "vintage," moving from the market place to the upper market boutique.

In London, dress has been persistently retailed as vintage since the early 1970s. Shopping guides of the mid-1970s note numerous vintage retailers, some offering in-house tailoring with vintage fabric, predating in practice (although quite possibly not in philosophy) the work of designers such as Martin Margiela, Russell Sage, Alice Temperley and Jessica Ogden. However, it was still not considered a wholly acceptable practice, and the clothing was predominantly worn by consumers affecting a rebellious challenge to the mores and propriety of previous generations.

The duality between thrift and economy on the one hand, and subversive practice on the other, made vintage fertile as a signifier for bohemian morality and practice, notably in the 1950s and 1960s. The hippie lifestyle was positioned as anticonsumerist, which sartorially was communicated through the wearing of old clothes. This interpretation continued throughout the following decades, as seen in the political stance of the Women's Environmental Network in the 1990s, but also in the work of designers such as Helen Storey, Komodo, and to a degree, Vivienne Westwood and the Punk movement.

The twenty-first century trend for vintage clothing has its roots more specifically in bohemianism—in the performance of individuality and artistic (rather than aristocratic) elitism. A number of specialist boutique retailers in London have acquired significant profile and status. A number of these (Virginia, Sheila Cook, Steinberg and Tolkein) are regularly credited and quoted in fashion magazines, and a steady flow of celebrities list them in "my favorite store/best-kept secret" questionnaires in Sunday supplements. Across Europe and North America, vintage retailers are no less conspicuous for their domination of fashion headlines. The owners of Resurrection and Mayle (New York) and Decades and Lily (Los Angeles), are considered important "women of fashion" and costumers to the stars. The vintage revival in the United States is due, in no small part, to the eclectic image that stylist and vintage retailer Patricia Fields created for Sarah Jessica Parker's character Carrie in the HBO comedy *Sex and the City*.

Retailers such as Selfridges, TopShop, and Jigsaw in London, A.P.C. in France, and Barneys and Henri Bendel in New York have all picked up on the trend, incorporating vintage offers or vintage-inspired collections into their ranges. Wearing vintage has become a distinguishing marker of cultural and economic capital—it's unique, it's expensive, and so on—that privileges the individual. More than money, it is free time that is required to invest in the laborious process of seeking, finding, repairing, and selling old clothing. In the latter half of the twentieth century and beyond, that free time was available predominantly to those who were wealthy or who were engaged in work that was flexible—principally, therefore, creative. Because the vintage garment is unique, it also suggests that the wearer is individual, separate from the increasingly and obviously shallow process of fashion.

Interestingly, many Hollywood celebrities have embraced vintage principally because it is outside fashion—suggestive either of anticonsumerist philosophy or of individual choice. Actresses allied with independent cinema such as Chloë Sevigny appear to have adopted the "trash" aesthetic to distinguish themselves from mainstream fashion. Sevigny's protégé designers Imitation of Christ are proponents of an anticorporate philosophy not dissimilar to Westwood's in the early 1970s. On the other hand, Nicole Kidman, one of the most prominent wearers of vintage in contemporary Hollywood, tends to purchase from retailers who position their stock as antique—timeless and culturally valuable—highlighting her sense of personal, individual style, which is supposedly sincere, authentic, and equally as timeless as the clothing she prefers.

One of the most pointed criticisms of vintage is that it is detrimentally nostalgic, particularly in its influence over contemporary design. Alongside the retailers, a cluster of designers have been steadily drawn toward old clothing, either literally, in the reworking of found fabrics or garments, or indirectly, in their plunder of the annals of dress history to create a modernized antiquity for the postmodern consumer. Designers as diverse as Ralph Lauren, John Galliano, Alexander McQueen, Donna Karan, and Miuccia Prada are all known to have invested heavily in vintage clothing to use as resource material. However, it is not necessarily a nostalgic practice since the selection of pieces is informed by the contemporary. Crucially, it is not necessarily the garment itself, but its positioning in a contemporary debate and context that reinvigorates the memories and meanings the garment contains.

See also **Actors and Actresses, Impact on Fashion; Bohemian Dress; Secondhand Clothes, Anthropology of.**

BIBLIOGRAPHY

Benjamin, Walter, trans. *Arcades Project.* Cambridge, Mass.: Belknap Press of Harvard University Press, 1999.

Bordieu, Pierre. *Distinction: A Social Critique of the Judgement of Taste.* London: Routledge and Kegan Paul, 1984.

Cicolini, Alice. "Vielle Couture: Authentic Display." Master's thesis. London College of Fashion, 2002.

Dyer, Richard. *Stars.* London: BFI Publishing, 1998.

Ewen, Stuart. "Varnished Barbarism." In *All Consuming Images: The Politics of Style in Contemporary Culture.* New York: Basic Books, 1988.

Ginsburg, Madeleine. "Rags to Riches: The Second-Hand Clothes Trade, 1700–1978." In vol. 14 of *Costume.* London: V&A Publishing for the Costume Society, 1980.

Joliffe, Kira. *Cheap Date: Antidotal Anti-Fashion.* Hove, U.K.: Slab-O-Concrete Publications, 2000.

Jones, Ann R., and P. Stallybrass. *Renaissance Clothing and the Materials of Memory.* Cambridge U.K.: Cambridge University Press, 2000.

Lemire, Beverly. *Dress, Culture, and Commerce: The English Clothing Trade before the Factory, 1660–1800.* London: Macmillan, 1997.

Silverman, Kaja. "Fragments of a Fashionable Discourse." In *Studies in Entertainment: Critical Approaches to Mass Culture.* Edited by Tania Modleski. Bloomington and Indianapolis: Indiana University Press, 1986.

Tolkein, Tracy. *Vintage: The Art of Dressing Up.* London: Pavilion, 2000.

Alice Cicolini

VINYL AS FASHION FABRIC Vinyl is a plasticized variation of Polyvinyl chloride (PVC). Although PVC is hard, with the addition of plasticizers it can be made pliable enough, for example, to coat fabrics in any thickness.

In 1926, Waldo L. Semon, a scientist working for BF Goodrich, accidentally discovered this compound while trying to form a synthetic rubber. At first he thought that the rubbery gel he created would work as a bonding agent to adhere rubber to metal. However, through further experimentation he found he had invented a highly versatile plasticized vinyl that, in the early 2000s, has hundreds of uses.

To present his discovery to the company, Semon applied the gel to curtains, creating a waterproof vinyl-coated shower curtain. It stirred a sensation! Vinyl was quickly adapted to umbrella and raincoat fabrics for its waterproof properties. Vinyl was also used to coat wires. Commercialized in 1931, the new technology was highly successful. During World War II, vinyl was turned to wartime use, and so it wasn't until the 1960s that vinyl again became a fashion item.

The 1950s were times for conformity, particularly in clothing. By the 1960s the public was ready to have fun with fashion, and clothes reflected the radical social change of that decade.

In the mid 1960s couture designers André Courréges, Pierre Cardin, and Paco Rabanne, noted for their modern and futuristic looks, seized upon the high-tech look of these fabrics. Vinyl-coated fabrics not only gave a new surface appeal to their designs, but lent a modern structural look to the designers' new vision of architectural shapes rather than fluid draped lines. Modern clean-lined geometric shapes characterized their designs. Garments were cut to suggest simple geometric forms, boxy with hard edges, angular straight lines, or circular in shape.

André Courréges, who claimed to have invented the miniskirt, made vinyl fashionable with his miniskirts, helmets, A-line dresses, and suits. Inspired by astronaut boots, he used vinyl in his "Moon Girl Collection" to create the shiny white boots that accessorized his designs. The "Courréges boot" was mid-calf length with open slots at the top and a tassel or bow in front. Soon the look was being copied everywhere. Popularized by teenagers wearing the boots on discotheque television shows, they were soon called "go-go boots" after the go-go dancers who wore them.

At the same time in England, the "Mod" fashion look first appeared on London's King's Road and Carnaby Street. The op art and pop art movements inspired the trendy English designer Mary Quant. She popularized the miniskirt, high vinyl boots, and shoulder bags. She used vinyl-coated fabrics to create what was called the "wet look" not just in raincoats, but in tight miniskirts and dresses as well.

Through the years vinyl coating was able to take on matte and textured surfaces to look more like leather for a cheaper alternative. Vinyl can also be produced in almost any color or can be crystal clear.

The downside of vinyl for cloth is that it does not "breathe." It also does not readily break down when discarded, lasting for decades. However, it can be recycled and converted to new applications.

After its first trendy appearance, vinyl's popularity in rainwear was only occasional because the vinyl coating rendered the fabric unbreathable. Wearing the coat, or other article of vinyl clothing, can become very uncomfortable, keeping heat and moisture trapped next to the skin. Also, although the fabric is waterproof, the garment isn't. In a heavy downpour water can get in through the seams. In the early twenty-first century, hi-tech fabrics and new construction methods have taken over the waterproof category in clothing, but the use of vinyl in other areas continues to grow.

See also **High-Tech Fashion; Rainwear; Umbrellas and Parasols.**

BIBLIOGRAPHY

Bernard, Barbara. *Fashion in the 60's.* New York: St. Martin's Press, 1978.

Carter, Ernestine. *With Tongue in Chic.* London: Joseph, 1974.

———. *The Changing World of Fashion: 1900 to the Present.* London: Weidenfeld and Nicolson, 1977.

De Pietri, Stephen, and Melissa Leventon. *New Look to Now: French Haute Couture, 1947–1987.* New York: Rizzoli International, 1989.

Fogg, Marnie. *Boutique: A '60s Cultural Icon.* London: Mitchell Beazley, 2003.

Lagassé, Paul. *The Columbia Encyclopedia.* 6th ed. New York: Columbia University Press, 2000.

Kamitsis, Lydia. *Paco Rabanne: A Feeling for Research.* Paris: Editions M. Lafon, 1996.

Kellogg, Ann T., et al. *In an Influential Fashion: An Encyclopedia of Nineteenth- and Twentieth-Century Fashion Designers and Retailers Who Transformed Dress.* Westport, Conn.: Greenwood Press, 2002.

Martin, Richard, ed. *The St. James Fashion Encyclopedia: A Survey of Style from 1945 to the Present.* Detroit: Visible Ink Press, 1997.

Moffitt, Peggy, et al. *The Rudi Gernreich Book.* New York: Rizzoli International, 1991.

O'Hara, Georgina. *The Thames and Hudson Dictionary of Fashion and Fashion Designers.* New York: Thames and Hudson, Inc., 1998.

Internet Resources

National Inventors Hall of Fame. 2004. Available from <http://www.invent.org/index.asp>.

Style.com. 2004. Available from <http://www.style.com>.

The Vinyl Institute. 2004. Available from <http://www.vinylinfo.org/index.html>.

"Waldo Simon—PVC Inventor." 2004. Available from <http://inventors.about.com/library/inventors/blpvc.htm>.

Mary Ann C. Ferro

VIONNET, MADELEINE Born in Chilleurs-aux-Bois in 1876, Madeleine Vionnet was apprenticed to a dressmaker while still a child. She began her career in fashion working for makers of lingerie, as well as dress-

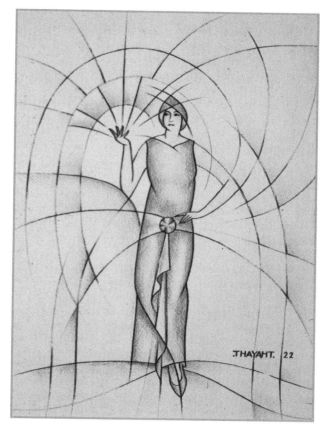

Illustration of a Vionnet dress. Madeline Vionnet helped to instigate fashion's exploration of private and public. Many found her designs controversial, and her main clients were stage performers. PHOTO BY JOHN S. MAJOR. REPRODUCED BY PERMISSION.

makers and couturiers in London and Paris. These early experiences of craft skills and, in particular, the relationship between body and fabric involved in making undergarments, influenced the future direction of her own designs. She learned to respect the intricate skills of craftspeople, who were able to produce delicate effects through, for example, drawn threadwork and fagoting, which created spatial patterns by moving and regrouping the fabric's threads. This fascination with minute detail and the possibilities of fabric manipulation formed the foundation of her approach. Her background in the couture trade was fundamental to her later status, since it distinguished her as a craftsperson who was knowledgeable about the various dressmaking skills and decorative trades that supported designers. She was therefore not only tutored in practical skills but was also aware of the status and treatment of young women who worked in the ateliers.

Birth of Vionnet's Design Philosophy

Around 1900 Vionnet moved to Callot Soeurs's celebrated couture house in Paris. There she began to understand the significance of garment design that sprang from draping fabric directly onto a live model, rather than sketching a design on paper and then translating it into fabric. This approach necessarily focused attention on the body and its relationship to the way fabric was draped and sculpted around its contours. Vionnet exploited this technique to the full. For Vionnet, draping—in her case on a miniature, eighty-centimeter mannequin—became crucial to her design philosophy. It enabled her to think of the body as a whole and to mobilize the full potential of the springy, malleable, silk crêpes she came to favor.

At Callot Soeurs these methods were combined with an acute awareness of fashion and style, as skillful designers and saleswomen sought to mold couture's elite tastes to each client's particular figure and requirements. Vionnet encountered high fashion and learned its seasonal rhythms, while she experimented with the dressmaking skills she had acquired over the years. An example of this was her adaptation of Japanese kimono sleeves to Western dress, which produced deeper armholes that made the silhouette less restrictive and enabled the fabric to flow and drape around the upper body. This early innovation incorporated several of what were to become Vionnet's trademarks. For example, her use of Asian and classical techniques freed fabric from established Western dressmaking methods that tended to fix the cloth, and therefore the body, into position. Her focus upon draping and wrapping rather than cutting and tailoring to the figure enabled her to achieve maximum fluidity, enhancing movement and flexibility. Her concentration on experimental construction techniques tested the boundaries of design and dressmaking and allowed her to create clothing that derived its significance from subtle reconfigurations of cloth, rather than from dramatic surface decoration. For Vionnet minute attention to detail was paramount.

Vionnet's career may have started during the late nineteenth century when fashion was predicated upon exaggeration, novelty, and decoration, but there were already intimations of new types of femininity and clothing that would enable greater physical freedom. These came partly from utopian dress reform movements, but also from other designers, such as Fortuny, who used historical dress as a source for comfortable yet luxurious dress.

Daring Designs

When Vionnet moved to the house of Doucet in 1907, she became more daring in her display of the female figure, inspired by avant-garde dancer Isadora Duncan's barefoot movements and by her own desire to strip fashion to its essential elements: fabric and body. She insisted that Doucet's models walk barefoot and corsetless into the couturier's salon for his seasonal fashion show. Her dramatic exposure of the models' skin enhanced the fall of the fabric as they moved and brought sudden focus onto the natural figure.

Vionnet helped to instigate modern fashion's exploration of private and public, with her designs' reliance upon a sophisticated interplay between sheer and opaque fabrics draped to swirl about the skin. Many found her work too controversial, and her main clients were stage performers, used to their public roles and more ready to experiment with avant-garde fashions. The *déshabillé*, a fashionable and fluid garment previously worn in private, became acceptable, if still daring, for entertaining at home. In Vionnet's hands its light drapes created a shimmering cocoon reminiscent of lingerie. For example, the French actress Lantelme was photographed in 1907 in a loose tea gown, the pastel tones and matte glow of its layered chiffon illuminated by beading and sequins.

Classical Influences and Cutting on the Bias

In 1912 Vionnet opened her own house in the rue de Rivoli. It was closed, however, at the outbreak of war in 1914, and Vionnet moved to Rome for the duration. Her experience there, as well as her studies of ancient Greek art in museum collections, became another crucial aspect of her work. Classicism, both as an aesthetic and design philosophy, provided Vionnet with a language to articulate her belief in geometrical form, mathematical rhythm, and the strength of proportion and balance as a basis for the garments she created.

During the late teens Vionnet focused on the process of wrapping lengths of fabric onto the body in the style of the Greek chiton. Through these experiments she exploited the advances made in fabric technology during World War I that had produced yarns that could be made into more supple fabrics, and she had extra wide lengths of material created for her to allow even greater drape. Vionnet was thus able to push her examination of construction methods that not only draped but twisted fabric still further than before; moreover, she formulated the potential of the bias cut for which she is so often remembered. To do this she cut the fabric diagonally, across the grain, to produce a springy, elastic drape. Although cutting on the bias had been used for accessories and had been applied to fixed, molded dress forms, it had not been used this extensively for the body of a garment. Vionnet took an experimental leap forward in her desire to release both fabric and figure from the tight-fitting ethos of traditional Western dressmaking.

Vionnet reduced the use of darts, often eliminating them completely and therefore allowing bias-cut fabric to hover freely around the body. She also introduced lingerie techniques—such as roll-tucked hems or fagoting to disguise the line of a seam—to both day and evening wear. Her designs aimed for simplicity of overall form and impact, while they frequently employed complex construction techniques.

One of the most dramatically minimal of her designs was a dress from 1919–1920, now in the collection of the Costume Institute at the Metropolitan Museum in New York. It demonstrates Vionnet's search during this period of her career for new ways to push the boundaries of the fabric while maintaining tight control over the ultimate hang of the garment. In this example she used four rectangles of ivory silk crêpe, two at the back and two at the front, held together at one point to form the shoulders of the dress. The rectangles hang down the body from these two points, to form two diamond forms of mobile fabric at front and back. Vionnet, in the act of turning the geometric shapes onto the diagonal for the final dress, swung the weave onto the bias. Thus the dress is stripped of dressmaking's usual devices to nip and sew the material for a "fit" with the body beneath; Vionnet instead used the movement released in the fabric to flow and drape around the wearer as she walked and danced. The deep drape of the fabric created vertical bands of light flowing down the figure. These elongated the silhouette, which was first blurred and then brought into relief as the wearer's movements caused the swathes of fabric to shift and form anew.

In Vionnet's hands the bias cut was a means to rethink the relationship between fabric and flesh. She constantly tested the methods she had learned during her early career, and her attention to anatomy led to her use of bias cutting not just to allow material to cocoon the figure, but to produce sophisticated forms of decoration. She varied the direction of the material's grain to encourage light to bounce off contrasting matte and shiny pattern pieces. The complexity of her construction techniques meant that her designs came alive only when worn or draped on the stand. They were conceived for the three dimensions of the body and cut to smooth over the figure: evening dresses dipped into the small of the back; day dresses slid under the clavicle to form a soft cowl neckline; and bias-cut fabric draped artfully to allow for the curve of the stomach or the arch of hip bones.

Futurist Influences
Such effects were only enhanced as the wearer moved, and Vionnet's interest in contemporary art, and in particular futurism, served to develop this exploration of movement as a further expression of modernism. The illustrations that artist Thayaht produced for the *Gazette du bon ton* in the 1920s expound futurism's view that art should represent the dynamics of the body in movement. His drawings show women in Vionnet outfits, with lines tracing the curves of the dress into the surrounding environment to suggest the flow of the body, and the fabric, as they walked. He wanted to express the sensation of the space between body and material, and between the material and the space the wearer inhabits, as alive with friction and loaded with the potential to blur air and matter.

Vionnet's approach explored women's modern lives and sought to express an adult, liberated femininity. Like modern artists she was interested in the integrity of the materials she used. She also exploited technology by experimenting with new ways to dye fabric, and she was driven to create clothes that broke away from highly decorative, constraining forms of fashion that relied upon historical notions of femininity. However, while she de-

"My efforts have been directed towards freeing material from the restrictions imposed on it, in just the same way that I have sought to liberate the female form. I see both as injured victims...and I've proved that there is nothing more graceful than the sight of material hanging freely from the body."

Madeleine Vionnet, quoted in Milbank 1985.

scribed her clothing as appropriate for any body size or shape, its revelatory exposure of the natural form, and the prevailing ideal of youth and athleticism, meant her designs can be seen as part of the twentieth century's shift toward bodies controlled from within, through diet and exercise, rather than through restrictive undergarments.

Classicism and Ornamentation
In 1923 Vionnet moved her couture house to 50 avenue Montaigne, where its salons were decorated in a classically inspired, modernist manner that formed a suitable backdrop to her work. The salon used for her seasonal shows contained frescoes that showed contemporary women clad in some of her most popular designs, intermingled with images of ancient Greek goddesses. Thus clients could measure themselves against classical ideals and see Vionnet's designs through the prism of a revered, idealized past. This placed her designs, which could seem so daring in their simplicity, within the context of classical antiquity's noble precedent and articulated the link between her own focus upon mathematical harmony and that of the past.

The various ateliers that produced her collections showed the diversity of her output and her ability to imbue a whole range of different types of clothing, from sportswear to furs, lingerie, and tailored clothes, with her ethos of creative pattern-cutting and subtle, supple silhouettes. Her daywear also relied upon the material's inherent properties and the possibilities to be explored in her integration of construction techniques and decoration. Discreet day dresses were pintucked in neat rows, whose spacing gently pulled fabric in toward the figure at the waist and curved diagonally across the body from shoulders, across the bust, around the hips, and round toward the small of the back to shape the dress. Thus Vionnet's garments were given shape while maintaining smooth, uncluttered silhouettes, and the tucks of materials created a pattern on the fabric's surface.

During the 1920s, when heavy beadwork and embroidery proliferated, Vionnet was committed to search for methods of ornamentation that took part in shaping the whole garment. Narrow pintucks were used to form her signature rose motif, its size subtly graduated to pull dresses toward the wearer's figure. For Vionnet such exact craftsmanship enabled her to challenge traditional methods continually. Even when she used beadwork, most famously on the 1924 Little Horses dress, she demanded an innovative approach. She commissioned couture embroiderer Albert Lesage to explore new ways to apply bugle beads to bias-cut silk, so that the flow of the fabric would not be interrupted and the images of glittering horses inspired by the stylized, representational forms on Grecian red figure vases would not be distorted by the beads' weight. Even thick furs and tweeds could be given greater fluidity and form through her manipulation of their drape and use of pattern pieces cut to sculpt and form around the figure.

Business Growth

Vionnet's couture house grew during the 1920s, and she opened a branch in Biarritz to provide everything from spectator sportswear and travel garments—a growing market as women led increasingly active lives—to her supple evening wear for dinners and dances. By 1932 her Paris establishment had grown, despite the impact of the Great Depression, to twenty-one ateliers. Her attitude toward her employees was as enlightened as her design approach. She remembered her own path through the studios' hierarchy and ensured that workers, while paid the same as in other couture houses, were provided with dental and medical care, had paid breaks and holidays, and were given help with maternity leave and proper teaching in her favored design techniques, such as bias cutting.

Vionnet set up her company, Vionnet et cie, in 1922, and with the support of her backers, she pursued a series of business schemes. These included several attempts during the mid-twenties to capitalize on America's reliance upon Parisian fashion for new trends and Vionnet's popularity there, through a number of deals with companies to produce ready-to-wear. Although innovative, these ventures were brief and did nothing to stem the tide of copyists, both in the United States and in France, who cost the couture industry large sums of money each season by plagiarizing original models and mass producing them at lower prices. This practice damaged Vionnet's profits and also reduced the cachet of particular outfits, since couture clients were paying, at least in part, for exclusivity. Despite Vionnet's involvement with a series of couture organizations pledged to track down copyists, and a landmark case in 1930, when Vionnet and Chanel successfully sued a French copyist, this plagiarism was a recurrent problem that haunted the couture industry.

Legacy and Influence on Fashion Design

The last collection Vionnet produced was shown in August 1939 and acknowledged the current vogue for romantic, figure-enhancing styles. Fragile-looking black laces were traced over palest silver lamé, with appliquéd velvet bows to pull out and shape the lighter weight lace overdress and add fashionable fullness to skirts. Vionnet closed her house on the outbreak of World War II. Her work had been hugely influential in both Europe and the Americas during the period between the wars. While she sought to stand outside fashion and create timeless clothing, her liquid bias cut became a defining emblem of 1930s sophistication and style and inspired Hollywood designers to use bias-cut gowns to create iconic images of actresses such as Jean Harlow. Her experiments with fabric control and manipulation and the advances she made in testing the boundaries of fabric construction left a complex legacy which has inspired designers as diverse as Claire McCardell, Ossie Clark, Azzedine Alaïa, Issey Miyake, Yohji Yamamoto, and John Galliano.

When Vionnet died in 1975, her place within the history of fashion in the early twentieth century was assured. Perhaps because of the lack of drama in her private life and her unwillingness to give many interviews, she was less well known than some of her contemporaries. However, Vionnet's focus on experimentation and her desire continually to redefine the relationship between body and fabric provided women with clothing that expressed the period's dynamic modernity.

Vionnet embraced the dressmaking skills she had learned as a child apprentice and elevated them to new levels of complexity, yet she always strove to produce finished garments that preserved, and indeed celebrated, the integrity of the materials she used and the natural shape of the wearer's body. She viewed couture as a testing ground for the new identities that the twentieth century created. Her clients became living embodiments of modern femininity, clad in garments inspired by contemporary art, Asian wrapping techniques, and classical antiquity. In Vionnet's hands these elements were united into dramatically simple silhouettes. Vionnet's intimate knowledge of cutting and draping enabled her to create clothing that expressed the dynamism and potential of women's increasingly liberated lives.

See also **Cutting; Embroidery; Film and Fashion; Lingerie; Tea Gown.**

BIBLIOGRAPHY
Chatwin, Bruce. *What Am I Doing Here.* London: Picador, 1990.
Demornex, Jacqueline. *Vionnet.* London: Thames and Hudson, Inc., 1991.
Evans, Caroline, and Minna Thornton. *Women and Fashion: A New Look.* London: Quartet, 1989.
Kirke, Betty. *Madeleine Vionnet.* San Francisco: Chronicle Books, 1998.
Koda, Harold, Richard Martin, and Laura Sinderbrand. *Three Women: Madeleine Vionnet, Claire McCardell, and Rei Kawakubo.* New York: Fashion Institute of Technology, 1987. Exhibition catalog.
Milbank Rennolds, Caroline. *Couture: The Great Designers.* New York: Stewart, Tabori, and Chang, Inc., 1985.

Rebecca Arnold

VOGUE *Vogue* is fashion's bible, the world's leading fashion publication. It was founded in 1892 as a weekly periodical focused on society and fashion, and was subscribed to by New York's elite. Condé Nast (1873–1942) bought the magazine in 1909 and began to transform it into a powerhouse.

Vogue delivered beautifully presented, authoritative content under the leadership and watchful eyes of a few talented editors-in-chief. One of the most notable, Edna Woolman Chase, became editor in 1914 and remained at its helm for thirty-eight years, until 1952. Caroline Seebohm, Nast's biographer, credits Chase with introducing new American talents to the fashion audience. Chase gave full coverage to European, and especially Parisian, fashions, but her approach also suggested that American women might exercise a certain independence of taste.

Chase's successor, Jessica Daves, served as editor in chief from 1952 to 1963 and is remembered primarily for her business acumen. She was followed by the flamboyant Diana Vreeland, whose eight-year tenure (1963–1971) documented "Youthquake," street-influenced youth fashions, and space age and psychedelic fashions. Vreeland's successor was her colleague Grace Mirabella, who served as editor-in-chief from 1971 to 1988. Mirabella was the antithesis of Vreeland; her watchwords for fashion were functionality and affordability. Whereas Vreeland wrote in 1970, "In the evening we go east of the sun and west of the moon—we enter the world of fantasy," Mirabella countered, in 1971, "When you come to evening this year, you do not come to another planet." Mirabella approached the "antifashion" 1970s with a levelheaded stance that addressed a growing constituency of the magazine: the working woman.

Anna Wintour became editor-in-chief of the magazine in 1988 and combined a shrewd and appealing mix of high and low. Her first cover for the magazine, in November 1988, featured model Michaela in a jeweled Lacroix jacket—worn with blue jeans.

A controlling interest in Condé Nast Publications was acquired in 1959 by S. I. Newhouse, who subsequently became the sole owner of the corporation. There are now more than twelve editions of *Vogue*: American, Australian, Brazilian, British, French, German, Greek, Italian, Japanese, Spanish, Taiwanese, Chinese, and Korean. *Teen Vogue* was launched in 2003. (Nast inaugurated the international editions with British *Vogue* in 1916 and French *Vogue* in 1920.)

Nast's original "formula" for *Vogue* was based on service, which Seebohm translates as disseminating fashion information to his readers as efficiently and clearly as possible. Clarity did not exclude creativity, and the magazine became well known for its own stylish look. *Vogue*'s most famous art and creative directors were M. F. (Mehmed Fehney) Agha, who started at *Vogue* in 1929, and Alexander Liberman, who joined the staff in 1941.

The magazine has employed the foremost illustrators and photographers of its times. (The first photographic cover appeared in 1932; color printing was introduced in the following year.) Its glossy pages maintain the highest standards for the visual presentation of fashion. *Vogue* is still the stuff that many dreams are made of.

See also **Fashion Editors; Vreeland, Diana.**

BIBLIOGRAPHY

Chase, Edna Woolman, and Ilka Chase. *Always in Vogue.* New York: Doubleday and Company, 1954.

Daves, Jessica. *Ready-Made Miracle.* New York: G. P. Putnam's Sons, 1967.

Dwight, Eleanor. *Diana Vreeland.* New York: William Morrow and Company, 2002.

Mirabella, Grace. *In and Out of Vogue: A Memoir.* New York: Doubleday and Company, 1995.

Seebohm, Caroline. *The Man Who Was Vogue: The Life and Times of Condé Nast.* New York: Viking Penguin, 1962.

Laird Borrelli

VON FURSTENBERG, DIANE Diane von Furstenberg was born Diane Simone Michelle Halfin in Brussels, Belgium, in 1946. Her introduction to fashion was as an assistant to a photographer and filmmaker's agent in Paris, her first job on leaving the University of Madrid and graduating in economics from the University of Geneva. Familiar with the 1960s jet-set life, she married Prince Egon von Furstenberg in 1969 and moved with him to New York. They were a glamorous couple, luminaries of society columns, and attended celebrity parties and balls. However, in keeping with the burgeoning feminist movement of the early 1970s, and wishing to be financially independent, von Furstenberg realized the significance of women's emergence into the world of work. She capitalized on women's desire for simple, wearable clothes that were flattering but also smart. From 1970 to 1977 she became the owner-designer of the Diane von Furstenberg Studio, which produced easy to wear polyester, cotton, and silk knit dresses in her signature prints. Her iconic wrap dress, however, which first appeared in 1973, established her reputation as the designer of the moment and promoted her name into a worldwide brand.

Von Furstenberg's wrap dress was practical, versatile, and sexy. Manufactured at the Ferretti factory in Italy, the dresses were initially stored and the orders processed in the dining room of her home. Cut to flatter, the dress wrapped in front and tied at the waist and was made from drip-dry cotton jersey. She remembers in her autobiography, "I had no focus groups, no marketing surveys, no plan. All I had was an instinct that women wanted a fashion option beside hippie clothes, bell-bottoms, and stiff pant-suits that hid their femininity."

Diane von Furstenberg. Sexy, flattering, and also easy-to-wear, von Furstenberg's styles responded to women's changing desires and needs in the era of women's liberation.

In 1975 she brought out a scent, Tatiana, named after her daughter. She expanded into home furnishings with The Diane von Furstenberg Style for Living Collection for Sears, and in 1977 she reorganized the company to deal solely with licensees for the fashion line, luggage, scarves, cosmetics, and jewelry. By the end of 1979 the combined retail sales of all the products bearing the von Furstenberg name came to $150 million. The extent of the licensing deals undermined the quality of the brand, however, and she closed her business in 1988.

The 1990s predilection for 1970s fashion meant that the wrap dress achieved cult status and was eagerly sought after from vintage shops. Following her success on the QVC home-shopping channel, von Furstenberg and her daughter-in-law, Alexandra, relaunched the business in 1997 and put the wrap dress back into production, this time in silk jersey with a new range of colors and prints.

Diane von Furstenberg will always be identified with the wrap dress; it typifies the era of women's sexual and political liberation. Its reemergence is evidence of the continuing desire of women for simple, one-stop dressing that is both flattering and versatile.

See also **Fashion Designer; Fashion Marketing and Merchandising.**

BIBLIOGRAPHY

Milbank, Caroline Rennolds. *New York Fashion: The Evolution of American Style.* Harry N. Abrams, 1989.

von Furstenberg, Diane. *Diane: A Signature Life.* New York: Simon and Schuster, 1998.

Marnie Fogg

VREELAND, DIANA Diana Vreeland (1903–1989) was, and continues to be, an iconic figure in fashion history, whose distinctive personal style and penchant for fantasy influenced her work at *Vogue* and the exhibitions she organized at the Costume Institute of the Metropolitan Museum of Art. Diana Vreeland was born in Paris in 1903 to Emily Key Hoffman and Frederick Young Dalziel. The Dalziels moved to New York in 1904, where the socially eminent family enjoyed a prosperous lifestyle. According to Vreeland's biographer, she was a vivacious child who was interested in fantasy and the transforming powers of artifice from a very young age. In 1924, Diana married Thomas Reed Vreeland, a socially prominent banker. The couple moved to London in 1929, where they remained until 1933. In London Vreeland started her career in fashion by opening a lingerie shop in the city, and her frequent visits to Paris familiarized her with haute couture. As a patron of designers such as Jean Patou, Elsa Schiaparelli, Madeleine Vionnet, and Mainbocher, Vreeland's flair for dressing, combined with her social standing, made her the subject of commentary in the social pages and in magazines such as American *Vogue*, *Harper's Bazaar* and *Town and Country*.

Harper's Bazaar and Vogue

The Vreelands moved back to New York in 1935. Diana began her first job in fashion editorial work at *Harper's Bazaar* in 1937. She was promoted to the position of fashion editor in 1939, working under editor-in-chief Carmel Snow, and remained at the magazine until 1962. Vreeland first came to the readership's attention with her 1936 column entitled "Why Don't You?" The feature encapsulated her personal belief in the ability of fashion to transform women by offering such extravagant and fantastic suggestions to her readers as "Why don't you … Turn your child into an Infanta for a fancy dress party?" (August 1936) and "Why don't you own, as does one extremely smart woman, twelve diamond roses of all sizes?"

"Mrs. Vreeland is unquestionably the Madame de Sévigné of fashion's court: witty, brilliant, intensely human, gifted like Madame de Sévigné with a superb flair for anecdotes that she communicates verbally rather than in epistles, Mrs. Vreeland is more of a connoisseur of fashion than anyone I know" (Beaton, p. 359).

(January 1937) Vreeland honed her editorial skills at *Harper's Bazaar* by working closely with such photographers as Richard Avedon and Louise Dahl-Wolfe to implement her ideas and transfer her imaginative vision to the fashion pages.

Vreeland became publicly known as the archetypal fashion editor, famous for such proclamations as "Pink is the navy blue of India" (Donovan). Her inimitable persona was further popularized when she was parodied in the 1957 film *Funny Face*.

In 1962, Vreeland moved to American *Vogue* as associate editor. In 1963, Sam Newhouse, the owner of Condé Nast, promoted her to editor-in-chief in an effort to re-invigorate the magazine. Having complete control over the look of the magazine, she imbued its pages with her distinctive style and flair for the fantastic. During Vreeland's tenure, the magazine's editorial spreads presented a popular audience with exoticism, aristocratic glamour, and such atypical models (atypical because of their youth, multicultural appearance, and unisex body types) as Veruschka, Penelope Tree, Twiggy, and Lauren Hutton. Vreeland firmly believed that the magazine had the ability to transport the reader, just as clothing had the ability to transform the wearer. The mundane realities of life did not interest her.

The Costume Institute

By the late 1960s, Vreeland's extravagant fashion editorials were deemed out of touch with the times and her position at *Vogue* was terminated in 1971; she was replaced by Grace Mirabella. In 1972, Vreeland became involved with the Costume Institute at the Metropolitan Museum of Art, the museum's acclaimed collection of historic costumes. Vreeland's fashionable and colorful personality was perceived as an opportunity to revitalize the costume exhibitions. Vreeland was brought in with the title of special consultant and acted as a creative director for twelve exhibitions from 1972 through 1985. Through these highly popular exhibitions, which included "Balenciaga," "The Eighteenth-Century Woman," "Romantic and Glamorous Hollywood Design," "The Glory of Russian Costume," "La Belle Époque," and "Yves Saint Laurent," Vreeland succeeded in placing her distinctive stamp upon the museum world. She transferred her unique style of fashion marketing to the museum gallery, taking inspiration from the runway, retail trends, fashion editorials, and her own fertile imagination. Her costume exhibitions were spectacular sensory experiences; as she herself admitted in her autobiography, she was interested more in effect than historical accuracy.

In 1976, she received the medal of the Legion d'Honneur from France for her contributions to the fashion industry. In 1984, she published her memoirs, entitled *D.V.* Vreeland died in New York City in 1989, but her status as an icon has had a lasting influence on the world of fashion. In 1993, the Costume Institute celebrated her memory with an exhibition entitled "Diana

Diana Vreeland, 1973. Vreeland stands with a Balenciaga coat at the Costume Institute at the Metropolitan Museum of Art in New York City. © BETTMANN/CORBIS. REPRODUCED BY PERMISSION.

Vreeland, Immoderate Style." She was the subject of a one-person off-Broadway play entitled *Full Gallop* in 1995. The repeated reexamination of Vreeland's impact on fashion attests to her impact as an arbiter of style who fostered the visibility of fashion on a popular level.

See also **Avedon, Richard; Dahl-Wolfe, Louise; Fashion Editors; Fashion Icons; Fashion Magazines; Fashion Models; Fashion Museums and Collections; Vogue.**

BIBLIOGRAPHY

Beaton, Cecil. *The Glass of Fashion*. Garden City, N.Y.: Doubleday, 1954.

Donovan, Carrie. "Diana Vreeland, Dynamic Fashion Figure, Joins *Vogue*." *New York Times* (28 March 1952).

Dwight, Eleanor. *Diana Vreeland*. New York: HarperCollins Publishers, Inc., 2002.

Martin, Richard, and Harold Koda. *Diana Vreeland: Immoderate Style*. New York: Metropolitan Museum of Art, 1993.

Silverman, Debora. *Selling Culture: Bloomingdale's, Diana Vreeland, and the New Aristocracy of Taste in Reagan's America*. New York: Pantheon Books, 1986.

Vreeland, Diana. *D.V.* Edited by George Plimpton and Christopher Hemphill. New York: Alfred A. Knopf, 1984.

Michelle Tolini Finamore

VUITTON, LOUIS Born in 1821 in Anchay, France, Louis Vuitton worked as an apprentice for the packing-case maker M. Maréchal, where he created personal luggage for Empress Eugénie before setting up his own business in 1854. Vuitton's career as a craftsman trunk maker quickly brought him an ever-expanding roster of clients, requiring him to move to workshops at Asnières, on the outskirts of Paris, in 1859. The workshops remain at the original site, and this is where all the luggage and accessories are still made. Annexed to the workshops is the family home, which is now a museum.

Vuitton's first innovation was to pioneer a gray, waterproof canvas (Trianon), which was stretched across the poplar wood structure of the trunk, eliminating the need for a dome-shaped lid, which had been essential for repelling rain from the trunk during transit atop a horse-drawn carriage. This innovation enabled porters to stack trunks one on top of the other, allowing travelers to take more luggage with them on trips.

Vuitton's success in the luxury luggage market was due to his willingness to modify and custom-build luggage that was adaptable to new forms of transportation. For example, cabin trunks for ocean liners were designed to fit under daybeds so as to maximize use of space. Yet what the luggage contained was never a secondary concern, but of equal value in the definition of first-class travel. To meet the needs of these elite travelers, Vuitton devised the wardrobe trunk with interior drawers and hanging space with the advice of the couturier Charles Frederick Worth.

As the company prospered, its products were widely imitated, forcing Vuitton to change the canvas design from a striped to a checkerboard (or Daumier) design. His son Georges created the famous monogram canvas in 1896. The design was intended primarily to combat commercial piracy, although its orientalist, decorative design also reflected the fashion for all things Japanese at the end of the nineteenth century. Beyond the initials that feature as a tribute to his father, Georges's design bears three abstracted flowers, based upon a Japanese *mon* or family crest that, not unlike a coat of arms, was traditionally used to identify items made for and owned by a particular family.

International stature was assured for the company by the opening of a London store in 1885, a French store opposite the Grand Hotel in 1871, and distribution in America through Wanamaker's department store in 1898. Design awards at the Exposition International d'Industrie et des Arts Decoratives of 1925 secured the company's reputation for grand luxe in the art deco style.

Later in the twentieth century, handbags, wallets, and other small leather goods became increasingly important parts of the company's product line, as luxe travel with numerous trunks and suitcases became largely a thing of the past. In 1997, the company hired the American fashion designer Marc Jacobs to design accessories and clothing. A commercial and critical success, the ready-to-wear collections have been central to the continued success of Louis Vuitton. Limited edition pieces produced in collaboration with other creative artists have resulted in some of the wittiest and shrewdest reworkings of brand identity. Fashion designer Stephen Sprouse (2001), British fashion illustrator Julie Verhoeven (2002), and Japanese artist Hideo Murakami (2003) have created some of the most popular designs.

The Stephen Sprouse collaboration was inspired by a visit Marc Jacobs made to Charlotte Gainsbourg's apartment, where he noticed a Louis Vuitton trunk that had once belonged to her father, the French singer Serge Gainsbourg. Gainsbourg had so disliked the status implied by the canvas design that he had tried to erase the symbols with black paint. Yet as the design is produced as a woven jacquard, he only made the design appear subtler, and in turn, more sophisticated. Sprouse was inspired to add graffiti over the monogram canvas in fluorescent colors as an ironic act of defilement. Yet the graffiti design only served to reinforce the status of the brand and its association with street credibility.

The consumption of luxury brands by American hip-hop performers, termed *bling-bling*, created a new and younger market for Louis Vuitton. This new market was memorably represented by the performing artist Lil' Kim, who posed on the cover of the November 1999 issue of *Interview* magazine naked, her body painted with the Louis Vuitton monogram.

Because they are such desirable status symbols, Louis Vuitton products are subject to intense counterfeiting, which the company vigorously combats. Vuitton remains the most prestigious and easily recognized brand of luggage.

See also **Leather and Suede; Logos.**

BIBLIOGRAPHY

Forestier, Nadege, and Nazanine Ravai. *The Taste of Luxury: Bernard Arnault and the Moët-Hennessy Louis Vuitton Story*. London: Bloomsbury Publishing, 1993.

Alistair O'Neill

WAFFLE-WEAVE. *See* **Weave, Jacquard.**

WAISTCOAT The waistcoat, or vest (as it is known in the United States), is a close-fitting sleeveless garment originally designed for men that buttons (or occasionally zips) down the front to the waist. Produced in either single or double-breasted styles, the waistcoat is designed to be worn underneath a suit or jacket, although it does not necessarily have to match. Similar garments are worn by women.

History
Originating in Persia, waistcoats first became fashionable in the middle of the seventeenth century. The new style was noticed by Samuel Pepys in 1666: "The King hath ... declared his resolution of setting a fashion for clothes which he will never alter," he wrote in his diary. "It will be a vest."

King Charles II was persuaded that, after the Great Plague and the Great Fire of London, a much more sober form of attire should be worn by gentlemen, particularly in view of the gross extravagance displayed in the French court at the time. The vest was a knee-length garment that would follow the cut of the coat but would be much tighter in fit. It was designed to discourage the use of lavish materials (such as lace) by covering much of the body in plainer and cheaper material. By 1670, vests had become one of the most important European fashion trends of the time, particularly among nobility who would soon forget the notion of sobriety in favor of opulence and excessive decoration.

1700 to 1900
By 1700, many waistcoats became much shorter, with skirts reaching above the knee, and few had collars or sleeves. Waistcoat styles designed for sporting purposes did away with any skirt almost completely. As the waistcoat became short it also became more and more cut away in a curve at the front to reveal the wearer's breeches. Whereas elaborately embroidered waistcoats were fastened with hooks and eyes, the majority were fastened with buttons that would match those of the coat being worn.

Double-breasted waistcoats were the most popular style during the first few decades of the eighteenth century and featured small pockets with flaps. By the middle of the century, rather than following the older style of having cuff-length sleeves, the majority of waistcoats were sleeveless; skirts were much shorter and by 1790 were cut square to the waist. Toward 1800, decorated single-breasted waistcoats with small lapels became fashionable; fabrics with horizontal or vertical stripes were particularly favored, especially if the waistcoat was finished with a silk trim.

By 1800, the waistcoat had become an increasingly decorative and flamboyant addition to the male wardrobe. Through various style trends at the time, the overriding principle was that as long as a waistcoat was highly conspicuous, ostentatious, and embroidered, it was deemed fashionable. Single-breasted, double-breasted, waist-length, square-cut, roll-collared, low stand-collared and flap-pocketed styles all were worn. Dandies at the time even took to wearing two waistcoats at once. One would be as elaborate as the other, with the upper unbuttoned to show the one underneath.

Generally speaking, after the mid-nineteenth century, waistcoats became much more sober. The majority were produced to match the jackets or suits they would be worn with, rather than being outward expressions of originality and wealth.

The 1900s and Onward
Although the waistcoat was still deemed fashionable at the beginning of the twentieth century, its popularity soon began to wane. Rather than being worn as a show of wealth or decadence, the waistcoat was considered little more than a functional item to house a pocket watch or to finish off a formal evening wear outfit. With suits becoming softer and men opting for the growing trend of the wristwatch, the waistcoat was deemed less than essential for the male wardrobe.

That is not to say that the waistcoat simply died. Many men continued to wear a knitted waistcoat in the winter and a lighter version in the summer; however, it was now seen as an item simply to accompany and harmonize the rest of the outfit.

After World War II, few businessmen were wearing waistcoats to work, and right up to the Peacock Revolution in the 1960s, they had become all but extinct except with the more conservative dressers and those of an older generation. The waistcoat began to revive among fashionable young men, however, who associated themselves with style tribes such as Neo-Edwardians and Teddy boys.

The 1960s also saw the waistcoat move away from being a formal item when it was adopted by the hippies and incorporated as part of their ethnic-inspired or countrified look. The hippy version of the waistcoat still followed the contours of the body, but it tended to be longer than the waistcoat of a business suit; some were knee-length and featured heavy floral embroidery, fringing, and patchwork; some were tie-dyed (a look that would be recreated for the spring/summer 1993 collection by Dolce & Gabbana).

In the early twenty-first century, the waistcoat is seldom worn, except by businessmen trying to show some form of individuality or personality with a suit. Among conservative members of some professions, such as corporate law and banking, a three-piece suit (i.e., trousers, jacket, and matching waistcoat) is still regarded as the most appropriate business attire. But aside from designers such as Jean Paul Gaultier and Dolce & Gabbana reviving waistcoats for men during the 1980s and early 1990s, they are now more likely to be worn as novelty items than to be part of a classic tailored look.

See also **Dandyism; Jacket; Trousers; Uniforms, Occupational.**

BIBLIOGRAPHY

Amies, Hardy. *A, B, C's of Men's Fashion*. London: Cahill & Company Ltd., 1964.

Byrde, Penelope. *The Male Image: Men's Fashion in England 1300–1970*. London: B. T. Batsford, Ltd., 1979.

Chenoune, Farid. *A History of Men's Fashion*. Paris: Flammarion, 1993.

De Marley, Diana. *Fashion For Men: An Illustrated History*. London: B. T. Batsford, Ltd., 1985.

Keers, Paul. *A Gentleman's Wardrobe*. London: Weidenfield and Nicolson, 1987.

Roetzel, Bernhard. *Gentleman: A Timeless Fashion*. Cologne, Germany: Konemann, 1999.

Schoeffler, O. E., and William Gale. *Esquire's Encyclopedia of 20th Century Men's Fashions*. New York: McGraw-Hill, 1973.

Tom Greatrex

WATCHES Watches are portable timepieces, used to measure time and intervals. Historically, watches were worn as decorative pendants or carried in the pocket. In modern times, they are branded accessories most frequently worn on the wrist.

A Period of Decoration
At the beginning of the eighteenth century, watches were still considered to be primarily decorative objects because of their poor functionality. Men who could afford them typically wore pocket watches, which hung from a short chain and easily slipped into a waistcoat pocket. Women's watches were traditionally more embellished and visibly worn as a pendant or on a chatelaine.

The century marked a period of rapid technical development. Pioneered by organizations and guilds in Germany, France, England, and Switzerland, inventors introduced new types of springs, encasements, and bearings that allowed for better accuracy and performance under vacillating temperature and position. They also replaced the key-winding watch with self-winding movement. Some English and Swiss watchmakers, who utilized jeweled bearings and newer escapements to control the rate of wheel movement, were able to equip watches with a minute hand, which until then was impossible.

These advancements influenced the design and stylistic components of watches, which became much smaller and slimmer. Greater attention was also paid to the protection of the watch, as they became more useful. Circular or oval faces were encased on either the front or back, sometimes both, by a hinged cover. These covers, made from brass, gold, or silver, often displayed intricate engravings or enamels of pastoral scenes, portraits, or other related designs. Fob watches, which were attached on a short chain or ribbon and often held other gold charms, became popular around this time as well. Although watches still lacked the accuracy they had in later years, they sometimes had calendar, moon phase, or alarm functions.

Advancements in Accuracy and Production
As innovations in springs and bearings continued, watches became more accurate. Watchmakers now tried to make very complicated pocket and pendant watches incorporating calendars, timers, dual time zones, and moon phases. As such, dials became larger and the watches heavier.

The development of mass-production practices and interchangeable parts made it possible to produce watches by machine and in volume. These practices made watches significantly less expensive. In 1892 Timex (then called Waterbury Watch Company) and Ingersoll introduced the Dollar or "Yankee" watch that eponymously expanded the ownership of watches. Although decorative, luxury watches were still popular for women during this period, the functionality and usefulness of the watch increasingly became the focal point of fashionability.

Wristwatches and Alternative Power Sources
There is evidence that watches adjusted for the wrist existed in the late 1500s in special creations for royalty, yet wristwatches were not used in large numbers until the

early twentieth century. The first designs were military in nature—they were introduced as chronographs offering multiple-timing capabilities. These wristwatches were used during the Boer War, and later during World War I for their practicality on the front lines. It was easier and quicker to glance at a watch on one's wrist than to rummage through pockets during battle operations.

Despite the wristwatch's legacy of military use, the style spread first to civilian women. Designs for women during the early twentieth century were jewelry-inspired. Art-deco faces, inlays of onyx and marcasite, and straps of black silk or satin joined the more traditional existing designs of silver and gold braceleting.

By the end of World War II, however, wristwatches were worn by both men and women. Pocket watches were now considered outmoded. Simpler and sleeker designs predominated, epitomized by the Movado Museum watch, which consisted of a black dial free from markers or numbers, characterized only by gold hands and a gold dot at the twelve o'clock position. The importance of fashionability continued into the 1960s with young, pop art designs influencing watch case and face designs. Triangles, octagons, and hexagons accompanied standard round cases, and straps came in a greater variety of colors and fabrics.

Simultaneously, technology dominated the accessory, and much of the development during this time centered around new sources of power. In 1957, the Hamilton Watch Company introduced the first battery-powered wristwatch, and in 1970, the use of quartz crystals to produce an integrated circuit resulted in a watch that was infinitely more reliable than mechanical versions. Omega was one of the first companies to bring the battery-operated watch to market, soon followed by the Hamilton Watch Company's introduction of the Pulsar LED digital watch, an expensive innovation in line with the Space-Age obsession dominating the later 1960s and early 1970s. Swiss watch manufacturers, who had long held a reputation in the industry for manufacturing high-quality, precision, mechanical watches saw integrated circuitry as a temporary fad. It was not until the early 1980s, when the Swiss-based Swatch Group embraced quartz technology, and paired it with designs that responded to consumers' desire for accessories that conveyed lifestyle and personality, that the Swiss industry regained its vigor within the watch-making market.

The Brand Speaks

Technological innovation remains an important component of the watch industry. Manufacturers market solar and kinetic watches, and some have introduced models equipped with global positioning systems, or those that link to computers or other portable electronic devices. Yet the wristwatch is also a fashion accessory for which aesthetics and brand are paramount. Fashion watches are associated with lifestyle, and many of the leading watch companies have positioned themselves to appeal to certain segments of the consumer market. Luxury companies such as Rolex, Cartier, Movado, Tissot, Patek, and Breitling, who market through word-of-mouth, high-end event sponsorship, or specialized high-end fashion and lifestyle magazines, still appeal to wealthy consumers. A Cartier watch may cost more than $10,000 and Rolexes or Movados are counterfeited as often as Gucci or Prada handbags. Mid-range watches, such as Fossil or Swatch, continue to sell in mid-priced jewelry and department stores, and Swatch remains well known for its wide range of strap and face styles. These companies have been joined by diversified companies, such as Nike, entering the watch market and promoting wristwatches designed for specific uses such as running or swimming. Lower-priced watches proliferate. Timex was one of the first companies to build its brand on selling through mass-market drugstores and stationery stores. In the early 2000s budget watches can be found almost anywhere: street markets, toy stores, and even inside fast-food kiddie meals. It is as uncommon not to own a watch in the twenty-first century as it was to own one at the beginning of the eighteenth. The watch has truly seen a revolution in time.

See also **Bracelets; Jewelry.**

BIBLIOGRAPHY

Bruton, Eric. *Collector's Dictionary of Clocks and Watches.* London: Robert Hale Limited, 1999. Comprehensive dictionary, but may be too advanced for new collectors.

———. *The History of Clocks & Watches.* London: Little, Brown, and Company, 2000.

Childers, Catherine. *Master Wristwatches.* New York: BW Publishing Associates in association with Rizzoli International Publications, 1999.

Doensen, Pieter. *Watch: History of the Modern Wristwatch: Design; 1950–1983.* Gent, Belgium: Snoeck, Ducaju and Zoon, 1994.

Milham, Willis. *Time & Timekeepers Including the History, Construction, Care, and Accuracy of Clocks and Watches.* London: Macmillan, 1923. Good straightforward overview.

Leslie Harris

WATERPROOFING. *See* **Performance Finishes.**

WEARABLE ART Individual, often extremely personal, and generally conforming to no unifying aesthetic criteria, wearable art is by its very nature difficult to define. It could be called artwork for the body, but this does not acknowledge its complex relationship to the art world, the fashion world, and the world of craft. Wearable art is separate from mainstream fashion, yet remains related to it. Although wearable art takes varied forms—sculptural or flat—and employs diverse techniques such as knitting, leather tooling, weaving, dyeing, and sewing, it shares a spirit of fantasy, craftsmanship, and commitment to personal vision.

The Wearable Art movement emerged at the close of the 1960s, flowered in the 1970s, and continues in the early 2000s. It is no accident that wearable art crystallized at the end of the tumultuous 1960s. The social, political, and cultural upheavals of that decade provided fertile ground for personal expression and explorations into body adornment.

During the 1970s "wearables" were generally unconventional works that celebrated the intimacy of creation through a highly individual artistic language. This intensely personal and narrative nature of wearable art distinguishes it from the earlier manifestations of artist-created garments that appeared beginning in the nineteenth century. Although it was not a direct linear development, wearable art owes its emergence to the climate of artistic expression cultivated by earlier avant-garde dress movements beginning a century before.

Nineteenth Century

The Pre-Raphaelite Brotherhood, formed in 1848 by John Everett Millais, William Holman Hunt, and Dante Gabriel Rossetti, was one of the first collective efforts by artists to create alternative dress. In response to an increasingly industrialized society and mass-produced, cheap goods, the Pre-Raphaelites deliberately sought inspiration in Medieval and Renaissance art; they encouraged their wives, mistresses, and models to wear clothing modeled after earlier styles. These historically inspired garments appeared in their paintings and provided a sharp visual contrast to the prevailing Victorian fashions of tightly corseted bodices with full, bell-shaped skirts suspended over petticoats and hoops.

Sharing in this disdain for the voluminous and constricting fashions of Victorian England was William Morris, the man most closely associated with the British Arts and Crafts Movement. Like the Pre-Raphaelites, Morris sought to revitalize art and dress through a return to simplicity and hand craftsmanship inspired by historic models. Morris admired the paintings and decorative arts of the Middle Ages and advocated simple, picturesque attire, which he felt was more complimentary to a woman's natural form. His wife, Jane, was known to have adopted a form of plain dress without corsets or hoops.

Efforts to create alternative dress for women without the armature of hoops, bustles, and corsets had been at the forefront of the concurrent Dress Reform Movement. This movement emerged in the mid-nineteenth century and concerned itself primarily with health and comfort, rather than the appearance of dress. In contrast, a number of artists linked to the Aesthetic Movement of the 1870s objected to contemporary fashion on the grounds of taste rather than health. In the 1870s and 1880s, advocates of Aesthetic Dress championed a natural line in dress formed from soft, drapable fabrics without corsets or bustles. Rejecting the garish colors produced by the aniline (synthetic) dyes prevalent in contemporary fashion, advocates of Aesthetic Dress preferred muted earth tones in moss greens, browns, yellows, and peacock blues.

Aesthetic dress took a variety of forms. Some garments incorporated smocking and puffed sleeves in vaguely Renaissance styles, while others suggested "classical" drapery. Another strong influence on artists during the late nineteenth century was Eastern art, particularly Japanese woodblock prints and stencil-printed fabrics. Fascination with Eastern goods went along with this Japonism. Alternative dress in the form of kimonos and caftans became a popular form of anti-fashion for artists and intellectuals. James McNeill Whistler had a strong hand in designing the fashion of his sitters and, in fact, created the Japonesque dress worn by Mrs. Frances Leyland in her 1873 portrait entitled *Symphony in Flesh Color and Pink*.

Aiding the efforts of the Aesthetes was Arthur Lazenby Liberty, whose emporium on Regent Street became a mecca for artists and enthusiasts seeking imported decorative arts from the Near and Far East, as well as fabrics in the soft greens, yellows, and browns so favored by Aesthetic dressers. In 1884, Liberty appointed the architect Edwin Godwin to direct a dress department thereby making artistic dress available to the public. Liberty's created a line of their own dresses with high waistlines and loose, puffed sleeves reminiscent of the Regency period of the early nineteenth century—a forecast of the direction that mainstream fashion would take in the early 1900s.

In the 1880s artistic dress gained a certain level of acceptance in mainstream fashion. Widespread acceptance of the tea gown, a loose, uncorseted informal gown worn at home, was one of the crowning achievements of Aesthetic Dress advocates. Moreover, the increasing influence of the British Arts and Crafts Movement led to efforts to expand reform and artistic dress. In 1890, The Healthy and Artistic Dress Union was formed and included Walter Crane, Henry Holiday, G. F. Watts, and A. F. Liberty. Their journal *Aglaia* featured several dresses designed in the classical mode by Walter Crane. The British Arts and Crafts Movement had a strong impact in America and stimulated a call for dress reform there. Gustav Stickley, chief spokesman for the American Arts and Crafts Movement, advocated beauty, comfort, and simplicity in dress in the journal *The Craftsman*, which had broad appeal to middle-class Americans.

A number of progressive artists and architects associated with art nouveau and art moderne espoused the belief that costume was the final frontier, an extension of the artistic effort to create unified interiors and exteriors. The Belgian architect Henry van de Velde designed dresses for his wife, as did the American architect Frank Lloyd Wright. In Vienna, Secessionist painter Gustav

Klimt collaborated with his wife, Emilie Floge, herself a dressmaker, to create costumes. Wiener Werkstätte co-founder Josef Hoffmann was known to design not only the interiors of his clients' homes, but also their clothing.

Early Twentieth Century

In the early twentieth century, unconventional artistic dress had achieved a certain level of acceptance. Wearing of artistic dress had even become a badge of distinction, bestowing upon the wearer an aura of progressive ideals, intellectualism, and good taste. These attributes were particularly accorded to the wearers of Fortuny dresses. Mario Fortuny y Madraz, born into a distinguished family of Spanish painters living in Venice, created Renaissance and medieval-inspired printed velvet gowns, as well as a simple columnar pleated silk dress inspired by ancient Greek sculpture. The latter dress, called the *Delphos*, was patented in 1909 and was produced, with slight variations, through the 1940s. Fortuny dresses became synonymous with simplicity, elegance, and timeless beauty and were favored by members of artistic and intellectual circles.

As the century progressed, a number of avant-garde painters also turned to the medium of fashion for artistic expression, viewing garments as the perfect form of kinetic, visual tableaux. Simultaneist and Rayonnist artists Sonia Delaunay and Natalia Goncharova tried their hand at fashion design and worked for the Parisian couture houses of Heim and Myrbor, respectively. Even more extreme were the 1913 dress designs of Italian Futurist Giacomo Balla and the mass-produced work clothes created by Russian Constructivists Varvara Stepanova and Alexander Rodchenko. Jean Cocteau, Pablo Picasso, and even Ferdinand Leger took turns designing garments in the first quarter of the twentieth century.

Greenwich Village, New York, became the epicenter for avant-garde thinking and dressing during the 1910s and 1920s. Poets, writers, artists, socialists, feminists, and philosophers flocked to this shabby neighborhood to share their progressive ideas on life and art, that found expression in the clothes they wore. Greenwich Village became synonymous with bohemian and alternative fashion that included uncorseted, straight tunic dresses, loose jackets, and bobbed hair for women. Greenwich Village artists appear to be particularly associated with the revival of the batik technique that became a popular form of artistic dress decoration during the late 1910s and 1920s. This "anti-fashion" provides a link with the European artistic dress movements of the previous century and set the stage for avant garde experiments in dress later in the twentieth century.

In the 1930s, a renewed interest in handweaving led to a revival in that and other textile crafts in America, particularly after World War II, and is linked to the wearable art movement of the late 1960s and 1970s. This weaving revival was particularly accelerated by the arrival of a number of Bauhaus-trained European émigrés in America during the 1930s and 1940s, such as Anni Albers and Marianne Strengell, who joined the teaching staffs of the Black Mountain College in North Carolina and Cranbrook Academy in Michigan, respectively. A generation later, their students pushed the boundaries of textile arts even further through their radical, off-loom woven sculptures of the late 1950s. Exploring the power of weaving, plaiting, dyeing, embroidery, knitting, and crochet, these fiber artists imbued the ancient techniques with new, expressive possibilities. Their creations paved the way for the wearable art movement that emerged ten years later. Wearable art carried on the exploration into textile techniques of the larger, inclusive fiber art movement.

Late Twentieth Century

Wearable art was also the product of a unique climate of cultural and social change that occurred at the end of the 1960s. It came during a period that witnessed the flourishing of performance and body art concurrent with the rejection of traditional haute couture in favor of more democratic fashions inspired by hippies and street style.

Makers of wearable art in the late 1960s and 1970s did not attempt to influence universal trends in fashion. Rather, they chose to express a singularly personal vision of dress—a notion that separates them from earlier artistic dress movements of the nineteenth and early twentieth centuries.

With New York City and San Francisco as hubs, artists engaged in wearable art pursued works that fused aesthetics with function. At the heart of the wearable art movement was the rejection of traditional hierarchies in art that elevated fine art over craft. In the 1970s, wearable art incorporated materials that had traditionally held craft associations, embracing the formerly "women's work" of textiles as fine art. Paramount to wearable art in this early phase was the utilization of traditional techniques in unconventional ways. In the 1970s, ancient techniques such as sewing, leather tooling, weaving, knitting, and dyeing were suddenly enriched by the dimension of storytelling, such as in the fantastical, painted and tooled-leather garments of Nina Vivian Huryn. Other artists such as Janet Lipkin, Sharon Hedges, and Norma Minkowitz reinvigorated traditional crochet and knitting, producing new, voluptuous, and organic wearables.

One of the most pervasive forms of wearable art that emerged in the 1970s was that of the kimono. With its wide, untailored panels it provided the ideal surface for showcasing two-dimensional treatments. Eschewing structure for surface effects, Katherine Westphal was one of the first to exploit the T-shape kimono form, creating complex visual collages by the photocopy heat-transfer print method. Tim Harding is another artist who has excelled in this format in the past three decades, producing rich garments from sandwiched fabrics, manipulated to reveal layers of color and texture.

Validation of this nascent art form arrived with the landmark exhibition "Art to Wear: New Handmade Clothing" held at the American Craft Museum in New York City in 1983. This came ten years after Julie Dale's had established her Artisan's Gallery in New York as the premier gallery for displaying and selling wearable art. Artisan's Gallery continues to showcase excellence in wearable art.

In the 1980s, wearable art became less organic and freewheeling. In keeping with concurrent developments in the visual arts, wearable works exhibited greater refinement in technique and a greater emphasis on surface imagery, rendered in a more controlled, graphic style. Crocheted and knitted garments by Jean Williams Caciededo illustrate this progression from the organic, sculptural works done in the 1970s to more graphic, flat appliqué works in the 1980s. Other artists such as Ana Lisa Hedstrom continue to explore and refine dyeing techniques inspired by Japanese traditional methods.

Wearable art in the 1990s and early twenty-first century continues to expand and gain greater acceptance in mainstream fashion. The exuberant and unwieldy forms of two decades past have been replaced with recent works that not only celebrate surface patterns, but also acknowledge the importance of comfort, drape, and fit. The work of Erman of Miami, Florida, embodies this new trend in wearables. Trained at several fashion houses on Seventh Avenue, Erman brings artistry and exquisite tailoring to his unique designs.

To some, the wearable art movement of the early 2000s is a splintered and unrecognizable entity, lacking the spirit of inquiry, exuberance, and integrity of the heady days of the 1970s and early 1980s. To others, wearable art has merely evolved into a larger, more diverse entity. Artists making wearables in the twenty-first century continue to explore techniques, but also show a new interest in computers and other technology. Moreover, wearable art has moved closer to mainstream contemporary fashion, revealing a stronger shared vision. As haute couture designers such as John Galliano and Alexander McQueen move increasingly into the "art-for-the-catwalk" realm, so wearable artists have exhibited greater practicality and business acumen in their garments, thereby appealing to a wider audience interested in craftsmanship, quality, and uniqueness in garments.

See also **Art and Fashion; Haute Couture.**

BIBLIOGRAPHY

Aimone, Katherine Duncan. *The Fiberarts Book of Wearable Art.* Asheville, N.C.: Lark Books, 2002.

American Craft Museum. *Art to Wear.* New York: American Craft Museum, 1983.

Cunningham, Patricia. "Healthful, Artistic and Correct Dress." In *With Grace and Favor: Victorian and Edwardian Fashions in America.* Cincinnati: Cincinnati Art Museum, 1993, pp. 14–25.

Dale, Julie Schafler. *Art to Wear.* New York: Abbeville Press, 1986.

Wollen, Peter. "Addressing the Century." In *Addressing the Century: 100 Years of Art and Fashion.* London: Haywood Gallery, 1998, pp. 6–77.

Lauren Whitley

WEAVE, DOUBLE Double weave is a family of weave styles in which the face of the fabric is effectively disengaged from the back except at specific connecting interlacings, yet with each side maintaining sufficient individual structural integrity to be identified as distinct fabrics in themselves. Fabrics in this category include the matelassés and tubular fabrics. These fabrics are encountered in both decorative and utilitarian roles and occupy interesting extremes at either end of those spectra.

The matelassé types of fabrics are decorative in nature and may be found in use as bed clothings and upholsteries. Utility double fabrics have been employed in roles as diverse as common garden gloves to highly technical, specialized end uses.

Double weaves are characterized by harness floats in paired or greater combinations on a face and different paired or greater float combinations on the back. The sets of floats are maintained as a distinct single fabric by warp yarns that alternate at long intervals between front and back of the cloth.

The simplest representations of double weave interlacings utilize both a point diagram and the filling cross section diagram to show alternations between top and bottom. In such diagrams, the warp yarns may be represented by each end to permit easier visualizations. Multiple repetitions of each end weaving pattern combine to permit the double face of a fabric.

Further considerations in double weaves include whether shuttle or shuttleless weaving techniques are used and whether simultaneous weft insertions in top and bottom sheds occur. If shuttle weaving is employed, a continuous loop of weft yarn is inserted across the width of the fabric. This technique permits the weaving of an unbroken, sealed tubular fabric. Technical uses of this fabric type include vascular grafts and spacesuit joints. In the latter role, a double weave tubular fabric was developed at Georgia Tech in the 1970s and 1980s by Dr. Howard Olson for elbow and knee joints as the first solution to prevent vascular destruction of astronauts' arms and legs during bending motions.

If shuttleless weaving techniques are used, discontinuous segments of weft are being inserted and therefore tubular structures cannot be made on these machines. On the other hand, multiple simultaneous insertions of weft by rapiers is easily practiced by these machines, so top and bottom shed formations and independent insertions are possible. A subtype of these double weaves are velvets, which are formed with a migrating binder warp that is cut after weaving to form a pile on the surface of either fabric base.

See also **Loom; Weave, Pile; Weave, Slack Tension; Weave Types; Weaving.**

BIBLIOGRAPHY

Collier, B., and P. Tortora. *Understanding Textiles.* Upper Saddle River, N.J.: Prentice-Hall Inc., 2001.

Emery, I. *The Primary Structures of Fabrics.* Washington, D.C.: The Textile Museum, 1980, pp. 156–160.

Gioello, D. A. *Understanding Fabrics: From Fiber to Finished Cloth.* New York: Fairchild Publishers, 1982. See Double Cloth and Double-faced Cloth, p. 101.

Howard Thomas

WEAVE, JACQUARD

Jacquard is a style of "figure weaving." It can be used to create elaborate designs and detailed images of objects such as flowers and birds. This is done on a Jacquard loom, a device invented in Lyons, France by Joseph-Marie Charles Jacquard in the early 1800s. Before that time, figure weaves could only be made by more labor-intensive techniques such as tapestry, adding extra yarns to the surface of another weaving by hand (supplementary weft), using different sizes of yarns to make parts of the pattern stand out (dobby weaving), or by using a draw loom.

Draw looms were invented more than two thousand years ago in China and are operated by two people. The weaver sits at the front of the loom, adds the filling yarns, and beats them in place. An assistant sits at the side of the loom and lifts combinations of dozens (or even hundreds) of harnesses. These are frames with "heddles" that hold one or more yarns in place. Joseph-Marie Jacquard modified the draw loom by replacing harnesses with individual heddles attached to small weights. He also used a series of metal punch cards that could tell the loom the order and number of heddles to lift, replacing the need for a human assistant. Until the invention of computers, Jacquard looms were the most complicated pieces of machinery in the world. In fact, the punch cards used by early computers were based on the Jacquard system. In a reversal of fortune, Jacquard looms now use computers instead of cards to keep track of the pattern.

Appearance and Use

Jacquard fabrics have a distinct front and backside. The front shows the design in crisp detail, but the back is covered with long "floats." These floats are yarns that were carried on the back of the fabric whenever they were not needed to form the design. Because the floats are easily snagged, the back of a jacquard fabric must be lined or hidden. An easy place to see floats is on the back of a clothing label—labels that are not printed are generally jacquard weavings.

As the design becomes more complex and the number of colors increases, more and more yarns have to be carried on the backside. This can make the cloth very heavy. For this reason, many jacquard fabrics are restricted for use in home furnishings. Brocade, made from silk or a synthetic material such as polyester, is one of the few figure weaves light enough for clothing. Although the mechanization of jacquard weaving has made it much less expensive to produce, brocade is still worn primarily for special occasions. Other figure weaves used in clothing, such as piqué and waffle weave, have a small textured pattern created by using a series of different yarn sizes. These patterns are less complicated than brocade and do not necessarily require a Jacquard loom.

Damask is a one-color, relatively lightweight cotton or linen jacquard fabric (originally produced on a draw loom) that is used for elegant curtains and tablecloths. Small floats on the surface are ironed or pounded flat (in a process called beetling) to make the cloth very smooth and lustrous. Heavier jacquard fabrics are used for upholstery and accessories such as shoes and handbags. Although these are sometimes called "tapestry," real tapestries are extremely expensive and are made by a very different process.

See also **Tapestry; Weaving; Weaving, Machinery.**

BIBLIOGRAPHY

Encyclopedia of Textiles. 3rd ed. Englewood Cliffs, N.J.: Prentice-Hall, Inc., 1980.

Kadolph, Sara J., and Anna L. Langford. *Textiles.* 9th ed. Upper Saddle River, N.J.: Prentice-Hall, Inc., 2001.

Tortora, Phyllis G., and Robert S. Merkel, eds. *Fairchild's Dictionary of Textiles.* 7th ed. New York: Fairchild Publications, 1996.

Heather Marie Akou

WEAVE, PILE

Pile weave is part of a family of woven fabrics created to produce pronounced or obvious protrusions of the constituent warp yarns within one set of the warp while a base structure of warp yarns maintains the tensile and structural integrity of the fabric in the machine delivery direction. The family of pile weaves includes terry cloth, velveteen, plush, and similar weaves in which a portion of the warp is extended to form an elongated, extended path from the flat plane of the fabric. Terry weave fabrics are traditionally used as houseware items for bath towels, mats, washcloths, and robes, but are occasionally used for apparel items such as beachwear. Other pile weave fabrics are usually associated with winterwear clothing items because of their softness and warmth.

The pile is defined as that set of yarns within the warp that is manipulated to allow large variations in the yarn interlacing lengths. The base structure of the warp that maintains a conventional mode of interlacings with the weft and provides structural binding and load integrity is known as the ground.

Ground warps and pile warps are provided to the shedding and weft insertion sections of the weaving machine in separate deliveries. Conventionally, the ground and pile yarns are wound separately onto warp beams, but direct delivery of the pile from package creels is also possible in specialty weaves such as carpets.

Pile formation is executed by formation of floats on either the face, back or both sides of the fabric. During this float formation, the interlacing frequency of the warp in the ground direction is much more frequent, creating higher tension in the ground warp than in the pile. The fabric take-up is actuated based on the ground warp advance rate, so the pile warp length becomes necessarily greater than that of the ground. The extra length of the pile is utilized to create loops, long floats, billowed structures, and similar protrusions from the fabric surface. In the case of terry pile weaves, the advance rate of the pile exceeds that of the ground to such an extent that relatively long loops are formed that are manipulated to form alternatively above and below the surface of the fabric during weaving.

Pile weaves may be further enhanced or manipulated by variation in reed beating motion or variation of the position of the cloth fell during beat-up. In the first case, the reed sweep motion is restricted after some insertions and occasionally driven fully forward to allow maximum pile loop formation. In the case of variable fell position, the reed position and motion remain constant through each pick insertion; the cloth support, which determines the fabric fell location, is maintained in a position further away from shedding motion and closer to the take-up until loop formation is required. At loop formation, the fell is advanced simultaneously with and in opposite direction to the beat of the reed. The combination of the opposing reed and fell motions form the pile loop.

See also **Loom; Weave, Double; Weave, Slack Tension; Weave Types; Weaving.**

BIBLIOGRAPHY

Collier, B., and P. Tortora. *Understanding Textiles.* Upper Saddle River, N.J.: Prentice-Hall Inc., 2001, pp. 312–316.

Emery, I. *The Primary Structures of Fabrics*, pp. 148–149. Washington, D.C.: The Textile Museum, 1980.

Gioello, D. A. *Profiling Fabrics: Properties, Performance, and Construction Techniques.* New York: Fairchild Publications, 1981.

Howard Thomas

WEAVE, PLAIN Plain weave (also known as tabby weave) is the most basic structure for producing cloth. When done by hand, the technique is like basket weaving: one filling (a crosswise or weft) yarn is drawn over, under, over, under, and so forth, through a series of warp (extended lengthwise) yarns. The next filling yarn takes the exact opposite path (under, over, under, over, ...) and the whole pattern is repeated. When using a loom, a weaver alternates between raising all of the even-numbered warp yarns and all of the odd-numbered warp yarns, laying down successive filling yarns in each opening (shed) to create the same pattern. Although this technique has been in use since the late Stone Age, *Fairchild's Dictionary of Textiles* estimates that 80 percent of all woven textiles are made using plain weave.

Simple Variations

The continuing popularity of plain weave is due to its simplicity as well as to the many possible variations in color, texture, and yarn count. Plain weave is the least expensive fabric to produce. At the same time, weavers often purposefully use this pattern to avoid visual competition with other aspects of the cloth: textured fibers (such as linen and silk dupioni); novelty yarns (such as tweed, chenille, and bouclé); printed patterns (on fabrics such as calico and chintz); and dyed patterns (on fabrics such as batik, ikat, and tie-dye). Textiles that have a specialty finish, including flannel (napped), organdy (parchmentized), ciré and moiré taffeta (embossed), are also frequently plain weaves.

Georgette, chiffon, and voile (sheer fabrics that are used for scarves, bridal veils, and decorative overlays on full skirts and dresses) are plain weave fabrics made with tiny, highly twisted silk or manufactured yarns. The twisted yarns create minute spaces in the fabric allowing light or another color to show through. Softer fabrics used for dresses and skirts, such as cotton lawn and rayon challis, are made with yarns that have a very light twist. This helps make the surface of the finished cloth feel very smooth. China silk, a popular fabric for women's blouses, is a fine cloth with a high yarn count (large number of threads per inch). Buckram and crinoline, plain weave fabrics with a low yarn count, are used as stiff linings in the construction of elaborate hats and dresses. Muslin is a cheap, medium-weight plain weave fabric that is often used by tailors and designers to make a test garment before working with more expensive material.

Striped and plaid fabrics, such as tartan, madras, and gingham, are made by changing the color on sections of filling and/or warp yarns. Gingham, for example, usually has thin stripes of red and white or blue and white threads in the warp and identical stripes in the filling. In the finished cloth the stripes create a checkerboard pattern. This look can be imitated by printing the same pattern on a plain weave fabric. Chambray, a popular cloth for button-down shirts, is made with filling yarns that are one color (frequently white) and warp yarns that are a different color. When the filling and warp have a high color contrast, the overall fabric seems to shift color as it moves on the body. This is known as iridescence. Ikat fabrics have a multicolored warp that is dyed before the weaving process begins. When the weaver uses plain weave and a neutral-colored filling yarn, the color and pattern of the warp yarns are allowed to stand out. A similar technique is used to produce fabrics such as tweed and chenille, where the goal is to highlight the texture of the novelty yarn. These bulky or fluffy yarns are usually in the filling. Simply using fewer yarns per inch in the warp and vice versa can also emphasize filling yarns.

Medium-weight plain weave fabrics are sometimes called "print cloth" because they're often used for printed fabrics such as chintz and calico. The smooth surface of plain weave is excellent for printing. These fabrics are also low-cost, which balances out the expense of printing a textile. One drawback to plain weave, however, is that other structures such as twill weave and double weave are much stronger. Plain weave fabrics are best used for clothing and household furnishings that do not take much abuse (such as curtains) or are periodically replaced (such as underwear and bedsheets).

Rib and Basket Weave

Changing the size or number of certain filling and/or warp yarns allows the creation of other variations of the plain weave. When several yarns are grouped together or larger yarns are used, a straight raised ridge called a rib or cord is formed. Poplin is a cotton or polyester fabric with very tiny ribs in the filling direction. This added thickness makes the cloth very crisp. Taffeta and faille, made of silk or a synthetic material such as acetate, are crisp fabrics with a slightly larger rib. Taffeta is often used to make ball gowns because the ribs make an elegant swishing sound when the fabric rubs together. Grosgrain ribbon is another fancy material with ridges in the filling direction. Bedford cord is a heavy fabric made as a lengthwise ribbed weave that resembles corduroy and is used for pants. Rip-stop nylon is a very strong fabric with noticeable ribs in both the filling and the warp direction. In this case, the ribs help prevent the fabric from tearing. Rip-stop is often used for sports gear such as windbreakers and athletic shoes.

Basket weave fabrics are made by having one or more filling yarns go over, under, over, ... more than one warp yarn at a time. This can be used to create a fabric that has a better drape and luster than standard plain weave, but the exposed yarns are more likely to be snagged. Oxford cloth, a popular fabric for men's dress shirts, is a basket weave that has one filling yarn going under and over two warp yarns at a time. Heavier basket weaves, such as canvas and sailcloth, have been used for shoes and outdoor clothing such as jackets and overalls for construction workers, sailors, and hunters. Monk's cloth, a very soft basket weave fabric that is easily damaged, has four yarns running together in both the filling and the warp direction.

See also **Batik; Calico; Chintz; Crinoline; Dyeing, Resist; Ikat; Muslin; Silk; Tartan; Tweed; Weave, Double; Weave, Satin; Weave, Twill; Weave Types; Weaving; Yarns.**

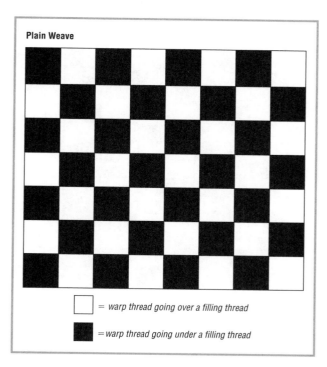

Plain weave. The most basic structure for producing cloth, the plain weave technique is known to have been in use as long ago as the Late Stone Age.

BIBLIOGRAPHY

Encyclopedia of Textiles. 3rd ed. Englewood Cliffs, N.J.: Prentice-Hall, Inc., 1980.

Kadolph, Sara J., and Anna L. Langford. *Textiles.* 9th ed. Upper Saddle River, N.J.: Prentice-Hall, Inc., 2001.

Tortora, Phyllis G., and Robert S. Merkel, eds. *Fairchild's Dictionary of Textiles.* 7th ed. New York: Fairchild Publications, 1996.

Heather Marie Akou

WEAVE, SATIN Along with plain and twill weave, satin is one of three basic weave structures that have been in use since ancient times. Associated with luxury, romance, and sensuousness, satin and sateen fabrics are made of fine silk and cotton yarns as well as manufactured fibers such as rayon, acetate, and polyester. Satin weaves have a smooth, lustrous surface and possess the best draping qualities out of all the weave structures. The pattern of a satin weave is similar to a twill, but the floats (yarns that go over multiple warp or filling yarns before they dip under the surface) are very long—covering up to eleven other yarns. Satin must be woven on a loom with at least six (and more commonly eight) harnesses. Instead of having diagonal lines, the floats are usually staggered to make the surface look as smooth and seamless as possible. This property is enhanced by packing the floats very close

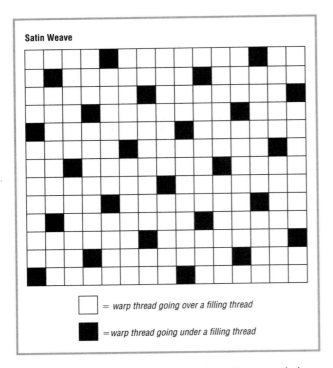

Satin Weave

☐ = warp thread going over a filling thread

■ = warp thread going under a filling thread

Satin weave. The staggered floats in the satin weave help to create a seemingly smooth surface, with a structure that can be difficult to see even under magnification.

together. Even under magnification, it can be difficult to see the structure of a very tight satin weave.

A History of Satin Weaving

Until the invention of manufactured fibers, satin fabrics were generally expensive to produce because they required large quantities of silk or very fine cotton yarns. (With yarns any thicker, the floats would be so long that the cloth would be too fragile to wear.) In the mythology surrounding silk weaving, the original source of the name for satin has been lost. One suggestion is that is comes from the ancient Chinese port of Zaytoun. Another is that satin was "called *sztun* until the Renaissance; then the Italian silk manufacturers changed the term to *saeta* to imply *hair* or *bristle*, a term which can be applied to fabrics of this type since they show a hairline and glossy surface" (American Fabrics, p. 198).

Satin weaving was invented in China more than two thousand years ago. Although elaborate textiles such as brocade (a figured satin produced on a draw loom) were expensive and in many cases restricted to the upper classes, the cultivation of silk was widespread. By the late second millennium B.C.E., "Ordinary peasant women were expert in the special techniques associated with silk weaving; silk was produced in quantity and worn, at least on some occasions, by a wide range of people, not just the aristocracy" (Steele and Major, p. 22). Silk weaving was a treasured secret, but eventually the technology

spread to Japan, Korea, India, Thailand, and other parts of southern Asia. Limited amounts of silk fabric were exported to the West as early as the time of ancient Greece, but satin was not produced in Europe until the Middle Ages. The scarcity of silk restricted the use of this material to the church, nobility, and upper classes.

During the late Renaissance, silk weaving expanded from Italy to Spain, the Netherlands, France, England, and the American colonies. Variations of satin acquired several new names including peau de soie (literally "skin of silk," a matte fabric with tiny diagonal lines) and charmeuse (a lightweight, pebbly satin, sometimes called crepe-backed satin). Sateen, made of finely spun cotton threads (often long-staple Egyptian cotton), has floats in the filling instead of the warp. These sideways floats drape in the opposite direction from a standard warp satin; when used for an elegant ball gown or full skirt they help the fabric stand away from the body. Slipper satin, a strong, compactly woven material is mainly used for footwear.

Uses of Satin in the West

Modern uses of satin in the West have been sacred and profane—it has been sewn into everything from bridal gowns, ballet slippers, and evening dresses to sexy corsets and lingerie. A contemporary book, *The Wedding Dress*, describes "silk, tulle, satin and lace" as the "heart of a romantic dream" (McBride-Mellinger, p. 9), but satin was not commonly used in bridal gowns until the late 1800s. Because the long floats on the surface of this fabric are easy to snag, it can be difficult to maintain the appearance of satin through repeated use. This was the first time that women outside of the upper classes could afford the luxury of a dress worn only for a single day. Before that time, dresses were used over and over again as "Sunday best."

As manufactured and synthetic fibers such as rayon (originally called "artificial silk"), acetate, and polyester were invented beginning in the 1920s and 1930s, satin gradually became available to an even larger number of women. Duchesse satin, a blend of rayon and silk, was invented as a less expensive, lightweight alternative to 100 percent silk satin. In the early 2000s, all varieties of satin are used for bridal gowns and bridesmaid dresses, evening gowns, prom dresses, and accessories at many different levels of price and quality.

Satin also made an appearance in the late 1800s in the undergarments of fashionable Parisian women. The sensuousness of satin—a prelude to the nude body underneath—was considered very erotic. Although colorful satin was first associated with prostitutes, "fashion journalism and advertising increasingly emphasized the importance of luxurious and seductive lingerie, including colorful, decorative corsets" (Steele, p. 133). In the early 1900s, satin became popular in other styles of lingerie as corselettes, girdles, brassieres, and panties were accepted as replacements for the petticoat and corset. "By 1910, brassieres were available in cotton tricotrine [a knit fabric], silk, satin; in 1920 *Vogue* advertised one in tulle; and in the 1930s sateen was particularly popular" (Carter, p. 89). New materials such as rayon, nylon, and polyester made it possible for women from nearly all walks of life to purchase sexy lingerie. These fabrics were rationed during World War II, but advertisements and pin-ups pictured women dressed in lustrous satin camisoles.

Satin has continued to be very popular. In the 1970s, the corset came back into fashion as members of punk and goth subcultures "began to reappropriate the corset as a symbol of rebellion and 'sexual perversity'" (Steele, p. 166). In her "Blond Ambition" tour in the early 1990s, Madonna wore a light pink satin corset designed by Jean-Paul Gaultier. An obvious symbol of her sexuality, the corset was not only flaunted as outerwear but had padded, cone-shaped breasts. Partly for reasons of nostalgia, these styles have come back into high fashion at the beginning of the twenty-first century.

See also **Cotton; Polyester; Rayon; Silk; Weave, Plain; Weave, Twill; Weave Types; Wedding Costume.**

BIBLIOGRAPHY

American Fabrics and Fashion editors. *Encyclopedia of Textiles.* 3rd ed. Englewood Cliffs, N.J: Prentice-Hall, Inc., 1980.

Carter, Alison. *Underwear: The Fashion History.* London: B.T. Batsford, Ltd., 1992.

McBride-Mellinger, Maria. *The Wedding Dress.* New York: Random House, 1993.

Steele, Valerie. *The Corset: A Cultural History.* New Haven, Conn.: Yale University Press, 2001.

Steele, Valerie, and John Major, eds. *China Chic: East Meets West.* New Haven, Conn: Yale University Press, 1999.

Heather Marie Akou

WEAVE, SLACK TENSION Slack tension weave is part of a family of weaves that rely on a variation in tension between top and bottom sheds to produce design effects on the surface of fabrics. Broadly speaking, terry, plisse, and pile fabrics fall within this definition, but other many other fabrics make use of the principle as well.

Fabric formation by weaving requires a tension balance between the top and bottom sheds of the warp prior to warp insertion. Common fabrics such as many twills, satins and plain weave variants utilize differences between top and bottom shed tensions to produce more dramatic face or back effects on a fabric surface. These types of shed geometry variations are sometimes colloquially known as "weaving in a sack" because the tension differences are reminiscent of a sack held open at the top while the bottom is allowed to be slack.

Slack sheds are produced by a smaller displacement from the horizontal or closed shed position by one shed opening than the other. Usually it is the top shed that is allowed to be slack while the bottom shed is held tight. The limiting factor to the tension in the tighter shed may be determined by one of two rules. In the first rule, the tightest shed may be no more than 10 percent tighter than the base tension of the warp during closed shed. By the second rule, the individual ends of the tighter shed should bear no more than 15 percent of the average single end break load of that warp yarn type.

Within the initial modulus region of the yarn's load-elongation profile, there is direct proportionality of the yarn tension to the shed opening angle. That tension or load may be determined either by dividing the base warp tension at closed shed by the cosine of the appropriate opening angle or it may be found by using the Pythagorean theorem to find the yarn extension during opening. It is important to note that the opening point of the rear shed is determined by the position of the stop motion and not by the whiproll of the weaving machine.

Since warp let-off is governed by reaction of the whiproll or tensioner rolls, the slack shed is advanced by the same length as that demanded by the more heavily loaded shed. As a result, longer floats are generated in the fabric than would be present in symmetrical shed weaves. These long floats create structural variations on a fabric surface that are utilized by designers to produce billows, waves, rows and similar textures.

Other variants of slack shed weave designs require the use of multiple warps advancing at different rates from different warp beam let-off systems on the same machine to produce pile and loop effects on the surface of a fabric. Such systems require exact feed measuring for the warps and often require variable beat-up systems to compact the picks into a warp of deliberately varying lengths.

See also **Loom; Weave, Double; Weave, Pile; Weave, Plain; Weave, Satin; Weave, Twill; Weaving; Weave Types; Weaving, Machines.**

BIBLIOGRAPHY

Emery, I. *The Primary Structures of Fabrics.* Washington, D.C.: The Textile Museum, 1980.

Gioello, D. A. *Profiling Fabrics: Properties, Performance, and Construction Techniques.* New York: Fairchild Publications, 1981.

Howard Thomas

WEAVE, TWILL Twill is an ancient weaving technique used to produce durable fabrics that have characteristically diagonal patterns called "wales." Twill fabrics are woven on looms using three or (more typically) four harnesses—frames with "heddles" (loops of string or wire) that hold individual warp yarns in place and are used to lift up every third or fourth warp yarn in a repeated pattern. On a four-harness loom, the weaver can

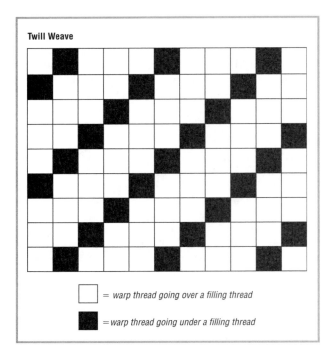

Twill Weave

☐ = warp thread going over a filling thread

■ = warp thread going under a filling thread

Twill weave. The twill weave technique produces fabrics that are stronger, thicker, and more durable than those made by other techniques. This is largely because the filling and warp yarns interlace less frequently.

alternatively lift up sets of two harnesses at once (1+2, 2+3, 3+4, …). This creates an even sturdier and more balanced twill weave.

Because the filling and warp yarns in a twill weave do not interlace as many times as they do in a plain weave, the yarns can be packed more tightly together. This makes the fabric stronger, thicker, and better able to hide soil than a plain weave made from the same materials. It also gives the fabric a better drape and resistance to wrinkling. Lightweight twills are commonly used for dresses, scarves, and neckties. Heavier weights are used for blue jeans, jackets, and outerwear for work such as carpentry and construction. Elegant variations of twill weave, including houndstooth and herringbone, are used for high-quality professional clothing.

Basic Twills

Lightweight twill fabrics for men's neckties are commonly called foulard or surah. Foulard is literally the French word for a necktie or scarf. These fabrics are made of silk or a manufactured material such as polyester. They can also be used for lingerie, slip dresses, or linings in other garments. Although the fabric is thin, the strength of a twill weave makes the final product fairly durable. Challis is a light- to medium-weight twill made of wool or rayon. This fabric has a luxurious drape, is resistant to wrinkling, and is often used for women's apparel.

A heavier twill known as serge has a smooth surface and is frequently used for stylish outerwear such as trench coats. Thicker versions made of wool and cotton are used for work clothing. Serge de Nîmes (serge from the city of Nîmes in southern France) was, some argue, the original name of denim, the heavy cotton twill now used for blue jeans. Levi Strauss, the inventor of blue jeans, was initially using tent canvas (a plain weave), but switched to denim because of its superior strength. For similar reasons, in 1908 the U.S. Army began to issue soldiers denim work uniforms. These were popular and widely used until they were phased out during World War II.

Denim generally has blue cotton yarns (dyed with indigo) in one direction and white cotton yarns in the other direction. A cheaper version can be made by substituting polyester for the white yarns.) This color difference emphasizes the diagonal wales of the cloth and gives denim its characteristically worn look. Trendier versions of denim can be woven with other colors of thread or dyed later as a whole garment. The strength of denim allows the garment to undergo harsh finishing treatments such as acid- and stonewashing, abrasion, and slashing. A lighter fabric that looks very similar is known as jean and is often used for casual button-down shirts, children's clothing, and home furnishings.

Other twill weaves that are frequently made into work clothing include drill (a heavy cotton fabric), cavalry twill (a smooth wool fabric with distinct diagonal lines), and chino (a relatively lightweight cotton fabric). Chino had its origins as a material for summer-weight military uniforms during World War I. Popularized by "casual Fridays" as well as Gap advertisements in the late 1990s, chino became a popular choice of fabric for casual pants, capris, and skirts. It was also part of the "Ivy League look" in the 1950s and early 1960s. Gabardine, an elegant material made from wool instead of cotton, is a common choice for professional suits and dress slacks. This fabric has distinct diagonal wales created by using many more warp threads per inch than filling threads. Different colors of thread in the warp and filling, such as brown and camel, can emphasize these lines further.

Variations

As with plain weave, there are many ways to alter the structure and appearance of a twill weave. Houndstooth is a classic twill fabric with a small, distinctive pattern that looks like a four-pointed star. This is created by alternating two different colors of warp and filling threads, often black and white to emphasize the pattern. Herringbone twills have diagonal lines that periodically change direction, creating zigzag patterns that look like subtle stripes from a distance. This pattern is made by changing either how the harnesses are threaded or the order in which they are lifted. Herringbone twills are generally made from smooth, medium-weight wool yarns and are used for professional clothing.

Other decorative twills that do not have specific names are called broken twills, pointed twills, or undulating twills. These patterns are created by using more harnesses and more complex systems of threading and of lifting the harnesses. Textile designers have an almost unlimited number of ways to change a twill pattern. These fancy twills are not very common and are generally used for either expensive home furnishings or couture apparel.

See also **Cotton; Denim; Gabardine; Indigo; Jean; Levi Strauss; Neckties and Neckwear; Polyester; Rayon; Silk; Weave, Plain; Weave, Satin; Wool.**

BIBLIOGRAPHY

American Fabrics and Fashion editors. *Encyclopedia of Textiles,* 3rd ed. Englewood Cliffs, N.J: Prentice-Hall, Inc., 1980.

Emerson, William K. *Encyclopedia of United States Army Insignia and Uniforms.* Norman: University of Oklahoma Press, 1996.

Finlayson, Iain. *Denim: An American Legend.* New York: Simon and Schuster, Inc., 1990.

Kadolph, Sara J., and Anna L. Langford. *Textiles.* 9th ed. Upper Saddle River, N.J.: Prentice-Hall, Inc., 2001.

Oelsner, G. Hermann, and Samuel S. Dale, eds. *A Handbook of Weaves.* Mineola, N.Y: Dover Publications, 1990. Original edition published in 1875.

Heather Marie Akou

WEAVE TYPES Names given to fabrics differ depending on who is naming them. One only has to walk through a museum collection and read the labels, to find out that even within the same institution, there is often no agreement on how to categorize a cloth. At different times, lampas, diasper, and tissue have all been used to describe the same type of cloth. Depending on when or who entered the piece into a collection, the label will reflect the terminology of that period. This can be confusing when one is standing next to two fabrics that appear to be similar, but have different labels (i.e., lampas for one and diasper for the other).

In a different textile circle, contemporary hand weavers might be heard talking about weaving using the Theo Moorman technique. The listener won't know, as the weavers themselves might not know, that this structure is identical with lampas, diasper, and tissue. Theo Moorman had the awareness to state that she suspected her technique had been used elsewhere, but since she didn't know where or when, it was not unreasonable for her to call it her own technique. Sometimes the magazines for handweavers have quite imaginative names for types of weaves that are invented by the authors, based only on their own sense of labeling.

The confusion increases when one looks at magazines and articles for the fashion or interior design market, where names are often created for marketing strategies rather than for clarification of terms. Marketers

often want to obscure the facts, making something very mundane appear exotic. It is much more exciting to label a cloth as microfiber than it is to remind the public of the negative connotations of polyester, even though they are, in fact, the same.

So it is important to realize that different constituencies in the world of textiles will use different labels for cloth. Even when the same word is being used, it may have a different meaning, depending on the viewpoint and education of the speaker. An interior designer might speak to another designer using the word "tapestry" to describe a wall hanging, and they understand they are discussing a pictorial textile, not necessarily referencing how the work was made. A weaver, however, who thinks in terms of weave structure for classification, overhearing their conversation, might take exception to this usage, unless the work being discussed was specifically a weft-faced plain weave using discontinuous wefts to create the pictorial elements. Thus, it is important to recognize that the classification of weave types reflects the needs and concerns of the group using the terms.

Codifying Weave Types

Perhaps textile historians, archaeologists, and curators are the most rigorous group trying to codify and clarify the labeling of weave types. After all, their need for clear communication is critical; their research is used by others, and perhaps spurs on further research. Thus textile scholars began an international movement to standardize terminology through the establishment of the Centre International d'Etude des Textiles Anciens (CIETA) in 1954. If one attends a symposium of scholars presenting papers on woven textiles today, or reads an exhibition catalog for a contemporary exhibit of historical textiles, most of the classification will try to follow the conventions of CIETA.

Another influential study on textile classification is Irene Emery's *The Primary Structures of Fabrics*, first published in 1966. Although she covers more than woven cloth, most of the book is focused on the structural classification of weaves (not on the process of making). Weaving falls under the heading of constructions using two or more elements, composed of the interlacement of vertical (warp) elements and horizontal (weft) elements. With concise language, clarified by magnified photographs of the structures, Emery details plain weave, float weaves, compound weaves, crossed-warp structures (gauze), twining, and weft wrapping.

Since Emery limits her discussion to structure, she does not include fabric names, which can take into account other characteristics such as fiber, color, finish, and texture. This type of classification, however, is critical to the worlds of fashion design and interior design. Thus taffeta, poplin, grosgrain, cheesecloth, ottoman, and broadcloth are just a few of the varieties of cloth sharing the same weave structure (plain weave), but each evokes

A weave draft documents the different components of a specific woven cloth. A diligent weaver can express, diagrammatically, all the pertinent information for another weaver to exactly re-create their fabric. Written for a shaft loom, these elements include the threading draft, which records the sequence used for threading each warp thread in a shaft; the tie-up, which records what shafts are connected to each peddle of the loom; the sequence of treadling, which documents the order in which the peddles are used; and the cloth diagram, which is the sum of the parts, and is another term for the weave structure. (The draft for a dobby loom assumes a direct tie-up [as if one shaft is tied to one peddle] and the ability to raise multiple shafts. The draft has one area called the liftplan, which combines the information that tie-up and treadling sequence give for a shaft loom.) Diagrams can also include the color sequence used for both warps and wefts; notations of different sizes of yarn used; and notations for denting instructions (how threads are clumped in the reed).

a distinct fabric with specific characteristics for the designer who uses these names. Cheesecloth is very open and soft (more open than gauze), and is a balanced plain weave, while broadcloth is of medium-weight with a ribbed effect caused by the warp being more dominant than the weft. These names can also refer to specific yarns being used; for example, taffeta is traditionally made with filament yarns and is very shiny, while broadcloth is traditionally made from cotton or a cotton blend.

Weave Types by Structure

The term weave structure refers specifically to the interlacement of the vertical and horizontal elements in a weave. As the vertical element, the warp, traverses the cloth, it dives over and under the horizontal element, the weft. Conversely, one can speak of the path the weft takes, moving over and under the warp ends, as it travels horizontally across the cloth. Structural diagrams of cloth can show slices of the cloth, depicting the paths of warp and weft in three-dimensional diagrams called cross sections. These diagrams are particularly helpful to remind the weaver that cloth, usually thought of as a flat, pliable plane, is really a three-dimensional form. More often, though, the diagram of a weave structure is rendered as a two-color grid format. Combined with other information needed to recreate the cloth, this diagram is called a weave draft.

The three most well-known categories of weave structure, using one warp system and one weft system, are plain weave, twills, and satin weaves. Each has a distinct type of interlacement that distinguishes it from the others. The path of a warp in plain weave is always over one weft, under one weft. The path of a warp thread in a twill can vary (for example, a 2,2 twill goes over two wefts and under two wefts, while a 5,3 twill would go over five wefts and under three), but it always has adjacent warp threads, in either the right or left direction, lifting, and following the same sequence of over and under. This causes distinct diagonal lines in the fabric. Satin structures, however, never have adjacent ends (warps) go under the same weft, and their appearance is of a smooth, unbroken surface.

These three weave types have been used throughout the history of textiles in all parts of the world. Whether on backstrap looms, draw looms, or floor looms, the majority of textiles created have used one of these three structures. Of course the sett of the warp (the density of the warp), the type of yarn used, the color of the warp and weft threads, and the texture of the yarn will affect the look of the fabric, and thus the classification of fabrics by name.

Weave structure can look different in the cloth. Since all weave structures can be modified in appearance through changes in sett, or yarn size, or color, using weave structure as the classification for weave type only tells part of the story.

Compound weave types. Weaves can also be classified in terms of dye processes done to the warp—thus ikat textiles, or painted warp textiles. Or they can be classified by finishing processes, such as fulled, felted, or shrunk; or stamped, incised, or watermarked. Whatever the classification, if one looks carefully, one can probably find a different name for the same weave type some time during the long and varied history of textiles.

See also **Polyester; Tapestry; Weave, Plain; Weave, Twill.**

BIBLIOGRAPHY

Burnham, Dorothy K. *Warp and Weft.* New York: Charles Scribner's Sons, 1980.

Emery, Irene. *The Primary Structures of Fabrics.* Washington, D.C.: The Textile Museum, 1966.

Collier, Billie J., and Phyllis G. Tortora. *Understanding Textiles.* Upper Saddle River, N.J.: Prentice Hall, 2001.

Grosicki, Z. *Watson's Textile Design and Colour.* London: Newnes-Butterworths, 1975.

———. *Watson's Advanced Textile Design.* London: Newnes-Butterworths, 1989.

Kadolph, Sara J., and Anna L. Langford *Textiles.* Upper Saddle River, N.J.: Prentice Hall, 2002.

Moorman, Theo. *Weaving as an Art Form.* West Chester, Pa.: Schiffer Publishing Ltd., 1975.

Oelsner, G. Hermann. *A Handbook of Weaves.* Translated and revised by Samuel S. Dale. New York: Dover Publications, Inc., 1952. Original edition was published in 1915.

van der Hoogt, Madelyn. *The Complete Book of Drafting for Handweavers.* Coupeville, Wash.: ShuttleCraft Books, 1993.

Bhakti Ziek

WEAVING Weaving, one of the oldest technologies practiced by humans, is the interlacement of two or more vertical and horizontal elements. The result of this action is that the individual elements form a shallow three-dimensional plane, which is usually flexible. In its simplest form, known as plain weave, the first warp (the vertical element) goes over and under each weft (the horizontal element); the second warp goes under and over each weft; and this sequence is repeated throughout the cloth. When the warp and weft are similar in size, and show up in equal amounts in the fabric, the cloth is known as a balanced plain weave. However, the scale of the elements and their density can vary, creating fabrics that show more warp or more weft.

The path that the interlacement of the threads takes can also vary. Weavers, historians, and others interested in weave structure, have developed systems for describing the various forms of interlacement—plain weave, twills, satins, and double cloth are some of the most common families of weave.

The first weavings were probably done through manual manipulation of the elements. Mat weavers in Nepal still create products using their hands and working on the ground. Looms were developed in all parts of the world to make the process of weaving easier and quicker. A loom holds the vertical warp threads under tension so the weft threads can be inserted with ease. The pot-holder loom that children use is such a device. The wefts are then inserted by manually going over and under the tensioned warps. Eventually looms were modified to aid the separating of the warp threads so the weft could easily be inserted in the resulting triangular space, known as the shed.

In most instances, when looking at a woven cloth, one will see the warp and weft crossing each other in a perpendicular manner. There are structures, however, where the 90-degree intersection is modified and leans one way or another, such as in the group of weaves known as deflected warp or weft. There are other processes that make planes of cloth, such as beating bark fibers or meshing animal fibers together (felting), that do not have the interlacement of elements found in weaving. Even when woven cloth is modified (shrunk and matted in a process called fulling or felting) until it loses the appearance of interlacement, the structure is still embedded in the fabric.

Some planes of fabric are made through the looping of single elements, using processes such as crochet, knit, and knotting. There are other two-element processes (including plaiting or braiding, macramé, and twining,) that differ from weaving in the manner of the interconnection of their elements.

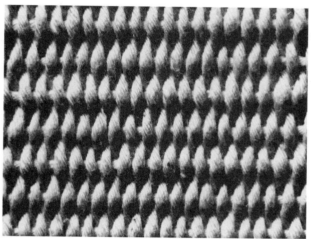

Weave types. *Top:* Balanced plain weave, warp and weft equal in size, spacing and count. *Center:* Warp-faced plain weave. *Bottom:* Weft-faced plain weave. PHOTOGRAPHS OF BALANCED, WARP-FACED AND WEFT-FACED PLAIN WEAVE FROM THE PRIMARY STRUCTURES OF FABRICS, BY IRENE EMERY, WASHINGTON, D.C.: THE TEXTILE MUSEUM, 1966, FIGURES 85, 86, 87, PAGE 76.

ENCYCLOPEDIA OF CLOTHING AND FASHION

Weaving, which can have more than one vertical or horizontal element, usually results in a plane of fabric that looks two-dimensional, but is actually a three-dimensional form. The strength and flexibility of this plane make it perfect for creating clothing, shelter, and furnishing fabrics. In recent times it has also been used as an art form.

See also **Loom; Weave, Plain; Weave, Twill; Weave, Satin; Weave Types; Weaving, Machinery.**

BIBLIOGRAPHY

Burnham, Dorothy K. *Warp and Weft*. New York: Charles Scribner's Sons, 1980.

Emery, Irene. *The Primary Structures of Fabrics*. Washington, D.C.: The Textile Museum, 1966.

Oelsner, G. Hermann. *A Handbook of Weaves*. Translated and revised by Samuel S. Dale. New York: Dover Publications, Inc., 1952. Original edition was published in 1915.

Bhakti Ziek

WEAVING MACHINERY The history of mechanization in the weaving industry is replete with stories of inventors whose ideas were untimely or impractical. The perseverance of inventors is a testimony to the importance of cloth in our culture and of the lucrative nature of the business. Mechanization of the weaving process began in earnest in the eighteenth century. Prior to developments in automation, one weaver was needed to operate one loom, and an assistant was necessary if a complex pattern was being woven. There were a few developments prior to 1700, but none of significance or permanent influence. One problem that inventors faced was violent opposition from textile workers who resented any innovations that would speed an individual's production capacity and therefore reduce the numbers of weavers needed. Improvements in the speed of weaving during the eighteenth century were given impetus by the invention of spinning machinery for the production of yarn necessary for weaving. Until mechanical spinning came into use, the output of three to four spinners was necessary to keep one weaver fully employed. Acceptance of advances in loom technology was also aided by continuing improvements in spinning and cloth finishing technologies. The first significant move toward automated weaving occurred when John Kay invented the flying shuttle in 1733. The flying shuttle was set in motion by the weaver pulling a cord or handle that propelled the shuttle across the width of the textile. Not only did this speed weaving by as much as four times, it also allowed a weaver to produce cloth wider than his arm's reach.

In 1785, a clergyman named Edmund Cartwright patented the first power loom. It was initially powered by an oxen, then by the new steam engine patented by James Watt in 1769. Cartwright's loom was slow to be accepted, but by the 1830s versions of his loom enabled one weaver and an assistant to operate four looms simultaneously. This machine was limited to producing plain textiles.

The automation of patterned fabric production began with the 1804 invention by Joseph Marie Jacquard. His so-called Jacquard mechanism could be mounted on any loom and controlled the lifting of the warp yarns that create the fabric's pattern. Previously, complex patterns had to be set up in advance on a loom and required an assistant to operate, but the Jacquard attachment allowed one weaver to control the shuttle and the pattern mechanism alone. Punched cards controlled the lift of the warp pattern yarns and a design could be changed very quickly by changing the punch cards that correspond to a particular design. This basic system remains in use in the early twenty-first century.

In 1835 the first automatic shuttle change machine enabled weft yarns of different colors to be inserted automatically in the weaving. 1895 saw the invention of the automatic pirn (weft supply) change in the shuttle, introduced by J. H. Northrop. Not until the 1950s did automatic weft winding directly on the weaving machine become commercially viable. It was introduced by the Leesona Company and known as the "Unifil" system.

Shuttleless looms appeared in the mid-twentieth century and employed various systems: grippers, rapier, and jets of water or air. Gripper machines use a small projectile that picks up a weft from a supply on the side and carries it to the other side; rapier machines use a long thin rod which travels from one side and grabs a weft which it pulls across as it returns (there are single and double rapier looms; the double rapiers meet in the center and pass off the weft thread); jet looms use a jet of air or water to propel the weft from side to side. Jet looms have the advantage of being particularly fast and can weave widths up to 85 inches. The rapier loom has the oldest history as the concept appears in a patent of 1678; the modern rapier loom was launched in 1963 by Dornier of Germany. A forerunner of the modern air jet loom first appeared in England in the 1860s, but the idea was finally commercially successful in the 1950s, introduced by Max Paabo of Sweden. The projectile (gripper) loom was invented in Switzerland by the Sulzer Brothers in 1924 but did not come into commercial use until 1953.

Fabrics from shuttleless looms do not have a selvage, as the weft is not a continuous yarn. The edges can be sealed with heat or resin. Until recently, these machines were limited to high volume weaving. Shuttle looms are still used for weaving basic constructions in low-wage economies and for specialist fabrics, which still comprise a large part of the market.

In the 1970s, the multiphase loom, in which all the actions of the loom take place simultaneously, was introduced. There are two types of multiphase looms: wave shed looms, in which the shed changes across the width of the textile as the weft travels, and parallel shedding, in which multiple sheds are formed along the length of the warp. One of the latest multiphase looms can produce 1.5 yards of fabric in one minute. In the early 1980s, computer-aided design and manufacture (CAD/CAM) became available and the design process, which could take weeks or months could be shortened drastically to as little as a twenty-four-hour period, if necessary. Computer generated design samples can also replace actual woven samples and can therefore be produced almost immediately and transmitted electronically to any point on the globe. This technology has also enabled designers to become partners in the manufacturing process, as changes can be introduced "virtually" without the cost of loom set-up and production time. Computers can also monitor the weaving process itself and can detect and automatically correct numerous mistakes.

Currently, designers have the possibility of working directly on systems where designs created on a computer screen are transferred directly to the controls of a computerized loom with the corresponding technology. The reaction to CAD/CAM has been mixed, as the ease of technology can lead to a disintegration of design.

See also **Loom; Weave, Double; Weave, Jacquard; Weave, Pile; Weave, Plain; Weave, Satin; Weave, Slack Tension; Weave, Twill; Weave Types; Weaving.**

BIBLIOGRAPHY

Benson, Anna, and Neil Warburton. *Looms and Weaving.* London: Shire Publications, Ltd., 1990.

Braddock, Sarah, and Marie O'Mahony, eds. *Textiles and New Technology: 2010.* London: Artemis Verlag, 1994.

Broudy, Eric. *The Book of Looms: A History of the Handloom from Ancient Times to the Present.* New York: Van Nostrand Company, 1979.

Kadolph, Sara. *Textiles.* Upper Saddle River, N.J.: Prentice Hall, 2002.

Omerod, A. *Modern Preparation and Weaving Machinery.* London: Butterworths, 1983.

Price, Arthur. *J.J. Pizzuto's Fabric Science.* New York: Fairchild Publications, 1994.

Melinda Watt

WEDDING COSTUME

WEDDING COSTUME A wedding dress is apparel used in conjunction with wedding ceremonies, including accessories that may differentiate nonmatrimonial dress from that worn specifically for weddings.

Contemporary Overview

As of the late twentieth and early twenty-first centuries, the global, urbanized standard of wedding apparel has followed the Western tradition of a bride dressed in white or off-white, with a head-covering, whether a veil or headpiece, and carrying flowers, a book, or some other object. The groom is attired in keeping with the degree of formality of the bride. Attendants are generally present, the number, gender, age, and dress of whom being peculiar to each culture. Family members usually attend, playing a prominent role, and are dressed in equally formal, but generally more subdued styles of clothing than the bridal party. Other accessories have become standard, some of which are mandated by religion or culture, and others of which are remnants of folk practice. The former may include specific types of headgear, for both bride and groom, and possibly all attendees. These range from yarmulkes at Jewish weddings, to crowns held over the heads of the bridal couple in Orthodox Christian ceremonies. Anglophone folkloric touches suggest the inclusion of "something old, something new, something borrowed, and something blue," as well as a single garter, a remnant of the days when the public removal of one's garters was a significant symbolic gesture. The throwing of the garter to the male attendants serves more or less the same function as the tossing of the bridal bouquet to the females: that of determining the next to wed, although the previous stipulation that all attendants be unmarried having disappeared, this old "good luck" charm is vitiated.

In contemporary non-western industrial societies, the situation is complex. There are generally local or national traditions, based on religious and/or societal norms that have developed over time to provide identifiable wedding apparel. This can range from Japanese kimonos to long body- and face-concealing robes in Islamic cultures, to elaborate saris in India, to hand-embroidered and metal-encrusted Hmong dress. However, the primacy of the "western wedding style"—that of a bride dressed in a white gown and a groom in typical western formal attire, has supplanted many local traditions, at least for the middle and upper classes. Even in countries with strong local traditions, if there are no specific religious strictures that would prohibit them and the economic resources are available, couples may opt to hold two ceremonies, one in the tradition of their own country and one of the western variety. This has been particularly popular in Japan and Korea, where the couple dresses according to the religion and architecture of the wedding chapel, or holds two separate ceremonies, and might change ensembles five to seven times during the course of the celebrations. Even in Islamic societies such as Saudi Arabia, this doubling up of wedding attire has proven popular among the upper classes.

History

It is not possible to determine from archaeological evidence whether or not prehistoric societies celebrated marital unions in a specific manner or marked those celebrations through the use of special garb. Information is nearly as scarce for the first great urban societies, where nothing is known of the wedding dress or practices of the bulk of the population and only dynastic marriages survive in the written record. However, it appears that even at the dynastic level, dress for weddings was less occasion-specific than a matter of showing off one's best garments and accessories.

The first clear references to specific wedding apparel, in the form of bridal crowns and veils, come from the Hellenistic period of Greece. These too, while specified for use in weddings, and ranging from simple flowers to elaborate metal tiaras, were accessories. It is not until many centuries later that most cultures adopted recognizable ensembles to mark the occasion. This stems, in part, from simple economics. In pre-industrial times, the idea of ceremony-specific clothing, particularly for a one-time event, was beyond the means of the vast majority of the population. Even at the court level, wardrobe inventories discuss the fact that royalty and courtiers alike tended to wear their most fashionable garments, with no real consideration of one-time use or symbolism of color or style. Again, it is the use of accessories that gives the garments their meaning.

It was during the long rule of Queen Victoria (1837–1901) that the Western notion of what the bride and her party should look like solidified, first in Britain, and subsequently the rest of the industrialized world. However, certain aspects, such as identically dressed attendants, appeared in many other cultures for more symbolic reasons than simply to honor, support, and, perhaps impress. The generation previous to Queen Victoria's introduced the white wedding gown, when Victoria's cousin, Crown Princess Charlotte, was married in 1816. According to reports, and a controversial garment in the collection of the Museum of London, her bridal gown consisted of a silver tissue and lace overgown worn over a white underdress. That this probably had more to do with the Regency fashion of white dresses than any symbolic intent did not stop it from exerting the same fashion influence of twentieth-century "royalty" such as Princess Grace of Monaco; Diana, Princess of Wales; or Carolyn Bessette Kennedy. The ideal of a white wedding dress was codified in 1840, when Queen Victoria wore a creamy white Spitalfields silk satin and lace gown. It was endlessly reproduced in fashion journals, setting a fashion standard for some appreciable time.

With the advent of industrialization in the West, the combination of readily available and comparatively cheap fabric meshed with the aspirations and needs of a no-longer self-sustaining population to acquire more garments, particularly those for festive occasions. Improved communication, in the form of newspapers, magazines, and their delivery methods of roads, railroads, and improved shipping speeds, as well as the establishment of dependable rural postal delivery at the turn of the twentieth century, allowed even isolated or working-class women to aspire to new fashion trends. However, economics and practicality continued to play a significant role, particularly among these populations. Societal norms decreed that appropriately formal dress be worn for significant occasions, from confirmation, to weddings, to church attendance, to funerals. Frequently, such a dress

was presented to a young woman at her coming of age; if funding permitted, another was obtained for her wedding. However, this dress would be expected to serve, not only for the festive occasion for which it was purchased, but also for all others in the foreseeable future, including funerals. It tended toward a conservative cut for this reason, and often had large seam allowances that could accommodate pregnancy and possible weight gain. With the long-standing tradition of black for funerals and mourning, most of these "good" dresses were black, and often worn for the first time at the woman's wedding. This tendency continued into the late nineteenth and even early twentieth century among rural women. Women of the higher classes wore colors; frequently, but not invariably, white. After a death in the family, when the period of strict mourning was over, marriage could take place, but the bride would wear either gray or lavender. Among the working classes, as soon as it was economically feasible, colors were adopted, although the white, one-time only dress was still a rarity. Even the more affluent often assumed their gowns would see use more than once, and colored wedding dresses were still common into the first decade of the twentieth century, after which the ideal of a white, often anachronistic gown, meant to be worn only once, was only supplanted by extraordinary conditions, such as war.

With nods to changes in silhouette and length, the now-immutable tradition of the bride in white, surrounded by equally formally dressed family and attendants, became the norm, not only in Western culture, but wherever Western fashion was emulated, and frequently in the face of centuries-old local tradition. Occasional vagaries of lifestyle, including nude hippie weddings and thematic concoctions ranging from period or folk evocations to camouflage in honor of a deploying soldier, did not dislodge the basic formal make-up of the wedding party, or its concentration on white or off-white and a fairly conservative cut. However, in the 1980s, this began to change, first among the attendants and guests, who began to wear colors such as black, previously considered taboo for twentieth-century weddings. New materials began to appear, including leather, sequins, and even tattoos, as part of the wedding ensemble which itself frequently displayed significantly more flesh than had previously been considered appropriate. Now even brides were sporting colors such as red and black, and indeed, even getting tattoos for the occasion.

The symbolism of both color and cut for the wedding party, solidified over the nineteenth century and even earlier in the case of many of the accessories, is accepted in the early 2000s with no understanding of origin or is ignored by many modern brides. The idea of wearing a one-time only dress is more prevalent, as most medium-priced gowns have their beaded or pearl decoration glued on rather than sewn. Alternatively the bride simply rents her gown, a tendency common in Japan, but that is making inroads in Europe and the United States.

Accessories and Their Symbolism

It is often the accessories that historically have provided clothing with bridal significance. Some can be traced to specific time periods while others appear to predate written records. One example of this is the headpiece. Depending on the culture, both men and women may have a specific type of head covering, but it is most unusual for the bride to be bareheaded. The earliest were undoubtedly simple wreaths of plant material: flowers, grain, or leaves, most of which appear to have had fertility symbolism, and possibly served to identify the wedding party. Later, head ornaments of cloth, metal, gems, and even wood began to be used. These were often accompanied by an additional piece of cloth, which might simply cover the hair or be draped over the entire head of the bride, obscuring her features. Certain religions dictate this kind of modesty, historically as well as in the early twenty-first century. However, in European culture, the veil also served as a disguise, a pre-Christian remnant of hiding the bride lest she be attacked by the forces of evil. Identically dressed attendants served not only to assist her, but to also confuse demonic presence.

Bouquets or other objects, such as fans or books, are also important accessories and are symbolic on several different levels. The carrying of flowers or other plants, such as wheat, is not only decorative, but refers to the fertility of the union. Flowers have been accorded symbolism in nearly every culture, but they also express wealth and taste in their choice and cost. In the early 2000s it is most common for Western brides to carry expensive flowers, with only very religious or economically prudent women opting for a prayer book. However, in earlier times, the owning and display of such a luxury item as a book would have lent the bride additional status, and frequently formed one of her betrothal gifts. The wedding ring, a token of affection, an exchange of property in the form of precious metal, and a none-too-subtle warning of future unavailability, is not a universal accessory. This is even more true of the engagement ring, a staple in North America, but not as common in other cultures, even in the West. Additionally, the finger or hand on which the rings are worn vary from culture to culture, as well as historically. Sixteenth-century examples of wedding portraits show the bride wearing a ring on her thumb.

Color symbolism did not play a role in weddings until relatively recently in the West, although now it signifies virginity, and, as mentioned above, the primacy of the white wedding dress flies directly in the face of many other cultures' norms. White is the color of mourning in most Asian cultures. Red, the one color still forbidden to most mainstream Western brides, due to its connotations of immorality ("scarlet woman," "red-light district"), is completely appropriate in other cultural settings. In India, it is the color of purity, and is often worn by brides. In much of East Asia, it is the color of celebration and luck, and therefore appropriate for bridal attire. However, the tendency toward adopting the Western white wedding, established only in the mid-nineteenth century, seems to be continuing throughout the world, sometimes alone, and sometimes in conjunction with local traditions. At the same time, the white wedding in the West is proving to be far less static than previously thought, evolving as fashions and societal norms do.

See also **Ceremonial and Festival Costumes; Religion and Dress.**

BIBLIOGRAPHY

Baker, Margaret. *Wedding Customs and Folklore.* Devon, U.K.: David and Charles, 1977. An early work exploring the symbolism of marriage and its dress.

Baldizzone, Tiziana, and Gianni Baldzonne. *Wedding Ceremonies: Ethnic Symbols, Costume, and Ritual.* Paris: Flammarian, 2002. One of many new studies that look at modern global practice.

Cunnington, Phillis, and Catherine Lucas. *Costume for Births, Marriages, and Deaths.* New York: A & C Black, 1972. One of the first, and still important studies of Western ceremonial clothing.

Foster, Helen Bradley, and Donald Clay Johnson. *Wedding Dress: Across Cultures.* Oxford: Berg, 2003. A rather good exploration of modern global wedding practices.

Kaivola-Bregenhøj, Annikki. *Bondebryllup.* Copenhagen, 1983. Excellent discussion of European peasant weddings.

Mordecai, Carolyn. *Weddings, Dating and Love: Customs and Cultures Worldwide, including Royalty.* Phoenix, Ariz.: Nittany, 1998. An imperfect but broad compendium of modern practices.

Newton, Stella Mary. *Fashion in the Age of the Black Prince: A Study of the Years 1340–1365.* Woodbridge, Suffolk: Boydell, 1980. Reprint, Totowa, N.J.: Rowman and Littlefield, 1999. One of the best studies of fourteenth-century dress, including weddings, using difficult to find primary sources.

Noss, Aagot. *Lad og Krone: frå jente til brur.* Oslo: Universitetsforlaget, 1991. The most careful case study to date of ethnic wedding traditions, focusing on those of Norway, by one of the pioneers of costume history fieldwork.

Piponnier, Françoise, and Perrine Mane. *Dress in the Middle Ages.* New Haven, Conn., and London: Yale University, 1997. A book that is significant because it presents much compressed information, and its discussion of garments signifying rites of passage is important.

Tobin, Shelley, Sarah Pepper, and Margaret Willes. *Marriage à la Mode: Three Centuries of Wedding Dress.* London: The National Trust, 2003.

Michelle Nordtorp-Madson

WESTWOOD, VIVIENNE Born Vivienne Swire in Glossop in Derbyshire in 1941, Vivienne Westwood originally set out to become a teacher. She married Derek Westwood in 1962; her first child was born a year later and she seemed destined to lead a quiet, suburban life. However, in 1965 she met Malcolm McLaren, a publicist and impresario, whose subversive ideas and alternative

Vivienne Westwood. Two models flank designer Vivenne Westwood, displaying her designs for the 1996 spring-summer pret-a-porter collection. Westwood's unconventional fashions often reference historical and traditional dress. © B.D.V./Corbis. Reproduced by permission.

lifestyle gave Westwood the opportunity and momentum to break free from her former life and embark on a highly successful career of fashion.

Vivienne Westwood's designs are a reaction against traditional British standards of morality—against petty bourgeois notions of etiquette and propriety. Since her early street style-based collaborations with McLaren, Westwood has defied the ideal of polite, anonymous clothes that express the wearer's ascribed social status. She seeks to transcend definitions of class, gender, ethnicity, and sexual orientation and create outfits that are dramatic—that encourage wearers to carry themselves confidently as they masquerade in theatrical assimilations of eighteenth-century aristocratic dress or traditionally tailored suits adorned with fetish bondage buckles. Westwood is a utopian. Through her work and the ideas she expresses in interviews, she strives to construct new personae for future cultures that draw upon idealized visions of the past inspired by portraiture and film.

During the early to mid-1970s, she and McLaren merged tough biker leather jackets with pornographic imagery and traditional tartans to produce the DIY (do-it-yourself) aesthetic that expressed the antiestablishment spirit of punk. Based in London's King's Road, they changed the name of their shop from time to time to enhance the current collection's ideals, from Let It Rock (1971) to Too Fast to Live, Too Young to Die (1973) to Sex (1974) and finally to Seditionaries (1976)—a name and anarchic style that coincided with the increased notoriety of the Sex Pistols, a punk rock band that McLaren managed. Punk enabled Westwood to break free from the suburbs she had felt trapped in and experiment with fashion's power to shock and challenge. Her sex shop-style plastic miniskirts worn with ripped fishnet stockings, buckles, and chains, fractured traditional notions of femininity and beauty. Along with her straggly-knit sweaters, Karl Marx portrait print shirts, and bondage trousers, they became emblems of pop cultural revolt.

Westwood's subsequent work with McLaren was just as closely linked to youth culture, music, and clubs. As her King's Road shop settled into its final incarnation as World's End in 1980, she embarked on a series of collections that explored historical construction techniques. One example was Pirates, presented at her first catwalk show in 1981. She continued to play with the relationship between body and fabric in the multilayered bulk of the Buffalo collection of 1982–1983 and the Witches collection of 1983–1984, which used sweatshirt fabric cut to pull away from the figure. These collections have inspired other designers; for example, punk was revisited in the early 1990s by Jean-Paul Gaultier and Karl Lagerfeld. Westwood's asymmetrical sportswear-based designs, highlighted with the neon colors that she used in her last collections with McLaren between 1983 and 1984, were seen on catwalks and in such High Street stores as Topshop and H & M in 2002–2003.

Westwood's split from McLaren prompted her shift away from pop culture and street style toward a more thorough exploration of history and tradition. She no longer wanted to be seen as a creator of subcultural dress, but rather as a designer of high fashion posing serious questions about culture, art, and identity. While her standing as one of the most significant British designers of the period was already established in mainland Europe, America, and Japan, she remained an outsider in Britain itself. It was not until the late 1980s that such high fashion magazines as *Vogue* began to feature her work on a regular basis. Before that time, her clothes were seen mainly in style magazines like *The Face* and *i-D*.

Westwood's first post-McLaren collection, Mini Crini (1986), indicated the direction she was to take, with its juxtaposition of eighteenth-century corsets, the "crini" (abbreviated 1860s-style crinolines), and huge curved wooden platform shoes that laced up the leg and rocked forward as the wearer walked in them. This collection was fashion created to make an impact; Westwood wanted to distinguish her wearers through references to grandeur, royalty, and the Establishment. In 1987 this dramatic aura was tempered by Westwood's ironic wit and her expertise with rich traditional fabrics: Harris tweed, John Smedley fine knits, and wool barathea were enlivened with such flourishes as a tweed crown worn with a tiny cape and crini. "You have a much better life if you wear impressive clothes," she remarked at the time (Jones, p. 57).

Westwood's philosophy, a mixture of contempt for late twentieth-century casual dress and reverence for the eighteenth-century Enlightenment's use of classical references, was encapsulated in her collections from 1988 through 1991 under the broad title Britain Must Go Pagan. These collections, like the punk fashions before them, sought to challenge existing ideas of status, gender, and display. In this case, however, Westwood strove for refinement and education rather than youthful rebel-

lion. She used togas to add grandeur to traditional suiting, and contrasted light, floating chiffons that evoked both ancient Greece and prerevolutionary France with thick Scottish tweeds and corsets photoprinted with Boucher paintings of rural idylls. The clothing that resulted from these combinations relied heavily upon an idealized vision of the past and required its wearers to take on new personae that suggested their awareness of the fine arts.

Westwood appropriated emblems of aristocratic status and elitism for their power and theatricality. She encouraged people to dress up in princess-style coats like those the Queen wore as a child, or in delicate silk coats with rose-strewn edges like an eighteenth-century gentleman's garment. She has continued to draw on these themes of heritage and culture in her subsequent work. While Westwood is always considered inherently British, and has undoubtedly drawn upon her own country's past, she has been equally transfixed by French art and style. This attraction was summarized in her autumn–winter 1993–1994 collection, Anglomania, which harked back to Parisians' fascination with Englishness in the 1780s.

Westwood has consolidated her label since the late 1990s. In 1993 she diversified her collections to appeal to different audiences: the Red Label for ready-to-wear styles, the Gold Label for made-to-measure garments, and in 1998, and the diffusion line Anglomania (a less expensive collection aimed at a younger market), which reinterprets such staples as the pirate shirts from her earlier collections. Along with her perfumes, Boudoir, launched in 1998, and Libertine, launched in 2000, this diversification has enabled her to widen her market and build upon her previous successes.

See also **Extreme Fashions; Gaultier, Jean-Paul; Lagerfeld, Karl; London Fashion; Perfume; Punk; Vogue.**

BIBLIOGRAPHY

Arnold, Rebecca. "Vivienne Westwood's Anglomania." In *The Englishness of English Dress*. Edited by Christopher Breward, Becky Conekin, and Caroline Cox. Oxford: Berg, 2002.

Evans, Caroline, and Minna Thornton. *Women and Fashion: A New Look*. London: Quartet, 1989.

Jones, Dylan. "Royal Flush: Vivienne Westwood." *i-D* (August 1987): 57.

Mulvagh, Jane. *Vivienne Westwood: An Unfashionable Life*. London: HarperCollins, 1998.

Rebecca Arnold

WIGS Wigs are artificial heads of hair, either cunningly concealing baldness or glaringly obvious fashion items in their own right. The Jewish *sheitel*, for instance, is worn for religious reasons where a woman's natural hair is shielded from the gaze of all men who are not her husband. The Talmud teaches that the sight of a woman's

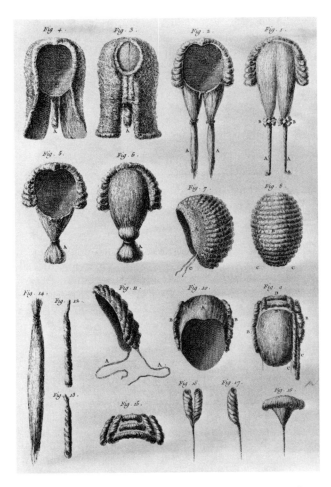

Illustration of eighteenth-century wigs. An engraving from the book *The Wigmaker III* shows the different styles of wigs popular during the eighteenth century. White wigs were most popular and were maintained with plaster of paris and starch. © BETTMANN/CORBIS. REPRODUCED BY PERMISSION.

hair constitutes an arousal or sexual lure; thus a woman hiding her hair helps protect the fabric of Jewish society. The entertainer Elton John's obvious ginger weave is, of course, completely different, worn to retain an air of youth and as a disguise for baldness.

Early Wigs

The earliest Egyptian wigs (c. 2700 B.C.E.) were constructed of human hair, but cheaper substitutes such as palm leaf fibers and wool were more widely used. They denoted rank, social status, and religious piety and were used as protection against the sun while keeping the head free from vermin. Up until the 1500s, hair tended to be dressed as a foundation for headdresses, but by the end of the century hairstyles became higher and more elaborate constructions in which quantities of false hair were used to supplement the wearer's own. Hair was gummed and powdered, false curls and ringlets were in fashion,

and, in some cases, a complete head of false hair called a *perruque*, was worn. The French perruque was colloquially known as a peruke, periwyk, periwig, and eventually the diminutive *wig* by 1675.

Seventeenth and Eighteenth Centuries

The seventeenth century saw the complete resurgence of the wig and it became the height of fashion for both men and women, with many shaving their heads beneath for both comfort and fit. Hair historian Richard Corson sees the ascendance of Louis XIV to the French throne as pivotal. The king supplemented his thinning hair with false pieces until "eventually he agreed to have his head shaved, which was done daily thereafter, and to wear a wig." (Corson, p. 215) By the eighteenth century, those who had the finances had a large wig for formal occasions and a smaller one for use in the home. The larger or more "full bottomed" the wig, the more expensive, thus they were also a mark of class and income and the target of wig snatchers. If one was unable to afford a wig, one made one's natural hair look as wiglike as possible. By the mid-eighteenth century, white was the favored color for wigs, and they were first greased then powdered with flour or a mixture of starch and plaster of paris in the house's wig closet using special bellows. Lucrative trades were constructed around their care and maintenance, such as hairdressing, so-called because hair was dressed rather than cut. Women's wigs were particularly high, powdered, and bejeweled, and the subject of much caricature. To achieve the look, hair was harvested from the heads of the rural working classes. Richard Corson noted that the full wig was disappearing by about 1790, however, "when there was a good deal of natural hair in evidence" (Corson, p. 298).

Nineteenth and Early Twentieth Centuries

After this brief period of respite during the French Revolution, when a natural look and thus natural hair was fashionable, the elaborately dressed hairstyles of the Victorian and Edwardian era demanded a myriad of false pieces or fronts and transformations. As the feminine ideal in the Edwardian era required enormous hairstyles, the natural bulk of the hair was padded out. Lady Violet Harvey recalled,

> Enormous hats often poised on a pyramid of hair, which if not possessed, was supplied, pads under the hair to puff it out were universal and made heads unnaturally big. This entailed innumerable hairpins. My sister and I were amazed to see how much false hair and pads were shed at 'brushing time.' (Hardy, p. 79)

The building of massive hairstyles was dependent on the use of *postiche*, the French word for "added hair" and styles included fringes, fronts, switches, pompadour rolls, and frizettes. All hairdressers had a workroom in which postiches were made for sale wherein the posticheur prepared hair. Hair combings were saved and then drawn through a hackle (a flat board with metal teeth sticking upward) to straighten them. Hair was sorted into bundles ready to be curled into false pieces or curled by a device called a *bigoudis* made of wood or hardened clay. Sections of hair were rolled up on the bigoudis and then dropped into water mixed with soda. After being boiled for several hours the dry hair was then unwound and stored—a method that dates back to the Egyptians. If too little hair was obtained from combings it came from other women. It was a commodity to be exploited and one famous source was the Hair Market at Morlans in the Pyrenees, one of a number of hiring fairs where dealers literally bought the hair from women's heads. Much hair was also imported from Asia Minor, India, China, and Japan and boiled in nitric acid to remove the color and vermin. Men wore wigs, too, but this was to hide baldness.

1920s to Present

With the introduction of the new bobbed hairstyle in the 1920s, wigs fell out of favor and were worn by older women who were not interested in the newly shorn look. Their use returned in the 1950s, but only as a way of having temporary fantasy hairstyles. The most renowned wigmakers and hairdressers in Europe were Maria and Rosy Carita. In black hairdressing, though, the wig was of supreme importance allowing for fashionable styles without undergoing the time-consuming, and in some instances painful, process of straightening. Black stars such as Diana Ross were known for their stylish wig collections in the mid-1960s. It was not really until the late 1960s that wigs underwent a massive renaissance in white hairdressing practices. Rapidly changing fashion, a space-age chic and the vogue for drip-dry clothes in new man-made fabrics led to a vogue for the artificial over the natural. By 1968 there was a wig boom and it is estimated that one-third of all European women wore what hairdressers called a "wig of convenience." Men still tended to wear wigs differently moving further toward the naturalism that many women were rejecting. Until the early 1950s, all wigs were made by hand. However, the invention of the machine-made, washable, nylon and acrylic wig in Hong Kong led to cheap, mass-produced wigs flooding the market. The novelty fashion wig or hairpiece became one of Hong Kong's fastest growing exports and by 1970 the industry employed 24,000 workers. In 1963 British imports of wigs and hairpieces from Hong Kong was worth £200,000 ($350,000); by 1968 it was almost £5 million ($8.78 million). By 1969 around forty percent of wigs were synthetic and the leading companies in wig development were the American firm Dynel and the Japanese Kanekalon, who both used modacrylics to create wigs that were easy to care for and held curl well. In the late twentieth century, many false forms of hair are used and the change from a long to a short hairstyle can be completed at a whim with extensions that have moved from black hairdressing to white hairdressing. Singers such as Beyoncé and Britney Spears use weaves of all styles and colors openly.

See also **Acrylic and Modacrylic Fibers; Caricature and Fashion; Hair Accessories; Hairdressers; Hairstyles; Headdress.**

BIBLIOGRAPHY

Corson, Richard. *Fashions in Hair: The First Five Thousand Years.* London: Peter Owen, 1965.

Cox, Caroline. *Good Hair Days: A History of British Hairstyling.* London: Quartet, 1999.

Hardy, Lady Violet. *As It Was.* London: Christopher Johnson, 1958.

Caroline Cox

WILDE, OSCAR Oscar Wilde (1854–1900) was one of the most prominent and influential figures of the fin de siècle. Playwright, author, journalist, dandy-aesthete, wit, and homosexual social critic, his life and work foreshadowed many of the features of twentieth-century popular and creative subcultures, not least their obsession with the cult of celebrity and the act of self-fashioning. Wilde's constant concern with surface appearance and its power also ensured that his distinctive and constantly changing personal image became a style-template for those who wish to dress in extravagant and innovative ways, from actors and artists to pop stars and clubbers.

Born in Dublin in 1854, Wilde was the second son of a leading surgeon, Dr. William Wilde, and Jane Francesca Speranza Elgee, an Irish nationalist poet and translator. Following the traditional route for a boy of his social background and aptitude, Wilde studied classics at Trinity College, Dublin before winning a scholarship to Magdalen College, Oxford in 1874. In photographs of this period Wilde appeared quite the student "masher" in loudly checked suits and bowler hats. There was little to indicate his later espousal of artistic fashions, though his hair was a little longer than the norm for the 1870s. During his time at Oxford Wilde immersed himself in the ideas of Walter Pater and John Ruskin, honing an acute appreciation of ancient and renaissance art on study visits to Greece and Italy. He graduated with a first class degree in 1878. Having established a reputation as a promising poet with the award of the Newdigate Prize for his poem "Ravenna" in the same year, Wilde launched himself on the London social and literary circuit, where he skillfully adapted the learned theories of Ruskin and Pater for a less erudite audience. His talent for self-publicizing soon earned him notoriety as the "Professor of Aesthetics" in such satirical publications as *Punch*, where his flowing hair, loosely tied collars, floral accessories, and velvet suits formed an obvious target for the caricaturists.

By 1881, Wilde's reputation was such that he found his opinions and appearance lampooned in the Gilbert and Sullivan operetta *Patience*, whose libretto ridiculed the current metropolitan taste for "aesthetic" clothing, interior design, and amateur philosophizing. Wilde turned this critique to his advantage by spearheading a promotional

Oscar Wilde. Wilde was recognized during his time for his literary works as well as for his outrageous fashion sense. Public Domain.

lecture tour for the operetta in the United States and Canada during the following year. Dressed in extreme aesthetic garb—which now included breeches, stockings and pumps, fur-trimmed overcoats, cloaks, and wide-brimmed hats—he delivered talks to American audiences on such subjects as "The House Beautiful." Wilde had his image from this period immortalized in a series of striking portraits by the society photographer Napoleon Sarony that idealized him as a romantic bohemian.

Back in London, Wilde married Constance Lloyd in 1884, setting up an elegant home with her in Chelsea where they raised two sons, Cyril (born 1885) and Vyvyan (born 1886). For the remainder of the 1880s, Wilde had a successful career as a reviewer and editor of the progressive magazine *Woman's World*, while honing his talents as an essayist and writer of exquisite short stories. During this time, he exchanged the long locks and soft velvets of the *Patience* era for dramatic "Neronian" curls—a subversive reference to the pagan moral code of imperial Rome—and urbane Savile Row tailoring, the better to represent himself as the epitome of cosmopolitan stylishness.

By the late 1880s Wilde was beginning to explore the then dangerous territory of male to male desire, both in his personal life and as a subject for artistic expression. He experienced his first homosexual relationship with a Cambridge undergraduate named Robert Ross in 1886, which partly inspired him to write an essay on Shakespeare's sonnets, "The Portrait of Mr. W. H.," exploring the thesis that Shakespeare's creativity was derived from his love for a boy actor. Wilde published the first version of his most explicit investigation of the demimonde in which he was now operating in 1890. *The Picture of Dorian Gray* was not only heavily informed by French decadent literature in terms of style and subject matter, but also contained expressions of the amoral outlook that would bring Wilde into contact in 1891 with his most infamous lover, Lord Alfred Douglas. In tandem with this search for hedonistic sensation, which was the ultimate outcome of the "art for art's sake" philosophy of aestheticism, Wilde was also a supporter of the socialism espoused by William Morris. He wrote his influential essay "The Soul of Man under Socialism" during the same period. In fashion terms, the ideals of socialism found a corollary in the rational Liberty style of "anti-fashion" dressing adopted by Constance Wilde and promoted by Oscar in his journalistic output.

Wilde's popularity as an author of astringent drawing-room comedies for the London stage peaked during the first half of the 1890s. Following the success of *Lady Windermere's Fan* in 1892, he went on to produce *A Woman of No Importance*, *An Ideal Husband*, and *The Importance of Being Earnest*. Besides opening the mores and hypocrisies of contemporary fashionable life to devastating scrutiny, these plays also afforded an opportunity for sophisticated costume designs that influenced the modes of the day. While the drawing-room plays enjoyed the critical acclaim of polite society, Wilde was also developing further his interest in decadent and erotic themes. These were represented most forcefully in Wilde's association with the avant-garde journal *The Yellow Book* and in his play *Salome*, which was refused a license for production in London on the grounds of obscenity.

The tension between Wilde's public and private interests snapped in 1895, when he rashly brought charges of criminal libel against the Marquess of Queensbury, who was enraged by Wilde's liaison with his son, Lord Alfred Douglas. The marquess had been accusing Wilde of "unnatural acts" to all who would listen. On the collapse of the libel trial Wilde was himself arrested for "acts of gross indecency with other male persons," for which he was eventually found guilty and sentenced to two years' imprisonment with hard labor. In 1897, during his incarceration, Wilde authored *De Profundis*, a confessional account of his fall. He published "The Ballad of Reading Gaol," a poem that captured the suffering of prison life, after his release and exile to Paris in 1898. Though the image of Wilde in convict's clothing provided a fitting costume for the final act of a drama that he himself might have written, he never fully recovered from the shame and physical discomfort caused by his punishment, and died a broken man in Paris in 1900. His remains were transferred to the Cimetière du Père-Lachaise in 1909, where they were marked by Jacob Epstein's powerful sculptured angel.

Following decades when his name, works and image were associated in the puritanical Anglo-Saxon world with "unmentionable vices," Wilde's reputation as a gifted writer was gradually restored from the 1950s onwards. Sympathetic film treatments of his life and plays helped bring his sparkling legacy to a new generation, and the counterculture of the 1960s interpreted Wilde as a sexual and aesthetic revolutionary. By the 1980s and 1990s Wilde's complex personality and self-contradictory proclamations made him once again the focus of intense study and speculation. For the fashion theorist and historian, Wilde's life and work undoubtedly offer a rich seam of material for further research.

See also **Aesthetic Dress; Dandyism; Fashion and Homosexuality; Fashion and Identity; Gender, Dress, and Fashion; Savile Row; Theatrical Costume.**

BIBLIOGRAPHY

Cohen, Ed. *Talk on the Wilde Side: Toward A Genealogy of a Discourse on Male Sexualities.* London: Routledge, 1993. An examination of the relevance of Wilde's trial to modern understandings of homosexual identities.

Ellmann, Richard. *Oscar Wilde.* London: Hamish Hamilton, 1987. The most authoritative and comprehensive biography of Wilde published to date.

Holland, Merlin. *The Wilde Album.* London: Fourth Estate Limited, 1997. An excellent visual resource for images of Wilde and his milieu.

Kaplan, Joel, and Sheila Stowell. *Theatre and Fashion: Oscar Wilde to the Suffragettes.* Cambridge, U.K.: Cambridge University Press, 1994. An innovative study of the relationship between the theater and sartorial culture in the 1890s.

Sinfield, Alan. *The Wilde Century: Effeminacy, Oscar Wilde and the Queer Movement.* London: Cassell, 1994. A sophisticated account of the political and theoretical afterlife of Wilde in the twentieth century.

Sloan, John. *Oscar Wilde.* Oxford, U.K.: Oxford University Press, 2003. A useful summary of the social and literary contexts of Wilde's life and work.

Christopher Breward

WINDBREAKER The windbreaker, or anorak, otherwise known as a windcheater in Great Britain, is a short, close-fitting garment with a hood, designed for the upper part of the body to give protection from the wind. The windbreaker, worn by men and women alike, is to casual dressing what the overcoat is to formal dress.

History

The windbreaker first became popular as an item of informal outerwear in the 1970s, but its history can be traced back almost 500 years. It is similar to, and descended from, the parkas worn by Inuits in arctic conditions. In fact, the word "anorak" is derived from the Danish interpretation of the Inuit word *annoraaq.*

In one version, the Inuit parka was made of two animal skins (either seal or caribou) sandwiched together, with the skin side of each facing outward and the hair side facing inward to trap warm air and retain it for insulation purposes. Although it was not a rain garment as such, it was generally waterproofed, using seal gut until other methods were introduced during the nineteenth century. These parkas were adapted by Western polar explorers in the late nineteenth and early twentieth centuries, and modified versions entered the twentieth-century sports wardrobe. Parkas became standard wear for skiing and other winter sports, and gradually were adopted for ordinary outdoor use in the winter. After World War II, nylon and other artificial-fiber textiles replaced animal skins in the production of parkas, and advances in the development of waterproof fabrics and efficient insulating materials led to the production of parkas that were thinner and less bulky than older versions. During the 1970s, anoraks and other forms of casual jackets grew in popularity among younger men searching for outerwear that was both functional and fashionable.

Modern windbreakers are usually made from nylon, poly-cotton, or nylon/cotton mixes. These fabrics may be rubberized, oiled, or treated with other waterproofing finishes; at the more expensive end of the market, the garments are designed with stormproof taping on all seams to make them impenetrable to the rain. The modern version is also cut slightly longer to cover the buttocks; cuffs are elasticized and pockets are often slanted for ease of entry, and are at hip level. The hood should fold down, close with a drawstring, and either fit into the collar or be detachable.

The windbreaker has had a significant impact on men's fashions. The rise of sportswear during the 1970s coincided with a boom in spectator sports, such as both soccer (known as football in Europe) and American football. Fans who filled stadiums in cold weather wanted good-looking protection from the elements, and numerous designers offered versions of the windbreaker to fill that demand. In the early twenty-first century, nearly every sportswear and casual-wear company has a version of a windbreaker in its collection. Most are produced to keep the wearer warm during sporting activities such as golf, boating, football, or tennis. More significantly, the windbreaker has taken the place of raincoats and overcoats in most younger men's wardrobes.

See also **Outerwear; Parka.**

BIBLIOGRAPHY

Amies, Hardy. *A, B, C of Men's Fashion.* London: Cahill and Co. Ltd., 1964.

Byrde, Penelope. *The Male Image: Men's Fashion in England 1300–1970.* London: B. T. Batsford, Ltd., 1979.

Chenoune, Farid. *A History of Men's Fashion*. Paris: Flammarion, 1993.

De Marley, Diana, *Fashion For Men: An Illustrated History*. London: B. T. Batsford, Ltd., 1985.

Keers, Paul. *A Gentleman's Wardrobe*. London: Weidenfield and Nicolson, 1987.

Roetzel, Bernhard. *Gentleman: A Timeless Fashion*. Cologne, Germany: Konemann, 1999.

Schoeffler, O. E., and William Gale. *Esquire's Encyclopedia of 20th Century Men's Fashions*. New York: McGraw-Hill, 1973.

Williams-Mitchell, Christobel. *Dressed for the Job: The Story of Occupational Costume*. Poole, England: Blandford Press, 1982.

Tom Greatrex

WINDOW DISPLAYS The eighteenth and early nineteenth centuries saw an evolution in shopping spurred by a faster turnover of manufactured "fashionable" goods and an increase in department stores selling them. These shops pioneered new techniques of window display. Rather than piling their stock up—as had been common in markets and bazaars—they sold goods in mannered and self-conscious window displays, intended to sell nonessential goods.

In cities, where competition was strongest, stores had larger windows and more frequently changing displays. A visitor to London in 1786 wrote of "A cunning device for showing women's materials whether they are silks, chintzes, or muslins, they hang down in folds behind the fine high windows so that the effect of this and that material, as it would be in the ordinary folds of a woman's dress, can be studied" (Adburgham, p. 6). This comment suggests that there was an awareness of sophisticated marketing techniques and a developing vocabulary for display in the late eighteenth century, which would be developed but not improved upon by later generations.

By the nineteenth century the small store with glass windows and some form of gas lighting dominated the main street. The arrival of department stores in the 1850s—multistoried buildings that utilized plate glass in long, uninterrupted window displays—would herald a new display aesthetic. Fashion goods began to be displayed in lifelike room settings, with mannequins. Known as "open displays," these windows relied on themes and narratives, rather than sheer quantity of goods, for visual impact. The window display was now contextualizing goods, giving them precise domestic or cultural settings and imparting qualities other than practicality and price. In these displays the fixtures, stands, and mannequins, came into their own. Unfashionable stock goods continued to be displayed as though they were on a market stall—piled high or stacked in rows in the windows in "massed displays."

Professionalization of Display Trade

These open displays were developed first in America, where the professionalization of the display trade had begun in the late nineteenth century. The display technocrat L. Frank Baum (who would later write *The Wizard of Oz*) began the first journal aimed at the display trade—*The Show Window* in 1897—and founded the National Association of Window Trimmers in 1898, which did much to raise the status of window trimmer to that of display manager. America had a large number of colleges teaching commercial design based upon the work of pioneering consumer psychologist Walter Dill-Scott, author of *Psychology of Advertising in* 1908. His theories for appealing to hidden desires of customers using particular colors, images, and formations in advertising layouts were applied to window display though numerous handbooks and journals detailing the creation of the "selling shop window."

This approach was brought over to England by Gordon Selfridge (a friend of L. Frank Baum) and his display manager, Ernst Goldsman. Both men had worked at Marshall Fields department store in Chicago in the 1890s, where Selfridge had introduced radical and innovative methods of display and marketing, starting the first window displays and display department. Selfridge's department store in London opened in 1909 with the longest window facade ever seen in Britain. The store achieved instant fame for its window displays: "They gaped in amazement at the American-style window-dressing with its life-like scenes and with wax models arranged in realistic poses" (Honeycombe p. 205). Goldsman was integral to the professionalization of the British display trade, founding the National Association of British Display Men in 1919. Such display organizations disseminated new ideas via lectures, display fairs, and their journals.

Art and Display

In Germany the design reform theories taught at the Deutsche Werkbund and later the Reimann School, in the first decades of the twentieth century, led to a new style of Modernist window display. The objects and fixtures were reduced to a bare minimum and arranged on strong geometric lines. These Modernist display ideals were disseminated when many window display managers left Germany for political reasons in the first decades of the twentieth century. The émigré designer Frederick Kiesler, for instance, was a Romanian architect, designer, and member of the De Stijl group who went to America in 1926. By 1928 he was working designing Modernist window displays at Saks and authoring the influential book *Contemporary Art Applied to the Store and Its Display* in 1929.

The photographer Eugène Atget had been documenting Parisian shop windows since the 1890s, and these images had been influential for succeeding generations of artists, particularly the Surrealists. Mass cultures, in-

Window shopping in Kuwait. First seen in eighteenth century Europe, window displays appeal to passersby in shopping malls worldwide. © Ed Kashi/Corbis. Reproduced by permission.

cluding window display, had become subject matter for artists such as Léger, Max Ernst, and Salvador Dali. Both Kiesler and Dali used the window itself as a frame in their commercial display work and in England commercial designers like Misha Black, Edward McKnight Kauffer, and Tom Eckersley also worked in display.

Hollywood

The extreme modernist displays would, for the most part, be confined to small designer boutiques. The rest of the retail industry was looking toward America and the film industry for inspiration. There was an obvious corollary between the brightly lit shop window display and the cinema screen and the new and "showy" style of window display developed in America. In the 1930s these displays drew on contained visual references from films and advertising to create windows that looked like stills from films: brightly lit, full of oversized props, shiny fixtures, and film-star-like mannequins. Film and magazine promotional "tie-in" displays became popular. Sometimes the shops were selling fashions copied from the film, but often these displays would only loosely link the goods in the window with the film, hoping that the merchandise would sell if it were associated with the glamour of Hol-

lywood. Advertising display agencies, which (on both sides of the Atlantic) mass-produced display campaigns for branded goods, were particularly well placed to take advantage of the mass appeal of film tie-ins.

World War II halted the progress of window display in Europe. As stores reopened for business after the war their windows were old fashioned and empty of goods. American display remained strong but uninspired. It was not until the 1960s, when display again became subject matter for artists such as Claes Oldenburg, Roy Lichtenstein, and Andy Warhol—particularly the bright spaces of food supermarkets—that creativity was revived. Warhol, who had begun his career in display, would combine the two when he introduced his pop paintings into windows commissioned by Bonwit Teller. American department stores would carry the creative banner of window display through much of the late twentieth century, working with artists such as Jasper Johns and Robert Rauschenberg.

Although some large stores continue to have display departments, shop windows across the world have been given over to the homogenous visual merchandising campaigns of the big brand names, often containing only tailor's dummies and photographic backdrops. It is the designer boutique that is pioneering truly creative work in the beginning of the twenty-first century. Shops such Prada and Comme des Garçons prove that the window display can still offer enough beauty, theatre, and spectacle to halt a passerby.

See also **Department Store; Mannequins; Shopping.**

BIBLIOGRAPHY
Adburgham, Alison. *Shops and Shopping, 1800–1914.* London: Allen and Unwin, 1964.

Honeycombe, Gordon Selfridge. *Seventy-five Years: The Story of the Store, 1909–1984.* London: Gordon Park Lane Press, 1984.

Kiesler, Frederick. *Contemporary Art Applied to the Store and Its Display.* London: Pitman and Sons, 1930.

Leach, William. *Land of Desire.* New York: Pantheon Books, 1993.

Marcus, Leonard S. *The American Store Window.* New York: Whitney Library of Design, 1978.

Walsh, Claire. "Shop Design and the Display of Goods in Eighteenth-Century London." *Journal of Design History* 8, no. 3 (1995): 157–176.

Ward, Janet. *Weimar Surfaces: Urban Visual Culture in 1920s Germany.* Berkeley: University of California Press, 2001.

Jane Audas

WINDSOR, DUKE AND DUCHESS OF If Bettina Zilkha's International Best Dressed List extended to couples, the Duke and Duchess of Windsor would be its king and queen. As individuals, their influence on twentieth century fashion was considerable, but combined it was unassailable. From the 1930s to the 1960s, the influence they exercised was all the more apparent for the media attention that magnified their sway on the public's imagination.

Biography
The Duke of Windsor was born Prince Edward of York on 23 June 1894. With the death of his grandfather, King Edward VII in 1910, his father was crowned King George V. Upon his father's accession, Prince Edward of York became Duke Edward of Cornwall, and on his sixteenth birthday, Prince Edward of Wales.

Bessie Wallis Warfield, who was to become the Duchess of Windsor, was born in Pennsylvania on 19 June 1896. Her upbringing, by her own admission, was modest and unexceptional. When she met Prince Edward of Wales for the first time around 1930, she had been married twice. Her first husband was Earl Winfield Spencer Jr., and her second was Ernest Aldrich Simpson, an American living in London.

It is generally accepted that the Prince of Wales and Mrs. Simpson began their affair in 1934. Following the death of King George V, the prince was crowned King Edward VIII on 20 January 1936. That summer, he took Mrs. Simpson on a yachting holiday in the Eastern Mediterranean. Press coverage of the trip created a scandal, complicating the king's decision to marry Mrs. Simpson. Parliament refused the king's marriage request on the grounds of Mrs. Simpson's status as a twice-divorced foreign commoner. A "Constitutional Crisis" ensued, which resulted in the king's abdication on 11 December 1936. In his abdication speech he explained, "You must believe me when I tell you that I have found it impossible to carry out the heavy burden of responsibility and discharge my duty as King as I would wish to do, without the support of the woman I love" (Ziegler, p. 331).

Upon his abdication, he became His Royal Highness the Duke of Windsor, and with his marriage to Mrs. Simpson on 3 June 1937, she became the Duchess of Windsor. The title Her Royal Highness, however, was never conferred upon her. Apart from spending time in the Bahamas during World War II, the Duke and Duchess of Windsor remained in exile in France for the rest of their lives. The duke died on 18 May 1972, while the duchess, who was last seen in public in 1975, died on 24 April 1986.

The Duke: Trend Setter
More than any other individual, the Duke of Windsor was responsible for a transformation of men's dress in the twentieth century. His personal preference for rejecting the received notions of Victorian and Edwardian "proprieties" not only influenced the men of his generation, but also—as Chanel is credited for having done with women—created a modern paradigm that persists to this day. What Nicholas Lawford said of him in the 1930s remained true of the Duke all his life, "In a world where men tend to look more and more alike, he seems more than ever endowed with the capacity to look like no one else" (Menkes, p. 95).

The Duke of Windsor preferred comfortable clothes that allowed freedom of movement, a style that he described as "dress soft" (The Duke of Windsor, 1960, p. 110). In the 1930s, he was one of the first men to wear unlined, unstructured jackets. From 1919–1959, these were made for him by Frederick Scholte, a Dutch-born, London-based tailor who disapproved of any form of exaggeration in the style of a jacket. As the duke commented in *A Family Album*, his treatise on style written in 1960, "Scholte had rigid standards concerning the perfect balance of proportions between shoulders and waist in the cut of a coat to clothe the masculine torso" (The Duke of Windsor, 1960, p. 99). The sleeves of the duke's jackets were usually adorned with four buttons, and he preferred welted pockets rather than pocket flaps.

Before World War II, Forster and Son in London tailored the duke's trousers. "I never had a pair of trousers made by Scholte," the duke explained. "I disliked the cut of them; they were made, as English trousers usually are, to be worn with braces high above the waist. So preferring as I did to wear a belt rather than braces with trousers, in the American style, I invariably had them made by another tailor" (The Duke of Windsor, 1960, p. 103). For every jacket the duke had made, two pairs of trousers were produced. These he wore in strict rotation. In 1934, along with his brother, the Duke of York, and his cousin, Lord Louis Mountbatten, he replaced the conventional button flies with zip flies. A heavy smoker all his life, the duke instructed Forster and Son to make his trousers with a slightly wider left pocket with no fastening, allowing him easy access to his cigarette case, which he always carried in his left pocket. The duke preferred trousers with cuffs or turn-ups. With the adoption of rationing restrictions in Britain during World War II, which banned turn-ups, he placed all subsequent orders with H. Harris, a tailor based in New York.

The London firm of Peal and Co. made the duke's shoes, Lock and Co. his hats, and Hawes and Curtis his shirts and ties. He favored shirts with soft, unstarched cuffs and collars and wore his ties, which he ordered with thick inner linings, with a wide "four-in-hand" knot. Despite popular opinion, the Duke of Windsor did not, in fact, wear a style known as the "Windsor knot." As he explains, "The so-called 'Windsor knot,' was I believe regulation wear for G.I.s during the war, when American college boys adopted it too. But in fact I was in no way responsible for this. The knot to which the Americans gave my name was a double knot in a narrow tie—a "Slim Jim" as it is sometimes called" (The Duke of Windsor, 1960, p. 116).

As a keen sportsman, the Duke of Windsor paid particular attention to his sporting attire. In the 1920s, he popularized the wearing of plus fours, which became his standard dress for hunting and sporting pursuits. Disliking the traditional style with fastenings below the knees, he developed a loose-fitting version with a soft cotton lining, which he wore slightly lower than the traditional four inches below the knee. When playing golf, he would wear them with brightly colored Argyle socks and Fair Isle sweaters. Commenting on the Prince at play, Lawford noted, "He was quite loud in the way he mixed his checks, but he represented style to his generation" (Menkes, p. 102).

Like his sportswear, the duke's highland dress expressed his theatrical and audacious use of color, pattern and texture. He wore kilts, often made by Chalmers of Oban or William Anderson and Sons in Scotland, in casual settings, usually at "The Mill," the Windsor's weekend retreat just outside Paris. These he would wear with a leather sporran, in which he would store his cigarettes. The duke preferred "tartans which I have the right to wear—Royal Stuart, Hunting Stuart, Rothesay, Lord of the Isles, Balmoral" (The Duke of Windsor, 1960,

The Duchess of Windsor, 1951. The duchess was known to have bought entire collections from a couture designer. Pictured here, she wears a flowered and beaded strapless Dior ball gown. © Condé Nast Archive/Corbis. Reproduced by permission.

p. 128). In *A Family Album*, the duke describes wearing a suit of Rothesay hunting tartan, originally belonging to his father, that triggered a vogue for tartan in the 1950s,

> I happened to wear it one evening for dinner at La Croe near Antibes, where the Duchess and I lived for a while after the last war. One of our guests mentioned the fact to a friend in the men's fashion trade, who immediately cabled the news to America. Within a few months tartan had become a popular material for every sort of masculine garment, from dinner jackets and cummerbunds to swimming-trunks and beach shorts. Later the craze even extended to luggage (The Duke of Windsor, p. 129).

One of the Duke of Windsor's most notable sartorial innovations was the introduction, in the 1920s, of the midnight blue evening suit, an alternative to the traditional black evening suit. Wanting to enhance his well-dressed standing in the popular press as well as soften men's formal wear, he explained,

> I was in fact 'produced' as a leader of fashion, with the clothiers as my showmen and the world as my audience. The middle-man in this process was the photographer, employed not only by the Press but by the trade, whose task it was to photograph me on every possible occasion, public or private, with an especial eye for what I happened to be wearing (The Duke of Windsor, 1960, p. 114).

The Prince of Wales understood that in black and white photography, unlike black, midnight blue allowed the subtle details of tailoring, such as lapels, buttons, and pockets, to become more apparent.

It is through these photographs that the Duke of Windsor influenced fashionable men of his generation, and, indeed, continues to influence fashionable men today. Through their designs, Ralph Lauren, Paul Smith, Sean John Combes, and a host of other men's wear designers pay homage to the Duke of Windsor's witty and idiosyncratic approach to self-presentation. As Diana Vreeland (1906–1989), editor of *Harper's Bazaar* and *Vogue*, said of him, "Did he have style? The Duke of Windsor had style in every buckle of his kilt, every check of his country suits" (Menkes, p. 126).

The Duchess: Trend Follower

Unlike the Duke of Windsor's innate sense of style, the Duchess of Windsor's self-presentation, as Suzy Menkes, fashion editor for the International Herald Tribune, has observed, was "a product of rigorous effort rather than inherited or natural taste" (p. 95). She was a picture of elegance, preferring simple, tailored clothes with no superfluous details or decoration. She remained on the International Best Dressed List for more than forty years, and upon her death in 1986, Elle commented, "She elevated sobriety to an art form" (Menkes, p. 95).

Being immaculate was the hallmark of the Duchess of Windsor's personal style. As Cecil Beaton (1904–1980), a British portrait photographer, commented, "She reminds one of the neatest, newest luggage, and is as compact as a Vuitton travelling-case" (Beaton, p. 27). Beaton's first impression of the Duchess, formed in 1930 before she had acquired her title, was less than favorable. He recalled her as "brawny and raw-boned in her sapphire blue velvet" (Tapert and Edkins, p. 92). Four years later, however, when they met again, the Duchess had changed. Beaton commented, "I liked her immensely. I found her bright and witty, improved in looks and chic" (Tapert and Edkins, p. 92). Lady Mendl (Elsie de Wolfe), who remained the Duchess of Windsor's friend and mentor throughout her life, was largely responsible for Mrs. Simpson's transformation. It was Lady Mendl who in-

troduced her to Mainbocher, who was to dress her until he retired in 1971. As Vreeland commented, "Mainbocher was responsible for the Duchess's wonderful simplicity and dash" (Menkes, p. 98).

Mainbocher was to make the Duchess of Windsor's wedding ensemble and trousseau. The wedding ensemble included a simple, floor-length dress and matching long-sleeved jacket in "Wallis Blue" silk crepe. The color was specially developed by Mainbocher to equal that of the Duchess of Windsor's eyes. The dress complemented the duchess's style of fashion austerity, being modest but not prudish. Shortly after her marriage, copies of the dress were sold at retailers for a small fraction of the original's cost, from $25 at Benwit Teller to a mere $8.90 at Klein's cash-and-carry. Within a few months, the "Wally" dress made its way to the United States, where it was available from department stores in a variety of styles, colors, and materials.

Cecil Beaton became the Duchess of Windsor's unofficial photographer. In this position, he was able to play an important role in the construction and depiction of her public image. Beaton, in fact, took photographs of the royal wedding the day before the actual ceremony. Several weeks before the marriage, he also took a series of famous photographs of the Duchess of Windsor wearing models from Elsa Schiaparelli's Spring/Summer 1937 collection, including the legendary "Lobster Dress" with a print designed by Salvador Dalí. Like Mainbocher's designs, Schiaparelli's clothes appealed to the Duchess of Windsor's rigorous, restrained aesthetic. She liked Schiaparelli's evening suits, in particular, and made them her trademark. Indeed, the duchess was at her most elegant in smart, impeccably tailored suits, a look that Cecil Beaton referred to as her "trim messenger-boy's suits" (Menkes, p. 102).

While the Duchess of Windsor's daywear tended to be plain and simple, her evening wear revealed a more feminine, romantic sensibility. As Danielle Porthault of Yves Saint Laurent commented, "Her Royal Highness's style was sobriety by day and fantasy and originality at night" (Menkes, p. 116). During the 1930s, the Duchess of Windsor favored Mainbocher, Schiaparelli, and Vionnet, while after World War II she preferred Dior, Givenchy, and Yves Saint Laurent. These she would wear with shoes by Roger Vivier, who began working for the House of Dior in 1953. According to Vreeland, one of the Duchess of Windsor's many sartorial innovations was the short evening dress.

The Duchess of Windsor's recipe of "sobriety by day and fantasy at night" included ingredients of wit and irony, often expressed in her exuberant use of jewelry. Her two favorite jewelers, Cartier and Van Cleef and Arpels, competed with each other to provide the Duchess with ever more lavish and innovative creations. The Duchess of Windsor's simple day suits proved the perfect backdrop for her flamboyant broaches, bracelets, earrings and necklaces, as did her more romantic confections worn at night. One of her more memorable pieces of jewelry was a bracelet made from jeweled crosses, which she wore at her wedding. Each cross represented "a stepping stone in their love story, and a cross they had to bear" (Menkes, p. 151).

The Duchess of Windsor once told her friend and confidante Elsa Maxwell, "My husband gave up everything for me … I'm not a beautiful woman. I'm nothing to look at, so the only thing I can do is dress better than anyone else" (Tapert and Edkins, p. 97). But she did much more than this. Not only did she dress to enhance the idiosyncrasies of her physicality, enhanced by her coiffure by Alexandre, but she dressed with a consciousness of how her image would be received by both the press and public. As Vreeland observed, "She had a position and dressed to it" (Menkes, p. 138). In this respect, she had a lasting influence on royal women and stateswomen alike, perhaps most notably Jacqueline Kennedy and Diana, Princess of Wales.

See also **Diana, Princess of Wales; Fashion Icons; Fashion Magazines; Formal Wear, Men's; Mainbocher; Neckties and Neckwear; Royal and Aristocratic Dress; Schiaparelli, Elsa; Tartan.**

BIBLIOGRAPHY

Beaton, Cecil. *Cecil Beaton's Scrapbook.* New York: Charles Scribner's Sons, 1937.

Duchess of Windsor. *The Heart Has Its Reasons.* New York: D. McKay Company, 1956.

Duke of Windsor. *A King's Story.* New York: Putnam, 1951.

———. *A Family Album.* London: Cassell, 1960.

Menkes, Suzy. 1988. *The Windsor Style.* Topsfield, Mass.: Salem House Publishers, 1988.

Sothebys. *The Duke and Duchess of Windsor.* New York: Sothebys, 1997.

Tapert, Annette, and Diana Edkins. *The Power of Style: The Women Who Defined the Art of Living Well.* New York: Crown, 1994.

Ziegler, Philip. *King Edward VIII.* London: Collins, 1990.

Andrew Bolton

WOMEN'S WEAR DAILY Its own motto is "the retailer's daily newspaper," but within the fashion industry, *Women's Wear Daily* is widely referred to as "the bible of the business." It is far more than just a trade publication serving an industry. With its unique mix of hard business, financial stories, society gossip, and biting fashion reviews, *WWD* (as it is commonly known) is a high-impact cultural voice.

Women's Wear first appeared as a supplement to the 21 May 1910 edition of the *Daily Trade Record*, a broadsheet that tracked the burgeoning, if rather dry, textiles imports and apparel manufacturing businesses. Both were products of Fairchild Publications, started by Edmund Wade (E.W.) Fairchild and his brother Louis E. Fairchild But with department stores booming and women's fashion becoming a business unto itself, it seemed obvious to the Fairchilds that the *Women's Wear* supplement could succeed as a stand-alone publication. "There is probably no other line of human endeavor in which there is so much change as in the product that womankind wears," opined an editorial in one of the first editions. *Women's Wear* became a daily on 15 July 1910, publishing every day but Sunday and selling for 15 cents.

The next year, E. W. Fairchild opened a Paris bureau, since that city's houses basically dictated the course of fashion; correspondents would wire stories about the trends in French fashion, such as the "universally repudiated hobble skirt," or Paul Poiret's scandalous Turkish trousers of 1913. In 1912, one of the paper's Paris correspondents, Edith L. Rosenbaum, happened to be on the maiden voyage of the Titanic; she survived and gave *Women's Wear* a version of the tragedy that noted which prominent retailers were on the ship (Isidore Straus, a founder of Abraham & Straus, perished with his wife) and what some of the survivors wore in the lifeboats ("Lady Duff-Gordon made her escape in a very charming lavender bathrobe").

The paper by then was based at 822 Broadway and had three Linotype machines dedicated to rolling out its copies. In 1927, Fairchild added the "Daily" to its name. Although the paper acknowledged world events, high society, Hollywood movies, and the like, its content was always within the context of the fashion industry. Coverage was always focused on business, not personalities. *WWD* adopted the mind-set of its readers slavishly following Paris designers like Christian Dior, Cristóbal Balenciaga, and Coco Chanel while essentially ignoring homegrown talents. It was first and foremost a trade paper, with a fairly narrow, albeit loyal and influential readership.

The second generation took over in 1948 when Louis E. Fairchild passed the president's title to his nephew, Louis W. But it wasn't until the charismatic, confident, worldly Princeton-educated John B. Fairchild (son of Louis W.) arrived in 1960, after a stint in the Paris office, that *WWD* shook off its old identity as a niche-market trade paper and became a cultural chronicler crackling with opinion. "It was as if a tornado hit 7 East 12th Street," recalled fashion journalist Etta Froio, then just starting her *WWD* career as a market editor. "In just a few weeks, he swept away every trace of the musty, stodgy newspaper we had known and set out to create a new era of style and status."

During his time in Paris, Fairchild had decided that the most interesting thing about fashion wasn't the clothes as much as the people who made and wore them. He began establishing the new tone of *WWD* there, as he befriended Coco Chanel, Christian Dior, Yves Saint Laurent, Pierre Bergé, and Pierre Cardin, among others.

Once back in New York, he expanded that vision to include the entire industry. Before John B., *WWD* had more or less ignored society, except as it pertained to the fashion business. Now, the paper began running on-the-street pictures of chic socialites and interviews with sexy young starlets like Julie Christie, Brigitte Bardot, Vanessa Redgrave, Jane Fonda, and Faye Dunaway. Even counterculture artists, rock stars, and scandalous trends (Andy Warhol, Patti Smith, braless women, the invasion of blue jeans), barely acknowledged in the mainstream press, were investigated and reported on.

Fairchild and *WWD* were instrumental in shifting the world's attention to the merits of American designers, giving their clothes and their personal style more attention than either had ever received. He covered designers such as Halston, Perry Ellis, Oscar de la Renta, and Calvin Klein as much for their social lives as for their collections. "We became fascinated with the personalities of the business executives and the social world," said John B. Fairchild in an interview he gave for *WWD*'s 90th Anniversary edition in 2001. "We were looking for people who made the world tick. That's what it has to be about. All the other coverage then was just endless descriptions of clothes. Nothing to me is more boring than that!" This new approach to fashion was seen in the paper's spin-off magazine *W*, founded in 1972, which combines edgy coverage of fashion with features such as celebrity interviews and news of society events.

When it came to modern women, Fairchild was particularly obsessed with Jacqueline Kennedy Onassis, sending photographers to wait outside restaurants like La Grenouille and Le Cote Basque where she regularly lunched. He also tracked chic young socialites like Babe Paley, Slim Keith, and CZ Guest. He had his editors write stinging reviews of collections that sometimes infuriated the designers (and occasionally resulted in banishment, which never lasted more than a season) but always delighted the readers. The phrases *WWD* invented to describe this gilded group have entered the common lexicon: the BPs (beautiful people), Nouvelle Society, Social Cyclones, Walkers (the men who escort Social Cyclones to events), and HotPants, coined in 1970 to describe indecently short shorts. The paper's power grew to the point that its decrees could make a trend or a designer; *Time* magazine put Fairchild on the cover of its 14 September 1970 issue, labeling him "The Man Behind Midi Mania."

WWD courted controversy, frequently needling designers—its review of Saint Laurent's first collection for Dior said the dresses looked like toothpaste tubes on top of a brioche—and occasionally banishing them from the pages. The most famous example was an estrangement lasting for several years between the paper and Geoffrey Beene. Under John B. Fairchild's editorship, *WWD* added theater, restaurant and movie reviews, lengthy interviews with celebrities such as Truman Capote, Barbra Streisand, Alfred Hitchcock, and Cassius Clay (pre-Muhammad Ali), and even coverage of the social doings of the White House. The paper's Washington coverage prompted Henry Kissinger to complain that it was giving his active social life too much attention. *WWD* became a must-read not just for retail and business executives, but also for socialites, public-relations people, talent agents, and even politicians.

A new round of conspicuous consumption in the 1980s fit perfectly with the paper's exuberant coverage of the worlds of fashion and society. *WWD* gave the Reagan White House ample play. Couture came back, exemplified by Christian Lacroix's bubble dress and the swept-up hairdo, and a new generation of celebrities designed and wore the high-end fashions of the decade. Designer Carolyne Roehm, for example, was married to the wealthy Henry Kravitz, and appeared in the pages of *WWD* both as a designer and a socialite. The recession of the late 1990s that accompanied the bursting of the dot-com bubble was like a morning-after hangover after the long party of the 1980s and early 1990s. The pages of *WWD* began to fill with news of liquidations and reorganizations in the fashion industry, and the flight of manufacturing to Asia and the developing world. But the paper remained the must-read publication for everyone connected with the world of fashion.

In 1968, the family decided to sell Fairchild Publications (which had grown to include trade papers dedicated to footwear, home furnishings, even electronics) to Capital Cities Broadcasting, thus becoming part of a publicly owned media empire. In 1986 *WWD* editors retired their typewriters and moved into the computer age. In 1991, Fairchild Publications moved from its woefully outdated Greenwich Village headquarters to modern offices in a more convenient, if less attractive, neighborhood across the street from the Empire State Building. John B. Fairchild retired in 1997 at age 70, naming Patrick McCarthy to be his successor as chairman and editorial director of Fairchild Publications. After a series of media mergers and acquisitions that gave Fairchild Publications various corporate parents in the 1980s and 1990s, the company was acquired in 1999 by Advance Publications Inc., the publishing empire (and publishers of *Vogue*), owned by the Newhouse family.

WWD remains one of the most influential voices in the world of fashion. It is famous as a sort of prep school for fashion journalists. Its alumni are on the masthead of almost every American consumer magazine, from *Condé Nast Traveller* to *Time*, although the concentration is heaviest, naturally, at fashion magazines. *New York Times* theater critic Ben Brantley and Bernadine Morris worked at *WWD*, as did former CNN correspondent Elsa Klensch, *Vogue* editor-at-large André Leon Talley, photographer Bill Cunningham, former French *Vogue* editor Joan Juliet Buck, and even Calvin Klein, who had a brief, unsuccessful stint as a copy boy in 1961.

See also **Fashion Advertising; Fashion Editors; Fashion Icons; Fashion Industry; Fashion Journalism; Fashion Magazines; Fashion Photography.**

BIBLIOGRAPHY

Agins, Teri. *The End of Fashion: How Marketing Changed the Clothing Business Forever.* New York: Quill, 2000.

Kelly, Katie. *The Wonderful World of Women's Wear Daily.* New York: Saturday Review Press, 1972.

Janet Ozzard

WOOL Wool is one of the oldest textile fibers used by humans. The term wool is generally used to describe fiber obtained from sheep or lambs. Legally the hair of a few other animals can also be called wool because its qualities are similar to sheep's wool. The United States government allows the fiber from alpaca, camel, llama, vicuña, Cashmere goat, and Angora goat to be labeled as wool, but these can also be labeled by their own fiber names.

Sheep were first domesticated in Central Asia about 10,000 years ago to provide a ready source of meat, milk, and hides for clothing. As humans worked with the hair from the sheep hides, they found that twisting thin strands of wool fiber together forms a continuous length of yarn. As time went on, they discovered that interlacing the yarn would form a fabric. Once yarn and fabric production were part of the knowledge base of humans, fabric became a second skin. The oldest surviving fragments of wool cloth were found in Egypt and date between 4000 and 3400 B.C.E.

The early, wild species of sheep had a two-layer coat. The coat closest to the body was a short wool undercoat of fine, downy fiber. This was protected by long, coarse

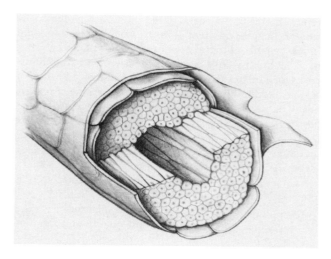

Cross section of a wool fiber. A wool fiber is made up of three layers: the cuticle, an outer layer of overlapping scales; the cortex which provides the bulk of the fiber; and the medulla, when present, is found in the middle of the cortex, and is a latticework of air-filled cells. REPRINTED WITH PERMISSION FROM *IN SHEEP'S CLOTHING* BY NOLA FOURNIER AND JANE FOURNIER. PUBLISHED BY INTERWEAVE PRESS, LOVELAND, COLORADO.

and straight guard hair. Since some sheep had better-quality fiber than others, people selected sheep for breeding that provided more undercoat and less guard hair. In the early 2000s, the majority of sheep growing wool for clothing produce mainly undercoat fiber.

A wool fiber is made up of three layers: the cuticle, cortex, and medulla. The cuticle is the outer layer of overlapping scales that comprises about 10 percent of the fiber. The cortex provides the bulk of the fiber, about 90 percent, and is composed of millions of long cells held together by a strong natural binding material. The cortex has two types of cells that behave differently to give wool fiber the characteristic "crimp" or waviness when a fiber is viewed from the side. The medulla, when present, is found in the middle of the cortex, and is a latticework of air-filled cells. A fiber with a large medulla is weak and doesn't dye easily.

Wool Production

Shearing. When human beings first used wool fiber, they gathered fiber that was shed from the sheep during their spring molt. As humans domesticated the sheep, they bred them to resist shedding so that the wool could be removed when it was convenient. In the early twenty-first century, the first step in wool production is removing the wool from the sheep by shearing (cutting). Once off the animal, the fleece of one sheep is bundled together with the clean side in.

Grading and sorting. Each fleece is examined, graded, and sorted. The tangled and dirty parts of the fleece are

TEASING OUT THE MEANING OF WOOL FIBER TERMS

Hair vs. Wool: Technically, hair differs from wool. Hair is a coarse and straight fiber, whereas wool is a fine and crimpy fiber with a scaly surface.

Fur fiber vs. fur: Fur fiber describes the hair of any animals other than sheep, lamb, Angora goat, Cashmere goat, camel, alpaca, llama, and vicuña. If hair or fur fiber is attached to the animal skin, it is also referred to as fur.

Fleece: The coat of fibers from one sheep is called a fleece.

removed and the fleece is graded for fiber fineness (diameter), length, crimp (a uniform waviness), color, kemp (thick hair fibers that dye poorly), strength, and elasticity. The finest wool's diameter is between 10 and 20 microns (one micron equals 1/20,000 of an inch). Fine wool is soft, like the fiber in a cotton ball, and is most luxurious. Coarse wool tends to be stiff and bristly, making it best for carpet. The length of wool fiber varies from 1 to about 14 inches. Fine combing wools measure 2.5 inches or more in length and coarse wools around 1.5 inches. While there are as many colors of sheep as there are colors of dogs and cats, white is the most common and has been the most valued over time. Sorting separates the individual fleece into various qualities, with the shoulders and sides giving the best quality and the legs the lowest quality.

Scouring. Wool needs to be cleaned of natural impurities before it is processed further. Impurities include a greasy substance called lanolin that oils the wool fiber and helps the sheep's coat shed water. Other impurities are dirt, vegetable matter, and perspiration or suint (pronounced *swint*). The wool is scoured by washing it with a detergent solution that carries the oil and dirt away from the wool. If some of the lanolin is left on the wool fibers to provide water repellency, it is called *grease wool*.

Blending. Sorted fleeces of a particular quality are thoroughly mixed together, in order to obtain a desired consistency of wool quality. Other types of fibers, such as spandex or nylon, may be added during this step to achieve an intimate blending of the fibers before they are spun into yarn.

Stock Dyeing. Clean fiber can be dyed before spinning it into yarn. This is referred to as stock dyeing. Dyed fiber may then be blended to obtain a yarn with a *heather effect*, which has many colors of fibers.

Carding. In order for an even yarn to be made, the fibers must be separated, spread into a uniform thickness, and encouraged to lie relatively parallel with one another. The carding step produces a continuous strand of untwisted fibers that are eventually drawn into a finer diameter strand before twisting the strand into yarn.

Woolen system. When a soft, fuzzy texture is desired in fabric, the woolen system of yarn production is used. In this process, the fiber is carded several times. Wool fibers of differing lengths and types may be processed with this system. Cloth made from yarn spun on the woolen system is correctly referred to as woolen. Typical fabrics include tweeds, sweater knits, and flannel.

Combing (worsted). In order to get a smooth and uniform textured fabric, the fiber must go through the combing process. Combing makes the fibers straight, in a parallel order. It removes short fibers and almost all of the foreign matter from the fiber matrix. Combed yarns are finer, cleaner, stronger, and more lustrous than carded yarns. Examples of worsted wool fabrics are gabardine and serge.

Spinning. The final step in the process of making yarn is spinning. This draws out the fiber mass, thinning it to the desired diameter, and then stabilizes the strand by twisting the fibers into a yarn.

Yarn dyeing. Coloring the wool in the yarn stage before it is woven or knitted into fabric is called yarn dyeing. Dyed yarn produces plaids, checks, and other color-effects in weaving and knitting.

Weaving. Interlacing two or more sets of yarns at right angles to one another forms a woven fabric. Both woolen and worsted yarns can be used in the weaving process. Fabrics made with woolen yarns can be classified as woolens, and those made with worsted yarns may be classified as worsteds.

Knitting. Inter-looping one yarn or a series of yarns forms a knitted fabric. Either woolen or worsted yarns may be used in the knitting process, but woolen yarns are most commonly used. Garments may be knit into shape or flat knitted fabric can be created, which must be cut and sewn into a garment.

Piece dyeing. After a fabric is woven or knitted, pieces of a fabric can be immersed in a dye bath to give color to that fabric. Piece dyeing generally results in a solid color fabric. If yarns of differing fibers are included in one fabric, multiple color effects are possible.

Finishing. A completed fabric needs additional treatment before being acceptable for use by consumers. Numerous finishes can be done to wool fabrics, including: mending to repair damage done in the weaving or knitting process, wet finishes to control shrinkage and to make the fabric more dense; napping to brush-up a fuzzy surface; and singeing (burning) to eliminate long yarn ends. Wool fabric is given a final press to smooth out the wrinkles from previous finishing processes.

The Properties of Wool

The natural qualities of wool are the reason it has been continually used for thousands of years. Its superior properties have not been totally duplicated by textile scientists. Wool remains a masterpiece of nature and provides a standard by which other fibers are compared.

Resiliency and elasticity. Wool fiber is resilient and elastic. It can bend 30,000 times without breaking or being damaged. Its natural elasticity is due to the cortex cells that naturally coil like springs to form crimp. The elasticity makes it comfortable to wear, because it conforms to the shape of the body and helps wrinkles disappear from wool garments when they are allowed to rest. Wool's resiliency is shown when it stretches and returns to its original shape. Dry wool fiber can be stretched about 30 percent without any damage. Wet wool can stretch between 60 and 70 percent, but is weaker, so washed wool must be handled carefully. The resiliency of wool helps it to wear longer and maintain its good appearance longer than many other fibers.

Comfort. Wool clothing provides superior comfort during both hot and cold weather. Its complex cellular structure enables it to absorb water vapor, but repel liquid. As wool absorbs the body's water vapor, a dry layer of air is left next to the skin to hold in body heat, thereby keeping the body warm. The crimp in the wool fibers keeps each fiber apart from one another, resulting in little pockets of air trapped between the fibers. This trapped air acts as a very good insulator.

Wool is comfortable in hot weather because it helps keep the body cooler by absorbing perspiration vapor from the body. The evaporation of perspiration allows the body to naturally cool. The crimp that helps keep the body warm in cold weather blocks out much of the outdoor heat with its insulating barrier of air pockets. This helps the body maintain an even temperature.

Wool's insulating properties protect against sudden changes of temperature and let the body breathe. While wool can absorb moisture, it repels liquids. The scales on the outside of the fiber keep the liquid on the surface of the wool fabric. If it rains, it will take some time before the raindrops penetrate wool clothing, so wool keeps the wearer drier. When wool eventually gets wet it releases the heat and keeps the wearer warm. Wool can absorb up to 30 percent of its own weight in moisture before feeling really damp.

Flame resistance. Wool is naturally fire resistant because it absorbs water vapor from the air. While wool will eventually burn, it will not support a flame. Once the flame source is removed, wool self-extinguishes and an ash is left that can easily be brushed away. Wool does not melt when burned, so it won't stick to the skin.

Resistance to static electricity. Because of wool's ability to absorb moisture from the air, its tendency to build-up static electricity is low. Wool garments are less likely to "spark" and cling to the body. Wool resists dirt and stays cleaner longer that other materials because static electricity doesn't attract dust from the air. Furthermore the scales of the wool keep dirt from penetrating the surface. These same qualities make wool easier to clean.

Felting. Felting occurs when wool fibers interlock with each other when they are subjected to a combination of heat, moisture, pressure, and agitation. The scales lie in one direction on the fiber, making it move more easily in one direction than another. This is the differential friction effect (DFE). As wool fiber is moistened, rubbed, and warmed, the fibers' scales become locked together. Felting allows wool fiber to be made directly into a fabric without first being made into a yarn. It also allows wool fabrics to be finished with a process called "fulling," a con-

trolled form of felting. "Fulling" makes a fabric thicker and more densely packed. Wool's ability to felt makes it tricky to wash, as heat, moisture, and agitation will encourage felting and permanent shrinking will occur.

See also **Alpaca; Angora; Camel Hair; Mohair; Worsted.**

BIBLIOGRAPHY

Fournier, Nola, and Jane Fournier. *In Sheep's Clothing: A Handspinner's Guide to Wool.* Loveland, Colo.: Interweave Press, 2001.

Harmsworth, Tom, and Graham Day. *Wool and Mohair.* 2nd ed. Victoria, Australia: Inkata Press, 1990.

Kadolph, Sara J., and Anne L. Langford. *Textiles.* 9th ed. Upper Saddle River, N.J.: Prentice Hall, Pearson Education, 2002.

Ryder, Michael L., and S. K. Stephenson. *Wool Growth.* London and New York: Academic Press, 1968.

Internet Resources

The American Wool Council. *Wool Fabrics Fact Sheet.* Available from <http://www.sheepusa.org/wool/genwool/woolfabrics.html>.

Federal Trade Commission. *Threading Your Way Through Labeling Requirements Under the Textile and Wool Acts.* Available from <http://www.ftc.gov/bcp/conline/pubs/buspubs/thread.htm>.

The Woolmark Company. *Natural Properties.* Available from <http://www.woolmark.com/about/naturalproperties.html>.

Ann W. Braaten

WORKING-CLASS DRESS

WORKING-CLASS DRESS For much of the period between the eighteenth century and the present, most people in western countries could be characterized as working class. Many occupations and styles of living are encompassed, ranging from independent skilled artisans in regular work to unskilled laborers or the unemployed. Despite a numerical majority and their central place in social, cultural, and economic history, working-class people, like women as a group, until recently have been hidden from written history and their clothing has been overlooked or subject to only generalized or romanticized interest. What they wore also remained under-represented in museums, due to a low survival rate caused by the thrifty reuse of clothing or its worn-out condition, and the tendency of museums to collect and preserve elite fashions rather than utilitarian clothing. In the early 2000s there is widespread interest in occupational dress, the clothing of the poor, and the role of working-class clothing consumption in the development of a consumer society during this period. Academic studies in this field make use of an array of sources including inventories, court records, and household accounts to pursue this interest in the earlier part of the period and the use of oral history, film, and photography helps ensure the more recent past is better documented.

"Everybody knows that good clothes, boots or furniture are really the cheapest in the end, although they cost more money at first; but the working classes can seldom or never afford to buy good things; they have to buy cheap rubbish which is dear at any price" (Tressell, p. 296).

Occupation, Social Position, and Clothing

One of the most marked gulfs between the appearance of working people and their employers was the use of livery for retainers and household servants. This practice of providing uniform clothing in the colors and style of a particular household was used to augment wages, and it served to embody hierarchy by distinguishing between employees and employer and between ranks of employees themselves. Livery was in widespread use during the period, as it had been since medieval times. It was far from universally popular with its recipients. By the nineteenth century it had become archaic in appearance, such as breeches and wigs for footmen, and had become very limited in use. It has been superseded to some extent by corporate uniforms. Domestic service was a major employer of women until World War I and generated styles of clothing representative of moral and practical notions of order and cleanliness.

Working people in the eighteenth and nineteenth centuries who did not get livery or other clothing as part of their employment often struggled not only to clothe themselves and their families at a basic level, but also to keep up certain levels of cleanliness and respectable appearances on which their continuing employment or their participation in local and church life depended. However, throughout these centuries, employers and the elite, in general, expressed anxiety about the consumption of clothing by working people. Increasing use, more styles, and a variety of available textiles, and the so-called democratization of fashion were judged to weaken conventional distinctions between social classes. Expenditure on clothing by working people was thought to indicate potential extravagance, vanity, and improvidence. There were numerous Victorian cartoons mocking both the domestic servant and her employer as the servant appeared in stylish crinolines or other finery. This was frequently observed in Britain, where social distinctions in dress are thought to have prevailed for longer than in the United States. In the twentieth century, new synthetic materials, simpler styles, affordable fashion magazines, dance halls, and the cinema especially, spurred greater access to fashionable clothing for working women. More recent adoption of homogeneous leisure wear means that social distinctions may be less visible than ever before outside work.

Working Clothes and Fashion

Modish and symbolic use of working-class dress entered general consumption in various ways and in general over the last three centuries; there has been a significant flow of garment types and textiles from utilitarian and occupational clothing into fashion. Examples include appropriation of military combat styles into everyday wear and the rough and thorn-proof warmth of local Scottish and Irish tweeds that were adopted for fashionable urban use in Victoria's reign. Sailors wore "trowsers" long before they entered fashionable male wardrobes. What was produced in nineteenth-century America as denim work wear for men is, in the early 2000s, universally available as fashionable leisure wear for men, women, and children alike and authentic antique jeans command high prices among collectors.

Doc Marten boots had a similar pattern of appropriation and cult status. English agricultural smocks of the nineteenth century were adopted and revived as artistic dress, popularized by Liberty's for well-off urban women and children at the end of the century, echoing nostalgia for a largely imagined idyll of rural England.

Politicians have made use of the symbolic value of materials or garments associated with working-class life, such as when Keir Hardy, elected as one of Britain's first working-class members of parliament, insisted on wearing a rough-spun tweed suit and a flat wool cap instead of the more formal garb usually seen in parliament. President Lyndon Johnson famously wore a cowboy hat to signify his allegiance, and President Jimmy Carter often wore a sweater rather than more formal attire.

In the arts, performers and actors such as Dolly Parton, James Dean, Marlon Brando, and Charlie Chaplin have used working and utilitarian dress to powerful effect. Subcultures, as disparate as Hell's Angels, hippies, punks, and New Agers, have often demonstrated their nonconformism by blending garments from a variety of sources, including working clothes. In the 1970s many pioneer feminists adopted dungarees as a sartorial rejection of fashion and conventional gender roles.

The making and wearing of replica working clothing from the past has become widespread through the popu-

"To imagine New York City in 1789 is to conjure up...tattered beggars, silk-stockinged rich men, pomadoured ladies and their liveried footmen, leather-aproned mechanics and shabby apprentice boys, sleek coach horses, pigs...where the riotous world of the labouring poor surrounded a small, self-enclosed enclave of the wealthy and urbane" (Stansell, p. 3).

larity of historical reenactment and the use of living history to interpret historic sites. The shift such clothing makes in its esteem and value may have no single explanation; rather, it may embody a complex range of social, cultural, and economic factors over time. Mass production of clothing, urbanization, and more recently, new attitudes to work and leisure, money, and credit, may change not only our clothing but the identities they represent.

Provision

Before the advent of systematic state support in the twentieth century, various local or parish bodies and charitable organizations took responsibility for those unable to help themselves, and clothing for such men, women, and children was often part of the provision. Outside this framework, provision was uncertain because it was dependent on income, locality, and luck.

Secondhand clothes were an important element in the clothing strategies of working people. These could be obtained as cast-offs from employers, or from markets and specialist shops in urban areas. There were large warehouses buying and selling secondhand clothing in bigger cities by the eighteenth century, and Henry Mayhew describes a vibrant trade in the wholesale and export of old clothes in 1850s London.

Where women possessed adequate sewing skills, much clothing was made over or recycled: For example, children's clothes were made from cut-down adult garments. The pawning of best clothes played a central part in many household economies. This provided regular cash, and often clothes left all week in the pawnshop were stored in better conditions than was possible in damp or overcrowded homes. In many working households, mothers were traditionally in charge of the budget, and there is evidence that they often clothed and shod working husbands, sons, and school-age children before meeting their own needs.

Sewing clothes at home was assisted by the advent of the sewing machine and effective paper patterns from the 1860s onward, but these were unaffordable for many women. Others sewed at home to earn cash by making or renovating garments for local customers.

Theft played its part in the provision of clothes for use or resale, and in the eighteenth century there are numerous records of vanished household servants who took quantities of clothing with them to pawn or sell. Peddlers traveled around selling clothing, accessories, and cloth to individual households in the eighteenth century before communications and transport improved.

Many working people continued to clothe themselves and their families in ways more suited to their circumstances than traveling to expensive shops. Local or workplace clothing clubs and, by the mid-nineteenth century, mail order with payment by installments played an important part in enabling them to be adequately and fashionably clothed.

Huge markets for slops and utilitarian clothing, including uniforms for the military, led to the development of the mass manufacture of ready-mades from the eighteenth century onward. In America the manufacture of jeans for men demonstrates the growth of factory-based specialist clothing companies. As urbanization coupled with expanding markets during the nineteenth century, new jobs grew up in service industries such as banking and insurance, which resulted in large numbers of low-paid white collar jobs for men and women. A big manufacturing sector developed for affordable clothes for this work, such as suits, blouses, collars, and shoes, which could be widely distributed through growth in urban retailing.

Specific Modes and Items

The common utilitarian dress for laboring men before the twentieth century was made up of breeches or trousers, jackets, and waistcoats of hard-wearing materials such as moleskin, fustian, or corduroy. In some situations, working women were the first women to don breeches or trousers. This occurred in the second half of the nineteenth century in Britain (in pits and mines, in work associated with fishing, and in brickworks), and in the United States (where women did agricultural work), and in some utopian communities.

In many manual occupations, until shorter skirts were widely accepted, women simply hitched up long skirts in various ways. Commonly, in many countries, they wore aprons and woolen shawls. In eighteenth- and early nineteenth-century Britain, the red woolen, hooded cloak was commonly worn by rural women. Women used boots instead of shoes; pattens and then clogs were valuable assets for workingmen and -women on dirt roads and later in factories and mills. Stout and durable footwear has always been a major investment for those undertaking physical labor. Similarly in the United States, denim became widely used by the second half of the nineteenth century for tough work by cattlemen, on the railways and in the mines. Roomy and rugged work shirts accompanied these. Leather and suede have been used in working garments for centuries and persists to the present day, providing hard-wearing and durable covering in the form of aprons for blacksmiths and chaps, gaiters, gloves, and various specialist items and outerwear for other occupations.

Although Britain differed from continental Europe in having no recognizable regional folk dress, two agricultural garments stand out as characteristic of rural workers, and these were worn either at work or as Sunday best. These were smocks for men, from the eighteenth century onwards, which provided a measure of protection and warmth; and the cotton sunbonnet for women, which was decorated with tucks and piping and had strikingly long panels to protect the neck. Fishermen have always had special clothing needs to protect them against the elements. In this context, oilskin was developed in the nineteenth century, and the woolen hand-knitted, close-fitting and ornamented upper garment for fishermen known variously as a gansy, jersey, Guernsey, knitfrock, and later sweater or jumper, became associated with the island fishing communities of Britain. Versions of it were later widely adopted as warm, informal attire for both sexes.

Occupational dress evolves as new occupations emerge, and innovative protective elements are introduced as new risks appear. In the industrializing period, boiler suits accompanied the use of steam power, and since the advent of forms of power that propel us into alien environments, special forms of clothing have been developed for, among others, pilots, divers, and astronauts. To an extent, occupational dress has often represented social and local or regional identities. In this sense, it has shown more style and commanded more loyalty than is strictly utilitarian. In 2002 in northern England a local bus driver was fired for refusing to exchange his habitual cloth cap for a baseball-style company cap. The dramatic fantail hats of the garbage collectors of early nineteenth century England or the intricate patterning on fishermen's knitwear have all testified to expressive and creative elements in occupational dress.

See also **Secondhand Clothes, History of; Uniforms, Occupational.**

BIBLIOGRAPHY

Crane, Diana. *Fashion and its Social Agendas: Class, Gender and Identity in Clothing.* Chicago: University of Chicago Press, 2000.

De Marly, Diana. *Working Dress: A History of Occupational Clothing.* London: B. T. Batsford, Ltd., 1986.

Hall, Lee. *Common Threads: A Parade of American Clothing.* London: Little, Brown and Company, 1992.

Kidwell, Claudia, and Margaret Christman. *Suiting Everyone: The Democratisation of Clothing in America.* Washington, D.C.: Smithsonian Institution Press, 1974.

Partington, Angela. "Popular Fashion and Working-Class Affluence." In *Chic Thrills: A Fashion Reader.* Edited by Juliet Ash and Elizabeth Wilson. London: Pandora, 1992.

Quennell, Peter, ed. *Mayhew's London: Henry Mayhew.* London: Bracken Books, 1984.

Severa, Joan. *Dressed for the Photographer: Ordinary Americans and Fashion, 1840–1900.* Kent, Ohio, and London: Kent State University Press, 1995.

Stansell, Christine. *City of Women: Sex and Class in New York 1789–1860.* Urbana: University of Illinois Press, 1987.

Textile History. Special Issue on the Dress of the Poor. Vol. 33, no. 1 (May 2002).

Tressell, Robert. *The Ragged Trousered Philanthropists.* London: Flamingo, 1993. The original edition was published in 1914.

Barbara Burman

WORSTED The term "worsted" identifies a yarn that has been processed on the worsted spinning system. This system of yarn production is designed to work with staple fiber lengths that range from 2.5 to 7 inches. It was originally designed for processing wool, but in the early twenty-first century any fiber or fiber blend of the appropriate length can be processed. This system of yarn production can utilize fibers with diameters that range from fine to coarse. While worsted wool in apparel fabrics generally uses fine diameter wool, worsted fabrics can use any diameter fiber so can vary in quality. "Worsted" also refers to a fabric woven from yarn processed on the worsted spinning system.

Both worsted and woolen spinning systems include the steps of opening, blending, carding, drawing, and spinning. Opening separates the fibers from their compact state. Blending mixes fibers from different fleeces to get a fixed level of quality. Carding works to organize the fiber into an even and fairly parallel strand. Drawing pulls the fiber into the desired diameter. Spinning twists the strand to hold the fibers in place.

What makes the worsted spinning system differ from yarns made on the woolen spinning system is an extra step in the yarn manufacturing process called "combing" or "gilling." To visualize what happens in the combing process think of the difference between brushing and combing tangled hair. The combing action removes snarls, short fibers, and any other waste matter from the fiber matrix. The short fibers are called *noils* and are recycled by blending them into woolen yarns. Combed yarns have their fibers lying parallel with each other, like spaghetti before being cooked. When the fibers are in this arrangement, they can be pulled to form a very thin yarn. This compact orientation and uniformity in fiber length makes worsted yarn smoother and stronger than similar yarns made on the woolen spinning system.

The worsted spinning system was originally developed in the English city of Worstead. (The term "worsted" is a Middle English derivation of the city's name.) The term "woolen" should not be used to describe worsted yarns or fabrics, as woolen refers to yarns manufactured on the woolen spinning system.

Worsted wool fabrics vary from woolen fabrics in several ways. Wool will be comfortable to wear in the hot summer months if the fabric is made with worsted wool yarns, as they are thinner and flatter yarns that trap less air than fuzzy woolen fabrics. The smooth surface helps worsted wool fabric repel soil and lint better. Worsted wool fibers will not shed from the fabric because the short fibers were removed in the combing step, unlike woolen fabrics. Worsted fabrics are longer wearing and stronger than woolen fabrics. They are also lighter weight than woolens, and will not sag.

Worsted wool fabrics for apparel can range from sheers to suitings. Worsteds made of fine diameter wool will provide sleek fabrics that show design details, and will take and hold a crisp press. Some common examples of worsted wool fabric include tropical worsted, wool crepe, wool broadcloth, wool gabardine, and wool serge. The word "worsted" may be pronounced in two different ways, *woo-sted* and *wer-sted.*

See also **Wool; Yarns.**

BIBLIOGRAPHY

James, John. *History of the Worsted Manufacture in England.* London: Cass; New York, A. M. Kelley, 1968.

Ann W. Braaten

WORTH, CHARLES FREDERICK

WORTH, CHARLES FREDERICK Four generations of Worths are associated with perhaps the most enduring name in fashion history. Indeed, without the house's contributions to fashion, the French Second Empire would not be remembered as an unending parade of luxurious confections in women's dress, and the Gilded Age would not seem so golden.

Charles Frederick Worth (1825–1895) was the founder of a fashion house usually credited with establishing the highest level of fashion creativity: haute couture. Originally the French phrase meant the highest level of sewing. Later it was employed to identify that portion of fashion—particularly French fashion—that both exemplified the pinnacle of dressmaking techniques and produced new styles. Unfortunately, the phrase *haute couture* has lost its original meaning through overuse.

Early Career

Charles Frederick Worth was uncommonly astute in recognizing that his talents were better directed toward artistic creativity rather than managing a business. Following a period of working in London dry-goods shops, Worth set out for Paris. In 1846 he found a position at the prominent dry-goods and dressmaking firm of Gagelin et Opigez. This position gave Worth the experience that later enabled him to build his own business. At Gagelin he was exposed to the best resources for fabrics and trims, and allowed to develop his design skills. He also learned the value of live models and met his future business partner, a Swede named Otto Bobergh (1821–1881). What eventually became the House of Worth was established in late 1856 or early 1857 as Worth and Bobergh at 7, rue de la Paix, with Worth as the artistic head and Bobergh as the financial director. The partnership dissolved in 1870–1871, when Bobergh decided to retire due to major political unrest in France.

Worth's wife, née Marie Vernet (1825–1898), was a former Gagelin model. Mme. Worth easily attracted the attention of the ladies of the French court and then the Empress Eugénie herself, by wearing Worth's creations. Taken with promoting French industries, including the once-dying silk industry of Lyon, the empress thrived on lavish gatherings and equally lavish dress at these events. The empress appointed Worth the court couturier in 1860. To make sure his house could keep up with the growing demand for his dresses, Worth introduced a new way of creating an outfit. Instead of designing a complete dress, he pioneered the concept of mixing and matching skirts

Charles Frederick Worth. Worth founded the House of Worth, which is credited as being the first producer of haute couture. THE LIBRARY OF CONGRESS. PUBLIC DOMAIN.

and bodices, which insured that ladies did not appear at a function in look-alike attire. Worth also developed interchangeable pattern pieces in constructing these garments, further insuring the uniqueness of a completed ensemble.

At the House, clients could preview evening attire in rooms illuminated by various forms of light—natural light, candlelight, gas lamps, and later, electric bulbs. While the House maintained the usual fitting and modeling rooms, it also offered rooms for fabric selection that were distinguished by color. An understanding of the play of colors and textures was one of the enduring achievements of the House, and was successfully passed from generation to generation. Charles Worth's sense of color was particularly noteworthy—he preferred nuanced hues to bold primary colors.

Merchandising Innovations

Throughout the House of Worth's existence, it catered to the rich and titled, although it also served those of more limited means. Garments could be ordered from afar with no personal fittings required. The client supplied a comfortably fitted garment from which appropriate measurements were taken. Worth's models also could be made from commercial paper patterns. The House initially advertised its creations in obscure but aesthetically interesting nineteenth-century publications before entering the mainstream at the end of the century with full-page images in *Harper's Bazaar* and *The Queen* as well as their French counterpart *La mode illustrée*. In the twentieth century, the House's models were advertised in such selective fashion publications as the *Gazette du bon ton*, and such newer entries as *Vogue*. The former type of publication carried on the centuries-old tradition of hand-drawn and hand-colored illustrations, while the latter featured modern photographs.

Late-nineteenth-century publicity images of Charles Frederick Worth depict a man who saw himself as an artist, wearing a bow at the neck or a beret. Many of the images of his son Jean-Philippe also show someone intent on conveying an impression of creativity. Like many classically trained painters and sculptors of their day, the Worths drew on historical prototypes. The House's designs included references to garments in historical paintings gleaned from museum visits, published descriptions of works of art, and personal familiarity with historic costume. Large numbers of Worth garments from the period of Charles and Jean-Philippe referenced seventeenth- and eighteenth-century styles, but none of them will ever be confused with their prototypes, thanks to construction detail and fabric choice. The Worths employed several distinguishing features in their garments beyond the waistband label that they first introduced in the mid-1860s. Although often credited with the innovation, Worth was not the first dressmaker to use a label. The earliest Worth examples were stamped in gold, but they became a woven signature in the late 1870s. This signature label would last the duration of the House. Attempts to defraud the public with spurious labels were made, especially in the United States in the early twentieth century.

Dress Construction and Materials
Contrary to Worth family mythology, the vast majority of the House's garments were trimmed with machine-made rather than handmade lace. Many Worth clients had collections of lace that had been acquired as investments. Sometimes such lace was used on a garment but almost always removed later and returned to the client. The same procedure was followed if gemstones were incorporated into a garment's design. An additional feature employed by the House was the use of selvage as a decorative touch as well as functional finishing.

Perhaps the House's most important contribution was the type of fabrics that it employed. Following the collapse of the Second Empire in 1870, Worth became an even more important client for the textile and trim producers of Lyon and its environs. There is evidence that Worth both used preexisting yard goods and worked with manufacturers to come up with patterns for new materials.

Charles Worth had begun his designing career by following the expansion of women's skirts in the 1850s, when they were supported by layer upon layer of petticoats. In the later 1850s Worth draped yards of fabric

over the skirts' increasing width, as the newly devised crinoline cage, or hoop, permitted expansion without increased bulk. Many Worth dresses from this period, sadly, were frothy, cloudlike confections in silk tulle that have now melted into oblivion. An impression of their impact, however, can be seen in portraits by such artists as Franz Xaver Winterhalter.

Worth introduced hooped dresses with flatter fronts in the early 1860s. It is evident, however, that he was careful not to diminish the amount of material needed; he merely pushed the fabric to the back of the dress. During this decade Worth is also credited with developing the princess-cut dress. These less expansive styles posed an economic challenge. Having been trained in dry-goods shops, Worth recognized the danger of weakening trades that contributed to the success of his own business. Therefore he had to either incorporate large quantities of material into his garments or support the production of costlier luxury goods. In order to maintain a high level of consumption, the House moved material throughout much of the 1870s and 1880s from draped overskirts to trains, bustled backs, and a variety of combinations of these styles. Just as the Empress Eugénie's patronage of the French textile industries had been crucial before 1870, so also was Worth's business vital for the looms of Lyon and Paris that created spectacular luxury materials afterward.

Many of the House's early garments had been constructed of unpatterned silks—tulles, taffetas, reps, and satins—or nominally patterned fabrics featuring stripes and small floral sprays—in other words, typical dress goods. Beginning in the 1870s, almost as a move to fill the void left by the departed French court, the house increasingly employed more expensive textiles usually associated with household furnishing in its garments. Worth boldly utilized grand-scale floral motifs designed for wall coverings in garments whose skirts were often not long enough to include a full repeat of the pattern. Such luxury fabrics, exhibiting astonishing richness of material and the highest level of technical skill, were a feature of the House's models into the first years of the twentieth century. With the exception of machine-made laces, Worth's trims and embroideries matched the ground fabric to which they were applied. The consensus among Worth's clients was that these costly toilettes were worth the price.

Charles Worth and his house did not merely purchase materials; they are also known to have worked closely with textile manufacturers. From such concerns as A. Gourd et Cie, J. Bachelard et Cie, and Tassinari et Chatel, the Worths either commissioned specific designs or ordered preexisting patterns. Often the fabrics they chose had been displayed at important international exhibitions. Many of the fabrics found in late-nineteenth- or early-twentieth-century Worth garments feature subjects that were especially popular with the House: feathers, stalks of grain, stars, butterflies, carnations, iris, tulips, chestnut and oak leaves, scallops and scales, and bowers of roses.

The First Couturier

Worth was not the first man to be an acclaimed creator of fashion. LeRoy had been held in similar esteem as a milliner and dressmaker to the Empress Josephine. Worth was, however, the first clothing designer to be called a couturier. Nevertheless, Worth had the good fortune to be a man entering a field that had become dominated by women, a position that automatically made him a curiosity in the 1850s. During the heady days of the Second Empire, the magic of the "man milliner" called Worth drew the fashion-conscious to the rue de la Paix. Worth's clients were decried as slaves to this dictatorial monarch. Nor was it lost on the House that the theater was an active agent for the propagation of fashion. Even when dressing actresses of the stature of Sarah Bernhardt, however, Worth would insist on full payment for garments. British actress Lillie Langtry was a faithful client, as were such other *grandes horizontales* (courtesans), actresses, and opera stars as Cora Pearl, Eleanora Duse, and Nellie Melba. Such Bostonians as Lillie Moulton, Isabella Stewart Gardner, and Mrs. J. P. Morgan were dressed by the House, as were their counterparts of the Vanderbilt, Astor, Hewitt, Palmer, McCormick, and Stanford families in New York, Chicago, and San Francisco. The House dressed members of the royal families of Russia, Italy, Spain, and Portugal as well as the noblewomen of numerous German principalities.

The first challenge to the house's primacy came with the founding of the House of Paquin in 1891. During the 1890s Worth began to lose clients to this concern. An analysis of the order numbers found in late nineteenth- and early twentieth-century garments reveals not only the year of manufacture but also the fact that orders were declining during this period. But for nearly fifty years, however, a Worth garment had been the most coveted of all apparel, particularly among American women. Perhaps this popularity developed because women from the United States felt at ease discussing their dressmaking needs with a man who could speak English. In return, Charles Worth appreciated his American clients because they had faith in him, figures that displayed his creations to advantage, and perhaps most importantly—francs to pay his bills.

Worth's Successors

Charles Frederick Worth was officially succeeded on his death by his sons Jean-Philippe and Gaston, who had established important roles within the House in the 1870s. Jean-Philippe (1856–1926) worked as a designer alongside his father, and Gaston (1853–1924) functioned as business manager. Throughout the years and over the span of four generations, the Worths never lost sight of the need for astute financial as well as artistic direction.

During the period when Charles and Jean-Philippe worked together as designers within the House it is im-

possible to separate their designs. Even though later house labels carry the signature of the elder Worth, others may have been responsible for the garment's inspiration.

World War I and the subsequent devaluations of European currencies were particularly devastating to the Worths, because the house had dressed so many female members of the royal families of Europe. In addition, many of the House's older clients died during this period, while fashions were making the transition from Edwardian modes to jazz age styles. When Jean-Philippe and Gaston retired in the early 1920s, they were succeeded by Gaston's sons; Jean-Charles Worth became the new designer, and his brother Jacques the financial director. Jean-Charles easily moved the House's designs from the more staid yet elaborate models of the prewar period into the simpler and more practical styles of the 1920s. In the process, however, fewer and fewer of the characteristics that had been exclusively associated with the House's production can be discerned in the garments that survive from this period.

Worth's grandsons were followed in the 1930s by his great-grandsons Maurice and Roger, the latter assuming the couturier role. They attempted to breathe new life into the House; in 1936 they moved the Paris store to 120, rue du Faubourg St.-Honoré. At the end of World War II, however, both the London and Paris branches of the house merged with Worth's old rival Paquin. The London branches, the first established in 1911, survived the Paris branch by eight years. Worth's heirs also shuttered the branches of the House that had been established in Cannes and Biarritz.

As of the early 2000s, the Worth name survived in perfume, although the company has long been out of direct family control.

See also **Crinoline; Fancy Dress; Fashion Marketing and Merchandising; Haute Couture; Paquin, Jeanne; Paris Fashion; Perfume; Royal and Aristocratic Dress.**

BIBLIOGRAPHY

Coleman, Elizabeth A. *The Opulent Era: Fashions of Worth, Doucet and Pingat.* New York: The Brooklyn Museum in association with Thames and Hudson, 1989.

De Marly, Diana. *Worth: Father of Haute Couture.* 2nd ed. New York: Holms and Meier, 1990.

Saunders, Edith. *The Age of Worth.* London and New York: Longmans, Green, 1954.

Internet Resources

Charles Frederick Worth Organization. Available from <http://www.charlesfrederickworth.org>.

House of Worth. Available from <http://www.houseofworth.co.uk>.

Elizabeth Ann Coleman

XULY BËT The Paris-based African fashion designer Lamine Kouyaté is the creator of the XULY.Bët brand. The company is best known for its use of recycled clothing to create high fashion, reshaping found garments by cutting, stitching, and silk-screening, or making modifications that range from the subtle shaping of a seam to the complete transformation of a garment's function. XULY.Bët's recycled clothing embodies several seemingly contradictory attributes: simultaneously mass-produced and unique, new and old, African and European, exclusive and accessible, emerging out of the rarified fantasy of fashion runways and the gritty practicality of the streets. This work turns the notion of haute couture inside out, since it relies on the creation of garments that are one of a kind because they are made of used clothing that has been discarded.

Personal Background
Lamine Badian Kouyaté is the product of the cosmopolitan African culture of both urban Africa and the African diaspora. He was born in Bamako, the capital of the West African country Mali, in 1962. His father was a government minister in the first postcolonial administration, and his mother was a doctor from Senegal. Kouyaté's father was imprisoned during the 1968 coup d'état, when President Modibo Keita was overthrown by Moussa Traoré, who led a repressive, dictatorial government until 1992. The family left the country, moving to Paris when Kouyaté was fourteen, then to Dakar when he was sixteen, where his father worked for the United Nations. Dakar and Bamako are cosmopolitan centers whose cultural influences draw upon African, European, American, and myriad other sources. Kouyaté described the global perspective of youth culture in the African cities: "I knew more about rock and funk in the 70's than any of the kids in Paris when I got here" (Spindler, p. 1). At age twenty-four, he left Dakar to study architecture at the University of Strasbourg in France.

Before completing his architecture degree, Kouyaté moved to Paris and began working as a clothing designer. He founded his XULY.Bët label in 1989. Kouyaté's background in architecture may in part explain his tendency to reveal and rework the structure of garments, often by disassembling them at the seams. Kouyaté's fashion sensibilities were also shaped by his interests in music and performance. He participated in the underground Parisian music and nightclub scene of the early 1980s and, as part of that environment, began designing clothes for performances and for his friends in the clubs. He continues to perform as a musician with his band, "This Is Not A Machine Gun." His attention to the expressive potential of music and performance continues to be manifested in his work, including most notably his presentation of designs at fashion shows.

Recycled Clothing
Kouyaté's line of recycled garments debuted in 1992 as part of the first major collection of the XULY.Bët brand. The garments were made of previously owned shirts, sweaters, dresses, pants, hosiery, and other clothing purchased in flea markets, charity shops, and low-end department stores. Kouyaté altered each garment, responding to the fabrics and the shape of the piece, cutting, removing, and restitching seams using bright red thread. His energetic technique is preserved in the threads left hanging at the end of seams, their red hue emphasizing the process of transformation from discarded garment to designer statement. Kouyaté's reshaping of garments includes the transformation of dresses into skirts, skirts into bags, stockings into halter tops, and sweaters stitched together to create dresses.

The previous lives of XULY.Bët recycled garments are deliberately preserved; Kouyaté leaves the original labels in the collars of used shirts and the waistbands of pants purchased at flea markets. These labels provide vivid evidence of the histories of clothing that has been used, discarded, and later returned to the fashion market by the designer. The original label alludes to the garment's first life; the bright red XULY.Bët label, usually placed on the outside of the garment, declares its current identity. The used garments Kouyaté works with provide an endless source of constantly changing raw material, like an archaeological record of past styles that are reintroduced into the fashion market.

Rethinking the Fashion Show
XULY.Bët's first major fashion show, held during the spring 1992 season in Paris, illustrates Kouyaté's interest

in the tension between the theatrical and the mundane. His debut fashion show's innovative staging emphasized the brand's raw, edgy aesthetic. Kouyaté presented the show outside the conventional precincts of the fashion industry, at a public park. He did not use a runway or a sound system. Instead, models emerged from a bus that pulled up at the site, each carrying a boombox that provided her own soundtrack to the event. No stage, no lights, no delineation of theatrical space separated the audience from the performers, just as the garments themselves were but subtly separated from their previous, mundane lives.

African Elements

Kouyaté's work incorporates aspects of his own biography, which encompasses contemporary, urban Africa as well as the fashion worlds of Paris and New York. His company's name draws immediate attention to his African origins. In Oulouf (or Wolof), the predominant language of Senegal, *xuly bët* is a colloquial term that can be roughly translated as "voyeur," or, in a more nuanced definition, as someone who breaks through appearances to see the reality beneath the surface. This notion, peeling back the exterior to reveal the often uneven surfaces layered beneath, is embodied by Kouyaté's exposed seams and loose threads. He has cited his roots in Africa as an important source of inspiration for his recycled fashion, reflecting a widespread African ethic of reusing resources that is born out of necessity. Kouyaté draws on Africa in a more literal sense, using African fabrics in several of his designs and, in the early twenty-first century, working with dyers in Mali to create fabrics that he uses in his other clothing lines.

International Presence

Kouyaté is among the few African designers to have achieved an international profile; XULY.Bët clothing and the designer himself have been featured in prominent publications, including French *Glamour*, the *New York Times*, *Le Figaro*, and *Essence*. His clothing played a prominent role in Robert Altman's film *Ready To Wear* (1994), in which a fashion show in an underground subway station presents XULY.Bët clothing as the work of one of the film's main characters. The designer's personal background as well as his work drew substantial attention from both the fashion and the popular press, particularly in the early 1990s. In the early 2000s Kouyaté continued to design actively, marketing his clothing through several shops in Paris and for international clients.

See also **Fashion Designer; Fashion Shows; Recycled Textiles; Textiles, African.**

BIBLIOGRAPHY

Jacobs, P. "Xuly Bet: A Brother from the 'Mother' Turns Fashion Inside Out." *Essence* 15 (May 1994): 26–27, 144. Introduction to Kouyaté's background and his work, with several illustrations.

Renaux, P. "Pari Dakar de Xuly Bët." *Glamour* (April 1994). Focuses on the designer's African background, documenting a trip home to Dakar to visit his family.

Revue Noire 27 (March 1998). Special issue on African fashion includes a large spread devoted to XULY.Bët, with generous illustrations of his recycled line of clothing. An important publication for readers seeking insight into African fashion design as an international phenomenon.

Spindler, A. M. "Prince of Pieces." *New York Times* (2 May 1993): section 9, pp. 1, 13. Most substantive coverage of the designer available, including an overview of his career and extensive quotations from interview with Kouyaté.

Van der Plas, E., and M. Willemsen, eds. *The Art of African Fashion.* Lawrenceville, N.J.: Africa World Press, 1998. Kouyaté is one of a handful of African designers featured in this important publication. Several essays by academics and fashion practitioners situate African fashion design within global markets.

Victoria L. Rovine

Y

YAMAMOTO, YOHJI Yohji Yamamoto is widely regarded as ranking among the greatest fashion designers of the late twentieth and early twenty-first centuries. He is one of the few in his profession who have successfully broken the boundaries between commodity and art, by creating clothing that ranges from basics like athletic shoes and denim jeans to couture-inspired gowns that are nothing short of malleable mobile sculptures. Lauded as a blend of master craftsman and philosophical dreamer, Yamamoto has balanced the seemingly incompatible extremes of fashion's competing scales.

Despite the magnitude of his talent and the importance of his work, however, Yamamoto has yet to be the subject of serious critical discourse among fashion journalists and historians. It is perhaps ironic that the only probing analysis of Yamamoto—both the man and the designer—came from someone who possessed little knowledge of or interest in fashion. Wim Wenders, the renowned German filmmaker, produced a documentary in 1989 entitled *Notebook on Cities and Clothes.* Throughout the film, Wenders dramatized Yamamoto's creative genius by setting the words of the late German philosopher Walter Benjamin against the urban backdrops of both Tokyo and Paris. Yet the director's probing failed to illuminate the crucial elements that constituted Yamamoto's fashions. Neither the elements particular to the art of dressmaking nor Yamamoto's particular aesthetic contributions were discussed.

Inspiration from the intangible, mainly images of historical dress from sources such as photographs, has been a mainstay in Yamamoto's work. The crumpled collar in a August Sander portrait, the gauzy dresses captured by Jacques-Henri Lartigue while vacationing on the Riviera, and the gritty realism of Françoise Huguier's travels among the Inuit of the Arctic Circle are but a few examples. It is not surprising that the riveting catalogs created for each of Yamamoto's high-end ready-to-wear women's collections have included the work of such notable photographers as Nick Knight, Paolo Roversi, Inez van Lamsweerde, and Vinoodh Matadin. Whether Yamamoto is evoking historicism via the ancien régime or the belle epoque, or ethnic garments made of richly woven silks and woolens, he has come to epitomize the vast range of creative possibilities in the art of dress.

Early Career

Yamamoto was born in Tokyo on 3 October 1943. He never knew his father, who died in Manchuria during World War II; he was reared by his widowed mother Yumi. A dressmaker by trade, Yumi suffered what Yamamoto recalls as the indignities of a highly skilled worker whose gender and station in life afforded her little opportunity to make a rewarding living or to obtain recognition for her talents. Yumi encouraged her son to become an attorney—he graduated with a law degree from Keio University but never practiced. The lure of becoming a designer, however, pulled Yamamoto into fashion.

After completing his university studies in 1966, Yamamoto studied fashion design at the famous Bunkafukuso Gakuin, a fashion institute in Tokyo. Despite his skills as a master craftsman, he started his career as an anonymous creator around 1970. Two years later he marketed his own designs under the label Y's. Clothing under this label is now considered to be Yamamoto's lower-priced, or "bridge," line. In 1977 he presented his Y's collection for the first time in Tokyo. Along with his compatriot Rei Kawakubo, he designed his first high-end women's ready-to-wear collection in 1981 and presented it in Paris. Over the next two years, Kawakubo and Yamamoto pioneered the idea of deconstructed fashions. Their revolutionary aesthetic shocked the world with clothing that appeared to be unfinished, tattered, and haphazardly put together. Yamamoto's loose, flowing silhouettes and ubiquitous use of black further enhanced his groundbreaking work, which became the favored look of the 1980s urban aesthetic. In 1984 Yamamoto presented a deluxe menswear line that incorporated many of these same elements.

Yamamoto's Aesthetic

From the moment Kawakubo and Yamamoto presented their first fashion collections to an international audience in the 1980s, they were defined as Japanese designers. Virtually every article about them as well as the critical reviews of their collections began by describing them as inseparable from and encapsulated in their Asian heritage. Many journalists inaccurately assumed that they produced clothing worn by all Japanese people. The reality was that the loose, dark-colored, and seemingly tattered garments were as startling to the average Japanese as they were to the Western audiences that first viewed them. Although Yamamoto's work changed and evolved over the next two decades, it retained several key elements—the ambiguities of gender, the importance of black, and the aesthetics of deconstruction.

Gender ambiguity. Yamamoto's professed love of and respect for women has not been evident to many because his clothes were often devoid of Western-style gender markers. He expressed an aversion to overtly sexualized females, and often dressed women in designs inspired by men's wear. Such cross-gender role-playing has long been a part of Japanese culture, and a persistent theme among performers and artists for centuries. The fact that Yamamoto on more than one occasion chose women as models for his menswear fashion shows was another small piece of his sexual identity puzzle.

Even when his later work embraced the sweeping romanticism of postwar Parisian haute couture, Yamamoto's historical recontextualizations contrasted sharply with the work of other marquee designers. Deliberately absent from his runway presentations were the requisites of the contemporary high-fashion wardrobe for women: high heels, rising hemlines, plunging necklines, and sheer fabrics. These characteristics might be the reason that Yamamoto's dark tailored suits and white shirts for both men and women have been some of his most enduring and compelling products. Worn by Western men of all classes for two centuries, the dark-colored suit and the white shirt have a combined ability to convey both sexuality and power through conformity. This blend of erotic appeal and strength was a perfect template for Yamamoto to express his postwar version of male and female sexuality.

Basic black. No color in the fashion palette has been as important in the work of Yohji Yamamoto as black. This early unrelenting black-on-black aesthetic earned his devotees the nickname *karasuzoku*, or members of the crow tribe. Black has certain associations in the history of the West that have been processed through a kaleidoscope of self-conscious modernist or postmodernist theories and assumptions. As a result of historical recontextualization, black had by the last quarter of the twentieth century acquired a range of meanings, such as poverty and devastation for some fashion critics, and sobriety, intellectualism, chic, self-restraint, and nobility in dress for others.

The aesthetic attributes of traditional Japan and contemporary culture, as well as the role black plays in fashion, can be seen in the color's association with poverty. For some observers, black is an illusion of—or perhaps an allusion to—rusticity, simplicity, and self-restraint. In Japan, black dyes may connote rural origin as well as noble warrior status. An important connection between black and the symbolic associations of old Europe, traditional Japan, and the modern urban landscape may also be derived from the couture atelier. Yamamoto, like

Cristóbal Balenciaga, often created day suits, dresses, ball gowns, and coats devoid of any ornament. Charcoal gray, navy blue, and of course black woolens were often molded and manipulated into pure sculptural forms that displayed both marvelous engineering and tailoring techniques as well as a love of dramatic form.

Deconstructed styles. The connection between deconstruction, originally a French philosophical movement, and contemporary fashion design has yet to be fully explored by fashion historians. There is no direct evidence that such ideas were the motivating force in the early designs of Yohji Yamamoto. It is more likely that he combined a mélange of influences: the devastation and rapid rebuilding of Japan in the postwar era; the revolt against bourgeois tastes; an affiliation with European street styles; and a desire, like that of the early proponents of abstraction in fine art, to find a universal expression of design by erasing elements that assign people to specific socioeconomic and gender roles.

Aesthetically, the dressmaking techniques that gave Yamamoto's work its deconstructed look were also related to traditional non-Western methods of clothing construction as well as to the concept that natural, organic, and imperfect objects can also be beautiful. Yamamoto's clothes masked the body with voluminous folds and layers of dark fabric; in addition, they diminished such evident elements of clothing as frontality and clear demarcations between the inside and outside of a garment.

Yamamoto's version of deconstruction fashion more likely began by questioning the very essence of his postwar existence. Japan's initial efforts to rebuild its physical and political infrastructure, and its later economic ascendancy, did provide the right environment to foster the talents of an amazingly creative generation that included the architects Tadao Ando, Arata Isozaki, and Kenzo Tange as well as the furniture designer Shiro Kuramata and the fashion designers Yamamoto and Kawakubo.

It seems more plausible that Yamamoto was fueled by the anger typical of the generation that spearheaded the social changes of the 1960s. Thus he arrived at a new vision for fashion that railed against the bourgeois conformity that resulted from what Yamamoto obliquely referred to as American colonialism. Though the exact elements that led him to the creation of his particular style may not be known, more than one journalist concluded that Yamamoto's clothing reflected a kind of anger that evoked images of nuclear holocaust survivors and were labeled the "Hiroshima bag lady" look by some. A few critics even made an alliance between his fashions and a coven of witches.

Despite such misunderstandings, the designs of Yamamoto paralleled the rise of punk fashions and street style, and their connection with mid-twentieth-century urban degradation. In fact, more than one writer noted that the look established by Yamamoto was neither a pure invention on his part nor a derivative of Asian culture.

Such London-based designers as Malcolm McLaren and Vivienne Westwood, like other disenfranchised English youth, turned clothing into a medium for political expression and were at the forefront of the punk movement.

Yamamoto's ability to see beauty in degradation, however, and to strip things to their foundation in a search for the inherent integrity of each object is profoundly Japanese. This aesthetic of imperfection, incompleteness, or poverty, is a hallmark of *wabi-sabi*. A worldview that originated in Zen Buddhism, *wabi-sabi* was later applied to the creation of objects characterized by external lack of ornamentation and internal refinement *(wabi)* and an emphasis on the ephemeral nature of all things that eventually leads to decay *(sabi)*. While Yamamoto did not formally study *wabi-sabi*, he is the product of his culture, one that is arguably the most aesthetically refined in the world.

Mature Work

The initial impact of Yamamoto's designs began to diminish as the 1980s came to a close; the designer fell into a self-professed decline for the next few years. By the mid-1990s, however, Yamamoto experienced a resurgence of creativity rare in contemporary fashion. His output was vastly different from his work of a decade earlier, in that it fully embraced the most lyrical and fleeting elements of historical modes. His designs became a blend of street-style realism and Victorian romanticism, reshaped and reconfigured for a contemporary audience. At both extremes, Yamamoto retained his very personal vision—creating clothes for an ideal woman who, according to the couturier, does not exist.

Perhaps the most potent quality that Yamamoto displayed was his brilliant ability to recontextualize the familiar into wearable creations that came as close to works of art as any clothing designed in the early 2000s. Although he created several lines of clothing for both men and women, it was his couture-inspired creations for women that manifested this concept most completely. One of the best fashion presentations in recent memory was the spring 1999 collection that Yamamoto created around the theme of a wedding. All the Yamamoto hallmarks were evident: the play on androgyny as seen through an array of masculine-tailored suits; the reliance on a neutral color scheme of black, white and khaki; and magnificent three-dimensional gowns that evoked both the Victorian era and the golden age of twentieth-century Parisian haute couture. The glory of the garments was further enhanced by the lyrical presentation itself, with the highlight being a young bride who performed a reverse striptease. Rather than disrobing, as is usually the case in fashion shows, the mannequin, dressed in an unadorned hoop-skirted wedding gown, pulled her mantle, a pair of sandals, a hat, gloves, and finally, a bouquet of flowers from pockets hidden in the gown. Fittingly, the usually jaded fashion journalists found themselves shedding tears before giving Yamamoto a standing ovation.

After the success of this collection, he was honored as international designer of the year by the Council of Fashion Designers of America in New York City in June 2000.

Yamamoto continued to evolve in the early 2000s. His spring 2003 collection was not shown during the Paris ready-to-wear fashion week in October of 2002, but instead during the haute couture presentations earlier that year. Simultaneously, he became the designer for a new line of clothing produced in conjunction with the Adidas sportswear company called Y's 3. This agreement came about after Yamamoto first designed an astoundingly successful set of trainers, athletic shoes, and sports shoes for Adidas in 2001.

See also **Benjamin, Walter; Fashion, Theories of; Film and Fashion; Japanese Fashion; Punk; Street Style; Westwood, Vivienne.**

BIBLIOGRAPHY

Armstrong, Lisa. "Deconstructing Yohji." British *Vogue* (August 1998): 134–137.

Chua, Lawrence. "Exploring the Yamamoto Cult." *Women's Wear Daily* (April 1988).

Hildreth, Jean C. *A New Wave in Fashion: Three Japanese Designers, March 1–April 24, 1983.* Phoenix, Ariz.: The Arizona Costume Institute of the Phoenix Art Museum, 1983.

Hirokawa, Taishi. *Sonomama Sonomama: High Fashion in the Japanese Countryside.* San Francisco: Chronicle Books, 1988.

Kondo, Dorinne. *About Face: Performing Race in Fashion and Theater.* New York: Routledge, 1997.

Koren, Leonard. *New Fashion Japan.* Tokyo: Kodansha International, 1984.

Martin, Richard. "Destitution and Deconstruction: The Riches of Poverty in the Fashions of the 1990s." *Textile and Text* 15 (1992): 3–12.

Takashina, Shuji. "Japonism: An Aesthetic of Shadow and Fragment." In *Japonism in Fashion.* Edited by A. Fukai. Tokyo: Kyoto Costume Research Foundation, 1996.

Wenders, Wim. *Aufzeichnungen zu Kleidern und Städten (Notebook on Cities and Clothes.)* Berlin: Road Movies Filmproduktion in cooperation with Centre National d'Art et du Culture Georges Pompidou, 1989.

Patricia Mears

YARNS Yarns are linear structures that are formed by collecting and twisting fibers together. Converting fibers into yarns is a necessary step for weaving or knitting fabrics. Yarns can be classified in a number of ways: by type, size, number of parts, or similarity of parts. These classifications determine the specification of yarns for end-use textile products with different properties. Yarn structure can affect fabric strength, appearance, comfort, feel or hand, and drape among other properties.

The two main types of yarns are staple and filament. Staple yarns, also called spun yarns, are made of fibers that come in short discrete lengths. All natural fibers except silk are staple fibers. Filament yarns are collections of long continuous filament fibers. Silk is such a fiber, and manufactured fibers are produced in filament form. The manufactured filaments can then be cut into staple lengths if staple yarns are desired.

Staple Yarns

Staple fibers are formed into yarns by a series of processing steps that have been developed over time for specific fibers. Cotton, wool, and linen yarns all have their distinctive processes. The cotton system is the most commonly used, for both cotton and cotton-blend yarns.

In the cotton system, fibers from bales are first run through rollers with spikes to pull the clumps apart, and are then further separated in an opening and cleaning step where trash is removed. This is followed by carding, in which the fibers are passed through fine wires or pins to individually separate and align them. They emerge as a loose collection of aligned fibers known as a sliver. The sliver can then be combed, an optional step in which the carded fibers are pulled through fine combs to remove shorter fibers and arrange the longer fibers into a parallel form. Cotton fabrics made from these yarns are smooth and soft and often labeled "fine combed cotton." As can be imagined, combed cottons are more expensive than yarns that are carded only. After several processes in which the carded or carded and combed fibers are drawn through rollers, they are slightly twisted to form a soft rope called a roving. The roving is tightly twisted in the final spinning step.

Preparation of wool fibers for spinning is similar. Fibers that are carded only are formed into woolen yarns, which are soft and bulky. Worsted yarns, on the other hand, are combed and also subjected to a special drawing process, gilling, where pins help to straighten the fibers. Worsted yarns are more tightly twisted in the final spinning step, making them smoother and more compact in appearance.

There are several techniques for inserting the final twist in staple yarns. Ring spinning is the most mature spinning method. The yarn is wound on a bobbin or spool that rotates at a high rate of speed. The rotation twists the loose rope of fibers into a strong yarn. Ring spinning gets its name from a ring that travels up and down the spindle. A small clip, the traveler, holds the yarn and moves around the ring. Ring-spun yarns are smoother and stronger than yarns made by other spinning techniques, and can also be made in finer sizes. Ring spinning is slower and therefore more expensive than other methods, prompting garment makers to identify ring-spun yarns in products such as cotton underwear and T-shirts.

Another process for twisting staple yarns is open-end spinning. In its most common manifestation, rotor spinning, the fiber roving is carried by an air stream into a rapidly spinning rotor with a V-shaped groove. The fibers are deposited by centrifugal force in the groove and then drawn off through a center delivery tube. The operation bears some resemblance to a cotton candy machine. As the fine candy fibers are formed they are caught and collected. In rotor spinning, fibers are caught by the "open end" of a previously formed yarn and the rapid rotation of the rotor twists the yarn. Rotor spun yarns are more uniform than ring-spun yarns, but not as strong. In addition, they cannot be made in very fine sizes. Most cotton yarns for denim are rotor spun.

Friction spinning is another open-end method. A mixture of air and fibers is fed between two drums rotating in opposite directions. This inserts twist into the fibers, much as spinners did in ancient times by rolling clumps of fibers between their fingers.

An increasingly popular spinning method is air-jet spinning. Yarns are formed by jets of air forcing the outer layers of fibers in a sliver to wrap around the interior fibers. Air-jet yarns are weaker than ring or open-end spun yarns, but can be made in finer sizes.

Filament Yarns

Filament yarns are made by gathering together long continuous fibers, with or without inserting twist. Filament yarns produce fabrics that are smooth and slippery to the touch. They are also stronger than staple yarns, which is why before the discovery of synthetic manufactured fibers parachutes were made of silk. Because of their value, the parachutes used during World War II were often retrieved by civilians and made into garments. Filament yarns are also associated with luxury fabrics such as satin and velvet, which were traditionally made with silk filament yarns.

To change their properties, filament yarns can be textured or "bulked." This makes them softer, stretchier, more resilient, and more like staple yarns. Textured yarn fabrics are also more permeable to moisture and air, increasing the comfort to the wearer. Common texturing methods are: false twist, in which the yarns are twisted, heated to set the twist, and then untwisted; and air jet, in which the slack filaments in the yarn are entangled and formed into loops by jets of air. False twist imparts stretch as well as the look and feel of staple yarn fabrics. Air jet yarns are soft and bulky but have little stretch. The polyester double-knit fabrics of the 1960s were made of textured filament yarns.

Yarn Size

Over the years different systems have emerged for designating the size of textile yarns. The oldest systems are "indirect," in that the higher the number is the smaller, or finer, the yarn. Cotton count is an indirect system for specifying the size of cotton and cotton-blend yarns. It is the number of 840-yard lengths of yarn in one pound. As spinning processes were developed for wool and linen, specific yarn numbering systems were created for these

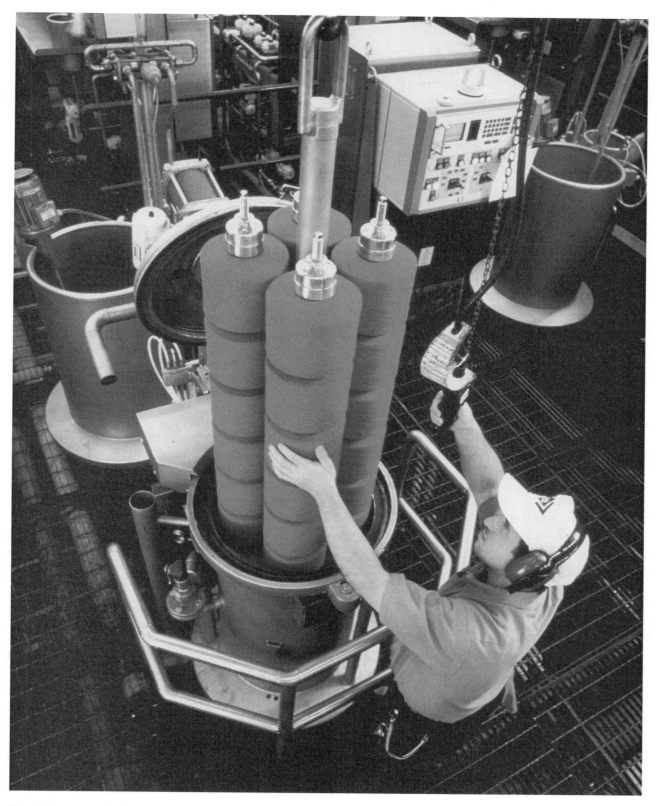

Yarn dyeing. A worker lowers four spoils of yarn into a dyeing vat with a remote control. Textile styles such as bouclé and tweed can be produced by blending different color yarns. © ROGER BALL/CORBIS. REPRODUCED BY PERMISSION.

fibers, differing in the lengths that are specified per pound of yarn.

These indirect systems for yarn size were based on English measuring units (yards, pounds); the move toward universally accepted metric units has resulted in yarn numbering systems in which the yarn count varies directly with the size. Tex is the weight in grams of 1,000 meters of yarn, while denier is the weight in grams of 9,000 meters. Tex is the more general term as it can be used for sizing both staple and filament yarns.

An understanding of the relative sizes of yarns can be used to determine appropriate end-uses for fabrics. Properties such as strength, smoothness, drape, and wrinkle resistance are affected by yarn size. For example, heavier yarns are used in denim fabrics for jeans and pants because both strength and some degree of wrinkle resistance are desired. Cotton blouses and shirts, however, would require smaller yarns for a smooth comfortable feel.

Number and Similarity of Parts

Yarns can be single, ply, or cord. Single yarns are made from staple or filament fibers twisted together. Ply yarns are two single yarns twisted together. They are stronger and smoother than singles. Most sewing threads are ply yarns. The strength and smoothness help the threads withstand the friction and mechanical action during sewing. Twisting two or more ply yarns together forms cord yarns, which are stronger still. Cords are mostly destined for industrial uses such as cables and ropes, although they can be used in apparel for different effects and textures.

If all parts of a yarn, be it single, ply, or cord, are uniform in size and have a regular surface, the yarn is termed a simple yarn. Varying the structure of one or more of the parts of a yarn produces a novelty yarn. An example of a novelty single yarn is a crepe yarn, which is over twisted to yield kinks and an irregular surface.

A great variety of novelty yarns can be made by plying two dissimilar singles or twisting similar singles in an irregular structure. In a bouclé yarn, one ply (the effect yarn) forms irregular loops around the base yarn. Ratiné yarns are similar in structure, but the loops are regularly spaced along the yarn. The loops are visible in fabrics made with bouclé or ratiné yarns. Another variation of this is twisting the effect yarn irregularly around the base yarn so that it creates knots or nubs in some places. These are called knot, spot, or nub yarns. Varying the degree of twist along single or ply yarn produces thick soft "slubs" in the yarn. Slub yarns show these irregularities in the fabric; one such fabric is shantung, often made of silk. Spiral or corkscrew yarns are made of two plies, one of which is heavy and soft, winding around a finer core yarn.

Chenille yarns are different from other structures in that a fabric is first woven, then cut into strips that form the yarn. The strips have fiber ends sticking out on all sides and the yarn resembles a caterpillar. These fluffy ends protrude in fabrics containing chenille yarns.

Color can be used to produce or enhance novelty effects. In plied yarns for example, single yarns of different colors can be twisted together. This effect is enhanced in bouclé, ratiné, or corkscrew yarns. Tweed fabrics are made from novelty single yarns; the novelty lies in combining different colored fibers in a single spun yarn.

Blended Yarns

Blended yarns, which contain mixtures of fibers, have several purposes. Self-blending is done to more thoroughly mix fibers, particularly natural fibers, from different sources. This minimizes the possibility of concentrating fiber defects in one section or batch of yarn. Another purpose of blending is to combine the properties of different fibers, for example the comfort and absorbency of cotton with the strength and wrinkle resistance of polyester. Cotton-polyester blends are popular fabrics and are usually made by mixing the fibers at some stage of processing.

Fibers can be blended when bales or boxes are opened and cleaned prior to carding. They can also be mixed by drawing several slivers together. Repeated drawing of blended slivers enhances the mixing. Yarns for Harris tweed fabrics are made by blending different colored wool fibers in large chambers supplied with air streams, prior to carding.

See also **Spinning; Spinning Machinery; Wool.**

BIBLIOGRAPHY

Demir, Ali, and Hassan Mohamed Behery. *Synthetic Filament Yarn.* Upper Saddle River, N.J.: Prentice Hall, 1997.

Goswami, Bhuvenesh Chandra, J. G. Martindale, and F. L. Scardino. *Textile Yarns: Technology, Structure, and Applications.* New York: Wiley-Interscience, 1977.

Billie J. Collier

YEOHLEE A native of Malaysia, Yeohlee Teng (1955–) came to the United States to study at the Parsons School of Design in New York City. She worked in New York since her graduation from Parsons, and opened her own house, Yeohlee Inc., in 1981.

Yeohlee's strong and consistent approach to clothing design has made her name synonymous with efficiency, striking geometrical designs, and concise functionalism. All of her clothing patterns have incorporated the principle of maximum utilization of fabric. Her signature garment was a one-size-fits-all hooded cape cut from a single 3.25-yard piece of 60-inch fabric, using all of the material with no waste whatsoever. This unique cape brought her widespread attention when it was included in her first collection in 1981, and it has been in every one of her collections since then. Yeohlee also pioneered the use of high-tech fabrics and surface treatments to produce wrinkle- and stain-resistant clothes that are easy to care for and easy to pack. She worked with a palette of colors that emphasized black, white, and earth tones, though her collections were also often accented with striking shades of green, red, and orange. Yeohlee designed for the urban nomad, a postmodern customer who demanded adaptable, functional, low-maintenance clothing that looked appropriate and made a powerful impression in a wide range of situations. The designer was associated with the phrases "clothing as shelter" and "intimate architecture."

The output of Yeohlee Inc. was aimed at a relatively small and loyal customer base rather than at the mass market; the company sold through a limited number of department stores and specialty shops in the early 2000s. Yeohlee's designs tended to be relatively uninfluenced by seasonal and annual fashion trends, but rather followed the evolution of her own design vision. Her clothes appealed to the sophisticated, design-conscious clientele of the early 2000s.

Yeohlee's work, often described as "architectural," attracted the attention of critics and professionals in other fields of design. To an extent unusual for fashion designers, her clothes were exhibited as design art in many museums and galleries in the 1990s and early 2000s. Her participation in the group show Intimate Architecture: Contemporary Clothing Design, presented at the Hayden Gallery at the Massachusetts Institute of Technology in 1982, won a great deal of favorable attention for her work and was an important factor in the early success of her company. Her clothes were also featured in solo shows at the Aedes East Gallery, Berlin; P.S. 1, New York City; the Netherlands Architecture Institute, Rotterdam; the London College of Fashion in association with the Victoria and Albert Museum, London; and the Museum at the Fashion Institute of Technology, New York, as well as in a number of other group shows. Her work was also placed in the permanent collections of the Costume Institute of the Metropolitan Museum of Art, the Museum at the Fashion Institute of Technology, and other major fashion museums worldwide.

In the words of the late fashion historian Richard Harrison Martin, Yeohlee "is one of the few practitioners of her art who has fully eschewed fashion hyperbole to engage in a critical discourse about clothing in space [and] on the body."

See also **Fashion Museums and Collections; High-Tech Fashion; Performance Finishes; Techno-Textiles.**

BIBLIOGRAPHY

Major, John S., and Yeohlee Teng, eds. *Yeohlee: Work—Material Architecture.* Mulgrave (Victoria), Australia: Peleus Press, 2003.

Steele, Valerie, and John S. Major. *China Chic: East Meets West.* New Haven, Conn., and London: Yale University Press, 1999.

John S. Major

YOUTHQUAKE FASHIONS A tag, a slogan, and a rallying cry, "Youthquake" exemplifies the slickness as well as the conviction, the spontaneous ebullience as well as the commercial aggression that during the 1960s marked the triumph of London ready-to-wear. Powered by the momentum of a cresting youth culture, a cadre of British designers, mostly women, wrenched dominance away from the Paris couture houses and profoundly altered global fashion.

Youthquake fashion cannot be explored or understood without acknowledging its social and political context. In *Fifty Years of Fashion*, Valerie Steele notes that the "narrow, apolitical approach," preferred by many fashion journalists "becomes insupportable when dealing with the 1960s" (p. 49). These clothes garbed armies of protagonists in the ongoing narrative of women's economic, sexual, and social independence, and the consequent and reciprocal expansion of men's personas. In 1988, Mary Quant recalled: "Women had been building to this for a long time, but before the pill there couldn't be a true emancipation. It's very clear in the look, in the exuberance of the time—a rather childlike exuberance. "Wow—look at me!—isn't it lovely? At last, at last!'" (Conversation with author, December, 1988).

Youthquake fashion was also a lever as well as a product of the increased social mobility engendered by the postwar Labor governments of Britain. Due to government-subsidized tuition, an unprecedented number of students of humble origin were now able to pursue careers in the fine and commercial arts. At the Royal College of Art, Madge Garland, formerly editor in chief of British *Vogue*, had developed a graduate program in fashion design. Professor Janey Ironside became the program's principal in 1956. "We were trained to see, to explore, to enjoy ourselves," recalled RCA alumna Sally Tuffin, one half of celebrated Youthquake design team (Marion) Foale and Tuffin. "We felt as though we could go off and do anything, without restriction." (Conversation with author, November, 1988).

Boutiques

Throughout the 1950s, British fashion was dominated by the Paris couture, and the long shadow it cast over London couturiers such as Norman Hartnell and Hardy Amies. British manufacturers followed the parameters laid out by the high end of fashion. But the emerging generation wanted something entirely different and entirely their own. They were out of sympathy with the mores of expensive made-to-order clothing. "The couture was for kept women," said Barbara Hulanicki, who opened the London boutique Biba after working as a fashion illustrator in the late 1950s and early '60s. As she sketched the couture for London newspapers, Hulanicki objected as well to "the snobbery that was designed to make everyone feel inferior." (Conversation with author, November, 1988)

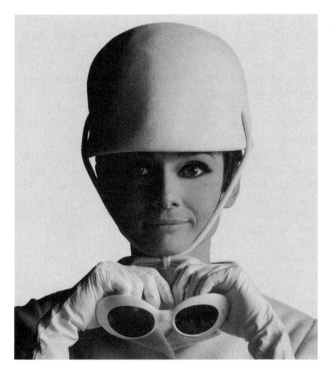

Audrey Hepburn wears a Courrèges hat, 1965. Youthquake designers pushed forward the mod look, which favored monochrome and streamlined outfits. © DOUGLAS KIRKLAND/CORBIS. REPRODUCED BY PERMISSION.

Youthquake fashion found its own staging ground as the boutique replaced the couture salon as fashion incubator. The Youthquake boutique was somewhere between a neighborhood dressmaker's atelier and the auxiliary shops maintained within some Paris couture strongholds, in which accessories and related bagatelles might be sold. Youthquake fashion could be said to have begun in November 1955, when Quant, recently graduated from art college, opened her boutique "Bazaar" in the London district of Chelsea. A year later she started designing because she couldn't find the type of clothes she wanted to stock her store.

"What was wrong at that stage was that fashion only came through one route," Quant recalled, "which designed for a way of life which was very much that of a minority."…She instead would design for "women who had a job and a fantasy life that took that job into account" (conversation with author, December 1988). The daughter of schoolteachers, Quant was married to Alexander Plunkett Greene, scion of an aristocratic lineage. Their marriage became emblematic of falling class barriers.

The Miniskirt Emerges

Chelsea had long been a magnet for London artists and bohemians, and during the 1950s it was a haunt for the city's Beatnik culture. Quant paid tribute to their mini-

mal and monochromatic uniforms. As the couture never could, Quant and her brethren acknowledged, even asserted defiantly, that a primary design inspiration was the clothes of the young wandering the streets outside their workrooms. Quant was enamored, too, of the look of tap dancing students she'd watched as a child, as they practiced wearing short skirts, black tights, and patent-leather shoes. She kept on raising hemlines, and eventually Quant became known as "Mother of the Miniskirt." Some accounts have her showing skirts above the knee by 1958, although Quant's claims to precedence were challenged by Paris couturier André Courrèges. But who was first, or if there indeed was a first, is of peripheral importance. As far back as the late 1920s, hemlines were almost above the knee, and it was inevitable that after the long skirts of the late 1940s, they would rise again. As well, the inexorable shifts in society provided an historical imperative. In 1968, British fashion historian James Laver described the miniskirt as "the final word in the emancipation of women—in proving her economic independence…Long, hampering skirts were fetters to keep a woman at home. The very short ones scream: 'I am stepping out'" (*WWD* March 22, 1968, p.8).

King's Road

Eventually, there were three Bazaars in London. They survived until 1968, by which time Quant was presiding over a vast wholesale and licensing empire. Bazaar was a catalyst in King's Road's transformation into a streaming, coursing artery of fashion and display. Kiki Byrne, who had worked as Quant's assistant, also opened a celebrated boutique there, where Hulanicki was enthralled by Byrne's "wonderful black dresses … shifts that weren't over-designed" (conversation with author, November 1988). Her generation wanted something much looser both philosophically and structurally even than the unfitted shape that was being shown in the Paris couture as the 1950s progressed. The Youthquake silhouette was less determined, less sculptural, less constructed, and usually less decorated. "Our clothes *had* to be comfortable," Tuffin recalled. "That was the main requirement" (conversation with author, November 1988).

While the Paris couture continued to take itself very seriously, the kingdom of Youthquake teemed with humor and irreverence. Quant gave droll names to her clothes and arranged gag tableau in her store windows. Foale and Tuffin put Y's across the front of shift dresses—"Y-fronts" were men's underwear briefs.

Where pants for women were concerned, London was more adventurous than the Paris couture or even the "ye-yes," the young ready to wear designers of Paris. The Foale and Tuffin trouser suit became a global prototype—"The cut was incredible," Betsey Johnson recalled, "the best I've ever seen" (conversation with author, August, 1987). They were strongly advocating trousers well before Courrèges's pants-dominated couture collections of the mid-1960s. Yet in 1961, when they first began teaming pants instead of skirts with jackets, the combination seemed so incongruous that "we actually fell about laughing," Tuffin recalled. Lines were straight, shoulders natural, the jacket semi-fitted like riding attire, but devoid of constructed reinforcement. The trouser suit was one of Youthquake fashion's most controversial provocations, but also one of its most enduring legacies.

Youthquake fashion at its most egalitarian and inclusive was represented by London's Biba boutique, which Hulanicki opened with her husband Stephen Fitz-Simon in 1964. "We practically gave our things away to the public," Hulanicki claimed. Biba practiced a rapid response to the trends of the street, alternately spurring and parrying the restless experimentation of the young. "I couldn't stand wholesale," Hulanicki said, "because it's just between you and the buyer, and the buyers are always wrong, anyway. They want what sold last year, but we were working right on the moment, all the time" (conversation with author, November 1988). Biba kept moving to larger and large quarters, its decor an iconoclastic mise-en-scène of oddments and antiques. With Biba, the Youthquake boutique reached its apogee as destination, event, parade ground, and crossroads.

Although at Biba the use of inexpensive synthetics was dictated by the need to keep prices down, synthetics were also championed by Youthquake fashion for reasons other than necessity. Rather then simply a pallid imitation of natural fibers, they could manifest novel textures and appearances. Machine-tooled fabrics were celebrated as a threshold to a utopia of increased leisure and lessened drudgery. Quant extolled their ability to look "like a delicious soufflé that happened with a pure kind of joy—without anybody's tears on them" (conversation with author, December 1988).

Youthquake designers were certainly gratified by the boggled attention their work received by mainstream manufacturers, journalists, and even the couture itself. But they were primarily concerned with designing for themselves and their contemporaries, and because of the exploding youth market, were able to do so without compromise. Certainly mature women could legitimately complain that the ubiquitous narrow armholes of the Youthquake silhouette were not easy to fit into. Women who'd been brought up on the postwar British rations were not robust. Hulanicki noted that the average women's shoe size during the 1960s was 3 1/2 or 4, while twenty years later it had jumped two sizes. The somewhat androgynous silhouette privileged by Youthquake fashion was also an aesthetic and sexual statement, however, a rejection of the overblown ideal of hourglass femininity that been promulgated during the 1950s by the couture and, perhaps more oppressively, by the imagery of popular culture.

Men's New Look

Women's reassessment of gender-specific clothes and behavior, unleashed from men a rejection of the dour

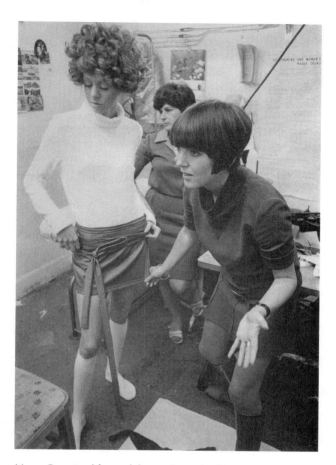

Mary Quant with model wearing miniskirt. Quant became known "the Mother of the Miniskirt," a garment that became very popular with young women in the late 1960s. © Bettmann/Corbis. Reproduced by permission.

clothes that had been obligatory since the Regency epoch of the nineteenth century. Young working-class men of the late 1950s organized themselves into coteries—The Teddy Boys, The Mods, the Rockers—each with its own odd and distinctive uniform. Around this time, Scottish-born retailer John Stephens began to transform London's Carnaby Street into a chockablock concentration of stores inviting men to cast off the fetters of old. Once all but completely polarized, men's and women's clothes could now converge into unisex outfits designed to be worn by either sex. A colony of men's and unisex boutiques sprung up around London, allowing men a selection unlike anything previously imaginable.

Clothing Anarchy

Biba's enveloping of new world fashions in the warm patina of vintage furnishings could be seen to anticipate the historical bent of late '60s London fashion. The city's archival closets were turned inside out and its streets became a fantastic masquerade. The rage for antique clothing, as well as the folklore and psychedelic panoply of the hippies dominated this second phase of Youthquake. The hippies' sartorial revolution evolved from the fashions of the Beats and the British ready-to-wear sisterhood; its founding mothers smoothly negotiated this second phase of Youthquake. The late '60s also saw the rise of designers like Ossie Clark and Zandra Rhodes, whose gossamer and fanciful creations recalled the romanticism of Arts and Crafts dress of the previous century. Vanguard London fashion of the late '60s was more anarchic than earlier in the decade. The laissez-faire of the hippies necessitated less homogeneous internal consistency to broadcast its sartorial and cultural message.

The End of an Era

By the mid-1970s, however, the very moniker Youthquake was superannuated. Many of the movers and shakers were in states of decompression or stately retreat. Quant was by now concentrating entirely on licensing. Foale and Tuffin disbanded. After Hulanicki and Fitz-Simon's alliance with outside capital, Biba suffered a bitter demise not long after reaching its apotheosis taking over a huge Art Deco department store. On the other hand, designers like Rhodes thrived amid a London fashion environment that continued to appreciate the eccentric. Conversely, the more muted and classic designs of Youthquake's Jean Muir became more popular than ever.

The plucky young firebrands of Youthquake had succeeded in radically upending global fashion markets. London itself has never returned to the fashion backwaters it was in the 1950s. The social and economic leveling proclaimed by Youthquake's habits and habiliments were not defeated by reactionary political developments during Britain in the 1980s. The Youthquake movement will always be an inspiration to those who seek to democratize fashion and tap the creative vitality of youth.

See also **Biba; Miniskirt; Quant, Mary.**

BIBLIOGRAPHY

Lobenthal, Joel. *Radical Rags: Fashions of the Sixties.* New York: Abbeville Press, 1990.

Mulvagh, Jane. *Vogue History of 20th Century Fashion.* London: Viking, 1988.

Quant, Mary. *Quant by Quant.* London: Cassell, 1966.

Steele, Valerie. *Fifty Years of Fashion: New Look to Now.* New Haven, Conn.: Yale University Press, 1997.

Joel Lobenthal

YUKATA The *yukata* of the early 2000s has remained, since the Edo period (1603–1868), an unlined cotton garment, with the traditional T-shape and overlapping lapels of the kimono. Purists may consider it more of a bathrobe than a true kimono. An ancestor of the modern yukata is the *katabira*, an unlined bast fiber (usually hemp or ramie) *kosode* worn in the summer by the upper classes. A *yukatabira* (*yu* is derived from the word for bathing) was

A Japanese woman wearing a floral *yukata*. Made of lightweight cotton, *yukata* are kimonos usually worn in the summer. © ROBERT ESSEL NYC/CORBIS. REPRODUCED BY PERMISSION.

put on after a bath as a way of drying the body; bath towels were not used in Japan at this time.

By the late Edo period cotton was abundant in Japan, having first been successfully cultivated as a commercial crop in the seventeenth century. As cotton, while still a bast fiber, is a softer and more absorbent fiber than hemp or ramie, it became the fiber of preference for the yukatabira. By the time cotton was readily available, the garment became known by its current abbreviated name, yukata.

Cotton is more easily dyed than other bast fibers, and indigo is one of the most colorfast of all natural dyes. It has the additional benefit of not requiring a separate mordanting process. Blue, therefore, became the dominant color for cotton yukata, and remains so, in spite of the prevalence of the more practical and versatile synthetic dyes, which can create virtually any desired color on cotton. Blue remains as popular a color for yukata as it was during the Edo period, when the color brought to mind coolness and water, welcoming thoughts during the hot Japanese summers.

The most common method employed for the dyeing of cotton fabric intended for yukata involved the use of paper stencils and a resist-paste made from rice. Stencils slightly wider than the width of a single bolt of cloth were cut with intricate designs, both figural and abstract. Rice paste was applied through the stencils, and the bolt of cloth would then be dyed by immersion in the indigo vat. The indigo dye would not penetrate the cloth in areas where the rice paste adhered; therefore, the designs would appear in white and the background in blue.

The custom of soaking in a wooden tub filled with hot water is relatively recent in Japanese history. Prior to the eighteenth century, bathing consisted of taking a steam bath. The rise of the public bathhouse (there were more than 500 in Edo [modern-day Tokyo] by the mid-nineteenth century) created a milieu for the wearing of yukata in a public place on a regular basis. Bathhouses were popular not only for reasons of hygiene and relaxation, but also because they often included rooms for eating, drinking, and having sex.

The most enthusiastic customers of the bathhouses came from the lowly merchant class, and they welcomed the opportunity to make a show of the latest in yukata designs. As with kosode, it was kabuki actors and other entertainers who often launched new fashions in yukata. Witty and amusing larger-scale motifs were most popular, and required the use of the *chûgata* stencil, as opposed to the tiny-scale repeats of the komon stencil. Komon patterns were typical of the dignified and conservative samurai class.

Another reason for the popularity of the yukata as a fashionable garment was the existence of sumptuary laws, which impacted most strongly on the merchant class. A yukata, being made of cotton rather than silk, and patterned by the inexpensive process of stencil dyeing, might be excessive in design, but was never very costly. Therefore, yukata escaped the scrutiny of the government authorities.

As Japan modernized in the Meiji period (1868–1912) and beyond, yukata became the one traditional garment that a man might wear in public. Hot spring resorts were, and still are, another popular venue for the yukata, as are traditional summer festivals, such as Obon. Foreign visitors to Japan, especially those who stay at a traditional inn (*ryōkan*), will find a yukata in their room, which conveniently presents the foreigner with an opportunity to wear a kimono-like garment.

See also **Japanese Fashion; Japanese Traditional Dress and Adornment; Japonisme; Kimono.**

BIBLIOGRAPHY

Gonick, Gloria Granz. *Matsuri! Japanese Festival Arts.* Los Angeles: UCLA Fowler Museum of Cultural History, 2002.

Kuo, Susanna Campbell. *Carved Paper: The Art of the Japanese Stencil.* Santa Barbara, New York, and Tokyo: Santa Barbara Museum of Art and Weatherhill, Inc., 1998.

Stevens, Rebecca T., and Yoshiko Iwamoto Wada, eds. *The Kimono Inspiration: Art and Art-to-Wear in America.* Washington, D.C.: The Textile Museum, 1996.

Alan Kennedy

ZIPPER More generically called a "slide fastener," the zipper is used as a closure in garments and a variety of other articles. Zippers were first introduced in a primitive form in the 1890s, but were not widely accepted in clothing until the 1930s.

The fastener that Americans most commonly call "zippers" can be traced to the invention of a Midwestern traveling salesman, Whitcomb Judson, in the early 1890s. Judson patented his device as a "clasp locker or unlocker" for shoes; this invention resembled the later zipper only superficially. It consisted of a series of hooks and eyes, each pair of which was engaged by the action of a key or slider. Over the next few years, Judson designed modifications of this device, none of which worked very effectively. The idea of an "automatic hook-and-eye," however, caught the attention of entrepreneurs, so Judson was given money and encouragement to continue engineering his invention, and in the first years after 1900, the first devices came to market under the aegis of the Universal Fastener Company of Hoboken, New Jersey.

After several years of futile design and sales efforts, the Hoboken company gained the services of a Swedish immigrant, Gideon Sundback. Trained as an electrical engineer, Sundback was a remarkably clever and astute mechanic. He analyzed with care the key elements of the automatic hook-and-eye, and concluded that the hook-and-eye model was not a suitable one for any kind of automatic fastener. Late in 1913, Sundback introduced his "Hookless Fastener," based on novel principles and resembling in all important respects the modern metal zipper.

Sundback's hookless fastener depended on the action of a series of closely spaced elements, technically called "scoops," whose precise spacing and ingenious shape are key to the fastener's success. Each scoop has a dimple on one side and a protruding nib on the other. The fastener consists of two opposing rows of scoops, spaced so that the scoops from one side engage in the spaces between the scoops on the other side. The nib from one scoop fits into the dimple in the facing scoop, whose nib in turn fits into the next dimple down the row. Sundback likened the action to a series of spoons in which the bowls of alternating spoons fitted into one another. If the spoons at each end of the rows are held in place, the intermediate spoons cannot disengage one another. The slider's function is simply to bring the two rows of scoops together (or to separate them) in a continuous, serial action.

The entrepreneurs who had backed Judson and then Sundback readily saw the efficacy of the hookless fastener design. Sundback's contributions went further to include the construction of machinery that made fastener manufacture rapid and economical. The Hookless Fastener Company was organized in Meadville, Pennsylvania, and efforts to market the novel device began in 1914. The fastener makers encountered challenges every bit as formidable as the technical ones they had overcome after such effort. The early hookless fastener was an unquestionably clever device, and it worked reasonably reliably and consistently. It was, however, expensive compared to the buttons or hooks and eyes that it was designed to replace, and it posed a host of difficulties for the designers and makers of most garments.

The clothing industry initially rejected the new fastener. It might, in fact, have died an ignominious early death if its salesmen had not cultivated small niche markets that sustained it for several years. Money belts for World War I sailors were followed by tobacco pouches, which in turn were followed, in the early 1920s, by rubber overshoes. The manufacturers of this last, the B. F. Goodrich Rubber Company, came up with a moniker for their new product, "Zippers," that became even more popular than the overshoes themselves, and the term "zipper" came to be the common American term for the fastener (despite Goodrich's trademark claims). Through most of the 1920s, expanding niche markets brought the fastener to a wider public, although garment makers still resisted wider adoption. Hookless Fastener adopted the trademark "Talon" in 1928 (and changed the corporate name to Talon, Inc., a decade later).

Only in the 1930s did zippers come to be accepted elements of men's and women's clothing, and even then only by steps. The famous haute couture designer, Elsa Schiaparelli, chose to set her designs of 1935 off by liberal use of zippers—even in places where no fastener was needed or expected. A couple of years later, in 1937, zippers began to appear widely in high fashion lines— Edward Molyneux's pencil-slim coats, for example, used zippers to emphasize the sleek silhouette. At about the same time, the designers of the best tailored men's clothing let it be known that zippered flies were acceptable, and by the end of the decade, zippers were common in the better men's trousers and were making their way into the ready-to-wear market. The combination of a reduction in prices (due to higher volume production) and the growing association of the zipper with modernity and fashion overcame the long-standing resistance of the garment makers and buyers. The widespread use of zippers in military uniforms during World War II was associated by many with the final popularization of the fastener, but its usage was already well on its way to becoming common before the war. By the 1950s, the zipper was the default fastener for everything from skirt plackets and trouser flies to leather motorcycle jackets and backpacks.

Even before the war, some manufacturers experimented with replacing the copper-nickel alloy standard in zippers with plastic, but this substitution was not very successful until Talon and the DuPont Company collaborated on a very new zipper design, in which the metal scoops were replaced by nylon spirals. The nylon zipper, after a few difficult years, became the standard appliance for lightweight applications, as garment makers were particularly attracted to the ease with which the nylon could be colored to match fabric dyes. Other materials were used for more specialized purposes: surgeons even adopted inert Teflon zippers for post-operative applications.

The zipper was by no means a strictly American phenomenon. Within only a few years of its introduction, British manufacturers sought to establish manufacture, and by the mid-1920s, French, German, and other suppliers followed. The chief British manufacturer, the Lightning Fastener Company of Birmingham, gave its name to the fastener itself in a wide range of languages; in France it became known as a "fermature éclair," and in Germany as a "Blitzverschluss" (*Reissverschluss* became the more common German word later).

As the zipper became increasingly common in the twentieth century, it acquired an unusual cultural status. It became a widely recognized and used symbol with a host of associations. Aldous Huxley used zippers throughout his 1932 novel, *Brave New World,* to allude to the impersonal and mechanical nature of sex in his nightmarish world of the future. Broadway and Hollywood began in the same decade to use the zipper to convey images of promiscuity: Rodgers and Hart's 1940 musical *Pal Joey* included a famous pantomime striptease with the refrain of "zip" throughout. Rita Hayworth, in her 1946 movie *Gilda,* used the zipper more than once as an instrument of sexual provocation. Even in the realm of urban legend, the zipper quickly became a common trope, conveying the awkwardness of relying on the mechanical in the intimate realms of daily life.

In the course of the twentieth century, the zipper became so ubiquitous as to become almost invisible. It has multiplied in form, size, style, and function; ranging from the simple plastic of the Ziploc bag to the zippers used in surgery and spacesuits. Arguably the most characteristic fastener of the twentieth century, the zipper has still not, even in the twenty-first century, lost its symbolic power to convey sexuality, opening and closing, separating and joining. And, despite the apparent allure of alternatives from old-fashioned buttons to modern Velcro, zippers appear in no danger of being displaced as the leading fastener.

See also **Fasteners; Uniforms, Military.**

BIBLIOGRAPHY

Friedel, Robert. *Zipper: An Exploration in Novelty.* New York: W. W. Norton, 1994.

Gray, James. *Talon, Inc.: A Romance of Achievement.* Meadville, Pa.: Talon Inc., 1963.

Robert Friedel

ZOOT SUIT The zoot suit cut a suave silhouette. Initially popularized by black "hipsters" in the mid- to late-1930s, but embraced more generally by swing jazz enthusiasts of all colors, the zoot suit jacket exaggerated the upper male body with wide padded shoulders and broad lapels, tapering dramatically down to the waist and flaring out to the knees. The pants were flowing, high waisted, and pleated, flaring at the knees and angling radically down to a tight fit around the ankles. The look was usually completed with a porkpie hat, long watch chain, thin belt, and matching shoes. It was a style androgynous enough to be worn by either men or women, but the fashion was most popular among men.

Eastern zooters favored eye-catching colors and patterns, but youth on the West coast preferred a more discreet appearance, possibly prompted by the March 1942 ruling of the War Production Board restricting the measurements for men's suits and rationing the availability of material for civilian use. Men's fashion in general became more moderate, and "the drape" was the more conservative version of the zoot suit. The length of the drape jacket was considerably shorter than the zoot jacket, falling at mid-thigh, and otherwise looked little different from a man's oversized business suit. Some women in Los Angeles took to wearing pleated skirts underneath the drape jacket with hosiery and huarache sandals.

Contemporary accounts placed the origins of the zoot suit in the African American communities of Gainesville, Georgia; Chicago; and Harlem, but the stylistic foundations of the zoot suit trace back to Edwardian fashion at the turn of the century. In the Northeast, the style was known as the "root suit," "suit suit," and "zoot suit"; in the South as "killer diller"; and in the West as "drape shape" or in Spanish as "el tacuche" (the wardrobe).

Jobs in war production allowed young people to experiment with consumption and a popular culture largely inspired by the African American jazz artists they admired. Jazz music, dance, clothing, and language that

Three men wearing zoot suits at a Los Angeles night club, 1942. Zoot suits were a trend carried by many Latino and black youth. Police and government authorities were often suspicious of the youth who wore it. © Bettmann/Corbis. Reproduced by permission.

boundaries. As people of color challenged racial barriers across the nation, many whites violently resisted integration. To them, the popularity of the zoot suit seemed to epitomize growing concerns over juvenile delinquency as young people of color increasingly refused to defer to white privilege.

In early June 1943, sailors, soldiers, and some civilians in Los Angeles rioted for a week, setting off a wave of race riots in cities large and small across the nation. The Zoot Suit Riot in Los Angeles was the longest, but the Detroit Race Riot in mid-June was the deadliest. Growing tensions over integration led to a day and a half of rioting, leaving twenty-five blacks and nine whites dead and more than 1,800 arrested. Conversely, in Los Angeles, no murders, rapes, deaths, or serious damage to property were reported in connection with the riot, and only a few cases of serious injury. The mob of mostly white military men seemed focused on reasserting segregation, breached by "uppity" young men of color, by destroying their public displays of wealth and beating those who refused to yield their drapes.

Jazz followed wherever American troops were stationed abroad, and for a moment zoot suits were fashionable among jazz enthusiasts in France, England, and

youth across the color line shared allowed for re-creations of social identities. For some, jazz music and the hipster style were audacious celebrations of life in spite of the difficulties blacks faced during the 1930s. For others, wearing the fashion was a show of newfound but modest wealth from wartime employment that signaled their move from square to cool or from "country" to urbane. At the same time, the zoot suit was a dashing if not scandalous image because of its association with hipsters, drugs, and sex. Such layered meanings promised rich possibilities for transforming cultural expression into a form of resistance to the social conventions of segregation.

Although a few saw the popularity of the zoot suit as a harmless development, many more had visceral reactions to it as a symbol of the breakdown of social convention. Critics of jazz fashion seemed unable to accept that working-class youth of color could afford such an expensive suit through honest means. Some saw the suit as a waste of rationed material and an unabashed disregard for community values of thrift and sacrifice. Others projected the antiwar sympathies that some black hipsters expressed to all jazz enthusiasts who wore the zoot suit.

In many communities, the zoot suit grew into a powerful symbol of subversion by the mid-1940s, transformed by different sources of tension over changing social

Jazz band members in zoot suits, 1942. Jazz band leader Lionel Hampton shortens a band member's zoot suit on stage. Zoot suits were popular with jazz enthusiasts. © Bettmann/Corbis. Reproduced by permission.

as far away as South Africa. The zoot suit fell out of fashion in the postwar years as the jazz world moved from swing to be-bop, but it served as the inspiration for the Teddy Boys' distinctive look in postwar London.

Decades later the zoot suiter arose immortalized in the dramatic and scholarly works of Chicano artists and intellectuals who saw the wartime generation as cultural nationalists. A zoot suit revival inspired by Luis Valdez's stage and screen musical continues in popular venues, and productions of *Zoot Suit* continue to draw large audiences in the Southwest. Some businesses and Internet sites cater to customers interested in zoot suits, and zoot-suited youth are a staple at some low rider car shows. For many Mexican American youth, putting on the zoot suit serves as a way to connect with a past that was self-assertive and stylish, pay homage to community elders, and assume a place in the continuum of cultural resistance and affirmation.

High-end designers such as Stacey Adams, Vittorio St. Angelo, and Gianni Vironi produce suits that could well be considered next-generation zoot suits. Updated zoot suits no longer elicit the public censure received in the 1940s, because the social context in which the fashion was first received has changed so dramatically.

See also **African American Dress; Latin American Fashion.**

BIBLIOGRAPHY

Capeci, Dominic J., and Martha Wilkerson. *Layered Violence: The Detroit Rioters of 1943.* Jackson: University of Mississippi, 1991.

Mazón, Mauricio. *The Zoot Suit Riots: The Psychology of Symbolic Annihilation.* Austin: University of Texas, 1984.

Pagán, Eduardo Obregón. *Murder at the Sleepy Lagoon: Zoot Suits, Race, and Riot in Wartime L.A.* Chapel Hill: University of North Carolina Press, 2003.

White, Shane, and Graham White. *Stylin': African American Expressive Culture From Its Beginnings to the Zoot Suit.* Ithaca, New York: Cornell University Press, 1998.

Eduardo Pagán

ZORAN Zoran Ladicorbic, born in 1947, was an architectural student from Yugoslavia who came to New York and launched an unconventional fashion business in 1976 that stood out for its simple formula of luxurious, casual basics. In contrast to the ornate frocks of Parisian couture that screamed "expensive," Zoran made stark minimalism his signature as he turned out spartan collections of tops, pull-on pants, shift dresses, sarong skirts, and sweaters in sumptuous cashmere, Tasmanian wool, cotton and silk taffeta, and lamé. Zoran's silhouettes never changed, so that a Zoran wardrobe defies the very notion of fashion trends. Zoran calls his fashion formula "jet pack" fashion: simple styles without zippers, fastenings, or other embellishments. The clothes can be folded flat and tossed into a carry-on suitcase stashed in the overhead compartment of an airplane. Zoran's business is as spare as his fashions; he has neither design assistants nor does he offer secondary lines like jeans and fragrances that round out other designer collections.

In the 1990s, Zoran's business exploded and became one of the top-selling high–fashion brands in stores such as Neiman Marcus, Bergdorf Goodman, and Saks Fifth Avenue. As a luxury brand, Zoran appealed to upscale businesswomen and movie stars such as Isabella Rossellini and Elizabeth Taylor, who preferred the low-key glamour of simple basics that allowed them—and not the clothes—to shine through. His most devoted fans are known as the Zoranians. Fashion observers regarded Zoran's minimalist formula as basics for the rich.

Fueling the mystique of Zoran's quirky fashions is his iconoclastic demeanor. As he wears his hair and busy beard long, he has been dubbed fashion's Rasputin. A chain smoker who loves Stolichnaya vodka, Zoran is a confrontational dictator who doesn't believe in fashion's usual conventions. He believes that confident women should simplify their lives and wear flat shoes, no jewelry, and a wash-and-wear haircut—along with his clothes.

Retailers say that the Zoran formula is luxury goods marketing 101. He only sells to one or two stores in every city, which makes his clothes hard to find, and therefore all the more coveted by his fans. As a result, retailers aren't compelled to mark down the goods to fuel sales, as Zoran repeats the same styles year after year so that nothing in his collections looks dated. Because he does no fashion shows and gets very little publicity in the press, shoppers regard his brand as having the ultimate snob appeal—the epitome of "dog whistle fashion," pitched so high that only insiders recognize it.

See also **Department Store; Fashion Designer; Fashion Marketing and Merchandising; Retailing.**

BIBLIOGRAPHY

Agins, Teri. "Uniquely Chic: If Zoran Doesn't Ring a Bell That's Fine with Quirky Designer." *Wall Street Journal*, (5 May 1995).

——. "Outside of the Box: Zoran." In *The End of Fashion: The Mass Marketing of the Clothing Business.* New York: William Morrow and Co., 1999, pp. 247–274.

Brantley, Ben. "Zoran Zeitgeist." *Vanity Fair*, (March 1992).

Teri Agins

ZORIS. *See* **Sandals.**

SYSTEMATIC OUTLINE OF CONTENTS

This systematic outline provides a general overview of the conceptual scheme of the *Encyclopedia*, listing the titles of each entry. The outline is divided into seven broad subject areas and then subsequent categories within the topic.

Because section headings are not mutually exclusive, certain entries in the *Encyclopedia* are listed in more than one section.

I. HISTORY OF CLOTHING
A. Regional Dress

First Ladies' Gowns
Godey's Lady's Book
Hollywood Style
Madonna
Supermodels
Trendsetters
Twiggy
Vogue
Wilde, Oscar
Windsor, Duke and Duchess of
Women's Wear Daily

J. Writing about Fashion
Balzac, Honoré de
Barthes, Roland
Baudelaire, Charles
Baudrillard, Jean
Benjamin, Walter
Best-Dressed Lists
Clothing, Costume, and Dress
Cunnington, C. Willett and Phillis
Demorest, Mme.
Fashion, Historical Studies of
Fashion, Theories of
Fashion Editors
Fashion Journalism
Fashion Magazines
Fashion Online
Fashion Plates
Flügel, J. C.
Future of Fashion
Godey's Lady's Book
Laver, James
Mallarmé, Stéphane
Marx, Karl
Moore, Doris Langley
Proust, Marcel
Simmel, Georg
Uzanne, Octave
Veblen, Thorstein
Vogue
Wilde, Oscar
Women's Wear Daily

K. Marketing and Merchandising
Boutique
Brands and Labels
Department Store
Economics and Clothing
Fads
Fashion Advertising
Fashion Editors
Fashion Magazines
Fashion Marketing and Merchandising
Fashion Online
Fashion Photography
Fashion Plates
Fashion Shows

Fashion Television
Film and Fashion
Logos
Ready-to-Wear
Retailing
Savile Row
Seventh Avenue
Shopping
Supermodels
Trendsetters
Trickle-Down
Twiggy
Vogue
Window Displays

L. Display
Cunnington, C. Willett and Phillis
Fashion Models
Fashion Museums and Collections
Fashion Online
Fashion Photography
Fashion Plates
Fashion Shows
Fashion Television
Mannequins
Moore, Doris Langley
Ready-to-Wear
Seventh Avenue
Supermodels
Twiggy
Vogue
Wearable Art
Window Displays

VI. DESIGNERS AND DESIGN HOUSES

Adrian
Alaïa, Azzedine
Albini, Walter
Amies, Hardy
Armani, Giorgio
Balenciaga, Cristóbal
Balmain, Pierre
Beaton, Cecil
Beene, Geoffrey
Bertin, Rose
Biba
Blahnik, Manolo
Blass, Bill
Brooks Brothers
Burberry
Burrows, Stephen
Callot Sisters
Capucci, Roberto
Cardin, Pierre
Cashin, Bonnie
Chalayan, Hussein

Chanel, Gabrielle (Coco)
Clark, Ossie
Comme des Garçons
Courrèges, André
de la Renta, Oscar
Delaunay, Sonia
Demeulemeester, Ann
Dior, Christian
Dolce & Gabbana
Doucet, Jacques
Ellis, Perry
Fath, Jacques
Fendi
Ferragamo, Salvatore
Fogarty, Anne
Fontana Sisters
Ford, Tom
Fortuny, Mariano
Galanos, James
Galliano, John
Gaultier, Jean-Paul
Gernreich, Rudi
Gigli, Romeo
Givenchy, Hubert de
Grès, Mme.
Gucci
Halston
Hartnell, Norman
Hawes, Elizabeth
Head, Edith
Hermès
Hilfiger, Tommy
Hugo Boss
James, Charles
Kamali, Norma
Karan, Donna
Klein, Calvin
Lacroix, Christian
Lagerfeld, Karl
Lang, Helmut
Lanvin, Jeanne
Lauren, Ralph
Leiber, Judith
Lesage, François
Levi Strauss & Co.
Liberty & Co.
Lucile
Mackie, Bob
Mainbocher
Margiela, Martin
Marimekko
Marks & Spencer
McCardell, Claire
McFadden, Mary
McQueen, Alexander
Missoni
Miyake, Issey

Mori, Hanae
Moschino, Franco
Mugler, Thierry
Muir, Jean
Norell, Norman
Paquin, Jeanne
Patou, Jean
Poiret, Paul
Prada
Pucci, Emilio
Quant, Mary
Rabanne, Paco
Rhodes, Zandra
Rykiel, Sonia
Saint Laurent, Yves
Schiaparelli, Elsa
Seydou, Chris
Smith, Paul
Smith, Willi
Steele, Lawrence
Sy, Oumou
Toledo, Isabel and Ruben
Treacy, Philip
Trigère, Pauline
Valentina
Valentino
Versace, Gianni and Donatella
Viktor & Rolf
Vionnet, Madeleine
von Furstenberg, Diane
Vreeland, Diana
Vuitton, Louis
Westwood, Vivienne
Worth, Charles Frederick
Xuly Bët
Yamamoto, Yohji
Yeohlee
Zoran

VII. DISTRIBUTION, MATERIALS, AND MANUFACTURING
A. Production and Distribution
Boutique
Department Store
Domestic Production
Economics and Clothing
Globalization
Milliners
Ready-to-Wear
Seamstresses
Secondhand Clothes, Anthropology of
Secondhand Clothes, History of
Sewing Machine
Shoemaking
Shopping
Sweatshops

Tailoring
Textiles and International Trade
Textile Workers

B. Labor
Domestic Production
Garments, International Trade in
Globalization
Labor Unions
Milliners
Seamstresses
Shoemaking
Sweatshops
Textile Workers
Working-Class Dress

C. Fibers, Fabrics, and Textiles
Acrylic and Modacrylic Fibers
Adinkra
Adire
Agbada
Alpaca
Appliqué
Angora
Animal Prints
Bark Cloth
Batik
Beads
Calico
Cambric, Batiste, and Lawn
Camel Hair
Camouflage Cloth
Cashmere and Pashmina
Chintz
Corduroy
Cotton
Crepe
Crinoline
Denim
Elastomers
Feathers
Felt
Fibers
Flannel
Fur
Gabardine
Handwoven Textiles
Hemp
Homespun
Ikat
Jersey
Kanga
Kente
Lace
Leather and Suede
Linen
Microfibers

Mohair
Muslin
Nonwoven Textiles
Nylon
Oilskins
Olefin Fibers
Paisley
Plaid
Polyester
Ramie
Rayon
Recycled Textiles
Ribbon
Rubber as Fashion Fabric
Silk
Spangles
Striped Cloth
Tapestry
Tartan
Techno-Textiles
Textiles, African
Textiles, Andean
Textiles, Byzantine
Textiles, Central Asian
Textiles, Chinese
Textiles, Coptic
Textiles, Japanese
Textiles, Middle Eastern
Textiles, Prehistoric
Textiles, South Asian
Textiles, Southeast Asian Islands
Textiles, Southeast Asian Mainland
Textiles and International Trade
Textile Workers
Trimmings
Tweed
Velvet
Vinyl as Fashion Fabric
Wool
Yarns

D. Garment Construction
Closures, Hook-and-Loop
Cutting
Fasteners
Hemlines
Mannequins
Needles
Patterns and Patternmaking
Pins
Pockets
Safety Pins
Sewing Machine
Skirt Supports
Tailored Suit
Tailoring
Trimmings
Zipper

DIRECTORY OF CONTRIBUTORS

Isabella A. Abbott
Bark Cloth

Thomas S. Abler
Department of Anthropology,
University of Waterloo
Uniforms, Military

Teri Agins
Wall Street Journal
Garments, International Trade in
Zoran

Heather Marie Akou
University of Minnesota, Twin Cities
Islamic Dress, Contemporary
Jilbab
Weave, Jacquard
Weave, Plain
Weave, Satin
Weave, Twill

Ann Ilan Alter
Masquerade and Masked Balls

Fiona Anderson
National Museums of Scotland
Plaid
Scottish Dress
Shawls
Shoes, Men's
Tartan
Tweed

Joanne Arbuckle
Fashion Institute of Technology
Closures, Hook-and-Loop

Rebecca Arnold
Senior lecturer in fashion and theory,
Central Saint Martins College of Art
and Design, London
Heroin Chic
Vionnet, Madeleine
Westwood, Vivienne

Linda B. Arthur
Washington State University
Asia, Southeastern Islands and
the Pacific: History of Dress
Hawaiian Shirt
Religion and Dress

Juliet Ash
Tutor in Fashion/Textiles Critical &
Historical Studies, Royal College of Art,
London, U.K.
Prison Dress

Sonia Ashmore
Research fellow, London College of
Fashion, University of the Arts, London
Liberty & Co.

Jane Audas
Royal College of Art, London
Mannequins
Window Displays

Patricia L. Baker
Iran, History of Pre-Islamic
Dress
Middle East: History of Islamic
Dress

Mukulika Banerjee
University College, London, U.K.
Sari

E. J. W. Barber
Professor of Archeology and Linguistics,
Occidental College, Los Angeles
Textiles, Prehistoric

Ruth Barcan
Department of Gender Studies,
University of Sydney, Australia
Nudism
Nudity

Ruth Barnes
Researcher, Department of Eastern Art,
Ashmolean Museum, Oxford
Ikat

Claire Barratt
Central Saint Martins, University of
the Arts, London
Shroud

Djurdja Bartlett
Independent scholar
Communist Dress

Beatrix Bastl
Royal and Aristocratic Dress

Reed Benhamou
Department of Apparel Merchandising
and Interior Design, Indiana
University
Sumptuary Laws

Lenore Benson
Fashion Editors
Professional Associations

Parminder Bhachu
Clark University, Massachusetts
Salwar-Kameez

Vandana Bhandari
Associate Professor, Fashion and
Textiles Department, National Institute
of Fashion Technology
Turban

Martin Bide
Department of Textiles, Fashion
Merchandising and Design, University
of Rhode Island
Acrylic and Modacrylic Fibers
Elastomers
Olefin Fibers

Thomas A. Bilstad
Professional copy editor, freelance author
Occult Dress

Anne Bissonnette
Curator, Kent State University Museum
Tea Gown

Sandy Black
Reader in Knitwear and Fashion, London College of Fashion, University of the Arts, London
Sweater

Whitney Blausen
Independent researcher
Costume Designer
Spangles
Theatrical Costume

Heidi Boehlke
Batik
Kain-kebaya
Sarong

Andrew Bolton
Associate Curator, The Costume Institute, The Metropolitan Museum of Art
Kilt
Windsor, Duke and Duchess of

Laird Borrelli
Senior Fashion Editor, Style.com
Fashion Illustrators
Fashion Online
Trendsetters
Vogue

Marie Botkin
Apparel Marketing and Design, Family and Consumer Science, California State University, Sacramento
Corduroy
Flannel
Jersey
Napping

G. Bruce Boyer
Fashion Writer and Editor
Brooks Brothers

Ann W. Braaten
North Dakota State University
Alpaca
Angora
Camel Hair
Mohair
Wool
Worsted

Archie Brennan
Tapestry

Christopher Breward
London College of Fashion
London Fashion
Savile Row
Wilde, Oscar

Claudia Brown
Arizona State University
Textiles, Chinese

Stella Bruzzi
Professor of Film Studies at Royal Holloway, University of London
Film and Fashion

Michele Wesen Bryant
Fashion Institute of Technology
Rubber as Fashion Fabric

Vern L. Bullough
Cross-Dressing
Plastic and Cosmetic Surgery

Barbara Burman
University of Southampton, U.K.
Domestic Production
Pockets
Seamstresses
Working-Class Dress

Jeffrey A. Butterworth
Shoes, Children's

Elizabeth K. Bye
University of Minnesota
High-Tech Fashion
Nautical Style

Colleen R. Callahan
Curator Emeritus, The Valentine Richmond History Center
Bloomer Costume
Children's Clothing
Godey's Lady's Book
Outerwear

Gillion Carrara
Director of the Fashion Resource Center
Ferragamo, Salvatore
Fortuny, Mariano
Gucci
Italian Fashion
Missoni
Moschino, Franco
Steele, Lawrence
Versace, Gianni and Donatella

Michael Carter
Department of Art History and Theory, University of Sydney
Flügel, J. C.
Laver, James
Veblen, Thorstein

Frank Cartledge
Senior Lecturer, Chelsea College of Art, University of the Arts, London
Punk

Anna Beatriz Chadour-Sampson
Freelance jewelry historian and scholarly author, England, U.K.
Jewelry
Rings

Gary Chaison
Professor of Industrial Relations, Clark University, Worcester, Massachusetts
Sweatshops

Angel Chang
Design Assistant: Fabric Development and Creative Direction, The Donna Karan Company
Delaunay, Sonia
Sport Shoes
Viktor & Rolf

Beth Dincuff Charleston
Klein, Calvin

Xavier Chaumette
Gaultier, Jean-Paul
Tailored Suit

Joyce Cheney
Focus Communications/American Association of Museums/National Association of Museum Exhibition
Aprons

Beverly Chico
Regis University, School for Professional Studies
    Beret
    Chador
    Hats, Women's
    Headdress
    Helmet

Kimberley Chrisman-Campbell
Huntington Library, San Marino, California
    Bertin, Rose

Alice Cicolini
Curator and Project Manager, Design, British Council
    Dandyism
    Historicism and Historical Revival
    Stockings, Women's
    Vintage Fashion

Shaun Cole
Victoria & Albert Museum
    Jockey Shorts
    Fashion and Homosexuality

Elizabeth Ann Coleman
Museum of Fine Arts
    Doucet, Jacques
    Fashion Dolls
    James, Charles
    Worth, Charles Frederick

Billie J. Collier
University of Tennessee
    Microfibers
    Nonwoven Textiles
    Performance Finishes
    Yarns

John R. Collier
University of Tennessee
    Spinning Machinery

Caroline Cox
Vidal Sassoon Advanced Academy
    Barbers
    Beards and Mustaches
    G-string and Thong
    Lingerie
    Panties
    Petticoat
    Underwear
    Wigs

Maxine Leeds Craig
California State University, Hayward
    Afro Hairstyle

Patricia Cox Crews
Cather Professor of Textiles and Director, International Quilt Study Center, University of Nebraska, Lincoln
    Quilting

Oriole Cullen
Museum of London
    Aesthetic Dress
    Fath, Jacques

Elyssa Schram Da Cruz
Research Associate, The Costume Institute, The Metropolitan Museum of Art
    Cocktail Dress

M. Catherine Daly
    Veils

Mary Lynn Damhorst
Department of Textiles and Clothing, Iowa State University
    Casual Business Dress

Alison Matthews David
Centre for the History of Textiles and Dress, University of Southampton
    Balzac, Honoré de
    Brummell, George (Beau)
    Equestrian Costume
    Tailoring

Kaat Debo
Curator Contemporary Fashion MoMu
    Belgian Fashion
    Demeulemeester, Ann
    Margiela, Martin

Amy de la Haye
London College of Fashion
    Chanel, Gabrielle (Coco)
    Muir, Jean
    Patou, Jean
    Quant, Mary

Marilyn Revell DeLong
University of Minnesota, Saint Paul
    Color in Dress
    Fashion, Theories of
    Korean Dress and Adornment

Marilee DesLauriers
The Goldstein Museum of Design, University of Minnesota
    Embroidery
    Marimekko

Jasleen Dhamija
    Asia, Central: History of Dress
    Asia, South: History of Dress
    Paisley
    Textiles, Central Asian

Kitty G. Dickerson
Department of Textile and Apparel Management, University of Missouri, Columbia
    Textiles and International Trade

Carol A. Dickson
Apparel Product Design and Merchandising, University of Hawaii-Manoa
    Bark Cloth
    Denim
    Hemp

Jean L. Druesedow
Kent State University Museum
    Ready-to-Wear
    Trigère, Pauline

Robin Dutt
    Formal Wear, Men's

Bronwen Edwards
    Department Store
    Shopping

Edwina Ehrman
Curator of Dress and Decorative Art, Museum of London
    Amies, Hardy
    Hartnell, Norman

Joanne B. Eicher
University of Minnesota
    Africa, Sub-Saharan: History of Dress
    Clothing, Costume, and Dress
    Ethnic Dress

Fadwa El Guindi
University of Southern California
    Djellaba
    Hijab
    Kaffiyeh

Julia Emberley
Professor in English, University of Western Ontario
    Fur

Joy Spanabel Emery
Theatre University of Rhode Island
    Patterns and Patternmaking

Joanne Entwistle
Lecturer, University of Essex
    Dress for Success
    Fashion, Attacks on

Caroline Evans
Reader in Fashion Studies, Central Saint Martins College of Art and Design, The University of the Arts, London
    Fashion Models
    McQueen, Alexander
    Schiaparelli, Elsa

Sandra Lee Evenson
University of Idaho
    Cache-Sexe
    Codpiece
    Penis Sheath

William Ewing
    Avedon, Richard
    Horst, Horst P.
    Hoyningen-Huene, George

Jane Farrell-Beck
Textiles and Clothing Program, Iowa State University
    Girdle

Brigitte Felderer
    Gernreich, Rudi

Gretchen Fenston
Registrar, Condé Nast Archive
    Klein, Calvin

Mary Ann C. Ferro
Associate Professor, Fashion Institute of Technology
    Vinyl as Fashion Fabric

Michelle Tolini Finamore
Rhode Island School of Design
    Callot Sisters
    Iribe, Paul
    Fashion Shows
    Vreeland, Diana

Aurora Fiorentini
    Armani, Giorgio
    Valentino

Lynda Fitzwater
M.A. in Fashion Theory from London College of Fashion
    Secondhand Clothes, History of

Marnie Fogg
M.A.
    De la Renta, Oscar
    McFadden, Mary
    Rhodes, Zandra
    Rykiel, Sonia
    Smith, Paul
    Smith, Willi
    Suit, Business
    Treacy, Philip
    von Furstenberg, Diane

Katherine Forde
    Nail Art

Helen Bradley Foster
University of Minnesota
    African American Dress

Ed Franquemont
    Textiles, Andean

Robert Friedel
University of Maryland
    Zipper

Phyllis Galembo
Professor, Fine Arts Department, University at Albany, State University of New York
    Halloween Costume

Lorraine Gamman
Reader Design Context, School of Graphic and Industrial Design, Central St. Martins College of Art and Design
    Laundry

Philippe Garner
    Newton, Helmut

Colleen Gau
Independent historian
    Brassiere
    Corset

Liz Gessner
Freelance fashion writer, formerly editor of W Magazine *and* Women's Wear Daily
    Blahnik, Manolo
    Karan, Donna
    Little Black Dress

Key Sook Geum
Hong-IK University, Seoul, South Korea
    Korean Dress and Adornment

Donna Ghelerter
Costume and Textile historian, NYC
    Future of Fashion
    Norell, Norman
    Scarf

Pamela Church Gibson
Senior Lecturer, London College of Fashion
    Actors and Actresses, Impact on Fashion
    Celebrities
    Fashion Icons
    Hollywood Style
    Proust, Marcel
    Twiggy

Madeleine Ginsberg
    Fashion Magazines
    Fashion Plates

Jessica Glasscock
Author of Striptease: From Gaslight to Spotlight
    Striptease

Pamela Golbin
Curator, The Musée de la Mode et du Textiles, Paris
    Lacroix, Christian
    Saint Laurent, Yves

Ch. Didier Gondola
Indiana University, Indianapolis
    Sapeurs

Tom Greatrex
London, U.K.
    Blazer
    Boxer Shorts
    Coat

Tom Greatrex (*continued*)
    Dress Shirt
    Duffle Coat
    Jacket
    Oilskins
    Parka
    Polo Shirt
    Raincoat
    Rainwear
    Shirt
    Sport Shirt
    Sports Jacket
    Waistcoat
    Windbreaker

Annette Green
President Emeritus, The Fragrance Foundation. Shipman School of Journalism, NYU, The New School
    Perfume

Rebecca L. Green
Associate Professor and Chair of Art History, Bowling Green State University
    Kanga

Susan W. Greene
American Costume Studies, Alfred Station, NY
    Calico
    Cambric, Batiste, and Lawn
    Crepe
    Indigo
    Muslin

Michael Gross
Contributing editor of Travel and Leisure, *contributing writer for* Radar
    Lauren, Ralph
    Supermodels

Irene Guenther
Professor, Department of History, Houston Community College-Northwest
    Fascist and Nazi Dress

Elisabeth Hackspiel-Mikosch
Lecturer at the Niederrhein University of Applied Sciences, Moenchengladbach, Germany
    Uniforms, Diplomatic
    Uniforms, Occupational

Nancy Hall-Duncan
Curator, Bruce Museum of Arts and Science, Greenwich, Conn.
    Beaton, Cecil
    Bourdin, Guy
    Dahl-Wolfe, Louise
    Fashion Photography
    Meisel, Steven

Karen Tranberg Hansen
Department of Anthropology, Northwestern University
    Colonialism and Imperialism
    Secondhand Clothes, Anthropology of

Marin F. Hanson
Assistant curator, International Quilt Study Center, University of Nebraska, Lincoln
    Quilting

Leslie Harris
Independent scholar, London, U.K.
    Canes and Walking Sticks
    Legal and Judicial Costume
    Watches

Avril Hart
Assistant Curator of the Department of Textiles and Dress, Victoria & Albert Museum
    Fans

H. Kristina Haugland
Philadelphia Museum of Art
    Blouse
    Bustle
    Crinoline
    Leotard
    Nightgown
    Skirt
    Skirt Supports
    Slip

Jana M. Hawley
Textile and Apparel Management, University of Missouri
    Recycled Textiles

Michaele Haynes
Curator of History and Textiles, Witte Museum of San Antonio
    Debutante Dress

Thomas Hecht
Central School of Speech and London College of Fashion
    Ballet Costume
    Dance and Fashion
    Dance Costume
    Hugo Boss
    Lang, Helmut
    Pointe Shoes

Joyce Heckman
    Fads

Jane E. Hegland
Department Head and Associate Professor, Apparel Merchandising and Interior Design, South Dakota State University
    Ball Dress
    Evening Dress
    Fashion Education

Barbara Perso Heinemann
University of Minnesota
    Jumper Dress

Paula Heinonen
IGS (CCCRW), University of Oxford
    Cosmetics, Non-Western

Janet Hethorn
University of Delaware
    Skating Dress

Robert Hillestad
University of Nebraska, Lincoln
    Appearance

Bette Hochberg
    Spinning

Paul Hodkinson
University of Surrey, England
    Goths

Susie Hopkins
London College of Fashion
    Crowns and Tiaras
    Hats, Men's
    Milliners

Catherine Horwood
Royal Holloway, University of London
    Tennis Costumes

Nancy Arthur Hoskins
Coptic researcher, former weaving instructor, and author of The Coptic Tapestry Albums *and the* Archaeologist of Antinoé
    Textiles, Coptic

Stephanie Day Iverson
University of California, Los Angeles
    Cashin, Bonnie

Anthea Jarvis
Curator, Gallery of Costume, Platt Hall, Manchester, U.K.
    Fancy Dress

Charlotte Jirousek
Cornell University
    Textiles, Middle Eastern

Paul Jobling
The School of Historical and Critical Studies, University of Brighton, U.K.
    Fashion Advertising

Anna Johnson
    Handbags and Purses

Kim K. P. Johnson
University of Minnesota
    Politics and Fashion

Lucy Johnston
Curator of nineteenth century fashion and wedding dress, Victoria & Albert Museum
    Ski Clothing

Alan Cannon Jones
F.FCDE (Fellow, Federation of Clothing Designers and Executives)
    Cutting

Esther Juhasz
Hebrew University, Israel
    Jewish Dress

Sara J. Kadolph
Textiles and Clothing, Department of Apparel, Educational Studies, and Hospitality Management, Iowa State University
    Chintz
    Dyeing
    Dyes, Natural
    Gabardine

Susan B. Kaiser
University of California at Davis
    Fads
    Fashion and Identity
    Trickle-Down

Lydia Kamitsis
Fashion historian; independent fashion curator
    Lesage, François
    Rabanne, Paco

Walter Karcheski
Chief curator of arms and armor, Frazier Historical Arms Museum, Louisville, Kentucky
    Armor

Denise Kastrinakis
    Fads

Yuniya Kawamura
State University of New York, Fashion Institute of Technology
    Japanese Fashion
    Miyake, Issey
    Mori, Hanae

Alan Kennedy
Independent researcher, contributing editor, Hali
    Japanese Traditional Dress and Adornment
    Kimono
    Yukata

Shirley Kennedy
Fashion Art Bank Inc., founding partner
    Pucci, Emilio

Claudia Kidwell
    First Ladies' Gowns

Raisa Kirsanova
    Russia: History of Dress

Rosanne Klass
Director, Afghanistan Information Center, Freedom House, New York, 1980–1991
    Burqa

Dorothy Ko
Barnard College, Columbia University
    Footbinding

Anna König
Associate Lecturer, London College of Fashion
    Neckties and Neckwear
    Umbrellas and Parasols

Désirée Koslin
Fashion Institute of Technology
    Textiles, Byzantine
    Velvet

Colleen E. Kriger
University of North Carolina at Greensboro
    Robe

Youn Kyung-Kim
    Recycled Textiles

Karen L. LaBat
University of Minnesota
    Asia, Southeastern Mainland: History of Dress
    Bicycle Clothing
    Fasteners
    High-Tech Fashion

John Lappe
President, Museum Quality Speciality Drycleaning Services
    Dry Cleaning

Babatunde Lawal
Department of Art History, Virginia Commonwealth University
    Agbada
    Carnival Dress

Seung-Eun Lee
University of Minnesota
    Retailing

Leedom Lefferts
Drew University, Madison, New Jersey
    Textiles, Southeast Asian Mainland

Ulrich Lehmann
Royal College of Art, Victoria & Albert Museum
    Art and Fashion
    Benjamin, Walter
    Futurist Fashion, Italian
    Mallarmé, Stéphane
    Simmel, Georg

Ann Marie Leshkowich
Assistant Professor of Anthropology,
College of the Holy Cross
 Ao Dai

Esther Leslie
Lecturer, School of English and
Humanities, Birkbeck, University of
London, U.K.
 Marx, Karl

Van Dyk Lewis
Assistant Professor, Textiles and
Apparel, Cornell University
 Afrocentric Fashion
 Hip-Hop Fashion
 Music and Fashion

Joel Lobenthal
Independent Writer
 Hippie Style
 Psychedelic Fashion
 Space Age Styles
 Youthquake Fashions

Linda Loppa
Director and Chief Curator MoMu
 Belgian Fashion
 Demeulemeester, Ann
 Margiela, Martin

Ingrid Loschek
Professor of history and theory of
fashion, University of Applied Sciences
in Pforzheim, Germany
 Twentieth-Century Fashion

Elizabeth D. Lowe
City University of New York, Queens
College
 Feathers
 Labeling Laws
 Polyester
 Ramie

Marylou Luther
Editor-in-chief of the International
Fashion Syndicate
 Fashion Journalism
 Retro Styles

Hazel Lutz
Independent scholar of textiles, dress
and South Asia
 India: Clothing and Adornment
 Nehru Jacket

Karmen MacKendrick
Department of Philosophy, Le Moyne
College
 Body Piercing

Phyllis Magidson
Curator of Costumes and Textiles,
Museum of the City of New York
 Mainbocher

Michele Majer
Assistant Professor, Bard Graduate
Center
 Barbier, Georges
 Boutique
 Demimonde
 Moore, Doris Langley

John S. Major
China Institute
 Asia, East: History of Dress
 Balmain, Pierre
 Blass, Bill
 Camouflage Cloth
 China, History of Dress
 Givenchy, Hubert de
 Lagerfeld, Karl
 Mugler, Thierry
 Paris Fashion
 Prada
 Striped Cloth
 Textiles, Japanese
 Yeohlee

Joanna Marschner
Kensington Palace, State Apartments
and Royal Ceremonial Dress Collection
 Court Dress

Margaret Maynard
The University of Queensland, Australia
 Australian Dress

Joanne McCallum
Bachelor of Design Studies Honours
Class 1, The University of Queensland
 Academic Dress
 Cuff Links and Studs

Aliecia R. McClain
 Distressing

Catherine McDermott
Art, Design, and Music, Kingston
University
 Diana, Princess of Wales

Elizabeth McLafferty
 Lipstick
 Makeup Artists
 Theatrical Makeup

Peter McNeil
University of New South Wales, Sydney,
School of Art History and Theory
 Caricature and Fashion
 Macaroni Dress

Brian J. McVeigh
University of Arizona
 Dress Codes
 Uniforms, School

Patricia Mears
 Grès, Mme.
 Japonisme
 Orientalism
 Yamamoto, Yohji

Beatrice Medicine
 America, North: History of
  Indigenous Peoples' Dress

Katalin Medvedev
 Social Class and Clothing

Lynn A. Meisch
Associate Professor of Anthropology,
Saint Mary's College of California
 America, South: History of
  Dress

Dean L. Merceron
M.A. from the Fashion Institute of
Technology, Museum Studies: Costume
and Textiles
 Lanvin, Jeanne

Susan O. Michelman
University of Kentucky
 Gender, Dress, and Fashion

Caroline Rennolds Milbank
 Ellis, Perry
 Hermès
 Poiret, Paul

Daniel Miller
 Sari

Lesley Ellis Miller
University of Southampton, U.K.
 Balenciaga, Cristóbal
 Spanish Dress

Kimberly A. Miller-Spillman
Gender, Dress, and Fashion

Josephine Moreno
University of California, Berkeley
Latino Style

David Muggleton
University College, Chichester, U.K.
Subcultures

Robert Muir
Penn, Irving

Hudita Mustafa
Department of Anthropology, Emory University
Sy, Oumou

Nan H. Mutnick
Chair, Department of Human Ecology, Marymount College of Fordham University
Appliqué

Michelle Nordtorp-Madson
University of St. Thomas, St. Paul, Minn.
Wedding Costume

Jill Oakes
Department of Environmental Studies and Geography, Faculty of Environment. University of Manitoba, Winnipeg, Canada
Inuit and Arctic Dress
Inuit and Arctic Footwear

Alden O'Brien
D.A.R. Museum
Empire Style
Maternity Dress
Travel Clothing

Sean O'Mara
Laundry

Alistair O'Neill
London College of Fashion
Burberry
Ford, Tom
Lucile
Tuxedo
Vuitton, Louis

Bill Osgerby
Teenage Fashion

Janet Ozzard
Women's Wear Daily

Eduardo Obregon Pagán
Arizona State University West
Zoot Suit

Alexandra Palmer
Nora Vaughan Fashion Costume Curator, Textile section, Royal Ontario Museum, Toronto, Canada
Haute Couture

Jennifer Park
Fashion Institute of Technology, Museum
Courrèges, André
Sweatshirt
Unisex Clothing

Pamela A. Parmal
Department of Textile and Fashion Arts, Museum of Fine Arts, Boston
Hemlines
Lace
Ribbon

Christopher M. Pastore
Philadelphia University
Techno-textiles

Kathleen Paton
Freelance writer and editor
Best-Dressed Lists
Paper Dresses
Trimmings

Jane M. Pavitt
University of Brighton, Victoria & Albert Museum
Brands and Labels
Logos

Kathy Peiss
University of Pennsylvania
Cosmetics, Western

Nicole Pellegrin
Barthes, Roland

Simioan Petrovan
University of Tennessee
Spinning Machinery

Lindsey Philpott
President, Pacific Americas Branch of the International Guild of Knot Tyers
Knotting

John Picton
School of Oriental and African Studies, University of London
Textiles, African

Uraiwan Pitimaneeyakul
King Mongkut's Institute of Technology
Asia, Southeastern Mainland: History of Dress

Ted Polhemus
Independent scholar, teacher and lecturer
Street Style

Shannon Bell Price
The Costume Institute, The Metropolitan Museum of Art
Grunge

Eric Pujalet-Plaà
Musée de la mode et du textile, Union centrale des arts décoratifs, Palais du Louvre
Dior, Christian
New Look

Bradley Quinn
Independent scholar and freelance curator
Activewear
Bodybuilding and Sculpting
Chalayan, Hussein

Leslie W. Rabine
University of California, Davis
Boubou
Globalization
Pagne and Wrapper

Erica Rand
Department of Art and Visual Culture, Bates College
Barbie

Jan Glier Reeder
Consultant, The Costume Institute, Metropolitan Museum of Art Appraisers Association of America
Paquin, Jeanne

Simona Segre Reinach
IULM University, Milan, Italy
    Albini, Walter
    Capucci, Roberto
    Dolce & Gabbana
    Fendi
    Fontana Sisters
    Gigli, Romeo

Elisha P. Renne
University of Michigan, Ann Arbor
    Ecclesiastical Dress

Victoria Z. Rivers
Design Program, University of California–Davis
    Textiles, South Asian

Janet Rizvi
Historian, freelance researcher, and writer specializing in the Western Himalaya, especially Kashmir and Ladakh
    Cashmere and Pashmina
    Paisley

Regina A. Root
College of William and Mary
    Latin American Fashion

Doran H. Ross
    Adinkra
    Kente

Fred Rottman
Executive VP of Picchi Mills (Italian textile company)
    Halston

Victoria L. Rovine
University of Iowa Museum of Art, Curator of the Arts of Africa, Oceania, and the Americas
    Bogolan
    Seydou, Chris
    Xuly Bët

Carol J. Salusso
International Textiles and Apparel Association; Washington State University
    Cotton
    Linen
    Nylon
    Rayon
    Silk

Clare Sauro
Curatorial Assistant, The Museum at the Fashion Institute of Technology
    Boots
    Flappers
    Head, Edith
    Jeans
    Pajamas
    Mackie, Bob

Margot Blum Schevill
Curator, San Francisco Airport Museums
    America, Central, and Mexico:
      History of Dress

Mark Schultz
Curatorial specialist, Goldstein Museum of Design, University of Minnesota
    Belts and Buckles

Lidia D. Sciama
Senior Associate of Queen Elizabeth House, Oxford, U.K.
    Beads

Karen Searle
    Handwoven Textiles

Dennita Sewell
    Animal Prints
    Burrows, Stephen
    Mantua
    T-Shirt

Julia Sharp
Centenary College, Hackettstown, N.J.; Queens College, N.Y.
    Felt

Rebecca Shawcross
Assistant Shoe Resources Officer, Northampton Museum and Art Gallery, U.K.
    High Heels

Lindsay Shen
Director, Goldstein Museum of Design, University of Minnesota
    Crochet
    Embroidery
    Knitting

Jody Shields
    Costume Jewelry

Margot Siegel
    Seventh Avenue

Lise Skov
Post-doctoral research fellow, Department of Sociology, Copenhagen University
    Ethnic Style in Fashion

Orpa Slapak
Israel Museum, Jerusalem
    Jewish Dress

Fred T. Smith
Kent State University
    Ceremonial and Festival
      Costumes
    Masks

Jan Rawdon Smith
The Braid Society
    Braiding

Susan L. Sokolowski
Nike, Inc. Beaverton, Oregon
    Sneakers
    Uniforms, Sports

Christopher Spring
Curator, Ethography Department British Museum
    Africa, North: History of Dress

Jo Ann C. Stabb
University of California–Davis
    Tie-Dyeing

Kristina Stankovski
    Dress Reform
    Gloves

Valerie Steele
Fashion Institute of Technology
    Baudelaire, Charles
    Corset
    Fashion
    Fashion Museums and
      Collections
    Fetish Fashion
    Italian Fashion
    Leiber, Judith
    Paris Fashion
    Tight-Lacing
    Toledo, Isabel and Ruben
    Uzanne, Octave

Francesca Sterlacci
Fashion Institute of Technology
    Fashion Designer
    Leather and Suede

Elaine Stone
Professor Emeritus, Fashion Institute of Technology
  Fashion Marketing and
    Merchandising

Mitchell D. Strauss
University of Northern Iowa
  Reenactors

Pauline Sullivan
  Recycled Textiles

Barbara Sumberg
Curator of Textiles and Costume, Museum of International Fold Art, Santa Fe, N.M.
  Traditional Dress

Anne Hartley Sutherland
Georgia State University
  Roma and Gypsy

Lou Taylor
Professor of dress and textile history, University of Brighton
  Art Nouveau and Art Deco
  Cunnington, C. Willett and
    Phillis
  Fashion, Historical Studies of
  Mourning Dress

Edward Tenner
Princeton University
  Pins
  Needles
  Safety Pins
  Sewing Machine

Howard Thomas
Auburn University
  Knitting Machinery
  Weave, Double
  Weave, Pile
  Weave, Slack Tension

Stefano Tonchi
  Military Style

Susan J. Torntore
Iowa State University, Ames, Iowa
  Breeches
  Brooches and Pins
  Doublet
  Hosiery, Men's
  Necklaces and Pendants

Phyllis Tortora
Author of Understanding Textiles, The Fairchild Encyclopedia of Fashion Accessories, and The Fairchild's Dictionary of Textiles
  Ancient World: History of
    Dress
  Europe and America, History of
    Dress (400-1900 C.E.)
  Fibers
  Toga

Jane Trapnell
  Adrian

Julianne Trautmann
  Bracelets
  Hair Accessories

Efrat Tseëlon
University College, Dublin
  Baudrillard, Jean

Marketa Uhlirova
Associate Lecturer and Research Assistant at Central Saint Martins College of Art and Design
  Galliano, John

Laurel Thatcher Ulrich
  Homespun

Jonathan Walford
Artistic director of Kirkshaw Productions
  Sandals
  Shoemaking
  Shoes
  Shoes, Women's

Myra Walker
University of North Texas
  Cardin, Pierre
  Miniskirt

Susan Ward
Research Fellow, Department of Textile and Fashion Arts, Museum of Fine Arts, Boston
  A-Line Dress
  Chemise Dress
  Earrings
  Eyeglasses
  Sunglasses
  Swimwear

Patricia Campbell Warner
University of Massachusetts, Amherst
  Golf Clothing
  Shirtwaist
  Sportswear

Susan M. Watkins
Professor Emeritus, Cornell University
  Fashion, Health, and Disease
  Protective Clothing
  Space Suit

Judith Watt
  Clark, Ossie
  Muffs

Melinda Watt
Metropolitan Museum of Art
  Beene, Geoffrey
  Buttons
  Extreme Fashions
  Hawes, Elizabeth
  Weaving Machinery

Tiffany Webber-Hanchett
Museum of Fine Arts, Boston
  Bikini
  Fashion Television
  Fogarty, Anne
  Hilfiger, Tommy
  Madonna

Linda M. Welters
Professor, Textiles, Fashion Merchandising and Design, University of Rhode Island
  Folk Dress, Eastern Europe
  Folk Dress, Western Europe
  Folklore Look

Lauren D. Whitley
Museum of Fine Arts, Boston
  Demorest, Mme.
  Galanos, James
  Kamali, Norma
  Levi Strauss & Co.
  Tanning of Leather
  Wearable Art

Clare Wilcox
Senior Curator, modern fashion, Victoria & Albert Museum, London
  Alaïa, Azzadine
  Comme des Garçons

Gloria M. Williams
University of Minnesota
Labor Unions
Textile Workers

Robyne Williams
North Dakota State University
Dyeing, Resist
Dyes, Chemical and Synthetic
Flocking
Fulling
Glazing

Elizabeth Wilson
*Professor Emeritus, London
Metropolitan University*
Biba
Bohemian Dress

Eric Wilson
Women's Wear Daily
Fashion Industry

Laurel E. Wilson
University of Missouri-Columbia
Cowboy Clothing

Verity Wilson
*Asian Department, Victoria & Albert
Museum, London, U.K.*
Qipao
Mao Suit

Geitel Winakor
*Mary B. Welch Distinguished Professor
in Family and Consumer Sciences, Iowa
State University*
Economics and Clothing

Theresa M. Winge
University of Minnesota
Branding
Implants
Modern Primitives
Occult Dress
Scarification
Tattoos

Norma H. Wolff
*Department of Anthropology, Iowa
State University*
Adire
Caftan
Dashiki

Gundula Wolter
Trousers

Rachel Worth
Marks & Spencer

Ann Wright-Parsons
Director, Anthropology Museum
Textiles, Southeast Asian
Islands

Kohle Yohannan
McCardell, Claire
Valentina

Steve Zdatny
*Associate Professor of History, West
Virginia University*
Hairdressers
Hairstyles

Bhakti Ziek
Cerrillos, N.M.
Loom
Weave Types
Weaving

INDEX

Bold page numbers (e.g. **1:10–11**) refer to the main entry on the subject. Page numbers in italics refer to illustrations, figures and tables.

Vionnet, Madeleine, **3:401–404**
  Alaïa, Azzedine and, 1:33
  art deco, 1:77
  body proportion and dress, 1:73
  Callot sisters, work with, 1:216
  celebrity, 2:51
  Chanel, as competitor to, 3:19
  Clark, Ossie, influence on, 1:268
  cocktail dresses, 1:274
  Doucet, House of, 1:377
  embroidery of Michonet, 2:350
  fashions of, *3:401*
  Japonisme, 2:271–272
  kimono style, 2:265
  neoclassicism, 2:220
  1930s fashion, 3:350
  revival of historical styles, 3:6
  Steele, Lawrence, influence on, 3:222
  Vreeland, Diana, patronage of, 3:406
  Windsor, Duchess of, 3:438
Viramontes, Tony, 2:49
Vironi, Gianni, 3:468
Viscose rayon, 3:82, 83
Visé, Donneau de, 2:54
Visual color mixing, 1:282
Vitucci, Angelo, 2:386
Vivier, Roger, *2:204*, 205
Vizé, Jean Donneau de, 2:66
Vladimir, Prince, 3:122, 123
Vocational and technical schools. *See* Fashion education
Vogel, Lucien, 2:55, 67
Vogue, **3:405**
  1929 cover, *2:56*
  Avedon, Richard and, 1:105
  Beaton, Cecil, 1:138–139
  Bourdin, Guy, 1:177–178
  caftans, 1:212
  costume jewelry, 1:304
  editorial slant, 2:54
  editorship, 2:40
  fashion illustration, 2:49, 67
  Horst, Horst P., 2:224–225
  Hoyningen-Huene, George, 2:228
  Klein, Calvin, fashions of, 2:306
  little black dress, 2:359
  Meisel, Steven, 2:401–402
  Penn, Irving, 3:30–31
  trendsetters, 3:335
  Twiggy, 3:355
  Vreeland, Diana, 3:407
Volt, 2:118
Von Boehn, Max, 2:18
Von Furstenberg, Diane, 1:78, 434, **3:405–406**, *406*
Von Runkle, Theodora, 3:323
Von Unwerth, Ellen, 2:65
Vreeland, Diana, **3:406–408**, *407*
  on bikinis, 1:156
  caftans, 1:212
  celebrity, 1:239
  Chanel, Gabrielle (Coco), fashions of,

1:252
  Clark, Ossie, influence on, 1:268
  Costume Institute of the Metropolitan Museum of Art, 2:60
  costume jewelry, 1:303–304, 305
  editorship of *Vogue*, 2:40, 3:405
  on military dress, 2:409
  Missoni style, 2:416
  Romantic and Glamorous: Hollywood Style exhibit, 2:221
  Saint Laurent exhibition, 3:132
  Windsor, Duchess of, 3:438, 439
  Windsor, Duke of, 3:438
  on youthquake, 2:61
Vrubel', M., 3:125
Vuitton, Louis, **3:408**
  accessories, 2:127
  celebrities, use of, 1:240
  logo, 2:360, 361
  luggage, 2:171
  military style, 2:410
Vulcanization of rubber, 3:120–121, 195, 214

W

W (magazine), 2:56
Wabi-sabi, 3:455
Wages
  clothing workers, 1:403–404
  garment workers at House of Chanel, 1:252
  immigrant garment workers, 2:144–145
Wahlberg, Mark, 3:361
Waifs, 3:244
Waistcoats, **3:409–410**
Wakabayashi, Yasuhiro, 2:64
Walden, George, 1:344
Wales, 2:98
Walker, Catherine, 1:363–364
Walker, Madame C. J., 1:15, 16, 297
Walker Wear, 2:216
Walking sticks and canes, **1:219–221**
Walking suits, 3:259
Wallace, Barbara Markey, 1:398
Wallets, 2:170
Wallpaper*, 2:49
Walpole, Horace, 2:219, 367
Waltzes, 1:334, 339
Wang, Vera, 3:36
War bonnets, 2:75, 194
War paint, 1:294
Ward, Jim, 1:167–168
Ward, Melanie, 2:203
Ward, Montgomery
  ready-to-wear, 3:87
  shirtwaists, 1:164–165
Warhol, Andy, 3:132, 396, 435
Warlocks. *See* Occult dress
Warm colors, 1:281–282
Warnings, fabric, 2:320

Warp-faced fabrics
  gabardine, 2:122
  twills, 1:359
Warp knits, 2:311
Warp stripes, 3:280
Warren, Lavinia, 1:359
Wash-and-wear
  Brooks Brothers, 1:199
  wrinkle resistance finishes, 3:32
Washing machines, 2:339–340
Wassau, Hinda, 3:230
Watanabe, Junya, 1:285, 2:208
Watch pockets, 3:41
Watches, **3:410–411**
Water-resistant clothing
  Burberry, 1:200–202
  health and, 2:45
  Inuit and arctic, 2:245, 247–248
  microfibers, 2:402
  rubber, 3:121
  techno-textiles, 3:272–273
Water spirit masks, 2:389
Waterbury Buttons, 1:208
Watkins, Liselotte, 2:49
Watteau pleats, 3:271
Waugh, Jacinta Numina, 1:102
Waugh, Nora, 2:19
Wax resist dyeing. *See* Batik
Wayfarer style sunglasses, 3:241
Wealth
  Bhutanese textiles, 3:311
  conspicuous consumption, 3:390–391
  jewelry as repository of, 2:278
  See also Social class and status
Wearable art, 2:305, **3:411–414**
Wearable electronics, *2:207, 209,* 3:273–274
Weather protection
  health and, 2:45
  microfibers, 2:402
  protective clothing, 3:58
  ski clothing, 3:189
  umbrellas and parasols, 3:357–360
Weave types, **3:421–422**, *423*
  See also Double weave; Jacquard weave; Pile weave; Plain weave; Satin weave; Slack Tension weave; Twill weave
Weaving, **3:423–424**
  ancient China, 3:292–294
  Baltic folk dress, 2:93–94
  Byzantine textiles, 3:286–287
  card weaving, 1:185
  Central America and Mexico, 1:38–40
  Central Asian textiles, 3:290–291
  Coptic textiles, 3:298
  double weaves, 3:414–415
  handweaving revival, 3:413
  Japanese textiles, 3:300–301
  looms, 2:362–364
  lurik, 3:314
  Middle East, 3:304
  prehistoric textiles, 3:305–307